EVALUATION GUIDE FOR CHEMISTRY: A MODERN COURSE

Chemistry: A Modern Course presents an up-to-date approach to teaching chemistry. Chemical concepts and principles are developed in a logical yet flexible order to make the study of chemistry interesting and challenging for students. Many features have been included to strengthen the presentation with the intent of increasing students' understanding and interest in chemistry.

To examine the features of *Chemistry: A Modern Course,* please turn to the following pages:

(p. 2)	A color photo and thought-provoking paragraph introduce each chapter.
(p. 17)	A Goal statement at the beginning of each chapter establishes a purpose for study.
(pp. 46-47)	Accurate diagrams, along with photographs, and line drawings help students visualize ideas presented in the text.
(pp. 66-67)	Student notes placed in the margin emphasize important information and aid students' review of the text material.
(p. 97)	New terms are presented in boldface type and defined in context.
(pp. 100-101)	Important laws and points of emphasis are printed in italic type.
(pp. 110-111)	Example problems, using the factor-label method, guide students through the mathematical concepts needed for chemical calculations.
(pp. 195-196)	Chemical Career and Technology features present additional relevant material related to the chapter.
(p. 218)	Biographies are included of scientists who have contributed to the principles discussed in each chapter.
(pp. 228-229)	Tables appear within the context of related material.
(pp. 294-295)	A Summary of main ideas, comprehensive Problems and questions, Review problems and questions covering preceding chapters, One More Step questions and projects, as well as suggested Readings appear at the end of each chapter.
(pp. 636-648)	The Appendices include supplementary information on careers and logarithms as well as numerous tables for general reference.
(pp. 649-658)	The Glossary includes all important terms used in the text.
(pp. 659-666)	Index.

CHEMISTRY

A MODERN COURSE

TEACHER'S ANNOTATED EDITION

ROBERT C. SMOOT

Chairman, Science Department
McDonogh School
McDonogh, Maryland

JACK S. PRICE

Superintendent, Vista Unified School District
Vista, California

RICHARD G. SMITH

Chairman, Science Department
Bexley High School
Bexley, Ohio

CHARLES E. MERRILL PUBLISHING CO.
A BELL & HOWELL COMPANY
COLUMBUS, OHIO

TORONTO • LONDON • SIDNEY

PREFACE

The *Teacher's Annotated Edition* for the sixth edition of **Chemistry: A Modern Course** is an integral part of the Merrill Chemistry Program. In one book, you have at your fingertips all of these important features: detailed solutions to all questions and problems in the text, a planning guide, suggested teaching aids, demonstrations, and teaching strategies and techniques for presenting text material.

Using this Annotated Edition, you will find that it is not necessary to carry with you two or more easily misplaced supplementary books. All of the materials you will need are in this Annotated text. Thus you eliminate the time consuming, frustrating, and often fruitless search for usable supplementary materials.

The comments, notes, and suggestions are concise and written with an awareness of the classroom situation. The *Teacher's Annotated Edition* is designed to make your teaching of chemistry effective.

The *Teacher's Annotated Edition* can be divided into two parts:

Annotated Pupil's Pages. The annotations are concise statements overprinted in red on the Pupil's text. Each annotation is directly applicable to the section or problem where it is located. Demonstrations are used to introduce chapters and sections where appropriate. Answers are provided for most problems (where space allows) for your convenience.

Teacher's Guide. The Teacher's Guide appears at the front of the *Teacher's Annotated Edition*. These pages have grey edges to set them off from the Pupil's text. The Teacher's Guide is a compilation of the complete problem solutions together with explanations and comments arranged in consecutive order as they appear within the text. The introductory section of the Teacher's Guide provides you with some insight as to our philosophy in teaching chemistry and the features of the text and other components of the Merrill Chemistry Program. The Teacher's Guide is organized to allow you to locate material quickly and check assignments. Performance objectives are included for each chapter. The introductory materials also include a discussion on using performance objectives, audiovisual aids, and literature references.

A questionnaire is included on the last page of the Teacher's Guide. It is our hope that you will take the time to complete it after you have thoroughly reviewed this text. It is our goal to consistently provide a text to meet your teaching needs.

The Authors

ISBN 0-675-06395-7

PUBLISHED BY

CHARLES E. MERRILL PUBLISHING CO.
A BELL & HOWELL COMPANY
COLUMBUS, OHIO 43216

CONTENTS

Includes: Teaching Techniques, Demonstration Information,
Detailed Solutions to all Questions and Problems

PHILOSOPHY

Chemistry: A Modern Course is organized around a central theme: the properties of matter are a consequence of its structure. We feel that before a detailed study of structure can be pursued, it is necessary to establish a working "vocabulary" between students and teacher. This vocabulary is established in the first seven chapters of the text. The organization of the early chapters allows you to begin quantitative lab work early in the course. Students get the motivational benefits of hands-on activity while studying the more concrete aspects of chemistry. Chapter 1 indicates the function of chemistry in society. Chapter 2 reviews basic measurement principles and mathematical techniques which are important in problem solving and laboratory work. In addition, the factor-label method of problem solving is introduced here. Note that the International System of measurement is used throughout the text after its introduction in Chapter 2. We believe students should learn these units as they are the proper foundation for communication among scientists all over the world. Chapter 3 outlines the basic classification system for matter. Chemical symbols and formulas are covered in Chapter 4. Chapter 5 begins an elementary study of the stoichiometry of compounds with an emphasis on the mole as the chemist's basic counting unit. Chapter 6 introduces the chemical equation as a shorthand representation of chemical change, while Chapter 7 covers the mass and energy relationships associated with chemical change. Thus, with the first seven chapters as a framework, students can now move on to more abstract concepts.

The study of structure begins with Chapters 8-11 concerning the atom. In Chapter 8, atomic theory, subatomic particles, and basic ideas about the structure of atoms are discussed. A more detailed look at the theory and behavior of electrons in atoms is the subject of Chapter 9. Atoms are classified, based on their structure, into the periodic system in Chapter 10. Properties of some elements as a consequence of their atomic structure comprise the subject matter of Chapter 11.

Combining atoms into compounds is covered in Chapters 12-14. Chapter 12 discusses the underlying principles of chemical bond formation, while Chapter 13 concerns the bonds themselves and their geometric arrangement in molecular structures. Properties of polar molecules as a consequence of their structure are discussed in Chapter 14.

Chapters 15-19 consider groups of molecules and ions beginning with their kinetic behavior. Chapter 15 presents the physical states of matter as a consequence of their thermal behavior. Chapters 16-19 introduce the basic principles of the three common physical states as a consequence of their structure. Solids are covered first as they are more familiar to students. Gases are covered last since their characteristics are less easily observed. The mole is reintroduced in Chapter 19 in connection with Avogadro's principle in developing the ideal gas equation.

Chapter 20 brings together various concepts of energy and disorder which have been introduced at appropriate points earlier in the text. These ideas are organized into a formal presentation of elementary thermodynamics.

Chapters 21-27 consider aggregates of molecules and ions of different kinds. Nonreacting homogeneous mixtures are covered in Chapter 21. The properties of solutions and colloids on the basis of their structure are covered in Chapter 22. Chapter 23 begins reacting mixtures on the basis of rate and establishing equilibrium. Heterogeneous mixtures are included. Acids and bases are discussed is Chapter 24 with emphasis on their behavior in water solution. The content of Chapter 25 concerns salts and their behavior in water. Chapter 26 presents reactions in which electron transfer takes place and Chapter 27 introduces the interaction of electricity and chemical species.

Chapter 28 introduces the specialized area of nuclear chemistry. This vital area of our present economy is a high interest subject for students. The nomenclature and structure of the simplest classes of organic compounds are covered in Chapter 29. The reactions of organic compounds with emphasis on petroleum products, synthetic materials, and biochemical systems concludes the text in Chapter 30.

Throughout this text, we have used the basic learning principle of proceeding from familiar or known information to the unknown. As you can see from the sequence of chapters, we recognize that a certain amount of repetition is a necessary part of the learning process. Thus, principles of structure, matter-energy relationships, the mole concept, thermodynamics, and chemical equilibrium are presented several times throughout the text with varying degrees of emphasis. We believe students will develop a sense of confidence when they recognize familiar concepts presented later in greater depth. Minimum emphasis has been placed on memorization of fact. Instead, our purpose is to foster understanding and the ability to predict consequences.

CHEMISTRY: A MODERN COURSE

AN INTRODUCTORY CHEMISTRY TEXT AND RELEVANT

Content that focuses on basic chemical principles while giving students a better understanding of their world.

Written by experienced educators in science and mathematics, *CHEMISTRY: A MODERN COURSE* reflects the preferences of science educators throughout the country.

The **sequence** of chapters provides for an understanding of chemical principles without the tedious memorization of equations and facts.

Chapters 1-7 provide the vocabulary to be used throughout the course. The study of atomic structure, bonding, kinetic theory, physical states, solutions, energy, equilibrium systems, redox, and analytical techniques comprise the bulk of the text. Chapters 28-30 are devoted to basic information on nuclear, organic, and biochemistry.

CONTENTS

iv

THAT IS BOTH COMPREHENSIVE

The Great Pyramid is a symbol of human ingenuity. The pyramid contains over 2 million stone blocks each having an average mass of 2300 kilograms. It stands 137 meters high with a base covering 50 000 square meters. In comparison, consider a diamond chip having a mass of 1 gram. This chip contains over 5×10^{23} carbon atoms. Think of the difficulty a chemist encounters in building molecules from single atoms. It is much more practical to work with a large amount as a single unit. The mole is a chemist's counting unit. What number of objects does a mole represent? Why was this particular number selected to represent a mole?

A format designed to motivate and provide a successful learning experience.

THE MOLE   5

Chapter 5 introduces the mole and the use of this concept in manipulating formulas. Students are expected to set up and solve quantitative problems.

Demonstration—Place some $CuSO_4 \cdot 5H_2O$ in a large test tube. Heat it over a flame until the blue color disappears. Place the white anhydrous $CuSO_4$ on a watch glass and add H_2O from a dropper. **CAUTION:** exothermic. Discuss how quantitative information can be used to completely describe our observations.

Chemical symbols and formulas (such as H and H_2O) are shorthand signs for chemical elements and compounds. The symbol of an element may represent one atom of the element. The formula of a compound may represent one molecule or one formula unit of the compound. Symbols and formulas may also represent a group of atoms or formula units. Since atoms are so very small, chemists deal with large groups of atoms. This chapter is about a group called a mole, containing a specific number of units.

GOAL: You will demonstrate your understanding of the mole concept by using it in calculations with chemical formulas, solutions, molecular formulas, and hydrates.

Point out that elements can have formulas such as I_2, S_8, and P_4.

5:1   MOLECULAR MASS

The masses of the atoms are compared by using the **atomic mass scale.** This scale has the "atomic mass unit" (amu) as a standard. The source of this standard will be discussed in Chapter 8. A list of atomic masses for the elements is found on the inside back cover of the book.

The atomic mass of hydrogen in atomic mass units is 1, and the atomic mass of oxygen is 16. Therefore, the total mass of a water molecule, H_2O, is $1 + 1 + 16$, or 18 amu. If the atomic masses of all the atoms in a molecule are added, the sum is the mass of that molecule. Such a mass is called a **molecular mass.** This name is incorrect when applied to an ionic substance. Sodium chloride, NaCl, is an ionic substance which does not exist in molecular form. A better name for the mass of ionic substances is formula mass. The sum of the atomic masses of all atoms in the formula unit of an ionic compound is called the **formula mass** of the substance. To calculate a formula mass add the masses of all the atoms in the formula.

The atomic mass unit is used to compare masses of atoms.

The data in the atomic mass table gives relative masses of the elements.

Molecular mass is the sum of the atomic masses of the atoms in the molecule.

Formula mass is the sum of the atomic masses of the atoms in a formula unit.

The Pupil's text is overprinted in red with **Teacher Annotations.** Thus, answers, points of emphasis, teaching strategies, and demonstrations are conveniently located with the text material.

The 30 chapters are subdivided into **numbered sections** allowing you to flexibly plan your assignments.

Full color chapter openings provide students with a purpose for studying the chapter.

Readability is enhanced by using a single column format leaving the margin free for student notes and annotations to highlight important information.

CHEMISTRY: A MODERN COURSE

Reading and study aids designed to remove any obstacles students may encounter in learning.

Student margin notes, printed in blue, highlight important points. Thus, students are not faced with the problem of discerning what is important from a mass of new material.

A **Goal,** found in statement form at the beginning of each chapter, identifies the major objective to be accomplished in studying the chapter.

Phrases and sentences to be emphasized are printed in italic type.

Numbered sections provide students with a ready outline of the chapter. Thus, students are better able to see the relationships among concepts.

New terms are highlighted in boldface type. They are used repeatedly allowing students to establish a familiarity with the term and its definition. All new terms are clearly defined in the Glossary.

COLLIGATIVE AND COLLOIDAL PROPERTIES 22

When a solute is dissolved in a solvent, there is a change in certain properties of the solvent. On the other hand, when particles too large to dissolve are dispersed throughout a liquid, the solvent's properties remain unchanged. In this chapter, we want to investigate those properties of solvents which are changed by solutes. We also want to look at the behavior of those particles which are too large to dissolve and have no effect on the liquid. Throughout the first six sections of this chapter, we will be dealing with an ideal solution. In Chapter 18, we were able to define an ideal gas. Unfortunately, we cannot define an ideal solution completely at this point. For the time being, we will just say that the particles of solute in an ideal solution have no effect on each other.

GOAL: You will gain an understanding of the properties of solutions that depend upon the number of particles, size of the particles, and the type of particles in the solution.

22:1 RAOULT'S LAW

Colligative properties are determined by the number of particles in solution rather than by the type of particle in solution. The properties so affected are vapor pressure, freezing point, boiling point, and the rate of diffusion through a membrane. Consider a solute dissolved in a liquid solvent. Some of the solute particles take up space on the liquid surface normally occupied by solvent particles. These solute particles decrease the opportunity for solvent particles to escape (evaporate) from the liquid surface. Thus, if the solute is nonvolatile, the vapor pressure of a solution is always less than that of the pure solvent at the same temperature. The lowering of the vapor pressure of the solvent varies directly as the mole fraction of dissolved solute. *Any nonvolatile solute at a specific concentration lowers the vapor pressure of a solvent by an amount which is characteristic of that solvent.* The characteristics of the solute are not involved. Ionic

Colligative properties depend on the number of particles in solution.

Colligative properties
1. vapor pressure
2. freezing point
3. boiling point
4. rate of diffusion through a membrane
All ionic and molecular solids having low vapor pressures are said to be nonvolatile.

427

An approach to problem solving that reinforces the content without the burden of memorization.

EXAMPLE: Volume of a Dry Gas

A quantity of gas is collected over water at 8°C in a 353-cm³ vessel. The manometer indicates a pressure of 84.5 kPa. What volume would the dry gas occupy at standard pressure and 8°C?

Solving process:

(a) We must determine what part of the total pressure is due to water vapor. Table 18-2 indicates that at 8°C, water has a vapor pressure of 1.1 kPa. To find the pressure of the collected gas:

$$P_{gas} = P_{total} - P_{water}$$
$$= 84.5 \text{ kPa} - 1.1 \text{ kPa}$$
$$= 83.4 \text{ kPa}$$

(b) Since this pressure is less than standard, the gas would have to be compressed to change it to standard. The pressure ratio by which the volume is to be multiplied must be less than 1. The correct volume is

$$\frac{353 \text{ cm}^3}{} \left| \frac{83.4 \text{ kPa}}{101.3 \text{ kPa}} \right. = 291 \text{ cm}^3$$

$$V_2 = V_1 \left(\frac{P_1}{P_2} \right)$$

Note that the temperature remains constant. See Table 18-2 page 362 for pressure corrections.

PROBLEM

5. The following gas volumes were collected over water under the indicated conditions. Correct each volume to the volume that the dry gas would occupy at standard pressure and the indicated temperature (T is constant).
   a. 888 cm³ at 14°C and 93.3 kPa
   b. 30.0 cm³ at 16°C and 77.5 kPa
   c. 34.0 m³ at 18°C and 82.4 kPa
   d. 384 cm³ at 12°C and 78.3 kPa
   e. 8.23 m³ at 27°C and 87.3 kPa

5. a. 804 cm³

18:4 CHARLES' LAW

Jacques Charles, a French physicist, noticed a simple relationship between the volume of a gas and the temperature. He found that, starting at 0°C, the volume of any gas would double if the temperature were raised to 273°C (pressure constant). For each Celsius degree increase in temperature, the volume of the gas increased by 1/273 of its volume at 0°C. If the original volume (at 0°C) is expressed as 273/273 = 1, an increase in temperature of 273° will result in a new volume of

For each 1 C° change, a gas changes 1/273 of its 0°C volume.

$$\frac{273 + 273}{273}, \text{ or } 2$$

Examples are used throughout the text as models for students in applying mathematical skill in solving chemical calculations.

Practice problems throughout each chapter enable students to review immediately the material just studied. Answers are provided to some problems allowing students to check their work.

SI units are used to provide students with the proper base for communicating in science. The simplicity of this measurement system drastically reduced the number of new units students will learn in the course.

CHEMISTRY: A MODERN COURSE

A strong graphic presentation to help students visualize new concepts.

Tables are used to organize text information and quantitative data. The use of a tabular format allows students to see relationships among ideas and data at a glance.

Illustrations provide the visual models needed to fully understand abstract topics such as bonding, atomic and molecular structure, and large scale chemical processes. Graphs are used to show relationships between measured quantities.

Photographs are used to directly illustrate the text information or present additional applications and analogies to help students visualize difficult concepts. The captions reinforce the text or provide additional relevant information.

Table 13-1

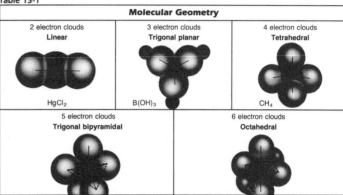

Molecular Geometry

2 electron clouds Linear	3 electron clouds Trigonal planar	4 electron clouds Tetrahedral
$HgCl_2$	$B(OH)_3$	CH_4

5 electron clouds Trigonal bipyramidal	6 electron clouds Octahedral

Iodine: Essential for the synthesis of thyroid hormones

Iron: Metallic center of hemoglobin; needed for the formation of vitamin A; component of some enzymes

Copper: Essential for hemoglobin synthesis; needed for bone formation and the production of melanin and myelin

Potassium: Maintains intracellular osmotic pressure and pH; needed for proper transmission of nerve impulses and muscle contraction

Zinc: Component of several enzymes involved in digestion, respiration, bone formation, liver metabolism; needed for a normal healing process and good skin tone

Manganese: Component of enzymes involved in the synthesis of fatty acids and cholesterol; needed for the formation of urea and the normal functioning of the nervous system

Doug Martin

discovered. As an example, lack of zinc in the diet prevents the pancreas from producing some digestive enzymes.

Metallic zinc, like chromium, is corrosion resistant. It is used extensively as a coating to protect iron. The coating can be applied in three ways. When the iron is dipped in molten zinc, the process is called **galvanizing**. The coating is also applied electrically. The third method is to allow gaseous zinc to condense on the surface of iron. Another major use for metallic zinc is in the production of alloys. Especially important is its combination with copper to form brass.

FIGURE 11-17. Zinc is one of many elements essential to proper body function. Vitamin tablets act as a supplement in the event that one does not receive adequate amounts from the daily diet.

Zinc is corrosion resistant.

A. Mercado/Jeroboam

FIGURE 11-18. Zinc discs are used on the underside of ships to prevent corrosion.

SUMMARY

1. A polar bond is one in which a shared pair of electrons is attracted more strongly to one of the atoms. 14:1
2. van der Waals forces are the net result of dipole-dipole, dipole-induced dipole, and dispersion effects. 14:2
3. A complex ion is composed of a central positive ion and molecular or negative ion ligands. 14:3
4. The number of ligands surrounding the central ion is the coordination number of a complex. 14:3
5. Complex ions which contain more than one type of ligand may exhibit geometric isomerism. 14:4
6. Small positive ions with a large nuclear attractive force form excellent central ions. The transition metal ions are good examples of these. 14:6
7. The bonds of complex ions have both ionic and covalent bonding characteristics. 14:6
8. Chromatography is a method of separating substances into identifiable chemical fractions by differences in their polarity. 14:8-14:11

PROBLEMS

7. The following pairs of atoms are all covalently bonded. Arrange the pairs in order of decreasing polarity of the bonds using Table 12-6.
   a. arsenic and oxygen   d. oxygen and fluorine
   b. chlorine and silicon   e. phosphorus and bromine

REVIEW

1. What shape would you predict for the NI_3 molecule? For CCl_4?
2. Describe the shapes of s and p orbitals.
3. Explain why carbon can form four equivalent bonds with a predicted outer configuration of $2s^2 2p^2$.
4. Why is benzene more stable than a compound with three single and three double bonds?
5. What shape would you predict for H_2Se? Why?
6. From molecular orbital theory, predict the stability of the He_2^+.
7. Draw as many isomers of C_5H_{10} as you can. Hint: There are 10 isomers and the compound contains one $C=C$ double bond.
8. Predict the $N—C=O$ bond angle in $(NH_2)_2CO$.
9. Draw isomers for compounds with the formula C_6H_6.
10. Draw resonance structures for SO_3.

ONE MORE STEP

1. In preparing paper chromatograms, identification of unknowns is aided by the measurement of R_f values. These values concern the distance an unknown has advanced compared to the distance the solvent has advanced. Research the chromatographic process to determine how these values are useful in identification.
2. Look up the structure of chlorophyll and hemoglobin. Determine the central ion and its coordination number. What is the coordinated group, and what is its spatial orientation about the central ion?
3. Medicine and industry use certain materials called chelating agents. What are they and how are they related to complexes?
4. A number of organic compounds are used in the analysis of inorganic ions because they form complex ions. Investigate the substances used in detecting nickel, aluminum, and zirconium by such a method.
5. Try to separate the pigments of spinach leaves using paper chromatography.

READINGS

Barth, Howard G., "Separations Using Liquid Chromatography." *Chemistry,* Vol. 50, No. 7 (September 1977), pp. 11-13.

Eliel, Ernest L., "Stereochemistry." *Chemistry,* Part I, Vol. 49, No. 1 (January-February 1976), pp. 6-10; Part II, Vol. 49, No. 3 (April 1976), pp. 8-13.

Kauffman, George B., "Left-handed and Right-handed Molecules." *Chemistry,* Vol. 50, No. 3 (April 1977), pp. 14-18.

Nassau, Kurt, "The Causes of Color." *Scientific American,* Vol. 243, No. 4 (October 1980), pp. 124-154.

Navratil, J. D., and Walton, H. F., "Ion Exchange and Liquid Chromatography." *Chemistry,* Vol. 50, No. 6 (July-August 1977), pp. 18-20.

A complete range of chapter review materials to meet your teaching needs.

Summary lists the major points presented in the chapter. Each statement is annotated for students allowing them to refer back to the section where the statement is presented.

Problems includes additional questions and practice problems enabling students to further check their understanding of the chapter before a test. The questions range from simple recall to the application of previously studied material to new situations.

Review includes questions and practice problems which cover material from previous chapters. Thus, students constantly build their knowledge base rather than treating each chapter as an isolated unit.

One More Step includes questions and activities which take students beyond the material in the chapter. These items are ideal for individualized study or extra credit.

Readings is a list of suggested references and high interest articles allowing students to explore chapter concepts in more depth.

CHEMISTRY: A MODERN COURSE

Additional features to provide a balanced approach to chemistry, thereby eliminating any need to supplement the text.

Appendices include a comprehensive set of reference data and supplementary information on logarithms and careers thereby eliminating the need to purchase expensive reference tables or handbooks.

Chemical Careers are short overviews of career choices requiring some knowledge of chemistry.

Biographies are brief insights into the lives and discoveries of scientists who have made a significant contribution to the field of chemistry.

Chemical Technology articles provide a brief insight into topics which supplement the chapter material or a current research problem.

APPENDIX B

LOGARITHMS

A logarithm or log is an exponent. We will work with exponents given in terms of base 10.

$$N = b^x$$

$$\text{number} = \text{base}^{\text{exponent or logarithm}}$$

$$100 = 10^{2.0000}$$

---

38   Measuring and Calculating

CHEMICAL CAREER: Chemical Engineering

Chemistry is a science. Engineering, on the other hand, is a particular approach to problem solving. The engineer uses the facts generated by scientists to solve everyday problems. Most engineers (and some chemists) deal with technology.

Though a chemical engineer performs many functions, a broad definition would be a person who designs, builds, and/or operates chemical plants or industrial plants using chemistry. The design function involves working with chemists who have investigated

---

352   Liquids

Norbert Rillieux (1806–1894)

Norbert Rillieux was born in the United States; however he received his education in Paris, France. At the age of 24, he was teaching applied engineering at École Centrale. It was his interest in chemistry and steam engineering which returned him to the United States and led him to a process that revolutionized the sugar industry.

The crystallization of sugar from cane syrup had been done by ladling the cane syrup from vat to vat until the liquid evaporated. In 1846, Rillieux made use of the reduced boiling point of a liquid under a vacuum evaporator. This process produced a cheaper, better, and more automated method of crystallizing sugar. The same concept is now used in the manufacture of condensed milk, soap, and glue. It is also useful in the recovery of wastes from distilleries and paper factories.

CHEMICAL TECHNOLOGY: Herbicides

As the population of the world increases, it becomes more and more difficult to feed everyone. Scientists are constantly searching for ways to increase crop yields from farmland.

One method of improving farm productivity is to remove weeds which crowd paying crops. Herbicides are chemicals which kill weeds without harming the cash crop. Almost 200 different herbicides are available commercially in the United States.

The most widely used herbicides are alachlor and atrazine. Another herbicide, one which has caused much controversy is 2,4,5-T (2,4,5-trichlorophenoxyacetic acid). This substance tends to accumulate in the ground and in water run-off from those fields where it has been used. Most herbicides used today are decomposed in the soil by bacteria within a year. Persistent herbicides, such as 2,4,5-T, can be a problem if they accumulate to levels that are harmful to animals and humans.

Scientists are constantly searching for microorganisms which can degrade these persistent herbicides. It is sometimes possible to control the evolution of such organisms over a long period of time by gradually changing their diets. Thus, organisms can be bred to naturally degrade some of these materials. There are many problems to be overcome in such research. For instance, a microorganism which thrives on a certain chemical in the laboratory may not be able to survive in the wild.

Ancillary materials to provide for hands-on learning, development of math skills, and evaluation of student progress.

Laboratory Program

Chemical concepts often appear abstract to students. *LABORATORY CHEMISTRY* provides students with an opportunity to investigate many of the concepts covered in *CHEMISTRY: A MODERN COURSE.* A teaching approach which combines lecture and textbook materials with practical laboratory experiences will enhance students' ability to comprehend new and difficult material.

The focus of *LABORATORY CHEMISTRY* is on a logical approach to investigating and analyzing problems. A wide variety of laboratory techniques which stress safety are presented. Accurate reporting of experimental data in a well organized laboratory report is emphasized. Students are then required to interpret their results in terms of the concepts being investigated.

LABORATORY CHEMISTRY is designed to be flexible for a variety of teaching needs. When time or cost is a prohibitive factor, teachers are encouraged to use experiments for class demonstrations. The Planning Guide on pages 14T-15T contains a suggested laboratory sequence which correlates the experiments with the text material.

Problem Solving

Students often encounter difficulty in applying their mathematical skills to chemical calculations. *SOLVING PROBLEMS IN CHEMISTRY* is designed to develop problem solving skills through the use of *Example* and practice problems. This paperback text contains a minimal amount of reading material and focuses strictly on problem solving. The factor-label method is used as in the text *CHEMISTRY: A MODERN COURSE.* Each Example problem has a carefully explained step-by-step solving process. Emphasis has been placed on the practical applications of problem solving in chemistry. Industrial and everyday uses of chemicals are discussed within the problems.

Solving Problems in Chemistry is an excellent source of supplementary problems and exercises for developing problem solving skills.

Evaluation of Student Progress

The *EVALUATION PROGRAM FOR CHEMISTRY: A MODERN COURSE* is designed to be used as a learning tool as well as an instrument in evaluating student progress. The spirit master book consists of a four-part test for each of the 30 chapters in *CHEMISTRY: A MODERN COURSE.* The four sections of each chapter test include:

Discovering Concepts—A set of multiple choice questions in which students demonstrate their ability to recall specific facts from the chapter.

Interpreting Concepts—A set of completion and matching items in which students demonstrate their ability to interpret basic concepts.

Using Concepts—A set of problems and/or essay questions which require students to apply their basic knowledge to related situations.

Completing Concepts—A set of completion items in which students demonstrate their understanding of chemical terms used in context.

The major focus of each test is to help students improve their knowledge of chemistry. Using these tests as a diagnostic tool you can decide what supplemental materials may be needed to help overcome any weaknesses in presentation and instruction which may become apparent.

USING
CHEMISTRY: A MODERN COURSE

Organization and Sequence

The *TEACHER'S ANNOTATED EDITION OF CHEMISTRY: A MODERN COURSE* is divided into two sections—the Teacher's Guide having grey edges along the pages and the red overprinted Pupil's text.

The Pupil's text is divided into 30 chapters. Each chapter is further divided into numbered sections. The numbering and headings of the sections aid students in locating specific topics and assist you in arranging class and homework assignments.

Chemistry: A Modern Course follows a logical, sequential development of major chemistry principles. The text begins with the "mechanics" of chemistry, the mole concept, and the structure of matter. The text then deals with the behavior of matter in terms of acidity, oxidation-reduction, and electric potential. It also includes descriptive material in nuclear, organic, biochemistry, and analytical chemistry.

Teacher's Guide

Overview

This section provides you with a short synopsis of the major themes of the chapter. You are also given an insight as to how the chapter material fits into the overall sequence.

Demonstrations

Good teacher demonstrations are important in helping students visualize abstract concepts and allow for the development of observational skills and proper lab techniques. Use the demonstrations in the text to emphasize safety rules and procedures. The approach you use in presenting a demonstration can be one of the following: begin with a clearly defined problem or use the demonstration as a silent type where your goal is to develop students' ability to observe and draw conclusions. These skills will be critical to their success in the laboratory portion of the course. Good demonstrations allow students to recognize and verbalize relationships based on their level of experience. The demonstration as a teaching technique allows you to present a maximum amount of text material in a concrete and visual manner. You will find numerous demonstrations printed in red throughout the Pupil's text. Any additional preparation and teaching strategies will be covered in the Teacher's Guide section for that chapter.

Performance Objectives

The major Goal of the chapter is followed by a list of specific objectives. Thus, you are aware of the points to emphasize in covering the chapter. When designing your chapter tests or course of study for beginning chemistry use these objectives as a framework. The Evaluation Program which is part of the Merrill Chemistry Program is written based on the chapter objectives. A thorough explanation on how to use performance objectives is found on pages 22T-24T.

Teaching Techniques

Section teaching techniques are provided when appropriate. These strategies include information concerning the authors' approach to a particular topic, additional science background, and suggestions as to how to achieve a better level of success in presenting a section to students.

Problem Solutions

Answers to most problems are found in red overprinted on the Pupil's page for convenience. However, note that some answers would not fit in the existing space on a page. The Teacher's Guide contains full solutions for all questions and problems in the Pupil's text.

Teacher Annotations

The red Teacher Annotations consist of answers to problems, demonstrations, science background, points of emphasis, and teaching strategies. They are conveniently located with the appropriate text material.

Pupil's Text

Readability

Readability plays a major role in determining the success of a textbook in the classroom. A text which can be comprehended by the majority of students promotes their interest and involvement in the subject area. This feature promotes teachability and helps facilitate classroom management.

In controlling reading level, careful attention has been given to vocabulary, sentence construction, paragraph structure, chapter organization, illustrations, and text format.

The vocabulary in the text is consistent with the developmental level of average high school students. Words with a large number of syllables have been avoided whenever possible. In addition, important science terms are printed in boldface or italic type when first presented. Some terms are followed by their phonetic spellings. Each term is then clearly defined and used repeatedly throughout the discussion to reinforce its meaning.

The open format is the result of appropriate spacing between sections, problems, and illustrations. The typeface and size in which the text is set is another aspect that enhances readability. The margin is used for supplemental information in the form of margin notes, captions, and annotations. Thus, the flow of ideas in the main body of the text is not disrupted. Highlighting and organizing important information using boldface type, student notes, tables, and Summary statements also enhances readability.

Photographs and Illustrations

We maintain that a visual presentation not only motivates students but certainly adds to their level of understanding. The use of material which provides students with visual links between chemistry principles and real-world happenings is a vital part of the learning process. Each chapter opening consists of a color photograph and a thought-provoking paragraph designed to stimulate student interest in the material to be presented in the chapter. In addition over 450 color photographs, illustrations, and graphs are included throughout the text to reinforce and clarify concepts presented in adjacent paragraphs. Use these graphics as part of your presentation as much as possible so students learn to think of them as an active part of the text.

Example Problems

Example problems are used extensively to present the mathematical concepts needed in studying chemistry. The factor-label method of problem solving is used and unit cancellation lines are printed in blue to aid students in setting-up problems. The Example problems provide students with clear, logical models they can use to achieve an answer. Each Example problem is titled and set-off from the body of the text for quick reference. Take the time in your presentation of a section to thoroughly review each Example with students.

Student Notes

Student notes are placed in the margin to aid in review. Using the section titles as a framework, these notes can be used to provide students with a ready outline of the concepts discussed within the chapter. They are also an excellent reading aid in providing students with a concise statement of a paragraph or concept.

Chemical Careers

These features are designed to give students an awareness of the many fields which draw on a knowledge of chemistry. These features should be used to emphasize the importance of this subject in students' overall education. Use the features as a starting point for students to do additional research into the many career options available. Emphasize that a doctorate in chemistry is not necessary to pursue a chemistry-related career. A basic chemistry course is adequate preparation for many jobs.

Chemical Technology

These features present supplemental discussions of chapter concepts and insights into current research problems. These pages should be used to motivate students to seek additional information concerning timely issues such as the use of scarce resources, energy alternatives, progress, and the environment. Some features highlight an additional application of some topic within the chapter. Thus, students are aware of how our knowledge of topics such as crystal structure, distance measurement, and ion activity was formulated.

Biographies

Each chapter includes a short biography of a scientist whose work has contributed to the principles presented in that chapter. The Biographies are designed to bring out the human aspects of scientists in general and to relate their work to the relevant problems of their times. In using the Biographies be sure to emphasize that many great scientists had to overcome numerous obstacles in the pursuit of their work.

Section- and Chapter-End Materials

Questions and problems follow many sections of the text. They are designed for students to check their understanding of the previously covered material. Answers are provided in blue for some questions and problems within a chapter to allow students to gain confidence in the mastery of new material.

The chapter-end materials begin with a Summary which concisely reviews the major concepts and principles in the chapter. Each Summary statement is numbered and keyed back to the chapter by a blue student note. You can begin the chapter using the Summary to determine how much your students know about a topic from previous science courses. The Summary is an excellent reading aid in that it helps students discern the important points from the mass of material in the chapter. It also gives you an insight as to the points the authors feel should be emphasized in presenting a chapter.

The Problems section provides questions and problems to review the major concepts of the chapter. Students' success depends greatly on their being given the opportunity to develop math skills and apply their chemical knowledge to new situations. Having students answer these items and then thoroughly reviewing each with them should be adequate preparation for a chapter test.

The Review section provides questions and problems where students recall the important principles and concepts from previous chapters.

Since many topics in this text build on the knowledge gained in a previous chapter, this section provides an excellent way of unifying information. It also gives students additional practice in problem solving and applying concepts.

The One More Step section presents questions and activities to lead students beyond the material covered in the text. This section is designed to provide a number of open-ended activities. Use these items to develop positive attitudes toward science, as extra credit projects, or as a means of individualizing the course for students having the ability to digest material at a higher level than that presented in the text. Note that these items provide for a wide range of activities from simple library research to designing a technical research problem. Thus, they can be assigned to students at all levels of ability.

The Readings provide interested students with references to expand their knowledge of some aspects of the chapter. Encourage students to read articles concerning science in the local newspaper and popular news magazines. At this point in their education you want to establish the idea that a study of science is not relegated to the classroom or laboratory. The success of new science magazines for the nonscientist exemplifies this idea.

Appendices

Appendix A contains twelve useful tables to provide students with all the necessary data to work the problems in the text. This comprehensive set of tables provides you with all of the necessary reference data in one volume.

Appendix B contains a section to review the use of logarithms in chemical calculations. A table of logarithms follows this review section.

Appendix C contains a partial listing and description of some chemistry related careers.

Glossary

The Glossary provides students with a quick reference to the key terms presented in the text.

PLANNING GUIDE FOR
CHEMISTRY: A MODERN COURSE

You are in the best position to design a chemistry course that meets the needs of your students. You will find the arrangement of *Chemistry: A Modern Course* allows for a certain amount of flexibility in planning. You may prefer to use the chapters in a different sequence to reflect your own philosophy of teaching chemistry. For example, if you prefer a historical approach, use Chapters 1, 8-18, 2-7, and 19-30 in that order. We have arranged the text so as to provide a background early in the course that permits a strong laboratory approach. This planning guide is provided to assist you with both long range and daily planning. We hope it helps in designing the best possible chemistry program.

The guide is organized to present a suggested number of class sessions for each chapter. The entire course is based on 180 class sessions in the school year, which is equivalent to 160 hours of combined class and laboratory time.

The sections of each chapter are classified as being of primary or secondary importance. We believe that a basic chemistry curriculum must include those sections designated as primary importance. The sections listed in this category provide a minimum program. After presenting the essential sections in each chapter, you may have the time to select from additional text topics and laboratory experiments. The planning guide shows the correlation between the experiments in *Laboratory Chemistry* and the content of the text.

The first sixteen chapters are considered to be the equivalent of a semester of study. You will want to complete them in 90 class sessions. We consider the first 27 chapters to be essential in an introductory high program which is designed to survey chemistry and prepare students for further study in science.

Once you have determined your goals for the year, use this guide to aid you in scheduling. The number of class sessions suggested includes time for laboratory experiments and testing. You may

find that some classes will take longer to cover a chapter than what is projected in the planning guide. Use the planning guide as a framework not as a rigid schedule that must be adhered to.

The following is a general guide to covering the chapters if you are on six or nine week reporting periods.

Six Week Periods		Nine Week Periods	
	Chapters		Chapters
First	1–6	First	1–8
Second	7–11	Second	9–16
Third	12–16	Third	17–23
Fourth	17–20	Fourth	24–30
Fifth	21–25		
Sixth	26–30		

Correlation for supplemental problems in *Solving Problems in Chemistry* © 1983

Chemistry: A Modern Course	*Solving Problems in Chemistry*
Chapter 2	Chapter 1
4	2
5	3, 4, 5, 6, 16
6	7
7	8
17	14
18	9
19	10, 11, 12, 13
20	15
21	16, 18
22	19
23	17
24	20
25	21, 22, 23
26	24
27	25
28	26
29	27

PLANNING GUIDE FOR CHEMISTRY: A MODERN COURSE

Chapter	Class Sessions	Emphasis Level Of Primary Importance	Of Secondary Importance	Suggested Experiments from LABORATORY CHEMISTRY
1	3	1:3–1:5	1:1, 1:2	Laboratory check-in OBSERVING, INVESTIGATING, ANALYZING, INTERPRETING: SCIENTIFIC METHOD INVESTIGATING THE LAW OF CONSERVATION OF MASS-ENERGY
2	5	2:1–2:7	2:8	INTRODUCTION TO QUANTITATIVE MEASUREMENT: DENSITY DETERMINATION
3	4	all sections		CHEMICAL AND PHYSICAL CHANGES IN MATTER
4	5	all sections		CHEMICAL FORMULAS AND OXIDATION NUMBERS
5	6	all sections		QUANTITATIVE DETERMINATION OF AN EMPIRICAL FORMULA HYDRATED CRYSTALS
6	5	all sections		CHEMICAL CHANGES AND EQUATIONS
7	10	7:1–7:4	7:5–7:7	QUANTITATIVE STUDY OF A REACTION MOLE RELATIONSHIP IN A CHEMICAL REACTION SPECIFIC HEAT OF A METAL HEAT OF A CHEMICAL REACTION
8	7	8:6–8:10 8:13–8:14	8:1–8:5 8:11–8:12, 8:15	FLAME TESTS INTRODUCTION TO THE SPECTROPHOTOMETER ENERGIES OF ELECTRONS
9	8	9:5–9:15	9:1–9:4	ELECTRON ARRANGEMENTS
10	7	10:2–10:13	10:1	THE PERIODIC LAW INTRODUCTION TO QUALITATIVE ANALYSIS
11	3		all sections	THE ACTIVITY OF GROUPS IA, IIA, AND VIIA
12	6	all sections		ENERGY RELATIONSHIPS OF METALLIC IONS CONDUCTIVITY AND CHEMICAL BONDING
13	8	13:1–13:8	13:9–13:12	SHAPES OF COVALENT MOLECULES AND POLARITY
14	4	14:1–14:2	14:3–14:11	INTRODUCTION TO CHROMATOGRAPHY
15	5	all sections		

16	6	16:1–16:2 16:5 16:8–16:10	16:3–16:4 16:6–16:7 16:11–16:15	ION OR ATOM ARRANGEMENT IN CRYSTALS ALLOTROPIC FORMS OF SULFUR
17	7	17:1–17:11	17:12	DETERMINATION OF HEAT OF FUSION
18	7	18:1–18:6 18:9	18:7–18:8	CHARLES' LAW: THE EFFECT OF TEMPERATURE ON VOLUME DIFFUSION OF GASES
19	6	19:1–19:7	19:8–19:10	THE MOLAR RELATIONSHIP INVOLVING MASS AND VOLUME STOICHIOMETRY: MASS-VOLUME
20	6	20:1–20:4 20:6–20:7	20:5	ENTROPY AND ENTHALPY
21	4	21:1–21:4 21:9–21:10	21:5–21:8	DETERMINING AND GRAPHING THE EFFECT OF TEMPERATURE ON SOLUBILITY DETERMINING SOLUTION CONCENTRATION USING A SPECTROPHOTOMETER
22	5	22:1 22:3–22:5 22:7	22:2, 22:6 22:8–22:10	MOLECULAR MASS DETERMINATION USING BOILING POINT AND FREEZING POINT
23	7	23:1–23:9	23:10, 23:11	REACTION RATES A STUDY OF CHEMICAL EQUILIBRIUM
24	7	24:1–24:5 24:7–24:8 24:10–24:11 24:13	24:6, 24:9 24:12, 24:14	QUALITATIVE ANALYSIS OF NET IONIC REACTIONS SOME REACTIONS BETWEEN IONS IN SOLUTION
25	9	25:1–25:4 25:6–25:7	25:5	QUANTITATIVE DETERMINATION OF THE SOLUBILITY PRODUCT CONSTANT HYDRONIUM ION CONCENTRATION INDICATORS HYDROLYSIS: WATER REACTIONS WITH NORMAL SALTS ACID-BASE TITRATION AND VOLUMETRIC ANALYSIS
26	7	26:1–26:8	26:9–26:12	OXIDATION-REDUCTION REACTIONS QUANTITATIVE TITRATION INVOLVING REDOX REACTIONS
27	6	27:1–27:9 27:14	27:10–27:13 27:15	MEASURING THE POTENTIAL OF ELECTROCHEMICAL CELLS CORROSION: AN ELECTROCHEMICAL PROBLEM
28	6	28:4–28:8	28:1–28:3 28:9–28:12	NATURAL RADIOACTIVITY
29	6	29:1–29:4 29:7–29:17	29:5–29:6	PREPARATION OF SOME ORGANIC COMPOUNDS
30	5	30:1–30:5	30:6–30:13	PREPARATION OF SOAP, SYNTHETIC RUBBER, AND NYLON BIOCHEMISTRY: IDENTIFICATION OF CARBOHYDRATES, FATS, AND PROTEINS

TEACHER REFERENCES

General references for demonstrations and laboratory practice.

Irgolic, Kurt, et al., *Fundamentals of Chemistry in the Laboratory*, Harper, 1977.

Langsjoen, Arne N., *Exercises in General, Organic, and Biological Chemistry*, Burgess, 1977.

Pease, Burton F., *Basic Instrumental Analysis*, Van Nostrand, 1980.

Reilley, Charles N., and Donald T. Sawyer, *Experiments for Instrumental Analysis*, Krieger, 1979.

White, John M., *Physical Chemistry Laboratory Experiments*, Prentice-Hall, 1975.

General references useful in several chapters, referred to hereafter by code numbers.

(1) DeKock, Roger L., et al., *Chemical Structure and Bonding*, Benjamin, 1980.

(2) Companion, Audrey L., *Chemical Bonding*, McGraw-Hill, 1979.

(3) Laidler, Keith J., *Physical Chemistry with Biological Applications*, Benjamin, 1978.

(4) HuHeey, James E., *Inorganic Chemistry: Principles of Structure and Reactivity*, Harper, 1978.

(5) Brown, William H., *Introduction to Organic Chemistry*, William Grant, 1975.

(6) Gutsche, C. David, and Daniel J. Pasto, *Fundamentals of Organic Chemistry*, Prentice-Hall, 1975.

(7) Shriner, Ralph L., et al., *The Systematic Identification of Organic Compounds*, Wiley, 1980.

(8) Tuma, Jan J., *Handbook of Physical Calculations*, McGraw-Hill, 1976.

(9) Trefil, James S., *From Atoms to Quarks*, Scribner's, 1980.

(10) Atkins, P. W., *Physical Chemistry*, Freeman, 1978.

(11) Harrison, Walter A., *Electronic Structure and the Properties of Solids*, Freeman, 1980.

(12) Solomons, T. W. G., *Organic Chemistry*, Wiley, 1978.

(13) Stumm, Werner, and James J. Morgan, *Aquatic Chemistry*, Wiley, 1981.

Chapter 1

Cantrell, Joseph S., "Solar Energy Concepts in the Teaching of Chemistry." *Journal of Chemical Education*, Vol. 55, No. 1 (January 1978), pp. 41-42.

Journal of Chemical Education Staff, "Energy Review." *Journal of Chemical Education*, Vol. 55, No. 4 (April 1978), pp. 263-264.

Schneider, Stephen H., and Richard L. Temkin, "Climatic Changes and Human Affairs," in *Climatic Change*, edited by John Gribben, Cambridge University Press, Cambridge, 1978.

Chapter 2

General Reference (8)

Dence, Joseph B., *Mathematical Techniques in Chemistry*, Wiley, 1975.

Chapter 4

Kolb, Doris, "The Chemical Formula." *Journal of Chemical Education*, Part I, Vol. 55, No. 1 (January 1978), pp. 44-47. Part II, Vol. 55, No. 2 (February 1978), pp. 109-112.

Chapter 6

Kolb, Doris, "The Chemical Equation." *Journal of Chemical Education*, Vol. 55, No. 3 (March 1978), pp. 184-189.

Chapter 8

General Reference (1), (2), and (10)

Brescia, Frank, "Negative Energies." *Journal of Chemical Education*, Vol. 53. No. 9 (September 1976), pp. 557-559.

Hänsch, Theodor W., "The Spectrum of Atomic Hydrogen." *Scientific American*, Vol. 240, No. 3 (March 1979), pp. 94-110.

Kleppner, Daniel, et al., "Highly Excited Atoms." *Scientific American*, Vol. 244, No. 5 (April 1981), pp. 130-149.

Kragh, Helge, "Chemical Aspects of Bohr's 1913 Theory." *Journal of Chemical Education*, Vol. 54, No. 4 (April 1977), pp. 208-210.

Chapter 9

General Reference (1), (2), (3), (4), and (10)

Christoudouleas, N. D., "Particles, Waves, and the Interpretation of Quantum Mechanics." *Journal of Chemical Education*, Vol. 52, No. 9 (September 1975), pp. 573-575.

Fano, Ugo, "Dynamics of Electron Excitation." *Physics Today*, Vol. 29, No. 9 (September 1976), pp. 32-41.

Goodisman, J., *Contemporary Quantum Chemistry*, Plenum, 1977.

Chapter 10

General Reference (4)

Chapter 11

General Reference (4)

Cotton, F. Albert, and Geoffrey Wilkinson, *Basic Inorganic Chemistry*, Wiley, 1976.

Chapter 12

General Reference (1), (2), (3), (4), and (11)

Chen, E. C. M., and W. E. Wentworth, "The Experimental Values of Atomic Electron Affinities." *Journal of Chemical Education*, Vol. 52, No. 8 (August 1975), pp. 486-489.

Goodisman, J., *Contemporary Quantum Chemistry*, Plenum, 1977.

Robinson, Edward A., and Ronald J. Gillespie, "Bent Bonds and Multiple Bonds." *Journal of Chemical Education*, Vol. 57, No. 5 (May 1980), pp. 329-333.

Chapter 13

General Reference (1), (3), (10), and (11)

Hoffman, D. K., et al., "A Novel Pictorial Approach to Teaching MO Concepts in Polyatomic Molecules." *Journal of Chemical Education*, Vol. 54, No. 10 (October 1977), pp. 590-595.

Liberles, Arno, "Delocalization." *Journal of Chemical Education*, Vol. 54, No. 8 (August 1977), pp. 479-482.

Robinson, Edward A., and Ronald J. Gillespie, "Bent Bonds and Multiple Bonds." *Journal of Chemical Education*, Vol. 57, No. 5 (May 1980), pp. 329-333.

Chapter 14

General Reference (1), (2), (4), (10), and (13)

Yoder, Claude H., "Teaching Ion-Ion, Ion-Dipole, and Dipole-Dipole Interactions." *Journal of Chemical Education*, Vol. 54, No. 7 (July 1977), pp. 402-408.

Chapter 15

General Reference (10)

Chapter 16

General Reference (1) and (11)

Adler, David, "Chemistry and Physics of Amorphous Semiconductors." *Journal of Chemical Education*, Vol. 57, No. 8 (August 1980), pp. 560-564.

Abrahams, Sidney C., and Jerome B. Cohen, "Role of Crystallography." *Physics Today*, Vol. 29, No. 11 (November 1976), pp. 34-42.

Cowley, John M., and Sumio Iijima, "Electron Microscopy of Atoms in Crystals." *Physics Today*, Vol. 30, No. 3 (March 1977), pp. 32-40.

Philipps, James C., "The Physics of Glass." *Physics Today*, Vol. 35, No. 2 (February 1982), pp. 27-33.

Rioux, Frank, "Simple Calculations of the Lattice Energy of Lithium Hydride." *Journal of Chemical Education*, Vol. 54, No. 9 (September 1977), pp. 555-556.

Chapter 17

General Reference (10)

Chapter 18

General Reference (10)

Chapter 20

General Reference (3), (10), and (13)

Hamori, Eugene, "Illustration of Free Energy Changes in Chemical Reactions." *Journal of Chemical Education*, Vol. 52, No. 6 (June 1975), pp. 370-373.

Redlich, Otto, "Entropy: A Modern Discussion." *Journal of Chemical Education*, Vol. 52, No. 6 (June 1975), pp. 374-376.

Chapter 21

General Reference (13)

Palombari, Roberto, "A Graphical Evaluation of the Solubility of Protolyzable Salts." *Journal of Chemical Education*, Vol. 54, No. 4 (April 1977), pp. 222-224.

Schrieffer, J. Robert, and Paul Soven, "Theory of the Electronic Structure." *Physics Today*, Vol. 28, No. 4 (April 1975), pp. 24-30.

Smith, Derek W., "Ionic Hydration Enthalpies." *Journal of Chemical Education*, Vol. 54, No. 9 (September 1977), pp. 540-542.

Chapter 22

Chang, Raymond, and Lawrence J. Kaplan, "The Donnan Equilibrium and Osmotic Pressure." *Journal of Chemical Education*, Vol. 54, No. 4 (April 1977), pp. 218-219.

Estrup, Peder J., "The Geometry of Surface Layers." *Physics Today*, Vol. 28, No. 4 (April 1975), pp. 33-41.

Tanaka, Toyoichi, "Gels." *Scientific American*, Vol. 244, No. 1 (January 1980), pp. 124-138.

Chapter 23

General Reference (3), (4), and (10)

Gibbard, H. Frank, and Michael R. Emptage, "Gas Phase Chemical Equilibria." *Journal of Chemical Education*, Vol. 53, No. 4 (April 1976), pp. 218-219.

Gilbert, H. F., "The 'Rule of Thumb' for Deriving Steady State Rate Equations." *Journal of Chemical Education*, Vol. 54, No. 8 (August 1977), pp. 492-493.

Lovett, G. H., "An Elementary View of Thermodynamics for Calculating Chemical Equilibria." *Journal of Chemical Education*, Vol. 53, No. 10 (October 1976), pp. 626-628.

Mickey, Charles D., "Chemical Equilibrium." *Journal of Chemical Education*, Vol. 57, No. 11 (November 1980), pp. 801-804.

Mickey, Charles D., "Chemical Kinetics: Reaction Rates." *Journal of Chemical Education*, Vol. 57, No. 9 (September 1980), pp. 659-663.

Treptow, Richard S., "Le Chatelier's Principle." *Journal of Chemical Education*, Vol. 57, No. 6 (June 1980), pp. 417-420.

Volk, L., et al., "Steady State and Equilibrium Approximations in Reaction Kinetics." *Journal of Chemical Education*, Vol. 54, No. 2 (February 1977), pp. 95-97.

Chapter 24
General Reference (4) and (13)

Lessley, Sim D., and Ronald O. Ragsdale, "Trends in the Acidities of Some Binary Hydrides in Aqueous Solution." *Journal of Chemical Education*, Vol. 53, No. 1 (January 1976), pp. 19-20.

Myers, R. Thomas, "The Strength of the Hydrohalic Acids." *Journal of Chemical Education*, Vol. 53, No. 1 (January 1976), pp. 17-19.

Pauling, Linus, "The Strength of the Hydrohalogenic Acids." *Journal of Chemical Education*, Vol. 53, No. 12 (December 1976), pp. 762-763.

Chapter 25

Burke, John D., "On Calculating $[H^+]$." *Journal of Chemical Education*, Vol. 53, No. 2 (February 1976), pp. 79-80.

Seymour, M. D., and Quintus Fernando, "Effect of Ionic Strength on Equilibrium Constants." *Journal of Chemical Education*, Vol. 54, No. 4 (April 1977), pp. 225-227.

Chapter 26
General Reference (10) and (13)

Kolb, Doris, "More on Balancing Redox Equations." *Journal of Chemical Education*, Vol. 56, No. 3 (March 1979), pp. 181-184.

Chapter 27
General Reference (3) and (10)

Bailey, D. N., et al., "On the Relationship between Cell Potential and Half-Cell Reactions." *Journal of Chemical Education*, Vol. 53, No. 2 (February 1976), pp. 77-78.

Burrows, Hugh D., "On the Relationship between Standard Electrode and Ionization Potentials of Metal Ions." *Journal of Chemical Education*, Vol. 53, No. 6 (June 1976), p. 365.

Friedel, A., and R. Murray, "Using Oxidation State Diagrams to Teach Thermodynamics and Inorganic Chemistry." *Journal of Chemical Education*, Vol. 54, No. 8 (August 1977), pp. 485-487.

Vincent, Colin A., "The Motion of Ions in Solution under the Influence of an Electric Field." *Journal of Chemical Education*, Vol. 53, No. 8 (August 1976), pp. 490-493.

Chapter 28
General Reference (3) and (9)

Georgi, Howard, "A Unified Theory of Elementary Particles and Forces." *Scientific American*, Vol. 224, No. 4 (April 1981), pp. 48-63.

Chapter 29
General Reference (5), (6), (7), and (12)

Chapter 30
General Reference (5), (6), (7), and (12)

STUDENT GENERAL REFERENCES

The following references should be accessible to students in the classroom or school library.

Himes, Gary K., et al., *Solving Problems in Chemistry*. Columbus, OH: Charles E. Merrill Publishing Co., 1983.

Strauss, Howard J., and Kaufman, Milton, *Handbook for Chemical Technicians*. New York: McGraw-Hill Book Co., 1976.

Magazines
DISCOVER
Time-Life Building
541 N. Fairbanks Court
Chicago, IL 60672

CHEMECOLOGY
Chemical Manufacturer's Association
2501 M St., NW
Washington, DC 20037

FDA CONSUMER
Superintendent of Documents
Government Printing Office
Washington, DC 20402

JOURNAL OF CHEMICAL EDUCATION
20th & Northampton Sts.
Easton, PA 18042

NATIONAL GEOGRAPHIC SOCIETY
1155 Sixteenth St., NW
Washington, DC 20036

OMNI
Omni Publications International Ltd.
909 Third Ave.
New York, NY 10022

PHYSICS TODAY
American Institute of Physics
S/F Division

335 East 45th St.
New York, NY 10017

POPULAR SCIENCE
Boulder, CO 80302

SCIENCE
American Association for the Advancement
of Science
1515 Massachusetts Ave., NW
Washington, DC 20005

SCIENCE DIGEST
P.O. Box 10076
Des Moines, IA 50350

SCIENCE NEWS
Science Service, Inc.

231 W. Center St.
Marion, OH 43302

SCIENCE 8
Subscription Department
Xerox Publications
Columbus, OH 43216

SCIENTIFIC AMERICAN
Scientific American Inc.
415 Madison Ave.
New York, NY 10017.

SCI QUEST
Circulation Manager
American Chemical Society
P.O. Box 2895
Washington, DC 20013

AUDIOVISUAL AIDS

Chapter 1
Ins and Outs of Energy, Learning Arts, Chemistry
#112, filmstrips/8 cassettes
Pollution: Problems and Prospects, National Geo-
graphic Society, #03244, 2 filmstrips
The Forms of Energy, Nova, #530-1724, filmstrips/
2 cassettes

Chapter 2
Basic Math for Science Students and Technicians,
Prentice-Hall, #WLC800FS, filmstrips/slides/10
cassettes
Density, Science Software Systems, #VCT-2, video-
cassette
Mathematical Techniques for Science Students,
Prentice-Hall, #WLC905FS, filmstrips/slides/3
cassettes
Metric System Tutor, Nova, #519-0500, computer
software (Apple)
Modern Measure: The SI Metric System, Prentice-
Hall, #WLC660, filmstrips/4 cassettes
Physics: Measurement of Scalars, Bergwall, #150,
filmstrips/4 cassettes
Stoichiometric Calculations, Prentice-Hall,
#WLC720FS, filmstrips/slides/4 cassettes

Chapter 3
All about Matter, Nova. #530-1710, filmstrips/4
cassettes

Chapter 4
Chemistry I Series, Science Software Systems,
#CI-2200, computer software (Apple)
Introduction to Chemical Nomenclature, Prentice-
Hall, #WLC840FS, filmstrips/slides/3 cassettes

Naming Chemical Substances, Prentice-Hall,
#WLC730FS, filmstrips/slides/2 cassettes
Symbols, Formulas, and Equations, Learning Arts,
Chemistry #101, filmstrips/4 cassettes

Chapter 5
Chemistry I Series, Science Software Systems,
#CI-2200, computer software (Apple)
Stoichiometric Calculations, Prentice-Hall,
#WLC720FS, filmstrips/slides/4 cassettes
Stoichiometry, Prentice-Hall, #WLC830FS, film-
strips/slides/4 cassettes
The Mole Concept, Inquiry Audio-Visuals, #67130,
filmstrip
Moles and Formulas, Carolina, #41-3532, computer
software (Apple)

Chapter 6
Balancing Chemical Equations, Prentice-Hall,
#WLC710FS, filmstrips/slides/4 cassettes
Chemical Equations, Carolina, #41-3542, computer
software (Apple)
Symbols, Formulas, and Equations, Learning Arts,
Chemistry #101, filmstrips/4 cassettes

Chapter 7
Chemical Equations, Carolina, #41-3542, computer
software (Apple)
Chemical Reaction Principles, Science Software
Systems, #480-0085, slides
Ins and Outs of Energy, Learning Arts, Chemistry
#112, filmstrips/8 cassettes
Moles and Formulas, Carolina, #41-3532, computer
software (Apple)

Stoichiometry, Prentice-Hall, #WLC830FS, film-strips/slides/4 cassettes

Chapter 8

Atomic Structure, Prentice-Hall, #WLC850FS, film-strips/slides/4 cassettes

Chemistry I Series, Science Software Systems, #CI-2200 computer software (Apple)

Definite Proportions: Electrolysis of Water, BFA Educational Media, #4B0672C, filmloop

Models of the Atom, Audio Visual Narrative Arts, Inc., #005C, filmstrips/5 cassettes

Spectroscopy, Modern Learning Aids, #140-4207, 16 mm film

The Atom: From Atomic Hypothesis to Atomic Fact, Audio Visual Narrative Arts, Inc., #441C, filmstrips/3 cassettes

Chapter 9

Atomic Structure, Prentice-Hall, #WLC850FS, filmstrips/slides/4 cassettes

Chemistry I Series, Science Software Systems, #CI-2200, computer software (Apple)

Electron Configurations, Science Software Systems, #VCT-4, videocassette

Electron Configurations and Orbital Diagrams, Science Software Systems, #475-0255, filmstrip/slides/cassette

Electron Structure, Carolina, #41-3812, computer software (Apple)

Light: The Wave That Wasn't—Quantum Theory, Audio Visual Narrative Arts, #425C, filmstrips/4 cassettes

Models of the Atom, Audio Visual Narrative Arts, #005C, filmstrips/5 cassettes

Particles and Waves—Quantum Theory, Audio Visual Narrative Arts, #429C, filmstrips/4 cassettes

Quantum Numbers, Science Software Systems, #VCT-5, videocassette

Chapter 10

Atomic Structure, Prentice-Hall, #WLC850FS, filmstrips/slides/4 cassettes

Quantum Numbers, Science Software Systems, #VCT-5, videocassette

Electron Structure, Carolina, #41-3812, computer software (Apple)

The Periodic Table, Science Software Systems, #480-0080, slides

The Periodic Table of the Elements, Prentice-Hall, #WLC740FS, filmstrips/slides/2 cassettes

Chapter 11

Chemical Elements, Science Software Systems, #480-0465F, #480-0475F, 7 filmstrips

Properties of the Elements, Kalmia, #7010, filmloop or 16 mm film

The Periodic Table, Science Software Systems, #480-0080, slides

The Periodic Table of the Elements, Prentice-Hall, #WLC740FS, filmstrips/slides/2 cassettes

Chapter 12

Bonding of Atoms, Learning Arts, Chemistry #104 series, 13 filmstrips

Chemical Bonding, Prentice-Hall, #WLC860FS, filmstrips/slides/5 cassettes

Forces in Solids, Liquids, and Gases, Learning Arts, Chemistry #109, filmstrips/5 cassettes

The Periodic Table, Science Software Systems, #480-0080, slides

Chapter 13

Bonding between Atoms of the Same Element: Nonmetals and the Covalent Bond, Science Software Systems, #475-0305, filmstrip/slides/cassette

Bonding of Atoms, Learning Arts, Chemistry #104 series, filmstrips/13 cassettes

Electron Configurations, Science Software Systems, #VCT-4, videocassette

Chapter 14

Bonding of Atoms, Learning Arts, Chemistry #104 series, filmstrips/13 cassettes

Chemical Bonding, Prentice-Hall, #WLC860FS, filmstrips/slides/5 cassettes

Coordination Compounds and Other Special Topics, Science Software Systems, #475-0245, filmstrip/slides/cassette

The Periodic Table, Science Software Systems, #480-0080, slides

Chapter 15

Properties of Gases, Learning Arts, Chemistry #106, filmstrips/6 cassettes

The States of Matter, CRM McGraw-Hill Films, #106656-X, 16 mm film

Chapter 16

Crystal Systems of Minerals, Science Software Systems, #480-0645, slides

Forces in Solids, Liquids, and Gases, Learning Arts, Chemistry #109, filmstrips/5 cassettes

Chapter 17

Forces in Solids, Liquids, and Gases, Learning Arts, Chemistry #109, filmstrips/5 cassettes

Vapor Pressure and Partial Pressure, Learning Arts, Chemistry #107, filmstrips/3 cassettes

Chapter 18

Gas Laws, Prentice-Hall, #WLC890FS, filmstrips/slides/4 cassettes

Properties of Gases, Learning Arts, Chemistry #106, filmstrips/6 cassettes

Vapor Pressure and Partial Pressure, Learning Arts, Chemistry #107, filmstrips/3 cassettes

Chapter 19
Chemistry I Series, Science Software Systems, #CI-2200, computer software (Apple)

Gaseous Volume and the Mole, Learning Arts, Chemistry #108, filmstrips/3 cassettes

Gas Laws, Prentice-Hall, #WLC890FS, filmstrips/slides/4 cassettes

Moles and Formulas, Carolina, #41-3532, computer software (Apple)

Properties of Gases, Learning Arts, Chemistry #106, filmstrips/6 cassettes

Stoichiometric Calculations, Prentice-Hall, #WLC720FS, filmstrips/slides/4 cassettes

Stoichiometry, Prentice-Hall, #WLC830FS, filmstrips/slides/4 cassettes

Chapter 20
Energy and Entropy in Chemical Reactions, Prentice-Hall, #WLC821, filmstrips/2 cassettes

Chapter 21
Looking at the Solution, Learning Arts, Chemistry #110 filmstrips/5 cassettes

Molarity of Solutions, Learning Arts, Chemistry #111, filmstrips/3 cassettes

Solution Problems, Prentice-Hall, #WLC895FS, filmstrips/slides/3 cassettes

Chapter 22
Looking at the Solution, Learning Arts, Chemistry #110, filmstrips/5 cassettes

Solution Problems, Prentice-Hall, #WLC895FS, filmstrips/slides/3 cassettes

Solution Process and Theory, Science Software Systems, #480-0485F, 3 filmstrips

Chapter 23
Chemical Equilibrium, Prentice-Hall, #WLC880FS, filmstrips/slides/8 cassettes

Chemical Reaction Principles, Science Software Systems, #480-0085, slides

Equilibrium: Le Chatelier's Principle, BFA Educational Media, #4B0678C, filmloop

Reaction Kinetics, Carolina, #41-4522, computer software (Apple)

Reaction Rates, BFA Educational Media, #4B0679C, filmloop

Reaction Rates: Molecules in Motion, Learning Arts, Chemistry #116, filmstrips/9 cassettes

Chapter 24
All about Acids and Bases, Nova, #530-1717, filmstrips/4 cassettes

Chemical Equilibrium, Prentice-Hall, #WLC880FS, filmstrips/slides/8 cassettes

Chapter 25
Acid Base Problems, Carolina, #41-3582, computer software (Apple)

All about Acids and Bases, Nova, #530-1717, filmstrips/4 cassettes

Chemical Equilibrium, Prentice-Hall, #WLC880FS, filmstrips/slides/8 cassettes

pH, pOH, and Buffers, Science Software Systems, #475-0340, filmstrip/slides/cassette

Solution Problems, Prentice-Hall, #WLC895FS, filmstrips/slides/3 cassettes

Chapter 26
Balancing Chemical Equations, Prentice-Hall, #WLC710FS, filmstrips/slides/4 cassettes

Oxidation Reduction, Carolina, #41-3552, computer software (Apple)

Oxidation-Reduction Reaction, Science Software Systems, #480-0460F, 4 filmstrips

Chapter 27
Chemical Reaction Principles, Science Software Systems, #480-0085, slides

Electrochemistry, Prentice-Hall, #WLC870FS, filmstrips/slides/4 cassettes

Galvanic Cells: Electrolytes and Electrodes, BFA Educational Media, #4B0675C, filmloop

Galvanic Cells: Half-Cell Reactions, BFA Educational Media, #4B0676C, filmloop

Oxidation-Reduction: Electrolytic Cells, BFA Educational Media, #4B0671C, filmloop

Chapter 28
Atomic Energy, Nova, #525-1615, 6 transparencies

Fermilab, Educational Audio Visuals Inc., #E1KF 1628, filmstrip/cassette

Nuclear Energy: Peril or Promise, Science and Mankind, #1-1051-2850, slides/cassette

Radioactivity, Prentice-Hall, #WLC855FS, filmstrips/slides/2 cassettes

Chapter 29
Nomenclature in Organic Chemistry, Prentice-Hall, #WLC9101, filmstrips/slides/3 cassettes

Organic Chemistry, Learning Arts, Chemistry #120, filmstrips/7 cassettes

Organic Chemistry, Nova, #519-0560, computer software (Apple)

Chapter 30
Organic Chemistry, Learning Arts, Chemistry #120, filmstrips/7 cassettes

Organic Chemistry, Nova, #519-0560, computer software (Apple)

Biochemistry, Nova, #519-0552, computer software (Apple)

AUDIOVISUAL SUPPLIERS

Audio Visual Narrative Arts, Inc.
Box 9
Pleasantville, NY 10570

Bergwall Productions Inc.
839 Stewart Ave.
Garden City, NY 11530

BFA Educational Media
2211 Michigan Ave.
Santa Monica, CA 90404

Carolina Biological
  Supply Company
2700 York Road
Burlington, NC 27215

CRM McGraw-Hill Films
110 Fifteenth St.
Del Mar, CA 92014

Educational Audio Visuals, Inc.
Pleasantville, NY 10570

Inquiry Audio-Visuals
1754 West Farragut Ave.
Chicago, IL 60640

Kalmia Company
Department C6
Concord, MA 01742

Learning Arts
P.O. Box 179
Wichita, KS 67201

Modern Learning Aids
Ward's Natural Science
  Establishment Inc.
P.O. Box 1712
Rochester, NY 14603

National Geographic Society
Educational Services
Washington, DC 20036

Nova Scientific Corporation
111 Tucker St.
P.O. Box 500
Burlington, NC 27215

Prentice-Hall Media
150 White Plains Rd.
Tarrytown, NY 10591

Science and Mankind Inc.
Communications Park
Box 2000
Mount Kisco, NY 10549

Science Software Systems Inc.
11899 West Pico Blvd.
West Los Angeles, CA 90064

PERFORMANCE OBJECTIVES

What Is a Good Performance Objective?

Statements of performance objectives can usually be divided into three distinct parts. First is a description of the conditions under which the desired behavior will be observed. Here are some examples which describe the condition:

"When presented with models of crystal structures. . . ."

"When asked to draw electron dot diagrams for . . ."

"When presented with the materials suggested on page. . . ."

"After having read and discussed. . . ."

"In groups of three students, given conductivity apparatus and several solutions. . . ."

A good performance objective includes a condition which tells what causes, stimulates, or motivates the student to perform the behaviors or under what circumstances those behaviors will be performed.

The second part of a well-stated performance objective is a clear description of exactly what behavior you're looking for. A good performance objective would avoid using such terms as "know about," "appreciate," or "sense the relationship between." Rather, a good performance objective will include terms which describe what you could observe students doing if they do "know about" or "appreciate." It's almost impossible to observe students "appreciating," but you can gather some evidence that they are appreciating science if they are:

reading science books instead of comic books;

staying late or coming to class early to work in the laboratory;

requesting that you repeat a demonstration or wanting to do it themselves;

In other words, a good performance objective uses verbs which express some type of observable action. Here are some examples of action verbs which describe observable behaviors:

states orally	manipulates
matches	measures
distinguishes between	expresses
constructs	observes
identifies	states hypotheses

The third part of a well-stated performance objective is a description of some level of performance or criteria which may help you to know if the student or class has performed to the degree which you hoped for.

For example, if you were teaching students to use a balance, would you want all of your class to be able to accurately measure the mass of a solid or liquid? Would you feel satisfied if 90% of your class could perform this skill? 80%? 50%? Would you be happy if just one student did it? Obviously, this level of performance would vary for each class, each student, each teacher, and each task.

What do we mean by accurately? Would you be satisfied if students could measure a mass to the nearest centigram? Half-centigram? Milligram? Just how accurately would be acceptable to you? Here then, is another aspect of a level of performance: A well-stated performance objective might also include some description of how precise, how accurate, how well the behavior should be performed in order for you to know that the student has really achieved the objective.

Another kind of a criterion measure or performance level which might be included in a performance objective is a statement of how often or how many times students must perform the behavior in order to demonstrate that they have learned something. For example, if a student measured a mass with a balance accurately just one time, would you conclude that the student has learned how to measure? What if you asked the student to measure the mass of 5 objects with a balance, and you were looking for the ability to measure them correctly to the nearest centigram? Would you be satisfied if the student measured four of them correctly? Three out of five? Or would you only be satisfied if the student measured all five of them correctly?

Again, this decision will have to be made on the basis of what you know about the student's ability, and the task at hand.

Now let's put all these parts together and see what a well-stated performance objective looks like.

Conditions—*tells you how to plan and organize your class and what materials you'll need*
Working individually, when presented with a laboratory balance, beaker, liquid, solid, and graduated cylinder, ...

Performance—*tells you what student behaviors to look for*
students will measure the masses of the liquid and solid to the nearest 0.01 g, measure the volume of liquid to the nearest 0.01 cm^3, measure the volume of the solid by liquid displacement. Students will be able to calculate the density of the solid and liquid to the correct number of significant digits.

Criterion Measure—*tells you to what degree the objective should be achieved*
Of all the students, 95% will achieve 100% of the above objectives.

How Do You Use the Performance Objectives in This Teacher's Guide?

Performance objectives are listed for each chapter of *CHEMISTRY: A MODERN COURSE.*

They are related to four broad goals of science education.

A **Attitudes:** To develop students' attitudes of curiosity and involvement with phenomena in their natural environment; to develop an appreciation for the contributions of science to daily living; and to develop the value and inclinations toward solving problems in a scientific manner.

P **Processes:** To develop those intellectual processes of inquiry by which scientific problems and phenomena are explained, predicted, and/or controlled.

K **Knowledge:** To develop knowledge of facts, terminology, concepts, generalizations, and principles which help students confront and interpret their environment.

S **Skills:** To develop students' ability to handle, construct, and manipulate materials and equipment in a productive and safe manner, and to develop their ability to measure, organize, and communicate scientific information.

Next to each performance objective you will find one or more of the following letters: A, P, K, S. They indicate the goal on which the objective is based—Attitudes, Processes, Knowledge, Skills. Keep in mind a balance among these four goals since they are all of equal priority.

Attitudes

The statements of performance objectives which are identified as ''A''—developing Attitude goals—are behaviors which you might observe as students increase their enjoyment of science activities, and as they demonstrate an interest in the scientific objects and events in their environment. You will find such statements as:

Students will request that the demonstration be repeated.

Students will volunteer to conduct outside research.

Students will request the use of the chemistry laboratory during free periods.

Students will volunteer to do research and report their findings in class.

As you can see, few of these behaviors are prompted by the teacher. They are voluntary behaviors which indicate an affinity for, an inclination toward, and a preference for science. You will find suggested attitudinal behaviors at the end of each area or chapter when students may have an opportunity to go beyond the information presented in the text.

Processes

The statements of performance objectives which are identified as ''P''—developing Process goals—are behaviors which you might observe as students use the thinking processes of analyzing, experimenting, applying, hypothesizing, theorizing, comparing and contrasting, classifying, observing, etc. You will find such statements as:

When presented with various objects, students will compare and contrast their similarities and differences and classify them as metallic or nonmetallic.

Given data from Appendix A, students will calculate the amount of heat needed to raise the temperature of 1000 kg of iron from 20°C to 1000°C.

Given a skeleton equation, students will balance a redox equation by the half-reaction method.

Knowledge

The statements of performance objectives which are identified as "K"—developing knowledge goals—are behaviors which you might observe as students demonstrate they have gained an understanding and use of certain terms, concepts, and generalizations of science. You will find such statements as:

When asked, students will define the term "ionization" correctly.

Students will correctly identify the triple point on a phase diagram.

Students will describe the effects of a catalyst on reaction rate.

Generally, a knowledge objective is one which calls upon the student to recall or explain information, concepts, or principles which have been learned in the past or which have been presented in the text and other materials.

Skills

The statements of performance objectives which are identified as "S"—developing Skills goals—are behaviors which you might observe as students gain skill in using scientific equipment correctly, and organizing, recording, or reporting information accurately. Some examples of such statements are:

Students will use a pipette to transfer a solution from one container to another.

While observing the demonstration, students will record their observations in their notebooks.

Using plastic spheres and toothpicks, students will construct models of crystal lattice types.

In the Teacher's Guide that follows, a specific statement of the goal for each chapter is given. A goal statement is also given at the beginning of each chapter in the student's text. Following the goal statement in the Teacher's Guide, the specific performance objectives for each section of the chapter are listed. There may be several objectives in each section. Each objective is numbered to correspond to that section of the chapter. For example, 22:5 is Chapter 22, Section 5. From these objectives you should be able to determine and plan for the achievement of the objectives for each section of a chapter.

Remember, these performance objectives are not meant to be all inclusive. You should supplement them with objectives from other sources and with those you create yourself.

You will also find that the criterion or level of performance for each objective is not included. The intent was to create guidelines and not to state levels of expectancies for you. Only you can decide if 100% or only 50% of your students should be able to accomplish each task. You will need to develop and insert these criterion levels for your own students based upon your materials, and your own situation.

How Do You Know You've Achieved Your Objectives?

When you try to find out if students have learned anything, you probably give some form of written test—true-false, completion, matching, or essay type of examination. All of these forms of evaluation are important in determining whether or not students have achieved their objectives. Evaluation materials are available to accompany *CHEMISTRY: A MODERN COURSE.* Each chapter test is based on the performance objectives in this Teacher's Guide.

Bibliography

Bloom, Benjamin, Hastings, J. Thomas, and Madaus, George, *Handbook on Formative and Summative Evaluation of Student Learning.* McGraw-Hill Book Co., New York, 1971.

Bloom, Benjamin and others, *Taxonomy of Educational Objectives, Handbook I: Cognitive Domain.* David McKay, New York, 1956.

Krathwohl, D. R., Bloom, Benjamin, and Masia, Bertram R., *Taxonomy of Educational Objectives, Handbook II: Affective Domain.* David McKay, New York, 1956.

Lindvall, C. M., ed., *Defining Educational Objectives.* University of Pittsburgh Press, Pittsburgh, 1964.

Mager, Robert, *Preparing Instructional Objectives.* Fearon Publishers, Inc., Palo Alto, Calif., 1962.

Popham, W. James, *The Teacher-Empiricist.* Aegeus Publishing Co., Los Angeles, 1965.

Popham, W. James, and Baker, Eva L., *Establishing Instructional Goals.* Prentice Hall, Inc., Englewood Cliffs, N.J., 1970.

NATURE, CHEMISTRY, AND YOU

1

An Overview

Chapter 1 demonstrates the relevance of chemistry to daily life. The chapter should leave the student with the realization that when voting on future scientific issues, the ballot must be cast after a detailed analysis of the facts. Chemistry will provide the student with the background needed to better understand the laws and relationships of the natural world. The first of these relationships is presented in chapter one, that of matter and energy ($E = mc^2$).

Demonstration Information

Before class prepare three solutions as follows: Dissolve 5 or 6 very small crystals of $KMnO_4$ in 500 cm^3 of water to make a pale wine-colored solution. Dissolve 1 g of $NaHSO_3$ in as little water as possible. Dissolve 1 g $BaCl_2 \cdot 2H_2O$ in a small amount of water. In class, pour the 500 cm^3 of "wine" ($KMnO_4$ soln) into a large beaker or flask. With stirring, add the $NaHSO_3$ solution. The "wine" changes into "water". Then with stirring, add the $BaCl_2$ solution. The "water" will change into "milk". Knowing the chemistry of this demonstration would be of little value to your students at this time. Your purpose should be to emphasize that the chemist has the experience to know how to change one substance into another with different properties.

Performance Objectives

Goal: Students will gain an understanding of the nature of chemistry through studying the relationship between science and human progress.

Objectives: Upon completion of the reading and problems, and when asked to demonstrate their understanding either orally or on a written test, students will

Intro.	P	list ways early civilizations have modified the environment for useful or destructive purposes.
1:1	P	list some major problems facing today's world.
1:2	P	differentiate between facts and value judgments.
1:3	K	define chemistry and state the role of chemists.
1:4	K	define matter in terms of the property of inertia.
1:5	K	differentiate among the three general forms of energy.
1:6	K/P	state the law of conservation of mass-energy and give examples of its application.
	A	exhibit an interest in science by completing voluntarily one or more of the One More Step activities at the end of the chapter.
	A	read unassigned literature related to the ideas presented in the chapter.

Teaching Techniques

Section 1:1

As you discuss the world's needs versus available space and resources, point out the role of chemists and research. Chemists are able to convert materials into substances that will be suitable substitutes for scarce resources.

Section 1:5

Discuss the necessity of including cost considerations in the decision making processes concerning energy alternatives. Have students bring in articles from the newspaper and magazines concerning alternative sources of power and the advantages and disadvantages of each. This approach reinforces the idea developed in Section 1:2 that applications of scientific knowledge involve considerations other than straight scientific facts. In considering alternate energy forms, the resource supply, economics, and values all play an important part.

A battery is an excellent example of chemical potential energy. If you connect one to a small electric motor, you can demonstrate the conversion to kinetic energy.

Be sure students understand the differences among kinetic, potential, and radiant energy. These terms will be used throughout the text in describing chemical behavior.

Chemical Career

Use this feature as the start of a year long project whereby students investigate the various branches and careers in chemistry. For example, you can assign reports on a weekly basis having a student report on biochemistry as a science and another student can focus on the duties of a biochemist. Appendix C—Careers can aid you in making these assignments. There are a number of popular science magazines available which highlight the branches of science and give personal insights into some of today's important scientists. Make arrangements to have these magazines made available to your students. A career bulletin board is another way of generating interest. Allow students to have an active part in putting the display together.

Chapter End Problems

Page 14.

1. potential, kinetic, electrical, mechanical, thermal, radiant

2. potential—energy due to position
   kinetic—energy due to motion
   mechanical—composed of potential and kinetic
   electric—energy due to electric charge in motion
   thermal—form of kinetic energy
   radiant—energy of electromagnetic wave
   sound—form of mechanical energy
   light, radio waves, etc.—all forms of radiant energy
   nuclear energy—energy due to the structure of the nucleus

3. agronomist—field crops and soil
   astronomer—stars, planets, other bodies of the universe
   biologist—living things
   botanist—plant life
   ecologist—living things and their environment
   entomologist—insects
   geochemist—chemical properties and changes in the earth's crust
   geologist—history of the earth's crust

geophysicist—physical properties of the earth's crust
horticulturalist—fruits, vegetables, decorative plants
limnologist—properties and conditions of fresh water areas
metallurgist—metals
meteorologist—weather
physicist—energy-matter relationships
zoologist—animal life

4. There are many that most students can name: pharmacist, doctor, farmer, foundry chemist, biologist. Accept what you wish.

5. Types of facts that may be mentioned: Should the lake be developed? How will it be developed? Will it harm the ecology of the area? What kind of development should it be: single homes, apartments, condominiums? This should produce much discussion regarding facts and value judgments.

One More Step

Page 15.

1. Nearly every student can list some of the more common industries. The list will vary with the community, but would include the chemical producing and consuming industries, institutions of higher education, government agencies, medical and pharmaceutical institutions.

2. Cockcroft and Walton bombarded ^7Li nuclei with protons and obtained two alpha particles as products. From the balancing of the mass-energy of the system before and after the change, the Einstein equivalence hypothesis was established.

3. Advantages—source of food and oil, source of employment
   Disadvantages—loss of several species of interest and beauty, upset ecological balance. See *Oceans*, Vol. 10, No. 4 (July-August 1977)

4. Advantages—source of power not dependent on dwindling oil supplies, does not pollute air
   Disadvantages—thermal pollution of cooling water source, radioactive waste disposal

5. See contemporary press reports and trial results. See also *NOAA* article in student readings.

MEASURING AND CALCULATING

2

An Overview

Chapter 2 reviews basic mathematical techniques and measuring principles which are important in problem solving and laboratory work. In addition, the factor-label method of problem solving is introduced and will be used throughout this book.

SI measurement units are used throughout the text with few exceptions. Regardless of trends in the United States, SI is being used to facilitate communication among scientists all over the world.

We encourage the use of calculators in high school chemistry. Stress to students that in chemistry they will begin to use, perhaps for the first time, the math skills they have learned over the years to solve practical, relevant problems. It is important that you approach measurement and calculations in a positive manner.

Performance Objectives

Goal: Students will gain knowledge and understanding of basic measurement and demonstrate proficiency in related calculations used by chemists.

Objectives: Upon completion of the reading and problems, and when asked to demonstrate their understanding either orally or on a written test, students will

Intro.	K	list the three requirements for making a measurement.
2:1	K	list the seven basic SI units.
2:2	K	state the difference between mass and weight.
2:3-5	K	list the standard and related measurements for length, time, and temperature.
2:6	K/S	combine SI units to form derived units used to express other quantities.
2:7	K/S	determine the number of significant digits for a given number or measurement.
2:8	P/S	determine the relative error of a measurement given its accuracy.
2:9	P/S	perform calculations using scientific notation.
2:10	P/S	demonstrate a logical approach to solving a problem.
2:11-12	P	use the factor-label method for solving numerical problems and SI conversions.
2:13	K/P/S	define density and perform calculations using the mathematical relationship among density, mass, and volume.
	A	exhibit an interest in science by completing voluntarily one or more of the One More Step activities at the end of the chapter.
	A	read unassigned literature related to the ideas presented in the chapter.

Teaching Techniques

Section 2:1

In using SI you will note many changes in the units and abbreviations in this book in comparison to older chemistry texts. All quantitative energy measurements (including heat) are expressed in joules (1 cal = 4.18 J). The degree symbol is not used in expressing kelvin temperatures. Pressure is measured in pascals and kilopascals. Commas are no longer used to group digits in long numbers. Rather a space is used instead to group digits in threes to the right and left of the decimal point. Teaching SI may require that you first familiarize yourself with the system. Supplemental materials can be obtained from the National Bureau of Standards and the American National Metric Council.

The seven base units are presented in this section to reinforce the simplicity of the system. Units which are combinations of these base units are covered later in the chapter. Emphasize that the changes do actually make learning chemistry less confusing by eliminating units having duplicate meaning.

Section 2:2

It is important to emphasize now and throughout the text that weight and mass are not the same. These terms will not be used interchangeably. Weight is rarely used in a chemistry laboratory. Students will probably notice many out of date materials which do not make this distinction. It is important that you as an educator set a good example.

Section 2:6

We are emphasizing the use of dm^3 and cm^3 for expressing volumes rather than mL and L. Liter and milliliter are not SI units. However, since they are in common use and part of the metric system they may appear in the text. Be sure students know the quantitative relationships among these units.

Section 2:7

It is important to develop the use of significant digits. Using a calculator or computer requires that students apply some rules in making calculations in order to obtain answers with reasonable numbers of digits. Calculated accuracy should at least resemble measured accuracy. There can be some disadvantages to being too strict in marking students' answers. They will encounter a number of new mathematical relationships throughout the course. It is important that they understand these relationships and can perform operations based on them. Being too critical of the number of digits in the answer can be frustrating for students. As a result of these limitations, we occasionally will express measurements as 20°C instead of 20.0°C, or 1000 cm^3 rather than

1000.0 cm^3. We maintain that it is more important to use realistic values rather than try to fill
the text with numbers.

Section 2:11

Using unfamiliar units in a problem will help
you evaluate students' mastery of the concept of
conversion factors and their use. For example,
1 wag = 12 zoom, 1000 warp = 1 bam, 3 zoom = 1
bam. Convert 8 wags to warps.

$$\frac{8 \text{ wag}}{} \left| \frac{12 \text{ zoom}}{1 \text{ wag}} \right| \frac{1 \text{ bam}}{3 \text{ zoom}} \left| \frac{1000 \text{ warp}}{1 \text{ bam}} \right. = \frac{32\,000}{\text{warp}}$$

Note the fraction bar used above is used in problem
set-ups throughout the text. It is a convenient way
to organize information and allows students to
manipulate units without having to memorize a
number of mathematical equations. Though it may
be difficult to use at first, in the long run it en-
courages a real understanding of how an answer is
obtained. You should also note that students will
show their work more neatly on tests, lab reports
and homework.

Section 2:12

Students commonly have trouble setting up
chemical problems. They must decide which math
operations to perform. They must analyze the
units. The best way to handle these questions is
to use a systematic approach; the factor-label
method. The biggest advantage to be gained from
this method is that the math operations needed to
convert a measurement from one set of units to
another are clearly indicated by the units of the
answer sought. In chemistry, units are carried
along with nearly every number used. Stress to
students that units are handled in division and
multiplication as though they are numbers.

Chemical Career

Emphasize the distinction between a career in
engineering versus science. Engineering is related
to technology and the use of scientific knowledge
for practical purposes. Other fields of engineering
(biomedical, mechanical, nuclear, and so on) also
involve a knowledge of chemistry. You can assign
reports concerning these careers.

Problem Solutions

Page 23.

1. $\dfrac{3.46 \text{ cg}}{} \left| \dfrac{1 \text{ g}}{100 \text{ cg}} \right| \dfrac{1000 \text{ mg}}{1 \text{ g}} = 34.6 \text{ mg}$

2. $\dfrac{1.00 \text{ km}}{} \left| \dfrac{1000 \text{ m}}{1 \text{ km}} \right| \dfrac{100 \text{ cm}}{1 \text{ m}} = 1.00 \times 10^5 \text{ cm}$

3. $\dfrac{91.6 \text{ ps}}{} \left| \dfrac{1 \text{ s}}{10^{12} \text{ ps}} \right. = 9.16 \times 10^{-11} \text{ s}$

4. $\dfrac{247 \text{ mg}}{} \left| \dfrac{1 \text{ g}}{1000 \text{ mg}} \right. = 0.247 \text{ g}$

5. $\dfrac{1.71 \text{ nm}}{} \left| \dfrac{1 \text{ m}}{10^9 \text{ nm}} \right| \dfrac{100 \text{ cm}}{1 \text{ m}} = 1.71 \times 10^{-7} \text{ cm}$

6. $\dfrac{405 \text{ mL}}{} \left| \dfrac{1000 \text{ cm}^3}{1000 \text{ mL}} \right. = 405 \text{ cm}^3$

7. $\dfrac{750 \text{ cm}^3}{} \left| \dfrac{1 \text{ dm}^3}{1000 \text{ cm}^3} \right. = 0.750 \text{ dm}^3$

8. $\dfrac{25.0 \text{ m}^2}{} \left| \dfrac{10\,000 \text{ cm}^2}{1 \text{ m}^2} \right. = 2.50 \times 10^5 \text{ cm}^2$

9. $\dfrac{35.5 \text{ mL}}{} \left| \dfrac{1 \text{ dm}^3}{1000 \text{ mL}} \right. = 0.0355 \text{ dm}^3$

10. $\dfrac{5.00 \text{ km}}{\text{h}} \left| \dfrac{1 \text{ h}}{3600 \text{ s}} \right| \dfrac{1000 \text{ m}}{1 \text{ km}} = 1.39 \text{ m/s}$

Page 25.

11. a. 4   d. 2   g. 2   j. 1
    b. 3   e. 3   h. 2
    c. 4   f. 2   i. 1

Page 26.

12. $\dfrac{0.1}{12.7} = 0.008$

13. $\dfrac{1}{50} = 0.02$

14. $\dfrac{0.0001}{236.0490} = 4 \times 10^{-7}$

Page 29.

15. a. 0.211
    b. 2.2×10^6
    c. 3400
    d. 0.2287
    e. 2800
    f. 0.0944
    g. 303
    h. 4.56

16. a. 5.53×10^5
    b. 8.65×10^3
    c. 5.23×10^{18}
    d. 26.0
    e. 169
    f. 166
    g. 1240
    h. 10.5
    i. 2.42×10^{-4}
    j. 1.07×10^4

Page 32.

17. a. $\dfrac{8.00 \text{ h}}{} \left| \dfrac{60 \text{ min}}{1 \text{ h}} \right| \dfrac{60 \text{ s}}{1 \text{ min}} = 2.88 \times 10^4 \text{ s}$

    b. $\dfrac{0.0200 \text{ m}}{} \left| \dfrac{100 \text{ cm}}{1 \text{ m}} \right. = 2.00 \text{ cm}$

c. $\dfrac{1.42\ \text{cm}^3}{}\ \Bigg|\ \dfrac{1\ \text{dm}^3}{1000\ \text{cm}^3} = 0.00142\ \text{dm}^3$

d. $\dfrac{51.2\ \text{mg}}{}\ \Bigg|\ \dfrac{1\ \text{g}}{1000\ \text{mg}} = 0.0512\ \text{g}$

e. $\dfrac{0.492\ \text{dm}^3}{}\ \Bigg|\ \dfrac{1000\ \text{cm}^3}{1\ \text{dm}^3} = 492\ \text{cm}^3$

Page 33.

18. a. $\dfrac{24.0\ \text{mg}}{}\ \Bigg|\ \dfrac{1\ \text{g}}{1000\ \text{mg}}\ \Bigg|\ \dfrac{1\ \text{kg}}{1000\ \text{g}} = 2.40 \times 10^{-5}\ \text{kg}$

b. $\dfrac{8.60\ \text{mg}}{}\ \Bigg|\ \dfrac{1\ \text{g}}{1000\ \text{mg}} = 8.60 \times 10^{-2}\ \text{g}$

c. $\dfrac{201\ \text{dm}^3}{}\ \Bigg|\ \dfrac{1\ \text{L}}{1\ \text{dm}^3} = 201\ \text{L}$

d. $\dfrac{88.7\ \text{cm}^3}{}\ \Bigg|\ \dfrac{(1\ \text{m})^3}{(100\ \text{cm})^3} = 8.87 \times 10^{-5}\ \text{m}^3$

e. $\dfrac{68.8\ \text{m}^3}{}\ \Bigg|\ \dfrac{(10)^3\ \text{dm}^3}{1\ \text{m}^3} = 68\ 800\ \text{dm}^3$

f. $\dfrac{6.4\ \text{nm}}{}\ \Bigg|\ \dfrac{1\ \text{m}}{1 \times 10^9\ \text{nm}}\ \Bigg|\ \dfrac{100\ \text{cm}}{1\ \text{m}}$
$= 6.4 \times 10^{-7}\ \text{cm}$

g. $\dfrac{0.279\ \text{mm}}{}\ \Bigg|\ \dfrac{1\ \text{cm}}{10\ \text{mm}} = 0.0279\ \text{cm}$

h. $\dfrac{7.64\ \text{kg}}{}\ \Bigg|\ \dfrac{1000\ \text{g}}{1\ \text{kg}} = 7640\ \text{g}$

i. $\dfrac{0.0492\ \text{g}}{}\ \Bigg|\ \dfrac{1000\ \text{mg}}{1\ \text{g}} = 49.2\ \text{mg}$

j. $\dfrac{8.00\ \text{dm}^3}{}\ \Bigg|\ \dfrac{1000\ \text{cm}^3}{1\ \text{dm}^3} = 8.00 \times 10^3\ \text{cm}^3$

k. $\dfrac{800\ \text{dm}^3}{}\ \Bigg|\ \dfrac{1\ \text{m}^3}{(10)^3\ \text{dm}^3} = 0.8\ \text{m}^3$

l. $\dfrac{2.80\ \text{h}}{}\ \Bigg|\ \dfrac{60\ \text{min}}{1\ \text{h}}\ \Bigg|\ \dfrac{60\ \text{s}}{1\ \text{min}} = 1.01 \times 10^4\ \text{s}$

Pages 36–37.

19. $D = \dfrac{m}{V} = \dfrac{8.76\ \text{g}}{3.07\ \text{cm}^3} = 2.85\ \text{g/cm}^3$

20. $D = \dfrac{m}{V} = \dfrac{0.650\ \text{g}}{2.71\ \text{cm}^3} = 0.240\ \text{g/cm}^3$

21. $m = DV = \dfrac{2.72\ \text{g}}{\text{cm}^3}\ \Bigg|\ 981\ \text{cm}^3 = 2670\ \text{g}$

22. $\dfrac{1.84\ \text{g}}{1\ \text{cm}^3}\ \Bigg|\ 6.96\ \text{cm}^3 = 12.8\ \text{g}$

23. $\dfrac{2.74\ \text{g}}{1\ \text{cm}^3}\ \Bigg|\ 610\ \text{cm}^3 = 1670\ \text{g}$

24. $\dfrac{6.32\ \text{g}}{1\ \text{cm}^3}\ \Bigg|\ 66.6\ \text{cm}^3 = 421\ \text{g}$

25. $\dfrac{3.37\ \text{g}}{}\ \Bigg|\ \dfrac{1\ \text{cm}^3}{2.15\ \text{g}} = 1.57\ \text{cm}^3$

26. $\dfrac{706\ \text{g}}{}\ \Bigg|\ \dfrac{1\ \text{cm}^3}{3.17\ \text{g}} = 223\ \text{cm}^3$

27. $\dfrac{13.4\ \text{g}}{}\ \Bigg|\ \dfrac{1\ \text{cm}^3}{5.50\ \text{g}} = 2.44\ \text{cm}^3$

Chapter End Problems
Page 39–41.

28. meter, kilogram, second, ampere, kelvin, mole, candela

29. Values for weight are subject to gravitational force. The mass of a substance is constant regardless of gravitational force.

30. Celsius temperature is defined by the freezing point of water as 0°C and the boiling point of water as 100°C.

31. the kilogram

32. A calculated answer cannot be any more accurate than the accuracy of the measurements used in the calculation.

33. a. 1
    b. 2
    c. 6
    d. 8

34. a. $\dfrac{0.1}{41.3} \times 100 = 0.2\%$

    b. $\dfrac{0.1}{67.9} \times 100 = 0.1\%$

    c. $\dfrac{0.0001}{0.0961} \times 100 = 0.1\%$

35. a. 3.68×10^1
    b. 3.87×10^{-2}
    c. 9.86963×10^7
    d. 5.1683×10^{11}

36. a. 0.009 14
    b. 0.000 035 0
    c. 952 000
    d. 46.6

37. a. 1.03×10^6
    b. 2.17×10^{-5}
    c. 3.8×10^{-1}
    d. 1.7×10^{-2}

38. a. 2
    b. 1
    c. 2
    d. 2

39. a. 52 (nearest whole number)
    b. 0.9 (nearest tenth)
    c. 156 (nearest whole number)
    d. 10 (nearest whole number)
    e. 2 (nearest whole number)

40. a. $V = lwh$
    $= 2.00 \times 2.00 \times 9.00 = 36.0\ \text{cm}^3$
    $\dfrac{108\ \text{g}}{36.0\ \text{cm}^3} = 3.00\ \text{g/cm}^3$

    b. $V = lwh$
    $= 5.00 \times 10.0 \times 23.0 = 1150\ \text{cm}^3$
    $\dfrac{3.22\ \text{kg}}{1150\ \text{cm}^3}\ \Bigg|\ \dfrac{1000\ \text{g}}{1\ \text{kg}} = 2.80\ \text{g/cm}^3$

c. $\dfrac{6120 \text{ g}}{9 \text{ L}} \Bigg| \dfrac{1 \text{ L}}{1000 \text{ cm}^3} = 0.680 \text{ g/cm}^3$

d. $\dfrac{2.06 \text{ kg}}{2.00 \text{ L}} \Bigg| \dfrac{1000 \text{ g}}{1 \text{ kg}} \Bigg| \dfrac{1 \text{ L}}{1000 \text{ cm}^3} = 1.03 \text{ g/cm}^3$

e. $V = lwh$
$= 23.0 \times 15.0 \times 15.5 = 5350 \text{ cm}^3$

$\dfrac{10.22 \text{ kg}}{5350 \text{ cm}^3} \Bigg| \dfrac{1000 \text{ g}}{1 \text{ kg}} = 1.91 \text{ g/cm}^3$

f. $\dfrac{411 \text{ g}}{384 \text{ cm}^3} = 1.07 \text{ g/cm}^3$

g. $\dfrac{233 \text{ g}}{97.0 \text{ cm}^3} = 2.40 \text{ g/cm}^3$

h. $\dfrac{535 \text{ g}}{62.3 \text{ cm}^3} = 8.59 \text{ g/cm}^3$

i. $\dfrac{49.2 \text{ g}}{27.3 \text{ cm}^3} = 1.80 \text{ g/cm}^3$

j. $\dfrac{171 \text{ g}}{1320 \text{ cm}^3} = 0.130 \text{ g/cm}^3$

k. $\dfrac{3.19 \text{ g}}{4.56 \text{ cm}^3} = 0.700 \text{ g/cm}^3$

l. $\dfrac{6.36 \text{ g}}{2.65 \text{ cm}^3} = 2.40 \text{ g/cm}^3$

m. $\dfrac{272 \text{ g}}{312 \text{ cm}^3} = 0.872 \text{ g/cm}^3$

41. $\dfrac{1590 \text{ kg}}{\text{m}^3} \Bigg| \dfrac{1000 \text{ g}}{1 \text{ kg}} \Bigg| \dfrac{\text{m}^3}{(100 \text{ cm})^3} = 1.59 \text{ g/cm}^3$

42. $\dfrac{30.0 \text{ km}}{1 \text{ h}} \Bigg| \dfrac{1000 \text{ m}}{1 \text{ km}} \Bigg| \dfrac{100 \text{ cm}}{\text{m}} \Bigg| \dfrac{1 \text{ h}}{60 \text{ min}} \Bigg| \dfrac{1 \text{ min}}{60 \text{ s}}$
$= 833 \text{ cm/s}$

43. $\dfrac{1.25 \text{ g}}{1 \text{ L}} \Bigg| \dfrac{1 \text{ L}}{1000 \text{ cm}^3} \Bigg| \dfrac{(100 \text{ cm})^3}{1 \text{ m}^3} \Bigg| \dfrac{1.00 \text{ m}^3}{}$
$= 1250 \text{ g}$

44. $\dfrac{9.80 \text{ g}}{1 \text{ cm}^3} \Bigg| \dfrac{9.40 \text{ cm}^3}{} = 92.1 \text{ g}$

45. $\dfrac{1 \text{ cm}^3}{7.87 \text{ g}} \Bigg| \dfrac{10 \text{ g}}{} = 1.27 \text{ cm}^3$

46. $\dfrac{1.2 \times 10^9 \text{ kg}}{1.0 \text{ km}^3} \Bigg| \dfrac{1000 \text{ g}}{1 \text{ kg}} \Bigg| \dfrac{1 \text{ km}^3}{(10^3 \text{ m})^3} \Bigg| \dfrac{1 \text{ m}^3}{(10^2 \text{ cm})^3}$
$= 1.2 \times 10^{-3} \text{ g/cm}^3$

47. $\dfrac{6.70 \text{ g}}{1 \text{ cm}^3} \Bigg| \dfrac{7.69 \text{ cm}^3}{} = 51.5 \text{ g}$

48. $\dfrac{19.3 \text{ g}}{1 \text{ cm}^3} \Bigg| \dfrac{0.402 \text{ cm}^3}{} = 7.76 \text{ g}$

49. $\dfrac{50.5 \text{ g}}{} \Bigg| \dfrac{1 \text{ cm}^3}{1.74 \text{ g}} = 29.0 \text{ cm}^3$

50. $\dfrac{7.57 \text{ kg}}{} \Bigg| \dfrac{1000 \text{ g}}{1 \text{ kg}} \Bigg| \dfrac{1 \text{ cm}^3}{7.28 \text{ g}} = 1040 \text{ cm}^3$

Review

Page 41.

1. To provide the facts as a basis for the application of value judgments.

2. kinetic and potential

3. To understand the structure and properties of matter sufficiently well to make predictions about unexamined substances.

4. Mass and energy are always conserved and their sum cannot be increased or decreased.

One More Step

Page 41.

1. Thermocouple: Measures the potential difference across the junction of two dissimilar metals in contact
Optical pyrometer: Measures temperature by determining the wavelength of the radiation given off by a glowing object
Thermister: An electric device whose resistance varies with temperature
Advantages—All three of the above devices can measure temperatures higher and lower than mercury thermometers. The thermister and thermocouple are small and compact.
Disadvantages—All three of the above devices must be carefully calibrated. The optical pyrometer can measure extremely high temperatures but it is not as accurate. In order to use the thermister and thermocouple, one must understand the mathematical and physical relationships involved.

2. $\text{viscosity} = \dfrac{\text{mass}}{\text{length} \times \text{time}}$

$\text{power} = \dfrac{\text{mass} \times \text{length}^2}{\text{time}^3}$

$\text{torque} = \dfrac{\text{mass} \times \text{length}^2}{\text{time}^2}$

$\text{rate of heat transfer} = \dfrac{\text{heat}}{\text{time}}$
$= \dfrac{\text{mass} \times \text{length}^2}{\text{time}^3}$

3. A computer is basically a series of "off-on" switches. Most high speed computers operate on the *binary system* which contains only two symbols, 0 and 1. It is possible to construct all of the integers (1, 2, 3, ...) using only these two symbols and the off and on positions of a series of switches or lights as follows:

decimal number	computer panel	binary number
0		
1	X	1
2	X	10
3	XX	11
4	X	100
5	X X	101
6	XX	110
7	XXX	111
8	X	1000
9	X X	1001
etc.		

Such a computer performs all mathematical operations by either adding or subtracting over and over in rapid succession in a manner determined by its program. For instance, 4 would be divided by 2 by adding two's until the sum was four and recording the number of times the number was added.

$$\frac{4}{2} = 2 + 2 = 2 \text{ additions}$$

$$\frac{8}{2} = 2 + 2 + 2 + 2 = 4 \text{ additions}$$

For more information, see *Algebra One* and *Two* by Foster, Rath, and Winters, Columbus, Ohio, Charles E. Merrill Publishing Co., 1983. *Algebra One* pp. 237, 243. *Algebra Two* pp. 550–551.

4. Calculators which round off properly are almost always more expensive than calculators which simply eliminate all digits after the display.

MATTER   3

An Overview

Chapter 3 outlines one basic classification system for matter. Keep in mind that this classification is intended to organize matter into categories for students. Several concepts mentioned in Chapter 3 are developed fully later in the text. For example, Chapter 17 covers change of state in more depth. Try not to anticipate the material in later chapters by going into too much detail in Chapter 3. Many new terms are introduced that students will use throughout the course. You may want to remind students that an understanding of chemical concepts involves the ability to use the vocabulary.

Demonstration Information

The chapter opening demonstration makes the student aware that a special vocabulary is used by scientists to describe a system and its surroundings. Use the demonstration to introduce such terms as: heterogeneous material (ore), phase (H_2O), interface (oil-H_2O), homogeneous material (PbO), solution, solute, solvent, substance.

Performance Objectives

Goal: Students will gain an understanding of the ways in which matter is classified and of the changes it undergoes.

Objectives: Upon completion of the reading and problems, and when asked to demonstrate their understanding either orally or on a written test, students will

3:1-2	K	distinguish between heterogeneous and homogeneous materials.
3:3	K	differentiate between elements and compounds.
3:4	P	list examples of extensive and intensive properties.
3:5-7	K	differentiate between physical and chemical changes.
3:5	P	explain the physical separation of a mixture.
3:5-7	P	list examples of physical and chemical changes.
	A	voluntarily complete one or more of the One More Step activities.
	A	read unassigned literature related to the chapter.

Teaching Techniques

Section 3:3

The terms atom, element, and compound are introduced but not defined precisely. Emphasize the particle nature of each of these substances. This section is the basis for proposing the presence of atoms in all matter. The proof of atomic theory will be presented in Chapter 8. Show some elements that are available in your stockroom such as C, Zn, Pb, Cu, Na, and Br_2. Use these substances to begin the discussions of physical properties (3:4) and physical changes (3:5).

Show the class some compounds such as baking soda, epsom salts, water, sugar, and alcohol. Avoid mixtures, minerals, and polymers as these are not good examples. Name the compounds, but do not give the formulas yet unless the class asks for them. Use these substances to begin the discussion of chemical properties (3:6) and chemical changes (3:7).

Section 3:4

Show students a piece of colored paper. Ask them about its length, mass, color, hardness, density, and conductivity. Is it malleable or ductile? These questions require a thorough understanding of some new terms. Begin Section 3:5 by tearing the paper into small pieces.

Section 3:5

Using the torn paper, ask students which properties have changed and which have remained the same. Now group these properties into extensive and intensive properties. Emphasize that changing the size of the pieces is a physical change. Relate this concept to dissolving as a physical change.

Section 3:7

Burn a piece of colored paper over the sink. Have students examine the ash and compare the properties before and after the reaction.

Chemical Career

You can use this feature to begin a project concerning food values and food labels. Food labels can be used to begin discussions of formulas in Chapter 4, and energy values in Chapter 7. Students should be more aware of the importance of chemistry to the food industry. The subject of food additives has received much bad publicity. However, ask students to consider the lack of nutritional value of many foods if they were not supplemented. Ask them to consider how without preservatives a decreased shelf life would affect the cost and availability of many foods.

Problem Solutions

Page 48.

1. **a.** solution (Gases in gases are homogeneous solutions rather than heterogeneous mixtures)
   b. heterogeneous mixture
   c. heterogeneous mixture
   d. compound
   e. compound
   f. heterogeneous mixture
   g. heterogeneous mixture (When homogenized, milk is an emulsion—a colloid.)
   h. element
   i. compound

2. **a.** inspection of "grain"
   b. see bubbles
   c. examine under a microscope
   d. see vessels
   e. evaporate liquid
   For all of these there is the possibility that the process of examination causes some chemical change, particularly in e. However, admission of this does not destroy the usefulness of the concept.

Page 52.

3. **a.** 38 g   **c.** 46 g
   b. 230 g   **d.** 95 g

Page 54.

4. **a.** physical   **g.** physical
   b. chemical   **h.** physical
   c. chemical   **i.** physical
   d. physical   **j.** physical
   e. physical   **k.** chemical
   f. chemical   **l.** chemical

5. **a.** chemical   **c.** chemical
   b. chemical   **d.** physical

6. **a.** chemical   **d.** physical
   b. physical   **e.** physical
   c. chemical

7. Some examples—carbonated beverages, noncarbonated beverages, wash water for clothes and dishes, saltwater solutions used for cooking vegetables and pasta, ammonia, cleaning fluids, paint thinner, air deodorizers.

8. Most cooking procedures (particularly baking), photography, explosives exploding, gasoline engine burning gasoline, any action of the body, and a dry cell or a battery discharging.

9. See the appropriate handbook.

Chapter End Problems

Pages 56–57.

10. **a.** heterogeneous mixture **d.** heterogeneous mixture
    b. compound   **e.** solution
    c. heterogeneous mixture **f.** element

11. **a.** chemical   **d.** physical
    b. physical   **e.** chemical
    c. physical   **f.** chemical

12. Suggested list of phases—soda, ice cream, cherry, straw, spoon, glass, CO_2, air, cream.
    Suggested list of interfaces—soda-glass, soda-ice cream, soda-straw, soda-spoon, soda-gas (two: in cream and "fizz"), ice cream-cream, ice cream-glass, ice cream-straw, ice cream-spoon, ice cream-gas (2), cream-gas, cream-cherry, cherry gas.

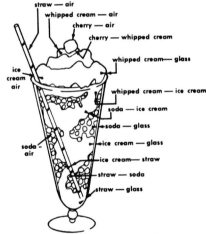

13. **a.** physical
    b. physical
    c. physical

Review

Page 57.

1. **a.** $\dfrac{2.84 \ \text{kg}}{} \left| \dfrac{1000 \ \text{g}}{1 \ \text{kg}} \right. = 2840 \ \text{g}$

   b. $\dfrac{544 \ \text{ms}}{} \left| \dfrac{1 \ \text{s}}{1000 \ \text{ms}} \right. = 0.544 \ \text{s}$

c. $\dfrac{0.0656 \cancel{g} \mid 1000 \text{ mg}}{1 \cancel{g}} = 65.6 \text{ mg}$

d. $\dfrac{1102 \cancel{cm} \mid 1 \text{ m}}{100 \cancel{cm}} = 11.02 \text{ m}$

e. $\dfrac{0.220 \cancel{g} \mid 1000 \text{ mg}}{1 \cancel{g}} = 220 \text{ mg}$

f. $\dfrac{3.6 \cancel{nm} \mid 1 \cancel{m} \mid 100 \text{ cm}}{1 \times 10^9 \cancel{nm} \mid 1 \cancel{m}}$

$= 3.6 \times 10^{-7} \text{ cm}$

2. a. $\dfrac{42.0 \text{ g}}{19.1 \text{ cm}^3} = 2.20 \text{ g/cm}^3$

b. $\dfrac{8.17 \text{ g}}{34.0 \text{ cm}^3} = 0.240 \text{ g/cm}^3$

c. $\dfrac{6120 \text{ g}}{5100 \text{ cm}^3} = 1.20 \text{ g/cm}^3$

d. $\dfrac{201 \text{ g}}{165 \text{ cm}^3} = 1.22 \text{ g/cm}^3$

e. $\dfrac{381 \text{ g}}{438 \text{ cm}^3} = 0.870 \text{ g/cm}^3$

3. mass—amount of matter, kilogram, balance
length—distance between two points, meter, meter stick
time—interval between two occurrences, second, clock
temperature—intensity of heat energy, kelvin, thermometer

4. inertia

5. 6

6. $\dfrac{0.002}{101.476} = 1.97 \times 10^{-5}$

One More Step
Page 57.

1. Action of salt water on bacteria is physical. Too high a concentration of salt causes the cells to lose water from their cytoplasm and to dry up. Too low a concentration of salt causes the cells to absorb water and to "explode."

2. Dissolve salt in water, filter, wash, dry copper in filter paper, evaporate filtrate.

3. There are several ways to convert oil shale to crude oil. One way involves preparation and retorting. Preparation involves breaking the shale into correct size pieces by crushing and screening. Primary crushing is with jaw crushers and gyratory crushers; secondary crushing is by roll crusher. One kind of retort procedure subjects shale to high pressure steam which vaporizes the oil. The steam also extracts ammonia and nitrogen gases as well as naphtha. The vapors are scrubbed to separate the crude oil vapor from the ammonia, naphtha, and other gases. Then the crude oil is refined.

4. Processes in use include solar distillation, conventional evaporators, flash evaporation, electrodialysis, vapor compression, reverse osmosis, and freezing.

5. Mineral: A naturally occurring crystalline substance with a definite small range in chemical composition and physical properties.
Rock: A natural aggregate of one or more minerals.

CHEMICAL FORMULAS   4

An Overview

Chemical symbols and oxidation numbers are presented in this chapter. These tools allow students to successfully write chemical formulas. We will not consider bonding or atomic structure at this time. Our purpose is to give students a working vocabulary as soon as possible in the course. This approach enables students to function in lab at an earlier stage. It also keeps the abstract topics of structure and bonding for a later period in the course when students are better able to handle them.

The chapter is short in that formula writing is a necessary skill that may require time to master. We recommend some memorization to give students greater confidence and success.

The quantitative aspects of formulas will be covered in Chapter 5. Chemical equations will be covered in Chapter 6. Do not rush students into equations if they have not mastered formula writing.

Demonstration Information

The reaction is dramatic and attracts students' attention. **CAUTION:** Good ventilation is a must in that a fair amount of poisonous fumes will be produced as a result of the reaction

$$Zn + I_2 \rightarrow ZnI_2$$

Have students turn to Table 4-3 in the text and ask them to predict the formula for zinc iodide. Use this demonstration to show students the need for a shorthand way to represent a chemical compound.

Performance Objectives

Goal: Students will learn to write formulas for and name chemical compounds.

Objectives: Upon completion of the reading and problems, and when asked to demonstrate their understanding either orally or on a written test, students will

4:1	K	list the symbols for common elements highlighted on Table 4-1.
4:2	K	differentiate between formulas and symbols.
4:3	P/S	write formulas for chemical compounds using oxidation numbers.
4:4	P	name compounds from given chemical formulas.
4:5	K/P	differentiate between molecular and empirical formulas.
4:6	K	define a formula unit.
	A	voluntarily complete one or more of the One More Step activities.
	A	read unassigned literature related to the chapter.

Teaching Techniques

Section 4:1

Point out that no rules have been followed in naming the elements. Some elements have names based on Latin or Greek roots. Silicon is named for the Latin word *silex* meaning flint. Some are named for geographic locations. Holmium (Stockholm), ytterium (Ytterby, Sweden), rhenium (Rhine river, Germany), and strontium (Strontian, Scotland) are examples. Some are named in honor of scientists such as einsteinium and fermium.

Section 4:3

Students come into chemistry with a basic knowledge about atoms gained in previous science courses. At this point, all they need to know is a nucleus is surrounded by electrons. It is not important that they know how oxidation numbers are assigned. This topic will be covered later in the text. Students should treat the oxidation state tables as given information used in solving an algebraic problem. Using this approach, we believe that formula writing can be taught before a detailed description of atomic structure is presented. It is recommended that charges for some ions be memorized. Daily quizzes will probably be helpful.

Section 4:4

Note that we do not present grid systems for formula writing or naming compounds. This method teaches by inference that all combinations are possible which is not actually the case. It is standard policy that compounds shown throughout this text do actually exist. We do not advocate using the technique that has students cross oxidation numbers to get subscripts. Again, this shortcut results in too many errors.

Chemical Career

Consider the number of new publications concerning science and technology that are presently on the market. As a result, the demand for skilled reporters, photographers, and illustrators in the science field is up. As a project, students could assemble science or science-related articles for the school newspaper.

Problem Solutions

Page 68.

1.
  a. $CaCl_2$
  b. $CaCO_3$
  c. $NaCN$
  d. MgO
  e. NaF
  f. $AlCl_3$
  g. SiO_2
  h. ZnI_2
  i. $CoCO_3$
  j. KH

2.
  a. barium chloride
  b. zinc nitrate
  c. cesium acetate
  d. hydrogen sulfide
  e. potassium carbonate
  f. iron(II) chloride
  g. aluminum nitrate
  h. ammonium acetate
  i. barium hydroxide
  j. copper(II) acetate

3.
  a. $CuCO_3$
  b. KOH
  c. CaI_2
  d. $RbCN$
  e. KF
  f. $Ca(OH)_2$

4.
  a. potassium chloride
  b. potassium bromide
  c. potassium iodide
  d. calcium nitrate
  e. mercury(II) iodide
  f. copper(II) nitrate

5.
  a. KNO_3
  b. $NaOH$
  c. $Pb(NO_3)_2$
  d. $ZnSO_4$
  e. Na_2S
  f. $FeCl_3$

6.
  a. ammonium nitrate
  b. sodium sulfate
  c. sodium oxide
  d. sodium phosphate
  e. ammonium chloride
  f. sodium chloride

Page 70.

7.
  a. 1 formula unit of silver carbonate
  b. 3 formula units of thallium(I) bromide
  c. 2 formula units of iron(II) nitrate
  d. 4 formula units of bismuth(III) bromide
  e. 6 formula units of barium arsenate
  f. 3 formula units of phosphoric acid
  g. 3 formula units of acetic acid

Chapter End Problems

Pages 73-75.

8. A definite amount of a compound as represented by its formula.

9. H_2, O_2, N_2, F_2, Cl_2, Br_2, I_2

10. b

11. Roman numerals are used to denote the oxidation state of elements having variable oxidation states.

12. To treat the phosphate ion as a single entity in that it occurs more than once in the formula.

13. iron(II) hydroxide also exists

14. a. $FeSO_4$
b. $Mn(NO_3)_2$
c. $Cr(NO_3)_3$
d. Tl_2Se
e. $Na_2C_2O_4$
f. $AgClO_4$

15. a. sodium nitrate
b. ammonium sulfate
c. iron(III) nitrate
d. sodium acetate
e. barium selenide
f. copper(II) sulfate

16. a. $RbC_2H_3O_2$
b. $CePO_4$
c. $Ca_3(AsO_4)_2$
d. $CuC_4H_4O_6$
e. CrN
f. $AgNO_3$

17. a. thallium(I) selenate
b. cadmium phosphide
c. cobalt(II) phosphate
d. lithium hydride
e. gallium(III) telluride
f. mercury(II) chloride

18. a. $Mg(OH)_2$ **e.** $Al_2(SO_4)_3$
b. $Cd(OH)_2$ **f.** KCN
c. $AgC_2H_3O_2$
d. $Mg(NO_3)_2$

19. a. $SnCl_4$
b. ThF_4
c. $Mg(IO_3)_2$
d. $(NH_4)_2S$
e. $Co(NO_3)_2$
f. $Ba(NO_3)_2$

20. a. copper(II) selenide
b. lead(II) cyanide
c. magnesium hydride
d. manganese(II) oxide
e. aluminum carbide
f. hydrogen chloride

21. a. $Cd(NO_3)_2$
b. $Co(NO_3)_2$
c. $Ni(NO_3)_2$
d. $Mg(ClO_4)_2$

22. a. strontium nitrate
b. calcium oxalate
c. cesium iodate
d. lithium selenide

23. a. $Co(OH)_2$
b. Cs_2CO_3
c. $MgCO_3$
d. CaO

e. $LiC_2H_3O_2$
f. $ZnTe$

24. a. thallium(I) oxalate
b. ammonium fluoride
c. barium selenate
d. silver sulfide
e. thallium(I) acetate
f. ammonium selenide

25. a. Al_2Se_3
b. $Ni_3(PO_4)_2$
c. $CaTe$
d. $Co(ClO_4)_2$
e. $MgSiF_6$
f. $Ba(ClO_4)_2$

26. a. aluminum arsenate
b. chromium(III) sulfate
c. mercury(II) iodate
d. cadmium bromide
e. cerium(III) chloride
f. bismuth(III) arsenate

Review

Page 75.

1. a. compound
b. heterogeneous mixture
c. solution
d. element
e. solution
f. heterogeneous mixture

2. a. 3   **d.** 6
b. 2   **e.** 3
c. 2

3. Accuracy = ± 0.0001 g
Relative error = $\dfrac{0.0001}{0.8320} = 1.2 \times 10^{-4}$

4. a. 9.55×10^{-1}
b. 6.80×10^{-1}
c. 5.35×10^{1}
d. 3.14×10^{2}
e. 6.25×10^{-2}
f. 2.23×10^{3}

5. a. 73 300 000
b. 904
c. 77 300
d. 0.00021
e. 0.000 074
f. 0.000 009 18

One More Step

Page 75.

1. Daltonides are compounds of definite composition. Bertholides are compounds of variable composition. Bertholides are possible because of the occurrence of interstitial atoms in crystal lattices. Transitional metal hydrides and copper(I) sulfide are well known Bertholides.

THE MOLE

5

An Overview

Chapter 5 begins with a strong emphasis on the mole as the chemist's basic measuring unit. The mole concept is developed through a logical progression. Formula mass is presented first. The mole and Avogadro's number are presented next. The remainder of the chapter provides students with applications of the mole concept. The problem solving sections of the chapter provide practice in using the mole concept with the factor-label method. Emphasis on these problems will give your students a better understanding of the quantitative aspects of chemistry.

Demonstration Information

Copper(II) sulfate pentahydrate loses water in an observable manner. You can determine the mass before and after heating. This procedure enables you to answer the question "how much water is lost?" Do not overheat the hydrate since it could decompose. Demonstrate proper safety procedure by wearing goggles or safety glasses. Stress the need for quantitative data (numbers of grams, moles, and molecules) to accurately describe what is happening.

Performance Objectives

Goal: Student will gain an understanding of the mole concept and will use it in connection with chemical formulas, solutions, molecular formulas, and hydrates.

Objectives: Upon completion of the reading and problems, and when asked to demonstrate their understanding either orally or on a written test, students will

5:1	P	calculate the formula mass for any substance.
5:2	K	state Avogadro's number.
5:3	K/P	define the mole and do simple conversions to find the number of moles in a given mass.
5:4	K	define molarity and determine molarities for given solutions.
5:5	P	calculate the percentage composition of any given compound.
5:6	P	determine the empirical formula of a substance from percentage composition data.
5:7	P	find the molecular formula given molecular mass and the empirical formula.
5:8	S/P	determine the percentage of water in a hydrate.
	A	voluntarily complete one or more of the One More Step activities.
	A	read unassigned literature related to the chapter.

Teaching Techniques

Section 5:1

The choice of the first atomic mass standard was arbitrary. For a long time chemists used an atomic mass scale based on oxygen. In 1961, it was agreed to use carbon-12 as the standard. This isotope is easy to measure in the mass spectrometer.

The terms molecular weight and atomic weight are incorrect even though these terms have been used for many years. Weight is measured in newtons.

Section 5:2

Perrin, a French physicist, made measurements of Brownian motion in natural gum. He found the number of molecules per mole to be 6.8×10^{23}. Perrin was the first to use the term Avogadro's number. Rutherford later did an experiment using He gas produced by the alpha decay of certain radioactive nuclides. He calculated N_A as 6.16×10^{23} atoms per mole. Millikan's oil drop experiment (covered in Chapter 8) gave the accepted value of 6.023×10^{23} electrons per mole.

Section 5:3

Since the mole as a counting unit is unfamiliar to students, it may help to relate the following:

1 dozen = 12 pieces of anything
1 mole = 6.02×10^{23} pieces of anything

Section 5:4

The mole concept is extended in calculating solution concentrations. Molarity is defined as the ratio of the moles of solute to the volume of solution in dm^3. The change in volume unit (dm^3) will not be noticed by your students since they are learning it for the first time. They will think of molarity as mol/dm^3. It is important to teach units in use throughout the world (SI) and those that will appear in the literature in the future in spite of the fact that we may be more familiar with outdated units.

Section 5:5

Some students have difficulty recalling how to calculate percentages. They may find it easier to remember the following:

part over the whole time 100 equals percent

We recommend that students read atomic masses to three significant digits.

Chemical Technology

Throughout the text, up-to-date analytical equipment is shown to emphasize the use of computers in chemistry. Many high schools are now using computers for independent learning and review. Students who are interested in programming could put your lab program calculations on computer as a project.

Problem Solutions

Page 78.

1. a. 30.1
   b. 136
   c. 193
   d. 424
   e. 310
   f. 484
   g. 266
   h. 110
   i. 245
   j. 58.1
   k. 899
   l. 46.1
   m. 342
   n. 60.1

Pages 81-82.

2. $\dfrac{1.00 \times 10^{23} \text{ formula units TlI}}{} \left| \dfrac{1 \text{ mol}}{6.02 \times 10^{23} \text{ formula units}} = 1.66 \times 10^{2} \text{ mol TlI}\right.$

3. $\dfrac{0.400 \text{ mol } H_2O}{} \left| \dfrac{6.02 \times 10^{23} \text{ molecules}}{1 \text{ mol}} = 2.41 \times 10^{23} \text{ molecules } H_2O\right.$

4. $\dfrac{76.0 \text{ g } CaBr_2}{} \left| \dfrac{1 \text{ mol } CaBr_2}{200 \text{ g } CaBr_2} = 0.380 \text{ mol } CaBr_2\right.$

5. $\dfrac{46.0 \text{ g } Ag_2Te}{} \left| \dfrac{1 \text{ mol } Ag_2Te}{343 \text{ g } Ag_2Te} \right| \dfrac{6.02 \times 10^{23} \text{ formula units}}{1 \text{ mol}} = 8.07 \times 10^{22} \text{ formula units } Ag_2Te$

6. $\dfrac{1.00 \times 10^{23} \text{ formula units } Mg(C_2H_3O_2)_2}{} \left| \dfrac{1 \text{ mol}}{6.02 \times 10^{23} \text{ formula units}} \right| \dfrac{142 \text{ g } Mg(C_2H_3O_2)_2}{1 \text{ mol } Mg(C_2H_3O_2)_2} = 23.6 \text{ g } Mg(C_2H_3O_2)_2$

7. $\dfrac{3.00 \text{ mol } Ce_2(CO_3)_3}{} \left| \dfrac{460 \text{ g } Ce_2(CO_3)_3}{1 \text{ mol } Ce_2(CO_3)_3} = 1380 \text{ g } Ce_2(CO_3)_3\right.$

8. $\dfrac{4.70 \times 10^{24} \text{ formula units } Ca(ClO_4)_2}{} \left| \dfrac{1 \text{ mol}}{6.02 \times 10^{23} \text{ formula units}} = 7.81 \text{ mol } Ca(ClO_4)_2\right.$

9. $\dfrac{18.0 \text{ g } HBr}{} \left| \dfrac{1 \text{ mol } HBr}{80.9 \text{ g } HBr} = 0.222 \text{ mol } HBr\right.$

10. $\dfrac{9.30 \text{ mol } SiH_4}{} \left| \dfrac{6.02 \times 10^{23} \text{ molecules}}{1 \text{ mol}} = 5.60 \times 10^{24} \text{ molecules } SiH_4\right.$

11. $\dfrac{8.00 \times 10^{19} \text{ molecules HCN}}{} \left| \dfrac{1 \text{ mol}}{6.02 \times 10^{23} \text{ molecules}} \right| \dfrac{27.0 \text{ g HCN}}{1 \text{ mol HCN}} = 0.003\ 59 \text{ g HCN}$

Page 83.

12. $\dfrac{145 \text{ g } (NH_4)_2C_4H_4O_6}{500 \text{ cm}^3 \text{ soln}} \left| \dfrac{1 \text{ mol } (NH_4)_2C_4H_4O_6}{184 \text{ g } (NH_4)_2C_4H_4O_6} \right| \dfrac{1000 \text{ cm}^3}{1 \text{ dm}^3} = 1.58M \ (NH_4)_2C_4H_4O_6$

13. $\dfrac{45.1 \text{ g } CoSO_4}{250 \text{ cm}^3 \text{ soln}} \left| \dfrac{1 \text{ mol } CoSO_4}{155 \text{ g } CoSO_4} \right| \dfrac{1000 \text{ cm}^3}{1 \text{ dm}^3} = 1.16M \ CoSO_4$

14. $\dfrac{41.3 \text{ g } Fe(NO_3)_2}{100 \text{ cm}^3 \text{ soln}} \left| \dfrac{1 \text{ mol } Fe(NO_3)_2}{180 \text{ g } Fe(NO_3)_2} \right| \dfrac{1000 \text{ cm}^3}{1 \text{ dm}^3} = 2.29M \ Fe(NO_3)_2$

15. $\dfrac{49.9 \text{ g } Pb(ClO_4)_2}{200 \text{ cm}^3 \text{ soln}} \left| \dfrac{1 \text{ mol } Pb(ClO_4)_2}{406 \text{ g } Pb(ClO_4)_2} \right| \dfrac{1000 \text{ cm}^3}{1 \text{ dm}^3} = 0.615M \ Pb(ClO_4)_2$

16. $\dfrac{35.0 \text{ g } MnSiF_6}{50.0 \text{ cm}^3 \text{ soln}} \left| \dfrac{1 \text{ mol } MnSiF_6}{197 \text{ g } MnSiF_6} \right| \dfrac{1000 \text{ cm}^3}{1 \text{ dm}^3} = 3.55M \ MnSiF_6$

17. $\dfrac{1000 \text{ cm}^3 \text{ soln}}{} \left| \dfrac{3.00 \text{ mol NiCl}_2}{1000 \text{ cm}^3 \text{ soln}} \right| \dfrac{130 \text{ g NiCl}_2}{1 \text{ mol NiCl}_2} = 390 \text{ g NiCl}_2$

18. $\dfrac{250 \text{ cm}^3 \text{ soln}}{} \left| \dfrac{4.00 \text{ mol RbOH}}{1000 \text{ cm}^3 \text{ soln}} \right| \dfrac{103 \text{ g RbOH}}{1 \text{ mol RbOH}} = 103 \text{ g RbOH}$

19. $\dfrac{500 \text{ cm}^3 \text{ soln}}{} \left| \dfrac{1.50 \text{ mol AgF}}{1000 \text{ cm}^3 \text{ soln}} \right| \dfrac{127 \text{ g AgF}}{1 \text{ mol AgF}} = 95.3 \text{ g AgF}$

20. $\dfrac{250 \text{ cm}^3 \text{ soln}}{} \left| \dfrac{0.0500 \text{ mol SrSiF}_6}{1000 \text{ cm}^3 \text{ soln}} \right| \dfrac{230 \text{ g SrSiF}_6}{1 \text{ mol SrSiF}_6} = 2.88 \text{ g SrSiF}_6$

21. $\dfrac{250 \text{ cm}^3 \text{ soln}}{} \left| \dfrac{0.00200 \text{ mol Tl}_2\text{CO}_3}{1000 \text{ cm}^3 \text{ soln}} \right| \dfrac{469 \text{ g Tl}_2\text{CO}_3}{1 \text{ mol Tl}_2\text{CO}_3} = 0.235 \text{ g Tl}_2\text{CO}_3$

Page 85.

22. 1 Cs @ 133
    $\underline{\text{1 F } @ \quad 19}$
    152

    $\text{Cs} = \dfrac{133}{152} \left| \dfrac{100}{1} \right. = 87.5\%$

    $\text{F} = \dfrac{19}{152} \left| \dfrac{100}{1} \right. = 12.5\%$

23. 1 Ni @ 58.7
    $\underline{\text{2 I } @ 254}$
    313

    $\text{Ni} = \dfrac{58.7}{313} \times 100 = 18.8\%$

    $\text{I} = \dfrac{254}{313} \times 100 = 81.2\%$

24. 2Bi @ 209 = 418
    $\underline{\text{3O } @ \quad 16 = \quad 48}$
    466

    $\text{Bi} = \dfrac{418}{466} \left| \dfrac{100}{1} \right. = 89.7\%$

    $\text{O} = \dfrac{48}{466} \left| \dfrac{100}{1} \right. = 10.3\%$

25. 1Cu @ 63.5 = 63.5
    2C @ 12   = 24.0
    $\underline{\text{4O } @ 16 \quad = 64.0}$
    152

    $\text{Cu} = \dfrac{63.5}{152} \left| \dfrac{100}{1} \right. = 41.8\%$

    $\text{C} = \dfrac{24}{152} \left| \dfrac{100}{1} \right. = 15.8\%$

    $\text{O} = \dfrac{64.0}{152} \left| \dfrac{100}{1} \right. = 42.1\%$

26. 1 Tl @ 204 = 204
    1 I @ 127 = 127
    $\underline{\text{3O } @ \quad 16 = \quad 48.0}$
    379

    $\text{Tl} = \dfrac{204}{379} \times 100 = 53.8\%$

    $\text{I} = \dfrac{127}{379} \times 100 = 33.5\%$

    $\text{O} = \dfrac{48.0}{379} \times 100 = 12.7\%$

27. $\text{Th} = 232 \ \dfrac{232}{264} \times 100 = 87.9\%$

$\quad 2\text{O} = 32.0 \ \dfrac{32.0}{264} \times 100 = 12.1\%$

28. $3\text{Co} = 177 \ \dfrac{177}{455} \times 100 = 38.9\%$

    $2\text{As} = 150 \ \dfrac{150}{455} \times 100 = 33.0\%$

    $8\text{O} = 128 \ \dfrac{128}{455} \times 100 = 28.2\%$

29. $\text{Ba} = \dfrac{137}{265} \times 100 = 51.8\%$

    $\text{Te} = \dfrac{128}{265} \times 100 = 48.2\%$

30. $\text{Zn} = 65.4 \ \dfrac{65.4}{141} \times 100 = 46.2\%$

    $\text{Si} = 28.1 \ \dfrac{28.1}{141} \times 100 = 19.9\%$

    $3\text{O} = 48.0 \ \dfrac{48.0}{141} \times 100 = 33.9\%$

31. $\text{Cd} = 112 \ \dfrac{112}{150} \times 100 = 74.7\%$

    $2\text{F} = 38 \ \dfrac{38}{150} \times 100 = 25.3\%$

32. $\text{Ba} = 137 \ \dfrac{137}{139} \times 100 = 98.6\%$

    $2\text{H} = 2.02 \ \dfrac{2.02}{139} \times 100 = 1.45\%$

33. $\text{Ca} = 40 \ \dfrac{40}{143} \times 100 = 28\%$

    $2\text{Cl} = 71 \ \dfrac{71}{143} \times 100 = 49.7\%$

    $2\text{O} = 32 \ \dfrac{32}{143} \times 100 = 22.4\%$

Page 87.

34. $\text{Ce} = \dfrac{1.67}{140} = 0.0119, \ \text{I} = \dfrac{4.54}{127} = 0.0358$
    $0.0119/0.0358 \approx 1:3$
    Therefore, CeI_3

35. $\text{Mg} = \dfrac{31.9}{24.3} = 1.31, \ \text{P} = \dfrac{27.1}{31.0} = 0.875$
    $1.31/0.875 \approx 3:2$
    Therefore, Mg_3P_2

36. $\text{Cs} = \dfrac{4.04}{133} = 0.0304, \ \text{Cl} = \dfrac{1.08}{35.5} = 0.0305$

$0.0304/0.0305 \approx 1:1$
Therefore, CsCl

37. $Ni = \dfrac{9.11}{58.7} = 0.155$, $F = \dfrac{5.89}{19.0} = 0.310$

$0.155/0.310 \approx 1:2$
Therefore, NiF_2

38. $Ca = \dfrac{6.27}{40.1} = 0.156$, $N = \dfrac{1.46}{14.00} = 0.104$

$0.156/0.104 \approx 3:2$
Therefore, Ca_3N_2

Page 88.
39. $CH = 12 + 1 = 13$

$\dfrac{78}{13} = 6$

$6(CH) = C_6H_6$

40. $CHOCl = 12 + 1 + 16 + 35.5 = 64.5$

$\dfrac{129}{64.5} = 2$

$2(CHOCl) = C_2H_2O_2Cl_2$

41. $CClN = 12 + 35.5 + 14 = 61.5$

$\dfrac{184.5}{61.5} = 3$

$3(CClN) = C_3Cl_3N_3$

42. $TlC_2H_2O_3 = 204 + 24 + 2 + 48 = 278$

$\dfrac{557}{278} \approx 2$

$2(TlC_2H_2O_3) = Tl_2C_4H_4O_6$

43. $(0.856)(42.1\ g) = 36.0\ g\ C$

$\dfrac{36.0}{12} = 3$

$(0.144)(42.1\ g) = 6.06\ g\ H$

$\dfrac{6.06}{1.01} = 6$

Therefore, C_3H_6

Page 89.
44. $\dfrac{0.391\ g\ Li_2SiF_6 \quad | \quad 1\ mol}{\quad | \quad 156\ g\ Li_2SiF_6} = 0.00251\ mol$

molecular mass $= 2(7) + 28 + 6(19)$
$14 + 28 + 114 = 156$

$\dfrac{0.0903\ g\ H_2O \quad | \quad 1\ mol}{\quad | \quad 18.0\ g\ H_2O} = 0.00501\ mol$

molecular mass $= 2(1) + 16 = 18$
$0.00251/0.00501 = 1/2$ $\therefore Li_2SiF_6 \cdot 2H_2O$

45. $\dfrac{0.737\ g\ MgSO_3 \quad | \quad 1\ mol}{\quad | \quad 104\ g\ MgSO_3} = 0.00706\ mol$

$\dfrac{0.763\ g\ H_2O \quad | \quad 1\ mol\ H_2O}{\quad | \quad 18.0\ g\ H_2O} = 0.0424\ mol\ H_2O$

$0.00706/0.0424 \approx 1:6$
Therefore, $MgSO_3 \cdot 6H_2O$

46. $\dfrac{95.3\ g\ LiNO_3 \quad | \quad 1\ mol\ LiNO_3}{\quad | \quad 68.9\ g\ LiNO_3} = 1.38\ mol\ LiNO_3$

Molecular mass $= 6.9 + 14 + 3(16) = 68.9$

$\dfrac{74.7\ g\ H_2O \quad | \quad 1\ mol}{\quad | \quad 18.0\ g\ H_2O} = 4.15\ mol\ H_2O$

$1.38/4.15 \approx 1/3$ $LiNO_3 \cdot 3H_2O$

47. Assume 100 g of material
$\therefore 76.9\ g\ CaSO_3,\ 23.1\ g\ H_2O$

$\dfrac{76.9\ g\ CaSO_3 \quad | \quad 1\ mol}{\quad | \quad 120\ g\ CaSO_3} = 0.640\ mol$

molecular mass $= 40 + 32 + 3(16) = 120$

$\dfrac{23.1\ g\ H_2O \quad | \quad 1\ mol}{\quad | \quad 18.0\ g\ H_2O} = 1.28\ mol$

$0.640/1.28 \approx 1/2$ $\therefore CaSO_3 \cdot 2H_2O$

48. Assume 100 g of material
$\therefore 89.2\ g\ BaBr_2,\ 10.8\ g\ H_2O$

$\dfrac{89.2\ g\ BaBr_2 \quad | \quad 1\ mol}{\quad | \quad 297\ g\ BaBr_2} = 0.300\ mol$

molecular mass $= 137 + 2(80) = 297$

$\dfrac{10.8\ g\ H_2O \quad | \quad 1\ mol}{\quad | \quad 18.0\ g\ H_2O} = 0.600\ mol$

$0.30/0.60 \approx 1/2$ $\therefore BaBr_2 \cdot 2H_2O$

Chapter End Problems

Pages 93-94.
49. The term formula mass should be used in speaking of the mass of ionic substances.

50. Avogadro's number of atoms has a mass in grams which is equal to the mass of a single atom in atomic mass units.

51. A mole is a counting unit equivalent to 6.02×10^{23} particles.
Molarity is the ratio of moles per cubic decimeter for a solution.

52. Empirical formula: Simplest ratio of atoms in a compound.
Molecular formula: The number of atoms in a molecule based on its molecular mass.

53. $Rb = \dfrac{63.0}{85.5} = 0.737$

$O = \dfrac{5.90}{16.0} = 0.369$

$0.737/0.369 \approx 2:1$
Therefore, Rb_2O

54. $Th = \dfrac{0.00495}{232} = 2.13 \times 10^{-5}$

$S = \dfrac{0.00137}{32.1} = 4.27 \times 10^{-5}$

$2.13 \times 10^{-5}/4.27 \times 10^{-5} \approx 1:2$
Therefore, ThS_2

55. $Co = \dfrac{1.39}{58.9} = 0.0236$

$I = \dfrac{5.98}{127} = 0.0471$

$O = \dfrac{2.26}{16.0} = 0.141$

$0.0236/0.0471/0.141 \approx 1:2:6$
Therefore, $Co(IO_3)_2$

56. $Na = \dfrac{2.13}{23.0} = 0.0926$

$As = \dfrac{2.32}{74.9} = 0.0310$

$O = \dfrac{1.98}{16.0} = 0.124$

$0.0926/0.0310/0.124 \approx 3:1:4$
Therefore, Na_3AsO_4

57. $N = \dfrac{30.0}{14.0} = 2.14$

$H = \dfrac{8.65}{1.01} = 8.58$

$Se = \dfrac{84.7}{79.0} = 1.07$

$O = \dfrac{68.6}{16.0} = 4.29$

$2.14/8.58/1.07/4.29 = 2:8:1:4$
Therefore, $(NH_4)_2SeO_4$

58. $Cr = \dfrac{32.8}{52.0} = 0.631$

$Cl = \dfrac{67.2}{35.5} = 1.90$

$0.630/1.90 \approx 1:3$
Therefore, $CrCl_3$

59. $Co = \dfrac{42.7}{58.9} = 0.725$

$Se = \dfrac{57.3}{79.0} = 0.726$

$0.725/0.726 \approx 1:1$
Therefore, $CoSe$

60. $Ba = \dfrac{78.3}{137} = 0.570$

$F = \dfrac{21.7}{19.0} = 1.14$

$0.570/1.14 = 1:2$
Therefore, BaF_2

61. $Tl = \dfrac{96.2}{204} = 0.471$

$O = \dfrac{3.77}{16.0} = 0.236$

$0.471/0.236 = 2:1$
Therefore, Tl_2O

62. $Rb = \dfrac{58.0}{85.5} = 0.679$

$N = \dfrac{9.50}{14.0} = 0.678$

$O = \dfrac{32.5}{16.0} = 2.03$

$0.679/0.678/2.03 = 1:1:3$
Therefore, $RbNO_3$

63. $Zr = \dfrac{32.2}{91.2} = 0.353$

$S = \dfrac{22.6}{32.1} = 0.705$

$O = \dfrac{45.2}{16.0} = 2.83$

$0.353/0.705/2.83 \approx 1:2:8$
Therefore, $Zr(SO_4)_2$

64. $Cd = \dfrac{48.8}{112} = 0.434$

$C = \dfrac{20.8}{12.0} = 1.73$

$H = \dfrac{2.62}{1.01} = 2.60$

$O = \dfrac{27.8}{16.0} = 1.74$

$0.434/1.73/2.60/1.74 \approx 1:4:6:4$
Therefore, $CdC_4H_6O_4$

65. $Fe = \dfrac{49.5}{55.8} = 0.886$

$F = \dfrac{50.5}{19.0} = 2.66$

$0.886/2.66 \approx 1:3$
Therefore, FeF_3

66. $Ni = \dfrac{42.6}{58.7} = 0.726$

$Se = \dfrac{57.4}{79.0} = 0.727$

$0.726/0.727 \approx 1:1$
Therefore, $NiSe$

67. $Al = \dfrac{8.29}{27.0} = 0.307$

$Cl = \dfrac{32.7}{35.5} = 0.922$

$O = \dfrac{59.0}{16.0} = 3.69$

$0.307/0.922/3.69 \approx 1:3:12$
Therefore, $Al(ClO_4)_3$

68. a. 174
b. 79.5
c. 233
d. 551
e. 350
f. 325

69. a. 134
b. 319
c. 143
d. 368
e. 350
f. 158

70. a. $\dfrac{10 \text{ g } Rb_2SeO_4}{} \left| \dfrac{1 \text{ mol } Rb_2SeO_4}{314 \text{ g } Rb_2SeO_4} \right. = 0.0318 \text{ mol } Rb_2SeO_4$

b. $\dfrac{1.00 \times 10^{25} \text{ molecules } I_2}{} \left| \dfrac{1 \text{ mol}}{6.02 \times 10^{23} \text{ molecules}} \right| \dfrac{254 \text{ g } I_2}{1 \text{ mol } I_2} = 4.22 \times 10^3 \text{ g } I_2$

c. $\dfrac{0.426 \text{ mol } HF}{} \left| \dfrac{6.02 \times 10^{23} \text{ molecules}}{1 \text{ mol}} \right. = 2.56 \times 10^{23} \text{ molecules } HF$

d. $\dfrac{26.8 \text{ mol } CO_2}{} \left| \dfrac{6.02 \times 10^{23} \text{ molecules}}{1 \text{ mol}} \right. = 1.61 \times 10^{25} \text{ molecules } CO_2$

e. $\dfrac{681 \text{ formula units } MnC_2O_4}{} \left| \dfrac{1 \text{ mol}}{6.02 \times 10^{23} \text{ formula units}} \right. = 1.13 \times 10^{-21} \text{ mol } MnC_2O_4$

71. a. $\dfrac{6.94 \text{ g } ZrF_4}{500 \text{ cm}^3 \text{ soln}} \left| \dfrac{1 \text{ mol } ZrF_4}{167 \text{ g } ZrF_4} \right| \dfrac{1000 \text{ cm}^3}{1 \text{ dm}^3} = 0.0830M \text{ } ZrF_4$

b. $\dfrac{48.5 \text{ g } NH_4Br}{250 \text{ cm}^3 \text{ soln}} \left| \dfrac{1 \text{ mol } NH_4Br}{97.9 \text{ g } NH_4Br} \right| \dfrac{1000 \text{ cm}^3}{1 \text{ dm}^3} = 1.98M \text{ } NH_4Br$

c. $\dfrac{23.5 \text{ g } CuF_2}{1000 \text{ cm}^3 \text{ soln}} \left| \dfrac{1 \text{ mol } CuF_2}{102 \text{ g } CuF_2} \right| \dfrac{1000 \text{ cm}^3}{1 \text{ dm}^3} = 0.230M \text{ } CuF_2$

d. $\dfrac{70.0 \text{ g } CdCl_2}{1000 \text{ cm}^3 \text{ soln}} \left| \dfrac{1 \text{ mol } CdCl_2}{183 \text{ g } CdCl_2} \right| \dfrac{1000 \text{ cm}^3}{1 \text{ dm}^3} = 0.383M \text{ } CdCl_2$

e. $\dfrac{50.0 \text{ g } Ce(C_2H_3O_2)_3}{250 \text{ cm}^3 \text{ soln}} \left| \dfrac{1 \text{ mol } Ce(C_2H_3O_2)_3}{317 \text{ g } Ce(C_2H_3O_2)_3} \right| \dfrac{1000 \text{ cm}^3}{1 \text{ dm}^3} = 0.631M \text{ } Ce(C_2H_3O_2)_3$

72. a. $\dfrac{1000 \text{ cm}^3 \text{ soln}}{} \left| \dfrac{4.00 \text{ mol } CsCl}{1000 \text{ cm}^3 \text{ soln}} \right| \dfrac{169 \text{ g } CsCl}{1 \text{ mol } CsCl} = 676 \text{ g } CsCl$

b. $\dfrac{1000 \text{ cm}^3 \text{ soln}}{} \bigg| \dfrac{6.00 \text{ mol LiBr}}{1000 \text{ cm}^3 \text{ soln}} \bigg| \dfrac{86.8 \text{ g LiBr}}{1 \text{ mol LiBr}} = 521 \text{ g LiBr}$

c. $\dfrac{500 \text{ cm}^3 \text{ soln}}{} \bigg| \dfrac{2.00 \text{ mol MgBr}_2}{1000 \text{ cm}^3 \text{ soln}} \bigg| \dfrac{184 \text{ g MgBr}_2}{1 \text{ mol MgBr}_2} = 184 \text{ g MgBr}_2$

d. $\dfrac{1000 \text{ cm}^3 \text{ soln}}{} \bigg| \dfrac{1.50 \text{ mol MnSO}_4}{1000 \text{ cm}^3 \text{ soln}} \bigg| \dfrac{151 \text{ g MnSO}_4}{1 \text{ mol MnSO}_4} = 227 \text{ g MnSO}_4$

e. $\dfrac{1000 \text{ cm}^3 \text{ soln}}{} \bigg| \dfrac{0.750 \text{ mol NiSO}_4}{1000 \text{ cm}^3 \text{ soln}} \bigg| \dfrac{155 \text{ g NiSO}_4}{1 \text{ mol NiSO}_4} = 116 \text{ g NiSO}_4$

73. a. Na @ 23.0
Br @ $\underline{79.9}$
103

$\text{Na} = \dfrac{23.0}{103} \times 100 = 22.3\%$

$\text{Br} = \dfrac{79.9}{103} \times 100 = 77.7\%$

b. 2C @ 12 = 24
4H @ 1 = 4
2O @ 16 = $\underline{32}$
60

$\text{C} = \dfrac{24.0}{60} \bigg| \dfrac{100}{1} = 40.0\%$

$\text{H} = \dfrac{4.03}{60} \bigg| \dfrac{100}{1} = 6.72\%$

$\text{O} = \dfrac{32.0}{60} \bigg| \dfrac{100}{1} = 53.3\%$

c. Th = 232 $\dfrac{232}{408} \times 100 = 56.9\%$

4C = 48.0 $\dfrac{48.0}{408} \times 100 = 11.8\%$

8O = 128 $\dfrac{128}{408} \times 100 = 31.4\%$

d. Zn @ 65.4
S @ $\underline{32.1}$
97.4

$\text{Zn} = \dfrac{65.4}{97.4} \times 100 = 67.1\%$

$\text{S} = \dfrac{32.1}{97.4} \times 100 = 32.9\%$

e. Cd @ 112 = 112
C @ 12.0 = 12.0
3O @ 16.0 = $\underline{48.0}$
172

$\text{Cd} = \dfrac{112}{172} \times 100 = 65.2\%$

$\text{C} = \dfrac{12.0}{172} \times 100 = 6.97\%$

$\text{O} = \dfrac{48.0}{172} \times 100 = 27.8\%$

f. 4C @ 12 = 48
10H @ 11 = 10
1O @ 16 = $\underline{16}$
74

$\text{C} = \dfrac{48}{74} \times 100 = 64.9\%$

$\text{H} = \dfrac{10}{74} \times 100 = 13.5\%$

$\text{O} = \dfrac{16}{74} \times 100 = 21.6\%$

74. $\text{Ca} = \dfrac{33.3}{40.1} = 0.831$

$\text{O} = \dfrac{40.0}{16.0} = 2.50$

$\text{S} = \dfrac{26.7}{32.1} = 0.833$

$0.831/2.50/0.833 \approx 1:3:1$
Therefore, CaSO_3

75. $\text{C} = \dfrac{92.3}{12.0} = 7.68$

$\text{H} = \dfrac{7.70}{1.01} = 7.64$

$7.68/7.64 = 1:1$
$(\text{CH})_n = 78 \text{ g}$
$n = 6$, therefore, C_6H_6

76. $\text{P} = \dfrac{26.7}{31.0} = 0.861$

$\text{N} = \dfrac{12.1}{14.0} = 0.864$

$\text{Cl} = \dfrac{61.2}{35.5} = 1.72$

$0.861/0.864/1.72 \approx 1:1:2$
$(\text{PNCl}_2)_n = 695 \text{ g}$
$n = 6 \therefore \text{P}_6\text{N}_6\text{Cl}_{12}$

77. Assume 100 g of the material
$\therefore 90.7 \text{ g SrC}_2\text{O}_4, \therefore 9.30 \text{ g H}_2\text{O}$

$\dfrac{90.7 \text{ g SrC}_2\text{O}_4}{} \bigg| \dfrac{1 \text{ mol}}{176 \text{ g SrC}_2\text{O}_4} = 0.515 \text{ mol SrC}_2\text{O}_4$

$\dfrac{9.30 \text{ g H}_2\text{O}}{} \bigg| \dfrac{1 \text{ mol}}{18.0 \text{ g H}_2\text{O}} = 0.516 \text{ mol H}_2\text{O}$

$0.515/0.516 \approx 1:1 \quad \therefore \text{SrC}_2\text{O}_4 \cdot \text{H}_2\text{O}$

Review

Pages 94-95.

1. $\dfrac{81.2 \text{ g}}{} \bigg| \dfrac{1000 \text{ mg}}{1 \text{ g}} = 81\ 200 \text{ mg}$

2. 4

3. $\dfrac{0.5}{12.0} = 0.0417$

4. **a.** HI
   b. $\text{Mn}_3(\text{PO}_4)_2$
   c. Rb_2SO_4
   d. GaBr_3

5. a. thorium(IV) phosphate
   b. sodium tartrate
   c. copper(II) hexafluorosilicate
   d. cesium nitrate
6. a. chemical
   b. physical
   c. chemical
   d. chemical
7. a. physical

b. chemical
c. physical
d. physical

One More Step

Page 95.

1. Experimental percentages are usually within 1-2% of the calculated values.
2. See Section 5:2 of the Teaching Techniques.

CHEMICAL EQUATIONS   6

An Overview

In Chapter 4, students learned how to name and write chemical formulas. In Chapter 5, they were made aware of the quantitative relationships involving chemical formulas. Chapter 6 builds on the techniques learned in the previous chapters. The ability to write and balance chemical equations is a basic goal of any introductory chemistry course. The chapter develops the following concepts:

1. The chemical equation represents chemical change. The system will be characterized by a whole new set of properties after the reaction has occurred.
2. In a balanced equation, equal numbers of each kind of atoms are present on both sides of the equation.
3. Reactions can be classified into four general types: single displacement, double displacement, decomposition, and synthesis. Products may be predicted once students learn the characteristics of the four general types.

Chapter 6 prepares students for quantitative relationships associated with a chemical equation in Chapter 7.

Demonstration Information

You may want to add a few drops of H_2O to the glycerol-liquid soap mixture. Once the soap bubble is free of the funnel, it rises quickly. It is best to have an assistant hold the meter stick with the candle attached above the funnel before you shake it free. The bubbles burn with a yellow-blue flame in mid air. **CAUTION:** Do not do this demonstration near any flammable materials (drapes, ceiling, and so on). As with any open flame, have a fire extinguisher close by. Note, the combustion will not leave any soot marks on the ceiling.

Performance Objectives

Goal: Students will complete and balance equations representing chemical reactions.

Objectives: Upon completion of the reading and problems, and when asked to demonstrate their understanding either orally or on a written test, students will

6:1	K	list the various parts of a chemical equation including symbols representing the physical state of substances in the reaction.
6:2	P/S	balance equations, given names or formulas for the reactants and products.
6:3	P/S	classify a given reaction as one of four general types.
6:3	P/S	predict the products and balance the equation when given the reactants for a reaction.
	A	voluntarily complete one or more of the One More Step activities.
	A	read unassigned literature related to the chapter.

Teaching Techniques

Section 6:1

Representing balanced chemical equations can best be done using models. If you do not have a commercial kit, obtain 18 plastic foam balls. Paint 4 black, 4 blue, and leave 10 white. Use pipe cleaners or toothpicks to build the molecules listed in the chapter introduction ($2C_2H_2$ and $5O_2$ molecules).

Explain the color coding to students. Ask them to rearrange the atoms, using all of them, to form

CO_2 and H_2O molecules. They should end up with $4CO_2$ and $2H_2O$ models. Without any discussion, students have balanced the equation and should see why it is necessary to have the same number of each kind of atom on both sides of the equation.

Section 6:3

Students should receive sufficient drill in predicting the products of a reaction. This skill will be used throughout the course especially in the lab where students will be writing equations to represent their observations.

We wish to make the point once again that our approach in teaching formula writing, balancing equations, and the quantitative aspects of the mole concept before structure and bonding allows you more freedom in scheduling laboratory experiments.

Chemical Career

This feature is designed to show the diverse types of careers that involve a knowledge of chemistry. You may want to have students bring in articles showing instances where regulatory groups (FDA or OSHA) have brought action to protect the public. *FDA Consumer* magazine has feature articles every month concerning product safety as well as a listing of seizures and actions brought against companies for unsanitary practices.

Problem Solutions

Page 100.
1. Balanced. $Te + H_2O \rightarrow TeO + H_2$
2. $La(NO_3)_3 + 3NaOH \rightarrow La(OH)_3 + 3NaNO_3$
3. Balanced. $RhO_3 \rightarrow RhO + O_2$
4. $3Hf + 2N_2 \rightarrow Hf_3N_3$
5. $2Ga + 3H_2SO_4 \rightarrow Ga_2(SO_4)_3 + 3H_2$
6. $PdCl_2 + 2HNO_3 \rightarrow Pd(NO_3)_2 + 2HCl$
7. Balanced. $RbBr + AgCl \rightarrow AgBr + RbCl$
8. $2PaI_5 \rightarrow 2Pa + 5I_2$
9. $5O_2 + Sb_2S_3 \rightarrow Sb_2O_4 + 3SO_2$
10. Balanced $Cu + Cl_2 \rightarrow CuCl_2$

Pages 101-102.
11. Balanced. $CuO + H_2 \rightarrow Cu + H_2O$ single displacement
12. $2Sb + 3H_2O \rightarrow Sb_2O_3 + 3H_2$ single displacement
13. $2Re + 3Br_2 \rightarrow 2ReBr_3$ synthesis
14. $2Ac(OH)_3 \rightarrow Ac_2O_3 + 3H_2O$ decomposition
15. $Ra + 2C \rightarrow RaC_2$ synthesis
16. $3HfCl_3 + Al \rightarrow 3HfCl_2 + AlCl_3$ single displacement
17. $Zn + 2CrCl_3 \rightarrow 2CrCl_2 + ZnCl_2$ single displacement
18. $Ca(AlO_2)_2 + 8HCl \rightarrow 2AlCl_3 + CaCl_2 + 4H_2O$ double displacement
19. $BaCO_3 + C + H_2O \rightarrow 2CO + Ba(OH)_2$ double displacement
20. $2CeO_2 + 2KI + 8HCl \rightarrow 2KCl + 2CeCl_3 + 4H_2O + I_2$ double displacement
21. $CuCO_3(c) \rightarrow CuO(c) + CO_2(g)$
22. $2Na(c) + 2H_2O(l) \rightarrow 2NaOH(aq) + H_2(g)$
23. $NH_4NO_2(c) \rightarrow 2H_2O(l) + N_2(g)$
24. $2Cu(c) + S(c) \rightarrow Cu_2S(c)$
25. $2AgNO_3(aq) + H_2SO_4(aq) \rightarrow Ag_2SO_4(c) + 2HNO_3(aq)$
26. $H_2SO_4(l) \rightarrow H_2O(l) + SO_3(g)$
27. $CaCO_3(c) \rightarrow 2HCl(aq) \rightarrow CaCl_2(aq) + H_2O(l) + CO_2(g)$
28. $NH_4NO_3(c) \rightarrow 2H_2O(l) + N_2O(g)$

Chapter End Problems

Pages 104-105.
29. $Cr(c) + 2HCl(aq) \rightarrow H_2(g) + CrCl_2(aq)$
30. $Ba(OH)_2(aq) + CO_2(g) \rightarrow BaCO_3(c) + H_2O(l)$
31. Changing a subscript changes the substance being represented. Balancing an equation involves changing the ratio of substances involved in the reaction not the substances themselves.
32. To accurately represent the ratio of substances involved in a reaction.

33. $4Na(c) + O_2(g) \rightarrow 2Na_2O(c)$

34. $AsCl_3(c) + 3H_2O(l) \rightarrow 3HCl(aq) + As(OH)_3(aq)$

35. $2Ho(c) + 6H_2O(l) \rightarrow 2Ho(OH)_3(aq) + 3H_2(g)$

36. $2IrCl_3(aq) + 3NaOH(aq) \rightarrow Ir_2O_3(c) + 3HCl(aq) + 3NaCl(aq)$

37. $2MoO_3(c) + 3Zn(c) + 3H_2SO_4(l) \rightarrow Mo_2O_3(c) + 3ZnSO_4(aq) + 3H_2O(l)$

38. Balanced. $NbI_3(c) + I_2(c) \rightarrow NbI_5(c)$

39. $Pb(C_2H_3O_2)_2(aq) + K_2CrO_4(aq) \rightarrow PbCrO_4(c) + 2KC_2H_3O_2(aq)$

40. $RbCl(c) + 2O_2(g) \rightarrow RbClO_4(c)$

41. $3SiF_4(c) + 3H_2O(l) \rightarrow 2H_2SiF_6(aq) + H_2SiO_3(c)$

42. $Sn(c) + 2KOH(aq) \rightarrow K_2SnO_2(c) + H_2(g)$

43. $2Ag_2O(c) \rightarrow 4Ag(c) + O_2(g)$

44. $Cu(c) + 2AgNO_3(aq) \rightarrow Cu(NO_3)_2(aq) + 2Ag(c)$

45. $2Mg(c) + O_2(g) \rightarrow 2MgO(c)$

46. $HCl(aq) + AgNO_3(aq) \rightarrow HNO_3(aq) + AgCl(c)$

47. $Mg(c) + 2HCl(aq) \rightarrow MgCl_2(aq) + H_2(g)$

48. $4Fe(c) + 3O_2(g) \rightarrow 2Fe_2O_3(c)$

49. $Fe(c) + S(c) \rightarrow FeS(c)$

50. $Ca(OH)_2(aq) + H_2SO_4(aq) \rightarrow CaSO_4(c) + 2H_2O(l)$

51. $Mg(c) + N_2(g) \rightarrow Mg_3N_2(c)$

52. $Zn(c) + H_2SO_4(aq) \rightarrow ZnSO_4(aq) + H_2(g)$

Review

Page 105.

1. a. $\dfrac{2.52 \times 10^{21} \text{ formula units } ZrS_2}{} \left| \dfrac{1 \text{ mol}}{6.02 \times 10^{23} \text{ formula units}} \right. = 0.00419 \text{ mol } ZrS_2$

b. $\dfrac{1.26 \times 10^{25} \text{ formula units } Al(C_2H_3O_2)_3}{} \left| \dfrac{1 \text{ mol}}{6.02 \times 10^{23} \text{ formula units}} \right| \dfrac{204 \text{ g } Al(C_2H_3O_2)_3}{1 \text{ mol } Al(C_2H_3O_2)_3} = 4270 \text{ g } Al(C_2H_3O_2)_3$

c. $\dfrac{6.06 \text{ g } Fe_2(SO_4)_3}{} \left| \dfrac{1 \text{ mol } Fe_2(SO_4)_3}{400 \text{ g } Fe_2(SO_4)_3} \right. = 0.0152 \text{ mol } Fe_2(SO_4)_3$

d. $\dfrac{88.4 \text{ g } MnI_2}{} \left| \dfrac{1 \text{ mol } MnI_2}{309 \text{ g } MnI_2} \right. = 0.286 \text{ mol } MnI_2$

e. $\dfrac{0.00202 \text{ mol } Ni(OH)_2}{} \left| \dfrac{92.7 \text{ g } Ni(OH)_2}{1 \text{ mol } Ni(OH)_2} \right. = 0.187 \text{ g } Ni(OH)_2$

2. $\dfrac{0.550 \text{ g } Ni(IO_3)_2}{1000 \text{ cm}^3 \text{ soln}} \left| \dfrac{1 \text{ mol } Ni(IO_3)_2}{409 \text{ g } Ni(IO_3)_2} \right| \dfrac{1000 \text{ cm}^3}{1 \text{ dm}^3} = 0.00135M \text{ Ni(IO}_3)_2$

3. $\dfrac{200 \text{ cm}^3 \text{ soln}}{} \left| \dfrac{0.00364 \text{ mol } Ag_2C_4H_4O_6}{1000 \text{ cm}^3 \text{ soln}} \right| \dfrac{364 \text{ g } Ag_2C_4H_4O_6}{1 \text{ mol } Ag_2C_4H_4O_6} = 0.265 \text{ g } Ag_2C_4H_4O_6$

4. $Sr = 87.6 \dfrac{87.6}{341} \times 100 = 25.7\%$

$2I = 254 \dfrac{254}{341} \times 100 = 74.3\%$

5. $Zn = \dfrac{45.3}{65.4} = 0.693, \ Se = \dfrac{54.7}{79.0} = 0.693$

$0.693/0.693 = 1:1$

Therefore, ZnSe

6. $\dfrac{79.0 \text{ g } Zr(NO_3)_4}{} \left| \dfrac{1 \text{ mol } Zr(NO_3)_4}{339 \text{ g } Zr(NO_3)_4} \right. = 0.233 \text{ mol } Zr(NO_3)_4$

$\dfrac{21.0 \text{ g } H_2O}{} \left| \dfrac{1 \text{ mol } H_2O}{18.0 \text{ g } H_2O} \right. = 1.17 \text{ mol } H_2O$

$0.233/1.17 \approx 1:5$

Therefore, $Zr(NO_3)_4 \cdot 5H_2O$

One More Step

Page 105.

1. a. $Cu(c) + 2H_2SO_4(l) \rightarrow CuSO_4(aq) + SO_2(g) + 2H_2O(l)$

b. $Cu_2S(c) + 12HNO_3(aq) \rightarrow Cu(NO_3)_2(aq) + CuSO_4(aq) + 10NO_2(g) + 6H_2O(l)$

c. $CH_4(g) + 2O_2(g) \rightarrow CO_2(g) + 2H_2O(l)$

d. $2Ce(IO_3)_4(aq) + 24H_2C_2O_4(aq) \rightarrow Ce_2(C_2O_4)_3(aq) + 4I_2(aq) + 42CO_2(g) + 24H_2O(l)$

e. $2KBr(c) + 3H_2SO_4(l) + MnO_2(c) \rightarrow 2KHSO_4(aq) + MnSO_4(aq) + Br_2(l) + 2H_2O(l)$

2. Double displacement

3. A metal carbonate may decompose when heated to form a metal oxide and CO_2 gas.
A metal hydroxide may decompose when heated to form a metal oxide and H_2O.
A metal oxide may decompose when heated to form the metal and O_2 gas.
An acid containing oxygen may decompose when heated to form a nonmetal oxide and H_2O.

QUANTITATIVE

RELATIONSHIPS   7

An Overview

Chapter 7 continues the application of the mole concept covered in Chapter 5 with balanced equations in Chapter 6 as the basis for mass-mass problems (stoichiometry). The chapter also presents the energy changes associated with reactions. Calculations involving the heat of reaction and heat of formation are used to introduce students to elementary thermodynamics. This presentation provides a basis for actual heat measurement (specific heat capacity) and heat calculations (calorimeter work) in the lab.

Demonstration Information

CAUTION: Safety glasses or goggles are a must while heating and breaking the test tube.

Performance Objectives

Goal: Students will gain a knowledge of mass and energy relationships in chemical reactions.

Objectives: Upon completion of the reading and problems, and when asked to demonstrate their understanding either orally or on a written test, students will

7:1	P/S	solve problems based on mass relationships in chemical reactions.
7:2	K	differentiate between the characteristics of endothermic and exothermic reactions.
7:3	K/P	define specific heat capacity and its relationship to calorimetric measurements.
7:4	P	calculate the change in enthalpy for a chemical reaction.
7:5-7	P	determine the heats of formation and reaction using enthalpy values and the law of conservation of energy.
	A	voluntarily complete one or more of the One More Step activities. read unassigned literature related to the chapter.

Teaching Techniques

Section 7:1

It is important to stress the coefficients of a balanced equation as being the ratio of moles for the mass-mass problem. Doing mass-mass problems in one step may be somewhat difficult for students to master at first. It is important that you emphasize using the factor-label method here to cut down on mistakes in problem solving. The proportion method of solving mass-mass problems is actually a form of factor-label in logic but the units are not expressed. As a result students memorize rather than understand the solving process.

Section 7:2

Use the diagrams in the text in discussing the differences between exothermic and endothermic reactions, Figure 7-6. The illustrations will help students see what we mean when we say the products are at a higher or lower energy state than the reactants.

Section 7:3

Specific heat capacities were studied by Dulong and Petit around 1820. They reported the following relationship for an element.

$$\text{specific heat} = \frac{25.5 \text{ J}}{\text{atomic mass}}$$

Their work was only an approximation.

Section 7:5

Students might question the usefulness of calculating heats of reaction since they can be measured in the laboratory directly. You can explain that some reactions take so long that the energy changes cannot be measured in a calorimeter. Students may ask where the heat in a reaction comes from or where it goes. If the question arises, make students aware of the energy in the various vibrational and rotational motions of the molecules and particles. Potential energy exists because of the relative positions of particles and molecules with respect to each other. Also, energy is stored in the nuclear structure of the atom. These concepts will be presented in detail in later chapters.

Section 7:6

Thermodynamics is introduced early in the course for two primary reasons.
1. Students should be aware that they are studying matter and energy and not just matter.
2. Calorimetry can be done earlier in the lab program and students should now be able to note as part of their observations in lab what reactions are exothermic and endothermic.

Chemical Career

The job description for a laboratory technician can vary widely. The educational requirements for this type of work can vary also. Have students investigate various programs at technical schools, junior colleges, and colleges. There may also be some on the job training programs sponsored by industries in your area.

Problem Solutions

Pages 111-112.

1. $2Na(c) + 2H_2O(l) \rightarrow 2NaOH(aq) + H_2(g)$

$$\frac{11.5 \text{ g Na}}{} \left| \frac{1 \text{ mol Na}}{23.0 \text{ g Na}} \right| \frac{1 \text{ mol H}_2}{2 \text{ mol Na}} \left| \frac{2.02 \text{ g H}_2}{1 \text{ mol H}_2} \right. = 0.505 \text{ g H}_2$$

2. $N_2(g) + 3H_2(g) \rightarrow 2NH_3(g)$

$$\frac{2.00 \text{ g H}_2}{} \left| \frac{1 \text{ mol H}_2}{2.02 \text{ g H}_2} \right| \frac{2 \text{ mol NH}_3}{3 \text{ mol H}_2} \left| \frac{17.0 \text{ g NH}_3}{1 \text{ mol NH}_3} \right. = 11.3 \text{ g NH}_3$$

3. $C(c) + O_2(g) \rightarrow CO_2(g)$

$$\frac{85.6 \text{ g C}}{} \left| \frac{1 \text{ mol C}}{12.0 \text{ g C}} \right| \frac{1 \text{ mol O}_2}{1 \text{ mol C}} \left| \frac{32.0 \text{ g O}_2}{1 \text{ mol O}_2} \right. = 228 \text{ g O}_2$$

4. $$\frac{85.6 \text{ g C}}{} \left| \frac{1 \text{ mol C}}{12.0 \text{ g C}} \right| \frac{1 \text{ mol CO}_2}{1 \text{ mol C}} \left| \frac{44.0 \text{ g CO}_2}{1 \text{ mol CO}_2} \right. = 314 \text{ g CO}_2$$

5. $2KClO_3(c) \rightarrow 2KCl(c) + 3O_2(g)$

$$\frac{64.2 \text{ g O}_2}{} \left| \frac{1 \text{ mol O}_2}{32.0 \text{ g O}_2} \right| \frac{2 \text{ mol KCl}}{3 \text{ mol O}_2} \left| \frac{74.6 \text{ g KCl}}{1 \text{ mol KCl}} \right. = 99.7 \text{ g KCl}$$

6. $$\frac{18.7 \text{ g Fe}}{} \left| \frac{1 \text{ mol Fe}}{55.8 \text{ g Fe}} \right| \frac{3 \text{ mol CO}}{2 \text{ mol Fe}} \left| \frac{28.0 \text{ g CO}}{1 \text{ mol CO}} \right. = 14.1 \text{ g CO}$$

7. $2HCl(aq) + Ca(OH)_2(c) \rightarrow CaCl_2(aq) + 2H_2O(l)$

$$\frac{75.1 \text{ g Ca(OH)}_2}{} \left| \frac{1 \text{ mol Ca(OH)}_2}{74.1 \text{ g Ca(OH)}_2} \right| \frac{2 \text{ mol HCl}}{1 \text{ mol Ca(OH)}_2} \left| \frac{36.5 \text{ g HCl}}{1 \text{ mol HCl}} \right. = 74.0 \text{ g HCl}$$

8. $2Al(c) + 6HCl(aq) \rightarrow 2AlCl_3(aq) + 3H_2(g)$

$$\frac{5.62 \text{ g Al}}{} \left| \frac{1 \text{ mol Al}}{27.0 \text{ g Al}} \right| \frac{3 \text{ mol H}_2}{2 \text{ mol Al}} \left| \frac{2.02 \text{ g H}_2}{1 \text{ mol H}_2} \right. = 0.631 \text{ g H}_2$$

Pages 116-117.

9. $H = m(\Delta T)C_p = \dfrac{91.4 \text{ g}}{} \left| \dfrac{51.1 \text{ C}}{} \right| \dfrac{0.874 \text{ J}}{\text{g} \cdot \text{C}} = 4080 \text{ J}$

10. $H = m(\Delta T)C_p = \dfrac{4.66\ \cancel{g}}{} \bigg| \dfrac{55.9\ \cancel{C^\circ}}{} \bigg| \dfrac{0.856\ \text{J}}{\cancel{g}\cdot\cancel{C^\circ}} = 223\ \text{J}$

11. $H = m(\Delta T)C_p = \dfrac{787\ \cancel{g}}{} \bigg| \dfrac{82.0\ \cancel{C^\circ}}{} \bigg| \dfrac{4.18\ \text{J}}{\cancel{g}\cdot\cancel{C^\circ}} = 2.70 \times 10^5\ \text{J}$

12. $H(\text{lost}) = H(\text{gained})$
    $m(\Delta T)C_p = m(\Delta T)C_p$

$$\dfrac{3.99\ \text{g}}{} \bigg| \dfrac{(100 - x)\ \text{C}^\circ}{} \bigg| \dfrac{0.0900\ \text{J}}{\text{g}\cdot\text{C}^\circ} = \dfrac{10.0\ \text{g}}{} \bigg| \dfrac{(x - 21.0)\ \text{C}^\circ}{} \bigg| \dfrac{4.18\ \text{J}}{\text{g}\cdot\text{C}^\circ}$$

$x = 27.3^\circ\text{C}$

13. $H(\text{lost}) = H(\text{gained})$
    $m(\Delta T)C_p = m(\Delta T)C_p$

$$\dfrac{37.6\ \text{g}}{} \bigg| \dfrac{(100 - x)\ \text{C}^\circ}{} \bigg| \dfrac{0.232\ \text{J}}{\text{g}\cdot\text{C}^\circ} = \dfrac{25.0\ \text{g}}{} \bigg| \dfrac{(x - 23.0)\ \text{C}^\circ}{} \bigg| \dfrac{4.18\ \text{J}}{\text{g}\cdot\text{C}^\circ}$$

$x = 28.9^\circ\text{C}$

14. $H(\text{lost}) = H(\text{gained})$
    $m(\Delta T)C_p = m(\Delta T)C_p$

$$\dfrac{5.19\ \text{g}}{} \bigg| \dfrac{76.17\ \text{C}^\circ}{} \bigg| x = \dfrac{10.0\ \cancel{g}}{} \bigg| \dfrac{1.83\ \cancel{C^\circ}}{} \bigg| \dfrac{4.18\ \text{J}}{\cancel{g}\cdot\cancel{C^\circ}}$$

$x = 0.193\ \text{J/g}\cdot\text{C}^\circ$

15. $H(\text{lost}) = H(\text{gained})$
    $m(\Delta T)C_p = m(\Delta T)C_p$

$$\dfrac{23.8\ \text{g}}{} \bigg| \dfrac{76.5\ \text{C}^\circ}{} \bigg| x = \dfrac{50.0\ \cancel{g}}{} \bigg| \dfrac{8.50\ \cancel{C^\circ}}{} \bigg| \dfrac{4.18\ \text{J}}{\cancel{g}\cdot\cancel{C^\circ}}$$

$x = 1.11\ \text{J/g}\cdot\text{C}^\circ$

Page 121.

16. $NH_3 + HBr \rightarrow NH_4Br$
$\Delta H = \Delta H_f^\circ\,(\text{products}) - \Delta H_f^\circ\,(\text{reactants})$

$$\Delta H^\circ = \left[\dfrac{1\ \text{mol } \cancel{NH_4Br}}{}\bigg|\dfrac{(-270)\ \text{kJ}}{1\ \text{mol } \cancel{NH_4Br}}\right] - \left[\dfrac{1\ \text{mol } \cancel{NH_3}}{}\bigg|\dfrac{(-46.2)\ \text{kJ}}{1\ \text{mol } \cancel{NH_3}} + \dfrac{1\ \text{mol } \cancel{HBr}}{}\bigg|\dfrac{(-36.2)\ \text{kJ}}{1\ \text{mol } \cancel{HBr}}\right]$$

$\Delta H^\circ = -188\ \text{kJ}$

$$\dfrac{193\ \text{g } \cancel{NH_4Br}}{}\bigg|\dfrac{1\ \text{mol } \cancel{NH_4Br}}{97.9\ \text{g } \cancel{NH_4Br}}\bigg|\dfrac{(-188)\ \text{kJ}}{1\ \text{mol } \cancel{NH_4Br}} = -370\ \text{kJ}$$

17. $CoCO_3 \rightarrow CoO + CO_2$
$\Delta H^\circ = \Delta H_f^\circ\,(\text{products}) - \Delta H_f^\circ\,(\text{reactants})$

$$\Delta H^\circ = \left[\dfrac{1\ \text{mol } \cancel{CoO}}{}\bigg|\dfrac{(-239)\ \text{kJ}}{1\ \text{mol } \cancel{CoO}} + \dfrac{1\ \text{mol } \cancel{CO_2}}{}\bigg|\dfrac{(-393.5)\ \text{kJ}}{1\ \text{mol } \cancel{CO_2}}\right] - \left[\dfrac{1\ \text{mol } \cancel{CoCO_3}}{}\bigg|\dfrac{(-723)\ \text{kJ}}{1\ \text{mol } \cancel{CoCO_3}}\right]$$

$\Delta H^\circ = 90.5\ \text{kJ}$

$$\dfrac{0.772\ \text{g } \cancel{CoCO_3}}{}\bigg|\dfrac{1\ \text{mol } \cancel{CoCO_3}}{119\ \text{g } \cancel{CoCO_3}}\bigg|\dfrac{90.5\ \text{kJ}}{1\ \text{mol } \cancel{CoCO_3}} = 0.587\ \text{kJ}$$

18. $Cl_2 + 2NaBr \rightarrow 2NaCl + Br_2$
$\Delta H^\circ = \Delta H_f^\circ\,(\text{products}) - \Delta H_f^\circ\,(\text{reactants})$

$$\Delta H^\circ = \left[\dfrac{2\ \text{mol } \cancel{NaCl}}{}\bigg|\dfrac{(-411)\ \text{kJ}}{1\ \text{mol } \cancel{NaCl}} + \dfrac{1\ \text{mol } \cancel{Br_2}}{}\bigg|\dfrac{0\ \text{kJ}}{1\ \text{mol } \cancel{Br_2}}\right] -$$

$$\left[\dfrac{1\ \text{mol } \cancel{Cl_2}}{}\bigg|\dfrac{0\ \text{kJ}}{1\ \text{mol } \cancel{Cl_2}} + \dfrac{2\ \text{mol } \cancel{NaBr}}{}\bigg|\dfrac{(-360)\ \text{kJ}}{1\ \text{mol } \cancel{NaBr}}\right]$$

$\Delta H^\circ = -102\ \text{kJ}$

$$\dfrac{0.0663\ \text{g } \cancel{Br_2}}{}\bigg|\dfrac{1\ \text{mol } \cancel{Br_2}}{160\ \text{g } \cancel{Br_2}}\bigg|\dfrac{(-102)\ \text{kJ}}{1\ \text{mol } \cancel{Br_2}} = -0.0423\ \text{kJ}$$

Chapter End Problems

Pages 124-125.

19. To obtain the ratio of moles of required substance to given substance.

20. $\dfrac{8.32 \text{ g AlCl}_3}{} \left| \dfrac{1 \text{ mol AlCl}_3}{133.5 \text{ g AlCl}_3} \right| \dfrac{1 \text{ mol NaAlO}_2}{1 \text{ mol AlCl}_3} \left| \dfrac{82.0 \text{ g NaAlO}_2}{1 \text{ mol NaAlO}_2} \right. = 5.11 \text{ g NaAlO}_2$

21. $\dfrac{1.74 \text{ g Ce}_2(\text{C}_2\text{O}_4)_3}{} \left| \dfrac{1 \text{ mol Ce}_2(\text{C}_2\text{O}_4)_3}{544 \text{ g Ce}_2(\text{C}_2\text{O}_4)_3} \right| \dfrac{42 \text{ mol CO}_2}{1 \text{ mol Ce}_2(\text{C}_2\text{O}_4)_3} \left| \dfrac{44.0 \text{ g CO}_2}{1 \text{ mol CO}_2} \right. = 5.91 \text{ g CO}_2$

22. Endothermic reactions take in heat while exothermic reactions give off heat.

23. Striking a match.

24. **a.** exothermic   **b.** released   **c.** lower

25. 1 joule $= 1 \text{ kg} \cdot \text{m}^2/\text{s}^2$

26. Specific heat is a measure of heat capacity for 1 gram of a substance. Molar heat capacity is a measure of the heat capacity for 1 mole of a substance.

27. ΔH_f° of a free element $= 0$

28. $\Delta H^\circ = m(\Delta T)C_p$

$= \dfrac{390\,000 \text{ g}}{} \left| \dfrac{(300 - 25) \text{ C}^\circ}{} \right| \dfrac{0.443 \text{ J}}{\text{g} \cdot \text{C}^\circ} = 4.75 \times 10^5 \text{ J}$

29. $\Delta H^\circ = m(\Delta T)C_p$

$= \dfrac{54.4 \text{ g}}{} \left| \dfrac{(100 - 24) \text{ C}^\circ}{} \right| \dfrac{0.220 \text{ J}}{\text{g} \cdot \text{C}^\circ} = 910 \text{ J}$

30. $2NO(g) + O_2(g) \rightarrow 2NO_2(g)$
$\Delta H^\circ = [2(33.2)] - [2(90.2) + (0)]$
$\Delta H^\circ = -114 \text{ kJ}$

31. $4FeO(c) + O_2(g) \rightarrow 2Fe_2O_3(c)$
$\Delta H^\circ = [2(-824)] - [4(-272) + 0]$
$\Delta H^\circ = -560 \text{ kJ}$

Review

Page 125.

1. assume a 100 g sample

$\dfrac{84.2 \text{ g (NH}_4)_2\text{CO}_3}{} \left| \dfrac{1 \text{ mol (NH}_4)_2\text{CO}_3}{96.1 \text{ g (NH}_4)_2\text{CO}_3} \right. = 0.876 \text{ mol (NH}_4)_2\text{CO}_3$

$\dfrac{15.8 \text{ g H}_2\text{O}}{} \left| \dfrac{1 \text{ mol H}_2\text{O}}{18 \text{ g H}_2\text{O}} \right. = 0.877 \text{ mol H}_2\text{O}$

$0.876/0.877 \approx 1:1 \quad \therefore (NH_4)_2CO_3 \cdot H_2O$

2. **a.** $2Na + 2H_2O \rightarrow 2NaOH + H_2$ **c.** $2Sb + 3Cl_2 \rightarrow 2SbCl_3$
   b. $Mg + 2HCl \rightarrow MgCl_2 + H_2$ **d.** $Cl_2 + 2KBr \rightarrow 2KCl + Br_2$

One More Step

Page 125.

1. Brown bottles delay the spoiling of foods in which the decomposition reaction is activated by light.

2. Exposing the film involves the light-sensitive reaction
AgBr (*light*) AgBr (*exposed*)
$\rightarrow$

Developing the exposed film replaces the exposed AgBr with Ag.
$AgBr + C_6H_4(OH)_2 \rightarrow 2Ag + C_6H_4O_2 + 2HBr$
(*exposed*)   (*image*)

Fixing the film involves removal of the unexposed AgBr.
$AgBr + 2Na_2S_2O_3 \rightarrow NaBr + Na_3Ag(S_2O_3)_2$
(*unexposed*)

3. The temperature at which a heated liquid will flash momentarily when exposed to "flame" is called the flash point.

4. The change in disorder of the reaction will also determine whether or not the reaction will take place. (Entropy change $= \Delta S$.)

5. Any changes of mass to energy (or vice versa) which are associated with ordinary chemical reactions are too small to be detectable with present instruments. In molecular rearrangements (for example, chemical reactions) it is the change in potential energy of the particles involved (for example, the relative positions of the particles) which manifests itself as ΔH.

6. Hess's law: The heat of reaction for a multistep process is the sum of the heats of reaction of the individual steps. The law may also be stated: The ΔH of a reaction depends only on the initial and final energy states, not on the path from the initial energy state to the final energy state.

7. The amount of heat per mole of a fuel is a determinant in the selection of a fuel. Other factors of selection are cost per mole of processing and use. Certainly given equal cost for obtaining and delivering two fuels, the one with greater heat content would provide more heat per dollar.

8. O_2: $6.15 + 0.00310(298) - 9.23 \times 10^{-7}(298)^2 = 6.99$
   $6.15 + 0.00310(500) - 9.23 \times 10^{-7}(500)^2 = 7.47$
   CO_2: $6.21 + 0.0104(298) - 3.55 \times 10^{-6}(298)^2 = 9.00$
   $6.21 + 0.0104(500) - 3.55 \times 10^{-6}(500)^2 = 10.52$

ATOMIC STRUCTURE   8

An Overview

The study of atomic structure begins with Chapter 8. The atomic theory, subatomic particles, and basic ideas about the structure of atoms are discussed using a historical approach. Students can follow logically the historical development of scientific knowledge about atoms. When teaching atomic theory, you should make students aware of the parts of the theory that are firmly grounded in experiment and the parts that are tentative. For example, the existence of a dense positive nucleus is firmly based upon experiment. Any description of a electron's location is not based on experiment. The chapter builds toward the structure of the hydrogen atom. However, do not stress the Bohr planetary model of the atom.

Demonstration Information

The demonstration offers students visual evidence that matter reacts in small units called atoms. Hg_2I_2 changes to HgI_2 with an observable color change.

Performance Objectives

Goal: Students will gain knowledge and understanding of atomic theory.

Objectives: Upon completion of the reading and problems, and when asked to demonstrate their understanding either orally or on a written test, students will

8:1-5	K	state a brief history of the development of the theory of atoms.
8:2	K	state the law of conservation of mass.
8:3	K	state the law of definite proportions.
8:4	K	list the points of Dalton's hypothesis.
8:5	K/P	list examples of the law of multiple proportions.
8:6	K	differentiate among electron, proton, and neutron.
8:7	K	define atomic number and mass number and their relationship to isotopes.
8:8	K	define the standard for atomic mass units.
8:9	K	explain how a mass spectrometer can be used to determine average atomic mass.
	S/P	calculate average atomic mass given percentage of isotopes and their masses.
8:10	K	describe the Rutherford-Bohr atom.
8:11-12	K	explain the use of spectroscopy to determine the structure of a substance.
8:13-14	K	state the relationship between quantum theory and the location of an electron.
8:15	K	define photoelectric effect.
	A	voluntarily complete one or more of the One More Step activities.
	A	read unassigned literature related to the chapter.

Teaching Techniques

Section 8:1

Students often ask why they have to study history in chemistry class. We have included a presentation of the origin of the atomic theory for two reasons. (1) To show that our present theory is the work of many scientists over many years. (2) To make students aware of the logic used in obtaining evidence to support an atomic theory. The chemical evidence includes

1. elements cannot be decomposed into simpler substances
2. compounds have a definite composition by mass (Proust)
3. Dalton's law of multiple proportions
4. gases react in simple whole number ratios by volume (Gay Lussac)

Point out to your students that our understanding of atomic theory will need to be modified in light of yet undiscovered information.

Section 8:7

The nuclear theory of the atom was first proposed by Rutherford on the basis of the scattering experiment described in Section 8:10. His theory was the basis of modern atomic structure. This work raised several questions.

1. How are electrons arranged about the nucleus? This question will be considered in the next several chapters.
2. How do atoms of different elements differ in structure? F. Soddy first used the term isotopes in 1913. The separation of isotopes in a lab occurred in 1913 by J. J. Thomson (neon-20 and 22)
3. What is the internal structure of the nucleus? This question is still unanswered.

Section 8:10

Bohr provided the model to explain why the hydrogen atom does not collapse. The Bohr model did predict successfully the energy levels of hydrogen. However, do not spend a great deal of time on the Bohr model. Experiments show that the electron does not move in circular or elliptical orbits. Spatial distribution described by quantum mechanics is covered in Chapter 9. Bohr calculations did not explain the energy levels of the multi-electron atom. The Bohr model also does not explain chemical bonding in terms of energy. Finally, his basic assumption concerning the angular momentum $n(h/2\pi)$ is incorrect. It is actually

$$\sqrt{l(l+1)}\,(h/2\pi)$$

For these reasons, this model is treated lightly in the text. It is surprising that the Bohr model is still retained and emphasized almost sixty years after the proposal of the wave equation.

Section 8:13

Planck first described light as a particle. He used this description to explain the frequency distribution of black body radiation. Planck proposed this model based on experimental facts. Section 8:15 describes the photoelectric effect which demonstrates the particle nature of light. Interpretation of spectroscopic data concerns the behavior of light as a particle.

Section 8:14

We have avoided illustrations of atoms using Bohr models. Beginning chemistry students have open minds and should not be given the impression that the atom is planetary. Refer to the electrons as a cloud and to their positions as probable positions. This concept will be expanded in Chapter 9.

Section 8:15

When light falls on a metal surface, there is a frequency of the light which will cause the ejection of electrons from the surface of the metal. Changing the intensity at this frequency causes more electrons to be emitted. Increasing the light intensity increases the number of photons but does not change the energy per photon. Light which strikes the metal surface which is below the minimum frequency has no effect on the metal. Emphasize the difference between increasing light intensity and increasing the frequency.

Chemical Technology

This section should be used as a supplement to the topic of light covered in Chapter 8. Students who go on to study physics will cover this information in more detail when studying relativity.

Problem Solutions

Page 134.
1. boron = 5 electrons, 6 neutrons, 5 protons
   curium = 96 electrons, 151 neutrons, 96 protons

Page 137.

2. $\dfrac{(5 \times 176)+(19 \times 177)+(27 \times 178)+(14 \times 179),+(35 \times 180)}{100}$

   $= 179$ amu

3. $\dfrac{(7.42 \times 6.02) + (92.58 \times 7.02)}{100} = 6.95$ amu

Chapter End Problems

Page 149.

4. a. Dalton reintroduced the atomic theory and gathered experimental evidence to support his theory.

b. Thomson, who made the Cavendish Laboratory famous, made several important advances. He discovered the electron and showed that canal rays actually consist of positively charged particles. Thomson also calculated the mass of the proton.

c. Rutherford demonstrated that the nucleus is a small heavy core in an atom which consists mostly of space.

d. Chadwick showed that rays discovered by Walter Bothe in 1930 were really a beam of uncharged particles. Chadwick is credited with discovery of the neutron.

e. Moseley did research which resulted in a modification of the atomic theory to include atomic number.

f. Bohr originated the idea that electrons travel in a definite energy level around the nucleus. He applied Planck's idea of small packets or quanta of energy to his electron model.

g. Planck introduced the idea that (electromagnetic) energy is radiated in small packets called quanta.

h. Avogadro formed a hypothesis regarding gases at the same temperature and pressure: Equal volumes of gases, at the same temperature and pressure, have the same number of molecules.

5. Dalton's Theory:
(1) All matter is composed of atoms which are indivisible.
(2) Atoms of the same element are identical, atoms of different elements are dissimilar.
(3) Atoms can unite with other atoms in simple numerical ratios.

6. Carbon

7. Demonstrate conservation of mass by burning a candle in a closed container. Measure the mass of the candle and container before and after burning. There should be no change in mass if mass is conserved.

8. Analyze a compound to determine what elements it is composed of and the percentage of each element present. Synthesize the same compound (such as water) being careful to measure the reactants and products accurately. If the same ratio of elements is always involved, you have demonstrated the law of definite proportions.

9. Equal volumes of gases at the same temperature and pressure contain the same number of particles.

10. The atomic number is equal to the number of protons in the nucleus of an atom. The atomic number is 18. The mass number would be $(18 + 22) = 40$.

11. $(0.6)(69) + (0.4)(71) = 41.4 + 28.4$
$\qquad\qquad\qquad\qquad = 69.8$ amu

or consider 100 atoms in a random sample 60 are 69 and 40 are 71

$$\frac{60 \times 69 + 40 \times 71}{100} = 69.8$$

12. $\dfrac{49.9(4.31) + 51.9(83.8) + 52.9(9.55) + 53.9(2.38)}{100}$

$= 52.0$ amu

13. $\dfrac{2.01 \ \cancel{cm}}{} \left| \dfrac{1 \ \cancel{m}}{100 \ \cancel{cm}} \right| \dfrac{10^9 \ nm}{1 \ \cancel{m}} = 2.01 \times 10^7$ nm

14. Modified Theory:
(1) Atoms are composed of electrons, protons, and neutrons.
(2) All atoms of the same element have the same number of protons in the nucleus but the number of neutrons may vary.
(3) Remains unchanged.

15.

	charge	relative mass	location
proton	+1	1	nucleus
neutron	0	1	nucleus
electron	−1	0	orbitals

16. 7 electrons, 7 neutrons, 7 protons
91 electrons, 140 neutrons, 91 protons

17. Rutherford interpreted the results of the experiment.

18. Lines in the spectrum corresponded to the energy differences between Bohr's orbits.

19. Only the ionized form of an element will be affected by electric and magnetic fields.

20. The energy of electrons depends on the wavelength of light (energy in a quantum) while the number of electrons depends on the intensity of light (number of quanta).

Review

Pages 149-150.

1. a. strontium acetate
b. manganese(II) hydroxide
c. cadmium oxalate
d. lithium arsenate
e. thorium(IV) nitride
f. cerium(III) carbonate

2. a. Na_3N
b. Ce_2S_3
c. $BaSiF_6$
d. H_2Te
e. Ag_2SO_4
f. Cs_2SiF_6

3. a. $2K + 2H_2O \rightarrow 2KOH + H_2$
b. $Ca + 2HCl \rightarrow CaCl_2 + H_2$
c. $Cl_2 + 2KI \rightarrow 2KCl + I_2$
d. $2Na_2O_2 + 2H_2O \rightarrow 4NaOH + O_2$

4. $\dfrac{0.633 \ \cancel{mol} \ Th(SeO_4)_2}{} \left| \dfrac{6.02 \times 10^{23} \ \text{formula units}}{1 \ \cancel{mol}} \right.$

$= 3.81 \times 10^{23}$ formula units

5. $\dfrac{0.0731 \ \cancel{mol \ Sr(CN)_2}}{} \left| \dfrac{140 \ g \ Sr(CN)_2}{1 \ \cancel{mol \ Sr(CN)_2}} \right. = 10.2$ g $Sr(CN)_2$

6. Ba = 137 $\quad \dfrac{137}{233} \times 100 = 58.8\%$

S = 32.1 $\quad \dfrac{32.1}{233} \times 100 = 13.8\%$

O = 64.0 $\quad \dfrac{64.0}{233} \times 100 = 27.5\%$

7. assume a 100 g sample

$$\dfrac{44.2 \text{ g Cd}}{} \quad \dfrac{1 \text{ mol Cd}}{112 \text{ g Cd}} = 0.393 \text{ mol Cd}$$

$$\dfrac{44.8 \text{ g F}}{} \quad \dfrac{1 \text{ mol F}}{19.0 \text{ g F}} = 2.36 \text{ mol F}$$

$$\dfrac{11.0 \text{ g Si}}{} \quad \dfrac{1 \text{ mol Si}}{28.1 \text{ g Si}} = 0.392 \text{ mol Si}$$

0.393/2.36/0.392 = 1:6:1

$CdSiF_6$

8. assume a 100 g sample

$$\dfrac{76.0 \text{ g SrI}_2}{} \quad \dfrac{1 \text{ mol SrI}_2}{341 \text{ g SrI}_2} = 0.223 \text{ mol SrI}_2$$

$$\dfrac{24.0 \text{ g H}_2\text{O}}{} \quad \dfrac{1 \text{ mol H}_2\text{O}}{18.0 \text{ g H}_2\text{O}} = 1.33 \text{ mol H}_2\text{O}$$

0.223/1.33 ≈ 1:6

Therefore, $SrI_2 \cdot 6H_2O$

9. $\dfrac{84.1 \text{ g MgO}}{} \quad \dfrac{1 \text{ mol MgO}}{40.3 \text{ g MgO}} \quad \dfrac{1 \text{ mol Mg(OH)}_2}{1 \text{ mol MgO}} \quad \dfrac{58.3 \text{ g Mg(OH)}_2}{1 \text{ mol Mg(OH)}_2} = 122 \text{ g Mg(OH)}_2$

10. $H = m(\Delta T)C_p$

$= \dfrac{91.0 \text{ g}}{} \quad \dfrac{26.8 \text{ C}^\circ}{} \quad \dfrac{0.469 \text{ J}}{\text{g} \cdot \text{C}^\circ} = 1144 \text{ J}$

11. $\Delta H^\circ = \Delta H_f^\circ \text{ (products)} - \Delta H_f^\circ \text{ (reactants)}$

$= \left[\dfrac{1 \text{ mol MnCl}_2}{} \; \middle| \; \dfrac{(-555) \text{ kJ}}{1 \text{ mol MnCl}_2} \right] - \left[2 \text{ mol HCl} \; \middle| \; \dfrac{(-167) \text{ kJ}}{1 \text{ mol HCl}} \right]$

$= -221 \text{ kJ}$

One More Step

Pages 150-151.

1. See: Glasstone, Samuel, *Sourcebook for Atomic Energy*, New York, D. Van Nostrand Co., Inc., 1958, pp. 227-230.

2. See: Richards, James A., Jr., et al., *Modern University Physics*, Reading, Addison-Wesley Pub. Co., Inc., 1960, pp. 747-749.

3. Note: Because research in this area is so current, only a partial list is given.

Particle	Mass	Charge	Lifetime
electron	1	±	∞
electron's neutrino	0	0	∞
muon	207	±	$2.20 \quad 10^{-6}$ s
muon's neutrino	0	0	∞
pion	273	±	2.60×10^{-8} s
pion	265	0	0.8×10^{-16} s

Particle	Mass	Charge	Lifetime
kaon	966	±	1.24×10^{-8} s
kaon	975	0	5.17×10^{-8} s 0.86×10^{-10} s
eta	1074	0	2.53×10^{-19} s
rho	1507	±, 0	$4 \quad \times 10^{-23}$ s
proton	1836	+	∞
neutron	1839	0	0.93×10^3 s
lambda	2183	0	2.5×10^{-10} s
sigma	2328	±, 0	8.0×10^{-11} s
delta	2410	α+, ±, 0	$4 \quad \times 10^{-23}$ s
xi	2583	0	3.0×10^{-10} s
sigma (1385)	2710	0, −	$1 \quad \times 10^{-10}$ s
omega	3287	−	1.3×10^{-10} s
tau meson	3522	±	?
D meson	3523	±, 0	?
psi/J	6062	0	$6 \quad \times 10^{-20}$ s
upsilon	18590	0	?
upsilon	19570	0	?

4.

Atomic Number	Mass Number	Atomic Number	Mass Number
1	1, 2, ③*	6	⑨, ⑩, ⑪, 12, 13, ⑭, ⑮, ⑯
2	3, 4, ⑥, ⑧	7	⑫, ⑬, 14, 15, ⑯, ⑰, ⑱
3	6, 7, ⑧, ⑨	8	⑬, ⑭, ⑮, 16, 17, 18, ⑲, ⑳
4	⑥, ⑦, 9, ⑩, ⑪		
5	⑧, 10, 11, ⑫, ⑬		

*Radioactive isotopes are circled

Atomic Number	Mass Numbers
9	17*, 18*, 19, 20*, 21*, 22*
10	17*, 18*, 19*, 20, 21, 22, 23*, 24*
11	20*, 21*, 22*, 23, 24*, 25*, 26*
12	20*, 21*, 23*, 24, 25, 26, 27*, 28*
13	24*, 25*, 26*, 27, 28*, 29*, 30*
14	25*, 26*, 27*, 28, 29, 30, 31*, 32*
15	28*, 29*, 30*, 31, 32*, 33*, 34*
16	29*, 30*, 31*, 32, 33, 34, 35*, 36, 37*, 38*
17	32*, 33*, 34*, 35, 36*, 37, 38*, 39*, 40*
18	33*, 34*, 35*, 36, 37*, 38, 39*, 40, 41*, 42*, 43*, 44*
19	36*, 37*, 38*, 39, 40*, 41, 42*, 43*, 44*, 45*, 46*, 47*
20	37*, 38*, 39*, 40, 41*, 42, 43, 44, 45*, 46, 47*, 48, 49*, 50*

5. The Japanese physicist Hantaro Nagaoka suggested the planetary model for the atom in 1904.

6. *Encyclopaedia Britannica,* "Proton: Characteristics;" also, Hofstadter's Nobel address, 1962. (The method is essentially electron diffraction.)

7. $\nu = \frac{c}{\lambda} = \frac{3.00 \times 10^{8}\ \cancel{m}}{s} \cdot \frac{1}{410\ \cancel{nm}} \cdot \frac{10^{9}\ \cancel{nm}}{1\ \cancel{m}}$

$= 7.32 \times 10^{14}$ Hz

8. $E = h\nu = \frac{6.63 \times 10^{-34}\ J}{\cancel{Hz}} \cdot 4.31 \times 10^{14}\ \cancel{Hz}$

$= 2.86 \times 10^{-19}$ J

9. $\lambda = \frac{c}{\nu} = \frac{3.00 \times 10^{8}\ \cancel{m}}{\cancel{s}} \cdot \frac{\cancel{s}}{6.62 \times 10^{14}} \cdot \frac{10^{9}\ nm}{1\ \cancel{m}}$

$= 453$ nm

$E = h\nu = \frac{6.63 \times 10^{-34}\ J}{\cancel{Hz}} \cdot 4.53 \times 10^{14}\ \cancel{Hz}$

$= 3.00 \times 10^{-19}$ J

10. $\nu = \frac{c}{\lambda} = \frac{3.00 \times 10^{8}\ \cancel{m}}{s} \cdot \frac{1}{662\ \cancel{nm}} \cdot \frac{10^{9}\ \cancel{nm}}{1\ \cancel{m}}$

$= 4.53 \times 10^{14}$ Hz

11. Energy of light = energy of photon + release energy: $(1.20 \times 10^{-19}) + (3.60 \times 10^{-19}) = 4.80 \times 10^{-19}$ J then determine the frequency:

$E = h\nu$

Therefore, $\nu = \frac{E}{h} = \frac{4.80 \times 10^{-19}\ \cancel{J}}{6.63 \times 10^{-34}\ \cancel{J}\cdot s}$

$= 7.24 \times 10^{14}$ Hz

We conclude:

$\lambda = \frac{v}{\nu} = \frac{3.00 \times 10^{8}\ \cancel{m}}{\cancel{s}} \cdot \frac{\cancel{s}}{7.24 \times 10^{14}} \cdot \frac{10^{9}\ nm}{1\ \cancel{m}}$

$= 414$ nm

12. Frequency has no effect on the number of electrons that leave the metal surface. Frequency affects the energy of the electrons leaving the surface—the higher the frequency, the greater the energy of the ejected electrons.

13. $\nu = \frac{v}{\lambda}$

$= \frac{3 \times 10^{8}\ \cancel{m}}{s} \cdot \frac{1}{413\ \cancel{nm}} \cdot \frac{10^{9}\ \cancel{nm}}{1\ \cancel{m}}$

$= 7.26 \times 10^{14}$ Hz

14. $\lambda = \frac{v}{\nu}$

$= \frac{3 \times 10^{8}\ \cancel{m}}{\cancel{s}} \cdot \frac{\cancel{s}}{6.26 \times 10^{14}} \cdot \frac{10^{9}\ nm}{1\ \cancel{m}}$

$= 479$ nm

15. $\frac{6.63 \times 10^{-34}\ J}{\cancel{Hz}} \cdot 7.25 \times 10^{14}\ \cancel{Hz}$

$= 4.81 \times 10^{-19}$ J

16. $\frac{6.63 \times 10^{-34}\ J}{\cancel{Hz}} \cdot 6.26 \times 10^{14}\ \cancel{Hz}$

$= 4.15 \times 10^{-19}$ J

17. Colorimetry is the analysis of colored solutions. A solution of unknown concentration can be compared to a solution of known concentration. When the colors are of equal intensity the concentration of the unknown solution can be determined.

    Fluorometry is the analysis of fluorescent substances, i.e., those substances which absorb light at one wavelength, usually UV, and then emit light at another longer wavelength. It is used for the analysis of steroids, amino acids, and vitamins.

    Nephelometry is the analysis of colloids or suspensions by their light-scattering ability. It is used in analysis of bacteria concentration, particle size in turbid water, concentration of ion producing colloidal precipitates with analytical reagents.

18. EPR (or ESR, Electron Spin Resonance) is completely analogous to NMR (Nuclear Magnetic Resonance). A spinning electron has a magnetic field. If an external field is imposed, the electron will tend to align with it. The energy required to "flip" the electron over can be measured. The energy required is related to the environment of the electron and helps deduce electronic structures.

ELECTRON CLOUDS AND PROBABILITY

9

An Overview

The study of structure continues in Chapter 9 with a more detailed look at the behavior of electrons in atoms. In the text, students follow along as scientists develop the wave-mechanical view of the atom. This historical approach allows students to understand the limitations of the Bohr atom. Students see how the work of de Broglie, Heisenberg, and Schrödinger led to the new atomic model. The order of filling of the electron energy levels, sublevels, and orbitals is presented as a result of the study of quantum numbers derived from spectra. The chapter concludes with electron dot diagrams. Chapter 9 provides the foundation needed for Chapters 10, 11, and 12.

Demonstration Information

If a hydrogen gas tube and spectroscope are not available, the colored flames of Sr, Li, Ba, Cu, and Na salts can be used to introduce students to Chapter 9. Radiant energy is found to have many of the particle properties. Use the demonstration to begin a discussion of energy levels and line spectra. Discuss how spectral observations are the basis of contemporary atomic theory. **CAUTION:** As with any open alcohol flame, use caution to avoid spilling the alcohol from the evaporating dish. For best results, dissolve a few grams of the salt in a few drops of water before adding 3 cm^3 of methanol. The color will be most noticeable in a darkened room just as the alcohol is almost consumed.

Performance Objectives

Goal: Students will gain an understanding of the electron structure of the atom.

Objectives: Upon completion of the reading and problems, and when asked to demonstrate their understanding either orally or on a written test, students will

9:1-3	K/P	explain the wave-particle duality of the electron and other particles.
9:3-4	K	define Heisenberg's uncertainty principle based upon momentum and position.
9:5-7	K/P	use Schrödinger's work to develop a mental model of the atom involving charge clouds.
9:5-12	K	define the four quantum numbers and explain the effect of each on the charge cloud.
9:13	K/P	write an electron configuration for any atom using the diagonal rule.

9:14	K/P	draw an electron dot diagram for any atom.
	A	voluntarily complete one or more of the One More Step activities.
	A	read unassigned literature related to the chapter.

Teaching Techniques

Section 9:1

In 1927, Davisson and Germer demonstrated that electrons show wave properties. The wave properties of fundamental particles are now recognized. Diffraction patterns have been demonstrated for fundamental particles just like those for light. The mathematics of quantum mechanics is based upon a modification of the mathematics of classical mechanics. The equations describe waves. They have a statistical nature in which variables are in terms of probabilities and averages. Quantum mechanics depends upon an acceptance of the wave description of fundamental particles.

Section 9:3

Substituting momentum for mv in de Broglie's wave equation alters the mathematical nature of the equation. It becomes the Schrödinger equation by substituting a second derivative where momentum appears. This equation is the basis of quantum mechanics. The electron must be accelerated as it moves in a curved path around a proton. The electron should radiate energy, slow down, and spiral into the nucleus. Classical mechanics predicts that the atom would collapse in a fraction of a second. Obviously, atoms do not follow the same physics equations as the planets. The equations that describe electron behavior are called quantum or wave mechanics equations.

Section 9:4

Use Heisenberg's uncertainty principle to stress that quantum theory tells us in probability terms how the electron occupies the space outside the nucleus. For example, an electron can be as far away as 0.224 nm from the hydrogen nucleus and as close as 0.01 nm. However, 90% of the time the electron will be between 0.142 nm and 0.029 nm from the nucleus. Probability distribution is an important concept in quantum mechanics because we do not know the exact position and momentum of an electron simultaneously.

Section 9:5

The following is a more detailed explanation of the Schrödinger wave equation found on page 158 of the text.

$$\frac{\partial^2 \Psi}{\partial x^2} + \frac{\partial^2 \Psi}{\partial y^2} + \frac{\partial^2 \Psi}{\partial z^2} + \frac{8\pi^2 m}{h^2}(E - V)\Psi = 0$$

∂ = The mathematical symbol indicating a partial derivative.

Ψ = the Greek letter *psi*. It is the symbol used to indicate the amplitude of a wave. Ψ is also called the wave function. Ψ^2 determines the probability of finding an electron in a specified region which can be represented on a three dimensional graph by the coordinates:

$$x \text{ and } x + dx,$$
$$y \text{ and } y + dy,$$
$$z \text{ and } z + dz.$$

x, y, z = the coordinates of probable wave location.
m = the mass of an electron = 9.11×10^{-28} g.
h = Planck's constant = 6.63×10^{-34} J·s.
E = total energy.
V = potential energy.

Section 9:6

The probability distribution of an electron in space is described by the wave function, ψ. If a time exposed photograph was taken of an atom, we would see where an electron spends more time and less time. The information contained in this picture is also contained in ψ. It gives us a time-averaged view of the electron's motion. The square of the wave function, $|\psi|^2$, gives us the probability distribution in space, an orbital. Each permitted set of quantum numbers defines an orbital. The electron motion around the nucleus in the Bohr model suggested an orbital. The true meaning of ψ conflicts with the term orbital.

Section 9:8

The value of the principle quantum number n can actually go to infinity, but in a practical sense, there are seven energy levels. The value of n describes an average distance from the nucleus of the electron cloud.

Section 9:9

The letters s, p, and d stand for sharp, principal and diffuse. These terms were originally spectroscopy labels for different series of spectral lines emitted by the elements. Other permitted values are names f, g, h, . . . and were added later in alphabetical order. The letter e was omitted because of its frequent use elsewhere.

Section 9:11

Students often ask how a complex electron probability cloud shape, such as a d orbital can be described by integers. You can stretch a rope between a doorknob and your hand to help answer the question. Begin to move the rope so as to induce a standing wave. At a low vibrating frequency there is one crest. At a higher frequency, there are two crests with a node in the center. An easy way to describe these waves is to represent the number of nodes with an integer. The quantum number is analogous to the integer. A nodal surface is a surface at which the probability of finding an electron is zero. When $n = 1$, the first energy level having a spherical shaped electron cloud, there is one nodal surface at infinity. When $n = 2$, there are two nodal surfaces, etc. The vibrating rope can be a helpful model to relate the abstract nature of Schrödinger's equation, the wave function, and the probability distribution.

Section 9:12

The values of n, l, and m are fixed values designating the energy level, sublevel, and orbital. The fourth quantum number has only two numerically permitted values. The fourth quantum number (s) is independent of the other three quantum numbers. It has a value of either $+\frac{1}{2}$ or $-\frac{1}{2}$. It describes the direction of rotation of an electron on its axis.

Only two electrons can occupy the same orbital according to the Pauli exclusion principle. If two electrons had the same set of four quantum numbers in an atom, they would have the same probability of being in the same place at the same time. That possibility is excluded considering the like charges.

You can summarize the quantum numbers as being analogous to an address. 123 Main St., Columbus, Ohio, consists of four parts: state = n, city = l, street = m, and lot number = s. The four quantum numbers give us an electron's address in an atom.

Chemical Career

Use the perfumer career as the beginning of a project to explore the various science-related careers in the cosmetics industry.

Problem Solutions

Page 154.

1. $x = \dfrac{h}{mv}$

$$\dfrac{6.67 \times 10^{-34}\,\text{kg}\cdot\text{m}^2}{s} \left|\dfrac{s}{9.11 \times 10^{-28}\,g}\right| \dfrac{1000\,g}{1\,kg} \left|\dfrac{s}{2.00 \times 10^8\,m}\right| \dfrac{10^9\,\text{nm}}{1\,m}$$

$= 3.66 \times 10^{-3}$ nm

Page 161.

2. The greatest number of electrons in a given energy level can be determined by finding the value of $2n^2$

where n is the energy level involved; for

$n = 2$, $2n^2 = 2(2)^2 = 8$
$n = 3$, $2n^2 = 2(3)^2 = 18$
$n = 5$, $2n^2 = 2(5)^2 = 50$
$n = 7$, $2n^2 = 2(7)^2 = 98$

Page 164.

3. **a.** A d sublevel contains 5 orbitals.
   b. An f sublevel contains 7 orbitals.

Page 168.

4. $z = 1$ $1s^1$
         2   $1s^2$
         3   $1s^2 2s^1$
         4   $1s^2 2s^2$
         5   $1s^2 2s^2 2p^1$
         6   $1s^2 2s^2 2p^2$
         7   $1s^2 2s^2 2p^3$
         8   $1s^2 2s^2 2p^4$
         9   $1s^2 2s^2 2p^5$
        10   $1s^2 2s^2 2p^6$
        11   $1s^2 2s^2 2p^6 3s^1$
        12   $1s^2 2s^2 2p^6 3s^2$
        13   $1s^2 2s^2 2p^6 3s^2 3p^1$
        14   $1s^2 2s^2 2p^6 3s^2 3p^2$
        15   $1s^2 2s^2 2p^6 3s^2 3p^3$
        16   $1s^2 2s^2 2p^6 3s^2 3p^4$
        17   $1s^2 2s^2 2p^6 3s^2 3p^5$
        18   $1s^2 2s^2 2p^6 3s^2 3p^6$
        19   $1s^2 2s^2 2p^6 3s^2 3p^6 4s^1$
        20   $1s^2 2s^2 2p^6 3s^2 3p^6 4s^2$

Page 169.

5. **a.** $1s^2 2s^2 2p^6 3s^2 3p^6 4s^2 3d^8$ Ni:
   b. $1s^2 2s^2 2p^6 3s^2 3p^6$:A̤r:
   c. $1s^2 2s^2 2p^6 3s^2 3p^4$ ·S̤:
   d. $1s^2 2s^2 2p^6 3s^2 3p^6 4s^2 3d^{10} 4p^6 5s^2 4d^9$ Ag:
   e. $1s^2 2s^2 2p^6 3s^2 3p^6 4s^1$ K·
   f. $1s^2 2s^2 2p^6 3s^2 3p^6 4s^2 3d^{10} 4p^2$ ·G̈e:

Chapter End Problems

Page 172.

6. He equated Einstein's expression for energy with Planck's expression for energy.

7. An inverse relationship $\lambda = \dfrac{h}{p}$

8. $2n^2 = 2(5)^2 = 50$

9. $+1/2, -1/2$

10. Electron configuration for uranium:
    Experimental (p. 184)
    $1s^2 2s^2 2p^6 3s^2 3p^6 3d^{10} 4s^2 4p^6 4d^{10}$
    $4f^{14} 5s^2 5p^6 5d^{10} 5f^3 6s^2 6p^6 6d^1 7s^2$

Diagonal rule (p. 167)
$1s^2 2s^2 2p^6 3s^2 3p^6 4s^2 3d^{10} 4p^6 5s^2$
$4d^{10} 5p^6 6s^2 4f^{14} 5d^{10} 6p^6 7s^2 5f^4$

Experimental Levels

1.	2	2
2.	2 + 6	8
3.	2 + 6 + 10	18
4.	2 + 6 + 10 + 14	32
5.	2 + 6 + 10 + 3	21
6.	2 + 6 + 1	9
7.	2	2
		92

Predicted (diagonal rule) Levels

1.	2	2
2.	2 + 6	8
3.	2 + 6 + 10	18
4.	2 + 6 + 10 + 14	32
5.	2 + 6 + 10 + 4	22
6.	2 + 6	8
7.	2	2
		92

Levels 5, 6, and 7 are not full.

11. a. Mn manganese
    b. Mo molybdenum

12. Nb, $Z = 41$ $1s^2 2s^2 2p^6 3s^2 3p^6 4s^2 3d^{10} 4p^6 5s^2 4d^3$
    Zn, $Z = 30$ $1s^2 2s^2 2p^6 3s^2 3p^6 4s^2 3d^{10}$

13. Po, $Z = 84$ $1s^2 2s^2 2p^6 3s^2 3p^6 4s^2 3d^{10} 4p^6 5s^2 4d^{10}$
    $5p^6 6s^2 4f^{14} 5d^{10} 6p^4$
    Tc, $Z = 43$ $1s^2 2s^2 2p^6 3s^2 3p^6 4s^2 3d^{10} 4p^6 5s^2 4d^5$

14. $Z = 33$, ·Äs: Note that this is
    $Z = 51$, ·S̈b: column VA of the
    $Z = 83$, ·B̈i: periodic table.

15. There are 4 paired electrons in a boron atom.
    Boron configuration = $1s^2 2s^2 2p^1$.
    There are 14 paired electrons in a sulfur atom.
    There are 8 paired electrons in a fluorine atom.
    Fluorine configuration = $1s^2 2s^2 2p^5$.

16. Two electrons are not shown in each electron dot diagram.

$Z = 3$	$1s^2 2s^1$	Li·	2
$Z = 4$	$1s^2 2s^2$	Be:	2
$Z = 5$	$1s^2 2s^2 2p^1$	B̈:	2
$Z = 6$	$1s^2 2s^2 2p^2$	·C̈:	2
$Z = 7$	$1s^2 2s^2 2p^3$	·N̈:	2
$Z = 8$	$1s^2 2s^2 2p^4$	·Ö:	2
$Z = 9$	$1s^2 2s^2 2p^5$	:F̈:	2
$Z = 10$	$1s^2 2s^2 2p^6$	:N̈e:	2

Review

Page 173.

1. Law of conservation of mass and law of definite proportions.

2. nuclide—an atom with a specific number of protons and a specific number of neutrons
   isotopes—two different nuclides of the same element

3. atomic number = number of protons in the nucleus of an atom
   atomic mass = average mass of the atoms of an element

4. $\Delta H° = \Delta H_f°$ (products) $- \Delta H_f°$ (reactants)

$$= \left[1\ mol\ MnS \left| \frac{(-214)\ kJ}{1\ mol\ MnS} \right| + 2\ mol\ NaNO_3 \left| \frac{(-447)\ kJ}{1\ mol\ NaNO_3} \right| \right] - \left[1\ mol\ Mn(NO_3)_2 \left| \frac{(-636)\ kJ}{1\ mol\ Mn(NO_3)_2} \right| + 1\ mol\ Na_2S \left| \frac{(-437)\ kJ}{1\ mol\ Na_2S} \right| \right]$$

$= -35$ kJ

5. $\dfrac{10.0\ g \quad | \quad 200\ C° \quad | \quad 0.220\ J}{\quad | \quad \quad | \quad g \cdot C°} = 440$ J

6. The regularity of the spacing in the lines of the hydrogen atom.

7. Planck proposed the quantum theory.

8. $\dfrac{(91.906808)(15.84) + (93.905090)(9.04) + (94.905837)(15.72) + (95.904674)(16.53) + (96.906023)(9.46) + (97.905409)(23.78) + (99.907478)(9.63)}{100}$

   $= 95.9$ amu

9. 101 electrons, 155 neutrons, 101 protons

10. The emission of electrons from a surface when it is exposed to radiant energy.

One More Step

Page 173.

1. First, change nm to meters:

$$\frac{0.01 \text{ nm}}{} \left| \frac{1 \text{ m}}{10^9 \text{ nm}} \right. = 1 \times 10^{-11} \text{ m}$$

then solve:

$$\Delta p = \frac{h}{\Delta x} = \frac{6.63 \times 10^{-34} \text{ kg} \cdot \text{m}^2}{\text{s}} \left| \frac{}{10^{-11} \text{ m}} \right.$$
$$= 6.63 \times 10^{-23} \text{ kg} \cdot \text{m/s}$$

2. In relativistic mechanics there is a fourth dimension—time. The experimental evidence indicating the fourth dimension is the splitting of spectral lines (Zeeman effect).

3. Wave properties: An electron beam which is passed through a crystal is diffracted and produces a pattern similar to that produced by light and water waves when they are passed through slits of the appropriate size.

   Particle properties: The cloud chamber, bubble chamber, cyclotron, synchrotron, and linear accelerator, mass spectrometer, electron gun and Milikan's apparatus all treat the electron successfully as a particle.

THE PERIODIC TABLE   10

An Overview

Classification of atoms into the periodic system on the basis of their structure is introduced in Chapter 10. The chapter begins with the historical development of the periodic table. This approach provides students with a rationale for the development of a classification system. The periodic table organizes a tremendous number of chemical facts and trends. The text shows students that the electron structure of atoms is the basis for the regularities observed in elements. In this chapter students are presented with many concepts and chemical facts. Center their attention on the chemistry which best illustrates the family relationships and periodicity. We will continue to use the periodic table in several later chapters.

Demonstration Information

$2Na(c) + 2H_2O(l) \rightarrow 2NaOH(aq) + H_2(g)$. The introductory paragraph in the text refers to the demonstration. Use the demonstration to introduce the activity trend found in group IA. Stress the ability of the chemist to make predictions based on a knowledge of such trends. **CAUTION:** Wear goggles or safety glasses and quickly cover the beaker with a wire screen to prevent the Na or K metal from flying out of the beaker. The H_2 gas will burn when potassium metal is dropped in the beaker. The flame will be more visible if you turn the overhead projector off.

Performance Objectives

Goal: Students will gain an understanding of the periodic table and the relationship between periodic properties of the elements and their electron structures.

Objectives:

Upon completion of the reading and problems, and when asked to demonstrate their understanding either orally or on a written test, students will

10:1-2	K	list early attempts at classification of the elements and their limitations.
10:3	K	explain the basis for the modern periodic law.
10:4-6	K/P	fill out a periodic table based on applying the diagonal rule.
10:7-8	K/P	determine whether an atom is unstable or stable using the octet rule or filled versus half-filled sublevels.
10:9	K/P	distinguish among metals, nonmetals, and metalloids.
10:10-12	P/S	use the periodic table to predict the sizes of atoms and ions.
10:13	P/S	predict oxidation numbers using an element's position on the periodic table.
	A	voluntarily complete one or more of the One More Step activities.
	A	read unassigned literature related to the chapter.

Teaching Techniques

Section 10:1

The history of some thought processes that went into the development of the periodic table is presented briefly. The emphasis of this section should be on gaining knowledge about the structure and properties of the elements and their compounds.

Section 10:2

The original paper presented by Mendeleev appears in English in

Newman, J. R., ed., *World of Mathematics*, Vol. II, Simon and Schuster, 1956, pp. 913-918.

Section 10:4

To impress students with the idea of classification, you can display a number of elements and compounds from the stockroom in random order. Students should be made aware of the difficulty of listing all the properties for each substance. A classification of the elements into metals and nonmetals allows us to generalize concerning some properties. Point out that electron configurations can be used to organize the elements into columns and rows. Review the Aufbau principle, the pattern in which the lowest electron levels fill first.

Section 10:8

Using Figure 10-4, students can write the electron configurations for most elements. Be sure students are aware that exceptions exist. You may want them to memorize Cr and Cu as examples of exceptions.

Section 10:12

To help students understand why the chloride ion is larger than the chlorine atom use the following model: Imagine a circle of seven students (an energy level) in a large room. There is distance between each of them. As the nuclear charge increases, atomic number increases, the students move closer to the center of the circle. Eventually their shoulders touch. They can go no closer without distorting the circle. In order to admit an eighth student to the circle, the students must back up, increasing the size.

You may wish to demonstrate the reaction of Na with Cl_2, Br_2, or I_2. **CAUTION:** Do not use potassium. It explodes with Br_2 and I_2.

Chemical Career

Emphasize the importance of analysis and analytical techniques to the study of chemistry. There are a number of analytical techniques covered briefly in the text (chromatography, mass spec, NMR, IR, electrophoresis, and so on). You can have students research these topics in more detail and present their findings in class. You may also want to consider having students research the analytical procedures used by a particular industry in your area (steel, pharmaceuticals, food processing, and so on).

Problem Solutions

Page 188.
1. a. metal   e. metal
   b. metal   f. metal
   c. metal   g. metal
   d. nonmetal

2. There are more metals than nonmetals in the periodic table.

Page 193.
3. a. Ne   d. Al   g. K
   b. Be   e. As   h. Se^{2-}
   c. N^{3-} f. Br   i. Sc

4. Be is larger because in boron the same outer level is attracted by 1 more proton. As has one more layer of electrons. K is larger because in calcium the same outer level is attracted by 1 more proton.

Page 194.
5. Gd 2+
   Ra 2+
   Nb 3+, 4+, 5+

6. 3+ should be more stable since the *d* sublevel is half-filled.

Chapter End Problems

Pages 197-198.
7. a. metal   e. metal   i. nonmetal
   b. nonmetal   f. metal   j. metal
   c. metal   g. nonmetal   k. nonmetal
   d. nonmetal   h. metal   l. nonmetal

8. decrease

9. increase

10. smaller

11. larger

12. a. 3+, 5+   f. 2+, 3+, 4+, 5+
    b. 2+   g. 2+
    c. 3−, 3+, 5+   h. 1+
    d. 2−, 4+, 6+   i. 1+, 2+
    e. 2+

13. a. $Z = 34$, selenium
    b. 4th period, Group VIA
    c. nonmetal
    d. tends to gain electrons, hard, brittle
    e. 2−
    f. $\cdot \overset{\cdot\cdot}{\underset{\cdot}{Se}} \colon$ $\colon \overset{\cdot\cdot}{\underset{\cdot\cdot}{Se}} \colon^{2-}$
    g. smaller

14. Cesium
    a. 6th period, Group IA
    b. metal
    c. malleable, conducts electricity, loses electrons
    d. $1s^2 2s^2 2p^6 3s^2 3p^6 4s^2 3d^{10} 4p^6 5s^2 5p^6 4d^{10} 6s^1$
    e. 1+
    f. Cs$\cdot$ Cs^{1+}
    Chromium
    a. 3rd period, Group VIB

b. metal
c. malleable, ductile, conducts heat and electricity, loses electrons
d. $1s^2 2s^2 2p^6 3s^2 3p^6 4s^1 3d^5$
e. 2+, 3+, 6+
f. Cr⁚   Cr²⁺

Cadmium
a. 5th period, Group IIB
b. metal
c. malleable, ductile, conducts heat and electricity, loses electrons
d. $1s^2 2s^2 2p^6 3s^2 3p^6 4s^2 3d^{10} 4p^6 5s^2 4d^{10}$
e. 2+
f. Cd⁚   Cd²⁺

Antimony
a. 5th period, Group VA
b. metalloid
c. loses or gains electrons, semiconductor

d. $1s^2 2s^2 2p^6 3s^2 3p^6 4s^2 3d^{10} 4p^6 5s^2 4d^{10} 5p^3$
e. 3+, 5+
f. ·Sb⁚   Sb⁚³⁺

Bromine
a. 4th period, Group VIIA
b. nonmetal
c. gains electrons, does not conduct
d. $1s^2 2s^2 2p^6 3s^2 3p^6 4s^2 3d^{10} 4p^5$
e. 1−
f. ⁚B̈r⁚   ⁚B̈r⁚¹⁻

Radon
a. 7th period, Group VIIIA
b. nonmetal
c. does not conduct
d. $1s^2 2s^2 2p^6 3s^2 3p^6 4s^2 3d^{10} 4p^6 5s^2 4d^{10} 5p^6 4f^{14}$
   $6s^2 5d^{10} 6p^6$
e. 0
f. ⁚R̈n⁚

Review

Pages 198-199.

1. frequency, wavelength, velocity, amplitude
2. Schrödinger considered the electron as a wave; Bohr as a particle.
3. n, l, m, s
   n represents energy level, l sublevel, m and s have no effect on energy
   n = cloud size, l = cloud shape, m = cloud spatial orientation, s = electron spin
4. a. $1s^2 2s^2 2p^6 3s^2 3p^1$ Äl⁚

   b. $1s^2 2s^2 2p^6 3s^2 3p^4$ ·S̈⁚

   c. $1s^2 2s^2 2p^6 3s^2 3p^6 4s^2$ Ca⁚

   d. $1s^2 2s^2 2p^6 3s^2 3p^6 4s^2 3d^2$ Ti⁚

   e. $1s^2 2s^2 2p^6 3s^2 3p^6 4s^2 3d^3$ V⁚

   f. $1s^2 2s^2 2p^6 3s^2 3p^6 4s^2 3d^5$ Mn⁚

   g. $1s^2 2s^2 2p^6 3s^2 3p^6 4s^2 3d^7$ Co⁚

   h. $1s^2 2s^2 2p^6 3s^2 3p^6 4s^2 3d^{10} 4p^2$ ·G̈e⁚

   i. $1s^2 2s^2 2p^6 3s^2 3p^6 4s^2 3d^{10} 4p^5$ ⁚B̈r⁚
5. λ = wavelength
   h = Planck's constant
   m = mass
   v = velocity
6. $$\frac{(1.14)(179.9467) + (26.41)(181.94825) + (14.40)(182.95027) + (30.64)(183.95097) + (28.41)(185.9544)}{100} = 185.64 \text{ amu}$$
7. 2
8. $\dfrac{0.01}{10.14} \times 100 = 0.09\%$
9. $\dfrac{42.5 \text{ g}}{} \Big| \dfrac{cm^3}{3.15 \text{ g}} = 13.5 \text{ cm}^3$
10. a. $Zn_3 P_2$
    b. $Zr(SeO_4)_2$

    c. AlF_3

    d. $BiCl_3$

11. a. zinc tartrate

    b. lead(II) selenide

    c. chromium(III) acetate

    d. manganese(II) phosphide

12. 291

13. $\dfrac{3.00 \; \cancel{\text{mol } Zn_3(PO_4)_2}}{} \left| \dfrac{386 \text{ g } Zn_3(PO_4)_2}{1 \; \cancel{\text{mol } Zn_3(PO_4)_2}} \right. = 1160 \text{ g } Zn_3(PO_4)_2$

14. $\dfrac{10.0 \; \cancel{cm^3 \text{ soln}}}{} \left| \dfrac{0.100 \; \cancel{\text{mol } ZrCl_4}}{1000 \; \cancel{cm^3 \text{ soln}}} \right| \dfrac{233 \text{ g } ZrCl_4}{1 \; \cancel{\text{mol } ZrCl_4}} = 0.233 \text{ g } ZrCl_4$

    add water to make 10 cm^3 of solution

15.   Co = 58.9

    4 C = 48.0

    6 H = 6.05

    4 O = $\dfrac{64.0}{177}$

    $\dfrac{58.9}{177} \times 100 = 33.3\%$ Co

    $\dfrac{48.0}{177} \times 100 = 27.1\%$ C

    $\dfrac{6.05}{177} \times 100 = 3.42\%$ H

    $\dfrac{64.0}{177} \times 100 = 36.2\%$ O

16. $\dfrac{40.1 \; \cancel{\text{g Co}}}{} \left| \dfrac{1 \text{ mol Co}}{58.9 \; \cancel{\text{g Co}}} \right. = 0.680 \text{ mol Co}$

    $\dfrac{16.3 \; \cancel{\text{g C}}}{} \left| \dfrac{1 \text{ mol C}}{12.0 \; \cancel{\text{g C}}} \right. = 1.36 \text{ mol C}$

    $\dfrac{43.5 \; \cancel{\text{g O}}}{} \left| \dfrac{1 \text{ mol O}}{16.0 \; \cancel{\text{g O}}} \right. = 2.72 \text{ mol O}$

    $0.680/1.36/2.72 \approx 1:2:4$ CoC_2O_4

17. $\dfrac{682}{341} = 2$ Thus, $Bi_2C_6O_{12}$

    or $Bi_2(C_2O_4)_3$

18. $\dfrac{66.3 \; \cancel{\text{g } Ga_2(SeO_4)_3}}{} \left| \dfrac{1 \text{ mol } Ga_2(SeO_4)_3}{568 \; \cancel{\text{g } Ga_2(SeO_4)_3}} \right. = 0.117 \text{ mol } Ga_2(SeO_4)_3$

    $\dfrac{33.7 \; \cancel{\text{g } H_2O}}{} \left| \dfrac{1 \text{ mol } H_2O}{18.0 \; \cancel{\text{g } H_2O}} \right. = 1.87 \text{ mol } H_2O$

    $0.117/1.87 \approx 1:16$ $\therefore Ga_2(SeO_4)_3 \cdot 16H_2O$

19. $Cr(NO_3)_3 + 3NaOH \rightarrow Cr(OH)_3 + 3NaNO_3$

20. $\dfrac{2.37 \; \cancel{\text{g NaOH}}}{} \left| \dfrac{1 \; \cancel{\text{mol NaOH}}}{40.0 \; \cancel{\text{g NaOH}}} \right| \dfrac{2 \; \cancel{\text{mol } AgNO_3}}{2 \; \cancel{\text{mol NaOH}}} \left| \dfrac{170 \text{ g } AgNO_3}{1 \; \cancel{\text{mol } AgNO_3}} \right. = 10.1 \text{ g } AgNO_3$

21. $\Delta H = m(\Delta T)C_p$

    $\dfrac{5.24 \; \cancel{\text{g}}}{} \left| \dfrac{1995 \; \cancel{°C}}{} \right| \dfrac{0.238 \text{ J}}{\cancel{\text{g} \cdot °C}} = 2490 \text{ J}$

22. $\Delta H° = \Delta H_f° \text{ (products)} - \Delta H_f° \text{ (reactants)}$

    $= \left[\dfrac{1 \; \cancel{\text{mol } ZnSO_4}}{} \left| \dfrac{(-1063) \text{ kJ}}{1 \; \cancel{\text{mol } ZnSO_4}} \right. \right] - \left[\dfrac{1 \; \cancel{\text{mol } H_2SO_4}}{} \left| \dfrac{(-908) \text{ kJ}}{1 \; \cancel{\text{mol } H_2SO_4}} \right. \right] = -155 \text{ kJ}$

23. 8 electrons, 8 protons, 8 neutrons

One More Step

Page 199.

1. Sections 10:1 and 10:2 give a start. See: Ihde, *The Development of Modern Chemistry*

2. Mendeleev's predictions about gallium and scandium were about as good as his predictions about germanium. However, his predictions about technetium, rhenium, and neptunium were not as accurate.

3. Mo *predicted* $5s^2 4d^4$
   actual $5s^1 4d^5$ (half-filled d sublevel)
   Pd *predicted* $5s^2 4d^8$
   actual $4d^{10}$ (full d sublevel)
   Gd *predicted* $4f^8$
   actual $4f^7 5d^1$ (half-filled f sublevel)

4. Au *predicted* $6s^2 4f^{14} 5d^9$
   actual $6s^1 4f^{14} 5d^{10}$ (full d sublevel)
   Cm *predicted* $5f^8$
   actual $5f^7 6d^1$ (half-filled f sublevel)
   Th *predicted* $5f^2$
   actual $6d^2$ (exception to the rules given in the text)

5. Ar 0 outer level already has 8 electrons
   Eu 2+ loss of the two $6s$ electrons
   Al 3+ loss of the two $3s$ and one $3p$ electron
   Sb 3+ loss of the three $5p$ electrons
   5+ loss of the two $5s$ electrons in addition to $5p$ loss
   Br 1− gain of one electron to complete outer level
   Ar as predicted
   Eu also a 3+ (no obvious explanation)
   Al as predicted
   Sb as predicted (sometimes considered to have a 3− in which the outer level is completed by gaining three electrons)
   Br as predicted

6. U 2+ loss of two $7s$ electrons
   Na 1+ loss of one $3s$ electron
   Si 4+ loss of two $3p$ and two $3s$ electrons
   4− gain of four electrons to fill outer level
   Ce 2+ loss of two $6s$ electrons
   Co 2+ loss of two $4s$ electrons
   U missing 2+ (no obvious explanation)
   Na as predicted
   Si as predicted
   Ce no 2+; 3+ and 4+ instead (no obvious explanation)
   Co also 3+ (no obvious explanation)

7. Element name origins:

   Named for Discoverer's Geographic Origin
   germanium
   lutetium
   polonium

   Named for Properties

Chemical	Physical
hydrogen	phosphorus
oxygen	iron(?)
sulfur	bromine
argon	tungsten
zinc	osmium

   arsenic
   antimony
   lead(?)
   astatine
   radium
   actinium
   protactinium

   Named to Honor

A Person	A Place
gadolinium	europium
curium	hafnium
einsteinium	francium
fermium	americium
mendelevium	berkelium
lawrencium	californium
nobelium	

   Named for Mythological Character

Due to Property	Due to Other Reason
titanium	vanadium
cobalt	niobium
nickel	tantalum

   Named for Color

Of Element	Of Compound	Of Spectra
chlorine	chromium	rubidium
silver	iridium	rhodium
iodine		indium
platinum		cesium
gold		thallium
bismuth		

   Named for Discovery

Location	Material	Process
helium	lithium	neon
scandium	carbon	krypton
copper	nitrogen	technetium
gallium	sodium	xenon
ruthenium	potassium	lanthanum
tin	calcium	promethium
holmium	radon	dysprosium
rhenium	samarium	thulium

   Named for Mineral

Color	Property	Location
beryllium	fluorine	strontium
boron	aluminum	yttrium
magnesium	silicon	cadmium
zirconium	manganese	terbium
praseodymium	neodymium	erbium
	molybdenum	ytterbium
	barium	thorium

   Named for Heavenly Body

Earth	Moon	Planet	Asteroid
tellurium	selenium	mercury	palladium
		uranium	cerium
		neptunium	
		plutonium	

8. Metalloids are semiconductors. Although Si and Ge have the same crystalline structure as diamond, they will conduct electrons. Heat energy at ordinary temperatures frees electrons from the valence band to the conducting band. The conductivity of semiconductors increases with temperature, and donor and acceptor impurities are easily introduced.

PERIODIC PROPERTIES

11

An Overview

Chapter 11 extends the concepts of Chapter 10 in a descriptive study of example elements and their chemistry. After concluding this chapter, your students will have the background necessary to make some fairly good predictions concerning properties and chemistry of other elements and compounds.

Performance Objectives

Goal: Students will learn properties common to members of the same chemical family and some differences which exist among family members.

Objectives: Upon completion of the reading and problems, and when asked to demonstrate their understanding either orally or on a written test, students will

11:1	K/P	list four ways in which hydrogen can bond.
11:2	K	describe the characteristics associated with shielding effect.
11:2-3	K/P	distinguish between the behavior of lithium and the other members of the alkali family.
11:2-16	K	list various families of elements along with specific similarities and differences of properties within each family.
11:6	K/P	describe the effect of catenation on carbon and silicon compounds.
11:7	K/P	state differences and similarities between nitrogen and phosphorous.
11:6-8	K/P	list examples of allotropes in groups IVA, VA, and VIA.
11:9-10	P	given two elements on a periodic table, determine which is more chemically active.
11:11	K	list some compounds of the noble gases.
11:12-14	K	list some properties of transition metals.
11:15-16	K	list some properties of lanthanides and actinides.
	A	voluntarily complete one or more of the One More Step activities.
	A	read unassigned literature related to the chapter.

Teaching Techniques

Section 11:1

Stress the fact that hydrogen is a unique element and can be included in either the alkali or halogen family. Experimental observations show that hydrogen does not fit exclusively into either of these families.

Section 11:2

Emphasize to the students that they are studying group behavior to accumulate knowledge. The characteristics and properties presented will become the foundation on which chemical bonding will be built in Chapter 12.

Section 11:11

If your physics department has a neon gas discharge tube, you may want to light it for your students. Two papers, published in 1962, by Bartlett and Chernick, altered a well established theory that the inert gases were not inert.

Chemical Career

You can use this feature as a starting point to have students research the chemistry involved in water treatment and sewage disposal. Use this topic to integrate their knowledge of biology from the previous year in discussing the chemical functions of bacteria in the breakdown of organic matter in sewage.

Chapter End Problems

Pages 221-222.

1. Hydrogen reacts by
   (1) gaining electrons
   (2) losing electrons
   (3) sharing electrons
   (4) acting as a bridge between other atoms
2. Shielding effect reduces the effect of the nucleus on the outer electrons due to electrons in between the nucleus and the outer electrons.
   Barium is more reactive since, with a greater shielding effect, it loses the outer electrons more readily.
3. Thallium has a similar charge density.
4. Lithium has a greater charge density than other members of the group.
5. Aluminum loses its electrons less readily than sodium and magnesium.
6. Catenation is the bonding of atoms to form long chains. Carbon catenates easily. This property is the basis of organic chemistry.

7. Tin and lead are corrosion resistant.

8. Allotropes are different forms of the same element. Carbon, oxygen, and phosphorus have allotropic forms.

9. Phosphorus is a component of nucleic acids and energy transfer compounds in the body.

10. nitrogen and phosphorus

11. Metal oxides are basic and ionic in nature. Non-metal oxides are acidic and involve the sharing of electrons.

12. Amphoteric oxides can react as acids or bases, while nonmetal oxides are acidic.

13. SO_3 is a nonmetallic oxide therefore the bonds involve electron sharing.

14. Halogen means salt former.

15. francium

16. The noble gases have a full outer level of electrons. Thus, they would not be expected to gain or lose electrons.

17. The transition metals have the highest energy electrons located in d sublevels.

18. These metals are generally strong, some are corrosion resistant. They are generally malleable, ductile, lustrous, conductors of heat and electricity.

19. Zinc is used to protect iron from corrosion.

20. 3+

21. Plutonium is used as a raw material in the production of curium.

22. a. iron
    b. nickel
    c. fermium
    d. fluorine
    e. barium
    f. hafnium
    g. potassium
    h. selenium
    i. sodium
    j. nitrogen

23. a. actinium
    b. plutonium
    c. berkelium
    d. gallium
    e. neptunium
    f. carbon
    g. fluorine
    h. oxygen
    i. cesium
    j. bromine

Review

Page 222.

1. a. $Cr + H_2SO_4 \rightarrow CrSO_4 + H_2$ or
      $2Cr + 3H_2SO_4 \rightarrow Cr_2(SO_4)_3 + 3H_2$
   b. $Mn + 2H_2O \rightarrow Mn(OH)_2 + H_2$ or
      $Mn + H_2O \rightarrow MnO + H_2$
   c. $CuSO_4 + 2NaOH \rightarrow Cu(OH)_2 + Na_2SO_4$
   d. $BaCrO_4 + 2HCl \rightarrow BaCl_2 + H_2CrO_4$

2. $\dfrac{38.7 \text{ g AgCNS}}{} \left| \dfrac{1 \text{ mol AgCNS}}{166 \text{ g AgCNS}} \right| \dfrac{1 \text{ mol AgNO}_3}{1 \text{ mol AgCNS}} \left| \dfrac{170 \text{ g AgNO}_3}{1 \text{ mol AgNO}_3} \right. = 39.6 \text{ g AgNO}_3$

3. $\dfrac{(50.54 \times 78.918332) + (49.46 \times 80.916292)}{100} = 79.91 \text{ amu}$

4. $Y:, Dy:, \overset{\cdot}{In}:$

5. $S = 2-$, $Ge = 4\pm$

One More Step

Page 222.

1. See *Science*, Vol. 138, October 12, 1962, for example of initial reports. XeF_4 is the compound most commonly reported.

2. Although its ionization energy is higher, the Li^+ ion is so highly hydrated that the entire process
   $$Li(c) \rightarrow Li(g) \rightarrow Li^+(g) \rightarrow Li^+(aq)$$
   is more exothermic than the process
   $$Na(c) \rightarrow Na(g) \rightarrow Na^+(g) \rightarrow Na^+(aq)$$

3. The addition of 14 protons to the nucleus without starting a new energy level causes a considerable contraction of the elements following the lanthanides in the periodic table. Consequently, elements in the 6th row are smaller than we would otherwise expect. As a result, their chemical behavior is altered somewhat. As an example, gold is less reactive than silver.

CHEMICAL BONDING   12

An Overview

Chapter 12 begins a series of chapters concerning the combination of atoms into molecules, (Chapters 12, 13, 14). In Chapter 12, we discuss the underlying principles of bond formation. The data on ionization energies reinforces the electronic structure discussed in Chapter 9. This unit presents chemical bonding and how it affects molecular structure and properties. The first five sections should develop naturally from the discussions of periodic properties in Chapter 10. Ionic and covalent bonding are presented in detail. Time is spent discussing the different radii between bonded atoms. The chapter concludes with a look at metallic properties as explained by the metallic bond model.

Demonstration Information

If gas cylinders are not available, the gases needed can be generated.

Oxygen gas can be prepared by reacting solid Na_2O_2 with H_2O, or 10 cm^3 of H_2O_2 can be decomposed by adding a pinch of MnO_2.

Bromine gas fumes can be "poured" from a bottle of liquid bromine. **CAUTION:** Use Br_2 in a fume hood and wear rubber gloves.

Chlorine gas can be prepared by adding 20 cm^3 of concentrated HCl to 6 g of MnO_2 and heating gently. **CAUTION:** Prepare Cl_2 in a fume hood.

A small piece of roll sulfur is placed in a deflagrating spoon and placed in a burner flame briefly, then it is lowered into a bottle of O_2 gas. **CAUTION:** Do not breathe the SO_2 gas produced. Use a fume hood.

Wear goggles when burning Mg or Na in O_2, Br_2, or Cl_2. Use a glass shield between the demonstration and the students. **CAUTION:** Students should not look directly at the Mg ribbon while it is burning. Place it inside a can while burning in a darkened room.

Performance Objectives

Goal: Students will gain understanding of the chemical bond and the characteristics of ionic, covalent, and metallic substances.

Objectives: Upon completion of the reading and problems, and when asked to demonstrate their understanding either orally or on a written test, students will

12:1-2	P	define ionization energy and explain the trends among the various families of the periodic table.
12:3	K	differentiate among subsequent ionization energies for various atoms.
12:4	K/P	compare electron affinity to ionization energy.
12:5-6	K/P	utilize electronegativity to explain bond character.
12:7-9	K/P	differentiate between ionic and covalent bonds and properties of ionic and covalent compounds.
12:8-10	P/S	determine bond lengths for ionic compounds and covalent molecules.
12:11	K	describe the bonding characteristics of polyatomic ions.
12:12	K	define van der Waals radius.
12:13	K/P	list and differentiate among the four radii.
12:14-15	K	explain metallic properties using the metallic bond concept.
	A	voluntarily complete one or more of the One More Step activities.
	A	read unassigned literature related to the chapter.

Teaching Techniques

Section 12:5

Linus Pauling interpreted the bond energy of unsymmetrical molecules. Pauling's electronegativity scale is derived from fluorine as 4.0. Using this scale, one can decide if electrons favor one atom over another. For unequal attraction, the center of negative charge is displaced, resulting in a dipole. The bond will then have some ionic character (Section 12:6). Using the electronegativity table, students can predict bond stability (large electronegativity difference) and dipole formation in the molecule (Section 14:2).

Section 12:7

Discuss with students that high melting points are not exclusive to ionic substances. Metals have high melting points, as do macromolecular solids. The high melting points in both cases result from three-dimensional attractions of each atom to its neighbors. This same factor occurs for ionic solids as well.

Section 12:14

Felix Bloch is credited with the band theory of the energy levels of solids. His theory provided an explanation of semiconductor behavior (Section 16:11). Inform students that Table 12-11 is a great review and study aid.

Chemical Technology

Use this feature as a starting point to have students research careers related to the ceramics industry such as ceramic engineers and technicians. Many of the uses of ceramics listed in the feature can be assigned as topics for reports (optical fibers, laser materials, heat resistant materials, and radioactive waste disposal using glass pellets).

Problem Solutions

Page 232.
1. **a.** Thallium, bismuth, tellurium, chlorine, neon
   b. Radium, gallium, germanium, arsenic, sulfur

2. Peaks for the noble gases are due to the breaking of the complete outer level.
The first peak *after* each alkali metal is due to the complete *s* sublevel.
The second peak after Li and Na is due to the half-filled *p* sublevel.
Peak at $Z = 30$, full $3d$ sublevel.
Peak at $Z = 33$, half-full $4p$ sublevel.
Peak at $Z = 48$, full $4d$ sublevel.
Peak at $Z = 80$, full $5d$ sublevel.

Page 233.

3. Ionic—b, c, f, g, h, i
Covalent—a, d, e, j

Page 237.

4. a. ionic
b. covalent
c. covalent
d. covalent
e. ionic
f. ionic

Chapter End Problems

Page 246.

5. Al, K, C, K, K, S:

6. Those electrons come from a lower energy level and are held more tightly.

7. The first four carbon electrons are the hybrids of $2s^2 2p^2$ and are in the outer energy level. Although each requires more energy to remove than the previous due to the factors which affect ionization energies, they are reasonably close in energy. The next two are in the first energy level and are most tightly held. The increased advantage of nuclear positive charge and no shielding electrons makes them most difficult to remove.

8. When a force is applied to the crystal the attempted deformation forces ions of like charge next to each other. The resultant repulsive forces cause the crystal to split.

9. Since xenon tends neither to gain nor to lose electrons, it must bond covalently.

10. a. 0.198 nm   d. 0.151 nm
b. 0.107 nm   e. 0.154 nm
c. 0.147 nm   f. 0.130 nm

11.

21	Sc	3
22	Ti	4
23	V	5
24	Cr	6
25	Mn	6
26	Fe	6
27	Co	6
28	Ni	6
29	Cu	5.5
30	Zn	4.5

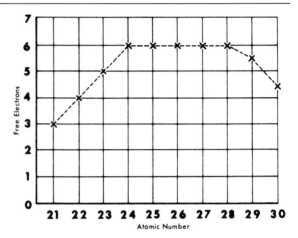

12. nuclear charge, shielding effect, radius, sublevel

13. Van der Waals radius concerns the distance between nonbonded adjacent atoms, while covalent radius concerns the distance between bonded adjacent atoms.

14. The atoms vibrate constantly. Thus an exact value for bond length cannot be determined.

15. high conductivity, lustrous, malleable, ductile, lose electrons

16. As the degree of delocalization of electrons increases the metal is harder, more dense, and exhibits a higher melting point.

Review

Pages 246-247.

1.

N	Se	I
P	Br	Ta
S	Nb	W
Cl	Mo	Re
Ti	Tc	Os
V	Ru	Ir
Cr	Rh	Pt
Mn	Te	

2. Dobereiner's triads → Newland's law of octaves → Mendeleev's and Meyer's tables based on properties and atomic mass → modern table based on electron configurations

3. a. astatine   7+, −1
germanium   4±
mercury   2+
polonium   6+, 2−
tin   2+, 4+
b. francium   1+
hafnium   2+, 3+, 4+
neodymium   2+
rubidium   1+
tellurium   6+, 2−

4. Elements with similar endings are in the same column (except H and He). Elements with the same principle quantum number for the outer level are in the same period.

5. a. 1+

b. 2+, 3+, 4+

c. 2+, 3+, 4+, 5+

d. 2−, 4+, 6+

e. 1−

6. a. metal

b. metal

c. metal

d. metalloid

e. nonmetal

7. a. alkali metals

b. alkaline earth metals

c. transition metals

d. halogens

e. noble gases

8. a. $1s^2 2s^2 2p^6 3s^2 3p^6 4s^2 3d^{10} 4p^6 5s^2 4d^4$

b. $1s^2 2s^2 2p^6 3s^2 3p^6 4s^2 3d^{10} 4p^6 5s^2 4d^{10} 5p^3$

c. $1s^2 2s^2 2p^6 3s^2 3p^6 4s^2 3d^{10} 4p^6 5s^2 4d^{10} 5p^6 6s^2 4f^1$

d. $1s^2 2s^2 2p^6 3s^2 3p^6 4s^2 3d^{10} 4p^6 5s^2 4d^5$

e. $1s^2 2s^2 2p^6 3s^2 3p^6 4s^2 3d^{10} 4p^6 5s^2 4d^{10} 5p^2$

One More Step

Page 247.

1. Pauling's equation:

$$Q = 23.06\Sigma(X_A - X_B)^2 - 55.1N_N - 24.2N_O$$

where $Q = \Delta H_f$ in kcal/mol

X_A = electronegativity of element A

X_B = electronegativity of element B

N_N = number of nitrogen atoms in compound

N_O = number of oxygen atoms in compound

Mulliken's equation:

$$\tfrac{1}{2}(I_A - E_A) - \tfrac{1}{2}(I_B - E_B) = 2.78(X_A - X_B)$$

where I_A and I_B = ionization potentials of A and B

E_A and E_B = electron affinities of A and B

Allred and Rochow's equation:

$$X = 0.359\frac{Zeff}{r^2} + 0.744$$

where X = electronegativity

$Zeff$ = effective nuclear charge

r = covalent radius

Liu's equation:

$$X = 0.313\left(\frac{n + 2.6}{r^{2/3}}\right)$$

where X = electronegativity

n = number of valence electrons

r = covalent radius

Gordy's equation:

$$X = 0.31\left(\frac{n + 1}{r}\right) + 0.50$$

where X = electronegativity

n = number of valence electrons

r = covalent radius

2. X-ray diffraction of crystals; electron diffraction of gases; neutron diffraction of crystals; microwave spectroscopy—From the energy absorbed, the mo-ment of inertia of the molecule can be calculated. Then, using known atomic masses, distances can be calculated.

3. Covalent—one-half length of X—X bond for elements forming diatomic molecules. Others from subtraction of known radius from bond length.

Assumptions: Additivity of radii in bond length

No pi bonding in simple compounds not involving known double or triple bonds

No ionic character

No effect of one atom on electron cloud of another

Ionic—subtract known radius from X-ray diffraction determined internuclear distance.

Assumptions: One set of values (usually lithium halides) has anions in contact

Additivity of radii in bond lengths

No covalent character

No effect of one ion on electron cloud of another

A precisely defined electron cloud

van der Waals—one half nonbonded distance in pure elements

Assumptions: No effect of one atom on electron of another

A precisely defined electron cloud

4. In complexes—number of ligands bonded to central ion

In crystals—number of ions of opposite sign surrounding a given ion

In metals—number of nearest neighbor atoms

5. Both carbon and silicon have all four of their outer electrons involved in bonding in the diamond arrangement. However, at room temperature, a few of the electrons in silicon are able to acquire enough energy to cross the forbidden zone (see metallic bond). The "holes" left by these electrons migrate counter-current to the electrons under the influence of an external field. Thus, silicon is an intrinsic semi-conductor. Carbon, on the other hand, has such a large forbidden zone, that none of its electrons can be excited enough to enter the conduction band.

6. In diamond, all four outer electrons of carbon are involved in bonding in stable, sigma bonds. For these electrons, the forbidden zone represents an enormous energy gap and they cannot cross to the conduction band. In graphite, however, each carbon atom is involved in one pi bond. The pi bonding electrons are at a much higher energy level than the sigma bonds. As a result, some of these pi electrons can be excited to "jump" the forbidden zone and enter the conduc-tion band.

MOLECULAR STRUCTURE   13

An Overview

Chapter 13 presents a study of chemical bonds and their geometric arrangement. Different ap-proaches to explain bonding in molecules are pre-sented in a sequence that proceeds from the simple to the sophisticated: electron pair repulsion theory, hybrid orbitals, resonance, and molecular orbital theory.

There are numerous ways to represent atoms and their combinations in molecules. Thus, students should realize that the pictures in the text are simply models. Different approaches to bonding may dictate different representations. Do not attach too much importance to pictorial aspects of the orbital representations. Emphasize that these models are useful because they provide a basis for the prediction of structure and properties. The ability to predict avoids the necessity of memorizing hundreds of individual molecular shapes. Chapter 13 ends with an elementary treatment of the molecular orbital theory. Students are certain to encounter this theory in more advanced chemistry courses.

Demonstration Information

Two balloons tied together make a convincing *p* orbital. Two or three of these pairs can be used to illustrate orbital arrangements. These models are more effective than chalkboard drawings in demonstrating special arrangements of the bonds. You may want to take slide pictures of the more complex models for use in future classes.

Performance Objectives

Goal: Students will learn four hypotheses regarding the structure and shape of molecules.

Objectives: Upon completion of the reading and problems, and when asked to demonstrate their understanding either orally or on a written test, students will

13:1-3	K	describe the directional characteristics of simple molecules due to electron pair repulsion.
13:3	K	differentiate between sigma and pi bonds.
13:4	K	describe the hybridization of orbitals available for bonding.
13:5-7	P	utilize hybridization theory to explain the directional characteristics of compounds with multiple bonds.
13:8	K/P	list and differentiate among the four types of isomers.
13:9	P	apply hybridization theory to inorganic compounds.
13:10	K/P	construct electron-dot resonance formulas to explain alternate structures for molecules and ''average'' bond length.
13:11	K	utilize molecular orbital theory to explain the behavior of some simple molecules.
	A	voluntarily complete one or more of the One More Step activities.
	A	read unassigned literature related to the chapter.

Teaching Techniques
Section 13:1

As you discuss electron repulsion, a balloon model of water is helpful. On the chalkboard, write the electron dot structure of water. Have two large pear-shaped balloons of one color (unshared pairs on oxygen) and two smaller ones of another color (shared pairs between O and H). Blow them up and attach them to the chalkboard with masking tape. Students can visualize the concept of unshared-unshared repulsion > unshared-shared > shared-shared using this model. If you wish, CH_4, NH_3 and HF can be demonstrated in the same way. Color slides of these models can serve well in future years. Students may also be willing to make them for extra credit.

Section 13:2

Using plastic foam balls and toothpicks, you can show the free rotation of a single bond. Ethane, C_2H_6, is a simple model to use. Point out to students that the double bond prevents this rotation. Demonstrate it by changing the C_2H_6 to C_2H_4, ethene. Emphasize the trigonal planar shape of the double bond.

Section 13:8

Emphasize that mixtures of isomers can be separated and each isomer has its own physical and chemical properties. Models help students visualize the concept better than the single dimension pictures in the text. Build the molecules shown in the text.

Section 13:10

Attach a thin rope to a point across the room. Show how the rope vibrates (resonates) between two extremes as you move your hand up and down to produce a standing wave. Relate this idea to the different electron dot structures that can be drawn for resonance structures. We average the extremes to get a structure of the molecule.

Chemical Technology

A study of the boranes is included in this chapter to reinforce the concepts of bonding and molecular structure previously studied. The 1976 Nobel Prize was awarded for research concerning the boranes. An excellent follow-up article for additional reading is the following.

Lipscomb, William N., "The Boranes and Their Relatives." *Science,* Vol. 196, No. 4294 (June 3, 1977), pp. 1047-1054.

Chapter End Problems

Pages 271-272.

1.   predicted   actual
   - **a.** $<109.5°$ 90°
   - **b.** $<109.5°$ 93°
   - **c.** $>$H—P—H in   99°
        b. because interference of methyls
   - **d.** $<109.5°$ 98°
   - **e.** $<109.5°$ 109°
   - **f.** $109.5°$ 109.5°

2. Sigma (σ) bonds are end-to-end overlaps of two orbitals. Pi (π) bonds result from the sideways overlap of two p orbitals.

3. Hybridization is the formation of equivalent orbitals by 2 or more orbitals from different energy sublevels. For example, one s and two p orbitals form three equivalent sp^2 hybrid orbitals.

4. The double bond (C=C) is formed by the σ overlap of two sp^2 orbitals and the π overlap of two p orbitals. The H—C bonds are formed by the σ overlap of sp^2 hybrid orbitals of the carbon with s orbitals of the hydrogens.

5. Benzene has a conjugated ring which in effect results in delocalization of the pi electrons, a very stable form.

6. **a.** trigonal planar, 120° bond angles

$$\begin{matrix} H \\ \diagdown \\ \quad\;\; C{=}O \\ \diagup \\ H \end{matrix}$$

   b. trigonal planar, 120° bond angle

$$O{=}\overset{\cdot\cdot}{S}\diagdown \longleftrightarrow O{-}\overset{\cdot\cdot}{S}\diagdown$$
$$\qquad\;\; O \qquad\qquad\qquad O$$

   c. trigonal planar

$$\begin{matrix} F \quad\;\; F \\ \diagdown\;\diagup \\ B \\ | \\ F \end{matrix}$$

   d. octahedral

$$\begin{matrix} F \;\; F \;\; F \\ \diagdown | \diagup \\ S \\ \diagup | \diagdown \\ F \;\; F \;\; F \end{matrix}$$

   e. $\underset{Cl}{\overset{\quad Cl}{S{\text{—}}S}}$ One Cl is 106° from plane of other three atoms.
      ←106°

---

   f. trigonal bipyramidal with one equatorial position occupied by the unshared pair

$$\begin{matrix} F \;\; F \\ | \diagup \\ :S \\ | \diagdown \\ F \;\; F \end{matrix}$$

7. Linear; sp; H—C bond is sigma, C≡N is one sigma and two pi bonds.

8.

Bond axes

Bond length

Bond angle 91.0°

van der Waals radius

Covalent radii

9. Hexane has five isomers:
   - (1) C—C—C—C—C—C
   - (2) $C{-}\overset{\overset{C}{|}}{C}{-}C{-}C{-}C$
   - (3) $C{-}C{-}\overset{\overset{C}{|}}{\underset{\underset{C}{|}}{C}}{-}C{-}C$
   - (4) $C{-}\overset{\overset{C}{|}}{C}{-}\overset{\overset{C}{|}}{C}{-}C$
   - (5) $C{-}\overset{\overset{C}{|}}{\underset{\underset{C}{|}}{C}}{-}C{-}C$

10. Geometric isomerism results from groups being able to take two different positions with respect to double bonds. Positional isomers are formed when a particle may bond at different points on a chain of carbons.
    Functional isomerism results when a particle may be bonded in two or more ways.

11. **a.**   **b.**

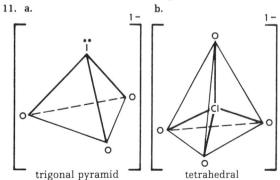

trigonal pyramid   tetrahedral

c.

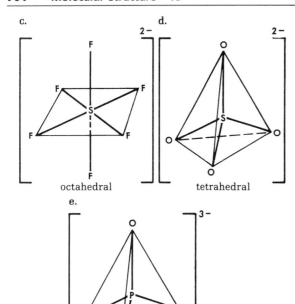

octahedral   tetrahedral

e.

tetrahedral

f.

the fluorines are planar, however including the unshared pairs the ion can be labeled as octahedral

12. PCl_5—trigonal bipyramid

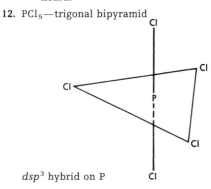

dsp^3 hybrid on P

PCl_4^+—tetrahedral, sp^3 hybrid on P
PCl_6^-—octahedral, d^2sp^3 hybrid on P

13. Both benzene and metals exhibit delocalization of electrons. For benzene, the delocalization occurs for each individual molecule. For metals, the delocalization exists throughout the entire piece of matter.

14. A 90° arrangement indicates all atoms are in the same plane. Electron pair repulsions result in 3-dimensional arrangements. Thus, the maximum distance of repulsion for four electron pairs results in a tetrahedral shape with bond angles of 109.5°.

15. NH_3 has a tetrahedral shape (see Figure 13-2) having three shared pairs and one unshared pair. The unshared pair causes the distortion which makes the bond angle less than 109.5°. BF_3 is a planar arrangement with three shared pairs. The maximum distance of repulsion for atoms in a single plane is 120°.

16.

17.

Benzene

Naphthalene

18. **a.** $\sigma 2s^2(2-0)/2 = 1$ bond, stable
b. $\sigma 2s^2\sigma^*2s^2\pi 2p^2(4-2)/2 = 1$ bond, stable
c. $\sigma 2s^2\sigma^*2s^2\pi 2p^4(6-2)/2 = 3$ bonds, stable
d. $\sigma 2s^2\sigma^*2s^2\pi 2p^4\sigma 2p^2(8-2)/2 = 3$ bonds, stable
e. $\sigma 2s^2\sigma^*2s^2\pi 2p^4\sigma 2s^2\pi^*2p^4(8-6)/2 = 1$ bond, stable

19. $\sigma 2s^2\sigma^*2s^2\pi 2p^4\sigma 2p^2, \left(\dfrac{8-2}{2}\right) = 3$ bonds, stable

Review

Pages 272–273.
1. francium, manganese, zinc, boron
2. **a.** ionic   **d.** covalent
   b. ionic   **e.** covalent
   c. ionic   **f.** covalent
3. Electrons are in the outer level band which is separated from the conduction band by only a narrow forbidden zone.

One More Step

Page 273.
1. **a.** 125°   **d.** 134°
   b. 108°   **e.** 115°
   c. 113°
2. octahedral; SF_6, $CdCl_6^{4-}$, ICl_4^-, BrF_4^-, BrF_5, IF_5, $Co(NH_3)_6^{3+}$, $PdCl_6^{2-}$, $Fe(CN)_6^{3-}$, and so on.

3. puckered ring; two shapes of C_6H_{12}:

Chair form   Boat form

The chair form is more stable because of the H—H interference found in boat form:

4. **a.** $H_2C=C=CH_2$ linear, planar on both ends, but one —CH_2 is in a plane perpendicular to the other —CH_2 group.
   b. $H_2C=C=C=CH_2$ linear; entire molecule planar.

5. Alfred Werner → Langmuir → G. N. Lewis → Sidgwick → Born → Pauling → Ingold
No one theory agrees with all experimental data. No one theory enables one to make sure predictions.

6. Because electrons, in the two bound atoms, with the same quantum numbers are no longer at the same energy. Therefore, the way in which they combine to form molecular orbitals is extremely difficult to predict.

7. There are three molecular orbitals for the six pi electrons. The lowest energy orbital encompasses all six carbon atoms. The other two MO's are equivalent in energy, and each exists in two parts. One orbital has half bonding carbons 1 and 6 while the other half bonds carbons 3 and 4. The other orbital has half bonding atoms 1, 2, and 3, while the other half bonds 4, 5, and 6. The net result of all MO's is two flat rings of electron cloud, half below the plane of the carbon and half above.

POLAR MOLECULES   14

An Overview

Properties of molecules which are a consequence of their structure are discussed in Chapter 14. The chapter begins with a study of polar molecules. Students investigate how some properties of similar compounds differ because of varying molecular shapes and structures.

Polarity shows the relationship between properties and electric dipoles in molecules. Before beginning the study of complex ions, students may find a brief review of solid geometrical figures helpful. In Section 14:3, students find that the presence of d orbitals gives no new bonding types, only some new shapes. A study of the weak van der Waals forces between molecules is important if students are to have a complete understanding of the relationship between structure and properties. Finally the knowledge of polarity is applied in learning how to separate the components of a mixture by chromatography. Several types of chromatography are discussed.

Demonstration Information

CAUTION: Both cyclohexane, and carbon tetrachloride, CCl_4, vapors are to be considered poisonous. Perform the demonstration in a fume hood. **CAUTION:** Do not use cyclohexane near open flames.

Performance Objectives

Goal: Students will gain an understanding of the relationship between molecular shape and structure.

Objectives: Upon completion of the reading and problems and when asked to demonstrate their understanding either orally or on a written test, students will

14:1	K	distinguish between polar and nonpolar bonds.
14:2	K/P	define and give examples of substances exhibiting dipole-dipole and dispersion forces as part of van der Waals forces.
14:3-4	K/P	relate coordination number to the structure of complex ions and their isomers.
14:5	K/P/S	name complex ions given their formulas and write formulas for complex ions given the names.
14:6	K/P	describe the coordinate covalent bond; list reasons why transition metals form complex ions.
14:7	K/S	write equations for reactions involving complex ions.
14:8-11	K	list and describe various chromatographic processes for chemical analysis.
	A	voluntarily complete one or more of the One More Step activities.
	A	read unassigned literature related to the chapter.

Teaching Techniques

Section 14:3

Ball and stick models are helpful to students as they attempt to visualize the coordination number of the central positive ion in a complex. The structures of complexes are usually either linear (*sp* bonding), tetrahedral (*sp*^{3}), square planar (*dsp*^{2}), or octahedral (*d*^{2}*sp*^{3}).

Section 14:9

Your students have probably seen paper chromatography before, but column chromatography may be new to them. You can purchase commercial resins, many of which are shipped slightly moist. Do not breathe any of the dust if you use a dry resin. Columns can be kept from year to year if kept moist and sealed. Old columns can be reconditioned by percolating 2M HCl through them. If you do not have a commercial resin, a list of acceptable substitutes is found on page 288. A flow rate that works well is 2-3 cm^3 per minute. If the rate is too slow, use either air pressure on top (rubber squeeze bulb) or an aspirator on the bottom of the tube. A good solution to separate can be prepared by dissolving 2.8 g FeCl$_3 \cdot$6H$_2$O, 2.5 g NiCl$_2 \cdot$6H$_2$O, and 2.5 g CoCl$_2 \cdot$6H$_2$O in 100 cm^3 of 9M HCl. Use 2 cm^3 of this solution for a column 10 mm × 20 cm long. A usual manner of separation is to begin with three aliquots of 5 cm^3 each of 9M HCl, then 4 portions of 5 cm^3 of 5M HCl then 5 portions of 5 cm^3 of 1M HCl.

Chemical Technology

This feature provides an introduction to many concepts introduced later in the text (freezing point depression (Chapter 22), saponification (Chapter 30), ion ratios in the body (Chapters 11 and 30). You may have students do further research on any of these topics as well as water softening and desalination processes.

Problem Solutions

Page 277.

1. d, a, e, f, c, b

Page 284.

2. a. hexiodoplatinate(IV) ion
   b. diamminecadmium ion
   c. hexafluorogermanate(IV) ion
   d. tetraquochromium(II) ion
   e. hexacyanoferrate(III) ion
   f. hexacyanoferrate(II) ion
   g. hexamminecobalt(II) ion
   h. hexachloroplatinate(IV) ion
   i. hexamminenickel(II) ion
   j. hexachloroiridate(IV) ion

3. a. PtBr$_6{}^{2-}$
   b. Pt(NH$_3$)$_4{}^{2+}$
   c. AuBr$_4{}^-$
   d. PdCl$_6{}^{2-}$
   e. AuCl$_4{}^-$
   f. Ir(NH$_3$)$_5$(H$_2$O)$^{3+}$
   g. W(CO)$_6$
   h. AlF$_6{}^{3-}$
   i. Co(NH$_3$)$_4$(H$_2$O)Cl^{2+}
   j. Cd(NH$_3$)$_4{}^{2+}$

4. a. chloropentammineiridium(III) ion
   b. tetramminepalladium(II) ion
   c. hexahydroxoantimonate(V) ion
   d. tetrachloropalladate(II) ion
   e. trioxalatoferrate(III) ion
   f. tetramminecopper(II) ion

5. a. FeCO(CN)$_5{}^{3-}$
   b. Ru(CO)$_5$
   c. Co(NH$_3$)$_6{}^{3+}$
   d. Cu(CN)$_2{}^-$
   e. Pd(NH$_3$)$_2$Cl$_2$
   f. Cr(NH$_3$)$_6{}^{3+}$

6. a. GaCl$_4{}^-$
   b. GaF$_6{}^{3-}$
   c. HgI$_4{}^{2-}$
   d. OsCl$_6{}^{2-}$
   e. IrBr$_6{}^{3-}$
   f. Fe(CN)$_6{}^{4-}$

Chapter End Problems

Page 294.

7. a, b, e, d, f, c
   note that d and f have the same electronegativity difference

8. van der Waals forces caused by dipole-dipole, dipole-induced dipole, and dispersion forces

9. octahedral

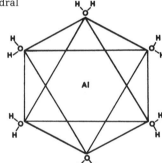

10. Central ion: Ion about which ligands cluster
    Coordination number: Number of ligands
    Ligand: Negative ion or polar molecule bonded to central ion

11. size and charge

12. The transition metals have partially filled *d* orbitals to accept *e*$^-$ and are relatively small, thus, they have large charge-to-radius ratio.

13. a. pentafluorogallate(III) ion
    b. tetrathioantimonate(V) ion
    c. dicyanoaurate(I) ion
    d. tetracyanoaurate(III) ion
    e. hexamminechromium(III) ion

14. Both depend upon selective adsorption. In the column, the solvent is run through the adsorbent, while on paper, the solvent moves by capillary action.

15. X$_2$A, X$_2$A

16. Due to filled orbitals, noble gas particles are held together only by dispersion forces. Since these forces are the weakest of those holding molecules together, we would expect Group VIIIA elements to be gases.

17. O=C=O

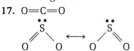

The linear shape of CO_2 accounts for a dipole moment of zero. The unshared pair and bent shape of SO_2 account for the dipole moment value and its resulting polarity.

Review

Page 295.

1. NI_3 pyramidal, CCl_4 tetrahedral

2. An s orbital is spherical and a p orbital is dumbbell shaped.

3. The s and p orbitals hybridize to four orbitals of equivalent energy each containing one electron.

4. The p orbital overlap is conjugated so that the electron cloud for the pi bond completely encircles the ring of carbon atoms. Such a delocalized system of electrons represents a more stable arrangement than isolated sigma and pi bonds.

5. Bent. The two unshared pairs of electrons push the shared pairs toward each other.

6. The He_2^+ ion would have a total of 3 electrons in the outer level. Their orbital arrangement would be $\sigma 1s^2 \sigma^* 1s^1$. The bonding would be $(2 -)/2 = 1/2$. In other words it should be a stable species.

7. C=C—C—C—C
   C—C=C—C—C (cis and trans)
   C=C—C—C
   |
   C

   C—C=C—C
   |
   C

   C=C—C—C
   |
   C

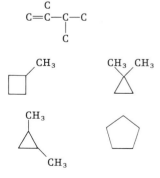

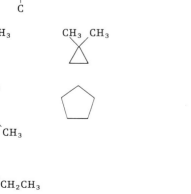

8. 120°

9.

10. O   O   O
    ‖   ‖   ‖

One More Step

Page 295.

1. R_f values must be found for a particular system with standards of known concentration. Once that piece of apparatus has been standardized for a substance, an unknown containing that substance can be analyzed. The volume of the chromatographic chamber, for instance, has a large effect on R_f values. Values from one chamber cannot be applied to another chamber of different geometry. Other factors affecting R_f values are the state of subdivision of the adsorbent, temperature, purity of the solvent, separation of a multi-component solvent, and evaporation. Solvents and/or adsorbents from the same manufacturer but from different batches will give different R_f values. However, the *relative* values are quite useful in analysis.

2. Mg, 4, phaeophorbide, planar
   Fe, 4, porphyrin, planar

3. The formation of a heterocyclic ring with a metal atom in the ring is the process of chelation.

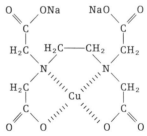

disodium ethylenediaminetetraacetate
copper chelate

4. Ni = dimethylglyoxime
   Al = ammonium aurin tricarboxylate
   Zr = sodium alizarin sulfonate

5. Extract the pigments from a few grams of spinach leaves by grinding them in a mortar with a little broken glass and acetone as the solvent. Filter the solution and spot the paper in the usual manner being certain to dry between each application. Develop the chromatogram using a solvent of 0.5% propanol in petroleum ether.

KINETIC THEORY   15

An Overview

Chapter 15 presents the physical states as a consequence of their thermal behavior. A model that treats gases as hard, round, perfectly elastic spheres in constant motion is discussed first. From Sections 15:4-5 students should get the idea that the temperature of a gas is a measure of the average kinetic energies of its molecules. It then follows that molecules of all gases at the same temperature must have the same kinetic energies. Section 15:5 presents a discussion of temperature. Students should be able to convert Celsius to kelvin and the reverse. At the end of the chapter students use the kinetic theory to explain the properties of gases, liquids, solids, and plasmas.

Performance Objectives

Goal: Students will gain an understanding of the kinetic theory and its relationship to the states of matter.

Objectives: Upon completion of the reading and problems, and when asked to demonstrate their understanding either orally or on a written test, students will

15:1	K	define and describe mean free path of a molecule in motion.
15:2	K	relate pressure to molecular motion.
15:3	P/S	describe the use of a manometer in measuring gas pressure and solve conversion problems.
15:4	K	define kinetic energy in terms of the motion and mass of particles.
15:5-6	P	relate temperature and heat transfer to molecular motion.
15:7	K	describe the three common states of motion in terms of kinetic theory.
15:8	K	describe the characteristics of the plasma state as a special case.
	A	voluntarily complete one or more of the One More Step activities.
	A	read unassigned literature on a topic related to the chapter.

Teaching Techniques

Section 15:1

Oxygen gas molecules have an average speed of 1900 km/h (about 1000 miles/h). You can relate mean free path to driving a car. An oxygen "car" would have a collision every 314 car lengths, or 4.5×10^9 collisions per second.

Section 15:2

If you have empty duplicating fluid cans, attach one to an aspirator or vacuum pump and let students observe its collapse.

Pressure in the laboratory is measured in mm of Hg and converted to pascals or kilopascals. The auto and tire industries have been using kilopascals for tire pressure measurements.

One atmosphere (760 mm Hg) of pressure is equal to 100 (101.325) kilopascals. Students will generally accept new units. Pascal is the unit of pressure used throughout the world. You may experience the most difficulty with this conversion.

Section 15:3

An open manometer can be prepared using two burets connected with rubber tubing. Two meter sticks can be used for quantitative measurements. Stopper one of the burets to provide a sample of gas (air). Place a little oil over the mercury in each buret. This equipment will help students better understand the diagrams in the text.

Section 15:5

The degree symbol associated with the K was dropped officially in 1968. The kelvin is the SI unit of temperature.

At absolute zero, theory predicts that all particle motion has stopped. Absolute zero has not yet been reached (see the Technology feature on cryogenics).

Section 15:7

This section serves only to introduce solids, liquids, and gases. Each of these will be covered in the next three chapters. Do not go into much detail here.

Chemical Technology

Since many of the materials used for replacement parts are organic, you may want to introduce some organic chemistry at this point. We have made it a point to use organic as well as inorganic examples throughout the text, so as not to relegate their study to the last two chapters.

Problem Solutions

Pages 300-301.

1. The gas pressure is 80 mm less than the pressure of the air on the tube.

$$\frac{80 \text{ mm} \mid 1 \text{ kPa}}{\mid 7.50 \text{ mm}} = 10.7 \text{ kPa}$$

Total pressure = 97.7 − 10.7 = 87.0 kPa

2. $$\frac{690 \text{ mm} \mid 1 \text{ kPa}}{\mid 7.50 \text{ mm}} = 92.0 \text{ kPa}$$

3. The gas pressure is 6 mm less than the pressure of the air on the tube.

$$\frac{6 \text{ mm} \mid 1 \text{ kPa}}{\mid 7.50 \text{ mm}} = 0.8 \text{ kPa}$$

Total pressure = 100 − 0.8 = 99.2 kPa

4. $$\frac{86.0 \text{ mm} \mid 1 \text{ kPa}}{\mid 7.50 \text{ mm}} = 11.5 \text{ kPa}$$

Page 302.
5. **a.** 360 K   **d.** 205 K
   b. 289 K   **e.** 346 K
   c. 332 K
6. **a.** −187°C   **d.** 45°C
   b. −82°C   **e.** 621°C
   c. 260°C
7. **a.** 296 K   **d.** 291 K
   b. 331 K   **e.** 298 K
   c. 363 K
8. **a.** 599°C   **d.** −253°C
   b. 417°C   **e.** −213°C
   c. 111°C

Chapter End Problems

Pages 308-309.
9. The gas pressure is 12 mm less than air.

$$\frac{12 \text{ mm} \mid 1 \text{ kPa}}{\mid 7.50 \text{ mm}} = 1.6 \text{ kPa}$$

Total pressure 98.7 − 1.6 = 97.1 kPa

10. $$\frac{400 \text{ mm} \mid 1 \text{ kPa}}{\mid 7.50 \text{ mm}} = 53.3 \text{ kPa}$$

11. **a.** 828 K − 273 = 555°C
    b. 751°C + 273 = 1024 K
    c. 16°C + 273 = 289 K
    d. 3 K − 273 = −270°C
    e. 62°C + 273 = 335 K

12. The molecular mass of ammonia is: 14 + 3 = 17. The molecular mass of chlorine gas is: 2(35.5) = 71.0. Since the velocity of gas molecules varies inversely as the square root of their mass, the *ammonia* which is composed of lighter molecules will be expected to cross the room first.

One More Step

Page 309.
1. Oxygen: $KE = (1/2)mv^2$ $v = 4.43 \times 10^2$ m/s (see page 297)

$$KE = \frac{1}{2} \mid \frac{32.0 \text{ g}}{6.02 \times 10^{23} \text{ molecules}} \mid \frac{1 \text{ kg}}{1000 \text{ g}} \mid \frac{(4.43 \times 10^2)^2 \text{ m}^2}{\text{s}^2}$$
$$= 5.22 \times 10^{-21} \text{ J/molecule}$$

13. The mean free path of an atom or molecule is the average distance it travels between collisions.
14. Each molecule moves independently of other molecules in a gas. A molecule appears to vibrate about a moving point in a liquid. Molecules appear to vibrate about fixed points in a solid.
15. Temperature is a measure of the average kinetic energy of particles.
16. Theoretically, at absolute zero all molecular motion would cease.
17. Kinetic energy is conserved in an elastic collision. In an inelastic collision, some kinetic energy is converted to another energy form (potential or radiant).

Review

Page 309.
1. **a.** RuF
2. Advantage—surface chromatography is a more rapid separation method.
   Disadvantage—surface chromatography is not as quantitative as column chromatography.
3. H_2O
4. trigonal bipyramidal (unshared pairs are equatorial)
5. A sigma bond involves the end-to-end overlap of orbitals. Pi bonds involve a sideways overlap of *p* orbitals.
6. linear
7. Molecules with multiple bonds are rigid with respect to rotation of the bonded atoms. These molecules are more reactive than those with single bonds. Multiple bonding always involves the *p* orbitals.
8.
9. At
10. Sc, Ti, Ni, C, F
11. a, c, d covalent
    b, e ionic
12. linear
13. $\sigma 2s^2 \sigma^* 2s^2 \pi 2p^4 \sigma 2p^2$
14. **a.** hexamminecobalt(II) ion
    b. diamminecopper(II) ion
    c. diaquotetramminenickel(II)
    d. diammineplatinum(IV) chloride
    e. diamminesilver ion
15. **a.** $RhCl_6^{3-}$ **c.** $Fe(CO)_6$
    b. BeF_4^{2-} **d.** $Ni(CO)_4$

Automobile:

$$KE = \frac{1}{2} \left| \frac{1500 \text{ kg}}{} \right| \frac{(50.0)^2 \cancel{\text{km}^2}}{\cancel{1 \text{ hr}^2}} \left| \frac{(1000)^2 \text{ m}^2}{1 \cancel{\text{km}^2}} \right| \frac{\cancel{1 \text{ hr}^2}}{(60)^2 \cancel{\text{min}^2}} \left| \frac{1 \cancel{\text{min}^2}}{(60)^2 \text{ s}^2} \right.$$

$$= 1.45 \times 10^5 \text{ J}$$

Remember that 1 joule $= 1 \text{ kg} \cdot \text{m}^2/\text{s}^2$

2. $\dfrac{v_{\text{hydrogen}}}{v_{\text{oxygen}}} = \sqrt{\dfrac{m_{\text{oxygen}}}{m_{\text{hydrogen}}}}, \quad \dfrac{v_{\text{hydrogen}}}{4.43 \times 10^2 \text{ m/s}} = \sqrt{\dfrac{32.0 \text{ g}}{2.02 \text{ g}}},$

$v_{\text{hydrogen}} = (4.43 \times 10^2 \text{ m/s})\sqrt{15.8}$
$= (4.43 \times 10^2 \text{ m/s})3.97$
$= 1.77 \times 10^3 \text{ m/s}$

3. Other instruments used to measure pressure: steam gauge, depth gauge, altimeter.

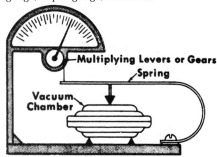

4. Plasma is the term applied to highly ionized gases in strong magnetic fields. This "state of matter" is used primarily to control thermonuclear reactions. The student may be interested in the "pinch effect." Further information can be found in the *Columbia Encyclopedia*; *Physics* by Gamow and Cleveland, Prentice-Hall, 1960; *Plasma Physics* by Chandrasekhar, University of Chicago Press, paperback.

5. Blaise Pascal (1623-1662). French mathematician and physicist. Early investigator of the mass of air and of the properties of a vacuum. 1 millibar = 100 pascal

SOLIDS

16

An Overview

In Chapter 16, students study particles bonded or attracted to one another in the solid state. The properties of solids are a direct consequence of their structures. Students are introduced to crystals by studying unit cells. If attention is given to size and charge, the packing arrangements can be used to explain the observed crystal structures. Students can apply this knowledge when studying transistor chemistry. The chapter concludes by showing a contrast between crystals and amorphous solids.

Demonstration Information

Section 16:4—**CAUTION:** Lead(II) acetate is poisonous. Use care to avoid contamination of the environment when disposing of the substance.

Performance Objectives

Goal: Students will gain an understanding of crystal structure and its relationship to properties of solids.

Objectives: Upon completion of the reading and problems, and when asked to demonstrate their understanding either orally or on a written test, students will

16:1	K/P	distinguish among the seven crystal systems.
16:2-5	K/P/S	identify examples of unit cells.
16:4-5	K/P	describe the relationship between particle size and unit cell arrangement.
16:6-7	K/P	differentiate between the packing arrangements and properties for metallic and nonmetallic crystals.
16:8	K/P	define and list characteristics of macromolecules.
16:9	P	distinguish among the properties of substances held together by various types of bonds.
16:10	K	identify the types of crystal defects.
16:11	K	describe the chemistry of transistors.
16:12	P	distinguish between isomorphism and polymorphism.
16:13	K/P	define and give examples of hygroscopic, deliquescent, and efflorescent compounds.
16:14	K/P	explain the characteristics of and give uses for liquid crystals.
16:15	K/P	define and give examples of amorphous materials.

A voluntarily complete one or more of the One More Step activities.

A read unassigned literature related to the chapter.

Teaching Techniques

Section 16:1

You may wish to add to the definition of a crystal as given in the text. Crystals have well defined melting points. They also have flat faces that meet at definite angles.

Section 16:2

Three-dimensional models of unit cells are of value in helping students to visualize the diagrams in the text. Students can construct permanent models for you. Glue them together and paint them using latex paint covered with enamel. Emphasize that the unit cells presented in the text are not all inclusive. There are many others.

Section 16:5

The hexagonal closest packed structure can be shown on an overhead projector using seven circles having the same diameter (coins). Show students that the next layer has only three particles, then seven, then three, repeating. This demonstration will help them understand that HCP has a coordination number of 12.

Section 16:6

The hair pins can be heat treated as indicated in the red annotation. Count the number of bends each will take before breaking. This count will show quantitatively that a change occurs in the metal. You may wish to have a student give a report on heat treated metals (tempering) and the career of metallurgy.

Section 16:7

Commercially prepared models of a diamond and graphite are good investments. They help students visualize important concepts, including the relationship between structure and melting point. Point out that graphite is a good dry lubricant under heat and pressure due to its structure. The layers don't break down, but slide over each other easily.

Section 16:15

Point out that glasses fracture and produce curved surfaces. Crystals cleave and produce flat faces and definite angles. A glass is a liquid with very high viscosity (a supercooled liquid). The particles have no orderly arrangement. If there is a glass factory in your area try to obtain a large piece of cullet (broken glass) that will show the curved surfaces.

Chemical Technology

You can use this feature as a starting point for a more in-depth study of crystals. If your students have sufficient math backgrounds, have them research the calculations used to determine the distances between particles in a crystal from X-ray diffraction data.

Chapter End Problems

Page 332.

1.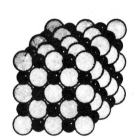

A one-to-one correspondence exists between the chlorine and sodium ions.

2. Na^+ 0.095 nm
Cl^- $\underline{0.181 \text{ nm}}$
      0.276 nm

3. The radius ratio of the positive ions and negative ions in one pair of compounds is the same as the positive to negative and negative to positive in the other pair.

4.   1 Cu @ 63.5 = 63.5
    1 S @ 32.1 = 32.1
    4 O @ 16.0 = 64.0
  5 H_2O @ 18.0 = $\underline{90.0}$
                249.6 = 250

  % $H_2O = \dfrac{90.0}{250} \times 100 = 36.0\%\ H_2O$

5. **a.** nickel sulfate heptahydrate
b.   1 Ni   58.7 = 58.7
      1 S   32.1 = 32.1
      4 O   16.0 = 64.0
    7 H_2O 18.0 = $\underline{126.0}$
                  280.8 = 281

  % $H_2O = \dfrac{126}{281} \times 100 = 44.8\%\ H_2O$

c. 11 O in $NiSO_4 \cdot 7\ H_2O$ @ 16.0 = 176

  % $O = \dfrac{176}{281} \times 100 = 62.6\%\ O$

6. **a.** barium hydroxide octahydrate
b.   1 Ba   137   = 137.
      2 O   16.0   = 32.0
      2 H   1.01 =   2.02
    8 H_2O 18.0   = $\underline{144.0}$
                    315.02 = 315

  % $H_2O = \dfrac{144}{315} \times 100 = 45.7\%\ H_2O$

c. 10 O in Ba(OH)$_2 \cdot$ 8 H$_2$O @ 16.0 = 160

$$\% \text{ O} = \frac{160}{315} \times 100 = 50.8\% \text{ O}$$

7. a. sodium carbonate decahydrate

b.
2 Na	23.0 =	46.0
1 C	12.0 =	12.0
3 O	16.0 =	48.0
10 H$_2$O	18.0 =	180.
		286.0

$$\% \text{ H}_2\text{O} = \frac{180}{286} \times 100 = 62.9\% \text{ H}_2\text{O}$$

c. 13 O in Na$_2$CO$_3 \cdot$ 10 H$_2$O @ 16.0 = 208

$$\% \text{ O} = \frac{208}{286} \times 100 = 72.7\% \text{ O}$$

8. Diamond has 3-dimensional network bonds. Thus, it is a very hard substance. Graphite has a 2-dimensional layered structure of covalent bonds. The bonds between layers are strictly van der Waals forces. Thus, its layers slide easily over one another.

9. The number and arrangement of particles differs for each.

10. the radius ratio of the ions involved

11. Sodium and cesium have different radius ratios.

12. The particles of most nonmetallic elements are held together by van der Waals forces.

13. generally hard, strong, high melting solids; diamond and silicate compounds exhibit these characteristics

14. Some defects cause color in substances (see Figure 14-11, page 285). Doping causes some substances to be better conductors.

15. The electric conductivity of silicon and germanium increases.

16. a. Mg(NO$_3$)$_2 \cdot$6H$_2$O
    b. FeSO$_4 \cdot$7H$_2$O
    c. Cu(NO$_3$)$_2 \cdot$3H$_2$O
    d. SnCl$_2 \cdot$2H$_2$O

17. Isomorphs have the same shape. Isomers have the same number and types of atoms but different arrangements.

18. Amorphous substances do not have a regular internal arrangement like that in crystalline solids.

Review

Pages 332.

1. The gas pressure is less in the gas than in the air.

$$\frac{64 \text{ mm}}{} \left| \frac{1 \text{ kPa}}{7.50 \text{ mm}} \right. = 8.5 \text{ kPa}$$

Total pressure of the gas = 92.7 − 8.5 = 84.2 kPa

2. $$\frac{421 \text{ mm}}{} \left| \frac{1 \text{ kPa}}{7.50 \text{ mm}} \right. = 56.1 \text{ kPa}$$

3. In plasma, the atoms are not intact, but rather, they are broken up into individual electrons and nuclei.

4. Because it depends upon selective adsorption as do all the other chromatographic methods.

One More Step

Page 333.

1. See the *Encyclopaedia Britannica* article on crystallography. This gives an excellent treatment of the history of X-ray probing.

2. One source is the Bell Telephone Laboratories book, *Conductors and Semiconductors*, by Alan Holden. Almost any elementary electronics text deals with the subject.

3. Cholesteric compounds have two dimensional order as do smectic compounds. However, in smectic compounds the molecules are arranged in layers in which the parallel molecules are oriented with their long axes perpendicular to the plane. In cholesteric compounds, on the other hand, although the molecules are still arranged in planes, the long axes of the molecules are in the plane. Although cholesterol itself is not mesomorphic, as an alcohol it forms many esters which are mesomorphic. Since these esters have their molecules aligned in the plane of order, the class name is cholesteric.

LIQUIDS

17

An Overview

Chapter 17 introduces the study of liquids by developing the idea of vapor pressure in relationship to phase diagrams. We present a brief systematic view of the interactions that hold matter in the liquid state. Chapter 17 is a logical extension of Chapters 15 and 16, with the kinetic theory applied to the interactions in liquids. Keep in mind that several topics mentioned in Chapter 17 are intended to be brief and will be developed in more detail later, i.e. Le Chatelier's principle and equilibrium. At this point in the course, emphasize the apparent unchanging aspect of observed properties at equilibrium. Vapor pressure leads students to an understanding of the definition of normal boiling point. The phase diagram is an important tool in that it graphically summarizes the first part of the chapter. The ability to interpret is an important skill for this chapter. The quantitative aspects of change of state are then covered. The chapter closes with the application of structure to understand the properties of liquids.

Demonstration Information

Safety glasses are a must for the demonstrator (such a system could implode).

Obtain a 500 cm³ round bottom flask (check carefully for hairline cracks) and a 2-hole rubber stopper. Place a thermometer in one hole and a short piece of glass tubing in the other. On the glass tube, connect a short piece of rubber tubing as shown. Fill the flask 1/4 full of water and boil unclamped at room pressure for 3-5 minutes. Have a student read the thermometer. Remove the burner and clamp the rubber tubing closed. Quickly wrap a towel around the neck of the flask, invert the flask and have a student hold 2-3 ice cubes on the bottom of the flask. Water will continue to boil in the neck of the flask. Have a student read the thermometer after a few minutes while the water is boiling in the neck of the flask under reduced pressure. Place a phase diagram on the board or overhead projector and ask students to explain their observations of the flask. Do not tell them about the reduced pressure. Let them discover the concept.

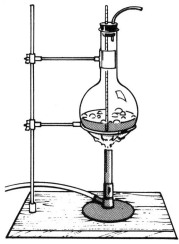

Performance Objectives

Goal: Students will gain an understanding of the properties of liquids and their relationship to molecular structure and the kinetic theory.

Objectives: Upon completion of the reading and problems, and when asked to demonstrate their understanding either orally or on a written test, students will

17:1	P/K	explain the causes of vapor pressure for a solid or liquid.
17:2	K/P	define Le Chatelier's principle and relate it to temperature and pressure.
17:3	K/P	relate vapor pressure to intermolecular forces.
17:4-6	K	define melting point and boiling point in terms of vapor pressure.
17:7	K	list conditions for liquefaction of gases.
	K	define and give examples of critical temperature and critical pressure.
17:8	S/K	using a phase diagram determine melting point, boiling point, critical temperature, critical and triple point for a substance.
17:9	K/P	determine the relationship between energy and change of state.
17:10-11	K	define and describe the properties of substances having hydrogen bonds.
17:12	K/P	explain surface tension and capillary rise on the basis of unbalanced surface forces.
	A	voluntarily complete one or more of the One More Step activities.
	A	read unassigned literature related to the chapter.

Teaching Techniques

Section 17:1

You can demonstrate vapor pressure and equilibrium using a 500 cm³ Florence flask fitted with a 3-hole stopper. Connect one side to the manometer you constructed in Chapter 15. The other side is fitted with rubber tubing and a clamp. In the center hole, insert a dropping funnel equipped with a stopcock. Partially evacuate the flask. A difference of 150 mm Hg in the manometer levels is satisfactory. Add a few cm³ of acetone to the dropping funnel. Open the stopcock and allow a few drops of acetone to enter the Florence flask. Have a student read the mercury level every minute for 8-10 minutes then add a few more drops of acetone to establish vapor equilibrium. The flask will be cooler than room temperature because of the evaporation. The vapor pressure of acetone at 15° is approximately 20 kPa.

Section 17:2

Discuss the ice skating example presented in the text in detail. Students can understand and remember it (See Teachers Guide 15:2). Stress that the expansion of water in forming the ice crystal is unique to water.

Section 17:6

The demonstration described on page 345 (boiling water in a paper container) can also be used effectively here. The constant temperature during a change of state is visually reinforced because the water prevents a temperature increase to the kindling temperature of paper. Emphasize that the energy is being used to overcome attractive forces between the molecules and is not available to increase the temperature. This conceptual model can be used to introduce molar heat of vaporization (Section 17:9). A definite amount of heat will be required to overcome a definite number of attractive forces.

Section 17:9

An interesting calculation for your students is to determine the number of joules given off to the air when a rain barrel full of water freezes. The rain barrel was placed in root cellars to keep the vegetables stored there from freezing. A rain barrel holds approximately 8.7×10^7 grams of H_2O. This amount of water releases 2.9×10^{10} J. The January thaw remelts the ice and it is ready to give off more heat. Ask your students if this concept could be used as an alternative heat source.

Section 17:10

To demonstrate hydrogen bonding while reinforcing the concepts of equilibrium and Le Chatelier's principle, dissolve 1.4 g of $CoCl_2 \cdot 2H_2O$ in 30 cm^3 of H_2O. Place this solution in a 100 cm^3 graduated cylinder and slowly pour 60 cm^3 of acetone down the inside of the graduate. Observe the blue layer on top.

$$Co(H_2O)_6{}^{2+} + 4Cl^- \rightleftharpoons CoCl_4{}^{2-} + 6H_2O$$
$$\text{pink} \qquad\qquad \text{blue}$$

The acetone forms hydrogen bonds with water and in effect decreases the concentration of water on the top of the solution. The equilibrium shifts to the right to form the blue chloro complex.

Chemical Technology

You can use this feature as an extension of the theme presented in Chapter 1 concerning the use of scientific knowledge. There has been much controversy concerning the use of chemical herbicides and their possible harmful effects. However, students should also consider the implications if no herbicides were used. How would this ban affect food supply, prices, and the availability of some foods?

Problem Solutions

Page 342.
1. a. 119°C   c. 66.3°C
   b. 99.6°C   d. −19.4°C

Page 344.
2. a. $T_c = 33$ K   d. $P_t = 5$ kPa
   b. $P_c = 1290$ kPa   e. $T_m = 14$ K
   c. $T_t = 13.8$ K   f. $T_b = 20.3$ K

3. a. gas   c. liquid
   b. solid   d. liquid

Pages 346-347.
4. a. $H = m(\Delta T)C_p = $
   $$\frac{23.0\,g \mid 46.0\,°C \mid 2.06\text{ J}}{g \cdot °C} = 2180 \text{ J}$$

   b. $$\frac{23.0\,g \mid 334 \text{ J}}{g} = 7680 \text{ J}$$

   c. $$\frac{23.0\,g \mid 100\,°C \mid 4.18 \text{ J}}{g \cdot °C} = 9610 \text{ J}$$

   d. $$\frac{23.0\,g \mid 2260 \text{ J}}{g} = 52\,000 \text{ J}$$

   e. $$\frac{23.0\,g \mid 9.00\,°C \mid 2.02 \text{ J}}{g \cdot °C} = 418 \text{ J}$$

5. $$\frac{25.4\,g \mid 61.7 \text{ J}}{g} = 1570 \text{ J}$$

6. $$\frac{4.24\,g \mid 162 \text{ J}}{g} = 687 \text{ J}$$

7. Cs melts at 28.4°C and boils at 678°C (Table A-3 of the Appendix)
   $$\frac{45.0\,g \mid 4.4\,°C \mid 0.246 \text{ J}}{g \cdot °C} = 48.7 \text{ J}$$

   $$\frac{45.0\,g \mid 15.7 \text{ J}}{g} = 707 \text{ J}$$

   $$\frac{45.0\,g \mid 650\,°C \mid 0.252 \text{ J}}{g \cdot °C} = 7370 \text{ J}$$

   $$\frac{45.0\,g \mid 514 \text{ J}}{g} = 23\,100 \text{ J}$$

   $$\frac{45.0\,g \mid 202\,°C \mid 0.156 \text{ J}}{g \cdot °C} = 1420 \text{ J}$$

   Summing all five steps and rounding off to the proper number of decimal places = 32 600 J

8. $$\frac{5.58 \text{ kg} \mid 980 \text{ C}° \mid 0.448 \text{ J}}{g \cdot C°} = 2450 \text{ J}$$

9. $$\frac{50.0\,g \mid 32\,°C \mid 2.06 \text{ J}}{g \cdot °C} = 3300 \text{ J}$$

   $$\frac{50.0\,g \mid 334 \text{ J}}{g} = 16\,700 \text{ J}$$

   $$\frac{50.0\,g \mid 100\,°C \mid 4.18 \text{ J}}{g \cdot °C} = 20\,900 \text{ J}$$

   $$\frac{50.0\,g \mid 2260 \text{ J}}{g} = 113\,000 \text{ J}$$

   $$\frac{50.0\,g \mid 300\,°C \mid 2.02 \text{ J}}{g \cdot °C} = 30\,300 \text{ J}$$

   Sum of all five steps = 184 000 J

Chapter End Problems

Pages 354-355.

10. Above the critical temperature, T_c, no amount of pressure will cause the gas to liquefy.
The critical pressure, P_c, is the pressure that will cause the gas to liquefy at the critical temperature.

11. The triple point is the temperature and pressure at which the vapor pressures of the three phases of a substance, gas, liquid, and solid, are in equilibrium. The triple point for water = 0.61 kPa at +0.01°C. NOTE: Students will probably overestimate the temperature of the triple point for water because the slant of the solid-liquid line in Figure 17-9 has been exaggerated to emphasize that the triple point is not at 0°C and that increased pressure lowers the freezing point of water.

12. Le Chatelier's principle: If stress is applied to a system at equilibrium, the system readjusts so that the stress is reduced.
As pressure is applied to one portion of a balloon surface, another portion bulges and the increased pressure is distributed evenly over the entire balloon surface.

13. Molecules appear to vibrate about points in a solid. By chance, a molecule near the surface may undergo a collision or series of collisions which result in a velocity (direction and speed) or kinetic energy sufficiently large enough to counterbalance the attractive forces of surrounding molecules. If these forces are weak enough, the molecule "escapes" from the surface. The loss of molecules from the surface of a liquid in this manner is called evaporation. The loss of molecules from the surface of a solid is called sublimation. Camphor is an excellent example.

14. See number 5 of the Summary on page 353. Sublimation is the change of state in which a substance passes directly from the solid to the gaseous state. Three examples: dry ice changes to a gas, naphthalene balls (mothballs) gradually disappear, and in cold weather, snow or ice sublimes. Frozen clothes hanging on a clothesline gradually become soft and flexible.

15. The boiling point is the temperature at which the vapor pressure of the liquid equals the atmospheric pressure. The melting point is the temperature at which the vapor pressure of the solid and liquid are equal.

16. The HBr molecule is not highly polar and does not form hydrogen bonds. HF does form hydrogen bonds and therefore has a higher boiling point.

17. In the ice crystal lattice, each oxygen atom touches four hydrogen atoms and each hydrogen atom touches two oxygen atoms (note that this follows from the formula, H_2O). In the solid, the repulsion of similar atoms results in the formation of an open lattice but as the molecular motion increases and becomes more random, the open crystal collapses, causing the molecules to move closer together and the ordered structure of the ice crystal is destroyed.

This results in a decrease in volume as the ice melts and as the temperature rises from 0°C to 4°C.

18. Volatile substances evaporate rapidly at room temperature. Nonvolatile substances evaporate slowly at room temperature. Volatile substances have a higher vapor pressure at a given temperature than nonvolatile substances. Ether is a volatile liquid, iodine a volatile solid. Oil is a nonvolatile liquid, iron a nonvolatile solid.

19. The temperature remains at 0°C because the energy added with the warm water is absorbed by the ice and simply causes the equilibrium to shift. Some of the ice melts and becomes liquid. The temperature does not change until all of the ice has melted. The equilibrium is then destroyed.
When the ice below 0°C is added some of the water freezes giving up energy to the ice. The ice is then warmed to 0°C. Again, the equilibrium is simply shifted, unless so much ice (low temperature) is added that all the water freezes. In that case, the equilibrium is destroyed.

20.

	x	y
B.P.	249 K	410 K
M.P.	133 K	300 K
T.P.	124 K	300 K
T_c	255 K	700 K
P_c	1200 kPa	12 kPa

21. $\dfrac{86.4 \cancel{g}}{} \left| \dfrac{5.59 \text{ kJ}}{\cancel{mol}} \right| \dfrac{1 \cancel{mol}}{69.7 \cancel{g}} = 6.93 \text{ kJ}$

22. $\dfrac{59.5 \cancel{g}}{} \left| \dfrac{95.4 \cancel{C°}}{} \right| \dfrac{2.06 \text{ J}}{\cancel{g \cdot C°}} = 11\,700 \text{ J}$

$\dfrac{59.5 \cancel{g}}{} \left| \dfrac{334 \text{ J}}{\cancel{g}} \right. = 19\,900 \text{ J}$

$\dfrac{59.5 \cancel{g}}{} \left| \dfrac{100 \cancel{C°}}{} \right| \dfrac{4.18 \text{ J}}{\cancel{g \cdot C°}} = 24\,900 \text{ J}$

$\dfrac{59.5 \cancel{g}}{} \left| \dfrac{2260 \text{ J}}{\cancel{g}} \right. = 134\,000 \text{ J}$

$\dfrac{59.5 \cancel{g}}{} \left| \dfrac{924 \cancel{C°}}{} \right| \dfrac{2.02 \text{ J}}{\cancel{g \cdot C°}} = 111\,000 \text{ J}$

Total of all five steps = 302 000 J

Review

Page 355.

1. A solid is a rigid body in which the constituent particles are arranged in a repeating pattern.

2. 1

3. FCC, BCC, HCP

4. A macromolecule is a network crystal in which each atom is bonded to its nearest neighbors throughout the entire crystal. diamond, graphite

5. A doped crystal is a better conductor of electricity than the same crystal in pure form.

6. 14

7. FCC

8. By proper heat treatment, its crystalline structure may be altered thereby altering its properties.

9. because of its collisions with the walls of its container

10. Distance = several hundred times the molecular diameter.

11. The pressure of the gas is less than that of the air.

$$\frac{97.1 \text{ mm}}{} \left| \frac{1 \text{ kPa}}{7.50 \text{ mm}} \right. = 12.9 \text{ kPa}$$

Total pressure for the gas = 98.5 − 12.9 = 85.6 kPa

12. $$\frac{409 \text{ mm}}{} \left| \frac{1 \text{ kPa}}{7.50 \text{ mm}} \right. = 54.5 \text{ kPa}$$

One More Step

Page 355.

1. The pressure exerted on the ice by the wire causes an equilibrium shift directly under the wire, the ice melts and the wire moves downward. The water remaining above the wire is at 0°C and is no longer under pressure so it refreezes. As the wire passes through the block of ice, the equilibrium shifts first from solid to liquid, then from liquid to solid. See pp. 337–338, Section 17:2.

2. Faraday sealed crystals of a chlorine compound in a closed bent glass tube and cooled one leg of the bent tube. He heated the crystals which released chlorine gas. As the gas was evolved, pressure in the tube increased and the chlorine gas condensed to a liquid in the cooled portion of the tube. Under these conditions of pressure and temperature, chlorine is a liquid.

3. The CO_2 is under pressure in the extinguisher. When the pressure is released, the gas expands and as a result is cooled due to the Joule-Thomson effect. Each molecule which escapes causes the average K.E. to decrease, thus cooling the gas. The CO_2 is at atmospheric pressure and reduced temperature (−78°C). Under these conditions, CO_2 is a solid.

4. Freezing points:

H_2O	0°C
H_2S	−85.5°C
H_2Se	−60.4°C
H_2Te	−49°C

Hydrogen bonding raises the freezing point to 0°C. Hydrogen bonding also causes ice at 0°C to be less dense than water. This lower density causes ice to float on top of water.

5. Antimony and bismuth expand on freezing. When melting, the metals change from crystalline form to a polyatomic molecular liquid which is a more compact arrangement.

6. $N = N_0 e^{-kT}$, where N is the number of molecules with the energy in question, N_0 is the original number of molecules, e is the base of natural logarithms, k is the Boltzmann constant (R/N_A), and T is the absolute temperature.

7. Arsenic, iodine, and many metals are required in high purity for special scientific applications, e.g., magnesium, selenium. Processes are described in texts on industrial chemistry, chemical engineering, and chemical technology.

GASES

18

An Overview

In Chapter 18, the ideal gas laws are developed with the aid of the kinetic theory model. The chapter begins with the introduction of the characteristics of an ideal gas. The behavior of an ideal gas is easy to predict. Do not allow students to finish the chapter thinking that real gases are ideal. Each ideal gas law is presented and then students are given the opportunity to develop their problem solving abilities. Students are encouraged to think through the problems rather than plugging numbers into formulas. Emphasize that STP (101.325 kPa and 0°C) has no special scientific basis, but was chosen for convenience. The chapter closes with application of the kinetic theory model to understand the properties of gases. Once again properties are seen as a consequence of a particular structure.

Demonstration Information

The flask will become the color of the balloon as the air pressure forces it into the flask. Students usually have no trouble explaining what happened. However, point out to them the compressibility of gases (water vapor) compared to liquids and solids which are considered to be noncompressible. This property can be related to the brake fluid in a car. You step on the brake pedal and the fluid transfers the force to the brake disc or shoe because it is noncompressible. Emphasize that gases are therefore unique in the way temperature, volume, and pressure are related. Ask students how they think pressure and volume are related based on the demonstration.

Performance Objectives

Goal: Students will gain an understanding of ideal gases based on the kinetic theory model and the actual behavior of real gases.

Objectives: Upon completion of the reading and problems, and when asked to demonstrate their understanding either orally or on a written test, students will

18:1-2   P/S   solve volume-pressure variation problems using Boyle's law.

18:3   P/S   utilize Dalton's law of partial pressures to find the dry volume of a gas collected over water.

18:4-5   P/S   solve volume-temperature variation problems using Charles' law.

18:6   P/S   determine the volume of a dry gas under changing conditions of temperature and pressure.

18:7   P/S/K   explain Graham's law and use it to determine relative rates of diffusion of various gases.

18:8   P/S   determine the density of a dry gas given original volume, mass and the changing conditions.

18:9   K   list properties of real gases which lead to deviations from the ideal gas behavior.

    A   voluntarily complete one or more of the One More Step activities.

    A   read unassigned literature related to the chapter.

Teaching Techniques

Section 18:2

Some of your students may find the ratio method of solving problems useful for calculations involving gases. The following explanation may help in presenting the ratio method.

Consider the equation for finding the area of a rectangle: $A = lw$. If we have a rectangle with width 3 and length 4, the area is 12. What will happen to the area if we double the length? The new area is 24. It was easy enough in this case to calculate the new area from the original equation. However, let us look at the problem a different way. We will use the basic equation to represent values of the original problem. That is, $A = 12$, $l = 4$, and $w = 3$. Now let the equation $A' = l'w$, where A' represents the new area and l' the new length. w remains the same because the width did not change. If we divide the first equation by the second we get

$$\left(\frac{A = lw}{A' = l'w} \right) = \left(\frac{A}{A'} = \frac{lw}{l'w} \right) \left(\frac{A}{A'} = \frac{l}{l'} \right)$$

We then solve the final equality for the new area, A'. Upon doing so we get

$$A' = A \frac{l'}{l}$$

In other words, we find the new area by multiplying the old area by the ratio of the two lengths. Should we then multiply the old area (12) by 4/8 or 8/4? Since the new length is greater than the old we can expect to get a new area that is greater than the old. Multiplying the old area by a fraction less than one (4/8) would give a new area less than the old. Multiplying by a fraction greater than one (8/4) will give us an area larger than the original area, so we choose the fraction greater than one.

In applying the relationships between volume, pressure, and temperature, the same kind of reasoning leads to easy solution for gas-related problems.

Section 18:3

The cubic decimeter and the liter differ by 28 parts in a million. In 1964 international metric organizations (CIPM and CGPM) recommended that the liter should not be used in volume measurements. The cubic decimeter was adopted as the volume unit to replace it, based on the m^3 which is the SI unit of volume. For this reason, we use cm^3, dm^3, and m^3 as volume units rather than mL and L.

Section 18:4

Have students take a small balloon, blow it up and measure the circumference with a tape measure. Then, place it in the freezer and remeasure in one hour. This procedure will help them remember Charles' law.

Section 18:7

For uniformity, have students use the first gas named in the problem as V_1 and the second one as V_2.

Section 18:9

An equation exists that takes into account the two major differences in real and ideal gases. Research conducted by van der Waals led to the equation $(P + a/V^2)(V - b) = RT$. The pressure of a real gas is less than ideal because the attractive forces delay the molecules. There are fewer collisions per second. The factor (a/V^2) is added to the pressure to correct for this change. The kinetic theory assumes that the molecules are point masses. However, they do have volume. The volume we calculate isn't totally available because some of it is occupied by the molecules. The variable (b) is the correction that is subtracted from the volume. These corrections allow us to calculate more accurate values for gases at high pressures.

Chemical Technology

Use this feature as a starting point in having students research current pollution standards and methods of eliminating pollutants.

Problem Solutions

Page 361.

1. a. $\dfrac{952 \text{ cm}^3}{} \left| \dfrac{86.4 \text{ kPa}}{101.3 \text{ kPa}} \right. = 812 \text{ cm}^3$

   b. $\dfrac{273 \text{ cm}^3}{} \left| \dfrac{59.4 \text{ kPa}}{101.3 \text{ kPa}} \right. = 160 \text{ cm}^3$

   c. $\dfrac{338 \text{ m}^3}{} \left| \dfrac{122 \text{ kPa}}{101.3 \text{ kPa}} \right. = 407 \text{ m}^3$

   d. $\dfrac{598 \text{ cm}^3}{} \left| \dfrac{94.4 \text{ kPa}}{101.3 \text{ kPa}} \right. = 557 \text{ cm}^3$

   e. $\dfrac{77.0 \text{ m}^3}{} \left| \dfrac{105.9 \text{ kPa}}{101.3 \text{ kPa}} \right. = 80.5 \text{ m}^3$

2. a. $\dfrac{930 \text{ cm}^3}{} \left| \dfrac{92.9 \text{ kPa}}{101.3 \text{ kPa}} \right. = 853 \text{ cm}^3$

   b. $\dfrac{50.0 \text{ m}^3}{} \left| \dfrac{55.1 \text{ kPa}}{101.3 \text{ kPa}} \right. = 27.2 \text{ m}^3$

   c. $\dfrac{36.0 \text{ m}^3}{} \left| \dfrac{65.9 \text{ kPa}}{101.3 \text{ kPa}} \right. = 23.4 \text{ m}^3$

   d. $\dfrac{329 \text{ cm}^3}{} \left| \dfrac{163 \text{ kPa}}{101.3 \text{ kPa}} \right. = 529 \text{ cm}^3$

   e. $\dfrac{231 \text{ cm}^3}{} \left| \dfrac{80.7 \text{ kPa}}{101.3 \text{ kPa}} \right. = 184 \text{ cm}^3$

3. a. $\dfrac{0.600 \text{ m}^3}{} \left| \dfrac{110 \text{ kPa}}{62.4 \text{ kPa}} \right. = 1.06 \text{ m}^3$

   b. $\dfrac{380 \text{ cm}^3}{} \left| \dfrac{66.0 \text{ kPa}}{42.1 \text{ kPa}} \right. = 596 \text{ cm}^3$

   c. $\dfrac{0.338 \text{ m}^3}{} \left| \dfrac{102.4 \text{ kPa}}{47.3 \text{ kPa}} \right. = 0.732 \text{ m}^3$

   d. $\dfrac{459 \text{ cm}^3}{} \left| \dfrac{153 \text{ kPa}}{231 \text{ kPa}} \right. = 304 \text{ cm}^3$

   e. $\dfrac{0.123 \text{ m}^3}{} \left| \dfrac{104.1 \text{ kPa}}{117.7 \text{ kPa}} \right. = 0.109 \text{ m}^3$

4. a. $\dfrac{388 \text{ cm}^3}{} \left| \dfrac{86.1 \text{ kPa}}{104.0 \text{ kPa}} \right. = 321 \text{ cm}^3$

   b. $\dfrac{0.951 \text{ m}^3}{} \left| \dfrac{82.1 \text{ kPa}}{114.6 \text{ kPa}} \right. = 0.681 \text{ m}^3$

   c. $\dfrac{31.5 \text{ cm}^3}{} \left| \dfrac{97.8 \text{ kPa}}{82.3 \text{ kPa}} \right. = 37.4 \text{ cm}^3$

   d. $\dfrac{524 \text{ cm}^3}{} \left| \dfrac{110.0 \text{ kPa}}{104.5 \text{ kPa}} \right. = 552 \text{ cm}^3$

   e. $\dfrac{171 \text{ cm}^3}{} \left| \dfrac{122.5 \text{ kPa}}{104.3 \text{ kPa}} \right. = 201 \text{ cm}^3$

Page 363.

5. a. $93.3 - 1.6 = 91.7$,

   $\dfrac{888 \text{ cm}^3}{} \left| \dfrac{91.7 \text{ kPa}}{101.3 \text{ kPa}} \right. = 804 \text{ cm}^3$

   b. $77.5 - 1.8 = 75.7$,

   $\dfrac{30.0 \text{ cm}^3}{} \left| \dfrac{75.7 \text{ kPa}}{101.3 \text{ kPa}} \right. = 22.4 \text{ cm}^3$

   c. $82.4 - 2.1 = 80.3$,

   $\dfrac{34.0 \text{ m}^3}{} \left| \dfrac{80.3 \text{ kPa}}{101.3 \text{ kPa}} \right. = 27.0 \text{ m}^3$

   d. $78.3 - 1.4 = 76.9$,

   $\dfrac{384 \text{ cm}^3}{} \left| \dfrac{76.9 \text{ kPa}}{101.3 \text{ kPa}} \right. = 292 \text{ cm}^3$

   e. $87.3 - 3.6 = 83.7$,

   $\dfrac{8.23 \text{ m}^3}{} \left| \dfrac{83.7 \text{ kPa}}{101.3 \text{ kPa}} \right. = 6.80 \text{ m}^3$

Page 366.

6. a. $\dfrac{617 \text{ cm}^3}{} \left| \dfrac{273 \text{ K}}{282 \text{ K}} \right. = 597 \text{ cm}^3$

   b. $\dfrac{609 \text{ cm}^3}{} \left| \dfrac{273 \text{ K}}{356 \text{ K}} \right. = 467 \text{ cm}^3$

   c. $\dfrac{942 \text{ cm}^3}{} \left| \dfrac{273 \text{ K}}{295 \text{ K}} \right. = 872 \text{ cm}^3$

   d. $\dfrac{7.12 \text{ m}^3}{} \left| \dfrac{273 \text{ K}}{988 \text{ K}} \right. = 1.97 \text{ m}^3$

   e. $\dfrac{213 \text{ m}^3}{} \left| \dfrac{273 \text{ K}}{372 \text{ K}} \right. = 156 \text{ m}^3$

   f. $\dfrac{7.16 \text{ m}^3}{} \left| \dfrac{273 \text{ K}}{280 \text{ K}} \right. = 6.98 \text{ m}^3$

   g. $\dfrac{4.40 \text{ m}^3}{} \left| \dfrac{273 \text{ K}}{280 \text{ K}} \right. = 4.29 \text{ m}^3$

   h. $\dfrac{819 \text{ cm}^3}{} \left| \dfrac{273 \text{ K}}{294 \text{ K}} \right. = 761 \text{ cm}^3$

   i. $\dfrac{5.80 \text{ m}^3}{} \left| \dfrac{273 \text{ K}}{514 \text{ K}} \right. = 3.08 \text{ m}^3$

   j. $\dfrac{5.94 \text{ m}^3}{} \left| \dfrac{273 \text{ K}}{352 \text{ K}} \right. = 4.61 \text{ m}^3$

7. a. $\dfrac{2.90 \text{ m}^3}{} \left| \dfrac{296 \text{ K}}{226 \text{ K}} \right. = 3.80 \text{ m}^3$

   b. $\dfrac{608 \text{ cm}^3}{} \left| \dfrac{346 \text{ K}}{158 \text{ K}} \right. = 1330 \text{ cm}^3$

   c. $\dfrac{7.91 \text{ m}^3}{} \left| \dfrac{538 \text{ K}}{325 \text{ K}} \right. = 13.1 \text{ m}^3$

   d. $\dfrac{880 \text{ cm}^3}{} \left| \dfrac{325 \text{ K}}{563 \text{ K}} \right. = 508 \text{ cm}^3$

   e. $\dfrac{5.94 \text{ m}^3}{} \left| \dfrac{290 \text{ K}}{317 \text{ K}} \right. = 5.43 \text{ m}^3$

   f. $\dfrac{2.97 \text{ m}^3}{} \left| \dfrac{502 \text{ K}}{345 \text{ K}} \right. = 4.32 \text{ m}^3$

   g. $\dfrac{19.0 \text{ cm}^3}{} \left| \dfrac{326 \text{ K}}{56.0 \text{ K}} \right. = 111 \text{ cm}^3$

   h. $\dfrac{5.18 \text{ m}^3}{} \left| \dfrac{279 \text{ K}}{349 \text{ K}} \right. = 4.14 \text{ m}^3$

   i. $\dfrac{994 \text{ cm}^3}{} \left| \dfrac{244 \text{ K}}{300 \text{ K}} \right. = 808 \text{ cm}^3$

   j. $\dfrac{833 \text{ cm}^3}{} \left| \dfrac{357 \text{ K}}{300 \text{ K}} \right. = 991 \text{ cm}^3$

Page 367.

8. a. $\dfrac{7.51 \text{ m}^3}{} \left| \dfrac{273 \text{ K}}{278 \text{ K}} \right| \dfrac{59.9 \text{ kPa}}{101.3 \text{ kPa}} = 4.36 \text{ m}^3$

   b. $\dfrac{149 \text{ cm}^3}{} \left| \dfrac{341 \text{ K}}{291 \text{ K}} \right| \dfrac{94.7 \text{ kPa}}{82.4 \text{ kPa}} = 201 \text{ cm}^3$

c. $\dfrac{7.03 \text{ m}^3}{} \;\bigg|\; \dfrac{273 \text{ K}}{304 \text{ K}} \;\bigg|\; \dfrac{111 \text{ kPa}}{101.3 \text{ kPa}} = 6.92 \text{ m}^3$

d. $\dfrac{955 \text{ cm}^3}{} \;\bigg|\; \dfrac{349 \text{ K}}{331 \text{ K}} \;\bigg|\; \dfrac{108 \text{ kPa}}{123 \text{ kPa}} = 884 \text{ cm}^3$

e. $\dfrac{960 \text{ cm}^3}{} \;\bigg|\; \dfrac{286 \text{ K}}{344 \text{ K}} \;\bigg|\; \dfrac{107.2 \text{ kPa}}{59.3 \text{ kPa}} = 1440 \text{ cm}^3$

9. a. $\dfrac{654 \text{ cm}^3}{} \;\bigg|\; \dfrac{277 \text{ K}}{279 \text{ K}} \;\bigg|\; \dfrac{65.3 \text{ kPa}}{108.7 \text{ kPa}} = 390 \text{ cm}^3$

b. $\dfrac{2.13 \text{ m}^3}{} \;\bigg|\; \dfrac{273 \text{ K}}{368 \text{ K}} \;\bigg|\; \dfrac{103 \text{ kPa}}{101.3 \text{ kPa}} = 1.61 \text{ m}^3$

c. $\dfrac{4.76 \text{ m}^3}{} \;\bigg|\; \dfrac{273 \text{ K}}{279 \text{ K}} \;\bigg|\; \dfrac{124.5 \text{ kPa}}{101.3 \text{ kPa}} = 5.72 \text{ m}^3$

d. $\dfrac{61.4 \text{ cm}^3}{} \;\bigg|\; \dfrac{273 \text{ K}}{340 \text{ K}} \;\bigg|\; \dfrac{96.8 \text{ kPa}}{101.3 \text{ kPa}} = 47.1 \text{ cm}^3$

e. $\dfrac{164 \text{ cm}^3}{} \;\bigg|\; \dfrac{294 \text{ K}}{273 \text{ K}} \;\bigg|\; \dfrac{101.3 \text{ kPa}}{98.0 \text{ kPa}} = 183 \text{ cm}^3$

Page 369.

10. $\dfrac{V_{\text{hydrogen}}}{V_{\text{oxygen}}} = \dfrac{\sqrt{m_{\text{oxygen}}}}{\sqrt{m_{\text{hydrogen}}}} = \dfrac{\sqrt{32.0 \text{ g}}}{\sqrt{2.02 \text{ g}}} = \sqrt{\dfrac{32.0}{2.02}}$

$= \sqrt{15.9} = 3.98$

11. $\dfrac{V_{\text{helium}}}{V_{\text{radon}}} = \dfrac{\sqrt{m_{\text{radon}}}}{\sqrt{m_{\text{helium}}}} = \dfrac{\sqrt{222 \text{ g}}}{\sqrt{4.00 \text{ g}}} = \sqrt{55.5} = 7.45$

12. $\dfrac{V_{\text{helium}}}{V_{\text{oxygen}}} = \sqrt{\dfrac{m_{\text{oxygen}}}{m_{\text{helium}}}}$

$\dfrac{V_{\text{helium}}}{0.0760 \text{ m/s}} = \sqrt{\dfrac{32.0 \text{ g}}{4.00 \text{ g}}} = \sqrt{8} = 2\sqrt{2}$

$V_{\text{helium}} = 2(\sqrt{2})(0.0760 \text{ m/s})$
$= (2.83)(0.0760 \text{ m/s})$
$= 0.215 \text{ m/s}$

13. $\dfrac{V_{\text{He}}}{V_{\text{Ar}}} = \sqrt{\dfrac{m_{\text{Ar}}}{m_{\text{He}}}} = \sqrt{\dfrac{39.9}{4.00}} = 3.16$

14. $\dfrac{V_{\text{Ar}}}{V_{\text{Rn}}} = \sqrt{\dfrac{m_{\text{Rn}}}{m_{\text{Ar}}}} = \sqrt{\dfrac{222}{39.9}} = 2.36$

Page 370.

15. a. $\dfrac{1.64 \text{ g}}{969 \text{ cm}^3} \;\bigg|\; \dfrac{1000 \text{ cm}^3}{1 \text{ dm}^3} \;\bigg|\; \dfrac{337 \text{ K}}{273 \text{ K}} \;\bigg|\; \dfrac{101.3 \text{ kPa}}{96.4 \text{ kPa}}$
$= 2.20 \text{ g/dm}^3$

b. $\dfrac{0.530 \text{ g}}{498 \text{ cm}^3} \;\bigg|\; \dfrac{1000 \text{ cm}^3}{1 \text{ dm}^3} \;\bigg|\; \dfrac{304 \text{ K}}{273 \text{ K}} \;\bigg|\; \dfrac{101.3 \text{ kPa}}{103.5 \text{ kPa}}$
$= 1.16 \text{ g/dm}^3$

c. $\dfrac{8.30 \text{ g}}{833 \text{ cm}^3} \;\bigg|\; \dfrac{1000 \text{ cm}^3}{1 \text{ dm}^3} \;\bigg|\; \dfrac{372 \text{ K}}{273 \text{ K}} \;\bigg|\; \dfrac{101.3 \text{ kPa}}{103 \text{ kPa}}$
$= 13.4 \text{ g/dm}^3$

d. $\dfrac{3.69 \text{ g}}{883 \text{ cm}^3} \;\bigg|\; \dfrac{1000 \text{ cm}^3}{1 \text{ dm}^3} \;\bigg|\; \dfrac{310 \text{ K}}{273 \text{ K}} \;\bigg|\; \dfrac{101.3 \text{ kPa}}{115 \text{ kPa}}$
$= 4.18 \text{ g/dm}^3$

e. $\dfrac{5.03 \text{ g}}{4750 \text{ cm}^3} \;\bigg|\; \dfrac{1000 \text{ cm}^3}{1 \text{ dm}^3} \;\bigg|\; \dfrac{299 \text{ K}}{273 \text{ K}} \;\bigg|\; \dfrac{101.3 \text{ kPa}}{92.5 \text{ kPa}}$
$= 1.27 \text{ g/dm}^3$

16. $\dfrac{2.97 \text{ g}}{\text{dm}^3} \;\bigg|\; \dfrac{273 \text{ K}}{300 \text{ K}} \;\bigg|\; \dfrac{100 \text{ kPa}}{101.3 \text{ kPa}} = 2.67 \text{ g/dm}^3$

17. $\dfrac{5.01 \text{ g}}{\text{dm}^3} \;\bigg|\; \dfrac{325 \text{ K}}{273 \text{ K}} \;\bigg|\; \dfrac{101.3 \text{ kPa}}{107 \text{ kPa}} = 5.65 \text{ g/dm}^3$

Chapter End Problems
Pages 374-375.

18. An ideal gas is composed of particles which are considered point masses. These particles have no attraction for each other.

19. low pressure, high temperature

20. The gas would disappear. In reality, the gas would condense to form a liquid.

21. The masses of the gases would be different. Thus, they would be traveling at different velocities.

22. A gas exhibits the Joule-Thomson effect in cooling when released through a small opening under high pressure.

23. $\dfrac{928 \text{ cm}^3}{} \;\bigg|\; \dfrac{273 \text{ K}}{300 \text{ K}} \;\bigg|\; \dfrac{106.0 \text{ kPa}}{101.3 \text{ kPa}} = 884 \text{ cm}^3$

24. $122.0 - 3.6 = 118.4$
$\dfrac{96.0 \text{ cm}^3}{} \;\bigg|\; \dfrac{343 \text{ K}}{300 \text{ K}} \;\bigg|\; \dfrac{118.4 \text{ kPa}}{127.0 \text{ kPa}} = 102 \text{ cm}^3$

25. $111.0 - 70.1 = 40.9$
$\dfrac{372 \text{ cm}^3}{} \;\bigg|\; \dfrac{275 \text{ K}}{363 \text{ K}} \;\bigg|\; \dfrac{40.9 \text{ kPa}}{98.0 \text{ kPa}} = 118 \text{ cm}^3$

26. $96.9 - 0.8 = 96.1$
$\dfrac{5.08 \text{ cm}^3}{} \;\bigg|\; \dfrac{317 \text{ K}}{276 \text{ K}} \;\bigg|\; \dfrac{96.1 \text{ kPa}}{117.6 \text{ kPa}} = 477 \text{ cm}^3$

27. $93.0 - 2.3 = 90.7$
$\dfrac{30.0 \text{ cm}^3}{} \;\bigg|\; \dfrac{272 \text{ K}}{293 \text{ K}} \;\bigg|\; \dfrac{90.7 \text{ kPa}}{101.3 \text{ kPa}} = 25.0 \text{ cm}^3$

28. a. $95.3 - 3.0 = 92.3$
$\dfrac{903 \text{ cm}^3}{} \;\bigg|\; \dfrac{92.3 \text{ kPa}}{101.3 \text{ kPa}} = 823 \text{ cm}^3$

b. $113.5 - 3.2 = 110.3$
$\dfrac{317 \text{ cm}^3}{} \;\bigg|\; \dfrac{110.3 \text{ kPa}}{101.3 \text{ kPa}} = 345 \text{ cm}^3$

c. $107 - 2.0 = 105$
$\dfrac{7.83 \text{ m}^3}{} \;\bigg|\; \dfrac{105 \text{ kPa}}{101.3 \text{ kPa}} = 8.12 \text{ m}^3$

d. $111.5 - 4.0 = 107.5$
$\dfrac{964 \text{ cm}^3}{} \;\bigg|\; \dfrac{107.5 \text{ kPa}}{101.3 \text{ kPa}} = 1020 \text{ cm}^3$

29. $\dfrac{325 \text{ cm}^3}{} \;\bigg|\; \dfrac{293 \text{ K}}{273 \text{ K}} \;\bigg|\; \dfrac{101.3 \text{ kPa}}{93.3 \text{ kPa}} = 379 \text{ cm}^3$

30. $101.3 - 0.6 = 100.7$
$\dfrac{8.00 \text{ cm}^3}{} \;\bigg|\; \dfrac{100.7 \text{ kPa}}{101.3 \text{ kPa}} = 7.95 \text{ cm}^3$

Review
Page 375.

1. It must be on the surface, heading away from the body of the liquid and have sufficient kinetic energy to overcome the attractive forces of its neighboring particles in the liquid.

2. A system at equilibrium will shift so as to relieve an outside stress.

3. change directly from solid to gas

4. The molecules must be brought close enough together for van der Waals forces to take effect, and they must be slowed sufficiently for the van der Waals forces to keep them together.

5.

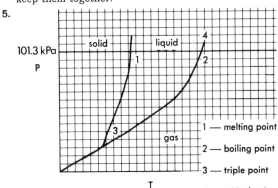

6. Changes are occurring, but they are the reverse of each other and are occurring at the same rate.

7. the temperature at which the vapor pressures of the solid and liquid phases are equal

8.
$$\frac{1.70\ \cancel{g}\ \left|\ 12\ \cancel{C^\circ}\ \right|\ 2.06\ J}{\cancel{g}\cdot\cancel{C^\circ}} = 42\ J$$

$$\frac{1.70\ \cancel{g}\ \left|\ 334\ J\right.}{\cancel{g}} = 568\ J$$

$$\frac{1.70\ \cancel{g}\ \left|\ 100\ \cancel{C^\circ}\ \right|\ 4.18\ J}{\cancel{g}\cdot\cancel{C^\circ}} = 711\ J$$

$$\frac{1.70\ \cancel{g}\ \left|\ 2260\ J\right.}{\cancel{g}} = 3840\ J$$

$$\frac{1.70\ \cancel{g}\ \left|\ 40\ \cancel{C^\circ}\ \right|\ 2.02\ J}{\cancel{g}\cdot\cancel{C^\circ}} = 140\ J$$

Sum of all 5 steps = 5300 J

One More Step

Page 375.

2. The most common equation is that of van der Waals.

$$\left(P + \frac{an^2}{V^2}\right)(V - nb) = nRT$$

For N_2:
$a = 141\ dm^6\cdot kPa/mol^2$, $b = 0.0394\ dm^3/mol$
Solving for V (assuming 1 mole) gives $0.0736\ dm^3$. Solving the ideal gas equation gives 0.0560. The % is then,

$$\frac{(0.0736 - 0.0560)}{0.0560}\ \left|\ \frac{100}{1}\right. = 31.4\%$$

Other equations are

Keyes $\left(P - \dfrac{a}{V - L_2}\right)(V - d) = RT$ for 1 mole

Berthelot $\left(P - \dfrac{n^2A}{TV^2}\right)(V - nB) = nRT$

3.

Height of Hg in closed arm	Height of Hg in open arm
0	0
0.5	1.4375
1	2.8125
1.5	4.375
2	6.1875
2.5	7.875
3	10.125
3.5	12.5
4	15.0625
4.5	17.9375
5	21.1875
5.5	25.1875
6	29.6875
6.25	32.1875
6.5	34.9375
6.75	37.9375
7	41.5625
7.25	45
7.5	48.75
7.75	53.6875
8	58.125
8.25	63.9375
8.5	71.3125
8.75	78.6875
9	88.4375

All measurements are in inches of mercury. The barometric pressure that day was 29.125 inches of mercury. The total length of the closed end of the tube was 12 inches.

GASES AND THE MOLE

19

An Overview

Chapter 19 continues the study of gases by comparing the gas laws with experimental results obtained from real gases. The mole is reintroduced in connection with Avogadro's principle in order to develop the ideal gas equation, $pV = nRT$. Point out to students that R as a constant provides evidence for the validity of our kinetic theory model. Remind students that there is nothing special about the value 22.4 dm^3, the molar volume. It is a result of the values that were selected for standard temperature and pressure. You may want to review stoichiometry problems (mass-mass) from Chapter 7 before introducing mass-volume and volume-volume problems. Emphasize the factor-label method. Attempt to get your students to ask themselves, "Is this answer reasonable?" It helps students understand what they are trying to accomplish in the answer. The student will need this ability to master the non 1 to 1 mole ratio problems. The chapter closes by introducing the concept that gases can do work or have work done on them.

Demonstration Information

$Mg(c) + 2HCl(aq) \rightarrow MgCl_2(aq) + H_2(g)$

This demonstration is often done as a laboratory experiment. Volume, temperature, and pressure measurements can be made and then used to introduce related calculations. A 50 cm^3 gas measuring tube works better than a graduated cylinder.

Performance Objectives

Goal: Students will gain an understanding of the concept of molar gas volume and its use in solving gas reaction problems.

Objectives: Upon completion of the reading and problems, and when asked to demonstrate their understanding either orally or on a written test, students will

19:1-2	K/P	determine the molar volume of a gas using Avogadro's principle.
19:3	P/S	given any three variables in the ideal gas equation—pressure, temperature, volume, or number of particles—determine the fourth.
19:4	P/S	determine the molecular mass of a gas from the ideal gas equation.
19:5-7, 9	P/S	determine the volume or mass of reactants or products in a reaction involving gases given one or more of the products or reactants under standard conditions or nonstandard conditions.
19:8	P/S	use the concept of limiting reactants to solve stoichiometric problems.
19:10	K/P	explain the relationship between gases and work.
	A	voluntarily complete one or more of the One More Step activities.
	A	read unassigned literature related to the chapter.

Teaching Techniques

Section 19:1

Small magnets representing molecules placed on a magnetic board can be used to represent a

chemical reaction. They can be moved together to simulate a reaction such as $H_2 + I_2 \rightarrow 2HI$. Stress the equal temperature and equal pressure part of Avogadro's principle.

Section 19:3

The value for R, is not constant when working with real gases. When it is experimentally determined, it varies in the third or fourth decimal place from the accepted value of R. You can determine R experimentally using a small disposable butane (C_4H_{10}) lighter. Submerge the lighter in water, shake it off, dry it and mass it. Fill a 100 cm^3 graduated cylinder with water and invert it in a large beaker of water. Release the gas and collect 100 cm^3 by water displacement. Shake and dry the lighter before massing it again. The difference is the mass of 100 cm^3 of butane. Correct the volume for water vapor and pressure levels. Substitute the pressure and corrected volume for P and V. Calculate the moles of butane using the mass of the gas and the molecular mass. Substitute for n in the equation. Convert the temperature of the gas to kelvin. ($PV/nT = R$) Using the units $kPa \cdot dm^3/mol \cdot K$, you will have a close experimental value for R. One butane lighter will last 5 or 6 demonstrations. Make students aware that R has many values depending on the units used to derive it.

Section 19:10

Ask your students how we use compressed gases to do work for us. They may name the air impact wrench used to change tires. Compressed air mixed with a liquid is used for quick response on airplane flight control surfaces. This brief discussion will help students relate to the text material.

Chemical Technology

With supplies dwindling for some resources ocean mining is becoming more economically feasible. You can have students do further research into the costs and benefits of deep sea mining.

Problem Solutions

Page 380.

1. $P = \dfrac{nRT}{V} = \dfrac{0.300 \text{ mol}}{8.00 \text{ dm}^3} \left| \dfrac{8.31 \text{ dm}^3 \cdot kPa}{\text{mol} \cdot K} \right| 291 K$

$= 90.7$ kPa

2. $n = \dfrac{PV}{RT} = \dfrac{66.7 \text{ kPa}}{} \left| \dfrac{0.486 \text{ dm}^3}{283 K} \right| \dfrac{\text{mol} \cdot K}{8.31 \text{ dm}^3 \cdot kPa}$

$= 0.0138$ mol

3. $V = \dfrac{nRT}{P} = \dfrac{0.362 \text{ mol}}{100.3 \text{ kPa}} \left| \dfrac{8.31 \text{ dm}^3 \cdot kPa}{\text{mol} \cdot K} \right| 281 K$

$= 8.43 \text{ dm}^3$

4. $T = \dfrac{PV}{nR} = \dfrac{100.4 \text{ kPa}}{0.0851 \text{ mol}} \Bigg| \dfrac{604 \text{ cm}^3}{} \Bigg| \dfrac{\text{mol} \cdot \text{K}}{8.31 \text{ dm}^3 \cdot \text{kPa}} \Bigg| \dfrac{1 \text{ dm}^3}{1000 \text{ cm}^3} = 85.8 \text{ K} = -187°\text{C}$

5. $P = \dfrac{nRT}{V} = \dfrac{0.00306 \text{ mol}}{25.9 \text{ cm}^3} \Bigg| \dfrac{8.31 \text{ dm}^3 \cdot \text{kPa}}{\text{mol} \cdot \text{K}} \Bigg| \dfrac{282 \text{ K}}{} \Bigg| \dfrac{1000 \text{ cm}^3}{1 \text{ dm}^3} = 277 \text{ kPa}$

Page 381.

6. $M = \dfrac{mRT}{PV} = \dfrac{0.800 \text{ g}}{106.7 \text{ kPa}} \Bigg| \dfrac{8.31 \text{ dm}^3 \cdot \text{kPa}}{\text{mol} \cdot \text{K}} \Bigg| \dfrac{373 \text{ K}}{0.372 \text{ dm}^3} = 62.5 \text{ g/mol}$

7. $\dfrac{m}{V} = \dfrac{MP}{RT} = \dfrac{32.0 \text{ g}}{\text{mol}} \Bigg| \dfrac{100.5 \text{ kPa}}{296 \text{ K}} \Bigg| \dfrac{\text{mol} \cdot \text{K}}{8.31 \text{ dm}^3 \cdot \text{kPa}} = 1.31 \text{ g/dm}^3$

8. $M = \dfrac{mRT}{PV} = \dfrac{6.71 \text{ g}}{100.4 \text{ kPa}} \Bigg| \dfrac{8.31 \text{ dm}^3 \cdot \text{kPa}}{\text{mol} \cdot \text{K}} \Bigg| \dfrac{302 \text{ K}}{2.12 \text{ dm}^3} = 79.1 \text{ g/mol}$

9. $M = \dfrac{mRT}{PV} = \dfrac{0.646 \text{ g}}{105.1 \text{ kPa}} \Bigg| \dfrac{8.31 \text{ dm}^3 \cdot \text{kPa}}{\text{mol} \cdot \text{K}} \Bigg| \dfrac{277 \text{ K}}{0.160 \text{ dm}^3} = 88.4 \text{ g/mol}$

10. $M = \dfrac{mRT}{PV} = \dfrac{8.11 \text{ g}}{109.1 \text{ kPa}} \Bigg| \dfrac{8.31 \text{ dm}^3 \cdot \text{kPa}}{\text{mol} \cdot \text{K}} \Bigg| \dfrac{283 \text{ K}}{2.38 \text{ dm}^3} = 73.5 \text{ g/mol}$

Page 383.

11. $3H_2(g) + N_2(g) \rightarrow 2NH_3(g)$

$\dfrac{14.0 \text{ g } N_2}{} \Bigg| \dfrac{1 \text{ mol } N_2}{28.0 \text{ g } N_2} \Bigg| \dfrac{2 \text{ mol } NH_3}{1 \text{ mol } N_2} \Bigg| \dfrac{22\,400 \text{ cm}^3}{1 \text{ mol}} = 22\,400 \text{ cm}^3 \text{ } NH_3$

12. $Zn(c) + H_2SO_4(aq) \rightarrow ZnSO_4(aq) + H_2(g)$

$\dfrac{28.0 \text{ g } Zn}{} \Bigg| \dfrac{1 \text{ mol } Zn}{65.4 \text{ g } Zn} \Bigg| \dfrac{1 \text{ mol } H_2}{1 \text{ mol } Zn} \Bigg| \dfrac{22\,400 \text{ cm}^3}{1 \text{ mol}} = 9590 \text{ cm}^3 \text{ } H_2$

13. $H_2(g) + Br_2(g) \rightarrow 2HBr(g)$

$\dfrac{5600 \text{ cm}^3 \text{ } H_2}{} \Bigg| \dfrac{1 \text{ mol}}{22\,400 \text{ cm}^3} \Bigg| \dfrac{2 \text{ mol } HBr}{1 \text{ mol } H_2} \Bigg| \dfrac{80.9 \text{ g } HBr}{1 \text{ mol } HBr} = 40.5 \text{ g } HBr$

14. $2Sb(c) + 3Cl_2(g) \rightarrow 2SbCl_3(c)$

$\dfrac{6720 \text{ cm}^3 \text{ } Cl_2}{} \Bigg| \dfrac{1 \text{ mol}}{22\,400 \text{ cm}^3} \Bigg| \dfrac{2 \text{ mol } SbCl_3}{3 \text{ mol } Cl_2} \Bigg| \dfrac{228 \text{ g } SbCl_3}{1 \text{ mol } SbCl_3} = 45.6 \text{ g } SbCl_3$

Pages 385-386.

15. $2C_4H_{10}(g) + 13O_2(g) \rightarrow 8CO_2(g) + 10H_2O(g)$

$\dfrac{401 \text{ cm}^3 \text{ } C_4H_{10}}{} \Bigg| \dfrac{13 \text{ cm}^3 \text{ } O_2}{2 \text{ cm}^3 \text{ } C_4H_{10}} = 2610 \text{ cm}^3 \text{ } O_2$

16. $\dfrac{75.2 \text{ dm}^3 \text{ } Cl_2}{} \Bigg| \dfrac{1 \text{ dm}^3 \text{ } Br_2}{1 \text{ dm}^3 \text{ } Cl_2} = 75.2 \text{ dm}^3 \text{ } Br_2$

17. $O_2(g) + 2NO(g) \rightarrow 2NO_2(g)$

$\dfrac{500 \text{ cm}^3 \text{ } NO}{} \Bigg| \dfrac{1 \text{ cm}^3 \text{ } O_2}{2 \text{ cm}^3 \text{ } NO} = 250 \text{ cm}^3 \text{ } O_2$

18. $\dfrac{941 \text{ m}^3 \text{ } C_6H_6}{} \Bigg| \dfrac{4 \text{ m}^3 \text{ } H_2}{1 \text{ m}^3 \text{ } C_6H_6} = 3760 \text{ m}^3 \text{ } H_2$

Page 388.

19. $\dfrac{2.10 \text{ g } NaBr}{} \Bigg| \dfrac{1 \text{ mol } NaBr}{103 \text{ g } NaBr} = 0.0204 \text{ mol } NaBr \text{ (limiting reactant)}$

$\dfrac{9.42 \text{ g } H_2SO_4}{} \Bigg| \dfrac{1 \text{ mol } H_2SO_4}{98.1 \text{ g } H_2SO_4} = 0.0960 \text{ mole } H_2SO_4$

$\dfrac{0.0204 \text{ mol } NaBr}{} \Bigg| \dfrac{1 \text{ mol } Br_2}{2 \text{ mol } NaBr} \Bigg| \dfrac{160 \text{ g } Br_2}{1 \text{ mol } Br_2} = 1.63 \text{ g } Br_2$

20. $\dfrac{4.14 \text{ g } Ca_3(PO_4)_2}{} \Bigg| \dfrac{1 \text{ mol } Ca_3(PO_4)_2}{310 \text{ g } Ca_3(PO_4)_2} = 0.0134 \text{ mol } Ca_3(PO_4)_2$

$\dfrac{1.20 \text{ g } SiO_2}{} \Bigg| \dfrac{1 \text{ mol } SiO_2}{60.1 \text{ g } SiO_2} = 0.0200 \text{ mol } SiO_2 \text{ (limiting reactant)}$

$\dfrac{0.0200 \text{ mol } SiO_2}{} \Bigg| \dfrac{10 \text{ mol } CO}{6 \text{ mol } SiO_2} \Bigg| \dfrac{22\,400 \text{ cm}^3}{1 \text{ mol}} = 747 \text{ cm}^3 \text{ } CO$

21. $\dfrac{4.11 \text{ g } I_2}{} \Bigg| \dfrac{1 \text{ mol } I_2}{254 \text{ g } I_2} = 0.0162 \text{ mol } I_2$

$$\frac{317 \text{ cm}^3 \text{ H}_2\text{S} \quad | \quad 1 \text{ mol}}{| \quad 22\,400 \text{ cm}^3} = 0.0142 \text{ mol H}_2\text{S (limiting reactant)}$$

$$\frac{0.0142 \text{ mol H}_2\text{S} \quad | \quad 1 \text{ mol S} \quad | \quad 32.1 \text{ g S}}{| \quad 1 \text{ mol H}_2\text{S} \quad | \quad 1 \text{ mol S}} = 0.456 \text{ g S}$$

22. $$\frac{116 \text{ cm}^3 \text{ Cl}_2 \quad | \quad 1 \text{ mol}}{| \quad 22\,400 \text{ cm}^3} = 0.00518 \text{ mol Cl}_2 \text{ (limiting reactant)}$$

$$\frac{7.62 \text{ g HgO} \quad | \quad 1 \text{ mol HgO}}{| \quad 217 \text{ g HgO}} = 0.0351 \text{ mol HgO}$$

$$\frac{116 \text{ cm}^3 \text{ Cl}_2 \quad | \quad 1 \text{ cm}^3 \text{ Cl}_2\text{O}}{| \quad 2 \text{ cm}^3 \text{ Cl}_2} = 58.0 \text{ cm}^3 \text{ Cl}_2\text{O}$$

Page 391.

23. a. $w = -2.303 nRT \log \dfrac{V_2}{V_1}$

$\quad\quad = -(2.303)(1)(8.31)(298) \log \dfrac{44.5}{9.92}$

$\quad\quad = -3720 \text{ J}$

b. $w = -P_{\text{ex}} \Delta V$

$\quad\quad = -(10.0)(44.5 - 9.92) = -346 \text{ J}$

24. $w = C_v \Delta T$

$\quad\quad = (12.5)(8.48) = 106 \text{ J/mol}$

25. $w = -2.303 nRT \log \dfrac{V_2}{V_1}$

$\quad\quad = -(2.303)(1.80)(8.31)(371) \log \dfrac{0.151}{0.492}$

$\quad\quad = 6230 \text{ J}$

26. $w = C_v \Delta T$

$\quad\quad = (34.2)(80.0)$

$\quad\quad = 2740 \text{ J/mol}$

Chapter End Problems

Pages 394–395.

27. $P = \dfrac{nRT}{V} = \dfrac{0.400 \text{ mol}}{10.0 \text{ dm}^3} \left| \dfrac{8.31 \text{ dm}^3 \cdot \text{kPa}}{\text{mol} \cdot \text{K}} \right| \dfrac{300 \text{ K}}{} = 99.7 \text{ kPa}$

28. $M = \dfrac{mRT}{PV} = \dfrac{1.00 \text{ g}}{1.05 \text{ kPa}} \left| \dfrac{8.31 \text{ dm}^3 \cdot \text{kPa}}{\text{mol} \cdot \text{K}} \right| \dfrac{250 \text{ K}}{0.500 \text{ dm}^3} = 39.6 \text{ g/mol}$

29. $2\text{C}_2\text{H}_6(g) + 7\text{O}_2(g) \rightarrow 4\text{CO}_2(g) + 6\text{H}_2\text{O}(g)$

$$\frac{10.0 \text{ dm}^3 \text{ C}_2\text{H}_6 \quad | \quad 4 \text{ dm}^3 \text{ CO}_2}{| \quad 2 \text{ dm}^3 \text{ C}_2\text{H}_6} = 20.0 \text{ dm}^3 \text{ CO}_2$$

30. $$\frac{10.0 \text{ dm}^3 \text{ C}_2\text{H}_6 \quad | \quad 7 \text{ dm}^3 \text{ O}_2}{| \quad 2 \text{ dm}^3 \text{ C}_2\text{H}_6} = 35.0 \text{ dm}^3 \text{ O}_2$$

31. $\text{CS}_2(g) + 3\text{O}_2(g) \rightarrow \text{CO}_2(g) + 2\text{SO}_2(g)$

$$\frac{7.00 \text{ dm}^3 \text{ CS}_2 \quad | \quad 2 \text{ dm}^3 \text{ SO}_2}{| \quad 1 \text{ dm}^3 \text{ CS}_2} = 14.0 \text{ dm}^3 \text{ SO}_2$$

32. $$\frac{7.00 \text{ dm}^3 \text{ CS}_2 \quad | \quad 1 \text{ dm}^3 \text{ CO}_2 \quad | \quad 1 \text{ mol}}{| \quad 1 \text{ dm}^3 \text{ CS}_2 \quad | \quad 22.4 \text{ dm}^3} = 0.313 \text{ mol CO}_2$$

33. $\text{Ni}(c) + \text{S}(c) \rightarrow \text{NiS}(c)$

$$\text{Ni} = \frac{10.0 \text{ g Ni} \quad | \quad 1 \text{ mol Ni}}{| \quad 58.7 \text{ g Ni}} = 0.170 \text{ mol}$$

$$\text{S} = \frac{4.00 \text{ g S} \quad | \quad 1 \text{ mol S}}{| \quad 32.1 \text{ g S}} = 0.125 \text{ mol (S is the limiting reactant)}$$

$$\frac{0.125 \text{ mol S} \quad | \quad 1 \text{ mol NiS} \quad | \quad 90.8 \text{ g NiS}}{| \quad 1 \text{ mol S} \quad | \quad 1 \text{ mol NiS}} = 11.4 \text{ g NiS}$$

34. $\text{CaO}(c) + \text{H}_2\text{O}(l) \rightarrow \text{Ca(OH)}_2(aq)$

$$\frac{7.00 \text{ g CaO} \quad | \quad 1 \text{ mol CaO}}{| \quad 56.1 \text{ g CaO}} = 0.125 \text{ mol CaO}$$

$$\frac{2.00 \text{ g H}_2\text{O} \quad | \quad 1 \text{ mol H}_2\text{O}}{| \quad 18.0 \text{ g H}_2\text{O}} = 0.111 \text{ mol H}_2\text{O (H}_2\text{O is the limiting reactant)}$$

$$\frac{0.111 \text{ mol H}_2\text{O} \quad | \quad 1 \text{ mol Ca(OH)}_2 \quad | \quad 74.1 \text{ g Ca(OH)}_2}{| \quad 1 \text{ mol H}_2\text{O} \quad | \quad 1 \text{ mol Ca(OH)}_2} = 8.23 \text{ g Ca(OH)}_2$$

35. $2Na(c) + Cl_2(g) \rightarrow 2NaCl(c)$

$$\frac{23.0 \text{ g Na}}{} \left| \frac{1 \text{ mol Na}}{23.0 \text{ g Na}} \right. = 1.00 \text{ mol Na (Na is limiting reactant)}$$

$$\frac{22.4 \text{ dm}^3 \text{ Cl}_2}{} \left| \frac{1 \text{ mol}}{22.4 \text{ dm}^3} \right. = 1.00 \text{ mol Cl}_2$$

$$\frac{1.00 \text{ mol Na}}{} \left| \frac{2 \text{ mol NaCl}}{2 \text{ mol Na}} \right| \frac{58.5 \text{ g NaCl}}{1 \text{ mol NaCl}} = 58.5 \text{ g NaCl}$$

36. $$\frac{16.0 \text{ g Fe}_2\text{O}_3}{} \left| \frac{1 \text{ mol Fe}_2\text{O}_3}{160 \text{ g Fe}_2\text{O}_3} \right. = 0.100 \text{ mol Fe}_2\text{O}_3 \text{ (Fe}_2\text{O}_3 \text{ limiting reactant)}$$

$$\frac{10.0 \text{ dm}^3 \text{ CO}}{} \left| \frac{1 \text{ mol}}{22.4 \text{ dm}^3} \right. = 0.446 \text{ mol CO}$$

$$\frac{0.100 \text{ mol Fe}_2\text{O}_3}{} \left| \frac{3 \text{ mol CO}}{1 \text{ mol Fe}_2\text{O}_3} \right| \frac{22.4 \text{ dm}^3}{1 \text{ mol}} = 6.72 \text{ dm}^3$$

37. $$\frac{6.72 \text{ dm}^3}{} \left| \frac{300 \text{ K}}{273 \text{ K}} \right| \frac{101.3 \text{ kPa}}{104.5 \text{ kPa}} = 7.16 \text{ dm}^3$$

38. $$\frac{44.0 \text{ g}}{22.4 \text{ dm}^3} \left| \frac{273 \text{ K}}{300 \text{ K}} \right| \frac{104.5 \text{ kPa}}{101.3 \text{ kPa}} = 1.84 \text{ g/dm}^3$$

39. $w = -2.303 nRT \log \dfrac{V_2}{V_1}$

$= -(2.303)(0.638)(8.31)(304) \log \dfrac{23.3}{10.1}$

$= -1350 \text{ J}$

40. $w = C_v \Delta T$

$= (20.8)(91.1) = 1.90 \times 10^3 \text{ J/mol}$

Review

Page 395.

1. $$\frac{642 \text{ cm}^3}{} \left| \frac{93.9 \text{ kPa}}{109.0 \text{ kPa}} \right. = 553 \text{ cm}^3$$

2. $114.9 - 12.3 = 102.6 \text{ kPa}$

$$\frac{62.5 \text{ cm}^3}{} \left| \frac{102.5 \text{ kPa}}{97.8 \text{ kPa}} \right. = 65.6 \text{ cm}^3$$

3. $$\frac{286 \text{ cm}^3}{} \left| \frac{333 \text{ K}}{315 \text{ K}} \right| \frac{98.1 \text{ kPa}}{42.2 \text{ kPa}} = 703 \text{ cm}^3$$

4. $\dfrac{v_{O_2}}{v_{Ar}} = \sqrt{\dfrac{m_{Ar}}{m_{O_2}}} = \sqrt{\dfrac{39.9}{32.0}} = 1.12 \text{ O}_2/\text{Ar}$

5. $$\frac{1.34 \text{ g}}{343 \text{ cm}^3} \left| \frac{1000 \text{ cm}^3}{1 \text{ dm}^3} \right| \frac{297 \text{ K}}{273 \text{ K}} \left| \frac{101.3 \text{ kPa}}{99.0 \text{ kPa}} \right.$$

$= 4.35 \text{ g/dm}^3$

6. The particles of an ideal gas occupy zero volume and have no attractive forces.

7. $\dfrac{v_{H_2}}{v_{He}} = \sqrt{\dfrac{m_{He}}{m_{H_2}}} = \sqrt{\dfrac{4.00}{2.02}} = \sqrt{1.98} = 1.41 \text{ H}_2/\text{He}$

8. $\dfrac{v_{Ne}}{v_{N_2}} = \sqrt{\dfrac{m_{N_2}}{m_{Ne}}} = \sqrt{\dfrac{28.0}{20.2}} = \sqrt{1.39} = 1.18 \text{ Ne}/\text{N}_2$

9. $$\frac{60.0 \text{ dm}^3}{} \left| \frac{585 \text{ K}}{280 \text{ K}} \right. = 125 \text{ dm}^3$$

One More Step

Page 395.

1. In 1858 Cannizzaro wrote a paper in an Italian scientific journal in which he explained how Avogadro's hypothesis could be used in teaching chemistry. At the Karlsruhe Congress in 1860, Cannizzaro argued persuasively for the adoption of Avogadro's hypothesis and won over a number of prominent chemists. Distribution of reprints of the earlier paper helped when some of the delegates had a chance to read it at length after the congress.

2. In a time-of-flight spectrometer, a burst or pulse of ionized particles is fired through a series of electrodes or grids. Ions of different masses require varying times to transit the path; by proper interpretation of the electrode currents, the sample may be analyzed for e/m values.

3. The amount of materials to be used in the iron foundry could be calculated. Analysis could be used to determine whether the iron had the correct amount of carbon, manganese, and other additives. Knowledge of reactions to produce a given amount of a product could be used. Mostly these would involve mass-mass rather than mass-volume problems, however. Students may wish to check into the chemistry of iron more closely.

4. too low

5. none

ENERGY AND DISORDER

20

An Overview

Chapter 20 brings together various concepts of energy and disorder which have been introduced at appropriate points earlier in the text. The purpose of Chapter 20 is to introduce students to thermodynamics through a study of state functions. Students have just completed a study of solids, liquids, and gases. Point out that mass-mass and mass-volume calculations allow laboratory results to be mathematically predicted. However, enthalpy and entropy factors must be considered in order to completely describe a system. The problem solving part of the chapter gives students the mathematical relationships among ΔH, ΔS, and ΔG and allows them to interpret the results in a practical way. The chapter ends with the presentation and calculation of the work performed by a chemical system.

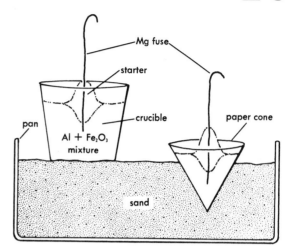

Demonstration Information

Commercially prepared thermite mixture and starter are available, however you can prepare your own. Fill a large pan with sand to protect the demonstration table. Place a small iron or clay crucible on top of the sand. You can also use a paper cone made from filter paper and place it in the sand. Place the thermite mixture in the crucible or cone (60 g of powdered Fe_3O_4 to 15 g Al powder, well mixed). Make a slight depression in the center of the thermite mixture and fill with the thermite starter. (10 parts barium peroxide and 1 part Al powder) Insert a Mg ribbon fuse into the starter. Mound up additional starter around the fuse. Finely powdered $KMnO_4$ sprinkled over glycerin can also be used as an ignition method. If you do not have a safety shield do the demonstration outside. The filter paper-in-the-sand method helps to prevent splattering.

Safety glasses are a must. Darken the room. Bend the end of the fuse over and light it with a burner. **CAUTION:** Move away quickly since the heat generated will produce molten iron. If the paper cone is used, cool the metal in water using tongs, then break off the crude ceramic that coats the iron metal. Use the demonstration to introduce terms such as enthalpy, entropy, and free energy.

Performance Objectives

Goal: Students will gain an understanding of enthalpy, entropy, and free energy and their relationship to chemical reactions.

Objectives: Upon completion of the reading and problems, and when asked to demonstrate their understanding either orally or on a written test, students will

20:1-2	K	define enthalpy and entropy and explain their relationship to exothermic and endothermic reactions.
20:3	K	define free energy in terms of enthalpy and entropy.
20:4	K	state standard states for measuring entropy, enthalpy, and free energy.
20:5	P/S	solve problems dealing with entropy, enthalpy, and free energy changes in chemical reactions.
20:6	K	define internal energy and give examples of different paths from one state to another with the same ΔE.
20:7	K	explain how enthalpy is related to internal energy.
	A	voluntarily complete one or more of the One More Step activities.
	A	read unassigned literature related to the chapter.

Teaching Techniques

Section 20:1

Remind students that the sign convention of ΔH is arbitrary. However, it is well established and accepted worldwide; $\Delta H = (heat\ content\ of\ products) - (heat\ content\ of\ reactants)$. You may think that thermodynamics is too sophisticated for high school students. However, it is presented in a logical manner at a low level of intensity. Most students are successful with Chapter 20 including the problem solving. We do not recommend a more detailed presentation for an introductory high school course. We will use these concepts in later chapters for reinforcement (Sections 23:11, 27:13).

Section 20:2

See the Teacher's Guide Section 17:3 for an introductory discussion topic.

Section 20:3

The first two sections of the chapter have prepared students to understand free energy.

$$\left(\begin{array}{c}reaction \\ trend\end{array}\right) = \left(\begin{array}{c}trend\ toward \\ min.\ energy\end{array}\right) = \left(\begin{array}{c}trend\ toward \\ max.\ energy\end{array}\right)$$
$$\Delta G \quad = \quad \Delta H \quad = \quad T\Delta S$$

Point out that the ability to predict the occurrence of a chemical reaction makes free energy an important concept and tool. Both the concentration and the nature of the reactants control the tendency for a reaction to occur.

You can evaluate students' comprehension of free energy by asking about a "dead" battery. The amount of useful work, free energy, is equal to zero. Thus, the system must be at equilibrium.

Section 20:4

Emphasize the difference in the standard temperature for gases, $0°C$, and for thermodynamic properties, $25°C$.

Section 20:5

Recommend to students that they use the table method to organize the data they obtain from Appendix A-6. Have them especially note the units (kJ versus J). Also remind them to multiply by the number of moles from the balanced chemical equation.

Chemical Technology

Emphasize the importance of liquid air as a raw material for the production of other gases (Group VIIIA elements) as well as oxygen and nitrogen.

Problem Solutions

Page 404.

1. $\Delta G° = \Delta G°_{f(products)} - \Delta G°_{f(reactants)}$

$= \left[\dfrac{1\ mol\ BaSO_4}{}\ \middle|\ \dfrac{(-1350)\ kJ}{1\ mol\ BaSO_4} + \dfrac{2\ mol\ HCl(aq)}{}\ \middle|\ \dfrac{(-131)\ kJ}{1\ mol\ HCl(aq)}\right]$

$- \left[\dfrac{1\ mol\ BaCl_2(aq)}{}\ \middle|\ \dfrac{(-823)\ kJ}{1\ mol\ BaCl_2(aq)} + \dfrac{1\ mol\ H_2SO_4(aq)}{}\ \middle|\ \dfrac{(-742)\ kJ}{1\ mol\ H_2SO_4(aq)}\right]$

$= -47\ kJ$ Yes, the reaction is spontaneous.

2. $\Delta G° = \Delta G°_{f(products)} - \Delta G°_{f(reactants)}$

$= \left[\dfrac{1\ mol\ H_2}{}\ \middle|\ \dfrac{0\ kJ}{1\ mol\ H_2} + \dfrac{1\ mol\ F_2}{}\ \middle|\ \dfrac{0\ kJ}{1\ mol\ F_2}\right] - \left[\dfrac{2\ mol\ HF}{}\ \middle|\ \dfrac{(-271)\ kJ}{1\ mol\ HF}\right]$

$= -542\ kJ$

3. $\Delta H° = \Delta H°_{f(products)} - \Delta H°_{f(reactants)}$

$= \left[\dfrac{1\ mol\ Ca(OH)_2}{}\ \middle|\ \dfrac{(-987)\ kJ}{1\ mol\ Ca(OH)_2} + \dfrac{1\ mol\ H_2}{}\ \middle|\ \dfrac{0\ kJ}{1\ mol\ H_2}\right] - \left[\dfrac{1\ mol\ Ca}{}\ \middle|\ \dfrac{0\ kJ}{1\ mol\ Ca} + \dfrac{2\ mol\ H_2O}{}\ \middle|\ \dfrac{(-286)\ kJ}{1\ mol\ H_2O}\right]$

$= -415\ kJ$

$\Delta G° = \Delta G°_{f(products)} - \Delta G°_{f(reactants)}$

$= \left[\dfrac{1\ mol\ Ca(OH)_2}{}\ \middle|\ \dfrac{(-897)\ kJ}{1\ mol\ Ca(OH)_2} + \dfrac{1\ mol\ H_2}{}\ \middle|\ \dfrac{0\ kJ}{1\ mol\ H_2}\right] - \left[\dfrac{1\ mol\ Ca}{}\ \middle|\ \dfrac{0\ kJ}{1\ mol\ Ca} + \dfrac{2\ mol\ H_2O}{}\ \middle|\ \dfrac{(-237)\ kJ}{1\ mol\ H_2O}\right]$

$= -423\ kJ$

$\Delta G° = \Delta H° - T\Delta S°$

$\Delta S° = \dfrac{\Delta H° - \Delta G°}{T}$

$\Delta S° = \dfrac{-415 - (-423)}{298}$

$= 26.8\ kJ/K = 26\ 800\ J/K$

4. $\Delta H° = \Delta H°_{f(products)} - \Delta H°_{f(reactants)}$

$$= \left[\frac{2 \text{ mol H}}{} \middle| \frac{218 \text{ kJ}}{1 \text{ mol H}} \right] - \left[\frac{1 \text{ mol H}_2}{} \middle| \frac{0 \text{ kJ}}{1 \text{ mol H}_2} \right]$$

$= 436 \text{ kJ}$

$$\Delta S° = \left[\frac{2 \text{ mol H}}{} \middle| \frac{115 \text{ J/K}}{1 \text{ mol H}} \right] - \left[\frac{1 \text{ mol H}_2}{} \middle| \frac{131 \text{ J/K}}{1 \text{ mol H}_2} \right]$$

$= 99 \text{ J/K}$

$\Delta G° = \Delta H° - T\Delta S°$

$$= 436 \text{ kJ} - \frac{298 \text{ K}}{} \middle| \frac{99 \text{ J}}{\text{K}} \middle| \frac{1 \text{ kJ}}{1000 \text{ J}}$$

$= 407 \text{ kJ}$

$\Delta S° = \Delta S°_{(products)} - \Delta S°_{(reactants)}$

$\Delta G° = \Delta G°_{f(products)} - \Delta G°_{f(reactants)}$

$$407 = \left[\frac{2 \text{ mol H}}{} \middle| \frac{x \text{ kJ}}{1 \text{ mol H}} \right] - \left[\frac{1 \text{ mol H}_2}{} \middle| \frac{0 \text{ kJ}}{1 \text{ mol H}_2} \right]$$

$x = 204 \text{ kJ}$

Page 406.

5. $\Delta E = q - w = 419 - 389 = 30 \text{ kJ}$

6. $\Delta E = q - w = -196 - (-420) = 224 \text{ kJ}$

Page 407.

7. $\Delta H = \Delta E + \Delta(PV) = 418 + (-616) = -198 \text{ kJ}$

8. $\Delta H = \Delta E + \Delta(PV) = -845 \text{ kJ} = -489 \text{ kJ} + \Delta(PV)$
$\Delta(PV) = -356 \text{ kJ}$

Chapter End Problems

Page 409.

9. $\Delta G = \Delta G°_{f(products)} - \Delta G°_{f(reactants)}$,
if ΔG is negative the reaction is spontaneous.
  a. $\Delta G = [(1)(-314)] - [(1)(-260)]$
  $= -54 \text{ kJ}$, spontaneous
  b. $\Delta G = [(1)(-229)] - [(1)(-237)]$
  $= 8 \text{ kJ}$, nonspontaneous
  c. $\Delta G = [(8)(-394) + (10)(-237)]$
  $- [(2)(-15.7)] = -5490 \text{ kJ}$, spontaneous
  d. $\Delta G = [(2)(-53.7)] - [(1)(-86.2)]$
  $= -21.2 \text{ kJ}$, spontaneous
  e. $\Delta G = [(1)(-662)] - [(1)(-53.7)]$
  $= -608 \text{ kJ}$, spontaneous

10. $\Delta G = \Delta H - T\Delta S$, $\Delta G = \Delta G°_{f(products)}$
  $- \Delta G°_{f(reactants)}$
  $\Delta H = \Delta H°_{f(products)} - \Delta H°_{f(reactants)}$
  $\Delta S = S°_{(products)} - S°_{(reactants)}$
  a. $\Delta G = [(2)(-177)] - [(1)(-211)] = -143 \text{ kJ}$
  $\Delta H = [(2)(-230)] - [(1)(-265)] = -195 \text{ kJ}$
  $\Delta S = \frac{-195 - (-143)}{298} = -0.174 \text{ kJ} = 174 \text{ J}$
  $\Delta S = -174 = [(2)(x)] - [(1)(196) + (1)(223)]$
  $x = 245 \text{ J/mol·K}$
  b. $\Delta G = -512 \text{ kJ}$
  $\Delta H = -568 \text{ kJ}$
  $\Delta S = \frac{-568 - (-512)}{298} = -0.188 \text{ kJ} = -188 \text{ J}$
  $-188 = [x] - [(3)(9.54) + (1)(192)]$
  $x = 32.6 \text{ J/mol·K}$
  c. $\Delta G = [(1)(-213) + (1)(-394)]$
  $- [(1)(-650)] = 43 \text{ kJ}$

$\Delta H = [(1)(-239) + (1)(-394)$
$- [(1)(-723)] = 90 \text{ kJ}$

$\Delta S = \frac{90 - 43}{298} = 0.158 \text{ kJ} = 158 \text{ J}$

$158 = [(1)(43.9) + (1)(214)] - [x]$
$x = 99.9 \text{ J/mol·K}$
  d. $\Delta G = [(2)(-237)] - [(2)(-118)] = -238 \text{ kJ}$
  $\Delta S = [(2)(70.0) + (1)(205)] - [(2)(110)] =$
  $125 \text{ J} = 0.125 \text{ kJ}$
  $\Delta H = -238 + (298)(0.125) = -201 \text{ kJ}$
  $-201 = [(2)(-286)] - [2x]$
  $x = -186 \text{ kJ/mol}$

11. $\Delta E = 622 - 813 = -191 \text{ kJ}$

12. $\Delta E = -262 - (-160) = -102 \text{ kJ}$

13. $\Delta H = \Delta E + \Delta(PV) = 632 + 681 = 1313 \text{ kJ}$

14. $-926 = \Delta E + 816$
$\Delta E = -1742 \text{ kJ}$

Review

Pages 410-411.

1. $\dfrac{163 \text{ cm}^3}{} \middle| \dfrac{52.4 \text{ kPa}}{68.7 \text{ kPa}} = 124 \text{ cm}^3$

2. $\dfrac{258 \text{ cm}^3}{} \middle| \dfrac{350 \text{ K}}{370 \text{ K}} = 244 \text{ cm}^3$

3. $\dfrac{94.5 \text{ dm}^3}{} \middle| \dfrac{316 \text{ K}}{319 \text{ K}} = 93.6 \text{ dm}^3$

4. CO_2

5. Real gas molecules occupy a finite volume and exert an attractive force on each other.

6. Equal volumes of gases at the same temperature and pressure contain the same number of molecules.

7. $V = \dfrac{nRT}{P}$ $\dfrac{0.161 \text{ mol}}{43.3 \text{ kPa}} \middle| \dfrac{8.31 \text{ dm}^3 \cdot \text{kPa}}{\text{mol·K}} \middle| \dfrac{325 \text{ K}}{}$

$= 10.0 \text{ dm}^3$

8. $\dfrac{4.90 \text{ dm}^3 \text{ Cl}_2}{22.4 \text{ dm}^3} \middle| \dfrac{1 \text{ mol}}{3 \text{ mol Cl}_2} \middle| \dfrac{2 \text{ mol Al}}{} \middle| \dfrac{27.0 \text{ g Al}}{1 \text{ mol Al}}$

$= 3.94 \text{ g Al}$

9. $\dfrac{49.5 \text{ g HCl}}{} \middle| \dfrac{1 \text{ mol HCl}}{36.5 \text{ g HCl}} = 1.36 \text{ mol HCl}$

$\dfrac{91.8 \text{ g NaOH}}{} \middle| \dfrac{1 \text{ mol NaOH}}{40.0 \text{ g NaOH}} = 2.30 \text{ mol NaOH}$

$\dfrac{1.36 \text{ mol HCl}}{} \middle| \dfrac{1 \text{ mol NaCl}}{1 \text{ mol HCl}} \middle| \dfrac{58.5 \text{ g NaCl}}{1 \text{ mol NaCl}}$

$= 79.6 \text{ g NaCl}$

10. $\dfrac{134 \text{ g Al(OH)}_3}{} \middle| \dfrac{1 \text{ mol Al(OH)}_3}{78.0 \text{ g Al(OH)}_3} = 1.72 \text{ mol Al(OH)}_3$

$\dfrac{635 \text{ g NaOH}}{} \middle| \dfrac{1 \text{ mol NaOH}}{40.0 \text{ g NaOH}} = 15.9 \text{ mol NaOH}$

$\dfrac{1.72 \text{ mol Al(OH)}_3}{} \middle| \dfrac{1 \text{ mol Na}_3\text{AlO}_3}{1 \text{ mol Al(OH)}_3} \middle| \dfrac{144 \text{ g Na}_3\text{AlO}_3}{1 \text{ mol Na}_3\text{AlO}_3}$

$= 248 \text{ g Na}_3\text{AlO}_3$

11. a. 54.4 K   **d.** 54.8 K
  b. 0.152 kPa   **e.** 155 K, 5040 kPa
  c. 90.2 K

12. $$\frac{8.16\,g \mid 16°C \mid 2.06\,J}{g\cdot °C} = 270\,J$$

$$\frac{8.16\,g \mid 334\,J}{g} = 2730\,J$$

$$\frac{8.16\,g \mid 100\,°C \mid 4.18\,J}{g\cdot °C} = 3410\,J$$

$$\frac{8.16\,g \mid 2260\,J}{g} = 18\,400\,J$$

$$\frac{8.16\,g \mid 2\,°C \mid 2.02\,J}{g\cdot °C} = 30\,J$$

Sum of all 5 steps = 24 800 J

13. $$\frac{37.0\,dm^3 \mid 78\,kPa}{103\,kPa} = 28.0\,dm^3$$

14. $$\frac{629\,cm^3 \mid 273\,K \mid 101.0\,kPa}{297\,K \mid 101.3\,kPa} = 576\,cm^3$$

15. $$\frac{8.02\,g \mid 101.3\,kPa \mid 281\,K}{1.20\,dm^3 \mid 103.1\,kPa \mid 273\,K} = 6.76\,g/dm^3$$

16. $$M = \frac{mRT}{PV} = \frac{2.20\,g \mid 8.31\,dm^3\cdot kPa \mid 293\,K}{107.1\,kPa \mid mol\cdot K \mid 2.13\,dm^3} = 23.5\,g/mol$$

17. $$\frac{21.0\,g\,Zn \mid 1\,mol\,Zn \mid 1\,mol\,H_2 \mid 22.4\,dm^3}{65.4\,g\,Zn \mid 1\,mol\,Zn \mid 1\,mol\,H_2} = 7.19\,dm^3$$

18. $$\frac{93.0\,dm^3\,Cl_2 \mid 2\,dm^3\,HCl}{1\,dm^3\,Cl_2} = 186\,dm^3\,HCl$$

19. $$\frac{10.1\,g\,Mn \mid 1\,mol\,Mn \mid 1\,mol\,H_2 \mid 22.4\,dm^3 \mid 279\,K \mid 101.3\,kPa}{54.9\,g\,Mn \mid 1\,mol\,Mn \mid 1\,mol\,H_2 \mid 273\,K \mid 123.0\,kPa} = 3.47\,dm^3$$

One More Step

Page 411.

1. Heat capacity is the heat required to raise the temperature of a certain amount of a substance a specified number of degrees, usually one.

    Heat content is used in two ways by chemists: (a) The total thermal (kinetic) energy of molecules determined by their mass and velocity. (b) The enthalpy, which is the heat lost (or gained) during an isothermal reaction.

2. Work function is usually known as the Helmholtz free energy. It is represented by the letter A and is defined by the equation $A = E - TS$. It is of use principally in constant-volume systems and is not as useful as G for chemists who are usually working at constant pressure. ΔA represents the maximum work obtainable from a constant-volume, isothermal process. If $\Delta A > 0$, then work must be done on the system. In a similar manner, ΔG is the maximum work at constant pressure and temperature.

3. constant volume

4. reversible

SOLUTIONS

21

An Overview

A study of nonreacting homogeneous mixtures is presented in Chapter 21. The mixtures of homogeneous aggregates are classified into nine groups of solutions. The properties of each group are discussed. We examine only one solvent in detail, water. Emphasize that many solvents are used in everyday practice. Solution equilibria and solution rate are studied in preparation for Chapter 23. Heat of solution is presented as an application of the thermodynamic topics in Chapter 20. Molarity is reviewed from Chapter 5. The concentration units of molarity and mole fraction are introduced and applied.

Performance Objectives

Goal: Students will gain an understanding of solutions, their formation, and their strengths expressed in various units.

Objectives: Upon completion of the reading and problems, and when asked to demonstrate their understanding either orally or on a written test, students will

21:1	K	explain the solvation process.
21:2	K	describe the characteristics of the four solvent-solute combinations.
21:3	K	list and give examples of the nine physical state solution combinations.
21:4	K/P	use the concept of solution equilibrium to explain degree of saturation.
21:5-7	K	describe factors which affect solution rate.
21:8-11	K/P/S	solve problems involving molar concentration, molal concentration, and mole fraction of solutions.
	A	voluntarily complete one or more of the One More Step activities.
	A	read unassigned literature related to the chapter.

Teaching Techniques

Section 21:4

Demonstration—A supersaturated solution can be prepared by adding sodium thiosulfate to hot H_2O and letting it cool slowly. Prepare several large test tubes before class. Scratching the test tube or adding a small seed crystal causes crystallization to occur.

Section 21:5

Obtain a sugar cube, mass it, and place it in a small beaker of water on the overhead projector. Mass the same amount of granulated and powdered sugar. Add these to the same volume of water and also place on overhead. Observe which dissolves first without stirring. Repeat the above set-ups but stir them equally the second time.

To demonstrate the temperature (kinetic energy) effect, place one sugar cube in a beaker of cold water and one in a beaker of hot water and observe on the overhead projector.

Section 21:7

To help students visualize Henry's Law, draw some circles on the chalkboard to represent solvent molecules. In the space between the molecules, draw small three dimensional boxes (cubes) to represent volumes of a gas. Ask students about the expansion or contraction ability of a liquid. (It is much less than 3% in most solvents.) If the pressure is halved, the volume doubles. Students will see quickly that the volumes of gas will no longer fit in the space between the solvent molecules. Thus, some of the gas leaves the solution according to the law.

Chemical Technology

Use this feature as a practical example of solution chemistry. Students could report on current processes being researched concerning desalination of ocean water.

Problem Solutions

Page 421.

1.a. $$\frac{316 \text{ g MgBr}_2}{859 \text{ cm}^3 \text{ soln}} \cdot \frac{1 \text{ mol MgBr}_2}{184 \text{ g MgBr}_2} \cdot \frac{1000 \text{ cm}^3}{1 \text{ dm}^3} \cdot \frac{2 \text{ mol Br}^-}{1 \text{ mol MgBr}_2} = 4.00M \text{ Br}$$

b. $$\frac{8.28 \text{ g Ca}(C_5H_9O_2)_2}{414 \text{ cm}^3 \text{ soln}} \cdot \frac{1 \text{ mol Ca}(C_5H_9O_2)_2}{242 \text{ g Ca}(C_5H_9O_2)_2} \cdot \frac{1000 \text{ cm}^3}{1 \text{ dm}^3} \cdot \frac{1 \text{ mol Ca}^{2+}}{1 \text{ mol Ca}(C_5H_9O_2)_2}$$
$$= 0.0826M \text{ Ca}^{2+}$$

Page 421.

2.a. $$\frac{199 \text{ g NiBr}_2}{500 \text{ g H}_2O} \cdot \frac{1 \text{ mol NiBr}_2}{219 \text{ g NiBr}_2} \cdot \frac{1000 \text{ g H}_2O}{1 \text{ kg H}_2O} = 1.82m \text{ NiBr}_2 \text{ (mol/kg} = m\text{)}$$

b. $$\frac{92.3 \text{ g KF}}{1000 \text{ g H}_2O} \cdot \frac{1 \text{ mol KF}}{58.1 \text{ g KF}} \cdot \frac{1000 \text{ g H}_2O}{1 \text{ kg H}_2O} = 1.59m \text{ KF}$$

Page 422.

3.a. $\dfrac{12.3 \text{ g } C_4H_4O}{} \bigg| \dfrac{1 \text{ mol } C_4H_4O}{68.1 \text{ g } C_4H_4O} = 0.181 \text{ mol } C_4H_4O$

$\dfrac{100 \text{ g } C_2H_6O}{} \bigg| \dfrac{1 \text{ mol } C_2H_6O}{46.1 \text{ g } C_2H_6O} = \dfrac{2.17 \quad \text{mol } C_2H_6O}{2.35 \quad \text{mol soln}}$

$\dfrac{0.181}{2.35} = 0.0770 \text{ mole fraction } C_4H_4O$

$\dfrac{2.17}{2.35} = 0.923 \text{ mole fraction } C_2H_6O$

b. $\dfrac{56.3 \text{ g } C_{12}H_{22}O_{11}}{} \bigg| \dfrac{1 \text{ mol } C_{12}H_{22}O_{11}}{342 \text{ g } C_{12}H_{22}O_{11}} = 0.165 \text{ mol } C_{12}H_{22}O_{11}$

$\dfrac{200 \text{ g } H_2O}{} \bigg| \dfrac{1 \text{ mol } H_2O}{18.0 \text{ g } H_2O} = \dfrac{16.7 \quad \text{mol } H_2O}{16.9 \quad \text{mol soln}}$

$\dfrac{0.165}{16.9} = 0.00976 \text{ mole fraction } C_{12}H_{22}O_{11}$

$\dfrac{16.7}{16.9} = 0.988 \text{ mole fraction } H_2O$

Chapter End Problems

Pages 424-425.

4. a. not soluble   d. not soluble
   b. not soluble   e. not soluble
   c. soluble   f. soluble
   Students may predict solubility in some cases because of the difference in electronegativities. Such answers are satisfactory.

5. a. slightly soluble   d. not soluble
   b. soluble   e. soluble
   c. soluble

6. a. $\dfrac{31.1 \text{ g } Al_2(SO_4)_3}{756 \text{ cm}^3 \text{ soln}} \bigg| \dfrac{1 \text{ mol } Al_2(SO_4)_3}{342 \text{ g } Al_2(SO_4)_3} \bigg| \dfrac{1000 \text{ cm}^3 \text{ soln}}{1 \text{ dm}^3} = 0.120M \text{ Al}_2(SO_4)_3$

   b. $\dfrac{59.5 \text{ g } CaCl_2}{100 \text{ cm}^3 \text{ soln}} \bigg| \dfrac{1 \text{ mol } CaCl_2}{111 \text{ g } CaCl_2} \bigg| \dfrac{1000 \text{ cm}^3 \text{ soln}}{1 \text{ dm}^3} = 5.36M \text{ CaCl}_2$

   c. $\dfrac{313.5 \text{ g } LiClO_3}{250 \text{ cm}^3 \text{ soln}} \bigg| \dfrac{1 \text{ mol } LiClO_3}{90.4 \text{ g } LiClO_3} \bigg| \dfrac{1000 \text{ cm}^3 \text{ soln}}{1 \text{ dm}^3} = 13.9M \text{ LiClO}_3$

7. a. $\dfrac{98.0 \text{ g } RbBr}{824 \text{ g } H_2O} \bigg| \dfrac{1 \text{ mol } RbBr}{165 \text{ g } RbBr} \bigg| \dfrac{1000 \text{ g } H_2O}{1 \text{ kg } H_2O} = 0.721m \text{ RbBr}$

   b. $\dfrac{85.2 \text{ g } SnBr_2}{140 \text{ g } H_2O} \bigg| \dfrac{1 \text{ mol } SnBr_2}{278 \text{ g } SnBr_2} \bigg| \dfrac{1000 \text{ g } H_2O}{1 \text{ kg } H_2O} = 2.19m \text{ SnBr}_2$

   c. $\dfrac{10.0 \text{ g } AgClO_3}{201 \text{ g } H_2O} \bigg| \dfrac{1 \text{ mol } AgClO_3}{191 \text{ g } AgClO_3} \bigg| \dfrac{1000 \text{ g } H_2O}{1 \text{ kg } H_2O} = 0.26m \text{ AgClO}_3$

8. a. $\dfrac{54.3 \text{ g } C_{10}H_8}{} \bigg| \dfrac{1 \text{ mol } C_{10}H_8}{128 \text{ g } C_{10}H_8} = 0.424 \text{ mol } C_{10}H_8$

   $\dfrac{600 \text{ g } C_4H_{10}O}{} \bigg| \dfrac{1 \text{ mol } C_4H_{10}O}{74.1 \text{ g } C_4H_{10}O} = \dfrac{8.10 \quad \text{mol } C_4H_{10}O}{8.52 \quad \text{mol soln}}$

   $\dfrac{0.424}{8.52} = 0.0498 \text{ mole fraction } C_{10}H_8$

   $\dfrac{8.10}{8.52} = 0.951 \text{ mole fraction } C_4H_{10}O$

b. $\dfrac{67.4\text{ g C}_9\text{H}_7\text{N}}{}\;\bigg|\;\dfrac{1\text{ mol C}_9\text{H}_7\text{N}}{129\text{ g C}_9\text{H}_7\text{N}} = 0.522\text{ mol C}_9\text{H}_7\text{N}$

$\dfrac{200\text{ g C}_2\text{H}_6\text{O}}{}\;\bigg|\;\dfrac{1\text{ mol C}_2\text{H}_6\text{O}}{46.1\text{ g C}_2\text{H}_6\text{O}} = \dfrac{4.34}{4.86}\;\dfrac{\text{mol C}_2\text{H}_6\text{O}}{\text{mol soln}}$

$\dfrac{0.522}{4.86} = 0.107$ mole fraction C_9H_7N

$\dfrac{4.34}{4.86} = 0.893$ mole fraction C_2H_6O

c. $\dfrac{5.48\text{ g C}_5\text{H}_{10}\text{O}_5}{}\;\bigg|\;\dfrac{1\text{ mol C}_5\text{H}_{10}\text{O}_5}{150\text{ g C}_5\text{H}_{10}\text{O}_5} = 0.0365\text{ mol C}_5\text{H}_{10}\text{O}_5$

$\dfrac{3.15\text{ g CH}_6\text{ON}_4}{}\;\bigg|\;\dfrac{1\text{ mol CH}_6\text{ON}_4}{90.1\text{ g CH}_6\text{ON}_4} = 0.0350\text{ mol CH}_6\text{ON}_4$

$\dfrac{21.2\text{ g H}_2\text{O}}{}\;\bigg|\;\dfrac{1\text{ mol H}_2\text{O}}{18.0\text{ g H}_2\text{O}} = \dfrac{1.18}{1.25}\;\dfrac{\text{mol H}_2\text{O}}{\text{mol soln}}$

$\dfrac{0.0365}{1.25} = 0.0292$ mole fraction $C_5H_{10}O_5$

$\dfrac{0.0350}{1.25} = 0.0280$ mole fraction CH_6ON_4

$\dfrac{1.18}{1.25} = 0.944$ mole fraction H_2O

9. a. $\dfrac{1000\text{ cm}^3\text{ soln}}{}\;\bigg|\;\dfrac{0.780\text{ mol Sc(NO}_3)_3}{1000\text{ cm}^3\text{ soln}}\;\bigg|\;\dfrac{231\text{ g Sc(NO}_3)_3}{1\text{ mol Sc(NO}_3)_3}$
$= 180\text{ g Sc(NO}_3)_3$

b. $\dfrac{200\text{ cm}^3\text{ soln}}{}\;\bigg|\;\dfrac{0.301\text{ mol Er}_2(\text{SO}_4)_3}{1000\text{ cm}^3\text{ soln}}\;\bigg|\;\dfrac{623\text{ g Er}_2(\text{SO}_4)_3}{1\text{ mol Er}_2(\text{SO}_4)_3}$
$= 37.5\text{ g Er}_2(\text{SO}_4)_3$

c. $\dfrac{100\text{ cm}^3\text{ soln}}{}\;\bigg|\;\dfrac{0.626\text{ mol VBr}_3}{1000\text{ cm}^3\text{ soln}}\;\bigg|\;\dfrac{291\text{ g VBr}_3}{1\text{ mol VBr}_3} = 18.2\text{ g VBr}_3$

d. $\dfrac{250\text{ cm}^3\text{ soln}}{}\;\bigg|\;\dfrac{0.0965\text{ mol DyCl}_3}{1000\text{ cm}^3\text{ soln}}\;\bigg|\;\dfrac{269\text{ g DyCl}_3}{1\text{ mol DyCl}_3} = 6.49\text{ g DyCl}_3$

e. $\dfrac{500\text{ cm}^3\text{ soln}}{}\;\bigg|\;\dfrac{0.0978\text{ mol IrCl}_4}{1000\text{ cm}^3\text{ soln}}\;\bigg|\;\dfrac{334\text{ g IrCl}_4}{1\text{ mol IrCl}_4}$
$= 16.3\text{ g IrCl}_4$

f. $\dfrac{1000\text{ cm}^3\text{ soln}}{}\;\bigg|\;\dfrac{0.0130\text{ mol YBr}_3}{1000\text{ cm}^3\text{ soln}}\;\bigg|\;\dfrac{329\text{ g YBr}_3}{1\text{ mol YBr}_3} = 4.28\text{ g YBr}_3$

g. $\dfrac{100\text{ cm}^3\text{ soln}}{}\;\bigg|\;\dfrac{0.528\text{ mol Li}_2\text{SO}_4}{1000\text{ cm}^3\text{ soln}}\;\bigg|\;\dfrac{110\text{ g Li}_2\text{SO}_4}{1\text{ mol Li}_2\text{SO}_4}$
$= 5.81\text{ g Li}_2\text{SO}_4$

h. $\dfrac{200\text{ cm}^3\text{ soln}}{}\;\bigg|\;\dfrac{0.0469\text{ mol KHC}_2\text{O}_4}{1000\text{ cm}^3\text{ soln}}\;\bigg|\;\dfrac{128\text{ g KHC}_2\text{O}_4}{1\text{ mol KHC}_2\text{O}_4}$
$= 1.20\text{ g KHC}_2\text{O}_4$

i. $\dfrac{250\text{ cm}^3\text{ soln}}{}\;\bigg|\;\dfrac{0.274\text{ mol UO}_2(\text{NO}_3)_2\cdot 6\text{H}_2\text{O}}{1000\text{ cm}^3\text{ soln}}\;\bigg|\;\dfrac{502\text{ g UO}_2(\text{NO}_3)_2\cdot 6\text{H}_2\text{O}}{1\text{ mol UO}_2(\text{NO}_3)_2\cdot 6\text{H}_2\text{O}}$
$= 34.4\text{ g UO}_2(\text{NO}_3)_2\cdot 6\text{H}_2\text{O}$

j. $\dfrac{500\text{ cm}^3\text{ soln}}{}\;\bigg|\;\dfrac{0.512\text{ mol HSO}_3\text{F}}{1000\text{ cm}^3\text{ soln}}\;\bigg|\;\dfrac{100\text{ g HSO}_3\text{F}}{1\text{ mol HSO}_3\text{F}} = 25.6\text{ g HSO}_3\text{F}$

10. a. $\dfrac{1000\text{ g H}_2\text{O}}{}\;\bigg|\;\dfrac{0.851\text{ mol Fe}_2(\text{C}_2\text{O}_4)_3}{1000\text{ g H}_2\text{O}}\;\bigg|\;\dfrac{376\text{ g Fe}_2(\text{C}_2\text{O}_4)_3}{1\text{ mol Fe}_2(\text{C}_2\text{O}_4)_3}$
$= 320\text{ g Fe}_2(\text{C}_2\text{O}_4)_3$

b. $\dfrac{1000\ \text{g H}_2\text{O}}{}\left|\dfrac{0.534\ \text{mol VOBr}_3}{1000\ \text{g H}_2\text{O}}\right|\dfrac{307\ \text{g VOBr}_3}{1\ \text{mol VOBr}_3} = 164\ \text{g VOBr}_3$

c. $\dfrac{200\ \text{g C}_2\text{H}_6\text{O}}{}\left|\dfrac{1\ \text{mol C}_2\text{H}_6\text{O}}{46.1\ \text{g C}_2\text{H}_6\text{O}}\right. = 4.34\ \text{moles C}_2\text{H}_6\text{O (solvent)}$

$\dfrac{4.34}{x + 4.34} = 0.510$

$x = 4.17\ \text{mol solute}$

$\dfrac{4.17\ \text{mol C}_7\text{H}_4\text{O}_2\text{Br}_2}{}\left|\dfrac{280\ \text{g C}_7\text{H}_4\text{O}_2\text{Br}_2}{1\ \text{mol C}_7\text{H}_4\text{O}_2\text{Br}_2}\right. = 1170\ \text{g C}_7\text{H}_4\text{O}_2\text{Br}_2$

d. $\dfrac{1000\ \text{g C}_4\text{H}_{10}\text{O}}{}\left|\dfrac{1\ \text{mol C}_4\text{H}_{10}\text{O}}{74.1\ \text{g C}_4\text{H}_{10}\text{O}}\right. = 13.5\ \text{mol C}_4\text{H}_{10}\text{O (solvent)}$

$\dfrac{x}{x + 13.5} = 0.363$

$x = 7.7\ \text{mol solute}$

$\dfrac{7.7\ \text{mol C}_{14}\text{H}_{16}\text{N}_2}{}\left|\dfrac{212\ \text{g C}_{14}\text{H}_{16}\text{N}_2}{1\ \text{mol C}_{14}\text{H}_{16}\text{N}_2}\right. = 1630\ \text{g C}_{14}\text{H}_{16}\text{N}_2$

e. $\dfrac{1000\ \text{g H}_2\text{O}}{}\left|\dfrac{0.614\ \text{mol LiMnO}_4}{1000\ \text{g H}_2\text{O}}\right|\dfrac{126\ \text{g LiMnO}_4}{1\ \text{mol LiMnO}_4} = 77.4\ \text{g LiMnO}_4$

11. Iodine and carbon tetrachloride are both nonpolar, while water is highly polar.

12. a. Cl^- will precipitate Ag^+ but not Na^+
    b. OH^- will precipitate Fe^{3+} but not Na^+
    c. $SO_4{}^{2-}$ will precipitate Ba^{2+} but not K^+
    d. S^{2-} will precipitate Cu^{2+} but not Kt^+

13. $\dfrac{3.5\ \text{g AgCl}}{}\left|\dfrac{170\ \text{g AgNO}_3\ \text{mixture}}{143.5\ \text{g AgCl}}\right. = 4.14\ \text{g AgNO}_3\ \text{in mixture}$

14. Most solids having positive heats of solution are more soluble in hot water than in cold. Gases with negative heats of solution are more soluble in cold water.

15. Molarity is the ratio of solute to solution by volume. Molality is the ratio of solute to solvent mass.
    molarity = mol/dm^3 soln
    molality = mol/kg solvent

Review

Page 425.

1. $\Delta H = \Delta H^\circ_{f(\text{products})} - \Delta H^\circ_{f(\text{reactants})}$
   $\Delta H = [(1)(-770) + (1)(-297) + (2)(-286)] - [(2)(-908)] = 177\ \text{kJ}$

2. $\Delta G = \Delta H - T\Delta S = -454\ 300 - 298(-3.76) = -453\ 000\ \text{J} = -453\ \text{kJ}$

3. The standard state for thermodynamic measurements is 101.325 kPa, $1M$ concentration, and 25°C. The standard state of a substance is its physical state under those conditions.

4. q = heat received from the surroundings
   w = work done on the surroundings

One More Step

Page 425.

1. See page 51, Figure 3-10, for solubility curves. Any of the compounds listed on the curve can be used. The student may use 50 g of water and the corresponding amount of solute. The temperature should be measured and then increased slowly as more solute is added. By plotting a solubility curve, the student should be able to determine the substance by comparison with Figure 3-10.

2. In a 400 cm^3 beaker, place about 80-90 cm^3 of distilled water. Heat to near boiling. Add about 200 g of $Na_2S_2O_3 \cdot 5H_2O$ (hypo) of reagent grade. Filter while hot into a very clean 250 cm^3 boiling flask. Allow the system to cool without disturbance.

3. The heat of solution increases with concentration. The curve is asymptotic to 54.3 kJ/mol for the anhydrous salt. The dodecahydrate is formed. If the $Na_3PO_4 \cdot 12H_2O$ is dissolved, the curve becomes asymptotic to -67.2 kJ/mol.

COLLIGATIVE AND COLLOIDAL PROPERTIES   22

An Overview

The chapter begins with a practical discussion of Raoult's law. The problem solving techniques presented enable students to calculate the freezing point depressions and boiling point elevations as well as determine experimentally the molecular mass of an unknown solute. Osmotic pressure as a colligative property is also introduced. An introduction to colloids concludes the chapter. This study focuses on the properties of colloids as a consequence of their structure.

Demonstration Information

Discuss the fact that the NaCl that was added is taking the place of solvent molecules at the surface of the water. This surface change results in a lowering of the vapor pressure. Point out that there are now additional attractive forces (ions and polar H_2O molecules) that lead to a reduction in the vapor pressure of the pure H_2O. Relate these changes to a phase diagram for water. Show on the diagram how the freezing point is lowered. Ask students what they think would happen to the boiling point. If you have time, you may want to boil both the H_2O and the saltwater and demonstrate the elevation.

Performance Objectives

Goal: Students will gain an understanding of the colligative and colloidal properties of solutions.

Objectives: Upon completion of the reading and problems, and when asked to demonstrate their understanding either orally or on a written test, students will

22:1-5	K/P/S	utilize Raoult's law to develop, explain, and solve problems related to
		a. fractional distillation
		b. boiling point elevation
		c. freezing point depression
		d. determination of molecular mass
22:6	K/P/S	relate osmosis to colligative properties and calculate osmotic pressure.
22:7	K	relate the concept of ion activity to deviations from ideal behavior.
22:8	K	describe the characteristics of colloids and their uses.
22:9	K/P	differentiate among the characteristics of solutions, suspensions, and colloids.
22:10	K	list the properties associated with colloids.
	A	voluntarily complete one or more of the One More Step activities.
	A	read unassigned literature related to the chapter.

Teaching Techniques

Section 22:5

In actual practice in organic chemistry, camphor is often used as the solvent in molecular mass determination because it has a freezing point constant of 39.7 C° (for water, this value is 1.86 C°). The temperature change is therefore easier to observe accurately.

Section 22:10

Demonstration—Into each of two tall cylinders, pour a solution of $NaHCO_3$. Add 2-3 g of licorice extract to one cylinder. Then add $Al_2(SO_4)_3$ solution to each and observe the stabilizing action of colloids as the CO_2 bubbles subside rapidly in one of the cylinders. This principle is used in fire extinguishers.

Chemical Technology

This feature provides some exposure to organic compounds as well as uses of nitrogen compounds.

Problem Solutions

Page 429.

1. v.p. H_2O @ $28°C = 3.78$ kPa
   v.p. soln $= (3.78$ kPa$)(1 - 0.181) = 3.10$ kPa

2. v.p. ethanal $= (86.3$ kPa$)(0.300) = 25.9$ kPa
   v.p. methanol $= (11.6$ kPa$)(0.700) = 8.12$ kPa
   v.p. soln $= 25.9 + 8.12 = 34.0$ kPa

Page 434.

3. $\Delta T_{FP} = mK_{FP}$, $\Delta T_{BP} = mK_{BP}$

   a. $\dfrac{47.7 \text{ g } C_7H_{11}NO_7S}{100 \text{ g } H_2O} \left| \dfrac{1 \text{ mol } C_7H_{11}NO_7S}{253 \text{ g } C_7H_{11}NO_7S} \right| \dfrac{1000 \text{ g}}{1 \text{ kg}} = 1.88m$

   $\Delta T_{FP} = (1.88)(1.86) = 3.50 \text{ C}°$
   $\Delta T_{BP} = (1.88)(0.512) = 0.964 \text{ C}°$
   $FP = 0 - 3.50 = -3.50°C$
   $BP = 100 + 0.964 = 100.964°C$

   b. $\dfrac{100 \text{ g } C_{10}H_8O_6S_2}{100.0 \text{ g } H_2O} \left| \dfrac{1 \text{ mol } C_{10}H_8O_6S_2}{288 \text{ g } C_{10}H_8O_6S_2} \right| \dfrac{1000 \text{ g}}{1 \text{ kg}} = 3.47m$

   $\Delta T_{FP} = (3.47)(1.86) = 6.45 \text{ C}°$
   $\Delta T_{BP} = (3.47)(0.512) = 1.78 \text{ C}°$
   $FP = 0 - 6.45 = -6.45°C$
   $BP = 100 + 1.78 = 101.78°C$

   c. $\dfrac{21.6 \text{ g } NiSO_4}{100 \text{ g } H_2O} \left| \dfrac{1 \text{ mol } NiSO_4}{155 \text{ g } NiSO_4} \right| \dfrac{2 \text{ mol ions}}{1 \text{ mol } NiSO_4} \left| \dfrac{1000 \text{ g}}{1 \text{ kg}} \right. = 2.79m$

   $\Delta T_{FP} = (2.79)(1.86) = 5.19 \text{ C}°$
   $\Delta T_{BP} = (2.79)(0.512) = 1.43 \text{ C}°$
   $FP = 0 - 5.19 = -5.19°C$
   $BP = 100 + 1.43 = 101.43°C$

   d. $\dfrac{100 \text{ g } Mg(ClO_4)_2}{200 \text{ g } H_2O} \left| \dfrac{1 \text{ mol } Mg(ClO_4)_2}{223 \text{ g } Mg(ClO_4)_2} \right| \dfrac{3 \text{ mol ions}}{1 \text{ mol } Mg(ClO_4)_2} \left| \dfrac{1000 \text{ g}}{1 \text{ kg}} \right. = 6.72m$

   $\Delta T_{FP} = (6.72)(1.86) = 12.5 \text{ C}°$
   $\Delta T_{BP} = (6.72)(0.512) = 3.44 \text{ C}°$
   $FP = 0 - 12.5 = -12.5°C$
   $BP = 100 + 3.44 = 103.44°C$

   e. $\dfrac{41.3 \text{ g } C_{15}H_9NO_4}{100 \text{ g } C_6H_5NO_2} \left| \dfrac{1 \text{ mol } C_{15}H_9NO_4}{267 \text{ g } C_{15}H_9NO_4} \right| \dfrac{1000 \text{ g}}{1 \text{ kg}} = 1.55m$

   $\Delta T_{FP} = (1.55)(8.1) = 12.5 \text{ C}°$
   $\Delta T_{BP} = (1.55)(5.24) = 8.10 \text{ C}°$
   $FP = 5.8 - 12.5 = -6.7°C$
   $BP = 211 + 8.10 = 219°C$

Page 435.

4. a. $\dfrac{0.430 \text{ C}°}{1.86 \text{ C}°} \left| \dfrac{1 \text{ mol solute}}{1 \text{ kg } H_2O} \right. = 0.231$ mol solute/kg H_2O

   $\dfrac{6.70 \text{ g solute}}{983 \text{ g } H_2O} \left| \dfrac{1000 \text{ g } H_2O}{1 \text{ kg } H_2O} \right. = 6.82$ g solute/kg H_2O,

   $\dfrac{6.82 \text{ g}}{0.231 \text{ mol}} = 29.5$ g/mol

   b. $\dfrac{0.680 \text{ C}°}{0.512 \text{ C}°} \left| \dfrac{1 \text{ mol solute}}{1 \text{ kg } H_2O} \right. = 1.33$ mol solute/kg H_2O

   $\dfrac{42.1 \text{ g solute}}{189 \text{ g } H_2O} \left| \dfrac{1000 \text{ g } H_2O}{1.33 \text{ mol solute}} \right. = 168$ g/mol

c. $\dfrac{3.1 \, \ell}{3.9 \, \ell} \quad \Bigg| \quad \dfrac{1 \text{ mol solute}}{1 \text{ kg } CH_3COOH} = 0.79 \text{ mol solute/kg } CH_3COOH$

$\dfrac{20.8 \text{ g}}{128 \text{ g } CH_3COOH} \quad \Bigg| \quad \dfrac{1000 \text{ g } CH_3COOH}{1 \text{ kg } CH_3COOH} = 163 \text{ g/kg } CH_3COOH$

$\dfrac{163 \text{ g}}{0.79 \text{ mol}} = 206 \text{ g/mol}$

d. $\dfrac{4.7 \, \ell}{7 \, \ell} \quad \Bigg| \quad \dfrac{1 \text{ mol solute}}{1 \text{ kg phenol}} = 0.67 \text{ mol solute/kg phenol}$

$\dfrac{10.4 \text{ g solute}}{164 \text{ g phenol}} \quad \Bigg| \quad \dfrac{1000 \text{ g phenol}}{1 \text{ kg phenol}} = 63.4 \text{ g solute/kg phenol}$

$\dfrac{63.4 \text{ g}}{0.67 \text{ mol}} = 94.6 \text{ g/mol}$

e. $\dfrac{2.4 \, \ell}{8.1 \, \ell} \quad \Bigg| \quad \dfrac{1 \text{ mol solute}}{1 \text{ kg nitrobenzene}} = 0.296 \text{ mol solute/kg nitrobenzene}$

$\dfrac{2.53 \text{ g}}{63.5 \text{ g nitrobenzene}} \quad \Bigg| \quad \dfrac{1000 \text{ g nitrobenzene}}{1 \text{ kg nitrobenzene}} = 39.8 \text{ g/kg nitrobenzene}$

$\dfrac{39.8 \text{ g}}{0.296 \text{ mol}} = 134 \text{ g/mol}$

Page 436.

5. $\pi = MRT$

$\pi = \dfrac{18.6 \text{ g } X}{1.00 \text{ dm}^3} \quad \Bigg| \quad \dfrac{1 \text{ mol } X}{8940 \text{ g } X} \quad \Bigg| \quad \dfrac{8.31 \text{ dm}^3 \cdot \text{kPa}}{\text{mol} \cdot K} \quad \Bigg| \quad 298 \, K$

$\pi = 5.15 \text{ kPa}$

6. $x \text{ g/mol } Y = \dfrac{\quad}{15.8 \text{ kPa}} \quad \Bigg| \quad \dfrac{96 \text{ g } Y}{1.00 \text{ dm}^3} \quad \Bigg| \quad \dfrac{8.31 \text{ dm}^3 \cdot \text{kPa}}{\text{mol} \cdot K} \quad \Bigg| \quad 298 \, K$

$x = 15 \, 000 \text{ g/mol}$

7. $\pi = MRT$

$\pi = \dfrac{81.0 \text{ g}}{1 \text{ dm}^3} \quad \Bigg| \quad \dfrac{1 \text{ mol}}{4010 \text{ g}} \quad \Bigg| \quad \dfrac{8.31 \text{ dm}^3 \cdot \text{kPa}}{\text{mol} \cdot K} \quad \Bigg| \quad 293 \, K = 49.2 \text{ kPa}$

8. $\pi = \dfrac{nRT}{V} = \dfrac{mRT}{MV}, \; M = \dfrac{mRT}{\pi V}$

$= \dfrac{200 \text{ g}}{1 \text{ dm}^3} \quad \Bigg| \quad \dfrac{8.31 \text{ dm}^3 \cdot \text{kPa}}{\text{mol} \cdot K} \quad \Bigg| \quad \dfrac{294 \, K}{100 \text{ kPa}} = 4890 \text{ g/mol}$

Chapter End Problems

Pages 442-443.

9. Colligative properties are those which depend only on the number of particles and not their nature (vapor pressure, freezing point, boiling point, osmotic pressure).

10. Ideal solutions obey Raoult's law.

11. A nonvolatile solute is one which does not evaporate.

12. These solute particles decrease the opportunity for the solvent particles to evaporate. Thus the vapor pressure of a solution with a nonvolatile solute is always less than the vapor pressure of the pure solvent.

13. The size of colloidal particles is smaller than suspension particles. Colloidal particles will not settle out and can pass through filter paper.

14. v.p. H_2O @ 60°C = 19.9 kPa

$$\frac{133 \text{ g } C_6H_8O_7}{} \left| \frac{1 \text{ mol } C_6H_8O_7}{192 \text{ g } C_6H_8O_7} \right. = 0.692 \text{ mol } C_6H_8O_7$$

$$\frac{100 \text{ g } H_2O}{} \left| \frac{1 \text{ mol } H_2O}{18.0 \text{ g } H_2O} \right. = \frac{5.56 \text{ mol } H_2O}{6.25 \text{ mol soln}}$$

$$x\ H_2O = \frac{5.56}{6.25} = 0.890$$

15. v.p. soln = (19.9)(0.890) = 17.7 kPa

$$\frac{6.05 \text{ g } C_6H_6}{} \left| \frac{1 \text{ mol } C_6H_6}{78.1 \text{ g } C_6H_6} \right. = 0.0775 \text{ mol } C_6H_6$$

$$\frac{1.60 \text{ g } CHCl_3}{} \left| \frac{1 \text{ mol } CHCl_3}{119 \text{ g } CHCl_3} \right. = \frac{0.0134 \text{ mol } CHCl_3}{0.0909 \text{ mol soln}}$$

$$x\ C_6H_6 = \frac{0.0775}{0.0909} = 0.853, \text{ v.p. } C_6H_6 = (12.1)(0.853) = 10.3 \text{ kPa}$$

$$x\ CHCl_3 = \frac{0.0134}{0.0909} = 0.147, \text{ v.p. } CHCl_3 = (25.2)(0.147) = 3.7 \text{ kPa}$$

v.p. soln = 10.3 + 3.7 = 14.0 kPa

16. a. $\dfrac{97.5 \text{ g } C_{12}H_{22}O_{11}}{185 \text{ g } H_2O} \left| \dfrac{1 \text{ mol } C_{12}H_{22}O_{11}}{342 \text{ g } C_{12}H_{22}O_{11}} \right| \dfrac{1000 \text{ g } H_2O}{1 \text{ kg } H_2O} = 1.54m$

BP = 100° + (1.54° × 0.512°) = 100.788°C
FP = 0° − (1.54° × 1.86°) = −2.86°C

b. $\dfrac{14.0 \text{ g } C_{10}H_8}{25.0 \text{ g } C_6H_6} \left| \dfrac{1 \text{ mol } C_{10}H_8}{128 \text{ g } C_{10}H_8} \right| \dfrac{1000 \text{ g } C_6H_6}{1 \text{ kg } C_6H_6} = 4.37m$

BP = 80.1° + (4.37 × 2.53°) = 91.2°C
FP = 5.5° − (4.37 × 4.90°) = −15.9°C

c. $\dfrac{500 \text{ g } X}{500 \text{ g } H_2O} \left| \dfrac{1 \text{ mol } X}{511 \text{ g } X} \right| \dfrac{1000 \text{ g } H_2O}{1 \text{ kg } H_2O} = 1.96m$

BP = 100°C + (1.96 × 0.512°) = 101.00°C
FP = 0°C − (1.96 × 1.86°) = −3.65°C

d. $\dfrac{250 \text{ g } Y}{500 \text{ g } C_6H_6} \left| \dfrac{1 \text{ mol } Y}{246 \text{ g } Y} \right| \dfrac{1000 \text{ g } C_6H_6}{1 \text{ kg}} = 2.03m$

BP = 80.1°C + (2.03 × 2.53°) = 85.2°C
FP = 5.5°C − (2.03 × 4.90°) = −4.5°C

e. $\dfrac{60.0 \text{ g } C_9H_{18}}{1 \text{ kg HAc}} \left| \dfrac{1 \text{ mole } C_9H_{18}}{126 \text{ g } C_9H_{18}} \right. = 0.475m$

BP = 117.9°C + (0.475 × 3.07°) = 119°C
FP = 16.604°C − (0.475 × 3.90°) = 14.7°C

17. $\dfrac{-0.603 \text{ C}°}{-1.86 \text{ C}°} = 0.324m$

$$\frac{5.60 \text{ g X}}{104 \text{ g } H_2O} \left| \frac{1000 \text{ g}}{1 \text{ kg}} \right| \frac{\text{kg } H_2O}{0.324 \text{ mol}} = 166 \text{ g X/mol}$$

18. $\pi = MRT$

$$= \frac{8.10 \text{ g}}{1 \text{ dm}^3} \left| \frac{\text{mol}}{1310 \text{ g}} \right| \frac{8.31 \text{ dm}^3 \cdot \text{kPa}}{\text{mol} \cdot \text{K}} \left| \frac{295 \text{ K}}{} \right. = 15.2 \text{ kPa}$$

Review

Page 443.

1. $\dfrac{20.0 \text{ g } Fe_2(C_2O_4)_3}{100 \text{ g } H_2O} \left| \dfrac{1 \text{ mol } Fe_2(C_2O_4)_3}{376 \text{ g } Fe_2(C_2O_4)_3} \right| \dfrac{1000 \text{ g}}{1 \text{ kg}} = 0.532m \ Fe_2(C_2O_4)_3$

2. $$\frac{250 \text{ cm}^3 \text{ H}_2\text{O}}{} \left| \frac{1 \text{ g H}_2\text{O}}{1 \text{ cm}^3 \text{ H}_2\text{O}} \right| \frac{0.560 \text{ mol Li}_2\text{S}}{1000 \text{ g H}_2\text{O}} \left| \frac{45.9 \text{ g Li}_2\text{S}}{1 \text{ mol Li}_2\text{S}} \right.$$

$$= 6.43 \text{ g Li}_2\text{S}$$

3. $$\frac{50.0 \text{ g CH}_3\text{COCH}_3}{} \left| \frac{1 \text{ mol CH}_3\text{COCH}_3}{58.1 \text{ g CH}_3\text{COCH}_3} \right. = 0.861 \text{ mol CH}_3\text{COCH}_3$$

$$\frac{50.0 \text{ g H}_2\text{O}}{} \left| \frac{1 \text{ mol H}_2\text{O}}{18.0 \text{ g H}_2\text{O}} \right. = \frac{2.78 \text{ mol H}_2\text{O}}{3.64 \text{ mol soln}}$$

$$\frac{0.861}{3.64} = 0.237 \text{ mole fraction CH}_3\text{COCH}_3$$

One More Step

Page 443.

1. See any elementary organic chemistry laboratory manual. Possible mixtures are CCl_4 and toluene, 1-butanol and 1-octanol, benzene and toluene, benzene and acetic acid, methanol and water. **Caution:** The mixtures are flammable. Collect five fractions and analyze by refractive index or density.

2. The ultracentrifuge was developed by the Swedish scientist, Svedberg. It can, through centrifugal force, produce an effective gravitational field about 500 000 times the earth's. Dissolved particles of large molecular mass settle out quickly and mass values can be determined by this rate. For further information consult *Encyclopaedia Britannica.*

3. Cyclone separators—stack gas forced into a spiral path. Centrifugal force throws dust against sides when it settles out.
   Cottrell precipitators—electrostatic precipitation of charged, colloidal dust particles.

Scrubbing towers—gas is bubbled through water, or other wash liquid, which strips out dust as well as noxious gases.

4. Gelatin forms most useful protective colloids. It is used with silver bromide emulsions in photography, to prevent ice crystals in ice cream, and as an emulsifying agent in many solutions. Egg is an emulsifier in foods such as salad dressings or mayonnaise. Detergents are special protective colloids.

5. A living cell is filled principally with water (75-85%). The inorganic salts and some of the smaller organic molecules (if hydrophilic) are in solution. However, the larger molecules in the colloidal range of size and hydrophobic materials are dispersed. The larger molecules would include proteins and nucleic acids; while the hydrophobic materials would include lipids. Many of the long molecules, particularly proteins, tend to align themselves in a degree of order which appears the same as in liquid crystals.

REACTION RATE AND CHEMICAL EQUILIBRIUM   23

An Overview

Chapter 23 is used to introduce both the qualitative and quantitative aspects of the factors affecting rates of chemical reactions. Emphasize the role of energy in affecting the rate of a chemical reaction. The concept of activation energy should be graphically contrasted to the heat of reaction. Reaction rates can be measured by observing the rate at which some property of the reaction changes. Some properties which change are index of refraction, rotation of polarized light, pH, volume, color, and pressure. Stress that the accurate prediction of reaction rates is one of the most important unsolved problems in chemistry. The quantitative study of equilibrium is then based on

the study of reaction rates. At equilibrium, the rates of the forward and reverse reactions are equal. Using Le Chatelier's principle, students may predict how changes in concentration, pressure, and temperature affect equilibrium concentrations. Stress that in many reactions some of the product molecules will have enough energy to cause the reverse reaction to occur. The chapter ends by relating small K_{eq} values to negative free energy changes.

Demonstration Information

The clock reaction: To 40 cm^3 of distilled H_2O in a small beaker, add 20 drops of saturated KIO_3 solution. Place 100 cm^3 of distilled H_2O into another small beaker, add 40 drops of a soluble starch solution (4 g/100 cm^3 boiling water), 12 drops of Na$_2$S$_2$O$_5$ solution (2.5 g/100 cm^3), and 4 drops of concentrated H$_2$SO$_4$. Pour the solutions in the two beakers together and time the reaction. If the reaction time is longer than 20 seconds, increase the amount of KIO$_3$ solution. Dilute the KIO$_3$ solution if the reaction time is too fast. Run the demonstration before class and adjust the concentrations accordingly. Vary the concentration of KIO$_3$ in the first beaker and run several trials. (Example: 15, 20, 15 and 30 drops) Record the time for each trial. Place the two solutions in large test tubes in an ice water bath and run a trial at the colder temperature. Record the time. Repeat in a hot water bath (35°C) and record the time for the reaction to take place. You may prefer to do this as a laboratory experiment for your students. Discuss how the rate of a reaction can vary without changing the temperature. Use the demonstration to introduce reaction mechanisms, rate determining step, and activation energy.

$$IO_3^-(aq) + H_3O^+(aq) + S_2O_5^{2-}(aq) \rightarrow$$
$$I^-(aq) + 2SO_4^{2-}(aq) + H_3O^+(aq)$$
$$I^-(aq) + 6H_3O^+(aq) + IO_3^-(aq) \rightarrow I_2(aq) + 3H_2O(l)$$

Performance Objectives

Goal: Students will gain an understanding of the factors which affect reaction rate and their relationship to quantitative chemical equilibrium.

Objectives: Upon completion of the reading and problems, and when asked to demonstrate their understanding either orally or on a written test, students will

23:1	K	define a reversible reaction.
23:2	K	define reaction rate.
23:3-6	K	list and describe the factors which influence rate of reaction.
23:7	K	explain reaction mechanism.
23:8	P/S	solve problems developing an equilibrium constant or the concentration of a reactant or product.
23:9	K/P	explain the relationship of Le Chatelier's principle to equilibrium systems.
23:10	K	explain the equilibria of gas phase reactions.
23:11	K/P	describe the relationship between, and solve problems dealing with, free energy and the equilibrium constant for a reaction.

A	voluntarily complete one or more of the One More Step activities.
A	read unassigned literature related to the chapter.

Teaching Techniques

Section 23:1

A reversible reaction can be demonstrated by dissolving 14 g NaOH in 700 cm^3 distilled H$_2$O, in a 1000 cm^3 Erlenmeyer flask. Add 14 g of dextrose or glucose and 1 or 2 cm^3 of methylene blue indicator solution to the NaOH solution and stopper tightly. Shake vigorously and the solution is blue in color. Allow it to sit and the color clears.

Section 23:4

Lycopodium powder can be purchased from chemical supply houses. Place a scoop full on a ceramic square. Try to light the powder using a burner. It does not burn. Then, lift the square containing the powder about 50 cm above the burner flame and turn the square over. The falling dust will produce a roaring flame which is best viewed in a darkened room. The surface area is directly proportional to concentration. Thus an increase in surface area increases the reaction rate. Relate this demonstration to a dust explosion in a grain elevator or cement plant.

Section 23:5

Figure 23-6 is a simplified diagram. The graph of a multistep reaction would have several valleys and peaks. The "controlling" step in such a reaction is the one with the highest peak.

Section 23:6

The demonstration in the margin shows a homogeneous catalyst. The cobalt(II) tartrate complex is oxidized to a green Co(III) tartrate compound. The green form is then reduced by tartaric acid and H$_2$O$_2$ to Co(II) tartrate with the evolution of CO$_2$ and O$_2$ gas. This demonstration shows a multistep mechanism (Section 23:7). The pink to green (oxidation) is faster than the green to pink (reduction). The short life of a collision product (activated complex) can also be discussed.

Section 23:9

A demonstration that helps students visualize Le Chatelier's principle is based on the equilibrium:

$$Co(H_2O)_6^{2+} + 4\ Cl^+ \rightarrow CoCl_4^{2-} + 6H_2O$$

pink   blue

Dissolve 2.0 g of $CoCl_2$ in 40 cm^3 of H_2O. Put the 40 cm^3 of solution in a 100 cm^3 graduated cylinder. Have the equilibrium equation on the chalkboard. Ask students to predict if a change will occur before adding 60 cm^3 of $12M$ HCl to the graduated cylinder. Observe the color change from pink to blue. Pour half of the blue solution into another graduated cylinder. Ask students to predict the color again before adding 35 cm^3 of water. Observe the color change back to pink. Point out to students that this is a reversible reaction (Section 23:1). To the graduated cylinder with blue solution, add 35 cm^3 of $0.1M$ $AgNO_3$ and observe the formation of the AgCl precipitate and a color change to pink. This reaction shows students that chlorides are removed by precipitation with $AgNO_3$. This precipitation causes the equilibrium to shift to the left (decreases concentration of Cl^-).

The relationship between equilibrium constants for short temperature ranges assuming $\Delta H°$ constant for the short range is

$$\ln \frac{K_{T_2}}{K_{T_1}} = \frac{\Delta H°}{R}\left(\frac{1}{T_2} - \frac{1}{T_1}\right)$$

where K_{T_2} and K_{T_1} are the values of the equilibrium constant at the second and first temperatures respectively.

Chemical Technology

This feature is an extension of the discussion concerning kelvin temperature. Emphasize to students that some of the research in this area concerns trying to reach absolute zero. For students to do additional literature research concerning absolute zero and the devices used to maintain low temperatures, some knowledge of physics may be required.

Problem Solutions

Pages 455-456.

1. **a.** doubled $[2H_2] = 2[H_2]$
   b. eight times faster
      $[2NO]^2[2H_2] = 8[NO]^2[H_2]$
   c. slows down

2. **a.** Rate $= k[H_2][I_2]$
      $0.2 = k(1)(1)$
      $k = 0.2$ dm^6/mol·s
      $0.4 = k(1)(2)$
      $k = 0.2$ dm^6/mol·s
      $0.8 = k(2)(2)$
      $k = 0.2$ dm^6/mol·s
   b. Rate $= 0.2(0.5)(0.5)$
      Rate $= 0.05$ mol/s

3. rate $= k[CH_3COCH_3]$ (Iodine has no effect)

$$H^+ + CH_3 - \overset{\overset{\displaystyle O}{\|}}{C} - CH_3 \rightarrow CH_3 - \overset{\overset{\displaystyle OH}{|}}{\underset{\oplus}{C}} - CH_3 \quad \text{slow}$$

$$CH_3 - \overset{\overset{\displaystyle OH}{|}}{\underset{\oplus}{C}} - CH_3 \rightarrow CH_3 - \overset{\overset{\displaystyle OH}{|}}{C} = CH_2 + H^+ \quad \text{fast}$$

$$CH_3 - \overset{\overset{\displaystyle OH}{|}}{C} = CH_2 + I_2 \rightarrow CH_3 - \overset{\overset{\displaystyle OH}{|}}{\underset{\oplus}{C}} - CH_2I + I^- \quad \text{fast}$$

$$CH_3 - \overset{\overset{\displaystyle OH}{|}}{\underset{\oplus}{C}} - CH_2I + I^- \rightarrow CH_3 - \overset{\overset{\displaystyle O}{\|}}{C} - CH_2I + HI \quad \text{fast}$$

Pages 458-459.

5. $[HI]^2 = \dfrac{[H_2][I_2]}{K_{eq}}$

   $[HI]^2 = \dfrac{(2.00 \times 10^{-4})(2.00 \times 10^{-4})}{1.40 \times 10^{-2}} = 2.86 \times 10^{-6}$

   $[HI] = 1.69 \times 10^{-3}M$

6. $K_{eq} = \dfrac{[H_2][CO_2]}{[CO][H_2O]} = \dfrac{(0.320)(0.420)}{(0.200)(0.500)} = 1.34$

7. $[CO] = \dfrac{[H_2][CO_2]}{K_{eq}[H_2O]}$

   $[CO] = \dfrac{(0.320)(0.420)}{(2.40)(0.500)} = 0.112M$

8. $K_{eq} = \dfrac{[H_2]^2[S_2]}{[H_2S]^2}$

   $= \dfrac{(2.22 \times 10^{-3})^2(1.11 \times 10^{-3})}{(7.06 \times 10^{-3})^2} = 1.10 \times 10^{-4}$

9. $K_{eq} = \dfrac{[NO_2]^2}{[N_2O_4]}$

   $[NO_2]^2 = K_{eq}[N_2O_4]$
      $= (8.75 \times 10^{-2})(1.72 \times 10^{-2})$
      $= 15.1 \times 10^{-4}$
   $[NO_2] = 3.88 \times 10^{-2}M$

Page 463.

10. $\log K_{eq} = -\dfrac{\Delta G}{2.30RT} = -\dfrac{28.95}{(2.30)(8.31 \times 10^{-3})(298)}$
      $= 5.0828$
    antilog $5.0828 = 8.26 \times 10^{-6}$

11. $\Delta G = -2.30RT \log K_{eq}$
      $= (-2.30)(0.00831)(900)(\log 3.16 \times 10^{-4})$
      $= 60.2$ kJ

Chapter End Problems

Pages 466-467.

12. a. $K_{eq} = \dfrac{[(NH_4)_2SO_4]}{[NH_3]^2[H_2SO_4]}$

b. $K_{eq} = \dfrac{4.00}{(2.00)^2(3.00)} = 0.333$

c. increases d. shifts right e. changes

13. $H_2(g) = Cl_2(g) \rightarrow 2\ HCl(g)$
Cl_2 is more active than Br_2

14. The reaction rate would increase.

15. The surface area of the log is less than the surface area of the paper. The match cannot raise the temperature of the log to its kindling point but can heat the paper.

16. See Figure 23-6, page 451 for an example of how to set up the uncatalyzed reaction. The catalyzed reaction should show a lower activation energy hill.

17. If [NO] is constant, rate $\propto$ [H]; thus the reaction rate doubles.

18. The reaction rate would increase.

19. $\Delta G = -RTlnK_{eq}$

$$= \dfrac{-8.31\ J}{mol \cdot K} \left| \begin{array}{c} 2000\ K \end{array} \right| \begin{array}{c} ln(6.45 \times 10^{-8}) \end{array}$$

$= 2.75 \times 10^5\ J = 275\ kJ$

20. $33\ 800\ J = \dfrac{-8.31\ J}{mol \cdot K} \left| \begin{array}{c} 1273\ K \end{array} \right| \begin{array}{c} ln\ x \end{array}$

$x = 1.33 \times 10^{-14}$

Review

Page 467.

1. Due to ion-dipole or van der Waals forces, solvent particles adhere to solute particles during the solvation process.

2. No. Water is highly polar. Butter is nonpolar.

3. crush solute, heat, stir

4. A constant volume of gas will dissolve in a given quantity of liquid.

5. $\dfrac{16.0\ g\ HIO_3}{100\ cm^3} \left| \dfrac{1\ mol\ HIO_3}{176\ g\ HIO_3} \right| \dfrac{1000\ cm^3}{1\ dm^3}$
$= 0.909M\ HIO_3$

6. It increases the boiling point.

7. The activity of the ions is slightly less than their concentration.

8. $\dfrac{98.1\ g\ C_{12}H_{22}O_{11}}{} \left| \dfrac{1\ mol\ C_{12}H_{22}O_{11}}{342\ g\ C_{12}H_{22}O_{11}} \right| = 0.287\ mol\ C_{12}H_{22}O_{11}$

$\dfrac{100\ g\ H_2O}{} \left| \dfrac{1\ mole\ H_2O}{18.0\ g\ H_2O} \right| = 5.55\ mol\ H_2O$

$\dfrac{5.55}{5.84}$ mol soln

$\dfrac{5.55}{5.84} = 0.950$ mole fraction water

vapor pressure of the solution $= x(v.p.\ solvent) = (0.950)(3.17\ kPa) = 3.01\ kPa$

9. $\dfrac{6.78\ g\ C_6H_{12}O_6}{30.0\ g\ H_2O} \left| \dfrac{1\ mol\ C_6H_{12}O_6}{180\ g\ C_6H_{12}O_6} \right| \dfrac{1000\ g}{1\ kg}$
$= 1.25m\ C_6H_{12}O_6$
$FP = 0° - (1.86\ C° \times 1.25) = -2.33°C$
$BP = 100° + (0.512\ C° \times 1.25) = 100.64°C$

10. $\dfrac{1.58}{1.86} = 0.849m$

$\dfrac{4.23\ g}{45.0\ g\ H_2O} \left| \dfrac{1000\ g}{1\ kg} \right| \dfrac{kg}{0.849\ mol} = 111\ g/mol$

11. $\pi = MRT$

$\dfrac{4.70\ g}{500\ cm^3} \left| \dfrac{1\ mol}{6870\ g} \right| \dfrac{1000\ cm^3}{1\ dm^3}$
$\left| \dfrac{8.31\ dm^3 \cdot kPa}{mol \cdot K} \right| 288\ K = 3.27\ kPa$

One More Step

Page 467.

1. $K_{eq} = \dfrac{[C]^2}{[A]^2[B]} = 8$

initial concentration of A $= \dfrac{0.5}{10} = 0.05M$

initial concentration of B $= \dfrac{0.5}{10} = 0.05M$

If x moles of B react per liter, then $2x$ moles of A must react per liter and $2x$ moles of C will be produced per liter. Therefore,

final concentration of A $= 0.05 - 2x$
final concentration of B $= 0.05 - x$
final concentration of C $= 2x$

Note: The final solution to this problem involves a "sticky" third-degree equation:

$$\dfrac{(2x)^2}{(0.05 - 2x)^2(0.05 - x)} = 8$$

$$\dfrac{4x^2}{(0.000125 - 0.0125x + 0.4x^2 - 4x^3)} = 8$$

$4x^2 = 0.001 - 0.1x + 3.2x^2 - 32x^3$
$32x^3 + 0.8x^2 + 0.1x - 0.001 = 0$
$x = 0.00910$
Since [C] $= 2x$, [C] $= 0.0182M$,
Then [A] $= 0.0318M$ and [B] $= 0.0409M$

2. $E_a = \Delta H^{\circ*} + RT$ for solid and liquid systems
   $E_a = \Delta H^{\circ*} - (\Delta n^* - 1) RT$ for gaseous systems
   $\Delta G^{\circ*} = H^{\circ*} - T\Delta S^{\circ*}$
   $\Delta G^{\circ*} = -RT \ln K^*$
   where E_a = activation energy
   $\Delta H^{\circ*}$ = enthalpy of activation
   R = gas constant
   T = kelvin temperature
   Δn^* = moles of complex minus number of moles
   of reactants
   $\Delta G^{\circ*}$ = free energy of activation
   $\Delta S^{\circ*}$ = entropy of activation
   $\ln$ = natural logarithm
   K^* = equilibrium constant for reactants $\leftrightarrows$
   complex in units of concentration

3. There are many multistep reactions listed in texts on kinetics and physical chemistry. For example:
   $2 O_3 \rightarrow 3 O_2$

   $2 H_2 O_2 \xrightarrow{I^-} 2 H_2 O + O_2$
   (The I^- is a catalyst for decomposing $H_2 O_2$.)
   $H_2 + Cl_2 \rightarrow 2 HCl$

$O_3 \leftrightarrows O_2 + O$ 　　fast
$O + O_3 \rightarrow 2 O_2$ 　　slow
$H_2 O_2 + H_3 O^+ \leftrightarrows H_3 O_3$ 　　fast
$H_3 O_2 + I^- \rightarrow H_2 O + HOI^+$ 　　slow
$HOI^+ + H_2 O_2 \rightarrow H_3 O^+ I^- + O_2$ 　　fast
$Cl_2 + h\nu \rightarrow 2 Cl$ 　　slow
chain $\quad$ $\begin{cases} Cl + H_2 \rightarrow HCl + H & \text{fast} \\ H + Cl_2 \rightarrow HCl + Cl & \text{fast} \end{cases}$
reaction
$\left.\begin{array}{l} H + HCl \rightarrow H_2 + Cl \\ Cl + HCl \rightarrow Cl_2 + H \end{array}\right\}$ inhibiting reactions
$\left.\begin{array}{l} 2 Cl \rightarrow Cl_2 \\ 2 H \rightarrow H_2 \end{array}\right\}$ chain-breaking reactions

4. $K_c = K_p \dfrac{1}{(RT)} \Delta n$ 　where Δn = the increase in moles in going from reactants to products.

5. See *Biology: Living Systems* © 1983, Oram, Charles E. Merrill Publishing Co., pp. 61-64.

6. Free energy (G) always decreases with temperature. The free energy change (ΔG) becomes more positive as temperature increases if ΔS is negative and vice versa.

ACIDS, BASES, AND SALTS 　　# 24

An Overview

The three classes of electrolytes—acids, bases, and salts are discussed in Chapter 24 with an emphasis on their behavior in water solution. The chapter begins with an introduction to three acid-base theories. Point out that the Arrhenius definitions are applicable only in water solution. Under the Brönsted-Lowry definitions we write $H_3 O^+$ as a convenience. However, a more exact representation we can use $H(H_2 O)n^+$. The Lewis theory is applicable to reactions carried out in the absence of solvents. After the students know the definition of an acid, teach them how to name them. The properties and behavior of acids, bases, and salts are discussed qualitatively and then expressed and applied in a quantitative manner. Students apply the knowledge gained in Chapter 23 on equilibrium to solve problems involving the ionization constant, percent of ionization, and common ion effect.

Performance Objectives

Goal: Students will gain an understanding of the acid-base theories; the general properties of acids, bases, and salts; and the procedures for naming them.

Objectives: Upon completion of the reading and problems, and when asked to demonstrate their understanding either orally or on a written test, students will

24:1-3	K	list the differences and similarities in the Arrhenius, Brönsted-Lowry, and Lewis acid-base theories.
24:4-5	K/P	name or write formulas for common acids and bases.
24:6	K	describe the properties of acidic and basic anhydrides.
24:7	P/S	determine acidic, basic, or amphoteric behavior for given elements.
24:8	K	define and give examples of common salts.
24:9	K	explain the factors that determine strengths of acids or bases.
24:10	K	write net ionic equations given a reaction taking place in water.
24:11-13	P	Use acid-base equilibrium constants to develop and explain
		a. ionization constant
		b. percent of ionization
		c. common ion effect

24:14   K   define and give examples of
                polyprotic acids.
        A   voluntarily complete one or more
                of the One More Step activities.
        A   read unassigned literature
                related to the chapter.

Teaching Techniques

Section 24:1

The first three sections of the chapter discuss the three popular theories regarding the definitions of acids and bases. Point out to students that each definition has two parts—descriptive and theoretical. All three theories describe acid properties as is shown in the chapter opening demonstration (sour taste, electrolyte, affect indicators, and react with metals to produce H_2). What makes each theory unique is the theoretical description of behavior (ionizable hydrogen, proton donor, or electron pair acceptor). Your students will ask, "which one is the right definition?" They all are. As in Chapter 13, different observations can be explained by different theories. Arrhenius' theory applies only to water solutions. The Brönsted-Lowry theory can be used with all solvents that will gain or lose a proton, including water. As a result, this theory is more widely applicable.

Section 24:9

Acids and bases can be grouped as either strong or weak with no intermediate groups. Orthophosphoric acid is an exception. This acid is intermediate between strong and weak acids. It is much weaker than strong acids like HCl and H_2SO_4 but much stronger than acetic acid.

Chemical Technology

This topic is included as it is somewhat controversial. In addition to focusing on the chemistry of acid rain, you may want to have students consider who is to accept the responsibility for reducing anhydride levels in the atmosphere and the costs associated with repairing the damage caused by acid rain.

Problem Solutions

Page 471.

1. **a.** acid − HNO_3
     base − NaOH
     conjugate acid − H_2O
     conjugate base − $NaNO_3$
b. acid − HCl
     base − $NaHCO_3$
     conjugate acid − H_2CO_3
     conjugate base − NaCl

Page 473.

2. **a.** Lewis base
    b. Lewis acid
    c. Lewis acid
    d. Lewis base

Page 474.

3. **a.** hydrobromic acid
    b. hydrofluoric acid

Page 475.

4. **a.** boric acid
    b. nitrous acid
    c. phosphoric acid
    d. arsenious acid
    e. iodic acid

5. **a.** H_2CO_3
    b. HNO_3
    c. H_3AsO_4
    d. H_2SeO_4
    e. HIO

Page 477.

6. **a.** basic
    b. basic
    c. acidic
    d. basic
    e. acidic

7. **a.** BaO
    b. I_2O_7
    c. TeO_3
    d. Al_2O_3
    e. ZnO

Page 479.

8. **a.** sodium hydrogen sulfate
    b. potassium hydrogen tartrate
    c. sodium dihydrogen phosphate
    d. sodium hydrogen sulfide

9. **a.** $NaHCO_3$
    b. Na_2HPO_4
    c. NH_4HS
    d. $KHSO_4$

Page 481.

10. **a.** $2Cl^-(aq) + 2Cr^{2+}(aq) + 2Hg^{2+}(aq) \rightarrow 2Cr^{3+}(aq) + Hg_2Cl_2(c)$
   b. $2Mn^{2+}(aq) + 5NaBiO_3(c) + 14H^+(aq) \rightarrow 2MnO_4^-(aq) + 5Bi^{3+}(aq) + 7H_2O(l) + 5Na^+(aq)$
   c. $2Ag^+(aq) + HSO_4^-(aq) \rightarrow Ag_2SO_4(c) + H^+(aq)$
   d. $H_4SiO_4(aq) + 4OH^-(aq) \rightarrow SiO_4^-(aq) + 4H_2O(l)$
   e. $2Cu^{2+}(aq) + SO_4^{2-}(aq) + 2CNS^-(aq) + H_2SO_3(aq) + H_2O(l) \rightarrow 2CuCNS(c) + 2HSO_4^-(aq) + 2H^+(aq)$

Page 484.

11. $HClO + H_2O \rightleftarrows H_3O^+ + ClO^-$
$$K_a = \frac{[H_3O^+][ClO^-]}{[HClO]} = 3.16 \times 10^{-8} = \frac{x^2}{0.01 - x}$$
$$x = 1.78 \times 10^{-5} M$$

12. $N_2H_4 + H_2O \rightleftarrows N_2H_5^+ + OH^-$
$$K_b = \frac{[N_2H_5^+][OH^-]}{[N_2H_4]} = \frac{(1.23 \times 10^{-3})^2}{0.499}$$
$$K_b = 3.03 \times 10^{-6}$$

Page 485.

13. $K_a = \dfrac{[CH_3COO^-][H_3O^+]}{[CH_3COOH]}$
$$1.76 \times 10^{-5} = \frac{x^2}{0.1 - \boxed{x}} \leftarrow \text{neglect}$$
$$x^2 = 1.76 \times 10^{-6}$$
$$x = 1.32 \times 10^{-3}$$
$$\% = \frac{1.33 \times 10^{-3}}{0.1} \left| \frac{100}{1} \right. = 1.33\%$$

14. $K_a = \dfrac{[A^-][H_3O^+]}{[HA]} = \dfrac{(0.0200)^2}{0.980} = 4.08 \times 10^{-4}$

Page 487.

15. $HNO_2 + H_2O \rightleftharpoons H_3O^+ + NO_2^-$

$K_a = \dfrac{[H_3O^+][NO_2^-]}{[HNO_2]}$

$4.60 \times 10^{-4} = \dfrac{x(\boxed{x} + 0.03)}{(0.15 - \boxed{x})} \leftarrow \text{neglect}$

$x = 2.3 \times 10^{-3} M$

16. $HBrO + H_2O \rightleftharpoons H_3O^+ + BrO^-$

$K_a = \dfrac{[H_3O^+][BrO^-]}{[HBrO]}$

$2.40 \times 10^{-9} = \dfrac{x(\boxed{x} + 0.00500)}{0.106 - \boxed{x}} \leftarrow \text{neglect}$

$x = 5.09 \times 10^{-8} M$

17. Add either HCO_3^- or CO_3^{2-} in the form of soluble salts.

18. oxalic acid $\dfrac{5.90 \times 10^{-2}}{6.40 \times 10^{-5}} = 9.22 \times 10^2$

carbonic acid $\dfrac{4.30 \times 10^{-7}}{5.61 \times 10^{-11}} = 7.66 \times 10^3$

phosphoric acid $\dfrac{7.52 \times 10^{-3}}{6.23 \times 10^{-8}} = 1.21 \times 10^5$

sulfurous acid $\dfrac{1.54 \times 10^{-2}}{1.02 \times 10^{-7}} = 1.51 \times 10^5$

boric acid $\dfrac{7.30 \times 10^{-10}}{1.80 \times 10^{-13}} = 4.06 \times 10^3$

selenious acid $\dfrac{3.50 \times 10^{-2}}{4.80 \times 10^{-9}} = 7.29 \times 10^6$

phosphorous acid $\dfrac{1.00 \times 10^{-2}}{2.60 \times 10^{-7}} = 3.85 \times 10^4$

Chapter End Problems

Pages 489-490.

19.

	Acid	Base	Conjugate acid	Conjugate base
a.	H_3O^+	NH_3	NH_4^+	H_2O
b.	CH_3OH	NH_2^-	NH_3	CH_3O^-
c.	H_3O^+	OH^-	H_2O	H_2O
d.	H_2O	NH_2^-	NH_3	OH^-
e.	$HClO_4$	H_2O	H_3O^+	ClO_4^-

20. a. :C̈l:
Al:C̈l: acid (electron-pair acceptor)
:C̈l:

b. :Ö:S::Ö: $\longleftrightarrow$:Ö::S:Ö: $\longleftrightarrow$:Ö:S:Ö: acid
   :Ö: :Ö: :Ö:

c. H
:P̈:H   base (electron-pair donor)
H

d. :Ẍe: base

e. Zn^{2+} acid

21. a. hydrobromic acid   d. selenious acid
b. hydroselenic acid   e. hyponitrous acid
c. iodic acid

22. a. H_3PO_3
b. H_3PO_2
c. H_2Te
d. HIO_4
e. HIO_3
f. HCl

23. a. $NaOH$
b. $Ca(OH)_2$
c. HNO_3
d. $RbOH$
e. H_2TeO_3
f. $CsOH$

24. a. Sc_2O_3
b. Cs_2O
c. I_2O_5
d. Ga_2O_3
e. CdO
f. K_2O

25. a. $6Cr^{2+} + 3Cu^{2+} \rightarrow 3Cu + 6Cr^{3+}$
b. $3H^+ + HSO_4^- + MnO_2 + 2Br^- \rightarrow Mn^{2+} + SO_4^{2-} + Br_2 + 2H_2O$
c. $H^+ + HSO_4^- \rightarrow H_2O + SO_3$
d. $P_4O_{10} + 6H_2O \rightarrow 4H_3PO_4$
e. $4CuCNS + 7IO_3^- + 14H^+ + 7Cl^- \rightarrow 4HCN + 4Cu^{2+} + 4SO_4^{2-} + 7ICl + 5H_2O$

26. a. sodium phosphate, Na_3PO_4
b. potassium borate, K_3BO_3
c. chromium(III) perchlorate, $Cr(ClO_4)_3$
d. cadmium bromide, $CdBr_2$
e. lithium silicate, Li_4SiO_4

27. A Lewis acid does not necessarily produce H^+ in water solution.

28. $CH_3CH_2Cl + AlCl_3 \rightarrow AlCl_4^- + CH_3CH_2^+$
$CH_3CH_2^+ + C_6H_6 \rightarrow C_6H_6CH_2CH_3^+$
$C_6H_6CH_2CH_3^+ + AlCl_4^- \rightarrow C_6H_5CH_2CH_3 + HCl + AlCl_3$

29. Metals have low electronegativities. Oxygen pulls shared electrons away from the metal keeping the hydrogen joined to the oxygen.

30. H_2SO_4 is completely ionized in solution, while H_2CO_3 is only partially ionized in solution.

31. Insoluble salts do not dissociate.

32. Two or more substances producing the same ion in an equilibrium system exhibit the common ion effect.

33. With each succeeding ionization, it becomes more difficult to remove a positive charge from an increasingly negative ion.

34. $KHSO_4 \rightarrow K^+ + HSO_4^-$ 100%
$H_2O + HSO_4^- \rightleftharpoons H_3O^+ + SO_4^{2-}$
$[SO_4^{2-}] = [H_3O^+] = x$

$K_a = \dfrac{[H_3O^+][SO_4^{2-}]}{[HSO_4^-]} = 1.20 \times 10^{-2}$

$= \dfrac{[H_3O^+]^2}{0.1 - [H_3O^+]} = \dfrac{x^2}{0.1 - x}$

The x in $0.1 - x$ is *not* negligible since the concentration (0.1) is so close to the K_a (1.2×10^{-2}).
Solving for x by the quadratic formula:
$1.2 \times 10^{-3} - 1.2 \times 10^{-2}x = x^2$
$x^2 + 1.2 \times 10^{-2}x - 1.2 \times 10^{-3} = 0$

$x = \dfrac{-1.2 \times 10^{-2}}{2}$

$\dfrac{\pm \sqrt{1.44 \times 10^{-4} + 4.8 \times 10^{-3}}}{2}$

$x = \dfrac{-1.2 \times 10^{-2} \pm \sqrt{49.4 \times 10^{-4}}}{2}$

$x = \dfrac{5.83 \times 10^{-2}}{2}$

$x = 2.92 \times 10^{-2} = [H^+] = [H_3O^+]$

35. % ionization $= \dfrac{[H_3O^+]}{[HSO_4^-]} \Big| \dfrac{100}{1}$

$= \dfrac{2.92 \times 10^{-2}}{0.1} \Big| \dfrac{100}{1} = 29.2\%$

36. $K_a = \dfrac{[H_3O^+][C_6H_5COO^-]}{[C_6H_5COOH]}$

$[H_3O^+] = [C_6H_5COO^-] = x$

$K_a = 6.46 \times 10^{-5} = \dfrac{x^2}{0.05 - \boxed{x}} \leftarrow$ neglect

$x^2 = 3.20 \times 10^{-6}$

$x = 1.80 \times 10^{-3} = [C_6H_5COO^-]$

$(1.77 \times 10^{-3}$ by quadratic)

37. $NaOH \rightarrow Na^+ + OH^-$ 100% ionization

$NH_3 + H_2O \rightleftharpoons NH_4^+ + OH^-$

$K_b = \dfrac{[NH_4^+][OH^-]}{[NH_3]}$

$NH_4^+ = x$

$OH^- = x + 0.1$ — from NaOH

— from NH_4OH

$K_b = 1.74 \times 10^{-5}$

$= \dfrac{x(\boxed{x} + 0.1)}{1 - \boxed{x}}$ — neglect

$x = 1.74 \times 10^{-4}$ (negligible compared to the amount from NaOH)

$[OH^-] = 0.1 = 10^{-1}$

$[H_3O^+] = \dfrac{10^{-14}}{10^{-1}} = 10^{-13} M$

38. $HOOC-COOH + H_2O \rightleftharpoons HOOC-COO^- + H_3O^+$

neglect second ionization (3 orders of magnitude less)

$K_a = \dfrac{[HOOC-COO^-][H_3O^+]}{[HOOC-COOH]}$

$[HOOC-COO^-] = [H_3O^+] = x$

$K_a = 5.90 \times 10^{-2} = \dfrac{x^2}{0.2 - x}$

$1.18 \times 10^{-2} - 5.90 \times 10^{-2}x = x^2$

$x^2 + 5.90 \times 10^{-2}x - 1.18 \times 10^{-2} = 0$

$= \dfrac{-5.90 \times 10^{-2} \pm \sqrt{3.48 \times 10^{-3} + 4.72 \times 10^{-2}}}{2}$

$= \dfrac{-5.90 \times 10^{-2} \pm \sqrt{5.07 \times 10^{-2}}}{2}$

$= \dfrac{-5.90 \times 10^{-2} \pm 2.25 \times 10^{-1}}{2}$

$= \dfrac{1.66 \times 10^{-1}}{2}$

$= 8.30 \times 10^{-2} M = [H_3O^+]$

Review

Page 491.

1. A reaction whose products will react to produce the original reactants.

2. molarity

3. increased number of collisions per unit time; more collisions have the requisite activation energy

4. homogeneous reactions—all reactants in the same phase

heterogeneous reactions—reactants in two or more phases

5. $\dfrac{k_f}{k_r} = K_{eq}$

6. shift left

7. No. nonpolar, low boiling point

8. unsaturated—more solute will dissolve

saturated—dissolved solute in equilibrium with undissolved solute

supersaturated—more solute per unit of solvent than in saturated solution

9. concentrated—high ratio of solute to solution

dilute—low ratio of solute to solution

10. positive

11. rate $= k[IO_3^-][Br^-]^2$

12. $K_a = \dfrac{[H_3O^+][C_6H_5O^-]}{[C_6H_5OH]}$

$1.02 \times 10^{-10} = \dfrac{x^2}{0.25 - x}$

$x = 5.05 \times 10^{-6} M$

13. $\log K_{eq} = \dfrac{\Delta G}{-2.30 RT}$

$= \dfrac{-55.6}{(-2.30)(0.00831)(298)}$

$= 9.7618$

$K_{eq} =$ antilog $9.7618 = 5.78 \times 10^9$

One More Step

Page 491.

1. All strong acids ionize completely in water because water is a strong enough base to remove all protons from an acid. However, in less basic solvents, these acids (for example, $HClO_4$, HCl, HNO_3) would not be completely ionized, and an order of relative strength can be set up. Because water is basic, it "levels" the effect of these acids to equality.

2. H_2SO_5 peroxysulfuric acid (contains $-O-O-$ peroxy group)

$H_2S_2O_7$ disulfuric acid (contains 2 sulfuric acid molecules condensed)

$H_2S_2O_8$ peroxydisulfuric acid (both of above reasons)

HNCO   isocyanic acid (HOCN is normal cyanic acid)

HSCN   thiocyanic acid (S substituted for O in normal cyanic acid)

3. acid = carboxylic acids (R—COOH)

base = amines (R—NH₂)

SOLUTIONS OF ELECTROLYTES

25

An Overview

Chapter 25 presents the practical side of acid, base, and salt behavior to students. Solubility product constant is described both qualitatively and quantitatively. Common ion effect is demonstrated mathematically. The sequence is for students to progress from the ionization of water, to pH, and then to the hydrolysis of salts. The concepts of hydrolysis and the common ion effect are linked in a practical study of buffers. Students are prepared for laboratory work with a study of indicators followed by titration calculations.

Demonstration Information

Prepare 50 cm^3 of 0.5M Pb(NO$_3$)$_2$ by dissolving 8.25 g in enough water to make 50 cm^3 of solution. Prepare 100 cm^3 of 0.5M Na$_2$SO$_4$ by dissolving 7.1 g anhydrous Na$_2$SO$_4$ in enough H$_2$O to prepare 100 cm^3 of solution. 0.5M Na$_2$S can be prepared by dissolving 12 g in 100 cm^3 of solution. The white to black color change is dramatic.

$$PbSO_4 \rightleftarrows Pb^{2+} + SO_4{}^{2-}$$
$$Pb^{2+} + S^{2-} \rightarrow PbS$$

Lead(II) sulfate is very slightly soluble with a K_{sp} of 1.9×10^{-8}. As the Pb^{2+} ion reacts with S^{2-} ion, the equilibrium shifts to produce more Pb^{2+}. Most Pb^{2+} cations will be converted from PbSO$_4$ to PbS.

Performance Objectives

Goal: Students will gain an understanding of the relationship of salts to acids and bases, and to their interaction with water.

Objectives: Upon completion of the reading and problems, and when asked to demonstrate their understanding either orally or on a written test, students will

25:1	K/P	use equilibrium constants to develop and explain solubility product constant for salts.
25:2	K/P	use equilibrium constant to develop and explain the ion product constant of water.
25:3	K/P	define the pH scale as $-\log$ [H$_3$O$^+$] and use it to determine pH and pOH of solutions.
25:4	P	write equations for hydrolysis reactions and predict the acidity or basicity of hydrolysis products.
25:5	K/P	describe and give examples of buffered solutions.
25:6	K	define indicators and give some examples of their use.
25:7	K/P/S	explain titration as a laboratory tool and solve for the concentration of an unknown acid or base using titration data.
	A	voluntarily complete one or more of the One More Step activities.
	A	read unassigned literature related to the chapter.

Teaching Techniques

Section 25:7
Normal Solutions

An older quantitative method of expressing the concentration of solutions is normality. A 1-normal (1N) solution contains one equivalent mass of solute per liter of solution.

For the moment, we may define the equivalent mass of a substance as the mass of a mole of the substance divided by the total positive charge in the compound. For instance, 1 mole of NaCl is 58.5 g; its total positive charge is 1. Therefore, its equivalent mass is 58.5 g. One mole of Bi(NO$_3$)$_3$ is 395 g; its total positive charge is 3. Therefore, its equivalent mass is 132. One mole of Al$_2$(SO$_4$)$_3$ is 342; its total positive charge is 6. Therefore, its equivalent mass is 57.

Equivalents

If 1 mole of NaOH is added to 1 mole of HCl, 1 mole of water and 1 mole of salt are formed: HCl + NaOH → NaCl + H$_2$O. What will happen if 1 mole of NaOH is added to 1 mole of H$_3$PO$_4$?

$$NaOH(aq) + H_3PO_4(aq) \rightarrow NaH_2PO_4(aq) + H_2O(l)$$

or, eliminating the spectator ion:

$$OH^-(aq) + H_3PO_4(aq) \rightarrow H_2PO_4{}^-(aq) + H_2O(l)$$

However, we can see that each H$_2$PO$_4{}^-$ ion has two more protons which can be liberated, so in order to neutralize all available protons, 3 moles of NaOH are needed.

$$3NaOH(aq) + H_3PO_4(aq) \rightarrow Na_3PO_4(aq) + 3H_2O(l)$$

One mole of H$_3$PO$_4$ is equivalent to 3 moles of NaOH.

The important reactants in the neutralization reaction are H$_3$O$^+$ and OH$^-$. But one mole of NaOH contains one mole of OH$^-$ while one mole of H$_3$PO$_4$

contains three moles of H^+. We could solve the problem by expressing concentration in terms of moles of H^+ and OH^-, or in terms of equivalents. One equivalent of acid is the amount of acid that can donate 1 mole of H^+ ions to a strong base. One equivalent of base can donate 1 mole of OH^- ions. One equivalent of acid will exactly neutralize one equivalent of base.

Normality and Equivalents

An equivalent of an acid must yield one mole of H^+ (H_3O^+) ions. One liter of a $1N$ solution of any acid will contain one mole of H^+ ions.

For example, the equivalent mass of HCl is

$$\frac{molecular\ mass}{total\ positive\ charge} = \frac{36.5\ g}{1} = 36.5\ g$$

A $1N$ HCl solution contains one mole of HCl and will yield one mole of H^+ ions. The equivalent mass of H_3PO_4, on the other hand, is the molecular mass divided by 3. Since one mole of H_3PO_4 would release 3 moles of H^+ ions, one equivalent mass would release 1 mole of H^+ ions. Equivalents of acid (or base) can be expressed in terms of normality. A $0.5N$ H_2SO_4 means that one liter of solution contains one-half mole of H^+ ions.

One advantage of this concentration unit is that we can then pour the amount of H^+ or OH^- ions that we want. If we need two equivalents of H_2SO_4, we can use 500 mL of $4N$ H_2SO_4, 1000 mL of $2N$ H_2SO_4, 2 liters of $1N$ H_2SO_4 or 8 liters of $0.25N$ H_2SO_4. Notice that in every case, the product of the volume in liters and the normality is 2, the number of equivalents needed.

$$0.5\ L \times 4N = 2\ equivalents$$
$$1\ L \times 2N = 2\ equivalents$$
$$2\ L \times 1N = 2\ equivalents$$
$$8\ L \times 0.25N = 2\ equivalents$$

Titration

The equivalents of acid can be calculated by multiplying the volume of acid solution by the normality of the acid solution.

$$(L) \times (eq/L) = eq$$
$$V_a \times N_a = equivalents\ of\ acid$$

The equivalents of base in the titrated solution are equivalent to the volume of the basic solution times the unknown normality of the solution.

$$V_b \times N_b = equivalents\ of\ base$$

Since we stop titrating exactly at the point of complete neutralization, the equivalents of acid are equal to the equivalents of base or:

$$V_a \times N_a = V_b \times N_b$$

We now know V_a, N_a, and V_b and we can solve the equation for N_b, the normality of the basic solution we have just titrated.

Suppose that we use 15.0 mL of NaOH and 25.0 mL of vinegar solution. What is the normality of the vinegar solution?

$$V_a \times N_a = V_b \times N_b$$
$$N_a = \frac{V_b \times N_b}{V_a}$$
$$N_a = \frac{15.0\ mL \times 0.5N}{25.0\ mL}$$
$$N_a = 0.3N$$

Notice that it is not necessary to convert mL to L as long as both volumes are in the same units.

Example: Titration

How many mL of $0.02N$ KOH will exactly neutralize 15 mL of $0.4N$ H_2SO_4?

$$V_b \times N_b = V_a \times N_a$$
$$V_b = \frac{V_a \times N_a}{N_b}$$
$$V_b = \frac{15\ mL \times 0.4N}{0.02N}$$
$$V_b = 300\ mL$$

Notice that the volume will have the same units as the known solution.

Chemical Technology

This feature is included to provide added insight into an important topic in the chapter—ion activity. You can have students research the mathematics associated with ion activity problems as this is a topic they will encounter if they proceed to college chemistry.

Problem Solutions

Page 496.

1. $AgI \rightleftharpoons Ag^+ + I^-$
   $$K_{sp} = [Ag^+][I^-]$$
   $$[Ag^+] = [I^-] = x$$
   $$x^2 = 1.50 \times 10^{-16}$$
   $$x = 1.22 \times 10^{-8}M = [Ag^+]$$

2. $D_2A \rightleftharpoons 2D^+ + A^{2-}$
   $$K_{sp} = [D^+]^2[A^{2-}]$$
   $$2[A^{2-}] = [D^+] = 2.00 \times 10^{-5}$$
   $$[A^{2-}] = 1 \times 10^{-5}$$
   $$K_{sp} = (2.00 \times 10^{-5})^2(1 \times 10^{-5})$$
   $$K_{sp} = 4.00 \times 10^{-15}$$

3. $Be(OH)_2 \rightleftharpoons Be^{2+} + 2OH^-$
   $$K_{sp} = [Be^{2+}][OH^-]^2$$
   $$1.60 \times 10^{-22} = x(2x)^2$$
   $$x = 3.42 \times 10^{-8}M$$

4. $PbI_2 \rightleftharpoons Pb^{2+} + 2I^-$
   $$K_{sp} = [PB^{2+}][I^-]^2$$
   $$K_{sp} = (1.21 \times 10^{-3})(2.42 \times 10^{-3})^2$$
   $$K_{sp} = 7.09 \times 10^{-9}$$

Page 498.

5. $H_2O + H_2O \rightleftharpoons H_3O^+ + OH^-$

$K_w = [H_3O^+][OH^-]$

$10^{-14} = x(6.80 \times 10^{-10})$

$x = 1.47 \times 10^{-5}M$

6. $H_2O + H_2O \rightleftharpoons H_3O^+ + OH^-$

$K_w = [H_3O^+][OH^-]$

$10^{-14} = x(5.21 \times 10^{-3})$

$x = 1.92 \times 10^{-12}M$

Page 501.

7. a. $-\log(1.00 \times 10^{-3}) = 3.00$

b. $-\log(1.00 \times 10^{-6}) = 6.00$

c. $-\log(6.59 \times 10^{-10}) = 9.18$

8. a. antilog$(-8) = 1.00 \times 10^{-8}$

b. antilog$(-4) = 1.00 \times 10^{-4}$

c. antilog$(-7.828) = 1.49 \times 10^{-8}$

d. $-\log(7.01 \times 10^{-6}) = 5.15$

e. $-\log(9.47 \times 10^{-8}) = 7.02$

f. $-\log(6.89 \times 10^{-14}) = 13.2$

d. antilog$(-9.821) = 1.51 \times 10^{-10}$

e. antilog$(-1.355) = 4.42 \times 10^{-2}$

f. antilog$(-3.68) = 2.09 \times 10^{-4}$

Page 503.

9. a. acidic

b. acidic

c. acidic

d. acidic

e. basic

Chapter End Problems

Pages 511-512.

10. $\dfrac{27.3 \text{ cm}^3}{} \left| \dfrac{0.413 \text{ mol HBr}}{1000 \text{ cm}^3} \right| \dfrac{1 \text{ mol LiOH}}{1 \text{ mol HBr}} \left| \dfrac{1000 \text{ cm}^3}{0.196 \text{ mol LiOH}} \right. = 57.5 \text{ cm}^3$

11. $\dfrac{75.0 \text{ cm}^3 \text{ acid}}{95.5 \text{ cm}^3 \text{ base}} \left| \dfrac{0.823 \text{ mol HClO}_4}{1000 \text{ cm}^3 \text{ acid}} \right| \dfrac{1 \text{ mol Ba(OH)}_2}{2 \text{ mol HClO}_4} \left| \dfrac{1000 \text{ cm}^3}{1 \text{ dm}^3} \right. = 0.323M \text{ Ba(OH)}_2$

12. Increase the Cl^- concentration by adding a soluble salt or acid producing Cl^- in solution.

13. 1×10^{-14}

14. These two scales are the reverse of each other.

15. Hydrolysis is the reaction of a salt with water.

16. The anion of the salt reacts with the H^+ of the water leaving OH^- in the solution. Thus, it is basic.

17. The type of solution formed depends on the degree of weakness of the acid and base. Thus, the solution could be acidic, basic, or neutral.

18. A buffer contains an ion in common between the acid or base, and its salt.

19. Rebreathing exhaled air increases the CO_2 concentration in the blood. Thus, the proper pH is restored.

20. $MnS \rightleftharpoons Mn^{2+} + S^{2-}$

$K_{sp} = [Mn^{2+}][S^{2-}]$

$1.40 \times 10^{-15} = 0.1[S^{2-}]$

$[S^{2-}] = 1.40 \times 10^{-14}$

21. $[H_3O^+] = \dfrac{10^{-14}}{[OH^-]} = \dfrac{10^{-14}}{2.77 \times 10^{-10}} = 3.61 \times 10^{-5}$

22. $pOH = -\log[OH^-] = 6.13$

$[OH^-] = 7.41 \times 10^{-7}$

23. $Mg(OH)_2 \rightleftharpoons Mg^{2+} + 2OH^-$

$K_{sp} = [Mg^{2+}][OH^-]^2$

$2[Mg^{2+}] = [OH^-]$

$[Mg^{2+}] = x$

$1.20 \times 10^{-11} = x(2x)^2$

$1.20 \times 10^{-11} = 4x^3$

$x^3 = 3.00 \times 10^{-12}$

$x = 1.44 \times 10^{-4}$

$[OH^-] = 2.88 \times 10^{-4}$

$[H^+] = \dfrac{10 \times 10^{-15}}{2.88 \times 10^{-4}} = 3.47 \times 10^{-11}$

$pH = 10.46$

24. $[OH^-] = 10^{-4}$ $[H^+] = 10^{-10}$

$pH = 10$

25. $K_a = \dfrac{[H_3O^+][CN^-]}{[HCN]}$

$K_a = 4.93 \times 10^{-10}$

$= \dfrac{[x](0.01\cancel{x})}{0.300 - \cancel{x}} \leftarrow \text{neglect}$

$[H_3O^+] = \dfrac{1.48 \times 10^{-10}}{0.01} = 1.48 \times 10^{-8}$

$pH = 7.83$

26. a. neutral

b. basic, $CO_3^{2-} + H_2O \rightarrow HCO_3^- + OH^-$

c. acidic, $Al(H_2O)_6^{3+} + H_2O \rightarrow Al(H_2O)_5(OH)^{2+} + H_3O^+$

d. acidic, $Hg^{2+} + H_2O \rightarrow HgOH^+ + H^+$

e. neutral

27. $HCN + H_2O \rightleftharpoons H_3O^+ + CN^-$

$K_a = \dfrac{[H_3O^+][CN^-]}{[HCN]}$

$4.93 \times 10^{-10} = \dfrac{x(0.15 + x)}{0.01 - x}$

$x = 3.29 \times 10^{-11}$

$pH = 10.48$

28. $NaOH + HCl \rightarrow NaCl + H_2O$

$\dfrac{21.2 \text{ cm}^3 \text{ acid}}{25.0 \text{ cm}^3 \text{ base}} \left| \dfrac{0.0800 \text{ mol HCl}}{1000 \text{ cm}^3 \text{ acid}} \right| \dfrac{1 \text{ mol NaOH}}{1 \text{ mol HCl}}$

$= 0.0678M \text{ NaOH}$

29. $\dfrac{96.2 \text{ cm}^3 \text{ NaOH}}{30.0 \text{ cm}^3 \text{ HCl}} \left| \dfrac{0.765 \text{ mol NaOH}}{1000 \text{ cm}^3 \text{ NaOH}} \right| \dfrac{1 \text{ mol HCl}}{1 \text{ mol NaOH}} \left| \dfrac{1000 \text{ cm}^3}{1 \text{ dm}^3} \right.$

$= 2.20M \text{ HCl}$

30. $2KOH + H_2SO_4 \rightarrow K_2SO_4 + 2H_2O$

$$\frac{40.8 \text{ cm}^3 \text{ H}_2\text{SO}_4}{61.8 \text{ cm}^3 \text{ KOH}} \left| \frac{0.106 \text{ mol H}_2\text{SO}_4}{1000 \text{ cm}^3 \text{ H}_2\text{SO}_4} \right| \frac{2 \text{ mol KOH}}{1 \text{ mol H}_2\text{SO}_4} \left| \frac{1000 \text{ cm}^3}{1 \text{ dm}^3} \right. = 0.140M \text{ KOH}$$

Review

Pages 512-513.

1. $\dfrac{46.6 \text{ g Hg(CN)}_2}{1 \text{ dm}^3 \text{ soln}} \left| \dfrac{1 \text{ mol Hg(CN)}_2}{253 \text{ g Hg(CN)}_2} \right. = 0.184M \text{ Hg(CN)}_2$

2. $\dfrac{0.944 \text{ g K}_3\text{AsO}_4}{10.0 \text{ g H}_2\text{O}} \left| \dfrac{1 \text{ mol K}_3\text{AsO}_4}{256 \text{ g K}_3\text{AsO}_4} \right| \dfrac{1000 \text{ g}}{1 \text{ kg}} = 0.368m \text{ K}_3\text{AsO}_4$

3. $\dfrac{100 \text{ g Rb}_2\text{C}_4\text{H}_4\text{O}_6}{} \left| \dfrac{1 \text{ mol Rb}_2\text{C}_4\text{H}_4\text{O}_6}{319 \text{ g Rb}_2\text{C}_4\text{H}_4\text{O}_6} \right. = 0.313 \text{ mol Rb}_2\text{C}_4\text{H}_4\text{O}_6$ $\dfrac{50.0 \text{ g H}_2\text{O}}{} \left| \dfrac{1 \text{ mol H}_2\text{O}}{18.0 \text{ g H}_2\text{O}} \right. = \dfrac{2.78 \text{ mol H}_2\text{O}}{3.09 \text{ mol soln}}$

$$\frac{0.313}{3.09} = 0.101 \text{ mole fraction Rb}_2\text{C}_4\text{H}_4\text{O}_6$$

4. $\dfrac{39.5 \text{ g C}_6\text{H}_{12}\text{O}_6}{} \left| \dfrac{1 \text{ mol C}_6\text{H}_{12}\text{O}_6}{180 \text{ g C}_6\text{H}_{12}\text{O}_6} \right. = 0.219 \text{ mol C}_6\text{H}_{12}\text{O}_6$

$$\frac{100 \text{ g H}_2\text{O}}{} \left| \frac{1 \text{ mol H}_2\text{O}}{18.0 \text{ g H}_2\text{O}} \right. = \frac{5.55 \text{ mol H}_2\text{O}}{5.77 \text{ mol soln}}$$

$\dfrac{5.55}{5.77} = 0.962$ mole fraction H_2O

v.p. soln = (v.p. solvent) (x)

v.p. soln = (4.2 kPa)(0.962) = 4.03 kPa

5. $\dfrac{42.4 \text{ g C}_6\text{H}_{12}\text{O}_6}{200 \text{ g H}_2\text{O}} \left| \dfrac{1 \text{ mol C}_6\text{H}_{12}\text{O}_6}{180 \text{ g C}_6\text{H}_{12}\text{O}_6} \right| \dfrac{1000 \text{ g}}{1 \text{ kg}}$

$= 1.18m \text{ C}_6\text{H}_{12}\text{O}_6$

$\Delta T_{FP} = m \cdot K_{FP} = (1.18)(1.86°) = 2.19 \text{ C}°$

$\Delta T_{BP} = m \cdot K_{BP} = (1.18)(0.512°) = 0.604 \text{ C}°$

$FP = 0° - 2.19 = -2.19°C$

$BP = 100° + 0.604 = 100.60°C$

6. $m = \dfrac{\Delta T_{FP}}{K_{FP}} = \dfrac{1.83}{1.86} = 0.984m$

mols solute $= (0.984)\left(\dfrac{250}{1000}\right) = 0.246$ $\dfrac{22.2}{0.246} = 90.3 \text{ g/mol}$

7. $\pi = MRT$

$$\pi = \frac{7.10 \text{ g}}{0.500 \text{ dm}^3} \left| \frac{1 \text{ mol}}{1000 \text{ g}} \right| \frac{8.31 \text{ dm}^3 \cdot \text{kPa}}{\text{mol} \cdot \text{K}} \left| 298 \text{ K} \right. = 35.2 \text{ kPa}$$

8. rate $= k[PCl_3][Cl_2]$

9. $K_{eq} = \dfrac{[CO_3^{2-}]}{[HCO_3^-][OH^-]}$

10. $\log K_{eq} = \dfrac{\Delta G}{-2.30RT}$

$= \dfrac{-8170 \text{ J}}{(-2.30)(8.31)(298)}$

$= 1.43$

$K_{eq} = $ antilog of $1.43 = 2.72$

11. acid $-$ LiH

base $-$ BH$_3$

conjugate base $-$ BH$_4^-$

conjugate acid $-$ Li$^+$

12. Tl$^+$ can be classified as either a Lewis acid or base. Since it has a positive charge, it can accept electrons, but it also retains two of its outer level electrons which it can donate.

One More Step

Page 513.

1. See Jensen, William B., "Lewis Acid-Base Theory: Part III Hard and Soft Acid-Base Theory," *Journal of Chemical Education*, Vol. 47 No. 5 (May 1974)

2. $Ac^- + H_2O \rightarrow HAc + OH^-$

$$K_{eq} = \frac{[H_3O^+][Ac^-]}{[HAc]} = \frac{\left(\dfrac{10^{-14}}{[OH^-]}\right)[Ac^-]}{[HAc]}$$

$$1.76 \times 10^{-5} = \frac{\left(\dfrac{10^{-14}}{x}\right)(0.1 - \cancel{x})}{x}$$

neglect

$1.76 \times 10^{-5} x = \dfrac{10^{-15}}{x}$

$1.76 \times 10^{-5} x^2 = 10^{-15}$

$x^2 = \dfrac{10 \times 10^{-16}}{1.76 \times 10^{-5}} = 5.68 \times 10^{-11}$

$= 56.8 \times 10^{-12}$

$x = 7.54 \times 10^{-6}$

$[H^+] = \dfrac{10 \times 10^{-15}}{7.54 \times 10^{-6}}$

$[H^+] = 1.33 \times 10^{-9}$

pH = 8.88

3. $AgCl \rightleftarrows Ag^+ + Cl^-$

$K_{sp} = [Ag^+][Cl^-]$

$1.56 \times 10^{-10} = (1)[Cl^-]$

$[Cl^-] = 1.56 \times 10^{-10}$

$PbCl_2 \rightleftarrows Pb^{2+} + 2Cl^-$

$K_{sp} = [Pb^{2+}][Cl^-]^2$

$1.62 \times 10^{-5} = (1)[Cl^-]^2$

$[Cl^-]^2 = 1.62 \times 10^{-5}$

$[Cl^-] = 4.02 \times 10^{-3}$

$PbCl_2$ will require a higher concentration of Cl^-, so $AgCl$ will precipitate first.

4. From Problem 3, we know that $4.02 \times 10^{-3} = [Cl^-]$ when $PbCl_2$ precipitates.

Therefore, $1.56 \times 10^{-10} = [Ag^+](4.02 \times 10^{-3})$

$[Ag^+] = \dfrac{1.56 \times 10^{-10}}{4.02 \times 10^{-3}}$

$[Ag^+] = 3.88 \times 10^{-8}M$

5. methyl violet

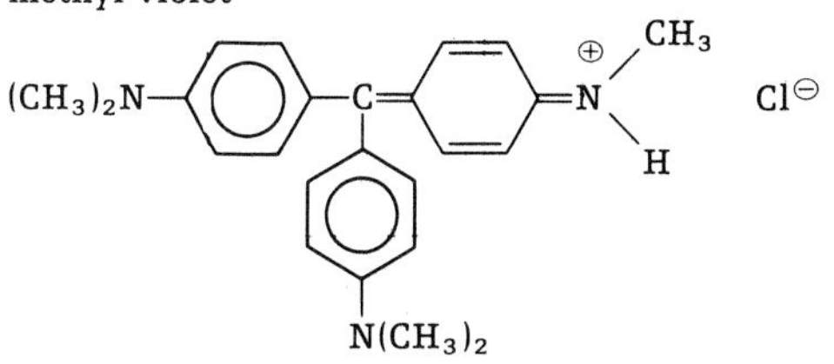

$(CH_3)_2N$—[ring]—C=[ring]=$\overset{\oplus}{N}$—CH_3 (with CH_3 and H), $Cl^{\ominus}$

N(CH_3)_2

acid

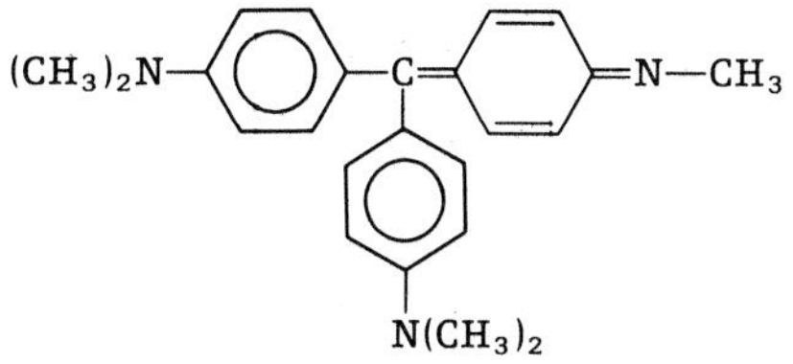

$(CH_3)_2N$—[ring]—C=[ring]=N—CH_3

N(CH_3)_2

base

cresol red

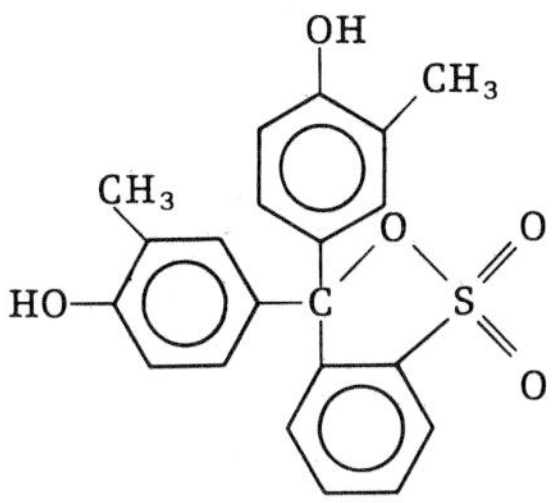

OH
CH_3
CH_3
HO
C
O
S
O
O

acid

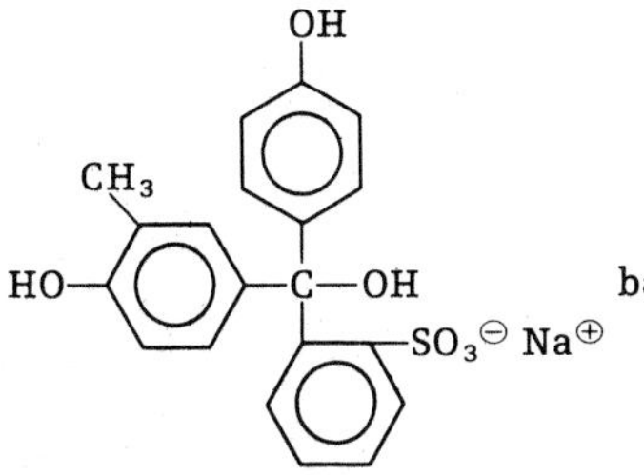

OH
CH_3
HO
C—OH
SO_3^{\ominus} Na^{\oplus}

base

4-nitrophenol

OH
NO_2

acid

O
NO_2^{\ominus}

base

methyl orange

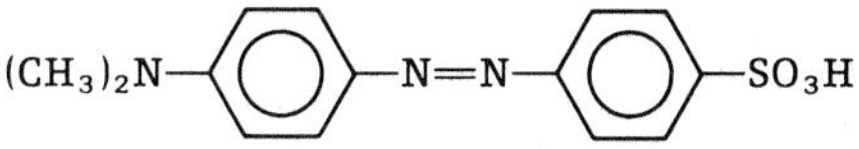

$(CH_3)_2N$—[ring]—N=N—[ring]—SO_3H

acid

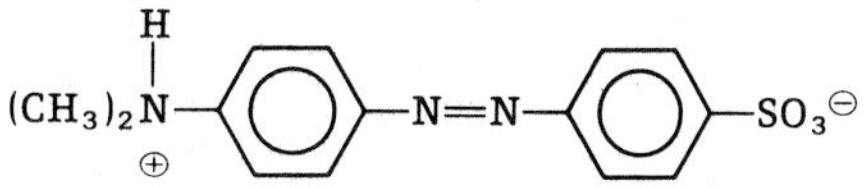

$(CH_3)_2\overset{H}{\underset{\oplus}{N}}$—[ring]—N=N—[ring]—$SO_3^{\ominus}$

base

bromothymol blue

CH_3
CH_3—CH
OH
Br
Br
CH_3
CH_3
OH
C
O
S
O
O
CH_3—CH
CH_3

acid

brilliant yellow

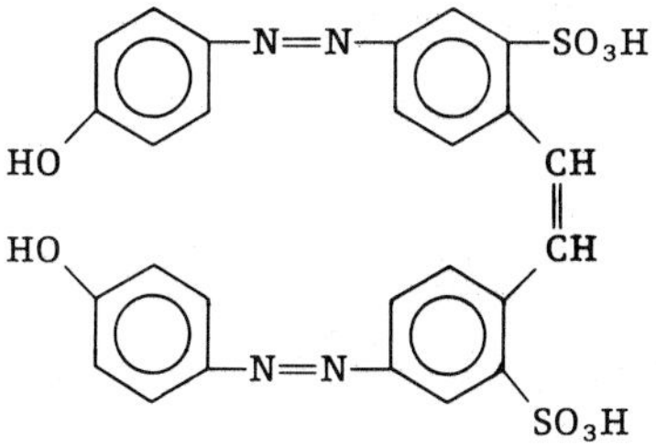

[ring]—N=N—[ring]—SO_3H
HO
HO
CH
CH
[ring]—N=N—[ring]
SO_3H

acid

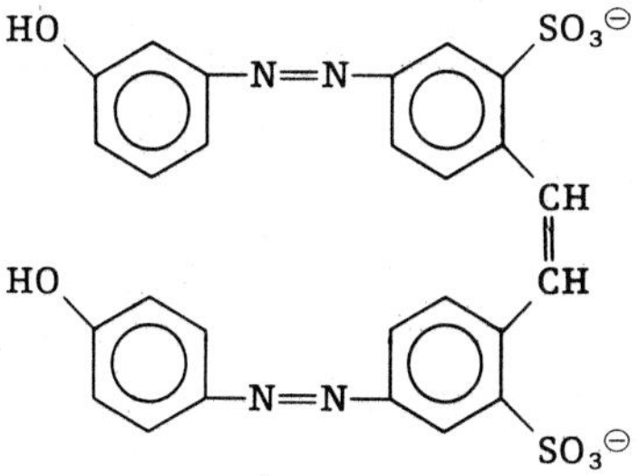

HO—[ring]—N=N—[ring]—SO_3^{\ominus}
CH
CH
HO—[ring]—N=N—[ring]
SO_3^{\ominus}

base

alizarin yellow R

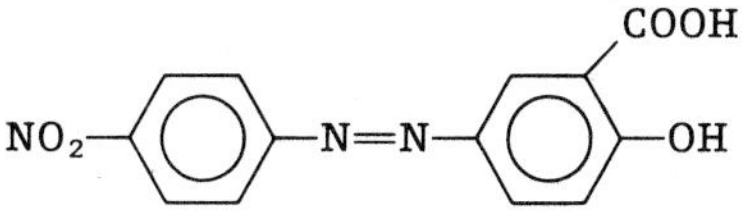

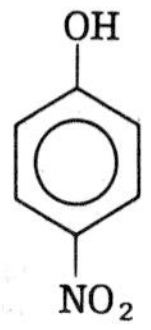

NO_2—[ring]—N=N—[ring]
COOH
OH

acid

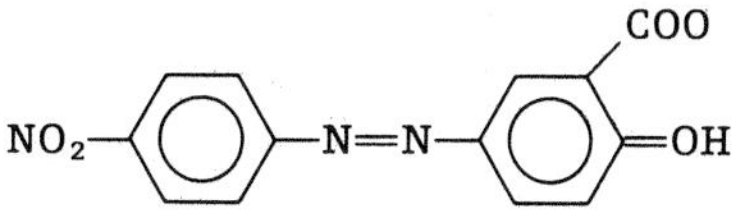

NO_2—[ring]—N=N—[ring]
COO
OH

base

CH_3
CH_3—CH
OH
Br
Br
CH_3
HO
CH_3
C—OH
CH_3—CH
SO_3^{\ominus} Na^{\oplus}
CH_3

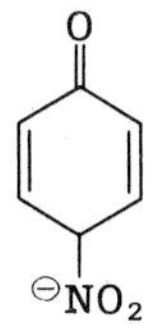

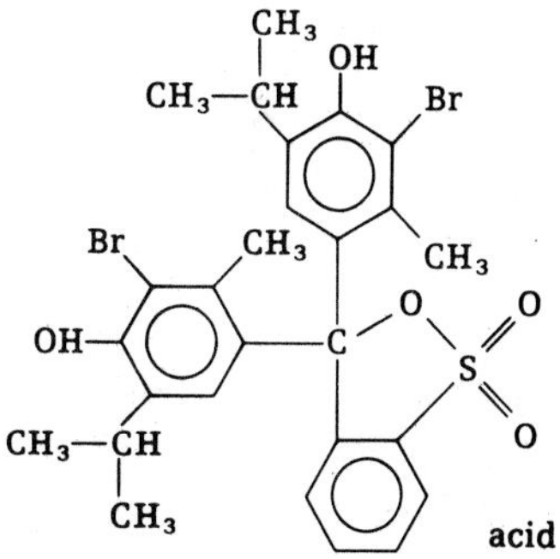

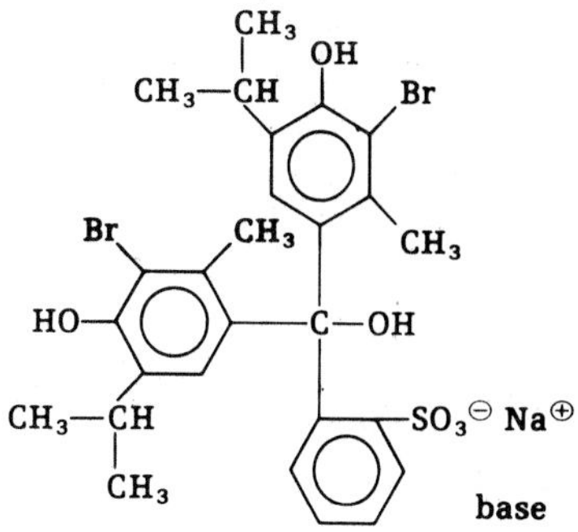

base

methyl red

$(CH_3)_2N$—⟨○⟩—N=N—⟨○⟩ with COOH

acid

$(CH_3)_2\overset{\oplus}{N}H$—⟨○⟩—N=N—⟨○⟩ with $COO^{\ominus}$

base

orange IV

HSO_3—⟨○⟩—N=N—⟨○⟩—NH—⟨○⟩

acid

$^{\ominus}O_3S$—⟨○⟩—N=N—⟨○⟩—$\overset{\oplus}{N}H_2$—⟨○⟩

base

OXIDATION—REDUCTION   **26**

An Overview

Chapter 26 presents electron transfer reactions. The chapter begins with the definitions of oxidation and reduction. This approach allows students to apply these definitions when assigning oxidation numbers. Balancing redox reactions is demonstrated using the half reaction method. The method demands that we conserve mass, electrons, and charge. We should emphasize that our use of this method does not imply that we really believe electronic charges are truly described by the concept. It is important to point out to students that the oxidation numbers used in balancing redox equations are arbitrary values obtained by using arbitrary rules. Students should be warned against thinking that the oxidation number represents the real ion charge in the molecule.

Demonstration Information

Students should respond that $CuCl_2(aq)$ cannot be shipped in an aluminum tank car. Later in Chapter 27, they will learn to predict whether a reaction will occur. At that time, you can refer to this demonstration and ask students if they would ship $Cl^-(aq)$ in an iron tank car (no); H_2O_2 in a nickel tank car (no); or $OH^-(aq)$ in a lead tank car (yes).

Performance Objectives

Goal: Students will gain an understanding of oxidation-reduction reactions and develop skill in balancing the equations which represent them.

Objectives: Upon completion of the reading and problems, and when asked to demonstrate their understanding either orally or on a written test, students will

26:1-3	K/P	define and give examples of oxidation, reduction, and oxidizing and reducing agents.
26:4-6	P	assign oxidation numbers to elements in common compounds.
26:7	K/P	identify reactions as redox or nonredox.
26:8-12	P/S	balance equations for oxidation-reduction reactions.
	A	voluntarily complete one or more of the One More Step activities.
	A	read unassigned literature related to the Chapter.

Teaching Techniques

Section 26:3

To help students with the concept that an oxidizing agent is itself reduced, you can discuss the action of a bleaching agent on clothing in a washing machine. A bleaching agent, which causes whitening to occur, does not itself become whiter. An oxidizing agent is not oxidized.

Section 26:6

Remind students that oxidation numbers do not necessarily represent the number of electrons gained or lost. They are arbitrary numbers assigned using arbitrary rules that enable us to make predictions.

Section 26:7

Corrosion—Obtain 2 petri dishes. Clean 4 iron nails with CCl_4 to remove any oil. Clean the nails with emery cloth. Cut a thin strip of zinc and obtain a clean piece of copper wire. Prepare 200 cm³ of plain agar-agar solution (2.0 g/200 cm³ boiling water). After the agar has dissolved add 10 drops of $0.1M$ $K_3Fe(CN)_6$ and 5 drops of phenolphthalein solution. While the agar cools, place a bent nail and a straight nail in one petri dish. In a second petri dish, place two nails, one wrapped with Cu, the other with Zn. Keep the nails separated and slowly pour the agar solution into the dishes to cover the metals. Observe the color changes, pink is reduction (OH^-) and blue is oxidation. Discuss ways to prevent the corrosion of metals.

Section 26:8

The oxidation number method of balancing redox equations is not presented in the text for simplicity. Students become confused in learning two methods to solve the same problem. We feel it is more valuable for students to be proficient using one technique at this level. The techniques taught in this chapter approximate more closely what actually happens in solvated reactions. This presentation results in maximum learning for minimum investment of student time and effort.

Chemical Technology

Students can do additional research into the career options in the field of metallurgy. It is important to emphasize to students that most metals are not found in pure form. Students may not have considered this point since they generally encounter metals in the pure state after refining.

Problem Solutions

Page 522.

1. **a.** 4+   **e.** 4+   **h.** 2−
   b. 7+   **f.** 6+   **i.** 2+
   c. 5+   **g.** 6+   **j.** 0
   d. 4+

Page 523.

2. no

3. yes
   H is oxidized and H_2 is the reducing agent.
   N is reduced and N_2 is the oxidizing agent.

4. yes
   C is oxidized and the reducing agent
   H is reduced
   H_2O is oxidizing agent

5. no

6. no

7. no

8. yes
   O is reduced
   S is oxidized
   H_2O_2 is oxidizing agent
   PbS is reducing agent

9. no

10. yes
    N is reduced
    P is oxidized
    HNO_3 is oxidizing agent
    H_3PO_3 is reducing agent

11. yes
    N is reduced
    I is oxidized
    HNO_3 is oxidizing agent
    I_2 is the reducing agent

12. no

13. yes
    N is reduced
    Fe^{2+} is oxidized and the reducing agent
    NO_3^- is oxidizing agent

14. yes
    Br_2 is reduced and the oxidizing agent
    Fe^{2+} is oxidized
    $FeBr_2$ is reducing agent

15. yes
    I^- is reduced
    S is oxidized
    $S_2O_3^{2-}$ is reducing agent
    I_2 is the oxidizing agent

16. yes
    Mn is reduced
    O is oxidized
    MnO_4^- is oxidizing agent
    H_2O_2 is reducing agent

Page 529.

17. $(8H^+ + 5e^- + MnO_4^- \rightarrow Mn^{2+} + 4H_2O) \times 2$
    $(H_2O + H_2SO_3 \rightarrow HSO_4^- + 2e^- + 3H^+) \times 5$
    $$\frac{16H^+ + 10e^- + 2MnO_4^- \rightarrow 2Mn^{2+} + 8H_2O}{5H_2O + 5H_2SO_3 \rightarrow 5HSO_4^- + 10e^- + 15H^+}$$
    $H^+ + 2MnO_4^- + 5H_2SO_3 \rightarrow 2Mn^{2+} + 5HSO_4^- + 3H_2O$

18. $(14H^+ + 6e^- + Cr_2O_7^{2-} \rightarrow 2Cr^{3+} + 7H_2O)$
    $(2I^- \rightarrow I_2 + 2e^-) \times 3$
    $$\frac{14H^+ + 6e^- + Cr_2O_7^{2-} \rightarrow 2Cr^{3+} + 7H_2O}{6I^- \rightarrow 3I_2 + 6e^-}$$
    $Cr_2O_7^{2-} + 14H^+ + 6I^- \rightarrow 2Cr^{3+} + 3I_2 + 7H_2O$

19. $(5OH^- + NH_3 \rightarrow NO + 5e^- + 4H_2O) \times 4$
    $4H_2O + 4e^- + O_2 \rightarrow 2H_2O + 4OH^-$
    Simplifying the 2nd equation gives:
    $2H_2O + 4e^- + O_2 \rightarrow 4OH^-$
    $(2H_2O + 4e^- + O_2 \rightarrow 4OH^-) \times 5$
    $$\frac{20OH^- + 4NH_3 \rightarrow 4NO + 20e^- + 16H_2O}{10H_2O + 20e^- + 5O_2 \rightarrow 20OH^-}$$
    $4NH_3 + 5O_2 \rightarrow 4NO + 6H_2O$

20. $(5H_2O + As_2O_3 \rightarrow 2H_3AsO_4 + 4e^- + 4H^+) \times 3$
$(4H^+ + 3e^- + NO_3^- \rightarrow NO + 2H_2O) \times 4$

$$15H_2O + 3As_2O_3 \rightarrow 6H_3AsO_4 + 12e^- + 12H^+$$
$$16H^+ + 12e^- + 4NO_3^- \rightarrow 4NO + 8H_2O$$
$$\overline{3As_2O_3 + 4H^+ + 4NO_3^- + 7H_2O \rightarrow 6H_3AsO_4 + 4NO}$$

21. $(2e^- + I_2 \rightarrow 2I^-) \times 1$
$(H_2O + H_2SO_3 \rightarrow HSO_4^- + 2e^- + 3H^+) \times 1$
$$\overline{I_2 + H_2SO_3 + H_2O \rightarrow 2I^- + HSO_4^- + 3H^+}$$

22. $(8H^+ + 8e^- + H_3AsO_4 \rightarrow AsH_3 + 4H_2O) \times 1$
$(Zn \rightarrow Zn^{2+} + 2e^-) \times 4$
$$8H^+ + 8e^- + H_3AsO_4 \rightarrow AsH_3 + 4H_2O$$
$$4Zn \rightarrow 4Zn^{2+} + 8e^-$$
$$\overline{H_3AsO_4 + 8H^+ + 4Zn \rightarrow AsH_3 + 4H_2O + 4Zn^{2+}}$$

23. $(MnO_4^{2-} \rightarrow MnO_4^- + e^-) \times 2$
$(4H^+ + 2e^- + MnO_4^{2-} \rightarrow MnO_2 + 2H_2O) \times 1$
$$2MnO_4^{2-} \rightarrow 2MnO_4^- + 2e^-$$
$$\overline{3MnO_4^{2-} + 4H^+ \rightarrow 2MnO_4^- + MnO_2 + 2H_2O}$$

24. $(8H^+ + 5e^- + MnO_4^- \rightarrow Mn^{2+} + 4H_2O) \times 2$
$(2H_2O + SO_2 \rightarrow SO_4^{2-} + 2e^- + 4H^+) \times 5$
$$16H^+ + 10e^- + 2MnO_4^- \rightarrow 2Mn^{2+} + 8H_2O$$
$$10H_2O + 5SO_2 \rightarrow 5SO_4^{2-} + 10e^- + 20H^+$$
$$\overline{2MnO_4^- + 5SO_2 + 2H_2O \rightarrow 2Mn^{2+} + 5SO_4^{2-} + 4H^+}$$

25. $e^- + NO_2 \rightarrow NO_2^-$
$$2OH^- + NO_2 \rightarrow NO_3^- + e^- + H_2O$$
$$\overline{2NO_2 + 2OH^- \rightarrow NO_2^- + NO_3^- + H_2O}$$

26. $(4Cl^- + HgS \rightarrow S + 2e^- + HgCl_4^{2-}) \times 3$
$(4H^+ + 3e^- + NO_3^- \rightarrow NO + 2H_2O) \times 2$
$$12Cl^- + 3HgS \rightarrow 3S + 6e^- + 3HgCl_4^{2-}$$
$$8H^+ + 6e^- + 2NO_3^- \rightarrow 2NO + 4H_2O$$
$$\overline{8H^+ + 3HgS + 12Cl^- + 2NO_3^- \rightarrow 3HgCl_4^{2-} + 3S + 2NO + 4H_2O}$$

Chapter End Problems

Page 532.

27. $(Cu \rightarrow Cu^{2+} + 2e^-) \times 3$
$(4H^+ + 3e^- + NO_3^- \rightarrow NO + 2H_2O) \times 2$
$$3Cu \rightarrow 3Cu^{2+} + 6e^-$$
$$8H^+ + 6e^- + 2NO_3^- \rightarrow 2NO + 4H_2O$$
$$\overline{3Cu + 8H^+ + 2NO_3^- \rightarrow 3Cu^{2+} + 2NO + 4H_2O}$$

28. $3Fe^{2+} \rightarrow 3Fe^{3+} + 3e^-$
$$4H^+ + 3e^- + NO_3^- \rightarrow NO + 2H_2O$$
$$\overline{3Fe^{2+} + 4H^+ + NO_3^- \rightarrow 3Fe^{3+} + NO + 2H_2O}$$

29. $(Zn \rightarrow Zn^{2+} + 2e^-) \times 1$
$(2H^+ + e^- + NO_3^- \rightarrow NO_2 + H_2O) \times 2$
$$Zn \rightarrow Zn^{2+} + 2e^-$$
$$4H^+ + 2e^- + 2NO_3^- \rightarrow 2NO_2 + 2H_2O$$
$$\overline{Zn + 4H^+ + 2NO_3^- \rightarrow Zn^{2+} + 2NO_2 + 2H_2O}$$

30. $(Sb \rightarrow Sb^{3+} + 3e^-) \times 2$
$(3H^+ + 2e^- + HSO_4^- \rightarrow SO_2 + 2H_2O) \times 3$
$$2Sb \rightarrow 2Sb^{3+} + 6e^-$$
$$9H^+ + 6e^- + 3HSO_4^- \rightarrow 3SO_2 + 6H_2O$$
$$\overline{2Sb + 9H^+ + 3HSO_4^- \rightarrow 2Sb^{3+} + 3SO_2 + 6H_2O}$$

31. $(H_2S \rightarrow S + 2e^- + 2H^+) \times 2$
$4H^+ + 4e^- + H_2SO_3 \rightarrow S + 3H_2O$
$$2H_2S \rightarrow 2S + 4e^- + 4H^+$$
$$\overline{H_2SO_3 + 2H_2S \rightarrow 3S + 3H_2O}$$

32. $(H_2O + Cl^- \rightarrow HClO + 2e^- + H^+) \times 3$
$(4H^+ + 3e^- + NO_3^- \rightarrow NO + 2H_2O) \times 2$
$$3H_2O + 3Cl^- \rightarrow 3HClO + 6e^- + 3H^+$$
$$8H^+ + 6e^- + 2NO_3^- \rightarrow 2NO + 4H_2O$$
$$\overline{3Cl^- + 5H^+ + 2NO_3^- \rightarrow 3HClO + 2NO + H_2O}$$

33. $(Cl^- + Ag \rightarrow AgCl + e^-) \times 6$
$6H^+ + 6e^- + ClO_3^- \rightarrow Cl^- + 3H_2O$
$(6Cl^- + 6Ag \rightarrow 6AgCl + 6e^-$
$$\overline{6H^+ + ClO_3^- + 5Cl^- + 6Ag \rightarrow 3H_2O + 6AgCl}$$

34. $(3I^- \rightarrow I_3^- + 2e^-) \times 2$
$$6I^- \rightarrow 2I_3^- + 4e^-$$
$$4H^+ + 4e^- + O_2 \rightarrow 2H_2O$$
$$\overline{6I^- + 4H^+ + O_2 \rightarrow 2I_3^- + 2H_2O}$$

35. $(4H^+ + 3e^- + NO_3^- \rightarrow NO + 2H_2O) \times 2$
$(2Hg + HSO_4^- \rightarrow H^+ + Hg_2SO_4 + 2e^-) \times 3$
$$8H^+ + 6e^- + 2NO_3^- \rightarrow 2NO + 4H_2O$$
$$3HSO_4^- + 6Hg \rightarrow 3Hg_2SO_4 + 6e^- + 3H^+$$
$$\overline{3HSO_4^- + 5H^+ + 2NO_3^- + 6Hg \rightarrow 2NO + 4H_2O + 3Hg_2SO_4}$$

36. $(H_2O + CO \rightarrow CO_2 + 2e^- + 2H^+) \times 5$
$10H^+ + 10e^- + I_2O_5 \rightarrow I_2 + 5H_2O$
$$5H_2O + 5CO \rightarrow 5CO_2 + 10e^- + 10H^+$$
$$\overline{I_2O_5 + 5CO \rightarrow I_2 + 5CO_2}$$

37. Oxidation is a loss of electrons; reduction is a gain of electrons.

38. $K_2SO_3 \rightarrow K_2SO_4$ lose $2e^-$ per atom S
$KMnO_4 \rightarrow MnO_2$ gain $3e^-$ per atom Mn
therefore, need 3 moles K_2SO_3 for 2 moles $KMnO_4$

$$\frac{7.90 \text{ g } KMnO_4}{} \left| \frac{1 \text{ mol } KMnO_4}{158 \text{ g } KMnO_4} \right| \frac{3 \text{ mol } K_2SO_3}{2 \text{ mol } KMnO_4} \left| \frac{158 \text{ g } K_2SO_3}{1 \text{ mol } K_2SO_3} \right. = 11.9 \text{ g } K_2SO_3$$

39. $KClO_3 \rightarrow Cl^-$ gain $6e^-$ per atom Cl
$Cr_2O_3 \rightarrow K_2CrO_4$ lose $3e^-$ per atom Cr; Cr_2O_3 gives up $6e^-$
Therefore, need one mole Cr_2O_3 for each mole $KClO_3$

$$\frac{20.0 \text{ cm}^3 \ Cr_2O_3}{} \left| \frac{0.1 \text{ mol } Cr_2O_3}{1000 \text{ cm}^3 \ Cr_2O_3} \right| \frac{1 \text{ mol } KClO_3}{1 \text{ mol } Cr_2O_3} \left| \frac{1000 \text{ cm}^3 \ KClO_3}{0.2 \text{ mol } KClO_3} \right. = 10.0 \text{ cm}^3 \ KClO_3$$

Review

Pages 532-533.

1. $Cd_3(PO_4)_2 \rightleftarrows 3Cd^{2+} + 2PO_4^{3-}$
$K_{sp} = [Cd^{2+}]^3[PO_4^{3-}]^2$
Let $[PO_4^{3-}] = 2x$, then $[Cd^{2+}] = 3x$
$2.50 \times 10^{-33} = (3x)^3(2x)^2 = (27x^3)(4x^2) = 108x^5$
$x^5 = 2.31 \times 10^{-35}$
$x = 1.18 \times 10^{-7}$
$[Cd^{2+}] = 3x = 3.54 \times 10^{-7}$

2. increases the rate

3. Slowest step is the rate determining step.

4. $Sr(OH)_2$, strontium hydroxide

5. $H_2PO_4^- + H^+ \rightarrow H_3PO_4$
$CH_3CH_2COOH + H_2O \rightleftarrows H_3O^+ + CH_3CH_2COO^-$

6. $K_a = \dfrac{[H_3O^+][CH_3CH_2COO^-]}{[CH_3CH_2COOH]}$

$K_a = \dfrac{(1.16 \times 10^{-3})(1.16 \times 10^{-3})}{(0.100 - 1.16 \times 10^{-3})} = 1.36 \times 10^{-5} M$

7. $\dfrac{1.16 \times 10^{-3}}{0.1} \times 100 = 1.16\%$

8. $HF + H_2O \rightleftarrows H_3O^+ + F^-$
$K_a = \dfrac{[H_3O^+][F^-]}{[HF]}$

$3.53 \times 10^{-4} = \dfrac{x(0.01 + x)}{0.1 - x}$

$x = 3.53 \times 10^{-3} M$ (by quadratic 2.70×10^{-3})

9. $K_{eq} = \dfrac{[H^+][CHCl_2COO^-]}{[CHCl_2COOH]}$

$K_{eq} = \dfrac{(0.200)(0.200)}{1.20}$
$= 0.0333$ or 3.33×10^{-2}

10. $\dfrac{0.200 \times 100}{1.20 + 0.200} = \dfrac{0.200}{1.40} \left| \dfrac{100}{1} \right. = 14.3\%$

11. $0.0333 = \dfrac{x(0.400)}{1.40 - x}$
$0.0466 - 0.0333x = 0.400x$
$0.433x = 0.0466$
$x = 0.108$
$1.40 - x = 1.29 M$

One More Step

Page 533.

1. a. Ba_3N_2
  b. CrO_3
  c. Ca_3P_2
  d. SrH_2
  e. Fr_4C
  f. Li_2O
  g. Fe_2S_3
  h. ScF_3
  i. $TiCl_4$

2. all the O atoms are $2-$
the central S is $5+$
the peripheral S is $1-$
The ion contains 2 atoms of the same element (S) in different oxidation states.

3. $3-$ NH_3 ammonia
  $2-$ N_2H_4 hydrazine
  $1-$ NH_2OH hydroxylamine
  0 N_2 the free element
  $1+$ N_2O nitrogen (I) oxide
  $2+$ NO nitrogen (II) oxide
  $3+$ N_2O_3 nitrogen (III) oxide
  $4+$ NO_2 nitrogen (IV) oxide
  $5+$ N_2O_5 nitrogen (V) oxide

4. Black; (O) $= 2-$, one Fe $= 2+$, two Fe $= 3+$; magnetic

5. The ore is crushed, dried, and dissolved in sulfuric acid. Iron (the principal impurity) is reduced to Fe^{2+} and crystallized out as the sulfate. The solution is filtered, concentrated by vacuum evaporation, and boiled to precipitate the TiO_2. The TiO_2 mixed with coke (C) is exposed to Cl_2 to convert the titanium to $TiCl_4$. The $TiCl_4$ is reduced to the metal by Mg or Na in an inert atmosphere. The metallurgy of most common metals may be found in encyclopedias, chemical engineering texts, or industrial chemistry texts.

ELECTROCHEMISTRY

27

An Overview

Chapter 27 introduces the interaction of electricity and chemical species. The chapter uses the concepts presented in Chapters 25 and 26 to develop an understanding of electrochemistry and its applications. Discuss with your classes the differences between experimental fact, model, and convention. In a voltaic cell, electrons flow from the negative pole to the positive pole; this statement is fact. We describe the chemical process that produces the electrons using half-reactions for each electrode; this description is our model. We name the oxidation electrode the anode; this labeling is convention. Definitions and vocabulary are developed first for students. Then, the concepts are applied to practical situations such as electrolysis and voltaic cells. Students should learn to use the table of standard reduction potentials to predict the products of a chemical reaction. Section 27:11 shows students that predictions made from the table without considering other factors may be wrong. The quantitative aspects of electrochemistry are practical and relevant.

Demonstration Information

Zn-Cu cell—In a 250 cm³ beaker, place 100 cm³ of $0.5M$ $Cu(NO_3)_2$ solution. In another 250 cm³ beaker, place 100 cm³ of $0.5M$ $Zn(NO_3)_2$ solution. Fill a U-tube with a $0.5M$ $NaNO_3$ solution, plugging both ends with cotton. Place a strip of Zn metal in the $Zn(NO_3)_2$ solution and Cu metal in the $Cu(NO_3)_2$ solution. Connect the Zn (anode) and Cu (cathode) electrodes to the terminals of a vacuum tube voltmeter. Invert the U-tube and connect the two beakers, completing the internal circuit. A voltage should register on the meter. Use this demonstration to introduce the vocabulary in Chapter 27.

Performance Objectives

Goal: Students will gain an understanding of the relationship among electrolytes, energy, and electron changes in electrochemical reactions.

Objectives: Upon completion of the reading and problems, and when asked to demonstrate their understanding orally or on a written test, students will

27:1-2	K	explain similarities and differences in electronic and electrolytic conduction.
27:3-4	P/K/S	write equations for the reactions occurring at the cathode and anode in electrolytic conduction.
27:5-6	K	explain the process of obtaining electricity from a chemical voltaic cell.
27:7-10	P	use redox potentials to predict electrolysis products and the electric potential of a cell.
27:11	K	describe the effect of nonstandard conditions on cell voltage.
27:12-13	K	define the relationship of pH and free energy to potential using modified Nernst equations.
27:14-15	P/S	solve simple problems dealing with electroanalyses.
	A	voluntarily complete one or more of the One More Step activities.
	A	read unassigned literature related to the chapter.

Teaching Techniques

Section 27:4

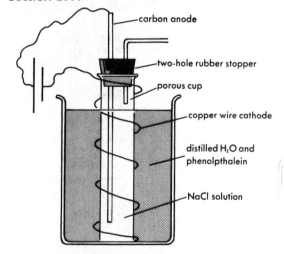

carbon anode

two-hole rubber stopper

porous cup

copper wire cathode

distilled H_2O and phenolphthalein

NaCl solution

Electrolysis of NaCl—This demonstration is a simulation of the industrial process for the preparation of sodium hydroxide, chlorine, and hydrogen. Fill a porous cup three-quarters full of sodium chloride solution. Insert a carbon rod, supported by a two-hole rubber stopper, into the solution in the porous cup. This rod serves as the anode. Wrap a copper wire around the porous cup to serve as the cathode. Place the porous cup in a 250 cm³ beaker half-full of water to which some phenolphthalein has been added. Connect the electrodes to a 4½ volt battery or power supply and note all changes that occur.

Section 27:5

A diagram of a voltaic cell can be duplicated and distributed to students to assist them in taking notes as you cover the electrochemical cell. They can label the anode (oxidation) and cathode (reduction). The direction of electron flow can be charted. The voltage can be calculated and written by the meter. Ion migration can be diagrammed and half reactions at the electrodes written and balanced. The oxidizing agent can be identified. The diagram needs to be large enough for students to draw and write information in the proper location.

Section 27:8

Table 27-1 conforms to IUPAC conventions in that it is a reduction table. The voltage becomes more positive as you go from top to bottom of the table. This convention may be unfamiliar to you, but it will not be difficult for your students since it is their first exposure to it.

Section 27:14

Plating Cu metal—The apparatus shown in the diagram can be used in the electrolysis of a variety of solutions. The electrodes are ordinary pencils with the wood covers peeled back about 1 cm at each end. The products of the reaction can be identified visually and by smell. The odor of chlorine is retained by the pencil for a short time. After copper has plated on one of the electrodes,

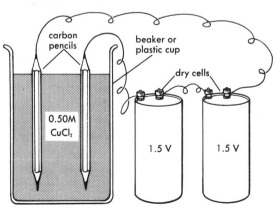

disconnect the power supply and measure the voltage between the electrodes. Students will now be able to observe an electrochemical cell. Short out the electrodes and watch the cell reach equilibrium. Reverse the polarity of the cell to show that the copper leaves one electrode and plates on the other.

Chemical Technology

This feature illustrates the practical application of a knowledge of electrochemistry. Have students do additional research concerning electroplating for protective and ornamental purposes (jewelry, silverplated objects).

Problem Solutions

Page 548.

1. **a.** $Zn \rightarrow Zn^{2+}$ 0.76 V, $Fe^{2+} \rightarrow Fe$ -0.44 V,
   sum = 0.32 V
   b. $Mn \rightarrow Mn^{2+}$ 1.18 V, $Br_2 \rightarrow Br^-$ 1.07 V,
   sum = 2.25 V
   c. $H_2C_2O_4 \rightarrow CO_2$ 0.49 V, $MnO_4^- \rightarrow Mn^{2+}$ 1.51 V,
   sum = 2.00 V
   d. $Ni \rightarrow Ni^{2+}$ 0.25 V, $Hg_2^{2+} \rightarrow Hg$ 0.79 V,
   sum = 1.04 V
   e. $Cu \rightarrow Cu^{2+}$ -0.34 V, $Ag^+ \rightarrow Ag$ 0.80 V,
   sum = 0.46 V
   f. $Pb \rightarrow Pb^{2+}$ $+0.13$ V, $Cl_2 \rightarrow Cl^-$ 1.36 V,
   sum = 1.49 V

2. **a.** H_2 and O_2—hydrogen reduction requires less energy than sodium, sulfate cannot be oxidized
   b. Cu and O_2—copper reduction requires less energy than hydrogen, oxygen oxidation requires less energy than chlorine
   c. Co and O_2—cobalt reduction requires less energy than hydrogen, oxygen oxidation requires less energy than fluorine
   d. Pb and O_2—lead reduction requires less energy than hydrogen, nitrate cannot be oxidized
   e. H_2 and O_2—hydrogen reduction requires less energy than lithium, oxygen oxidation requires less energy than bromine
   f. H_2 and Cl_2—hydrogen reduction requires less energy than sodium, chloride oxidation requires less energy than oxygen.

Page 552.

3. $Pb + Sn^{4+} \rightarrow Pb^{2+} + Sn^{2+}$
$$E = E^\circ - \frac{0.0592}{n} \log K = E^\circ - \frac{0.0592}{n} \log \frac{[Pb^{2+}][Sn^{2+}]}{[Sn^{4+}]}$$
$$E = 0.28 - \frac{0.0592}{2} \log \frac{(0.100)(1.00)}{(0.150)} = 0.285 \text{ V}$$

4. $Ni + Cu^{2+} \rightarrow Ni^{2+} + Cu$
$$E = E^\circ - \frac{0.0592}{n} \log K = E^\circ - \frac{0.0592}{n} \log \frac{[Ni^{2+}]}{[Cu^{2+}]}$$
$$E = 0.59 - \frac{0.0592}{2} \log \frac{(1.00)}{(0.100)} = 0.531 \text{ V}$$

5. $Fe + 2Ag^+ \rightarrow Fe^{2+} + 2Ag$

$$E = E^\circ - \frac{1.98 \times 10^{-4} T}{n} \log K = E^\circ - \frac{1.98 \times 10^{-4} T}{n} \log \frac{[Fe^{2+}]}{[Ag^+]^2}$$

$$E = 1.24 - \frac{(1.98 \times 10^{-4})(291)}{2} \log \frac{(0.152)}{(0.120)^2} = 1.21 \text{ V}$$

Page 553.

6. $E^\circ = 1.46$ V
$\Delta G = -nFE^\circ = (-2)(96\ 500)(1.46) = -282$ kJ

7. $E^\circ = 1.68$ V
$\Delta G = -nFE^\circ = (-2)(96\ 500)(1.68) = -324$ kJ

Page 555.

8. $Ag^+(aq) + e^- \rightarrow Ag(c)$

1.00 A̶	9650 s̶	1 mol e̶⁻	1 mol Ag̶	108 g Ag	
		96 500 A̶·s̶	1 mol e̶⁻	1 mol Ag̶	= 10.8 g Ag

9. $Ag^+(aq) + e^- \rightarrow Ag(c)$

5.00 A̶	10.0 min̶	60 s̶	1 mol e̶⁻	1 mol Ag̶	108 g Ag	
		1 min̶	96 500 A̶·s̶	1 mol e̶⁻	1 mol Ag̶	= 3.36 g Ag

10. $Cu^{2+}(aq) + 2e^- \rightarrow Cu(c)$

2.00 mol Cu̶	2 mol e̶⁻	96 500 A·s̶	1 min̶	
3.00 min̶	1 mol Cu̶	1 mol e̶⁻	60 s̶	= 2140 A

11. $2Cl^-(aq) \rightarrow Cl_2(g) + 2e^-$

1.00 mol Cl̶₂	2 mol e̶⁻	96 500 A̶·s	
5.00 A̶	1 mol Cl̶₂	1 mol e̶⁻	= 3.86 × 10⁴ s = 643 min = 10.7 h

12. $Ca^{2+}(aq) + 2e^- \rightarrow Ca(c)$

0.400 g Ca̶	1 mol Ca̶	2 mol e̶⁻	96 500 A̶·s	1 min	
10.0 A̶	40.1 g Ca̶	1 mol Ca̶	1 mol e̶⁻	60 s̶	= 3.21 min

Page 556.

13. new mass 28.273 g
  original mass 26.203 g
   mass copper   2.070 g

$$\% \text{ copper} = \frac{2.07}{2.36} \times 100 = 87.7\%$$

Chapter End Problems

Pages 559-560.

14. a, e, and f will proceed spontaneously
b, c, and d do not proceed spontaneously

15. The anode is the site of oxidation and the cathode is the site of reduction.

16. If an insulator develops a high enough electric potential to break down its electronic structure, it can be made to conduct.

17. The structure of an ionic solid is such that the ions cannot migrate. Thus, they are "locked" in the crystal lattice.

18. Electrolysis involves a chemical change. Electrolytic conduction is a physical change.

19. The outer electrons of the active metal are held less tightly.

20. **a.** Fe   **c.** Zn
b. Ca   **d.** Cu

21. **a.** Ca^{2+} **c.** Cl_2
b. Hg_2^{2+} **d.** Cu^+

22. Electronic conduction consists of the movement of electrons through a conductor, electrolytic conduction consists of the migration of ions through a solution or an ionic melt.

23. $Al(c) \rightarrow Al^{3+} + 3e^-$
$3Ag^+ + 3e^- \rightarrow 3Ag(c)$
$Al + 3Ag^+ \rightarrow Al^{3+} + 3Ag$
1.66 V   (Al)
0.80 V   (Ag)
2.46 V

24. cathode: $2H_2O + 2e^- \rightarrow 2OH^- + H_2$
anode: $2Cl^- \rightarrow Cl_2 + 2e^-$

25. $(2e^- + 2H_2O \rightarrow H_2 + 2OH^-) \times 2$
$2H_2O \rightarrow O_2 + 4H^+ + 4e^-$
$4e^- + 4H_2O \rightarrow 2H_2 + 4OH^-$
$6H_2O \rightarrow O_2 + 2H_2 + 4H_2O$
$2H_2O \rightarrow O_2 + 2H_2$

10.0 g H₂O̶	1 mol H₂O̶	1 mol O₂	22 400 cm³
	18.0 g H₂O̶	2 mol H₂O̶	1 mol̶

$= 6220 \text{ cm}^3 \text{ O}_2 \text{ STP}$

26. $Mg + Cl_2 \rightarrow Mg^{2+} + 2Cl^-$

$$E = E^\circ - \frac{0.0592}{n} \log K = E^\circ - \frac{0.0592}{n} \log [Cl^-]^2 [Mg^{2+}]$$

$$E = 3.73 - \frac{0.0592}{2} \log (0.100)^2(0.170) = 3.82 \text{ V}$$

27. $Cd \rightarrow Cd^{2+}$ 0.40 V, $Fe^{3+} \rightarrow Fe^{2+}$ 0.77 V, $E = 1.17$ V

$$E = E° - \frac{0.0592}{n} \log \frac{[Cd^{2+}][Fe^{2+}]^2}{[Fe^{3+}]^2}$$

$$E = 1.17 - \frac{0.0592}{2} \log \frac{(0.500)(0.200)^2}{(0.100)^2}$$

$$E = 1.16 \text{ V}$$

28. $Sn^{4+} \rightarrow Sn^{2+}$ 0.15 V, $Fe \rightarrow Fe^{2+}$ 0.44 V, sum = 0.59 V

$$\Delta G = -nFE° = -(2)(96\ 500)(0.59)$$
$$= -114 \text{ kJ}$$

29. $\Delta G = -2.30RT \log K = -114$ kJ

$$= -(2.30)(0.00831)(\log K)$$

$$K = 10^{5960} \equiv \infty$$

30. $-30\ 000 = -n(96\ 500)E°$

$E° = 0.311$ V per electron transferred

31. $9.417 - 7.493 = 1.924$ g (mass of nickel)

$$\frac{1.924}{4.871} \times 100 = 39.5\% \text{ Ni}$$

32. $2NaCl(aq) + 2H_2O(l) \rightarrow 2NaOH(aq) + H_2(g) + Cl_2(g)$

See page 540.

40.0 g NaOH	1 mol NaOH	1 mol e⁻	96 500 A·s	
20.0 A	40.0 g NaOH	1 mol NaOH	1 mol e⁻	= 4825 s = 1.34 h

a. $Ag^+(aq) + e^- \rightarrow Ag(c)$

b.

5.00 A	2.00 h	60 min	60 s	1 mol e⁻	1 mol Ag	108 g Ag	
	1 h	1 min	96 500 A·s	1 mol e⁻	1 mol Ag	= 40.3 g Ag

Review

Pages 560-561.

1. loss of electrons
2. gains electrons
3. **a.** 6+   **c.** 7+
   b. 4+   **d.** 5+
4. $(Fe^{2+} \rightarrow Fe^{3+} + e^-) \times 6$

   $14H^+ + 6e^- + Cr_2O_7^{2-} \rightarrow 2Cr^{3+} + 7H_2O$

   $\underline{6Fe^{2+} \rightarrow 6Fe^{3+} + 6e^-}$

   $14H^+ + Cr_2O_7^{2-} + 6Fe^{2+} \rightarrow 2Cr^{3+} + 7H_2O + 6Fe^{3+}$
5. proton acceptor
6. hydrotelluric acid
7. hypochlorous acid
8. metallic
9. $H_2P_2O_7^{2-} + H_2O \rightarrow H_3O^+ + HP_2O_7^{3-}$

   $$K_a = \frac{[H_3O^+][HP_2O_7^{3-}]}{[H_2P_2O_7^{2-}]}$$

   $$= \frac{(1.58 \times 10^{-4})^2}{0.100 - (1.58 \times 10^{-4})}$$

   $$= 2.50 \times 10^{-7}$$
10. $\dfrac{1.58 \times 10^{-4}}{0.100} \times 100 = 0.158\%$
11. $H_4IO_6^-$
12. $[OH^-] = \dfrac{10^{-14}}{|H_3O^+|} = \dfrac{10^{-14}}{3.61 \times 10^{-6}}$

    $$= 2.77 \times 10^{-9}$$
13. 5.44

One More Step

Page 561.

1. *Encyclopaedia Brittanica* is a good source. Start with Thales → Franklin → nuclear reactors. Another good source is the Bell Telephone Laboratories book, *Conductors and Semiconductors*.

2. $E = 0 - \dfrac{0.0592}{0} \log \dfrac{10^{-1}}{10^0}$

   $$= -\frac{0.0592}{2} \log 10^{-1}$$

   $$= \frac{0.0592}{2} = 0.0296 \text{ volts}$$

3. $E = E° - \dfrac{RT}{nF} \ln \dfrac{[C][D]}{[A][B]}$

   $E = 0.76 - \dfrac{0.0592}{2} \log 2$

   $= 0.76 - (0.0296)(0.301)$

   $= 0.76 - 0.00888 = 0.75$ volts

4. The danger is the explosion of hydrogen gas generated by electrolysis of the moisture present during recharging.

5. Fuels are combined with oxygen to release energy directly in the form of electricity rather than heat. Information on the hydrogen-oxygen cells used in space craft is available from NASA.

NUCLEAR CHEMISTRY 28

An Overview

Chapter 28 presents the specialized area of nuclear chemistry. This material continues the theme of the book because the emphasis is on properties as a consequence of structure. Chapter 28 introduces elementary particles, accelerators, radioactivity, half-life, and reactions involving nuclear change. Fusion and fission processes are presented in relation to their development, use, and control.

Demonstration Information

Cloud chambers may be purchased from commercial sources. You can construct your own using a clear plastic sandwich box or other similar container. Paint the bottom of the box black. Wet two pieces of blotter paper with alcohol and place them on opposite sides of the box. Place the box on dry ice. Keep the box level for best results. Place a radioactive source in the middle of the box and cover it with the plastic lid. After a few minutes, shine a high-intensity light beam through the box. If the room is darkened, the vapor tracks will be more visible.

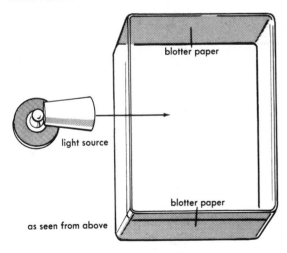

blotter paper

light source

blotter paper

as seen from above

Performance Objectives

Goal: Students will gain an understanding of natural and artificial nuclear reactions and the instruments used by chemists to study, control, and utilize radioactive materials and nuclear processes.

Objectives: Upon completion of the reading and problems, and when asked to demonstrate their understanding either orally or on a written test, students will

28:1	K	list the factors explaining nuclear structure.
28:2	K/P	list and classify elementary subatomic particles.
28:3	K	explain the principles utilized in accelerators.
28:4	K	differentiate among the three forms of radiation from natural radioactive nuclei.
28:5	K/P	define half-life and solve simple problems using the concept.
28:6	K	list the three factors which affect the stability of nuclides.
28:7-8	K/P/S	describe natural and synthetic transmutations and write balanced equations to represent nuclear reactions.
28:9	K	list some practical uses for radioactive nuclides.
28:10-11	K	differentiate between fission and fusion reactions and reactors; give examples of uses and problems in their use.
	A	voluntarily complete one or more of the One More Step activities.
	A	read unassigned literature related to the chapter.

Teaching Techniques

Section 28:4

Emphasize that natural radioactivity is a natural occurrence. Students are aware of the amount of heat produced by nuclear bombs and nuclear reactors. Radium undergoes natural radioactive decay producing heat, 552 J/h for each gram. Thus 1.0 gram of radium produces 1.00×10^{10} J of heat in its lifetime. This energy is equivalent to the heat produced by half a ton of coal when it burns. The heat, from natural radioactivity, can be detected deep within the earth. Nuclear energy and geothermal energy are related. Solar energy is from a great nuclear furnace also.

Section 28:10

Demonstration—Staple or tape books of paper matches to a board with the heads over the edge. Hold the board upright and light the bottom match. The others will follow in turn demonstrating a chain reaction. Place the board in sink and use small rubber tubing connected to water to extinguish the flame.

Chemical Technology

Use this feature to reinforce nuclear reactions and as an extension of Chapters 3 and 11 concerning the elements. Students can research other theories as to the origins of the elements.

Problem Solutions

Page 569.

1. $\dfrac{5.32 \times 10^9}{5.20 \times 10^6} = 1024 = 2^{10} = 10$ half lives

   $10(32.1 \text{ h}) = 321 \text{ h} = 13.4 \text{ days}$

2. $\dfrac{3.03 \times 10^6}{3.79 \times 10^5} = 8$ half lives

   $2^8 = 256 \quad \dfrac{5.80 \times 10^{28}}{256} = 2.27 \times 10^{26}$ atoms

3. Time required for one-half the atoms in a sample to decay.

Pages 574-575.

4. $^{27}_{12}\text{Mg} \rightarrow {}^{0}_{-1}e + {}^{27}_{13}\text{Al}$

5. $^{49}_{24}\text{Cr} \rightarrow {}^{0}_{+1}e + {}^{49}_{23}\text{V}$

6. $^{76}_{36}\text{Kr} + {}^{0}_{-1}e \rightarrow {}^{76}_{35}\text{Br}$

7. $^{213}_{88}\text{Ra} \rightarrow {}^{4}_{2}\text{He} + {}^{209}_{86}\text{Rn}$

8. $^{231}_{90}\text{Th} \rightarrow {}^{4}_{2}\text{He} + {}^{227}_{88}\text{Ra}$

Chapter End Problems

Page 584.

9. Alpha particles are helium nuclei; beta particles are electrons; gamma rays are electromagnetic radiation. α and β radiation consists of particles while γ radiation consists of electromagnetic waves. α particles are positively charged and several thousand times as heavy as the negatively charged β particles.

   increasing penetration

   $\longrightarrow$

   α β γ

   $\longleftarrow$

   increasing ionizing power

10. Stability tests:
    (a) Binding energy. A greater binding energy per particle indicates greater stability.
    (b) Neutron-proton ratio. The more closely the ratio approximates 1, the more stable the atom, for light atoms.
    (c) In general, the atoms having an even number of neutrons and protons are more stable than those having an odd number of neutrons and protons.

11. Radioactive isotopes are used to:
    (a) gauge wear of pistons in automobile engines.
    (b) determine location of certain substances in the human body.
    (c) produce γ-rays.
    (d) trace the progress of radioactive chemicals in plants.

12. Fusion is the joining of small nuclei to form one large nucleus.
    Fission is the splitting of a large nucleus into smaller nuclei.

13. a. $^{3}_{1}\text{H} \rightarrow {}^{3}_{2}\text{He} + {}^{0}_{-1}e$
    b. $^{61}_{30}\text{Zn} \rightarrow {}^{61}_{29}\text{Cu} + {}^{0}_{+1}e$
    c. $^{9}_{3}\text{Li} \rightarrow {}^{9}_{4}\text{Be} + {}^{0}_{-1}e$
    d. $^{240}_{96}\text{Cm} \rightarrow {}^{236}_{94}\text{Pu} + {}^{4}_{2}\text{He}$
    e. $^{199}_{84}\text{Po} + {}^{0}_{-1}e \rightarrow {}^{199}_{83}\text{Bi}$

14. $\dfrac{6.00 \times 10^{20}}{1.88 \times 10^{19}} = 32 = 2^5 = 5$ half lives

    $5(2.4 \text{ min}) = 12 \text{ min}$

Review

Pages 584-585.

1. it is reduced

2. Otherwise the reactants would transfer electrons directly between particles instead of through the external wire.

3. No

4. $\text{Co} \rightarrow \text{Co}^{2+}$ 0.28 V, $\text{Pb}^{2+} \rightarrow \text{Pb}$ −0.13 V, sum = 0.15 V

5. $\dfrac{0.506\ \cancel{A} \quad | \quad 22.0\ \cancel{\text{min}} \quad | \quad 60\ \cancel{s}\quad | \quad 1\ \cancel{\text{mol } e^-}}{ \quad\quad\quad\quad | \quad 1\ \cancel{\text{min}} \quad | \quad 96\,500\ \cancel{A\text{-}s}}$

   $\dfrac{1\ \cancel{\text{mol Sn}} \quad | \quad 119 \text{ g Sn}}{2\ \cancel{\text{mol } e} \quad | \quad 1\ \cancel{\text{mol Sn}}} = 0.412 \text{ g Sn}$

6. Cu, O_2

7. $E = E° - \dfrac{0.0592}{n} \log [\text{Pb}^{2+}][\text{F}^-]^2$

   $E = 3.00 - \dfrac{0.0592}{2} (0.282)(0.0400)^2$

   $E = 3.10 \text{ V}$

8. $\Delta G = -nFE°$

   $E° = \dfrac{\Delta G}{-nF} = (-26.6)/96\,500n$

   $= 0.276 \text{ V/e}^-$ transferred

9. gain of electrons

10. 5+

11. 2+

12. At least one element changes oxidation number

13. $\text{Pb} + \text{SO}_4^{2-} \rightarrow \text{PbSO}_4 + 2e^-$

    $\dfrac{\text{PbO}_2 + 2e^- + \text{SO}_4^{2-} + 4\text{H}^+ \rightarrow \quad \text{PbSO}_4 + 2\text{H}_2\text{O}}{\text{Pb} + 2\text{SO}_4^{2-} + \text{PbO}_2 + 4\text{H}^+ \rightarrow 2\text{PbSO}_4 + 2\text{H}_2\text{O}}$

14. $(8\text{H}^+ + 5e^- + \text{MnO}_4^- \rightarrow \text{Mn}^{2+} + 4\text{H}_2\text{O}) \times 2$

    $(2\text{Cl}^- \rightarrow \text{Cl}_2 + 2e^-) \times 5$

    $16\text{H}^+ + 10e^- + 2\text{MnO}_4^- \rightarrow 2\text{Mn}^{2+} + 8\text{H}_2\text{O}$

    $\dfrac{10\text{Cl}^- \rightarrow 5\text{Cl}_2 + 10e^-}{16\text{H}^+ + 2\text{MnO}_4^- + 10\text{Cl}^- \rightarrow 2\text{Mn}^{2+} + 8\text{H}_2\text{O} + 5\text{Cl}_2}$

15. $(2H_2O + 3e^- + MnO_4^- \rightarrow MnO_2 + 4OH^-) \times 2$
$(2I^- \rightarrow I_2 + 2e^-) \times 3$

$\underline{4H_2O + 6e^- + 2MnO_4^- \rightarrow 2MnO_2 + 8OH^-}$
$6I^- \rightarrow 3I_2 + 6e^-$

$\overline{4H_2O + 2MnO_4^- + 6I^- \rightarrow 2MnO_2 + 8OH^- + 3I_2}$

One More Step

Page 585.

1. **a.** Intensity varies inversely as the square of the distance between source and detector.

   b. Relative effectiveness for equal thicknesses of: paper 1, masonry 16, iron 50, lead 100. (Figures will vary with type of paper and type of masonry.)

2. weak—slow processes (on a nuclear time-scale, $>10^{-10}$ s) such as beta decay of nuclei, and decay of muons, kaons, and λ particles.
   strong—forces responsible for holding the nucleus together.

3. Cyclotron—makes use of magnetic fields and electrostatic charges to accelerate charged particles.
   Betatron—accelerates electrons by means of magnetic fields alone.
   Synchrotron—synchronizes an electric field and a magnetic field in order to accelerate the particles.
   See: Wilson, Robert R., and Littauer, Raphael, *Accelerators: Machines of Nuclear Physics*. Garden City, Doubleday and Co., 1960.

4. For about 30 years physicists have been working toward the goal of harnessing the nuclear fusion process to obtain power. One of the systems studied is the magnetohydrodynamic (MHD) generator in which the fusion reaction is confined by magnetic means. Another system involves laser fusion which is based on ignition of a pellet of fuel by focused laser beams.

5. In the upper atmosphere, ^{14}C is formed as a result of bombardment of ^{14}N in the upper atmosphere by cosmic rays. This radioactive carbon soon reacts with oxygen to form $^{14}CO_2$. Through mixing by winds, the distribution of $^{14}CO_2$ in the atmosphere remains virtually uniform. Carbon dioxide containing $^{14}CO_2$ is constantly being removed from the air by plants. All living plants have a constant concentration of ^{14}C in their composition because they use the radioactive ^{14}C in photosynthesis. However, when the plant dies, no more $^{14}CO_2$ is replaced by photosynthesis. Now, only disintegration is occurring. The ^{14}C concentration in the plant begins to decrease. By measuring the ^{14}C level in the dead plant and comparing it with the ^{14}C level in a living plant, it is possible to tell how long a plant has been dead. If an archeologist unearths logs in an excavation of an ancient city, *radio-carbon dating* of the timbers will indicate approximately when the trees were cut down.

6. By measuring the ratio of parent radioactive nuclide to daughter nuclide, the number of half-lives that have past since the mineral was formed can be found. The assumption is made that all of the daughter nuclide came from the parent. Common parent-daughter pairs in use are $^{238}U–^{206}Pb$, $^{235}U–^{207}Pb$, $^{40}K–^{40}Ar$, $^{87}Rb–^{87}Sr$. Of course, the half-life of the parent must be known.

7. The first tests of the Shiva laser were completed in late 1977. The laser is used in inertial confinement fusion experiments at the Lawrence Livermore Laboratory. The laser produced 10 200 J in a pulse lasting 10^{-9} second. Its 11.3 trillion watt pulse is used in fusion power experiments with deuterium and tritium targets. Other experiments use 12 lasers aimed at the same target.

CLASSES OF ORGANIC COMPOUNDS

29

An Overview

Organic chemistry is presented through a systematic study of hydrocarbons and their derivatives.

You should tell students that the chemical principles which govern the behavior of organic reactions are the same ones used in inorganic chemistry. The importance of structure is presented early in the chapter. Students should be made aware of the systematic way many compounds can be grouped according to similarities in their properties as a consequence of their structure. While teaching nomenclature, stress the pronunciation since compounds have similar names. It is important to make students aware of the 3-dimensional structure of organic compounds.

Demonstration Information

Many students think of hydrocarbons only as fuels. Use the demonstration to introduce a discussion about different fuels. Point out in the discussion that many other uses of carbon compounds are part of organic chemistry. Ask your students to name materials made from organic compounds.

Performance Objectives

Goal: Students will gain an understanding of the properties and preparation of hydrocarbons and halogen, oxygen, and nitrogen derivative compounds.

Objectives: Upon completion of the reading and problems, and when asked to demonstrate their understanding either orally or on a written test, students will

29:1	K	distinguish between chain and ring compounds.
29:2-4	K/P	define, name, and give formulas for representative alkanes and their isomers.
29:5-6	K/P	describe the use of optical activity and NMR to identify organic compounds.
29:7	K	list examples and names of cycloalkanes.
29:8-9	K	identify and name representative alkenes and their isomers.
29:10	K	list representative alkynes and differentiate them from alkanes and alkenes.
29:11	K	define, identify, and give uses for representative aromatic hydrocarbons.
29:12	K/P	describe halogen substituted hydrocarbons and list some of their uses.
29:13-16	K	list the classes of organic oxygen compounds, and describe some uses for each class.
29:17	K	list the classes of important organic nitrogen compounds.
	A	voluntarily complete one or more of the One More Step activities.
	A	read unassigned literature related to the chapter.

Teaching Techniques

Section 29:10

Demonstrate the reactivity of the triple bond by producing ethyne. Place some calcium carbide in water and cover with an inverted, water-filled test tube. Collect the gas by H_2O displacement. Collect three tubes: one 100% gas, one 50% gas (half filled with water, half air), and one 10% gas. Ignite each, keeping the mouth of the test tube down.

Section 29:14

Esters can be prepared by placing 6 cm^3 of each reactant into a test tube with 5 drops of concentrated H_2SO_4. Heat the test tubes in a water bath.

butyric acid	+ ethanol	pineapple
acetic acid	+ amyl alcohol	banana
salicylic acid	+ methanol	wintergreen

Place a few drops of each ester on separate pieces of numbered filter paper and pass around the room. Ask students to identify the odor. Discuss the difference in price of natural oils (esters) and synthetic esters in perfumes and flavorings.

Section 29:15

Demonstrate the oxidation of an aldehyde by slowly adding $1.0M$ NH_3(aq) dropwise to 5 cm^3 of $1.0M$ $AgNO_3$(aq) in a very clean test tube. A precipitate will form but will dissolve as more NH_3(aq) is added. Add NH_3(aq) until the precipitate is almost completely dissolved, then add 5 drops of 40% formaldehyde. Shake the test tube and warm (do not boil). A silver mirror will be deposited on the inside of the test tube. Silver ions are reduced to silver metal while the aldehyde is oxidized. Aldehydes oxidize to form acids. Discard all unused material because it can form an explosive.

Chemical Technology

Use this feature as a starting point for a project concerning research on synthetic fuels. It is important to emphasize to students that there are many options for synthetic fuels, however the conversion costs associated with some of these options do not make them feasible. The economics of energy is an important topic in discussing the total energy picture.

Problem Solutions

Page 592.

1. **c.** 2,3-dimethylpentane
2. **a.** 2,2-dimethylbutane   **c.** 3-methylpentane
   b. hexane   **d.** 3-ethyl-2-methylhexane

3. **a.**
$$CH_3-\overset{\overset{\displaystyle CH_3}{|}}{CH}-CH_3$$

   b.
$$CH_3-\overset{\overset{\displaystyle CH_3}{|}}{CH}-\overset{\overset{\displaystyle CH_3}{|}}{CH}-\overset{\overset{\displaystyle CH_3}{|}}{CH}-CH_2-CH_2-CH_2-CH_3$$

   c.
$$CH_3-\overset{\overset{\displaystyle CH_3}{|}}{CH}-\overset{\overset{\displaystyle CH_2}{|}}{CH}-CH_2-CH_2-CH_3$$

$$CH_2CH_3$$
$$|$$
$$CH_2$$
$$|$$

d. $CH_3-CH_2-CH_2-CH-CH_2-CH_2-CH_2-CH_3$

Pages 593-594.
4. a. 2,3-dimethylpentane
   b. octane
   c. 2,2,3-trimethylheptane
   d. 2,3,4-trimethylhexane
   e. 2,2-dimethylbutane

5. a.
$$CH_3$$
$$|$$
$$CH_3-CH-CH_2-CH_2-CH_2-CH_2-CH_3$$

   b.
$$CH_3\ CH_3$$
$$|\ \ \ |$$
$$CH_3-C-\!-C-CH_3$$
$$|\ \ \ |$$
$$CH_3\ CH_3$$

   c.
$$CH_3\ \ \ \ CH_3$$
$$|\ \ \ \ \ \ \ |$$
$$CH_3-C-CH_2-CH-CH_3$$
$$|$$
$$CH_3$$

   d.
$$CH_3\ \ \ \ CH_3$$
$$CH_3\ CH_2$$
$$|\ \ \ |$$
$$CH_3-CH-CH-CH_2-CH_3$$

   e.
$$CH_3-CH_2-CH-CH_2-CH_2-CH_3$$
$$|$$
$$CH_2$$
$$|$$
$$CH_3$$

6. C—C—C—C—C—C

C— C —C—C—C
(structures)

7. hexane
   2-methylpentane
   3-methylpentane
   2,2-dimethylbutane
   2,3-dimethylbutane

Chapter End Problems

Pages 610-613.
8. A homologous series is a group of compounds which differ by a specific structural unit.
9. C_nH_{2n}
10. a. C_6H_{12}
    b. C_8H_{18}
    c. $C_{10}H_{18}$
11. C_nH_{2n+1}

12. Longer molecules have more surface area over which weak forces can interact and heavier molecules travel more slowly than light molecules at the same temperature.
13. $CH_3-CH_2-CH_2-CH_2-CH_2-CH_2-CH_3$
    $CH_3-CH_2-CH_2-CH_2-CH_2-CH_2-CH_2-CH_3$
14. C_7H_{15}
15. a. 2
    b. 2
16. a nonhydrocarbon or branch to the parent chain
17. Position numbers are assigned to give the lowest possible numbers to the substituents. Radicals appear in the name in alphabetical order.
18. $C_8H_{16}, C_7H_{14}, C_{10}H_{20}$
19. heptyne contains a triple bond
20. $C_7H_5N_3O_6$ 21. C_8H_{10}

22. C_nH_{2n-2}
23. a. amide   c. nitrile
    b. amine   d. amino acid
24. a. alcohol   c. aldehyde
    b. alcohol   d. ketone
25. a. ether   c. carboxylic acid
    b. alcohol   d. ether
26. methane   undecane   heneicosane
    ethane   dodecane   docosane
    propane   tridecane   tricosane
    butane   tetradecane tetracosane
    pentane   pentadecane pentacosane
    hexane   hexadecane   hexacosane
    heptane   heptadecane heptacosane
    octane   octadecane   octacosane
    nonane   nonadecane   nonacosane
    decane   eicosane   triacontane

27. (structures)

28. nonane = 35 isomers
decane = 75 isomers

29. a. 2,6-dimethyl-4-ethyloctane
b. 2-pentene
c. 1,2-diethylbenzene
d. 1,1,4-trimethylcyclohexane
e. 3,3-dimethyl-1-butyne

30. a.

$$CH_3-CH_2-\overset{\overset{\displaystyle CH_2-CH_3}{|}}{CH}-CH_2-CH_2-CH_3$$

b.

$$CH_3,\ CH_3,\ CH_3,\ CH_3,\ CH_3,\ CH_3$$ (substituted cyclohexane)

c.

$$CH_2=\overset{\overset{\displaystyle CH_3}{|}}{C}-CH_3$$

d. $CH\equiv C-CH_2-CH_2-CH_2-CH_3$

e. (naphthalene with CH_3)

31. $C_{40}H_{82}$
40(12) + 82(1) = 562

32. a. 1-propanol
b. 2-methyl-2-propanol
c. 1-pentoxyhexane
d. butanal
e. 2-hexanone
f. butanoic acid
g. hexyl propanoate
h. 1-propanamine (1-aminopropane)

33. a. $CH_3-CH_2-CH_2-CH_2-OH$

b.

$$CH_3-\overset{\overset{\displaystyle CH_3}{|}}{CH}-\overset{\overset{\displaystyle OH}{|}}{CH_2}$$

c. $CH_3-CH_2-CH_2-O-CH_2-CH_2-CH_2-CH_3$

d.

$$CH_3-\overset{\overset{\displaystyle O}{\|}}{CH}$$

e.

$$CH_3-CH_2-\overset{\overset{\displaystyle O}{\|}}{C}-CH_2-CH_3$$

f.

$$CH_3-CH_2-CH_2-O-\overset{\overset{\displaystyle O}{\|}}{C}-H$$

g.

$$CH_3-\overset{\overset{\displaystyle CH_3}{|}}{N}-CH_3$$

h.

$$CH_3-CH_2-\overset{\overset{\displaystyle O}{\|}}{C}-OH$$

i.

$$CH_3-CH_2-\overset{\overset{\displaystyle O}{\|}}{C}-NH_2$$

j. CH_3-NO_2

34. The inductive effect is the electron withdrawing (or donating) power of an atom away from the functional group.

35. If the functional group exhibits the inductive effect or is an atom of high electronegativity the acid strength increases.

36. The chlorine is closer to the functional group in 2-chlorobutanoic acid.

37. a. (cyclopentanone with O)

b.

$$CH_3-\overset{\overset{\displaystyle O}{\|}}{C}-CH=CH-CH_3$$

c.

$$CH_3-\overset{\overset{\displaystyle CH_3}{|}}{C}=CH-CH_3$$

d.

$$CH_3-CH_2-O-\overset{\overset{\displaystyle O}{\|}}{C}-CH_2-Cl$$

e. CH_3-CN

f.

$$\overset{\overset{\displaystyle CH_2-CH-CHO}{|}}{\underset{NH_2}{(benzene)}}$$

g.

$$Br-CH-CH_2-Br\ (benzene)$$

h. $CH_3-CH_2-CH_2-CH_2-CH_2-CH_2-CH_2-CH_2$

$-CH_2-CH_2-CH_2-CH_2-CH_2-CH_2-CH_2-CH_3$

38. a. 2-methylpropanal
b. 2-methylbutanal
c. methanoic acid (formic acid)
d. ethandioic acid (oxalic acid)
e. methylamine
f. chloromethane

39. a. $CH=CH-CH_3$ (benzene)
b. (benzene with CH_3, CH_3, CH_3)
c. (benzene with I)

d. $CH_3-CH_2-CH_2-CH_2-CH_2-Br$

e.

$$CH_3-CH_2-\overset{\overset{\displaystyle OH}{|}}{\underset{CH_3}{C}}-CH_2-CH_3$$

f. (benzene with OH and CH_3)

Review

Page 613.

1. Nuclear force exists as a result of trading or sharing of pions between nucleons.

2. alpha—2+, mass of He atom (about 4 amu)
beta—1−, negligible mass

3. It represents the amount of energy necessary to break up the nucleus.

4. The products of one fission include one or more neutrons which can initiate one or more additional fissions.

5. bombard Cf nuclei with Ne nuclei

6. $Co \rightarrow Co^{2+}$ 0.28 V, $Cu^{2+} \rightarrow Cu$ 0.34 V,
   sum $(E°)$ = 0.62 V

$$E = E° - \frac{0.0592}{n} \log \frac{[Co^{2+}]}{[Cu^{2+}]}$$

$$= 0.62 - \frac{0.0592}{2} \log \frac{(0.1)}{(2)} = 0.66 \text{ V}$$

7. $2.30RT \log K = nFE°$
   $(2.30)(8.31)(298) \log K = (1)(96\ 500)(1)$
   $K = 8.76 \times 10^{16}$
   $\Delta G = -nFE° = -(1)(96\ 500)(1) = -96\ 500$ J

8. $12.6731 - 12.3247 = 0.3484$ g Ni
   $\frac{0.3483}{0.8128} \times 100 = 42.86\%$

9. $\frac{6.30 \times 10^{11}}{2.46 \times 10^9} = 256 = 2^8$
   $8(74.2) = 594$ days $= 1.63$ years

10. $^{240}_{92}U \rightarrow {}^{0}_{-1}e + {}^{240}_{93}Np$

One More Step

Page 613.

1. ethylene—Some is a by-product of petroleum processing. The remainder is made principally from ethane. Ethane and steam are run through a cracking tower at 700–900°C. The output is cooled to condense high-boiling products and remove water. The product is then fractionally distilled to recover ethane, ethylene, propane, propylene, and methane.
   Uses—Manufacture of polyethylene plastic, ethylene oxide, ethylene dichloride, ethanol, ethylbenzene, acetaldehyde, ethyl chloride

benzene—Recovered by liquid-liquid extraction from by-products of petroleum cracking and reforming operations
   Uses—manufacture of styrene, phenol, decylbenzene, fibers, plastics
propylene—By-product of petroleum processing. See also under ethylene.
   Uses—Manufacture of polypropylene plastic, isopropyl alcohol, detergents, cumene, glycerine, gasoline
toluene—same source as benzene
   Uses—gasoline, manufacture of other chemicals
urea—The principle process for the production of urea is the combining of ammonia and carbon dioxide under high pressure. The ammonium carbamate (NH_2COONH_4) thus formed is decomposed to urea and water.
   Uses—principally in fertilizer and plastics (e.g., urea-formaldehyde). Also in wood treatment, glues, and the production of other chemicals.

2. Silicon is prepared from silica (SiO_2) and coke in an electric furnace. Treatment of the silicon with HCl produces $HSiCl_3$. Reaction with Grignard reagents (see problem 1) produces R_2SiCl_2. Hydrolysis of these produces the polymer ($R_2SiO)_n$. There is an excellent outline of silicon chemistry in the first few pages of the Petrarch Systems catalog (P. O. Box 141, Levittown, Pa. 19059).
   Depending upon the degree of polymerization and the R- groups, silicones can be oils, resins, or elastomers. They are used for surface coatings, electrical insulation, rubber, lubricating oil and grease, antifoam agents, water repellants, and glues.
   They are heat-stable, pliable, and have a nearly constant viscosity with changing temperature.

ORGANIC REACTIONS AND BIOCHEMISTRY

30

An Overview

Chapter 30 presents the common types of organic chemical reactions. Reaction patterns lead students to an understanding of basic organic chemistry. Reaction patterns allow us to predict the products of similar processes. The chapter then describes some of the common products of organic reactions. Soap, petroleum products, synthetic rubber, plastics, and synthetic fibers are studied. The properties studied are a consequence of structure. The chapter concludes with a presentation of introductory biochemistry.

Demonstration Information

Preparation of nylon—Goggles are a must because the solution can easily splash into eyes. In a 250 cm^3 beaker place 50 cm^3 of carbon tetrachloride. **CAUTION:** Vapors hazardous, use a fume hood for this demonstration. Add 1 cm^3 of sebacyl chloride to the CCl$_4$ and stir vigorously. It is important that the solution be thoroughly mixed. In a 100 cm^3 beaker, dissolve 1.1 g of 1,6-diaminohexane and 2.5 g of anhydrous sodium carbonate in 25 cm^3 H$_2$O. Pour the water solution in the CCl$_4$ solution without mixing the two. Using forceps, pick up the center of the "film" that forms at the interface of the two liquids. Slowly pull the nylon fiber from the beaker and roll it up on a graduated cylinder that has a paper towel taped around it. A crank can be made from a glass bend with two 90° angles. Insert the tubing in a stopper placed in the end of the graduated cylinder.

Performance Objectives

Goal: Students will gain an understanding of various industrial and biochemical organic reactions.

Objectives: Upon completion of the reading and problems, and when asked to demonstrate their understanding either orally or on a written test, students will

30:1-5	K/P	identify, describe, and differentiate among oxidation, substitution, addition, elimination, esterification, and saponification reactions.
30:6-9	K	describe the manufacture of products derived from organic compounds such as gasoline, synthetic rubber, plastics, and synthetic fibers.
30:10-13	K	list, differentiate among, and describe the biochemical functions of proteins, carbohydrates, lipids, and nucleic acids.
	A	voluntarily complete one or more of the One More Step activities.
	A	read unassigned literature related to the chapter.

Teaching Techniques

Section 30:5

Soap—Place 25 g of a solid vegetable oil in a 250 cm^3 beaker. Add 10 cm^3 of ethanol and 5 cm^3 of 6M NaOH solution. Heat the mixture and stir constantly for 15 minutes. Cool the mixture in a water bath, then add 25 cm^3 of hot distilled water and 25 cm^3 of a saturated NaCl solution. The soap should now appear as curds. Collect the soap and press it into an evaporating dish to mold it.

Section 30:6

Gasolines are rated on a scale known as octane rating. The basis for this scale is the property of some fuels to cause "knocking" in engines. The knocking occurs when some of the fuel explodes suddenly instead of burning evenly. To rate a gasoline, a "standard" engine is required. Heptane is given an arbitrary octane rating of zero, and 2,2,4-trimethylpentane is given a rating of 100. The standard engine is run on the test fuel as well as on various mixtures of heptane and 2,2,4-trimethylpentane. When one of the mixtures of the two standards causes the same degree of knocking as the test fuel, the test is complete. The octane rating for the test fuel is the percentage of 2,2,4-trimethylpentane in the mixture with heptane.

Section 30:7

Synthetic Rubber—**CAUTION:** Wear your safety glasses. Place 75 cm^3 of distilled water in a 250 cm^3 beaker. Dissolve 7 g of Na_2S and 4 g of NaOH in the H_2O. Bring to a boil before adding 10 g of flowers of sulfur while stirring. Cool the solution, then filter. Add another 200 cm^3 of distilled H_2O and heat to 70-80°C. Add 15 cm^3 of a hot 5% soap solution. Cool in a water bath to 60°C. Then add 10 cm^3 of ethylene dichloride (dichloroethane) slowly while stirring. **CAUTION:** Vapors hazardous, use a fume hood. The color will change to a light yellow. Add 8 cm^3 of concentrated NH_3(aq). Allow this solution to stand overnight. The next day, pour off the top layer. Add 200 cm^3 of H_2O containing 8 cm^3 of concentrated NH_3(aq). Add 60 cm^3 of 20% acetic acid solution while stirring. The rubber will be seen in the bottom of the beaker. Rinse well. The rubber will leave an odor on your hands if you handle it.

Section 30:10

Use clothes pins to present a visual model of the monomer-polymer relationship. Clip one clothes pin onto the leg of another one and continue this process to form a polymer chain. Each clothes pin acts as a monomer.

Chemical Technology

There has been much controversy surrounding the topic of genetic engineering. Use this feature as a starting point. Have students investigate the advantages and disadvantages of continuing research in this area.

Problem Solutions

Page 616.

1. $2C_6H_{14} + 19O_2 \rightarrow 12CO_2 + 14H_2O$

Page 617.

2. $HOH + (CH_3)_3CI \rightarrow (CH_3)_3COH + HI$

Page 618.

3. CH_3—CH_2—CH=CH_2 + Br_2 → CH_3—CH_2—CH—CH_2
                                                        | |
                                                       Br   Br

4. $CH_3—CH_2—CH_2—CH_2—OH \xrightarrow{H_2SO_4} CH_3—CH_2—CH=CH_2 + H_2O$

Page 619.

5. $CH_3—CH_2—OH + CH_3—CH_2—CH_2—COOH \rightarrow CH_3—CH_2—O—\overset{\overset{O}{\|}}{C}—CH_2—CH_2—CH_3 + H_2O$

Page 620.
6. petroleum ether, ligroin, gasoline, kerosine, gas oil, lubricating oil

Page 623.
7. cellulose

Page 625.
8. nylon

9.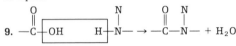

Page 627.
10. energy source and reserve

Page 628.
11. fats, vitamins, steroids, porphyrins (hemoglobin and chlorophyll)

12. Animal fats contain saturated fatty acid residues. Plant oils contain unsaturated fatty acid residues.

Page 629.
13. DNA contains thymine; RNA contains uracil. DNA is used to make RNA and to pass genetic information between generations. RNA is used to make proteins and enzymes.

Chapter End Problems

Page 631-632.
14. $CH_2=CH_2(g) + HI(g) \rightarrow CH_3—CH_2I(l)$

15. 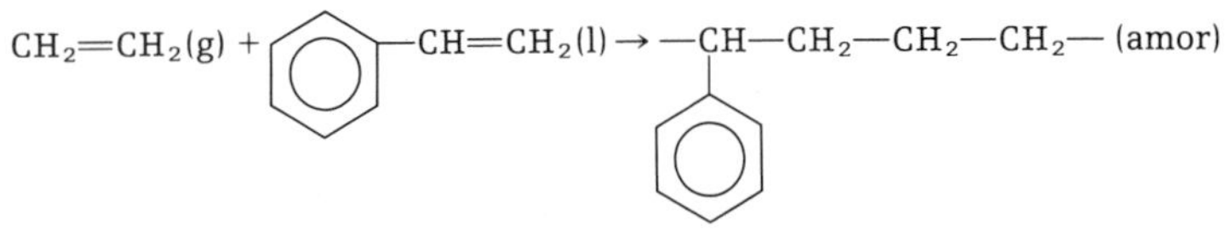 $CH_2=CH_2(g) +$ ⬡$—CH=CH_2(l) \rightarrow —CH—CH_2—CH_2—CH_2—$ (amor) ⬡

16. **a.** $Cl_2(g) + CH_2=CH—CH_3(g) \rightarrow Cl—CH_2—\underset{\underset{Cl}{|}}{CH}—CH_3(l)$

b. $CH_3—CH_2—CH_2—CH_2—CH_2—OH(l) + CH_3—\overset{\overset{O}{\|}}{C}—OH(l) \rightarrow CH_3—\overset{\overset{O}{\|}}{C}—O—CH_2—CH_2—CH_2—CH_2—CH_3(l) + H_2O(l)$

c. $2C_6H_6(l) + 15O_2(g) \rightarrow 12CO_2(g) + 6H_2O(l)$

d. $HO—CH_2—CH_2—CH_2—CH_3(l) \xrightarrow{H_2SO_4} CH_2=CH—CH_2CH_3(g) + H_2O(l)$

e. $\begin{matrix} CH_2—O—\overset{\overset{O}{\|}}{C}—(CH_2)_{17}—CH_3 \\ | \quad\quad \overset{O}{\|} \\ CH—O—C—(CH_2)_{17}—CH_3 \quad\quad + 3NaOH(aq) \rightarrow \\ | \quad\quad \overset{O}{\|} \\ CH_2—O—C—(CH_2)_{17}—CH_3 \text{(amor)} \end{matrix}$

$\underset{\underset{OH \quad OH \quad OH}{| \quad\quad | \quad\quad |}}{CH_2—CH—CH_2} + 3[CH_3—(CH_2)_{17}—\overset{\overset{O}{\|}}{C}—O^{\ominus} \ Na^{\oplus}](aq)$

17. Addition polymerization is a result of the "adding on" to each other of monomers containing double bonds. Condensation polymerization is the result of monomers reacting by eliminating a small molecule between them.

18.
$$NH_2-CH-C(=O)-NH-CH-C(=O)-NH-CH-C(=O)-OH$$

(with side chains: CH_3 on first carbon; $CH-CH_3$ / CH_3 on second; CH_2—indole ring with NH on third)

19.
$$NH_2-CH_2-C(=O)-NH-CH-C(=O)-NH-CH-C(=O)-NH-CH-C(=O)-OH$$

(side chains: CH_2—SH; CH_2—(phenol ring with OH); CH_2—CH_2—CH_2—CH_2—NH_2)

20. Proteins contain hundreds or thousands of amino acid residues. Thus, the number of possible combinations are enormous.

21. Enzymes act as catalysts and are structural components.

22. adenosine triphosphate—ATP

23. assist enzymatic reactions, and act as coenzymes

Review

Pages 632-633.

1.
$$Bi \rightarrow Bi^{3+} + 3e^-$$
$$4H^+ + 3e^- + NO_3^- \rightarrow NO + 2H_2O$$
$$\overline{Bi + 4H^+ + NO_3^- \rightarrow Bi^{3+} + NO + 2H_2O}$$

2. $0.28 + 0.63 = 0.91$ V

3. H_2, SO_2

4. $E = E° - \dfrac{0.0592}{n} \log \dfrac{[Cu^+]^5[Mn^{2+}]}{[MnO_4^-][H^+]^8}$

$= 0.99 - \dfrac{0.0592}{5} \log \dfrac{(1)^5(0.01)}{(1)(1)^8}$

$= 1.01$ V

5. $\Delta G = -nFE° = (-n)(96\,500)(1.94) = -187$ kJ/mol e^- transferred

6. $2Br^- \rightarrow Br_2 + 2e^-$

2.60 A̶	2.17 h̶	60 m̶i̶n̶	60 s̶	1 m̶o̶l̶ e̶⁻	1 m̶o̶l̶ B̶r̶₂	160 g Br₂	
	1 h̶	1 m̶i̶n̶	96 500 A̶·s̶	2 m̶o̶l̶ e̶⁻	1 m̶o̶l̶ B̶r̶₂		$= 16.8$ g Br₂

7. $\dfrac{16}{4} = 4$ half lives; $2^4 = 16$

$\dfrac{270}{16} = 16.9$ g

8. $^{129}_{55}Cs + \,^{0}_{-1}e \rightarrow \,^{129}_{54}Xe$

9. **a.** 2-bromobutane
   b. propene
   c. 1,1,2,2-tetramethylcyclohexane
   d. 1-bromo-3,4-dimethylbenzene (4-bromo-1,2-xylene)

10. **a.** $Br-C(Cl)=CH-CH_3$ **d.** $Br-CH-(phenyl)\ -CH-CH_3 (phenyl)$
    b. CH_2-CH_2
    c. Cl (cyclopropene with Cl)

One More Step

Page 633.

1. **Grignard Reagents.** In 1901, the French chemist Victor Grignard made the important observation that alkyl halides dissolved in diethyl ether ($C_2H_5-O-C_2H_5$) will react with metallic magnesium to form ether-soluble alkylmagnesium halides. These halides are now called Grignard reagents. The reaction producing them will be illustrated here by the formation of methylmagnesium iodide from methyl iodide. The diethyl ether solvent must be very pure, and the apparatus and reagents must be moisture free.

$$CH_3I + Mg \rightarrow CH_3MgI$$

methylmagnesium iodide

Grignard reagents react with water to produce alkanes. Since the step leading to the formation of the Grignard reagent and the hydrolysis process both produce a good yield, this reaction sequence is an attractive one for the conversion of alkyl halides to the corresponding alkanes. The hydrolysis of methylmagnesium iodide produces methane in the following manner:

$$CH_3MgI + HOH \rightarrow CH_4 + MgI(OH)$$

This type of reaction sequence may be generalized as:

$$R-X + Mg \rightarrow RMgX \quad R\boxed{MgX + H-O}H \rightarrow R-H + MgX(OH)$$

The following equations summarize the preparation and reactions of some Grignard reagents. The symbol R is used here both for alkyl and aryl groups.

(1) $RX + Mg \xrightarrow{\text{ether}} RMgX$

    (2) $RMgX + H_2O \rightarrow RH + Mg(OH)X$

    (3) $RMgX + CO_2 \rightarrow RCO_2MgX \xrightarrow{H_2O} RCO_2H + Mg(OH)X$

    (4) $RMgX + CH_2{-}CH_2$

              $\overset{\diagdown \ \ \diagup}{O} \rightarrow RCH_2CH_2OMgX \xrightarrow{H_2O} RCH_2CH_2OH + Mg(OH)X$

    (5) $RMgX + CH_2O \rightarrow RCH_2OMgX \xrightarrow{H_2O} RCH_2OH + Mg(OH)X$

    (6) $RMgX + R'CHO \rightarrow R{-}\underset{|}{C}H{-}R' \xrightarrow{H_2O} R{-}\underset{|}{C}H{-}R' + Mg(OH)X$

                               OMgX   OH

    (7) $RMgX + R'\underset{\|}{C}R' \rightarrow R\underset{|}{C}(R')R' \xrightarrow{H_2O} R\underset{|}{C}(R')R' + Mg(OH)X$

                      O   OMgX   OH

    (8) $2RMgX + R'CO_2R' \rightarrow R'\underset{|}{C}R_2 \rightarrow R'\underset{|}{C}R_2 + Mg(OH)X$

                          OMgX   OH

The Wurtz Synthesis. Some years prior to the work of Grignard, another famous French chemist, Charles Wurtz, became interested in the reactions of alkyl halides with metals. In 1855, he reported that the treatment of two moles of alkyl halide with an equivalent amount of sodium produced an alkane containing twice the number of carbons as the halide. The reaction is illustrated here by the preparation of butane from ethyl bromide.

$2CH_3{-}CH_2{-}Br + 2Na \rightarrow CH_3{-}CH_2{-}CH_2{-}CH_3 + 2NaBr$

The Wurtz synthesis has greater limitations than the Grignard reaction, and not all alkyl halides produce useful yields of alkanes. The general equation for the reaction is

$R{-}X + 2Na + X{-}R \rightarrow R{-}R + 2NaX$

The reaction between two different alkyl halides and sodium leads to a mixture of alkanes which limits the usefulness of this synthesis to the preparation of symmetrical alkanes.

2. Saran®—copolymer of vinyl chloride and vinylidene chloride.

    Kodel®—copolymer of ethylene glycol and terephthalic acid.

    Acrilan®—acrylonitrile.

    Dynel®—copolymer of acrylonitrile and vinyl chloride.

    Mylar®—copolymer of ethylene glycol and terephthalic acid.

    vinyl chloride $CH_2{=}CH{-}Cl$

    vinylidene chloride $CH_2{=}CCl_2$

    ethylene glycol $HO{-}CH_2{-}CH_2{-}OH$

    terephthalic acid

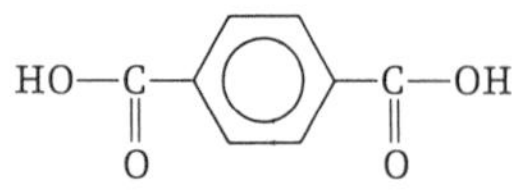

         $HO{-}\underset{\underset{O}{\|}}{C}{-}\bigcirc{-}\underset{\underset{O}{\|}}{C}{-}OH$

    acrylonitrile $CH_2{=}CH{-}C{\equiv}N$

3. A dipolar ion; e.g., an amino acid in a solution acidic
enough to produce

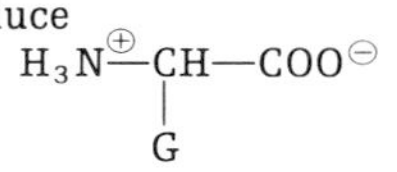

$$H_3\overset{\oplus}{N}-\underset{\underset{G}{|}}{C}H-COO^{\ominus}$$

4. for an α-helix, imitate Fig. 3-7, p. 37, in Kilgour,
Fundamentals of Biochemistry
for a β-pleat, imitate Fig. 3-5, p. 35, Kilgour, *Fundamentals of Biochemistry*

5. During the "burning" of glucose, NAD acts as the
oxidizing agent (it is reduced) in converting glyceraldehyde-3-phosphate to glyceric acid-1,3-diphosphate.

6.

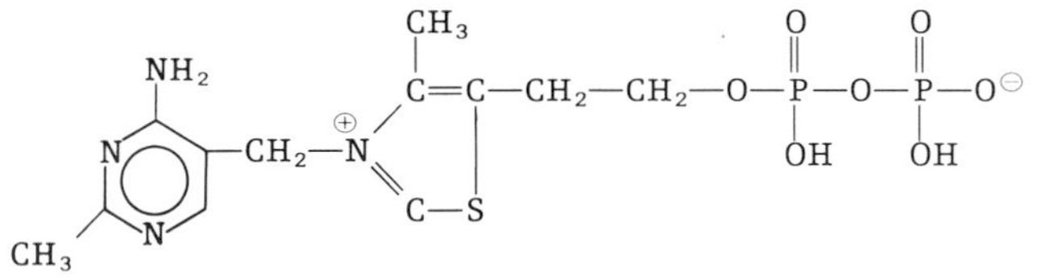

7. for the citric acid cycle, imitate the right-hand front
end paper of Kilgour, *Fundamentals of Biochemistry*

8. As the liver attempts to regulate glucose levels in the
blood, amino acid and fatty acid metabolism upset
the citric acid cycle resulting in an accumulation of
acetoacetic acid. The body cannot excrete the acid
and neutralizes it with various cations. The remaining H^+ builds up and the pH of the blood dips into
the acid range.

9.

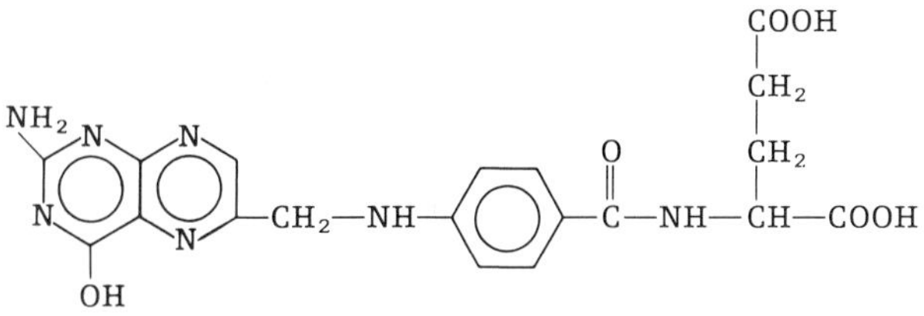

TEACHER'S NOTES

TEACHER'S NOTES

TEACHER QUESTIONNAIRE

Perhaps one of the best ways to ensure that effective educational materials are produced is to let authors and publishers know how you feel concerning the texts you are using. Please help us plan revisions and new programs to meet your needs. Complete and return the form provided. Please attach any additional comments to the questionnaire form. After removing the questionnaire from the book, form and staple it so that the address label shows. We would certainly appreciate hearing from you.

CHEMISTRY: A MODERN COURSE

Circle the number which corresponds to your opinion of each of the following items for the Merrill Chemistry Program. Please also star (*) those three factors which most influence your evaluation or choice of a text.

Student Text	Excellent	Very Good	Satisfactory	Fair	Poor	Comments
1. Readability	5	4	3	2	1	_____
2. Approach	5	4	3	2	1	_____
3. Organization	5	4	3	2	1	_____
4. Factual accuracy	5	4	3	2	1	_____
5. Coverage of chemical principles	5	4	3	2	1	_____
6. Concept development	5	4	3	2	1	_____
7. Visual impact	5	4	3	2	1	_____
8. Chapter end materials	5	4	3	2	1	_____
9. Tables	5	4	3	2	1	_____
10. Illustrations	5	4	3	2	1	_____
11. Technology career features	5	4	3	2	1	_____
12. Biographies	5	4	3	2	1	_____
13. Student notes	5	4	3	2	1	_____
14. Example problems	5	4	3	2	1	_____
15. Appendices	5	4	3	2	1	_____
16. Glossary	5	4	3	2	1	_____

Teacher's Annotated Edition	Excellent	Very Good	Satisfactory	Fair	Poor	Comments
1. Teachability	5	4	3	2	1	_____
2. Effective program use	5	4	3	2	1	_____
3. Demonstrations	5	4	3	2	1	_____
4. Chapter suggestions	5	4	3	2	1	_____
5. Planning guide	5	4	3	2	1	_____
6. Chapter end answers	5	4	3	2	1	_____
7. Audiovisual aids	5	4	3	2	1	_____
8. Annotations	5	4	3	2	1	_____
9. Suggested readings	5	4	3	2	1	_____

Supplements	Excellent	Very Good	Satisfactory	Fair	Poor	Comments
1. *Laboratory Chemistry*	5	4	3	2	1	_____
2. *Laboratory Chemistry TAE*	5	4	3	2	1	_____
3. *Evaluation Program for Chemistry: A Modern Course*	5	4	3	2	1	_____
4. *Solving Problems in Chemistry*	5	4	3	2	1	_____

Circle the appropriate information:

1. Grade level of your students   9   10   11   12
2. Average number of students in your chemistry classes   5-10   11-20   21-30   31-40   40+
3. Total number of students enrolled in chemistry   under 100   101-200   201-300   300+
4. Total school enrollment   under 200   201-500   501-1000   1000+
5. Locale of the school   rural   small town   suburban   city
6. Ability level of the students   below avg.   average   above avg.
7. Appropriateness of the text for your class   easy   about right   difficult
8. The number of years the text will be used   1   2   3   4   5
9. May we quote you?   yes   no

Please feel free to attach an additional sheet to make further comments.

Name _____ Date _____

School _____ City _____ State _____ Zip _____

- -

- -
Fold

CHEMISTRY
A MODERN COURSE

ROBERT C. SMOOT
Chairman, Science Department
McDonogh School
McDonogh, Maryland

Robert C. Smoot is a chemistry teacher and Chairman of the Science Department at McDonough School. He has taught chemistry at the high school level for 24 years. He has also taught courses in physics, mathematics, engineering, oceanography, and electronics. He earned his B.S. degree in Chemical Engineering from Pennsylvania State University and his M.A. in Teaching from Johns Hopkins University. He is a member of many national professional organizations including the American Chemical Society and the National Science Teachers Association. In addition, Mr. Smoot is editor of the science section of *Curriculum Review* and a coauthor of other Merrill senior high science textbooks.

JACK S. PRICE
Superintendent, Vista Unified School District
Vista, California

Jack S. Price taught chemistry and mathematics for 13 years before becoming Math/Science Coordinator for the San Diego County Department of Education. He earned his B.A. degree at Eastern Michigan University and M. Ed. and Ed. D. degrees at Wayne State University. While at Wayne State, Dr. Price did original research in organometallic compounds. He has participated in NSF summer institutes at New Mexico State University and the University of Colorado. Presently, he is Superintendent of Schools in Vista, California where he periodically teaches semester courses at Vista High School. He is also a coauthor of other Merrill science and mathematics textbooks at the junior and senior high levels.

RICHARD G. SMITH
Chairman, Science Department
Bexley High School
Bexley, Ohio

Richard G. Smith has been teaching chemistry at the high school level for 17 years. Presently, he is also the Science Department Chairman at Bexley High School. He received a regional outstanding teacher award from the American Chemical Society in 1978 and has participated in NSF summer institutes in chemistry. Mr. Smith earned his B.S. degree in Education from Ohio University and his M.A.T. in Chemistry from Indiana University. He is a member of the American Chemical Society and the National Science Teachers Association as well as other national professional organizations.

CHARLES E. MERRILL PUBLISHING CO.
A BELL & HOWELL COMPANY
COLUMBUS, OHIO
TORONTO   LONDON   SIDNEY

A MERRILL SCIENCE PROGRAM

CHEMISTRY: A MODERN COURSE
CHEMISTRY: A MODERN COURSE, TEACHER'S ANNOTATED EDITION
CHEMISTRY: A MODERN COURSE, SPIRIT DUPLICATING EVALUATION PROGRAM
LABORATORY CHEMISTRY
LABORATORY CHEMISTRY, TEACHER'S ANNOTATED EDITION
SOLVING PROBLEMS IN CHEMISTRY

Reviewers:

Peter F. Cardamone, Science Supervisor; Webster Central School District, Webster, NY

Thomas Custer, Coordinator of Science; Anne Arundel County Public Schools, Annapolis, MD

Laurel Dieskow, Chemistry/Physics Teacher; Oak Forest High School, Oak Forest, IL

Gary E. Dunkleberger, Supervisor of Science; Carroll Country Public Schools, Westminster, MD

Frank M. Hammock, Chemistry Teacher; Cocoa Beach High School, Cocoa Beach, FL

Margaret Henley, Chemistry Teacher; Los Angeles Unified School District, Los Angeles, CA

Paul Herzberg, Chemistry Teacher; Mankato West High School, Mankato, MN

Donald J. Holderread, Science Dept. Chairman; Evergreen High School, Jefferson County, CO

Harold Lathrop, Science Dept. Chairman; Hinsdale Twp. High School, South Darien, IL

Wayne Mikach, Science Coordinator; North Hills High School, Pittsburgh, PA

Warren Montgomery, Chemistry Teacher; Bremen High School, Midlothian, IL

Richard J. Parsons, Science Dept. Chairman; Wilcox High School, Santa Clara, CA

William S. Talbott, Science Educational Specialist; Baltimore City Schools, Baltimore, MD

John Zimelis, Chemistry Teacher; East Grand Rapids High School, Grand Rapids, MI

Project Editor; Ellen M. Lappa; **Editor:** Mary E. Kremer; **Book Design:** Larry P. Koons; **Project Artist:** Michael T. Henry; **Artists:** Becky Vilasineekul, Karen P. Johnson; **Illustrators:** Lew Bolen, Don Robison, Jim Robison, Jim Shough; **Biography Art:** Lloyd Ostendorf; **Photo Editor:** Susan Marquart; **Production Editor:** Janice Wagner

Cover photo: Larry Hamill

ISBN -0-675-06394-9

PUBLISHED BY

CHARLES E. MERRILL PUBLISHING CO.

A BELL & HOWELL COMPANY

COLUMBUS, OHIO 43216

PREFACE

The 1983 Edition of **Chemistry: A Modern Course** is an introductory chemistry program which is comprehensive as well as relevant. The aim of the program is to enable students to develop a better understanding of their physical world. The central theme of the text is the basic principle that the properties of matter are a consequence of the structure of matter. A balanced approach is presented in combining chemical theories and concepts with quantitative problems. Students will find this material challenging and will be encouraged to think independently throughout the course.

The content is presented in a logical manner which is flexible enough so that later chapters may be studied in a variety of sequences. The initial chapters present some descriptive chemistry as well as the "mechanics" and basic vocabulary needed to move on to more complex concepts. Introduction of the mole concept early in the text enables students to perform quantitative and qualitative laboratory experiments within the first few weeks of the course. Several chapters are then devoted to the structure of matter and the periodicity of the elements. The principles developed in these chapters provide the foundation for the remainder of the text. The chapters that follow cover matter in terms of acidity, oxidation-reduction, and electric potential. The text concludes with descriptive material in nuclear, organic, and biochemistry.

Each chapter is introduced with a photograph and a thought-provoking paragraph which sets the theme of the chapter. The *Goal* statement gives an overall purpose for studying the chapter so students will know from the first page of the chapter what they are expected to learn. Within each chapter, *margin notes* appear beside the text to highlight important ideas and to assist students in organizing information for study and review.

Sections are kept short to present only one or two main ideas in each. Thus, the pace at which new material is introduced is carefully controlled. The section titles provide an outline of the basic framework for each chapter. *New terms* are highlighted using boldface type. The *Glossary* at the back of the text will assist students in learning the definitions of these terms.

The development of a systematic approach to problem solving should be a major aim of any beginning course in chemistry. The *factor-label method* exemplifies this philosophy and is used throughout the text. Many *Example* problems are provided within chapters. Each *Example* includes a step-by-step solving process to guide students in mastering problem solving. *Practice problems* are also included within each chapter. Answers are provided for some of these in-chapter problems to enable students to check their understanding of the material just studied.

Each chapter includes a *Biography* of a scientist whose work is related to the material presented in the chapter. *Chemical technology* and *careers* are highlighted as feature sections.

Each chapter ends with an extensive *Summary* covering the major points of the chapter. A comprehensive set of *questions* and *problems* is included to test understanding of the chapter material. *Review problems* are included to keep material from previous chapters fresh in students' minds. Another feature is the series of *problems* and *projects* under the heading *One More Step*. This section may be used to further students' knowledge of the chapter material by having them prepare projects, papers, or talks which can benefit the entire class.

The text takes into consideration a realistic appraisal of the capabilities and maturities of typical students. We wish to express our sincere thanks to the many chemistry students, teachers, and science educators who have made suggestions for changes based on their use of **Chemistry: A Modern Course.**

The Authors

CONTENTS

Camping is a recreational activity where you compete with the elements of nature. Technological advancements have given you the advantage in surviving outdoors. The materials shown have been produced as a result of applying a knowledge of chemistry. Think of the vast number of products you use each day. Most of them were originally produced in a chemical laboratory. What is the role of chemistry in today's society? What situations have arisen where chemical knowledge may have been used unwisely?

Hanson Carroll/Alpha

NATURE, CHEMISTRY, AND YOU

1

Chapter 1 covers the necessity of being informed in order to make intelligent decisions concerning the environment and quality of life. Chemistry is defined and the mass-energy relationship is introduced.

Throughout recorded history (and even before), people have tried to alter their environment to improve their way of life. Such "tinkering" has often had unexpected results.

Some of the earliest examples we have of people altering their environment involve farming. More than 4000 years ago, the Sumerians of the lower Tigris-Euphrates valley built a system of canals and dikes. This system was used to control yearly floodwaters and to carry water to crops in dry areas. However, as the water flowed down from the mountains, it picked up salts in the hills. When it reached the fields, some of the water was used by the plants. The rest evaporated and left salts in the soil where they collected over centuries. In time, the salt content of the soil became so high that crops could not grow. The Babylonians, who next occupied the land, paid the price for such "tinkering."

When the early Egyptian pharoahs built the pyramids about 4500 years ago, they had to quarry huge amounts of stone. The Great Pyramid alone needed over five million metric tons of stone! In the process of obtaining this stone, the landscape was badly scarred.

In India, about 400 A.D., a method for making rust-resistant iron was discovered. This method was later used by the Persians and then by the Arabs. The fine "Damascus" steel in swords which were used in many "holy wars" was an unexpected later application of this Indian discovery.

GOAL: You will gain an understanding of the nature of chemistry by looking at the relationship between science and human progress.

Farming is an example of how people have altered their environment in an attempt to improve the quality of life.

Discuss other examples in which the environmental impact has not been thoroughly studied in advance.

About 600 A.D., the Chinese discovered an explosive mixture containing potassium nitrate. They used it to make fireworks for amusement. Five centuries later, this same mixture was being used as a gunpowder.

There is nothing good or bad about water, salt, stone, steel, or potassium nitrate. People determine whether these things are helpful or harmful. The people of Sumeria, India, and China could not have foreseen the damage their discoveries would bring. They did not intend for their work to lead to undesirable results. Their aim was simply to improve the quality of their lives.

Photri

The Granger Collection

a

b

FIGURE 1-1. Rust resistant iron (a) was used in the construction of this ancient pillar in Delhi, India. The ancient painting (b) depicts the flood control system developed by the Egyptians along the Nile river.

We must plan for the future with care while using our existing resources wisely.

1:1 LIMITATIONS AND OPPORTUNITIES

Today we face many problems resulting from past attempts to "tinker" with nature. We have learned that we must plan for the future with care. However, planning for the future requires making choices.

Livable space on our planet is limited. Space travel is enormously expensive. It seems unlikely that people will colonize space stations in the near future. Therefore, we must use our existing resources wisely. An increasing world population leads to greater needs for housing, food, and water. Housing and farming

ENERGY PRODUCTION IN THE UNITED STATES

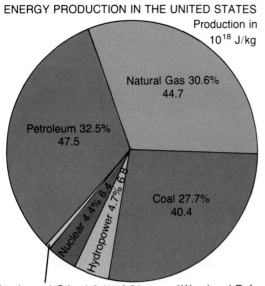

Production in
10^{18} J/kg

Natural Gas 30.6%
44.7

Petroleum 32.5%
47.5

Coal 27.7%
40.4

Nuclear 4.4% 6.4

Hydropower 4.7% 6.8

a Geothermal/Other* 0.1% 0.21   *Wood and Refuse

ENERGY CONSUMPTION IN THE UNITED STATES

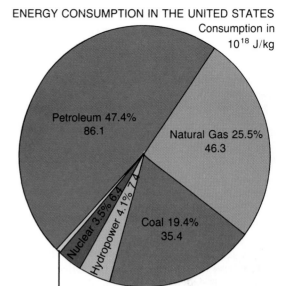

Consumption in
10^{18} J/kg

Petroleum 47.4%
86.1

Natural Gas 25.5%
46.3

Coal 19.4%
35.4

Nuclear 3.5% 6.4

Hydropower 4.1% 7.4

b Geothermal/Other* 0.1% 0.21   *Wood and Refuse

both require suitable space. How is the available space to be divided? How is the available water supply to be divided?

Machines make our lives easier and more fun. However, machines need energy to run. The demand for energy is growing rapidly, yet our energy resources are limited. How should known energy resources be used? There is no single "best" answer to this question.

FIGURE 1-2. In comparing graphs (a) and (b), we see that the relative percentages for energy produced are lower than the amounts consumed.

1:2 FINDING OUT AND MAKING CHOICES

People and their leaders make daily decisions which affect the use of the environment and natural resources. To make an intelligent choice, one must know the facts on each side of a question. The decision a person makes involves a value judgment. That is, the person must apply his or her own values and beliefs to the facts at hand.

Values vary from country to country. Moral and ethical standards differ from person to person. You may judge a person as "good" or "bad" on the basis of how that person behaves. You are really comparing their behavior to your own set of standards. This kind of judgment is called a value judgment.

The facts of nature, however, are neither good nor bad. Established facts are the same for everyone. For example, table salt dissolves in water. A diamond is hard. Neither of these statements can be labeled as good or bad. Neither is the process of determining these facts good or bad.

To make an intelligent choice, one must be aware of the available facts.

How we use facts involves value judgments.

A collection of facts is neither good nor bad.

Discussion topic: Science is not "good" or "bad." What people do with science may be.

Ask students what "trade-offs" they consider when making decisions on a daily basis.

When making choices, we must consider the risks and the benefits.

FIGURE 1-3. The use of nuclear reactions as an energy source is a controversial issue. Both pro-nuclear (a) and anti-nuclear groups (b) have strong arguments for their positions. You should be well informed in order to make wise decisions concerning this issue.

It is the way facts are used which may be good or bad. For example, scientists have learned the fact that sudden movements of the earth's crust can cause earthquakes. Can we hold scientists responsible for the destruction of life and property by an earthquake? Scientists have also learned the fact that huge amounts of energy are released by changes in certain atomic nuclei. It is the use of this fact to make a nuclear bomb, not the fact itself, which involves a value judgment.

Even when the facts are known, making choices can be difficult. In making one choice, we decide against others. Usually, an advantage is traded for a disadvantage. For example, we may choose to develop more efficient car engines to save energy. However, this development will also mean more expensive cars. We choose to ship oil in huge tankers in order to lower shipping costs. However, if one of these tankers is involved in an oil spill, the resulting damage to the environment is beyond measurement in dollars. Science cannot provide the values a person uses to make such choices.

Science deals with learning facts about the universe. The scientist uses many methods to try to obtain facts free from human bias. However, methods of learning facts and applying them cannot be freed from human values.

a   Artie Grace/Sygma   b   Richard Choy/Peter Arnold, Inc.

Science is always changing. Science is not a set of procedures or a certain group of people. It is not a collection of facts which never changes and should not be viewed as a subject forever a mystery to you. Someday you may decide to pursue a career as a scientist and seek facts about our world. As a scientist, you will make observations. You will also hypothesize (make predictions based on your observations) and then experiment to test your hypotheses. In this way, you will add to the collection of facts that scientists have already recorded. This collection of facts is a product of science. The information it provides may help us make wiser choices in planning for our future.

Science continually changes as our knowledge of the universe increases.

Scientists observe, hypothesize, and experiment to expand the collection of facts.

Be sure students are aware of the distinction between science and technology.

NASA

FPG

1:3 CHEMISTRY

Chemistry is the study and investigation of the structure and properties of matter. Thousands of such studies have been made. As a result, certain properties are found to be related to the internal structure of matter. Knowledge of the relationship between structure and properties can be useful. For example, an engineer may tell a chemist that a new material with certain properties is needed for a job. With this information, the chemist can predict what structure that material should have. For example, many new materials had to be developed for space exploration. These materials had to fit exacting specifications. An attempt was then made to produce the needed material.

FIGURE 1-4. Oil spills such as that of the Argo Merchant in 1976 have caused extensive environmental damage. The damage done to the aquatic life in the area may be difficult to measure.

Chemistry is the study and investigation of the structure and properties of matter.

The Granger Collection

FIGURE 1-5. This painting depicts an alchemist's laboratory during the Middle Ages. Alchemists were mainly concerned with changing abundant materials into precious or rare metals. They never reached their goal.

Point out that many disciplinary boundaries, such as biochemistry, physical chemistry, and biophysics, overlap. (Refer to Appendix C—Chemistry Related Careers)

A chemist may study many things. Such studies could be as different as the structure of the human brain or the bonding of rubber in a car tire. To make these studies, a chemist must be familiar with all of the sciences, including physics and mathematics. A chemist expresses the results of these studies as characteristics of the materials being examined.

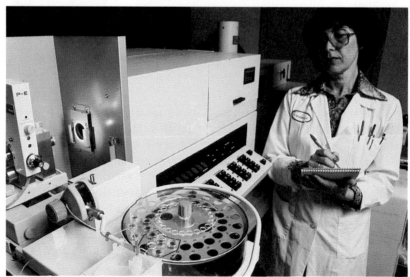

Jim Howard/FPG

FIGURE 1-6. Today's chemistry laboratory is highly mechanized. Many analytical procedures are run completely by computerized machines. The chemist monitors the machines and analyzes the data produced.

Certain basic principles and facts relate the properties of materials to their structure. These basic facts and principles are the foundations of chemistry. Therefore, it is not necessary for a person to study the properties of all known materials in order to gain a knowledge of chemistry.

1:4 MATTER

All material is called **matter** by scientists. Matter may be as difficult to observe as the particles which produce the odor of perfume. It may be as easy to observe as a block of lead. Matter is defined by scientists as anything which has the property of inertia. What is inertia? **Inertia** (in UHR shuh) is the resistance of matter to any change in motion. This change can be in either the direction or the rate of motion, or in both. For example, suppose you are riding in a moving car. When the car is stopped suddenly, your body tends to continue to move forward. If the car makes a sharp turn, your body tends to continue to move in its original direction. Thus, you are thrown against the side of the car opposite from the direction of the turn. In both cases, your body is showing the property of inertia. All matter has the property of inertia.

1:5 ENERGY

In the study of science, an important concept to understand is energy. For many years, energy has been defined as work or as the capacity to do work. This definition is not always useful since energy takes so many forms. For instance, think about the battery-alternator system of a car. As the starter switch is turned on, the chemical energy in the battery is converted to electrical energy. The car starts and chemical energy in the gasoline is converted into the energy of the moving car. As the crankshaft gains speed, its mechanical energy is transferred by belt and pulley to the alternator. In the alternator, the mechanical energy is converted into electric energy. This electric energy is transferred to the battery where it is converted to chemical energy. The battery is thus "recharged." During this time, other kinds of energy such as heat and sound are also produced as by-products.

At first, we shall define energy as a property of all matter. Under certain conditions, energy can be changed into work. We also know that energy can be converted from one kind to another. Energy can also be transferred directly from one particle of matter to another. For example, when two billiard balls collide, energy is transferred from one ball to the other. With the exception of nuclear change, all such transfers of energy occur without an observable loss or gain in the total amount of energy.

FIGURE 1-7. Energy may be transferred from one object to another as seen by the motion of these billiard balls.

Potential energy depends upon the position of an object with respect to another object.

Kinetic energy depends upon the motion of an object with respect to another object.

An object, or sample of matter, will have two general forms of energy: potential energy and kinetic energy. **Potential energy** depends upon the position of the object with respect to another object. **Kinetic energy** refers to the motion of one object with respect to another object. A book on a table has a greater potential energy relative to the earth than a book on the seat of a chair. The book on the table is further from the earth than the book on the chair. Therefore, it can do more work in falling to the floor than the book on the chair. An airplane traveling 700 kilometers per hour has a greater kinetic energy with reference to the earth than a bus traveling 88 kilometers per hour.

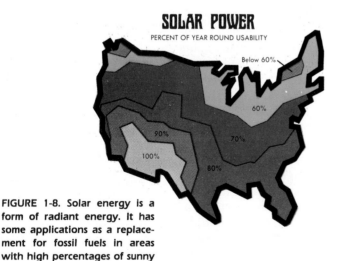

FIGURE 1-8. Solar energy is a form of radiant energy. It has some applications as a replacement for fossil fuels in areas with high percentages of sunny days.

When two billiard balls collide, kinetic energy is transferred directly from one ball to the other. Often, energy is transferred between objects not in contact. An example is the transfer of energy from the sun to Earth. Energy being transferred through empty space is called **radiant energy.** Unlike potential energy and kinetic energy, *radiant energy is not the property of an object.* Light is a kind of radiant energy. All other types of energy (chemical, mechanical, electrical, etc.) are special cases or combinations of kinetic, potential, and radiant.

1:6 MATTER AND ENERGY

For years, scientists thought that the total amount of matter and the total amount of energy in the universe were each constant. They stated this belief in the form of two laws. These laws are the law of conservation of matter and the law of conservation of energy.

The **law of conservation of matter** *states that matter is always conserved.* This statement means that the total amount of matter in the universe remains constant. Matter is neither created nor destroyed. It is only changed in form.

The **law of conservation of energy** *states that energy is always conserved.* This statement means that the total amount of energy in the universe remains the same. Energy is neither created nor destroyed. It too, is only changed in form.

Albert Einstein, in the early 1900's, showed that, in fact, matter can be changed to energy. He also showed that energy can be changed to matter. Einstein expressed this relationship in his famous equation:

$$E = mc^2$$

In this equation, E is energy, m is mass, and c is the speed of light (a constant).

According to Einstein's equation, mass and energy are equivalent. Thus we see that the two conservation laws are really just one law. This law is known as the law of conservation of matter-energy. Because mass is a measure of the amount of matter, this law is usually called the law of conservation of mass-energy. The **law of conservation of mass-energy states** *that mass and energy are always conserved and that their sum cannot be increased or decreased.* Mass and energy can, however, be changed from one to the other. Changes of energy to mass and mass to energy are observable only in nuclear reactions. In our laboratory work and in our discussions, we will always assume the original laws of conservation of matter and energy to be correct.

Radiant energy is transferred through empty space, and is not a property of an object.

Demonstration—Half fill a 150 cm³ beaker with sugar. Carefully pour concentrated H_2SO_4 on top of the sugar. Ask students for signs that energy is involved in the change they observe. Have a student touch the outside of the beaker. **CAUTION:** The beaker will be quite hot.

Matter can be changed to energy; energy can be changed to matter.

Mass and energy are equivalent.

Law of conservation of mass-energy: Mass and energy are always conserved.

Mass-energy conversions are observed in nuclear reactions.

Ellen H. Richards   (1842–1911)

In 1871 Ellen Swallow entered Massachusetts Institute of Technology as the first woman ever admitted to a technical school in the United States. Her major interest in research and teaching was in public health in the fields of nutrition and sanitation. For more than thirty years, Mrs. Richards worked to establish standards for pure food, clean air and water, and safe sewage. At one time in her career she tested over 40 000 samples of the water in Massachusetts making certain that the citizens had a safe water supply. She taught sanitary chemistry at MIT for 27 years and served as consultant in public health to many communities. During her research, she encountered a certain material which she believed to contain new elements. Her work, however, did not allow her the time to find samarium and gadolinium which were later discovered in the same material by two French chemists. The health and well-being of people were more important to her than the fame she would have received from the discovery.

CHEMICAL CAREER: Chemists

We have defined chemistry as the science of matter. Chemists, then, must work with matter. That statement, however, is too broad for a definition. In the Preface of this text, the theme of the book is stated as: The properties of matter are a consequence of its structure. Using this theme, chemists can be described as those scientists concerned chiefly with the interrelationship of the structure and properties in matter.

Some chemists are primarily concerned with finding the internal atomic structure of matter. Once the structure for a number of related compounds is determined, the chemist looks for patterns of behavior. In other words, the chemist tries to determine if a particular structural feature always leads to the same property or properties.

Other chemists take advantage of what is already known about structure and properties. These chemists "design" new compounds and predict the properties these compounds may have. They then try to produce these new compounds and check for the properties which were predicted. This work involves research in the library as well as the laboratory. Some chemists spend their entire lifetime making new compounds. Often these compounds are desired for a specific application. You will see in Chapter 5 how chemists design new drugs. Other times the compounds are produced merely to check the predictions made about their behavior.

Photri

Doug Martin

FIGURE 1-9. Chemists are involved in synthesizing new compounds as well as follow-up testing to ensure product safety. The chemists shown are running analytical tests on pesticide compounds.

A third group of chemists spends little time in the laboratory. This group uses the information produced by chemists in the lab to combine chemical facts into broad, useful theories concerning the structure and behavior of matter.

A fourth group of chemists devotes its efforts to finding out the composition of materials. That is, they determine the compounds and elements present in a material as well as the proportions in which these substances occur.

In addition to chemists, many other persons with various backgrounds and training work with matter. Some deal with the science of chemistry. Others are more concerned with the technological applications of chemical principles to the solution of practical problems. In the following chapters, we will examine in detail, some of the careers and technological applications which involve chemistry.

SUMMARY   Point out that the Summary is an excellent aid in reviewing the chapter.

1. For thousands of years, people have altered their physical environment. Their work has led to both helpful and harmful results. Intro

2. Today, people face many decisions which will affect their environment and the use of natural resources. In order to make intelligent decisions, people must obtain the facts related to the decision to be made. 1:1

3. The function of science is to provide the facts needed to make informed, intelligent decisions. 1:2

4. Chemistry is the science of materials. A chemist studies the properties and structures of materials. 1:3

5. Matter is anything with the property of inertia. Inertia is the resistance of an object or particle to a change in either its direction or rate of motion, or in both. 1:4

6. The energy of an object consists of potential energy and kinetic energy.

7. Energy being transferred through empty space between objects is in the form of radiant energy. 1:5

8. Under certain conditions, any form of energy can be transferred from one object to another or made to do work on an object. 1:5

9. The law of conservation of mass-energy states that mass and energy are always conserved and that the sum of mass and energy is always the same. 1:6

Detailed discussions and answers to problems are given in the Teacher's Guide at the front of this book.

PROBLEMS

1. Make a list of at least five different forms of energy. Use reference materials in your school library, particularly physics texts, to help you.

2. Define each of the forms of energy that you listed in your answer to Problem 1.

3. Using a dictionary, find out what phases of nature are investigated by each of the following scientists: agronomist, astronomer, biologist, botanist, ecologist, entomologist, geochemist, geologist, geophysicist, horticulturist, limnologist, metallurgist, meteorologist, physicist, and zoologist.

4. Find out what kinds of careers require a knowledge of chemistry. Use the career appendix in the back of this book as a starting point. Obtain the career education materials that your counselor may have, including the *Dictionary of Occupational Titles* and the *Occupational Outlook Handbook*.

5. Assume that there is a remote mountain lake that can be developed as a vacation spot for city dwellers. What facts must be determined before development starts? What value judgments must be made?

ONE MORE STEP The One More Step section is intended to provide impetus to research topics related to the chapter.

1. Make a list of the industries and institutions in your community which make use of the services of a chemist.

2. Investigate the Cockcroft-Walton experiment which confirmed Einstein's matter-energy hypothesis. Use reference materials from your library.

3. Investigate the advantages and disadvantages of continuing the whaling industry.

4. Investigate the advantages and disadvantages of expanding the nuclear power industry.

5. In December, 1976, the tanker "Argo Merchant" went aground off Massachusetts. A very large oil spill resulted. Try to find out what decisions led to the disaster, and why the decisions were made as they were.

6. Obtain college catalogues from your guidance counselor or library. Make a list showing those fields of study which require some background in chemistry.

READINGS Suggested Readings for teachers are found in the Teacher's Guide.

Baeder, D. L., "Love Canal—What Really Happened," *Chemtech,* Vol. 10, No. 12 (December 1980), pp. 740-743.

Cromie, William J. "Which is Riskier—Windmills or Reactors." *SciQuest,* Vol. 53, No. 3 (March 1980) pp. 6-10.

Fetter, Steven A., and Kosta Tsipis, "Catastrophic Releases of Radioactivity," *Scientific American,* Vol. 244, No. 4 (April 1981), pp. 41-47.

Gray, Charles L., Jr., and Frank von Hippel, "Fuel Economy of Light Vehicles," *Scientific American,* Vol. 244, No. 5 (May 1981), pp. 48-59.

Jackson, Thomas C., "PCB Time Bomb." *Oceans,* Vol. 9, No. 4 (July-August 1976), pp. 58-63.

Lowenstein, Jerold M., "Nuclear Pollution of the Seas." *Oceans,* Vol. 9, No. 3 (May-June 1976), pp. 60-65.

Paint, Roland D., "NOAA and the Nantucket Oilspill." *NOAA,* Vol. 7, No. 2 (April 1977), pp. 9-20.

Piver, Warren T., "Perspectives on Energy," *SciQuest,* Vol. 53, No. 1 (January 1980), pp. 17-21.

Taylor, Harriet V., "Conservation Energy," *Journal of Chemical Education,* Vol. 58, No. 2 (February 1981), pp. 185-188.

Weaver, Kenneth F., et al., *Energy,* Washington, D.C.: National Geographic Society, 1981.

Construction requires an in-depth knowledge of the structure and properties of materials. Measurement and design are key factors in using materials wisely. Design specifications for a building must conform to specific standards. In this chapter, you will learn how measurements and calculations using measurements will be important in gaining chemical knowledge. What standards are required in making a measurement? What measurement standards are used throughout the world?

Larry Hamill

MEASURING AND CALCULATING

2

Chapter 2 introduces scientific measurement and the mathematical concepts used in this text. These concepts include scientific notation, SI measurement, and the factor-label method of problem solving.

Thus far, we have discussed two properties of matter: inertia and energy. We refer to properties as we describe materials. Thus, it is helpful to learn how to measure properties of matter.

In order to make a measurement, we must meet three basic requirements.

1. We must know exactly what we are trying to measure.
2. We must have some standard with which to compare whatever we are measuring.
3. We must have some method of making this comparison.

When we describe a property in words, we are characterizing the object **qualitatively.** When the property can be measured and described by a number of standard units, we have characterized the object **quantitatively.**

GOAL: You will gain a knowledge of and demonstrate a proficiency in using SI measurement and related calculations used by chemists.

Qualitative—described with words.

Quantitative—a description based on measurements.

2:1 THE INTERNATIONAL SYSTEM (SI)

The standard units of measurement in science are part of a measuring system called the International System (SI). The letters are reversed in the symbol for the system because they are taken from the French name *Le Système International d' Unites.* SI is used by all scientists throughout the world and is used in everyday life in almost all countries. SI is a modern version of an older system called the metric system.

SI will be used throughout the text as it is the accepted system of measurement in science.

SI is a modern version of the metric system.

Larry Hamill

FIGURE 2-1. Information concerning breakthroughs and advances in chemistry is published in journals from all over the world. Thus, scientists must have a standardized system of presenting measurement data. Since many products are imported and exported, standardized measurements for specifications have become a necessity.

SPECIFICATIONS (Hatchback Model)
Dimensions

Length 4210 mm	Wheelbase 2450 mm
Width 1650 mm	Ground clearance 165 mm
Height 1355 mm	

Capacity

Fuel tank 60 L	Power steering fluid 1.4 L
Radiator coolant 5.0 L	Manual transmission oil 2.5 L
Engine oil 4.0 L	Windshield washer fluid 2.5 L

Valve Clearance

Intake and Auxiliary 0.12 0.17 mm
Exhaust 0.25 0.30 mm

Engine

Type Water cooled 4-stroke OHC gas engine
Bore × Stroke 77.0 × 94.0 mm
Displacement 1751 cm^3

Most countries have converted or are in the process of converting to SI. This measurement system will be used throughout the text. One important feature of SI is its simplicity. Seven basic units are the foundation of the International System. These units are shown in Table 2-1

Table 2-1

SI Base Units		
Quantity	**Name**	**Symbol**
Length	meter	m
Mass	kilogram	kg
Time	second	s
Electric current	ampere	A
Thermodynamic temperature	kelvin	K
Amount of substance	mole	mol
Luminous intensity	candela	cd

The International System (SI) is based on seven units of measurement.

Detailed definitions of these units are found in Table A-1 of the Appendix. We will discuss length, mass, time, and temperature in this chapter. Amount of substance will be discussed in Chapter 5 and electric current in Chapter 27. Luminous intensity will not be used in this book. The seven base units are shown so you can see the simplicity of SI.

Order of magnitude is indicated by a prefix.

In SI, prefixes are used to obtain different units for measuring the same property. SI prefixes and their equivalents are listed in Table 2-2.

Table 2-2

Prefix	Symbol	Meaning	Multiplier (Numerical)	Multiplier (Exponential)
		SI Prefixes		
		Greater than 1		
tera	T	trillion	1 000 000 000 000	10^{12}
giga	G	billion	1 000 000 000	10^{9}
mega	M	million	1 000 000	10^{6}
*kilo	k	thousand	1 000	10^{3}
hecto	h	hundred	100	10^{2}
deka	da	ten	10	10^{1}
		Less than 1		
*deci	d	tenth	0.1	10^{-1}
*centi	c	hundredth	0.01	10^{-2}
*milli	m	thousandth	0.001	10^{-3}
*micro	μ	millionth	0.000 001	10^{-6}
*nano	n	billionth	0.000 000 001	10^{-9}
pico	p	trillionth	0.000 000 000 001	10^{-12}
femto	f	quadrillionth	0.000 000 000 000 001	10^{-15}
atto	a	quintillionth	0.000 000 000 000 000 001	10^{-18}

*These prefixes are commonly used in this book and should be memorized. Spaces are used to group digits in long numbers. In some countries, a comma indicates a decimal point. Therefore, commas will not be used.

2:2 MASS

In chemistry, finding the amount of matter is very important. For instance, we may wish to measure the amount of wood in a small block. One way of measuring is to weigh the block. Suppose we weigh such a block on a spring scale and find that its weight is one newton* (N). Now suppose we take the scale and the block to the top of a high mountain. There we weigh the block again. The weight now will be slightly less than one newton. The weight has changed because the weight of an object depends on its distance from the center of the earth. Weight is a measure of the force of gravity between two objects. For our purposes, these two objects are the block and the earth. This force of gravity changes when the distance from the center of the earth changes.

We have seen that the weight of an object can vary from place to place. In scientific work, we need a measurement which does not change from place to place. This measurement is called mass. **Mass** is a measure of the quantity of matter.

The standard for mass is a piece of metal kept at the International Bureau of Weights and Measures in Sèvres, France. This object is called the International Prototype Kilogram. Its mass is defined as one kilogram (kg).

National Bureau of Standards

FIGURE 2-2. The international standard for mass is the Prototype Kilogram.

*The newton is the measurement standard for weight or force.

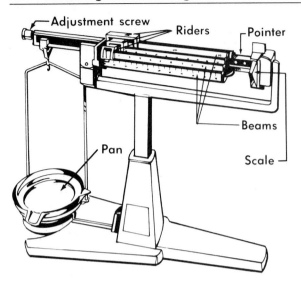

—Adjustment screw
Riders
Pointer
Beams
Scale
Pan

FIGURE 2-3. A balance measures mass by comparing the mass of an object to standard masses.

It is important to use the terms mass and massing correctly so students make the distinction between mass and weight.

Standard for mass is one kilogram (kg).

1 650 763.73 times the wavelength of orange-red light of krypton-86 at 101.3 kPa and 15°C is 1 meter. Other standards are defined in Table A-1 of the Appendix.

Standard for length is the meter (m).

The second is now defined as the duration of 9 192 631 770 periods of the radiation corresponding to the transition between two hyperfine levels of the fundamental state of the atom of cesium-133.

We have completed the first two requirements for making a measurement. We know what property we are going to measure and what our standard of comparison will be. Now we must compare the object with our standard. To compare, we use a balance. A **balance** is an instrument used to determine the mass of an object by comparing unknown mass to known mass. To compare these masses, we first place the object with unknown mass on the left side of the balance. Then we add standard masses to the right side until the masses on both sides are equal. In this comparison, the known masses and the unknown mass (the object) are the same distance from the center of the earth. They are, therefore, subject to the same attraction by the earth. At the top of the mountain, the unknown mass and known masses will still be equally distant from the center of the earth. Thus, the earth's attraction for each mass will still be equal, the mass of the object as compared to the standard will be the same. The balance will indicate no change in mass.

The process of measuring mass by comparing masses on a balance is called massing. Unfortunately, many terms which apply to the measurement of weight are often incorrectly applied to the measurement of mass. For example, standard masses used on the balance are often incorrectly called "weights." Also, the process of using a balance to compare masses is often incorrectly called "weighing." The SI standard of mass is the **kilogram** (kg). However, the kilogram is too large a unit for everyday use in the chemical laboratory. For this reason, the gram (g), one-thousandth of a kilogram, is commonly used.

2:3   LENGTH

A second important measurement is that of length. **Length** is the distance covered by a line segment connecting two points. The standard for measuring length is defined in terms of the wavelength of a particular color of light (Table A-1 of the Appendix). The standard unit of length is the **meter** (m). Length is usually measured with a ruler or similar device.

2:4   TIME

A third basic measurement is time. **Time** is the interval between two occurrences. Our present standard of time, like our standard of length, is defined in terms of an electron transition in an atom. The unit of time, the **second** (s), is 1/86 400 of an average day. The most common device for measuring time is a watch or clock. More precise time pieces include the chronometer, the atomic clock, and the solid state digital timer.

a

The Bettmann Archive

b

National Bureau of Standards

FIGURE 2-4. Early time measurements made by a sundial (a) were not nearly as precise as those made by a cesium clock (b).

2:5 TEMPERATURE

"What a hot day it is!" What does this expression mean? It means that the heat content per unit volume of air that day is greater than usual. What is heat? Heat is a form of energy. **Heat** always flows from a region of higher intensity to one of lower intensity. **Temperature** is a measure of heat intensity. Heat flows until the heat intensity (temperature) is the same everywhere. If one end of a metal rod is heated, the other end eventually becomes warm.

A thermometer is the most common instrument used to measure temperature. When the bulb is heated, the mercury expands and rises in the tube. When the bulb is cooled, the mercury contracts and the height of the mercury column decreases. The height of the mercury column can thus be used to measure temperature. The temperature can be read directly from the scale on the tube.

The unit of temperature is the **kelvin** (K). We will not define this unit until Chapter 15. However, the kelvin has a direct connection with a more familiar unit, the Celsius degree (C°).

The Celsius temperature scale is based on the fact that the freezing and boiling temperatures of pure water under normal atmospheric pressure are constant. The difference between the boiling and freezing points is divided into 100 equal intervals.

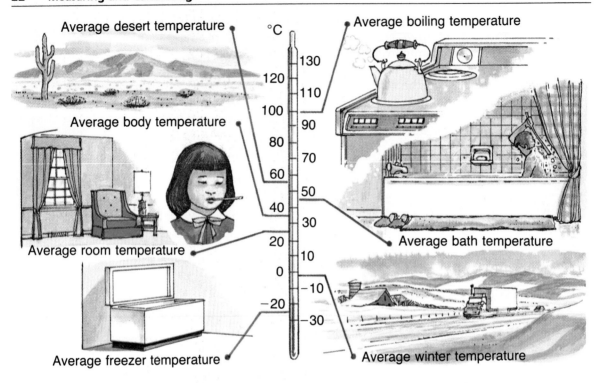

Average desert temperature

°C

Average boiling temperature

Average body temperature

Average room temperature

Average bath temperature

Average freezer temperature

Average winter temperature

130
120
110
100
90
80
70
60
50
40
30
20
10
0
−10
−20
−30

FIGURE 2-5. Familiar reference points for estimating Celsius temperatures are shown.

The Celsius degree is exactly equal to the kelvin.

Each interval is called a Celsius degree. The point at which water freezes is labeled zero degrees Celsius (0°C). The point at which water boils is labeled 100°C. The Celsius degree is exactly equal to the kelvin. We will use both units in our study of chemistry.

2:6 DERIVED UNITS

By combining the fundamental SI units, we obtain measurement units used to express other quantities. Distance divided by time equals speed. If we multiply length by length, we get area. Area multiplied by length produces volume. The SI unit of volume is the cubic meter (m^3). However, this quantity is too large to be practical for the laboratory. Chemists often use cubic decimeters (dm^3) as the unit of volume. One cubic decimeter is given another name, the liter (L). The liter is a unit of volume. One liter equals 1000 milliliters (mL) and 1000 cubic centimeters (cm^3). From these facts, you can see that

SI unit of volume is cubic meter (m^3).

1 liter (L) = 1 cubic decimeter (dm^3).

$$1000 \text{ cm}^3 = 1000 \text{ mL} = 1L = 1 \text{ dm}^3$$

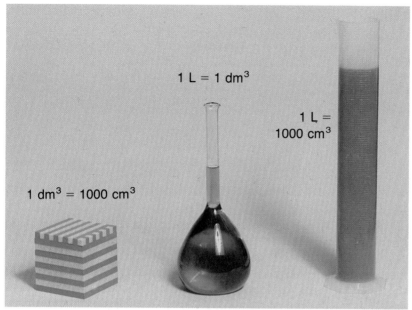

1 L = 1 dm³

1 L = 1000 cm³

1 dm³ = 1000 cm³

Tim Courlas

FIGURE 2-6. The volumes shown here are equivalent.

The units used to express measurements of speed, area, and volume are called derived units. You saw that area and volume measurements are expressed using length units. The units used to express speed, such as kilometers per hour or meters per second, combine fundamental units of length and time.

Derived units combine fundamental units. For example speed = meters per second (m/s).

Students may have difficulty setting up these problems. The factor-label method will be introduced in Section 2:11. Students will then come to realize how valuable a systematic method of problem solving is.

PROBLEMS

Convert.

1. 3.46 centigrams to milligrams
2. 1.00 kilometers to centimeters
3. 91.6 picoseconds to seconds
4. 247 milligrams to grams
5. 1.71 nanometers to centimeters
6. 405 mL to cm³
7. 750 cm³ to dm³
8. 25.0 m² to cm²
9. 35.5 mL to dm³
10. 5.00 km/h to m/s

1. 34.6 mg
2. 1.00×10^5 cm
3. 9.16×10^{-4} s
4. 0.247 g
5. 1.71×10^{-7} cm
6. 405 cm³
7. 0.750 dm³
8. 2.50×10^5 cm²
9. 0.0355 dm³
10. 1.39 m/s

2:7 SIGNIFICANT DIGITS

Suppose we want to measure the length of a strip of metal. We have two rulers. One ruler is graduated in centimeters. The other is graduated in millimeters. With which ruler can we obtain a better measurement of length? The length of the strip measured in millimeters is the more significant measurement since it is closer to the actual length of the strip. We say that the measurement in millimeters has more significant digits than the measurement in centimeters.

Suggestion: Have students actually measure the length of several objects using a ruler with a centimeter and millimeter scale.

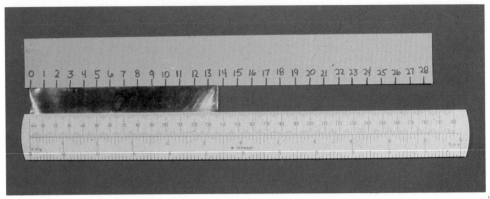

Janet Adams

FIGURE 2-7. The number of significant digits in the length measurement of the metal strip depends on the precision of the ruler used.

The last digit of a measurement is considered an approximation.

Significant digits indicate the exactness of a measurement.

Look at Figure 2-7. The measurement on the centimeter scale lies approximately 6/10 of the way from the 13-cm mark to the 14-cm mark. This length is recorded as 13.6 cm. On the millimeter ruler, the length lies approximately 3/10 of the way from the 13.6-cm mark to the 13.7-cm mark. This length is recorded as 13.63 cm. The measurement 13.6 cm has three significant digits. The measurement 13.63 cm has four significant digits. The last digit is uncertain (an estimate).

The exactness of measurements is an important part of experimentation. The exactness of a measurement is indicated by the number of **significant digits** in that measurement. The observer and anyone reading the results of an experiment want to know the number of significant digits in any observation. The following rules are used to determine the number of significant digits in a recorded measurement.

1. *Digits other than zero are always significant.*

967	3 significant digits
96.7	3 significant digits
9.6	2 significant digits

2. *Any final zero or zeros used after the decimal point are significant.*

9.670 0   5 significant digits

3. *Zeros between two other significant digits are always significant.*

9.067   4 significant digits

4. *Zeros used solely for spacing the decimal point are not significant.*

7000	1 significant digit
0.00967	3 significant digits

Additional examples

30.4	3 sig. dig.
2700	2
5.10	3
0.023	2
7.0200	5
0.04010	4
3.00	3
2.700	4
0.0304	3
51.0	3

The zeros are placeholders only.

PROBLEM

11. How many significant digits are there in each of the following?
    a. 903.2   c. 900.0   e. 0.090 0   g. 0.008 8   i. 0.02
    b. 90.3   d. 0.009 0   f. 99   h. 0.049   j. 70

11. a. 4
    b. 3
    c. 4   g. 2
    d. 2   h. 2
    e. 3   i. 1
    f. 2   j. 1

2:8 ACCURACY AND PRECISION

The terms accuracy and precision are often used in discussing measurements. **Accuracy** refers to quality of the measuring instrument as compared with the standard for that measurement. A micrometer used to measure engine parts may approximate the standard very closely. The micrometer has a high degree of accuracy. A plastic ruler has a low degree of accuracy.

Accuracy depends on how closely an instrument's measurement agrees with the standard for that measurement.

Precision refers to uncertainty in measurement. If we use a ruler marked off in divisions of 0.1 centimeter to measure a textbook, we might obtain the following data.

Precision is uncertainty in measurement.

Dimension	Measurement	Accuracy
Length	24.3 cm	± 0.1 cm
Width	18.7 cm	± 0.1 cm
Depth	4.4 cm	± 0.1 cm

The absolute uncertainty in each case is ±0.1 centimeter. However, that uncertainty is a different proportion of each dimension. A better reflection of uncertainty is the relative error. **Relative error** is often expressed as the percentage uncertainty in the measurement.

FIGURE 2-8. An analytical balance (a) is a highly precise tool for measuring mass. The data obtained should have a high degree of accuracy. The accuracy of an archer's aim is shown by the number of hits to the target (b).

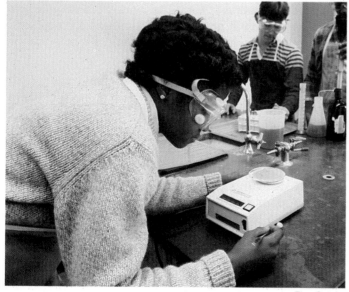

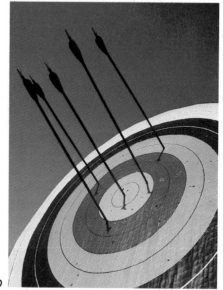

a   Tim Courlas   b   Doug Martin

Measurement	Accuracy	Relative Error	Precision (Percentage Uncertainty)
24.3 cm	±0.1 cm	$\dfrac{0.1 \text{ cm}}{24.3 \text{ cm}} = 0.004$	0.4%
18.7 cm	±0.1 cm	$\dfrac{0.1 \text{ cm}}{18.7 \text{ cm}} = 0.005$	0.5%
4.4 cm	±0.1 cm	$\dfrac{0.1 \text{ cm}}{4.4 \text{ cm}} = 0.02$	2%

In this case, we see that length and width are far more precise measurements than depth.

PROBLEMS

Compute the relative error of each of the following measurements.

12. 12.7 cm (accuracy of measurement = ±0.1 cm).
13. 50 cm^3 (accuracy of measurement = ±1 cm^3).
14. 236.0490 g (accuracy of balance = ±0.0001 g).

12. 0.008

13. 0.02

14. 4×10^{-7}

2:9   HANDLING NUMBERS IN SCIENCE

In this course we will sometimes use very large numbers. For example, Avogadro's number is 602 217 000 000 000 000 000 000. We will also use very small numbers. The distance between particles in a salt crystal is 0.000 000 002 814 cm. In working with such numbers it is easy to drop a zero or to lose a decimal place.

Scientific notation makes it easier to work with very large or small numbers. In **scientific notation,** all numbers are expressed as the product of a number between 1 and 10 and a whole-number power of 10.

Scientific notation is a convenient system of expressing very large or very small numbers.

$$M \times 10^n$$

In this expression, $1 \le M < 10$, and n is an integer. This number is read as M times ten to the nth.

One advantage of scientific notation is that it removes any doubt about the number of significant digits in a measurement. Suppose the volume of a gas is expressed as 2000 cm^3. We do not know whether the measurement was made to one or to four significant digits. Suppose the measurement was actually made to the nearest cm^3. Then the volume 2000 cm^3 is expressed to four significant digits. In scientific notation, we can indicate the additional significant digits by placing zeros to the right of the decimal point. Thus, 2×10^3 cm^3 has only one significant digit, while 2.000×10^3 cm^3 has four significant digits.

In scientific notation, only significant digits are shown.

Scientific notation allows the entry of very large and very small numbers into a calculator.

~ 2 080 000 000 000 000 000 000 000 m
from earth

~0.000 025 m in diameter

a

b

David Scharf/Peter Arnold, Inc.

Tersch

FIGURE 2-9. Expressing numbers in scientific notation for extremely small and large measurements such as the diameter of a moth's eye (a) or the distance to another galaxy (b) is less confusing than showing all digits.

Once we have recorded measurements to the correct number of significant digits and expressed them in scientific notation, if appropriate, we are ready to use these measurements in calculations.

To determine the number of digits that should appear in the answer to a calculation, we will use two rules.

1. *In addition and subtraction, the answer may contain only as many decimal places as the least accurate value used in finding the answer.* For example, if 345 is added to 27.6 the answer must be given to the nearest whole number. In adding a column of figures such as

$$
\begin{array}{r}
677 \\
39.2 \\
\underline{6.23} \\
722.43
\end{array}
$$

the answer should be rounded off to the nearest whole number. The answer to the problem above is 722.

2. *In multiplication and division, the answer may contain only as many significant digits as the least accurate value used to arrive at the answer.* For example, in the following problem

$$(1.133\ 0)(5.126\ 000\ 00) =$$

the answer has five significant digits. The answer to this division problem has four significant digits.

$$\frac{49.600\ 0}{47.40} =$$

Emphasize that a calculated answer cannot exceed the accuracy of a measurement in the problem.

Problem entered into the calculator

$$\frac{49.600}{47.40}$$

Calculator answer readout

1.046 413 5

Uncertain digits in each value

49.60<u>0</u>   47.4<u>0</u>

FIGURE 2-10. When using a calculator, it is important to express your answers to the proper number of significant digits. Therefore, you will not always use all the values shown on the readout.

Answer should be correctly stated as

1.046

In multiplication and division, the answer should have the same number of significant digits as the term having the least number of significant digits in the problem.

Emphasize that an answer can be as precise as the least precise digit in the problem.

If you are using a calculator to obtain your numerical answer, you must be very careful. The calculator may give you an answer with eight or ten digits. For example, in the problem 49.600 0/47.40, the answer may appear as 1.046 413 502. The answer must be rounded to the proper number of significant digits. In this case, the number of significant digits is four. Thus, the answer is 1.046. Always double-check your answer against the data given. Report the answer only to the number of significant digits justified by the data.

EXAMPLE: Multiplying in Scientific Notation

Find the product of $(4.0 \times 10^{-2})(3.0 \times 10^{-4})(2.0 \times 10^{1})$.

Solving process:

To multiply numbers expressed in scientific notation ($M \times 10^n$), multiply the values of M and add the exponents. The exponents do not need to be alike.

Multiply the values of M. $4.0 \times 3.0 \times 2.0 = 24$

Add the exponents. $-2 + (-4) + 1 = -5$

$$= (4.0 \times 3.0 \times 2.0) \times 10^{-2-4+}$$
$$= 24 \times 10^{-5} = 2.4 \times 10^{-4}$$

Standard position for the decimal point is after the first significant digit.

EXAMPLE: Dividing in Scientific Notation

Divide. $$\frac{(4 \times 10^3)(6 \times 10^{-1})}{(8 \times 10^2)}$$

Solving process:
Division is similar to multiplication except the exponents are subtracted. To divide numbers in scientific notation ($M \times 10^n$), divide the values of M and subtract the exponents of the denominator from the exponents of the numerator.

$$\frac{(4 \times 10^3)(6 \times 10^{-1})}{(8 \times 10^2)} = \frac{(4 \times 6) \times 10^{3-1}}{8 \times 10^2} = \frac{24}{8} \times \frac{10^2}{10^2}$$

$$= 3 \times 10^0 = 3$$

PROBLEMS

15. Perform the following operations. Express your answers to the correct number of significant digits.

Remember to observe rules of significant digits when solving problems.

a. $(35.72)(0.005\ 90) =$

e. $\dfrac{6810.12}{2.4} =$

b. $(707\ 000)(3.1) =$

f. $\dfrac{0.4832}{5.12} =$

c. $(0.054\ 32)(62\ 000) =$

g. $201 + 3.57 + 98.493 =$

d. $(0.005\ 900\ 0)(38.76) =$

h. $5.32 - 0.759\ 38 =$

16. Perform the following operations.

a. $(6.09 \times 10^{-1})(9.08 \times 10^5)$

g. $\dfrac{(7.79 \times 10^4)(6.45 \times 10^4)}{(5.44 \times 10^6)(7.45 \times 10^{-1})}$

b. $(1.65 \times 10^1)(5.24 \times 10^2)$

h. $\dfrac{(7.69 \times 10^2)(6.56 \times 10^6)}{(2.92 \times 10^4)(1.65 \times 10^4)}$

c. $(1.10 \times 10^9)(4.75 \times 10^9)$

i. $\dfrac{(9.19 \times 10^7)(1.79 \times 10^1)}{(8.17 \times 10^4)(8.32 \times 10^7)}$

d. $(1.18 \times 10^{-2})(2.20 \times 10^3)$

j. $\dfrac{(6.40 \times 10^2)(9.97 \times 10^4)}{(6.12 \times 10^{-2})(9.71 \times 10^4)}$

e. $\dfrac{(8.17 \times 10^1)(8.70 \times 10^5)}{4.20 \times 10^5}$

f. $\dfrac{(4.87 \times 10^6)(9.69 \times 10^1)}{2.84 \times 10^6}$

15. a. 0.211
 b. 2.2×10^6
 c. 3400
 d. 0.2287
 e. 2800
 f. 0.0944
 g. 303
 h. 4.56
16. a. 5.53×10^5
 b. 8.65×10^3
 c. 5.23×10^{18}
 d. 26.0
 e. 169
 f. 166
 g. 1240
 h. 10.5
 i. 2.42×10^{-4}
 j. 1.07×10^4

2:10 A GENERAL APPROACH TO PROBLEMS

One trait shared by most chemists is the ability to solve problems. You will need to develop this ability during your study of chemistry. Skill in solving problems can be developed by practice.

A good way to practice solving problems is to break the problem into three parts. In Part One, decide what information you are given. Locate the starting material with which you will be working. Another way of expressing Part One is "Where am I?"

In Part Two, decide what is required of you. Make certain you know what you are to find. Another way of expressing Part Two is "Where do I want to be?" In Part Three, find a "bridge" which connects what you are given to what is required of you. Part Three could also be expressed, "How do I get from where I am to where I want to be?"

Parts One and Two require a careful reading and rereading of the question or problem. The first time you read the problem, concentrate on finding the starting point. Concentrate the second time on what you are required to find.

The "bridge" mentioned in Part Three comes from two sources. Your background of general knowledge is the first source. The second source is the knowledge you will gain in your study of chemistry. Perhaps your chemical knowledge will not lead you to an immediate method of solving the problem. However, the knowledge you already have will be a guide to using the textbook including the Table of Contents, the Appendices, and the Index. The text contains Example problems and descriptions which you can use in solving problems. Learn to look for patterns in solving different types of problems. Then apply the pattern to solving the problem at hand.

The solving of problems in chemistry is not an inherited talent. Everyone can learn the skill with practice. Be patient, concentrate, and you will develop the skill.

2:11 CONVERSION FACTORS

Conversion factors are ratios with a value equal to one.

In Section 2:1, the relationships between various prefixes were described. For example, the relationship between the centimeter and the meter is 1 m = 100 cm. The kilogram and the gram are related by the equation 1 kg = 1000 g. Using these and similar relationships, we can convert a unit to any other related unit.

EXAMPLE: Conversion

Spend time on conversions as they will be used throughout the book.

How many cubic centimeters are there in 5 cubic decimeters?

Solving process:

The given quantity is 5 dm^3. The required quantity is cm^3. The "bridge" we must find is that which will take us from cm^3 to dm^3.

(a) We know that 1 dm is equal to 10 cm. The relationship between dm and cm is

$$1 \text{ dm} = 10 \text{ cm}$$

(b) If we cube both sides of the equation we get

$$1 \text{ dm}^3 = 1000 \text{ cm}^3$$

(c) Both sides of the equation can be divided by the quantity 1 dm³. Now the equation appears as

$$1 = \frac{1000 \text{ cm}^3}{1 \text{ dm}^3}$$

(d) Using the known quantity of 5 dm³ that is given in the problem, we can write the equation

$$5 \text{ dm}^3 = 5 \text{ dm}^3$$

(e) We can now multiply the right side of the expression in (d) by the fraction

$$\frac{1000 \text{ cm}^3}{1 \text{ dm}^3}$$

1 dm³ = 1000 cm³

Since this fraction equals one, the value of the right side of the equation is not changed. (Recall that the value of any quantity multiplied by 1 is unchanged.) The equation then becomes

The value of any quantity multiplied by 1 is unchanged.

$$5 \text{ dm}^3 = 5 \text{ dm}^3 \left(\frac{1000 \text{ cm}^3}{1 \text{ dm}^3} \right)$$

$$= \frac{(5 \text{ dm}^3)(1000 \text{ cm}^3)}{(1 \text{ dm}^3)}$$

The equation then reduces to

$$5 \text{ dm}^3 = (5)(1000 \text{ cm}^3)$$

$$= 5000 \text{ cm}^3$$

Such a procedure is far too involved for finding the number of cm³ in dm³. However, these principles can be used to solve many kinds of problems.

In order to simplify the working of problems, we will use the following notation. In the sample problem just given, we had the equation

$$5 \text{ dm}^3 = 5 \text{ dm}^3 \left(\frac{1000 \text{ cm}^3}{1 \text{ dm}^3} \right)$$

That equation is equivalent to the equation

$$5 \text{ dm}^3 = \left(\frac{5 \text{ dm}^3}{1} \right) \left(\frac{1000 \text{ cm}^3}{1 \text{ dm}^3} \right)$$

Instead of enclosing every factor in parenthesis, we will simply set off each factor by a vertical line. Our equation is now written as

$$5 \text{ dm}^3 = \frac{5 \text{ dm}^3}{} \left|\, \frac{1000 \text{ cm}^3}{1 \text{ dm}^3} \right. = 5000 \text{ cm}^3$$

The fraction bar eliminates the need for parentheses.

EXAMPLE: Conversion

Convert 72 cm to meters.

Solving process:

(a) We know that

$$72 \text{ cm} = 72 \text{ cm} \qquad \text{and} \qquad 100 \text{ cm} = 1 \text{ m}$$

(b) By dividing both sides of the second equation by 100 cm, the equation becomes

$$1 = \frac{1 \text{ m}}{100 \text{ cm}}$$

Always make certain the unit you wish to eliminate is properly placed in the fraction that equals one.

(c) Multiplying both sides of the equation by 72 cm, we get

$$72 \text{ cm} \times 1 = \frac{72 \text{ cm}}{} \left| \frac{1 \text{ m}}{100 \text{ cm}} \right.$$

$$= \frac{72 \text{ m}}{100} = 0.72 \text{ m}$$

PROBLEM

17. *Convert.*

    a. 8.00 hours (h) to seconds   **d.** 51.2 milligrams to grams

    b. 0.0200 meter to centimeters   **e.** 0.492 dm^3 to cm^3

    c. 1.42 cm^3 to dm^3

17. a. 2.88×10^4 s
   b. 2.00 cm
   c. 0.00142 dm^3
   d. 0.0512 g
   e. 492 cm^3

2:12   FACTOR-LABEL METHOD

Unit labels are treated as factors.

Labels may be regarded as factors and "divided" out.

    The problem-solving method discussed in Sections 2:10 and 2:11 is called the **factor-label method.** In effect, unit labels are treated as factors. As common factors, these labels may be divided out. The solution to a problem depends upon having the correct unit label. Thus, this method aids in solving a problem and provides a check on mathematical operations. The individual conversion factors (ratios whose value is equivalent to one) may usually be written by inspection. Let us see how the method can be applied to more complex measurements.

The factor label method is used throughout the text. Spend a considerable amount of time familiarizing students with it. This time is an important factor in their success throughout the course.

    Many measurements are simply combinations of the elementary measurements as discussed in Section 2:6. We are all familiar with the measurement of speed. Speed is the distance covered in a single unit of time. It is length per unit time. The speed of an automobile is measured in kilometers (length) per hour (time). Most scientific measurements of speed are made in centimeters or meters per second. These units are in keeping with the use of SI for scientific work.

EXAMPLE: Conversion of Units

Express 60 kilometers per hour in terms of centimeters per second.

Solving process:

(a) Write 60 kilometers per hour as a ratio

$$\frac{60 \text{ km}}{1 \text{ h}}$$

Most conversion factors have an unlimited number of significant digits because they are definitions.

(b) We wish to convert kilometers to meters. Since 1000 m = 1 km, we can use the ratio

$$\frac{1000 \text{ m}}{1 \text{ km}}$$

(c) In the same manner, we will use

$$1 \text{ m} = 100 \text{ cm, or } \frac{1 \text{ m}}{100 \text{ cm}}$$

$$1 \text{ h} = 60 \text{ min, or } \frac{1 \text{ h}}{60 \text{ min}}$$

$$1 \text{ min} = 60 \text{ s, or } \frac{1 \text{ min}}{60 \text{ s}}$$

(d) All these ratios equal 1. Since any number may be multiplied by 1 or its equivalent without changing its value, we can now write

$$\frac{60 \text{ km}}{1 \text{ h}} = \frac{60 \text{ km}}{1 \text{ h}} \left| \frac{1000 \text{ m}}{1 \text{ km}} \right| \frac{100 \text{ cm}}{1 \text{ m}} \left| \frac{1 \text{ h}}{60 \text{ min}} \right| \frac{1 \text{ min}}{60 \text{ s}} = 1700 \text{ cm/s}$$

Notice that ratios are arranged so that units can be divided out as factors. This procedure leaves the correct units in the answer and provides a check on the method used.

Unit cancellation marks will be shown in blue for all Example problems. Use these as a guide in working on your own problems. They act as a check as to whether the problem has been set up correctly.

Unit cancellation marks act as a check as to whether the problem has been set up correctly.

PROBLEMS

18. Make the following conversions.

   a. 24.0 milligrams to kilograms
   b. 8.60 milligrams to grams
   c. 201 dm^3 to liters
   d. 88.7 cm^3 to cubic meters
   e. 68.8 m^3 to cubic decimeters
   f. 6.4 nm to centimeters

   g. 0.279 mm to cm
   h. 7.64 kg to g
   i. 0.0492 g to mg
   j. 8.00 dm^3 to cm^3
   k. 800 dm^3 to m^3
   l. 2.80 h to s

18. a. 2.4×10^{-5} kg
   b. 8.6×10^{-2} g
   g. 0.0279 cm
   h. 7 640 g
   i. 49.2 mg
   j. 8.00×10^3 cm^3
   k. 0.8 m^3
   l. 1.01×10^4 s

c. 201 L   e. 68 800 dm^3
d. 8.87×10^{-5} m^3 f. 6.4×10^{-7} cm

2:13 DENSITY

A less familiar, but common, scientific measurement is density. **Density** is mass per unit of volume. To measure density, we must be able to measure both mass (m) and volume (V). Mass can be measured on a balance. The volume of a solid can be measured in different ways. For instance, the volume of a cube is the length of one edge cubed (multiplied by itself three times). The volume of a rectangular solid is the length times the width times the height. The volume of a liquid can be measured in a clear container graduated to indicate units of volume. You will use graduated cylinders in lab to measure liquid volumes. In density measurements of liquids and solids, volume is usually measured in cubic centimeters (cm³). Density, then, is expressed in grams per cubic centimeter (g/cm³). The units used to express density are derived units. In equation form, density can be expressed as

$$D = \frac{m}{V}$$

Densities of common materials are listed in Table 2-3. Such a table offers a convenient and accurate means of comparing the masses of equal volumes of different materials. Note that the values given for gases are quite small. It is more practical to express gas density in g/m³. People sometimes say that lead is heavier than feathers. However, a truckload of feathers is heavier than a single piece of lead buckshot. To be exact, we should say that the density of lead is greater than the density of feathers. The density of a substance changes with changes in temperature. Ice floats in a glass of ice water because it is less dense than the liquid.

Hickson-Bender Photography

FIGURE 2-11. Though the volumes of the wood and sponge are equal, the balance shows the masses are not the same. Wood has more mass per unit volume.

Table 2-3

Densities of Some Common Materials	
Material	**Density**
natural gas	0.000 555 g/cm³
air	0.001 22 g/cm³
blood	1.06 g/cm³
sucrose (table sugar)	1.59 g/cm³
sodium chloride (table salt)	2.16 g/cm³
stainless steel	7.86 g/cm³
copper	8.92 g/cm³
mercury	13.59 g/cm³

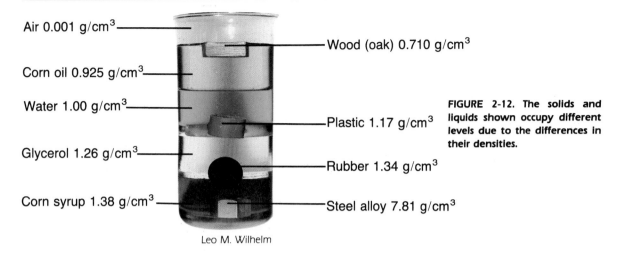

Air 0.001 g/cm^3

Corn oil 0.925 g/cm^3

Water 1.00 g/cm^3

Glycerol 1.26 g/cm^3

Corn syrup 1.38 g/cm^3

Wood (oak) 0.710 g/cm^3

Plastic 1.17 g/cm^3

Rubber 1.34 g/cm^3

Steel alloy 7.81 g/cm^3

FIGURE 2-12. The solids and liquids shown occupy different levels due to the differences in their densities.

Leo M. Wilhelm

EXAMPLE: Conversion of Units

Express 0.053 cubic centimeters as cubic meters.

Solving process:

$$0.053 \text{ cm}^3 = \frac{0.053 \text{ cm}^3}{} \left| \frac{1 \text{ m}^3}{(10^2 \text{ cm})^3} \right. = 5.3 \times 10^{-8} \text{ m}^3$$

Express 0.20 kg/m^3 as g/cm^3.

Solving process:

$$0.20 \text{ kg/m}^3 = \frac{0.20 \text{ kg}}{1 \text{ m}^3} \left| \frac{10^3 \text{ g}}{1 \text{ kg}} \right| \frac{1 \text{ m}^3}{(10^2 \text{ cm})^3}$$

$$= \frac{0.20}{1} \left| \frac{10^3 \text{ g}}{1} \right| \frac{1}{10^6 \text{ cm}^3} = \frac{0.20 \text{ g}}{10^3 \text{ cm}^3} = 2.0 \times 10^{-4} \text{ g/cm}^3$$

a *b*

F. Bernard Daniel

FIGURE 2-13. The volume of an irregular solid can be determined by water displacement (a). The density of a battery acid solution is measured using a hydrometer (b).

EXAMPLE: Factor Label

Calcium has a density of 1.54 g/cm³. What mass would 3.00 cm³ of calcium have?

Solving process:

Density is mass per unit volume, or

$$D = \frac{m}{V}$$

Solving this equation for mass by multiplying each side by V, we obtain

$$m = D \times V$$

Substituting the known information, we obtain

$$\frac{1.54 \text{ g}}{\text{cm}^3} \left| \frac{3.00 \text{ cm}^3}{} \right. = 4.62 \text{ g}$$

Correct units for the answer act as a check that the problem is set up correctly.

The fact that the answer is expressed in grams is another check on the work. If the unit is correct, chances are the problem was done correctly.

EXAMPLE: Factor Label

Cobalt has a density of 8.90 g/cm³. What volume would 17.8 g of cobalt have?

Solving process:

We know that density can be expressed as

$$D = \frac{m}{V}$$

Solving this equation for volume and substituting the known information in the resulting equation, we obtain

$$V = \frac{m}{D}$$

$$= \frac{17.8 \text{ g}}{8.90 \text{ g/cm}^3} \quad \text{or} \quad \frac{17.8 \text{ g}}{} \left| \frac{1 \text{ cm}^3}{8.90 \text{ g}} \right. = 2.00 \text{ cm}^3$$

The answer is in cm³, a unit of volume, which is another check on the accuracy of the problem solving approach.

PROBLEMS

19. 2.85 g/cm³

19. What is the density of a piece of cement which has a mass of 8.76 g and a volume of 3.07 cm³?

20. What is the density of a piece of cork which has a mass of 0.650 g and a volume of 2.71 cm^3?

21. Limestone has a density of 2.72 g/cm^3. What is the mass of 981 cm^3 of limestone?

Solve the following problems for mass.

22. Ammonium magnesium chromate has a density of 1.84 g/cm^3. What is the mass of 6.96 cm^3 of this substance?

23. Barium perchlorate has a density of 2.74 g/cm^3. What is the mass of 610 cm^3 of this substance?

24. Bismuth phosphate has a density of 6.32 g/cm^3. What is the mass of 66.6 cm^3 of this substance?

Solve the following problems for volume.

25. Calcium chloride has a density of 2.15 g/cm^3. What is the volume of 3.37 g of this substance?

26. Cerium sulfate has a density of 3.17 g/cm^3. What is the volume of 706 g of this substance?

27. Chromium silicide has a density of 5.50 g/cm^3. What is the volume of 13.4 g of this substance?

20. 0.240 g/cm^3
21. 2670 g
22. 12.8 g
23. 1670 g
24. 421 g
25. 1.57 cm^3
26. 223 cm^3
27. 2.44 cm^3

Marie Curie (1867–1934)

A Nobel Prize usually caps the career of a scientist. Marie Curie won two! In 1903, she was awarded the prize in physics for her joint research with her husband Pierre on the radiation phenomenon discovered by Becquerel. In 1911, she won the chemistry prize for the discovery of the elements radium and polonium, and for the study of radium compounds. Madame Curie was devoted not only to scientific research but also to the applications of the research. The use of the radioactive rays of radium in the treatment of cancer is but one example of this concern. In spite of the honors and her fame in the scientific community and the world, she remained modest and unassuming until her death at age 67. In 1935, one year after her death, her daughter, Irene Joliot-Curie (1897–1956) was awarded a Nobel Prize with her husband for the discovery of artificial radioactivity.

CHEMICAL CAREER: Chemical Engineering

Chemistry is a science. Engineering, on the other hand, is a particular approach to problem solving. The engineer uses the facts generated by scientists to solve everyday problems. Most engineers (and some chemists) deal with technology.

Though a chemical engineer performs many functions, a broad definition would be a person who designs, builds, and/or operates chemical plants or industrial plants using chemistry. The design function involves working with chemists who have investigated the process for which the plant is being built. The design engineer may call on other engineers to research certain aspects of the design. Typically, one problem which must be solved is the types of materials to be used in construction. Raw materials, intermediate substances, and the final product may be corrosive and require special handling. Stainless steel piping and titanium pumps may be needed for their ability to resist corrosion.

Before a chemical plant is built, a small scale duplicate, called a pilot plant, is constructed. In general, full-scale plants cannot be designed simply by multiplying a process performed in the lab by some appropriate number. Doubling the amount of raw materials and the size of the reaction vessel may not produce the desired result. Development of a new process takes place in several stages before final production. The chemical engineer monitors all aspects of this process.

Chemical engineers oversee the construction of the plant to ensure that all specifications are met. They also direct the operations of the plant after it goes into production. In both of these functions, the engineer may well have to use his or her knowledge of economics and business to make decisions about sources of raw materials, selling price of the product, and value of overtime work. Since the chemical engineers are involved in the production of chemicals, it is also important that they be aware of the environmental factors involved. The costs of scrubbers and other antipollution devices must be considered. Decisions must be made as to how to preserve the environment while supplying a price competitive product.

Some chemical engineers are involved in selling chemical process machinery to chemical-producing companies. The chemical engineer in sales "talks the language" of the purchasing firm and can help in designing new and more specialized equipment for the customer.

Most chemical engineers eventually reach management positions in a company. The actual operation of a chemical-producing company is usually in the hands of an experienced company member who started as an engineer and therefore understands intimately the processes run by the company.

SUMMARY

1. Scientific work requires a quantitative approach. In other words, to investigate a phenomenon, certain characteristics must be measured. Intro
2. Scientists use SI measurements. This system of measurement consists of seven fundamental units. SI units are particularly convenient because they are based on multiples of 10. 2:1
3. The most elementary measurements in science are those of mass, length, time, and temperature. 2:2–2:5
4. The SI unit of volume is the cubic meter (m^3). Speed is length per unit time. Density is the mass of a substance in a unit volume of that substance. All three of these quantities are compound or derived. 2:6
5. Accuracy of a measurement is determined by the quality of the measuring instruments. Precision of a measurement is the relative error. 2:8
6. Any number can be expressed in scientific notation as $M \times 10^n$. Where M is some number ≥ 1 and <10 and n is an integer. 2:9
7. Scientific notation indicates clearly the number of significant digits. This notation is particularly helpful in multiplication and division. 2:9
8. In the factor-label method of problem solving, unit labels are treated as factors. This method makes conversion of units easier. 2:12

PROBLEMS

28. What are the seven base units in SI?   m, kg, s, A, K, mol, cd
29. Why is mass used instead of weight for scientific work?   Mass does not vary.
30. How is the Celsius temperature scale defined?   100 equal intervals between boiling and freezing points of H_2O
31. What is the SI fundamental unit of mass? kg
32. Why is it important to maintain the correct number of significant digits in calculations? to indicate the exactness of a measurement
33. List the number of significant digits for each of the following:
    a. $1. \times 10^8$ 1
    b. 6.8×10^8 2
    c. $4.930\ 00 \times 10^9$ 6
    d. $8.420\ 000\ 0 \times 10^8$ 8
34. Compute the precision of each of the following measurements:
    a. 41.3 s (accuracy of stopwatch = ±0.1 s).   0.2%
    b. 67.9°C (accuracy of thermometer = ±0.1°).   0.1%
    c. 0.0961 km (accuracy of pedometer = ±0.0001 km).   0.1%
35. Express in scientific notation.
    a. 36.8 3.68×10^1
    b. 0.0387 3.87×10^{-2}
    c. 0.000 216 5 2.165×10^{-4}
    d. 516 830 000 000 5.168×10^{11}
36. Express as a whole number or decimal.
    a. 9.14×10^{-3} 0.009 14
    b. 3.50×10^{-5} 0.000 035 0
    c. 9.52×10^5 952 000
    d. 4.66×10^1 46.6

37. a. 1.03×10^6
  b. 2.17×10^{-5}
  c. 3.8×10^{-1}
  d. 1.7×10^{-2}

37. Perform the following operations.
  a. $9.43 \times 10^5 + 8.82 \times 10^4$ **c.** $(1.6 \times 10^2)(2.4 \times 10^{-3})$
  b. $2.78 \times 10^{-5} - 6.12 \times 10^{-6}$ **d.** $(75.4 \times 10^2)(0.774 \times 10^{-2}) \div (3.4 \times 10^3)$

38. List the number of significant digits that should appear in the answers to the following problems.
  a. $(0.50)(0.005\ 5)$ 2   **c.** 0.30 divided by 0.058 2
  b. $(0.7)(9.48 \times 10^1)$ 1   **d.** 0.6 divided by 9.59×10^1 1

39. Solve the following problems. Round off your answers to the proper number of decimal places.

a.	**b.**	**c.**	**d.**	**e.**
0.089 90	0.9	63	4	0.06
+ 52.	− 0.000 05	+ 93	+ 6	+ 2.
52	0.9	156	10	2

40. a. 3.00 g/cm³
  b. 2.80 g/cm³
  c. 0.680 g/cm³
  d. 1.03 g/cm³
  e. 1.91 g/cm³
  f. 1.07 g/cm³
  g. 2.40 g/cm³
  h. 8.59 g/cm³
  i. 1.80 g/cm³
  j. 0.130 g/cm³
  k. 0.700 g/cm³
  l. 2.40 g/cm³
  m. 0.872 g/cm³

40. Find the density in g/cm³ of the following:
  a. cement, if a rectangular piece 2.00 cm × 2.00 cm × 9.00 cm has a mass of 108 g
  b. granite, if a rectangular piece 5.00 cm × 10.0 cm × 23.0 cm has a mass of 3.22 kg
  c. gasoline, if 9.00 liters have a mass of 6120 g
  d. milk, if 2.00 liters have a mass of 2.06 kg
  e. ivory, if a rectangular piece 23.0 cm × 15.0 cm × 15.5 cm has a mass of 10.22 kg
  f. evaporated milk, if 411 g occupy 384 cm³
  g. asbestos, if 233 g occupy 97.0 cm³
  h. brass, if 535 g occupy 62.3 cm³
  i. brick, if 49.2 g occupy 27.3 cm³
  j. balsa wood, if 171 g occupy 1320 cm³
  k. cardboard, if 3.19 g occupy 4.56 cm³
  l. chalk, if 6.36 g occupy 2.65 cm³
  m. butter, if 272 g occupy 312 cm³

41. 1.59 g/cm³
42. 833 cm/s
43. 1250 g
44. 92.1 g
45. 1.27 cm³
46. $0.001\ 2$ g/cm³
47. 51.5 g
48. 7.76 g

41. What is the density of sugar in g/cm³ if its density is 1590 kg/m³?

42. An automobile is traveling at the rate of 30.0 kilometers per hour. What is its rate in centimeters per second (cm/s)?

43. The density of a sample of nitrogen gas is 1.25 g/L. What is the mass of 1.00 m³ of the gas?

44. Bismuth has a density of 9.80 g/cm. What is the mass of 9.40 cm³ of bismuth?

45. Iron has a density of 7.87 g/cm³. What volume would 10.0 g of iron occupy?

46. If 1.0 km³ of air has mass 1 200 000 000 kg, what is the density of air in g/cm³?

47. Antimony has a density of 6.70 g/cm³. What is the mass of 7.69 cm³ of antimony?

48. Gold has a density of 19.3 g/cm³. What is the mass of 0.402 cm³ of gold?

49. Magnesium has a density of 1.74 g/cm^3. What is the volume of 50.5 g magnesium?

50. Tin has a density of 7.28 g/cm^3. What is the volume of 7.57 kg of tin?

49. 29.0 cm^3
50. 1040 cm^3

REVIEW   1. To provide the facts as the basis for making value judgments.

1. What is the role of science in making environmental decisions?

2. What are the two general forms of energy an object can possess? potential and kinetic

3. What is the principal aim of chemists in their work?

4. State the law of conservation of mass-energy. Matter and energy are always conserved and their sum cannot be increased or decreased.

ONE MORE STEP

1. Thermometers are not the only instruments used to measure temperature. Other temperature measuring devices are the thermocouple, the optical pyrometer, and the thermister. Prepare a report for your class on operation and advantages and disadvantages of each of these instruments.

2. A procedure used by many scientists and engineers is dimensional analysis. Look up this term in an unabridged dictionary in the school library. After you have familiarized yourself with the meaning of the term, predict the units associated with the measurement of the following phenomena: viscosity, power, torque, and rate of heat transfer.

3. Determine how a computer makes computations with large numbers.

4. Some hand-held calculators round off. Others merely drop all digits after the last one shown. Investigate the calculators in your class to see which round off and which do not. Compare prices on the two groups.

5. Some personal microcomputers can do calculations in "double precision mode." Find the meaning of that phrase.

6. Research how surveyors use lasers in making measurements.

READINGS

Himes, Gary K., *Solving Problems in Chemistry*. Columbus, Ohio: Charles E. Merrill Publishing Company, 1983.

Strauss, Howard J., and Kaufman, Milton, *Handbook for Chemical Technicians*. New York: McGraw-Hill Book Co., 1976.

Tuma, Jan J., *Handbook of Physical Calculations*. New York: McGraw-Hill Book Co., 1976.

Weaver, Kenneth F., "How Soon Will We Measure in Metric?" *National Geographic*, Vol. 152, No. 2 (August 1977), pp. 287-294.

Every object in the photograph can be labeled as matter. However, it would seem to be an impossible task to study the characteristics of all matter. Classifying matter into smaller groups with similar characteristics can make this study easier. Knowing the characteristics and properties of some members of a group allows us to generalize about others. Consider the properties of some materials in the photograph. The clothing is designed to allow for movement and allows the body to breathe. The materials in the athletic shoes provide support, comfort, and allow for quick and agile movements.

MATTER

3

Chapter 3 introduces atoms, molecules, elements, compounds, and mixtures. It also describes the general properties of matter and the changes it undergoes.

Demonstration—Mix sand and PbO to simulate an ore. Place the ore in a large test tube, add water and mineral oil, shake well. Note the separation of the ore. Use this demonstration to introduce the vocabulary in this chapter.

The world around us is filled with objects of many kinds. There are people, chairs, books, trees, lumps of sugar, ice cubes, drinking glasses, doorknobs, and an endless number of other familiar objects. Each of these objects may be characterized by its size, shape, use, color, and texture. Many unlike objects have certain things in common. For example, a tree and a chair are both made of wood. Millions of other objects with different shapes and purposes may also be made of wood. The word **material** is used in referring to a specific kind of matter (such as wood). Familiar materials include wood, steel, copper, sugar, salt, nickel, marble, concrete, and milk.

GOAL: You will gain an understanding of the ways in which matter is classified by properties and changed by physical and chemical processes.

Material refers to a specific kind of matter.

3:1 HETEROGENEOUS MATERIALS

Most of the things we see around us contain two or more different materials. Sometimes it is necessary to use a microscope to distinguish between these different materials. Wood, granite, concrete, and milk are examples. If we look closely at granite, we can see at least three minerals. These minerals are quartz, biotite, and feldspar. If a piece of granite is crushed into sand-sized particles, it is possible to pick out the quartz, biotite, or feldspar. Milk appears to be uniform. Under a microscope, however, we can see particles suspended in water. Milk is not uniform. Such nonuniform materials are called heterogeneous (het uh roh JEE nee uhs) materials. One type of material can be separated from the other material in milk. Fat globules can be removed by a cream separator.

A heterogeneous material is not uniform throughout.

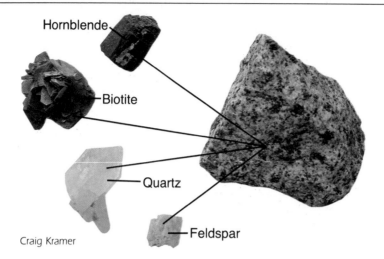

Hornblende

Biotite

Quartz

Feldspar

Craig Kramer

**FIGURE 3-2. Milk (a) is a hetero-
geneous material as can be
seen from this microscopic view
(b). A microscopic view of cream
is shown in (c).**

Any physically separate part of a material is called a phase. A **phase** is any region with a uniform set of properties. We can distinguish between different phases of the same material. For example, ice and water are different phases of the same material. All the material in the water region has the same set of properties. Likewise, all the material in the ice region has the same set of properties. Ice and water are different states (solid and liquid) of the same material.

We may now define a **heterogeneous material** as one that is composed of more than one phase. The different phases in a heterogeneous material are separated from each other by definite boundaries called **interfaces**. In the two-phase system of ice and water, the surfaces of the ice and water are the interfaces.

a

Larry Hamill

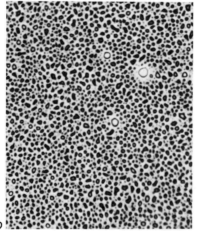

b

c

J. Gnau and A. Ottolenghi at Ohio State Univ.

Corn syrup

Water

Gasoline

Mercury

Water vapor

Ice

Water

Tim Courlas

FIGURE 3-3. The layered liquids on the left compose a four-phase system in the liquid state. The container on the right is a three-phase system at three different physical states.

3:2 HOMOGENEOUS MATERIALS

Materials which consist of only one phase are called **homogeneous** (hoh moh JEE nee uhs) **materials.** Since they are homogeneous, there must be a uniform distribution of the particles within the material. If you break a piece of homogeneous matter into smaller pieces, each piece will have the same properties as every other small piece. If you look at one of the pieces under a microscope, it is impossible to distinguish one part as being a different material from any other part. Examples of homogeneous materials are sugar, salt, seawater, quartz, and window glass.

Some homogeneous matter can be classified as mixtures. A **mixture** contains more than one kind of material. Heterogeneous matter is always composed of more than one phase and is always a mixture. Homogeneous matter composed of more than one material is called a **solution.**

Solutions such as seawater, window glass, and gold-silver alloys vary in composition from sample to sample. If we put a small amount of pure salt into pure water and let it stand, we get a solution, or homogeneous mixture. If we add a larger amount of pure salt to the same amount of pure water, we again get a solution. The composition of the second sample would differ from the first. The second sample contains more salt in an equal volume of water. Homogeneous mixtures, or solutions, have variable compositions. For example, we may add 5, 10, or 15 grams of salt to 100 grams of water. In each case, the resulting material is homogeneous. A solution may also be defined as a single phase which can vary in composition. Solutions are not necessarily liquid. Air is a homogeneous material composed of nitrogen, oxygen, and smaller quantities of other gases. Its composition

Homogeneous materials consist of only one phase.

A mixture contains more than one kind of material.

A solution is a homogeneous mixture whose composition varies.

Students should understand the distinction between mixing and combining. Natural gas and air can mix, but when they combine CO_2 and H_2O are produced.

Solutions may be solids, liquids, or gases.

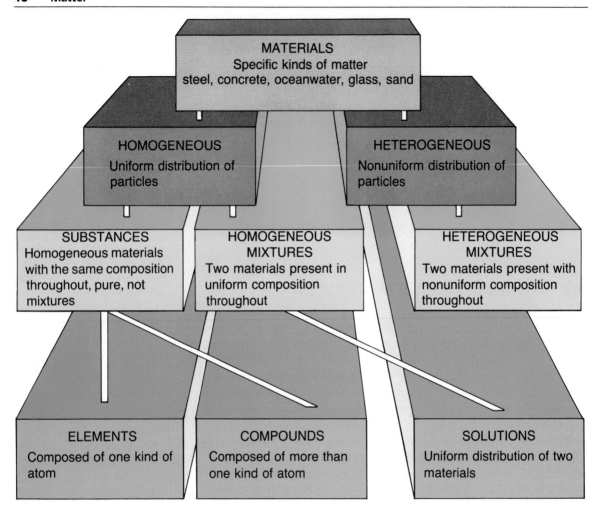

FIGURE 3-4. Matter can be classified from general to specific types by characteristic properties.

A solution has a solute dispersed uniformly in a solvent.

varies from place to place. However, each sample of air is a homogeneous mixture. Different types of window glass have different compositions, yet each type is homogeneous. Both air and glass are solutions.

A solution consists of a **solute** (dissolved material) in a **solvent** (dissolving material). In the case of two liquids in solution, the solvent is the component which is the larger proportion of the whole solution. The solute is scattered in the solvent in very small particles (molecular or smaller). Because of this scattering, the solution appears uniform, even under the most powerful optical microscope. Since the scattering of particles appears to be completely uniform, solutions are classified as homogeneous materials.

In your laboratory work, you will be using solutions labeled with a number followed by the letter "*M.*" The symbol represents the term molarity. The exact meaning of molarity will be studied

2.9 grams   291 grams   1746 grams

Hickson-Bender Photography

When discussing molarity, prepare $KMnO_4$ solutions of different concentrations to show students color-concentration relationship.

FIGURE 3-5. The flasks contain a cobalt compound in solution. The relative amounts of solid needed to prepare $0.01M$, $1M$, and $6M$ solutions are shown.

in Chapter 5. In the meantime, you should keep in mind that **molarity** is used to indicate the amount of solute in a specific amount of solution. A $6M$ (six molar) solution contains 60 times as much solute as a $0.1M$ (tenth molar) solution of the same volume.

Molarity, M, indicates the amount of solute in a specific amount of solution.

3:3   SUBSTANCES

Some homogeneous materials such as pure salt, pure sugar, or pure sulfur always have the same composition. Such materials are called **substances.** A large part of chemistry is the study of the processes by which substances may be changed into other substances.

Materials which always have the same composition are substances.

According to the atomic theory, matter is made of very tiny particles called **atoms.** Substances are divided into two classes. Substances composed of only one kind of atom are called **elements.** Examples are sulfur, oxygen, hydrogen, nitrogen, copper, gold, and chlorine. Substances composed of more than one kind of atom are called **compounds.** The atoms in the particles of compounds are always in definite ratios. Thus, water contains hydrogen atoms and oxygen atoms in a ratio of 2 to 1. To summarize, all matter can be classified as heterogeneous mixture, solution, compound, or element.

An element is composed of only one kind of atom.

Elements and compounds are substances.

A compound is made of more than one kind of atom.

The development of this system of classification played a significant role in the early development of chemistry. Early chemists spent much time and energy sorting the pure substances from the mixtures.

Tc and Pm do not occur naturally. At and Fr are present in such negligible amounts that they can be ignored as contributing to the earth's mass.

Chemists know of 88 naturally-occurring elements. A complete list of the elements is found on page 60. Uranium is the natural element with the most complex atoms. Two elements, technetium and promethium, which have simpler atoms than uranium are not found in nature. Astatine and francium have been detected in nature. However, they are present in such small amounts that they cannot be easily separated from their ores. These four elements are not normally counted among the natural elements. These synthetic elements, and over a dozen others, can be produced by scientists through nuclear reactions. Synthetic elements and nuclear reactions will be discussed in Chapter 28.

Chemists today are interested in reactions of elements and compounds, the analysis of compounds into their component elements, and the synthesis of compounds from elements or other compounds. These properties and processes depend upon the structure of the elements and compounds. Thus, chemists are very much interested in these structures.

a

Oak Ridge National Laboratory

b   Hickson-Bender Photography   c   Hickson-Bender Photography

FIGURE 3-6. Curium (a) is a synthetic element. Mercury (b) and iron (c) appear quite different from the compounds they form.

PROBLEMS

1. Classify the following materials as heterogeneous mixtures, solutions, compounds, or elements. Use a dictionary to identify any unfamiliar materials.
   - **a.** air
   - **b.** India ink
   - **c.** paper
   - **d.** table salt
   - **e.** wood alcohol
   - **f.** apple
   - **g.** milk
   - **h.** plutonium
   - **i.** water

2. Indicate how you would demonstrate that each of the following is a heterogeneous mixture or a homogeneous mixture.
   - **a.** a piece of lumber
   - **b.** a glass of soda pop
   - **c.** a piece of cloth advertised as 50% wool and 50% synthetic fiber
   - **d.** a piece of calf's liver
   - **e.** shaving cream

3:4 PHYSICAL PROPERTIES

The properties of a substance can be divided into two classes. One class depends on the substance itself. The other depends for the most part on the action of the substance in the presence of other substances. The first class of properties is called **physical properties.** Length, color, and temperature are physical properties. Physical properties may be divided into groups: extensive properties and intensive properties. **Extensive properties** depend upon the amount of matter present. Some of these properties are mass, length, and volume.

Intensive properties do not depend upon the amount of matter present. For example, each sample of a substance, regardless of its size, has the same density throughout. Other intensive properties include malleability (mal ee uh BIHL uht ee), ductility and conductivity. For example, copper can be hammered quite easily into thin sheets. It is more malleable than iron, which resists this pounding. Copper can also be drawn out into a fine wire; it is quite ductile. Both copper and silver have high heat and electrical conductivity. A high heat conductivity or electrical conductivity means that a substance offers little resistance to the flow of heat or electricity. Silver has a high heat conductivity and a silver spoon will become hot if left in a hot pan of soup.

In addition to density, the intensive properties most important to the chemist are color, crystalline shape, melting point, boiling point, and refractive index (ability to bend light).

Extensive properties depend on the amount of material.

Intensive properties depend upon the nature of material itself.

Tom Flynn/Taurus Photos

FIGURE 3-7. Copper is quite malleable and ductile. These properties make it useful for a variety of products including sheeting, tubing, and wire.

3:5 PHYSICAL CHANGES

Changes like pounding, pulling, or heating do not change the chemical character of a substance. Pounded copper is still copper. Only its physical appearance is changed. Thus, these changes are called **physical changes.** Dividing a piece of material into smaller pieces, tearing paper, dissolving sugar in water, and pouring a liquid from one container to another, are other examples of physical changes.

Physical changes affect only physical properties.

Physical changes occur when a substance melts or boils. At the melting point, a solid changes to a liquid. At the boiling point, a liquid changes to a gas. Such physical changes are called changes of state, since the substance is not altered except for its physical state. A knowledge of physical properties and changes can be applied to separating mixtures. Separating substances by **distillation** is a change-of-state operation. It is used to separate substances with different boiling points. For instance, you can separate a solution of salt in water by heating the solution to a temperature equal to the boiling point of the solution. The water will then be turned to steam and escape from the container. The salt, whose boiling point has not yet been reached, will remain.

Distillation is a means of separating substances by boiling point differences.

FIGURE 3-8. A distillation apparatus is used to separate the components of a mixture by differences in boiling points.

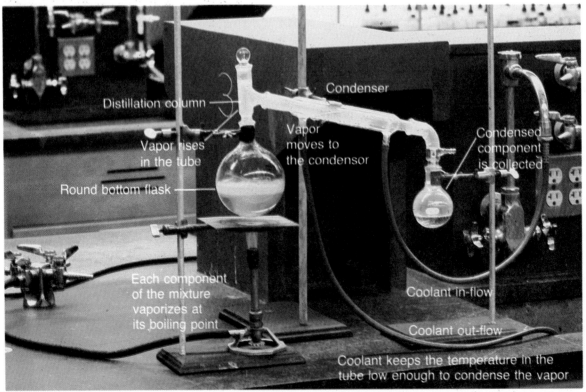

a   Manfred Kage/Peter Arnold, Inc.

b   Hickson-Bender Photography

FIGURE 3-9. An electron micro-scope was used to photograph the crystallization of palladium (a). The yellow precipitate formed in this reaction is lead(II) chromate (b).

Another separation based on phase difference depends upon the solubility of one substance in another. Most substances have a specific solubility (amount of solute that dissolves) in water at a given temperature. Therefore, it is usually possible to separate two sub-stances in the same solution by a process called **fractional crystallization.** The insoluble substance which forms from a solution is called a **precipitate.** This pro-cess may be called crystallization since most substances form crystals when they precipitate.

Notice in Figure 3-10 that, at 70°C, potassium bromide (KBr) is less soluble than potassium nitrate (KNO_3). If a water solution containing equal amounts of both substances is allowed to evapo-rate at 70°C, the potassium bromide will crystallize first. This process is used quite often by chemists to purify labora-tory chemicals. It is also used in industry in the production of many crystalline items, such as sugar, salt, and drugs.

Both distillation and crystallization are useful in separating mixtures. As a rule, any mixture can be separated by physical changes. In some cases, how-ever, such separations are not practical.

FIGURE 3-10. A solubility graph shows the amount of solid that will dissolve at a given tempera-ture.

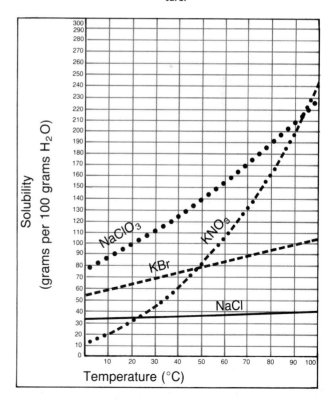

PROBLEM

3. Using Figure 3-10, determine the solubility of the following.
   a. NaCl at 70°C   **c.** KNO_3 at 30°C
   b. $NaClO_3$ at 100°C   **d.** KBr at 80°C

3:6 CHEMICAL PROPERTIES

Chemical properties are determined by observing the behavior of a substance in the presence of other substances.

Some properties of matter depend upon the action of substances in the presence of other substances. These properties are called **chemical properties.** In order to determine the chemical properties of a substance we must know the kinds of chemical changes that the substance can undergo. Does it burn? Does it help other substances to burn? Does it react with water? Does it react with acids and/or bases? With what other kinds of substances does it react? Such questions help to determine the chemical properties of a substance.

FIGURE 3-11. Information concerning the chemical and physical properties of a substance can be found in a chemical handbook. The chemical and physical properties of uranium are highlighted.

☐ Physical property

▨ Chemical property

Uranium. U: atomic mass 238.029; atomic number 92; oxidation states 6+, 5+, 4+, 3+. Occurrence in the earth's crust 2×10^{-5}%; melting point 1132.3°C; boiling point 3818°C; density 19.05 g/cm^3. Silver-white radioactive metal, softer than glass. Uranium is malleable, ductile, and can be polished. Half-life of the U-238 isotope is 4.51×10^9 years. Specific heat is 0.117 J/g·C°; heat of fusion 12.1 kJ/mol; heat of vaporization 460 kJ/mol. Burns in air at 150–175°C to form U_3O_8. When finely powdered, it slowly decomposes in cold water, more quickly in hot water. Burns in fluorine to form a green, volatile tetrafluoride; also burns in chlorine, bromine, and iodine. Reacts with acids with the liberation of hydrogen and the formation of salts with the 4+ oxidation state. Not attacked by alkalies.

3:7 CHEMICAL CHANGES

Suppose you are given two test tubes containing colorless liquids. One test tube contains water. The other contains nitric acid. If you place a pinch of sugar in the water, it will disappear and the liquid remains colorless. The sugar has dissolved and you now have a sugar-water solution. A physical change has occurred. If you put a small piece of copper into the other test tube, it will also disappear. However, the liquid will turn blue and a brown gas will be given off. You now have a solution of copper nitrate and some nitrogen dioxide gas. A chemical change has occurred. Let us take another example. Sodium is a silvery, soft metal which reacts violently with water. Chlorine is a greenish-yellow gas, which is highly corrosive and poisonous. However, if these two dangerous elements are allowed to combine, they produce a white crystalline solid which neither reacts with water nor is poisonous. It is common table salt—sodium chloride. In this case, the properties of the reactants have disappeared. The new substance formed has different properties.

Whenever a substance undergoes a change so that one or more new substances with different properties are formed, a **chemical change** (reaction) has taken place. Burning, digesting, and fermenting are examples of chemical changes.

The separation of compounds into their component elements always requires a chemical change. Such a separation is one type of analysis. Mixtures can always be separated by physical means. However, it is sometimes more convenient to separate mixtures by a chemical change.

Demonstration—Add AgNO$_3$ solution to NaCl solution to give precipitate, or Pb(NO$_3$)$_2$ and K$_2$CrO$_4$ solutions give a precipitate that is yellow in color.

You may wish to do this as a demonstration. **CAUTION:** Vent the fumes from the Cu + HNO$_3$ reaction.

Chemical changes produce new substances with new properties.

FIGURE 3-12. The reaction of copper with nitric acid (a) produces a copper compound and reddish gas. The combustion of steel wool in pure oxygen (b) is also a chemical change.

a

Tim Courlas

b

Courtesy of Kodansha Ltd.

PROBLEMS

4. a. physical
   b. chemical
   k. chemical
   l. chemical

c. chemical   e. physical   g. physical   i. physical
d. physical   f. chemical   h. physical   j. physical

4. Classify the following properties as chemical or physical. Use a dictionary to identify any unfamiliar properties.

   a. color
   b. reactivity
   c. flammability
   d. odor
   e. porosity
   f. stability
   g. ductility
   h. solubility
   i. expansion
   j. melting point
   k. rusting
   l. reacts with air

5. a. chemical
   b. chemical
   c. chemical
   d. physical
6. a. chemical
   b. physical
   c. chemical
   d. physical
   e. physical

5. Classify the following changes as chemical or physical.
   a. digestion of food
   b. fading of dye in cloth
   c. growth of a plant
   d. melting of ice

6. Classify the following changes as chemical or physical.
   a. explosion of gasoline in an automobile engine
   b. formation of clouds in the air
   c. healing of a wound
   d. making of rock candy by evaporating water from a sugar solution
   e. production of light by an electric lamp

7. ammonia, soft drink, cleaning fluid, window cleaner, paint thinner, air deodorizer.

7. Make a list of five solutions commonly found in the home.

8. explosion, battery discharging, muscular contraction, cooking (particularly baking), gasoline burning in a gasoline engine.

8. List five chemical changes familiar to you in which the energy transfer that occurs is important.

9. Using a chemical dictionary, the *Handbook of Chemistry and Physics*, or *Lange's Handbook of Chemistry* prepare a report on the properties of an element as assigned by your teacher.

St. Elmo Brady   (1884–1966)

St. Elmo Brady was the first black student to receive a doctorate in chemistry. He spent the rest of his life making certain that other black students would have the same opportunity. After finishing his degree at the University of Illinois in 1916, he went to Tuskegee Institute to develop what became the first chemistry department there. He moved in 1920 to Howard University and accomplished the same task. In 1927 he moved to Fisk University and served 25 years building both undergraduate and graduate programs. After retirement, when he was nearly 70 years old, Brady was again asked to build a chemistry department, this time at Tougaloo, Mississippi. As a result of his efforts, thousands of students have had the opportunity for an education in chemistry. He studied and wrote until his death at 82.

CHEMICAL CAREER: Nutritionists

The human body is an extremely complex chemical factory. Several sciences are involved in the study of the body, but nutrition is one of the most practical. Knowledge gained in nutrition science can be put to immediate use in a number of career positions.

Nutritionists are concerned with the raw materials fed into the human chemical factory. A thorough study of chemistry, biochemistry, and human physiology is required. Some nutritionists make a career of researching medical and health-related nutritional problems. Others choose to apply their knowledge on a daily basis in maintaining the health of individuals or communities.

The nutritionist is an essential part of the health care team, whether it be in a hospital, rural clinic, food industry, or government agency. In that role, he or she must be able to cooperate with other health care professionals (doctors, food chemists, food standards boards) as well as communicate with a patient. In addition, the nutritionist must be aware of the legal limitations to which he or she is subject, the cultural biases of a patient, and the economic realities of a particular situation. The nutritional problems of rural areas or undeveloped nations are not easily solved.

The food intake of humans varies as an individual grows. Not all individuals grow at the same rate and nutritionists adjust diets to account for individual differences in physiology and metabolism. They must have a thorough knowledge of the chemical needs of the body and how these needs can be met by the chemical substances present in foods. In addition, nutritionists provide specialized diets to minister to individuals with particular medical problems such as obesity, high blood pressure, or ulcers.

FIGURE 3-13. The varied duties of a nutritionist require adequate background in chemistry.

Nutritionists also supervise food preparation, plan menus, recognize and treat dietary-based diseases, purchase food, and develop new recipes.

The principle employers of nutritionists are hospitals, school systems, restaurant and hotel chains, food producers, and government agencies.

Joseph Sterling/Click, Chicago

SUMMARY

1. A phase consists of uniform matter. One phase is separated from other phases by boundaries called interfaces. 3:1

2. Heterogeneous matter is made of more than one phase. The phases usually can be separated by physical means. 3:1

3. A mixture is a combination of two or more substances which retain their individual properties. 3:2

4. Homogeneous matter is made of only one phase. 3:2

5. A solution is a homogeneous mixture consisting of a solute dissolved in a solvent. The component parts need not be present in any specific ratios. 3:2

6. Compounds are substances made of more than one kind of atom. The component atoms are present in definite ratios. 3:3

7. Elements are made of one kind of atom and are the basic substances of the universe. They cannot be broken down into simpler substances by ordinary chemical means. 3:3

8. Physical properties depend upon the substance itself. 3:4

9. Extensive physical properties, such as mass and length, depend upon the amount of matter present. Intensive properties, such as ductility and melting point, depend on the nature of matter itself. 3:4

10. A physical change in a substance does not alter its chemical character. A change of state is a physical change from one state—solid, liquid, or gas—to another. 3:5

11. The chemical properties of a substance depend upon the action of the substance in the presence of other substances. 3:6

12. A chemical change in a substance involves the formation of new substances with different properties. Chemical changes must be used to separate the elements composing a compound. 3:7

PROBLEMS

solution
element

10. Use reference materials to classify the following materials as heterogeneous mixture, solution, compound, or element. Use a dictionary to identify any unfamiliar materials.
    a. paint heterogeneous mixture   c. granite heterogeneous mixture e. corn syrup
    b. orthoclase compound   d. leather heterogeneous mixture f. gold

11. a. chemical
    b. physical
    c. physical
    d. physical
    e. chemical
    f. chemical

11. Classify the following changes as chemical or physical.
    a. burning of coal   d. excavating of earth
    b. tearing of a piece of paper e. exploding of TNT
    c. kicking of a football   f. contracting a muscle

12. Estimate the number of phases present in an ice cream soda complete with whipped cream and candied cherry. How many interfaces would there be in this system? 9 phases, approximately 13 interfaces

13. Classify the following properties as chemical or physical.
    a. density   **b.** melting point   **c.** length

13. a. physical
    b. physical
    c. physical

REVIEW

1. Make the following conversions.
    a. 2.84 kilograms to grams
    b. 544 milliseconds to seconds
    c. 0.0656 grams to milligrams
    d. 1102 centimeters to meters
    e. 0.220 grams to milligrams
    f. 3.6 nanometers to centimeters

2. Compute the density of the following materials.
    a. clay, if 42.0 grams occupy 19.1 cm^3
    b. cork, if 8.17 grams occupy 34.0 cm^3
    c. linoleum, if 6120 grams occupy 5100 cm^3
    d. ebony wood, if 201 grams occupy 165 cm^3
    e. turpentine, if 381 grams occupy 438 cm^3

3. State the four basic measurements you have studied so far. Define these quantities. State the standards for each and the instrument used to measure each.

4. What is the one property possessed by all matter?

5. How many significant digits are in the measurement 101.476 g?

6. What is the relative error of the measurement in the previous problem if the measurement is precise to ±0.002 grams?

1. a. 2840 g
   b. 0.544 s
   c. 65.6 mg
   d. 11.02 m
   e. 220. mg
   f. 3.6×10^{-7} cm
2. a. 2.20 g/cm^3
   b. 0.240 g/cm^3
   c. 1.2 g/cm^3
   d. 1.22 g/cm^3
   e. 0.870 g/cm^3
3. mass, length, time, temperature
4. inertia
5. 6
6. 1.97×10^{-5}

ONE MORE STEP

1. The doctor sometimes recommends gargling with salt water to relieve a sore throat. Determine whether the action of the salt water on bacteria is chemical or physical. physical

2. Devise an experiment which will allow you to separate a mixture of copper filings and salt. Dissolve mixture in water and filter.

3. Find out how crude oil may be obtained from shale through physical and chemical means.

4. The shortage of drinkable water has become critical in many parts of the world. Investigate various methods of separating drinkable water from seawater. Pay particular attention to phase changes and other physical processes involved in the methods.

5. Find out how rocks and minerals differ. Rocks are mixtures, minerals are substances.

READINGS

Kolb, Doris, "What is an Element?" *Journal of Chemical Education,* Vol. 54, No. 11 (November 1977), pp. 696-700.

Seaborg, Glenn T., "Charting the New Elements." *SciQuest,* Vol. 53, No. 8 (Óctober 1980), pp. 7-11.

Artistic expression is considered a form of communication. The clear glass globe has appeared in various art exhibits. It contains krypton gas. Electric impulses cause the lightning flashes you see throughout the globe. Chemists like artists, have their own means of expression. The chemical changes you see here can be described by a lengthy paragraph or by using symbols and formulas. These shorthand forms provide the same information in much less space. You learned about the standardized system of expressing measurements in Chapter 2. What standardized system is used to describe matter using symbols and formulas?

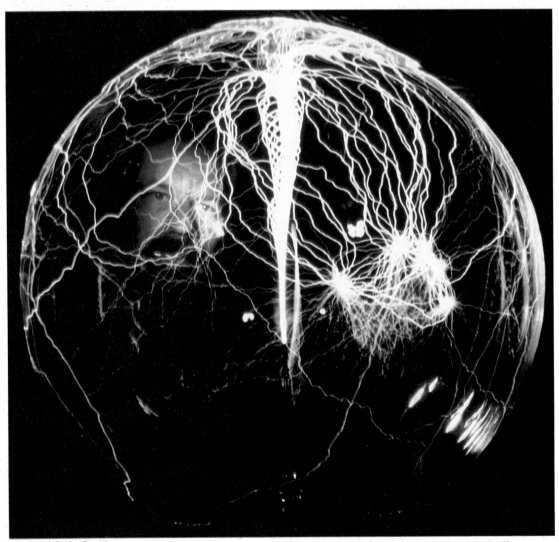

Sebastian Giefer-Bastel

CHEMICAL FORMULAS

4

Chapter 4 introduces symbols and their use as a means of writing chemical formulas.

Demonstration—Mix 1 gram of powdered zinc with 4 grams of iodine crystals on a watch glass. With a dropper add 5 to 10 cm^3 of water, one drop at a time. ZnI$_2$ is formed. **CAUTION:** Do this demonstration in a fume hood or near open window. It is very effective done on an overhead projector. Discuss the name and need for a formula to represent zinc iodide.

Although there are only a few more than 100 elements, there are literally millions of compounds known to chemists. It is convenient to represent elements and compounds by the use of symbols. These representations of substances are another way to help us to classify these substances quickly. This ability to classify simplifies the study of the vast number of substances with which chemists work.

GOAL: You will demonstrate a proficiency in writing chemical formulas and naming compounds.

4:1 SYMBOLS

The **chemical symbols** of the elements are a form of shorthand. They take the place of the complete names of the elements. A symbol may represent one atom of an element. Scientists throughout the world have agreed to represent one atom of aluminum by the symbol Al.

A symbol may be used in place of the name of an element.

Ancient symbols for some elements are shown in Figure 4-1. J. J. Berzelius, a Swedish chemist, is generally given credit for creating the modern symbols for elements. Berzelius proposed that all elements be given a symbol corresponding to the first letter of their names. In the case of two elements which began with the same letter, a second letter or a letter outstanding in the name was added. In some cases, the Latin name of the element was used. Thus, the symbol for sulfur is S; selenium, Se; strontium, Sr; and sodium, Na (Latin *natrium* = sodium).

Symbols consist of either one or two letters.

The symbols that have been agreed upon for 103 elements are listed in Table 4-1. Notice that they are capital and lowercase letters. Names for elements 104, 105, 106, and 107 have not yet been approved by the International Union of Pure and Applied Chemistry (IUPAC).

The first letter of a symbol is always capitalized.

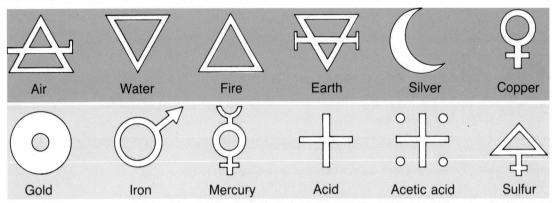

FIGURE 4-1. Picture symbols were once used for substances believed to be elements.

Table 4-1

Elements and Their Symbols

Actinium	Ac	Hafnium	Hf	Praseodymium	Pr
* Aluminum	Al	* Helium	He	Promethium	Pm
Americium	Am	Holmium	Ho	Protactinium	Pa
Antimony	Sb	* Hydrogen	H	Radium	Ra
* Argon	Ar	Indium	In	Radon	Rn
Arsenic	As	* Iodine	I	Rhenium	Re
Astatine	At	Iridium	Ir	Rhodium	Rh
* Barium	Ba	* Iron	Fe	* Rubidium	Rb
Berkelium	Bk	Krypton	Kr	Ruthenium	Ru
* Beryllium	Be	Lanthanum	La	Samarium	Sm
* Bismuth	Bi	Lawrencium	Lr	Scandium	Sc
* Boron	B	* Lead	Pb	Selenium	Se
* Bromine	Br	* Lithium	Li	* Silicon	Si
* Cadmium	Cd	Lutetium	Lu	* Silver	Ag
* Calcium	Ca	* Magnesium	Mg	* Sodium	Na
Californium	Cf	* Manganese	Mn	* Strontium	Sr
* Carbon	C	Mendelevium	Md	* Sulfur	S
Cerium	Ce	* Mercury	Hg	Tantalum	Ta
* Cesium	Cs	* Molybdenum	Mo	Technetium	Tc
* Chlorine	Cl	Neodymium	Nd	Tellurium	Te
* Chromium	Cr	* Neon	Ne	Terbium	Tb
* Cobalt	Co	Neptunium	Np	* Thallium	Tl
* Copper	Cu	* Nickel	Ni	Thorium	Th
Curium	Cm	Niobium	Nb	Thulium	Tm
Dysprosium	Dy	* Nitrogen	N	* Tin	Sn
Einsteinium	Es	Nobelium	No	Titanium	Ti
Erbium	Er	Osmium	Os	Tungsten	W
Europium	Eu	* Oxygen	O	Uranium	U
Fermium	Fm	Palladium	Pd	Vanadium	V
* Fluorine	F	* Phosphorus	P	Xenon	Xe
Francium	Fr	* Platinum	Pt	Ytterbium	Yb
Gadolinium	Gd	Plutonium	Pu	Yttrium	Y
Gallium	Ga	Polonium	Po	* Zinc	Zn
Germanium	Ge	* Potassium	K	Zirconium	Zr
Gold	Au				

Students should memorize those symbols marked with an asterisk as they will be used often throughout the text.

*Symbols for these elements will appear most frequently throughout the text.

4:2 CHEMICAL FORMULAS

Chemists also use combinations of symbols to represent compounds. Compounds are substances in which two or more elements are chemically combined. Compounds are represented by chemical formulas.

A **chemical formula** is a combination of symbols which represents the composition of a compound. Formulas often contain numerals to indicate the proportions in which the elements occur within a compound. For example, we have learned from experiments that water is composed of the elements hydrogen and oxygen. We also know that two atoms of hydrogen will react (combine chemically) with one atom of oxygen to form one molecule of water. As a formula for water, we write "H_2O." The small subscript, $_2$, after the H indicates that there are two atoms of hydrogen in one molecule of water. Note that there is no subscript after the oxygen. If a symbol for an element has no subscript, it is understood that only one atom of that element is present. A formula shows two things. It indicates the elements present in the compound and the relative number of atoms of each element in the compound. How many atoms of each element are present in each compound in Table 4-2?

Chemical formulas represent compounds.

Chemical formulas indicate the relative number of atoms for each element present in a compound.

Table 4-2

Some Common Compounds and Their Formulas		
Compound	**Formula**	**Elements**
ammonia	NH_3	nitrogen, hydrogen
rust	Fe_2O_3	iron, oxygen
sucrose	$C_{12}H_{22}O_{11}$	carbon, hydrogen, oxygen
table salt	NaCl	sodium, chlorine
water	H_2O	hydrogen, oxygen

Most compounds containing the element carbon are classed as organic compounds. Formulas for organic compounds are written according to a different set of rules. These rules will be studied in detail in Chapter 29. For example, the formula for acetic acid is written as CH_3COOH*. The actual structure of the acetic acid molecule is represented by

Compounds containing carbon are organic compounds.

$$\begin{array}{ccc} & H & O \\ & | & \| \\ H- & C-C & -O-H \\ & | & \\ & H & \end{array}$$

*The formula for acetic acid is also written as $HC_2H_3O_2$.

From this structural formula you can see how the shorthand formula is derived. It shows how the atoms are joined as well as the kind and number of atoms present.

4:3 OXIDATION NUMBER

Through experiments, chemists have determined the ratios in which most elements combine. They have also learned that these combining ratios depend upon the structure of their atoms. This relationship will be explored fully in Chapters 8-10. In the meantime, you should know that the atoms can acquire an electric charge. They may also attach themselves to other atoms so that the entire group acquires an electric charge. Such charged atoms are called **ions.** An ion made of more than one atom, for example OH^-, is called a **polyatomic ion.** When a single atom acquires a charge, that charge is known as its **oxidation number.**

Table 4-3 lists the oxidation numbers of some common elements. Table 4-4 lists the charges of some common polyatomic ions. We may use this information to write correct chemical formulas. Atoms and ions combine chemically in definite ratios. Oxidation numbers of elements and the charges on polyatomic ions tell us these combining ratios. The way to determine the ratio of elements in a compound is to add the charges algebraically. If the charges add up to zero, the formula for the compound is correct.

An ion is a charged atom or group of charged atoms.

Oxidation numbers represent apparent charge on an atom.

Table 4-3

Oxidation Numbers of Common Monatomic Ions					
1+	**2+**		**3+**	**4+**	
cesium, Cs^+	barium, Ba^{2+}	magnesium, Mg^{2+}	aluminum, Al^{3+}	germanium(IV), Ge^{4+}	
copper(I), Cu^+	cadmium, Cd^{2+}	manganese(II), Mn^{2+}	bismuth(III), Bi^{3+}	lead(IV), Pb^{4+}	
hydrogen, H^+	calcium, Ca^{2+}	mercury(II), Hg^{2+}	cerium(III), Ce^{3+}	silicon(IV), Si^{4+}	
lithium, Li^+	cobalt(II), Co^{2+}	nickel(II), Ni^{2+}	chromium(III), Cr^{3+}	thorium(IV), Th^{4+}	
potassium, K^+	copper(II), Cu^{2+}	strontium, Sr^{2+}	gallium(III), Ga^{3+}	tin(IV), Sn^{4+}	
rubidium, Rb^+	iron(II), Fe^{2+}	tin(II), Sn^{2+}	iron(III), Fe^{3+}	zirconium(IV), Zr^{4+}	
silver, Ag^+	lead(II), Pb^{2+}	zinc, Zn^{2+}			
sodium, Na^+					
thallium(I), Tl^+					
1−	**2−**		**3−**	**4−**	
bromide, Br^-	oxide, O^{2-}		nitride, N^{3-}	carbide, C^{4-}	
chloride, Cl^-	selenide, Se^{2-}		phosphide, P^{3-}		
fluoride, F^-	sulfide, S^{2-}				
hydride, H^-	telluride, Te^{2-}				
iodide, I^-					

Table 4-4

Charges of Common Polyatomic Ions*		
1+ ammonium, NH_4^+		
1−	**2−**	**3−**
acetate, $C_2H_3O_2^-$	carbonate, CO_3^{2-}	arsenate, AsO_4^{3-}
chlorate, ClO_3^-	hexafluorosilicate, SiF_6^{2-}	phosphate, PO_4^{3-}
cyanide, CN^-	oxalate, $C_2O_4^{2-}$	
hydroxide, OH^-	selenate, SeO_4^{2-}	
hypochlorite, ClO^-	silicate, SiO_3^{2-}	
iodate, IO_3^-	sulfate, SO_4^{2-}	
nitrate, NO_3^-	tartrate, $C_4H_4O_6^{2-}$	
nitrite, NO_3^-		
perchlorate, ClO_4^-		

*Table A-4 of the Appendix lists additional polyatomic ions and their charges.

Common table salt NaCl is made from sodium, Na, and chlorine, Cl. Table 4-3 shows a 1+ charge for sodium ions and a 1− charge for chloride ions.

$$Na^+Cl^-$$

Adding these charges, we see that $1 + (1-) = 0$. Therefore, the formula for salt is NaCl. This formula indicates that a one-to-one ratio exists between sodium ions and chloride ions in a crystal of salt. Sodium chloride is an **ionic compound,** that is, it is composed of charged particles called ions. Elements also combine in another way. Neutral atoms combine to form neutral particles called **molecules.** The compounds formed are called molecular compounds. In Chapter 12, we will study distinct differences in properties between ionic and molecular substances.

Ionic compounds are composed of charged particles; molecular compounds are composed of neutral particles.

a

David Scharf/Peter Arnold, Inc.

b

Craig Kramer

FIGURE 4-2. The microscopic view of salt (a) shows a cubic structure. A salt crystal model (b) shows the sodium and chlorine ions in a one to one ratio.

The element chlorine is a gas composed of molecules which are diatomic. A diatomic molecule is made of two atoms. One chlorine molecule contains two chlorine atoms. Chlorine gas is represented by the formula Cl_2. Six other common elements also occur as diatomic molecules. Hydrogen (H_2), nitrogen (N_2), oxygen (O_2), and fluorine (F_2) are diatomic gases under normal conditions. Bromine (Br_2) is a gas above 58.8°C. Iodine (I_2) is a gas above 184°C.

EXAMPLE: Writing Formulas

Write a formula for a compound of calcium and bromine.

Solving process:
With the exception of ammonia, NH_3, the element with the positive oxidation number is always written first. Using Table 4-3, we see the oxidation states of calcium and bromine are as follows

$$Ca^{2+} \qquad Br^-$$

Since the sum of the charges must equal zero, two Br^- are needed to balance Ca^{2+}.
The correct formula is $CaBr_2$.

Write the formula for a compound made from aluminum and sulfur atoms.

Solving process:
Using Table 4-3, we see the oxidation states of aluminum and sulfur are as follows:

$$Al^{3+} \qquad S^{2-}$$

To make the sum of the charge equal zero, we must find the least common multiple of 3 and 2. The least common multiple is 6. Thus, two Al^{3+} and three S^{2-} must combine for the charges to equal zero. The formula is written Al_2S_3.

Write the formula for a compound made from aluminum and the sulfate ion.

Solving process:
Using Tables 4-3 and 4-4, we see the oxidation states of aluminum and the sulfate ion are as follows:

$$Al^{3+} \qquad SO_4{}^{2-}$$

It is necessary to have two Al^{3+} and three $SO_4{}^{2-}$ in the compound to maintain neutrality. Writing aluminum ions in the formula is simple.

$$Al_2$$

For the sulfate, the entire polyatomic ion must be placed in parenthesis to indicate that three sulfate ions are required.

$$(SO_4)_3$$

Thus, aluminum sulfate has the formula $Al_2(SO_4)_3$. Note that parentheses are used in a formula only when you are expressing multiples of a polyatomic ion. If only one sulfate ion were needed in writing a formula, parenthesis would not be used. For example, the formula for the compound made from calcium and the sulfate ion is $CaSO_4$.

The formula of a substance represents a specific amount of a compound. If a substance is composed of molecules, the formula represents one molecule.

4:4 NAMING COMPOUNDS

Unfortunately, some compounds have many names, both common and chemical. However, there is a systematic method of naming practically all the compounds which we will use. The names of only a few compounds, particularly acids, will not be included in this system.

Compounds containing only two elements are called **binary compounds.** To name a binary compound, first write the name of the element having a positive charge. Then add the name of the negative element. The name of the negative element must be modified to end in *-ide.* For example, the compound formed by aluminum (Al^{3+}) and nitrogen (N^{3-}), with the formula AlN, is named aluminum nitride.

Table 4-5

Formulas and Names of Some Binary Compounds	
Formula	**Name**
Al_2S_3	aluminum sulfide
$CaBr_2$	calcium bromide
H_2O	hydrogen oxide (water)
H_2O_2	hydrogen peroxide
H_2Se	hydrogen selenide
NaCl	sodium chloride (table salt)

In looking at Table 4-3 we see that some elements have more than one possible charge. Therefore, they may form more than one compound with another element. For instance, nitrogen and oxygen form five different binary compounds with each other!

Hickson-Bender Photography

FIGURE 4-3. Iron(II) bromide, FeBr₂ (a) is different in appearance and properties than iron(III) bromide, FeBr₃ (b).

a   b

We must have a way of distinguishing the names of these compounds.

We tell the difference by writing the oxidation number of the element having positive charge after the name of that element. Roman numerals in parentheses are used. Examples of some compounds named according to this system are listed in Table 4-6.

Roman numerals are used in naming compounds that contain elements with more than one oxidation number.

Table 4-6

Formulas and Names of Some Binary Molecular Compounds having Variable Oxidation States			
Formula	**Name using Roman Numerals**	**Formula**	**Name using Roman Numerals**
N_2O	nitrogen(I) oxide	Cu_2S	copper(I) sulfide
NO	nitrogen(II) oxide	CuS	copper(II) sulfide
N_2O_3	nitrogen(III) oxide	FeF_2	iron(II) fluoride
NO_2	nitrogen(IV) oxide	FeF_3	iron(III) fluoride
N_2O_5	nitrogen(V) oxide	$PbCl_2$	lead(II) chloride
SO_2	sulfur(IV) oxide	$PbCl_4$	lead(IV) chloride
SO_3	sulfur(VI) oxide		

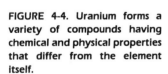

FIGURE 4-4. Uranium forms a variety of compounds having chemical and physical properties that differ from the element itself.

U.S. Department of Energy

There are many compounds that have been named by an older system in which prefixes indicate the number of atoms present. These names have been in use for so long that these more common names are usually used. Examples are listed in Table 4-7.

Table 4-7

Formulas and Common Names of Some Binary Molecular Compounds			
Formula	**Common Name**	**Formula**	**Common Name**
CS_2	carbon disulfide	SF_2	sulfur difluoride
CO	carbon monoxide	SF_4	sulfur tetrafluoride
CO_2	carbon dioxide	SF_6	sulfur hexafluoride
CCl_4	carbon tetrachloride	SO_2	sulfur dioxide
PBr_3	phosphorus tribromide	SO_3	sulfur trioxide
PBr_5	phosphorus pentabromide		

Prefix	*Number of atoms*
mono-	1
di-	2
tri-	3
tetra-	4
penta-	5
hexa-	6
hepta-	7
octa-	8

Not all compounds ending in -*ide* are binary. A few negative polyatomic ions have names ending in -*ide*. Examples are OH^- (hydrox*ide*), NH_2^- (am*ide*), $N_2H_3^-$ (hydraz*ide*), and CN^- (cyan*ide*).

A few compounds whose names end in -*ide* are not binary.

For naming compounds containing more than two elements, several rules apply. The simplest of these compounds are formed from one element and a polyatomic ion. These compounds are named in the same way as binary compounds. However, the ending of the polyatomic ion is not changed. An example is $AlPO_4$, which is named aluminum phosphate. Other examples are listed in Table 4-8.

In naming compounds containing polyatomic ions, the name of the polyatomic ion is not changed.

Table 4-8

Formulas and Names for Some Compounds containing Polyatomic Ions			
Formula	**Name**	**Formula**	**Name**
$AlAsO_4$	aluminum arsenate	$CuSO_4$	copper(II) sulfate
$(NH_4)_2SO_4$	ammonium sulfate	$Ni(OH)_2$	nickel(II) hydroxide
$Cr_2(C_2O_4)_3$	chromium(III) oxalate	$ZnCO_3$	zinc carbonate

Polyatomic ions which contain oxygen (other than OH^-) have the ending -*ite* or -*ate*. Thus, H_2SO_4 is hydrogen sulf*ate* not hydrogen sulf*ide* which is H_2S, a binary compound.

Other rules for naming compounds and writing formulas will be discussed when the need arises. The names of the common acids, for example, do not normally follow these rules. Table 4-9 lists names and formulas for acids which you should memorize.

The term *polyatomic ion* is used throughout this text in place of the term *radical*. We reserve the term radical for the free radical of organic chemistry.

Table 4-9

Acids			
Formula	**Name**	**Formula**	**Name**
CH_3COOH	acetic	$H_2C_2O_4$	oxalic
H_2CO_3	carbonic	$HClO_4$	perchloric
HCl	hydrochloric	H_3PO_4	phosphoric
HNO_3	nitric	H_2SO_4	sulfuric

The names and formulas for acids commonly used in the lab should be memorized.

PROBLEMS

1. a. $CaCl_2$ f. $AlCl_3$
   b. $CaCO_3$ g. SiO_2
   c. NaCN   h. ZnI_2
   d. MgO   i. $CoCO_3$
   e. NaF   j. KH

1. Write the formula for each of the following compounds. Table A-3 of the Appendix contains additional oxidation states of some elements.
   a. calcium chloride   f. aluminum chloride
   b. calcium carbonate   g. silicon(IV) oxide
   c. sodium cyanide   h. zinc iodide
   d. magnesium oxide   i. cobalt(II) carbonate
   e. sodium fluoride   j. potassium hydride

2. a. barium chloride
   b. zinc nitrate
   c. cesium acetate
   d. hydrogen sulfide
   e. potassium carbonate
   f. iron(II) chloride
   g. aluminum nitrate
   h. ammonium acetate
   i. barium hydroxide
   j. copper(II) acetate

2. Write the name for each of the following compounds.
   a. $BaCl_2$ f. $FeCl_2$
   b. $Zn(NO_3)_2$ g. $Al(NO_3)_3$
   c. $CsC_2H_3O_2$ h. $NH_4C_2H_3O_2$
   d. H_2S i. $Ba(OH)_2$
   e. K_2CO_3 j. $Cu(C_2H_3O_2)_2$

3. a. $CuCO_3$ f. $Ca(OH)_2$
   b. KOH   g. $Bi_2(SO_4)_3$
   c. CaI_2 h. $Mg_3(PO_4)_2$
   d. RbCN   i. $Hg(CN)_2$
   e. KF   j. $Ni_3(AsO_4)_2$

3. Write the formula for each of the following compounds.
   a. copper(II) carbonate   f. calcium hydroxide
   b. potassium hydroxide   g. bismuth sulfate
   c. calcium iodide   h. magnesium phosphate
   d. rubidium cyanide   i. mercury(II) cyanide
   e. potassium fluoride   j. nickel(II) arsenate

4. a. potassium chloride
   b. potassium bromide
   c. potassium iodide
   d. calcium nitrate
   e. mercury(II) iodide
   f. copper(II) nitrate
   g. phosphorus(V) oxide
   h. phosphorus(V) chloride
   i. sulfur(VI) fluoride
   j. phosphorus(III) chloride

4. Write the name for each of the following compounds.
   a. KCl   f. $Cu(NO_3)_2$
   b. KBr   g. P_2O_5
   c. KI   h. PCl_5
   d. $Ca(NO_3)_2$ i. SF_6
   e. HgI_2 j. PCl_3

5. a. KNO_3 d. $ZnSO_4$
   b. NaOH   e. Na_2S
   c. $Pb(NO_3)_2$ f. $FeCl_3$

5. Write the formula for each of the following compounds.
   a. potassium nitrate   d. zinc sulfate
   b. sodium hydroxide   e. sodium sulfide
   c. lead(II) nitrate   f. iron(III) chloride

6. a. ammonium nitrate
   b. sodium sulfate
   c. sodium oxide
   d. sodium phosphate
   e. ammonium chloride
   f. sodium chloride

6. Write the name for each of the following compounds.
   a. NH_4NO_3 d. Na_3PO_4
   b. Na_2SO_4 e. NH_4Cl
   c. Na_2O f. NaCl

4:5 MOLECULAR AND EMPIRICAL FORMULAS

The formulas for compounds that exist as molecules are called **molecular formulas.** For instance, one compound of hydrogen and oxygen is hydrogen peroxide (H_2O_2). The formula H_2O_2 is a molecular formula because one molecule of hydrogen peroxide contains two atoms of hydrogen and two atoms of oxygen. However, there is another kind of formula chemists also use. The atomic ratio of hydrogen to oxygen in hydrogen peroxide is one to one. Therefore, the simplest formula that would indicate the ratio between hydrogen and oxygen is HO. This simplest formula is called an **empirical formula.** As another example, both benzene (C_6H_6) and ethyne (C_2H_2) have the same empirical formula CH. Chemists can determine the empirical formula of an unknown substance through analysis. The empirical formula may then be used to help identify the molecular formula of the substance.

For many substances, the empirical formula is the only formula possible. We will discuss these substances later. Note that the molecular formula of the compound is always some whole-number multiple of the empirical formula. The actual calculation of empirical formulas will be covered in Chapter 5.

A molecular formula describes the composition of a molecule.

An empirical formula indicates the simplest whole-number ratio of atoms or ions in a compound.

A molecular formula is a whole number multiple of an empirical formula.

	NAME	1-hexene	ethene
	Empirical formula	CH_2	CH_2
	Molecular formula	C_6H_{12}	C_2H_4
TYPE OF FORMULA	Structural formula	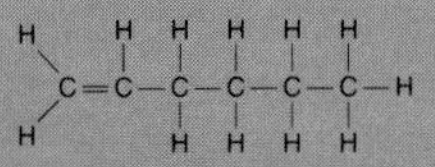 $H_2C=CH-CH_2-CH_2-CH_2-CH_3$	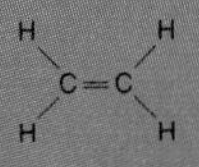 $H_2C=CH_2$
	Physical properties:	Colorless liquid	Colorless gas
		Molecular mass 84.16 amu	Molecular mass 28.05 amu
		Melting pt. 68–70°C	Melting pt. −169.2°C
		Boiling pt. 179°C	Boiling pt. −103.7 C

FIGURE 4-5. Hexene and ethene have the same empirical formula but different molecular formulas, structural formulas, and physical properties.

4:6   COEFFICIENTS

The formula of a compound represents a definite amount of that compound. This amount may be called a **formula unit.** It may be one molecule or the smallest number of particles giving the true proportions of the elements in the compound. One molecule of water is represented by H_2O. How do we represent two molecules of water? We use the same system as we would use in mathematics: coefficients. When we wish to represent two *x*, we write $2x$. When we wish to represent two molecules of water we write $2H_2O$. Three sodium ions combined with three chloride ions is represented as $3NaCl$. We will discuss the use of coefficients in Chapter 6.

Coefficients are used to represent the number of formula units.

PROBLEM

7. a. 1 formula unit of silver carbonate
   b. 3 formula units of thallium(I) bromide

7. Write the number of formula units represented by each of the following.

   a. Ag_2CO_3

   b. $3TlBr$

   c. $2Fe(NO_3)_2$ 2 formula units

   d. $4BiBr_3$ 4 formula units

   e. $6Ba_3(AsO_4)_2$ 6 formula units

   f. $5SnBr_4$ 5 formula units

   g. $3H_3PO_4$ 3 formula units

   h. $3CH_3COOH$ 3 formula units

Joseph Louis Proust   (1754–1826)

Joseph Proust received much of his early training in his father's apothecary shop in Angers, France. He taught for a while in France, and then moved to Spain where he was appointed director of the Royal Laboratory in Madrid.

The Law of Definite Proportions is Proust's greatest contribution to science. He held that compounds have definite composition, no matter how they are prepared. For example, 2.016 grams of hydrogen are found combined with 16.00 grams of oxygen in the compound water. This ratio holds true whether the water is prepared by burning hydrogen in oxygen, by decomposing gaseous nitrous acid, or by any other process.

In addition to this work, Proust was the first chemist to isolate and identify as distinct, more than one sugar (three in all). He is credited with the discovery of grape sugar.

CHEMICAL CAREER: Scientific Writing and Illustration

There are many people who have a strong interest in science and who also enjoy writing. A fascinating career for these people is scientific journalism. There are a variety of career positions requiring a knowledge of science and the ability to use the language in a clear, coherent manner.

Most major newspapers and magazines have one or more employees whose sole or primary function is the reporting of scientific news. The chance to be an accredited press representative to a Space Shuttle launch or an international scientific exchange is an enviable position. However, such a reporter would also probably spend most of his or her time investigating and reporting on local issues such as a source of pollution or a dramatic improvement in community health care facilities. Radio and television science journalists follow the same pattern in their careers.

Another career for a science writer is in the field of technical writing. These people work for companies producing chemicals, instruments, or machinery as well as large research foundations. New products and processes are usually accompanied by data sheets, instruction manuals, and maintenance and repair guides written by the company's technical writers. In these publications, it is important that ideas be conveyed clearly and unambiguously. Improper directions can lead to legal problems for the company. Some consumers consistently buy products from a particular firm because their product is reliable and their publications can be counted on to be written clearly.

Government agencies such as the Department of Energy and the Food and Drug Administration employ a number of scientific

Doug Martin

FIGURE 4-6. A career as a technical writer or photographer involves learning of new developments and breakthroughs as they are happening. The writer and photographer shown are interviewing a NASA representative. The science illustrator combines a knowledge of science with creativity in producing highly technical drawings.

writers. These people may be involved in converting highly technical research data to a form that can be understood by the average person.

Professional organizations such as the American Chemical Society and trade associations such as the Chemical Manufacturers' Association, produce journals and trade magazines. In addition, there are now a number of popular magazines concerned wholly or to a large extent with science. Most of these publications have a staff of science writers. Almost all of them will buy articles which are informative and well-written.

FIGURE 4-7. The science illustrator must have some basic background in science.

Janet Adams

A "free-lance" writer earns a living by selling articles to publications. The advantage of free-lancing is being your own boss. The disadvantage is the difficulty in getting started, and writers may experience some lean economic times until well established.

The technical illustrator is another position tied to scientific publications. It combines the creative aspects of art with the technical aspects of science. The tasks performed by the technical illustrator are in some ways similar to those of a scientific writer. The technical illustrator must be able to present clear, accurate drawings to be used in instruction manuals, research reports and as general information for the public in magazines and newspapers. As we saw in Chapter 1, many advances in research are based on the refinement of work published by another research team. The accurate communication of information through graphics is vitally important.

The technical illustrator must have some knowledge or background in the subject being illustrated to do an accurate job. He or she must be aware of the reader's knowledge level to provide drawings which are understandable but, more importantly, scientifically accurate. An undergraduate degree in one of the sciences is generally a prerequisite.

Any government agency or private industry involved in producing technical information will have a staff of in-house or free-lance illustrators.

SUMMARY

1. A chemical symbol for an element represents one atom of that element when it appears in a formula. 4:1
2. A chemical formula is a statement in chemical symbols of the composition of one formula unit of a compound. A subscript in a formula represents the relative number of atoms of an element in the compound. 4:2
3. A polyatomic ion is a stable, charged group of atoms. 4:3
4. The combining capacity of an atom or polyatomic ion is indicated by its oxidation number or charge. 4:3
5. In chemical compounds, atoms combine in definite ratios. Their combined charges add to zero. 4:3
6. A binary compound is composed of two elements. Its name is the name of the positive element followed by the name of the negative element modified to end in -*ide.* 4:4
7. Some elements can have more than one possible oxidation number. A compound containing such an element is named by showing the oxidation number in Roman numerals in parentheses after the element. 4:4
8. A compound formed from one element and one polyatomic ion is named in the same way as a binary compound. However, the ending of the name of the polyatomic ion is not changed. 4:4
9. An empirical formula represents the simplest whole number ratio between atoms in a compound. 4:5
10. A molecular formula shows the actual number of each kind of atom in one molecule of a compound. It is always a whole-number multiple of the empirical formula. 4:5
11. A formula unit represents a definite amount of a compound. 4:6
12. The coefficient of a formula indicates the number of molecules or the number of formula units of a nonmolecular substance. 4:6

PROBLEMS

8. Define formula unit.   the amount of a substance represented by the formula
9. What elements exist as diatomic molecules? H_2, N_2, O_2, F_2, Cl_2, Br_2, I_2
10. Which of the following is not a binary compound? b. $Mg(OH)_2$
    a. potassium chloride
    b. magnesium hydroxide
    c. calcium bromide
    d. carbon dioxide
11. Copper forms two different compounds with the chloride ion. In writing their formulas, how do we distinguish between them?
12. Why is it necessary to use parenthesis in writing the formula for zinc phosphate? the phosphate ion occurs more than once in the formula
13. Why is it necessary to use Roman numerals in writing the formula for iron(III) hydroxide? iron forms more than one compound with the hydroxide ion

14. Write the formula for each of the following compounds.
   a. iron(II) sulfate $FeSO_4$ **d.** thallium(I) selenide Tl_2Se
   b. manganese(II) nitrate $Mn(NO_3)_2$ **e.** sodium oxalate $Na_2C_2O_4$
   c. chromium(III) nitrate $Cr(NO_3)_3$ **f.** silver perchlorate $AgClO_4$

15. a. sodium nitrate
   b. ammonium sulfate
   c. iron(III) nitrate
   d. sodium acetate
   e. barium selenide
   f. copper(II) sulfate

15. Write the name for each of the following compounds.
   a. $NaNO_3$ **c.** $Fe(NO_3)_3$ **e.** BaSe
   b. $(NH_4)_2SO_4$ **d.** $NaC_2H_3O_2$ **f.** $CuSO_4$

16. Write the formula for each of the following compounds.
   a. rubidium acetate $RbC_2H_3O_2$ **d.** copper(II) tartrate $CuC_4H_4O_6$
   b. cerium(III) phosphate $CePO_4$ **e.** chromium(III) nitride CrN
   c. calcium arsenate $Ca_3(AsO_4)_2$ **f.** silver nitrate $AgNO_3$

17. a. thallium(I) selenate
   b. cadmium phosphide
   c. cobalt(II) phosphate
   d. lithium hydride
   e. gallium(III) telluride
   f. mercury(II) chloride

17. Write the name for each of the following compounds.
   a. Tl_2SeO_4 **c.** $Co_3(PO_4)_2$ **e.** Ga_2Te_3
   b. Cd_3P_2 **d.** LiH   **f.** $HgCl_2$

18. Write the formula for each of the following compounds.
   a. magnesium hydroxide $Mg(OH)_2$ **d.** magnesium nitrate $Mg(NO_3)_2$
   b. cadmium hydroxide $Cd(OH)_2$ **e.** aluminum sulfate $Al_2(SO_4)_3$
   c. silver acetate $AgC_2H_3O_2$ **f.** potassium cyanide KCN

19. Write the formula for each of the following compounds.
   a. tin(IV) chloride $SnCl_4$ **d.** ammonium sulfide $(NH_4)_2S$
   b. thorium(IV) fluoride ThF_4 **e.** cobalt(II) nitrate $Co(NO_3)_2$
   c. magnesium iodate $Mg(IO_3)_2$ **f.** barium nitrate $Mg(NO_3)_2$

20. a. copper(II) selenide
   b. lead(II) cyanide
   c. magnesium hydride
   d. manganese(II) oxide
   e. aluminum carbide
   f. hydrogen chloride

20. Write the name for each of the following compounds.
   a. CuSe   **c.** MgH_2 **e.** Al_4C_3
   b. $Pb(CN)_2$ **d.** MnO   **f.** HCl

21. Write the formula for each of the following compounds.
   a. cadmium nitrate $Cd(NO_3)_2$ **c.** nickel(II) nitrate $Ni(NO_3)_2$
   b. cobalt(II) nitrate $Co(NO_3)_2$ **d.** magnesium perchlorate $Mg(ClO_4)_2$

22. a. strontium nitrate
   b. calcium oxalate
   c. cesium iodate
   d. lithium selenide

22. Write the name for each of the following compounds.
   a. $Sr(NO_3)_2$ **c.** $CsIO_3$
   b. CaC_2O_4 **d.** Li_2Se

23. Write the formula for each of the following compounds.
   a. cobalt(II) hydroxide $Co(OH)_2$ **d.** calcium oxide CaO
   b. cesium carbonate Cs_2CO_3 **e.** lithium acetate $LiC_2H_3O_2$
   c. magnesium carbonate $MgCO_3$ **f.** zinc telluride $ZnTe$

24. a. thallium(I) oxalate
   b. ammonium fluoride
   c. barium selenate
   d. silver sulfide
   e. thallium(I) acetate
   f. ammonium selenide

24. Write the name for each of the following compounds.
   a. $Tl_2C_2O_4$ **d.** Ag_2S
   b. NH_4F **e.** $TlC_2H_3O_2$
   c. $BaSeO_4$ **f.** $(NH_4)_2Se$

25. Write the formula for each of the following compounds.
   a. aluminum selenide Al_2Se_3 **d.** cobalt(II) perchlorate $Co(ClO_4)_2$
   b. nickel(II) phosphate $Ni_3(PO_4)_2$ **e.** magnesium hexafluorosilicate $MgSiF_6$
   c. calcium telluride $CaTe$ **f.** barium perchlorate $Ba(ClO_4)_2$

26. Write the name for each of the following compounds.
    a. $AlAsO_4$
    b. $Cr_2(SO_4)_3$
    c. $Hg(IO_3)_2$
    d. $CdBr_2$
    e. $CeCl_3$
    f. $BiAsO_4$

    26. a. aluminum arsenate   d. cadmium bromide
    b. chromium(III) sulfate   e. cerium(III) chloride
    c. mercury(II) iodate   f. bismuth arsenate

REVIEW

1. Classify each object or material as a heterogeneous mixture, solution, compound or element.
    a. plastic garbage bag compound
    b. automobile heterogeneous mixture
    c. seawater solution
    d. hydrogen element
    e. maple syrup solution
    f. newsprint paper heterogeneous mixture

2. List the number of significant digits in each of the following measurements.
    a. 0.558 g   3
    b. 7.3 m   2
    c. 410 cm   2
    d. 0.0094 mg   2
    e. 19.0000 g   6
    f. 75.0 s   3

3. A student masses out 0.8320 grams of salt. Compute the relative error of this mass measurement if it is accurate to ±0.0001g.

4. Express in scientific notation.
    a. 0.955 9.55×10^{-1}
    b. 0.680 6.80×10^{-1}
    c. 53.5 5.35×10^1
    d. 314 3.14×10^2
    e. 0.0625 6.25×10^{-2}
    f. 2230 2.23×10^3

5. Express as whole numbers or decimals.
    a. 7.33×10^7 73 300 000
    b. 9.04×10^2 904
    c. 7.73×10^4 77 300
    d. 2.1×10^{-4} 0.000 21
    e. 7.4×10^{-5} 0.000 074
    f. 9.18×10^{-6} 0.000 009 18

6. Calculate the density of a material that has a mass of 7.13 grams and occupies a volume of 7.77 cm^3.   0.918 g/cm³

ONE MORE STEP

1. Investigate the difference between compounds known as Daltonides and those known as Bertholides.

2. Look through the medicine cabinet at home and find a bottle that lists ingredients. Using a chemical dictionary, handbook, or the Merck Index, find the formula for each ingredient.

READINGS

Kolb, Doris, "The Chemical Formula." *Journal of Chemical Education,* Vol. 55, No. 1 (January 1978), pp. 44-47.

The Great Pyramid is a symbol of human ingenuity. The pyramid contains over 2 million stone blocks each having an average mass of 2300 kilograms. It stands 137 meters high with a base covering 50 000 square meters. In comparison, consider a diamond chip having a mass of 1 gram. This chip contains over 5×10^{23} carbon atoms. Think of the difficulty a chemist encounters in building molecules from single atoms. It is much more practical to work with a large amount as a single unit. The mole is a chemist's counting unit. What number of objects does a mole represent? Why was this particular number selected to represent a mole?

Frank Siteman/Rainbow

THE MOLE 5

Chapter 5 introduces the mole and the use of this concept in manipulating formulas. Students are expected to set up and solve quantitative problems.

Demonstration—Place some $CuSO_4 \cdot 5H_2O$ in a large test tube. Heat it over a flame until the blue color disappears. Place the white anhydrous $CuSO_4$ on a watch glass and add H_2O from a dropper. **CAUTION:** exothermic. Discuss how quantitative information can be used to completely describe our observations.

Chemical symbols and formulas (such as H and H_2O) are shorthand signs for chemical elements and compounds. The symbol of an element may represent one atom of the element. The formula of a compound may represent one molecule or one formula unit of the compound. Symbols and formulas may also represent a group of atoms or formula units. Since atoms are so very small, chemists deal with large groups of atoms. This chapter is about a group called a mole, containing a specific number of units.

GOAL: You will demonstrate your understanding of the mole concept by using it in calculations with chemical formulas, solutions, molecular formulas, and hydrates.

Point out that elements can have formulas such as I_2, S_8, and P_4.

5:1 MOLECULAR MASS

The masses of the atoms are compared by using the **atomic mass scale.** This scale has the "atomic mass unit" (amu) as a standard. The source of this standard will be discussed in Chapter 8. A list of atomic masses for the elements is found on the inside back cover of the book.

The atomic mass of hydrogen in atomic mass units is 1, and the atomic mass of oxygen is 16. Therefore, the total mass of a water molecule, H_2O, is $1 + 1 + 16$, or 18 amu. If the atomic masses of all the atoms in a molecule are added, the sum is the mass of that molecule. Such a mass is called a **molecular mass.** This name is incorrect when applied to an ionic substance. Sodium chloride, NaCl, is an ionic substance which does not exist in molecular form. A better name for the mass of ionic substances is formula mass. The sum of the atomic masses of all atoms in the formula unit of an ionic compound is called the **formula mass** of the substance. To calculate a formula mass add the masses of all the atoms in the formula.

The atomic mass unit is used to compare masses of atoms.

The data in the atomic mass table gives relative masses of the elements.

Molecular mass is the sum of the atomic masses of the atoms in the molecule.

Formula mass is the sum of the atomic masses of the atoms in a formula unit.

EXAMPLE: Formula Mass

Find the formula mass of sodium sulfate, Na_2SO_4.

Solving process:
Add the atomic masses of all the atoms in the Na_2SO_4 formula unit.

2 Na atoms	$2 \times 23 =$ 46 amu
1 S atom	$1 \times 32 =$ 32 amu
4 O atoms	$4 \times 16 =$ $\underline{64}$ amu
formula mass of Na_2SO_4	142 amu

EXAMPLE: Formula Mass

Find the formula mass of calcium nitrate, $Ca(NO_3)_2$.

Solving process:
Add the atomic masses of all the atoms in the $Ca(NO_3)_2$ formula unit. Remember that the subscript applies to the entire poly-atomic ion.

1 Ca atom	$1 \times 40 =$ 40 amu
2 N atoms	$2 \times 14 =$ 28 amu
6 O atoms	$6 \times 16 =$ $\underline{96}$ amu
formula mass of $Ca(NO_3)_2$	164 amu

PROBLEM

1. Calculate the molecular or formula masses of the following compounds.

a. C_2H_6
b. KH_2PO_4
c. TaC
d. $Th(SO_4)_2$
e. $Ca_3(PO_4)_2$
f. $Na_2Al_2(SO_4)_4$
g. $TlNO_3$

h. K_2S
i. $LaCl_3$
j. CH_2CHCH_2OH *(propenol)*
k. $Pb_3(AsO_4)_2$
l. CH_3CH_2OH *(ethanol)*
m. $C_{12}H_{22}O_{11}$ *(sucrose)*
n. $CH_3CH_2CH_2OH$ *(propanol)*

1. a. 30.1 amu   h. 110 amu
   b. 136 amu   i. 245 amu
   c. 193 amu   j. 58.1 amu
   d. 424 amu   k. 899 amu
   e. 310 amu   l. 46.1 amu
   f. 484 amu   m. 342 amu
   g. 266 amu   n. 60.1 amu

5:2   AVOGADRO'S NUMBER

There is one problem in using the molecular masses of substances. These masses are in atomic mass units. An atomic mass unit is only 1.66×10^{-24} gram. The mass of a single molecule is so small that it is impossible to measure in the laboratory. For everyday use in chemistry, a larger unit, such as a gram, is needed.

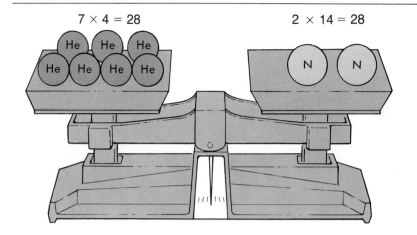

7 × 4 = 28   2 × 14 = 28

FIGURE 5-1. If it were possible to mass single atoms, the mass of two nitrogen atoms would equal the mass of seven helium atoms. Thus, the ratio of nitrogen to helium is 2 to 7.

One helium atom has a mass of 4 amu, and one nitrogen atom has a mass of 14 amu. The ratio of the mass of one helium atom to one nitrogen atom is 4 to 14, or 2 to 7. Let us compare the mass of two helium atoms to that of two nitrogen atoms. The ratio would be 2 × 4 to 2 × 14, or 2 to 7. If we compare the mass of 10 atoms of each element, we will still get a 2 to 7 ratio. No matter what number of atoms we compare, equal numbers of helium and nitrogen atoms will have a mass ratio of 2 to 7. In other words, the numbers in the atomic mass table give us the relative masses of the atoms of the elements.

The laboratory unit of mass you will use is the gram. We would like to choose a number of atoms which would have a mass in grams equivalent to the mass of one atom in atomic mass units. The same number would fit all elements since equal numbers of different atoms always have the same mass ratio. Chemists have found that 6.02×10^{23} atoms of an element have a mass in grams equivalent to the mass of one atom in amu. For example, one atom of hydrogen has a mass of 1.0079 amu; 6.02×10^{23} atoms of hydrogen have a mass of 1.0079 g. This number, **6.02×10^{23}** is called **Avogadro's number** in honor of a 19th century Italian scientist.

The mass of one atom of H is 1.0079 amu. The mass of 6.02×10^{23} atoms of H is 1.0079 g.

5:3 THE MOLE

Avogadro's number is an accepted SI standard. We may add it to the others we have studied: the kilogram, the meter, the second, and the kelvin. The symbol used to represent Avogadro's number is N_A. This quantity can be expressed as $6.022\ 17 \times 10^{23}$ to be more precise. This number of things is called one **mole** (mol) of the things. Recall that the mole is an SI base unit representing

Since the mole concept is central to much of chemistry, do not proceed quickly to the next section. Instead, give extra time to this section. Emphasize its importance, and give the students a chance to become familiar with it.

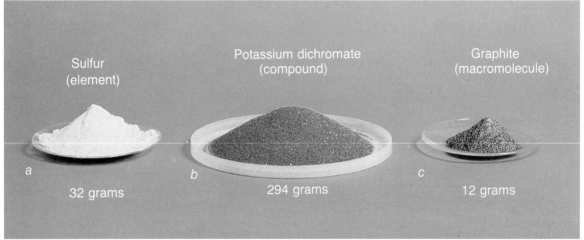

Sulfur
(element)

Potassium dichromate
(compound)

Graphite
(macromolecule)

a

b

c

32 grams

294 grams

12 grams

Tim Courlas

FIGURE 5-2. One mole of sulfur (a), potassium dichromate (b), and graphite (c) has a mass in grams which equals the mass of a single particle of each substance. Each amount shown here contains 6.02 × 10²³ particles for that substance.

For our purposes, Avogadro's number (N_A) = 6.02 × 10²³.

Avogadro's number (N_A) of anything is a mole of those things.

the amount of substance. One mole of particles (atoms, ions, molecules) has a mass in grams equivalent to that of one particle in atomic mass units. Thus, if a mole of any particle has a mass of 4.02 grams, then a single particle has a mass of 4.02 amu. In the same manner, if a single particle has a mass of 54.03 amu, then a mole of particles will have a mass of 54.03 grams.

N_A is a number that has been experimentally determined. If a mole of iodine molecules is inspected by X-ray diffraction, the actual number of I_2 molecules can be determined. This number has been found to be 6.02 × 10²³ molecules. Avogadro's number has also been determined by the scattering of light, by use of radioactive materials, and by Millikan's oil drop experiment which is covered in Chapter 8.

It is important to note that *one mole of atoms contains 6.02 × 10²³ atoms. One mole of molecules contains 6.02 × 10²³ molecules. One mole of formula units contains 6.02 × 10²³ formula units. One mole of ions contains 6.02 × 10²³ ions. N_A,* therefore, can have any of these units.

$$\frac{\text{molecules}}{\text{mole}}, \frac{\text{atoms}}{\text{mole}}, \frac{\text{ions}}{\text{mole}}$$

EXAMPLE: Conversion to Moles

How many moles are represented by 11.5 grams of C_2H_5OH? Use the factor-label method.

Solving process:
We have grams, we wish to convert to moles. Using the atomic mass table on the inside back cover, we see that one mole of C_2H_5OH has a mass of 46.1 grams.

Therefore,

$$1 \text{ mol} = 46.1 \text{ g} \quad \text{or} \quad \frac{1 \text{ mol}}{46.1 \text{ g}} = 1$$

$$\frac{11.5 \text{ g } C_2H_5OH}{} \left| \frac{1 \text{ mol } C_2H_5OH}{46.1 \text{ g } C_2H_5OH} = 0.249 \text{ mol } C_2H_5OH \right.$$

EXAMPLE: Conversion to Moles and Grams

1.20×10^{25} molecules of NH_3 will be how many moles? What mass is this number of molecules?

Solving process:

(a) We have molecules and wish to go to moles. One mole equals 6.02×10^{23} molecules. Use the ratio

$$\frac{1 \text{ mol}}{6.02 \times 10^{23} \text{ molecules}}$$

$$\frac{1.20 \times 10^{25} \text{ molecules } NH_3}{} \left| \frac{1 \text{ mol}}{6.02 \times 10^{23} \text{ molecules}} = 0.199 \times 10^2 \text{ mol} = 19.9 \text{ mol} \right.$$

(b) Using the table on the inside back cover, the molecular mass of NH_3 is 17.0, use

$$\frac{17.0 \text{ g } NH_3}{1 \text{ mol } NH_3}$$

$$\frac{19.9 \text{ mol } NH_3}{} \left| \frac{17.0 \text{ g } NH_3}{1 \text{ mol } NH_3} = 338 \text{ g of } NH_3 \right.$$

EXAMPLE: Conversion to Atoms

How many atoms are in a 10.0 gram sample of calcium metal?

Solving process:

1 formula mass of calcium is 40.1. Therefore, use the ratios

$$\frac{1 \text{ mol Ca}}{40.1 \text{ g Ca}} \quad \text{and} \quad \frac{6.02 \times 10^{23} \text{ atoms}}{1 \text{ mol}}$$

$$\frac{10.0 \text{ g Ca}}{} \left| \frac{1 \text{ mol Ca}}{40.1 \text{ g Ca}} \right| \frac{6.02 \times 10^{23} \text{ atoms}}{1 \text{ mol}} = 1.50 \times 10^{23} \text{ atoms}$$

PROBLEMS

Make the following conversions.

2. 1.00×10^{26} formula units of TlI to moles

3. 0.400 mole H_2O to molecules

4. 76.0 grams $CaBr_2$ to moles

5. 46.0 grams Ag_2Te to formula units

2. 166 mol

3. 2.41×10^{23} molecules
4. 0.380 mol
5. 8.07×10^{22} formula units

6. 23.6 g
7. 1380 g
8. 7.81 mol
9. 0.222 mol
10. 5.60 × 10²⁴ molecules
11. 0.003 59 g

6. 1.00×10^{23} formula units of $Mg(C_2H_3O_2)_2$ to grams

7. 3.00 moles $Ce_2(CO_3)_3$ to grams

8. 4.70×10^{24} formula units $Ca(ClO_4)_2$ to moles

9. 18.0 grams HBr to moles

10. 9.30 moles SiH_4 to molecules

11. 8.00×10^{19} molecules HCN to grams

5:4   MOLES IN SOLUTION

The SI unit of volume is the cubic meter (m³). Although liquid volume is often expressed in liters this unit is not SI. Thus, cubic decimeter (dm³) is used primarily throughout the text.

$$M = \frac{\text{mol of solute}}{\text{dm}^3 \text{ of solution}}$$

Many, if not most, chemical reactions take place in water solution. There are several methods of expressing the relationship between the dissolved substance and the solution. The method most often used by chemists is molarity (M). **Molarity** is the ratio between the moles of dissolved substance and the volume of solution in cubic decimeters. Remember that 1 dm³ = 1 L = 1000 cm³. A one-molar ($1M$) solution of nitric acid contains one mole of nitric acid molecules in one dm³ of solution. A $0.372M$ solution of $Ba(NO_3)_2$ contains 0.372 moles of $Ba(NO_3)_2$ in 1 dm³ of solution.

For a known molarity, a measurement of volume is a measure of the number of particles.

Assume that you wish to try a reaction using 0.1 mole of glucose ($C_6H_{12}O_6$). If the solution of glucose in your laboratory is $1M$, then 0.1 mole would be contained in 0.1 dm³, or 100 cm³ of solution. You can see that expressing the composition of solutions in units of molarity is a convenient way of measuring a number of particles.

It is important to be able to compute the molarity of solutions if you are given their composition. It is also important to be able to compute the amount of substance you need to produce a specific solution. You will be using these calculations in your laboratory work and later in solving problems in this book.

A 1 formal (1F) solution contains one gram-formula mass of solute per liter of solution. Some references reserve the term molar for solutions of substances which actually occur as molecules (sugar). We will not use the term formal.

EXAMPLE: Molarity

What is the molarity of 250 cm³ of solution containing 9.46 g CsBr?

Solving process:
The units of molarity are moles of substance per (divided by) dm³ of solution. Thus, to obtain molarity we must divide the substance, expressed in moles, by the solution, expressed in dm³. The table on the inside back cover is used to determine the formula mass of CsBr.

$$\frac{9.46 \text{ g CsBr}}{} \left| \frac{1 \text{ mol CsBr}}{213 \text{ g CsBr}} \right. = 0.0444 \text{ mol CsBr}$$

$$\frac{250 \text{ cm}^3}{} \left| \frac{1 \text{ dm}^3}{1000 \text{ cm}^3} \right. = 0.250 \text{ dm}^3$$

$$\frac{0.0444 \text{ mol CsBr}}{0.250 \text{ dm}^3} = 0.178M \text{ CsBr}$$

To save time and to reduce the chance for error, these calculations can be combined in one continuous chain. Note that the factors are arranged to yield an answer in mol/dm^3 which is molarity.

$$\frac{9.46 \text{ g CsBr}}{250 \text{ cm}^3} \mid \frac{1 \text{ mol CsBr}}{213 \text{ g CsBr}} \mid \frac{1000 \text{ cm}^3}{1 \text{ dm}^3} = 0.178M \text{ CsBr}$$

EXAMPLE: Making a Solution

How would you make 500 cm^3 of a 0.133M solution of MnSeO$_4$?

Solving process:
First, use the given quantity of solution, 500 cm^3, to find the part of a dm^3 desired. Then use the molarity to convert from solution to moles of substance. Finally, convert the moles of substance to grams.

$$\frac{500 \text{ cm}^3}{} \mid \frac{1 \text{ dm}^3}{1000 \text{ cm}^3} \mid \frac{0.133 \text{ mol MnSeO}_4}{1 \text{ dm}^3} \mid \frac{198 \text{ g MnSeO}_4}{1 \text{ mol MnSeO}_4} = 13.2 \text{ g MnSeO}_4$$

To make the solution, then, you would dissolve 13.2 g MnSeO$_4$ in sufficient water to make 500 cm^3 of solution.

PROBLEMS

Compute the molarity of the following solutions.
12. 145 g (NH$_4$)$_2$C$_4$H$_4$O$_6$ in 500 cm^3 of solution
13. 45.1 g CoSO$_4$ in 250 cm^3 of solution
14. 41.3 g Fe(NO$_3$)$_2$ in 100 cm^3 of solution
15. 49.9 g Pb(ClO$_4$)$_2$ in 200 cm^3 of solution
16. 35.0 g MnSiF$_6$ in 50.0 cm^3 of solution

Describe the preparation of the following solutions.
17. 1000 cm^3 of 3.00M NiCl$_2$
18. 250 cm^3 of 4.00M RbOH
19. 500 cm^3 of 1.50M AgF
20. 250 cm^3 of 0.0500M SrSiF$_6$
21. 250 cm^3 of 0.00200M Tl$_2$CO$_3$

12. 1.58M
13. 1.16M
14. 2.29M
15. 0.615M
16. 3.55M

17. Dissolve 390 g NiCl$_2$ in enough water to make 1000 cm^3 of solution.
18. Dissolve 103 g RbOH in enough H$_2$O to make 250 cm^3 of solution.
19. Dissolve 95.3 g
20. Dissolve 2.88 g
21. Dissolve 0.235 g

5:5 PERCENTAGE COMPOSITION

A chemist often compares the percentage composition of an unknown compound with the percentage composition calculated from an assumed formula. If the percentages agree it will help confirm the identity of the unknown. *The percentage of the total mass of a compound contributed by an element is the percentage of that element in the compound.* Consider the percentage composition of the following substances: copper, sodium chloride, and ethanol. For copper, the percentage composition is 100 percent Cu because it is composed of a single element. Salt is composed of two elements, sodium and chlorine. We know they are always present in the same ratio by mass. The ratio in which they are present is the ratio of their atomic masses. Therefore, the percentage of sodium in any sample of sodium chloride would be the atomic mass of the element divided by the formula mass and multiplied by 100.

$$\frac{Na}{NaCl} = \frac{23.0 \text{ amu}}{(23.0 + 35.5) \text{ amu}} \times 100 = 39.4\%$$

Consider a compound such as ethanol where more than one atom of an element appears. The formula for ethanol is C_2H_5OH and its molecular mass is 46.1 amu. It can be seen that one ethanol molecule, contains two carbon atoms with a combined atomic mass of 24.0 amu. Therefore, the percentage of carbon in the compound is

$$\frac{2C}{C_2H_5OH} = \frac{24.0 \text{ amu}}{46.1 \text{ amu}} \times 100 = 52.1\%$$

The percentage of hydrogen is (6.05 amu/46.1 amu) × 100, and that of oxygen is (16.0 amu/46.1 amu) × 100. The three percentages should add to 100%. Often, because we round off answers we may find that the percentages total one or two-tenths more or less than 100%.

FIGURE 5-3. The graph shows the percentages of each element present in lead(II) chromate (a) and nickel acetate (b).

64.1% Pb

19.8% O

16.1% Cr

Tim Courlas

36.2% O

33.3% Ni

3.4% H

27.1% C

a   b

EXAMPLE: Percentage Composition

Find the percentage composition of aluminum sulfate.

Solving process:

The formula for aluminum sulfate is $Al_2(SO_4)_3$. The formula mass is

2 Al atoms	$2 \times 27 =$	54 amu
3 S atoms	$3 \times 32 =$	96 amu
12 O atoms	$12 \times 16 =$	192 amu
		342 amu

The percentage of Al is $\dfrac{2Al}{Al_2(SO_4)_3} = \dfrac{54\ amu}{342\ amu} \times 100 = 15.8\%$

The percentage of S is $\dfrac{3S}{Al_2(SO_4)_3} = \dfrac{96\ amu}{342\ amu} \times 100 = 28.1\%$

The percentage of O is $\dfrac{12O}{Al_2(SO_4)_3} = \dfrac{192\ amu}{342\ amu} \times 100 = 56.1\%$

30. 46.2%, 19.9%, 33.9%
31. 74.7%, 25.3%
32. 98.6%, 1.45%

PROBLEMS
38.9%, 33.0%, 28.2% — 33. 28%, 49.6%, 22.4%

Find the percentage composition of the following.

22. CsF
23. NiI_2
24. Bi_2O_3
25. CuC_2O_4
41.8%, 15.8%, 42.1%

26. $TlIO_3$ 53.8%, 33.5%, 12.7%
27. ThO_2 87.9%, 12.1%
28. $Co_3(AsO_4)_2$ —
29. BaTe 51.7%, 48.3%

30. $ZnSiO_3$
31. CdF_2
32. BaH_2
33. $Ca(ClO)_2$

22. Cs = 87.5%
    F = 12.5%
23. Ni = 18.8%
    I_2 = 81.2%
24. Bi = 89.7%
    O = 10.3%

5:6 EMPIRICAL FORMULAS

Using experimental data we can find the empirical formula for a substance. We need only know the mass of each element in the substance. Elements are made of atoms, and compounds are made of elements. Half an atom does not exist. Therefore, we can state that the elements in a compound combine in simple whole number ratios, such as 1 to 1, 1 to 2, 2 to 3, and so on. If the atoms of the elements are present in simple ratios, then the moles of atoms for each element in the substance will be in small whole number ratios.

Consider the following example. We find a 2.5-gram sample of a certain substance contains 0.9 gram of calcium and 1.6 grams of chlorine. The substance is composed of only two elements. We can calculate the number of moles of calcium and the number of moles of chlorine in the compound. Then, we can find the ratio of the number of moles of calcium atoms to the number of moles of chlorine atoms. From this ratio, we can find the **empirical formula,** which is the simplest ratio of atoms in a compound.

Elements in compounds combine in simple whole number ratios.

An empirical formula is the simplest ratio of the atoms in a compound.

EXAMPLE: Empirical Formula

What is the empirical formula for a compound if a 2.50-gram sample contains 0.900 gram of calcium and 1.60 grams of chlorine?

Solving process:

(a) We must determine the number of moles of each element in the compound. Calcium in the sample has a mass of 0.900 g, and the atomic mass of Ca is 40.1. Chlorine in the sample has a mass of 1.60 g, and the atomic mass of Cl is 35.5 g. The sample contains

The ratio of moles is the same as the ratio of atoms for a given formula unit because there are exactly N_A atoms in one mole of any element.

$$\frac{0.900 \text{ g Ca}}{} \quad \frac{1 \text{ mol Ca}}{40.1 \text{ g Ca}} = 0.0224 \text{ mol of Ca}$$

$$\frac{1.60 \text{ g Cl}}{} \quad \frac{1 \text{ mol Cl}}{35.5 \text{ g Cl}} = 0.0451 \text{ mol of Cl}$$

(b) Dividing both numbers of moles by the smaller one (0.0224), we get 1.00 and 2.01. Since we know the ratio must be in whole numbers, we round off to 1 to 2. This calculation shows that for each mole of calcium, there are 2 moles of chlorine. The empirical formula is $CaCl_2$. We can also calculate empirical formulas from percentage composition.

EXAMPLE: Percentage Composition

A compound has a percentage composition of 40.0% carbon, 6.71% hydrogen, and 53.3% oxygen. What is the empirical formula?

Solving process:

Point out that any mass could be used: 45 g, 93.7 g, or any other. We use 100 g to simplify arithmetic.

We know that every sample of the compound, no matter how small or how large, will have this composition. To calculate the ratio of moles of these elements, we use a convenient amount of compound, usually 100 g. Then the percentages of the elements have the same numerical value in grams. In the present example, we would find 40.0 g of carbon, 6.71 g of hydrogen, and 53.3 g of oxygen in a 100-gram sample. We then change the quantities to moles.

$$\frac{40.0 \text{ g C}}{} \quad \frac{1 \text{ mol C}}{12.0 \text{ g C}} = 3.33 \text{ mol of carbon}$$

To determine an empirical formula, change grams to moles and find the ratio of the moles.

$$\frac{6.71 \text{ g H}}{} \quad \frac{1 \text{ mol H}}{1.01 \text{ g H}} = 6.64 \text{ mol of hydrogen}$$

$$\frac{53.3 \text{ g O}}{} \quad \frac{1 \text{ mol O}}{16.0 \text{ g O}} = 3.33 \text{ mol of oxygen}$$

Dividing each result by 3.33, we get 1 to 1.99 to 1, or 1 to 2 to 1. Thus, the empirical formula is CH_2O.

EMPIRICAL FORMULA OF A COMPOUND
40.0% Carbon, 6.71% Hydrogen, 53.3% Oxygen

	Percent		Grams in 100 g sample		Moles	Mole ratio	Empirical formula
C		40.0%		40.0 g	$\frac{40.0}{12.0} = 3.33$	$\frac{3.33}{3.33} = 1$	
H		6.71%		6.71 g	$\frac{6.71}{1.01} = 6.64$	$\frac{6.64}{3.33} = 2$	CH_2O $CHOH$
O		53.5%		53.3 g	$\frac{53.3}{16.0} = 3.33$	$\frac{3.33}{3.33} = 1$	

EXAMPLE: Empirical Formula

What is the empirical formula of a compound which is 66.0% Ca and 34.0% P?

Solving process:
Assume a 100-g sample so that we have 66.0 g Ca and 34.0 g P. Convert these quantities to moles of atoms.

$$\frac{66.0 \text{ g Ca}}{} \left| \frac{1 \text{ mol Ca}}{40.1 \text{ g Ca}} \right. = 1.65 \text{ mol Ca}$$

$$\frac{34.0 \text{ g P}}{} \left| \frac{1 \text{ mol P}}{31.0 \text{ g P}} \right. = 1.10 \text{ mol P}$$

FIGURE 5-4. This picture representation shows the steps in calculating an empirical formula from percentage composition.

Dividing both results by 1.10, we obtain 1.50 to 1. This result is not close to a whole number. Substituting the fractional form of 1.5, we get ³⁄₂. That ratio is 3 to 2. Thus, the ratio of Ca atoms to P atoms is 3 to 2 and the empirical formula is Ca_3P_2. Suppose we have an empirical formula problem which produces a ratio of 1 to 2.33. What is the correct whole number ratio? We can say 2.33 ≈ 2⅓. Since 2⅓ is ⁷⁄₃, the ratio is 7 to 3.

PROBLEMS

Find the empirical formulas of the following compounds.
34. 1.67 g Ce, 4.54 g I
35. 31.9 g Mg, 27.1 g P
36. 4.04 g Cs, 1.08 g Cl
37. 9.11 g Ni, 5.89 g F
38. 6.27 g Ca, 1.46 g N

34. CeI_3
35. Mg_3P_2
36. $CsCl$
37. NiF_2
38. Ca_3N_2

5:7   MOLECULAR FORMULAS

We have, thus far, calculated empirical formulas from experimental data. In order to calculate a molecular formula, we need one additional piece of data, the molecular mass. In one of the examples in the previous section, the empirical formula calculated was CH_2O. If we know that the molecular mass of the compound is 180, how can we find the molecular formula? The **molecular formula** shows the number of atoms of each element in a molecule. Knowing that the elements will always be present in the ratio 1:2:1, we can calculate the mass of the empirical formula. Then we can find the number of these empirical units present in one molecular formula. In the substance CH_2O, the empirical unit has a mass of

$$12 + 2(1) + 16, \text{ or } 30.$$

It will, therefore, take six of these units to equal 180 or one molecular formula. Thus, the molecular formula is $C_6H_{12}O_6$.

PROBLEMS

39. The molecular mass of benzene is 78 and its empirical formula is CH. What is the molecular formula for benzene?

40. What is the molecular formula of dichloroacetic acid, if the empirical formula is CHOCl and the molecular mass is 129?

41. What is the molecular formula of cyanuric chloride, if the empirical formula is CClN and the molecular mass is 184.5?

42. What is the molecular formula of a substance with empirical formula $TlC_2H_2O_3$ and molecular mass 557?

43. Find the molecular formula for a compound with percentage composition 85.6% C, 14.4% H, and molecular mass 42.1.

5:8   HYDRATES

There are many compounds which crystallize from a water solution with water molecules adhering to the particles of the crystal. These **hydrates,** as they are called, usually contain a specific ratio of water to compound. Chemists use heat to dry these compounds and then calculate the ratio of compound to water. An example of a hydrate is $NiSO_3 \cdot 6H_2O$. The dot shows that 6 molecules of water adhere to 1 molecule of formula unit. To calculate the formula mass, we add the formula mass of the compound and water. For $NiSO_3$ we obtain 139. We multiply the 18 for water by 6 and add to the 139. The formula mass of $NiSO_3 \cdot 6H_2O$ is then 139 + 6(18), or 247.

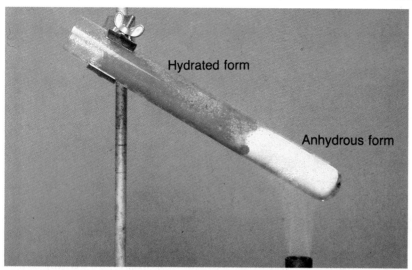

Hydrated form

Anhydrous form

Tim Courlas

FIGURE 5-5. The difference in color between the anhydrous and hydrated forms of a compound are shown. Heating drives off water molecules which causes the color change.

EXAMPLE: Hydrate Calculation

We have a 10.407 gram sample of hydrated barium iodide. The sample is heated to drive off the water. The dry sample has a mass of 9.520 grams. What is the ratio between barium iodide, BaI_2, and water, H_2O? What is the formula of the hydrate?

Solving process:
The difference between the initial mass and that of the dry sample is the mass of water that was driven off.

$$10.407 - 9.520 = 0.887 \text{ g}$$

The mass of water and mass of dry BaI_2 are converted to moles.

$$\frac{9.520 \text{ g } BaI_2}{} \left| \frac{1 \text{ mol } BaI_2}{391.2 \text{ g } BaI_2} \right. = 0.024\ 34 \text{ mol } BaI_2$$

$$\frac{0.887 \text{ g } H_2O}{} \left| \frac{1 \text{ mol } H_2O}{18.0 \text{ g } H_2O} \right. = 0.0492 \text{ mol } H_2O$$

The ratio between BaI_2 and H_2O is seen to be 1 to 2. The formula for the hydrate is written as $BaI_2 \cdot 2H_2O$.

PROBLEMS

Find the formulas for the following hydrates.
44. 0.391 g Li_2SiF_6, 0.0903 g H_2O
45. 0.737 g $MgSO_3$, 0.763 g H_2O
46. 95.3 g $LiNO_3$, 74.7 g H_2O
47. 76.9% $CaSO_3$, 23.1% H_2O
48. 89.2% $BaBr_2$, 10.8% H_2O

44. $Li_2SiF_6 \cdot 2H_2O$
45. $MgSO_3 \cdot 6H_2O$
46. $LiNO_3 \cdot 3H_2O$
47. $CaSO_3 \cdot 2H_2O$
48. $BaBr_2 \cdot 2H_2O$

Stanislao Cannizzaro (1826–1910)

As a pioneer in the development of modern atomic theory, Stanislao Cannizzaro insisted on the distinction between molecular and atomic masses. He determined atomic masses of elements in volatile compounds from the molecular masses of those compounds. He also found atomic masses of elements from a knowledge of their specific heat capacities.

Cannizzaro was devoted to organic chemistry, particularly the study of compounds containing a benzene ring. Cannizzaro's investigations were interrupted many times because of his political interests. In 1848, he became involved in a Sicilian revolution and was forced to flee to Paris. He returned to Italy and was eventually elected vice president of the senate.

CHEMICAL TECHNOLOGY: Computers in Chemistry

Many of the calculations described in this chapter are used regularly by analytical chemists. These problems are sometimes solved using hand-held calculators just as you do. However, there are times when such calculations can be handled automatically.

Not long ago, the analytical laboratory looked similar to your school chemistry lab. Analytical chemists used much of the same equipment that you use in lab. Today, much of the apparatus in an analytical laboratory is electronically operated and controlled by a microprocessor. A microprocessor is similar to the "works" of your hand-held calculator. However, the microprocessor has been set up, or "programmed", to do a specific job: run an analytical instrument and record data.

Some microprocessors have been programmed to perform certain calculations from the results obtained by an analytical instrument. The microprocessor is, in effect, acting as a microcomputer. The chemist is relieved of the job of performing calculations on the analytical results.

Computers are used by theoretical chemists to do complex and lengthy calculations which test ideas about molecular structure, stability of compounds, and possible reaction pathways.

Doug Martin

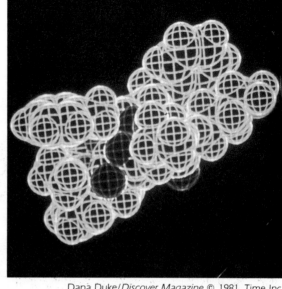

Dana Duke/*Discover Magazine* © 1981, Time Inc.

The use of a computer in the laboratory can be applied to safety as well as analysis. Sensors can be placed in reaction vessels and other sensitive locations. The sensor output is then directed to a computer. If temperatures or pressures exceed safe limits, the computer will decide what action is necessary and carry out that action. Remember, the computer must already have been programmed to make the appropriate decision and take the appropriate action. Typical actions include sounding alarms, turning off heaters, opening sprinkler system valves or safety valves, or starting cooling fans.

FIGURE 5-6. Computers are used to monitor and collect data from analytical testing equipment as in this gas chromatograph (a). The compound shown in (b) is a drug that was designed by chemists using a computer.

FIGURE 5-7. The action of a substrate and enzyme can be shown on a computer. Chemists can then work on synthesizing this enzyme for people who do not naturally produce it.

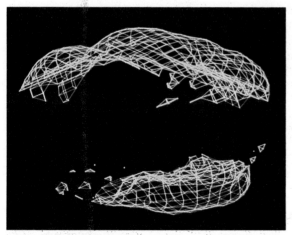

Dana Duke/*Discover Magazine* © 1981, Time Inc.

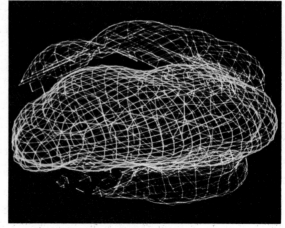

Dana Duke/*Discover Magazine* © 1981, Time Inc.

FIGURE 5-8. The control room for a nuclear reactor is highly computerized. Temperature and radiation sensors keep personnel informed as to conditions in the reactor.

Chemists also use computers for instructional purposes. Many laboratory experiments can be simulated on a computer equipped with a cathode-ray tube terminal. By running a simulated experiment before entering the laboratory, students can work more effectively once the experiment is actually performed.

Dan McCoy/Rainbow

SUMMARY

1. The symbol for an element represents one atom of the element or one mole of the element when it stands alone. Intro

2. The formula for a compound can represent one molecule or formula unit. It can also represent one mole of the compound. Intro

3. Masses of atoms are based on the atomic mass unit (amu). An atom of the lightest element, hydrogen, has a mass of approximately 1 amu, or 1.660×10^{-24} g. 5:1, 5:2

4. The molecular mass of a molecule is found by adding the atomic masses of all the atoms in one molecule. 5:1

5. Not all substances exist normally as molecules. Therefore, the term molecular mass is not used for all substances. The mass of the empirical formula unit of an ionic substance such as sodium chloride is called the formula mass. 5:1

6. There are 6.02×10^{23} particles in 1 mole. This quantity is known as Avogadro's number. 5:2

7. The number of moles in a given mass of substance can be found by dividing the total mass by the formula mass expressed in units of g/mol. 5:3

8. The percentage of the total mass of a compound contributed by an element is the percentage of that element in the compound. 5:5

9. The empirical formula indicates the simplest whole number ratio of atoms present in a compound. 5:6

10. The molecular formula of a compound is some whole number multiple of the empirical formula. 5:7

PROBLEMS

49. To what substances does the term formula mass refer? ionic
50. Why do chemists use 6.02×10^{23} as the number of things in a mole?
51. Explain the difference between the terms mole and molarity.
52. Explain the difference between an empirical formula and a molecular formula.

Find the empirical formulas of the following compounds.

53. 63.0 g Rb, 5.90 g O Rb_2O
54. 0.00495 g Th, 0.00137 g S ThS_2
55. 1.39 g Co, 5.98 g I, 2.26 g O $Co(IO_3)_2$
56. 2.13 g Na, 2.32 g As, 1.98 g O Na_3AsO_4
57. 30.0 g N, 8.65 g H, 84.7 g Se, 68.6 g O $(NH_4)_2SeO_4$
58. 32.8% Cr, 67.2% Cl $CrCl_3$
59. 42.7% Co, 57.3% Se $CoSe$
60. 78.3% Ba, 21.7% F BaF_2
61. 96.2% Tl, 3.77% O TlO_2
62. 58.0% Rb, 9.50% N, 32.5% O $RbNO_3$
63. 32.2% Zr, 22.6% S, 45.2% O $Zr(SO_4)_2$
64. 48.8% Cd, 20.8% C, 2.62% H, 27.8% O $Cd(C_2H_3O_2)_2$
65. 49.5% Fe, 50.5% F FeF_3
66. 42.6% Ni, 57.4% Se $NiSe$
67. 8.29% Al, 32.7% Cl, 59.0% O $Al(ClO_4)_3$

50. This number of particles has a mass in grams which is equivalent to the mass of one particle in amu.

51. mole = certain number of objects
molarity = unit of concentration

52. molecular formula describes the contents of a molecule; empirical formula describes the simplest whole number ratio between the different atoms in a compound

68. Calculate the formula mass of the following.
    a. K_2SO_4 174 amu
    b. CuO 79.5 amu
    c. $CsClO_4$ 233 amu
    d. Tl_2SiF_6 551 amu
    e. $Mg_3(AsO_4)_2$ 350 amu
    f. $Pb(C_2H_3O_2)_2$ 325 amu

69. Calculate the molecular or formula mass of the following.
    a. $CuCl_2$ 134 amu
    b. $Hg(C_2H_3O_2)_2$ 319 amu
    c. CeH_3 143 amu
    d. $Cr_2(C_2O_4)_3$ 368 amu
    e. $PbSeO_4$ 350 amu
    f. $KMnO_4$ 158 amu

70. Convert.
    a. 10.0 g of Rb_2SeO_4 to moles 0.0318 mol
    b. 1.00×10^{25} molecules of I_2 to grams 4220 g I_2
    c. 0.426 mole of HF to molecules 2.56×10^{23} molecules
    d. 26.8 moles of CO_2 to molecules 1.61×10^{25} molecules
    e. 681 formula units of MnC_2O_4 to moles 1.13×10^{-21} mol

71. Compute the molarity of the following solutions.
    a. 6.94 g ZrF_4 in 500 cm^3 of solution 0.083M
    b. 48.5 g NH_4Br in 250 cm^3 of solution 1.98M
    c. 23.5 g CuF_2 in 1000 cm^3 of solution 0.230M
    d. 70.0 g $CdCl_2$ in 1000 cm^3 of solution 0.383M
    e. 50.0 g $Ce(C_2H_3O_2)_3$ in 250 cm^3 of solution 0.631M

72. Describe the preparation of the following solutions.
    a. 1000 cm^3 of 4.00M $CsCl$ 676 g
    b. 1000 cm^3 of 6.00M $LiBr$ 521 g
    c. 500 cm^3 of 2.00M $MgBr_2$ 184 g
    d. 1000 cm^3 of 1.50M $MnSO_4$ 227 g
    e. 1000 cm^3 of 0.750M $NiSO_4$ 116 g

73. Find the percentage composition of each element in the following.
    a. $NaBr$ 22.3%, 77.7%
    b. CH_3COOH *(acetic acid)*
    c. $Th(C_2O_4)_2$ 56.9%, 11.8%, 31.4%
    d. ZnS 67.1%, 32.9%
    e. $CdCO_3$ 65.2%, 6.97%, 27.8%
    f. $CH_3CH_2CH_2CH_2OH$ *(butanol)*

b. 40% C, 53.3% O, 6.7% H

f. C 64.9%, H 13.5%, O 21.6%

74. Find the empirical formula for a compound containing 33.3% calcium, 40.0% oxygen, and 26.7% sulfur. $CaSO_3$

75. The percentage composition of a compound is 92.3% C and 7.70% H. If the molecular mass is 78, what is the molecular formula? C_6H_6

76. Find the molecular formula of a compound with percentage composition 26.7% P, 12.1% N, and 61.2% Cl and molecular mass 695. $P_6N_6Cl_{12}$

77. What is the formula for a hydrate which consists of 90.7% SrC_2O_4 and 9.30% H_2O? $SrC_2O_4 \cdot H_2O$

REVIEW

1. Convert 81.2 g to mg.

2. How many significant digits are in the measurement 41.02 m?

1. 81 200 mg

2. 4

3. What is the relative error of a measurement of 12.0 seconds if the stop watch is precise to ± 0.5 second?

3. 0.0417

4. Write the formulas for the following compounds.
   a. hydrogen iodide
   b. manganese(II) phosphate
   c. rubidium sulfate
   d. gallium(III) bromide

4. a. HI
   b. $Mn_3(PO_4)_2$
   c. Rb_2SO_4
   d. $GaBr_3$

5. Write the names for the following compounds.
   a. $Th_3(PO_4)_4$ thorium(IV) phosphate
   b. $Na_2C_4H_4O_6$ sodium tartrate
   c. $CuSiF_6$ copper(II) hexafluorosilicate
   d. $CsNO_3$ cesium nitrate

6. Classify the following properties as physical or chemical.
   a. flammability
   b. electrical conductivity
   c. displaces hydrogen from water
   d. reacts with acids

6. a. chemical
   b. physical
   c. chemical
   d. chemical

7. Classify the following changes as physical or chemical.
   a. distillation
   b. fermentation
   c. crystallization
   d. dissolving

7. a. physical
   b. chemical
   c. physical
   d. physical

ONE MORE STEP

1. Investigate the report of a new compound as reported in the *Journal of the American Chemical Society.*
   Duplicate the calculations of the researcher in computing the theoretical percent composition of the compound. Do you think the experimental percentages reported are close enough to the theoretical to justify the proposed formula for the new compound?

2. Investigate the methods scientists have used in determining Avogadro's number.

When you think of chemical reactions you usually picture an occurrence that happens immediately. However the chemical reactions involved in making this petrified wood have taken place over a very long period of time. The decaying wood cells are displaced by minerals so that the wood eventually turns to stone. In this chapter, you will study the characteristics of displacement reactions. What system is used to classify reactions? What conditions affect the speed of a reaction?

Michael Collier

Demonstration—Mix 25 cm³ glycerine with 25 cm³ liquid dish soap. Connect rubber tubing to natural gas outlet and other end to a small funnel. Invert funnel into beaker of soap mixture. Make a bubble using the gas. Dislodge bubble by turning funnel upright and shaking gently. As bubble rises, ignite with candle taped to meter stick. Discuss how equations are used to represent observations in a concise form. $CH_4(g) + O_2(g) \rightarrow CO_2(g) + 2H_2O(g)$

CHEMICAL EQUATIONS

6

Chapter 6 covers using chemical formulas to write and balance chemical equations.

You have already seen that chemists have a shorthand method for writing the formulas of substances. They also use this shorthand for describing the changes which substances undergo. Consider the following statement: "Two molecules of ethyne gas will react with five molecules of oxygen gas to produce four molecules of carbon dioxide gas and two molecules of liquid water. How much easier it is to write

$$2C_2H_2(g) + 5O_2(g) \rightarrow 4CO_2(g) + 2H_2O(l)$$

to express the burning of ethyne.

GOAL: You will demonstrate a proficiency in writing and balancing chemical equations.

6:1 REPRESENTING CHEMICAL CHANGES

The formulas of compounds are used to represent the chemical changes that occur in a chemical reaction. A **chemical reaction** is the process by which one or more substances are changed into one or more different substances. A chemical reaction may be represented by an equation. A correct chemical equation shows what changes take place. It also shows the relative amounts of the various elements and compounds that take part in these changes. The starting substances in a chemical reaction are called **reactants.** The substances which are formed by the chemical reaction are called **products.**

Chemical equations are used to represent chemical reactions.

$$2C_2H_2(g) + 5O_2(g) \rightarrow 4CO_2(g) + 2H_2O(l)$$
$$\underbrace{\qquad\qquad\qquad}_{\text{Reactants}} \qquad \underbrace{\qquad\qquad}_{\text{Products}}$$

Reactants are the starting substances and products are the substances formed in chemical reactions.

The letters in parentheses indicate the physical state of each substance involved. The symbol (g) after a formula means that the substance is a gas. Liquids are indicated by the symbol (l), and solids by the symbol (c). The symbol (c) for solid indicates that the solid is crystalline. We can see that in the reaction described above, C_2H_2, O_2, and CO_2 are gases. The H_2O is a liquid.

Physical state symbols in an equation:
(g) gas
(l) liquid
(c) crystalline solid

97

The symbol (aq) indicates a water solution of the substance.

Since many chemical reactions take place in water solution, a substance in water solution is shown by the symbol (aq). This symbol comes from the word aqueous (Latin *aqua* = water). For example, if a water solution of sulfurous acid is warmed, it decomposes. The products of this reaction are water and sulfur dioxide, a gas.

$$H_2SO_3(aq) \rightarrow H_2O(l) + SO_2(g)$$

6:2 BALANCING EQUATIONS

A chemical reaction can be represented by a chemical equation. To write an equation which accurately represents the reaction, we must perform correctly three steps.

Step 1. *Determine exactly what are the reactants and the products.* For example, when propane gas burns in air, the reactants are propane (C_3H_8) and oxygen (O_2). The products formed are carbon dioxide (CO_2) and water (H_2O).

Reactants are written on the left side of chemical equations; products are written on the right.

Step 2. *Assemble the parts of the chemical equation.* Write the formulas for the reactants on one side of the equation, usually on the left, and connect them with plus signs. Write the formulas for the products on the other side of the equation. Connect the two sides using an arrow to show the direction of the reaction. Thus,

$$C_3H_8 \quad + \quad O_2 \quad \rightarrow \quad CO_2 \quad + \quad H_2O$$

propane   oxygen   yield   carbon dioxide   water

reactants   yield   products

FIGURE 6-1. The reaction of propane with oxygen produces carbon dioxide, water, and a tremendous amount of energy. Thus, propane is used as a fuel in torches, lanterns, and camping stoves.

The symbols and formulas must be correct. If not, Step 3 will be useless. Refer to the oxidation tables in Chapter 4 when attempting to write correct formulas. We will ignore the symbols which indicate physical state while we learn to balance equations.

Step 3. *Balance the equation.* Balancing means showing an equal number of atoms for each element on both sides of the equation. Recall that the law of conservation of mass states that the same amount of matter must be present both before and after all chemical reactions. Therefore, the same number and kinds of atoms must be present on both sides of the equation. Check the preceding equation. It is not balanced. There are three carbon atoms on the left, but only one carbon atom on the right. To put the carbon in balance, we place the coefficient 3 before the carbon dioxide on the right. In balancing an equation, *change only the coefficients. Never change the subscripts.* To do so would change the substance represented. Our equation is now

Balanced equations have the same kind and number of atoms on each side.

Coefficients, not subscripts, may be changed to balance an equation.

$$C_3H_8 + O_2 \rightarrow 3CO_2 + H_2O$$

The carbon atoms are balanced, but the hydrogen atoms are not. There are eight hydrogen atoms on the left and only two on the right. By placing the coefficient 4 in front of the water, both the carbon and hydrogen atoms will be in balance. The equation is now

$$C_3H_8 + O_2 \rightarrow 3CO_2 + 4H_2O$$

Only the oxygen remains to be balanced. There are two oxygen atoms on the left and ten oxygen atoms on the right. To balance the oxygen, place the coefficient 5 in front of the oxygen. The equation is now balanced.

$$C_3H_8 + 5O_2 \rightarrow 3CO_2 + 4H_2O$$

In the commercial production of hydrogen, steam reacts with carbon in the form of coke to produce hydrogen and carbon monoxide. The equation is

$$H_2O + C \rightarrow H_2 + CO$$

2 hydrogen atoms		2 hydrogen atoms
1 oxygen atom	yield	1 carbon atom
1 carbon atom		1 oxygen atom

Because we have equal numbers of each kind of atom on both sides of the equation, the equation is balanced.

Be careful not to confuse subscripts and coefficients in balancing equations. *Never change the subscript in a formula in an attempt to balance an equation.* Changing a subscript changes the substance that is taking part in the reaction. The resulting equation will not represent the chemical change which actually takes place.

Never change a subscript to balance an equation.

1. balanced
2. La(NO$_3$)$_3$ + 3NaOH → La(OH)$_3$ + 3NaNO$_3$

PROBLEMS

Balance each of the following equations.

1. Te + H$_2$O → TeO + H$_2$
2. La(NO$_3$)$_3$ + NaOH → La(OH)$_3$ + NaNO$_3$
3. RhO$_3$ → RhO + O$_2$ balanced
4. Hf + N$_2$ → Hf$_3$N$_4$ 3Hf + 2N$_2$ → Hf$_3$N$_4$
5. Ga + H$_2$SO$_4$ → Ga$_2$(SO$_4$)$_3$ + H$_2$ 2Ga +3H$_2$SO$_4$ → Ga$_2$(SO$_4$)$_3$ + 3H$_2$
6. PdCl$_2$ + HNO$_3$ → Pd(NO$_3$)$_2$ + HCl   PdCl$_2$ + 2HNO$_3$ → Pd(NO$_3$)$_2$ + 2HCl
7. RbBr + AgCl → AgBr + RbCl   balanced
8. PaI$_5$ → Pa + I$_2$ 2PaI$_5$ → 2Pa + 5I$_2$
9. O$_2$ + Sb$_2$S$_3$ → Sb$_2$O$_4$ + SO$_2$ 5O$_2$ + Sb$_2$S$_3$ → Sb$_2$O$_4$ + 3SO$_2$
10. Cu + Cl$_2$ → CuCl$_2$ balanced

FIGURE 6-2. The hydrogen gas bubbles in this tube were produced by the single displacement reaction of magnesium and hydrochloric acid (a). The silver bromide precipitate shown was produced by the double displacement reaction of silver nitrate and zinc bromide (b).

a

Tim Courlas

b

Hickson-Bender Photography

6:3   CLASSIFYING CHEMICAL CHANGES

There are hundreds of different "kinds" of chemical reactions. For now, we will consider only four general types. Of these four, three are often used to make, or synthesize, new compounds.

Single Displacement. In this type of reaction, one element displaces another in a compound. For example, in the reaction

$$Cl_2(g) + 2KBr(aq) → 2KCl(aq) + Br_2(l)$$

chlorine displaces bromine from potassium bromide. In the reaction

$$3Li(c) + CmF_3(c) → 3LiF(c) + Cm(c)$$

lithium displaces curium from curium(III) fluoride. This type of reaction is recognized and predicted by its general form:

element + compound → element + compound

Double Displacement. There are hundreds of reactions in which the positive and negative portions of two compounds are interchanged.

$$PbCl_2(c) + Li_2SO_4(aq) → 2LiCl(aq) + PbSO_4(c)$$
$$ZnBr_2(aq) + 2AgNO_3(aq) → Zn(NO_3)_2(aq) + 2AgBr(c)$$
$$BaCl_2(aq) + 2KIO_3(aq) → Ba(IO_3)_2(c) + 2KCl(aq)$$

The form of these reactions is easy to recognize,

compound + compound → compound + compound

Decomposition. Many substances will break up into simpler substances when energy is supplied.

$$CdCO_3(c) → CdO(c) + CO_2(g)$$
$$Pb(OH)_2(c) → PbO(c) + H_2O(g)$$
$$N_2O_4(g) → 2NO_2(g)$$

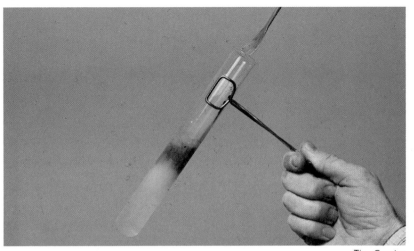

Tim Courlas

You may wish to use some of the indicated reactions as demonstrations.

FIGURE 6-3. Hydrogen peroxide decomposes on standing to form water and oxygen. This reaction proceeds slowly therefore a catalyst (MnO_2) is used to speed the process.

$$PCl_5(c) \rightarrow PCl_3(c) + Cl_2(g)$$
$$H_2CO_3(aq) \rightarrow H_2O(l) + CO_2(g)$$
$$2KClO_3(c) \rightarrow 2KCl(c) + 3O_2(g)$$
$$2Ag_2O(c) \rightarrow 4Ag(c) + O_2(g)$$

Products of a decomposition are not necessarily elements.

Energy may be supplied in the form of heat, light, mechanical shock, or electricity. The general form for this type of reaction is,

compound → two or more elements or compounds

Synthesis. In synthesis reactions two or more substances combine to form one new substance.

$$NH_3(g) + HCl(g) \rightarrow NH_4Cl(c)$$
$$CaO(c) + SiO_2(c) \rightarrow CaSiO_3(c)$$
$$2H_2(g) + O_2(g) \rightarrow 2H_2O(g)$$

Reactants of a synthesis are not necessarily elements.

From the name, one might expect that synthesis reactions would be the most common method of preparing new compounds. However, these reactions are rarely as practical as one of the three preceding methods. Here the general form is,

element or compound + element or compound → compound

Not all reactions take one of the general forms we have described. Other classes of reactions will be considered later. Until then, we will deal chiefly with displacement (single or double), decomposition, or synthesis reactions.

Four simple chemical reactions are: single displacement, double displacement, decomposition, synthesis.

PROBLEMS

Balance each of the following. Then classify 11-15 as single or double displacement, decomposition, or synthesis.

11. $CuO + H_2 \rightarrow Cu + H_2O$

12. $Sb + H_2O \rightarrow Sb_2O_3 + H_2$

Remind students about the diatomic gases. Acid formulas can be found on page 68.

11. balanced
single displacement

12. $2Sb + 3H_2O \rightarrow$
$Sb_2O_3 + 3H_2$
single displacement

13. $Re + Br_2 \rightarrow ReBr_3$ $2Re + 3Br_2 \rightarrow 2ReBr_3$ synthesis

14. $Ac(OH)_3 \rightarrow Ac_2O_3 + H_2O$ $2Ac(OH)_3 \rightarrow Ac_2O_3 + 3H_2O$ decomposition

15. $Ra + C \rightarrow RaC_2$ $Ra + 2C \rightarrow RaC_2$ synthesis

16. $HfCl_3 + Al \rightarrow HfCl_2 + AlCl_3$ $3HfCl_3 + Al \rightarrow 3HfCl_2 + AlCl_3$

17. $Zn + CrCl_3 \rightarrow CrCl_2 + ZnCl_2$ $Zn + 2CrCl_3 \rightarrow 2CrCl_2 + ZnCl_2$

$Ca(AlO_2)_2 + 8HCl \rightarrow 2AlCl_3 + CaCl_2 + 4H_2O$

18. $Ca(AlO_2)_2 + HCl \rightarrow AlCl_3 + CaCl_2 + H_2O$

19. $BaCO_3 + C + H_2O \rightarrow CO + Ba(OH)_2$ $BaCO_3 + C + H_2O \rightarrow 2CO + Ba(OH)_2$

$2CeO_2 + 2KI + 8HCl \rightarrow 2KCl + 2CeCl_3 + 4H_2O + I_2$

20. $CeO_2 + KI + HCl \rightarrow KCl + CeCl_3 + H_2O + I_2$

Substitute symbols for names, then balance each of the following equations.

21. copper(II) carbonate decomposes to copper(II) oxide and carbon dioxide gas $CuCO_3(c) \rightarrow CuO(c) + CO_2(g)$

22. sodium reacts with water to produce sodium hydroxide and hydrogen gas $2Na(c) + 2H_2O(l) \rightarrow 2NaOH(aq) + H_2(g)$

23. ammonium nitrite decomposes to nitrogen gas and water

$NH_4NO_2(c) \rightarrow 2H_2O(l) + N_2(g)$
$2Cu(c) + S(c) \rightarrow Cu_2S(c)$

24. copper combines with sulfur to form copper(I) sulfide

25. silver nitrate reacts with sulfuric acid to produce silver sulfate and nitric acid $2AgNO_3(aq) + H_2SO_4(aq) \rightarrow Ag_2SO_4(c) + 2HNO_3(aq)$

26. sulfuric acid decomposes to water and sulfur trioxide

$H_2SO_4(l) \rightarrow H_2O(l) + SO_3(g)$
$CaCO_3(c) + 2HCl(aq) \rightarrow CaCl_2(aq) + H_2O(l) + CO_2(g)$

27. calcium carbonate reacts with hydrochloric acid to produce calcium chloride, water, and carbon dioxide gas

28. ammonium nitrate decomposes to water and nitrogen(I) oxide
$NH_4NO_3(c) \rightarrow 2H_2O(l) + N_2O(g)$

Jons Jakob Berzelius   (1779–1848)

Jons Jakob Berzelius was one of many medical doctors who became interested in chemistry and contributed greatly to its progress. His early studies rarely took him very far from his native Swedish village near Stockholm.

One of his endeavors included a 10-year analysis of some 2 000 simple and compound materials to determine the proportions of their various elements.

He developed a system of nomenclature—our present system of symbols and formulas. He also discovered several new elements, including selenium, silicon, and thorium. Throughout his life, Berzelius served on national committees and commissions dealing with science, agriculture, and education in an effort to better the life of his fellow Swedes.

CHEMICAL CAREER: Health and Safety Inspectors

We take for granted that food we purchase is safe to eat. Most of the time it is because people and companies handling food are subject to many laws and regulations designed to protect the public. Federal, state, and local governments all employ investigators and inspectors to see that laws and regulations regarding health and safety are obeyed.

Much of the food we eat contains a number of additives used to enhance flavor, color, and prolong shelf life. Before any additive is approved for use by the Food and Drug Administration, a food processor must submit the results of a number of biochemical and analytical tests on the additive. Inspectors obtain samples from the field so the FDA can run their own set of tests to be sure the industry test data is accurate and complete. Inspectors must have a background in analytical procedures in that they are also responsible for on-site inspections of food processors' laboratories to be sure they are run in an appropriate manner. Thus, the FDA can rely on the industry data as being accurately determined.

Restaurants are frequently visited by health inspectors. The inspector looks for proper storage of food to make sure no insect pests or rodents can contaminate it. The inspector also observes the employees at work to ensure that the food is being handled in a clean and sanitary manner.

Food processing plants are also subject to on-site inspections of their facilities. Labeling of products is also examined to be sure a label complies with government standards. Inspectors have the power to seize and destroy any products which are improperly labeled, spoiled, contaminated, or processed under unsanitary conditions. The agency may take court action which could result in fines as well as an injunction prohibiting a business from resuming operations.

The Occupational Health and Safety Administration has many inspectors who visit industrial and commercial establishments. OSHA inspectors check for the observance of accepted procedures and safe physical arrangements of equipment and personnel. One of their major tasks is to check for fire hazards and the availability and maintenance of fire-fighting equipment.

These people are also concerned with many aspects of the workplace which may not appear potentially dangerous. For instance, they will check sound levels in a factory to see if the workers' hearing could be damaged. They check air quality inside the plant to ensure the prevention of occupational respiratory diseases. They also check radiation levels and worker exposure around nuclear power plants and medical facilities.

SUMMARY

1. Chemists use equations to describe the changes which substances undergo. 6:1

2. The physical state of substances in equations is shown by (g) for gas, (l) for liquid, (c) for solid, and (aq) for a water solution. 6:1

3. A chemical reaction is the process by which one or more substances are changed into one or more new substances. 6:1

4. Reactants are the starting substances in a reaction. Products are the substances resulting from a reaction. 6:1

5. A chemical equation represents changes that take place in a reaction. It also shows relative amounts of reactants and products. 6:2

6. Balancing an equation means adjusting coefficients so that there are the 6:2 same number of atoms of each element on both sides of the equation.

7. In a single displacement reaction, one element displaces another element. In a double displacement reaction, ions from two compounds are interchanged. 6:3

8. In a decomposition reaction, a compound breaks down into two or more simpler substances. 6:3

9. In a synthesis reaction, two or more substances combine to form a more complex substance. 6:3

PROBLEMS

Substitute symbols for names and balance.

29. chromium displaces hydrogen from hydrochloric acid, with chromium(II) chloride as the other product $Cr(c) + 2HCl(aq) \rightarrow H_2(g) + CrCl_2(aq)$

30. barium hydroxide reacts with carbon dioxide to form barium carbonate and water $Ba(OH)_2(aq) + CO_2(g) \rightarrow BaCO_3(c) + H_2O(l)$

31. Why is it that subscripts never change when balancing an equation? It would change the type of substances present in the reaction.

32. Why is it necessary to balance equations? Matter is conserved in chemical reactions.

Balance each of the following equations.

33. $Na(c) + O_2(g) \rightarrow Na_2O(c)$ $4Na(c) + O_2(g) \rightarrow 2Na_2O(c)$

34. $AsCl_3(c) + H_2O(l) \rightarrow HCl(aq) + As(OH)_3(aq)$ $AsCl_3(c) + 3H_2O(l) \rightarrow 3HCl(aq) + As(OH)_3(aq)$

35. $Ho(c) + H_2O(l) \rightarrow Ho(OH)_3(aq) + H_2(g)$ $2Ho(c) + 6H_2O(l) \rightarrow 2Ho(OH)_3(aq) + 3H_2(g)$

36. $2IrCl_3(aq) + 3NaOH(aq) \rightarrow Ir_2O_3(c) + 3HCl(aq) + 3NaCl(aq)$

37. $2MoO_3(c) + 3Zn(c) + 3H_2SO_4(l) \rightarrow Mo_2O_3(c) + 3ZnSO_4(aq) + 3H_2O(l)$

38. $NbI_3(c) + I_2(c) \rightarrow NbI_5(c)$ balanced

39. $Pb(C_2H_3O_2)_2(aq) + K_2CrO_4(aq) \rightarrow PbCrO_4(c) + 2KC_2H_3O_2(aq)$

40. $RbCl(c) + O_2(g) \rightarrow RbClO_4(c)$ $RbCl(c) + 2O_2(g) \rightarrow RbClO_4(c)$

41. $SiF_4(c) + H_2O(l) \rightarrow H_2SiF_6(aq) + H_2SiO_3(c)$ $3SiF_4(c) + 3H_2O(l) \rightarrow 2H_2SiF_6(aq) + H_2SiO_3(c)$

42. $Sn(c) + KOH(aq) \rightarrow K_2SnO_2(c) + H_2(g)$ $Sn(c) + 2KOH(aq) \rightarrow K_2SnO_2(c) + H_2(g)$

Balance each of the following reactions after predicting the products.

43. silver oxide decomposes $2Ag_2O(c) \rightarrow 4Ag(c) + O_2(g)$

44. copper plus silver nitrate (displacement; copper(II) compound is formed) $Cu(c) + 2AgNO_3(aq) \rightarrow$ $Cu(NO_3)_2(aq) + 2Ag(c)$

45. magnesium plus oxygen (synthesis) $2 Mg(c) + O_2(g) \rightarrow 2MgO(c)$

46. hydrochloric acid plus silver nitrate (double displacement) $HCl(aq) + AgNO_3(aq) \rightarrow HNO_3(aq) + AgCl(c)$

47. magnesium plus hydrochloric acid (displacement) $Mg(c) + 2HCl(aq) \rightarrow MgCl_2(aq) + H_2(g)$

48. iron plus oxygen (synthesis; iron(III) compound is formed) $4Fe(c) + 3O_2(g) \rightarrow 2Fe_2O_3(c)$

49. iron plus sulfur (synthesis; iron(II) compound is formed) $Fe(c) + S(c) \rightarrow FeS(c)$

50. calcium hydroxide plus sulfuric acid (double displacement) $Ca(OH)_2(aq) + H_2SO_4(aq) \rightarrow$ $CaSO_4(c) + H_2O(l)$

51. magnesium plus nitrogen (synthesis) $3Mg(c) + N_2(g) \rightarrow Mg_3N_2(c)$

52. zinc plus sulfuric acid (single displacement) $Zn(c) + H_2SO_4(aq) \rightarrow ZnSO_4(aq) + H_2(g)$

REVIEW

1. Make the following conversions.
   a. 2.52×10^{21} formula units of ZrS_2 to moles. 0.004 19 mol
   b. 1.26×10^{25} formula units of $Al(C_2H_3O_2)_3$ to grams. 4270 g
   c. 6.06 grams $Fe_2(SO_4)_3$ to moles. 0.0152 mol
   d. 88.4 grams MnI_2 to moles. 0.286 mol
   e. 0.002 02 mole $Ni(OH)_2$ to grams. 0.187 g

2. What is the molarity of a 1000-cm^3 solution containing 0.550 g $Ni(IO_3)_2$? 0.001 76M

3. How would you prepare a 0.00364M solution of $Ag_2C_4H_4O_6$? Assume you need 200 cm^3 of solution. 0.265 g dissolved in enough water to make 200 cm^3 of solution

4. Find the percentage composition of each element in SrI_2. 25.6%, 74.3%

5. Find the empirical formula for a substance with the following composition: 45.3% Zn and 54.7% Se. ZnSe

6. Find the formula for the hydrate with the composition 79.0% $Zr(NO_3)_4$ and 21.0% H_2O. $Zr(NO_3)_4 \cdot 5H_2O$

ONE MORE STEP

1. Try balancing each of the following equations.
   a. $Cu(c) + H_2SO_4(aq) \rightarrow CuSO_4(aq) + SO_2(g) + H_2O(l)$
   b. $Cu_2S(c) + HNO_3(aq) \rightarrow Cu(NO_3)_2(aq) + CuSO_4(aq) + NO_2(g) + H_2O(l)$
   c. $CH_4(g) + O_2(g) \rightarrow CO_2(g) + H_2O(l)$
   d. $Ce(IO_3)_4(aq) + H_2C_2O_4(aq) \rightarrow Ce_2(C_2O_4)_3(aq) + I_2(aq) + CO_2(g) + H_2O(l)$
   e. $KBr(c) + H_2SO_4(l) + MnO_2(c) \rightarrow KHSO_4(aq) + MnSO_4(aq) + H_2O(l) + Br_2(g)$

2. What kind of reaction is a methathesis reaction?

3. There are a number of general rules for predicting the products of decomposition reactions. Try to find at least four of these rules.

The burning of propane fuel in the outdoor stove provides the energy needed to cook the eggs. Both the combustion and cooking processes are chemical changes. Every chemical change occurs with the release or absorption of energy. What kind of energy is absorbed by the eggs? What term is used to describe reactions that absorb energy? What types of energy are released by the propane? Why are some substances more efficient fuel sources than others?

Philip Jon Bailey/Jeroboam

QUANTITATIVE RELATIONSHIPS

7

Chapter 7 presents background information on mass-mass relationships in a manner that allows the student to gain confidence in solving mass-mass problems. Also covered is the concept of energy as an important component in any chemical reaction, as well as calculations involving heat.

Demonstration—Mass 3.5 g of iron filings onto watch glass. Demonstrate magnetic property. Mass 2.0 g of sulfur onto watch glass. Mix and place in test tube. Heat until contents of tube glow red. Place test tube in cold water to break glass. Remove contents and demonstrate the absence of yellow color, and lack of magnetism. Mass the product. Write the equation for the reaction, $Fe(c) + S(c) \rightarrow FeS(c)$, and discuss the masses used as being $1/16$ of a mole. Use data to introduce mass-mass problems.

Chemists are constantly faced with the question, "How much?" How much of an element is present in a compound? How much water is contained in a hydrate? How much of each element or compound is required to prepare a new compound?

The mass relationships between reactants and products in chemical changes are an important concern to chemists. Several questions arise here. How much of one reactant is needed to combine with a given amount of another reactant? How much product is produced from a specific amount of reactant? There are other, similar, questions. Fortunately, all these questions can be answered using the same procedure.

GOAL: You will demonstrate your understanding of the mass-energy relationship in chemical reactions by using it to perform mass-mass and mass-heat calculations.

7:1 MASS-MASS RELATIONSHIPS

A chemical equation is simply a shorthand expression which gives information about a reaction. Once a balanced equation is written, it can be used to help solve problems involving the reaction. The coefficients of a balanced equation give the relative amounts (in moles) of reactants and products. Calculations to find the masses of materials involved in reactions are called **mass-mass problems.**

The coefficients of a balanced equation give the relative amounts (in moles) of reactants and products.

EXAMPLE: Mass-Mass

How many grams of silver chloride can be produced from the reaction of 17.0 g of silver nitrate with excess sodium chloride solution?

Solving process:

Step 1. We are given silver nitrate and requested to find silver chloride. What do we know which would connect two different substances? A chemical equation would relate them in a quantitative way. We then write a balanced equation to represent the reaction which occurs. Silver nitrate is reacting with sodium chloride. Since we have compound plus compound, we predict that a double displacement reaction will occur.

$$AgNO_3(aq) + NaCl(aq) \rightarrow AgCl(c) + NaNO_3(aq)$$

Step 2. In Chapter 6, we thought of equations as written in terms of individual atoms and formula units. However, we can also consider the coefficients in the equation as indicating the number of moles of formula units which take part in the reaction. The equation above indicates that one formula unit of silver nitrate will produce one formula unit of silver chloride. It also indicates that one mole of silver nitrate formula units will produce one mole of silver chloride formula units. The problem states that an excess of sodium chloride is used. This statement shows us that all the silver nitrate will react.

Let us review where we are. We are given grams of silver nitrate. We are asked to find grams of silver chloride. Silver nitrate and silver chloride are related by the equation. The equation is read in units of moles.

Step 3. Our solution begins by converting the grams of silver nitrate to moles. We use the table on the inside back cover to determine the formula mass of $AgNO_3$, which is 170 g.

$$\frac{17.0 \text{ g AgNO}_3}{} \left| \frac{1 \text{ mol AgNO}_3}{170 \text{ g AgNO}_3} \right. \ldots$$

Step 4. We have now converted the silver nitrate to units that will enable us to relate it to the silver chloride. We use the equation to find the conversion factor to use in going from silver nitrate to silver chloride. The equation tells us that one mole of silver nitrate will produce one mole of silver chloride. Using this fact gives us a partial solution which appears as:

$$\frac{17.0 \text{ g AgNO}_3}{} \left| \frac{1 \text{ mol AgNO}_3}{170 \text{ g AgNO}_3} \right| \frac{1 \text{ mol AgCl}}{1 \text{ mol AgNO}_3} \ldots$$

Step 5. We have now arrived at silver chloride which is the substance we were asked to find. However, we were to find the answer

A balanced equation is necessary for obtaining correct answers to chemical problems.

First step.
Write the balanced equation.

Second Step.
Find the number of moles of reactant and product.

Third Step.
Convert the grams of given to moles.

Fourth step.
Determine mole ratio from the balanced equation.

in grams. To complete the problem, we must convert the moles of silver chloride to grams. The final solution then appears as:

Fifth step.
Express the moles of required substance in terms of grams.

$$\frac{17.0 \text{ g AgNO}_3}{} \left| \frac{1 \text{ mol AgNO}_3}{170 \text{ g AgNO}_3} \right| \frac{1 \text{ mol AgCl}}{1 \text{ mol AgNO}_3} \right| \frac{144 \text{ g AgCl}}{1 \text{ mol AgCl}} = 14.4 \text{ g AgCl}$$

This problem involves finding the mass of one substance from a given mass of another substance. Problems of this type are called mass-mass problems. All mass-mass problems can be solved in this way. This example and other quantitative studies of chemical reactions are called stoichiometry (stoh kee AHM uh tree). Let us review the process.

Stoichiometry is the quantitative study of chemical reactions.

Step 1. *Write the balanced equation.*
The first step in the solution of any problem is to write a balanced equation for the correct reaction. In this section, we will always assume that only one reaction occurs and that all of one reactant is used. In practice, several reactions may occur, the actual reaction may not be known, or all the reactant may not react.

Step 2. *Find the number of moles of the given substance.*
Express the mass of the given substance in moles by dividing the mass of the given substance by its formula mass.

$$\text{grams of given substance} \left| \frac{1 \text{ mole}}{\text{formula mass of given substance}} \right. \ldots$$

Step 3. *Inspect the balanced equation to determine the ratio of moles of required substance to moles of given substance.*
For example, look at the following equation.

$$2H_2(g) + O_2(g) \rightarrow 2H_2O(g)$$

In this reaction, 1 mole of oxygen reacts with 2 moles of hydrogen. From the same equation, 1 mole of oxygen will produce 2 moles of water. Also, 2 moles of water are produced by 2 moles of hydrogen. Once the equation is balanced, only the reactants and products directly involved in the problem should be in your calculations. Multiply the moles of given substance by the ratio:

$$\ldots \frac{\text{moles of required substance}}{\text{moles of given substance}} \ldots$$

Step 4. *Express the moles of required substance in terms of grams.*

$$\ldots \frac{\text{formula mass of required substance}}{1 \text{ mole}} = \text{grams of required substance}$$

Notice that, as you work through a problem of this kind, you first convert grams of given substance to moles, and then convert moles of required substance back to grams.

start with grams given	→ grams to moles →	use mole ratio	→ moles to grams →	end with grams required

This method is used because the balanced equation relates the number of moles of given substance to the number of moles of required substance. Now try the following two problems.

EXAMPLE: Mass-Mass

How many grams of Cu_2S could be produced from 9.90 g of $CuCl$ reacting with an excess of H_2S gas?

Solving process:

(a) We must write the balanced equation. $CuCl$ and H_2S are reactants, Cu_2S is one product.

$$2CuCl(aq) + H_2S(g) \rightarrow Cu_2S(c) + 2HCl(aq)$$

If we use the wrong reaction or do not balance the equation properly, we cannot get a correct answer.

(b) Find the number of moles of the given substance.

$$\text{1 mole of } CuCl \text{ has mass:} \quad \begin{array}{l} \text{1 Cu } 1 \times 63.5 = 63.5 \text{ g} \\ \text{1 Cl } 1 \times 35.5 = \underline{35.5 \text{ g}} \\ \text{formula mass} = 99.0 \text{ g} \end{array}$$

$$\frac{9.90 \text{ g } CuCl}{} \left| \frac{1 \text{ mol } CuCl}{99.0 \text{ g } CuCl} \right. \cdots$$

(c) Determine the mole ratio of the required substance to the given substance. Notice that, although H_2S and HCl are part of the reaction, we do not consider them in this problem.

$$2CuCl + H_2S \rightarrow Cu_2S + 2HCl$$

$$\frac{9.90 \text{ g } CuCl}{} \left| \frac{1 \text{ mol } CuCl}{99.0 \text{ g } CuCl} \right| \frac{1 \text{ mol } Cu_2S}{2 \text{ mol } CuCl} \cdots$$

(d) We must convert moles of Cu_2S into grams of Cu_2S.

$$\text{1 mole of } Cu_2S \text{ has mass:} \quad \begin{array}{l} 2Cu \quad 2 \times 63.5 = 127 \text{ g} \\ 1S \qquad 1 \times 32 = \underline{32 \text{ g}} \\ \text{formula mass} = 159 \text{ g} \end{array}$$

$$\frac{9.90 \text{ g } CuCl}{} \left| \frac{1 \text{ mol } CuCl}{99.0 \text{ g } CuCl} \right| \frac{1 \text{ mol } Cu_2S}{2 \text{ mol } CuCl} \left| \frac{159 \text{ g } Cu_2S}{1 \text{ mol } Cu_2S} \right. = 7.95 \text{ g of } Cu_2S$$

Thus, we predict 9.90 g of CuCl will react to produce 7.95 g of Cu_2S. If the problem is set up correctly, all the factor labels will divide out except the final result. The final result should be the correct label for the answer.

Use the label in your solution as a check on the answer.

EXAMPLE: Mass-Mass

How many grams of calcium hydroxide will be needed to react completely with 10.0 grams of phosphoric acid? Note that we are asked to find the mass of one reactant which will react with a given mass of another reactant.

Solving process:
(a) Write a balanced equation.

$$3Ca(OH)_2 + 2H_3PO_4 \rightarrow Ca_3(PO_4)_2 + 6H_2O$$

(b) Change 10.0 g phosphoric acid to moles of phosphoric acid.

$$\frac{10.0 \text{ g } H_3PO_4}{} \left| \frac{1 \text{ mol } H_3PO_4}{98.0 \text{ g } H_3PO_4} \right. \cdots$$

(c) From the equation, 2 moles of H_3PO_4 will require 3 moles $Ca(OH)_2$

$$\frac{10.0 \text{ g } H_3PO_4}{} \left| \frac{1 \text{ mol } H_3PO_4}{98.0 \text{ g } H_3PO_4} \right| \frac{3 \text{ mol } Ca(OH)_2}{2 \text{ mol } H_3PO_4} \cdots$$

(d) Change moles of calcium hydroxide into grams (mass) of calcium hydroxide.

$$\frac{10.0 \text{ g } H_3PO_4}{} \left| \frac{1 \text{ mol } H_3PO_4}{98.0 \text{ g } H_3PO_4} \right| \frac{3 \text{ mol } Ca(OH)_2}{2 \text{ mol } H_3PO_4} \left| \frac{74.1 \text{ g } Ca(OH)_2}{1 \text{ mol } Ca(OH)_2} \right. = 11.3 \text{ g } Ca(OH)_2$$

PROBLEMS

1. How many grams of H_2 can be produced from the reaction of 11.5 grams of sodium with an excess of water?

2. An excess of nitrogen reacts with 2.00 grams of hydrogen. How many grams of ammonia are produced?

3. How many grams of oxygen are required to burn completely 85.6 grams of carbon?

4. In Problem 3, how many grams of CO_2 will be formed?

5. In the decomposition of potassium chlorate, 64.2 grams of O_2 are formed. How many grams of potassium chloride are produced?

6. The action of carbon monoxide on iron(III) oxide can be represented by the equation, $Fe_2O_3(c) + 3CO(g) \rightarrow 2Fe(c) + 3CO_2(g)$. What would be the minimum amount of carbon monoxide used if 18.7 grams of iron were produced?

1. 0.505 g H_2
2. 11.2 g NH_3
3. 228 g O_2
4. 314 g CO_2
5. 99.7 g KCl
6. 14.1 g CO

Heat energy is absorbed in endothermic reactions.
Heat energy is given off in exothermic reactions.

7. How many grams of hydrochloric acid are required to react completely with 75.1 grams of calcium hydroxide?   74.0 g HCl

8. How many grams of hydrogen are produced when 5.62 grams of aluminum react with excess hydrochloric acid?   0.631 g H₂

7:2 ENERGY AND CHEMICAL CHANGE

Chemical changes are always accompanied by a change in energy. If heat energy is absorbed in a reaction, the reaction is **endothermic.** The products, therefore, are higher in energy than the reactants. On the other hand, if heat energy is given off by a reaction, the reaction is **exothermic.** In this case, the products are lower in energy than the reactants. For example, the calcium hydroxide-phosphoric acid reaction is exothermic. If a thermometer is placed in the reaction vessel, the temperature will rise as the reaction occurs. Heat energy is given off. The products, calcium phosphate and water, are at a lower energy state than the reactants.

FIGURE 7-1. Friction is the source of activation energy when a match is struck (a). When electricity is supplied to a tungsten filament, heat and light are produced (b).

FIGURE 7-2. The reaction between substances in a cold compress is endothermic.

a   Larry Hamill   b   Hager/Alpha

Quantitative measurements of energy changes are expressed in **joules.** The joule (J) is an SI unit. It is a derived unit rather than a base unit.

Both endothermic and exothermic reactions require a certain minimum amount of energy to get started. This minimum amount of energy is called the **activation energy.** Without it, the reactant atoms or molecules will not unite to form the product and the reaction does not occur.

Chemical reactions have many possible sources for their activation energy. When a match is struck, friction produces enough heat to activate the reactants on the match head. As a result the match ignites. In photography, light is the source of the activation energy.

Greg Miller

a

b

U.S. Food and Drug Administration   U.S. Food and Drug Administration

7:3   HEAT MEASUREMENT

Experimentally, the energy changes of chemical reactions are measured in a **calorimeter,** Figure 7-4. The energy quantities involved in various physical changes can also be measured in a calorimeter. To change the temperature of a substance, heat must be added or removed. Some substances require little heat to cause a change in their temperature. Other substances require a great deal of heat to cause the same temperature change. For example, one gram of water requires 4.18 joules of heat to cause a temperature change of one Celsius degree. It takes only 0.903 joule to raise the temperature of one gram of aluminum one Celsius degree. The amount of heat needed to raise the temperature of 1 g of a substance by 1C° is called the **specific heat capacity** (C_p) of the substance. Every substance has its own specific heat capacity. The amount of heat required to raise the temperature of one gram of water one Celsius degree is 4.18 joules. The specific heat capacity of water is 4.18 J/g·C°.

Specific heat capacities are given in joules per gram-Celsius degree (J/g·C°). Tables A-3 and A-5 of the Appendix list the specific heat capacity of some substances. The specific heat capacity can be used in calculations involving the change in temperature of a specific amount of substance. For example, to heat 40.0 g of water from 20.0°C to 36.0°C requires:

$$\frac{4.18 \text{ J}}{g \cdot C°} \left| \frac{40.0 \text{ g}}{} \right| \frac{16.0 \text{ C}°}{} = 2680 \text{ J}$$

One kilojoule equals 1000 joules. 4.18 joules is the amount of heat required to raise the temperature of one gram of water one

A calorimeter is used to measure energy changes in chemical reactions.

FIGURE 7-4. A bomb calorimeter is used to measure the heat of a reaction. Energy produced in the reaction vessel is absorbed by the water.

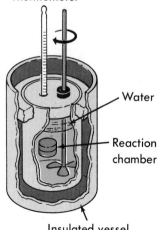

Thermometer

Water

Reaction chamber

Insulated vessel

4.18 joules is the amount of heat needed to raise the temperature of one gram of water 1 C°.

Molar heat capacity is the quantity of heat needed to raise the temperature of one mole of a substance 1 C°.

Celsius degree. Therefore, 4.18 kilojoules is the amount of heat required to raise the temperature of 1000 grams (one kilogram) of water one Celsius degree.

Another heat quantity, often used by chemists is the **molar heat capacity.** This quantity is the heat needed to raise the temperature of 1 mole of a substance by 1C°. In the case of a monatomic element, the term **atomic heat capacity** is used instead of molar heat capacity. The molar (or atomic) heat capacity of a substance is found by multiplying the specific heat capacity of the substance by its formula (or atomic) mass. All of the heat changes we have discussed are measured in calorimeters.

Doug Martin

Emphasize that the heat produced by a reaction must equal the heat gained by the water in an adiabatic system

FIGURE 7-5. The energy values of different foods can be determined by burning them in a calorimeter such as the one shown here.

There are several kinds of calorimeters. A calorimeter containing water is often used to measure the heat absorbed or released by a chemical reaction. Heat energy from a chemical reaction in the cup in the calorimeter causes a change in temperature of the water in the calorimeter. The temperature change of the water is used to measure the amount of heat absorbed or released by the reaction. The product of the specific heat capacity of the water, the temperature change of the water, and the mass of the water gives the change in heat energy. The heat energy released or absorbed by water is calculated using the following equation.

It is assumed that no heat is lost or absorbed by the calorimeter.

Heat flows from warmer to cooler areas.

Heat lost = Heat gained

$$\frac{\Delta T}{} \left| \frac{4.18\ \text{J}}{\text{g} \cdot \text{C}°} \right| \frac{\text{g of } H_2O}{} = \text{J}$$

$\Delta T = T_{final} - T_{initial}$

The same method can be used to calculate the change in heat energy when two dilute solutions react. The solutions are placed in a cup in the calorimeter. As the chemical reaction occurs, the temperature change is measured. Because the solutions are dilute, we can assume that the mixture has the same specific heat capacity as water, 4.18 J/g·C°. By multiplying the specific heat capacity by the temperature change, and the mass of the solutions, we can calculate the heat change of the reaction.

$H = m(\Delta T)C_p$

7:4 HEAT CALCULATIONS

Notice that throughout our discussion of calorimetry, we have assumed that the calorimeter itself does not absorb any heat. We also have assumed that no heat escapes from the calorimeter. Neither of these assumptions is completely true. However, we will assume them so in order to simplify our calculations. The error from actual losses of heat should be considered in any laboratory exercise using calorimeters.

The law of conservation of energy means that in an insulated system, any heat lost by one quantity of matter must be gained by another. The transfer of energy takes place between two quantities of matter which are at different temperatures. Energy flows from one to the other until the two reach the same temperature. Further, the amount of energy transferred can be calculated from the relationship:

$$\left(\begin{array}{c}\text{heat gained}\\\text{or lost}\end{array}\right) = \left(\begin{array}{c}\text{mass}\\\text{in grams}\end{array}\right) \left(\begin{array}{c}\text{change in}\\\text{temperature}\end{array}\right) \left(\begin{array}{c}\text{specific heat}\\\text{capacity}\end{array}\right)$$

$$H = (m)(\Delta T^*)(C_p)$$

EXAMPLE: Heat Calculation

How much heat is lost when a solid aluminum ingot with mass 4110 g cools from 660°C to 25°C?

Solving process:
From Table A-5 of the Appendix, we find that the specific heat capacity of aluminum is 0.903 J/g·C°. We also know that

$$H = (m)(\Delta T)(C_p) \qquad \Delta T = 660°C - 25°C$$

so

$$H = \frac{4110\ g}{} \left| \frac{635\ C°}{} \right| \frac{0.903\ J}{g \cdot C°} = 2.36 \times 10^6\ J$$

EXAMPLE: Heat Calculation

Suppose a piece of iron with a mass of 21.5 grams at a temperature of 100.0°C is dropped into an insulated container of water. The

*ΔT may be represented as $T_f - T_i$ when heat is gained and $T_i - T_f$ when heat is lost.

mass of the water is 132 grams and its temperature before adding the iron is 20.0°C. What will be the final temperature of the system?

Solving process:
We know the heat lost must equal the heat gained. Since the iron is at a higher temperature than the water, the iron will lose energy. The water will gain an equivalent amount of energy. (a) The heat lost by the iron is

$$H = (m)(\Delta T)(C_p) = \frac{21.5 \text{ g}}{} \left| \frac{(100.0°C - T_f)}{} \right| \frac{0.448 \text{ J}}{\text{g} \cdot \text{C}°}$$

(b) The heat gained by the water is

$$H = (m)(\Delta T)(C_p) = \frac{132 \text{ g}}{} \left| \frac{(T_f - 20.0°C)}{} \right| \frac{4.18 \text{ J}}{\text{g} \cdot \text{C}°}$$

(c) The heat gained must equal the heat lost

$$\frac{132 \text{ g}}{} \left| \frac{(T_f - 20.0°)}{} \right| \frac{4.18 \text{ J}}{\text{g} \cdot \text{C}°} = \frac{21.5 \text{ g}}{} \left| \frac{(100.0°C - T_f)}{} \right| \frac{0.448 \text{ J}}{\text{g} \cdot \text{C}°}$$

$$T_f = 21.4°C$$

The same type of calculation may be used to measure the specific heat capacity of an unknown metal. We must have the masses of the two substances and the initial and final temperatures of both. The only unknown factor is the specific heat capacity of the metal.

The specific heat capacities of metals are fairly constant over a wide range of temperatures. In fact, the specific heat capacities of all solids and liquids are fairly constant.

In contrast, the specific heat capacities of gases vary widely with temperature. They also depend on whether the gas is heated at constant volume or constant pressure. When performing heat calculations on gases, then, we must be careful to use correct data. We must use figures which give a good average of the heat capacities of a substance over the temperature range involved. We must also check the conditions of volume and pressure stated for the change.

C_p of solids and liquids are nearly constant over a temperature range.

C_p of gases vary with temperature.

PROBLEMS

9. 4080 J

10. 223 J

9. How much heat is required to raise the temperature of 91.4 g PCl_3 from 25.0°C to 76.1°C? (See Table A-5 of the Appendix).

10. How much heat is required to raise the temperature of 4.66 g CCl_4 from 20.9°C to 76.8°C? (See Table A-5 of the Appendix).

11. How much heat is required to raise the temperature of 787 g H_2O from 18.0°C to 100.0°C? 2.70 × 10⁵ J

12. If a piece of aluminum with mass 3.99 g and a temperature of 100.0°C is dropped in 10.0 cm³ of water at 21.0°C, what will be the final temperature of the system? 27.3°C

13. If a piece of cadmium with mass 37.6 g and a temperature of 100.0°C is dropped into 25.0 cm³ of water at 23.0°C, what will be the final temperature of the system? 28.9°C

14. A piece of an unknown metal with mass 5.19 g is heated to 100.00°C and dropped in 10.0 mL of water at 22.00°C. The final temperature of the system is 23.83°C. What is the specific heat capacity of the metal? Using the data in Table A-3 of the Appendix, what might this metal be? 0.193 J/g·C°, Pr

15. A piece of an unknown metal with mass 23.8 g is heated to 100.00°C and dropped in 50.0 cm³ of water at 24.0°C. The final temperature of the system is 32.50°C. What is the specific heat capacity of the metal? 1.11 J/g·C°

7:5 HEAT OF CHEMICAL REACTION

Balanced chemical equations can be used to predict the relative amounts of reactants and products in a reaction. A balanced chemical equation can also be used to calculate the energy absorbed or released during a chemical reaction.

Heat of reaction is the energy absorbed or released during a chemical reaction.

When carbon (in the form of coal) is burned, heat is released.

$$C(c) + O_2(g) \rightarrow CO_2(g) + heat \text{ (393.5 kJ)}$$

One mole of carbon reacts with one mole of oxygen to produce one mole of carbon dioxide and 393.5 kJ of heat. The heat released (393.5 kJ) is called the **heat of reaction.**

FIGURE 7-6. The graph in (a) shows the energy changes for an exothermic reaction. The graph in (b) shows the energy changes for an endothermic reaction. Note that the enthalpy of the products related to the enthalpy of the reactants determines the sign for ΔH.

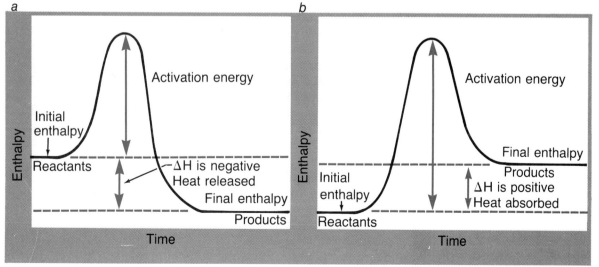

Since heat is released during this reaction, the product (CO_2) must contain less energy than the reactants (C and O_2). Because we think of the heat as coming from the reactants, we can assign each reactant a heat content. The heat content or **enthalpy** is represented by the symbol H.

H = heat content or enthalpy

We cannot measure enthalpy (heat content) in absolute terms. We can only measure changes in enthalpy. The height of a hill cannot be measured in absolute terms either. We can describe the level of the surrounding plain or we say it is a certain number of meters above sea level. The figure we give depends upon what standard of reference is used. In measuring heat content, we use the heat content of a free element at atmospheric pressure and 25°C as our standard. We arbitrarily define this heat content as zero. If carbon is burned in oxygen, chemical potential energy is converted into heat. We assign zero heat content to the elements carbon and oxygen. Therefore, the molar heat content of carbon dioxide must be −393.5 kJ/mol. Thus, carbon dioxide has a heat content or enthalpy of −393.5 kJ/mol.

The heat content of a free element is defined as zero, at standard atmospheric pressure and 25°C.

Different substances have differing enthalpies because their atoms are joined in different ways. When a reaction takes place, the atoms are rearranged. The new arrangement may represent more or less enthalpy than the original arrangement. Thus, energy must be given off or absorbed.

When referring to a table of heat of formation, check to determine which convention applies. All tables in this book employ the current convention; that is, a compound produced by an endothermic reaction will have a positive heat of formation.

7:6 HEAT OF FORMATION

The preceding reaction involves the formation of a compound from its elements. The change in enthalpy (ΔH) when one mole of a compound is produced from the free elements is known as the **heat of formation.** This quantity is usually expressed in terms of kilojoules per mole. A negative sign is given to the heat of formation of compounds produced in an exothermic reaction. This sign is used because such compounds are thought of as containing less energy than the elements from which they are formed. For the same reason, a compound produced by an endothermic reaction will have a positive heat of formation.

Heat of formation is the change in enthalpy when one mole of a compound is produced from free elements.

This is important. It is necessary if an exothermic reaction is to show a positive production of heat.

In Section 7:5, we found the enthalpy of CO_2 to be −393.5 kJ/mol. This quantity is the heat of formation of CO_2. Compounds like CO_2 with large negative heats of formation are thermodynamically stable. **Thermodynamics** is the study of the flow of energy, especially heat. **Thermodynamic stability** is due to the amount of energy that would be required to decompose the compound. One mole of CO_2 would require 393.5 kJ of energy to decompose to the elements. On the other hand, mercury fulminate, $Hg(OCN)_2$, produces 268 kJ when one mole decomposes. It is explosive and is used in making detonator caps.

Thermodynamically stable compounds have large negative heats of formation.

Table A-6 of the Appendix lists the enthalpies of formation for some compounds. The symbol used for enthalpy of formation is $\Delta H°_f$. The superscript "°" is used to indicate that the values given are those at atmospheric pressure and 25°C. The subscript "f" designates the value as enthalpy of formation.

7:7 CALCULATION OF ENTHALPY OF REACTION

Let us apply the law of conservation of energy to a reaction. The enthalpy of the products, $\Delta H°_{f(products)}$, must equal the enthalpy of the reactants, $\Delta H°_{f(reactants)}$, plus any change in enthalpy ($\Delta H°$).

$$\Delta H°_{f(products)} = \Delta H°_{f(reactants)} + \Delta H°$$

Solving for $\Delta H°$ we get

$$\Delta H° = \Delta H°_{f(products)} - \Delta H°_{f(reactants)}$$

If the enthalpy of formation of each reactant and product is known, we can calculate the amount of heat produced or absorbed. We can then predict whether a reaction will be exothermic or endothermic.

$\Delta H_f° = $ heat of formation

$\Delta H° = $ change in enthalpy

A positive $\Delta H°$ indicates an endothermic reaction.
A negative $\Delta H°$ indicates an exothermic reaction.

EXAMPLE: Enthalpy Change

Calculate the enthalpy change in the following chemical reaction.

carbon monoxide + oxygen → carbon dioxide

Solving process:
First, write a balanced equation. Include all the reactants and products.

$$2CO(g) + O_2(g) \rightarrow 2CO_2(g)$$

Each formula unit represents one mole. Remember that free elements have zero enthalpy by definition. Using the table of enthalpies of formation, Table A-6 of the Appendix, the total enthalpy of the reactants (2CO and O_2) is

$$\Delta H°_{f(reactants)} = \frac{2 \text{ mol CO}}{} \left| \frac{-110.5 \text{ kJ}}{\text{mol CO}} \right. + 0 \text{ kJ} = -221.0 \text{ kJ}$$

The total enthalpy of the product ($2CO_2$) is

$$\Delta H°_{f(products)} = \frac{2 \text{ mol CO}_2}{} \left| \frac{-393.5 \text{ kJ}}{\text{mol CO}_2} \right. = -787.0 \text{ kJ}$$

The difference between the enthalpy of the reactants and the enthalpy of the product is

$$\Delta H° = \Delta H°_{f(products)} - \Delta H°_{f(reactants)}$$
$$\Delta H° = -787.0 \text{ kJ} - (-221.0 \text{ kJ}) = -566.0 \text{ kJ}$$

This difference between the enthalpy of the products and the reactants (-566.0 kJ) is released as the heat of reaction.

$$2CO(g) + O_2(g) \rightarrow 2CO_2(g) + \textit{heat of reaction}$$

Notice that a release of heat is equivalent to a negative change in enthalpy. The negative sign for $\Delta H°(\Delta H° = -566.0$ kJ$)$ indicates that the two moles of carbon monoxide have released 566.0 kJ of heat. Since there are two moles of reactant, each mole has released half (566.0/2) or 283.0 kJ of heat. The $\Delta H°$ for each mole of carbon monoxide is -283.0 kJ.

If heat is absorbed during a reaction, the products must have a greater enthalpy than the reactants; the enthalpy change must be positive ($\Delta H°$ is positive). A positive enthalpy change indicates that a reaction is endothermic. A negative enthalpy change indicates that a reaction is exothermic. The products have less enthalpy than the reactants. Since an enthalpy change causes a change in temperature, we can measure $\Delta H°$ in a calorimeter.

EXAMPLE: Mass-Heat

How much heat is produced (or absorbed) by the reaction of 6.20 grams of sodium hydroxide with excess sulfuric acid?

Solving process:
(a) Begin with a balanced equation.

$$2NaOH(aq) + H_2SO_4(aq) \rightarrow Na_2SO_4(aq) + 2H_2O(l)$$

(b) We need the enthalpies of formation for each reactant and product, Table A-6, Appendix A.

$$NaOH(aq) = -425.6 \text{ kJ/mol}$$
$$H_2SO_4(aq) = -909.3 \text{ kJ/mol}$$
$$Na_2SO_4(aq) = -1384.5 \text{ kJ/mol}$$
$$H_2O(l) = -285.8 \text{ kJ/mol}$$

Note: There are two values listed for H_2O in Table A-6. Make sure the enthalpy of formation you use corresponds to the physical state shown in the equation.

(c) Multiply each enthalpy of formation by the number of moles (coefficient) from the balanced equation.

$$\frac{2 \text{ mol NaOH}}{} \left| \frac{-425.6 \text{ kJ}}{\text{mol NaOH}} = -851.2 \text{ kJ}\right.$$

$$\frac{1 \text{ mol H}_2\text{SO}_4}{} \left| \frac{-909.3 \text{ kJ}}{\text{mol H}_2\text{SO}_4} = -909.3 \text{ kJ}\right.$$

$$\frac{1 \text{ mol Na}_2\text{SO}_4}{} \left| \frac{-1384.5 \text{ kJ}}{\text{mol Na}_2\text{SO}_4} = -1384.5 \text{ kJ}\right.$$

$$\frac{2 \text{ mol H}_2\text{O}}{} \left| \frac{-285.8 \text{ kJ}}{\text{mol H}_2\text{O}} = -571.6 \text{ kJ}\right.$$

(d) We can now calculate the heat of the reaction.

$\Delta H° = \Delta H°_{f(products)} - \Delta H°_{f(reactants)}$
$\Delta H° = [(-1386.8 \text{ kJ}) + (-571.0 \text{ kJ})] - [(-939.2 \text{ kJ}) + (-907.5 \text{ kJ})]$
$\Delta H° = -111.1 \text{ kJ}$

Since $\Delta H° < 0$, the reaction is exothermic, and 111.1 kJ are produced. However, this amount of heat is for the equation as written. That is, 111.1 kJ are produced when one mole of sulfuric acid reacts with two moles of sodium hydroxide. In the problem at hand, only 6.20 g of sodium hydroxide reacted giving us the following solution.

$$\frac{6.20 \text{ g NaOH}}{} \left| \frac{1 \text{ mol NaOH}}{40.0 \text{ g NaOH}} \right| \frac{-111.1 \text{ kJ}}{2 \text{ mol NaOH}} = -8.61 \text{ kJ}$$

PROBLEMS

16. Compute the change in enthalpy for the formation of 193 grams of ammonium bromide from ammonia and hydrogen bromide.   *16. −370 kJ*

17. Compute the change in enthalpy for the decomposition of 0.772 grams of cobalt(II) carbonate into cobalt(II) oxide and carbon dioxide. **0.587 kJ**

18. Compute the change in enthalpy for the displacement of 0.0663 grams of bromine from sodium bromide by chlorine. **−0.0423 kJ**

James Prescott Joule   (1818–1889)

James Joule was a self-educated scientist. His only formal education consisted of a somewhat brief tutorship under John Dalton. Most of Joule's experiments were conducted as a hobby. As the owner of an English brewery, he did not have to concern himself with financial support and was free to experiment at leisure.

Throughout his life, Joule aimed at precise, quantitative measurements. After establishing that heat was a form of energy, he proceeded to investigate the quantitative relationships between electricity and heat, and between mechanical work and heat.

Joule discovered the mathematical relationship between the amount of current passed in a conductor and the amount of heat generated by its passage. He also determined the relationship between the amount of mechanical work performed and the amount of heat generated. The First Law of Thermodynamics is credited to Joule.

FIGURE 7-7. Chemical technicians run a variety of tests on cosmetics and related substances to ensure their safety for consumer use.

U.S. Food and Drug Administration

CHEMICAL CAREER: Laboratory Technicians

Not all workers in chemical laboratories are professional chemists. Most companies having one or more chemical laboratories employ laboratory technicians or assistants.

Laboratory technicians are involved with a number of aspects of laboratory operation. However, some of their principal work consists of carrying out routine analyses of materials. These procedures are tied to maintaining or improving product quality. If a company should receive a shipment of returned goods due to poor quality or shipment damage, the technician will run tests to determine the source of any manufacturing or packaging problems. They may measure the concentration of solutions using the titration process. They may separate mixtures using various analytical techniques such as distillation and chromatography.

In running an analytical procedure, the technician usually employs a number of delicate instruments designed to give very precise measurements. The maintenance and repair of those instruments is usually the responsibility of the technician. It may also be his or her responsibility to calibrate the instrument periodically, that is, to check its accuracy.

Some technicians spend considerable time preparing solutions or other materials for use by a professional chemist. Grinding coarse solids, obtaining samples from large batches of raw materials throughout the stages of production, and thorough testing of the final product are all routine tasks for a technician.

The technician must have sufficient background knowledge to read and interpret technical manuals. In addition, he or she may be called upon to write reports based on the work or to assist a chemist in writing a report on a project on which they have worked jointly.

Technicians employed by drug manufacturers must master some biological techniques as well as chemical. They monitor incubators, use microscopes, and run sterilizers, all of which require a knowledge of the equipment and analytical procedure being performed.

Argonne National Laboratory

FIGURE 7-8. Some technicians run simple analytical procedures with equipment similar to that in your chemistry lab.

U.S. Food and Drug Administration

FIGURE 7-9. Biological enzyme studies are being carried out in these flasks. The technician will interpret the resulting data.

A laboratory technician in a petroleum refinery may move throughout the plant reading temperatures and pressures from meters and gauges. The data gathered in the plant may be an important part of his or her report on the analytical sample taken at a particular time.

Laboratory technicians can be involved in a wide variety of jobs. After gaining experience, the technician could well move into a position as an important part of a research and development team.

To prepare to be a laboratory technician, at least two years of college training in a science is required. Most technicians receive further on the job training in procedures and equipment which are specialized to their particular job.

FIGURE 7-10. This technician is preparing a gas chromatograph.

Hickson-Bender Photography

SUMMARY

1. The balanced equation indicates the ratio of moles of reactants and products in the reaction and is used as the basis for solving mass-mass problems. 7:1

2. A chemical change is always accompanied by an energy change. Heat energy is absorbed in an endothermic reaction and given off in an exothermic reaction. 7:2

7:2 3. Activation energy is the energy required to start a chemical reaction.

4. The specific heat capacity of a substance is the heat required to raise the temperature of 1 g of the substance $1 C°$. 7:3

5. The heat energy transferred when a quantity of matter changes temperature is $\Delta H = (m)(\Delta T)(C_p)$. This value is expressed using an energy unit called joules. 7:3, 7:4

6. The specific heat capacity of water is 4.18 $J/g \cdot C°$. 7:3

7. The change in enthalpy of a system is the energy absorbed or produced during a chemical reaction. This change is represented by $\Delta H°$. 7:5

8. The heat of formation $\Delta H°_f$ of a compound is the heat released or 7:6 absorbed when 1 mole of the compound is formed from its elements.

9. A thermodynamically stable compound has a large negative heat of formation. 7:6

10. The enthalpy change $(\Delta H°)$ for a reaction is the difference between the enthalpy of the products and the enthalpy of the reactants. 7:7

$$\Delta H° = \Delta H°_{f(products)} - \Delta H°_{f(reactants)}$$

PROBLEMS

19. Why is it necessary to use a balanced equation in solving a mass-mass problem? to obtain the ratio of moles of required substance to moles of given substance

20. How many grams of $NaAlO_2$ can be obtained from 8.32 g of $AlCl_3$ according to the reaction: $AlCl_3(aq) + 4NaOH(aq) \rightarrow NaAlO_2(aq) + 3NaCl(aq) + 2H_2O(l)$? 5.11 g

21. How many grams of CO_2 are obtained when 1.74 g of $Ce_2(C_2O_4)_3$ are formed according to the reaction:
$2Ce(IO_3)_4(aq) + 24H_2C_2O_4(aq) \rightarrow Ce_2(C_2O_4)_3(aq) + 4I_2(aq) + 42CO_2(aq) + 24H_2O(l)$? 5.91 g

22. What is the difference between endothermic reactions and exothermic reactions? endothermic—absorbs energy exothermic—releases energy

23. Give an example of the use of activation energy in everyday life.

24. In an experiment, two clear liquids are combined. A white precipitate forms and the temperature of the substances in the beaker rises.
   a. Is this reaction endothermic or <u>exothermic</u>?
   b. Is heat <u>released</u> or absorbed?
   c. Are the products higher or <u>lower</u> in energy than the reactants?

25. The joule is an SI derived unit. Express joules in terms of SI base units.
26. How does specific heat capacity differ from molar heat capacity?
27. What reference standard is used in measuring enthalpy? ΔH_f° of a free element = 0
28. How many joules would be required to heat 390 kg of nickel from 25°C to 300°C? 4.75 × 10⁷ J
29. How many joules would be required to heat 54.4 g of tin from 24.0°C to 100.0°C? 910 J
30. Compute ΔH° for the following reaction. $2NO(g) + O_2(g) \rightarrow 2NO_2(g)$ −114 kJ
31. Compute ΔH° for the following reaction. $4FeO(c) + O_2(g) \rightarrow 2Fe_2O_3(c)$ −560 kJ

REVIEW

1. Find the formula for the hydrate which has a composition of 84.2% $(NH_4)_2CO_3$ and 15.8% H_2O. ($(NH_4)_2CO_3 \cdot H_2O$)
2. Balance the following equations.
   a. $Na + H_2O \rightarrow NaOH + H_2$ c. $Sb + Cl_2 \rightarrow SbCl_3$
   b. $Mg + HCl \rightarrow MgCl_2 + H_2$ d. $Cl_2 + KBr \rightarrow KCl + Br_2$

2. a. $2Na + 2H_2O \rightarrow 2NaOH + H_2$
   b. $Mg + 2HCl \rightarrow MgCl_2 + H_2$
   c. $2Sb + 3Cl_2 \rightarrow 2SbCl_3$
   d. $Cl_2 + 2KBr \rightarrow 2KCl + Br_2$

ONE MORE STEP

1. Why are some foods and beverages stored in brown bottles? Spoiling caused by exposure
2. Find out how light affects the emulsion on a photographic film. Obtain to light is delayed. a book on photography to determine what chemical reactions are involved in developing film.
3. Find out what is meant by the term "flash point."
4. The heat of a reaction gives only an indication of whether or not a reaction will take place. Consult other references to determine what other factor or factors must be taken into consideration.
5. If neither matter nor energy is created or destroyed in an ordinary chemical reaction before the reaction occurs, where is the energy that is given off or absorbed by the reaction?
6. Find out what the Law of Hess is and how to use it in energy calculations. Be prepared to report to the class on your findings.
7. How would heat capacity affect selection of fuels?
8. The heat capacities of gases are often expressed in the form $C_p = a + bT + cT^2$. For oxygen the constants a, b, and c are 6.15, 0.003 10, and -9.23×10^{-7}, respectively. For CO_2 the corresponding figures are 6.21, 0.0104, and -3.55×10^{-6}. Find the heat capacities of both O_2 and CO_2 at $T = 298$ K and $T = 500$ K. C_p O_2^{298} = 6.99, C_p O_2^{500} = 7.47
C_p CO_2^{298} = 9.00, C_p CO_2^{500} = 10.52

READING

Strauss, Howard J., and Kaufman, Milton, *Handbook for Chemical Technicians.* New York: McGraw-Hill Book Co., 1976, Chapter 5.

The building can be thought of as a simple model for the atom. A scientific model is a verbal description or visual representation for something which cannot be observed directly. You may already have the idea that atoms consist of hard spheres. However, like the building, the atom is much more complex on the inside than originally appears. How did early chemists describe the atom? What advances in technology caused scientists to change the model? What evidence do we have that atoms actually exist?

ATOMIC STRUCTURE

8

Chapter 8 contains a short historical summary of the development of atomic theory, introduces subatomic particles, and presents Bohr's atomic model.

Demonstration—Law of multiple proportions. Place 10 g of Hg in a mortar. Add 6.32 g of iodine a little at a time and grind the mixture after each addition. Hg_2I_2 forms. Now add another 6.32 g of iodine to the Hg_2I_2 product. Add a little at a time and grind thoroughly after each addition. A reddish-yellow powder, HgI_2, forms. **CAUTION:** Use mercury only in a fume hood. Do not let the mercury or the mercury compounds come in contact with the skin. Discuss how atoms react as units.

The first seven chapters have been devoted to learning the language of chemistry. We will now look at the structure and properties of matter. Much of the world depends on electricity. Most of our electricity travels from place to place along wires made of the element copper. Let us take a closer look at some copper. Suppose that we take a piece of copper wire and cut it into very small pieces. Would these pieces still be copper? How many times could we continue to divide a piece of copper and still have particles of copper? What do we have when we have divided the copper into smallest possible pieces? We found earlier that the smallest piece of matter which would still be copper is called an atom. This atom, in turn, is made of smaller particles such as electrons, protons, and neutrons. Why do we believe that such small particles actually exist? What evidence do we have that they exist? Our modern concept of the atom is a result of generations of work. Even today, our knowledge of the atom is not yet complete.

GOAL: You will gain a knowledge and understanding of the historical development for our present day model of the atom.

Yes. Until one atom is left.

We will devote this chapter to the study of atoms and their parts. In learning about the structure of the atom we will gain a better understanding of the properties of atoms taking part in chemical reactions.

8:1   EARLY ATOMIC THEORY

Democritus proposed the first atomic theory.

Early thoughts concerning atoms were proposed by the Greek philosopher, Democritus, about 400 B.C. He suggested that the world was made of two things—empty space and tiny particles which he called "atoms." This word comes from the Greek word *atomos,* meaning indivisible. Thus, he thought of atoms as the smallest possible particles of matter. He also thought there were different types of atoms for each material in the world. His theory was very general and was not supported by experimental evidence.

The belief in the existence of atoms was not accepted for centuries because it contradicted the teachings of Aristotle. Aristotle believed that matter was continuous and made of only one substance called hyle. Aristotle's teachings were accepted until the 17th century. Then, many people began to express doubts and objections to his theory.

Isaac Newton and Robert Boyle published articles stating their belief in the atomic nature of elements. Their works offered no proof, they were explanations of the known, with no predictions of the unknown. It was up to an English chemist, John Dalton, to offer a logical hypothesis about the existence of atoms.

FIGURE 8-1. The sum of the masses for the reactants equals the sum of the masses for the products as shown by the balance.

8:2   LAW OF CONSERVATION OF MASS

During the early 1800's, Dalton studied certain experimental observations made by others concerning chemical reactions. Antoine Lavoisier, a French chemist, had made one of these discoveries. He found that when a chemical change occurred in a closed system, the mass of the reactants before a chemical change equals the mass of the products after the change. In all tests of chemical changes in a closed system, he found that mass remains constant. He proposed that, *in ordinary chemical reactions, matter can be changed in many ways, but it cannot be created or destroyed.* Today this law is called the **law of conservation of mass.**

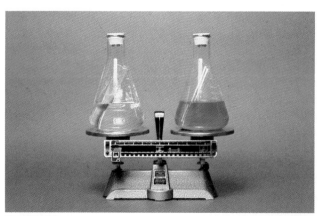

Tim Courlas

8:3 LAW OF DEFINITE PROPORTIONS

The work of another French chemist, Joseph Proust, also came to the attention of Dalton. Proust had observed that *specific substances always contain elements in the same ratio by mass.* For example, table salt is made of sodium and chlorine. The ratio of the mass of sodium to the mass of chlorine in any sample of pure salt is always the same. No matter where the sample is obtained, how it is obtained, or how large it is, the ratio of the mass of sodium to the mass of chlorine is always the same. This principle is known as the **law of definite proportions.**

Proust stated that substances have definite proportion by mass.

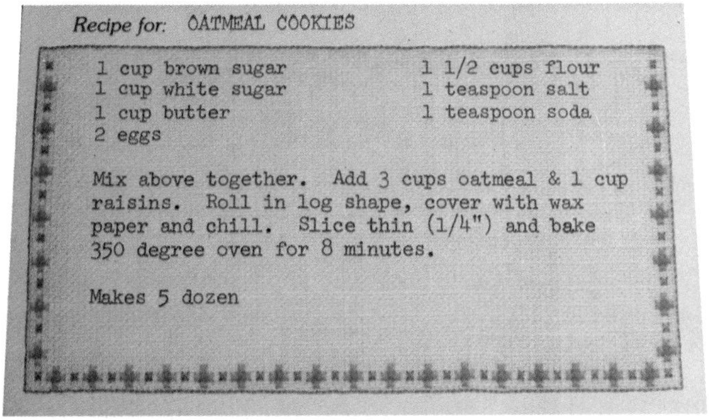
Recipe for: OATMEAL COOKIES

1 cup brown sugar
1 cup white sugar
1 cup butter
2 eggs

1 1/2 cups flour
1 teaspoon salt
1 teaspoon soda

Mix above together. Add 3 cups oatmeal & 1 cup raisins. Roll in log shape, cover with wax paper and chill. Slice thin (1/4") and bake 350 degree oven for 8 minutes.

Makes 5 dozen

Gerard Photography

FIGURE 8-2. A recipe shows the relative proportions of ingredients just as a balanced equation shows that substances combine in fixed ratios.

8:4 DALTON'S HYPOTHESIS

Dalton was trying to explain the findings of Lavoisier and Proust when he formed the basis of our present atomic theory. He stated that all matter is composed of very small particles called atoms, and that these atoms could not be broken apart. Dalton's ideas were like those of Democritus. However, Dalton believed that atoms were simpler than particles of air or rock, and that atoms of different elements were quite unlike but each element was made of atoms that were exactly alike. He stated that atoms can unite with other atoms in simple ratios to form compounds.

Dalton believed that each element is composed of like atoms.

Atoms unite in simple whole number ratios to form compounds.

These last two sentences are the key to the atomic theory. We can see how Dalton's ideas explain the two laws of Lavoisier and Proust. If atoms could not be destroyed, then they must simply be rearranged in a chemical change. The total number and kind of atoms must remain the same. Therefore, the mass before a reaction must equal the mass after a reaction. If the atoms of an element are always alike, then all atoms of a particular element must have the same mass.

According to Dalton, all sodium atoms have the same mass and all chlorine atoms have the same mass. When a sodium atom combines with a chlorine atom, salt is formed. The same is true of any pair of these atoms. Therefore, the ratio of the mass of sodium to the mass of chlorine must be the same for any sample of salt. He believed this reasoning would hold true for any given material. Experiments have shown that Dalton's ideas are not entirely correct. As we will see later, not all atoms of the same element have exactly the same mass. However, by changing the word "mass" to "average mass," we can use Dalton's ideas today.

Atoms of one element may differ in mass. Thus we use "average mass" rather than "mass."

8:5 LAW OF MULTIPLE PROPORTIONS

Dalton stated a second law based on his own atomic theory but not based on experimental data. *The ratio of masses of one element which combines with a constant mass of another element can be expressed in small whole numbers.* This statement is called the **law of multiple proportions.** Look at Table 8-1. Do you see why these numbers cannot be fractions? Atoms cannot be divided. A fraction of an atom does not exist.

The law of multiple proportions states that the combining masses of one element with a constant amount of another element are in the ratio of small whole numbers.

Table 8-1

Proportions of Tin to Oxygen			
	Mass of Sn in 1 mole	Mass of O in 1 mole	Ratio of O masses combined with constant mass (119 g) of tin.
tin(II) oxide, SnO	119 g	16 g	1
tin(IV) oxide, SnO$_2$	119 g	32 g	2

At about the same time that Dalton formed his atomic theory, J. L. Gay-Lussac, a French chemist, made an interesting observation. He was working with gas reactions at constant temperature and pressure. He noted that, under constant conditions, the volumes of reacting gases and gaseous products were in the ratio of small whole numbers.

Under constant temperature and pressure combining volumes of gases are related by small whole numbers.

A few years later, Amadeo Avogadro, an Italian physicist, explained Gay-Lussac's work using Dalton's theory. Avogadro's hypothesis also concerned gases at the same temperature and pressure. He stated that *equal volumes of gases, under the same conditions, had the same number of molecules.* These observations sped the acceptance of Dalton's theory.

The atomic theory and the law of multiple proportions, as stated by Dalton, have been tested and are accepted as correct. There are however major exceptions to some of Dalton's statements. These differences will be considered as we form our modern model of the atom in the sections that follow.

8:6 PARTS OF THE ATOM

Experiments by several scientists in the middle of the 19th century led to the conclusion that the atom consisted of smaller particles. Using a tube such as the one in Figure 8-3, it was possible to learn a great deal about atoms. In each end of the tube, there was a metal piece called an electrode. The positive terminal was called the **anode.** The negative terminal was called the **cathode.** Careful observation revealed rays in the tube. Since these rays appeared to begin at the cathode and travel toward the anode, they were called **cathode rays.**

Demonstration—Borrow this equipment from the physics lab to demonstrate the various discharge tubes.

Courtesy of Kodansha Ltd.

The same principles apply to both the cathode ray tube and the TV tube.

FIGURE 8-3. Thomson used a cathode ray tube to determine the properties of electrons. Note how the path of the ray is affected by the magnet.

In 1897, J. J. Thomson, an English scientist, did some skillful research on the cathode rays. As a result, Thomson is generally credited with the discovery that the rays consisted of electrons. Thomson built a cathode ray tube to subject the rays to both a magnetic field and an electric field. He measured the bending of the path of the cathode rays and was then able to determine the ratio of the electron's charge to its mass.

Robert Millikan, an American, obtained the first accurate measurement of an electron's charge. He used a device like the

Cathode rays are streams of electrons.

Thomson measured the ratio of charge to mass of the electron.

Millikan determined the charge on an electron.

one in Figure 8-4. Electrons were transferred from the brass atomizer to oil droplets. These negatively charged droplets, under the influence of gravity, fell through a vacuum chamber. The charge on the plates was adjusted to just offset the gravitational force on the droplet. Millikan could calculate the charge on the droplet. He found that the charges on the droplets varied. However, each charge was a multiple of one small charge. He concluded (correctly) that this small charge must be the charge on a single electron. This charge is now the standard unit of negative charge $(1-)$. The electron and charge on the electron may be represented by the symbol e^-.

Charge on electron = 1.6022×10^{-19} coulombs.

e^- is the symbol for an electron, which has a charge of $1-$.

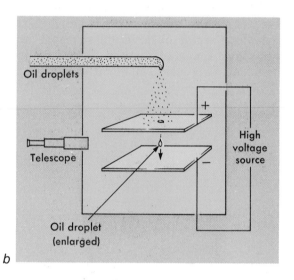

a

F. Bernard Daniel

b

Oil droplets

Telescope

+

High voltage source

−

Oil droplet (enlarged)

FIGURE 8-4. The charge on an electron can be determined using the apparatus in (a). A cross-sectional view of the apparatus is shown in (b).

To obtain protons, the gas discharge tube must be charged with hydrogen.

A proton has a charge equal in size but opposite in sign to that of an electron.

A proton has a mass 1836 times that of an electron.

Using the data of Thomson and Millikan, it was possible to calculate the actual mass of the electron. Its mass was only $\frac{1}{1837}$ the mass of the lightest atom known, the hydrogen atom.

Protons were also discovered in an experiment involving a cathode ray tube modified such as the one in Figure 8-5. Rays were discovered traveling in the direction opposite to that traveled by the cathode rays. Later it was shown that these rays possessed a positive charge and J. J. Thomson showed they consisted of particles. The particles he found have the same amount of electric charge as an electron. However, the charge is opposite in sign to that on the electron. These particles are now called protons. The atoms of hydrogen gas he used in the tube consist of a single proton and a single electron. Thomson calculated that the mass of the proton was just about 1836 times that of the electron. The proton is now the standard unit of positive charge $(1+)$.

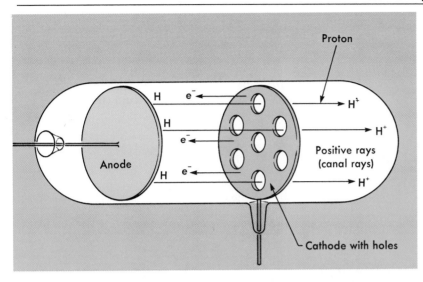

FIGURE 8-5. Using a modified cathode ray tube, Goldstein discovered rays that traveled in a direction opposite to that of cathode rays.

A third particle remained unobserved for a long time. However, its existence had been predicted by Lord Rutherford, an English physicist, in 1920. The first evidence of the particle was obtained by Walter Bothe in 1930. Another English scientist, James Chadwick, repeated Bothe's work in 1932. He found high energy particles with no charge and with essentially the same mass as the proton. These particles are now known as neutrons. We now know of a number of other subatomic particles. Scientists have predicted the existence of others. Subatomic particles will be studied in greater detail in Chapter 28.

Chadwick discovered the neutron.

A neutron has no charge and has approximately the same mass as a proton.

Dalton had assumed that atoms could not be broken into smaller particles. The discovery of subatomic particles led to a major revision of Dalton's atomic theory to include this new information.

8:7 ISOTOPES AND ATOMIC NUMBER

While working with neon, J. J. Thomson observed what seemed to be two kinds of neon atoms. They were exactly alike chemically, but slightly different in mass. **Isotope** is used to describe different atoms of the same element. Isotopes possess the same number of protons but a different number of neutrons.

Isotopes contain the same number of protons but a different number of neutrons.

Another English scientist, Henry Moseley found the wavelength of X rays produced in an X-ray tube was characteristic of the metal used as the anode. The wavelength depended on the number of protons in the nucleus of the atom and was always the same for a given element. This number of protons is known as the **atomic number** of the element and is represented by the symbol Z. Since an atom is electrically neutral, the number of electrons must equal the number of protons. The mass difference of isotopes is due to different numbers of neutrons in the nucleus. Thus, *the number of protons determines the identity of the element* and *the number of neutrons determines the particular isotope* of the element.

Courtesy of Kodansha Ltd.

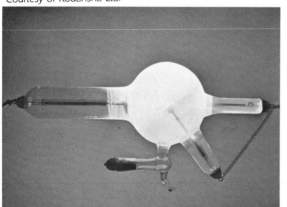

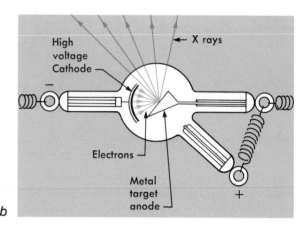

a   *b*

FIGURE 8-6. This tube is similar to that used by Moseley in studying X rays (a). The metal target in the X ray tube can be changed to produce X rays of different wavelengths (b).

The mass number (*A*) of an atom is the sum of the nucleons.

Dalton's atomic theory was again changed. It now states that all atoms of an element contain the same number of protons but they can contain different numbers of neutrons. The particles which make up the nucleus (protons and neutrons) are called **nucleons.** The total number of nucleons in an atom is called the **mass number** of that atom. The symbol for the mass number is A. A particular kind of atom containing a definite number of protons and neutrons is called a **nuclide.** The number of neutrons for any nuclide may be found by using the following.

$$number\ of\ neutrons = A - Z$$

Table 8-2

Isotopes of Hydrogen			
Name	**Protons**	**Neutrons**	**Mass Number**
protium	1	0	1
deuterium	1	1	2
tritium	1	2	3

PROBLEM

1. B = 5 electrons, 6 neutrons, 5 protons, Cm = 96 electrons, 151 neutrons, 96 protons

1. Use Table 8-3 on page 140 to compute the number of electrons, neutrons, and protons in the nuclide of boron with $A = 11$ and curium with $A = 247$.

8:8 ATOMIC MASS

The proton and neutron are essentially equal in mass. The mass of the electron is extremely small, therefore, almost all of the mass of an atom is located in the nucleus. Even the simplest atom, which contains only one proton and one electron, has 1836/1837 of its mass in the nucleus. In other atoms which have neutrons in the nucleus, an even higher fraction of the total mass of the atom is in the nucleus.

Nearly all the mass of an atom is in the nucleus.

It is possible to discuss the mass of a single atom. However, chemists have continued to use the masses of large groups of atoms. They do so because of the very small size of the particles in the atom. Chemists have chosen one mole, which is Avogadro's number of atoms, as a standard unit for large numbers of atoms. Chemists chose this number so that the mass of N_A atoms in grams is equivalent to the mass of one atom in atomic mass units. We know that the unit gram was defined as $\frac{1}{1000}$ the mass of the International standard kilogram. What is an atomic mass unit? To measure atomic masses, an atom of one element was chosen as a standard, and the other elements were compared with it. Scientists used a carbon nuclide, carbon-12, as the standard for the atomic mass scale. The carbon-12 atom is the nuclide of carbon with 6 protons and 6 neutrons in the nucleus. *One carbon-12 atom is defined as having a mass of 12 atomic mass units.* An atomic mass unit is defined to be $\frac{1}{12}$ the mass of the carbon-12 nuclide.

Chemists generally deal in moles of atoms rather than in individual atoms.

Carbon-12 was selected for its isotopic purity.

One amu is defined as 1/12 the mass of one carbon-12 atom.

The particles which make atoms are called **subatomic particles.** The subatomic particles which we have studied thus far have the following masses.

$$\text{electron} = 9.11 \times 10^{-28} \text{ g} = 0.000\ 549 \text{ amu}$$
$$\text{proton} = 1.673 \times 10^{-24} \text{ g} = 1.0073 \text{ amu}$$
$$\text{neutron} = 1.675 \times 10^{-24} \text{ g} = 1.0087 \text{ amu}$$

If it were possible to take exactly 12 grams of carbon-12 atoms and count them, we would have Avogadro's number of atoms. Look carefully at Table 8-3. Notice that many of the elements have a mass in atomic mass units which is close to the total number of protons and neutrons in their nuclei. However, some do not. What causes the mass of chlorine or copper, for example, to be about halfway between whole numbers? The numbers in the table are based on the "average atom" of an element. Most elements have many isotopic forms which occur naturally. It is difficult and expensive to obtain a large amount of a single nuclide of an element. Thus, for most calculations, the average atomic mass of the element is used.

Avogadro's number (N_A) of atoms is contained in 12 grams of carbon-12.

The average atomic mass of an element is used in calculations.

8:9 AVERAGE ATOMIC MASS

Using a standard nuclide, there are two ways of determining masses for atoms of other elements. One method is by reacting the standard element with the element to be determined. Using accurate masses of the two elements and a known mole ratio, the atomic mass of the second element may be calculated as a mass-mass problem.

A mass spectrometer measures the masses and amounts of isotopes.

Greater accuracy can be obtained by using a physical method of measurement in a device called a **mass spectrometer.** Its development was based on the early tubes of J. J. Thomson. It is similar in design to the tube used by Thomson to find the charge/mass ratio of the electron. Using a mass spectrometer, we can determine the relative amounts and masses of the nuclides for all isotopes of an element.

The element sample, which is in the form of a gas, enters a chamber where it is ionized by hitting it with electrons. These ions are then propelled by electric and magnetic fields. As in the Thomson tube, the fields bend the path of the charged particles as shown in Figure 8-7. The paths of the heavy particles are bent slightly as they pass through the fields. The paths of the lighter particles are curved more. Thus, the paths of the particles are separated by relative mass. The particles are caught and recorded electronically. One drawback of the instrument is that the ionization chamber, field tube, and detection device must all be in a vacuum. This vacuum must be equal to about one hundred-millionth (1/100 000 000) of normal atmospheric pressure.

FIGURE 8-7. In the mass spectrometer, the ion beam is subjected to a magnetic field. Massive ions are affected less by the magnet than lighter particles.

Magnetic field separates ions by mass

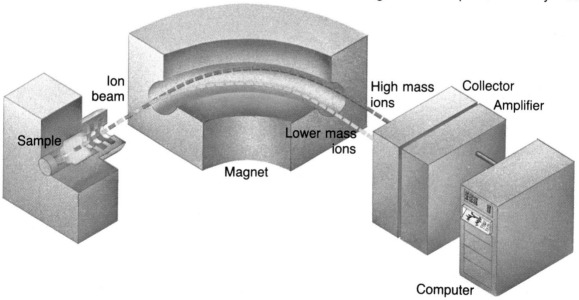

Sample

Ion beam

Magnet

Lower mass ions

High mass ions

Collector

Amplifier

Computer

Since the strength of the fields, and the speed and paths of the particles are known, the mass of the particles can be calculated. Once the masses of the isotopes and their relative amounts have been found, the average atomic mass can be calculated. For example, it has been found that neon has two isotopes. They have masses of 19.992 and 21.991 amu. They are present in every neon sample in the ratio of 9:1. In a sample of ten atoms, nine will be neon-20 and one will be neon-22. The average mass can then be found.

Average atomic mass can be determined from relative amounts of each isotope.

$$\frac{(9 \times 19.992 \text{ amu}) + (1 \times 21.991 \text{ amu})}{10} = \frac{201.92}{10} = 20.192 \text{ amu}$$

This average mass is called the **atomic mass** of an element. It is represented by the symbol M. The mass spectrometer has other uses. Geologists, biologists, petroleum chemists, and many other research workers use the mass spectrometer as an analytical tool.

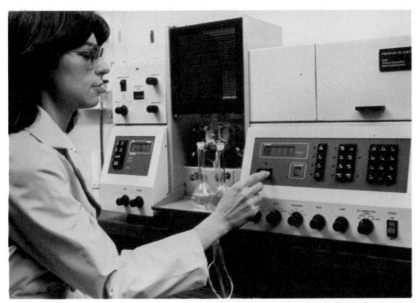

Photo Courtesy of The Perkin-Elmer Corporation

FIGURE 8-8. A chemist uses the data obtained from a mass spectrometer in chemical analysis.

PROBLEMS

2. What is the atomic mass of hafnium if, out of every 100 atoms, 5 have mass 176, 19 have mass 177, 27 have mass 178, 14 have mass 179, and 35 have mass 180?

2. 179 amu

3. What is the atomic mass of lithium if 7.42% of its atoms have mass 6.02 amu and 92.58% of its atoms have mass 7.02 amu?

3. 6.95 amu

8:10   RUTHERFORD-BOHR ATOM

During the period 1912-1913, Lord Rutherford brought together a brilliant team of physicists. Included in this group was Niels Bohr, a young Dane. The beginnings of our modern concept of atomic structure were developed by this group through experiment and hypothesis. Experiments designed to reveal the structure of atoms were performed under Rutherford's direction. These experiments showed that the atom consists of a central, positively charged nucleus surrounded in some manner by electrons. Hans Geiger and Ernest Marsden subjected a very thin sheet of gold foil to a stream of subatomic particles. They found that most of the particles passed right through the sheet. From this observation Rutherford concluded that the atom is mostly empty space. They also found a few particles (about 1 in 8000) bounced back in almost the opposite direction from which they started. Rutherford explained this observation as meaning that there was a very small "core" to the atom. The "core" contained all the positive charge and almost all the mass of the atom. This "core" is now called the nucleus.

Rutherford's experiments showed that the atom has a central positive nucleus surrounded by electrons.

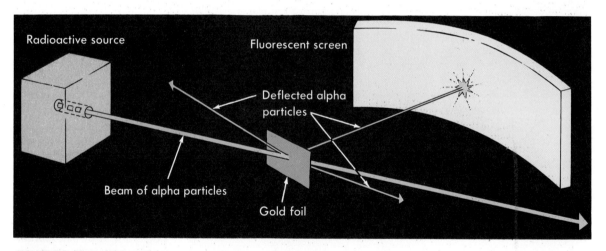

FIGURE 8-9. Most alpha particles pass through the gold foil. The deflections of particles indicate a collision has occurred between an alpha particle and gold nucleus.

The centimeter and meter are too large to be applied easily to the sizes of individual atoms. Therefore, the nanometer (nm) is used among scientists working with small dimensions. Most atoms have a diameter between 0.1 and 0.5 nm.

Geiger and Marsden found that most of the atom is empty space. The radii of the nuclei of atoms vary between 1.2×10^{-6} and 7.5×10^{-6} nm. The radius of the electron is about 2.82×10^{-6} nm. In small atoms, the distance between the nucleus and the nearest electron is about 0.05 nm. Thus, the nucleus occupies only about one trillionth (10^{-12}) of the volume of an atom.

To help you think about this relationship, imagine the hydrogen nucleus as the size of a ping-pong ball. Thus the electron is roughly the size of a tennis ball, and about 1.35 km away.

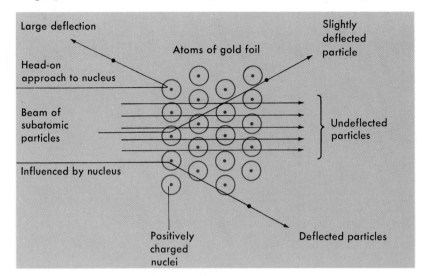

FIGURE 8-10. The gold foil experiment indicates that the gold atom consists of a central positively charged nucleus surrounded by electrons.

Electrons are negatively charged and attracted to the larger positive nucleus. What prevents the electrons from falling into the nucleus? The discussion of this question led by Rutherford and Bohr, resulted in a new idea. They thought of electrons in "orbit" around the nucleus in much the same manner as the earth is in orbit around the sun. They suggested that the relationship between the electrons and the nucleus is similar to that between the planets and the sun. The Rutherford-Bohr model of the atom is sometimes called the planetary atomic model. Thus according to the **planetary model,** the hydrogen atom should be similar to a solar system consisting of a sun and one planet.

Rutherford and Bohr thought the electrons "orbit" the nucleus.

The Rutherford-Bohr atom is a planetary model.

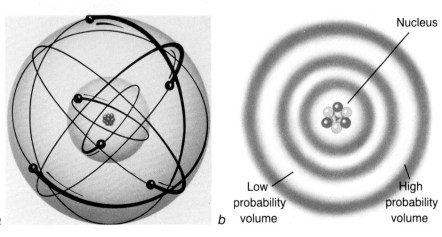

FIGURE 8-11. Bohr's planetary model (a) consists of a central nucleus surrounded by electrons traveling in fixed orbits. The modern model (b) shows a positive nucleus surrounded by electrons which occupy probability volumes of specific energy.

Table 8-3

International Atomic Masses							
Element	Symbol	Atomic number	Atomic mass	Element	Symbol	Atomic number	Atomic mass
Actinium	Ac	89	227.02779*	Neodymium	Nd	60	144.24
Aluminum	Al	13	26.98154	Neon	Ne	10	20.179
Americium	Am	95	243.06139*	Neptunium	Np	93	237.0482
Antimony	Sb	51	121.75	Nickel	Ni	28	58.71
Argon	Ar	18	39.948	Niobium	Nb	41	92 9064
Arsenic	As	33	74.9216	Nitrogen	N	7	14.0067
Astatine	At	85	209.98704*	Nobelium	No	102	255.093*
Barium	Ba	56	137.33	Osmium	Os	76	190.2
Berkelium	Bk	97	247.07032*	Oxygen	O	8	15.9994
Beryllium	Be	4	9.01218	Palladium	Pd	46	106.4
Bismuth	Bi	83	208.9808	Phosphorus	P	15	30.97376
Boron	B	5	10.81	Platinum	Pt	78	195.09
Bromine	Br	35	79.904	Plutonium	Pu	94	244.06424*
Cadmium	Cd	48	112.41	Polonium	Po	84	208.98244*
Calcium	Ca	20	40.08	Potassium	K	19	39.0983
Californium	Cf	98	251.07961*	Praseodymium	Pr	59	140.9077
Carbon	C	6	12.011	Promethium	Pm	61	144.91279*
Cerium	Ce	58	140.12	Protactinium	Pa	91	231.0359*
Cesium	Cs	55	132.9054	Radium	Ra	88	226.0254
Chlorine	Cl	17	35.453	Radon	Rn	86	222*
Chromium	Cr	24	51.996	Rhenium	Re	75	186.2
Cobalt	Co	27.	58.9332	Rhodium	Rh	45	102.9055
Copper	Cu	29	63.546	Rubidium	Rb	37	85.4678
Curium	Cm	96	247.07038*	Ruthenium	Ru	44	101.07
Dysprosium	Dy	66	162.50	Samarium	Sm	62	150.4
Einsteinium	Es	99	254.08805*	Scandium	Sc	21	44.9559
Erbium	Er	68	167.26	Selenium	Se	34	78.96
Europium	Eu	63	151.96	Silicon	Si	14	28.0855
Fermium	Fm	100	257.09515*	Silver	Ag	47	107.868
Fluorine	F	9	18.998403	Sodium	Na	11	22.9898
Francium	Fr	87	223.01976*	Strontium	Sr	38	87.62
Gadolinium	Gd	64	157.25	Sulfur	S	16	32.06
Gallium	Ga	31	69.737	Tantalum	Ta	73	180.9479
Germanium	Ge	32	72.59	Technetium	Tc	43	96.9062*
Gold	Au	79	196.9665	Tellurium	Te	52	127.60
Hafnium	Hf	72	178.49	Terbium	Tb	65	158.9254
Helium	He	2	4.00260	Thallium	Tl	81	204.37
Holmium	Ho	67	164.9304	Thorium	Th	90	232.0381
Hydrogen	H	1	1.0079	Thulium	Tm	69	168.9342
Indium	In	49	114.82	Tin	Sn	50	118.69
Iodine	I	53	126.9045	Titanium	Ti	22	47.90
Iridium	Ir	77	192.22	Tungsten	W	74	183.85
Iron	Fe	26	55.847	Uranium	U	92	238.029
Krypton	Kr	36	83.80	Vanadium	V	23	50.9415
Lanthanum	La	57	138.9055	Xenon	Xe	54	131.30
Lawrencium	Lr	103	256.099*	Ytterbium	Yb	70	173.04
Lead	Pb	82	207.2	Yttrium	Y	39	88.9059
Lithium	Li	3	6.941	Zinc	Zn	30	65.38
Lutetium	Lu	71	174.967	Zirconium	Zr	40	91.22
Magnesium	Mg	12	24.305	Element 104†		104	257*
Manganese	Mn	25	54.9380	Element 105†		105	260*
Mendelevium	Md	101	258*	Element 106†		106	263*
Mercury	Hg	80	200.59	Element 107†		107	258*
Molybdenum	Mo	42	95.94				

*The mass of the isotope with the longest known half-life.

†Names for elements 104–107 have not yet been approved by the IUPAC. The USSR has proposed Kurchatovium (Ku) for element 104, and Bohrium (Bh) for element 105. The United States has proposed Rutherfordium (Rf) for element 104, and Hahnium (Ha) for element 105.

8:11 SPECTROSCOPY

When a substance is exposed to a certain intensity of light, heat, or some other form of energy, the atoms absorb some of the energy. Such atoms are said to be **excited.** When atoms and molecules are in an excited state, energy changes occur. Each excited atom or molecule produces unique energy changes which can be used to identify it. Radiant energy of several different types can be emitted (given off) or absorbed (taken up) by excited atoms and molecules. The methods of studying substances that are exposed to some sort of continuous exciting energy are called **spectroscopy.**

Atoms are said to be excited when they absorb some energy.

Spectroscopy depends on continuous exciting energy.

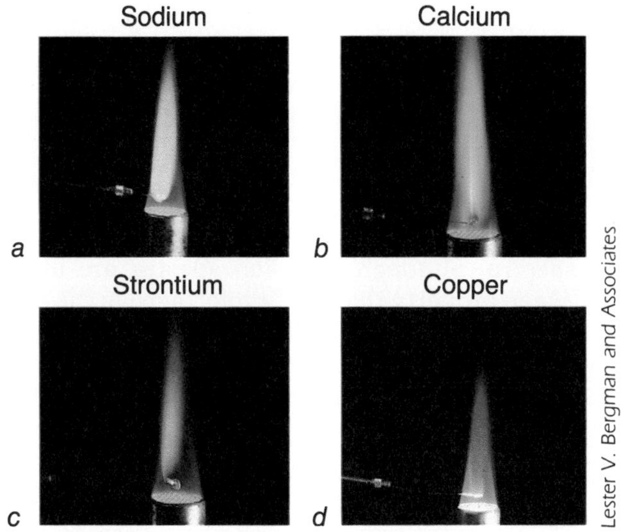

Flame tests illustrate emission of light as excited electrons return to lower energy states.

Element	Color
Na^+	Yellow
K^+	Violet
Ca^{2+}	Yellow-red
Sr^{2+}	Deep red
Li^+	Crimson
Ba^{2+}	Green-yellow
Cu^{2+}	Blue-green

Sodium | Calcium

Strontium | Copper

Lester V. Bergman and Associates

FIGURE 8-12. When exposed to a flame, these compounds emit colored light which is characteristic of the metal element in the compound. The flame tests for sodium (a), calcium (b), strontium (c), and copper (d) can be used to identify each.

Light is one form of radiant, or electromagnetic energy. Other forms of **electromagnetic energy** are radio, infrared, ultraviolet, and X ray. This energy consists of variation in electric and magnetic fields. The variation takes place in a regular, repeating fashion. If we plot the strength of the variation against time, our graph shows the "waves" of energy. The number of wave peaks which occur in a unit of time is called the **frequency** of the wave. Frequency is represented by the Greek letter *nu* (ν). All electromagnetic energy travels at the speed of light. The speed of light is 3.00×10^8 m/s in a vacuum and is represented by the symbol *c.* A third important characteristic of waves is the physical distance between peaks. This characteristic is called the **wavelength** and is represented by *lambda* (λ). In spectroscopy, the wavelength of light absorbed is characteristic of the substance being excited. The unique set of wavelengths absorbed by a substance is called the **spectrum** of that substance. This set would be emitted

Frequency (ν) is the number of cycles per unit of time.

Wavelength (λ) is the physical distance between peaks.

The spectrum of a substance is the set of wavelengths absorbed or emitted by that substance.

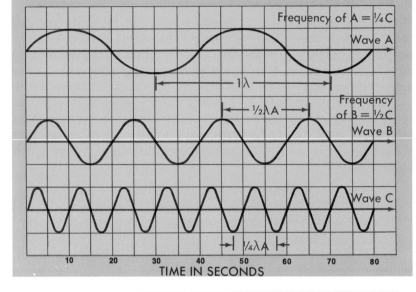

FIGURE 8-13. Wave A has the longest wavelength, however wave C has the largest frequency. Short electromagnetic waves have higher frequencies than long electromagnetic waves.

by all excited particles of the same substance. We will work with absorption spectra, although emission spectra are also useful.

Another wave property that is of importance is the **amplitude** of a wave, or its maximum displacement from zero. In Figure 8-14, two waves are plotted on the same axes. Note that the amplitude of wave A is twice that of wave B, even though they have the same wavelength.

Amplitude of a wave is its maximum displacement from a base line.

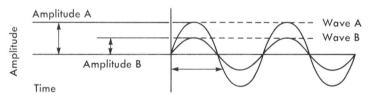

FIGURE 8-14. Waves having different amplitudes can have the same wavelength.

8:12 VISIBLE AND ULTRAVIOLET SPECTROSCOPY

Each element has a characteristic spectrum.

Absorption and emission spectra are the fingerprints of the elements. Each element has its own unique set of wavelengths that it absorbs or emits. Electromagnetic energy with a wavelength between 700 and 400 nanometers lies in the visible spectrum. This small band of visible radiation has given chemists and physicists much information about the elements. Some elements (rubidium, cesium, helium, and hafnium) were actually discovered through its use. The visible spectrum may also be used for finding the concentration of substances, for analyzing mixtures, and for analyzing complex ions. Almost any change involving color can be measured using visible spectroscopy.

Spectroscopy is used to find the concentration and identity of substances.

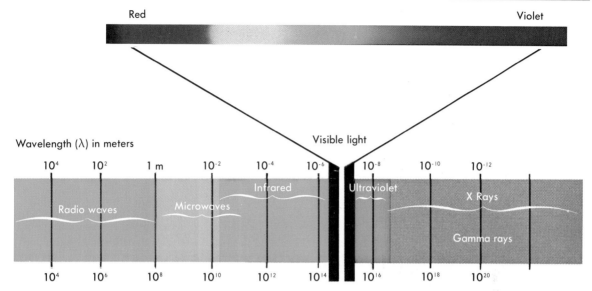

Wavelength (λ) in meters

| 10^4 | 10^2 | 1 m | 10^{-2} | 10^{-4} | 10^{-6} | 10^{-8} | 10^{-10} | 10^{-12} |

Visible light

Radio waves   Microwaves   Infrared   Ultraviolet   X Rays   Gamma rays

| 10^4 | 10^6 | 10^8 | 10^{10} | 10^{12} | 10^{14} | 10^{16} | 10^{18} | 10^{20} |

Frequency (ν) in Hertz

FIGURE 8-15. Visible light is only a small part of the electromagnetic spectrum. Note that the high frequency waves have short wavelengths.

Ultraviolet radiation (400-200 nm) can also be used to study atomic and molecular structure. Both ultraviolet spectra and visible spectra are produced by electron changes. The ultraviolet spectrum of an element or compound consists of bands rather than lines. Ultraviolet radiation has such high energy, it violently excites the electrons. The transition of the electrons from the ground state to such highly excited states causes changes in the molecule being studied. Bonds between atoms may even be broken. Visible radiations are not as destructive because they have less energy than UV radiation. Ultraviolet spectroscopy is used for the same types of analyses as visible spectroscopy. In order to describe completely the electronic structure of a substance, both types of analysis must be used.

a

Courtesy of Kodansha Ltd.

b

Courtesy of Kodansha Ltd.

FIGURE 8-16. The emission (a) and absorption (b) spectrum of sodium are used to identify the presence of sodium in a substance.

8:13 PLANCK'S HYPOTHESIS

Once Bohr had developed the basic outline of his planetary model of the atom, he used the **quantum theory** which had been stated by a German, Max Planck. Planck assumed that energy,

Planck proposed that light was radiated in little packets called quanta or photons.

instead of being given off continuously, is given off in little packets, or **quanta.** Quanta of radiant energy are often called **photons.** He further stated that the amount of energy given off is directly related to the frequency of the light emitted.

Hertz (Hz), the frequency unit, is one cycle per second.

The unit of frequency is the **hertz** (Hz) which is one peak, or cycle, per second. The wavelength and frequency of light are related by the statement $c = \lambda\nu$. With frequency in hertz and the speed of light in meters per second, the wavelength is in meters.

Energy of a quantum:
$E = h\nu$

Planck's idea was that one quantum of energy (light) was related to the frequency by the equation $E = h\nu$, where h is a constant. The constant is known as Planck's constant. Its value

Planck's constant $(h) = 6.63 \times 10^{-34}$ J/Hz

is 6.63×10^{-34} joules per hertz.

8:14 THE HYDROGEN ATOM AND QUANTUM THEORY

Planck's hypothesis stated that energy is given off in quanta instead of continuously. Bohr pointed out that the absorption of light by hydrogen at definite wavelengths means definite changes in the energy of the electron. He reasoned that the orbits of the electrons surrounding a nucleus must have a definite diameter. According to Bohr, electrons could occupy only certain orbits. The only orbits allowed were those whose differences in energy equaled the energy absorbed when the atom was excited. Bohr thought that the electrons in an atom could absorb or emit energy only in whole numbers of photons. In other words, an electron could emit energy in one quantum or two quanta, but not in 1¼ or 3½ quanta.

Each wavelength corresponds to a definite change in the energy of an electron.

Electrons absorb or emit only whole numbers of quanta.

Bohr pictured the hydrogen atom as an electron circling a nucleus at a distance of about 0.053 nm. He also imagined that this electron could absorb a quantum of energy and move to a larger orbit. Since a quantum represents a certain amount of energy, the next orbit must be some definite distance away from the first. If still more energy is added to the electron, it moves into a still larger orbit, and so on.

An electron moves farther from the nucleus as it absorbs energy.

When an electron drops from a larger orbit to a smaller one, energy is emitted. Since these orbits represent definite energy levels, a definite amount of energy is radiated.

The ground state of an electron is the level of least energy.

The size of the smallest orbit which an electron can occupy, the one closest to the nucleus, can be calculated. This smallest orbit is called the **ground state** of the electron. Bohr calculated the ground state of the hydrogen electron. Using quantum theory, he calculated the frequencies for the lines that should appear in the hydrogen spectrum. His results agreed almost perfectly with

Courtesy of Kodansha Ltd.

FIGURE 8-17. The actual hydrogen spectrum consists of many closely spaced lines. Bohr used quantum theory to calculate the frequencies for four of these lines.

Modern atomic theory differs from Bohr's in describing the path of the electron.

the actual hydrogen spectrum. Although today we use a model of the atom which differs from the Bohr model, many aspects of his theory are still retained. The difference is that electrons do not move around the nucleus as the planets orbit the sun. We will explore this difference in the next chapter. However, the idea of energy levels is still the basis of atomic theory. The energy level values calculated by Bohr for the hydrogen atom are still basically correct.

We can restate the discussion as follows: A wave of a certain frequency has only one possible wavelength, given by $\lambda = c/v$. It has only one possible amount of energy, given by $E = hv$, since both c and h are constants. If any one of the three quantities, frequency, wavelength, or energy, is known, we can calculate the other two.

The visible and ultraviolet spectra produced by a compound can be used to determine the elements in the compound. Each line in a spectrum represents one frequency of light. Because the velocity of light is always constant, each frequency means a certain energy. This energy is determined by the movement of electrons between energy levels which are specific for each element. The same set of energy levels will always produce the same spectrum.

8:15 PHOTOELECTRIC EFFECT

Before leaving quantum theory, we will consider another observation explained by this theory. Recall that quanta of light energy are referred to as photons. It had been known for some time that light falling on the surface of certain substances would cause electrons to be emitted. There was, however, a puzzling fact about this change. When the intensity of light (the number of photons per unit time) was reduced, the electrons had the same energy. However, there were fewer electrons emitted. Albert Einstein pointed out that Planck's hypothesis explained this observation.

A certain amount of energy is needed to remove an electron from the surface of a substance. If a photon of greater energy strikes the electron, the electron will move away from the surface. Since it is in motion, the electron has some kinetic energy. Some of the energy of the photon is used to free the electron from the surface. The remainder of the energy becomes the kinetic energy of the electron. If light of one frequency is used, then the electrons escaping from the surface of the substance will all have the same energy. This emission of electrons is called the **photoelectric effect.** If the light intensity is increased, but the frequency remains the same, the number of electrons being emitted will increase. If the frequency of the light is increased, the energy of the photon is increased. The amount of energy that must be used to free the electron from the atom is constant for a given substance. The electrons now leave the surface with a higher kinetic energy than they did with the other frequency. Planck's hypothesis, together with Einstein's explanation, confirmed the particle nature of light.

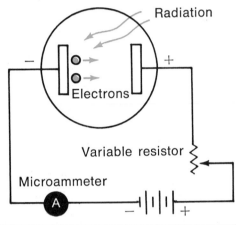

FIGURE 8-18. This diagram of a photocell circuit shows light causing the ejection of electrons from a metal's surface. The circuit is completed as electrons move toward the opposite plate.

Ernest Rutherford (1871–1937)

Ernest Rutherford was one of the most brilliant scientists involved in the investigation of atomic structure. He won the Nobel Prize in chemistry for his study of radioactivity. The theories he proposed in this area serve as a basis for our modern theory of radioactivity.

In his principle of atomic transmutation, Rutherford contended a radioactive atom emits electrically charged particles and forms a new atom of a different chemical element.

In 1911, Rutherford worked out the nuclear theory of the atom which led him to be known as the "father of nuclear science." From his experiments, he constructed a model for the atom in which the electrons were outside a positively charged center or nucleus. This model is the basis of our modern view of atomic structure.

CHEMICAL TECHNOLOGY: Using Light to Measure Distance

Some of the shortest and longest measurements of distance have been made using light as a measuring device. An interferometer is used to measure small distances. In the interferometer, light from source S passes to a partially silvered mirror P. Some light passes through to a fixed mirror F. The remainder of the light reflected by mirror F strikes mirror P and some of it is reflected to the detector D. Light from mirror M is reflected to mirror P and some of it passes through mirror P to the detector. Thus, the detector is receiving light which has traveled by two different paths: $S \rightarrow P \rightarrow F \rightarrow P \rightarrow D$ and $S \rightarrow P \rightarrow M \rightarrow P \rightarrow D$.

One characteristic of light is that if the path lengths of two light samples differ by exactly one-half wavelength, the two samples cancel each other and no light is detected at D. If the moveable mirror is shifted exactly one-half wavelength, the detector indicates a maximum of light. Since the wavelengths of visible light are short (4×10^{-7} to 7×10^{-7} m), the movement of mirror M can be used to measure short distances.

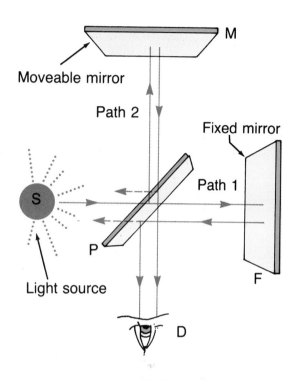

FIGURE 8-19. The path of light through an interferometer is shown.

At the other extreme of measurement, light can also be used to determine large distances. The light emitted by celestial objects such as stars is characteristic of the elements in the object. As you know, light can be spread into a spectrum. The wavelengths in the spectrum show a unique pattern for each element. The wavelengths associated with each pattern, however, are determined by the relative motion between the object and the earth. If the object is moving away from the earth, it takes longer for each successive cycle of the wave to arrive. The wavelength thus appears longer. The star's spectrum is then shifted toward the red, or longer wavelength, end of the electromagnetic spectrum. An object approaching the earth would have a blue-shifted spectrum. The faster an object is traveling with respect to the earth, the more its spectrum is shifted away from the normal spectrum for the elements on earth. By measuring the red or blue shift, scientists can determine the rate at which an object is moving to or from the earth.

SUMMARY

1. Democritus proposed the earliest recorded atomic theory. 8:1

2. Modern atomic theory dates from John Dalton's hypothesis. He made use of the law of conservation of mass and the law of definite proportions to state that all matter is formed of indivisible particles called atoms; all atoms of one element are the same; atoms of different elements are unlike; and atoms can unite with one another in simple whole-number ratios. 8:2–8:5

3. Modern atomic theory differs from Dalton's atomic theory due to the discovery of subatomic particles and isotopes. 8:6, 8:7

4. An electron is a negatively charged particle with a very small mass. A proton is a positively charged particle with a mass 1836 times the mass of an electron. A neutron is an uncharged particle with a mass about the same as the mass of a proton. 8:6

5. All atoms of an element contain the same number of protons in their nuclei. 8:6

6. Atoms containing the same number of protons but different numbers of neutrons are isotopes of the same element. 8:7

7. The atomic number (Z) of an element is the number of protons in its nucleus. The mass number (A) of an atom is the number of particles in its nucleus. 8:7

8. The atomic mass of an element is the weighted average mass, (M) of all the natural isotopes of the element. It is the mass of an average individual atom of the element compared with $\frac{1}{12}$ the mass of the carbon-12 atom. 8:8

9. Atomic mass can be measured with the mass spectrometer. 8:9

10. Atoms are extremely small and consist mostly of space. 8:10

11. Rutherford and Bohr pictured the atom as consisting of a central nucleus surrounded by electrons in orbits. 8:10

12. Substances excited by an energy source emit light in definite wavelengths called a spectrum. 8:11

13. Visible and ultraviolet spectroscopy are used to study the wavelengths of light absorbed and emitted by electrons in atoms. 8:12

14. Planck stated that energy is radiated in discrete units called quanta. A photon is a quantum of light energy. 8:13

15. The energy of a quantum of radiation varies directly as the frequency of the radiation $(E = h\nu)$. 8:13

16. Quantum theory helped Bohr explain the hydrogen spectrum, and thus, to calculate the orbits for the hydrogen atom. 8:14

17. The photoelectric effect is the loss of electrons from a substance, caused by photons striking its surface. 8:15

PROBLEMS

4. What did each of the following contribute in forming the atomic theory?
  a. Dalton   c. Rutherford   e. Moseley   g. Planck
  b. Thomson   d. Chadwick   f. Bohr   h. Avogadro

5. List the major points in Dalton's atomic theory.

6. What element is used as the reference standard in defining atomic mass units? carbon

7. How would you show the law of conservation of mass with a burning candle?

8. Design an experiment to demonstrate the law of definite proportions.

9. State Avogadro's hypothesis.

10. A particular atom of argon contains 18 protons, 18 electrons, and 22 neutrons. What is the atomic number of this atom? What is its mass number? $Z = 18, A = 40$

11. Compute the average atomic mass of gallium, if 60% of the gallium atoms occurring in nature have mass number 69 and 40% of the atoms have mass number 71. 69.8 amu

12. Compute the average atomic mass of chromium if the relative amounts are as follows. 52.0 amu

isotopic mass	percentage
49.9	4.31
51.9	83.8
52.9	9.55
53.9	2.38

13. How many nm are in 2.01 cm? 2.01×10^7 nm

14. How did the discovery of subatomic particles and isotopes affect Dalton's theories?

15. What are the basic differences among protons, neutrons, and electrons?

16. How many electrons, neutrons, and protons are in the isotope of nitrogen with mass number 14? How many of each are in the isotope of protactinium with mass number 231? N = 7 electrons, 7 neutrons, 7 protons
Pa = 91 electrons, 140 neutrons, 91 protons

17. What was Rutherford's role in the Geiger-Marsden experiment?

18. How did Bohr use spectroscopic data to formulate his model of the atom?

19. Why is it necessary to ionize an element sample before it can be separated into its isotopic components?

20. How does quantum theory explain the photoelectric effect?

REVIEW

1. Write names for the following compounds.
  a. $Sr(C_2H_3O_2)_2$ strontium acetate   c. CdC_2O_4 cadmium oxalate   e. Th_3N_4 thorium(IV) nitride
  b. $Mn(OH)_2$ manganese(II) hydroxide   d. Li_3AsO_4 lithium arsenate   f. $Ce_2(CO_3)_3$ cerium(III) carbonate

2. Write formulas for the following compounds.

Na_3N **a.** sodium nitride

Ce_2S_3 **b.** cerium(III) sulfide

$BaSiF_6$ **c.** barium hexafluorosilicate

d. hydrogen telluride H_2Te

e. silver sulfate Ag_2SO_4

f. cesium hexafluorosilicate Cs_2SiF_6

3. Balance the following equations.

$Cl_2 + 2KI \rightarrow 2KCl + I_2$

$2Na_2O_2 + 2H_2O \rightarrow 4NaOH + O_2$

$2K + 2H_2O \rightarrow 2KOH + H_2$ **a.** $K + H_2O \rightarrow KOH + H_2$

$Ca + 2HCl \rightarrow CaCl_2 + H_2$ **b.** $Ca + HCl \rightarrow CaCl_2 + H_2$

c. $Cl_2 + KI \rightarrow KCl + I_2$

d. $Na_2O_2 + H_2O \rightarrow NaOH + O_2$

4. Convert 0.633 mole $Th(SeO_4)_2$ to formula units. 3.81×10^{23} formula units

5. Convert 0.0731 mole $Sr(CN)_2$ to grams. 10.2 g

6. Find the percentage composition of each element in $BaSO_4$. $Ba = 58.8\%$, $S = 13.8\%$, $O = 27.5\%$

7. Find the empirical formula for a compound with composition: 44.2% Cd, 44.8% F, and 11.0% Si. $CdSiF_6$

8. Find the formula for a hydrate with composition: 76.0% SrI_2 and 24.0% H_2O. $SrI_2 \cdot 6H_2O$

9. What mass of magnesium hydroxide is obtained from 84.1 grams of magnesium oxide in accordance with the reaction: 122 g
$$MgO + H_2O \rightarrow Mg(OH)_2?$$

10. How much heat is required to raise the temperature of 91.0 grams ZnS from 8.9°C to 35.7°C? 1144 J

11. Compute ΔH for the following reaction.
$$Mn + 2HCl(aq) \rightarrow MnCl_2 + H_2 \quad 221 \text{ kJ}$$

ONE MORE STEP

1. The mass spectrometer is used to separate isotopes for use as nuclear fuel. Investigate this process and see how it differs from other processes used for the same purpose.

2. James Franck and Gustav Hertz performed an experiment to test the quantum theory. Prepare a report on their experiment and its results.

3. Make a table listing as many subatomic particles as you can. For each particle, list its mass, charge, and lifetime.

4. Use a handbook to make a list of the mass numbers of all known isotopes of the first twenty elements. Show those that are unstable (radioactive) in red.

5. Although Bohr was the first to use experimental evidence to support his hypothesis, he was not the first person to propose a planetary model for the atom. Look into the history of this idea prior to Bohr.

6. Find a description of an experiment used for determining the size of a proton or a neutron.

7.32×10^{14} Hz 7. What is the frequency of light with a wavelength of 410 nm?

2.86×10^{-19} J 8. What is the energy of a quantum of light of frequency 4.31×10^{14} Hz?

453 nm 9. What is the wavelength of light with frequency 6.62×10^{14} Hz?

3.00×10^{-19} J 10. What is the energy of light with wavelength 662 nm?

11. What would be the wavelength of light necessary to cause electrons to leave the surface of a substance with an energy of 1.20×10^{-19} J? Assume the energy necessary to release the electron from the surface is 3.60×10^{-19} J. **414 nm**

12. In considering the photoelectric effect, what is the relationship between the frequency of a photon striking the metal surface and the number and energy of the electrons leaving that surface?

13. A certain violet light has a wavelength of 413 nm. What is its frequency? The velocity of light is equal to 3.00×10^8 m/s. **7.26×10^{14} Hz**

14. A certain green light has a frequency of 6.26×10^{14} Hz. What is its wavelength? **479 nm**

15. What is the energy content of one quantum of the light in Problem 13? **4.81×10^{-19} J**

16. What is the energy content of one quantum of the light in Problem 14? **4.15×10^{-19} J**

17. Three techniques for analysis which are closely allied with spectroscopy are colorimetry, fluorimetry (floh uh RIHM ih tree), and nephelometry (nef uh LAHM ih tree). Investigate the uses of these procedures.

18. Prepare a report for your class on the topic of electron paramagnetic resonance (EPR), one of the newer methods in analysis.

READINGS

David, Jeff C., Jr., "Introduction to Spectroscopy." *Chemistry,* Part II, Vol. 48, No. 1 (January 1975), pp. 11-14; Part III, Vol. 48, No. 5 (May 1975), pp. 19-22; Part IV, Vol. 48, No. 7 (July-August 1975), pp. 15-18; Part V, Vol. 48, No. 11 (December 1975), pp. 5-9; Part VI, Vol. 49, No. 2 (March 1976), pp. 17-20; Part VII, Vol. 49, No. 9 (November 1976), pp. 18-21; Part VIII, Vol. 50, No. 9 (November 1977), pp. 17-20.

"Educated Guess". *SciQuest,* Vol. 54, No. 4 (April 1981), p. 25.

Ekstrom, Philip, and David Wineland, "The Isolated Electron." *Scientific American,* Vol. 242, No. 8 (August 1980), p. 104.

Kolb, Doris, "But if Atoms Are So Tiny . . .?" *Journal of Chemical Education,* Vol. 54, No. 9 (September 1977), pp. 543-547.

Pett, Virginia B., "Whole Numbers and Atomic Theory." *Chemistry,* Vol. 51, No. 1 (January-February 1978), pp. 16-18.

Suchow, Lawrence, "The Failings of the Law of Definite Proportions." *Journal of Chemical Education,* Vol. 52, No. 6 (June 1975), pp. 367-368.

The structure and behavior of atoms could not be fully explained by the solar system model. Therefore, it became necessary to formulate a new model for the atom. In some ways the galaxy shown is a more accurate representation of an atom. Think of this cloudlike mass as the volume occupied by electrons. Note that the edges of the galaxy are not clearly defined. Some areas appear more dense than others. In what other ways is the galaxy similar to an electron cloud? What are the other characteristics of the modern model of the atom?

Jack Zehrt/Alpha

ELECTRON CLOUDS AND PROBABILITY

9

Chapter 9 develops the wave mechanical model of the atom by introducing Schrödinger's probability equation and Heisenberg's uncertainty principle.

Demonstration—Using five evaporating dishes, dissolve small amounts of Sr, Li, Ba, Cu, and Na salts separately in each dish by adding a few drops of water and then a few cm³ of methanol. Ignite the alcohol solutions and observe the colors in a dark room. Discuss how improved spectral data have advanced the modern atomic theory. See additional information in front of text.

In the attempts to refine our model of the atom, we see the division between matter and energy has become less clear. Radiant energy is found to have many properties of particles. Small particles of matter are found to display the characteristics of wave motion. The purpose of this chapter is to look more closely at this wave-particle problem.

We have seen in Chapter 8 that the frequencies predicted by Bohr for the hydrogen spectrum are "essentially" correct. Note that we did not use the word "exactly." Improved equipment has shown that the hydrogen spectrum lines predicted by Bohr are not single lines. If we were to reexamine the hydrogen spectrum with a better spectroscope, we would see that what seemed to be single lines are really several lines closely spaced. Scientists have had to change many of their ideas about the behavior of the particles in an atom. They have done so because of the discovery of the "fine structure" of spectral lines. Bohr's use of quantum theory in the study of atomic structure has been revised to include the fine structure.

GOAL: You will gain an understanding of the electron structure of the quantum mechanical model of the atom.

Bohr's theory of the atom was revised to include the fine lines of the hydrogen spectrum.

9:1 DE BROGLIE'S HYPOTHESIS

In 1923, a French physicist, Louis de Broglie, proposed a hypothesis which led the way to the present theory of atomic structure. De Broglie knew of Planck's ideas concerning radiation being made of discrete amounts of energy called quanta. This theory seemed to give waves the properties of particles. De Broglie thought if Planck were correct, then it might be possible for particles to have some of the properties of waves.

De Broglie suggested that particles have characteristics of waves.

According to Einstein, the relationship between matter and energy is given by the equation

$$E = mc^2$$

Recall the Law of Conservation of Mass-Energy from Section 1:6.

It is also known that every quantum of a wave has a discrete amount of energy given by the equation

$$E = h\nu$$

De Broglie thought if particles had wave characteristics, the two expressions for energy would be equivalent.

$$mc^2 = h\nu$$

Since real particles do not travel at the speed of light, he substituted v, a general velocity, for c, the velocity of light.

$$m\text{v}^2 = h\nu$$

De Broglie substituted v/λ for ν since the frequency of a wave is equal to its velocity divided by its wavelength. He obtained an expression for the wavelength associated with a moving particle.

$$m\text{v}^2 = \frac{h\text{v}}{\lambda}$$

$$\lambda = \frac{h\text{v}}{m\text{v}^2} = \frac{h}{m\text{v}}$$

The Davisson-Germer experiment

The final expression was de Broglie's prediction of the wavelength of a particle of mass m and velocity v. Within two years, de Broglie's hypothesis was proven correct. Scientists found by experiment that, in some ways, an electron stream acted in the same way as a ray of light. They further showed that the wavelength of the electrons was exactly that predicted by de Broglie.

PROBLEM

1. 3.66×10^{-3} nm

1. What is the wavelength of an electron of mass 9.11×10^{-28} g traveling at 2.00×10^8 m/s? (Planck's constant = 6.63 $\times 10^{-34}$ J/Hz, 1 Hz = 1/s, 1J = N·m, 1N = 1 kg·m/s^2)

9:2   THE APPARENT CONTRADICTION

Light has properties of both particles and waves.

Waves can act as particles, and particles can act as waves. We saw how the photoelectric effect and Bohr's atom model explained light in terms of particle properties. Now let us look at a light property which can be explained by wave behavior.

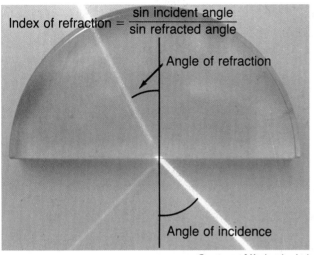

Index of refraction = $\dfrac{\text{sin incident angle}}{\text{sin refracted angle}}$

Angle of refraction

Angle of incidence

a

Courtesy of Kodansha Ltd.

b

Larry Hamill

FIGURE 9-1. Light is refracted as it passes through this piece of glass (a). Due to refraction, the thermometer appears bent (b).

Light waves travel at different speeds in different substances. When a light wave passes from one substance into another it changes speed. If a light wave strikes a surface at an angle, it also changes direction (is bent or refracted).

Refraction occurs when light strikes a surface and changes direction.

The **index of refraction** of a substance is determined by the bending of a light wave as it passes from a vacuum into that substance. We measure the angle between the ray and the surface both before and after the ray passes through the surface. Each substance has a characteristic index of refraction, Figure 9-1. We can identify a substance by its index of refraction. The instrument used to measure index of refraction is called a refractometer (ree frak TOM uh tuhr).

Index of refraction is a characteristic of all transparent materials. (Section 3:4)

Index of refraction is measured with respect to a vacuum. However, the index with respect to air will be negligibly different in most cases.

Like light, electrons also have properties of both waves and particles. However, one cannot observe both the particle and wave properties of an electron by the same experiment. If an experiment is done to show an electron's wave properties, the electron exhibits the properties of a wave. Another experiment, carried out to show the electron as a particle, will show that the electron exhibits the behavior of a particle. The whole idea of the two-sided nature of waves and particles is referred to as the **wave-particle duality of nature.** The duality applies to all waves and all particles. Scientists are not always interested in duality. For example, when scientists study the motion of an artillery shell, wave characteristics do not enter into their study. They are only interested in the shell as a particle. However, with very small particles we cannot ignore wave properties. For an electron, a study of its wave characteristics can tell as much about its behavior as a study of its particle characteristics.

Electrons have wave-particle duality.

9:3 MOMENTUM

The product of the mass and velocity of an object is called the momentum of the object. In equation form, $m\vec{v} = \vec{p}$*, where m is the mass, v is the velocity, and p is the symbol for momentum. You should note that velocity includes not only the speed but also the direction of motion. Recall de Broglie's equation for the wavelength of the wave associated with a particle in motion.

$$\lambda = \frac{h}{m\vec{v}}$$

Substituting momentum (p) for mv, we can then write

$$\lambda = \frac{h}{\vec{p}}$$

Notice that the equation is written in a form which shows that the wavelength varies inversely as the momentum. An object may have a large momentum because of a large mass or a large velocity. In either case, it would have a small wavelength. Therefore, the wave properties of all objects in motion are not always of interest to the scientist. There is a basic difference between Newtonian and quantum mechanics. **Newtonian mechanics** describes the behavior of visible objects traveling at ordinary velocities. **Quantum mechanics** describes the behavior of extremely small particles traveling at velocities near that of light.

To the chemist, the behavior of the electrons in an atom is of greatest interest. To be able to give a full description of an electron, we must know two things: where it is, and where it is going. In other words, we must know the electron's present position and its momentum. From the velocity and position of an electron at one time, we can calculate where the electron will be some time later.

9:4 MEASURING POSITION AND MOMENTUM

Werner Heisenberg further improved the ideas about atomic structure. He pointed out that *it is impossible to know both the exact position and the exact momentum of an object at the same time.* Let us take a closer look at Heisenberg's ideas. To locate the exact position of an electron, we must be able to "look" at it. When we look at an object large enough to see with our eyes, we actually see the light waves which the object has reflected.

*The symbol $\rightarrow$ above a quantity means it is a vector quantity. Vectors have both magnitude and direction.

Eric Hoffhines

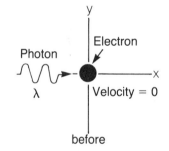

FIGURE 9-2. Radar is used in detecting weather patterns. The reflections of radar waves are picked up by a detector to form the image on the screen.

FIGURE 9-3. If an electron were in a fixed position and a photon collided with it, the velocity of the electron would change. Thus, there is always some uncertainty as to the position and momentum of the electron.

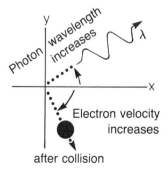

When radar detects an object, the radar receiver is actually "seeing" the radar waves reflected by the object. In other words, for us to see an object, it must be hit by some kind of radiant energy. However, a collision between a photon and an electron results in a large change in the energy of the electron. Let us assume we have "seen" an electron, using some sort of radiant energy as "illumination." We have found the exact position of the electron. However, we would have little idea of the electron's velocity. The collision between it and the photons used to see it has caused its velocity to change. Thus, we would know the position of the electron, but not its velocity. On the other hand, if we measure an electron's velocity, we will change the electron's position. We would know the velocity fairly well, but not the position. Heisenberg stated that there is always some uncertainty as to the position and momentum of an electron. This statement is known as **Heisenberg's uncertainty principle.**

The uncertainty of the position and the uncertainty of the momentum of an electron are related by Planck's constant. If Δp^* is the uncertainty in the momentum and Δx is the uncertainty in the location, then

$$\Delta p \Delta x \geqq h$$

Thus, since h is constant, the more certain we are of the position of the electron, the less certain we are of its momentum. The more certain we are of its momentum, the less certain we are of its position.

*Recall the Greek letter delta (Δ) means change in.

9:5 SCHRÖDINGER'S WORK

Chemists and physicists now found themselves unable to describe the exact structure of the atom. Heisenberg had, in effect, stated that the exact motion of an electron was unknown and could never be determined. Notice, however, that Heisenberg's principle of uncertainty treats the electron as a particle. What happens if the electron is treated as a wave? The wave nature of the electron was investigated by the Austrian physicist, Erwin Schrödinger.

Schrödinger mathematically treated the electron as a wave.

Schrödinger treated the electron as a wave and developed a mathematical equation to describe its wave-like behavior. Schrödinger's equation related the amplitude of the electron-wave ψ (psi) to any point in space around the nucleus. He pointed out that there is no physical meaning to the values of ψ. You should avoid trying to assume one. Terms for the total energy and for the potential energy of the electron are also part of this equation. In computing the total energy and the potential energy, certain numbers must be used. For example, the term for the total energy is

$$\frac{\partial^2 \Psi}{\partial x^2} + \frac{\partial^2 \Psi}{\partial y^2} + \frac{\partial^2 \Psi}{\partial z^2} + \frac{8\pi^2 m}{h^2}(E - V)\Psi = 0 \qquad\qquad 2\pi^2 me^4/h^2 n^2$$

Here, m is the mass of the electron, e is the charge on the electron, h is Planck's constant, and n can take positive whole number values. The symbol n represents the first of four quantum numbers. These four **quantum numbers** are used in describing electron behavior. They will be studied in detail in later sections. The actual wave equation involves mathematics with which you are probably not familiar and so it will not be given.

The four quantum numbers in Schrödinger's equation are used in describing electron behavior.

The physical significance of all this mathematics was pointed out by Max Born. He worked with the square of the absolute value of the amplitude, $|\psi|^2$. He showed that $|\psi|^2$ gave the probability of finding the electron at the point in space for which the equation was solved. By **probability**, we mean the ratio between the number of times the electron is in that position divided by the total number of times it is at all possible positions.

Probability =

No. of times in position X

Σ times in all positions

9:6 WAVE-MECHANICAL VIEW OF THE HYDROGEN ATOM

Schrödinger's wave equation is used to determine the probability of finding the hydrogen electron in any given place. The probabilities can be computed for finding the electron at different points along a given line away from the nucleus. One point will have a higher probability than any other, Figure 9-4. To carry the process even further, the probabilities for thousands

Schrödinger's equation can be used to describe the more probable positions of the hydrogen electron.

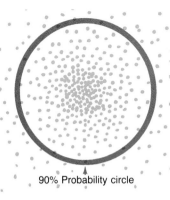

90% Probability circle

a

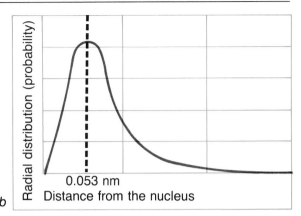

0.053 nm
Distance from the nucleus

b

FIGURE 9-4. Probability plots for a hydrogen electron are shown in (a). Note the area represented by 90% probability. The point of highest probability for a hydrogen electron occurs at about 0.053 nm from the nucleus (b).

of points in space may be calculated. There will be many points of equal probability. If all the points of highest probability are connected, some three dimensional shape is formed. These shapes will be shown later in the chapter. The most probable place to find the electron will be some place on the surface of this calculated shape. Remember that this shape is only a "mental model" and does not actually exist. It is something we use in our minds to help locate the electron.

There is another way of looking at probability. The electron moves about the nucleus in such a way as to pass through the points of high probability more often than through any other points. The electron is traveling at a high rate of speed. If the electron were visible to the eye, its rapid motion would cause it to appear as a cloud. Think of an auto fan as shown in Figure 9-5. When the fan is turning, it appears to fill the complete circle

FIGURE 9-5. The fan blades (a) appear to occupy the total volume through which they turn. An electron occupies a 3-dimensional volume to form a cloud of negative charge (b).

a

Larry Hamill

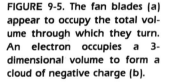

b **Electron cloud**

through which it turns. We cannot place an object between the blades while the fan is turning. If we do, the result will show that the fan is effectively filling the entire circle! So it is with the electron. It effectively fills all the space. At any given time, it is more likely to be somewhere on the surface of the shape described by the points of highest probability. The probability of finding the propeller outside its volume is zero. However, it is possible to find the electron outside of its high probability surface. Therefore, since the volume occupied by an electron is somewhat vague, it is better to refer to it as an **electron cloud.** Let us now look more closely at this electron cloud to learn more about its size and shape.

An electron effectively occupies all the space around a nucleus.

The position of an electron can best be represented by a cloud.

9:7 SOLVING SCHRÖDINGER'S EQUATION

Solutions to the Schrödinger equation proved difficult for even the best mathematicians. It has been solved exactly only for simple cases involving the hydrogen atom. The use of quantum numbers in the solution of the wave equation was mentioned in Section 9:5. These numbers represent different energy states of the electron. In Schrödinger's atomic model, changes between energy states must take place by emission or absorption of whole numbers of photons. For the simple hydrogen atom, solution of the wave equation gives us accurate energy states. The differences between these energy states correspond to the lines observed in the hydrogen spectrum. With more complex atoms, however, the interaction of electrons makes solution of the equation impossible. Recall that electrons all have the same charge which causes them to repel each other. In spite of this difficulty, scientists can come close to finding the electronic structure of atoms by making an assumption. They first calculate the various single energy states in the simple hydrogen atom. A different quantum number is used to arrive at a value for each state. They then assume that the various electrons in a multielectron atom occupy these same energy states without affecting each other. There are four quantum numbers, n, l, m, and s. Each electron within an atom can be described by a unique set of four quantum numbers. We will discuss each quantum number separately starting with n.

Quantum numbers represent different electron energy states.

Each electron within an atom can be described by a unique set of four quantum numbers.

9:8 PRINCIPAL QUANTUM NUMBER

An electron can occupy only specific energy levels. These energy levels are numbered, starting with 1 and proceeding to the higher integers. The **principal quantum number** (n) corresponds to the energy levels (1, 2, 3, . . . n) calculated for the hydrogen atom. The number of the energy level, referred to as n, is called the principal quantum number.

Principal quantum number, n, describes energy level. Maximum number of electrons in energy level = $2n^2$.

Electrons may be found in each energy level of an atom. The greatest number of electrons possible in any one level is $2n^2$. Thus, in the first level ($n = 1$), there may be at most two electrons (2×1^2). In the fourth energy level, there can be no more than 32 electrons (2×4^2). Figure 9-6 shows the relative energies of the various levels. It also indicates the maximum number of electrons possible in each level.

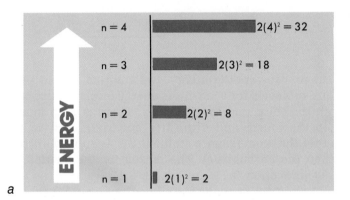

$n = 4$ $2(4)^2 = 32$

$n = 3$ $2(3)^2 = 18$

$n = 2$ $2(2)^2 = 8$

$n = 1$ $2(1)^2 = 2$

ENERGY

a

$n = 1$

$n = 2$

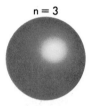

$n = 3$

b n determines effective volume

FIGURE 9-6. The relationship between energy and principal quantum number is shown in (a). The relationship between size of the charge cloud and principal quantum number is shown in (b).

PROBLEM

2. Calculate the maximum number of electrons that can occupy the levels when $n = 2, 3, 5,$ and 7. 8, 18, 50, 98

9:9 ENERGY SUBLEVELS

The second quantum number is *l*. In a hydrogen atom, all electrons in one level have the same energy. This statement is not true for any other atom. Spectrum studies have shown that an energy level is actually made of many energy states closely grouped together. We can refer to these states as **sublevels.**

Each level has a number of sublevels equal to the value of the principal quantum number. You can expect to find one sublevel in the first level, two sublevels in the second level, and three sublevels in the third level. The lowest sublevel in each level has been named *s*; the second, *p*; the third, *d*; and the fourth, *f*. Thus, the first level has only an *s* sublevel. The second energy level has *s* and *p* sublevels, while the third energy level has *s*, *p*, and *d* sublevels.

As an example, consider the $n = 4$ level. Instead of the single energy line as was shown in Figure 9-6, the $n = 4$ level should look as shown in Figure 9-7 with all sublevels shown.

Second quantum number, *l*, describes sublevels.

The number of sublevels in an energy level equals the value of *n*, the principal quantum number.

Sublevels are named *s, p, d,* and *f.*

The letters *s, p, d,* and *f* stand for sharp, principal, diffuse, and fundamental. These terms were originally spectroscopy labels for different series of spectral lines emitted by the elements.

FIGURE 9-7. The relationship between energy and the sublevels in $n = 4$ is shown.

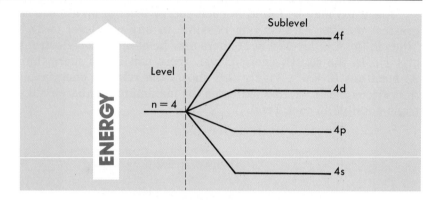

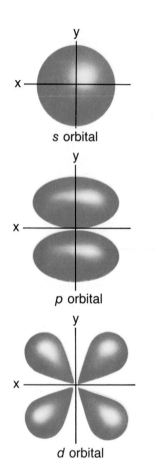

s orbital

p orbital

d orbital

f orbital

FIGURE 9-8. The relationship between sublevel number and orbital shape is shown.

We can now rework the energy level diagram. Figure 9-9 shows the various sublevels for each of the energy levels. Notice the overlapping in the third and fourth levels. There is even more overlapping in the fourth and fifth, fifth and sixth, and so on. The effect is that the atom is more stable if the 4s sublevel is of lower energy than the 3d sublevel. The reason for the overlap will be considered in Section 9:11. In Section 9:12 we will see why the overlap is important in understanding atomic structure.

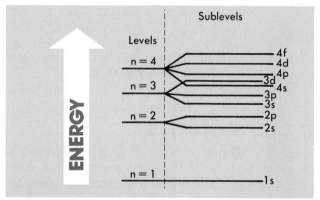

FIGURE 9-9. This energy level diagram shows the overlapping of orbitals that occurs between $n = 3$ and $n = 4$.

9:10   ORBITALS

The third quantum number is m. Calculation has shown that any s sublevel may contain one pair of electrons; any p sublevel, three pairs; and d sublevel, five pairs; and any f sublevel, seven pairs. Each pair in a given sublevel has a different place in space. This space occupied by one pair of electrons is called an **orbital.**

We can now redraw the energy level diagram with the orbitals shown. Each short line in Figure 9-10 represents an orbital that can hold a pair of electrons.

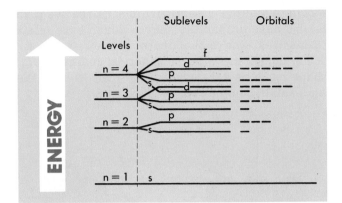

FIGURE 9-10. This energy level diagram shows the distribution of orbitals for each sublevel.

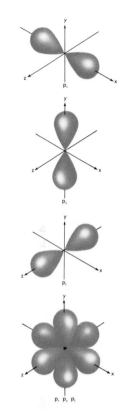

FIGURE 9-11. The probability shapes for each *p* orbital with a composite of their orientation in space.

9:11 SHAPE OF THE CHARGE CLOUD

We now want to see how these various energy levels and sublevels affect the electron charge cloud described in Section 9:6. In general, the size of the charge cloud is related to n, the principal quantum number. The larger the value of n, the larger the cloud. However, there are also other factors which govern the size of the cloud. Electrons are repelled by each other; they are also attracted by the positively charged nucleus. At the same time, other electrons serve to screen the effect of the nucleus. Picture an electron *A* between the nucleus and electron *B*. Electron *A* reduces the attraction of the nucleus for electron *B*. Thus, the size of the charge cloud is not controlled by any single factor.

The sum of all electron clouds in any sublevel (or energy level) is a spherical cloud. However, orbitals have characteristic probability shapes of their own. For example, look at Figure 9-11. The three *p* orbitals can be directed along the three mutually perpendicular *x, y,* and *z* axes. They are sometimes labeled as p_x, p_y, and p_z.

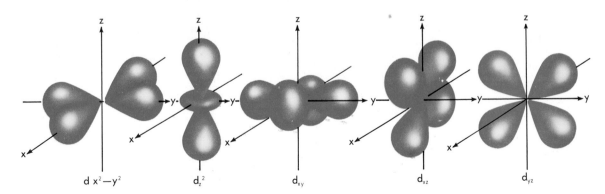

FIGURE 9-12. The probability shapes of the *d* orbitals.

As shown in Figure 9-12 and Figure 9-13, the five d and seven f orbitals also have probability shapes which have relationships among themselves. Notice that these, as well as the p orbitals, when filled and combined, form a spherical charge cloud. A large, simple shape (such as $4s$) represents a lower energy state in an atom than a small, complex shape (such as $3d$).

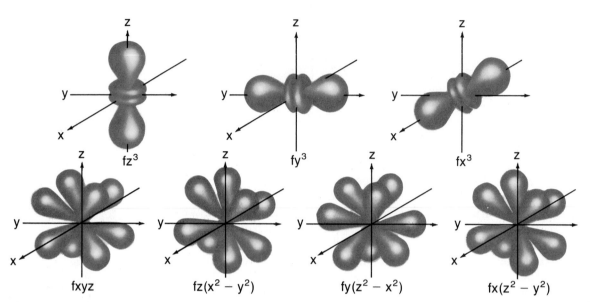

FIGURE 9-13. One set of probability shapes for the f orbitals.

The direction of the orbital in space depends on m.

Degenerate orbitals are occupied by electrons having the same energy.

The third quantum number, m, defines each orbital more precisely by indicating its direction in space. There are three possible values for m when discussing a p sublevel. The numbers designate orbitals aligned along the x, y, and z axes. There are five values for m in a d sublevel and seven values for m in an f sublevel. Orbitals which are alike in size and shape and differ only in direction have the same energy. Orbitals of the same energy are said to be degenerate. When atoms react, degenerate orbitals may change energy by different amounts. If this energy change occurs, the orbitals will no longer be degenerate.

PROBLEM

3. How many orbitals are in a(n)
   a. d sublevel 5 orbitals   b. f sublevel 7 orbitals

9:12 DISTRIBUTION OF ELECTRONS

How are electrons arranged among the energy levels? The atom is electrically neutral. For each proton in the nucleus, there is one electron in the charge cloud. Thus, as the atomic number increases, the number of electrons increases.

The energy levels in an atom can be thought of as a rooming house in which the choice double rooms are on the ground level. Electrons, as tenants, will tend to fill the better (lower) rooms first, one at a time. Then, they double up in these better rooms before going to the next level. In other words, electrons occupy the energy level and sublevel that produces the arrangement with the lowest energy. Let us consider as the first "tenant," the electron from the hydrogen atom. It will occupy the position of least energy, the $1s$ orbital. What about a different set of room tenants, the two electrons of the helium atom?

Before we can answer this question, we must consider a principle which helps to explain the arrangement of electrons. It has been found that *no two electrons in an atom have the same set of quantum numbers.* This behavior was first observed and stated by Wolfgang Pauli and is called the **Pauli exclusion principle.** The quantum numbers n, l, and m describe relative cloud size (n), shape of the cloud (l), and direction of the cloud (m). The fourth quantum number, s, describes the spin of the electron, clockwise or counterclockwise. If two electrons occupy the same orbital, they have opposite spins. Otherwise their quantum numbers would be identical, Figure 9-14.

Each orbital may contain a pair of electrons.

Pauli's exclusion principle: No two electrons in an atom can have the same set of four quantum numbers.

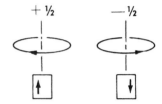

FIGURE 9-14. The fourth quantum number depicts the difference in spin for two electrons occupying the same orbital.

Two electrons can occupy the same orbital only if they have opposite spins. The magnetic fields of force produced by a moving charge can be used to explain this.

Table 9-1

Quantum States for the Hydrogen Atom									
n	l	m	s		n	l	m	s	
1	0	0	$\pm\frac{1}{2}$	1s	4	0	0	$\pm\frac{1}{2}$	4s
2	0	1	$\pm\frac{1}{2}$	2s	4	1	−1	$\pm\frac{1}{2}$	
2	1	−1	$\pm\frac{1}{2}$				0	$\pm\frac{1}{2}$	4p
		0	$\pm\frac{1}{2}$	2p			1	$\pm\frac{1}{2}$	
		1	$\pm\frac{1}{2}$		4	2	−2	$\pm\frac{1}{2}$	
3	0	0	$\pm\frac{1}{2}$	3s			−1	$\pm\frac{1}{2}$	
3	1	−1	$\pm\frac{1}{2}$				0	$\pm\frac{1}{2}$	4d
		0	$\pm\frac{1}{2}$	3p			1	$\pm\frac{1}{2}$	
		1	$\pm\frac{1}{2}$				2	$\pm\frac{1}{2}$	
3	2	−2	$\pm\frac{1}{2}$		4	3	−3	$\pm\frac{1}{2}$	
		−1	$\pm\frac{1}{2}$				−2	$\pm\frac{1}{2}$	
		0	$\pm\frac{1}{2}$	3d			−1	$\pm\frac{1}{2}$	
		1	$\pm\frac{1}{2}$				0	$\pm\frac{1}{2}$	4f
		2	$\pm\frac{1}{2}$				1	$\pm\frac{1}{2}$	
							2	$\pm\frac{1}{2}$	
							3	$\pm\frac{1}{2}$	

Now consider the helium atom. Both electrons of a helium atom take positions in the $1s$ orbital, and thus have opposing spins. We call this arrangement a $1s^2$ (read as *one-s-two*) electron configuration. We can represent the electron configuration

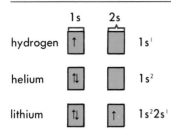

FIGURE 9-15. The orbital filling diagram and electron configuration for hydrogen, helium, and lithium.

Electrons in the same sublevel tend to occupy empty orbitals rather than pair with another electron.

Hund's Rule: Show a maximum number of unpaired electrons in a sublevel.

by a diagram like that in Figure 9-15. In the diagram, each box stands for an orbital. Arrows are used to indicate the direction of the spin of the electrons in the orbital.

The electron configuration of lithium ($Z = 3$) shows both positions in the $1s$ orbital and one position in the $2s$ orbital filled. We designate this arrangement as $1s^2 2s^1$, Figure 9-15.

Let's move on to the nitrogen atom and see how the seven electrons are distributed. We would expect two electrons in the $1s$ orbital, two in the $2s$, and three in the $2p$. This arrangement can be indicated as in Figure 9-16, where each arrow represents an electron. The opposing arrows indicate opposite spins. Notice that, each electron takes an empty orbital within a sublevel, if possible, rather than pair with another. This arrangement is reasonable because the negative electrons repel each other. It requires no more energy since all orbitals in a sublevel of an atom are degenerate. Since each orbital has a different orientation in space, electrons in different orbitals are farther apart than electrons in the same orbital. The electrons in the oxygen atom are arranged as shown in Figure 9-16. The eighth electron enters the partially filled $2p$ orbital.

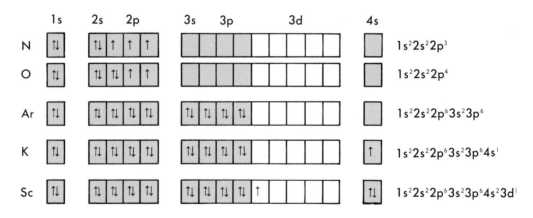

FIGURE 9-16. The orbital filling diagram and configuration for some representative elements.

The $4s$ level fills before the $3d$ level.

9:13 DIAGONAL RULE

Everything works well until we finish the electron configuration of argon: $1s^2 2s^2 2p^6 3s^2 3p^6$. Where will the electrons of the next element, potassium ($Z = 19$), go? You may remember that in the first energy level diagram Figure 9-9, the $4s$ level was shown below the $3d$ level. Thus, in this case, the $4s$ level fills first, because that order produces an atom with lower energy. The potassium configuration, therefore, is $1s^2 2s^2 2p^6 3s^2 3p^6 4s^1$. Calcium ($Z = 20$) has the configuration $1s^2 2s^2 2p^6 3s^2 3p^6 4s^2$. Scandium, however, begins filling the $3d$ orbitals, and has a configuration of $1s^2 2s^2 2p^6 3s^2 3p^6 4s^2 3d^1$.

In many atoms with higher atomic numbers, the sublevels are not regularly filled. It is of little value to memorize each configuration. However, there is a rule of thumb which will give a correct configuration for most atoms in the ground state. It is a thumb rule because we make an assumption that is not always true. The order of increasing energy sublevels is figured for the one-electron hydrogen atom. In a multielectron atom, each electron affects the energy of the others. Consequently, there are a number of exceptions to the rule of thumb. We will explore these exceptions more fully in the next chapter. This rule of thumb is called the **diagonal rule** and is shown in Figure 9-17. *If you follow the diagonals, listing the orbitals passed, you can find the electron configuration of most atoms.* As an example, suppose you are to find the electron configuration of zirconium $(Z = 40)$. Begin with the $1s$ level, drop to the $2s$ and move over to the $2p$. Follow the diagonal to $3s$ and move to $3p$. Follow the diagonal to $4s$. Move back up to the tail of the next diagonal at $3d$ and follow it through $4p$ and $5s$. Move back to the tail of the next diagonal $4d$, and place the remaining two electrons there. Thus, the electron configuration is

$$1s^2 2s^2 2p^6 3s^2 3p^6 4s^2 3d^{10} 4p^6 5s^2 4d^2$$

A quick addition of the superscripts gives a total of 40, which is the atomic number.

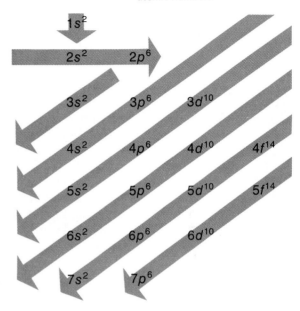

FIGURE 9-17. Use this model for the diagonal rule in writing electron configurations.

The atomic number (Z) is equal to the sum of the superscripts in the electron configuration.

To make clear that this rule is only an approximation, cite some exceptions: Cr, Cu, Nb, Mo, Tc, Ru, Rh, Pd, Ag, La, Ir, Pt, Au, Ac.

Levels n	Sublevels l	Orbitals m	Spin + −
3	d	5	
	p	3	
	s	1	
2	p	3	
	s	1	
1	s	1	

FIGURE 9-18. This complete energy level diagram depicts the relationships among the four quantum numbers.

4. $Z = 1$, $1s^1$
   $Z = 10$, $1s^2 2s^2 2p^6$
   $Z = 20$, $1s^2 2s^2 2p^6 3s^2 3p^6 4s^2$

PROBLEM

4. Write the electron configurations of the elements with $Z = 1$ through $Z = 20$.

9:14   ELECTRON DOT DIAGRAMS

Usually only the electrons in the outer level of atoms are involved in chemical change.

In studying electrons in atoms in the following chapters, our primary concern will be the electrons in the outer energy level. It is often useful to draw these outer electrons around the symbol of an element. This notation is referred to as an **electron dot diagram.**

The procedure for drawing electron dot diagrams follows.

In the electron dot diagram, the symbol represents the nucleus and all electrons except those in the outer level.

Step 1. We let the symbol of the element represent the nucleus and all electrons except those in the outer level.

Step 2. We write the electron configuration of the element. From the configuration we select the electrons which are in the outer energy level. Those in the outer level are the ones with the largest principal quantum number. Remember that n represents electron cloud size.

In the electron dot diagram, dots indicate outer level paired or unpaired electrons.

Step 3. Each "side" (top, bottom, left, right) of the symbol represents an orbital. We draw dots on the appropriate "sides" to represent the electrons in that orbital. It is important to remember which electrons are paired and which are not. *It is not important which side represents which orbital.*

EXAMPLE: Electron Dot Diagrams

Write the electron dot diagrams for hydrogen, helium, oxygen, calcium, and cadmium.

Solving process:

(a) Begin with the symbols for the elements required.

H, He, O, Ca, and Cd

(b) Write the electron configurations for each and determine the number of outer electrons

H $= 1s^1$	(outer electron $= 1s^1$)
He $= 1s^2$	(outer electrons $= 1s^2$)
O $= 1s^2 2s^2 2p^4$	(outer electrons $= 2s^2 2$
Ca $= 1s^2 2s^2 2p^6 3s^2 3p^6 4s^2$	(outer electrons $= 4s^2$)
Cd $= 1s^2 2s^2 2p^6 3s^2 3p^6 4s^2 3d^{10} 4p^6 5s^2 4d^{10}$	(outer electrons $= 5s^2$)

(c) Use the outer configuration to determine the number of dots required for each element.   H·, He:, :Ö·, Ca:, and Cd:

Note the following special considerations. First, when choosing the outer electrons for cadmium, we ignored the $4d$ electrons.

These $4d$ electrons are the highest energy electrons in the atom, but they are not in the outermost energy level. Their principal quantum number is less than that of the $5s$ electrons. Second, note that the s electrons are always shown as paired, that is, on the same "side" of the symbol. Note that in oxygen the four p electrons are distributed as one pair and two single electrons. Remember from Section 9:12 that electrons, being negative, will occupy an empty degenerate orbital before pairing with other electrons. For oxygen, no pairing takes place until the fourth electron in the p sublevel enters.

Table 9-2

Electron Dot Diagrams for Some Elements					
Element	Configuration Ending	Dot Diagram	Element	Configuration Ending	Dot Diagram
carbon	$2s^2 2p^2$	$\cdot\overset{\cdot}{C}:$	bromine	$4s^2 3d^{10} 4p^5$	$:\overset{\cdot\cdot}{Br}:$
sodium	$3s^1$	$Na\cdot$	xenon	$5s^2 4d^{10} 5p^6$	$:\overset{\cdot\cdot}{Xe}:$
magnesium	$3s^2$	$Mg:$	cerium	$6s^2 4f^2$	$\overset{\cdot}{Ce}:$
aluminum	$3s^2 3p^1$	$\overset{\cdot}{Al}:$	tungsten	$6s^2 4f^{14} 5d^9$	$W:$
phosphorus	$3s^2 3p^3$	$\cdot\overset{\cdot}{P}:$	osmium	$6s^2 4f^{14} 5d^6$	$Os:$
zinc	$4s^2 3d^{10}$	$\overset{\cdot}{Zn}:$	uranium	$7s^2 4f^9$	$U:$

PROBLEM

5. Write electron configurations and draw electron dot diagrams for the following elements. c. $1s^2 2s^2 2p^6 3s^2 3p^4$ $\cdot\overset{\cdot\cdot}{S}:$
   - a. $Z = 28$
   - b. $Z = 18$
   - c. $Z = 16$
   - d. $Z = 47$
   - e. $Z = 19$ e. $1s^2 2s^2 2p^6 3s^2 3p^6 4s^1$ $K\cdot$
   - f. $Z = 32$ f. $1s^2 2s^2 2p^6 3s^2 3p^6 4s^2 3d^{10} 4p^2$ $\cdot\overset{\cdot}{Ge}:$

   b. $1s^2 2s^2 2p^6 3s^2 3p^6$ $:\overset{\cdot\cdot}{Ar}:$ d. $1s^2 2s^2 2p^6 3s^2 3p^6 4s^2 3d^{10} 4p^6 5s^2 4d^9$ $Ag:$

9:15   ELECTRON SUMMARY

We have treated the electron as particle, wave, and cloud of negative charge. Which one is right? They all are. As pointed out in Section 9-2, electrons can behave as particles or as waves. There are times when the chemist considers the electron as a particle. At that time, the electron is exhibiting its particle characteristics. At other times, the chemist will be working on an experiment where the wave properties of the electron are of the greatest importance. At still other times, the chemist will consider the electrons in an atom as a cloud of negative charge. Scientists do not have a single, completely satisfactory description of the structure of atoms. Consequently, they make use of more than one explanation for the properties they observe. The particular explanation which best fits each situation is the one which is applied in that situation.

The electron can be thought of as a particle, a wave, or a negatively charged cloud.

Scientists do not have a single, completely satisfactory description of the structure of atoms.

We are now able to describe the electron configurations of the atoms of the elements. Our next study will be of a system of arranging elements based on their electronic structure—the periodic table.

Wolfgang Pauli (1900–1958)

As theorists, few physicists could match Vienna-born Wolfgang Pauli. As a young man he had the opportunity to study with Max Born and Niels Bohr.

In 1945, Pauli was awarded the Nobel Prize for his exclusion principle which enabled physicists to prepare a more useful description of the electronic structure of atoms. His interest in the electron and statistics led him to the study of other elementary particles. Some of his work concerned the theory of mesons and he predicted the existence of the neutrino.

Some of his other theories helped explain atomic spectra, the behavior of electrons in metals, and how metals are affected by magnetic fields.

In 1940, he was appointed to the chair of theoretical physics at the Institute for Advanced Studies in Princeton, New Jersey. He became a naturalized citizen of the United States in 1946, but later he returned to Zurich, Switzerland to live.

CHEMICAL CAREER: Perfumers

The manufacture of perfume is part science and part a creative art. One phase of perfume development is the evaluation of the odors from various sources as well as those from different mixtures. Such evaluations are subjective and comprise the creative art aspect of perfumery and the job of a perfumer.

One component of perfumes is the vehicle, or solvent. It usually contains ethanol or other similar alcohol. The solvent vaporizes readily and thus acts as the vehicle for transporting the scent. However, solvents have odors of their own. Perfumers are constantly looking for substances that will reduce any objectionable odors from the solvent without interfering with its other desirable properties.

Most perfumes are mixtures of many different compounds. The particular odor desired is achieved by the perfumer through blending several odoriferous substances. Each of these substances tends to evaporate at a different rate. As a result, the odor of the perfume tends to change with time after being applied to the skin. Perfumers add a material called a fixative to perfumes. A fixative, such as musk, tends to even out evaporation rates and therefore, maintains the quality of the odor.

The odorous substances are the most important parts of perfumes. Perfumers are constantly searching for new scents. Many odorous substances are extracts from plant parts (flowers, bark, leaves, fruits). Perfumers not only look for new plant extracts, but, using chemical analysis, they try to duplicate synthetically the particular substance or substances providing the odor. These substances can then be used directly in compounding perfumes, in place of the extracts, at much less cost. Perfumers, in conjunction with chemists, also work to develop new odorous substances. A thorough knowledge of solutions and organic chemistry is an important part of a perfumer's training.

The development of new fragrances is a highly competitive business. Consequently, the research and development function of a perfumer is quite important. An experienced perfumer may also be involved in the supervision of perfume production, quality control, marketing, and personnel administration.

Perfumers are not only involved in the production of substances used in perfumes. Many are also employed by soap and cosmetic industries. The scent associated with a soap or cosmetic product is a critical factor in its marketability. The plastics industry also employs perfumers whose job it is to deodorize plastics and other synthetic polymers. Once again the marketability of a product is at stake. You may have stored food in a plastic container and later detected the odor of the container in the food. Such a product has little appeal to the consumer at any price.

Rothwell/FPG

FIGURE 9-19. A perfumer combines a knowledge of chemistry with an acute sense of smell to produce pleasing fragrances.

SUMMARY

1. De Broglie first pointed out the wave-particle duality of nature. His idea was that all particles exhibit some wave characteristics, and vice versa. 9:1

2. The momentum of an object is the product of its mass and velocity. Wavelength varies inversely as momentum. 9:3

3. Heisenberg's uncertainty principle concerns the process of observing an electron's position or its velocity. It is impossible to know accurately both the position and the momentum of an electron at the same time. 9:4

4. Schrödinger developed a mathematical equation which describes the behavior of the electron as a wave. The solution set of the wave equation can be used to calculate the probability of finding an electron at a particular point. 9:5

5. Because of the electron's high velocity, it effectively occupies all the volume defined by the path through which it moves. This volume is called the electron cloud. 9:6

6. The principal quantum number (n = 1, 2, 3, . . .) is the number of the energy level and describes the relative electron cloud size. 9:8

7. Each energy level has as many sublevels as the principal quantum number. The second quantum number (l = s, p, d, f . . .) describes the shape of the cloud. 9:9

8. The third quantum number, m, describes the orientation in space of each orbital. 9:10, 9:11

9. The fourth quantum number, s, describes the spin direction of the electron. 9:12

10. Each orbital may contain a maximum of one pair of electrons. Electrons in the same orbital have opposite spins. 9:12

11. Pauli's exclusion principle states that no two electrons in an atom can have the same set of quantum numbers. 9:12

12. Electrons occupy first the empty orbital giving the atom the lowest energy. 9:12

13. The diagonal rule can be used to provide the correct electron configuration for most atoms. 9:13

14. The chemist is primarily concerned with the electrons in the outer energy level. Electron dot diagrams are useful in representing these outer level electrons. 9:14

PROBLEMS

$\lambda = \dfrac{h}{m\bar{v}}$

6. How did de Broglie show the relationship between waves and particles?

7. What is the relationship between momentum and wavelength? $\lambda = \dfrac{h}{p}$

8. How many electrons can exist in the fifth energy level? 50

9. What are the actual values for the fourth quantum number (s)? $\pm\frac{1}{2}$

10. Write the electron configuration for uranium. Compute the number of electrons in each level. Calculate the levels which are not full of electrons.

11. What elements are composed of atoms having the following electron configurations:

Mn a. $1s^2 2s^2 2p^6 3s^2 3p^6 4s^2 3d^5$

Mo b. $1s^2 2s^2 2p^6 3s^2 3p^6 4s^2 3d^{10} 4p^6 5s^2 4d^4$ Nb $1s^2 2s^2 2p^6 3s^2 3p^6 4s^2 3d^{10} 4p^6 5s^2 4d^3$

Zn $1s^2 2s^2 2p^6 3s^2 3p^6 4s^2 3d^{10}$

12. Write the electron configurations for niobium and zinc.

13. Write the electron configurations for polonium and technetium.

14. Draw electron dot diagrams for the elements with Z equal to 33, 51, and 83. ·A̤s: ·S̤b: ·B̤i: 4 (or 2 pairs)

15. How many pairs of electrons are there in an atom of boron? an atom of sulfur? an atom of fluorine? 8 (or 4 pairs)

14 (or 7 pairs)

16. How many electrons are not shown in the electron dot diagrams of the elements from Z = 3 to Z = 10? 2e$^-$

Margin answers:

10. $Z = 92$

e$^-$ in each level

$n = 1, 2$
$n = 2, 8$
$n = 3, 18$
$n = 4, 32$
$n = 5, 22$
$n = 6, 8$
$n = 7, 2$

Levels 5, 6, and 7 are not full.

Po $1s^2 2s^2 2p^6 3s^2 3p^6 4s^2 3d^{10} 4p^6 5s^2 4d^{10} 5p^6 6s^2 4f^{14} 5d^6 6p^4$

Tc $1s^2 2s^2 2p^6 3s^2 3p^6 4s^2 3d^{10} 4p^6 5s^2 4d^5$

Actual configurations may differ from those predicted by the diagonal rule.

REVIEW

1. What observations led John Dalton to formulate his atomic theory?
2. What is a nuclide? What are isotopes?
3. What is the difference between atomic number and atomic mass?
4. Compute ΔH for the reaction
$$Mn(NO_3)_2 + Na_2S \rightarrow MnS + 2NaNO_3 \quad -35\ kJ$$
5. How much energy is needed to heat 10.0 g of tin from 25°C to 225°C? 440 J
6. What data led Bohr to formulate the planetary model of the atom?
7. What is Planck's contribution to the development of atomic theory?
8. What is the atomic mass of molybdenum if it has the following isotopic composition? 95.9 amu

isotope	mass	abundance
92	91.906808	15.84%
94	93.905090	9.04%
95	94.905837	15.72%
96	95.904674	16.53%
97	96.906023	9.46%
98	97.905409	23.78%
100	99.907478	9.63%

9. How many electrons, neutrons, and protons are in mendelevium of mass number 256? 101 electrons, 155 neutrons, 101 protons
10. What is the photoelectric effect?

ONE MORE STEP

1. What is the uncertainty in the momentum of an electron if its position has been determined to an accuracy of ± 0.01 nm? 6.63×10^{-23} kg · m/s
2. Classical physics would predict that only the three quantum numbers should be necessary to describe the motion of the electron in three-dimensional space. What necessitates a fourth?
3. Look up experiments which have been performed with the electron. Select one demonstrating its properties as a wave, and one demonstrating its properties as a particle. Prepare a report to your class on the procedure and results of these experiments.

READINGS

David, Carl W., "On Orbital Drawings." *Journal of Chemical Education,* Vol. 58, No. 5 (May 1981), p. 377.

Greenberger, Daniel M., and Albert W. Overhauser. "The Role of Gravity in Quantum Theory." *Scientific American,* Vol. 242, No. 5 (May 1980) p. 66.

Hofstadter, Douglas R., "Mathematical Themas." *Scientific American,* Vol. 245, No. 1 (July 1981), pp. 18-30.

The market scene contains matter of various sizes, colors, and textures. In Chapter 3, you saw how matter could be classified into smaller groupings with similar characteristics. This chapter will focus on one of those smaller groups, the elements. Chemistry is based on studying the physical and chemical properties of over 100 elements. What system is used to classify the elements to make their study easier? How is this classification system related to properties? Devise your own system to classify the objects in the market scene.

Kent Oppenheimer/Alpha

Chapter 10 introduces the periodic table and reveals some of the periodic characteristics of the elements based upon their electronic structures.

PERIODIC TABLE

10

The element sodium reacts violently with water. Potassium reacts still more violently with water. An experienced chemist can predict that the elements rubidium, cesium, and francium will react in a similar manner. How can this prediction be made? Such predictions can be made because all of these elements have similar outer energy level structures. They have been placed in the first column of the periodic table because they have a similar structure.

GOAL: You will gain an understanding of how the periodic table is organized by studying the relationship between periodic properties and electron configuration.

10:1   EARLY ATTEMPTS AT CLASSIFICATION: DOBEREINER AND NEWLANDS

Early in the 19th century, scientists began to seek ways to classify the elements. One attempt at classification was by Johann Dobereiner, a German chemist, in 1817. Dobereiner found that the properties of the metals calcium, barium, and strontium were very similar. He also noted that the atomic mass of strontium was about midway between those of calcium and barium. He formed what he termed a **triad** of these three elements. Later, Dobereiner found several other groups of three elements with similar properties.

Properties of elements are in Appendix A, Table A-3.

Dobereiner discovered groups of three related elements which he termed a triad.

Table 10-1

Some of Dobereiner's Triads					
Name	Atomic Mass	Name	Atomic Mass	Name	Atomic Mass
Calcium	40	Chlorine	35.5	Sulfur	32
Barium	137	Iodine	127	Tellurium	127.5
Average	88.5	**Average**	81.3	**Average**	79.8
Strontium	87.6	Bromine	79.9	Selenium	79.2

Newlands' law of octaves was proposed to explain the property similarities which occurred with every eighth element when the elements were arranged in order of increasing atomic mass.

In 1863, John Newlands, an English chemist, suggested another classification. He arranged the elements in order of their increasing atomic masses. He noted that there appeared to be a repetition of similar properties every eighth element. Therefore, he arranged the elements known at that time into seven groups of seven each.* Newlands referred to his arrangement as the **law of octaves.**

Table 10-2

Newlands' Law of Octaves							
1	2	3	4	5	6	7	8
Li	Be	B	C	N	O	F	Na
Na	Mg	Al	Si	P	S	Cl	K
K							

10:2 MENDELEEV'S PERIODIC TABLE

Mendeleev suggested periods of varying lengths based on atomic masses.

Just six years after Newlands' proposal, Dmitri Mendeleev, a Russian chemist, proposed a similar idea. He suggested, as had Newlands, that the properties of the elements were a function of their atomic masses. However, Mendeleev felt that similar properties occurred after periods (horizontal rows) of varying length. Although he placed seven elements each in his first two periods, he placed seventeen elements in the next two.

Table 10-3

Mendeleev predicted the existence of six undiscovered elements:

ekaboron (scandium)
ekaaluminum (gallium)
ekasilicon (germanium)
ekamanganese (technetium)
dvimanganese (rhenium)
ekatantalum (polonium)

Mendeleev's Predictions	
Ekasilicon* *Predicted properties*	**Germanium** *Actual properties*
1. Atomic mass = 72	1. Atomic mass = 72.60
2. High melting point	2. Melting point = 958°C
3. Density = 5.5 g/cm^3	3. Density = 5.36 g/cm^3
4. Dark gray metal	4. Gray metal
5. Will obtain from K_2EsF_6	5. Obtain from K_2GeF_6
6. Slightly dissolved by HCl	6. Not dissolved by HCl
7. Will form EsO_2	7. Forms oxide (GeO_2)
8. Density of EsO_2 = 4.7 g/cm^3	8. Density of GeO_2 = 4.70 g/cm^3

*One of the blank spaces in Mendeleev's table was below silicon. Mendeleev assumed such an element existed but had not yet been discovered. He called this element (later named germanium) ekasilicon and predicted some of its properties.

*Note: Noble gases were not known at this time.

			Ti = 50	Zr = 90	? = 180
			V = 51	Nb = 94	Ta = 182
			Cr = 52	Mo = 96	W = 186
			Mn = 55	Rh = 104,$_4$ (103)	*Pt = 197,$_4$
			Fe = 56	Ru = 104,$_4$ (101)	*Ir = 198 (193)
			Ni, Co = 59*	Pd = 106,$_6$	*Os = 199 (191)
H = 1			Cu = 63,$_4$	Ag = 108	*Hg = 200
	Be = 9,$_4$	Mg = 24	Zn = 65,$_2$	Cd = 112	
	B = 11	Al = 27,$_4$	? = 68	*Ur = 116 (238)	*Au = 197?
	C = 12	Si = 28	? = 70	Sn = 118	
	N = 14	P = 31	As = 75	Sb = 122	Bi = 210
	O = 16	S = 32	Se = 79,$_4$	Te = 128?	
	F = 19	Cl = 35,$_5$	Br = 80	I = 127	
Li = 7	Na = 23	K = 39	Rb = 85,$_4$	Cs = 133	*Tl = 204
		Ca = 40	Sr = 87,$_6$	Ba = 137	*Pb = 207
		? = 45	*Ce = 92 (138)		
		*Er = 56 (166)	*La = 94 (137)		
		*Yt = 60 (88)	*Di = 95 (140)		
		*In = 75,$_6$ (113)	*Th = 118 (231)		

Sovfoto

Таблица I.   *Elements added after original publication in 1869.

Первая попытка Менделѣева найти естественную систему элементовъ. Перепечатана изъ „Журнала Химическаго Общества", т. I, стр. 70 (1869г.). Жирнымъ шрифтомъ и звѣздочками я обозначилъ элементы, попавшіе не на свое мѣсто, по причинѣ неточнаго опредѣленія ихъ атомнаго вѣса, а въ скобкахъ я привелъ ихъ дѣйствительные вѣса. У Менделѣева жирнаго шрифта и звѣздочекъ не было совсѣмъ. Все было однимъ шрифтомъ.

In 1871, Mendeleev and the German chemist Lothar Meyer, each working alone, made an eight-column table of the elements. However, Mendeleev had to leave some blank spots in order to group all the elements with similar properties in the same column. To explain these blank spots, Mendeleev suggested there must be other elements that had not yet been discovered. On the basis of his arrangement, Mendeleev predicted the properties and atomic masses of several elements which were unknown at the time. Today, these elements have been discovered, and Mendeleev's predictions have been found to be very nearly correct. Table 10-3 shows Mendeleev's predictions for the properties of germanium.

In Mendeleev's table, the elements were arranged in order of their increasing atomic masses. The table showed that the properties of the elements are repeated in an orderly way. Mendeleev regarded the properties of the elements as a periodic function of their atomic masses. This statement was called the periodic law.

FIGURE 10-1. Mendeleev's arrangement of the elements as published in 1869.

Mendeleev left blanks in his table for undiscovered elements.

Mendeleev predicted properties and masses of unknown elements correctly.

Mendeleev's predictions made his proposal seem superior to Meyer's.

Mendeleev's periodic law: Properties of elements are periodic functions of their atomic masses.

Periodic Table

(Based on Carbon 12 = 12.0000)

Metals

Transition Elements

IA								
1 H Hydrogen 1.0079								

IIA								VIIIB

		IIIB	IVB	VB	VIB	VIIB		
3 Li Lithium 6.941	**4** Be Beryllium 9.01218							
11 Na Sodium 22.9898	**12** Mg Magnesium 24.305							
19 K Potassium 39.0983	**20** Ca Calcium 40.08	**21** Sc Scandium 44.9559	**22** Ti Titanium 47.90	**23** V Vanadium 50.9415	**24** Cr Chromium 51.996	**25** Mn Manganese 54.9380	**26** Fe Iron 55.847	**27** Co Cobalt 58.9332
37 Rb Rubidium 85.4678	**38** Sr Strontium 87.62	**39** Y Yttrium 88.9059	**40** Zr Zirconium 91.22	**41** Nb Niobium 92.9064	**42** Mo Molybdenum 95.94	**43** Tc Technetium 96.9062*	**44** Ru Ruthenium 101.07	**45** Rh Rhodium 102.9055
55 Cs Cesium 132.9054	**56** Ba Barium 137.33	**71** Lu Lutetium 174.967	**72** Hf Hafnium 178.49	**73** Ta Tantalum 180.9479	**74** W Tungsten 183.85	**75** Re Rhenium 186.2	**76** Os Osmium 190.2	**77** Ir Iridium 192.22
87 Fr Francium 223.01976*	**88** Ra Radium 226.0254	**103** Lr Lawrencium 256.099*	**104** ___ 257*	**105** ___ 260*	**106** ___ 263*	**107** ___ 258*		

LANTHANIDE SERIES

57 La Lanthanum 138.9055	**58** Ce Cerium 140.12	**59** Pr Praseodymium 140.9077	**60** Nd Neodymium 144.24	**61** Pm Promethium 144.91279*	**62** Sm Samarium 150.4

ACTINIDE SERIES

89 Ac Actinium 227.02779*	**90** Th Thorium 232.0381	**91** Pa Protactinium 231.0359*	**92** U Uranium 238.029	**93** Np Neptunium 237.0482	**94** Pu Plutonium 244.06424

Gases—green, Liquids—blue, Solids—yellow, Synthetics—orange

Noble Gases
VIIIA

Nonmetals

IIIA	IVA	VA	VIA	VIIA	2 **He** Helium 4.00260
5 **B** Boron 10.81	6 **C** Carbon 12.011	7 **N** Nitrogen 14.0067	8 **O** Oxygen 15.9994	9 **F** Fluorine 18.998403	10 **Ne** Neon 20.179
13 **Al** Aluminum 26.98154	14 **Si** Silicon 28.0855	15 **P** Phosphorus 30.97376	16 **S** Sulfur 32.06	17 **Cl** Chlorine 35.453	18 **Ar** Argon 39.948

IB	IIB						

28 **Ni** Nickel 58.71	29 **Cu** Copper 63.546	30 **Zn** Zinc 65.38	31 **Ga** Gallium 69.737	32 **Ge** Germanium 72.59	33 **As** Arsenic 74.9216	34 **Se** Selenium 78.96	35 **Br** Bromine 79.904	36 **Kr** Krypton 83.80
46 **Pd** Palladium 106.4	47 **Ag** Silver 107.868	48 **Cd** Cadmium 112.41	49 **In** Indium 114.82	50 **Sn** Tin 118.69	51 **Sb** Antimony 121.75	52 **Te** Tellurium 127.60	53 **I** Iodine 126.9045	54 **Xe** Xenon 131.30
78 **Pt** Platinum 195.09	79 **Au** Gold 196.9665	80 **Hg** Mercury 200.59	81 **Tl** Thallium 204.37	82 **Pb** Lead 207.2	83 **Bi** Bismuth 208.9808	84 **Po** Polonium 208.98244*	85 **At** Astatine 209.98704*	86 **Rn** Radon 222*

Rare Earth Elements

63 **Eu** Europium 151.96	64 **Gd** Gadolinium 157.25	65 **Tb** Terbium 158.9254	66 **Dy** Dysprosium 162.50	67 **Ho** Holmium 164.9304	68 **Er** Erbium 167.26	69 **Tm** Thulium 168.9342	70 **Yb** Ytterbium 173.04
95 **Am** Americium 243.06139*	96 **Cm** Curium 247.07038*	97 **Bk** Berkelium 247.07032*	98 **Cf** Californium 251.07961*	99 **Es** Einsteinium 254.08805*	100 **Fm** Fermium 257.09515*	101 **Md** Mendelevium 258*	102 **No** Nobelium 255.093*

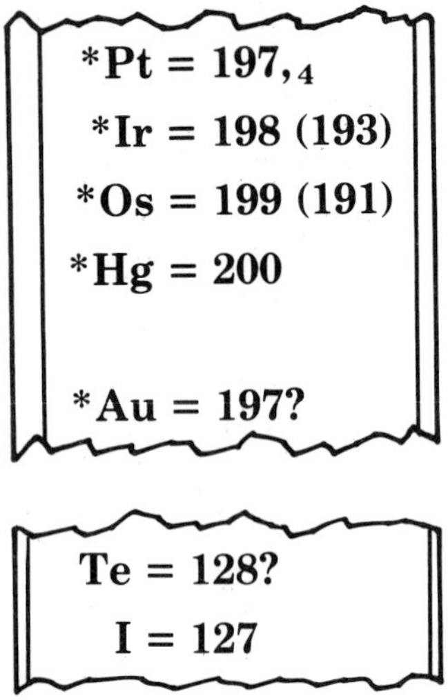

*Pt = 197,₄

*Ir = 198 (193)

*Os = 199 (191)

*Hg = 200

*Au = 197?

Te = 128?

I = 127

FIGURE 10-2. Discrepencies in Mendeleev's arrangement of some elements resulted in the revision of Mendeleev's periodic law.

10:3 MODERN PERIODIC LAW

There was a problem with Mendeleev's table. If the elements were arranged according to increasing atomic masses, tellurium and iodine seemed to be in the wrong columns. Their properties were different from those of other elements in the same column. However, they were next to each other. Switching their positions put them in the columns where they belonged according to their properties. If the switch were made, Mendeleev's basic assumption that the properties of the elements were a periodic function of their atomic masses would be wrong. Mendeleev assumed that the atomic masses of these two elements had been poorly measured. He thought that new mass measurements would prove his hypothesis to be correct. However, new measurements simply confirmed the original masses.

Soon, new elements were discovered, and two other pairs showed the same kind of reversal. Cobalt and nickel were known by Mendeleev, but their atomic masses had not been accurately measured. When such a determination was made, it was found that their positions in the table were also reversed. When argon was discovered, the masses of argon and potassium were reversed.

Henry Moseley found the reason for these apparent exceptions to the rule. As a result of Moseley's work, the periodic law was revised. It now has as its basis the atomic numbers of the elements instead of the atomic masses. Today's statement of the **periodic law** is *the properties of the elements are a periodic function of their atomic numbers.*

Moseley's revision: Properties of the elements are periodic functions of their atomic numbers.

Suggestion: Obtain blank periodic tables and have the students fill them in as this section is discussed.

Elements with similar electron configurations are listed in columns.

10:4 MODERN PERIODIC TABLE

The atomic number of an element indicates the number of protons in the nucleus of each atom of the element. The atomic number also indicates the number of electrons surrounding the nucleus.

Certain electron arrangements are periodically repeated. We can place elements with similar electron configurations in the same column. We can also list the elements in the column in order of their increasing principal quantum numbers. Thus, we can form a table of the elements similar to that on pages 178 and 179. This table is called the **periodic table** of the elements.

We construct our periodic table in this manner. We will use the diagonal rule (Section 9:13) to determine the order of filling the sublevels. Each *s* sublevel contains two electrons. Each *p* sublevel contains six electrons arranged in three pairs, or orbitals. Each *d* sublevel contains ten electrons in five orbitals. Each *f* sublevel contains fourteen electrons in seven orbitals. We then align the elements with similar electron configurations.

sublevel	e^- capacity
s	2
p	6
d	10
f	14

Table 10-4

Elements 1-10			
		1	**2**
Z	Element	s	s p
1	H	1	
2	He	2	
3	Li	2	1
4	Be	2	2
5	B	2	2 1
6	C	2	2 2
7	N	2	2 3
8	O	2	2 4
9	F	2	2 5
10	Ne	2	2 6

The first configuration in Table 10-4, hydrogen ($Z = 1$), consists of one electron in the $1s$ sublevel. The second configuration, helium ($Z = 2$), consists of two electrons in the $1s$ sublevel. These two electrons completely fill the $1s$ sublevel. The third element, lithium ($Z = 3$), has two electrons in the $1s$ sublevel and one electron in the $2s$ sublevel. Lithium is similar to hydrogen in that it has only one electron in its outermost sublevel. Therefore, we will place it in the same column as hydrogen. The next element, beryllium ($Z = 4$), has two electrons in the $1s$ sublevel and two electrons in the $2s$ sublevel. It might seem to belong in the column with helium. However, the two electrons in helium's outermost level fill that level.

The two electrons in the $2s$ sublevel of beryllium do not fill the second level. Recall that the $n = 2$ level has a p sublevel, as well as its s sublevel. Even though the beryllium and helium configurations are similar, beryllium starts a new column next to lithium. Boron ($Z = 5$) has a configuration composed of two $1s$ electrons, two $2s$ electrons, and one $2p$ electron. It heads a new column. Carbon ($Z = 6$), nitrogen ($Z = 7$), oxygen ($Z = 8$), and fluorine ($Z = 9$) atoms come next. They have structures containing two, three, four, and five electrons, respectively, in the $2p$ sublevel. Each of these elements heads a new column. The atoms of neon ($Z = 10$), the tenth element, contain six $2p$ electrons. The second level ($n = 2$) is now full, so neon is placed in the same column as helium.

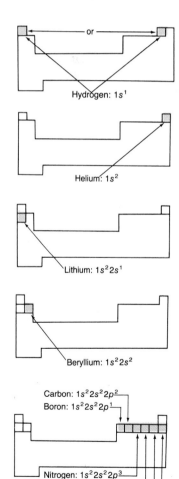

or

Hydrogen: $1s^1$

Helium: $1s^2$

Lithium: $1s^2 2s^1$

Beryllium: $1s^2 2s^2$

Carbon: $1s^2 2s^2 2p^2$
Boron: $1s^2 2s^2 2p^1$

Nitrogen: $1s^2 2s^2 2p^3$
Oxygen: $1s^2 2s^2 2p^4$
Fluorine: $1s^2 2s^2 2p^5$
Neon: $1s^2 2s^2 2p^6$

Table 10-5

		1	2		3			4
Z	Element	s	s	p	s	p	d	s
11	Na	2	2	6	1			
12	Mg	2	2	6	2			
13	Al	2	2	6	2	1		
14	Si	2	2	6	2	2		
15	P	2	2	6	2	3		
16	S	2	2	6	2	4		
17	Cl	2	2	6	2	5		
18	Ar	2	2	6	2	6		
19	K	2	2	6	2	6		1
20	Ca	2	2	6	2	6		2

Elements 11-20

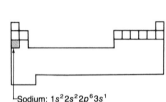

Sodium: $1s^2 2s^2 2p^6 3s^1$

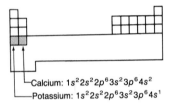

Calcium: $1s^2 2s^2 2p^6 3s^2 3p^6 4s^2$
Potassium: $1s^2 2s^2 2p^6 3s^2 3p^6 4s^1$

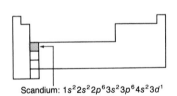

Scandium: $1s^2 2s^2 2p^6 3s^2 3p^6 4s^2 3d^1$

The transition elements fill the B columns.

Sodium atoms ($Z = 11$) have the same outer level configuration as lithium atoms, one s electron ($3s^1$). Thus, sodium is placed under lithium. The elements magnesium ($Z = 12$) through argon ($Z = 18$) have the same outer structures as the elements beryllium through neon. They are also placed in the appropriate columns. Atoms of potassium ($Z = 19$) and calcium ($Z = 20$) have outer structures that are similar to the atoms of sodium and magnesium.

10:5 TRANSITION ELEMENTS

The scandium ($Z = 21$) configuration introduces a new factor into the arrangement. It has two electrons in the outer level ($4s^2$) and is similar to the calcium configuration. However, the scandium atom has, in addition to a filled $4s$ sublevel, one electron in the $3d$ sublevel. It is, therefore, placed in a new column, which is labeled (IIIB). For the atoms of elements titanium ($Z = 22$) through nickel ($Z = 28$), additional electrons are added in the $3d$ sublevel. For all these elements, however, the outer level is the 4th level so they are placed in the fourth row. Each of these elements heads a new column (column IIIB to VIIIB). Note that the atoms of copper and zinc have filled inner levels. All structures in column IB have filled inner levels and one electron in the outer level. All structures in column IIB have filled inner levels and two electrons in the outer level. In columns IIIA through VIIIA, electrons are added to the p sublevel until there are a total of eight electrons in the outer level. The next electron is added to the next s sublevel whether the inner level is filled or not. The process is continued until all of the elements are placed in the main part of the table.

Table 10-6

		1	2		3			4				5				6			7
Transition Elements																			
Z	Element	s	s	p	s	p	d	s	p	d	f	s	p	d	f	s	p	d	s
21	Sc	2	2	6	2	6	1	2											
22	Ti	2	2	6	2	6	2	2											
23	V	2	2	6	2	6	3	2											
24	Cr	2	2	6	2	6	5	1											
25	Mn	2	2	6	2	6	5	2											
26	Fe	2	2	6	2	6	6	2											
27	Co	2	2	6	2	6	7	2											
28	Ni	2	2	6	2	6	8	2											
29	Cu	2	2	6	2	6	10	1											
30	Zn	2	2	6	2	6	10	2											
39	Y	2	2	6	2	6	10	2	6	1		2							
40	Zr	2	2	6	2	6	10	2	6	2		2							
41	Nb	2	2	6	2	6	10	2	6	4		1							
42	Mo	2	2	6	2	6	10	2	6	5		1							
43	Tc	2	2	6	2	6	10	2	6	5		2							
44	Ru	2	2	6	2	6	10	2	6	7		1							
45	Rh	2	2	6	2	6	10	2	6	8		1							
46	Pd	2	2	6	2	6	10	2	6	10									
47	Ag	2	2	6	2	6	10	2	6	10		1							
48	Cd	2	2	6	2	6	10	2	6	10		2							
71	Lu	2	2	6	2	6	10	2	6	10	14	2	6	1		2			
72	Hf	2	2	6	2	6	10	2	6	10	14	2	6	2		2			
73	Ta	2	2	6	2	6	10	2	6	10	14	2	6	3		2			
74	W	2	2	6	2	6	10	2	6	10	14	2	6	4		2			
75	Re	2	2	6	2	6	10	2	6	10	14	2	6	5		2			
76	Os	2	2	6	2	6	10	2	6	10	14	2	6	6		2			
77	Ir	2	2	6	2	6	10	2	6	10	14	2	6	7		2			
78	Pt	2	2	6	2	6	10	2	6	10	14	2	6	9		1			
79	Au	2	2	6	2	6	10	2	6	10	14	2	6	10		1			
80	Hg	2	2	6	2	6	10	2	6	10	14	2	6	10		2			
103	Lr	2	2	6	2	6	10	2	6	10	14	2	6	10	14	2	6	1	2
104		2	2	6	2	6	10	2	6	10	14	2	6	10	14	2	6	2	2?
105		2	2	6	2	6	10	2	6	10	14	2	6	10	14	2	6	3	2?

The elements in both columns IA & IB contain only one e^- in the outer level. However, column IA metals contain 8 e^- in the next to outer level and column IB metals contain 18 e^- in this level. The column IA metals (alkali metals) easily lose the single outer electron and form extremely stable ions which have a stable noble gas configuration. Column IB metals (coinage metals) are noncorrosive and relatively unreactive because loss of the single outer level electron does not result in the formation of an appreciably more stable ion.

10:6 THE LANTHANIDES AND ACTINIDES

The **lanthanide series** contains the elements lanthanum ($Z = 57$) through ytterbium ($Z = 70$). All of these elements have a predicted structure with two electrons in the outer level. In this series, electrons are being added to the $4f$ sublevel instead of to a sublevel of the sixth or outer level as shown in Table 10-7.

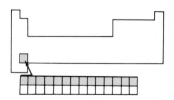

Table 10-7

Lanthanides add electrons to the 4f sublevels.

		1	2		3			4				5			6
Z	Element	s	s	p	s	p	d	s	p	d	f	s	p	d	s
57	La	2	2	6	2	6	10	2	6	10		2	6	1	2
58	Ce	2	2	6	2	6	10	2	6	10	1	2	6	1	2
59	Pr	2	2	6	2	6	10	2	6	10	3	2	6		2
60	Nd	2	2	6	2	6	10	2	6	10	4	2	6		2
61	Pm	2	2	6	2	6	10	2	6	10	5	2	6		2
62	Sm	2	2	6	2	6	10	2	6	10	6	2	6		2
63	Eu	2	2	6	2	6	10	2	6	10	7	2	6		2
64	Gd	2	2	6	2	6	10	2	6	10	7	2	6	1	2
65	Tb	2	2	6	2	6	10	2	6	10	9	2	6		2
66	Dy	2	2	6	2	6	10	2	6	10	10	2	6		2
67	Ho	2	2	6	2	6	10	2	6	10	11	2	6		2
68	Er	2	2	6	2	6	10	2	6	10	12	2	6		2
69	Tm	2	2	6	2	6	10	2	6	10	13	2	6		2
70	Yb	2	2	6	2	6	10	2	6	10	14	2	6		2

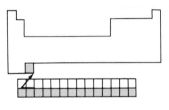

Actinides add electrons to the 5f sublevels.

The **actinide series** contains actinium ($Z = 89$) through nobelium ($Z = 102$). In this series, the $5f$ sublevel is being filled as shown in Table 10-8.

The atoms of some elements do not have the exact electron configurations predicted for them. However, the differences involve only one or two electrons. Note the configuration for gadolinium. For purposes of constructing the table, we will assume that all elements have the predicted configurations.

Table 10-8

		1	2		3			4				5				6			7
Z	Element	s	s	p	s	p	d	s	p	d	f	s	p	d	f	s	p	d	s
89	Ac	2	2	6	2	6	10	2	6	10	14	2	6	10		2	6	1	2
90	Th	2	2	6	2	6	10	2	6	10	14	2	6	10		2	6	2	2
91	Pa	2	2	6	2	6	10	2	6	10	14	2	6	10	2	2	6	1	2
92	U	2	2	6	2	6	10	2	6	10	14	2	6	10	3	2	6	1	2
93	Np	2	2	6	2	6	10	2	6	10	14	2	6	10	4	2	6	1	2
94	Pu	2	2	6	2	6	10	2	6	10	14	2	6	10	6	2	6		2
95	Am	2	2	6	2	6	10	2	6	10	14	2	6	10	7	2	6		2
96	Cm	2	2	6	2	6	10	2	6	10	14	2	6	10	7	2	6	1	2
97	Bk	2	2	6	2	6	10	2	6	10	14	2	6	10	8	2	6	1	2?
98	Cf	2	2	6	2	6	10	2	6	10	14	2	6	10	10	2	6		2
99	Es	2	2	6	2	6	10	2	6	10	14	2	6	10	11	2	6		2
100	Fm	2	2	6	2	6	10	2	6	10	14	2	6	10	12	2	6		2
101	Md	2	2	6	2	6	10	2	6	10	14	2	6	10	13	2	6		2
102	No	2	2	6	2	6	10	2	6	10	14	2	6	10	14	2	6		2

The blocks representing these elements are shown below the main table. Their proper position would be between 56 and 71 and 88 and 103. If we were to split the table there and insert the lanthanides and actinides the table would be too wide to print reasonably.

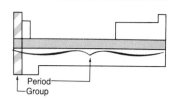

Period
Group

All elements in a horizontal line are referred to as a **period.** All elements in the same vertical column are referred to as a **group** and are labeled IA through VIIIA and IB through VIIIB.

Periods are horizontal rows of elements.

Groups are vertical columns of elements.

10:7 OCTET RULE

When an *s* electron is the highest energy level electron in an atom, it is in the outer level. The same is true of a *p* electron. However, *d* and *f* electrons, theoretically, can never be in the outer level of a neutral atom (see diagonal rule, page 167). Since *s* sublevels hold two electrons and *p* sublevels hold six, the largest number of electrons normally in an outer level is eight. One of the basic rules in chemistry is that an atom with eight electrons in its outer level is particularly stable. This rule is called the **octet rule.** Although the helium atom has only two electrons in its outer level, it, too, is one of these stable elements. Its outer level is the first level and can hold only two electrons. Thus, it has a full outer level. We will then consider the octet rule to include helium.

The octet rule should be learned as "four pairs" of electrons.

Eight electrons in the outer level of an atom represent a stable arrangement.

Helium is included in the octet rule.

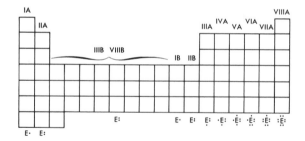

FIGURE 10-3. The relationship between electron dot structure and group number is shown.

10:8 SURVEYING THE TABLE: ELECTRON CONFIGURATIONS

The periodic table was originally constructed by placing elements with similar properties in a column. We now know that an atom's chemical properties are determined by its electron configuration. By reversing the procedure in which the table was constructed, the table may be used to "read" the configuration of an element. Thus, the written configuration of any element in Group IA will end in s^1. This configuration means that the outer level of each atom of Group IA elements contains one electron. The coefficient of s^1 is easily found from the table because the number

The periodic table can be used to determine electron configuration of an element.

of the period indicates the energy level. For example, potassium is in the fourth period of Group IA. Thus, the written electron configuration for the outer level of potassium is $4s^1$. The superscript, in s^1, indicates the group number. The coefficient, in $4s^1$, indicates the period number. Find lithium in the periodic table. How does its written electron configuration end? Find Group IIA in the periodic table. How does the written electron configuration for all elements in this group end? The same procedure can be used for Groups IIIA through VIIIA. There the endings, instead of s^1 or s^2, are p^1 through p^6 preceded by a coefficient which is the same as the number of the period.

Atoms in the same period have the same principal quantum number (n).

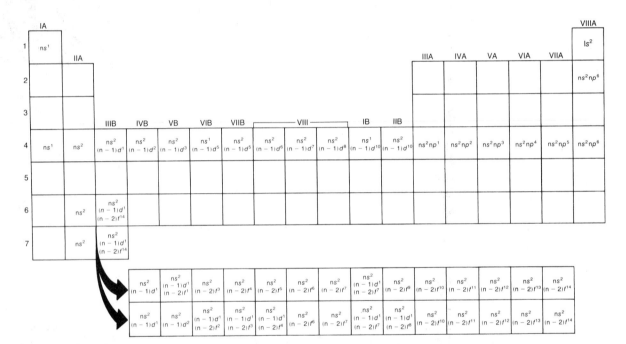

FIGURE 10-4. An element's position in the table can be used to determine its electron configuration.

Some deviations from the diagonal rule are periodic and explainable.

Full or half-full sublevels are particularly stable.

For Groups IIIB through IIB, the endings are d^1 through d^{10} preceded by a coefficient which is one less than the period number. For the lanthanides, the endings are f^1 through f^{14} preceded by a coefficient which is two less than the period number. For transition elements, remember that the d sublevel is always preceded by an s sublevel that is one quantum number higher.

To understand some of the exceptions to the diagonal rule, it is necessary to know that there is a special stability associated with certain electron configurations in an atom. You already know that an atom with eight electrons in the outer level has this stability. *An atom having a filled or half filled sublevel is also stable.* Thus, chromium is predicted to have two electrons in its $4s$ sublevel and four electrons in its $3d$ sublevel. Actually, it has one electron in its $4s$ sublevel and five electrons in its $3d$ sublevel. Note that one electron is shifted between two very closely spaced sublevels. The atom thus has two half-full sublevels instead of one full sublevel and one with no special arrangement. Copper has a similar change. Copper is predicted to have two $4s$ electrons and nine $3d$ electrons. Actually, it has one electron in its $4s$ sublevel and ten electrons in its $3d$ sublevel. One full and one half-full sublevel make an atom more stable than one full sublevel and one with no special arrangement as predicted. Most of the exceptions from predicted configurations can be explained in this way.

10:9 METALS AND NONMETALS

Groups IA and IIA of the periodic table contain the most active metals. Many of the columns in the table have family names. Group IA, except hydrogen, is called the *alkali metal family*. Group IIA is called the *alkaline earth metal family*.

On the other side of the table are the nonmetals, in Groups VIA, VIIA, and VIIIA. Group VIA is called the *chalcogen* (KAL kuh juhn) family. Group VIIA is known as the *halogen family*. The elements of Group VIIIA are called the *noble gases.*

We are all familiar with typical metallic properties. **Metals** are hard and shiny. They conduct heat and electricity well. **Nonmetals** are generally gases or brittle solids. Their surfaces are dull and they are insulators. Chemists use the electron structure of elements to classify them as metals or nonmetals.

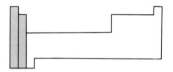

Most active metals: groups IA and IIA.

Suggestion: Ask students to list typical metallic and nonmetallic properties they are familiar with, such as: electrical conductivity, hardness, and metallic lustre. This will set the stage for later development of these properties in terms of bonding and electrons.

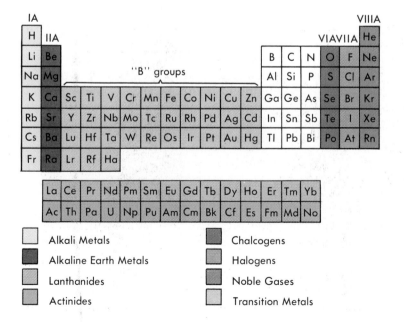

FIGURE 10-5. Groups of elements are often referred to as families.

Metals generally have fewer electrons in the outer level than nonmetals.

Metalloids are elements which have both metallic and non-metallic properties.

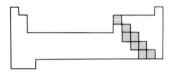

One characteristic of metals is that they have only a few electrons in the outer level. Nonmetals have more electrons in the outer level. There are exceptions. However, as a general rule, *elements with three or less electrons in the outer level are considered to be metals. Elements with five or more electrons in the outer level are considered to be nonmetals.* There are some elements which have properties of both metals and nonmetals. These elements are called the **metalloids.** Silicon, an element used in the manufacture of microcomputer chips, is a metalloid. On the periodic table, you will note a heavy, stairstep line on the right side. This line is a rough dividing line between metals and nonmetals. As you might expect, the elements along the line are generally metalloids.

Young/Hoffhines

Young/Hoffhines

Hickson-Bender Photography

a   b   c

FIGURE 10-6. Calcium (a) has properties characteristic of metals. Silicon (b) is a metalloid. Sulfur (c) is a nonmetal.

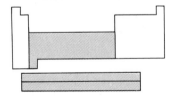

The elements of Groups IB through VIIIB are called the *transition elements.* Since all atoms of transition elements have one or two electrons in the outer level, they all show metallic properties. The elements 57 through 70, and 89 through 102 have a similar characteristic. These atoms have two electrons in the outer level as predicted and are therefore classified as metals.

The elements of Groups IIIA through VA include both metals and nonmetals. At the top of the table, each of these groups contains nonmetallic elements. The metallic character of the elements increases toward the bottom of the table, and the last member of each family is distinctly metallic.

Metallic character increases down the table.

1. a. metal

PROBLEMS

1. Classify the following elements as metals, metalloids, or nonmetals.
   a. cadmium
   b. calcium metal
   c. californium metal
   d. carbon nonmetal
   e. dysprosium metal
   f. praseodymium metal
   g. thallium metal

2. Are there more <u>metals</u> or nonmetals in the periodic table?

10:10 REVIEW: PERIODIC TABLE

We can now look at the periodic table as a whole. Metals are located on the left and nonmetals on the right. Note again that most of the elements are metallic; that is, their atoms contain one, two, or three electrons in the outer energy level. The most stable atoms are those of the noble gases.

Covalent and ionic bonds are discussed in Chapter 12. It would probably be advisable to avoid consideration of bond formation in this chapter. Concentrate instead on the properties of atoms as a function of their structure.

IA																	VIIIA
	H	IIA		metals				nonmetals					VIA	VIIA		He	
He	Li	Be									B	C	N	O	F	Ne	
Ne	Na	Mg				"B" groups					Al	Si	P	S	Cl	Ar	
Ar	K	Ca	Sc	Ti	V	Cr	Mn	Fe	Co	Ni	Cu	Zn	Ga	Ge	As	Se	Br	Kr
Kr	Rb	Sr	Y	Zr	Nb	Mo	Tc	Ru	Rh	Pd	Ag	Cd	In	Sn	Sb	Te	I	Xe
Xe	Cs	Ba	Lu	Hf	Ta	W	Re	Os	Ir	Pt	Au	Hg	Tl	Pb	Bi	Po	At	Rn
Rn	Fr	Ra	Lr	Rf	Ha												

La	Ce	Pr	Nd	Pm	Sm	Eu	Gd	Tb	Dy	Ho	Er	Tm	Yb
Ac	Th	Pa	U	Np	Pu	Am	Cm	Bk	Cf	Es	Fm	Md	No

FIGURE 10-7. Metal ions have stable outer levels which are of the same configuration as the noble gas to the left. Nonmetal ions have stable outer levels with the same configuration as the noble gas to the right.

As you look at the periodic table from top to bottom each period represents a new, higher principal quantum number. *As the principal quantum number increases, the size of the electron cloud increases.* Therefore, the size of atoms in each group increases as you look down the table. Chemists discuss the size of atoms by referring to their radii. As you look across the periodic table, all the atoms in a period have the same principal quantum number. However, the positive charge on the nucleus increases by one proton for each element. As a result, the outer electron cloud is pulled in a little tighter. Consequently, atoms generally decrease slightly in size from left to right across a period of the table. In summary, *atomic radii increase top to bottom and right to left in the periodic table.* If you look at Table 10-9 you can see the general trends and the few exceptions to the rule.

Atomic size increases down a group.

In general, atomic size decreases from left to right across a period.

10:11 SODIUM ATOMS AND CHLORINE ATOMS

Sodium and chlorine are located at opposite ends of the third period. Sodium is found at the left side of the table and is a metal. Chlorine is on the right side of the table in Column VIIA and is a nonmetal.

The variation in atomic and ionic radii can be explained in terms of:
1. Shielding effect
2. Distance of outer electrons from the nucleus
3. Size of nuclear charge

Table 10-9
Atomic and Ionic Radii
(in nanometers)

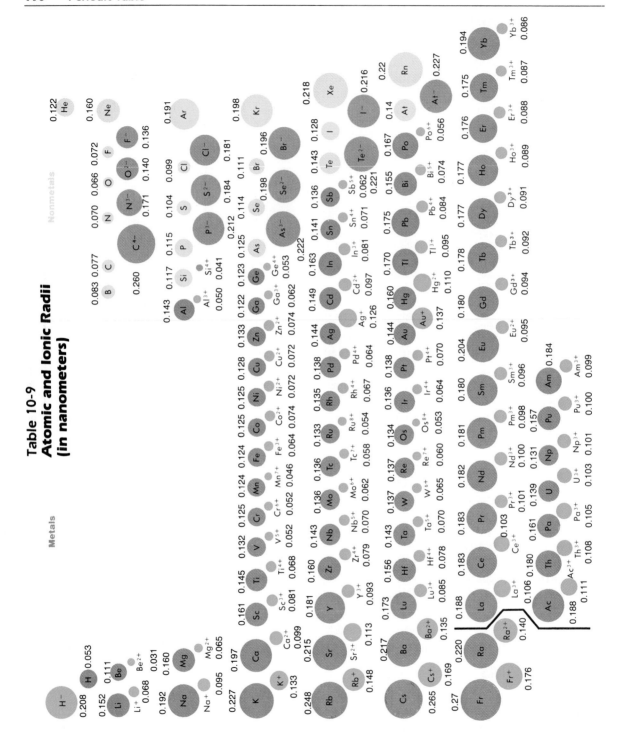

Both sodium and chlorine have partially filled third levels. The outer electrons which take part in reactions are separated from the positively charged nucleus by two inner energy levels. These two inner levels are filled (ten electrons). The chlorine nucleus contains seventeen protons; the sodium nucleus contains only eleven protons. The outer electrons of the chlorine atom are attracted by six more protons than are the outer electrons of the sodium atom. Therefore, the chlorine electrons are held more tightly, and the chlorine atom is smaller than the sodium atom. These two atoms, follow the general rule developed in Section 10:10.

The chlorine atom is smaller than the sodium atom.

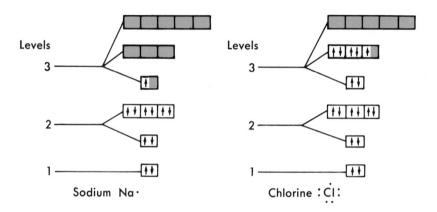

FIGURE 10-8. The orbital filling diagrams for sodium and chlorine show they have partially filled outer levels.

10:12   SODIUM IONS AND CHLORIDE IONS

In general, when atoms unite to form molecules or compounds, their structures become more stable. Sodium and chlorine form the compound sodium chloride, or common table salt. The sodium atom holds its single outer $3s$ electron loosely. When chlorine and sodium react, the more positive chlorine nucleus removes the outer electron from the sodium atom. The sodium ion has eleven protons, but only ten electrons, so it has a $1+$ charge. Since the positively charged nucleus is now attracting fewer electrons, the sodium ion is smaller than the sodium atom. The sodium ion is stable because its new outer level ($2s^2 2p^6$) is the same as the outer level of the stable noble gas, neon.

The sodium ion is smaller than the sodium atom.

The configuration of Na^+ is similar to neon.

The chlorine atom has gained an electron. The seventeen protons in its nucleus are now attracting eighteen electrons. The chloride ion thus has a $1-$ charge. Also, the chloride ion is larger than the chlorine atom. The ion is stable because it has the same outer level configuration as the noble gas, argon.

The configuration of Cl^- is similar to argon.

The chloride ion is larger than the chlorine atom.

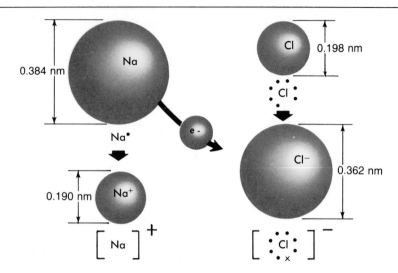

FIGURE 10-9. The sodium ion is smaller than the sodium atom because 11 protons are attracting only 10 electrons in the ion. The chlorine ion is larger than the chlorine atom because 17 protons are attracting 18 electrons in the ion. The chlorine atom is smaller than the sodium atom because the electrons in the outer energy level of chlorine are attracted by 6 more protons than in sodium.

Ions which are free to move can conduct an electric current.

The compound formed from sodium ions and chloride ions does not consist of sodium chloride molecules. Instead, each cube of sodium chloride is a collection of equal numbers of Na^+ and Cl^- ions. When salt is dissolved or melted, it will carry a current since the ions are free to move. However, a solid salt crystal will not carry an electric current because the individual ions are tightly bound. The mobility of electric charge completes a circuit. Thus, the substance is able to conduct a current.

We have noted that the sodium ion is smaller than the sodium atom. The magnesium ion is even smaller than its atom. In losing two outer electrons, the unbalanced nuclear positive charge is larger than the negative charge on the electron cloud. The cloud shrinks in size. The nonmetals, sulfur and chlorine, form ions

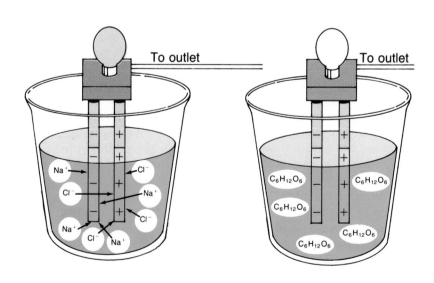

FIGURE 10-10. When salt dissolves, the ions are free to move. Thus, salt conducts an electric current. A molecular substance such as sugar does not conduct since there are no ions in solution.

which are larger than their respective atoms. These elements gain electrons to form ions. The elements silicon and phosphorus do not gain or lose electrons readily. They tend to form compounds by sharing their outer electrons.

We can now look at some trends which will apply to any row of the periodic table. In general, *metallic ions, on the left and in the center of the table, are formed by the loss of electrons. They are smaller than the atoms from which they are formed. Non-metallic ions are located on the right side of the table, they are formed by the gain of electrons and are larger than the atoms from which they are formed.* The metallic ions have a stable outer level which resembles the noble gas at the end of the preceding period. Nonmetallic ions have an outer level resembling the noble gas to the right in the same period.

Metallic atoms lose electrons to form smaller ions.

Nonmetallic atoms gain electrons to form larger ions.

PROBLEMS

3. From each of the following pairs of particles, select the particle which is larger in radius.

   a. He, Ne
   b. Be, B
   c. N, N^{3-}
   d. Al, Al^{3+}
   e. P, As
   f. S, Br
   g. K, Ca
   h. Se, Se^{2-}
   i. Sc, Sc^{3+}

4. State the reasons for your answers to Problems 3b, e, and g.

3. a. Ne

10:13 PREDICTING OXIDATION NUMBERS

Those electrons which are involved in the reaction of atoms with each other are the outer and highest energy electrons. You now know about electron configurations and the stability of atoms with noble gas structures. Thus, it is possible for you to predict what oxidation numbers atoms will have.

Oxidation numbers can be predicted from electron configurations.

Consider the metals in Group IA. Each atom has one electron in its outer level. The loss of this one electron will give these metals the same configuration as a noble gas. Group IA metals have an oxidation number of 1+. Note that the hydrogen atom could attain the helium configuration by gaining one electron. If this change occurred, we would say that hydrogen has a 1− oxidation number. Hydrogen does indeed exhibit a 1− oxidation number in some compounds. In Group IIA we would expect the loss of the two *s* electrons for the atom to achieve the same configuration as the prior noble gas. That loss leads to a prediction of 2+ oxidation number for the alkaline earth metals. These two columns exhibit the oxidation numbers predicted for them.

Inform students that our knowledge about scandium and other elements comes from actual observation and does not always follow patterns or rules.

Beginning with Group IIIB, we have atoms in which the highest energy electrons are not in the outer level. For instance, scandium has the configuration $1s^2 2s^2 2p^6 3s^2 3p^6 4s^2 3d^1$. Scandium's outer level is the fourth level containing two electrons. Its highest energy electron, however, is the one in the $3d$ sublevel. For the transition elements, it is possible to lose not only the outer level electrons, but also some lower level electrons. The transition elements exhibit oxidation numbers varying from 2+ (representing loss of the two outer s electrons) up to 7+. We would predict scandium to show only 2+ and 3+ oxidation numbers. In actual practice, the element shows only the 3+ oxidation number. Titanium, which has one more $3d$ electron than scandium, should show 2+, 3+, and 4+, and it does. As we continue across the fourth row, vanadium has a maximum oxidation number of 5+, chromium 6+, and manganese 7+. Iron, which has the configuration $1s^2 2s^2 2p^6 3s^2 3p^6 4s^2 3d^6$, has only 2+ and 3+ oxidation numbers. Recall that an atom with a half-full sublevel represents a particularly stable configuration. To take iron higher than 3+ would mean breaking up a half-full $3d$ sublevel.

Group IIIA elements lose three electrons and have an oxidation number of 3+. Thallium, in addition to the 3+ oxidation number, exhibits a 1+ oxidation number. If we look at its configuration, we can understand why. The thallium configuration ends $6s^2 4f^{14} 5d^{10} 6p^1$. The large energy difference between the $6s$ and the $6p$ electrons, makes it possible to lose only the $6p$ electron. That loss leads to an oxidation number of 1+. If stronger reaction methods are used, thallium also has an oxidation number of 3+. For the same reason, tin and lead in Group IVA may have a 2+ or 4+ oxidation number.

In Groups VA, VIA, and VIIA, there is a general tendency to gain electrons to complete the octet. The outside level is already more than half filled. These elements show oxidation numbers of 3− (Group VA), 2− (Group VIA), and 1− (Group VIIA). It is also possible for these elements to lose electrons and have positive oxidation numbers. The tendency to lose electrons increases as we move down a column. This tendency will be discussed in more detail later.

Metals	
Group	Oxidation Number
IA	1+
IIA	2+
Transition (B Groups)	tend to have more than one
IIIA	3+
IVA	2+ or 4+

Nonmetals	
Group	Oxidation Number
VA	3−
VIA	2−
VIIA	1−

PROBLEMS

5. Gd 2+
  Ra 2+
  Nb 3+, 4+, 5+
6. 3+, d sublevel is half-filled

5. Predict the oxidation numbers for gadolinium, radium, and niobium.

6. Would you predict iron to be more stable at the 2+ or 3+ oxidation state? Provide a reason for your answer.

Henry Gwyn-Jeffreys Moseley (1887–1915)

Henry Moseley was the first to discover a definite way of determining the atomic numbers of the elements. He accomplished this task by using different metals as targets in an X-ray tube. His research enabled scientists to determine the atomic number of elements which were unknown at the time and to correct the order in Mendeleev's periodic table.

As a teacher at the University of Manchester, Moseley also spent time investigating radioactivity. His efforts in this field were halted, however, when the British government sent him to serve as an ordinary foot soldier in the First World War. He was killed in the fighting in Gallipoli at the age of 28. Because of this loss, the British government later restricted its scientists to noncombatant duties during World War II.

CHEMICAL CAREER: Analytical Chemists

Analytical chemists are concerned chiefly with identifying the substances present in a material and in what proportions they occur. Quality control is one of the jobs performed by analytical chemists. Chemical processes must be checked each step of the way to ensure that the process is proceeding properly. The product must be analyzed to see that governmental and industrial standards are met.

Some analytical chemists devote their efforts to research in two areas. One area is the characterization of substances never before analyzed. The other area of research is the development of new techniques, methods, and procedures in analysis. This area also includes the development of new instrumentation for analysis. One problem which arises in setting standards of purity for commercial products is the result of the recent improvement in analytical procedures and equipment. Analytical chemists can now detect the presence of substances at extremely low concentrations. Unfortunately, no one knows the actual effects of some substances. Consequently, it is difficult to decide whether a substance should be banned at the 0.000 000 1% level if it is toxic at 1%.

Analytical chemists may also investigate the chemical and physical properties of substances. These investigations may involve the determination of the molecular or ionic structure of a substance. Structure and property determinations usually require the use of many instruments, many of which you will study throughout this book. Many analytical devices are controlled by microcomputer. The analytical chemist must have a knowledge of computer programming and operation to use these devices effectively.

FIGURE 10-11. The analytical chemist must have an in-depth knowledge of analytical methods to interpret data.

Courtesy of Milliken & Company

SUMMARY

1. There have been many attempts to classify the elements in a systematic manner. These attempts include Dobereiner's triads, Newlands' law of octaves, and Mendeleev's and Meyer's tables. 10:1–10:2

2. The modern periodic law states: The properties of the elements are a periodic function of their atomic numbers. 10:3

3. Today's periodic table is based on the electron configurations of atoms. All elements in a horizontal line of the table are called a period; all elements in a vertical line are called a group or family. 10:4–10:8

4. The most stable atoms, the noble gases, have eight electrons in the outer level. Helium atoms are stable with two electrons in the outer level. 10:7

5. Full and half-full sublevels represent atoms in states of special stability. 10:8

6. Elements with one, two, or three electrons in the outer level tend to be metals. Elements with five, six, seven, or eight outer electrons tend to be nonmetals. 10:9

7. The periodic table, together with the octet rule, may be used to predict oxidation numbers. 10:13

PROBLEMS

7. Classify the following elements as metals or nonmetals.
   a. chromium metal
   b. fluorine nonmetal
   c. gold metal
   d. helium nonmetal
   e. iron metal
   f. neodymium metal
   g. nitrogen nonmetal
   h. tantalum metal
   i. hydrogen nonmetal
   j. lithium metal
   k. phosphorus nonmetal
   l. silicon nonmetal

8. What happens to the size of the atoms as you move from left to right across a horizontal row of the periodic table? decrease

9. What happens to the size of the atoms as you move from the top to the bottom of a column of the periodic table? increase

10. How does the size of a positive ion compare to the size of the atom from which it was formed? smaller

11. How does the size of a negative ion compare to the size of the atom from which it was formed? larger

12. Predict the oxidation numbers for the following elements.
   a. arsenic 3+, 5+
   b. gadolinium 2+
   c. phosphorus 3+, 5+ 3−
   d. tellurium 2−, 4+, 6+
   e. cadmium 2+
   f. vanadium $^{2+,3+,4+,}_{5+}$
   g. strontium 2+
   h. cesium 1+
   i. copper 1+, 2+

13. Element X has the following electron configuration
$$1s^2 2s^2 2p^6 3s^2 3p^6 4s^2 3d^{10} 4p^4$$
   a. Locate its position on the periodic table. selenium no. 34
   b. To what group and to what period does this element belong? VIA, 4
   c. Classify the element as a metal, nonmetal, or metalloid. nonmetal
   d. List the properties associated with the classification you chose. hard, brittle
   e. Predict the oxidation number of the element. 2−
   f. Draw the electron dot diagram for an atom of Element X. Draw the electron dot diagram for an ion of Element X. $\cdot\ddot{Se}\!:, \;\; :\ddot{Se}\!:$
   g. How does the size of an atom of Element X compare to that of an ion of Element X? smaller

14. The positions of some elements are highlighted on the periodic table Figure 10-12, page 198. For each element highlighted answer the following.
   a. To what group and what period does this element belong?
   b. Classify the element as a metal, nonmetal, or metalloid.
   c. List the properties this element should exhibit based on the classification you chose in **b**.
   d. Write the electron configuration of the element.

e. Predict the oxidation number of the element.

f. Draw the electron dot diagram for both an atom and an ion of this element.

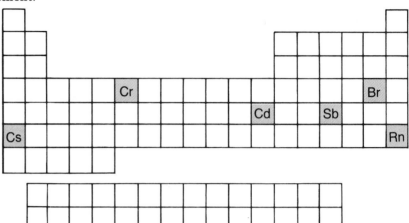

FIGURE 10-12. Use with Problem 14.

REVIEW

frequency, wavelength, velocity, amplitude

n = cloud size

l = cloud shape

m = cloud spatial orientation

s = electron spin

Schrödinger considered electron as a wave, Bohr as a particle.

1. What are the four characteristics of waves that we have studied?

2. How does Schrödinger's analysis of the atom differ from that of Bohr?

3. What are the four quantum numbers associated with each electron in an atom? What does each represent in terms of energy? In terms of the electron cloud? *n* represents energy level *l*, sublevel *m* and *s* have no effect on energy

4. Write the electron configurations and draw electron dot diagrams for the following elements.

   a. Al ($Z = 13$)   d. Ti ($Z = 22$)   g. Co ($Z = 27$)

   b. S ($Z = 16$)   e. V ($Z = 23$)   h. Ge ($Z = 32$)

   c. Ca ($Z = 20$)   f. Mn ($Z = 25$)   i. Br ($Z = 35$)

h = Planck's constant

m = mass   *v* = velocity

λ = wavelength

5. Explain the meaning of each symbol in the de Broglie equation.

6. Compute the atomic mass of tungsten if its isotopes occur as follows. 1.14% 179.9467, 26.41% 181.948 25, 14.40% 182.950 27, 30.64% 183.950 97, and 28.41% 185.954 40. 185.64 amu

7. How many significant digits are in the measurement 26°C? 2

8. What is the relative precision of the measurement 10.14 g if the balance is accurate to 0.01 g? 0.09%

9. What volume is occupied by 42.5 g of a substance of density 3.15 g/cm³? 13.5 cm³

10. Write formulas for the following compounds.

   a. zinc phosphide Zn_3P_2 c. aluminum fluoride AlF_3

   b. zirconium(IV) selenate $Zr(SeO_4)_2$ d. bismuth(III) chloride $BiCl_3$

11. Write names for the following compounds.

   a. $ZnC_4H_4O_6$ zinc tartrate   c. $Cr(C_2H_3O_2)_3$ chromium(III) acetate

   b. PbSe lead(II) selenide   d. Mn_3P_2 manganese(II) phosphide

12. Compute the formula mass of Sr_3N_2. 291 amu

4. a. $1s^2 2s^2 2p^6 3s^2 3p^1$ Al$\dot{:}$ d. $1s^2 2s^2 2p^6 3s^2 3p^6 4s^2 3d^2$ Ti$\dot{:}$ g. $1s^2 2s^2 2p^6 3s^2 3p^6 4s^2 3d^7$ Co$\dot{:}$

  b. $1s^2 2s^2 2p^6 3s^2 3p^4$ $\cdot\ddot{S}\!:$ e. $1s^2 2s^2 2p^6 3s^2 3p^6 4s^2 3d^3$ V$\dot{:}$ h. $1s^2 2s^2 2p^6 3s^2 3p^6 4s^2 3d^{10}4p^2$ $\cdot$Ge$\dot{:}$

  c. $1s^2 2s^2 2p^6 3s^2 3p^6 4s^2$ Ca$\dot{:}$ f. $1s^2 2s^2 2p^6 3s^2 3p^6 4s^2 3d^5$ Mn$\dot{:}$ i. $1s^2 2s^2 2p^6 3s^2 3p^6 4s^2 3d^{10}4p^5$ $\!:$Br$\dot{:}$

13. What is the mass of 3.00 mol $Zn_3(PO_4)_2$?

14. How would you prepare 10.0 cm³ of a 0.100M solution of $ZrCl_4$? dissolve 0.233 g in enough H_2O to make 10 cm³ of solution

15. Find the percentage composition of $Co(C_2H_3O_2)_2$. 33.3%, 27.1%, 3.42%, 36.2%

16. What is the empirical formula for a compound with the following composition: 40.1% Co, 16.3% C, and 43.5% O? CoC_2O_4

17. What is the molecular formula for a compound with empirical formula BiC_3O_6 and molecular mass 682? $Bi_2C_6O_{12}$

18. What is the formula for a hydrate which is 66.3% $Ga_2(SeO_4)_3$ and 33.7% H_2O? $Ga_2(SeO_4)_3 \cdot 16H_2O$

19. Balance the following equation.
$$Cr(NO_3)_3 + NaOH \rightarrow Cr(OH)_3 + NaNO_3 \quad Cr(NO_3)_3 + 3NaOH \rightarrow Cr(OH)_3 + 3NaNO_3$$

20. What mass of silver nitrate will react with 2.37 g NaOH?
$$2AgNO_3 + 2NaOH \rightarrow Ag_2O + 2NaNO_3 + H_2O \quad 10.1 \text{ g}$$

21. How much energy is needed to heat 5.24 g of Ru from 25°C to 2020°C? 2490 J

22. Compute ΔH for the reaction
$$Zn + H_2SO_4 \rightarrow ZnSO_4 + H_2$$

23. How many electrons, neutrons, and protons are found in oxygen of mass number 16? 8, 8, 8

ONE MORE STEP

1. Make a chart showing the history of the classification of elements. Include date, person, and contribution.

2. Mendeleev made predictions about five elements in addition to germanium. Find out what these elements were and how accurate his predictions were.

3. Explain why the following elements do not follow the diagonal rule for electron configurations: molybdenum, palladium, and gadolinium.

4. Explain the deviations from the diagonal rule for the electron configurations of gold, curium, and thorium.

5. Predict possible oxidation numbers for the following elements and state your evidence: argon, europium, aluminum, antimony, and bromine. Check the actual oxidation numbers and explain any deviations from your predictions.

6. Predict possible oxidation numbers for the following and state your evidence: uranium, sodium, silicon, cerium, and cobalt. Check the actual oxidation numbers and explain any deviations.

7. The names of the elements have an interesting history. Develop a table showing how each name was derived.

8. What property of metalloids has led to their use in transistors? Metalloids are semiconductors.

READING

Seaborg, Glenn T., "Charting the New Elements." *SciQuest*, Vol. 53, No. 8 (October 1980), pp. 7-11.

An artist specializes in a knowledge of color and design. A chemist specializes in the properties and structure of matter. One characteristic property of the transition metals is their ability to form colored compounds. You may have heard the terms cobalt blue or cadmium yellow to describe the color of an object. These pigments are used in many paints. They are actually transition metal compounds. What causes color in these compounds? How is color related to the electron structure of a metal? What are some of the characteristic properties of the other element groups?

Linda Young

PERIODIC PROPERTIES

11

Chapter 11 concerns how properties can be predicted after looking at the periodic nature of the elements in groups and periods.

Demonstration—Show the trend in solubility for Group II by dissolving 3 g of $MgSO_4$, $CaSO_4$, and $BaSO_4$ each in 25 cm^3 of water in separate test tubes (25 × 250 mm). Ask students how trends in properties such as solubility can be used to predict the solubility of other elements in Group II.

We can see the periodic nature of the elements in groups as well as in periods of the table. The elements in the first group-hydrogen through francium all contain one s electron in the outer level. A group is often called a **family** because of the similarity of the elements within it. Some families have a common name. We have already mentioned the alkali metal family and the halogen family. The members of a family have a similar arrangement of outer electrons and thus tend to react similarly. For instance, lithium, sodium, and potassium all lose one electron to chlorine and form chlorides (LiCl, NaCl, KCl). Hydrogen is also found in this group. It forms a chloride, hydrogen chloride. Let us take a closer look at some elements. From studying the properties of a few, we can predict the properties of many more.

GOAL: You will expand your knowledge of the periodic table by looking at similarities and differences among elements in various families.

Members of a chemical family (group) react similarly.

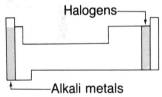

Hydrogen is generally considered a "family" by itself.

11:1 HYDROGEN

Hydrogen, like the alkali metals, has only one outer electron. Because of its unique properties, it is usually considered as a family by itself. There are four ways in which the hydrogen atom can react. It may lose its one electron to become a positive hydrogen ion. A positive hydrogen ion is simply a bare proton. Remember from Section 8:10 that a proton is about one trillionth the size of an atom. Because of its small size, the hydrogen ion has some unique characteristics. These characteristics will be considered in studying hydrogen bonding and acids later in this text.

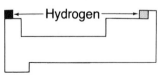

The second way a hydrogen atom can react is by sharing its single outer electron. Most nonmetals react with hydrogen to form compounds involving shared electrons. Examples of these compounds are HCl and H_2O. These compounds and their formation will be studied in more detail in Chapter 13.

The third way hydrogen can react is to gain an electron. When this change occurs, the atom becomes a **hydride ion,** H^-. Such a reaction can take place only between hydrogen and atoms of elements which give up electrons easily. The most reactive metals, Groups IA and IIA, form ionic hydrides. In these compounds, the radius of the hydride ion averages about 0.142 nm. From Table 10-7 we can see that the hydride ion is larger than the fluoride ion. Such a radius indicates that the single proton of the hydride ion has a very weak hold on the two electrons. We would expect, then, that the ionic hydrides would not be highly stable. Experiment confirms this conclusion. Ionic hydrides are found to be quite reactive compounds. By sharing or gaining electrons, hydrogen attains the stable outer level configuration of helium. Hydrogen gas is used in the manufacture of other chemicals such as ammonia and methanol. One interesting use is the conversion of a vegetable oil such as corn oil into shortening, or oleo margarine. The reaction which takes place involves the addition (Chapter 30) of hydrogen atoms to double bonds (Chapter 13) in the oil molecules.

Hydrogen reacts in four different ways.
1. *by losing an electron*
2. *by sharing an electron*
3. *by gaining an electron*
4. *by forming bridges with hydrogen atoms*

FIGURE 11-1. This experimental vehicle is powered by hydrogen released from a storage battery (a). The metal hydride fuel (b) contains a number of cracks where the metal surface has reacted with hydrogen.

a

Photo Courtesy of the Billings Corp.

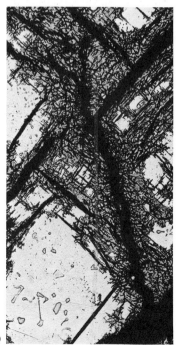

b

G. D. Sandrock/Inco Research & Development Center, Inc.

A fourth type of bonding involves the formation of bridges between two atoms by hydrogen atoms. The best examples of these compounds are found with the element boron and some of the transition metals. A study of such compounds is beyond the scope of this book. Since they are not common compounds, their behavior is only a small fraction of the chemistry of hydrogen.

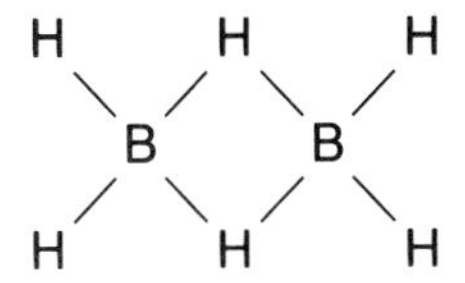

FIGURE 11-2. Hydrogen acts as a bridge between boron atoms. Compounds, such as the one shown, are discussed in detail on page 269.

11:2 ALKALI METALS

The metals in Group IA are reactive. If one member of a family forms a compound with an element or ion, we can predict that the other members will do the same. However, the members of a family are not the same in every way. The outer electron of lithium occupies a volume closer to the nucleus than the outer electron of sodium. The sodium atom has many more electrons between the outer electron and the nucleus than lithium. An increasing number of electrons between the outer level and the nucleus has a **shielding effect.** This effect blocks the attraction of the nucleus for the outer electrons. Larger atoms tend to lose their outer electrons more readily. This tendency is due to the increased distance of the electrons from the nucleus as well as the shielding effect.

Alkali metals are the Group IA elements.

The shielding effect occurs when electrons between the outer level and the nucleus partially block the nuclear attraction for the outer level electrons.

FIGURE 11-3. Increasing the number of energy levels between the outer level and the nucleus results in the shielding effect. Therefore, cesium loses its outer electron more readily than the other members of Group I.

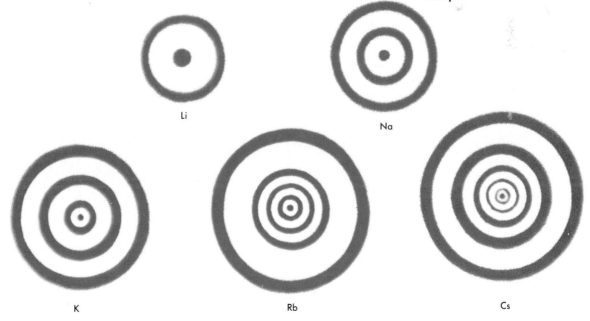

Li

Na

K

Rb

Cs

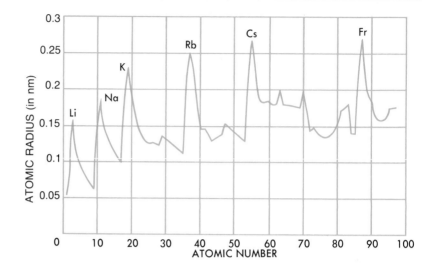

FIGURE 11-4. The peaks in the graph show that atomic radius is a periodic property.

As the atomic numbers of the alkali metals increase
1. the atoms become larger
2. the outer electron is farther from the nucleus
3. the lower level electrons shield the effect of the larger nucleus
4. the outer electrons are held less tightly
5. the atoms become more active.

As the atoms of the alkali metals increase in size, the nucleus increases in positive charge. However, the force of the increased positive charge is more than offset by the outer electron's distance from the nucleus and the shielding effect. As a result, we find that the alkali metals lose their outer electrons more readily as we proceed down the group. This trend indicates that the most active metal would be francium, which is in the lower left corner of the periodic table.

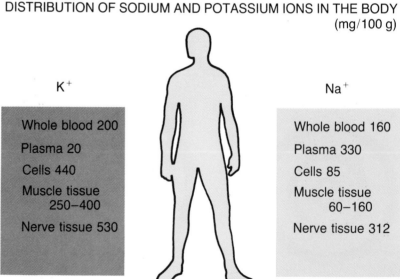

DISTRIBUTION OF SODIUM AND POTASSIUM IONS IN THE BODY
(mg/100 g)

K^+

Whole blood 200

Plasma 20

Cells 440

Muscle tissue
250–400

Nerve tissue 530

Na^+

Whole blood 160

Plasma 330

Cells 85

Muscle tissue
60–160

Nerve tissue 312

FIGURE 11-5. The biological importance of sodium and potassium are highlighted by showing their average concentrations throughout the body. Maintaining these levels is essential to proper body function.

Sodium and potassium ions are important biologically. The ratio of their concentrations in the body is vital to the transmission of nerve impulses.

Na^+ and K^+ ion concentrations are vital to nerve impulse transmission.

Sodium compounds are among the most important in the chemical industry. Millions of tons of sodium hydroxide are consumed each year in producing other chemicals, paper, and petroleum products. Sodium carbonate is also produced in millions of tons and used in manufacturing glass and other chemicals. Sodium sulfate is another substance used in manufacturing glass as well as paper and detergents. Sodium silicate is widely used as a catalyst in addition to being consumed in making soaps, detergents, paper, and pigments. A **catalyst** speeds up a reaction. Sodium tripolyphosphate ($Na_5P_3O_{10}$) is used as a food additive, in softening water, and in making detergents.

Sodium compounds are used as catalysts and in the production of paper, glass, detergents, soaps, pigments, and petroleum products.

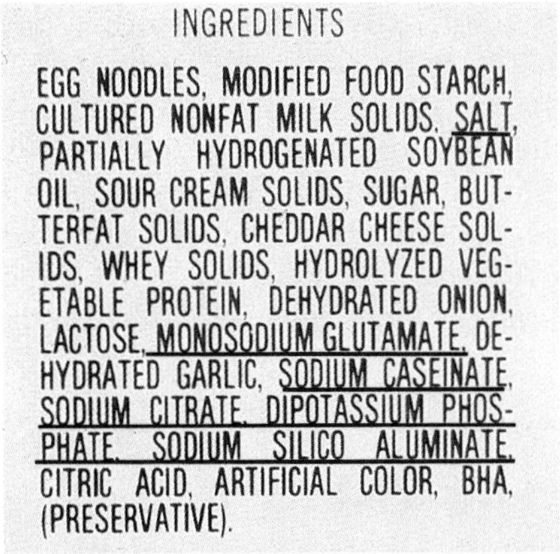
INGREDIENTS
EGG NOODLES, MODIFIED FOOD STARCH, CULTURED NONFAT MILK SOLIDS, SALT, PARTIALLY HYDROGENATED SOYBEAN OIL, SOUR CREAM SOLIDS, SUGAR, BUTTERFAT SOLIDS, CHEDDAR CHEESE SOLIDS, WHEY SOLIDS, HYDROLYZED VEGETABLE PROTEIN, DEHYDRATED ONION, LACTOSE, MONOSODIUM GLUTAMATE, DEHYDRATED GARLIC, SODIUM CASEINATE, SODIUM CITRATE, DIPOTASSIUM PHOSPHATE, SODIUM SILICO ALUMINATE, CITRIC ACID, ARTIFICIAL COLOR, BHA, (PRESERVATIVE).

a

Janet Adams

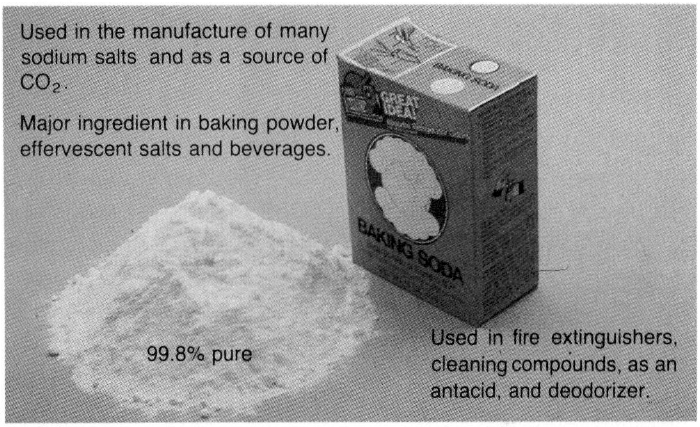
Used in the manufacture of many sodium salts and as a source of CO2.
Major ingredient in baking powder, effervescent salts and beverages.
BAKING SODA
99.8% pure
Used in fire extinguishers, cleaning compounds, as an antacid, and deodorizer.

b

Janet Adams

FIGURE 11-6. Many sodium and potassium compounds are used as food additives (a). Sodium hydrogen carbonate has a variety of everyday uses (b).

There are two other 1+ ions which, because of their size, behave in a similar fashion to the alkali ions. These are the ammonium ion (NH_4^+) and the thallium(I) ion (Tl^+). Their compounds follow much the same patterns as the alkali metal compounds.

11:3 LITHIUM

The reactions of the alkali metals involve mainly the formation of 1+ ions. In general, the reactivity increases with increasing atomic number, with an exception. Lithium reacts more vigorously with nitrogen than any other alkali metal. Lithium is exceptional in other ways, too. Its ion has the same charge as the other alkali metals, but the unusual behavior is due to its smaller size. The ratio of charge to radius is often a good indication of the behavior of an ion. The charge/radius ratio of lithium more closely resembles the magnesium ion (Mg^{2+}) of Group IIA. Its behavior

Charge to radius ratio is a good indicator of ion behavior.

Lithium exhibits a diagonal relationship. The lithium ion reacts similarly to the Mg^{2+} ion.

resembles Mg^{2+} more closely than the next member of its own family, sodium (Na^+). This diagonal relationship is not unusual among the lighter elements. One example of this relationship is that lithium burns in air to form the oxide, Li_2O, as does magnesium to form MgO. The other alkali metals form the peroxide, M_2O_2, or the superoxide, MO_2 (where $M =$ Na, K, Rb or Cs). Another example of this relationship concerns the solubilities of compounds. The solubility of lithium compounds is similar to that of magnesium compounds, but not to that of sodium compounds.

Solubility of Li compounds is similar to that of Mg compounds.

The lithium atom also differs from the other alkali metal atoms in some physical properties. Unlike the other alkali metals which dissolve in each other in any proportions, lithium is insoluble in all but sodium. It will dissolve in sodium only above 380°C. In other respects, lithium metal is like the other members of its family. For example, it is a soft, silvery metal with a low melting point, as are the other alkali metals except cesium which is yellow. All of the alkali metals will dissolve in liquid ammonia to give faintly blue solutions. These solutions conduct electricity.

Alkali metals form binary compounds with most nonmetals.

The alkali metals form binary compounds with almost all nonmetals. In these compounds, nonmetals are in the form of negative ions. In solution, the lithium ion, because of its high charge/radius ratio, attracts water molecules more strongly than any other alkali ion.

11:4   ALKALINE EARTH METALS

Alkaline earth metals are reactive and form the 2+ ion. Most Group IIA compounds are soluble.

The alkaline earth metals are quite similar to the alkali metals except that they form the 2+ ion. Most of their compounds exist as ions and are soluble except for some hydroxides, carbonates, and sulfates. Beryllium is used in making nonsparking tools and magnesium is widely used in lightweight alloys. The other metals are too reactive to be used as free elements.

Two calcium compounds find large markets. Lime (calcium oxide) is used to make steel, cement, and heat-resistant bricks. It is also applied to soils which are too acidic to farm without treatment. Calcium chloride is used in a wide range of applications. One interesting use is in controlling road conditions through de-icing in the winter and keeping down dust in the summer.

11:5   ALUMINUM

Aluminum has 3 outer electrons which it tends to share.

Aluminum is the only metal of practical importance in Group IIIA. With three electrons in the outer level, it is less metallic than the elements of Groups IA and IIA. For instance, in forming compounds it tends to share electrons rather than form ions. It is also less reactive than Group IA and IIA metals. Large quantities of aluminum are consumed each year in producing lightweight alloys to make everything from soda cans to aircraft. Aluminum sulfate finds applications in water purification, paper manufacture, and fabric dyeing.

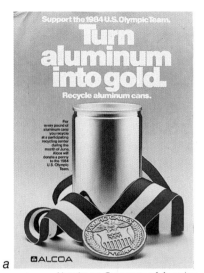

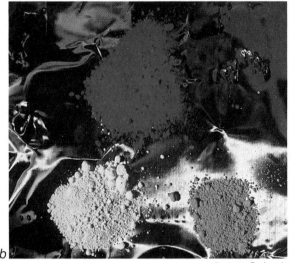

a Aluminum Company of America

b Barbara Probstein

FIGURE 11-7. Aluminum products are being recycled as a conservation measure (a). "Aluminum lake" compounds are complex organic substances used extensively as colorants in the food industry.

11:6 GROUP IVA

The elements of Group IVA have atoms with four electrons in the outer level. These elements generally react by sharing electrons. However, the tendency to lose electrons increases as atomic number of Group IVA elements increases. There are a few compounds in which carbon in the form of a **carbide ion** (C^{4-}) can be considered to exist. Silicon, the next member of this family, although nonmetallic, does not form 4− ions under any conditions. However, there are compounds in which silicon exists as a 4+ ion.

Group IVA members generally react by sharing electrons.

The major part of carbon chemistry is classed as organic chemistry. Carbon itself, carbonic acid and its salts, carbides, cyanides, and the oxides and sulfides of carbon are considered **inorganic.** Most **organic compounds** involve sharing electrons between a carbon atom and one or more other carbon atoms. The tendency to form "chains" of similar atoms is called **catenation** (kat uh NAY shuhn). Only carbon exhibits catenation to any great extent.

Organic chemistry: The chemistry of carbon.

Catenation: The tendency to form "chains" of similar atoms.

Carbon is found in nature in two different molecular forms— diamond and graphite. In diamond, each carbon atom shares electrons with the four nearest carbon atoms. In graphite, the sharing is to the nearest three carbon atoms. The difference in structure results in different properties for these two forms of carbon. We will study these differences in Chapter 16. Different forms of the same element are called **allotropes.**

Different forms of the same element are called allotropes.

$$CH_3-CH_2-CH_2-CH_2-CH_2-CH_2-CH_2-CH_2-CH=CH-CH_2-CH_2-CH_2-CH_2-CH_2-CH_2-CH_2-C\overset{\displaystyle O}{\underset{\displaystyle OH}{}}$$

Oleic acid

FIGURE 11-8. Carbon compounds exhibit catenation as shown by the structure for oleic acid. Silicon also exhibits this property as shown by the structure of this methyl silicon polymer.

$$\cdots-\underset{\underset{CH_3}{|}}{\overset{\overset{CH_3}{|}}{Si}}-O-\underset{\underset{CH_3}{|}}{\overset{\overset{CH_3}{|}}{Si}}-O-\underset{\underset{CH_3}{|}}{\overset{\overset{CH_3}{|}}{Si}}-O-\underset{\underset{CH_3}{|}}{\overset{\overset{CH_3}{|}}{Si}}-O-\underset{\underset{CH_3}{|}}{\overset{\overset{CH_3}{|}}{Si}}-O-\underset{\underset{CH_3}{|}}{\overset{\overset{CH_3}{|}}{Si}}-C-\cdots$$

Methyl silicon polymer chain

Industrially, carbon is used in a form called "carbon black" made by burning natural gas or other fuel. Carbon black is often referred to as "soot" when it has accumulated in a place where it is unwanted. It is actually a microcrystalline form of graphite, and is used as a black pigment and wear-resistant additive in rubber tires. Carbon dioxide gas is a by-product of several chemical processes. It is collected, compressed, and sold as a liquid in steel cylinders. Customers use it for refrigeration, carbonating beverages, and producing other chemicals.

Silicon shows only a slight tendency toward catenation, much less so than carbon. However, the chemistry of silicon, like that of carbon, is characterized by electron sharing. Silicon is

FIGURE 11-9. Natural latex is a white liquid (a). Graphite is added as a colorant to latex in making rubber tires (b). Carbonated beverages are solutions of CO_2 gas in liquid. The CO_2 tanks in a vending machine must be replaced periodically (c).

a

b

c

George Linyear

Janet Adams

the second most plentiful element in the earth's crust. (Oxygen is the most plentiful.) It is found in a large number of minerals.

Silicon is bound to oxygen atoms in a variety of ways. In these compounds, called silicates, each silicon atom is surrounded by four oxygen atoms with which it shares electrons. Transistors, computer chips, and synthetic motor oils are three developments of silicon chemistry. Carbon and silicon differ more than any other two vertically neighboring elements in the periodic table.

Transistors are discussed more fully in Section 16:11.

Carbon and silicon differ more than other vertically neighboring elements.

a Smithsonian Institution *b* Dan McCoy/Rainbow

Tin and lead are distinctly metallic members of Group IVA. They are quite similar except that for tin the 4+ state is more stable than the 2+ while the reverse is true for lead. These two metals are easily produced from their ores and have both been known since early times. In general, their uses are based on their lack of chemical reactivity. They are common components of alloys which are mixtures of metals. Examples of alloys are solder, which contains lead and tin, and bronze, which contains copper and tin.

FIGURE 11-10. Silicon is a component of the mineral quartz (a). Since it is a semiconductor, silicon is used extensively in the manufacture of computer chips (b).

Tin and lead are common components of alloys which are mixtures of metals.

11:7 NITROGEN AND PHOSPHORUS

Nitrogen and phosphorus differ quite a good deal for adjacent members of the same family. Nitrogen occurs in all oxidation states ranging from 3− through 5+; phosphorus shows only 3−, 0, 3+, and 5+. Liquid nitrogen is used to maintain very low temperatures. The unreactive gas is used to surround reactive materials which would otherwise react with oxygen in the air. Elemental nitrogen, N_2 gas, is one of the most stable substances known. Most nitrogen compounds are relatively unstable, tending to decompose to N_2. Conventional high explosives, for example, trinitrotoluene (TNT) and dynamite, utilize nitrogen compounds. Nitrogen compounds are produced naturally from atmospheric

Nitrogen and phosphorus differ greatly for being adjacent members of Group VA.

N_2 gas is one of the most stable substances known but many nitrogen compounds are relatively unstable.

nitrogen by nitrogen-fixing bacteria. These bacteria convert molecular nitrogen to a form which can be used readily by plants. This process is essential to plant life. Nitrogen compounds serve a vital function in living systems in amino acids, essential components of proteins.

CH_3 group and NO_2 substituents on a benzene ring:

$$O_2N \qquad \overset{CH_3}{\underset{NO_2}{\bigcirc}} \qquad NO_2$$

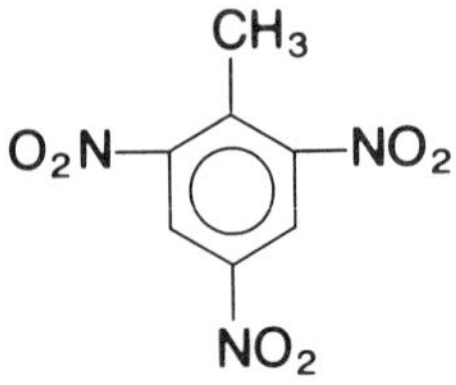

2,4,6-Trinitrotoluene
TNT

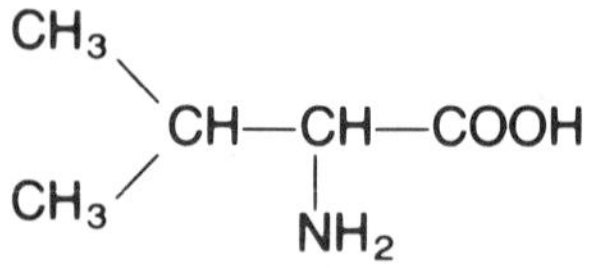

$$\overset{CH_3}{\underset{CH_3}{\diagdown}} CH—CH—COOH \\ \qquad \qquad \underset{NH_2}{|}$$

Valine
An amino acid

However, most nitrogen compounds are produced from atmospheric nitrogen by synthetic processes. Huge quantities of liquid N_2, obtained from the air, are used in the Haber Process, Section 23:9, or other similar processes to produce ammonia. The most common use for ammonia is as a fertilizer. Much of the ammonia not used directly as a fertilizer is converted to other nitrogen compounds which are themselves fertilizers. An example is ammonium nitrate, which is also used in explosives. Some ammonia is converted to nitric acid. Nitric acid itself is widely used in the manufacture of fertilizer and explosives. Large quantities of ammonium sulfate are obtained from the steel industry's conversion of coal to coke. The $(NH_4)_2SO_4$ by-product is then used as a fertilizer.

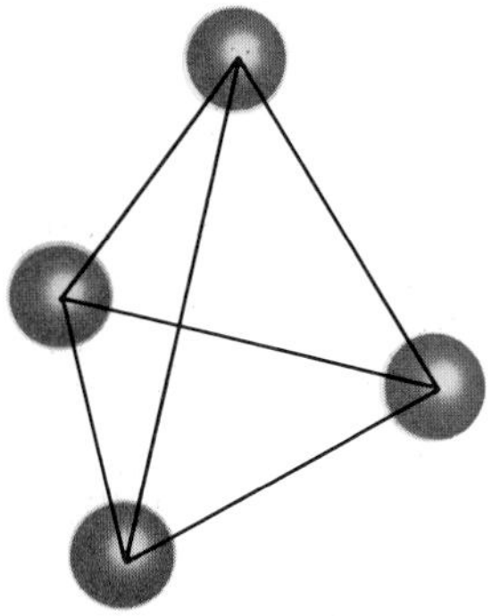

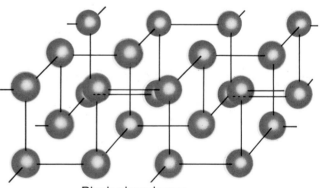

White phosphorus   Black phosphorus

Elemental phosphorus occurs as P_4 molecules and is solid at room temperature. The P_4 molecules "stack" in different ways to form several allotropes. One allotrope, white phosphorus, is so reactive that it ignites spontaneously on contacting air. Red phosphorus must be exposed to a flame to ignite. The principal source for phosphorus in nature is phosphate rock, $Ca_3(PO_4)_2$. Most phosphate rock is used in producing $Ca(H_2PO_4)_2$ and $CaHPO_4$ for use as fertilizer. Some phosphate rock is converted to phosphoric acid which is also used primarily in making fertilizer, but has other applications in industry.

Organic compounds of phosphorus are vital to living organisms. Utilization of energy by living systems involves a compound called adenosine triphosphate (ATP). The transfer of genetic information from generation to generation involves deoxyribonucleic acid (DNA). Each DNA molecule contains hundreds of phosphate groups. Ribonucleic acid (RNA), used by cells in metabolism, also contains phosphate groups.

Phosphorus occurs naturally in phosphate rock.

ATP, DNA, and RNA are biologically important compounds which contain phosphate groups.

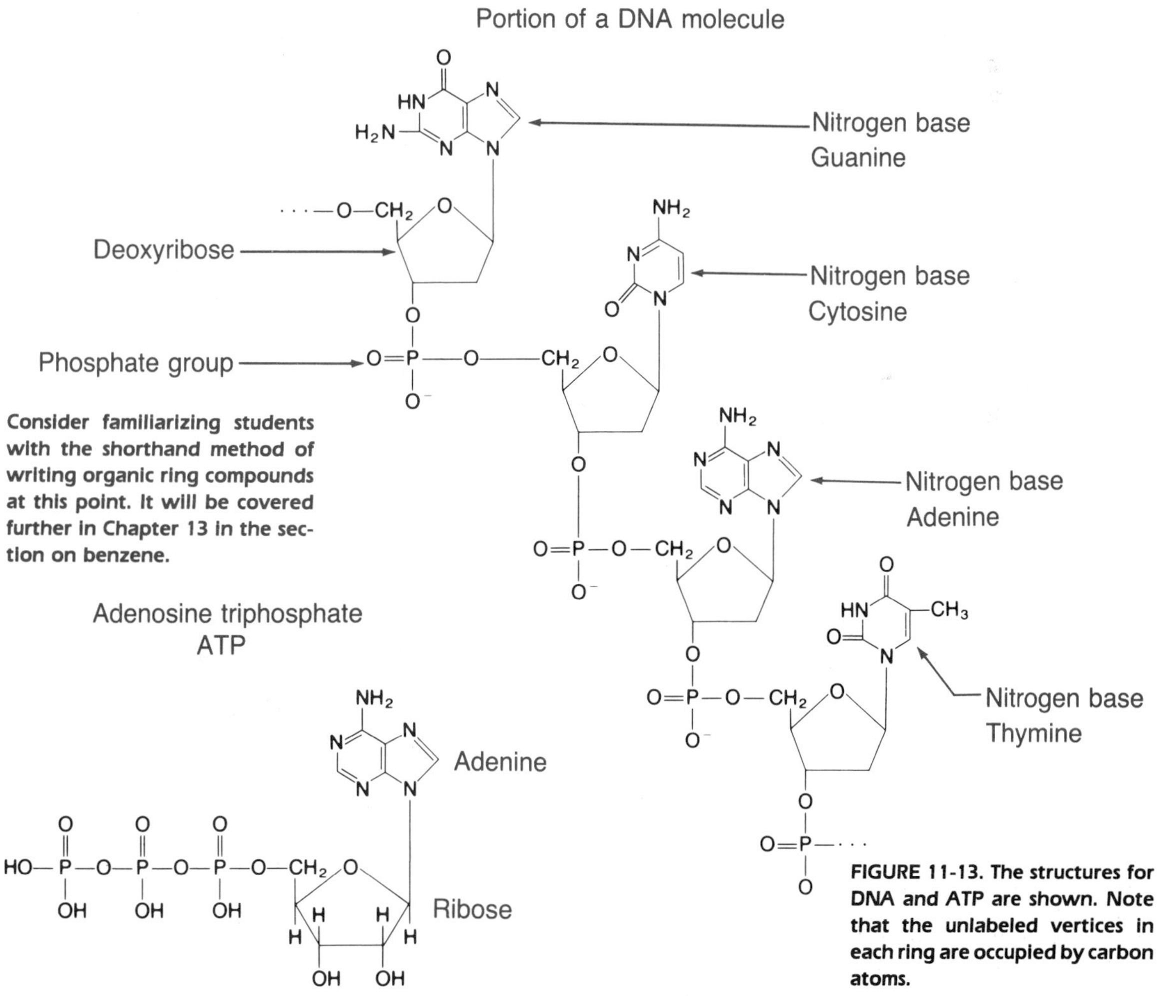

Consider familiarizing students with the shorthand method of writing organic ring compounds at this point. It will be covered further in Chapter 13 in the section on benzene.

FIGURE 11-13. The structures for DNA and ATP are shown. Note that the unlabeled vertices in each ring are occupied by carbon atoms.

11:8 OXYGEN

Oxygen is the most plentiful element in the earth's crust.

Oxygen is the most plentiful element in the earth's crust. It combines with all other elements except helium, neon, and argon. Since the atom has six electrons in its outer level, it can gain two electrons to achieve the stable octet configuration of neon. In so doing, it becomes the oxide ion, O^{2-}. It can also react by sharing electrons. With metals which tend to lose electrons readily, oxygen forms ionic oxides. With nonmetals, oxygen tends to share electrons. The behavior of these oxides when dissolved in water depends on their structure. Ionic oxides generally react with water to produce basic solutions. However, oxides formed by the sharing of electrons tend to react with water to form acidic solutions. There are some oxides which can produce either acidic or basic solutions, depending on the other substances present. Such oxides are called **amphoteric** (am foh TER ik) oxides.

Oxygen reacts by gaining or sharing 2 electrons.

Amphoteric oxides produce either acidic or basic solutions.

Like carbon, oxygen has allotropes. Oxygen usually occurs in the form of diatomic oxygen molecules, O_2. The free oxygen you breathe from air is O_2. There is another allotrope of oxygen called ozone. Ozone is the triatomic form of oxygen, O_3, and is highly reactive. Ozone can be synthesized by subjecting O_2 to a silent electric discharge. It is formed naturally in small amounts by lightning, and in the upper atmosphere by ultraviolet radiation from the sun. That layer of ozone protects living things on the earth from the sun's harmful ultraviolet radiation. In Europe, ozone is the main chemical used in water purification.

O_3 is ozone, a highly reactive allotrope of oxygen.

Pure oxygen is extracted from air, compressed, and sold in cylinders. Its largest uses are the production of steel, artificial breathing atmospheres, rocket engines, and welding torches.

The chemistry of sulfur is similar to the chemistry of oxygen.

The chemistry of sulfur is similar to the chemistry of oxygen, especially in the behavior of the 2− ion. The S^{2-} ion shows similar characteristics to oxygen in solubility and acid-base behavior. Unlike oxygen whose longest chain is O_3, sulfur can form long chains of atoms attached to the S^{2-} ion. These ions, for example S_6^{2-}, are called polysulfide ions. Sulfur exhibits two important positive oxidation states represented by the oxides SO_2 and SO_3. When sulfur or sulfur compounds are burned in an ample supply of air, SO_2 is produced. Using a catalyst, SO_2 can be converted to SO_3. When SO_2 is dissolved in water, sulfurous acid (H_2SO_3) is produced. If SO_3 is combined with water, sulfuric acid (H_2SO_4) is produced. The combination of SO_3 and water is done by dissolving the SO_3 in H_2SO_4 and then adding water. Sulfuric acid is produced in huge quantities. Twice as much H_2SO_4 (by mass) is produced as the next most common chemical. The principal sulfuric acid-consuming industries in the United States are fertilizer, petroleum refining, steel, paints, and pigments.

When sulfur or sulfur compounds are burned in air, SO_2 is produced.

Twice as much H_2SO_4 is produced as the next most common chemical.

11:9 HALOGENS

Group VIIA contains fluorine, chlorine, bromine, iodine, and astatine. The elements of this group are called the halogen (salt forming) family. In many chemical reactions, halogen atoms gain one electron. They become negatively charged ions with a stable outer level of eight electrons. As in other families already discussed, three factors determine the reactivity of the halogens. They are the distance between the nucleus and the outer electrons, the shielding effect of inner level electrons, and the size of the positive charge on the nucleus. Fluorine atoms contain fewer inner level electrons than the other halogens, so the shielding effect is the least. The distance between the fluorine nucleus and its outer electrons is less than the other halogens. Thus, the fluorine atom has the greatest tendency to attract other electrons. This attraction makes fluorine the most reactive nonmetal.

The astatine nucleus has the largest number of protons and the largest positive charge. However, the increased charge on the nucleus is not enough to offset the distance and shielding effects. Thus, of all halogen atoms, the astatine nucleus has the least attraction for outer electrons.

Notice that fluorine is active because the atoms of fluorine have a great tendency to gain one electron and become negative ions. The active metals are active because they hold the single outer electron loosely and it is easily removed. The groups between IA and VIIA vary between these two extremes. In general, *on the right side of the table, the nonmetallic elements become more active as we move from the bottom to the top. On the left-hand side of the table, the metals become more active as we move from the top to the bottom.* The most active elements are located at the upper right-hand and lower left-hand corners of the periodic table.

Halogens react by forming negative ions or by sharing electrons.

As the atomic numbers of the halogens increase
1. *the atoms become larger*
2. *the outer levels are farther from the nucleus*
3. *the intervening electrons shield the effect of a larger nucleus*
4. *the nucleus has less attraction for electrons of other atoms*
5. *the atoms becomes less active.*

The effective nuclear charge of all elements in a column is roughly the same.

The most active elements are in the upper right and lower left of the periodic table.

11:10 FLUORINE AND CHLORINE

The halogens are the most reactive nonmetallic family. They usually react by forming negative ions or sharing electrons. Fluorine is the most reactive of all the chemical elements. It reacts with all other elements except helium, neon, and argon. Fluorine is obtained from the mineral fluorspar, CaF_2. Like hydrogen, halogen atoms can form bridges between two other atoms. An example of such a compound is BeF_2. The halogens also form a large number of compounds among themselves. Examples are ClF, ClF_5, BrF_5, IF_5, IF_7, $BrCl$, and ICl_3.

Chlorine, though less abundant than fluorine in the earth's crust, is more commonly found in both the laboratory and industry. Chlorides of most elements are available commercially.

Halogens are the most reactive nonmetallic family.

Fluorine is the most reactive chemical element.

These compounds are quite often used in the laboratory as a source of positive metal ions bound with the chloride ions.

Chlorine is produced primarily to make other chemicals, but some is consumed in paper manufacture. Hydrochloric acid is a by-product of many industrial processes. Its uses include steel manufacture, dye production, food processing, and oil well drilling.

The commercial preparation of chlorine led to one of the major water pollution crises of the early 1970s. The chlorine was produced by running an electric current through a solution of sodium chloride in water. One of the substances used to conduct current in the apparatus was mercury. The leakage of mercury into nearby water sources caused a public outcry. Industries had to remove the mercury from their waste before dumping, or switch to another method of producing chlorine. Chemists solved the problem by designing new cells. There are many other pollution problems which must be given special attention by chemists in the near future.

FIGURE 11-14. Xenon tetra-fluoride is the easiest xenon compound to prepare. However, it is quite unstable and decomposes when added to water.

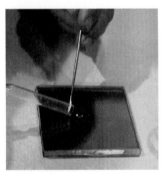

From the CHEM Study Film,
A Research Problem:
Inert Gas (?) Compounds

11:11 NOBLE GASES

For many years after their discovery Group VIIIA, the noble gases, were believed to be chemically unreactive or inert. However, in 1962, the first "inert" gas compound was synthesized. Since these gases are not inert, we will refer to them as the noble gases. The first compound made was xenon hexafluoroplatinate $(XePtF_6)$.

Other compounds of xenon were soon produced. Once the techniques were known, the compounds could be made with increasing ease. Xenon difluoride (XeF_2) was first made by combining xenon and oxygen difluoride (OF_2) in a nickel tube at 300°C under pressure. The same compound can now be made from xenon and fluorine. An evacuated glass container of fluorine and xenon is exposed to daylight. The equation can be written as

$$Xe(g) + F_2(g) \rightarrow XeF_2(c)$$

Compounds of xenon with oxygen and nitrogen have also been synthesized. Krypton and radon compounds have also been produced. Argon and helium are used to protect active metals during welding. Aluminum, for example must be welded in an argon or helium atmosphere. Argon is also widely used to fill light bulbs. Neon, krypton, and xenon are used to fill brightly colored gas discharge tubes for advertising.

11:12   TRANSITION METALS

The transition metals ("B" groups) are those elements who highest energy electrons are in the d sublevels. In all groups except IIB, the d orbitals are only partially filled. These partially filled d orbitals make the chemical properties of the transition metals different from the "A" group metals.

The major uses of the transition metals are as structural elements. The fourth period elements, titanium through zinc, are our principal structural metals. These metals are used either alone or as alloys. The only important transition metal compound produced commercially is titanium(IV) oxide, TiO_2. The TiO_2 is used extensively as a white paint pigment.

Transition elements have electrons filling d sublevels.

Transition metals, used alone or as alloys, are our principal structural metals.

FIGURE 11-15. The map shows major concentrations of high technology materials throughout the world. Note most of these materials are transition metals.

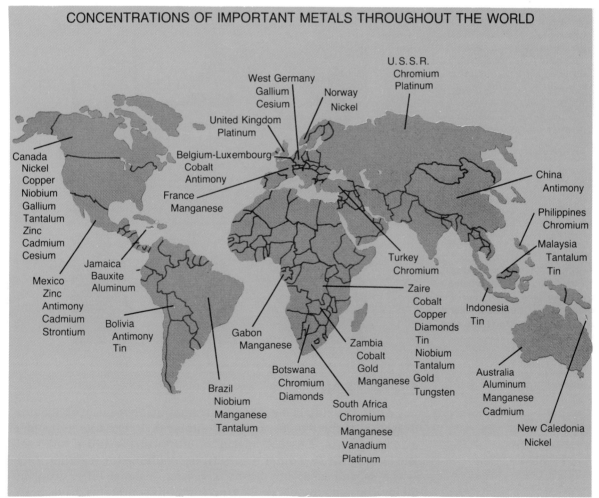

CONCENTRATIONS OF IMPORTANT METALS THROUGHOUT THE WORLD

You can begin a discussion of how political issues and relations can affect our supply of these materials. Many industries such as electronics, aerospace, and nuclear depend on the supply of high technology materials.

11:13 CHROMIUM

Chromium exhibits the typical properties of a transition metal. One property of chromium which is industrially important is its resistance to corrosion. Large quantities are used to make stainless steel and to "chromeplate" regular steel. In both cases, the chromium protects the iron in steel from corrosion.

Chromium usually reacts by losing three electrons to form the Cr^{3+} ion. Also of importance is the 6+ oxidation state. This state is formed when chromium loses all five of its $3d$ electrons, as well as its outer level $4s$ electron. Two polyatomic ions are important examples of the 6+ state. These ions are the chromate ion, CrO_4^{2-} and the dichromate ion, $Cr_2O_7^{2-}$. Chromium also forms a Cr^{2+} ion. However, this ion is easily converted by oxygen in air to Cr^{3+}. Consequently, the 2+ state is not of great importance. The 4+ and 5+ states are so unstable, they are just laboratory curiosities.

Chromium resists corrosion.

Chromium forms polyatomic ions like CrO_4^{2-} and $Cr_2O_7^{2-}$.

Chromium has multiple oxidation numbers.

FIGURE 11-16. Chrome plating is a chemical process whereby chromium ions in solution are changed to chromium metal which is deposited on the object to be plated.

Tom Pantages

11:14 ZINC

Zinc's behavior differs slightly from the other transition elements due to a full d sublevel $(3d^{10})$.

Although zinc is classed as a transition element, its behavior differs slightly due to a full d sublevel. It exhibits only one oxidation state, 2+. The special stability of the full d sublevel leaves only the two outer $4s$ electrons available for reacting. Zinc is the second most important transition element (after iron) in biological systems. Over 25 zinc-containing proteins have been

Iodine: Essential for the synthesis of thyroid hormones

Iron: Metallic center of hemoglobin; needed for the formation of vitamin A; component of some enzymes

Copper: Essential for hemoglobin synthesis; needed for bone formation and the production of melanin and myelin

Potassium: Maintains intracellular osmotic pressure and pH; needed for proper transmission of nerve impulses and muscle contraction

Each tablet contains: Vitamins		%U.S. RDA*
Vitamin A	5,000 Int. Units	100
Vitamin E	15 Int. Units	50
Vitamin C	60 mg	100
Folic Acid	400 mcg	100
Thiamine	1.2 mg	80
Riboflavin	1.7 mg	100
Niacin	14 mg	70
Vitamin B-6	2 mg	100
Vitamin B-12	6 mcg	100
Pantothenic Acid	10 mg	100
Minerals		
Iodine	150 mcg	100
Iron	10 mg	56
Copper	2 mg	100
Zinc	15 mg	100
Manganese	1 mg	†
Potassium	5 mg	†

Percentage of U.S. Recommended Daily Allowances.
†No U.S. Recommended Daily Allowance (U.S. RDA) has been established for this nutrient.

Ingredient List: Calcium Sulfate, Sucrose, Lactose, Sodium Ascorbate (Vit. C), Ferrous Sulfate, Zinc Oxide, Vitamin E Acetate, Niacinamide, Calcium Pantothenate, Potassium Sulfate, Cupric Sulfate, Artificial Color, Lacca, Gelatin, Povidone, Magnesium Stearate, Manganese Sulfate, Pyridoxine HCl (B-6), Vitamin A Acetate, Silica, Riboflavin (B-2), Thiamine Mononitrate (B-1), Folic Acid, Sodium Benzoate, Potassium Iodide, Carnauba and White Wax, Sesame Oil, Cyanocobalamin (B-12).

Doug Martin

Zinc: Component of several enzymes involved in digestion, respiration, bone formation, liver metabolism; needed for a normal healing process and good skin tone

Manganese: Component of enzymes involved in the synthesis of fatty acids and cholesterol; needed for the formation of urea and the normal functioning of the nervous system

FIGURE 11-17. Zinc is one of many elements essential to proper body function. Vitamin tablets act as a supplement in the event that one does not receive adequate amounts from the daily diet.

Zinc is corrosion resistant.

discovered. As an example, lack of zinc in the diet prevents the pancreas from producing some digestive enzymes.

Metallic zinc, like chromium, is corrosion resistant. It is used extensively as a coating to protect iron. The coating can be applied in three ways. When the iron is dipped in molten zinc, the process is called **galvanizing.** The coating is also applied electrically. The third method is to allow gaseous zinc to condense on the surface of iron. Another major use for metallic zinc is in the production of alloys. Especially important is its combination with copper to form brass.

A. Mercado/Jeroboam

FIGURE 11-18. Zinc discs are used on the underside of ships to prevent corrosion.

11:15 NEODYMIUM

The electron configuration of neodymium (knee o DIM ee um) ends $6s^2 4f^4$. From that configuration we would predict a 2+ oxidation state. However, Nd, as all the lanthanides, shows 3+ as its most stable state. The 3+ ion is pale violet in solution. The metal itself is soft and quite reactive. It tarnishes when exposed to air and has little practical use. The compound Nd_2O_3, is used in glass filters and in some lasers. Neodymium is the second most abundant lanthanide metal. Its compounds are separated from the other lanthanides by a chromatographic technique (Chapter 14). The metal is obtained from the fluoride by a single displacement reaction.

The lanthanides show 3+ as the most stable oxidation state.

$$3Ca + 2NdF_3 \rightarrow 3CaF_2 + 2Nd$$

11:16 CURIUM

Curium's predicted electron configuration ends $7s^2 5f^8$. However, its actual configuration is $7s^2 5f^7 6d^1$. Plainly, the stability of the half-full f sublevel more than offsets the promotion of one electron to the $6d$. The element exhibits a 3+ oxidation state in its compounds, and the ion is pale yellow in solution. The element itself is a silvery, hard metal of medium density and high melting point. It does not occur in nature. All curium (multigram quantities) has been produced by the slow neutron bombardment of the artificial element plutonium. It is reactive and highly toxic to the human organism. This metal is used as the energy source in nuclear generators in satellites.

Curium has a half-full f sublevel which is very stable.

Lise Meitner (1878–1968)

Lise was able to overcome the discriminatory practices against women and Jewish people to become an honored scientist. She received her doctorate at the University of Vienna. She then worked as an assistant to Otto Hahn in the field of radioactivity. Together, they researched the concept of isotopes until their study was interrupted by World War I. At the end of the war, Lise and Otto were responsible for the discovery of the radioactive element Protactinium ($^{231}_{91}Pa$).

Later she worked on Ida Noddack's presumptions (page 248), and was credited with predicting the products of a fission reaction. With her nephew, Otto Fritsch, she is credited with the first published work on fission in 1939.

CHEMICAL CAREER: Sanitary Engineers

Water is one of the most precious resources we have on the earth. Some areas are already faced with water shortages. Water is used by industry as a solvent, raw material, and as a coolant. However, water used for drinking is the most important use and the most critical problem.

The sanitary engineer is involved in two phases of the process of providing good water to the public. One phase is the treatment of water supplies to ensure the potability of the water. The first step is to analyze the water to find out what contaminants, if any, are present. The engineer must then decide what treatment is necessary. Chemicals may have to be added to precipitate minerals and neutralize acidic or basic compounds. Other substances might be added to cause suspended impurities to settle so they can be removed easily. The water may then be filtered through sand and gravel. Finally, it is treated with chlorine to destroy harmful organisms. Analyses are continued at each stage to ensure a consumable water supply.

A sanitary engineer is also concerned with preventing the introduction of pollutants into the water supply. This important task covers the treatment of industrial and domestic wastes. Garbage and trash are often disposed in land fills. It is the sanitary engineer's job to control the operation of such a site. This job may include supervising an incinerator which burns all flammable wastes. The design, construction, and supervision of sewage disposal plants becomes even more important as the population grows and government regulations become more stringent.

James Westwater

FIGURE 11-19. Sanitary engineers are primarily involved in the processes necessary to maintain a safe water supply.

Sewage treatment is divided into three stages. Primary treatment consists of the separation of solids and liquid waste. The solid material, or sludge, usually goes to a land fill, while the liquid is treated with chlorine and dumped in a nearby river or stream. Unfortunately, primary treatment is the only treatment received by much waste in the United States. Qualified sanitary engineers are needed to upgrade inadequate treatment plants.

Secondary treatment consists of using the liquid from the primary stage and treating it with bacteria which consume almost all the organic matter. The liquid is then treated with chlorine and released to a stream or river. The best plants provide tertiary treatment which subjects the water from secondary treatment to filtration through activated charcoal and oxidation using ozone. Sanitary engineers are steadily improving the treatment methods to preserve the purity of our water.

SUMMARY

1. The most active metals are listed toward the lower left-hand corner of the table. The most active nonmetals are listed toward the upper right-hand corner. 11:2, 11:9

2. Hydrogen is often considered as a family by itself because of the unique ways in which it reacts. 11:1

3. The alkali metals (Group IA) are the most active metals and react by losing one electron to form 1^+ ions. 11:2

4. The alkaline earth metals (Group IIA) are second only to alkali metals in terms of reactivity. They form 2+ ions. 11:4

5. Aluminum (Group IIIA) is less reactive than the alkaline earth metals and forms 3+ ions. 11:5

6. In Group IVA, carbon and silicon have four electrons in the outer level and react by sharing electrons. Tin and lead, in the same family, are distinctly metallic. 11:6

7. Nitrogen and phosphorus (Group VA) form compounds by sharing electrons, but differ from each other considerably. 11:7

8. In Group VIA, oxygen is distinctly nonmetallic and reacts by gaining two electrons or by sharing electrons. Sulfur is similar to oxygen but also exhibits positive oxidation states. 11:8

9. The halogens (Group VIIA) are the most active nonmetallic elements and usually react by gaining one electron. 11:9

10. The noble gases (Group VIIIA) have very stable outer electron configurations and are much less reactive than most of the other elements. 11:11

11. Chromium is a typical, corrosion resistant transition metal exhibiting more than one oxidation number. 11:12-11:13

12. Zinc is corrosion resistant. However, because of its full d sublevel, it does not exhibit more than one oxidation state as do most transition metals. 11:14

13. Lanthanides exhibit the 3+ oxidation state. Curium, an actinide, also exhibits the 3+ oxidation state. 11:15-11:16

PROBLEMS

1. Describe the four ways hydrogen can react.
2. What is the shielding effect? How does it explain the difference in reactivity between calcium and barium?
3. Why does thallium(I), a member of Group IIIA, have characteristics similar to those of the alkali ions?
4. What properties of lithium account for the differences in behavior that it exhibits in relation to the other alkali metals?
5. Why is aluminum considered less metallic than sodium and magnesium?
6. What is catenation? Why is it important to the study of carbon?
7. What chemical property accounts for the use of tin and lead as alloys?
8. What are allotropes? What elements discussed in this chapter exist in allotropic forms?
9. What is the importance of phosphorus to body systems?
10. What elements are particularly important in producing fertilizers?
11. How does the chemical behavior of oxygen differ when it combines with a metal rather than a nonmetal?
12. How does the chemical behavior of an amphoteric oxide differ from that of a nonmetal oxide?
13. Is the compound SO_3 produced by the transfer or sharing of electrons?
14. Why is Group VIIA labeled as the halogens?
15. Which element on the periodic table would you predict to have the least attraction for its outer level electrons?
16. Why would you predict the noble gases to be inert?
17. How does the electronic structure of the transition elements differ from the elements in the "A" Groups of the periodic table?
18. What properties are typical of transition metals?
19. Why is zinc important in the production of materials made from iron?
20. What oxidation state is common to all of the lanthanides?
21. What is the importance of plutonium to the production of curium?

22. Which elements from the following pairs would you predict to be more active?
    a. cobalt, <u>iron</u>
    b. copper, <u>nickel</u>
    c. <u>fermium</u>, mendelevium
    d. <u>fluorine</u>, oxygen
    e. <u>barium</u>, strontium
    f. hafnium, zirconium
    g. <u>potassium</u>, calcium
    h. arsenic, <u>selenium</u>
    i. lithium, <u>sodium</u>
    j. nitrogen, <u>phosphorus</u>

23. From their relative positions in the periodic table, predict which element from the following pairs is more active.
    a. <u>actinium</u>, lanthanum
    b. <u>americium</u>, plutonium
    c. <u>berkelium</u>, terbium
    d. <u>gallium</u>, germanium
    e. <u>neptunium</u>, plutonium
    f. carbon, <u>silicon</u>
    g. chlorine, <u>fluorine</u>
    h. nitrogen, <u>oxygen</u>
    i. rubidium, <u>cesium</u>
    j. <u>bromine</u>, iodine

REVIEW

1. Balance the following equations.
    a. $Cr + H_2SO_4 \rightarrow$
    b. $Mn + H_2O \rightarrow$
    c. $CuSO_4 + NaOH \rightarrow$
    d. $BaCrO_4 + HCl \rightarrow$

1. a. $2Cr + 3H_2SO_4 \rightarrow Cr_2(SO_4)_3 + 3H_2$
   b. $Mn + H_2O \rightarrow MnO + H_2$
   c. $CuSO_4 + 2NaOH \rightarrow Cu(OH)_2 + Na_2SO_4$
   d. $BaCrO_4 + 2HCl \rightarrow H_2CrO_4 + BaCl_2$

2. How many grams of $AgNO_3$ are required to produce 38.7 grams of $AgCNS$?
    $AgNO_3 + KCNS \rightarrow AgCNS + KNO_3$ 39.6 g $AgNO_3$

3. Compute the atomic mass of bromine from the following data.

isotopic mass	abundance
78.918332	50.54%
80.916292	49.46%

    79.91 amu

Y: Dy: In:
4. Draw electron dot diagrams for yttrium, dysprosium, and indium.
5. Predict oxidation numbers for sulfur and germanium.

ONE MORE STEP

1. Since 1962, research has been done on compounds of the noble gases. Find an article about one of these projects and report on it to the class.
2. Lithium is often listed as more reactive than sodium, contrary to predictions. See if you can find out why.
3. Investigate the lanthanide contraction and see what effect it has on the behavior of the elements exhibiting it.

READINGS

Dye, James L., "Anions of the Alkali Metals." *Scientific American,* Vol. 237, No. 1 (July 1977), pp. 92-105.

Firsching, F. H., "Anomalies in the Periodic Table." *Journal of Chemical Education,* Vol. 58, No. 6 (June 1981), pp. 478-479.

McCreery, Helen I., "Sodium." *Chemistry,* Vol. 49, No. 7 (September 1976), pp. 11-13.

Reilly, J. J., Sandrock, G. D., "Hydrogen Storage in Metal Hydrides." *Scientific American,* Vol. 242, No. 2 (February 1980), p. 118.

Robinson, Paul R., "A Gas for When the Oil is Gone," *SciQuest,* Vol. 54, No. 2 (February 1981), pp. 10-14.

Ternstrom, Torolf, "Subclassification of Lanthanides and Actinides." *Journal of Chemical Education,* Vol. 53, No. 10 (October 1976), pp. 629-631.

Tosteson, Daniel C., "Lithium and Mania," *Scientific American,* Vol. 244, No. 4 (April 1981), pp. 164-174.

Young, Gordon, "Salt." *National Geographic,* Vol. 152, No. 3 (September 1977), pp. 381-401.

One basic chemical concept is the study of how atoms join to form compounds. Because atoms are too small to see, models are used to help us visualize how atoms combine. The dancers can be thought of as a model for chemical bonding. Like a chemical bond the dancer model is 3-dimensional. Keep in mind that atoms and ions are also 3-dimensional. What forces link the dancers? What forces hold particles together in a chemical bond? How is the motion of the dancers related to chemical bonds? How are bonds formed?

Bevilacqua/Sygma

CHEMICAL
BONDING

12

Chapter 12 introduces chemical bonding and examines the factors which help determine the nature of the bond, and the properties characteristic of ionic, covalent, and metallic bonds.

Demonstration—Do one or more: Burn magnesium in air, burn magnesium in Br_2, or add sodium to Cl_2. See the Teacher's Guide for preparation details. Use your demonstration as an introduction to the process of ionic bonding.

In Chapter 10, we looked at the ways atoms are classified. We found that some atoms tend to give up electrons and become positive ions, while other atoms tend to gain electrons and become negative ions. We also discovered that some atoms tend to share electrons. In this chapter, we want to look at these processes in detail.

GOAL: You will gain an understanding of various bonding processes and the properties associated with each.

12:1 DETERMINING IONIZATION ENERGY

Our model of the atom was developed partly from determining the energy needed to remove the most loosely held electron from an atom. The experiments involve shooting electrons through a vapor. A substance is vaporized in a space between two electrodes as shown in Figure 12-1. No current flows through the vapor between the electrodes because the vapor particles have no charge. When this vapor is bombarded with a stream of electrons, some of the bombarding electrons will collide with atoms. The collision will result in "knocking off" electrons from atoms. This process produces positively charged ions. The positive ions will move toward the negative electrode, and a current will be detected. This current indicates that the vapor has been ionized.

In order to determine the necessary energy for ionization, the energy of the electron stream is increased slowly. When a

Ionization energy is determined by bombardment of a vapor by electrons.

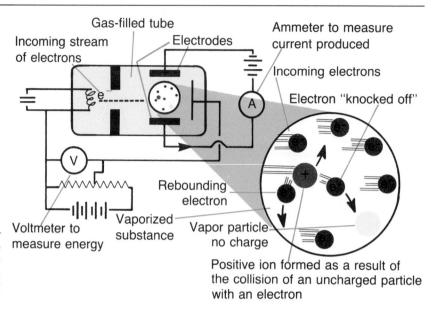

FIGURE 12-1. Ionization energy is determined by monitoring the energy of the incoming stream of electrons. When ionization occurs, a current will be detected by the ammeter.

current is detected, the energy of the electrons which first caused the ionization is noted. That value is the energy necessary to remove completely the most loosely held electron from an atom of the element being bombarded. This energy is called the **first ionization energy** of that element. It is measured in kilojoules per mole (kJ/mol).

First ionization energy: Energy needed to remove the most loosely held electron in an atom.

12:2   FIRST IONIZATION ENERGIES

The first ionization energies of the first ninety-five elements are graphed in Figure 12-2. Note that the ionization energies, like many other properties of the elements, are periodic. In fact, the relative ionization energies of two elements can be predicted by referring to their positions in the periodic table.

The *ionization energy tends to increase as atomic number increases in any horizontal row or period. In any column or group, there is a gradual decrease in ionization energy as atomic number increases.* Note, for example, the gradual decrease in ionization energy in the alkali metal series, lithium through cesium. The same trend is seen in the noble gas series, helium through radon.

Ionization energies increase across rows or periods. Ionization energies decrease down columns or groups.

A metal is characterized by a low ionization energy. Metals are located at the left side of the table. *An element with a high ionization energy is a nonmetal.* They are found at the right side of the table.

Metals have low ionization energy; nonmetals have high ionization energy.

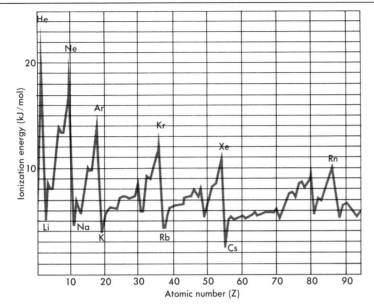

The energies shown on the graph are first ionization energies. Subsequent ionization energies give experimental evidence for the existence of energy levels and sublevels.

Note that the colored areas are maximum nodes and that the ionization energy falls off immediately as each node is passed and gradually builds up to the next maximum. This corresponds to the formation and filling of each new level.

FIGURE 12-2. The peaks in the graph indicate that ionization energy is a periodic property.

These ionization energies provide strong evidence for the existence of energy levels in the atom. Our theories of structure are based on experimental results such as ionization energies and atomic spectra. The experimental evidence came first, then the model of structure.

This experimental data gives evidence for:
1. Effect of increasing nuclear charge.
2. Stability of octet.
3. Effect of increased radius.
4. s & p sublevel in outer level.

Table 12-1

First Ionization Energies (in kilojoules per mole)							
H 1312.1							He 2372.5
Li 520.3	Be 899.5	B 800.7	C 1086.5	N 1402.4	O 1314.0	F 1681.1	Ne 2080.8
Na 495.9	Mg 737.8	Al 577.6	Si 786.5	P 1011.8	S 999.7	Cl 1251.2	Ar 1520.6
K 418.9	Ca 589.9						

Look at Table 12-1. Notice that the ionization energies decrease as you go down a column of the periodic table (for instance, lithium, sodium, potassium). The increased distance of the outer electrons from the nucleus and the shielding effect of the inner electrons tend to lower the ionization energy. Though it appears that the increased nuclear charge of an element with a greater atomic number tends to increase ionization energy, the lowering tendency is greater. Remember that the number of electrons in the outermost sublevel is the same for all elements in a column or group.

In passing across a period of the periodic table, we see some deviations from the expected trend of increasing ionization energy. This increase in ionization energy in going from left to right across the table is a result of the increasing nuclear charge. Look at the second row. There is a small decrease from beryllium $(1s^2 2s^2)$ to boron $(1s^2 2s^2 2p^1)$. In beryllium, the first ionization energy is determined by removing an s electron from a full s sublevel. In boron, it is determined by removing the lone p electron.

There is another slight decrease from nitrogen $(1s^2 2s^2 2p^3)$ to oxygen $(1s^2 2s^2 2p^4)$. The nitrogen p sublevel is half-full (a state of special stability) and a large amount of energy is needed to remove an electron from the sublevel. Thus, oxygen has a lower ionization energy than nitrogen.

The patterns in ionization energy values can be explained by the same factors which we discussed in detail in Chapter 10 in connection with the periodic table.

The fourth factor, the effect of s & p sublevels, causes the slight drop from beryllium to boron and from magnesium to aluminum. Electrons in the p sublevel have slightly more energy and therefore require less additional energy to be removed from the atom.

Ionization energies are determined by the same factors as activity.

Table 12-2

Factors Affecting Ionization Energy
1. **Nuclear charge**—the larger the nuclear charge, the greater the ionization energy.
2. **Shielding effect**—the greater the shielding effect, the less the ionization energy.
3. **Radius**—the greater the distance between the nucleus and the outer electrons of an atom, the less the ionization energy.
4. **Sublevel**—an electron from a full or half-full sublevel requires additional energy to be removed.

12:3 MULTIPLE IONIZATION ENERGIES

It is possible to measure other (second, third, and so on) ionization energies of an atom. These measurements give us the same evidence for atomic structure as first ionization energies. For example, the second ionization energy of aluminum is about three times as large as the first, as shown in Table 12-3. The difference can be explained by the fact that the first ionization removes a p electron and the second removes an s electron from a full s sublevel. The third ionization energy is about one and two-thirds times as large as the second. The second and third

Ionization energy increases with the removal of each additional electron.

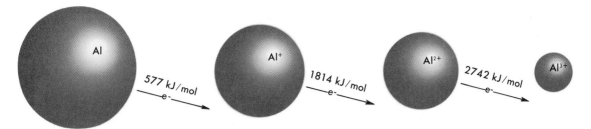

electrons are in the same sublevel. Yet, the third electron's ionization energy is greater because the nuclear charge remains constant as we remove electrons. As a result, the remaining electrons are more tightly held. The fourth ionization energy is about four times as large as the third. Why is the jump so large between the third and fourth ionization energies? Let us look at the electron configuration. Aluminum has the configuration $1s^2 2s^2 2p^6 3s^2 3p^1$. The fourth electron would come from the full second energy level which is closer to the nucleus. The $2s^2 2p^6$ level with eight electrons is stable. Thus a large amount of energy will be required to remove that fourth electron.

We have looked only at the aluminum atom, but the same reasoning can be used to explain similar data for other elements. This information can be applied as evidence for our theories of atomic structure.

FIGURE 12-3. The second, third, and fourth ionization energies of aluminum are higher than the first because the inner electrons are more tightly held by the nucleus.

Emphasize that the theories came from experimental evidence.

Table 12-3

Ionization Energies (in kilojoules per mole)					
Element	1st	2nd	3rd	4th	5th	6th
H	1312.1					
He	2372.5	5250.7				
Li	520.3	7298.5	11 815.6			
Be	899.5	1752.2	14 849.5	21 007.6		
B	800.7	2427.2	3 660.0	25 027.0	32 828.3	
C	1086.5	2352.8	4 620.7	6 223.0	37 832.4	47 279.4

12:4 ELECTRON AFFINITIES

Now consider an atom's attraction for additional electrons. The attraction of an atom for an electron is called **electron affinity**. The same factors which affect ionization energy will also affect electron affinity. In general, as electron affinity increases, an increase in ionization energy can be expected. *Metals have low electron affinities. Nonmetals have the high electron affinities* as shown in Table 12-4.

Electron affinity: Attraction of an atom for an electron.

Metals have low electron affinities; nonmetals have high electron affinities.

Table 12-4

Electron Affinities (in kilojoules per mole)							
H 72.8							**He** (−21.3)
Li 59.8	**Be** (−241)	**B** 23.2	**C** 123	**N** 0	**O** 141	**F** 322	**Ne** (−28.9)
Na 52.9	**Mg** (−232)	**Al** 44.4	**Si** 120	**P** 74.3	**S** 200	**Cl** 349	**Ar** (−34.7)
K 49.0							

( ) indicates a calculated rather than an experimental value.

FIGURE 12-4. As the difference in electronegativity increases, so does the strength of the bond between two atoms. In the case of these hydrogen-halogen compounds, the smaller molecule has a stronger bond than the larger molecule.

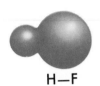

H—F

H—Cl

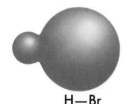

H—Br

H—I

12:5 ELECTRONEGATIVITY

Both electron affinity and ionization energy deal with isolated atoms. Chemists need a comparative scale relating the abilities of elements to attract electrons when their atoms are combined. The relative tendency of an atom to attract electrons to itself when bound with another atom is called its **electronegativity.** The elements are assigned electronegativities on the basis of many experimental tests.

Many chemical properties of the elements can be organized in terms of electronegativities. For example, the strength of the bond between two atoms increases with the difference in their electronegativities.

Table 12-5

Bonds between Hydrogen and Halogens		
Bond	**Bond Strength (kJ/mol)**	**Electronegativity Difference**
H—F	569	1.80
H—Cl	432	0.80
H—Br	366	0.62
H—I	299	0.28

Electronegativities of elements are influenced by the same factors affecting ionization energies and electron affinities. It is possible to construct an electronegativity scale using first ionization energies and electron affinities of the elements. Examine Table 12-6 which represents average values from several calculations. It shows that the variation in electronegativity follows the same trends as the ionization energies and the electron affinities. *The most active metals* (lower left) *have the lowest electronegativities.* Fluorine has the highest electronegativity of all the elements. Consider a reaction between two elements. Their relative attraction for electrons determines how they react. We can use the electronegativity scale to determine this attraction. Since electronegativity represents a comparison of the same property for each element, it is a dimensionless number.

Bond strength increases as the electronegativity difference increases.

Most active metals have low electronegativities; most active nonmetals have high electronegativities.

Table 12-6

Electronegativities																	
H 2.20																	
Li 0.96	Be 1.50											B 2.02	C 2.56	N 2.81	O 3.37	F 4.00	
Na 0.96	Mg 1.29											Al 1.63	Si 1.94	P 2.04	S 2.46	Cl 3.00	
K 0.84	Ca 1.02	Sc 1.28	Ti 1.44	V 1.54	Cr 1.61	Mn 1.57	Fe 1.74	Co 1.79	Ni 1.83	Cu 1.67	Zn 1.60	Ga 1.86	Ge 1.93	As 2.12	Se 2.45	Br 2.82	
Rb 0.85	Sr 0.97	Y 1.16	Zr 1.27	Nb 1.23	Mo 1.73	Tc 1.36	Ru 1.42	Rh 1.87	Pd 1.78	Ag 1.57	Cd 1.52	In 1.69	Sn 1.84	Sb 1.83	Te 2.03	I 2.48	
Cs 0.82	Ba 0.93	*Lu 1.20	Hf 1.23	Ta 1.33	W 1.88	Re 1.46	Os 1.52	Ir 1.88	Pt 1.86	Au 1.98	Hg 1.72	Tl 1.74	Pb 1.87	Bi 1.76	Po 1.76	At 1.96	
Fr 0.86	Ra ** 0.97																
	*La 1.09	Ce 1.09	Pr 1.10	Nd 1.10	Pm 1.07	Sm 1.12	Eu 1.01	Gd 1.15	Tb 1.10	Dy 1.16	Ho 1.16	Er 1.17	Tm 1.18	Yb 1.06			
	**Ac 1.00	Th 1.11	Pa 1.14	U 1.30	Np 1.29	Pu 1.25	Am 1.2 ←	Cm	Bk	Cf — estimated	Es	Fm	Md → 1.2				

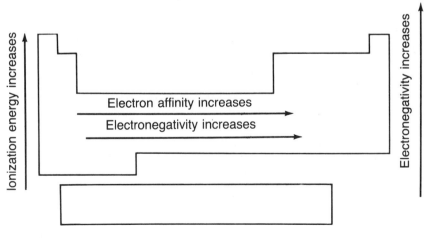

FIGURE 12-5. The general trends for ionization energy, electron affinity, and electronegativity are shown.

PROBLEMS

1. TI, BI, Te, Cl, Ne

1. Arrange the following elements in order of increasing force of attraction between the nucleus and the outer electrons.
   a. bismuth, chlorine, neon, tellurium, thallium.
   b. arsenic, gallium, germanium, radium, sulfur. Ra, Ga, Ge, As, S

2. Explain each of the peaks in the graph in Figure 12-2.

12:6   BOND CHARACTER

Electrons are transferred between atoms when the difference in electronegativity between the atoms is quite high. If the electronegativity difference between two reacting atoms is small, we might expect a sharing of electrons. At what point in electronegativity difference does the changeover occur? The answer is not simple. For one thing, the electronegativity of an atom varies slightly depending upon the atom with which it is combining. Another factor is the number of other atoms with which the atom is combining. Therefore a scale showing the percent of transfer of electrons (percent ionic character) has been constructed. The amount of transfer depends on the electronegativity difference between two atoms. Such a scale is shown in Table 12-7.

Bond character between atoms depends upon electronegativity differences.

Table 12-7

Character of Bonds									
Electronegativity Difference	0.00	0.65	0.94	1.19	1.43	1.67	1.91	2.19	2.54	3.03
Percent Ionic Character	0%	10%	20%	30%	40%	50%	60%	70%	80%	90%
Percent Covalent Character	100%	90%	80%	70%	60%	50%	40%	30%	20%	10%

Ionic bonds:
Transfer of electrons.

Covalent bonds:
Sharing of electrons.

Nearly all bonds have both covalent and ionic characteristics.

Emphasize that the character of the bonds—ionic to covalent—is on a continuum. The use of 1.67 as the breaking point is simply a convenience for working with compounds. Most covalent bonds will have some ionic character and vice versa.

When two atoms combine by transfer of electrons, ions are produced. The opposite charges of the ions hold them together. When two elements combine by electron transfer, they are said to form an ionic bond. If two elements combine by sharing electrons, they are said to form a covalent bond.

From Table 12-7 we see that two atoms with electronegativity difference of about 1.67 would form a bond that is 50% ionic 50% covalent. For our purposes, we will consider an electronegativity difference of less than 1.67 as indicating a covalent bond. A difference of 1.67 or greater indicates an ionic bond. However, almost all bonds have some of both sets of characteristics.

Think of magnesium reacting with oxygen. Magnesium has an electronegativity of 1.29 and oxygen is 3.37. The difference is 2.08. We would predict the formation of an ionic bond between these two elements. On the other hand, consider boron and

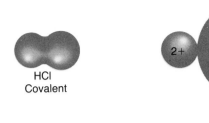

FIGURE 12-6. Covalent molecules, such as HCl, are held together by a mutual sharing of electrons. Note there is an overlap of the electron clouds. Ionic substances, such as MgO, are held together by the attractive force between oppositely-charged ions.

nitrogen. Boron has an electronegativity of 2.02 and nitrogen is 2.81. The difference is 0.79. We would predict boron and nitrogen to form a covalent bond.

12:7 IONIC BONDS

We have discussed sodium chloride, an excellent example of a compound with an ionic bond (an ionic compound). Most of the properties of ionic compounds are best explained by assuming a complete transfer of electrons.

$$2Na\cdot + \;:\!\ddot{C}l\!:\!\ddot{C}l\!: \rightarrow 2Na^+ + 2:\!\ddot{C}l\!:^-$$

If a chloride ion and a sodium ion are brought together, there will be an attractive force between them. If the ions are brought almost into contact, the force will be great enough to hold the two ions together. The electrostatic force which holds two ions together due to their differing charges is the **ionic bond.**

Elements can be assigned oxidation numbers for ionic bonding. Sulfur, for example, with six electrons in the outer level, will tend to gain two electrons. Thus, it attains the stable octet configuration. The oxidation number of sulfur for ionic bonding is 2−. The negative two is its electric charge after gaining two electrons.

Ionic compounds are characterized by high melting points and the ability to conduct electricity in the molten state. They tend to be soluble in water and usually crystallize as sharply defined particles.

Elements are assigned oxidation numbers for ionic bonding based on the number of electrons they must gain or lose in order to obtain a stable octet.

Characteristics of compounds with ionic bonds.
1. high melting point
2. soluble in water
3. well-defined crystals
4. molten form conducts electricity

PROBLEM

3. Classify the bonds between the following pairs of atoms as principally ionic or covalent.
   a. boron and carbon
   b. cesium and fluorine
   c. fluorine and silicon
   d. hydrogen and chlorine
   e. magnesium and nitrogen
   f. beryllium and fluorine
   g. bromine and strontium
   h. chlorine and lithium
   i. chlorine and sodium
   j. hydrogen and iodine

   ionic: b, c, f, g, h, i
   covalent: a, d, e, j

12:8   IONIC RADII

We saw in Chapter 10 that a sodium ion is smaller than a sodium atom. We also found that a chloride ion is larger than a chlorine atom. Values for the radii of many ions have been determined, Table 10-9. These values are found from a combination of experimental data and simplifying assumptions. By adding the radii of two ions in a compound we may find their **internuclear distance** in a crystal. Remember that the radii are not fixed values. One reason for their variability is the "fuzziness" of the electron cloud. Another reason is the effect each ion has on its neighbor ions.

Radii values are not fixed.

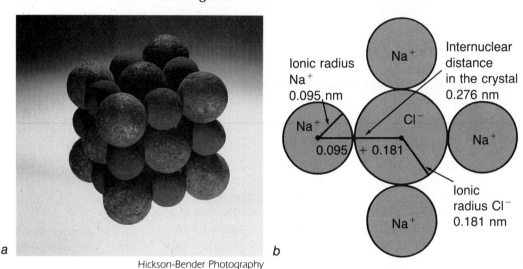

Ionic radius
Na$^+$
0.095 nm

Na$^+$

Cl$^-$

0.095 + 0.181

Na$^+$

Internuclear distance in the crystal
0.276 nm

Na$^+$

Ionic radius Cl$^-$
0.181 nm

Na$^+$

a

b

Hickson-Bender Photography

FIGURE 12-7. Sodium chloride consists of a regular arrangement of sodium and chloride ions as shown by the model (a). The ionic radius is the sum of the radii for both ions (b).

12:9   COVALENT BONDS

Atoms with the same or nearly the same electronegativities tend to react by sharing electrons. The shared pair or pairs of electrons constitute a **covalent bond.** Covalent compounds typically have low melting points, do not conduct electricity, and are brittle.

When two or more atoms bond covalently, the resulting particle is called **a molecule.** The line joining the nuclei of two bonded atoms in a molecule is called the **bond axis** as shown in Figure 12-13. If one atom is bonded to each of two other atoms, the angle between the two bond axes is called the **bond angle.** The distance between nuclei along the bond axis is called the **bond length.** This length is not really fixed, because the bond acts much as if it were a stiff spring. The atoms vibrate as though the bond were alternately stretching and shrinking as shown in Figure 12-8.

A molecule is formed with covalent bonds.

Bonds also undergo bending, wagging, and rotational vibrations. These movements cause the bond angles and length to vary. The amplitudes of these vibrations are not large and the bond lengths and bond angles which we measure are average values.

Bond angle and bond length are averaged values.

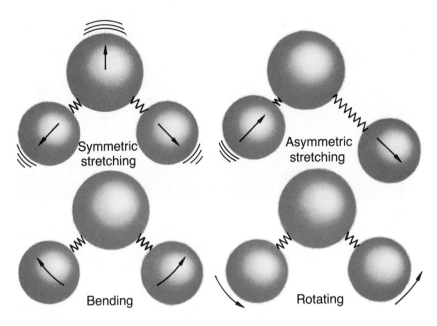

Symmetric stretching

Asymmetric stretching

Bending

Rotating

FIGURE 12-8. Molecules exhibit a variety of motions. Therefore, bond lengths and bond angles should be considered as average values.

We may think of them as the values for a molecule completely at rest. However, molecular motion never entirely ceases.

We have learned much of what we know about the structure of molecules from infrared spectroscopy. Recall from Figure 8-14 that infrared wavelengths lie in a region of the electromagnetic spectrum between radio waves and visible light waves. The wavelengths vary from 700 nm to over 50 000 nm. A molecular compound can be identified by the infrared radiation it absorbs or transmits. Each molecular compound has its own infrared spectrum which is different from that of any other compound.

The infrared (IR) spectrum indicates energy changes in the bonding between the particles of the molecule. At specific frequencies the atoms of the molecule stretch, twist, wag, and bend around the bonds joining them. Radiation of the wavelengths corresponding to those frequencies will be absorbed. The energy absorbed must agree in frequency with the natural frequency of vibration of the molecule.

In using the IR spectrophotometer, a sample of the compound is subjected to varied wavelengths of IR radiation. The various wavelengths absorbed by the compound are measured and recorded graphically. A unique continuous absorption spectrum

Point out IR spectroscopy as one more experimental process available to help understand the structure of the atom. Stress its usefulness as an identifying process.

The IR spectrum indicates energy changes in the bonding between particles of the molecule.

FIGURE 12-9. Most infrared spectrophotometers now provide video readouts. Hard copies of peak values can be obtained by computer. A chemist uses this information in comparing the spectra of an unknown substance to those of known substances to determine the identity of the unknown.

FIGURE 12-10. For the infrared spectra shown, note that the composition of both compounds is similar. However, the difference in the way the atoms are arranged causes different stretching motions in each molecule. Characteristic peaks in each graph can be used to identify the compound.

Photo Courtesy of the Perkin-Elmer Corporation

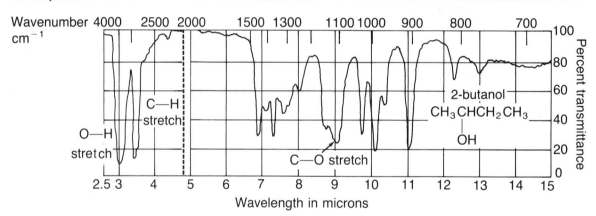

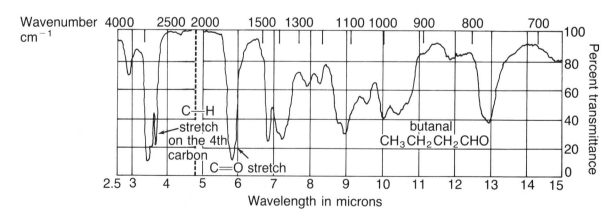

can be plotted for each molecular compound. Comparison with known spectra will reveal the identity of the compound, just as fingerprints reveal the identity of a person.

PROBLEM

4. For each atom pair listed below, decide whether an ionic or a covalent bond would form between the elements.
  a. fluorine - astatine   **d.** lanthanum - selenium
  b. boron - thorium   **e.** strontium - chlorine
  c. gadolinium - astatine   **f.** iodine - sodium   Ionic: a, e, f
                                                            covalent: b, c, d

12:10 COVALENT RADII

It is possible, by experiment, to determine the internuclear distance between two bonded atoms. For example, consider iodine(VII) chloride, ICl. What are the radii of the iodine and chlorine atoms in this molecule? The internuclear distance in ICl is found to be 0.230 nm. The internuclear distance in Cl_2 is 0.198 nm, and in I_2 it is 0.266 nm as shown in Figure 12-11. One half of each of these values might be taken as the radii of the chlorine and iodine atoms in a covalent bond: 0.099 nm and 0.133 nm. The sum of the iodine and chlorine radii would then be 0.232 nm. This sum is in good agreement with the observed bond distance in ICl. Covalent radii are only approximates; the value for hydrogen is less reliable than that for other atoms. Nevertheless, these radii are very useful in predicting bond lengths in molecules. Table 12-8 gives the covalent radii for some common atoms; Table 12-9 gives the bond lengths for some molecules. See for yourself how well the predicted bond lengths agree with the measured ones.

Approximate bond length can be determined by adding the radii of 2 bonded atoms.

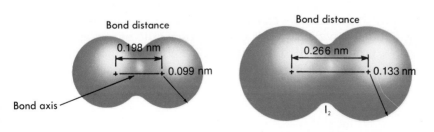

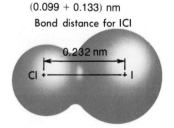

(0.099 + 0.133) nm
Bond distance for ICl

FIGURE 12-11. The internuclear distance is the sum of the covalent radii for each atom. Recall that bond distances are not fixed values.

Remember that covalent radii are used to find the internuclear distance between atoms bonded to each other. Like electronegativities covalent radii are average values. The radius of a particular atom is not constant. Its size is influenced by the other atom or atoms to which it is bonded.

Table 12-8

Covalent Radii (in nanometers)			
Atom	Radius	Atom	Radius
Al	0.125	I	0.133
As	0.121	N	0.070
B	0.088	O	0.066
Be	0.089	P	0.110
Bi	0.152	Pb	0.144
Br	0.114	S	0.104
C	0.077	Sb	0.141
Cl	0.099	Se	0.117
F	0.064	Si	0.117
Ga	0.125	Sn	0.140
Ge	0.122	Te	0.140
H	0.037		

These radii are averages obtained from a number of different compounds.

Table 12-9

Experimental Bond Lengths (in nanometers)		
Molecule	Bond	Length
BCl_3	B—Cl	0.174
B_2H_6	B—H	0.132
Diamond	C—C	0.154
CH_4	C—H	0.110
CH_3I	C—H	0.110
	C—I	0.221
ClBr	Cl—Br	0.214
HF	H—F	0.092
H_2O	H—O	0.096
NH_3	N—H	0.101
OF_2	O—F	0.141
O_3	O—O	0.128
H_2SAlBr_3	S—Al	0.243
$(H_3Si)_2NN(SiH_3)_2$	Si—N	0.173

12:11   POLYATOMIC IONS

The term *polyatomic ion* is used throughout this text in place of the term *radical*. We reserve the term radical for the free radical of organic chemistry.

There are a large number of ionic compounds made of more than two elements. In these compounds, one ion consists of two or more atoms covalently bonded. However, the particle as a whole possesses an overall charge.

For example, consider the hydroxide ion (OH^-). The oxygen atom is bonded covalently to the hydrogen atom. The hydrogen atom is stable with two electrons in its outer level. The hydrogen atom contributes only one electron to the octet of oxygen. The other electron required for oxygen to have a stable octet is the one which gives the 1− charge to the ion. Although the two atoms are bonded covalently, the combination still possesses charge. Such a group is called a polyatomic ion. Polyatomic ions form

A polyatomic ion contains covalently bonded atoms which together have a charge.

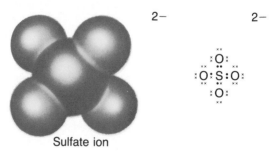

FIGURE 12-12. The sulfate ion contains S—O covalent bonds. The electron dot structure shows a stable octet for each atom. However, the particle as a whole has a net negative charge.

Sulfate ion

ionic bonds just as other ions do. Table 4-4 gives some of the more common polyatomic ions with their charges.

12:12 VAN DER WAALS RADII

A certain minimum distance must be maintained between atoms that are not bonded to each other. This limitation exists because the electron cloud of one atom repels the electron cloud of other atoms.

In effect, colliding free atoms and molecules act as if they had a rigid outer shell. This shell limits the closeness with which they may approach other atoms or molecules. Since the covalent bond consists of shared electrons, bonded atoms can come closer than atoms which are not bonded as shown in Figure 12-13. The radius of this imaginary rigid shell of an atom is called the **van der Waals radius.** It is named for the Dutch physicist Johannes van der Waals.

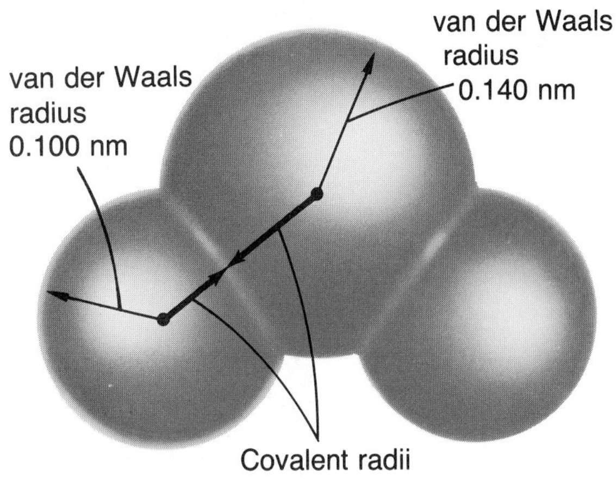

van der Waals radius 0.100 nm

van der Waals radius 0.140 nm

Covalent radii

FIGURE 12-13. The van der Waals radius is the minimum distance between nuclei for atoms on adjacent molecules. Note that the van der Waals radius will be larger than the covalent radius of a bonded atom.

Table 12-10

van der Waals Radii (in nanometers)			
Atom	Radius	Atom	Radius
As	0.200	O	0.140
Br	0.195	P	0.190
C	0.185	S	0.185
Cl	0.181	Sb	0.220
F	0.135	Se	0.200
H*	0.120	Si	0.200
I	0.215	Te	0.220
N	0.154		

*The van der Waals radius for hydrogen when it is hydrogen-bonded (Section 17:10) is 0.100 nm.

12:13 SUMMARY OF RADII

Thus far, we have studied four radii—atomic, ionic, covalent, and van der Waals. How do these various measurements differ? How are they the same? Atomic radii are measured in one of two ways. First, they may be measured on individual atoms in the gaseous state. On the other hand, they may be measured on atoms in metallic crystals. These atoms have special characteristics which will be discussed in Section 12:14. Note that in the first method, the atoms are unaffected by neighboring atoms. In the second case, neighboring atoms have a major effect. Measurements made on the same atom by the two methods will not give exactly the same results. The values given in Figure 12-13 are drawn from both methods and adjusted to give a consistent set of values.

Ionic radii differ from atomic radii because of the loss or gain of electrons. This difference was discussed in Section 10:12. Since most ionic radii are determined from ionic crystals, their values are consistent from the data. Covalent radii and van der Waals radii are quite variable due to the wide range of atoms to which the subject atom may be bonded. We would expect covalent radii to be less than an atomic radius. However, if an atom is bonded to more than one other atom, its electron cloud may be distorted. The distortion may make its covalent radius larger than the atomic radius. The same situation occurs with van der Waals radii. For both of these radii the data given in the tables in this chapter represent average values for the atom bonded to its usual number of neighboring atoms. In every case, we can use the radii to predict the internuclear distance between atoms.

Radii are used to predict internuclear distances between atoms.

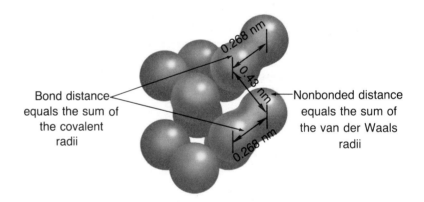

Bond distance equals the sum of the covalent radii

Nonbonded distance equals the sum of the van der Waals radii

FIGURE 12-14. The relationships among covalent radii, internuclear distances, and van der Waals radii are shown for an iodine crystal.

12:14 SPECIAL PROPERTIES OF METALS

The properties of metals are not explained by any of the bonding properties already considered. One of these properties is the ability to conduct electricity quite readily. Good electric conductivity indicates a ready source of electrons in metals.

We can use the following model to describe a piece of metal. Imagine metal atoms without their outer level electrons. These positive ions are packed together and their empty outer-level orbitals interact with each other. Each outer level is split into several closely-spaced energy levels. These splits are so small that we actually have bands of possible energies. These energy bands are separated from each other by small energy gaps called **forbidden zones** as shown in Figure 12-15.

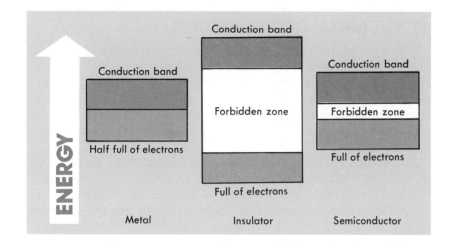

Let us now replace the outer level electrons in the metal. These electrons enter the lowest available energy band. However, there is another band representing a just slightly higher energy. This higher energy band is called the **conduction band.** If an outside energy source is applied, the electrons could jump to the conduction band. An electric field would be such an energy source. The orbitals of the atoms in the conduction band overlap. Once the electrons are in this conduction band, they can travel anywhere in the piece of metal. Under the influence of the electric field they will flow from one end of the piece of metal to the other. In other words, the metal is now conducting electrically. Since these electrons can travel anywhere, they are referred to as free or **delocalized electrons.** The electrons are called delocalized because they are not held in one "locality" as part of a specific atom or bond. The delocalized electrons act as a negative cloud surrounding and holding the positive ions. It is this negative cloud which constitutes the metallic bond.

In nonmetals, the forbidden zone represents a large quantity of energy. As a result, nonmetals do not conduct electricity. They are called **insulators** since they block the passage of an electric current.

There is another class of elements, called **semiconductors.** In these elements, all the outer electrons form covalent bonds. However, the forbidden zone in these elements is small. It is possible, therefore to excite the electrons enough to cause these materials to conduct under the proper conditions. We will look at semiconductors more closely in Chapter 16.

12:15 METALLIC PROPERTIES

The number of electrons available for metallic bonding determines the properties of metals.

The properties of metals are determined by the number of outer electrons available. Group IA metals have only one outer electron per atom. These metals are soft. Group IIA metals have two outer electrons and are harder than Group IA metals. In the transition elements however, electrons from the partially filled d orbitals may take part in the metallic bond. Many of these metals are very hard.

Groups IIIB through VIB elements have three through six delocalized electrons. In the elements of Groups VIIB and VIIIB, the number of delocalized electrons remains at six because all of the d sublevel electrons of these elements are not involved in the metallic bond. The number of delocalized electrons per atom begins to decrease with the metals of Groups IB and IIB. Going from Groups IIIA through VIIIA, the nonmetals, the metallic properties decrease rapidly.

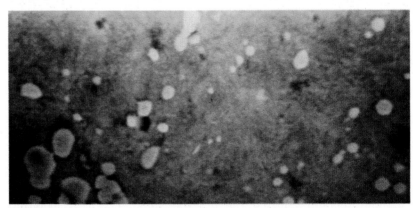

FIGURE 12-16. The scanning electron micrograph shows the internal structure of a molybdenum-steel alloy.

Tom Pantages

Alloys have properties different from those of pure metals.

The strong metallic bond of our structural metals, such as iron, chromium, and nickel, makes them hard and strong. In general, the transition elements are the hardest and strongest elements. It is possible to strengthen some of the elements with fewer delocalized electrons by combining them with other metals to form alloys. These alloys have properties different from those of pure elements.

Table 12-11

		Chemical Bond Summary			
	Bond Type	**Generally Formed between**	**Bond Formed by**	**Properties Associated with Bond Type**	**Examples of Substances Utilizing Bond Type**
INTER ATOMIC BONDS	Covalent	Atoms of nonmetallic elements of similar electronegativity	Sharing of electron pairs	Stable nonionizing molecules-not conductors of electricity in any phase	OF_2, C_2H_6, $AsCl_3$, $GeCl_4$, C, SiC, Si
	Ionic	Atoms of metallic and nonmetallic elements of widely different electronegatives	Electrostatic attraction between ions resulting from transfer of electrons	Charged ions in gas, liquid, and solid. Solid is electrically nonconducting. Gas and liquid are conductors. High melting points.	NaCl, K_2O, BaS, LiH, CdF_2, $BaBr_2$, $ErCl_3$, CdO, Ca_3N_2
	Metallic	Atoms of metallic elements	Delocalized electron cloud around atoms of low electronegativity	Electrical conductors in all phases-lustrous-very high melting points	Na, Au, Cu, Zn, Ac, Be, Gd, Fe, Dy

Ida Tacke Noddack (1896–)

Ida Tacke Noddack was intensely interested in the structure and organization of the periodic table. This interest led to two important discoveries. A gap in the table under manganese had led most researchers to assume that the new element would have properties similar to manganese.

Ida and her fiance, Walter Noddack, investigated the properties of the elements surrounding manganese. In 1925, using X-ray spectra, they were able to identify the element rhenium. This element was discovered in a sample of the mineral columbite. Further research allowed them to determine the properties of rhenium.

In 1934, Ida proposed that heavy nuclei bombarded by neutrons break down into isotopes of known elements but not neighboring elements or transuranium elements. This proposal was in direct opposition to the beliefs held by the great Enrico Fermi. Five years later Ida's proposal was confirmed by others in the scientific community.

CHEMICAL TECHNOLOGY: Ceramics

Your home or school may be a brick building. Brick is classified as a ceramic. Ceramics are materials formed by heating nonmetallic matter to a high temperature. Chinaware, porcelain, firebrick, cement, tile, abrasives, and glass are also classified as ceramics.

Pottery has been made for thousands of years. However, the field of ceramic chemistry is growing rapidly as a result of new technological advancements and applications. Some of our most recently developed materials are ceramics. In attempting to harness the energy produced by fusion reactions, scientists are having problems developing reaction containers that will withstand the extremely high temperatures involved. Zirconium oxide and silicon carbide ceramics have properties which may make them useful for this application. Lasers are being used to reach the high temperatures necessary for fusion reactions to occur. New glasses containing fluorine compounds such as beryllium fluoride have been developed for these lasers. These materials operate at high power levels, absorb less energy, and show less distortion of the laser beam than current laser materials.

Engineers have been trying to develop nonmetallic rotors for engines as an energy conservation measure. Silicon nitride and silicon carbide rotors are now close to the production stage. These rotors are lighter, cheaper to produce, and made of readily available materials.

The practical transmission of information through glass fibers has been achieved by coating the fibers with a resin augmenting their strength. Incorporating glass fibers and graphite fibers in plastics has allowed the use of these reinforced plastics to replace metal parts on automobiles. Thus, lighter automobiles can be produced resulting in lower fuel consumption.

Medical scientists are constantly searching for new materials which can be implanted in the human body without causing biological problems. The materials must be compatible with existing tissue to prevent rejection by the body's immune system. A calcium phosphate ceramic has been developed for repairing bones. As the body heals, the ceramic is gradually replaced by new, natural bone.

One drawback to the use of nuclear fission as a power source is the disposal of radioactive waste materials. One solution to this problem is the incorporation of radioactive wastes into special, stable glass pellets. The glass can then be stored underground in deep abandoned mines for thousands of years.

Another ceramic development of interest is the properties and design of the tiles covering the Space Shuttle. These tiles protect the craft from the tremendous heat generated by friction between the returning Shuttle and the atmosphere. These tiles are strong, tough, and have a low heat conductivity.

SUMMARY

1. Ionization energy is the energy necessary to remove an electron from an atom, leaving a positive ion. First ionization energy is the energy required to remove the first electron from an atom. 12:1

2. Ionization energies also provide evidence for our theories of atomic structure. 12:2-12:3

3. Electron affinity is the attraction of an atom for electrons. 12:4

4. Metals have low ionization energies and electron affinities. Nonmetals have high ionization energies and electron affinities. 12:4

5. The relative tendency of a bonded atom to attract shared electrons to itself is called its electronegativity. 12:5

6. As the difference in electronegativity between two covalently bound atoms increases, the strength of the bond between them increases. 12:5-12:6

7. Ionic compounds are characterized by high melting points, solubility in water, and crystal formation. 12:7

8. Ionic bonds are formed between atoms with a large difference in electronegativity. This bond involves a transfer of electrons. 12:6-12:7

9. The ionic radius is the best estimate chemists can make of the effective size of an ion. 12:8

10. Covalent bonds are formed between atoms with slight differences in electronegativity. This bond involves sharing of electrons. 12:9

11. The bond axis is a line joining the nuclei of two bonded atoms. The length of the bond axis is called the bond length. The angle between two bond axes is called the bond angle. 12:9

12. The infrared (IR) spectrophotometer can be used to determine molecular structure. Radiation with wavelengths 700 to 50 000 nm is absorbed in characteristic patterns by molecular bonds. 12:9

13. Covalent radii can be used to predict the distance between bonded atoms. 12:10

14. Polyatomic ions possess an overall charge just as other ions. However, they are composed of groups of atoms bonded covalently. 12:11

15. Compounds containing polyatomic ions are bonded ionically. 12:11

16. Electron clouds act as hard spheres when two nonbonded atoms approach each other. The radius of this imaginary sphere is called the van der Waals radius of the atom. 12:12

17. A metallic bond is formed between atoms with few electrons in the outer level. These electrons circulate as delocalized electrons and allow metals to carry an electric current. 12:14

18. The high number of delocalized electrons of such metals as iron, chromium, and nickel makes these metals very hard and strong. In general, the transition elements are the hardest and strongest elements. 12:15

PROBLEMS

5. Which atom in each of the following pairs of atoms would have the lower first ionization energy?
   a. Al, B
   b. Na, K
   c. O, C

   d. Ar, K
   e. K, Ca
   f. Si, C

   6. Those electrons come from a lower energy level and are held more tightly.

6. Using the data in Table 12-3, why does the ionization energy change so much for the fourth boron electron and the fifth carbon electron?

7. Explain the differences in the six ionization energies of carbon (Table 12-3).

8. Why are most ionic compounds brittle?

9. What type of bond would you expect to find between xenon and fluorine in XeF_4? Ionic

10. Using Table 12-8, predict the bond lengths indicated for the following substances.
    a. Cl—Cl in Cl_2 0.198 nm
    b. N—H in NH_3 0.107 nm
    c. C—N in $(CH_3)_3 N$ 0.147 nm

    d. H—Br in HBr 0.151 nm
    e. C—C in $CH_3 CH_3$ 0.154 nm
    f. F—O in OF_2 0.130 nm

11. Construct a graph of the number of delocalized electrons versus the atomic number for the elements $Z = 21$ through $Z = 30$.

12. What four factors affect the values obtained for ionization energies of an element? nuclear charge, shielding effect, radius, sublevel

13. How does van der Waals radius differ from covalent radius?

14. Why is it difficult to give exact values for bond lengths and bond angles?

15. List three characteristic properties of metals. conductors, malleable, ductile

16. How does the number of delocalized electrons in a metal affect its properties?

REVIEW

1. Make a list of ten elements having more than two possible oxidation states.

2. Briefly describe the development of classification for elements from Dobereiner to the modern periodic table.

3. Predict the oxidation number of the following elements, using only the periodic table as a guide.
   a. astatine, germanium, mercury, polonium, tin
   b. francium, hafnium, neodymium, rubidium, tellurium.

4. Describe the structure of the modern periodic table.

5. Predict oxidation numbers for the following elements using the periodic table as a guide.
   a. rubidium   metal 1+
   b. zirconium   metal 2+
   c. niobium   metal 2+
   d. tellurium   metalloid 6+, 2−
   e. iodine   nonmetal 1−

6. Classify each of the elements in Problem 5 as metal or nonmetal.

7. What are the family names of the elements in the following groups?
   a. IA   alkali metals
   b. IIA   alkaline earth metals
   c. IB through VIIIB   transition metals
   d. VIIA   halogens
   e. VIIIA   noble gases

8. Write electron configurations for the following elements.
   a. molybdenum
   b. antimony
   c. lanthanum
   d. technetium
   e. tin

ONE MORE STEP

1. Find an equation used to calculate electronegativities and try it on several elements.

2. Investigate the methods used by chemists for determining bond lengths.

3. What experimental data are used in determining covalent, ionic, and van der Waals radii? What assumptions are made in each case?

4. One factor affecting ionic radius, bond energy, and electronegativity of an atom is the coordination number of the atom. Prepare a report on this concept.

5. Carbon, in the form of diamond, is an insulator. Silicon, carbon's nearest neighbor in Group IVA, is a semiconductor. Find out why.

6. Carbon, in the form of diamond, is an insulator. Carbon, in the form of graphite, is a conductor. Find out why.

READINGS

Myers, R. Thomas, "Electronegativity, Bond Energy, and Chemical Reactivity," *Journal of Chemical Education,* Vol. 56 No. 11, (November 1979), pp. 711-712.

Myers, R. Thomas, "Physical and Chemical Properties and Bonding of Metallic Elements," *Journal of Chemical Education,* Vol. 56 No. 11, (November 1979), pp. 712-713.

"Synthetic Metal," *SciQuest,* Vol. 53, No 7 (September 1980), p. 28.

The properties and uses of a material are dependent on its structure. The internal atomic structure of materials is an important part of the design of this amusement park ride. The external design is based on chemical structure and geometric principles. What aspects of geometry are used in studying molecular structure? What theories are used to explain molecular structure? How does the geometry of a molecule determine its properties?

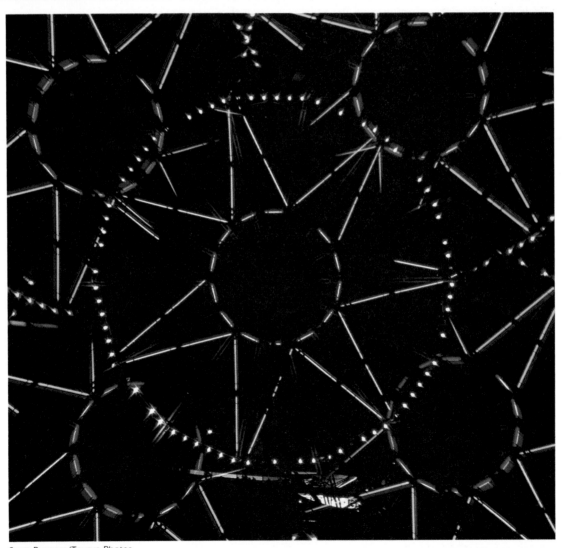

Scott Ransom/Taurus Photos

MOLECULAR STRUCTURE 13

Chapter 13 focuses on the relationship between chemical bonding and molecular structure in introducing four ways of explaining the apparent structural features of molecules. Valence shell electron pair repulsion (VSEPR), hybridization, resonance, and molecular orbital theory are presented.

Demonstration—Round and egg-shaped rubber balloons can be used to represent *s* and *p* electron clouds. They can be deformed when pushed together to demonstrate orbital overlap. When suspended by threads, charged balloons can be used to demonstrate *e*⁻ cloud repulsion. Rub balloons on wool cloth to charge.

There are several ways of looking at the structure of molecules in order to describe their shape. We will consider four of these hypotheses. The first of these ideas takes into account the repulsive forces of electron pairs surrounding an atom. The second method considers different ways in which atomic orbitals can combine to form orbitals surrounding more than one nucleus. The electrons occupying these combined orbitals then serve to bind the atoms together. The third method considers molecules with more than one possible structure. The fourth method considers orbitals for molecules as a whole instead of atoms.

In order to describe the shape of a molecule or polyatomic ion, it is useful to draw an electron dot diagram for it. Consider the water molecule. It is composed of one oxygen and two hydrogen atoms. The electron dot diagrams are $\cdot \ddot{O} \colon$ and $H \cdot$ for these elements. All electrons are identical. We use different symbols here only to help us understand how we arrive at the final structure. By combining an oxygen and two hydrogens, we obtain the following electron dot diagram.

$$H \colon \ddot{O} \colon$$
$$\ddot{H}$$

It is the only arrangement of electrons in which all three atoms can achieve a full outer level. Note that two pairs of electrons in the outer level of oxygen are involved in bonding the hydrogens. They are called **shared pairs.** The other two pairs of electrons are not involved in bonding. They are called **unshared pairs.**

GOAL: You will study four hypothesis explaining the structure and resulting properties of certain molecules.

Outer electron pairs attracted by two nuclei are called shared pairs.
Outer electron pairs attracted to one nucleus are called unshared pairs.

13:1 METHOD 1: PAIR REPULSION

One way of looking at molecules is to consider electron repulsion. Each bond and each unshared pair in the outer level of an atom form a charge cloud which repels all other charge clouds. In part, this repulsion is due to all electrons having the same charge. Another more important factor is the Pauli exclusion principle. Although electrons of opposite spin may occupy the same volume of space, electrons of the same spin may not do so. The repulsions resulting from the Pauli principle are much greater than the electrostatic ones at small distances. Because of these repulsions, atoms cannot be compressed.

The repulsions between the charge clouds in the outer level of atoms determine the arrangement of the orbitals. The orbital arrangement, in turn, determines the shape of molecules. As a result, the following rule may be stated: *Electron pairs spread as far apart as possible to minimize repulsive forces.* If there are only two electron pairs in the outer level, they will be on opposite sides of the nucleus. The arrangement is called linear. If there are three electron pairs, the axes of their charge clouds will be 120° apart. This arrangement is called trigonal planar and the electron pairs lie in the same plane as the nucleus. If there are four electron pairs, the axes of the charge clouds will be farthest apart when they intersect at an angle of 109.5°. Of course, these axes will not all lie in the same plane. The easiest way to see them is to imagine a regular tetrahedron. A tetrahedron is a figure having four faces, each of which is an equilateral triangle.

Electron pairs spread as far apart as possible to minimize repulsions.

FIGURE 13-1. Electron pairs spread as far apart as possible resulting in linear, trigonal planar, and tetrahedral arrangements for molecules containing two, three, and four bonding pairs.

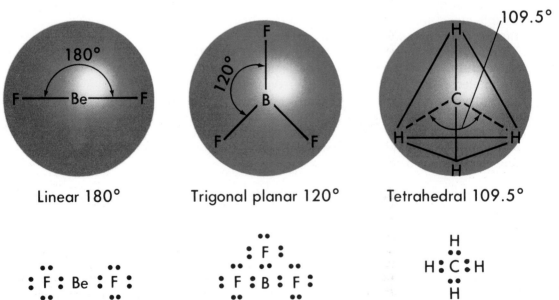

Linear 180°   Trigonal planar 120°   Tetrahedral 109.5°

The nucleus is at the center and the axes extend out to the corners. Figure 13-1 shows some examples in which each electron pair in the outer level is used in bonding to another atom. Can you see a relationship between the number of bonds formed and the resulting molecular shapes?

The bonds and unshared electron pairs determine the shape of a molecule. An unshared pair is acted upon by only one nucleus. Its charge cloud is like a very blunt pear, Figure 13-2, with its stem end at the nucleus. A shared pair of electrons moves within the field of two nuclei. The cloud is more slender.

The electron pair repulsions in a molecule may not all be equal. The repulsion between two unshared pairs is greatest because they occupy the most space. The repulsion between two shared pairs is least because they occupy the least space. The repulsion between an unshared pair and a shared pair is an intermediate case.

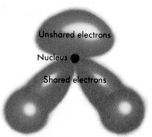

FIGURE 13-2. The charge clouds occupied by shared and unshared electron pairs are different shapes.

$$\underset{\text{repulsion}}{\text{unshared-unshared}} > \underset{\text{repulsion}}{\text{unshared-shared}} > \underset{\text{repulsion}}{\text{shared-shared}}$$

Electron pair repulsion strengths may not be equal.

Let us look at the molecular shapes of the compounds CH_4, NH_3, H_2O, and HF to illustrate this repulsion. In each of these compounds, the central atom has four clouds around it. We expect the axes of all four charge clouds to point approximately toward the corners of a tetrahedron.

In CH_4 molecules, all clouds are shared pairs, so their sizes are equal and each bond angle is in fact 109.5°. In NH_3 molecules, there are one unshared pair and three bonds. The unshared pair occupies more space than the other three, so the bonding clouds are at an angle of 107° to each other. In H_2O molecules, two unshared pairs are present, both of these clouds are larger than the bonds. This additional cloud size results in a still greater reduction in the bond angle which is, in fact, 104.5°. In the HF molecule, there is only one bond axis and consequently no bond angle. Note that in the four molecules discussed, each has four electron clouds. The differences in molecular shape result from the unequal space occupied by the unshared pairs and the bonds.

The shapes for different numbers of clouds can be predicted in the same way and are listed in Table 13-1.

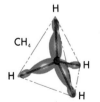

Tetrahedron

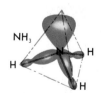

Trigonal pyramid

Angular

FIGURE 13-3. The central atom in each molecule is surrounded by four electron pairs. The influence of shared and unshared pairs accounts for the different shapes.

Table 13-1

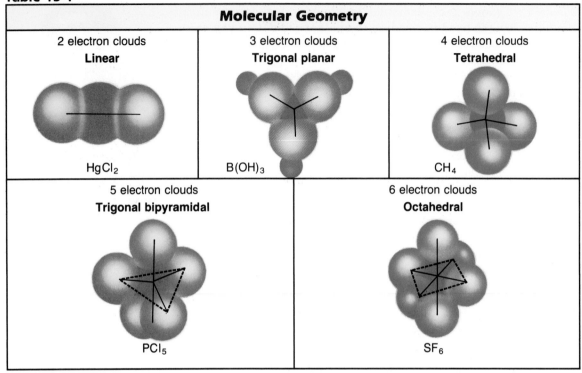

Molecular Geometry		
2 electron clouds **Linear**	3 electron clouds **Trigonal planar**	4 electron clouds **Tetrahedral**
$HgCl_2$	$B(OH)_3$	CH_4
5 electron clouds **Trigonal bipyramidal**		6 electron clouds **Octahedral**
PCl_5		SF_6

13:2   MULTIPLE BOND REPULSIONS

When two atoms combine by forming a covalent bond, it is sometimes possible for them to share more than one pair of electrons. For example, the organic compound methanal contains a double bond. The carbon atom and the oxygen atom share two pairs of electrons. The electron dot diagram for methanal is

Two atoms can form covalent bonds by sharing more than one pair of electrons.

$$\begin{array}{c} H \\ \overset{\bullet\bullet}{H\!:\!C}\!:\!\!:\!\overset{\times\times}{\underset{\bullet}{O}}\!: \end{array}$$

In the diatomic molecule, N_2, the two nitrogen atoms share three pairs of electrons. They are bound to each other by a triple bond. The electron dot diagram for the nitrogen molecule is

$$:N:::N:$$

How does the electron-pair repulsion theory predict the shapes of molecules containing multiple bonds?

A **double bond** can be considered as a single electron cloud made of two orbitals. However, because the bond consists of four electrons occupying the space, the cloud will occupy more space than a single bond. A triple bond, by the same reasoning, would occupy still more space. In the case of methanal, there are three clouds around the carbon atom, two single bonds and one double bond. We anticipate that the clouds will assume a trigonal planar shape. The double bond will occupy somewhat more space. As a result, the H—C—H bond angle should be a little less than 120°, and the H—C=O bond angle a little more. Experiment shows a H—C—H bond angle of 116° and a H—C=O angle of 122°.

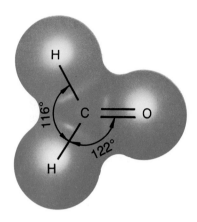

FIGURE 13-4. The methanal molecule contains a double bond. Thus the H—C—H bond angle is smaller than predicted, since a double bond occupies more space than a single bond.

Consider three electron pairs in the outer level arranged as a double bond with one atom and a single bond with another atom. Here we have three pairs forming two bonds and we get a linear molecule. This arrangement is only found in some unstable organic molecules. With two double bonds, each to a separate atom, we also get a linear molecule. The organic compound, ketene, illustrates two double bonds as well as a double bond with two singles. The structure of the ketene molecule is

$$\begin{array}{c} H \\ \diagdown \\ \diagup \quad C{=}C{=}O \\ H \end{array}$$

The C=C=O bond angle is 180°, while the H—C=C bond angle is slightly greater than 120°. The one remaining case is that of eight electrons shared as a triple bond and a single bond. As you might expect, such an arrangement gives rise to a linear shape. Another organic compound, ethyne, illustrates this arrangement. Ethyne has the structure

$$H{-}C{\equiv}C{-}H$$

The H—C≡C bond angles are 180°. When individual molecules are investigated in detail, the experimental bond angles are not always exactly as we would predict. There are other factors influencing bond angles which we will not pursue in this course.

In most compounds, the outer level is considered full with four pairs or eight electrons. The outer level in some atoms can contain more than eight electrons (if the outer level is the third or higher). In this case it is possible to force more than eight electrons into that level under the proper conditions. A number of nonmetals, mainly the halogens, form compounds in which the outer level is expanded to 10, 12 or 14 electrons. Such an arrangement would also explain noble gas compounds. An example is xenon tetrafluoride, XeF_4. The structure for this compound is shown in Figure 13-5. Xenon has eight electrons of its own in its outer level together with four from the fluorine atoms (one from each).

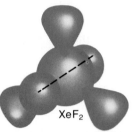

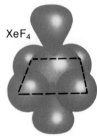

XeF$_4$

XeF_2

Trigonal bipyramidal shape
Linear molecule

Octahedral shape
Square planar molecule

FIGURE 13-5. XeF$_2$ and XeF$_4$ are two examples of compounds where the central atom has an expanded octet of electrons.

Table 13-2

Experimental Molecular Shapes		
Cl—B, Cl Cl 120°	I—C—H H H 107° 112°	H—C—H H H 109.5°
H C=C F F 125° 109°	:O: F F 103°	NH$_2$ C=S NH$_2$ 116° 122°
	H O H 104.5°	
C C C C C C C C C C C C C 109.5°	N H H H 107°	H Si H H H H 130° N—N 130° H H Si H H H H Si H H H Si H
	O O O 117°	

13:3 SIGMA AND PI BONDS

A covalent bond is formed when an orbital of one atom overlaps an orbital of another atom and they share the electron pair in the bond. For example, a bond may be formed by the overlap of two *s* orbitals. A bond formed by the direct overlap of two orbitals is called a **sigma bond** and is designated σ. A sigma bond is also formed by the overlap of an *s* orbital of one atom with a *p* orbital of another atom.

A sigma bond is formed by the direct overlap of two *s* orbitals or the direct overlap of an *s* and *p* orbital.

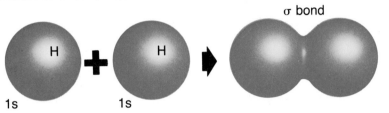

FIGURE 13-6. The overlap of two *s* orbitals is a sigma bond. The H—H bond in hydrogen gas is a sigma bond.

When two *p* orbitals overlap, there are two possibilities since *p* orbitals are not spherical. If two *p* orbitals overlap along an axis in an end-to-end fashion a sigma type (σ) bond is formed as shown in Figure 13-7. If, however, the two *p* orbitals overlap

A sigma bond is also formed by the direct overlap of two *p* orbitals.

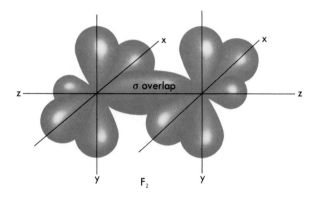

FIGURE 13-7. The direct overlap of two *p* orbitals is also a sigma bond.

sideways with their axes parallel, as in Figure 13-8, they form what is called a **pi (π) bond.** Ethene contains one sigma and one pi bond. Ethyne has one sigma and two pi bonds.

Two *p* orbitals with parallel overlap is a *pi* bond.

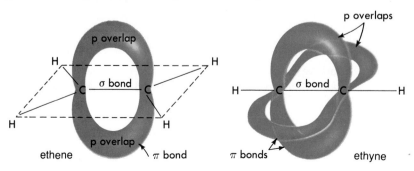

The orbitals are distorted to form pi bonds.

FIGURE 13-8. The C=C double bond in ethene consists of one sigma and one pi bond. The C≡C triple bond in ethyne is one sigma and two pi bonds.

13:4   METHOD 2: HYBRID ORBITALS

We would expect the carbon atom with four outer electrons to have two p orbitals available for bonding. However, it has been discovered that carbon does not usually form two p orbital bonds. Instead, according to theory, the s and p orbitals of carbon merge to form four equivalent **hybrid orbitals.** If one s and three p orbitals merge, four sp^3 hybrid orbitals are formed. The sp^3 orbitals are arranged in tetrahedral fashion.

These are 3-dimensional averages of the component orbitals.

Carbon can form four equivalent sp^3 hybrid orbitals, which are arranged as a tetrahedron.

This shape has also been explained by method 1 pair repulsion.

FIGURE 13-9. Carbon can form four equivalent sp^3 hybrid orbitals which are arranged in a tetrahedral shape.

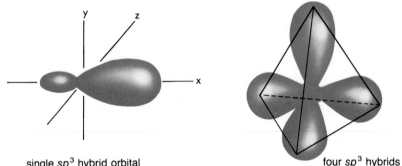

single sp^3 hybrid orbital   four sp^3 hybrids

A second way of looking at molecular shape is by considering the different ways s and p orbitals can overlap when electrons are shared. This method can best be seen by looking at the element carbon. However, the same principles can be applied to any atom forming covalent bonds.

A carbon atom can form four equivalent bonds. Carbon atoms can link covalently to other carbon atoms. Carbon atoms can also link covalently to atoms of many other elements. However, it is the linking of carbon atom to carbon atom which gives rise to the large number of carbon compounds. There are more carbon compounds than the total of noncarbon compounds.

13:5   GEOMETRY OF CARBON COMPOUNDS

Carbon can form four single sp^3 hybrid bonds. The bond angle between the bond axes is 109.5°.

The bonding of four hydrogen atoms to one carbon atom forms methane. The bonds involve the overlap of the s orbital of each hydrogen atom with one of the sp^3 hybrid orbitals of a carbon atom.

A three dimensional representation of the formula of methane is shown in the following diagram.

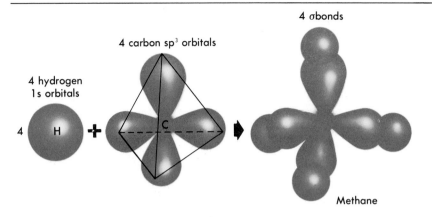

FIGURE 13-10. The methane structure can be explained by combining a hydrogen *s* orbital with each of the *sp³* hybrid orbitals of carbon.

There is an angle of 109.5° between each carbon—hydrogen bond axis.

Carbon atoms may bond to each other by the overlap of an orbital of one carbon atom with an orbital of another carbon atom. The carbon—carbon single bond is a sigma type bond. Many carbon atoms may bond in this manner to form a chain or ring. Recall from Chapter 11 that carbon exhibits catenation.

The other three *sp³* orbitals of each carbon atom may bond with hydrogen *s* orbitals. The compound C_2H_6 is called ethane. A three dimensional structure of this compound called ethane is shown to the right.

13:6 MULTIPLE BONDS

Carbon can also form compounds where one *s* orbital and two *p* orbitals merge to form *sp²* hybrid orbitals. The three *sp²* hybrid orbitals are arranged in a plane with 120° bond angles.

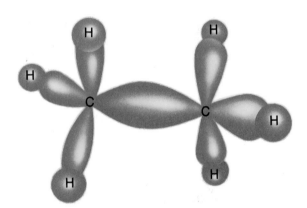

FIGURE 13-11. The shape of ethane is explained by combining two *sp³* hybrid carbon atoms. The single bond is a direct overlap of one hybrid orbital from each carbon atom.

The *sp²* hybrid orbitals are in a plane with 120° bond angles.

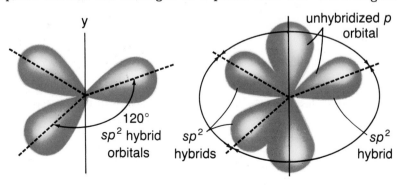

FIGURE 13-12. Carbon can form three equivalent *sp²* hybrid orbitals. The remaining *p* orbital is not hybridized and its lobes are 90° from the *sp²* hybrids. Note the hybrid orbitals are smaller than the *p* orbital.

The third p orbital is not hybridized. It is perpendicular to the plane of the sp^2 hybrids.

There is a double bond in ethene, H_2C═CH_2. It is formed by the σ overlap of two sp^2 orbitals and the π overlap of two pure p orbitals. Thus, the two carbon atoms are sharing two pairs of electrons. The six atoms of ethene lie in one plane. The structural formula shows the bond angles in the plane.

A double bond is one sigma bond and one pi bond.

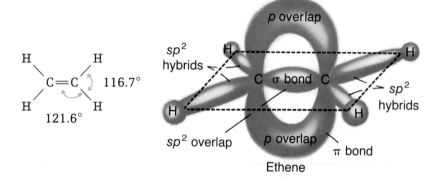

FIGURE 13-13. The shape of ethene is explained by combining two sp^2 hybrid carbon atoms. The C—H sigma bonds all lie in the same plane. The unhybridized p orbitals of the carbon atoms combine to form the pi bond.

The triple bond in ethyne (HC≡CH) is formed when one s orbital and one p orbital merge to form an sp hybrid. This change leaves two pure p orbitals perpendicular to each other and the hybrids. Two of the sp orbitals overlap head-on to form a σ type bond. The two p orbitals in each atom overlap sideways to form π type bonds.

A triple bond is one sigma bond and two pi bonds.

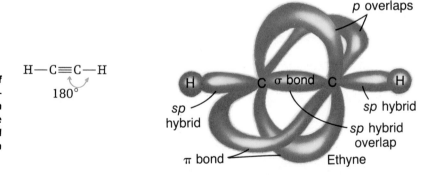

FIGURE 13-14. The shape of ethyne is explained by combining two sp hybrid carbon atoms. The two pi bonds are formed from the unhybridized p orbitals of both carbon atoms.

Double and triple bonds are less flexible than single bonds. Pi bonds are more easily broken than sigma bonds. As a result, molecules containing multiple bonds are usually more reactive than molecules containing only single bonds. However, a multiple bond between two atoms is stronger than a single bond between them. It also holds the atoms closer than a single bond would.

Molecules containing multiple bonds are usually more reactive than similar molecules containing only single bonds.

A multiple bond has a shorter bond length and is stronger than a single bond.

13:7 BENZENE

Each of the six carbon atoms in a benzene ring, C_6H_6, has three sp^2 hybrid orbitals and one p orbital. Sigma bonds are formed by the overlap of the sp^2 orbitals of six carbon atoms forming a ring of single bonds. The double bonds of the benzene ring are formed by the π overlap of the p orbitals of the carbon atoms.

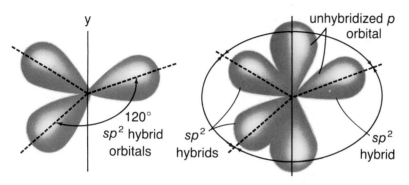

FIGURE 13-15. Each atom in a benzene ring is an sp^2 hybrid. The unhybridized p orbitals will form pi bonds.

However, one of the characteristics of benzene is that the π electrons can be shared all around the ring. Since the π electrons are shared equally among all the carbon atoms and not confined to one atom or bond, they are delocalized. This delocalization of π electrons among the carbon atoms in benzene results in greater stability of the compound.

Benzene has delocalized π electrons.

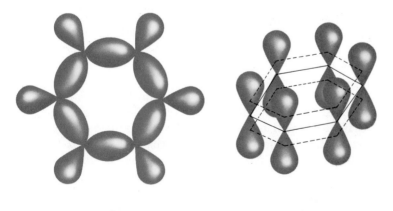

σ bonds with sp^2 hybrid orbitals   unhybridized p orbitals

FIGURE 13-16. The benzene ring results from the overlap of six sp^2 hybrid carbon atoms. The unhybridized p orbitals form two pi clouds allowing electrons to be shared around the ring.

Benzene is such an important compound it has been given a structural symbol. The symbol for benzene is

Unsaturated compounds contain double or triple carbon-to-carbon bonds.

A conjugated system makes the molecule very stable.

Isomers have the same molecular formula but different structures.

The inner circle indicates the unsaturated character of all the carbon atoms of the benzene ring. **Unsaturated compounds** are those containing double or triple bonds between carbon atoms.

Whenever multiple p orbital overlap can occur, the molecule is said to contain a **conjugated system.** Conjugated systems can occur in chains as well as in rings of atoms. 1,3-butadiene, $CH_2{=}CH{-}CH{=}CH_2$, is an example. Again, the conjugated system imparts a special stability to the molecule.

13:8 ISOMERS

The existence of two or more substances with the same molecular formula, but different structures, is called **isomerism** (i SOHM eh rihz uhm). The different structures are called **isomers** (i SOH muhrs). Since isomerism is so common in organic chemistry, we will study the isomers of carbon compounds.

Consider the compound with the formula C_4H_{10}. There are two structures which can be written for this formula.

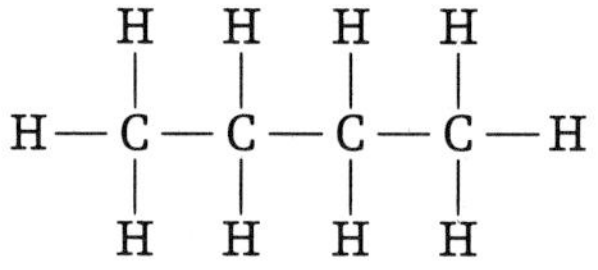

butane 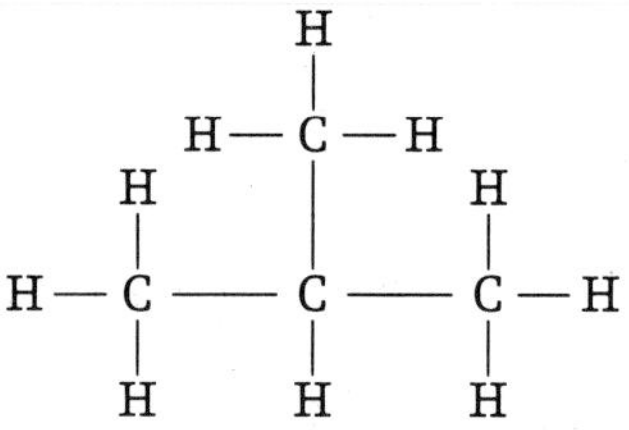   isobutane

Butane and isobutane are examples of **structural isomers** or skeleton isomers, since it is the carbon chain which is altered.

Look at the two structures shown for butene. Note that the formation of a π bond prevents the atoms on each end of the bond from rotating with respect to each other. Some compounds containing double bonds exhibit a kind of isomerism called **geometric isomerism.** We will use the compound 2-butene (C_4H_8) to illustrate geometric isomers. Note that in the *cis* form of 2-butene, the CH_3 groups and the hydrogen atoms are on the same side of the double bond. In the *trans* form, they are on opposite sides.

A double bond prevents free rotation of the atoms on each end of the bond.

Cis- and *trans*- are two forms of geometric isomerism.

Cis form: Like atoms are on the same side of the double bond.

Trans form: Like atoms are on opposite sides of the double bond.

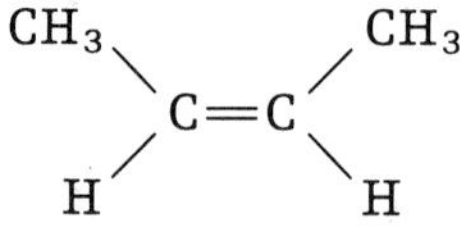

cis-2-butene 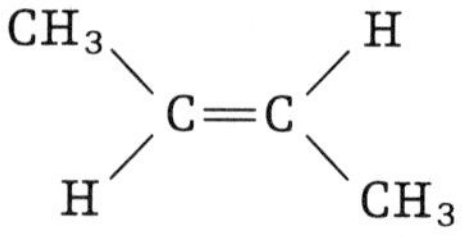   *trans*-2-butene

If we introduce another element into a hydrocarbon molecule, we find two more kinds of isomers, **positional** and **functional.** The newly introduced particle may occupy two or more positions in the molecule. Each different position produces a positional isomer. The positional isomers for propanol are shown. Note both compounds have the same molecular formula but differ in the position of the OH group.

Positional isomers are formed in hydrocarbon molecules where particles can occupy 2 or more different positions.

$$
\begin{array}{ccc}
\text{H} & \text{H} & \text{H} \\
| & | & | \\
\text{H}-\text{C}-\text{C}-\text{C}-\text{OH} \\
| & | & | \\
\text{H} & \text{H} & \text{H}
\end{array}
\qquad
\begin{array}{ccc}
\text{H} & \text{OH} & \text{H} \\
| & | & | \\
\text{H}-\text{C}-\text{C}-\text{C}-\text{H} \\
| & | & | \\
\text{H} & \text{H} & \text{H}
\end{array}
$$

1-propanol   2-propanol

The possibility of a new element being bonded in two different ways illustrates functional isomerism. Ethanol is a liquid while methoxymethane is a gas at room temperature.

Functional isomers are formed when the new element can be bonded in two different ways.

$$
\begin{array}{cc}
\text{H} & \text{H} \\
| & | \\
\text{H}-\text{C}-\text{C}-\text{OH} \\
| & | \\
\text{H} & \text{H}
\end{array}
\qquad
\begin{array}{cc}
\text{H} & \text{H} \\
| & | \\
\text{H}-\text{C}-\text{O}-\text{C}-\text{H} \\
| & | \\
\text{H} & \text{H}
\end{array}
$$

ethanol   methoxymethane

The mass spectrometer can be used to distinguish between isomers which have very similar properties. During the analysis, the sample being studied is ionized and divided into ion fragments. Each fragment has an m/e value (mass to charge ratio). In Figure 13-17, the mass spectrogram for hexane shows peaks

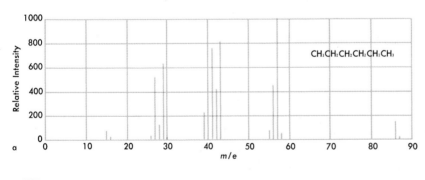

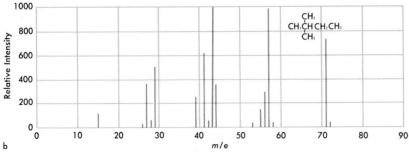

FIGURE 13-17. The mass spectrogram for hexane (a) and 2,2-dimethylbutane (b) show the same number of peaks. However, the differences in m/e values for each peak can be used to identify each compound in a mixture of unknown substances.

at 17 different m/e values. The hexane molecule can be broken into 17 fragments which each have a different mass. Note the spectrogram for 2,2-dimethylbutane also shows 17 fragments. However, you can see that the relative intensities for 2,2-dimethylbutane are significantly different from those shown for hexane.

13:9   INORGANIC COMPOUNDS

The ground state electron configuration of carbon ends in $2s^2 2p^2$. In Section 13:4 we saw that each of the four electrons was placed in a separate orbital. We treated the carbon atom as if it were in the state $2s^1 2p^3$. We assumed that this was the configuration in order that hybridization of orbitals could occur.

What about other atoms? For example, beryllium has two outer electrons $2s^2$ and only two orbitals need be hybridized. We would expect sp hybridization to lead to linear bonding orbitals. Analysis bears out this prediction with molecules having a central atom ending in an s^2 configuration. For boron, $2s^2 2p^1$, and other atoms with three outer electrons, we would predict sp^2 hybridization. Again, analysis bears out the prediction of trigonal planar bond arrangements.

Atoms other than carbon atoms may have hydridized orbitals.

Point out to students that the electron dot structures for Be and B do not follow the octet rule.

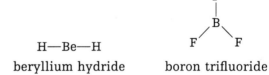

H—Be—H
beryllium hydride   boron trifluoride

We can, in fact, apply all our principles of molecular geometry and isomerism to inorganic compounds as well.

13:10   METHOD 3: RESONANCE

We have been looking at compounds that can be represented by a single structural formula. However, analysis shows that many molecules and polyatomic ions cannot be described by one formula. We will now consider another way of looking at molecules.

Compounds cannot always be represented by a single structural formula.

Consider the nitrate ion (NO_3^-). The theory of electron cloud spacing would predict 120° O—N—O bond angles and a trigonal planar ion. Experiments have shown this prediction to be true.

Now, suppose we attempt to draw an electron dot diagram for the nitrate ion. If we let electrons originally associated with oxygen atoms be represented by ($\times$), the electron dot structure for an oxygen atom would be:

$$\times \overset{\times \times}{\underset{\times}{O}} \times$$

Likewise, if nitrogen electrons are represented by (∘), the electron dot structure for nitrogen would be:

$$\circ \overset{\circ}{\underset{\circ}{\text{N}}} \circ$$

A possible electron dot diagram for the nitrate ion shows an ion with a 1⁻ charge. The extra electron is shown by the symbol (·).

$$\overset{\times \times}{\underset{\times \times}{\text{O}}} \quad -$$
$$\overset{}{\underset{}{:}}\overset{\times \times}{\underset{\times \times}{\text{O}}} \overset{\circ \circ}{\underset{\circ \circ}{\text{N}}} \overset{\times \times}{\underset{\times \times}{\text{O}}}\overset{}{:}$$

Note that the nitrogen atom has only six electrons in its outer level. We know that most atoms tend to satisfy the octet rule in compound formation. How, then, can we properly explain the structure of the nitrate ion?

Another electron dot diagram can be shown which satisfies our requirements. One of the oxygen atoms shares two pairs of electrons with the nitrogen. Suppose the nitrate ion was actually constructed. Then we would expect the doubly-bonded oxygen atom to be a little closer to the nitrogen than the other two oxygen atoms. However, analysis has shown that all three N—O bonds are the same length.

In NO_3^-, all bond lengths are equal.

$$: \text{O} : \quad -$$
$$: \text{O} : \text{N} : \text{O} :$$

To account for this observation, chemists have formulated a concept called resonance. Using the idea of **resonance**, we can draw several equivalent diagrams for the distribution of electrons in a molecule or ion. In fact, we draw all possible diagrams which obey the rules about full outer levels and the number of bonds an atom can form. We then consider the actual structure of the particle to be the average of all these possibilities. Thus the following structures can be drawn for the nitrate ion.

Resonance: Equivalent alternative structures for a molecule or polyatomic ion which lead to "average" bond lengths.

$$\begin{array}{ccccc} & - & & - & & - \\ \text{O} & & \text{O} & & \text{O} & \\ \text{N} :: \text{O} & \leftrightarrow & \text{N} : \text{O} : & \leftrightarrow & \text{N} : \text{O} : \\ \text{O} & & \text{O} & & \text{O} & \end{array}$$

If we "average" these three structures in our minds, we can see that we will end up with three equal N—O bonds. Each of these bonds will be about one and one third times the normal single bond strength. Because each bond is slightly stronger than a single bond, each bond length is slightly shorter than a single N—O bond. Since they are equivalent, the bond lengths will be the same, and the bond angles will be equal, 120°. Note that the different forms are shown to be equivalent by the double-ended arrows between them.

13:11   METHOD 4: MOLECULAR ORBITAL THEORY

The structure and properties of some molecules and ions cannot be explained by any of the methods we have studied. Another approach to structure makes use of **molecular orbitals.** These orbitals belong to the molecule as a whole, not to a particular atom. By combining atomic orbitals from the outer levels of bonding atoms, we get an equal number of molecular orbitals.

Molecular orbitals belong to the molecule as a whole, not to a particular atom.

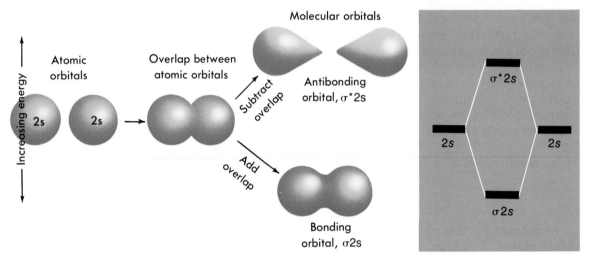

FIGURE 13-18. Two molecular orbitals are formed from two *s* atomic orbitals. The low energy molecular orbital is more stable than both atomic orbitals.

Consider the bonding of two atoms whose outer level is the second energy level. Each atom has four orbitals in its outer level,

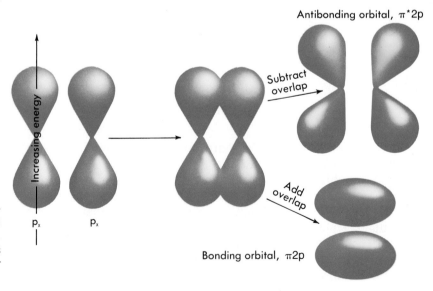

FIGURE 13-19. Four molecular orbitals are formed from the pi overlap of four atomic *p* orbitals. Two of these molecular orbitals are more stable than the four atomic orbitals.

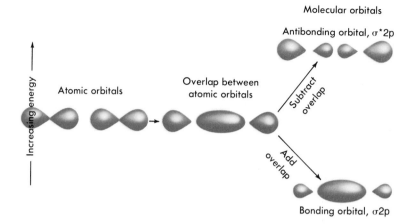

FIGURE 13-20. Two molecular orbitals are formed from the sigma overlap of two atomic *p* orbitals. The low energy molecular orbital is more stable than the atomic orbitals.

one *s* and three *p* orbitals. By combining the two atomic 2*s* orbitals we get two molecular orbitals. One of these two molecular orbitals represents less energy and is therefore more stable than the two atomic orbitals from which it was made. The other molecular orbital represents more energy and is less stable than its atomic orbitals. The more stable orbital is designated σ2*s* (sigma two ess) and the less stable σ*2*s* (sigma two ess star). Electrons in the σ2*s* orbital bond the two atoms together. As a result the σ2*s* is called a bonding orbital. Electrons in the σ*2*s* repel each other and the σ*2*s* is called an antibonding orbital.

Molecular orbitals result from combining outer atomic orbitals.

Two atomic orbitals combine to form two molecular orbitals; one is more stable, and one is less stable than the atomic orbitals.

The more stable molecular orbital is called a bonding orbital.

The less stable molecular orbital is called an antibonding orbital.

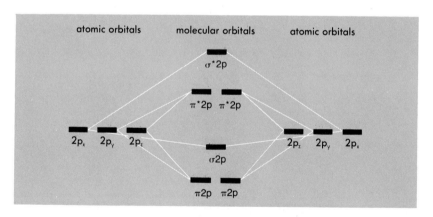

FIGURE 13-21. The energy diagram for the formation of molecular orbitals shows the lowest energy orbitals to be the bonding molecular orbitals. The highest energy and least stable orbitals are the antibonding molecular orbitals.

In a similar fashion, the 2*p* atomic orbitals are combined to form six molecular orbitals. The lowest energy molecular orbitals formed from the 2*p* atomic orbitals are two π2*p* orbitals. At a slightly higher energy, one σ2*p* orbital is formed. At still higher energy, two π*2*p* orbitals are formed. At the highest energy, one σ*2*p* orbital is formed. Again the starred orbitals represent antibonding orbitals.

Electrons in the outer level of the atoms enter the newly formed molecular orbitals. These electrons obey the same rules of filling molecular orbitals that they obeyed for atomic orbitals. Specifically, they enter the lowest-energy available orbital first. If two or more orbitals of the same energy are available, one electron will enter each before any pairing is done. Electron configurations for molecules can be written just as we write configurations for atoms, for example, $\sigma 2s^2$, $\sigma *2s^2$, $\pi 2p^4$, and so on. The bonding between atoms is found by subtracting antibonding electrons from bonding electrons and dividing by two. The number obtained is called the bond order. We divide by two because a bond consists of a shared pair of electrons.

One molecule which is successfully treated by molecular orbital theory is the oxygen molecule. Let us first consider the O_2 molecule by the other method. Each oxygen atom has six electrons in its outer level. To satisfy the octet rule, the electron dot diagram for oxygen would be

$$:\ddot{O}::\ddot{O}:$$

That diagram indicates a double bond between oxygen atoms, with all electrons paired. Study of the oxygen molecule indicates that there is a double bond present (bond order = 2). However, behavior of the oxygen molecule in the magnetic field indicates two unpaired electrons!

Electrons enter the lowest-energy molecular orbital available first. (aufbau principle)

If two or more orbitals of the same energy are available, one electron will enter each before pairing. (Hund's Rule)

You may wish to introduce the terms paramagnetic (unpaired e^-) and diamagnetic (all e^-'s are paired).

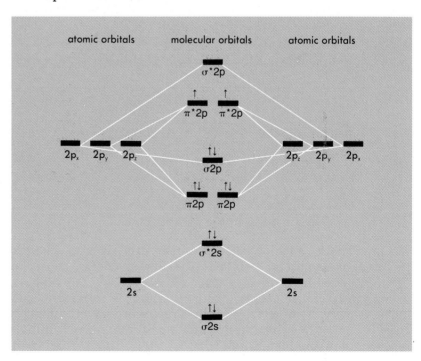

FIGURE 13-22. In filling the molecular orbital diagram for oxygen, electrons are placed in the lowest energy orbitals first.

How does molecular orbital theory describe the oxygen molecule? Molecular orbital theory predicts the formation of the molecular orbitals as mentioned earlier in this section. We then position the twelve outer electrons (six from each O atom). The first two enter the two $\sigma 2s$ orbital and the next two enter the $\sigma *2s$ orbital as shown in Figure 13-22. Four electrons enter the two $\pi 2p$ orbitals and two enter the $\sigma 2p$ orbital. The last two electrons enter the $\pi *2p$ orbitals. Since there are two of these orbitals, one electron enters each. Thus, there are the two unpaired electrons as observed by experiment. Eight electrons have entered bonding orbitals ($\sigma 2s^2$, $\pi 2p^4$, $\sigma 2p^2$). Four electrons have entered anti-bonding orbitals ($\sigma 2s^2$, $\pi *2p^2$). We calculate the bond order as

$$\frac{8-4}{2} = 2$$

$$\text{Bond order} = \frac{\substack{\text{bonding} \\ \text{electrons}} - \substack{\text{anti-} \\ \text{bonding} \\ \text{electrons}}}{2}$$

In agreement with experiment, molecular orbital theory shows the two oxygen atoms to be doubly bonded.

Again experimental evidence backs up or precedes theory.

EXAMPLE: Molecular Orbitals

Is the Be_2 molecule stable as described by molecular orbital theory?

Solving process:
If the two beryllium atoms were to combine, their atomic orbitals would form the molecular orbitals shown in Figure 13-23. Each

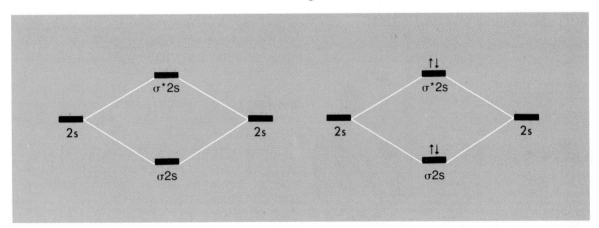

beryllium atom has two electrons in the outer level. Therefore, there would be four electrons to place in molecular orbitals. The first two electrons would enter the $\sigma 2s$ orbital and the second two would enter the $\sigma *2s$ orbital. The bond order is

$$\frac{2-2}{2} = 0$$

FIGURE 13-23. The molecular orbital model for Be_2 contains two molecular orbitals formed from two 2s atomic orbitals. Filling the diagram shows two electrons in the antibonding orbital resulting in a bond order of zero.

No bond forms. Therefore, the Be_2 molecule would be unstable, and, in fact, does not exist.

The band structure of metals, the delocalized electrons of benzene, and "averaged" resonance structures are all ideas that can be explained by molecular orbital theory. We will not go into the details of any of these derivations. They have, however, proved to be very useful concepts.

13:12   BOND SUMMARY

In studying atomic structure we treated the electron as particle, wave, and negative cloud. In studying bonding we have also studied several different approaches to explain what we observe. It is plain that chemists do not have a complete understanding of all factors in bonding. Therefore, more than one explanation is often needed to account for observations.

Chemists use several different approaches to explain bonding.
1. **electron pair repulsion theory**
2. **hybrid orbital theory**
3. **resonance**
4. **molecular orbital theory**

When faced with multiple explanations, scientists follow a basic rule. That rule is to try the simplest explanation first. If that method does not suffice, then the more complex ideas are applied until one is found to fit. The various ideas on structure presented in this chapter are arranged roughly in order of increasing complexity. Consequently, electron-pair repulsion is the simplest and should be applied first.

Friedrich August Kekulé   (1829–1896)

Quadrivalence of carbon and the linkage of carbon atoms formulae

1. *Ethyl chloride*
2. *Ethyl alcohol*
3. *acetic acid*
4. *acetamide*
5. *methyl formate*
6. *methyl cyanide*

German chemist, Friedrich Kekulé was considered by many as the most brilliant of his day. His work centered around ideas on the linking of atoms and the structure of molecules. He was the first to speculate on the existence of bonds between atoms and he drew structural diagrams similar to those we use now.

Kekulé explained that in substances containing several carbon atoms, it must be assumed that some of the bonds of each carbon atom are bonded to other carbon atoms.

This concept led Kekulé to propose a ring structure as the logical arrangement for the atoms composing benzene. At this time, many scientists felt that this proposal was the "most brilliant piece of prediction in all of organic chemistry."

Many of our present theories on the structures of compounds were formulated by Kekulé.

CHEMICAL TECHNOLOGY: The Boranes

Boron and hydrogen form several compounds with unusual bonding arrangements. From the electron configurations of boron and hydrogen, we would predict boron hydride, BH_3, to be a planar molecule with 120° H—B—H bond angles. Instead, the two elements form a whole series of compounds called boranes. The simplest compound in the series is diborane (6), B_2H_6.

In naming boranes, a prefix is used to indicate the number of boron atoms in the molecule. The number of hydrogen atoms is shown by Arabic numerals in parentheses after the name. In addition to diborane (6), some other boranes are tetraborane (10), pentaborane (9), pentaborane (11), hexaborane (10), and deca-borane (14).

All of these compounds are said to be electron deficient. That is, there are not enough electrons in the outer levels of the atoms to form any electron dot diagram to satisfy the octet rule.

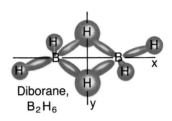

Diborane,
B_2H_6

FIGURE 13-24. The structure of diborane shows four hydrogen atoms in the same plane. The two bridging hydrogen atoms are at a 90° angle to this plane.

Boron $1s^2 2s^1$ $\dot{B}:$

Hydrogen $1s^1$ H·

As a result, chemists have developed a three-center, two-electron bond model. In this model, a pair of electrons occupies an orbital spread over three atoms, so that the middle atom acts as a bridge between the other two atoms.

In the structural diagrams shown, note that each contains bridging hydrogen atoms in three-center, two-electron bonds. In addition, all boranes having five or more boron atoms have at least one boron atom acting as a bridge between other boron atoms.

FIGURE 13-25. The structures of more complex diboranes are shown.

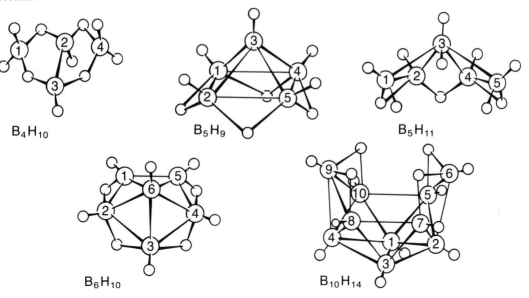

B_4H_{10}

B_5H_9

B_5H_{11}

B_6H_{10}

$B_{10}H_{14}$

Most boranes are unstable. Several, including diborane (6), are spontaneously flammable. Diborane (6) is used as a reactant in making other chemicals since it is an excellent Lewis acid. (Lewis acids will be covered in Chapter 24.) Diborane (6) has also been used on an experimental basis as a rocket fuel. The best rocket fuels are composed of low atomic mass elements. Lighter atoms travel faster than heavy atoms at the same temperature. The combustion of boranes produces higher velocity gases in the rocket motor nozzle. In addition, these compounds have higher heats of combustion than similar molecular mass organic fuels. For example, the heat of combustion of diborane, B_2H_6, is 2010 J/mol while ethane, C_2H_6, is 970 J/mol.

It is possible to produce similar compounds in which one or more boron atoms have been replaced by carbon atoms. These compounds are called carboranes. Their chemistry has been studied extensively in the hope that they too can be used as rocket fuels. Carborane polyesters have been used as ablative materials. An ablative material has the ability to carry away heat by gradually peeling away in layers. Space capsules use ablative materials in their heat shields. The peeling occurs when the capsule reenters the earth's atmosphere.

SUMMARY

1. The shape of molecules can be approximated by assuming the mutual exclusion of electron pairs. This repulsion of electron pairs has two sources. All electrons have the same electrostatic charge and are subject to the Pauli exclusions principle. Electron pairs spread as far apart as possible. 13:1

2. The shape of a molecule containing three or more atoms is determined by the number of electron clouds in the outer level. 13:1

3. If the central atom has two bonds and no unshared pairs, the molecule is linear. 13:1

4. If there are three bonds and no unshared pairs, the molecule is trigonal planar. 13:1

5. If there are four bonds, the molecule is tetrahedral. 13:1

6. The actual bond angles may vary from predicted angles. Unshared electron pairs occupy the most space. Shared pairs occupy the least space. 13:1

7. Two atoms sometimes share more than one pair of electrons forming double and triple bonds. This possibility must be considered when discussing molecular geometry. 13:2

8. Molecular covalent bonds are formed by overlap of atomic orbitals: *s-s*, *s-p*, and *p-p*. 13:3

9. If two *s* orbitals or *s* and *p* orbitals overlap, a sigma (σ) bond is formed. If two *p* orbitals overlap end-to-end, a sigma (σ) bond is formed. If two *p* orbitals overlap sideways, a pi (π) bond is formed. 13:3

10. *s* and *p* orbitals of the same atom can combine to form hybrid orbitals. One *s* and three *p* orbitals merge to form four tetrahedral *sp*³ hybrids. One *s* and two *p* orbitals merge to form three planar *sp*² hybrid orbitals. One *s* and one *p* orbitals merge to form two linear *sp* hybrid orbitals. 13:4-13:6, 13:9

11. A double bond is formed by the sigma overlap of two *sp*² orbitals and the π overlap of the two *p* orbitals. 13:6

12. A triple bond is formed by the sigma overlap of two *sp* orbitals and the π overlap of four *p* orbitals. 13:6

13. Delocalization of π electrons in conjugated chain and ring compounds produces stability. 13:7

14. Isomers are compounds with the same formula but a different arrangement of atoms and bonds. 13:8

15. There are several types of isomers: structural, geometric, positional, and functional. 13:8

16. In the concept of resonance, we consider all correct structures that can be written for that compound. We assume that the actual distribution of electrons in a particle is the average of all these structures. 13:10

17. Molecular orbital theory combines atomic orbitals to form molecular orbitals. Electrons fill molecular orbitals under the same rules as atomic orbitals. Molecular orbitals can be bonding or antibonding. Bond order is one-half the difference between bonding and antibonding electrons. 13:11

18. Scientists may use a number of theories as they seek the simplest possible explanation for the phenomena they observe. 13:12

PROBLEMS See Teacher's Guide.

1. Predict the bond angles indicated in the following compounds.
   a. H—Te—H in H_2Te
   b. H—P—H in PH_3
   c. C—P—C in $P(CH_3)_3$
   d. Cl—As—Cl in $AsCl_3$
   e. F—C—F in $CClF_3$
   f. C—Pb—C in $Pb(C_2H_5)_4$

2. What is the major difference between σ and π bonds?

3. What is meant by the term "hybridization"? Hybridization is the formation of equivalent orbitals by electrons from different energy sublevels.

4. What kinds of orbital arrangements contribute to the bonding in ethene $(H_2C=CH_2)$?

5. Why is benzene a particularly stable compound? The pi electrons are delocalized.

6. Predict the shapes of the following molecules:
   a. H_2CO
   b. SO_2
   c. BF_3
   d. SF_6 (see Table 13-1)
   e. S_2Cl_2
   f. SF_4

7. In the HCN molecule, the H—C bond is a single bond and the C—N bond is a triple bond. Predict the shape of the molecule, the hybridization of the carbon atom, and the type (σ, π) of each bond.

8. The substance H_2Se is a molecular compound. Sketch a cross-sectional view of the molecule and label its various dimensions.

9. Draw the isomers of the compound with the formula C_6H_{14}.

10. Define geometric, positional, and functional isomers.

11. Predict shapes for the following ions.
   a. IO_3^- trigonal pyramid
   b. ClO_4^- tetrahedral
   octahedral c. SiF_6^{2-} (see Table 13-1)
   d. SO_4^{2-} tetrahedral
   e. PO_4^{3-} tetrahedral
   f. ClF_4^- planar

12. The substance phosphorus pentachloride occurs as PCl_5 molecules in the gaseous state. As a solid, it is an ionic compound, $PCl_4^+ PCl_6^-$. Describe the shape and bonding in each of these species. (see Table 13-1)

13. How does the conjugated bonding arrangement in benzene compare to the bonding in metals?

14. One might expect the bond angle for each C—H bond in methane to be 90°. Why is this prediction incorrect?

15. Why is the bond angle in NH_3 only 107° when the bond angle for BF_3 is 120°?

16. Draw electron dot diagrams to show the resonance structures for the carbonate ion (CO_3^{2-}).

17. Conjugated systems, such as benzene, are often considered as "averages" of resonant forms. Draw the resonance forms for benzene and a

related compound, naphthalene $C_{10}H_8$.

18. Write the molecular orbital configurations for the following molecules. Compute the bonding in each molecule and decide whether the molecule would be stable or not.
   a. Li_2 b. B_2 c. C_2 d. N_2 e. F_2

19. When dissimilar atoms combine, the energy level diagram for the molecular orbital interpretation of the bond is much more complex than for two identical atoms. For the molecule CO, however, the two atoms are close enough to assume an energy diagram following Figures 13-18 and 13-21. Describe the bonding in the CO molecule.

REVIEW

1. Arrange the following elements in order of increasing attractive force between nucleus and outer electrons. Fr, Mn, Zn, B
   a. boron
   b. francium
   c. manganese
   d. zinc

2. Classify the bonds between the following pairs of atoms as principally ionic or principally covalent.
   a. barium and fluorine
   b. bromine and rubidium
   c. cesium and oxygen
   d. iodine and antimony
   e. nitrogen and sulfur   Ionic: a, b, c
   f. silicon and carbon   covalent: d, e, f

3. Explain briefly why metals conduct electricity.
   Electrons are in the outer level band which is separated from the conduction band by only a narrow forbidden zone.

ONE MORE STEP

1. Using library resources, find the following bond angles.
   a. C—C=C in CH_3CHCH_2
   b. F—C—F in CF_3I
   c. H—N—N in HN_3
   d. O—N—O in NO_2
   e. O—N—O in NO_2^-

   1. a. 125°
      b. 108°
      c. 113°
      d. 134°
      e. 115°

2. Find out the geometry of d^2sp^3 hybrid orbitals. See if you can discover some compounds or ions containing such hybrids. octahedral

3. Predict the shape of cyclohexane (C_6H_{12}). From references, determine the two shapes of cyclohexane. Make models of the two shapes to illustrate why one form is more stable than the other. puckered ring, chair, and boat forms

4. Predict shapes for the following molecules.
   a. $H_2C=C=CH_2$
   b. $H_2C=C=C=CH_2$

5. Read the story of the development of molecular structure theories.

6. Find out why the molecular orbital theory is difficult to apply to molecules composed of atoms from two different elements.

7. Investigate the molecular orbital structure of the benzene molecule.

READINGS

Fackler, John P., "Symmetry in Molecular Structure." *Journal of Chemical Education,* Vol. 55, No. 2 (February 1978), pp. 79-83.

Mickey, Charles D., "Molecular Geometry." *Journal of Chemical Education,* Vol. 57, No. 3 (March 1980), pp. 210-212.

Ramsay, O. Bertrand, "Molecules in Three Dimensions." *Chemistry,* Vol. 47, No. 1 (January 1974), pp. 6-9.

Most of our knowledge concerning the structure and properties of matter is derived from using analytical techniques. The computerized system shown is a gas chromatogram. The chromatographic separation of a mixture is an analytical technique based on the rates at which particles adhere to a substance. If molecules are neutral, what forces cause them to adhere? How are these forces related to the physical state of a substance? How are the forces between molecules used in chemical analysis?

Doug Martin

POLAR MOLECULES $\qquad$ 14

Chapter 14 describes the interrelationship of the attractive forces between molecules, molecular structure, and physical and chemical properties. The structures and properties of complex ions are introduced. The discussion of polarity is carried further in describing chromatography as an analytical process.

Demonstration—Fill two burets, one with a polar liquid (H_2O) and the other with a nonpolar liquid (cyclohexane). Allow the liquids to run out of the burets in a thin stream. Use a charged rod (plastic rubbed with fur) to deflect the polar stream. Use this demonstration as an introduction to the differences between polar and nonpolar molecules.

Think for a moment about the salt and sugar on your dinner table. They look alike. They both dissolve in water. Yet, to a chemist, they are quite different. Salt is made of ions; sodium ions and chlorine ions are oppositely charged and attract each other. Knowing the properties of ionic substances, we know why salt is a solid. Sugar, on the other hand, is made of molecules. Each molecule of sugar contains twelve atoms of carbon, twenty-two atoms of hydrogen, and eleven atoms of oxygen. These atoms are bonded to each other covalently. However, since a sugar molecule is neutral, what holds sugar molecules together? Why don't the sugar molecules just float away from each other and become a gas?

Substances composed of discrete molecules exhibit a wide range of melting and boiling points. There must be, therefore, a wide range in the forces holding molecules to each other. These forces are determined by the internal structure of a molecule. In this chapter we want to take a closer look at the aspects of internal structure that affect the forces holding molecules to each other.

GOAL: You will gain an understanding of the relationship between molecular structure and the properties of molecular compounds.

There is a wide range of forces holding molecules together.

14:1 POLARITY

Recall that electronegativity is an atom's ability to attract the electrons involved in bonding. Since the electronegativity of each element differs, we should consider that in a covalent bond one of the atoms attracts the shared pair more strongly than the other. The resulting bond is said to be **polar covalent.** Since one atom in the bond will attract the electrons more strongly, there will be a partial negative charge near that end of the bond. In the bond, the atom with the higher electronegativity will have a partial negative charge. The other atom will have a partial positive charge. Polar bonds, unless symmetrically arranged, produce polar molecules. In CCl_4, the four C—Cl bonds are polar but their symmetrical arrangement (tetrahedral) produces a nonpolar molecule.

A polar covalent bond occurs when a shared pair of electrons is attracted more strongly to one of the atoms.

Polar bonds, unless symmetrically arranged, produce polar molecules.

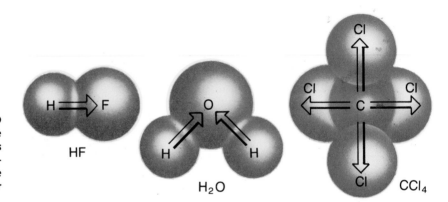

FIGURE 14-1. Both HF and H_2O are polar molecules because the arrangement of polar bonds is not symmetrical. The CCl_4 molecule is nonpolar in spite of the fact that it contains four polar bonds.

Substances composed of nonpolar molecules are generally gases or low-boiling liquids. Substances composed of polar molecules generally have higher boiling points than nonpolar compounds. Many polar molecules are solids under normal conditions.

A polar molecule is sometimes called a dipole. A **dipole** has asymmetrical charge distribution. Partial charges within a molecule are indicated by δ (delta). A water molecule would be represented as follows:

Dipole: A polar molecule.

$$\delta^+ \; H\!:\!\ddot{\underset{\displaystyle \underset{\delta^+}{\overset{\displaystyle H}{H}}}{O}}\!:\!\delta^- \qquad \text{bond angle } 104.5°$$

You may wish to introduce vectors and vector addition to show why a nonsymmetrical molecule has a dipole moment.

The strength of a dipole can be described by its dipole moment, μ. The dipole moment depends upon the size of the partial charges and the distance between them. In symbols

Dipole moment, μ, describes the strength of the dipole.

$$\mu = Qd$$

where Q is the size of the partial charge in coulombs and d is the distance in meters. Dipole moment is then expressed in coulomb · meters*. The higher the dipole moment, the stronger the inter-molecular forces; and, consequently, the higher the melting point and boiling point. Table 14-1 lists a number of common solvents in order of increasing polarity. (The first three are nonpolar.)

Melting point and freezing point are directly related to dipole moment.

Table 14-1

Polarity of Solvents		
Name	**Formula**	**$\mu \times 10^{30}$**
Cyclohexane	C_6H_{12}	0
Carbon tetrachloride	CCl_4	0
Benzene	C_6H_6	0
Toluene	$C_6H_5CH_3$	1.20
Ethoxyethane	$CH_3CH_2OCH_2CH_3$	3.84
1-Butanol	$CH_3CH_2CH_2CH_2OH$	5.54
1-Propanol	$CH_3CH_2CH_2OH$	5.61
Ethanol	CH_3CH_2OH	5.64
Methanol	CH_3OH	5.67
Ethyl acetate	$CH_3CH_2OOCCH_3$	5.94
Water	HOH	6.14
Propanone	CH_3COCH_3	9.61

PROBLEM

1. The following pairs of atoms are all covalently bonded. Arrange the pairs in order of decreasing polarity of the bonds. (See Table of Electronegativities, Chapter 12.)
   a. boron and nitrogen
   b. carbon and sulfur
   c. hydrogen and selenium
   d. iodine and technetium
   e. nitrogen and oxygen
   f. aluminum and phosphorus

1. d a e f c b

14:2 WEAK FORCES

Covalent compounds show a melting point range of over 3000 C°! How can we account for such a wide variation? The forces involved in some of these cases are called **van der Waals forces.** Johannes van der Waals was the first to account for these forces in calculations concerning gases. These forces are some-times referred to as weak forces because they are much weaker

*Older tables of dipole moments may be expressed in debyes (D) where 1 D = 3.338×10^{-30} C·m.

than chemical bonds. They involve the attraction of the electrons of one atom for the protons of another.

FIGURE 14-2. Dipole-dipole attraction exists between molecules which are permanent dipoles.

The first source of van der Waals attraction which we will consider is **dipole-dipole forces.** Two molecules, of the same or different substances, which are both permanent dipoles will be attracted to each other, Figure 14-2. Such would be the case between two trichloromethane molecules $CHCl_3$, or between a trichloromethane and an ammonia molecule.

Dipole-dipole attractions occur between two permanent polar molecules.

We can also have the attraction of a dipole for a molecule that is ordinarily not a dipole. When a dipole approaches a nonpolar molecule, its partial charge either attracts or repels the electrons of the other particle. For instance, if the negative end of the dipole approaches a nonpolar molecule, the electrons of the nonpolar molecule are repelled by the negative charge. The electron cloud of the nonpolar molecule is distorted by bulging away from the approaching dipole as shown in Figure 14-3. As a

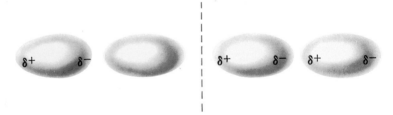

FIGURE 14-3. Dipole-induced dipole attraction occurs when a molecule which is a dipole causes a nonpolar molecule to become an induced dipole.

result, the nonpolar molecule is itself transformed into a dipole. We say it has become an **induced dipole.** Since it is now a dipole, it can be attracted to the permanent dipole. Interactions such as these are called **dipole-induced dipole forces.** An example of this force occurs in a water solution of iodine. The I_2 molecules are nonpolar while the water molecules are highly polar.

A nonpolar molecule may become an induced dipole.

Two nonpolar molecules may be attracted to each other.

The case of two nonpolar molecules being attracted must also be taken into account. For instance, there must be some force between hydrogen molecules; otherwise it would be impossible to form liquid hydrogen. Consider a hydrogen molecule with its molecular orbital including both nuclei. We know intuitively that the electrons occupying that orbital must have a specific location. If they are both away from one end of the molecule for an instant, then the nucleus is exposed for a short time. That end of the molecule has a partial positive charge for an instant; a temporary dipole is set up. For that time, the **temporary dipole** can induce a dipole in the molecule next to it and an attractive force results as shown in Figure 14-4. The forces generated in this way are called **dispersion forces.**

FIGURE 14-4. Dispersion forces exist between nonpolar molecules and are the result of the formation of temporary dipoles.

The various kinds of interactions making van der Waals forces affect each other, but we are only interested in the net result. The liquid and solid states of many compounds exist because of these intermolecular forces. These forces are effective only over very short distances. They vary roughly as the inverse of the sixth power of distance. In other words, if the distance is doubled, the attractive force is only 1/64 as large.

The van der Waals forces are effective only over very short distances.

Of the three contributing factors to van der Waals force, dispersion forces are the most important. They are the only attractive forces that exist between nonpolar molecules. Even for most polar molecules, dispersion forces account for 85% or more of the van der Waals forces. Only in some special cases, such as NH_3 and H_2O, do dipole-dipole interactions become more important than dispersion forces. We will examine these special cases in Chapter 17.

van der Waals attraction can result from
1. dipole-dipole forces
2. dipole-induced dipole forces
3. dispersion forces

While chemical bonds range from about 200 to 800 kJ/mol, dipole-dipole forces are < 125 kJ/mol.

Table 14-2

Weak Forces Summary					
INTERMOLECULAR BONDS — Molecules contain covalently bonded atoms	**Type of Force**	**Substances Exhibiting Force**	**Source of the Force**	**Properties Due to the Force**	**Example**
	Dipole	Polar covalent molecules	Electric attraction between dipoles resulting from polar bonds	Substances have higher boiling and melting points than those having nonpolar molecules of similar size $100° < mp < 600°$	ICl, SO_2, $BiBr_3$, AlI_3, SeO_3
	Dispersion Forces	Nonpolar molecules	Weak electric fluctuations which destroy spherical symmetry of electronic fields about atoms	Substances have low melting and boiling points	Cl_2, CH_4, N_2, O_2, F_2, Br_2, Cl_2, He, Ar

14:3 LIGANDS

As an ionic compound dissolves in water, its ions become hydrated. The surface ions of the crystal become surrounded by polar H_2O molecules which adhere to the surface. The water molecule-ion clusters formed enter solution. The stability of these clusters is greatest when they have at their center a small ion of high charge. Since positive ions are usually smaller than negative ions, the clusters with which we are concerned have a positive ion at the center. When polar molecules or negative ions cluster around a central ion, a **complex ion** is formed. Complex ions are widely used in analytical chemistry.

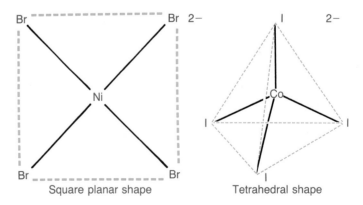

FIGURE 14-5. When an ionic substance dissolves in water, the molecules cluster around the ions forming complex ions.

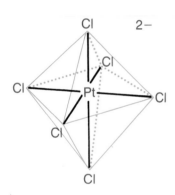

FIGURE 14-6. $PtCl_6^{2-}$ is a complex ion having an octahedral shape. Chloride ions are the ligands.

The molecules or negative ions which are attached to the central positive ion are known as **ligands.** The number of ligands around a central positive ion in a complex is called the **coordination number.** By far, the most common coordination number found in complexes is 6. These complex ions are described as octahedral. The ligands may be thought of as lying at the vertices of a regular octahedron with the central positive ion in the middle. $PtCl_6^{2-}$ is an example of an octahedral complex.

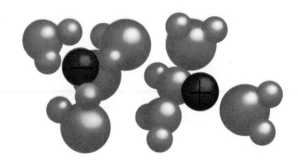

Square planar shape   Tetrahedral shape

FIGURE 14-7. Complexes with a coordination number of four may be square planar or tetrahedral.

The coordination number 4 is also common. These complexes may be square-planar, with the ligands at the corners of a square and the central positive ion in the center. Others may be tetrahedral, with the ligands at the vertices of a regular tetrahedron and the central positive ion in the middle. Complexes of Ni^{2+}, Pd^{2+}, and Pt^{2+} are usually planar if the coordination number is four. These elements all have electron configurations ending in d^8. They should have five orbitals available: one s, three p, and one d. However, the d orbital turns out to be an antibonding orbital and is oriented perpendicular to the plane of the other four orbitals. An example of a square planar complex is $NiBr_4^{2-}$. A typical tetrahedral complex is CoI_4^{2-}, Figure 14-7.

The number of coordinated groups is determined in part by the size and charge of the central ion. However, coordination numbers cannot at present be predicted from purely theoretical considerations.

The coordination number 2 is found in complexes of Ag^+, Au^+, and Hg^{2+}. Complex ions with coordination number 2 are always linear. The ligands are always located at the ends and the positive ion in the middle of a straight line. An example is $Ag(CN)_2^-$.

Complexes with a coordination number of 2 are always linear.

$$NC—Ag—CN^-$$

Ligands can be either molecules or negative ions. Molecular ligands are always polar and always have an unshared pair of electrons which can be shared with the central ion. The most common ligand is water. The hydrated compounds mentioned in Chapter 5 are composed of positive ions surrounded by water ligands and the negative ions. Ammonia, NH_3, is also a common ligand. Many negative ions can also act as ligands in complexes. Some of the most important are the following: fluoride, F^-; chloride, Cl^-; bromide, Br^-; iodide, I^-; cyanide, CN^-; thiocyanate, CNS^-; and oxalate $C_2O_4^{2-}$.

Water is the most common ligand.

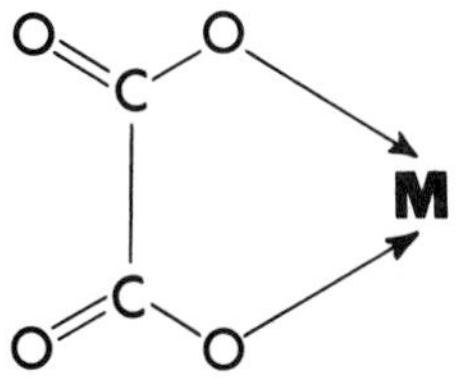

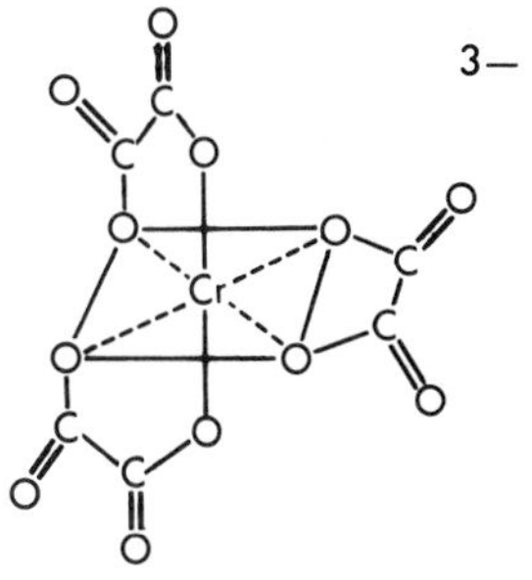

FIGURE 14-8. The oxalate ion is a bidentate ligand. Three oxalate ions surrounding a central ion form an octahedral complex.

Oxalate ion as bidentate ligand.

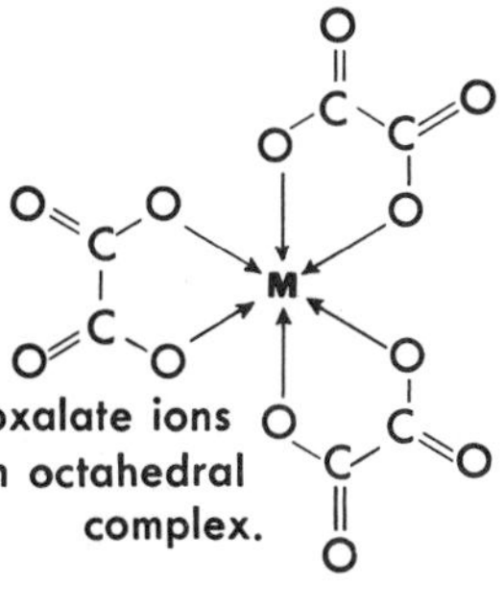

Three oxalate ions in octahedral complex.

The oxalate ion has two of its oxygen atoms attached to the positive ion. Such a ligand is called bidentate ("two-toothed"). A bidentate ligand attaches at two points, therefore two bidentate ligands can form a tetrahedral complex. Three bidentate ligands can form an octahedral complex. Tridentate and quadridentate ligands are also known, Figure 14-9.

A bidentate ligand attaches at two points.

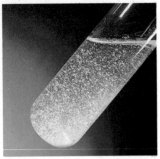

Hickson-Bender Photography

FIGURE 14-9. The EDTA ion (ethylenediamminetetraacetic acid) is hexadentate. When added to hard water, EDTA forms a complex with Ca^{2+}. This procedure is used as a test for water hardness.

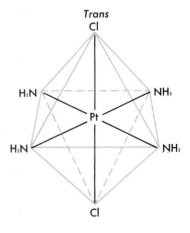

$Ca(EDTA)^{2-}$

EDTA ion

14:4   ISOMERS OF COMPLEXES

It is possible to have more than one kind of ligand in the same complex. For example, platinum(IV) may form an octahedral complex with four ammonia molecules and two chloride ions. This complex ion has the formula $[Pt(NH_3)_4Cl_2]^{2+}$. The coordination number is 6. Since two ligands are of one kind and four are of another kind, there are two uniquely different ways of arranging the ligands. These arrangements are shown in Figure 14-10. Note that in one structure, the chloride ions are at opposite corners of the octahedron, while in the other they are at adjacent corners. Thus, there are *cis* and *trans* isomers of $[Pt(NH_3)_4Cl_2]^{2+}$. The two complexes differ slightly in color and solubility.

Complex ions can exhibit isomerism because different ligands can have uniquely different arrangements.

Another example of isomerism in complexes is $Co(NH_3)_4Cl_2$.

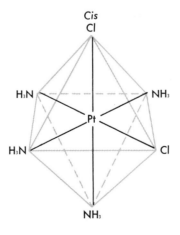

FIGURE 14-10. The $[Pt(NH_3)_4Cl_2]^{2+}$ complex exhibits *cis-trans* isomerism.

14:5 NAMING COMPLEXES

In naming a complex ion, the ligands are named first, followed by the name of the central ion. Each type of ligand is preceded by a prefix designating the number of molecules or ions of that particular ligand present in the complex. The prefixes used are *di-*, *tri-*, *tetra-*, *penta-*, and *hexa-*. The names of some of the common ligands are given in Table 14-3.

Table 14-3

Some Common Ligands			
Ligand	**Name**	**Ligand**	**Name**
OH^-	hydroxo	CN^-	cyano
Br^-	bromo	$S_2O_3^{2-}$	thiosulfato
Cl^-	chloro	$C_2O_4^{2-}$	oxalato
F^-	fluoro	H_2O	aquo
I^-	iodo	NH_3	ammine
S^{2-}	thio	CO	carbonyl
		NO	nitrosyl

A more extensive list may be found in the IUPAC report, *Nomenclature of Inorganic Chemistry*.

The order given in the table represents the order in which the ligands appear in a name. Note that negative ions are named before molecules. The name of the complex ion ends in *-ate* if the complex as a whole possesses a negative charge. If the central ion has more than one possible oxidation number, a roman numeral in parentheses must follow the name of the central ion. For example, in the complex ion $Cr(NH_3)_5Cl^{2+}$, the two ligands are the chloride ion and ammonia molecules. The chloride is placed first, then the ammonia, then the name of the central ion, chromium. Chromium has more than one possible oxidation number, so its oxidation number is given in parentheses after its name. The ending on the word chromium remains unchanged since the ion as a whole is positive. The name of the complex ion is written as one word. Thus, the name is chloropentammine-chromium(III) ion. If two more chloride ions are added, we obtain a compound with the formula $[Cr(NH_3)_5Cl]Cl_2$. Note that when a question about composition could arise, the whole complex is placed in brackets. This compound would be named chloropentamminechromium(III) chloride. The following examples further illustrate this method.

Complex ions are named in the following order.
1. negative ligands
2. molecular ligands
3. central ion
4. Roman numeral, if needed
5. *-ate* ending, if the ion is negative

SiF_6^{2-}	hexafluorosilicate(IV) ion
$PtCl_6^{2-}$	hexachloroplatinate(IV) ion
$Ni(NH_3)_6Br_2$	hexamminenickel(II) bromide
$Na_2Sn(OH)_6$	sodium hexahydroxostannate(IV)
$Ag_3Fe(CN)_6$	silver hexacyanoferrate(III)

Note that it is possible to have a complex with a net charge of zero in a coordination compound.

Note that Latin stems are used for some metals. Some of these Latin stems are given in Table 14-4.

Table 14-4

Latin Stems Used in Some Metal Complexes			
Metal	Latin Stem	Metal	Latin Stem
copper	cuprate	lead	plumbate
gold	aurate	silver	argentate
iron	ferrate	tin	stannate

PROBLEMS

2. a. hexiodoplatinate(IV) ion
   b. diamminecadmium ion
   c. hexafluorogermanate(IV) ion
   d. tetraquochromium(II) ion
   e. hexacyanoferrate(III) ion

2. Name the following complex ions.
   a. PtI_6^{2-}
   b. $Cd(NH_3)_2^{2+}$
   c. GeF_6^{2-}
   d. $Cr(H_2O)_4^{2+}$
   e. $Fe(CN)_6^{3-}$
   f. $Fe(CN)_6^{4-}$ hexacyanoferrate(II) ion
   g. $Co(NH_3)_6^{2+}$ hexamminecobalt(II) ion
   h. $PtCl_6^{2-}$ hexachloroplatinate(IV) ion
   i. $Ni(NH_3)_6^{2+}$ hexamminenickel(II) ion
   j. $IrCl_6^{2-}$ hexachloroiridate(IV) ion

3. a. $PtBr_6^{2-}$
   b. $Pt(NH_3)_4^{2+}$
   c. $AuBr_4^-$
   d. $PdCl_6^{2-}$
   e. $AuCl_4^-$
   f. $Ir(NH_3)_5H_2O^{3+}$
   g. $W(CO)_6$
   h. AlF_6^{3-}
   i. $Co(NH_3)_4(H_2O)Cl^{2+}$
   j. $Cd(NH_3)_4^{2+}$

3. Write formulas for the following complex ions.
   a. hexabromoplatinate(IV)
   b. tetrammineplatinum(II)
   c. tetrabromoaurate(III)
   d. hexachloropalladate(IV)
   e. tetrachloroaurate(III)
   f. aquopentammineiridium(III)
   g. hexacarbonyltungsten(0)
   h. hexafluoroaluminate
   i. chloroaquotetramminecobalt(III)
   j. tetramminecadmium

4. a. chloropentammineiridium (III) ion
   b. tetrammminepalladium(II) ion
   c. hexahydroxoantimonate (V) ion

4. Name the following complex ions.
   a. $Ir(NH_3)_5 Cl^{2+}$
   b. $Pd(NH_3)_4^{2+}$
   c. $Sb(OH)_6^-$
   d. $PdCl_4^{2-}$ tetrachloropalladate(II) ion
   e. $Fe(C_2O_4)_3^{3-}$ trioxalatoferrate(III) ion
   f. $Cu(NH_3)_6^{2+}$ tetramminecopper(II) ion

5. Write formulas for the following complex ions.
   a. pentacyanocarbonylferrate(II)
   b. pentacarbonylruthenium(0)
   c. hexamminecobalt(III)
   d. dicyanocuprate(I)
   e. dichlorodiamminepalladium(II)
   f. hexamminechromium(III)

5. a. $FeCO(CN)_5^{3-}$
   b. $Ru(CO)_5$
   c. $Co(NH_3)_6^{3+}$
   d. $Cu(CN)_2^-$
   e. $Pd(NH_3)_2Cl_2$
   f. $Cr(NH_3)_6^{3+}$

6. a. $GaCl_4^-$
   b. GaF_6^{3-}
   c. HgI_4^{2-}
   d. $OsCl_6^{2-}$
   e. $IrBr_6^{3-}$
   f. $Fe(CN)_6^{4-}$

6. Write formulas for the following complex ions.
   a. tetrachlorogallate(III)
   b. hexafluorogallate(III)
   c. tetriodomercurate(II)
   d. hexachloroosmate(IV)
   e. hexabromoiridate(III)
   f. hexacyanoiron(II)

14:6 BONDING IN COMPLEXES

Almost any positive ion might be expected to form complexes. In practice, the complexes of the metals of the first two groups in the periodic table have little stability. By far the most important and most interesting complexes are those of the transition metals. The transition metals have partially filled d orbitals which can become involved in bonding. These positive ions are small because of the strong attractive force of the nucleus for the inner electrons. They also have high oxidation numbers. The combination of small size and high charge results in a high charge density on the central ion. Such a high charge density is particularly favorable to complex ion formation.

Transition metals form complex ions.

Transition metals have partially filled d orbitals and high charge density.

FPG

Ray Halin/Tom Stack & Associates

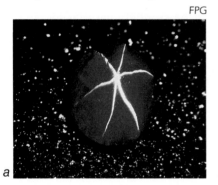

a

b

FIGURE 14-11. The color of a ruby (a) is the result of chromium impurities. Cr^{3+} ions are surrounded by oxygen atoms in an octahedral complex. Aquamarine (b) derives its color from an iron impurity having a structure similar to that for chromium ions in rubies.

In an isolated ion of one of the metals of the first transition series, the five $3d$ orbitals are degenerate (have the same energy). No energy is absorbed if an electron is transferred from one of the $3d$ orbitals to another. However, in the complex, the ligands affect the energies of the different $3d$ orbitals. In an octahedral complex, the d orbitals are split into a higher energy group of two orbitals and a lower energy group of three orbitals. Many complex ions have intense colors. The blue color which is typical

FIGURE 14-12. The copper tetrammine complex is highly colored as the result of the splitting of the d orbitals. Light energy is absorbed as electrons move from the lower to higher energy orbitals.

Robert C. Smoot

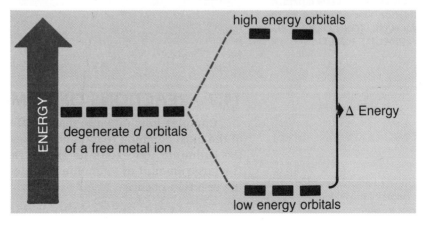

of solutions of copper(II) compounds is an example. This blue color is due to the $Cu(H_2O)_6^{2+}$ ion. The colors of complexes arise from electron transitions between the split d orbitals. The split represents only a small energy gap and as the electrons move from the lower to the higher energy group, they absorb light energy.

Ligands are either negative ions or polar molecules, while the central atom is a positive ion. These facts suggest that the bonding forces in a complex are electrostatic, just as they are in a salt crystal. In fact, there are strong similarities between the structures of salts and the structures of complex ions. On the other hand, the ligands have an unshared pair of electrons which they are capable of donating. The central ion always has unoccupied orbitals into which electron pairs might be placed. This combination suggests that the bonds are covalent. The name **coordinate covalent bond** has been given to covalent bonds in which both of the electrons in the shared pair come from the same atom. The coordinate covalent bond is exactly like any other covalent bond. The bonds of most complex ions have characteristics of both covalent and ionic bonding types. The covalent character dominates.

FIGURE 14-13. The color change for the reaction is caused by the replacement of water ligands by chloride ions according to the equation: $[Co(H_2O)_6]^{2+} + 4Cl^-$ $\rightarrow [CoCl_4]^{2-} + 6H_2O$.

Robert C. Smoot

14:7 REACTIONS OF COMPLEXES

Complex ions undergo many different kinds of reactions. One of the most common reactions is an exchange of ligands. In water, the cadmium ion exists as the tetraaquo complex, $Cd(H_2O)_4^{2+}$. If a large amount of ammonia is added to the solution, the following reaction occurs.

$$Cd(H_2O)_4^{2+} + 4NH_3 \rightleftarrows Cd(NH_3)_4^{2+} + 4H_2O$$

The reaction takes place in four steps.

$$Cd(H_2O)_4{}^{2+} + NH_3 \rightleftarrows Cd(NH_3)(H_2O)_3{}^{2+} + H_2O$$
$$Cd(NH_3)(H_2O)_3{}^{2+} + NH_3 \rightleftarrows Cd(NH_3)_2(H_2O)_2{}^{2+} + H_2O$$
$$Cd(NH_3)_2(H_2O)_2{}^{2+} + NH_3 \rightleftarrows Cd(NH_3)_3(H_2O)^{2+} + H_2O$$
$$Cd(NH_3)_3(H_2O)^{2+} + NH_3 \rightleftarrows Cd(NH_3)_4{}^{2+} + H_2O$$

The double arrow indicates the reaction is reversible.

Since each step can go in either direction, a measurement for the tendency for each step can be made. However, the tendency for the reaction to occur, called an equilibrium constant (Section 23:8) is usually given for the overall reaction. For example, the equilibrium constant for the reaction

$$Cd^{2+} + 4CN^- \rightleftarrows Cd(CN)_4{}^{2-}$$

is 1.23×10^{50}. That number is enormous meaning that there is a strong attraction between Cd^{2+} and CN^-. The tendency for the reaction to occur is enormous.

Multiple step reaction mechanisms and equilibrium constants will be studied in Chapter 23.

14:8 FRACTIONATION

Sometimes it is necessary to separate several materials from a mixture and identify them individually. A convenient method of separation based on the polarity of substances is a process called chromatography (kroh muh TAHG ruh fee). In chromatography, a mobile phase containing a mixture of substances is allowed to pass over a stationary phase which has an attraction for polar materials. The **mobile phase** consists of the mixture to be separated dissolved in a fluid (liquid or gas). The **stationary phase** consists of a solid or liquid adhering to the surface of a solid. The different substances in the mixture will travel at different rates due to their varying polarity. There are several polarity considerations in determining the rate at which each component of the mixture will migrate. A polar substance will have some attraction for the solvent as well as an attraction for the stationary phase. The stationary phase will attract some of the substances more strongly than others. The slowest migrating substance will be the one with the greatest attraction for the stationary phase. The fastest migrating substance will be the one with the least attraction for the stationary phase. Thus, they can be separated. These separations are called fractions because they are parts of the whole. The overall separation of parts from a whole by any process may be called **fractionation.**

Often, the fractions are different colors. For this reason, this separation method is called chromatography (writing with color). Gas chromatography does not involve color. However, since it also depends upon fractionation, the name chromatography is still applied.

Chromatography is a separation method which depends on polarity of substances.

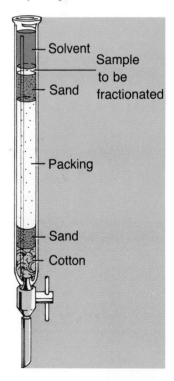

FIGURE 14-14. The packing components for a typical chromatography column are shown.

Suggestions for adsorbents: Aluminum oxide, Fuller's earth, calcium oxide, calcium carbonate, calcium phosphate, talc, and starch.

Suggested solvents, beginning with the least polar: Petroleum ether, CCl_4, cyclohexane, CS_2, ether, acetone, benzene, chloroform, alcohol, water, pyridine, and acid.

In column chromatography a solvent percolates through a packing substance.

FIGURE 14-15. The chemist in (a) is using column chromatography to separate the components of a cosmetic. The column chromatogram in (b) shows the separation of plant pigments into chlorophylls and xanthrophylls.

FIGURE 14-16. A mixture of dichromate and permanganate ions can be separated by column chromatography.

Robert C. Smoot

14:9 COLUMN CHROMATOGRAPHY

In column chromatography, a glass column is used to carry out the separation. The glass tube is packed with a stationary phase such as calcium carbonate. Other packings now in use are magnesium or sodium carbonate, activated charcoal, ion exchange resins, clays, gels, and many organic compounds.

The mobile phase with the material to be fractionated is added to the top of the column. Then fresh solvent is caused to percolate through the column. The solvent may be water, ammonia, an acid, an alcohol, or other organic or inorganic substance.

a

b

U.S. Food and Drug Administration   Robert C. Smoot

Each substance in the mobile phase migrates down the tube at a different rate and the substances are separated. The rate of travel depends upon the attraction of each substance for the stationary phase, its attraction for the solvent, and the solvent concentration. If the substance has a high attraction for the stationary phase, only a high concentration of solvent will dislodge it. As the solvent moves down the tube, it becomes less concentrated, and the solute becomes more attracted to the stationary phase again. Those substances with less attraction for the stationary phase are carried farther, even by the less concentrated solvent. By constant percolation, the substances are separated into zones. A sample chromatogram is shown in Figure 14-16. In the column shown, dichromate ions and permanganate ions are being separated on a packing of aluminum oxide. The solvent being used is dilute nitric acid. As you can see, the dichromate is more strongly attracted to the stationary phase so it moves down the column more slowly.

After separation, it may be necessary to recover the material in each separate zone for identification. One method involves forcing the zones out the bottom of the tube, one at a time. The substance in each zone is dissolved and then recovered by evaporation. A second method uses solvents of increasing polarity until each zone comes out the bottom along with the solvent. Identification is then made by any number of methods. Column chromatography is used now for extremely delicate separations. Complex substances such as vitamins, proteins, and hormones, not easily separated by other methods, can be separated by chromatography.

14:10 SURFACE CHROMATOGRAPHY

Paper chromatography is a form of chromatography in which the separations are carried out on paper rather than in glass columns.

Strips of paper are placed in a box or bell jar in which the atmosphere is saturated with water vapor or solvent vapor. A drop of the solution to be separated is placed at the top of the paper. The paper is then overlapped into solvent at the top of the box. The solvent moves down the paper by capillary action, separating the constituents of the drop. The paper may be placed into solvent at the bottom of the box. In this case, the drop of the solution would be placed at the bottom of the paper and the solvent would ascend the paper. In either case, the separations are seen as a series of colored spots on the paper strip. If the separated fractions happened to be colorless, they can be sprayed with

Paper chromatography uses strips of paper rather than columns.

Demonstration—Obtain a large test tube and a cork. Attach a strip of filter paper to the cork. Place a little water in the bottom of the test tube. Arrange the filter paper so the bottom tip is immersed in the water at the bottom of the test tube when the cork is inserted. Place a drop of ink on the filter paper just above the water level and let the tube stand upright. Observe.

FIGURE 14-17. The paper chromatographic separation of Ag^+, Pb^{2+}, and Hg_2^{2+} using 1-butanol/water in the ratio of 85/15 as the solvent. The paper was sprayed with a potassium chromate solution to highlight the metal ions.

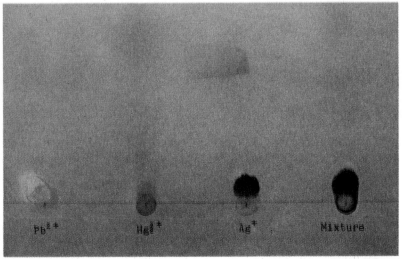

Robert C. Smoot

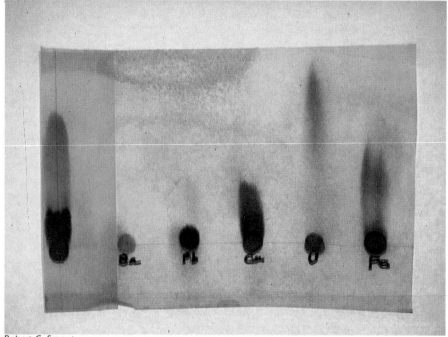
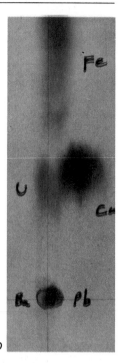

a

b

Robert C. Smoot

FIGURE 14-18. The paper chromatographic migration of Ba^{2+}, Pb^{2+}, UO_2^{2+}, and Fe^{3+} ions is shown in (a). Compare this chromatograph with that in (b) showing the migration of the same ions from a mixture.

solutions which will produce colored compounds. Some of these compounds may fluoresce under ultraviolet light.

For example, consider the separation of Ag^+, Pb^{2+}, Hg_2^{2+}. Let us see how it might be done with a paper chromatogram. The chromatogram is prepared, using 1-butanol and H_2O at a ratio of 85/15 solvent and a drop of the solution to be separated. The solvent will move to within 1 or 2 cm of the end of the paper. Then the chromatogram is sprayed with potassium chromate. A brick-red spot (Ag_2CrO_4) which fades to a pale yellow when held over ammonia indicates Ag^+. A bright yellow spot ($PbCrO_4$) which becomes orange with ammonia indicates Pb^{2+}. An orange or brown spot which blackens with ammonia indicates Hg_2^{2+}.

If further separation between spots is needed, the paper can be turned 90°. Each spot is then used as an originating spot. The same solvent, or a second solvent, may be used. For example, a solution containing Ba, Pb, Cu, U, and Fe ions could be resolved by the use of 1-butanol/water first. Then the paper may be turned and ethanol/$6M$ HCl at a solvent ratio of 90/10 used as the second solvent.

Paper chromatography is simple, fast, and has a high resolving power. This method can be used to separate the constituents of blood, urine, and antibiotics.

One great difficulty with paper chromatography separation arises out of its extremely small scale. Quantitative determinations are difficult. In addition, a control is needed to determine

The development of specially treated papers such as cellulose phosphate has made this method even more valuable.

which spots belong to which compound. Even with these difficulties, the method is still extremely useful. One way of extending the usefulness of paper chromatography is to combine it, when possible, with an electric field. By using both solvent and electric field, it is possible to separate substances which are inseparable by either method alone.

Thin layer chromatography combines some of the techniques of both column and paper chromatography. A glass plate is coated with a very thin layer of stationary phase, as is used in column chromatography. A spot of an unknown mixture is applied as in paper chromatography. The glass plate is placed in an atmosphere of solvent vapor and solvent. The procedure from this point is just the same as that for paper chromatography.

A number of reagent manufacturers presently produce excellent demonstration kits for thin layer chromatography.

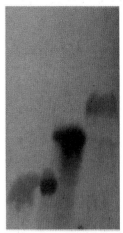

Robert C. Smoot

FIGURE 14-19. The thin-layer chromatogram shows the separation of four amino acids on cellulose using 1-butanol/acetic acid/water in the ratio of 12/3/5.

Gas chromatography is used to analyze volatile liquids and mixtures of gases.

14:11 GAS CHROMATOGRAPHY

Volatile liquids and mixtures of gases or vapors can also be analyzed by a chromatographic process. The gases to be analyzed are carried along by an inert gas such as helium in the mobile phase. The gases are fractionated on a stationary phase by a method similar to column chromatography. They are then carried by the inert helium through a tube fitted with an electrocouple. The varying amounts of contamination in the helium produce varying amounts of current. These variations are recorded by a needle on a moving sheet of graph paper. The amount of gas present in each fraction can be determined from the area under the curve produced.

TYPICAL CHROMATOGRAPHS

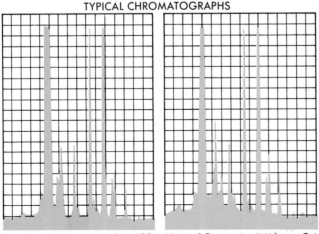

Synthesized Spearmint 0:1 600   Natural Spearmint (Midwest Origin)

FIGURE 14-20. These drawings of gas chromatograms show how closely synthetic spearmint flavoring matches natural spearmint oil.

Gas chromatography has been used mostly in organic chemistry because inorganic substances vaporize at higher temperatures.

A common test performed by environmental scientists is analysis of agricultural run-off for pesticide residues. Figure 14-21 shows such a chromatogram.

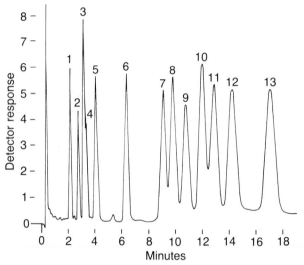

1. α-BHC
2. Lindane
3. β-BHC
4. Heptachlor
5. Aldrin
6. Heptachlor epoxide
7. p,p'-DDE
8. Dieldrin
9. o,p'-DDD (TDE)
10. Endrin
11. o,p'-DDT
12. p,p-DDD (TDE)
13. p,p-DDT

FIGURE 14-21. This drawing shows the pesticides present in a sample of run-off water.

Jokichi Takamine (1854–1922)

It is not often that industrial chemists receive the same fame that research chemists do. However, Jokichi Takamine, a Japanese industrial chemist had many "firsts" in the field of chemistry. He was the first to make a successful separation of the starch-hydrolyzing enzyme called diastase. As a result of this accomplishment, he made enzyme production commercially feasible.

At the age of 30, while in the United States, he learned of the use of superphosphate as a fertilizer. He returned to his native country and soon started an artificial fertilizer company to use the process in Japan. In 1901, he was the first to isolate pure adrenalin, which he added to the product line of his manufacturing laboratory.

Eleven years later, as a tribute both to his native country and his adopted country, the United States, he convinced the mayor of Tokyo to send the first cherry trees as a gift to the United States. Each year when these trees bloom along the Potomac, they reflect the social consciousness of a chemist who loved both countries.

CHEMICAL TECHNOLOGY: Salt

When we use the word salt in normal conversation, we generally mean sodium chloride. In addition to its use with food, salt is consumed for a variety of purposes by nearly all chemical industries. Its physical and chemical properties as well as its availability make it suitable for a variety of uses.

When salt is scattered on an icy sidewalk, the salt lowers the freezing point of water. Thus, ice melts as long as the air temperature is not too low. Salt is not effective at extremely low temperatures. (See Chapter 22.)

Water softening involves replacing hard water ions such as Ca^{2+} and Fe^{2+} with Na^+ ions. When the sodium ions in the softening agent are depleted, they may be restored by soaking the material in a concentrated brine or $NaCl$ solution.

Salt is applied to the flesh side of animal skins as the first step in making leather. The salt destroys any bacteria which could rot the skins.

Salt is an essential component of the diet. Most body fluids contain sodium ions, although the concentration inside cells is low. The ratio between sodium ions and potassium ions must be maintained within fairly narrow limits for good health. The ratio between these two ions is considerably different inside and outside nerve cells. See Figure 11-5. Nerve impulses are transmitted in part by varying these ratios.

During competition, athletes tend to perspire freely. That process is a normal function which cools the body. Perspiration consists of salt as well as water. A perspiring athlete will often drink water to replace lost fluid. Failure to replace lost salt causes an upset in the Na^+/K^+ ratio. As a result, the nerve impulses are disrupted and the athlete suffers muscle spasms or cramps. Many athletes now consume specially prepared drinks designed to maintain the ion balance and restore lost fluids.

Though most salt is produced as the result of mining, about 12% comes from the evaporation of salt water. Mines in Louisiana and Texas produce about half the total salt mined in the United States. Though some salt is mined as a solid, most is obtained by pumping water into the mine. The water dissolves the salt and the solution is piped to the surface. The salt solution, called brine, is then evaporated to recover the solid. The recovery process typically produces 98-99% pure sodium chloride.

The abundance of sodium chloride makes it a readily available raw material for the production of many other chemicals such as sodium carbonate, sodium hydroxide, sodium sulfate, chlorine, and hydrochloric acid.

SUMMARY

1. A polar bond is one in which a shared pair of electrons is attracted more strongly to one of the atoms. 14:1
2. van der Waals forces are the net result of dipole-dipole, dipole-induced dipole, and dispersion effects. 14:2
3. A complex ion is composed of a central positive ion and molecular or negative ion ligands. 14:3
4. The number of ligands surrounding the central ion is the coordination number of a complex. 14:3
5. Complex ions which contain more than one type of ligand may exhibit geometric isomerism. 14:4
6. Small positive ions with a large nuclear attractive force form excellent central ions. The transition metal ions are good examples of these. 14:6
7. The bonds of complex ions have both ionic and covalent bonding characteristics. 14:6
8. Chromatography is a method of separating substances into identifiable chemical fractions by differences in their polarity. 14:8-14:11

PROBLEMS

7. a, b, e, d, f, c
(d and f have the same value)

7. The following pairs of atoms are all covalently bonded. Arrange the pairs in order of decreasing polarity of the bonds using Table 12-6.
   a. arsenic and oxygen
   b. chlorine and silicon
   c. nitrogen and chlorine
   d. oxygen and fluorine
   e. phosphorus and bromine
   f. antimony and sulfur

van der Waals forces 8. What forces hold molecular substances in the liquid and solid states?

octahedral 9. What shape would you expect the $[Al(H_2O)_6]^{3+}$ complex to have? Sketch it.

10. Identify: central ion, ligand, coordination number.

11. What factors determine coordination number? size and charge

12. Why do transition metals make good central ions? empty d orbitals to accept e^-; large charge-to-radius ratio

13. Name the following complex ions.
   a. GaF_5^{2-} b. SbS_4^{3-} c. $Au(CN)_2^-$ d. $Au(CN)_4^-$ e. $Cr(NH_3)_6^{3+}$

14. How are column and paper chromatography similar? How are they different?

15. X_2A, X_2A

15. The dipole moment of compound X_2A equals 1.84×10^{-30} C·m. Compound X_3D has a dipole moment of 1.50×10^{-30} C·m. Which compound is more polar? If they have approximately the same formula mass, which compound would you predict to have the higher melting point?

16. Considering what you know about forces between molecules, why do all of the elements in Group VIII exist as gases at room temperature?

17. Carbon dioxide has a dipole moment of 0. The dipole moment of sulfur dioxide is 1.6×10^{-30} C·m. Draw structural diagrams for both molecules and use them to explain the difference in polarity.

13. a. pentafluorogallate(III) ion   c. dicyanoaurate(I) ion
    b. tetrathioantimonate(V) ion   d. tetracyanoaurate(III) ion
                                     e. hexamminechromium(III) ion

REVIEW

1. What shape would you predict for the NI_3 molecule? For CCl_4? pyramidal, tetrahedral

2. Describe the shapes of s and p orbitals. *s*-spherical *p*-dumbbell

3. Explain why carbon can form four equivalent bonds with a predicted outer configuration of $2s^2 2p^2$. The s and p orbitals hybridize to four orbitals of equivalent energy, containing one electron each.

4. Why is benzene more stable than a compound with three single and three double bonds? The π electrons are delocalized among the carbon atoms.

5. What shape would you predict for H_2Se? Why? bent. The two unshared pairs of electrons push the shared pairs toward each other.

6. From molecular orbital theory, predict the stability of the He_2^+.

7. Draw as many isomers of C_5H_{10} as you can. Hint: There are 10 isomers and the compound contains one $C=C$ double bond.

8. Predict the $N-C=O$ bond angle in $(NH_2)_2CO$. 120°

9. Draw isomers for compounds with the formula C_6H_6.

10. Draw resonance structures for SO_3.

ONE MORE STEP

1. In preparing paper chromatograms, identification of unknowns is aided by the measurement of R_f values. These values concern the distance an unknown has advanced compared to the distance the solvent has advanced. Research the chromatographic process to determine how these values are useful in identification.

2. Look up the structure of chlorophyll and hemoglobin. Determine the central ion and its coordination number. What is the coordinated group, and what is its spatial orientation about the central ion?

3. Medicine and industry use certain materials called chelating agents. What are they and how are they related to complexes?

4. A number of organic compounds are used in the analysis of inorganic ions because they form complex ions. Investigate the substances used in detecting nickel, aluminum, and zirconium by such a method.

5. Try to separate the pigments of spinach leaves using paper chromatography.

READINGS

Barth, Howard G., "Separations Using Liquid Chromatography." *Chemistry,* Vol. 50, No. 7 (September 1977), pp. 11-13.

Eliel, Ernest L., "Stereochemistry." *Chemistry,* Part I, Vol. 49, No. 1 (January-February 1976), pp. 6-10; Part II, Vol. 49, No. 3 (April 1976), pp. 8-13.

Kauffman, George B., "Left-handed and Right-handed Molecules." *Chemistry,* Vol. 50, No. 3 (April 1977), pp. 14-18.

Nassau, Kurt, "The Causes of Color." *Scientific American,* Vol. 243, No. 4 (October 1980), pp. 124-154.

Navratil, J. D., and Walton, H. F., "Ion Exchange and Liquid Chromatography." *Chemistry,* Vol. 50, No. 6 (July-August 1977), pp. 18-20.

A particle of a solid, liquid, or gas can be compared to a tennis ball in constant motion. A particle of matter constantly collides with other particles and the walls of its container just as the tennis ball collides with the court surface and rackets. The velocity of a tennis ball can be changed if a player increases the force on the ball. How can the velocity of a particle be increased? How does a change in velocity affect a particle?

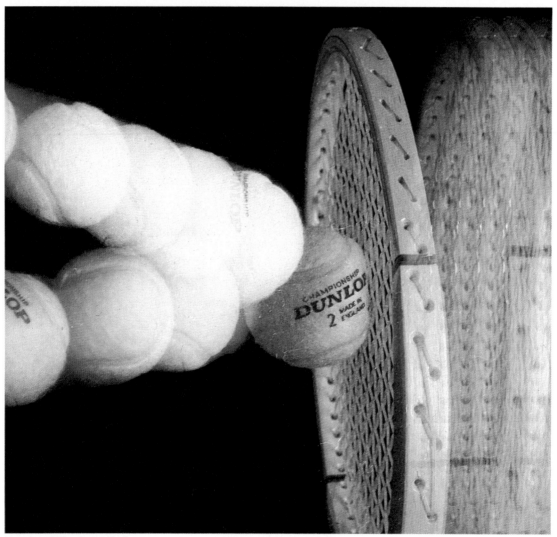

Don Carroll/The Image Bank

KINETIC THEORY

15

Chapter 15 uses the kinetic theory to describe the effects of heat and pressure on the four states of matter.

The **kinetic theory** explains the effect of heat and pressure on matter. First, let us consider some basic assumptions of the theory. *All matter is composed of particles* (atoms, ions, or molecules). *These small particles are in constant motion.* Finally, *all collisions are perfectly elastic.* Perfectly elastic means that there is no change in the total kinetic energy of two particles before and after their collision. It may be difficult to imagine that all particles in a great structure such as the Golden Gate Bridge are in constant motion. However, as we shall see, many of the properties of matter are the result of such motion. As early as the mid-seventeenth century, the English inventor Robert Hooke proposed a kinetic theory. He predicted that there were particles in nature which were in constant motion. In order to have some concept of size for the quantities involved, we will first discuss oxygen.

GOAL: You will gain an understanding of the kinetic theory and how it is used to describe the behavior of the four states of matter.

The kinetic theory is based on three assumptions.
1. All matter is composed of particles.
2. The particles of matter are in constant motion.
3. All collisions are perfectly elastic.

15:1 OXYGEN MOLECULES IN MOTION

At room temperature (25°C), the average velocity of an oxygen molecule is 443 m/s. This speed is equivalent to just over 1700 kilometers per hour. At this speed, the molecules collide with each other frequently. We can determine the average number of collisions a molecule undergoes in a unit of time. We do so by finding the average distance a molecule travels before colliding with another molecule. This distance is called the **mean free path** of the molecule. For oxygen at 25°C, the mean free path is 106 nm. The diameter of the oxygen molecule is about 0.339 nm. Thus, an oxygen molecule at 25°C will travel, on the average, about 314 times its own diameter before colliding with another molecule.

Even at room temperature molecules are moving extremely fast.

The mean free path of a molecule is the average distance a molecule travels between collisions.

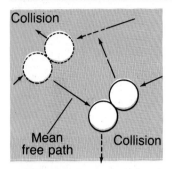

FIGURE 15-1. The mean free path of a molecule is the distance it travels between collisions.

Gas pressure results from collision of molecules with the walls of a container.

This travel corresponds to a little over four and a half billion collisions per second per molecule. We give these figures for oxygen as examples of the speed, the distance of travel, and the number of molecular collisions in a gas. These factors vary with the temperature and the mass of the particles composing the gas.

15:2 PRESSURE

Besides colliding with each other gas molecules collide with the walls of the container in which the gas is confined. When a gas molecule collides with the wall of a container, it exerts a force on the container. It is the force of collision and the number of collisions with the walls of a container that cause gas **pressure,** Figure 15-2. This pressure is measured in terms of the force per unit area.

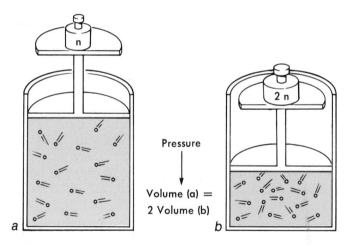

FIGURE 15-2. If the volume of a gas is halved, the number of collisions with the walls of the container doubles. Thus, the pressure in container (b) is twice that of container (a).

Emphasize that air pressure is equal in all directions in a container.

101.325 kPa is the average normal air pressure at sea level.

1 newton (N) = 1 kg·m/s^2

The molecules and atoms of the gases present in the air are constantly hitting the surface of the earth and everything on it. As a result, you and everything surrounding you are subject to a certain pressure from the molecules of the air. Air pressure has been used as a scientific standard of pressure. The standard is defined as the average pressure of the air at sea level under normal conditions. Since conditions in the air depend upon many weather factors, it is difficult to define "normal" conditions at sea level. Therefore, the standard has been defined in terms of a system which can be reproduced in the laboratory. It is 101.325 kilopascals (kPa). One **pascal** is a pressure of one newton per square meter (N/m^2). We will generally employ units of kilopascals.

15:3 MEASURING PRESSURE

In measuring gas pressure, an instrument called a **manometer** (mah NAHM uh tuhr) is used. Two types of manometers are shown in Figure 15-3. In the "open" type, air exerts pressure on the column of liquid in one arm of the U-tube. The gas being studied exerts pressure on the other arm. The difference in liquid level between the two arms is a measure of the gas pressure relative to the air pressure. If you know the density of the liquid in the manometer, you can calculate the pressure difference between the gas and the air.

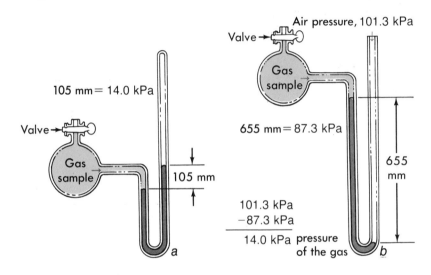

FIGURE 15-3. Closed (a) and open arm (b) manometers can be used to measure gas pressure.

The "closed" type of manometer has a vacuum above the liquid in one arm. The pressure measured with an instrument of this type does not depend on the pressure of the air and is called the absolute pressure. This manometer can be used to measure the pressure of the air itself. Such a manometer (one used to measure atmospheric pressure) is called a **barometer.** Most barometers are manufactured with a scale calibrated to read the height of a column of mercury in millimeters. The average pressure of the air will support a column of mercury 760 mm high. Since average air pressure is defined as 101.325 kPa, then 101.325 kPa = 760 mm. By dividing both sides of the equation by 101.325 we find that 1 kPa = 7.50 mm.

Even with an open manometer it is possible to calculate the absolute pressure of a gas. However, a barometer must be available to measure the atmospheric pressure on the outside arm of the manometer.

The following examples show some typical calculations involving gas pressure.

FIGURE 15-4. The mercury barometer is commonly used in the laboratory to measure air pressure.

Larry Hamill

EXAMPLE: Pressure

The open manometer in Figure 15-3 is filled with mercury. The difference between mercury levels in the two arms is 6 mm. What is the total pressure, in kilopascals, of the gas in the container? The air pressure is 101.3 kPa.

Solving process:
The mercury is higher in the arm connected to the gas. Thus, the pressure exerted by the gas must be less than that of the air. As a result, we must subtract the pressure of the mercury from the air pressure to get the gas pressure. Before subtracting, however, we must convert the 6 mm difference in height to kilopascals.

$$\frac{6 \text{ mm}}{} \; \left| \; \frac{1 \text{ kPa}}{7.50 \text{ mm}} \right. = 0.8 \text{ kPa}$$

Now we can subtract the two pressures. $101.3 - 0.8 = 100.5$ kPa

EXAMPLE: Pressure

Suppose the difference in height of the two mercury levels in the closed manometer in Figure 15-3 is 238 mm. What is the pressure in kilopascals of the gas in the container?

1 kPa = 7.50 mm

Solving process:
Since the column of mercury is 238 mm high and 7.50 mm of mercury equals 1 kPa, the pressure is

$$\frac{238 \text{ mm}}{} \; \left| \; \frac{1 \text{ kPa}}{7.50 \text{ mm}} \right. = 31.7 \text{ kPa}$$

PROBLEMS

1. An open manometer such as the one in Figure 15-3, is filled with mercury and connected to a container of hydrogen. The mercury level is 80 mm higher in the arm of the tube connected to the gas. Air pressure is 97.7 kPa. What is the pressure of the hydrogen in kilopascals?

1. 87.0 kPa

2. A closed manometer like the one in Figure 15-3 is filled with mercury and connected to a container of nitrogen. The difference in the height of mercury in the two arms is 690 mm. What is the pressure of the nitrogen in kilopascals? 92.0 kPa

3. An open manometer is filled with mercury and connected to a container of oxygen. The level of mercury is 6 mm higher in the arm of the tube connected to the container of oxygen. Air pressure is 100.0 kPa. What is the pressure, in kilopascals, of the oxygen? 99.2 kPa

4. A closed manometer is filled with mercury and connected to a container of helium. The difference in the height of mercury in the two arms is 86.0 mm. What is the pressure, in kilopascals, of the helium? **11.5 kPa**

15:4 KINETIC ENERGY

The average speed of the particles in a gas depends only on the temperature and the mass of the particles. How are temperature and particle mass related?

F. Bernard Daniel

Kinetic energy is the energy an object possesses because of its motion. Temperature is a measure of that kinetic energy. Therefore, the average kinetic energy of molecules or atoms in a gas is the same for all particles at a particular temperature. The kinetic energy of a particle is equal to $1/2\ mv^2$, where m is its mass and v its velocity. This equation shows that, at a given temperature, a particle with small mass will move faster than a particle with large mass.

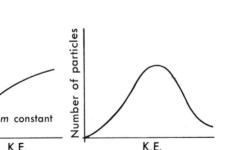

15:5 TEMPERATURE

A decrease in the temperature of a substance means the particles of the substance are moving more slowly. An increase in temperature means the particles are moving faster. Temperature is a measure of the average kinetic energy of the particles of a substance.

Molecular motion of a gas decreases as the temperature decreases. Therefore, it should in theory be possible to lower the

FIGURE 15-5. The cotton on one end of the tube is saturated with concentrated HCl. The cotton at the other end is saturated with NH_3(aq). The formation of NH_4Cl is shown by the white ring in the tube. By noting the postion of the ring, can you determine which end of the tube contains HCl?

Particles of samples of gases at the same temperature have the same average kinetic energy.

$$K.E. = \frac{1}{2}\ mv^2$$

FIGURE 15-6. The graphs show the relationships among mass, velocity, and kinetic energy. The third graph shows that in any given sample some particles will have more or less energy than the average.

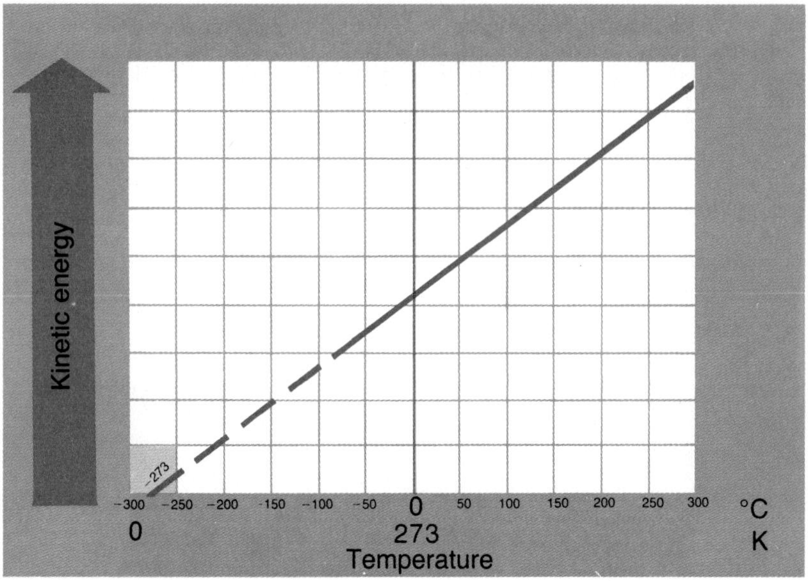

This section of the graph is an extrapolation. It is not verified by experimental evidence.

FIGURE 15-7. Theoretically, the point at which molecular motion ceases (KE = 0) is absolute zero (−273°C).

temperature to a point where all molecular motion ceases. This temperature, the temperature at which all molecular motion should cease, is known as **absolute zero.** It is −273.15°C. This value is usually rounded to −273°C.

A consequence of this derivation will be discussed in Section 18:8.

Absolute zero is −273°C or 0 K.

Remind students that the K does not have a degree symbol.

To make a temperature scale based on absolute zero scientists have agreed on a system known as the absolute, or **kelvin scale.** The zero point of the kelvin scale is absolute zero. The divisions, or degrees, are the same size as those of the Celsius scale. Therefore,

$$K = °C + 273$$

The kelvin is the SI unit of temperature.

PROBLEMS

5a. 360 K
6a. −187°C
7a. 296 K
8a. 599°C

5. Convert the following temperatures from Celsius to kelvin.
   a. 87°   **b.** 16° 289   **c.** 59° 332   **d.** −68° 205 **e.** 73° 346
6. Convert the following temperatures from kelvin to Celsius.
   a. 86   **b.** 191 −82°   **c.** 533 260°   **d.** 318 45°   **e.** 894 621°
7. Convert the following temperatures from Celsius to kelvin.
   a. 23°   **b.** 58° 331   **c.** 90° 363   **d.** 18° 291   **e.** 25° 298
8. Convert the following temperatures from kelvin to Celsius.
   a. 872   **b.** 690 417°   **c.** 384 111°   **d.** 20 −253°   **e.** 60 −213°

15:6 HEAT TRANSFER

Temperature can be used to determine the direction of flow of heat energy. Heat energy always flows from a warmer object to a cooler one. Kinetic theory explains the flow of heat energy in terms of particle collisions. The particles of the warmer object and the cooler object have unequal kinetic energy. The excess kinetic energy of the particles in the warmer object is passed on to the particles of the cooler object as they collide, Figure 15-8. The particles of the cooler object gradually receive more kinetic energy until the average kinetic energy of both objects is the same.

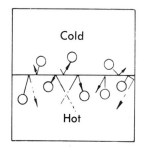

FIGURE 15-8. Heat flows from hot objects to cooler ones through a transfer of kinetic energy when particles collide.

15:7 STATES OF MATTER

Matter exists in four states—solid, liquid, gas and plasma. Thus far, our discussion of the kinetic theory has been limited to gases. However, kinetic theory can also be used to explain the behavior of solids and liquids. Plasmas are treated as a special case.

Gas particles are independent of each other and move in a straight line. Change of direction occurs only when one particle collides with another, or when a particle collides with the walls of the container. Gas particles, then, travel in a completely random manner. Since they travel until they collide with a neighbor or with the walls of their container, gases assume the shape and volume of their container.

The particles of a liquid have what appears to be a vibratory type of motion. Actually, they are traveling a straight-line path between collisions with near neighbors. The point about which the seeming vibration occurs often shifts as one particle slips past another. These differences in the amount of space between particles allow the particles to change their relative positions continually. Thus, liquids, although they have a definite volume, assume the shape of their container.

In solids, a particle occupies a relatively fixed position in relation to the surrounding particles. A particle of a solid appears to vibrate about a fixed point. Again, the particle is actually traveling a straight-line path between collisions with very near neighbors. For example, a molecule of oxygen gas at 25°C travels an average distance equal to 314 times its own diameter before colliding with another molecule. In a solid, however, the particles are closely packed and travel a distance equal to only a fraction of their diameters before colliding. Unlike liquids, solids have their particles arranged in a definite pattern. Solids, therefore, have both a definite shape and a definite volume.

Four states of matter: solid, liquid, gas, plasma.

Gas particles travel in random paths.

Gases assume the shape and volume of their container.

Liquid particles travel in straight-line paths between collisions, but appear to vibrate about moving points.

Liquids have definite volume but assume the shape of their container.

Solid particles are arranged in a definite pattern.

Solid particles appear to vibrate about fixed points.

Solids have both definite shape and definite volume.

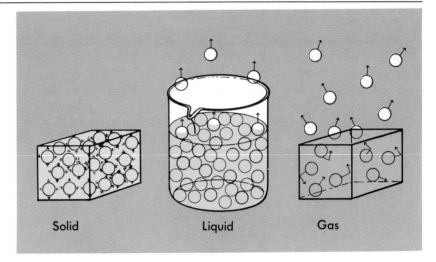

Solid   Liquid   Gas

FIGURE 15-9. The particles of a solid vibrate about fixed points. The particles of a liquid vibrate about moving points. The particles of a gas travel in straight lines between collisions.

The physical state of a substance depends mostly on its bonding structure (at room temperature and standard pressure).

The physical state of a substance at room temperature and standard atmospheric pressure depends mostly on the bonding in the substance. Ionic compounds have strong electric charges holding the ions together and exist as solids. Molecular substances are attracted to each other by van der Waals forces. Molecular compounds of high molecular mass tend to be solids. Nonpolar molecules of low molecular mass tend to be gases. Greater molecular mass and greater polarity both tend to make substances form a condensed state, either liquid or solid.

The arrangement of particles is important to the chemist. In the following chapters we will discuss some of the special characteristics of solids, liquids, and gases.

15:8   PLASMA

When matter is heated to very high temperatures (>5000°C), the collisions between particles are so violent that electrons are knocked away from atoms. Such a state of matter, composed of electrons and positive ions, is called a plasma.

A plasma state is composed of electrons and positive ions at very high temperatures.

Most of the universe is made of plasma. Stars are in a plasma state. Outer space is not really empty. It is composed of extremely thin plasma. The Van Allen radiation belts which surround the earth are made of plasma. Matter in a neon tube or in a cyclotron is in the form of plasma. Scientists are working on the character of plasmas because a nuclear reaction, called fusion, occurs only in plasmas. The fusion reaction, if it can be controlled, promises to be an energy source second only to the sun.

Electric and magnetic fields affect the plasma state.

Since plasma consists of charged particles traveling at high speeds, it is greatly affected by electric and magnetic fields.

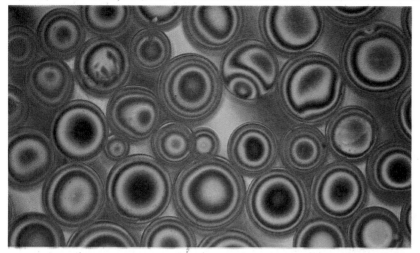

Dan McCoy/Rainbow

FIGURE 15-10. These fusion pellets are made of glass and contain tritium and deuterium to be used as fuel for the fusion reaction. When hit by a laser, the fuel changes to the plasma state. The pellets shown here are greatly magnified.

Therefore, the study of plasma is called magnetohydrodynamics (mag NET oh hy droh dy NAM iks). Magnetohydrodynamics (MHD) is involved in confining the plasma which scientists hope can be used as an energy source through nuclear fusion reactions. It is also involved in designing an advanced propulsion unit for space vehicles.

The study of plasma is called magnetohydrodynamics, MHD.

Plasma can be contained in a "magnetic bottle". (It is contained by magnetic fields.)

George Washington Carver   (1864–1943)

George Washington Carver was born in slavery in the United States. However before he died, he became one of the foremost agricultural chemists in the world. Largely self-educated, Carver was 35 years old when he received his masters degree from Iowa State University.

Carver is probably best known for his work with sweet potatoes and peanuts. However, he also made use of other agricultural products to develop building materials and household goods. For example, he prepared imitation marble from sawdust, and rugs from vegetable stalks. He was probably the forerunner of today's recycling movement. In addition to being an accomplished scientist Carver was also a pianist and an artist. Although many of his contemporaries scoffed because he failed to produce any scholarly papers, his experiments and practical contributions have benefited people all over the world.

CHEMICAL TECHNOLOGY: Artificial Body Parts

Biomedical engineers have made and continue to make replacements for various parts of the human body. Artificial limbs have been under development for a long time. However, other artificial body parts such as eyes, ears, and livers have only been attempted recently. One problem to be overcome by the design engineer is the tendency of the body to reject foreign substances. The body treats an artificial organ as an invader and reacts as if the organ were a bacterium or germ. Good materials for artificial organs must not trigger any of the body's defense systems.

The biggest problem in using biomaterials concerns the formation of bonds between natural tissue and the replacement part. Many of the substances used cause the growth of fibrous tissue which separates the natural tissue from the implant. This fibrous tissue may harden causing inflammation, pain, and the destruction of normal tissue.

Most biomaterials research concerns controlling any chemical reactions that may occur at the interface between the biomaterial and natural tissue.

One material which has found wide usage in medicine is silicone rubber (Silastic®). It contains very long molecules made of repeating units. Such molecules are called polymers. A simple structure for a silicone could be represented as

$$\left[\begin{array}{c} CH_3 \\ | \\ -O-Si- \\ | \\ CH_3 \end{array} \right]_n$$

Many other tissue-compatible materials are polymers. Their molecular shapes are such that they imitate safe biological materials. Some polymers are almost shapeless, that is their surfaces are relatively smooth. Thus, they are ignored by the body's defenses.

$$\left[\begin{array}{c} O \qquad\quad CH-CH \qquad\quad O \\ \parallel \qquad\quad \diagup\quad\diagdown \qquad\quad \parallel \\ -O-C-C \qquad\qquad C-C-O-CH_2-CH_2- \\ \diagdown\quad\diagup \\ CH=CH \end{array} \right]_n$$

Polyethylene terephthalate
(Dacron®)

$$\left[\begin{array}{c} CH_3 \\ | \\ -CH_2-C- \\ | \\ C=O \\ | \\ O \\ | \\ CH_3 \end{array} \right]_n$$

Polymethyl methacrylate
(Plexiglass®)

$$\left[\begin{array}{c} F \quad F \\ | \quad | \\ -C-C- \\ | \quad | \\ F \quad F \end{array} \right]_n$$

Polytetrafluoroethylene
(Teflon®)

$$\left[\begin{array}{c} O \quad H \\ \parallel \quad | \\ -C-N-CH_2-CH_2-CH_2-CH_2-CH_2-CH_2-N-C-O-CH_2-CH_2-CH_2-CH_2-O- \end{array} \begin{array}{c} H \quad O \\ | \quad \parallel \\ \end{array} \right]_n$$

Polyurethane

Currently, researchers have been attempting to produce materials by imitating or reusing natural body materials. One example is collagen, which is a protein material making the tendons and cartilage in the body. The collagen structure consists of three strands of protein twisted together to form a material called tropocollagen. These strands are then aligned to form collagen fibers. To align correctly, the third amino acid in each protein must be glycine. Collagen is also known to have a high content of hydroxyproline.

Table 15-1

Some Biomaterials and Their Uses	
Material	**Use**
Aluminum oxide	vertebrae spacers, dental reconstruction, tooth replacement
Co-Cr alloys	heart valves; joint reconstruction; plates, pins, and screws used in fracture repairs
Collagen	tumorous tissue replacement, artificial skin, internal shunts for dialysis
Dacron®	breast prosthesis, tissue patches
Polyethylene	artificial catheters and shunts, filling in bone defects
Polymethyl methacrylate	corneas used in correcting cataracts, replacing bones in the middle ear
Polyurethane	vessel replacements, artificial cartilage
Silicone rubber	artificial eustachian tubes, pacemakers, vessel replacements, tumorous tissue replacements
Stainless steel	filling in bone defects; joint reconstruction; tooth replacement; plates, pins, and screws used in fracture repair
Teflon®	artificial eustachian tubes; vessel replacements; artificial ureters, bladders, and intestinal walls
Ti alloy/Silastic®	heart valves

SUMMARY

1. The kinetic theory explains the effects of heat and pressure on matter. This theory assumes that (1) all matter is composed of particles; (2) these particles are in constant motion; (3) collisions between these particles are perfectly elastic. Intro.

2. At 25°C, an oxygen molecule travels at just over 1700 kilometers per hour in straight lines. At this temperature it has more than four and a half billion collisions per second. 15:1

3. A gas exerts pressure on its container because the gas molecules are constantly colliding with the walls of the container. 15:2

4. The average pressure of the atmosphere at sea level is 101.325 kilopascals under normal conditions. 15:2

5. The pressure necessary to support a column of mercury 760 mm high is 101.325 kilopascals. Therefore 7.50 mm = 1 kPa. 15:3

6. A manometer is an instrument used to measure gas pressure. 15:3

7. Kinetic energy is the energy an object possesses because of its motion. It is related to the mass and the velocity of the object. 15:4

8. Temperature is a measure of the average kinetic energy of the particles of a substance. 15:5

9. The kelvin temperature scale is based on absolute zero. It has the same unit as the Celsius scale degree, but a zero point at absolute zero (K = °C + 273). 15:5

10. Heat energy flows from an object of higher temperature to one of lower temperature until both reach the same temperature. 15:6

11. The particles of a gas travel at random in a straight-line manner. 15:7

12. The particles of a solid appear to be vibrating about a point which is fixed with respect to neighboring particles. 15:7

13. The particles of a liquid appear to be vibrating about a point which is moving with respect to neighboring particles. 15:7

14. A plasma consists of electrons and positive ions in random motion. It is strongly affected by electric and magnetic fields. 15:8

PROBLEMS

9. The open manometer in Figure 15-3 is filled with mercury. The difference in the mercury level in the arms is 12 mm. The mercury level is higher in the gas sample arm. What is the pressure, in kilopascals, of the gas in the container if the air pressure is 98.7 kilopascals? 97.1 kPa

10. In the closed manometer in Figure 15-3, assume that the height of the levels differs by 400 mm Hg. What is the pressure in kPa of the gas in the container? 53.3 kPa

11. Convert the following temperatures from one temperature scale to another as indicated.
   a. 828 K to °C 555°C   c. 16°C to K 289 K   e. 62°C to K 335 K
   b. 751°C to K 1024 K   d. 3 K to °C −270°C

12. Suppose you have two vials, one containing ammonia and the other containing chlorine. When they are opened across the room from you, which would you expect to smell first? ammonia

13. What is the mean free path of a particle? average distance it travels between collisions

14. With regard to particle motion, what are the differences in the states of matter?

15. How does temperature affect the kinetic energy of a particle? Temperature and kinetic energy are directly related.

16. In terms of the kinetic theory, what is the significance of absolute zero?

17. What is an elastic collision? How does it differ from an inelastic collision? Use a dictionary to define these terms.

REVIEW

1. Which of the following bonds has a greater polarity?
   a. Ru—F   b. Be—Br

2. What advantage does surface chromatography have over column chromatography? What disadvantage? advantage—rapid, disadvantage—not quantitative

3. What is the most common ligand? H_2O

4. Predict the shape of the molecule ICl_3. trigonal bipyramidal

5. What is the difference between a sigma bond and a pi bond? ⎦ A sigma bond involves end-to-end overlap of orbitals. Pi bonds involve sideways overlap of p orbitals.

6. What spatial orientation is taken by sp hybrid orbitals? linear

7. What properties are associated with multiple bonds? ⎤ rigid with respect to rotation of the bonded atoms; more reactive than single bonds and always formed from p orbitals

8. Draw resonance structures for the SO_2 molecule.

9. Which element is more reactive, At or Po? At

10. Arrange in order of increasing force on the outer electrons: Ni, F, Ti, C, Sc. Sc Ti Ni C F

11. Label each of the following as ionic or covalent.
    a. Au—Cl covalent   c. B—C covalent   e. Bi—F ionic
    b. Li—Cl ionic   d. Pb—Cl covalent

12. Predict the shape of CS_2. linear

13. Describe the electronic structure of NO^+ using molecular orbital theory.

14. Name the following complexes.
    a. $Co(NH_3)_6^{2+}$ c. $Ni(NH_3)_4(H_2O)_2^{2+}$ e. $Ag(NH_3)_2^+$
    b. $Cu(NH_3)_2^{2+}$ d. $Pt(NH_3)_2Cl_4$

    a. hexamminecobalt(II) ion
    b. diamminecopper(II) ion
    c. diaquotetramminenickel (II) ion
    d. diammineplatinum(IV) chloride
    e. diamminesilver ion

15. Write formulas for the following complex ions.
    a. hexachlororhodate(III) $RhCl_6^{3-}$ c. hexacarbonyliron(0) $Fe(CO)_6$
    b. tetrafluoroberyllate BeF_4^{2-} d. tetracarbonylnickel(0) $Ni(CO)_4$

ONE MORE STEP

1. Compute the kinetic energy of an oxygen molecule at 25°C, and of an automobile with a mass of 1500 kg traveling at 50 km/h. oxygen molecule – 5.22×10^{-21} J

2. Calculate the velocity of a hydrogen molecule at 25°C.   automobile – 1.45×10^5 J

3. Investigate the workings of an aneroid barometer. Are there other instruments used to measure pressures in addition to manometers?

4. Prepare a report for your class on the topic of plasmas.

5. The SI unit of pressure is the pascal. Find out who Pascal was. Also investigate the relationship between the millibar and the pascal. 1 mbar = 0.750 mm = 0.1 kPa

A study of the solid state is the study of the structure and properties of crystalline substances. When we think of a solid, we imagine an orderly arrangement of particles. However, as the photograph shows most crystals are not perfectly ordered structures. There are advantages to having defective arrangements in crystals. What are the types of crystal defects? Why are defects added purposely to some crystals? How do these defects affect the properties of the crystal?

Mrs. George T. Butts

SOLIDS

16

Chapter 16 introduces crystals through a study of unit cells. The relationship between packing arrangement and properties is covered for various substances. The distinction between crystalline solids and amorphous materials is emphasized.

Demonstration—Place a shallow glass dish on the overhead projector. Add 10 cm³ of H_2O and 10–15 drops of liquid dishwashing detergent to the dish. Gently blow bubbles with a straw or glass tube. The bubbles will arrange themselves like the unit cells in a crystal. Emphasize the definition of a crystal as having particles arranged in a repeating fashion.

Wooden models of the various crystal structures are available and can be helpful in the study of this chapter. It is also possible to have one or more students construct such models from foam spheres.

Have you ever examined table salt under a magnifying glass? If so, you would have seen that the crystals appear to be little cubes. The lengths of the edges may vary, but the angles between the surfaces are always exactly 90°.

The systematic study of crystals began with Nicolaus Steno, in 1669. He observed that corresponding angles between faces on different crystals of the same substance were always the same. This fact was true regardless of the size or source of the crystals.

Steno's observation has been extended to all intensive properties (density, refractive index, face angles, and other similar properties. For example, a single crystal of the mineral beryl, $Be_3Al_2Si_6O_{18}$, weighing more than 40 tons was once unearthed in New Hampshire. This huge crystal was found to be identical in intensive properties with any other beryl crystal. The size or mass of the crystal is not important. It can now be stated that the extensive properties of crystals vary while the intensive properties remain the same. (See Section 3:4 to refresh your memory on the difference between intensive and extensive properties.)

GOAL: You will gain an understanding of crystal structure and its relationship to the properties of solids.

All crystals of the same substance have the same angles between faces.

Extensive properties of crystals of the same substance may vary, but intensive properties remain the same.

No exceptions have been found to Steno's Law.

16:1 CRYSTALS

All true solid substances are crystalline. Apparent exceptions to this statement can be explained in either of two ways. In some cases, substances we think of as solids are not solids at all. In other cases, the crystals are so small that the solid does not appear crystalline to the unaided eye. The study of the solid state is really a study of crystals.

Suggestion: Obtain a microscope and allow students to observe salt crystals under low power, use a microprojector.

A study of crystals is a study of the solid state.

FIGURE 16-1. True crystalline substances such as beryl (a), sugar (b), and celestite (c) are made of regular repeating units.

A crystal is a rigid body in which the particles are arranged in a repeating pattern.

Properties of crystals are partially determined by the bonding.

Repeating patterns of atoms, molecules, or ions are caused by bonding.

All crystals of a certain substance must be made of similar small units. These units are then repeated over and over again as the crystal grows. Thus a **crystal** is defined as a rigid body in which the particles are arranged in a repeating pattern. The shape and properties of these units are determined by the bonds between the particles. Therefore, the bonding in the crystal partially determines the properties of the crystal.

The units which compose a crystal are too small to be seen. Yet before any methods existed for studying crystal structure, scientists suggested that crystals form by repetition of identical units. Consider the patterns on wallpaper or drapery fabrics. These patterns are applied by rollers which repeat the design with each revolution. In a crystal, the forces of chemical bonding play the same role that the roller does in printing. They cause the basic pattern to be repeated over and over again. However, the "design" of a crystal must be composed of atoms, molecules, or ions instead of ink. The major difference between crystals and wallpaper is that the units in crystals are three-dimensional. Those on wallpaper are only two-dimensional.

FIGURE 16-2. Crystal structures exhibit a repeating pattern just as that shown for the wallpaper and honeycomb.

Table 16-1

	Seven Crystal Systems		
	Lengths of the Unit Cell Axes	**Angles Between the Unit Cell Axes**	**Crystal System**
	all equal	all = 90°	cubic
	2 equal 1 unequal	all = 90°	tetragonal
	3 equal 1 unequal	1 = 90° 3 = 60°	hexagonal
	all equal	all ≠ 90°	rhombohedral
	all unequal	all = 90°	orthorhombic
	all unequal	2 = 90°, 1 ≠ 90°	monoclinic
	all unequal	all ≠ 90°	triclinic

There is a relationship between the repeating units and the external shape of the crystal. Long ago, crystallographers (kris tuh LAHG ruh fuhrs) classified crystals on the basis of their external shapes into seven "crystal systems."

Crystal structure is often determined by studying X-ray and electron diffraction patterns.

16:2   UNIT CELLS

Each substance which crystallizes does so according to a definite geometric arrangement. The simplest repeating unit in this arrangement is called the **unit cell.** It is possible to have more than one kind of unit cell with the same shape.

Consider the different kinds of three-dimensional unit cells. Fourteen such cells are possible, Table 16-2.

Table 16-2

Unit Cells	
Crystal System	**Unit Cell**
Cubic	simple, body-centered, face-centered
Tetragonal	simple, body-centered
Orthorhombic	simple, single face-centered, body-centered, face-centered
Monoclinic	simple, single face-centered
Triclinic	simple
Trigonal	simple
Hexagonal	simple

FIGURE 16-3. The three unit cells of the cubic system have the same shape.

Cubic

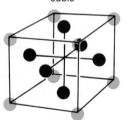

Face-centered cubic

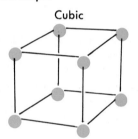

Body-centered cubic

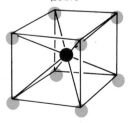

16:3   TYPICAL UNIT CELLS

Three of the simplest unit cells are the **cubic, face-centered cubic** (FCC), and **body-centered cubic** (BCC). There are many familiar substances which have the cubic structures listed above. Iron, for example is generally found as BCC. However, when it is heated between approximately 900°C and 1400°C, it becomes FCC.

Note the packing arrangement of the particles in each unit cell. In the simple cubic cell, each particle has six immediate neighbors. In the face-centered cell, each has twelve; and in the body-centered, each has eight. The three-dimensional arrangement of unit cells repeated over and over in a definite geometric arrangement is called a **space lattice.**

Keep in mind that the particles in the cells are not as far apart as indicated in the diagrams. They are represented as dots simply for clarity in those diagrams. Actually, the particles are extremely close.

It should also be pointed out that space lattices and unit cells have no real physical existence. The crystal is built of atoms, ions, or molecules. The space lattice is a mental model, or frame of reference, which helps us understand the facts of crystal structure.

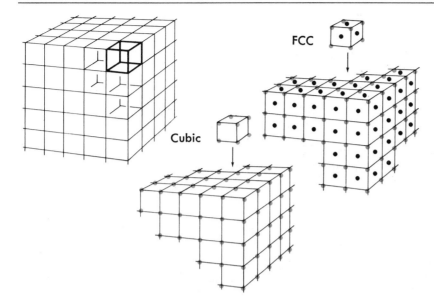

The space lattice and unit cell are mental models. Neither actually exists within the crystal. Important!

FIGURE 16-4. The space lattice is a regular arrangement of unit cells. Space lattices and unit cells are merely mental models.

There are fourteen different unit cells.
1. Triclinic
2. Monoclinic
3. Side-centered monoclinic
4. Orthorhombic
5. End-centered orthorhombic
6. Face-centered orthorhombic
7. Body-centered orthorhombic
8. Hexagonal
9. Rhombohedral
10. Tetragonal
11. Body-centered tetragonal
12. Cubic
13. Face-centered cubic
14. Body-centered cubic

16:4 COMPOUND UNIT CELLS

Sodium chloride crystallizes in a structure similar to that pictured in Figure 16-5. If you study the illustration, you can see that the Na^+ and Cl^- ions occupy different positions relative to each other.

How would you classify this unit cell? It apparently is some form of cubic, but which one? Look more closely. Each Cl^- ion is surrounded by six Na^+ ions. Each Na^+ ion in turn is surrounded by six Cl^- ions. If you consider either alone, you can see that the

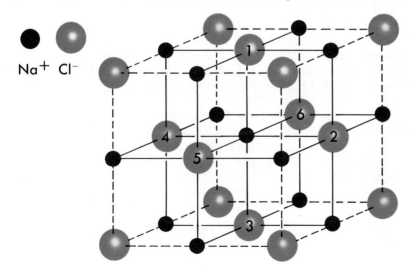

Na^+ Cl^-

FIGURE 16-5. The sodium chloride unit cell is face-centered cubic. Each ion is surrounded by six ions of opposite charge.

unit of repetition is face-centered cubic. Thus, the unit cell can be considered FCC, even though more than one kind of particle is present.

The particles of matter which lie within the cells are arranged in a symmetrical fashion. This symmetry is related to the symmetry of the cell itself. When the combinations of space lattices and symmetry arrangements are analyzed mathematically, it turns out that there are only 230 different kinds of internal arrangements in crystals. Crystals can have axes, planes, or points of symmetry.

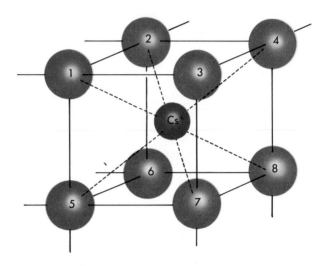

FIGURE 16-6. The cesium chloride unit cell is body-centered cubic. Each ion is surrounded by eight ions of opposite charge.

The particular crystal structure of an ionic compound such as salt is determined principally by the ratio of the radii of the ions. Since negative ions are larger than positive ions, the positive ions tend to fit in the spaces between negative ions. The positive ions must be large enough to keep the negative ions from coming into contact with each other, but small enough not to come into contact with neighboring positive ions.

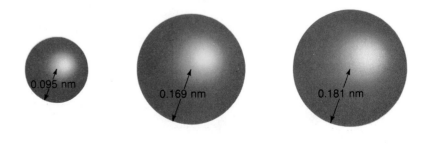

FIGURE 16-7. The size difference between the sodium ion and cesium ion accounts for the difference in unit cell arrangement.

16:5 CLOSEST PACKING

Let us examine in detail some of the simpler and more common types of arrangement in crystals. The elements usually have rather simple structures. Let us place a group of spheres as close as we can on a table and hold them so that they cannot roll apart. We can then place another layer upon the first one in an equally close arrangement. If we continue with more layers, a close-packed structure results. This structure is the kind found in the majority of metals. It is difficult to visualize the lattice in such a structure, since the lattice is really only a system of imaginary lines. However, the experienced eye will detect that the lattice is either hexagonal or face-centered cubic in the close-packed arrangement. They are often called **hexagonal closest packing** (HCP) and **cubic closest packing**, Figure 16-8. HCP is the one most frequently found in metals. Another structure, found particularly in the metals of group IA of the periodic table, is based on a body-centered cubic lattice. This structure is not quite so closely packed as the other two. In BCC, while the openings between the atoms are smaller, there are more openings.

The closest packed arrangements are hexagonal and FCC.

Cubic closest packing and face-centered cubic are the same arrangement.

FIGURE 16-8. The similarity in arrangement for the first two layers of a HCP and FCC lattice are shown. The dots represent the positions of particles in the second layer of the FCC arrangement. Differences in the arrangement are more apparent as subsequent layers are added as shown by the top and side views.

Layering progression

2 layer system

Subsequent layers (top view)

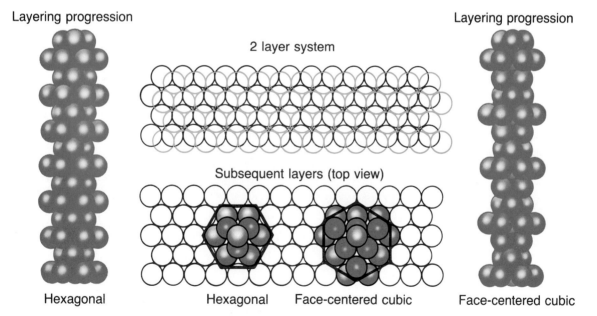

Hexagonal   Hexagonal   Face-centered cubic   Face-centered cubic

Layering progression

Iron has a body-centered structure at ordinary temperatures. At higher temperatures, it has a face-centered cubic structure. This fact is of great practical importance. Iron, in its common

a

Hickson-Bender Photography

b

Courtesy of Morton Salt "Division
of Morton-Norwich"

FIGURE 16-9. A salt crystal model is based on the FCC lattice (a). This structure gives salt its cubic shape as shown in the microscopic view of the crystal (b).

form of steel, always contains a small amount of carbon. Carbon atoms are smaller than iron atoms, and at high temperatures they fit into the open spaces in the face-centered structure. When the iron cools, it changes to the body-centered cubic form. In that form, the carbon atoms cannot fit into the smaller spaces. Either the iron lattice is distorted by the oversize carbon atoms, or the carbon separates out of the iron as iron carbide, Fe_3C.

Iron and Fe_3C crystals exist in many sizes and shapes. The final structure of the crystal is determined by the percentage of iron and the rate of cooling. These differences in crystal structure result in the great versatility of steel as an industrial material. They also account for the fact that the properties of steel can be changed greatly by heat treatment.

Simple salts are those formed by the elements of Group IA (the alkali metals except for Cs) and the elements of Group VIIA (the halogens). These salts always have structures based on the FCC lattice. Figure 16-5 shows a model of the sodium chloride structure, which is typical of this class of compounds. The same model would serve for other members of the group and also for many other binary compounds, like MgO and CaO. Note that it is impossible to distinguish an individual molecule of NaCl.

Figure 16-6 shows a body-centered cubic arrangement for CsCl. The Cs ion is too large to assume a face-centered cubic arrangement.

FIGURE 16-10. Stable unit cell packing arrangements for metals are shown on this coded periodic table.

CRYSTALLINE FORMS OF METALS

IA																	VIIIA
H	IIA														VIA VIIA	He
Li	Be											B	C	N	O	F	Ne
Na	Mg				"B" groups							Al	Si	P	S	Cl	Ar
K	Ca	Sc	Ti	V	Cr	Mn	Fe	Co	Ni	Cu	Zn	Ga	Ge	As	Se	Br	Kr
Rb	Sr	Y	Zr	Nb	Mo	Tc	Ru	Rh	Pd	Ag	Cd	In	Sn	Sb	Te	I	Xe
Cs	Ba	Lu	Hf	Ta	W	Re	Os	Ir	Pt	Au	Hg	Tl	Pb	Bi	Po	At	Rn
Fr	Ra	Lr	Rf	Ha													

La	Ce	Pr	Nd	Pm	Sm	Eu	Gd	Tb	Dy	Ho	Er	Tm	Yb
Ac	Th	Pa	U	Np	Pu	Am	Cm	Bk	Cf	Es	Fm	Md	No

Body-centered cubic

Face-centered cubic

Hexagonal closest packed

16:6 METALLIC ELEMENTS

In Chapter 12 we discussed the metallic bond. At that point, we just "packed together" the positive metal ions before adding the electrons. How are the metal ions packed? Almost all metals are packed in one of three kinds of unit cells. These three are body-centered cubic (BCC), cubic closest packed (FCC), or hexagonal closest packed (HCP). Figure 16-10 lists the unit cell arrangements for metals. The form given is the most stable at room temperature. Many metals, like iron, change their packing as the temperature rises. The general, though not universal, trend is toward the HCP arrangement.

Most metals are packed in one of three kinds of unit cells: BCC, FCC, or HCP.

Many metals change their packing as the temperature rises.

Demonstration—Take three hair pins and heat two of them until they turn red. Cool one quickly in H_2O. Allow the other one to cool slowly in air. Compare the flexibility of the three hair pins. Discuss the effect of heat treatment and tempering on metals.

16:7 NONMETALLIC ELEMENTS

There are two crystal forms of carbon—diamond and graphite. Their structures are illustrated in Figure 16-11. You can see that in graphite, the atoms within each layer have a hexagonal arrangement. The atoms within each layer are held close by strong covalent bonds. The layers themselves are relatively far apart and are held together only by weak van der Waals forces.

Diamond and graphite are different crystalline forms of carbon.

In diamond, each carbon atom is bonded covalently to four other carbon atoms. The four atoms are at the vertices of a tetrahedron. This arrangement forms a face-centered cubic lattice.

To melt diamond or other compounds having a covalent lattice crystalline structure, the individual covalent bonds must be broken. This requires energy and such compounds melt at high temperatures.

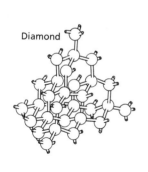

Diamond

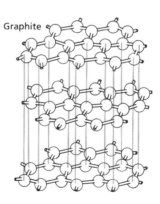

Graphite

FIGURE 16-11. The difference in crystalline structure of diamond and graphite accounts for the differences in physical properties.

Nonmetallic elements have relatively low melting points. Elements like sulfur or iodine form crystals in which the lattice positions are occupied by molecules. The atoms within the molecules are held together by covalent bonds. The molecules are attached to each other by weak van der Waals forces.

Molecules are held in crystal lattices by van der Waals forces.

The repulsion of bonding and nonbonding electron pairs causes the sulfur ring to pucker.

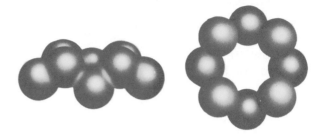

FIGURE 16-12. The sulfur molecule is a puckered ring of eight atoms.

In sulfur crystals, the S_8 molecule contains eight atoms arranged in a ring as shown in Figure 16-12. The atoms within the molecule are much closer to each other (0.208 nm) than they are to the atoms of neighboring molecules (0.37 nm). This lattice is orthorhombic.

16:8   MACROMOLECULES OR NETWORK CRYSTALS

In order to melt most molecular solids, we need overcome only the van der Waals forces. Observations in the laboratory show that discrete molecular compounds have very low melting points. They range from $-272°C$ to about 400°C. There are some very large molecules which melt at even higher temperatures, but here we are concerned with the rule, not the exception. Still, we have not accounted for covalently bound substances with melting points in the range 1000°C to 3000°C. An example is silicon carbide which melts at about 2700°C. In silicon carbide, each carbon atom is surrounded by four silicon atoms to which it is covalently bonded. Each of these silicon atoms, in turn, is surrounded by four carbon atoms to which it is covalently bonded.

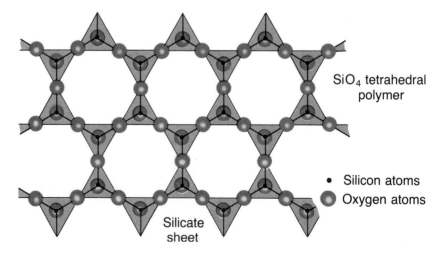

SiO_4 tetrahedral polymer

• Silicon atoms

◉ Oxygen atoms

Silicate sheet

FIGURE 16-13. Silicate compounds generally have high melting points. The macromolecule shown consists of repeating SiO_4 units. This substance melts at a high temperature since covalent bonds must be broken to liquefy the crystal.

Thus, each atom in the crystal network is bonded to its four nearest neighbors. Silicon carbide has the same structure as diamond except every other atom is silicon. We may think of the entire crystal as one giant molecule. In fact, this type of structure is often called a **network crystal** or a **macromolecule.** There are many substances composed of macromolecules. All of these substances have very high melting points. In order to melt the substance, you must break covalent bonds. These bonds are, on the average, about ten times stronger than van der Waals forces.

A macromolecule or network crystal consists of a single molecule with all component atoms bonded in a network fashion.

16:9 BONDING AND MELTING POINT: A SUMMARY

Crystals composed of ions are held together by the electrostatic attraction of oppositely charged ions. These substances generally have high melting points. In metallic crystals, the delocalized electrons bond the atoms tightly. Most metals have very high melting points. Other covalently bonded substances can have low or very high melting points. If the atoms are part of a macromolecule such as diamond, the melting point will be high. To melt a macromolecule, an enormous number of covalent bonds must be broken. On the other hand, if atoms are covalently bonded in small, discrete molecules, the melting point will be low. These molecules are held to each other only by van der Waals forces which are easily overcome.

Crystal Type	Melting Point
ionic	high
metallic	high
network	high
molecular	low

16:10 CRYSTAL DEFECTS

You should not assume that the repetition of the unit cell arrangement is perfect in all crystals. Actually, a perfect crystal is rare. Most crystals contain defects of one or more types. We will cover two basic types of defects.

The first type of defect occurs within the unit cell structure. Look at a plane of a simple crystal such as sodium chloride. The positive and negative ions alternate in such a crystal lattice. However, it is entirely possible that one of the ions may be missing from its proper position and occupy a space where no ion usually occurs. This change causes an imperfect crystal. Another possibility is that an ion may be missing completely from its position in the lattice. If a defect of this type occurs, for every positive ion missing there must be a negative ion missing. This arrangement preserves the electrical neutrality of the crystal. It is sometimes possible for foreign ions, atoms, electrons, or molecules to occupy these spaces vacated by the normal ions of the crystal.

Defects in crystals are common.

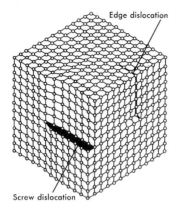

Edge dislocation

Screw dislocation

FIGURE 16-14. Edge and screw dislocations are defects in the way unit cells are joined.

Doping is important in the production of transistors. For instance, arsenic- and indium-doped germanium crystals can be made which have the correct structure for developing semiconducting (transistor) properties.

The second basic type of defect concerns the manner in which the unit cells are joined. These defects are called **dislocations.** In some crystals, an extra layer of atoms extends part of the way into a crystal. The resulting crystal is said to have an **edge dislocation** as shown in Figure 16-14. It is also possible for the particles to be slightly out of position. This defect is due to unequal growth while the crystal forms. Such a defect is termed a **screw dislocation.**

16:11 TRANSISTORS

Sometimes, defects in crystals are valuable. For example, in the manufacture of transistors, perfect crystals are "doped." That is, impurities are added deliberately. Silicon and germanium (Group IVA) are the most common elements used in transistors. A pure crystal of either of these elements will conduct very little electricity. However, if a small amount of another element is added, current will readily flow through the resulting "doped" crystal.

A closer look at the bonding of these elements reveals why they behave as they do. Silicon and germanium, each with four electrons in the outer level, crystallize in a structure similar to that of the diamond. Thus, all four electrons are involved in bonding. Recall from Chapter 12 that substances such as silicon and germanium are classed as semiconductors. The forbidden zone for semiconductors is small.

Arsenic atoms have five electrons available for bonding and gallium atoms have three. If arsenic atoms are introduced into a crystal of germanium, extra electrons are present. When a voltage is applied, the extra electrons in the lattice will move, Figure 16-15. If on the other hand, gallium atoms are introduced, the crystal will be short of electrons. The resulting electron deficient lattice, however, will also conduct electricity. It does so by moving electrons into the "holes" created by the gallium atom. Note that in both types of doping, the crystal is still electrically neutral.

Transistors are crystals which are deliberately "doped", causing imperfections.

Transistors depend upon an excess or shortage of electrons in the crystal lattice.

Since their development in the late 1940's, transistors have been used in place of vacuum tubes in electronic circuits. Because of their small size, long life, and resistance to shock, they have revolutionized the communications industry. Computers, transistor radios, heart pacemakers, space probes, and microwave ovens are only a few of the many devices that transistors have either made possible or improved. Today's silicon microprocessor chips contain thousands of transistors.

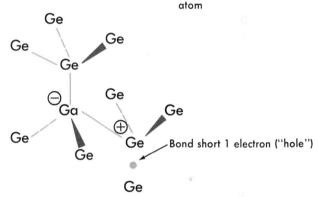

(a) Normal Ge crystal

(b) Arsenic-doped Ge crystal

(c) Arsenic-doped Ge crystal after application of an electrical field has caused the extra electron to move one atom

(d) Gallium-doped Ge crystal

(e) Gallium-doped Ge crystal after application of an electrical field has caused the "hole" to move two bonds

16:12 ISOMORPHISM AND POLYMORPHISM

There are many solid compounds and only a few ways they may crystallize. Therefore, it is not surprising that many substances have the same crystalline structure. Crystals of different solids with the same structure and shape are **isomorphous.**

It is also possible that the same substance may crystallize into two or more different patterns. A single substance which has two or more crystalline shapes is said to be **polymorphous.** Calcium carbonate, $CaCO_3$, has two crystalline forms: calcite, which is rhombohedral; and aragonite, which is orthorhombic. Surprisingly, calcite is isomorphous with crystalline $NaNO_3$, while aragonite is isomorphous with crystalline KNO_3. Aragonite is the normal form for $CaCO_3$. If aragonite is subjected to a high temperature, it rearranges to calcite.

FIGURE 16-15. Doped crystals are good electric conductors due to the fact that they contain an extra electron or an electron hole. Both arrangements allow electrons to move through the crystal.

Crystals of different substances with the same structure and shape are ismorphous.

A polymorphous substance has two or more crystalline shapes.

16:13 HYDRATED CRYSTALS

If solids crystallize from water solutions, molecules of water may be incorporated into the crystal structure. For some ionic substances, the attraction for water molecules is so high that the water molecules become chemically bonded to the ions. Ions which are chemically bonded to water atoms are called **hydrated ions.** Crystals containing hydrated ions are called **hydrated crystals.** As we saw in Chapter 14, it is also possible for ions to be surrounded by, or coordinated with, solvent molecules other than water.

Many common chemical compounds are normally hydrated. It is possible to remove the water molecules from some hydrated crystals. It can be done by raising the temperature or lowering the pressure, or both. The resulting compound, without the water molecules, is said to be anhydrous. **Anhydrous** means without water. Some anhydrous compounds gain water molecules so easily that they can be used to remove water from other substances. They are called drying agents. Chemists refer to drying agents as dehydrating agents or **desiccants** (DES ih kants).

Hydrated ions are chemically bonded to water molecules.

Hydrated crystals contain hydrated ions.

Common drying agents: Calcium chloride, conc. H₂SO₄, sodium hydroxide, magnesium chloride.

a

Courtesy of Kodansha Ltd.

b

Courtesy of Kodansha Ltd.

FIGURE 16-16. Hydrated copper(II) sulfate, CuSO₄·5H₂O, (a) can be changed to the anhydrous form (b) by heating the sample to drive off the water.

Formulas for hydrated compounds place the water of hydration following a dot after the regular formula. For example, $CuSO_4 \cdot 5H_2O$ is the formula for a hydrate of copper sulfate that contains 5 moles of water for each mole of copper sulfate. The name of the compound is copper(II) sulfate pentahydrate. Such compounds are named just as regular compounds except that the water is included. The regular name is followed by the word hydrate to which a prefix has been added to indicate the relative molar proportions of water and compound. The prefixes are listed in Table 16-3.

Table 16-3

Prefixes Used in Naming Hydrates			
Prefix	Moles of Water	Name	Formula
mono-	1	monohydrate	$XY \cdot H_2O$
di-	2	dihydrate	$XY \cdot 2H_2O$
tri-	3	trihydrate	$XY \cdot 3H_2O$
tetra-	4	tetrahydrate	$XY \cdot 4H_2O$
penta-	5	pentahydrate	$XY \cdot 5H_2O$
hexa-	6	hexahydrate	$XY \cdot 6H_2O$
hepta-	7	heptahydrate	$XY \cdot 7H_2O$
octa-	8	octahydrate	$XY \cdot 8H_2O$
nona-	9	nonahydrate	$XY \cdot 9H_2O$
deca-	10	decahydrate	$XY \cdot 10H_2O$

The ions of some anhydrous substances have such a strong attraction for water molecules that the dehydrated crystal will recapture and hold water molecules from the air. Such a substance is called a **hygroscopic** (hi gruh SKAHP ihk) substance. Some substances are so hygroscopic that they take up enough water from the air to dissolve and form a liquid solution. These substances are said to be **deliquescent** (del ih KWES uhnt). The opposite process can also occur. Water of hydration may be spontaneously released to the air. A substance which releases water molecules to the air from the crystal is said to be **efflorescent** (ef luh RES uhnt).

Special care is required in storing hygroscopic substances. You may have noticed that some reagents in the laboratory stockroom have hardened in the bottle. This action can be prevented by making sure bottles are closed tightly.

Hygroscopic substances pick up water from the air.

Deliquescent substances take up enough water to form a liquid solution.

Efflorescent substances release water of hydration to the air.

Demonstration—NaOH pellets are hygroscopic. Place a few on a watch glass and have students observe them for a few minutes. Discuss the effect on a quantitative lab experiment if NaOH were allowed to remain uncovered for a long period of time.

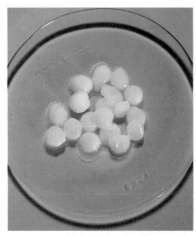

a

b

Hickson-Bender Photography   Hickson-Bender Photography

FIGURE 16-17. Sodium hydroxide (a) has a strong attraction for water molecules. Thus, it will begin to dissolve (b) if left exposed to the air.

16:14   LIQUID CRYSTALS

A crystalline solid is highly ordered.

As we have seen, true solids are crystalline. Their constituent particles are arranged in a highly ordered manner. The arrangement is called "ordered" because the particles are spaced in a regular, repeating fashion in all three dimensions.

A liquid has disorder in all three dimensions.

In Chapter 15, we saw that the structure of liquids was much less regular. Particles can actually change their positions in a liquid. The structure of a liquid is less ordered than the structure of a solid. The disorder of the liquid extends to all three dimensions. In general, when a pure solid is heated, it has a sharp melting point at a specific temperature. At that temperature the solid changes to a liquid and the order in all three dimensions is destroyed.

Solids which lose their crystalline order in only 1 or 2 dimensions at the melting point form liquid crystals.

However, there are some solid materials which can lose their crystalline order in only one or two dimensions at the melting point. At a specific higher temperature, the remaining order will also be destroyed. Between these two transition temperatures, these materials retain some degree of order. These substances are called liquid crystals. If they retain two dimensional order, they are usually called **smectic substances.** If they retain only one dimensional order, they are called **nematic substances.** There is a third class of liquid crystals (with two-dimensional order) which will not be considered here.

Smectic substances retain two dimensional order.

Nematic substances retain order in only one dimension.

The structure leading to such properties has been determined. **Liquid crystals** are formed by long, rodlike molecules arranged in a parallel manner. When the attractive force between layers of the molecules is overcome by heat energy, a smectic material results, with the layers remaining intact. If heat energy overcomes both layer attraction and end-to-end attraction, only parallel orientation remains. We then have a nematic material.

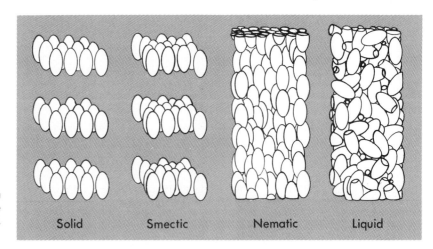

FIGURE 16-18. This diagram shows the differences in the degree of order for a solid, liquid crystal, and liquid.

Solid   Smectic   Nematic   Liquid

Substances in liquid crystal form are said to be **mesomorphic;** that is, between solid and liquid. Mesomorphic materials exhibit anisotropy. **Anisotropic materials** show different properties in different directions. We have already seen that graphite is anisotropic because of its bonding structure. Liquid crystals have optical and electrical anisotropy. Interestingly, along with several other biological systems, both muscle fibers and nerve fibers exhibit liquid crystal properties.

Some liquid crystals become transparent when subjected to a pulse of high-frequency current. Then if subjected to a low-frequency pulse, they become opaque. This property has led to the widespread use of liquid crystals for digital displays in watches and calculators.

A liquid crystal is mesomorphic (between solid and liquid).

Anisotropic materials have different properties in different directions.

Liquid crystals have optical and electrical anisotropy.

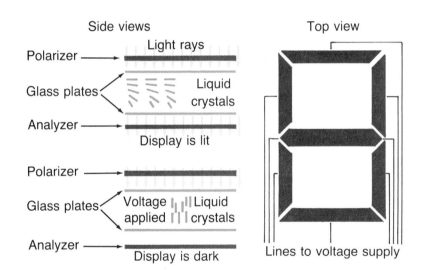

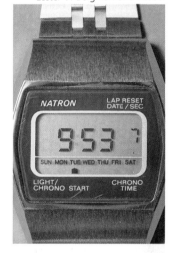

Lester V. Bergman and Assoc.

FIGURE 16-19. When a voltage is applied to a liquid crystal, the arrangement of particles prevents the passage of light through the crystal. The watch display will be dark. In the absence of the voltage, light passes through the crystal to light the display.

16:15 AMORPHOUS MATERIALS

There are many substances which appear to be solids, but are not crystalline. Examination of their structure reveals a disordered arrangement of particles. These materials are said to be **amorphous,** or without crystalline form.

Glass is an excellent example of an amorphous material. When glass is heated, it does not reach a point at which it suddenly becomes liquid. Glass does not have a fixed melting point as ice has. Rather, as glass is heated, it softens more and more and melts gradually over a wide temperature range. The hotter it gets, the more easily the glass flows. The resistance of a liquid to flow is called its **viscosity** (vis KAHS uh tee). Glass and cold molasses are good examples of viscous materials. Water and

An amorphous solid has a disordered arrangement of particles.

Viscosity is the resistance of a liquid to flow.

Crystals are said to undergo cleavage. Glasses are said to fracture.

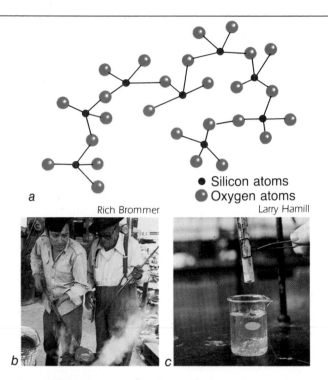

● Silicon atoms
◉ Oxygen atoms

a

Rich Brommer   Larry Hamill

b   *c*

FIGURE 16-20. Amorphous materials have a disordered arrangement of particles as shown by this structural model for glass (a). As a result, glass softens over a temperature range (b). Plastic sulfur is an amorphous form of that element (c). It will later change back to its crystalline form.

carbon tetrachloride are good examples of nonviscous liquids with low viscosities. Upon cooling, glass does not reach a specific temperature at which it turns into a solid. As it cools, it becomes more viscous and it flows more slowly. Amorphous substances are called super-cooled liquids. Butter is another good example. For equations in the chapters that follow, true crystalline solids will retain the symbol (c), and amorphous materials will be designated by (amor).

One form of sulfur contains long chains. It is an amorphous form and is called plastic sulfur. A few hours after it is prepared it changes back into the stable orthorhombic form. This change is characteristic of most amorphous substances. In these substances the amorphous form is unstable. Many substances, such as glass, remain in the amorphous form for long periods instead of changing to a more stable crystalline form as sulfur does. Substances which can occur in a long-lasting amorphous form are said to be **metastable.** Although a metastable form is not the most stable form, a substance in this form is not likely to change unless subjected to some outside disturbance. Glass is a metastable substance. It normally occurs in the amorphous form, but even glass may be crystallized under the proper conditions. The crystallizing times for many metastable substances have been calculated. These times range from centuries to millions of years.

Dorothy Crowfoot Hodgkin (1910–   )

In the early 1930's X-ray analysis of crystal structure was a new and limited field of study. Yet in 1933, a young British chemist and crystallographer, Dorothy Crowfoot made the first X-ray diffraction photograph of a protein molecule. The application of this technique set the stage for her later work.

By 1948, Dorothy, in working with other scientists, had determined the structure of penicillin. Her work in finding the crystalline structure of vitamin B_{12} won her the 1964 Nobel Prize for Chemistry and the British Order of Merit in 1965. Later, in 1969, she determined the three-dimensional structure of insulin.

A recipient of more than a dozen honorary doctorate degrees, Dorothy Hodgkin currently lives in England. Her husband is a noted authority on Africa.

CHEMICAL TECHNOLOGY: Inside Crystals

Light waves can be spread into a spectrum using a diffraction grating. The grating consists of a transparent or reflective plate containing a pattern of closely spaced lines. When a spectrum is produced by a grating, the process is called diffraction. You can see light diffraction by looking at a distant, bright light through a fine fabric or the space between two fingers. The diffraction pattern will be a multitude of little rainbows.

In 1912, Max von Laue got the idea that if the current theories concerning X rays and crystal structure were correct, a crystal ought to behave toward X rays in much the same way a diffraction grating behaves toward light. An experiment was performed whereby a narrow beam of X rays passed through a crystal. Von Laue was interested in the diffraction experiment primarily because of its application to the measurement of X-ray wavelengths. However, W. E. Bragg and his son, W. L. Bragg immediately recognized the value of this technique as a powerful tool for studying the solid state.

We now know that each unit cell in a crystal diffracts an X ray just as a slit in a grating diffracts light. A crystal is more complex and the resulting diffraction pattern is 3-dimensional. The greatest part of the radiation passes through undeflected. However, some of the X rays are diffracted. The diffraction pattern obtained possesses a symmetry related to the symmetry of the external faces of the crystal. The exact pattern of diffraction is determined by the dimensions of the unit cell. For crystals possessing a highly symmetrical arrangement, the interpretation of the data requires only a basic knowledge of physics and geometry. For less symmetrical arrangements, the calculations to determine the distances between cell layers may require the use of a computer.

The determination of the structure of biologically important molecules is a current application of X-ray analysis. The structure of hemoglobin was determined by combining X-ray diffraction with several other analytical techniques.

Present commercial methods of reacting atmospheric nitrogen require large amounts of energy. The molecules used by nitrogen-fixing bacteria are currently being investigated by X-ray diffraction. If a chemical process using a plant-like molecule could be developed, energy and money could be saved.

X-ray diffraction is also being used in determining the structures of new ceramic materials. By gaining a better understanding of the relationship between structure and properties in ceramics, even better products may be developed.

FIGURE 16-21. Using the proper orientation, X rays will be deflected by unit cells in a crystal (a). The resulting diffraction pattern can be used to determine the distances between layers of a crystal (b).

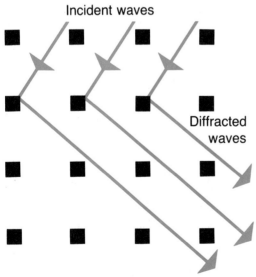

Incident waves

Diffracted waves

Each box represents a unit cell

a

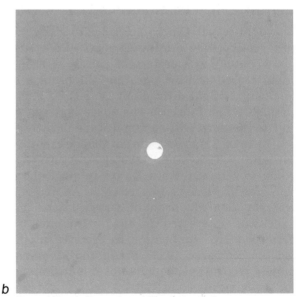

b

General Electric Research and Development Center

SUMMARY

1. Steno's law states that the corresponding angles between faces on different crystals of the same substance are always the same. Intro.

2. A crystal is a rigid body in which particles are arranged in a repeating pattern. The smallest unit of the repeating pattern is called the unit cell. 16:1-16:2

3. The repetition of the unit cell in a crystal forms an imaginary lattice of particles called a space lattice. 16:3

4. Many substances form crystals with a close-packed structure composed of layers of spheres packed closely. 16:4-16:6

5. Molecular substances form crystals in which the molecules are held together by weak van der Waals forces. These substances have low melting points and low boiling points. 16:7, 16:9

6. Some substances form macromolecular crystals which are characterized by very high melting points. 16:7-16:9

7. Crystal defects are lapses in the regular repetition of the unit cell arrangement. Defects can be a result of either missing particles which leave a hole or extraneous particles. Other defects are edge dislocations and screw dislocations. 16:10

8. The transistor is an example of a practical application of a crystal defect. 16:11

9. Crystals which have the same structure and shape but different components are said to be isomorphous. 16:12

10. A single substance which has two or more crystalline shapes is said to be polymorphous. 16:12

11. Anhydrous compounds which gain water molecules easily are called dessicants because they remove water from other substances. 16:13

12. A hygroscopic substance has such a strong attraction for water molecules that it will capture water molecules from the air. 16:13

13. A deliquescent substance is so hygroscopic that it takes enough water from the air to dissolve itself. 16:13

14. A substance which spontaneously releases water of hydration to the air from a crystal is called an efflorescent substance. 16:13

15. Liquid crystals are substances which retain some degree of order at their melting point. If they retain two-dimensional order they are called smectic. If they retain order in only one dimension they are called nematic. 16:14

16. Substances which seem to be solids but do not have a crystalline form are called amorphous substances. 16:15

17. The resistance of a liquid to flow is called its viscosity. The viscosity of substances usually decreases as the temperature increases. 16:15

PROBLEMS

1. From the photo of the NaCl lattice, show why NaCl is the simplest formula. There is a 1:1 correspondence between Na$^+$ and Cl$^-$ ions.

2. From a table of ionic radii, determine the distance between the Na$^+$ ion and the Cl$^-$ ion in the NaCl crystal. 0.276 nm

3. In Section 16:12, calcium carbonate is shown to have two crystalline forms, each isomorphous with different compounds. What explanation could you offer for this situation?

4. Find the percentage of water in a crystal of $CuSO_4 \cdot 5H_2O$. 36.0% H_2O

5. For $NiSO_4 \cdot 7H_2O$, determine the following information.
   a. the name of the compound nickel sulfate heptahydrate
   b. the percentage of water   44.8% H_2O
   c. the percentage of oxygen   62.6% O

6. barium hydroxide octahydrate 45.7% H_2O 50.8% O

6. Answer Parts a, b, and c in Problem 5 for $Ba(OH)_2 \cdot 8H_2O$.

7. sodium carbonate decahydrate 62.9% H_2O

7. Answer Parts a, b, and c in Problem 5 for $Na_2CO_3 \cdot 10H_2O$. 72.7% O

8. Use diamond and graphite to explain how bonding affects the properties of a crystal.

9. Simple cubic, body-centered cubic, and face-centered cubic unit cells all have the same shape. How are they different?

charge and radius

10. What determines the crystal structure of an ionic compound?

11. Explain why NaCl has a face-centered cubic unit cell, while CsCl is body-centered cubic.

12. weak van der Waals attractions

12. Cite reasons why nonmetallic elements have low melting points.

13. What are the characteristics of macromolecules?

14. How do the properties of a defective crystal differ from a perfect crystal?

15. How does doping change the properties of silicon and germanium?

16. Write formulas for the following hydrates

15. electric conductivity increases

   a. magnesium nitrate hexahydrate $Mg(NO_3)_2 \cdot 6H_2O$
   b. iron(II) sulfate heptahydrate $FeSO_4 \cdot 7H_2O$
   c. copper(II) nitrate trihydrate $Cu(NO_3)_2 \cdot 3H_2O$
   d. tin(II) chloride dihydrate $SnCl_2 \cdot 2H_2O$

17. How do isomorphs differ from isomers?

18. How do amorphous substances differ from crystalline substances?
disordered versus ordered arrangement

REVIEW

1. If an open manometer shows a mercury level 64 mm higher in the arm connected to the confined gas, what is the pressure of that gas? The pressure of the air is 92.7 kPa. 84.2 kPa

2. If a closed type manometer shows a mercury level difference of 421 mm, what is the pressure of the gas in kilopascals? 56.1 kPa

3. How does plasma differ from the other three states of matter?
In plasma, the atoms are not intact. They are broken up into individual electrons and nuclei.

4. Why is gas chromatography called a chromatographic method even though it doesn't involve color? It depends upon selective adsorption as do all other chromatographic methods.

ONE MORE STEP

1. Look up the lives of W. E. Bragg and W. L. Bragg. Write a report on the processes they used to determine crystal structure.

2. Write a report on how transistors work.

3. In this chapter it was mentioned that there is another class of liquid crystals with two-dimensional order in addition to smectic. This other class consists of cholesteric compounds. Find out the source of the name for the class and how smectic and cholesteric compounds differ.

READINGS

Adler, David, "Amorphous-Semiconductor Devices." *Scientific American,* Vol. 236, No. 5 (May 1977), pp. 36-48.

Bennett, Lawrence H., et al., "Interstitial Compounds." *Physics Today,* Vol. 30, No. 9 (September 1977), pp. 34-41.

Chaudhari, Praveen, et al., "Metallic Glasses." *Scientific American,* Vol. 242, No. 4 (April 1980), pp. 98-117.

Double, D. D., and Hellawell, A., "The Solidification of Cement." *Scientific American,* Vol. 237, No. 1 (July 1977), pp. 82-90.

Harris, William F., "Disclinations." *Scientific American,* Vol. 237, No. 6 (December 1977), pp. 130-145.

Suchow, Lawrence, "Other Views of Unit Cells." *Journal of Chemical Education,* Vol. 53, No. 4 (April 1976), pp. 226-227.

Wells, A. F., "Some Structural Principles for Introductory Chemistry." *Journal of Chemical Education,* Vol. 54, No. 5 (May 1977), pp. 273-276.

One property of liquids is their ability to flow. Water is a liquid which flows easily. This property is based on the internal structure of the liquid and the forces between molecules. What are some liquids that do not flow easily? What term is used to describe the ability to flow? What are some other properties that are characteristic of the liquid state?

Vernon Sigl/Alpha

LIQUIDS 17

Chapter 17 introduces liquids by developing the concept of vapor pressure through the use of phase diagrams. Students will be expected to calculate the energy associated with changes of physical state.

Demonstration—Water can be boiled at less than 100°C in a Florence flask at reduced pressure. See the Teacher's Guide in the front of this text for complete preparation details. This demonstration can be used to begin a discussion of constant temperature during a change of state, vapor pressure, and boiling.

According to the kinetic theory, if the temperature of a solid is raised, the velocity of the particles should increase. As the temperature increases, the particles collide with each other with a greater force. Thus, they are forced farther apart. Almost all solids and liquids expand when they are heated because of this increase in velocity. If the temperature of a solid is raised sufficiently, the particles will move far enough apart to slip over one another. The ordered arrangement of the solid state breaks down. When such a change takes place, we say the solid has melted.

If particles are in the liquid state, there will be a certain temperature (and pressure) at which the particles travel so slowly that they can no longer slip past one another. All pure liquids have a definite freezing point and all pure solids have a definite melting point. For a substance, the freezing point of the liquid form is the same temperature as the melting point of the solid form.

> **GOAL:** You will gain an understanding of the properties of liquids as explained by the kinetic theory and a study of their molecular structure.

> For a substance, the freezing point of the liquid state = melting point of solid state.

17:1 VAPOR EQUILIBRIUM

The average kinetic energy of atoms or molecules in a gas is a constant for all substances at a given temperature. This average kinetic energy can be calculated for any particular temperature. If we were to measure the kinetic energy of individual atoms or molecules in a gas, we would find that few had the predicted kinetic energy. Some molecules would have more and some would have less kinetic energy than the average. Most would have a

> Average K.E. of particles is constant for a given temperature.

> Boltzmann distribution law.

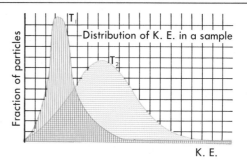

FIGURE 17-1. If it were possible to measure the kinetic energy of every gas particle in a sample at T_1, most would have a kinetic energy corresponding to T_1. Some particles would have more or less than the average kinetic energy. The particle distribution covers a wider range at T_2.

Few gas molecules have the average K.E. Most have a K.E. close to the calculated average.

Molecules having enough kinetic energy to overcome the attractive forces of neighboring molecules escape from the surface to form a vapor.

In a closed container, the vapor phase is in dynamic equilibrium with its solid or liquid phase.

kinetic energy close to the calculated amount. However, we would sometimes find a molecule with a kinetic energy considerably above or below the average.

All that has been said about the collisions of particles in a gas is also true of particles in a solid or a liquid. A molecule in a liquid, because of several rapid collisions with other molecules, might gain kinetic energy considerably above the average value. Imagine that molecule on the surface of the liquid. If it has enough kinetic energy to overcome the attractive force of nearby molecules, it may escape from the liquid surface. The same process may also occur at the surface of a solid. The molecules which escape from the surface of a solid or a liquid form a vapor. This vapor is made of molecules or atoms of the substance in the gaseous state. A gas and a vapor are the same. We usually use the word gas for those substances which are gaseous at room temperature. **Vapor** is used for the gaseous state of substances which are liquids or solids at room temperature.

A molecule of a solid or liquid which has escaped the surface behaves as a gaseous molecule. It is possible for this molecule to collide with the surface of the liquid it left. If its kinetic energy is sufficiently low at the time of such a collision, the molecule may be captured and again be a part of the liquid. However, in an open container, there is little chance of the molecule returning to the surface it left.

If the solid or liquid is in a closed container, then there is an increased chance of the molecule returning to the surface. In fact, a point will be reached where just as many molecules return to the surface as leave the surface. There will be a constant number of molecules in the solid or liquid phase, and a constant number of molecules in the vapor phase. Such a situation is known as an **equilibrium** condition. It is a special kind of equilibrium, called **dynamic equilibrium.** It is called dynamic because molecules are continuously escaping from and returning to the surface. However, the overall result remains constant. When a substance is in equilibrium with its vapor, the gaseous phase of the system is said to be **saturated** with the vapor of that substance.

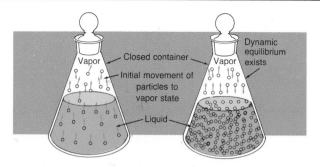

FIGURE 17-2. When the flask is sealed initially, most of the particle movement is away from the liquid surface. The system reaches dynamic equilibrium when the number of molecules leaving the liquid surface equals the number reentering the liquid.

The physical change from liquid to vapor is represented in equation form as

$$X_{(l)} \rightarrow X_{(g)}$$

where X represents any vaporizable substance, such as water.

The opposite process can be represented by

$$X_{(l)} \leftarrow X_{(g)}$$

The two equations can be combined

$$X_{(l)} \rightleftarrows X_{(g)}$$

A change such as this is called a **reversible change.** The reversible change has reached equilibrium when the change is occurring at the same rate in both directions.

Le Chatelier's principle applies to any equilibrium system. It is introduced here in relation to a solid-liquid equilibrium system.

In dynamic equilibrium molecules escape and return to the solid or liquid surface continuously, and at the same rate.

An equilibrium is expressed by arrows $\rightleftarrows$.

Equilibrium is an important concept in chemistry. We introduce the equilibrium concept here. Closely related to this concept is Le Chatelier's principle. For further development, see Chapter 23.

17:2   LE CHATELIER'S PRINCIPLE

The vapor phase exerts a pressure which is dependent on the temperature. The higher the temperature, the higher the vapor pressure. A liquid and its vapor will reach equilibrium at a specific pressure for any particular temperature. This shifting of the equilibrium was observed and described by the Frenchman Le Chatelier in 1884.

Le Chatelier's principle is expressed as: *If stress is applied to a system at equilibrium, the system readjusts so that the stress is reduced.* The stress may be a change in temperature, pressure, concentration, or other external force.

For example, an ice skater can skim over the ice with little effort. The skate blades are not really touching the ice but are traveling on a thin film of liquid water. The presence of this water can be explained by Le Chatelier's principle.

Both pressure and temperature must be considered in this example. We will discuss pressure first. The entire weight of the

Vapor pressure is directly dependent on temperature.

Emphasize: For a given substance the vapor pressure is determined solely by the temperature.

Le Chatelier's principle: A system at equilibrium will adjust to relieve outside stress.

Thomas Zimmermann/FPG

FIGURE 17-3. A skater glides across the ice due to the formation of a thin film of water on the ice.

Stress: increased pressure
ice   →   water
greater volume → less volume

Stress: increased temperature
ice   →   water
melting uses heat

skater is directed onto the ice through the blades on the skates. The surface area of the blades in contact with the ice is probably less than 15 cm^2. Thus, the blades exert a great pressure on the ice at the points of contact. A piece of ice (solid) occupies a greater volume than an equal mass of water (liquid). Therefore, the change of ice to water will tend to reduce the pressure (stress) caused by the blades. Increased pressure causes a reduction in volume. As a result the blades travel on a film of liquid water.

Temperature also plays an important role in skating. Friction between the ice and the blades of the skates warms the blades. This increased temperature (stress) will be relieved by the flow of heat into the ice. Increased temperature causes an increase in molecular motion. The low energy ice molecules are changed into more energetic water molecules. The blades will be cooled by this change. Both the increased pressure and the increased temperature enable the skater to glide over the ice with very little friction.

17:3 MEASURING VAPOR PRESSURE

Many techniques are available to measure vapor pressure. Figure 17-4 shows two methods of finding the vapor pressures of substances. The apparatus in Figure 17-4 is especially useful for finding the vapor pressure of solids at elevated temperatures. Table 17-1 gives the vapor pressures of some substances near room temperature. *Substances with low vapor pressure have strong intermolecular forces. Those with high vapor pressures have weak intermolecular forces.*

High vapor pressures are the result of weak intermolecular forces.

Table 17-1

Vapor Pressures of Some Liquids at 25°C			
Substance	**Vapor Pressure** (kPa)	**Substance**	**Vapor Pressure** (kPa)
Mercury (Hg)	0.000 247	Bromine (Br_2)	30.10
Turpentine ($C_{10}H_{16}$)	0.679	Acetone (CH_3COCH_3)	30.70
Water (H_2O)	3.17	Carbon disulfide (CS_2)	48.10
Carbon tetrachloride (CCl_4)	15.30	Sulfur dioxide (SO_2)	392.00

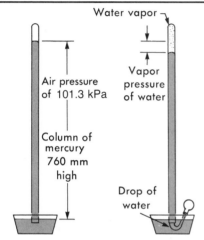

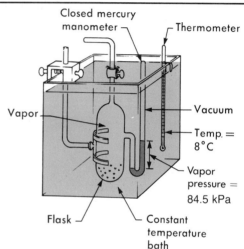

Section 17:4 is the first of several sections which lead toward the development of the phase diagram.

FIGURE 17-4. Two devices used for measuring vapor pressure are shown. In each, the vaporized liquid exerts a force (pressure) on the mercury in the tube.

17:4 MELTING POINT

Consider the phenomenon of melting in a closed container. In a mixture of solid and liquid states, there will be a dynamic equilibrium between the molecules of the solid and liquid. Remember, though, that each state is also in equilibrium with its vapor. Since there is only one vapor, the solid and liquid have the same vapor pressure, Figure 17-5a. At the melting point of

FIGURE 17-5. The graph (a) shows the melting point of a substance to be that temperature where the vapor pressures of the solid and liquid phases are equal. The apparatus in (b) is used for melting point determinations.

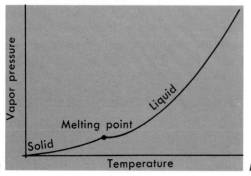

a

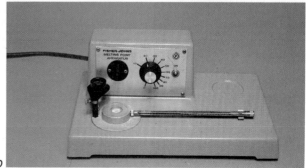

b

Hickson-Bender Photography

Temperature at which the vapor pressure of the solid and vapor pressure of the liquid are equal is the melting point.

any substance, the vapor pressure of the solid and the vapor pressure of the liquid must be equal. In fact, melting point is defined as the temperature at which the vapor pressure of the solid and the vapor pressure of the liquid are equal.

17:5 SUBLIMATION

Some solids have a vapor pressure large enough at room temperature to vaporize rapidly if not kept in a closed container. Such a substance will change directly from a solid to a gas, without passing through the liquid state. This process is known as **sublimation.** Dry ice (solid CO_2) and moth crystals are two examples of substances which sublime.

Sublimation: Change directly from solid to gas.

Examples of sublimation: Snow disappears from ground on a cold day without melting. Frozen clothes gradually become soft and flexible as ice sublimes. Dry ice sublimes to CO_2 gas.

a   Hickson-Bender Photography   *b*   Hickson-Bender Photography

FIGURE 17-6. Dry ice (a) and iodine (b) are two substances which sublime.

17:6 BOILING POINT

A liquid and its vapor can be at equilibrium only in a closed container. The molecules leaving the surface of a liquid have little chance of returning if the liquid container is open to the air. When a liquid is exposed to the air, it may gradually disappear. The disappearance is due to the constant escape of molecules from its surface. The liquid is said to evaporate.

Evaporation is the escape of molecules from the surface of a liquid.

As the temperature of a liquid is increased, the vapor pressure of that liquid increases because the kinetic energy of the molecules increases. Eventually, the kinetic energy of the molecules becomes large enough to overcome the internal pressure of the liquid. The internal pressure is due to the air pressing on the liquid surface. When this pressure is overcome, the molecules are colliding violently enough to push each other apart. They are pushed far enough apart, in fact, to form bubbles of gas within the body of the liquid. These bubbles rise to the surface of the

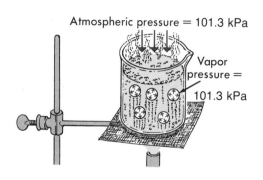

Atmospheric pressure = 101.3 kPa

Vapor pressure = 101.3 kPa

FIGURE 17-7. Boiling occurs when the kinetic energy of the liquid molecules is high enough to overcome the air pressure exerted on the surface of the liquid.

liquid because the vapor of which they are composed is less dense than the surrounding liquid. At this point, the liquid is boiling. The **normal boiling point** is the temperature at which the vapor pressure is equal to standard atmospheric pressure, or 101.325 kPa. Boiling point is a function of pressure. At lower pressures, the boiling point is lower.

Note carefully the difference between evaporation and boiling. Evaporation occurs only at the surface. Boiling, on the other hand, takes place throughout the body of a liquid.

Adding heat to a liquid at its boiling point will cause it to change to a gas rapidly by boiling. In a like manner, if we remove heat from a gas at the boiling point of that substance, the gas will change to a liquid. The boiling point of a liquid is also the condensation point of the vapor state of the liquid.

Different liquids boil at different temperatures. A liquid which boils at a low temperature and evaporates rapidly at room temperature is said to be **volatile** (VAHL uht uhl). Examples of volatile liquids are alcohol and ether. Liquids which boil at high temperatures and evaporate slowly at room temperature are said to be nonvolatile. Two such liquids are molasses and glycerol. Volatile substances have high vapor pressures; nonvolatile substances have low vapor pressures at room temperature.

Boiling occurs when the vapor pressure of a liquid is equal to atmospheric pressure.

FIGURE 17-8. The boiling point of a substance is lowered when atmospheric pressure is lowered. At any temperature, the vapor pressure of $CHCl_3$ is greater than that of H_2O.

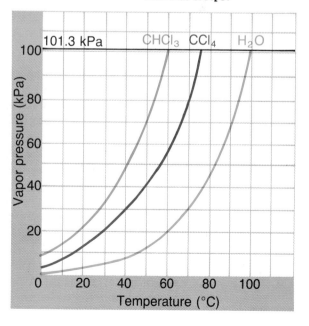

PROBLEM

1. Using Figure 17-8, determine boiling points of the following under the conditions listed.

   a. $CHCl_3$ at 50.0 kPa   c. CCl_4 at 75.0 kPa
   b. H_2O at 100.0 kPa   d. H_2O at 11.0 kPa

17:7 LIQUEFACTION OF GASES

We have considered the condensation of gases to liquids only for substances which are normally solids or liquids at room temperature. What about substances that are normally gases at room temperature? Can they be condensed? Yes, under the correct conditions. The condensation of substances which are normally gases is called **liquefaction** (lik wuh FAK shuhn). A gas must be below a certain temperature before it can be liquefied. Cooling reduces the kinetic energy of the molecules to the point where the van der Waals attraction is sufficient to bind the molecules together. It is also necessary to compress some gases. The van der Waals forces are effective for only short distances. Compression forces the molecules of these gases close enough for the van der Waals forces to take effect.

For every gas, there is a temperature above which no amount of pressure will result in liquefying the gas. This point is called the critical temperature (T_c) of the gas. The critical pressure (P_c) is the pressure that will cause the gas to liquefy at the critical temperature.

Table 17-2

Critical Temperature and Pressure		
Substance	Critical temperature (K)	Critical pressure (kPa)
Water (H_2O)	647.3	22.10
Sulfur dioxide (SO_2)	430.6	7.89
Carbon dioxide (CO_2)	304.4	7.39
Oxygen (O_2)	154.2	5.08
Nitrogen (N_2)	126.0	3.39
Hydrogen (H_2)	33.2	1.30

Many gases have critical temperatures above normal room temperature. Sulfur dioxide, for example, has a critical temperature of 430.6 K. It can be liquefied by increased pressure alone, if the temperature is not allowed to exceed 430.6 K. The critical temperature of a gas is an indication of the strength of the attractive forces between its atoms or molecules. The low critical

---

Liquefaction is the condensation of gases.

Gases may be liquefied by cooling and/or increased pressure.

T_c = Temperature above which no pressure will liquefy the gas.

P_c = Pressure needed to liquefy a gas at T_c.

Suggestion: Have students attempt to explain why the attractive forces differ (as indicated by the varying T_c and P_c) on the basis of the structure of these molecules. Note that this is fairly complicated; the higher T_c for SO_2 is due to both van der Waals attraction and polarity.

T_c indicates the relative strength of attractive forces between particles.

temperature of hydrogen indicates weak forces between its molecules. The high critical temperature of water indicates the existence of strong attractive forces between molecules.

Low T_c indicates weak attractive forces between gas particles.

17:8 PHASE DIAGRAMS

Much of the information we have discussed can be shown in graphic form called a phase diagram. The phase diagram shows the relationship among temperature, pressure, and physical state. Figure 17-9 is a phase diagram for water. The line labeled Solid-Vapor represents the vapor pressure of ice at temperatures from −100°C to point Y. The line labeled Liquid-Vapor represents the vapor pressure of the liquid at temperatures from point Y to 374°C. Point Y is called the **triple point.** All three states are in equilibrium at this temperature and pressure (0.01°C and 0.611 kPa). Above the critical point, X, there is no vapor pressure curve. The liquid and gaseous states are the same at pressures and temperatures above this point.

T_b is the boiling point and T_m is the melting point. The melting point occurs where the Solid-Liquid equilibrium line is cut by the standard atmospheric pressure line. It is important to realize that the vapor pressure of the liquid and solid (see point T_m in Figure 17-9) is not equal to atmospheric pressure at this point. The line YZ simply indicates the pressure-temperature conditions under which the solid and liquid can be in equilibrium. Only the solid-vapor and liquid-vapor lines represent vapor pressure information. The boiling point is that temperature at which the liquid-vapor equilibrium curve is cut by the pressure line of 101.325 kPa (see dotted lines crossing at T_b in Figure 17-9).

Note that the solid-liquid equilibrium line for water has a negative slope. A negative slope indicates that a rise in pressure will lower the freezing point. As was pointed out in Section 17:2 about the ice skater, water expands when it freezes. Such a change is unusual. Most substances contract when they freeze and their solid-liquid equilibrium line has a positive slope. Figure 17-10 shows the phase diagram for hydrogen. Note the positive slope for the Solid-Liquid equilibrium line.

Phase diagrams graphically represent changes of state at varying temperatures and pressures.

At a given pressure the triple point is the temperature at which all three phases of a substance are in equilibrium.

Note: The slope of the solid-liquid line is exaggerated slightly to emphasize that the triple point is slightly above 0°C.

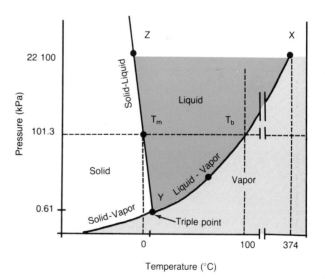

FIGURE 17-9. The phase diagram for water shows the relationships among pressure, temperature, and physical state.

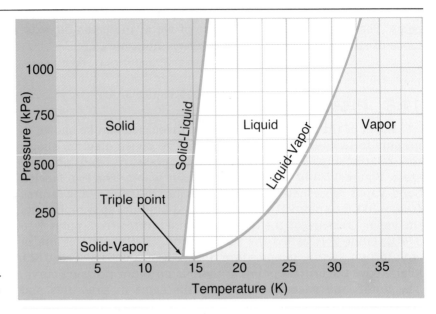

FIGURE 17-10. The phase diagram for hydrogen is shown.

PROBLEMS

2. Using Figure 17-10, determine the following for hydrogen.
   a. critical temperature
   b. critical pressure
   c. triple point temperature
   d. triple point pressure
   e. normal melting point
   f. normal boiling point
3. Using Figure 17-9, determine the state of matter that exists under the following conditions.
   a. 50°C and 0.1 kPa
   b. −10°C and 75.0 kPa
   c. 105°C and 1000 kPa
   d. 50°C and 60 kPa

17:9 ENERGY AND CHANGE OF STATE

We have seen that the loss or gain of heat energy from a system has an effect upon the equilibrium which exists between states. It is important for the chemist to be able to treat these energy changes quantitatively in order to describe completely a change which has taken place in a system.

When heat is added to a solid substance, the temperature of the object increases until the melting point of the substance is reached. Upon the addition of more heat, the substance begins to melt. The temperature, however, remains the same until all of the substance has melted. Before the melting point is reached, the added energy increases the kinetic energy of the molecules. In other words, the temperature is raised. At the actual melting point, the position of the particles is changed. In other words, the physical state was changed and the potential energy is increased. The heat required to melt 1 g of a specific substance at its melting point is called the heat of melting, or **heat of fusion** (H_f) of that substance. A similar phenomenon takes place at the boiling point. The heat required to vaporize 1 g of a substance at its boiling point is called the **heat of vaporization** (H_v) of the substance.

H_f is the heat required to melt one gram of a substance at its melting point.

H_v is the heat required to vaporize one gram of a substance at its boiling point.

EXAMPLE: Heats of Fusion and Vaporization

How much heat is necessary to convert 10.0 g of ice at $-10.0°C$ to steam at $150°C$?

Solving process:
It is often helpful in problems of this type to draw a graph to indicate the steps in changing the ice to steam.

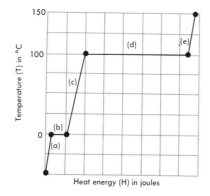

There is no increase in kinetic energy during melting and boiling because the temperature remains constant. Any additional energy is changed to potential energy which causes the particles to move farther apart and become more disorganized.

FIGURE 17-11. The graph shows the energy changes involved in heating ice at $-10°C$ to $150°C$.

(a) The ice must be warmed to its melting point, $0.0°C$. The energy that must be absorbed for the ice to reach $0.0°C$ is calculated by

$$H = m(\Delta T)C_p$$

The specific heat capacity of ice is $2.06 \text{ J/g} \cdot \text{C}°$.

$$H = \frac{10.0 \text{ g}}{} \left| \frac{10.0 \text{ C}°}{} \right| \frac{2.06 \text{ J}}{\text{g} \cdot \text{C}°} = 206 \text{ J}$$

Refer to Section 7:3 for a discussion of specific heat capacity. Tables A-3 and A-5 of the Appendix contain C_p values for the elements and several compounds.

(b) The ice must be melted. The heat of fusion of ice is 334 J/g. The change of state energy is calculated as follows:

$$H = mass \times heat\ of\ fusion = m(H_f)$$

$$H = \frac{10.0 \text{ g}}{} \left| \frac{334 \text{ J}}{\text{g}} \right. = 3340 \text{ J}$$

Demonstration—Have a student give you a piece of notebook paper. Fold it into a box and staple the corners. Place it on a wire screen above a bunsen burner. Fill the paper container with water to a depth of 2 cm. Light the burner. The water will boil but the paper will not burn. Ask the students why?

(c) The water must now be heated from 0.0°C to its boiling point, 100.0°C. The specific heat capacity of water is 4.18 J/g·C°.

$$H = \frac{10.0\ g \mid 100.0\ C° \mid 4.18\ J}{\mid \mid g·C°} = 4180\ J$$

(d) The water must now be vaporized. The heat of vaporization of water is 2260 J/g. The change of state energy is calculated as follows:

$$H = mass \times heat\ of\ vaporization = m(H_v)$$

$$H = \frac{10.0\ g \mid 2260\ J}{\mid g} = 22\ 600\ J$$

(e) Finally, the steam must be heated from 100.0°C to 150.0°C. The C_p of steam is 2.02 J/g·C°.

$$H = \frac{10.0\ g \mid 50.0\ C° \mid 2.02\ J}{\mid \mid g·C°} = 1010\ J$$

The total heat that must be absorbed is the sum of each of the five steps.

Remind students to express answers to the proper number of significant figures.

$$206\ J + 3340\ J + 4180\ J + 22\ 600\ J + 1010\ J = 31\ 300\ J$$

PROBLEMS

4. a. 2180 J
   b. 7680 J
   c. 9610 J
   d. 52 000 J
   e. 418 J

4. You have a sample of H_2O with mass 23.0 g at a temperature of −46.0°C. How many joules of heat energy are necessary to:
   a. heat the ice to 0°C?
   b. melt the ice?
   c. heat the water from 0°C to 100°C?
   d. boil the water?
   e. heat the steam from 100°C to 109°C?

5. 1570 J

6. 687 J

7. 32 600 J

5. How much heat is needed to melt 25.4 g of I_2 (H_f = 61.7 J/g)?
6. How much heat is needed to melt 4.24 g of Pd (H_f = 162 J/g)?
7. From the following data and that of Table A-3 of the Appendix, calculate the heat required to raise 45.0 g of cesium metal from room temperature (24.0°C) to 880°C. Specific heat capacity of solid Cs = 0.246 J/g·C°, specific heat capacity of liquid Cs = 0.252 J/g·C°, specific heat capacity of gaseous Cs = 0.156 J/g·C°, heat of fusion = 15.7 J/g, heat of vaporization = 514 J/g.

Introduce molar heat of fusion and vaporization before assigning these problems.

8. 2450 J

8. Using data from Table A-3 of the Appendix, calculate the amount of heat needed to raise the temperature of 5.58 kg of iron from 20°C to 1000°C.

9. Using information from the Example problem in Section 17:9, calculate the heat required to change 50.0 g of ice at −32°C to steam at 400°C.

17:10 HYDROGEN BONDING

In a number of substances, the predicted melting and boiling points differ from the observed ones. Remember that these changes of state can be predicted from a knowledge of atomic and molecular structure. It is the structure which affects interatomic and intermolecular forces. Many of the substances which do not behave as predicted have two things in common. First, their molecules contain hydrogen, and second, the hydrogen is covalently bonded to a highly electronegative atom. Under these conditions, the electronegative atom has almost complete possession of the electron pair shared with the hydrogen atom. The molecule is therefore highly polar. This polarity leaves the hydrogen atom with a strong partial positive charge. In fact, at the point of attachment of the hydrogen atom, there is a nearly bare hydrogen nucleus, or proton. The only elements electronegative enough to cause bonded hydrogen to behave in this manner are nitrogen, oxygen, and fluorine.

Consider the size of a proton compared to the size of the next largest ion with a 1+ charge, Li^+. The H^+ ion has a full positive charge in about one trillionth of the space. It simply will not exist near other particles without interacting with them. We will discuss this phenomenon again when we study the hydronium ion in Chapter 24.

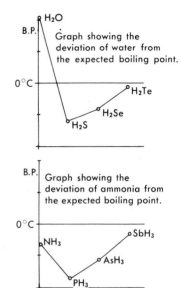

FIGURE 17-12. Molecules containing hydrogen bonded to an atom with a high electronegativity have boiling points which are higher than would be predicted.

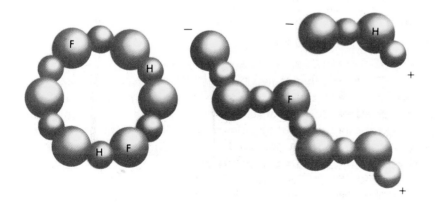

FIGURE 17-13. The high electronegativity of fluorine leaves hydrogen with a partial positive charge in HF. As a result, the HF molecules form chains linked by hydrogen bonds.

In a molecule containing hydrogen bonded to a highly electronegative element, the proton is not completely bare. However, the partial charge on the hydrogen end of the molecule is much more concentrated than that at the positive end of an average dipole. Hydrogen is the only element to exhibit this property because all other positive ions have inner levels of electrons shielding their nuclei. In a substance composed of polar molecules containing hydrogen, the hydrogen atom is attracted to the negative portion of other molecules. Since the hydrogen atom has been reduced to a proton with almost no electrons, the attractive force is strong. However, it is not nearly as strong as an actual chemical bond. The attractive force in such substances is called the hydrogen bond. The result of the hydrogen bond is that the hydrogen atom tends to hold the two molecules firmly to each other.

Because of its special properties, the hydrogen bond has a greater effect than another dipole with the same electronegativity difference. **Hydrogen bonding** is really just a subdivision of the large class of interactions called dipole attractions. However, it is considered apart from other dipole attractions because it has a greater effect on the properties of substances.

Hydrogen bonded to a strongly electronegative element causes some substances to differ from predicted behavior.

Hydrogen "bonds" have energies in the range of 8 to 36 kJ/mol.

The hydrogen bond is weaker than an actual chemical bond.

Guanine   Cytosine   Adenine   Thymine

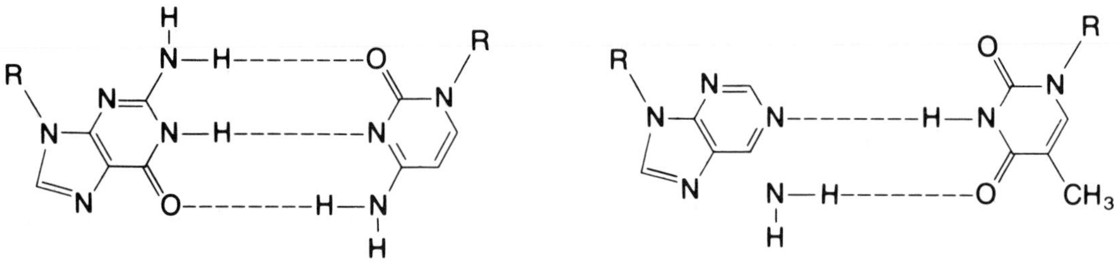

FIGURE 17-14. Hydrogen bonding occurs between the nitrogen bases in DNA.

17:11 HYDROGEN BONDING IN WATER

The effects of hydrogen bonding can be seen in water. For example, when frozen, a molecule of water is hydrogen bonded to four other water molecules, Figure 17-15. The two hydrogen atoms that are part of the central water molecule are attracted to the oxygen atoms of two other water molecules. Hydrogen atoms from two other water molecules are attracted to the oxygen atom of the central water molecule. This open crystalline structure occupies a large amount of space.

When ice melts, many, but not all, of the hydrogen bonds are broken. As some of the bonds are broken, the lattice collapses. The water molecules move closer. The same number of molecules occupy less space. Thus, water is more dense than ice. As water is heated above 0°C, more hydrogen bonds are broken, and the molecules continue to move closer. Finally, at 3.98°C, most of the hydrogen bonds have been broken. Above 3.98°C, the water

A hydrogen bond is a dipole attraction.

Question: What would happen if ice were more dense than water?

Ans. Ice would sink to the bottom of oceans and lakes. It would freeze from the bottom up.

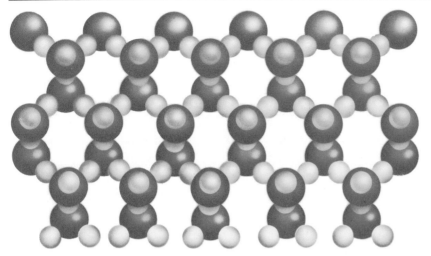

The energy due to hydrogen bonding in water is about 50 kJ per mol of water (or 25 kJ/mole of bonds since each water molecule forms 2 bonds).

FIGURE 17-15. Hydrogen bonding causes water to expand as the temperature falls below 3.98°C. This expansion is seen by the model for ice.

expands with increased temperature. At this temperature, the density of water starts to decrease. Now, we can understand why water has its maximum density at 3.98°C.

Water is the most dense at 3.98°C.

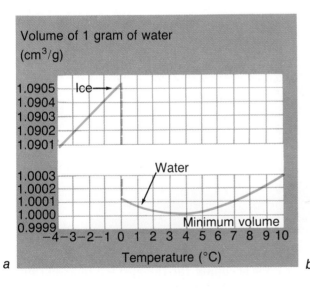

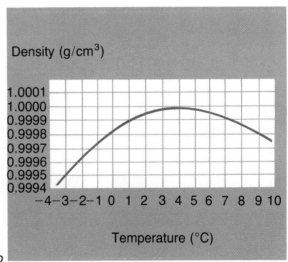

a   *b*

FIGURE 17-16. The temperature at which water reaches its minimum volume in graph (a) corresponds to the maximum density of water in graph (b).

17:12   SURFACE TENSION AND CAPILLARY RISE

Obtain a needle and a glass of water. With tweezers, place the needle carefully on the surface of the water. Be sure there is no soap on your hands, the tweezers, or the needle. With a little practice, you will be able to float the needle on the surface of the water. Why does the needle float? Have you ever poured a drink into a glass so that the surface of the liquid was higher than the rim of the glass?

The particles at the surface have special properties because they are subjected to unbalanced forces as shown in Figure 17-17.

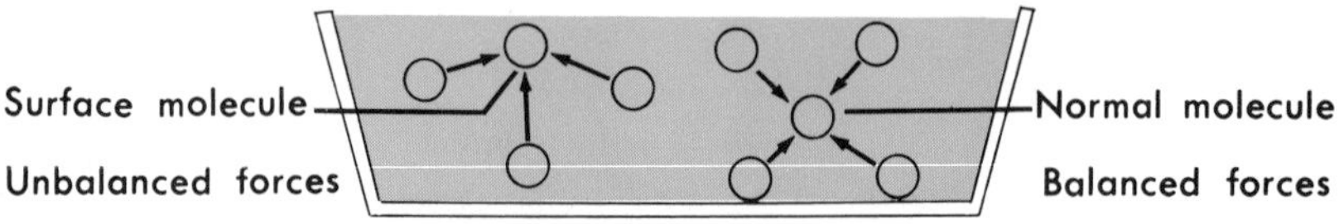

Surface tension of liquids is due to unbalanced forces on surface particles.

FIGURE 17-17. The particles at the surface of a liquid are subjected to unbalanced forces causing surface tension.

Surface molecule — Normal molecule

Unbalanced forces — Balanced forces

These unbalanced forces help explain the **surface tension,** or apparent elasticity of the surface. You know that jarring the overfilled glass destroys the forces at the surface and the liquid overflows.

FIGURE 17-18. Surface tension causes the needle to float (a) and the splashing liquid to form spherical drops (b).

a

Hickson-Bender Photography

b

Dow-Corning Corp.

Surface tension causes drops of liquid to be spherical.

The net force not only accounts for the surface tension, but also helps explain why liquids form spheres when dropped. The net force acting on a surface particle is directed perpendicularly into the liquid. Thus, the body of a liquid is pulling the surface molecules inward. Since a sphere has the least surface area for any given bulk, liquids tend to assume a spherical shape when dropped. Quantitatively, surface tension is expressed as force per unit volume.

The unbalanced force also accounts for the phenomenon known as capillary rise. If there is an attractive force between a

a   b

Hickson-Bender Photography   Hickson-Bender Photography

FIGURE 17-19. Water has a high surface tension as seen by the fact that it rises in the capillary tube (a). The low surface tension of mercury is shown by the fact that it is depressed in the tube (b).

liquid and the solid wall of the capillary tube, the liquid will rise in the tube. Capillary rise for water is shown in Figure 17-19. The attractive force relieves the unbalanced force on the surface molecules. Capillary rise is one method used for measuring surface tension. For example, water has a high surface tension at room temperature. It will rise quite readily in a capillary tube. Mercury, on the other hand, is depressed in a capillary tube as shown in Figure 17-19. It does not "wet" the glass of the tube. That is, there is not enough attractive force between the mercury and the glass to overcome the surface tension of mercury. Compare the meniscus of water and the meniscus of mercury in Figure 17-20. Can you think of an explanation for the difference in behavior?

Capillary rise is one method for measuring surface tension.

Surface tension causes the inverted meniscus of Hg and the almost spherical shape of liquid drops in a vacuum.

FIGURE 17-20. Compare the meniscus of water (a) with that of mercury (b).

Demonstrate this capillary rise by the use of a number of capillary tubes in liquids with various surface tensions, such as alcohol, water, mercury, and concentrated salt solution.

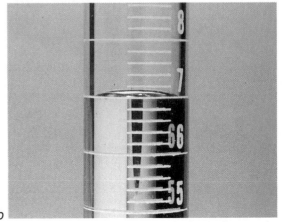

a   b

Hickson-Bender Photography   Hickson-Bender Photography

Norbert Rillieux (1806–1894)

Norbert Rillieux was born in the United States; however he received his education in Paris, France. At the age of 24, he was teaching applied engineering at École Centrale. It was his interest in chemistry and steam engineering which returned him to the United States and led him to a process that revolutionized the sugar industry.

The crystallization of sugar from cane syrup had been done by ladling the cane syrup from vat to vat until the liquid evaporated. In 1846, Rillieux made use of the reduced boiling point of a liquid under a vacuum evaporator. This process produced a cheaper, better, and more automated method of crystallizing sugar. The same concept is now used in the manufacture of condensed milk, soap, and glue. It is also useful in the recovery of wastes from distilleries and paper factories.

CHEMICAL TECHNOLOGY: Herbicides

As the population of the world increases, it becomes more and more difficult to feed everyone. Scientists are constantly searching for ways to increase crop yields from farmland.

One method of improving farm productivity is to remove weeds which crowd paying crops. Herbicides are chemicals which kill weeds without harming the cash crop. Almost 200 different herbicides are available commercially in the United States.

The most widely used herbicides are alachlor and atrazine. Another herbicide, one which has caused much controversy is 2,4,5-T (2,4,5-trichlorophenoxyacetic acid). This substance tends to accumulate in the ground and in water run-off from those fields where it has been used. Most herbicides used today are decomposed in the soil by bacteria within a year. Persistent herbicides, such as 2,4,5-T, can be a problem if they accumulate to levels that are harmful to animals and humans.

Scientists are constantly searching for microorganisms which can degrade these persistent herbicides. It is sometimes possible to control the evolution of such organisms over a long period of time by gradually changing their diets. Thus, organisms can be bred to naturally degrade some of these materials. There are many problems to be overcome in such research. For instance, a microorganism which thrives on a certain chemical in the laboratory may not be able to survive in the wild.

There are a number of mechanisms by which herbicides kill weeds. Some cause the weed to grow very rapidly so the plant's cells never mature as is the case with 2,4,5-T. Others inhibit the reactions associated with photosynthesis. For example, atrazine prevents the activation of water molecules by sunlight. Alachlor inhibits protein synthesis.

Herbicides are developed to protect cash crops. Farmers must choose their herbicides carefully to see that the product selected kills weeds only. Plants unaffected by a herbicide usually contain enzymes which render the chemical ineffective. The altered molecules are then metabolized quickly to eliminate them from the plant.

SUMMARY

1. The vapor pressure of a substance is the pressure exerted by the gaseous phase in equilibrium with the liquid or solid phase. 17:1

2. At the melting or freezing point of any substance, the vapor pressure of the liquid and the vapor pressure of the solid are equal. 17:4

3. In a gas-liquid dynamic equilibrium, the number of molecules in both the liquid and gaseous phases remains constant. 17:1

4. If stress is applied to a system at equilibrium, the system tends to readjust so that the stress is reduced (Le Chatelier's principle). 17:2

5. Sublimation is the change of state in which a substance passes directly from the solid to the gaseous state. 17:5

6. The boiling point of a liquid is the temperature at which the vapor pressure of the liquid is equal to the atmospheric pressure. 17:6

7. Evaporation is the process whereby molecules escape from the surface of a liquid or solid. 17:6

8. For every gas there is a critical temperature (T_c) above which no amount of pressure will result in liquefying the gas. The critical pressure (P_c) is the pressure which will produce liquefaction at T_c. A low critical temperature indicates weak van der Waals forces between molecules. 17:7

9. A phase diagram is a graph showing the relationship between temperature, pressure, and physical state. 17:8

10. The triple point is that temperature and pressure at which all three states of a substance are in equilibrium. 17:8

11. Adding heat to a substance may change its kinetic energy or its potential energy. If the kinetic energy is increased, the temperature of the substance will rise. If the potential energy is raised, the substance will change state (melt or boil). 17:9

12. The heat of fusion is the heat required to melt 1 gram of a solid substance at its melting point. The heat of vaporization is the heat required to vaporize 1 gram of a liquid at its boiling point. 17:9

13. Compounds containing hydrogen bonded to fluorine, oxygen, or nitrogen have unusual properties. These properties occur because of the formation of hydrogen bond. 17:10

14. Ice is less dense than water, which is most dense at 3.98°C. The expansion of ice upon freezing occurs because of hydrogen bonding between the highly polar water molecules 17:11

15. Unbalanced forces account for the surface tension of liquids. Capillary rise of liquids in small tubes is due to surface tension. 17:12

PROBLEMS

10. What is critical temperature? What is critical pressure?

11. What is a triple point? Look at the phase diagram in Figure 17-9. Determine the triple point.

12. What is Le Chatelier's principle? How does pressing on a partially filled balloon demonstrate this principle?

13. Describe how a molecule could leave the surface of a solid. (How do solids evaporate?)

14. What is sublimation? List three practical examples of a substance which sublimes.

15. Define boiling point and melting point in terms of vapor pressure.

16. Why would you expect the boiling point of HF to be higher than that of HBr?

17. Describe what happens to the crystal lattice as ice melts.

18. What is the difference between volatile and nonvolatile substances? Give a solid and a liquid example of each.

19. A well-stirred mixture of ice and water is at equilibrium. If a small amount of warm water or ice is added, the temperature doesn't change. Why?

20. Use the two phase diagrams shown in Figure 17-21. Determine the boiling point, melting point, triple point, and the critical temperature and pressure for substances x and y.

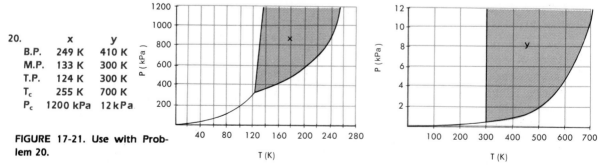

20.	x	y
B.P.	249 K	410 K
M.P.	133 K	300 K
T.P.	124 K	300 K
T_c	255 K	700 K
P_c	1200 kPa	12 kPa

FIGURE 17-21. Use with Problem 20.

21. Calculate the energy in joules required to melt 86.4 g of gallium. 6.93 kJ

22. Calculate the energy in joules required to change 59.5 g of ice at $-95.4°C$ to steam at $1024°C$. 302 000 J

REVIEW

1. What is a crystal? A rigid body in which the constituent particles are arranged in a repeating pattern.
2. How many particles are found in a simple cubic unit cell? 1
3. What are the most common crystal structures found in metals? FCC, BCC, HCP
4. What is a macromolecule? Name one substance that has a macromolecular crystal. A macromolecule is a network crystal in which each atom is bonded to its nearest neighbors throughout the entire
5. How does doping affect the physical properties of some crystals? crystal. diamond, graphite
6. How many kinds of unit cells have been identified? 14
7. What is the usual unit cell for the simplest salts? FCC

5. The doped crystal will conduct electricity.

8. Why is steel such a versatile material?
9. Why does a gas exert a pressure? 9. because of its collisions with the walls of its container
10. Compare the distance between molecules in a gas at room temperature with the size of the molecules themselves.
11. An open manometer shows a mercury level of 97.1 mm higher in the arm connected to the confined gas. The air pressure is 98.5 kPa. What is the pressure of the confined gas? 85.6 kPa
12. A closed manometer shows a mercury level difference of 409 mm. What is the pressure of the gas in kilopascals? 54.5 kPa

ONE MORE STEP

1. A particular physics experiment consists of a block of ice and two heavy weights at the ends of a thin wire. The ice is placed on a table and the wire is placed over the ice so that the weights hang over the edges of the table. Eventually, the wire has moved through the ice but the block of ice is still whole. Explain.
2. Find out how Michael Faraday (1791–1867) liquefied chlorine.
3. Why does carbon dioxide "snow" form when a CO_2 fire extinguisher is used?
4. Look up the freezing points of the hydrogen compounds of the oxygen family. Of what significance are these values?
5. There are substances other than water which expand on freezing. Find the names of some of them. Why do they behave as they do?
6. Investigate the equation describing the distribution of kinetic energies among molecules at a specific temperature.
7. Some substances are purified commercially by sublimation. Find out what two of them are and obtain a description of the process.

READING

Mermin, N. David, and Lee, David M., "Superfluid Helium 3." *Scientific American*, Vol. 235, No. 6 (December 1976), pp. 56-71.

Filling a hot air balloon requires a thorough knowledge of the properties of gases. The temperature and density of the gas in the balloon are critical in getting the balloon off the ground. Once in the air, changing atmospheric pressures must be considered or the balloon could burst. What are the effects of pressure on a gas? How does changing the temperature of a gas affect its volume? How can the laws governing gases be applied to the flight of a balloon?

James Westwater

GASES

Chapter 18 introduces the characteristics of an ideal gas. Gas behavior is covered through a discussion of Boyle's law, Charles' law, and the combined gas law.

Demonstration—Place a small amount of H_2O into a 250 cm³ Florence flask and boil the H_2O for several minutes. After removing the flask from the heat, immediately place a balloon over the mouth of the flask. Cool the flask under a stream of water. The balloon will be sucked into the flask. Heat the flask again and the balloon will expand and come out of the flask. Use this demonstration to introduce gas pressure, volume, and temperature relationships.

You already know many characteristics of gases because air is composed of gases. When we speak of a cubic centimeter of a solid or a hundred cubic centimeters of a liquid, we are referring to a definite amount of matter. Both solids and liquids expand and contract with temperature changes. However, the change is usually small enough to ignore. This statement is not true for gases. The kinetic theory, as well as common experience, shows that a given amount of gas will occupy the entire volume of its container. When gases are heated, the change in their volume is large. Most solids and liquids subjected to the same temperature change would change very little in comparison.

According to the kinetic theory, a gas is made of particles which are in constant random motion. Gas particles are not held in a fixed position by the attraction of other particles as are those in a solid. These particles do not behave like those found in a liquid either. In a liquid, particles may change their relative position easily but their motion is restricted. This restriction occurs because particles of a liquid are held relatively close by van der Waals forces.

The size of a gas molecule is insignificant when compared with the distance between molecules. Thus, we assume that the particles of a gas have no effect on each other. They are called **point masses** since they are considered to have no volume or diameter.

A gas composed of point masses does not actually exist. This imaginary gas, composed of molecules with mass but with no volume and no mutual attraction, is called an ideal gas. In the latter part of this chapter, you will study about real gases, and how they differ in behavior from ideal gases.

GOAL: You will gain an understanding of the behavior of ideal gases based on a study of kinetic theory and the behavior or real gases.

Changes in temperature have a greater effect on the volume of a gas than on the volume of a liquid or solid.

Gas particles are in constant random motion.

An ideal gas is composed of point masses with no volume and no mutual attraction.

Molecules of an ideal gas are considered to be points with no attractive or repulsive force. Emphasize that this is not actually true of real gases.

357

The number of gas particles in a volume of gas depends upon the pressure and temperature of the gas. Therefore, in discussing quantities of gas, it is necessary to specify not only the volume but also the pressure and the temperature. Scientists agreed that standards of pressure and temperature were needed in order to compare volumes of gas. **Standard pressure** is 101.325 kilopascals and **standard temperature** is 0°C. We indicate that a gas has been measured at standard conditions by the capital letters **STP** (standard temperature and pressure). Gas volumes are best reported in the scientific literature as so many m³ or dm³ at STP. The system is convenient but what can we do if we must actually measure a gas in the laboratory when the pressure is 98.7 kilopascals and the temperature is 22°C? In this chapter, we will describe how a measured gas volume can be adjusted to the volume the gas would occupy at STP.

STP = 101.325 kPa and 0°C

The standard temperature for electrochemical and thermodynamic values is 25°C.

Help students develop a mental picture of these relationships. Encourage them to reason through each gas law rather than to memorize a formula.

Pressure exerted by a gas depends on
1. number of particles/unit volume
2. average kinetic energy of particles

18:1 BOYLE'S LAW

We have seen that a gas exerts pressure on the walls of its container because gas molecules collide with the walls. The pressure exerted by a gas will then depend on two factors. The two factors are the number of molecules per unit of volume and the average kinetic energy of the molecules. A change in either of these factors will change the pressure exerted by the gas. If the number of molecules in a constant volume increases, the pressure increases. If the number of molecules and the volume

FIGURE 18-1. The number of molecules in flask (a) equals that in (b). The average kinetic energy of the molecules in (b) is increased by the warm water bath. Note the difference in pressure between the two flasks. *a*   *b*

Courtesy of Kodansha Ltd.   *Courtesy of Kodansha Ltd.*

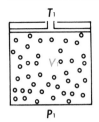

V_2 contains twice as many molecules per unit volume as V_1 per unit volume

N = number of molecules

$N_1 = N_2$

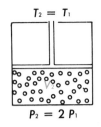

FIGURE 18-2. At constant temperature, an increase in pressure decreases the volume.

remain constant but the kinetic energy of the molecules increases, the pressure increases.

Consider a container of gas with a movable piston in the top, as shown in Figure 18-2. Now imagine that the piston is lowered (without change in the number of molecules) and the temperature is kept constant. If the piston is lowered until it is half the original distance from the bottom, there will be only half as much space as before. The same number of molecules will occupy half the volume. The molecules will hit the walls of the container twice as often and with the same force per collision. Since the same number of molecules in half the space is equivalent to twice as many in the same space, the pressure is doubled. We conclude that, at constant temperature, pressure varies inversely as volume. The product of pressure and volume is then a constant.

The British chemist, Robert Boyle, arrived at this principle by experiment 300 years ago. This relationship is called Boyle's law. Boyle's law states: *If the temperature of a gas remains constant, the pressure exerted by the gas varies inversely as the volume.* By putting the relationships into mathematical form, we obtain the following relationship:

$$P = k' \frac{n}{V} \text{ and if } k'n = k \ (n \text{ is constant}),$$

$$\text{then } P = \frac{k}{V}$$

In this equation, P is the pressure, V the volume, and n is the number of molecules. The k is a constant which takes into account the number of molecules and the temperature. Thus, pressure varies directly as the number of molecules, and inversely as the volume.

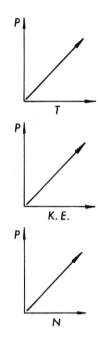

FIGURE 18-3. These graphs show the relationships among pressure, temperature, kinetic energy, and the number of molecules per unit volume.

18:2 APPLYING BOYLE'S LAW

It usually is not convenient to experiment with gases under standard conditions. Experiments are often carried out at room temperature and pressure. Since the temperature and pressure vary from day to day, experimental results cannot be compared

Boyle's Law: At constant temperature, $PV = k$. (Volume varies inversely with pressure.)

easily. It is desirable, therefore, to adjust all results mathematically to standard conditions. If P_1 = measured pressure and V_1 = measured volume, P_2 is standard pressure and V_2 is volume at standard pressure, then:

$$V_1 = \frac{k}{P_1} \text{ and } V_2 = \frac{k}{P_2}$$

In the first equation $k = V_1 P_1$. Since k is a constant, we may substitute $k = V_1 P_1$ into the second equation:

$$V_2 = \frac{V_1 P_1}{P_2} \quad \text{or} \quad V_2 = \frac{V_1}{} \, \bigg| \, \frac{P_1}{P_2}$$

Note that the original volume is simply multiplied by the ratio of the two pressures to find the new volume. We have derived this relationship by using Boyle's law.

EXAMPLE: Pressure Correction

A gas is collected in a 242-cm^3 container. The pressure of the gas in the container is measured and determined to be 87.6 kPa. What is the volume of this gas at standard pressure? (Assume that the temperature remains constant.)

Solving process:
Standard pressure is 101.325 kPa. Thus, a change to standard pressure would compress the gas. Therefore, the gas would occupy a smaller volume. If the volume is to decrease, then the ratio of pressures by which the original volume is to be multiplied must be less than 1. The two possible ratios by which the original volume could be multiplied are

$$\frac{101.3 \text{ kPa}}{87.6 \text{ kPa}} \quad \text{and} \quad \frac{87.6 \text{ kPa}}{101.3 \text{ kPa}}$$

The latter value is the proper one in this case because it is less than 1 and will decrease the volume. The corrected volume is

$$V_2 = V_1 \left(\frac{P_1}{P_2} \right)$$

$$242 \text{ cm}^3 \, \bigg| \, \frac{87.6 \text{ kPa}}{101.3 \text{ kPa}} = 209 \text{ cm}^3$$

The same process can be used to change the volume of a gas to correspond to a pressure other than standard. For instance, if we wish to compare the volume of a gas measured at 16.0 kPa with another quantity measured at 8.8 kPa, the mathematical operations would be as follows: Correcting for a pressure change from 16.0 kPa to 8.8 kPa is equivalent to expanding the gas. The new volume would be greater, and the ratio of pressures must be greater than 1. The proper ratio is 16.0 kPa/8.8 kPa. Do not fall into the habit of "plugging" numbers into equations. Visualize the change to be made in the volume, and then multiply by the appropriate ratio.

$$V_2 = \frac{V_1}{} \, \bigg| \, \frac{16.0 \text{ kPa}}{8.8 \text{ kPa}}$$
$$V_2 = (1.8) V_1$$

PROBLEMS

1. Correct the following volumes of gas from the indicated pressures to standard pressure.
   a. 952 cm³ at 86.4 kPa
   b. 273 cm³ at 59.4 kPa
   c. 338 m³ at 122 kPa
   d. 598 cm³ at 94.4 kPa
   e. 77.0 m³ at 105.9 kPa

2. Correct the following volumes of gas from the indicated pressures to standard pressure.
   a. 930 cm³ at 92.9 kPa
   b. 50.0 m³ at 55.1 kPa
   c. 36.0 m³ at 65.9 kPa
   d. 329 cm³ at 163 kPa
   e. 231 cm³ at 80.7 kPa

3. Make the indicated corrections in the following gas volumes.
   a. 0.600 m³ at 110.0 kPa to 62.4 kPa
   b. 380 cm³ at 66.0 kPa to 42.1 kPa
   c. 0.338 m³ at 102.4 kPa to 47.3 kPa
   d. 459 cm³ at 153 kPa to 231 kPa
   e. 0.123 m³ at 104.1 kPa to 117.7 kPa

4. Make the indicated corrections in the following gas volumes.
   a. 388 cm³ at 86.1 kPa to 104.0 kPa
   b. 0.951 m³ at 82.1 kPa to 114.6 kPa
   c. 31.5 cm³ at 97.8 kPa to 82.3 kPa
   d. 524 cm³ at 110.0 kPa to 104.5 kPa
   e. 171 cm³ at 122.5 kPa to 104.3 kPa

18:3 DALTON'S LAW OF PARTIAL PRESSURE

Chemists often obtain samples of gases by bubbling the gas through water. This procedure is known as collecting a gas over water. It is a useful system for collecting many gases, but the gas must be practically insoluble in water. Water vapor will be present in the gas sample.

How much pressure is exerted by a particular gas in a mixture of gases? John Dalton was the first to form a hypothesis about partial pressures. After experimenting with gases, he concluded that: *The total pressure in a container is the sum of the partial pressures of the gases in the container.* This statement is called Dalton's law of partial pressure. In other words, each gas exerts the same pressure it would if it alone were present at the same temperature. When a gas is one of a mixture, the pressure it exerts is called its partial pressure. Gases in a single container are all at the same temperature and have the same volume. Therefore, the difference in their partial pressures is due only to the difference in the numbers of molecules present.

For example, we add 1000 cm³ of O_2 and 1000 cm³ of N_2, both at room temperature and 101.325 kilopascals. The volume of the

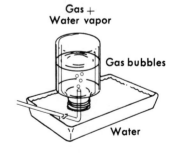

Gas +
Water vapor

Gas bubbles

Water

FIGURE 18-4. The total pressure of a gas collected over water is the sum of the pressure exerted by the gas and the pressure exerted by water vapor.

Dalton's Law: The sum of the partial pressures equals the total pressure in the container.

mixture is then adjusted to 1000 cm^3 with no change in temperature. The pressure exerted by this mixture will be 202.650 kilopascals. However, the pressure exerted by the oxygen will still be 101.325 kilopascals (one half the pressure). Also, the pressure exerted by the nitrogen will be 101.325 kilopascals (one half of the pressure). Air is an example of such a mixture. The air contains nitrogen, oxygen, argon, carbon dioxide, and other gases in small amounts. The total pressure of the atmosphere at standard conditions is 101.325 kilopascals. If 78% of the molecules present are nitrogen molecules, then 78% of the pressure is due to nitrogen. The partial pressure of nitrogen in the air at standard conditions is, then, 0.78 × 101.325 kilopascals or 79 kilopascals.

Doubling the number of particles (K.E. to remain constant) results in a doubling of the number of collisions. Therefore, the pressure doubles.

Each gas in a mixture exerts its own partial pressure.

Table 18-1

Composition of Air (dry)	
Gas	**Partial pressure** (kPa)
nitrogen	79.119
oxygen	21.224
argon	0.946
carbon dioxide	0.030
neon	0.002
Traces of helium, krypton, hydrogen, and xenon	

The assumption that the gas is saturated with water vapor is not always valid. The error, however, is very small, usually less than 0.1 kPa.

If a gas is collected over water, the pressure in the container actually includes the sum of the partial pressures of the gas and the water vapor. We know that each of the gases exerts the same pressure it would if it alone were present in the container. Therefore, if we subtract the value for water vapor pressure from the total pressure, the result will be the pressure of the gas alone. The vapor pressure of water at various temperatures has been measured. We need only to consult Table 18-2 to determine the partial pressure of water.

The volume of a gas collected over water must be corrected for water vapor pressure.

Pressure of dry gas = total pressure − water vapor pressure.

$$P_{gas} = P_{total} - P_{water}$$

Table 18-2

Vapor Pressure of Water					
Temperature (°C)	**Pressure** (kPa)	**Temperature** (°C)	**Pressure** (kPa)	**Temperature** (°C)	**Pressure** (kPa)
0	0.6	21	2.5	30	4.2
5	0.9	22	2.6	35	5.6
8	1.1	23	2.8	40	7.4
10	1.2	24	3.0	50	12.3
12	1.4	25	3.2	60	19.9
14	1.6	26	3.4	70	31.2
16	1.8	27	3.6	80	47.3
18	2.1	28	3.8	90	70.1
20	2.3	29	4.0	100	101.3

EXAMPLE: Volume of a Dry Gas

A quantity of gas is collected over water at 8°C in a 353-cm^3 vessel. The manometer indicates a pressure of 84.5 kPa. What volume would the dry gas occupy at standard pressure and 8°C?

Solving process:

(a) We must determine what part of the total pressure is due to water vapor. Table 18-2 indicates that at 8°C, water has a vapor pressure of 1.1 kPa. To find the pressure of the collected gas:

$$P_{gas} = P_{total} - P_{water}$$
$$= 84.5 \text{ kPa} - 1.1 \text{ kPa}$$
$$= 83.4 \text{ kPa}$$

(b) Since this pressure is less than standard, the gas would have to be compressed to change it to standard. The pressure ratio by which the volume is to be multiplied must be less than 1. The correct volume is

$$\frac{353 \text{ cm}^3 \mid 83.4 \text{ kPa}}{101.3 \text{ kPa}} = 291 \text{ cm}^3$$

PROBLEM

5. The following gas volumes were collected over water under the indicated conditions. Correct each volume to the volume that the dry gas would occupy at standard pressure and the indicated temperature (T is constant).
   a. 888 cm^3 at 14°C and 93.3 kPa
   b. 30.0 cm^3 at 16°C and 77.5 kPa
   c. 34.0 m^3 at 18°C and 82.4 kPa
   d. 384 cm^3 at 12°C and 78.3 kPa
   e. 8.23 m^3 at 27°C and 87.3 kPa

Sidebar

Demonstration — Rinse an empty duplicator fluid can, then boil 150 cm^3 of H_2O in the can. Remove the burner and immediately stopper the can. Run a thin stream of cold water on the outside of the can. Outside air pressure will cause the can to collapse. Ask the students to explain why. Discuss pressure-volume relationships, and partial pressure of the water vapor.

$$V_2 = V_1 \left(\frac{P_1}{P_2} \right)$$

Note that the temperature remains constant. See Table 18-2 page 362 for pressure corrections.

5. a. 804 cm^3
   b. 22.4 cm^3
   c. 27.0 m^3
   d. 292 cm^3
   e. 6.80 m^3

18:4 CHARLES' LAW

Jacques Charles, a French physicist, noticed a simple relationship between the volume of a gas and the temperature. He found that, starting at 0°C, the volume of any gas would double if the temperature were raised to 273°C (pressure constant). For each Celsius degree increase in temperature, the volume of the gas increased by 1/273 of its volume at 0°C. If the original volume (at 0°C) is expressed as 273/273 = 1, an increase in temperature of 273° will result in a new volume of

$$\frac{273 + 273}{273}, \text{ or } 2$$

For each 1 C° change, a gas changes 1/273 of its 0°C volume.

Charles' Law: At constant pressure, $V = kT$. (Volume varies directly with the kelvin temperature.)

An increase in temperature of 1 C° will result in a new volume of 274/273, or a 1/273 increase in volume. Similarly, Charles found that a gas will decrease by 1/273 of its 0°C volume for each Celsius degree decrease in temperature. This finding would suggest that at −273°C, a gas would have no volume, or would disappear. This temperature is called absolute zero. However, all gases become liquid before they are cooled to this low temperature, and Charles' relationship does not hold for liquids or solids. *The volume of a quantity of gas, held at a fixed pressure, varies directly with the kelvin temperature.* This relationship is called Charles' law.

This experimental information led to the formation of the absolute or kelvin temperature scale. Thus far, we have always defined the kelvin scale in terms of the Celsius scale. Now we are in a position to define the kelvin scale directly. The zero point of the kelvin scale is absolute zero. The other reference point in defining the kelvin scale is the triple point of water which is defined as 273.16 K. You must remember that temperatures given in Celsius must be converted to kelvin to work with gases. The relationship is K = °C + 273.

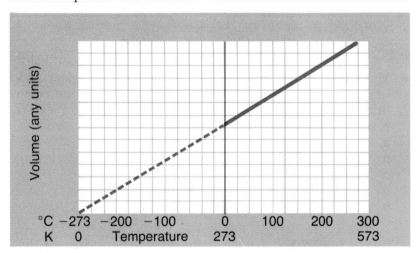

FIGURE 18-5. The volume of a gas at zero kelvin is theoretically zero.

18:5 APPLYING CHARLES' LAW

Charles' law states that volume varies directly as the absolute temperature: $V = k'T$. For any original volume, $V_1 = k'T_1$. A change in volume, with pressure constant, could be indicated at $V_2 = k'T_2$. Since $k' = V_1/T_1$, substituting would give:

$$\frac{V_1}{T_1} = \frac{V_2}{T_2} \quad \text{or} \quad V_2 = \frac{V_1 \ \bigg| \ T_2}{\bigg| \ T_1}$$

To correct the volume for a change in temperature, you must, as in pressure correction, multiply the original volume by a ratio. For temperature changes, the ratio is expressed in kelvin temperatures.

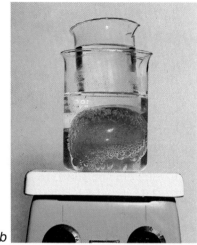

a

Hickson-Bender Photography

b
Hickson-Bender Photography

FIGURE 18-6. Note how the volume of the balloon changes from the ice bath (a) to the hot water bath (b).

EXAMPLE: Temperature Correction

A 225 cm³ volume of gas is collected at 57°C. What volume would this sample of gas occupy at standard temperature?

Solving process:
The temperature decreases and the pressure remains constant. Charles' law states that if the temperature of gas decreases at constant pressure, the volume will decrease. Therefore, the original volume must be multiplied by a fraction less than 1. Convert both the initial (57°C) and the final (0°C) temperatures to the kelvin scale (330 K and 273 K). The two possible temperature ratios are the following.

$K = °C + 273$

$$\frac{330 \text{ K}}{273 \text{ K}} \quad \text{and} \quad \frac{273 \text{ K}}{330 \text{ K}}$$

The correct ratio is 273 K/330 K because it is less than 1. The corrected gas volume is

$$\frac{225 \text{ cm}^3}{} \; \Big|\; \frac{273 \text{ K}}{330 \text{ K}} = 186 \text{ cm}^3$$

PROBLEMS

6. Correct the following volumes of gases for a change from the temperature indicated to standard temperature (P is constant).
   a. 617 cm³ at 9°C
   b. 609 cm³ at 83°C
   c. 942 cm³ at 22°C
   d. 7.12 m³ at 988 K
   e. 213 m³ at 99°C
   f. 7.16 m³ at 280 K
   g. 4.40 m³ at 7°C
   h. 819 cm³ at 21°C
   i. 5.80 m³ at 514 K
   j. 5.94 m³ at 79°C

7. Correct the following volumes of gases for the temperature changes indicated (P is constant).
   a. 2.90 m³ at 226 K to 23°C
   b. 608 cm³ at 158 K to 73°C
   c. 7.91 m³ at 52°C to 538 K
   d. 880 cm³ at 563 K to 52°C
   e. 5.94 m³ at 44°C to 17°C
   f. 2.97 m³ at 72°C to 502 K
   g. 19.0 cm³ at 56.0 K to 53°C
   h. 5.18 m³ at 76°C to 6°C
   i. 994 cm³ at 27°C to 244 K
   j. 833 cm³ at 27°C to 84°C

18:6   COMBINED GAS LAW

Introduce the combined gas law as a two step procedure—the second step being a correction of the result of the first step.

Laboratory experiments are almost always made at temperatures and pressures other than standard. It is sometimes necessary to correct the laboratory volumes of gases for temperature and pressure. The correction is made by multiplying the original volume by two ratios, one for temperature and the other for pressure.

A change in volume resulting from a change in both temperature and pressure can be found by combining the temperature and pressure ratios.

Since multiplication is commutative, it does not make any difference which ratio is used first. We may think of the process as correcting the volume for a pressure change while the temperature is held constant. Then, we correct for the temperature change while the pressure is held constant. The two changes do not have any effect on each other.

EXAMPLE: Volume Correction to STP

The common sense approach used here simplifies use of gas laws in mass-volume problems at nonstandard conditions.

The volume of a gas measured at 75.6 kPa pressure and 60°C is to be corrected to correspond to the volume it would occupy at STP. The measured volume of the gas is 10.0 cm³

Solving process:
The pressure must be increased from 75.6 kPa to 101.3 kPa. The volume must decrease. The correct pressure ratio is 75.6 kPa/ 101.3 kPa.

The temperature must be decreased from 333 K to 273 K. This change would also decrease the volume. Therefore, the correct temperature ratio is 273 K/333 K. The problem then becomes

$$\frac{10.0 \text{ cm}^3 \quad | \quad 75.6 \text{ kPa} \quad | \quad 273 \text{ K}}{\qquad\qquad | \quad 101.3 \text{ kPa} \quad | \quad 333 \text{ K}} = 6.12 \text{ cm}^3 \text{ at STP.}$$

PROBLEMS

8. Correct the volumes of the following gases as indicated.
  a. 7.51 m³ at 5°C and 59.9 kPa to STP
  b. 149 cm³ at 18°C and 94.7 kPa to 68°C and 82.4 kPa
  c. 7.03 m³ at 31°C and 111 kPa to STP
  d. 955 cm³ at 58°C and 108.0 kPa to 76°C and 123.0 kPa
  e. 960 cm³ at 71°C and 107.2 kPa to 13°C and 59.3 kPa

9. Correct the volumes of the following gases as indicated.
  a. 654 cm³ at 6°C and 65.3 kPa to 4°C and 108.7 kPa
  b. 2.13 m³ at 95°C and 103 kPa to STP
  c. 4.76 m³ at 6°C and 124.5 kPa to STP
  d. 61.4 cm³ at 67°C and 96.8 kPa to STP
  e. 164 cm³ at STP to 21°C and 98.0 kPa

8. a. 4.36 m³
   b. 201 cm³
   c. 6.92 m³
   d. 884 cm³
   e. 1440 cm³

9. a. 390 cm³
   b. 1.61 m³
   c. 5.72 m³
   d. 47.1 cm³
   e. 183 cm³

Demonstration—Stuff two cotton plugs that are saturated with HCl and $NH_3(aq)$ respectively into the ends of a large glass tube. Discuss why the NH_4Cl forms where it does. (Graham's Law)

18:7 DIFFUSION AND GRAHAM'S LAW

One of the basic ideas of the kinetic theory is that gas molecules travel in straight lines. However, a molecule is always colliding with other molecules. Therefore, its actual path is a series of straight lines connected end to end in no particular pattern. If a bottle of a substance with a strong odor is opened on one side of the room, its odor can later be detected on the other side of the room. The molecules of the substance have traveled across the room by traveling in straight lines between collisions. However, they did not necessarily travel straight across the room. It took some time for them to reach the other side because they were colliding with air molecules. This random scattering of the gas molecules is called **diffusion.** As the gas molecules diffuse, they become more and more evenly distributed throughout the room.

Emphasize that the rate of diffusion of gases varies directly with the velocity of the molecules. In two samples of the same gas, the rate of diffusion will be higher for the one having a higher temperature because the velocity of the molecules will be higher.

Diffusion is the random scattering of gas particles.

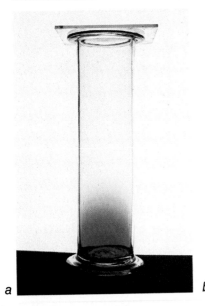
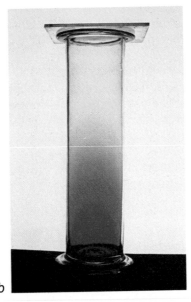
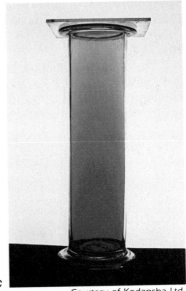

a   b   c

Courtesy of Kodansha Ltd.

FIGURE 18-7. This series of photos shows the diffusion of bromine vapor.

Molecules of large mass diffuse more slowly than molecules of small mass.

Effusion is the passage of gas molecules through small openings.

Particles of samples of gases at the same temperature have the same average kinetic energy.

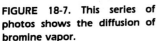

$$K.E. = \frac{1}{2}mv^2$$

Stress that kinetic energy relates to *average* **speed of molecules in a sample.**

Stress that at equal temperatures the average kinetic energies of different kinds of molecules are equal; however, their velocities may be different depending upon the molecular mass of each.

Graham's Law: The relative rates of diffusion of two gases under identical conditions vary inversely as the square roots of their molecular masses.

All gases do not diffuse at the same rate. We will assume that the rate of diffusion varies directly as the velocity of the molecules. This assumption is supported by experimental evidence. At the same temperature, molecules of low mass diffuse faster than molecules of large mass because they travel faster. They also will pass through a small hole (effuse) more rapidly than the molecules of higher mass.

In Section 15:4 we found that if two substances are at the same temperature their kinetic energies must be the same. Thus,

$$KE_1 = KE_2$$

$$1/2 \, m_1 v_1^2 = 1/2 \, m_2 v_2^2$$

$$m_1 v_1^2 = m_2 v_2^2 \quad \text{or} \quad \frac{v_1^2}{v_2^2} \quad \frac{m_2}{m_1}$$

which is equivalent to

$$\frac{v_1}{v_2} = \sqrt{\frac{m_2}{m_1}}$$

From this equation, we see that the relative rates of diffusion of two gases vary inversely as the square roots of their molecular masses. This relationship is true only when the temperature is the same for each. This principle was first formulated by a Scottish chemist, Thomas Graham, and is known as Graham's law. Graham's law states: *The relative rates at which two gases under identical conditions of temperature and pressure will pass through a small hole varies inversely as the square roots of the molecular masses of the gases.*

PROBLEMS

10. What is the ratio of the speed of hydrogen molecules to that of oxygen molecules when both gases are at the same temperature? Remember that both elements are diatomic.

11. What is the ratio of the speed of helium atoms to the speed of radon atoms when both gases are at the same temperature?

12. At a certain temperature, the velocity of oxygen molecules is 0.0760 m/s. What is the velocity of helium atoms at the same temperature?

13. Compute the relative rate of diffusion of helium to argon.

14. Compute the relative rate of diffusion of argon to radon.

10. 3.98

11. 7.45

12. 0.215 m/s

13. 3.16

14. 2.36

18:8   GAS DENSITY

The density of gases and vapors is most often expressed in grams per cubic decimeter. We express it in these units because the usual density units, g/cm^3, lead to very small numbers for gases. It is possible to calculate the density of a gas at any temperature and pressure from data collected at any other temperature and pressure. Assuming that the number of particles remains the same, a decrease in temperature would decrease the volume and increase the density. An increase of pressure would decrease the volume and increase the density. The following problem illustrates this calculation. (Remember 1000 cm^3 equals 1 dm^3.)

density = mass per unit volume

If the number of particles remains the same:
1. density increases as pressure increases
2. density decreases as temperature increases

Demonstration—Set a short, lighted candle in the center of a 400 cm^3 beaker. Fill a 1000 cm^3 beaker with CO_2 gas and proceed to pour it into the one with the lighted candle. Discuss gas densities. Relate to CO_2 fire extinguisher.

EXAMPLE: Density at STP

It is found that 981 cm^3 of a gas collected at 47°C and 98.1 kPa has mass 3.40 g. What is its density at STP?

Solving process:

(a) The temperature is decreased from 47°C (320 K) to 0°C (273 K). This change decreases the volume and increases the density. We would use

$$\frac{320 \text{ K}}{273 \text{ K}}$$

(b) The pressure is increased from 98.1 kPa to 101.3 kPa. This change decreases the volume and increases the density. Thus, we would use

$$\frac{101.3 \text{ kPa}}{98.1 \text{ kPa}}$$

Use a logical approach. Do not merely "plug" values into an equation.

The solution therefore, is

$$\frac{3.40 \text{ g}}{981 \text{ cm}^3} \, \bigg| \, \frac{1000 \text{ cm}^3}{1 \text{ dm}^3} \, \bigg| \, \frac{320 \text{ K}}{273 \text{ K}} \, \bigg| \, \frac{101.3 \text{ kPa}}{98.1 \text{ kPa}} = 4.20 \text{ g/dm}^3$$

| Original Density | Unit Correction | T Correction | P Correction |

PROBLEMS

15. a. 2.20 g/dm³
  b. 1.16 g/dm³
  c. 13.4 g/dm³
  d. 4.18 g/dm³
  e. 1.27 g/dm³

16. 2.67 g/dm³

17. 5.65 g/dm³

15. Compute the gas density at STP for the following.
   a. 969 cm³ of gas at 64°C and 96.4 kPa has mass 1.64 g
   b. 498 cm³ of gas at 31°C and 103.5 kPa has mass 0.530 g
   c. 833 cm³ of gas at 99°C and 103 kPa has mass 8.30 g
   d. 883 cm³ of gas at 37°C and 115.0 kPa has mass 3.69 g
   e. 4750 cm³ of gas at 26°C and 92.5 kPa has mass 5.03 g

16. The density of a gas is 2.97 g/dm³ at STP. What would its density be at 27°C and 100.0 kPa?

17. At 325 K and 107.0 kPa, a gas has a density of 5.01 g/dm³. What would be its density at STP?

18:9 DEVIATIONS OF REAL GASES

In Sections 18:1 through 18:8, we made two assumptions. The first was that gas molecules had no volume. The second was that gas molecules had no attraction for each other. These assumptions are not really true. However, for many gases at low pressure, the molecules closely approach the behavior of ideal gas molecules.

At low pressures, the molecules of both ideal and real gases are far apart. The volume occupied by the molecules is small when compared to the total gas volume. Most of the total volume is empty space. As the pressure is increased, the gas molecules are forced closer. Ideal gas molecules still remain relatively far apart but real gas molecules begin to occupy a significant portion of the total volume. A further increase in pressure does not always cause the predicted decrease in volume. If the molecules are slowed down enough, the van der Waals forces will have an effect.

Not all gases behave as ideal gases.

When the molecules are slowed down, van der Waals forces have an effect on the behavior of real gases.

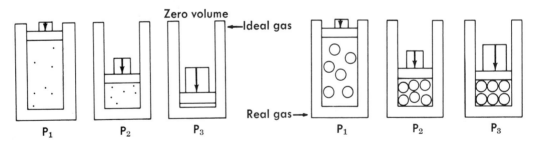

FIGURE 18-8. An increase in pressure increases the number of molecules per unit volume. Thus, the density of the gas increases.

Roughly, you reduce only the space not occupied by gas molecules.

For most common gases, the ideal gas laws are accurate to 1% at normal laboratory temperatures and pressure. It will be assumed, for convenience, that these gases have ideal gas properties. Generally, the lower the critical temperature of a gas the more closely the gas obeys the ideal gas laws. Using this knowledge, we can estimate the degree to which the gases listed in Table 18-3 approach the ideal gas.

Table 18-3

Critical Temperature	
Gas	Critical Temperature (K)
He	5.19
H$_2$	33.2
N$_2$	126.0
O$_2$	154.2
CO$_2$	304.4
SO$_2$	430.6
H$_2$O	647.3

Critical temperature is the temperature above which no amount of pressure will liquefy a gas.

Gases with low critical temperatures approximate ideal gases.

The ideal gas would have T_c = 0 K.

There is a property of real gases which depends upon the attractive forces which exist between molecules. If a highly compressed gas is allowed to escape through a small opening, its temperature decreases. This phenomenon is known as the Joule-Thomson effect, after the two scientists who first investigated it. In order to expand, the molecules of the gas must do some work in order to overcome the attractive forces between them. The energy used to do this work comes from their kinetic energy. As their kinetic energy decreases, the temperature falls. Consider the apparatus shown in Figure 18-9. The system shown is completely insulated so that no heat exchange can take place with the surroundings. Such a system is known as an **adiabatic** (ayd ee uh BAT ik) **system.** The temperature of the gas in (b) will be less than its temperature in (a) before the expansion.

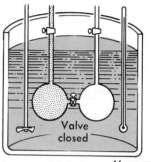

(a) Before Vacuum

(b) After

FIGURE 18-9. For an adiabatic system, the temperature of the gas in (a) is higher than that in (b).

Push button

Valve held closed by can pressure and coil spring, opened by applying pressure to the push button

Gaseous propellant occupies this volume

Gas pressure

Dip tube

Temperature of can decreases as product and propellant are released

Curved bottom to resist pressure

Product and propellant

FIGURE 18-10. The temperature of the material released from an aerosol can decreases as the material is forced through the nozzle.

Robert Boyle (1627–1691)

One of seven sons of the Earl of Cork, Robert Boyle distinguished his family by entering Eton at the age of eight. His chief contribution to science is his law concerning the behavior of a quantity of gas subjected to a change in pressure when the temperature is held constant.

Boyle also distinguished between a chemical element and a compound and was the first to define chemical reaction and analysis.

An intensely religious man, Boyle also pursued studies and responsibilities in this area. As a director of the East India Company, he worked for the propagation of Christianity in the East and circulated, at his own expense, translations of the Scriptures.

In the scientific realm, he helped found the Royal Society in England. Membership in this society became the ultimate honor for a British scientist.

CHEMICAL TECHNOLOGY: Photochemical Smog

The word smog was coined in 1905 as a combination of smoke and fog. Today, it is often used as a synonym for air pollution of any kind. A chemist will specify photochemical smog to mean those air pollutants produced by chemical reaction induced by sunlight.

Some of the reactants producing photochemical smog are natural components of the air, such as oxygen and water vapor. The principal source of other reactants is automobile engine exhaust. Industrial factories and electric power generating stations also contribute a significant amount.

Gasoline consists almost entirely of saturated hydrocarbons. Saturated hydrocarbons are chain compounds in which all the carbon-carbon bonds are single bonds. In the combustion of gasoline in the engine cylinder, some hydrocarbons do not react completely and are expelled in the exhaust as unsaturated hydrocarbons. Unsaturated hydrocarbons contain double and triple bonds between carbon atoms. The compound ethene, $CH_2\!\!=\!\!CH_2$ is produced in this way. In addition, some of the nitrogen in the air combines with oxygen to form oxides of nitrogen, such as NO and NO_2.

Small quantities of ozone, O_3, occur naturally in the air as a result of the action of sunlight on oxygen molecules.

$$O_2 + h\nu \rightarrow 2O \qquad O + O_2 \rightarrow O_3$$

The ozone is split by a quantum of sunlight into an oxygen molecule and a free oxygen atom which is highly reactive. The oxygen atom reacts with water vapor to form the highly reactive hydroxyl radical. The ozone oxidizes NO to NO_2.

$$O + H_2O \rightarrow 2OH \qquad O_3 + NO \rightarrow NO_2 + O_2$$

The hydroxyl radical* reacts with the unsaturated hydrocarbons to produce a number of products. These products are eventually oxidized to CO_2 if they do not react with other compounds in the meantime. However, some intermediate products react with NO_2 to produce peroxyacetyl nitrate, PAN, which is poisonous to plants and animals alike. It is especially irritating to the eyes.

$$CH_3-\overset{\overset{\displaystyle O}{\|}}{C}-O-O-NO_2$$
PAN

There are also other smog products which irritate and poison. Sunlight provides the activation energy for reactions of oxygen, unsaturated hydrocarbons, and nitrogen oxides to produce pernitric acid, carbon monoxide, ozone, organic peroxycompounds, and aldehydes.

The long term effects of photochemical smog on humans are unknown. However, research seems to indicate an increased susceptibility to bronchitis, emphysema, and lung cancer for people living in high smog areas.

The introduction of catalytic converters to automobile exhaust systems has helped reduce photochemical smog in some areas. The converter causes the hydrocarbons to be oxidized to CO_2 before they leave the automobile.

Photochemical smog is a significant problem in areas which experience a phenomenon known as temperature inversion. This effect is said to occur when air temperature increases with height. The density of the air at ground level is greater than that at higher elevations. The pollutants then tend to remain at ground level rather than be dispersed into the upper air. As a result of temperature inversion, the concentration of pollutants increases.

*A radical is a part of a molecule which lacks a complete octet of electrons.

SUMMARY

1. An ideal gas is an imaginary gas whose particles have no diameter and no mutual attraction. Intro.

2. The volume of a gas depends not only on the number of particles but also on temperature and pressure. Intro.

3. Standard temperature and pressure (STP) are 0°C and 101.325 kilopascals. Gas volumes are usually reported in m^3 or dm^3 at STP. Intro.

4. Gas pressure depends on the number of molecules per unit volume and the average kinetic energy of the molecules. 18:1

5. Boyle's law states that, at constant temperature, the volume of a gas varies inversely as its pressure $(V = k/P)$. 18:1-18:2

6. Dalton's law states that the total pressure in a container is the sum of the partial pressures of the individual gases in the container. 18:3

7. Charles' law states that, at constant pressure, the volume of a gas varies directly with the absolute temperature $(V = k'T)$. 18:4-18:5

8. The absolute temperature scale is defined by two points. One point is 18:4 absolute zero (0 K). The other point is the triple point of water (273.16 K).

9. When applying the combined gas laws, the correction for temperature and pressure have no effect upon each other. 18:6

10. Diffusion is the process by which gases spread to become evenly distributed throughout the entire space in which they are confined. All gases do not diffuse or effuse at the same rate. 18:7

11. Graham's law states that, under constant temperature and pressure, the relative velocities of two gases vary inversely as the square roots of their molecular masses. 18:7

12. Gas density varies directly as pressure and inversely as temperature. It is usually expressed in grams per cubic decimeter (g/dm^3). 18:8

13. The particles of real gases, as opposed to ideal gases, have both volume and mutual attraction. At high pressure and low temperatures, these two factors take effect. 18:9

14. At normal laboratory temperatures and pressures, most common gases behave nearly as ideal gases. The lower the critical temperature of a gas, the more nearly it behaves as an ideal gas. 18:9

PROBLEMS

18. What are the characteristics of an ideal gas?

19. Under what condition do real gases behave in a similar manner to ideal gases? **low pressure**

20. Theoretically, what would happen to a gas which is cooled to absolute zero? In reality, what occurs?

21. Why is it that if the kinetic energies of two different gases at the same temperature are equal, their rates of diffusion are not equal?

22. What is the Joule-Thompson effect?

23. Find the volume of a dry gas at STP if it measures 928 cm^3 at 27°C and 106.0 kPa. **884 cm³**

24. A chemist collects 96.0 cm^3 of gas over water at 27°C and 122.0 kPa. What volume would the dry gas occupy at 70°C and 127.0 kPa? **102 cm³**

25. A chemist collects 372 cm^3 of gas over water at 90°C and 111.0 kPa. What volume would the dry gas occupy at 2°C and 98.0 kPa? **118 cm³**

26. A chemist collects 5.08 cm^3 of gas at 3°C and 96.9 kPa over water. What volume would the dry gas occupy at 44°C and 117.6 kPa? **477 cm³**

27. 30.0 cm^3 of a gas are collected over water at 20°C and 93.0 kPa. What volume would the dry gas occupy at STP? **25.0 cm³**

28. The following gas volumes were collected over water under the indicated conditions. Correct each volume to the volume that the dry gas would occupy at standard pressure and the indicated temperature (T is constant).

   a. 903 cm^3 at 24°C and 95.3 kPa   **c.** 7.83 m^3 at 20°C and 107 kPa
   b. 317 cm^3 at 25°C and 113.5 kPa   **d.** 964 cm^3 at 29°C and 111.5 kPa

   28. a. 823 cm³
       b. 345 cm³
       c. 8.12 m³
       d. 1020 cm³

29. At STP, a gas measures 325 cm^3. What will it measure at 20°C and 93.3 kPa? **379 cm³**

30. A chemist collects 8.00 cm^3 of gas over water at STP. What volume would the dry gas occupy at STP? **7.95 cm³**

REVIEW

1. When a liquid at room temperature evaporates, what requirements must be met by the molecules escaping?

   2. A system at equilibrium will shift so as to relieve an outside stress.

2. State Le Chatelier's principle.

3. What is meant by sublimation?   direct solid to vapor phase change

4. What requirements must be met to liquify a gas?   high pressure, low temperature

5. Sketch a sample phase diagram, labeling all parts.

6. What is meant by the word "dynamic" in the phrase, "dynamic equilibrium"?

7. Define melting point in terms of vapor pressure.

8. How much energy is required to change 1.70 grams of ice at −12°C to steam at 140°C? **5300 J**

   6. Changes that are the reverse of each other are occurring at the same rate.

   7. The temperature at which the vapor pressures of the solid and liquid phases are equal.

ONE MORE STEP

1. Using a bicycle tire pump or a football inflating pump and an air pressure gauge such as is used on auto tires, see if you can demonstrate Boyle's law. Don't forget that the air in the pump is already at atmospheric pressure before you depress the plunger.

2. There are a number of approximate equations which deal with the behavior of real gases. Using one of these equations, calculate the percent deviation from ideal of nitrogen gas at 0°C and 40 000 kPa pressure.

3. Using Robert Boyle's original data, plot the pressure against the reciprocal of the volume. The pressure will be the difference in height of mercury in the two arms of the J-tube. The volume can be plotted directly from the difference between 12 and the height Boyle obtained in the closed arm, since he was using a tube of uniform bore. Draw a line through the points to make the best fit possible. Do you think Boyle did accurate work considering the primitive nature of his equipment?

The production of baked goods depends on a chemical reaction producing carbon dioxide. Bread and similar products can have different textures depending on the amount of gas produced. This quantity is controlled by the amounts of ingredients used in a particular recipe. How are the ingredients in bread similar to the reactants in an equation? How is it possible to control the amount of gas produced in a reaction? What is a limiting reactant?

Jeffry W. Myers/Alpha

Chapter 19 continues the study of gases focusing on the ideal gas law and gas reaction calculations in conjunction with varying conditions studied in the previous chapter.

GASES AND THE MOLE

19

In Chapter 18, we examined the effect of temperature and pressure on the volume of a constant mass of gas. The principles hold true for any gas exhibiting ideal behavior. Different gases, however, have molecules and atoms of different masses. In this chapter, we will look at the effect of the number of particles on the other gas variables, particularly volume. We will also find out how to obtain mass measurements of gases at various temperatures and pressures.

GOAL: You will gain an understanding of the relationship between the mole and gas volumes and use this relationship in solving gas reaction problems.

19:1 DEVELOPING AVOGADRO'S PRINCIPLE

Suppose we place two different gases at exactly the same temperature and pressure in separate containers which have exactly the same volume. At a given temperature, all gas molecules will have the same average kinetic energy regardless of size or mass. Massive molecules will travel slowly, lighter molecules will travel more rapidly. However, the average kinetic energy $(1/2\ mv^2)$ will be the same for all. If the kinetic energies are equal, any difference in pressure exerted by the gases is determined by the number of molecules of each gas. Since we have already said the two gases are at the same pressure, there must be an equal number of molecules in the two containers. *At equal temperatures and equal pressures, equal volumes of gases contain the same number of molecules.* This statement is called **Avogadro's principle,** after Amadeo Avogadro. When he proposed the principle, in 1811, the kinetic theory had not been developed. As we read in Section 5:2, Avogadro developed his principle to explain some of the observations made by Gay-Lussac. Gay-Lussac had observed that two gases always react in such a way that the combining volumes can be expressed in small whole numbers.

The number of gas molecules in a container determines the pressure at a given temperature.

Avogadro's principle states that under similar conditions, equal volumes of gases contain the same number of molecules.

Proust had previously stated his law of definite proportions. Avogadro knew that one molecule of chlorine always united with one molecule of hydrogen. He also knew that two molecules of hydrogen chloride were formed. He therefore concluded that equal volumes of gases must contain equal numbers of molecules. Avogadro's principle has been verified so often that it is sometimes called a law. One consequence of Avogadro's principle is that the value of the constant k, in

$$V = \frac{k}{P}$$

is the same for all gases. Similarly, the value of the constant in $V = kT$ does not change. It is the same for all gases.

19:2 MOLAR VOLUME

Let n represent the number of moles of a gas, and let V represent the volume. Then, for two gases under similar conditions, Avogadro's principle states: If $V_1 = V_2$, then $n_1 = n_2$. Conversely, if the number of moles of two gases under similar conditions is equal, then their volumes are equal. Thus, we can

FIGURE 19-1. The average kinetic energies of the molecules in the two gas samples are equal regardless of size or mass.

Gas 1  Gas 2

$$n_1 = n_2$$
$$V_1 = V_2$$
$$\frac{V_1}{n_1} = \frac{V_2}{n_2}$$

conclude that 1 mole of any gas at STP will occupy the same volume as 1 mole of any other gas at STP. For example, 1 mole of oxygen has mass 32.0 g and 1000 cm^3 of oxygen has mass 1.43 g. Therefore, a mole of oxygen will occupy

$$\frac{32.0 \text{ g}}{1 \text{ mol}} \left| \frac{1000 \text{ cm}^3}{1.43 \text{ g}} \right| \frac{1 \text{ dm}^3}{1000 \text{ cm}^3} = 22.4 \text{ dm}^3/\text{mol}$$

One mole of hydrogen gas has mass 2.016 g and 1000 cm^3 of hydrogen has mass 0.0899 g. We again find that 1 mole of hydrogen occupies

$$\frac{2.016 \text{ g}}{1 \text{ mol}} \left| \frac{1000 \text{ cm}^3}{0.0899 \text{ g}} \right| \frac{1 \text{ dm}^3}{1000 \text{ cm}^3} = 22.4 \text{ dm}^3/\text{mol}$$

This volume, 22.4 dm^3, the volume occupied by 1 mole of any gas under standard conditions, is called the **molar volume** of the gas.

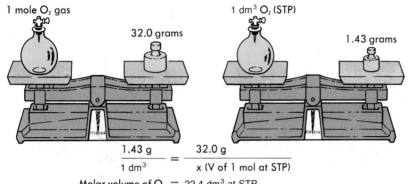

1 mole O₂ gas   32.0 grams   1 dm³ O₂ (STP)   1.43 grams

$$\frac{1.43 \text{ g}}{1 \text{ dm}^3} = \frac{32.0 \text{ g}}{x \text{ (V of 1 mol at STP)}}$$

Molar volume of O_2 = 22.4 dm³ at STP

FIGURE 19-2. One mole of oxygen gas occupies 22.4 dm³ at STP.

19:3 IDEAL GAS EQUATION

We are now in a position to combine all four variables concerned with the physical characteristics of gases. These variables are pressure, volume, temperature, and number of particles. Charles' law states that volume varies directly as the absolute temperature. Boyle's law states that volume varies inversely as the pressure. We have combined the two as

$$V = k'' \left(\frac{T}{P} \right), \text{ or } PV = k''T$$

The constant, k'', depends upon the number of particles present. Therefore, it will change if we add or remove molecules (if n is increased or decreased). We can write the equation using two constants, n and R, to replace the k''.

$$k'' = nR$$

therefore,

$$PV = nRT$$

The equation $PV = nRT$ is called the **ideal gas equation.** The value of the new constant R can be obtained by substituting into the equation a set of known values of n, P, V, and T. We know that standard pressure P is 101.325 kPa, molar volume V is 22.4 dm³, standard temperature T is 273 K, and the number of moles n is 1.

The ideal gas equation is $PV = nRT$.

$$(101.325 \text{ kPa})(22.4 \text{ dm}^3) = (1 \text{ mol})(R)(273 \text{ K})$$

$$R = \frac{(101.325 \text{ kPa})(22.4 \text{ dm}^3)}{(1 \text{ mol})(273 \text{ K})}$$

$$R = 8.31 \text{ dm}^3 \cdot \text{kPa/mol} \cdot \text{K}$$

This value for R is constant and can always be used if the units of the other quantities are not changed. We can determine the number of moles in a quantity of a substance by dividing its mass by its formula mass. Any problem that can be solved by this equation can also be solved by direct application of the gas laws.

R is a constant = 8.31 dm³ · kPa/mol · K

PROBLEMS

1. What pressure will be exerted by 0.300 mol of gas contained in an 8.00 dm^3 vessel at 18°C?

2. How many moles of gas will occupy a 486 cm^3 flask at 10°C and 66.7 kPa pressure?

3. What volume will be occupied by 0.362 mol of gas at 100.3 kPa and 8°C?

4. At what temperature is a gas if 0.0851 mol of it are found in a 604 cm^3 vessel at 100.4 kPa?

5. What pressure is exerted by 0.00306 mol of gas in a 25.9 cm^3 container at 9°C?

19:4   MOLECULAR MASS DETERMINATION

Molecular mass of a gas can be found from laboratory measurements.

The ideal gas equation can be used to solve a variety of problems. One type, which we will illustrate here, is the calculation of the molecular mass of a gas from laboratory measurements. Such calculations are of importance to the chemist in determining the formulas and structures of unknown compounds.

EXAMPLE: Molecular Mass from Gas Measurements

Suppose we measure the mass of the vapor of an unknown compound contained in a 273 cm^3 gas bulb. We find that the bulb contains 0.750 g of gas at 97.2 kPa pressure and 60°C. What is the molecular mass of the gas?

Solving process:

Note that this simple procedure includes an application of
Boyle's law
Charles' law
Avogadro's hypothesis
The kinetic-molecular theory
and—if the gas is collected over water—Dalton's law.

The number of moles n of a substance is equal to mass m divided by the molecular mass M. Therefore, the ideal gas equation may be written

$$PV = \frac{mRT}{M}, \text{ or } M = \frac{mRT}{PV}$$

Before we can substitute the known values into the ideal gas equation, °C must be converted to K. We get the following expression

The correct unit on an answer is a good check that the correct answer has been found.

$$\frac{\overset{m}{0.750 \text{ g}}}{\underset{P}{97.2 \text{ kPa}}} \left| \frac{\overset{R}{8.31 \text{ dm}^3 \cdot \text{kPa}}}{\text{mol} \cdot \text{K}} \right| \frac{\overset{T}{333 \text{ K}}}{\underset{V}{273 \text{ cm}^3}} \left| \frac{1000 \text{ cm}^3}{\underset{\text{conversion to dm}^3}{1 \text{ dm}^3}} \right. = 78.4 \text{ g/mol}$$

The solution is, therefore, 78.4 g/mol. Note that all other units in the problem divide out. The units remaining at the end of the problem serve as a check on the answer itself. In this problem, an answer with units of °C/kPa, or any other except g/mol, would be wrong. If we solve a problem and the units of our answer are not the units of the quantity which we set out to determine, we have made an error. The wrong units can often serve as a starting point in locating an error.

This modified form of the ideal gas equation,

$$PV = \frac{mRT}{M}$$

This equation should be memorized.

$$PV = \frac{mRT}{M}$$

may be used in many other types of problems.

PROBLEMS

6. What is the molecular mass of a gas if 372 cm^3 have mass 0.800 g at 100°C and 106.7 kPa?
7. What will be the density of oxygen at 100.5 kPa and 23°C?
8. What is the molecular mass of a gas if 6.71 g of it occupy 2.12 dm^3 at 100.4 kPa and 29°C?
9. What is the molecular mass of a gas if 0.646 g of it occupy 160 cm^3 at 105.1 kPa and 4°C?
10. What is the molecular mass of a gas if 8.11 g of it occupy 2.38 dm^3 at 109.1 kPa and 10°C?

6. 62.5 g/mol
7. 1.31 g/dm^3
8. 79.1 g/mol
9. 88.4 g/mol
10. 73.5 g/mol

19:5   MASS-GAS VOLUME RELATIONSHIPS

In Section 7:1, we discussed a method of finding the mass of one substance produced by a specific mass of another substance. It is usually awkward to measure the mass of a gas. It is easier to measure the volume under existing conditions and convert to the volume under standard conditions. One mole of gas molecules occupies 22.4 dm^3 (STP). This knowledge enables us to determine the volume of gas in a reaction by using the balanced equation for the reaction.

Stoichiometry is the quantitative study of chemical reactions.

EXAMPLE: Mass-Gas Volume

What volume of hydrogen at STP can be produced from the reaction of 6.54 grams of zinc with hydrochloric acid?

Solving process:
(a) Write a balanced equation.

$$2HCl(aq) + Zn(c) \rightarrow H_2(g) + ZnCl_2(aq)$$

A balanced equation is necessary for obtaining correct answers to chemical problems.

(b) Express the mass (6.54 g) of zinc in moles.

$$\frac{6.54 \text{ g Zn}}{} \bigg| \frac{1 \text{ mol Zn}}{65.4 \text{ g Zn}} \ldots$$

Find the number of moles of
reactant and product.

(c) Determine the mole ratio. Note that 1 mole of zinc yields 1 mole of hydrogen gas.

$$2HCl(aq) + Zn(c) \rightarrow H_2(g) + ZnCl_2(aq)$$
$$1 \text{ mole} \rightarrow 1 \text{ mole}$$

Find the moles of hydrogen produced.

$$\frac{6.54 \text{ g Zn}}{} \left| \frac{1 \text{ mol Zn}}{65.4 \text{ g Zn}} \right| \frac{1 \text{ mol H}_2}{1 \text{ mol Zn}} \cdots$$

One mole of gas occupies 22.4
dm³ at STP.

(d) Express the volume of hydrogen in terms of dm^3 of hydrogen, since 1 mole of hydrogen occupies 22.4 dm^3.

$$\frac{6.54 \text{ g Zn}}{} \left| \frac{1 \text{ mol Zn}}{65.4 \text{ g Zn}} \right| \frac{1 \text{ mol H}_2}{1 \text{ mol Zn}} \left| \frac{22.4 \text{ dm}^3}{1 \text{ mol}} \right. = 2.24 \text{ dm}^3 \text{ H}_2$$

We conclude that 2.24 dm^3 of hydrogen will be produced when 6.54 g of zinc react completely with hydrochloric acid. All mass-gas volume problems in this book can be solved in a manner similar to that shown in the Example.

Try to keep in mind the following four steps.
Step 1. *Write a balanced equation.*
Step 2. *Find the number of moles of the given substance.*
Step 3. *Find the ratio of the moles of given substance to the moles of required substance.*
Step 4. *Express moles of gas in terms of volume of gas.*
Remember that 1 mole of gas occupies 22.4 dm^3 at STP.

19:6   GAS VOLUME-MASS RELATIONSHIPS

It is also possible to determine the mass of one substance formed in a reaction when the volume of a gaseous substance is known.

EXAMPLE: Gas Volume-Mass

How many grams of NaCl can be produced by the reaction of 112 cm^3 of chlorine at STP with an excess of sodium?

Solving process:
(a) Determine the balanced equation.

$$2Na(c) + Cl_2(g) \rightarrow 2NaCl(c)$$

(b) Express the volume of chlorine as moles of chlorine at STP.

$$\frac{112 \text{ cm}^3 \text{ Cl}_2}{} \left| \frac{1 \text{ dm}^3}{1000 \text{ cm}^3} \right| \frac{1 \text{ mol Cl}_2}{22.4 \text{ dm}^3} \cdots$$

(c) Determine the mole ratio.

$$2Na(c) + Cl_2(g) \rightarrow 2NaCl(c)$$
$$1 \text{ mole} \rightarrow 2 \text{ moles}$$

$$\frac{112 \text{ cm}^3 \text{ Cl}_2}{} \left| \frac{1 \text{ dm}^3}{1000 \text{ cm}^3} \right| \frac{1 \text{ mol}}{22.4 \text{ dm}^3} \left| \frac{2 \text{ mol NaCl}}{1 \text{ mol Cl}_2} \right. \ldots$$

(d) Convert moles of NaCl to grams of NaCl (since NaCl is a solid, not a gas).

1 mole of NaCl has mass: Na 1(23.0 g) = 23.0 g
Cl 1(35.5 g) = 35.5 g
formula mass of NaCl = 58.5 g

$$\frac{112 \text{ cm}^3 \text{ Cl}_2}{} \left| \frac{1 \text{ dm}^3}{1000 \text{ cm}^3} \right| \frac{1 \text{ mol Cl}_2}{22.4 \text{ dm}^3} \left| \frac{2 \text{ mol NaCl}}{1 \text{ mol Cl}_2} \right| \frac{58.5 \text{ g NaCl}}{1 \text{ mol NaCl}} = 0.585 \text{ g NaCl}$$

We conclude that 112 cm^3 of Cl$_2$, plus enough sodium to react completely with the Cl$_2$, will yield 0.585 g of NaCl.

Note that the solution varied from the steps given in our mass-gas volume procedure. We began with gas volume and found the mass of solid produced. In the first example, we started with the mass of solid and found the volume of gas produced. However, we are still concerned with the mole relationships. The procedure followed in the second Example is

Step 1. *Write a balanced equation.*
Step 2. *Change volume of gas to moles of gas.*
Step 3. *Determine the ratio of moles of given to moles of required substance.*
Step 4. *Express moles of solid as grams of solid.*

After you have worked enough problems to become familiar with these procedures, you should be able to vary your approach to suit the problem.

PROBLEMS

11. An excess of hydrogen reacts with 14.0 grams of nitrogen. How many cm^3 of ammonia will be produced at STP?

12. How many cm^3 of hydrogen at STP will be produced from 28.0 grams of zinc with an excess of sulfuric acid?

13. Bromine will react with 5600 cm^3 of hydrogen to yield what mass of hydrogen bromide at STP?

14. How many grams of antimony(III) chloride can be produced from 6720 cm^3 of chlorine at STP reacting with an excess of antimony?

Place the conversion factor so a previous unit divides out.

You may wish to give the students the equations so that they can concentrate on the stoichiometry.

11. 22 400 cm^3 NH$_3$
12. 9590 cm^3 H$_2$
13. 40.5 g HBr
14. 45.6 g SbCl$_3$

19:7   VOLUME-VOLUME RELATIONSHIPS

The equation for the complete burning of methane is

$$CH_4(g) + 2O_2(g) \rightarrow CO_2(g) + 2H_2O(g)$$

Gas is more easily measured by volume than by mass.

Notice that all reactants and all products are gases. Gas is more easily measured by volume than by mass. Therefore, we will solve problems involving gases by converting moles to dm^3, instead of converting moles to grams.

EXAMPLE: Volume-Volume

How many dm^3 of oxygen are required to burn 1.00 dm^3 of methane? (All of these substances are gases measured at the same temperature and pressure.)

Solving process:
(a) Write a balanced equation.

$$CH_4(g) + 2O_2(g) \rightarrow CO_2(g) + 2H_2O(g)$$

(b) Change to moles.

$$\frac{1.00 \text{ dm}^3 \text{ CH}_4}{} \left| \frac{1 \text{ mol}}{22.4 \text{ dm}^3} \right. \cdots$$

In volume-volume problems, the coefficients of the balanced equation are used to determine the ratio of combining gas volumes.

(c) Determine the ratio of moles from the equation.

$$CH_4 + 2O_2 \qquad \rightarrow (\underline{\hspace{2cm}}) + (\underline{\hspace{2cm}})$$
$$1 \text{ mole} + 2 \text{ moles}$$

$$\frac{1.00 \text{ dm}^3 \text{ CH}_4}{} \left| \frac{1 \text{ mol}}{22.4 \text{ dm}^3} \right| \frac{2 \text{ mol O}_2}{1 \text{ mol CH}_4} \cdots$$

(d) Change moles to dm^3.

$$\frac{1.00 \text{ dm}^3 \text{ CH}_4}{} \left| \frac{1 \text{ mol}}{22.4 \text{ dm}^3} \right| \frac{2 \text{ mol O}_2}{1 \text{ mol CH}_4} \left| \frac{22.4 \text{ dm}^3}{1 \text{ mol}} \right. = 2.00 \text{ dm}^3 \text{ O}_2$$

We conclude that 1.00 dm^3 of methane will be completely burned by 2.00 dm^3 of O_2. This problem is no different from the gas volume-mass problems we discussed in the previous section, except that we start and end with volume.

There is an easier way to solve volume-volume problems. The volume of one mole of a solid or liquid may be larger or smaller than the volume of 1 mole of a different solid or liquid. One mole of any gas, however, occupies the same volume, 22.4 dm^3. It is, therefore, possible to eliminate the second and third steps of our procedure. We can find the ratio of moles of given to moles of required by inspecting the balanced equation.

EXAMPLE: Volume-Volume

We will solve the preceding example by a different method.

Solving process:
(a) Write a balanced equation.

$$CH_4(g) + 2O_2(g) \rightarrow CO_2(g) + 2H_2O(g)$$

(b) One mole of CH_4 unites with 2 moles of O_2, or 22.4 dm^3 of CH_4 unites with 44.8 dm^3 of O_2, or 1 dm^3 of CH_4 unites with 2 dm^3 of O_2.

The ratio of combining gas volumes is the same as the ratio of combining moles.

$$\frac{1.00 \text{ dm}^3 \text{ CH}_4}{} \left| \frac{2 \text{ dm}^3 \text{ O}_2}{1 \text{ dm}^3 \text{ CH}_4} = 2.00 \text{ dm}^3 \text{ O}_2 \right.$$

Note that the ratio of CH_4 to O_2 is 1/2, or of O_2 to CH_4 is 2/1. Both 2 and 1 are whole numbers. A fractional coefficient would indicate a fractional atom or molecule, and these do not exist.

The ratio of the combining volumes is the same as the ratio of the combining moles. Thus, you can make use of the coefficients of the balanced equation as the ratios of the combining volumes.

EXAMPLE: Volume-Volume

How many dm^3 of CO_2 will be produced by burning completely 5.00 dm^3 of ethane C_2H_6? (All of these substances are gases measured at the same temperature and pressure.)

Solving process:
(a) Write a balanced equation.

$$2C_2H_6(g) + 7O_2(g) \rightarrow 4CO_2(g) + 6H_2O(g)$$

(b) Note that 2 moles or 2 dm^3 of ethane yield 4 moles or 4 dm^3 of CO_2. Therefore,

$$\frac{5.00 \text{ dm}^3 \text{ C}_2\text{H}_6}{} \left| \frac{4 \text{ dm}^3 \text{ CO}_2}{2 \text{ dm}^3 \text{ C}_2\text{H}_6} = 10.0 \text{ dm}^3 \text{ CO}_2 \right.$$

We conclude that 5.00 dm^3 of ethane will yield 10.0 dm^3 of CO_2.

PROBLEMS

15. What volume of oxygen is required to burn completely 401 cm^3 of butane, C_4H_{10}? (All substances are gases measured at the same temperature and pressure.)

16. What volume of bromine gas is produced if 75.2 dm^3 of Cl_2 react with excess HBr? (All substances are gases measured at the same temperature and pressure.) $Cl_2(g) + 2HBr(g) \rightarrow Br_2(g) + 2HCl(g)$

15. 2610 cm^3 O_2
16. 75.2 dm^3 Br_2

17. What volume of O$_2$ is required to oxidize 500 cm^3 of NO to NO$_2$? (Assume STP.)

18. $C_6H_{14}(g) \rightarrow C_6H_6(g) + 4H_2(g)$. What volume of hydrogen is produced when 941 m^3 of C$_6$H$_6$ are produced? (All substances are gases measured at the same temperature and pressure.)

19:8 LIMITING REACTANTS

Suppose 4.00 dm^3 of hydrogen and 1.00 dm^3 of oxygen are placed in a container and ignited by means of a spark. An explosion occurs and water is formed.

$$2H_2(g) + O_2(g) \rightarrow 2H_2O(g)$$

We know that two volumes of hydrogen are all that can combine with one volume of oxygen, so 2.00 dm^3 of hydrogen are left unreacted. To take another example, let us drop nine moles of sodium into a vessel containing four moles of chlorine. If we warm the container slightly, the sodium will burn with a bright yellow flame, and crystals of sodium chloride will be formed.

$$2Na(c) + Cl_2(g) \rightarrow 2NaCl(c)$$

We know that one mole of Cl$_2$ will react completely with two moles of Na, so it is clear that one mole of sodium will remain unreacted. We say that the hydrogen and sodium are in "excess" and that the oxygen and chlorine are "limiting reactants." In a chemical reaction, the **limiting reactant** is the one which is completely consumed in the reaction. It is not present in sufficient quantity to react with all of the other reactant(s). The reactants which are left are said to be in **excess.**

A "limiting reactant" is completely used in a reaction.

Emphasize that the number of moles is the basis on which judgment is made.

EXAMPLE: Limiting Reactants

How many grams of CO$_2$ are formed if 10.0 g of carbon are burned in 20.0 dm^3 of oxygen? (Assume STP.)

Solving process:
(a) Write a balanced equation.

$$C(c) + O_2(g) \rightarrow CO_2(g)$$

(b) Change both quantities to moles.

$$\frac{10.0 \text{ g C} \mid 1 \text{ mol C}}{12.0 \text{ g}} = 0.833 \text{ mol C}$$

$$\frac{20.0 \text{ dm}^3 \text{ O}_2 \mid 1 \text{ mol O}_2}{22.4 \text{ dm}^3 \text{ O}_2} = 0.893 \text{ mol O}_2$$

(c) The equation indicates that

$$1 \text{ mole C} + 1 \text{ mole O}_2 \rightarrow 1 \text{ mole CO}_2$$

Because there are fewer moles of carbon, the carbon limits the reaction. Some oxygen (0.060 mole) is left unreacted. We call carbon the limiting reactant.

(d) Complete the problem on the basis of the limiting reactant.

$$\frac{0.833 \text{ mol C}}{} \left| \frac{1 \text{ mol CO}_2}{1 \text{ mol C}} \right| \frac{44.0 \text{ g}}{1 \text{ mol CO}_2} = 36.7 \text{ g CO}_2$$

We conclude that 10.0 g of carbon will react with excess O_2 to form 36.7 g of CO_2. Notice that in the Example, all coefficients are 1. When coefficients other than 1 are introduced, as in the following problem, an additional calculation is necessary.

EXAMPLE: Limiting Reactants

How many grams of aluminum sulfide are formed if 9.00 grams of aluminum react with 8.00 grams of sulfur?

Solving process:

(a) $\qquad\qquad 2\text{Al}(c) + 3\text{S}(c) \rightarrow \text{Al}_2\text{S}_3(c)$

(b) $\qquad \frac{9.00 \text{ g Al}}{} \left| \frac{1 \text{ mol Al}}{27.0 \text{ g Al}} \right. = 0.333 \text{ mol Al}$

2 moles Al yield 1 mole Al_2S_3.

$$\frac{0.333 \text{ mol Al}}{} \left| \frac{1 \text{ mol Al}_2\text{S}_3}{2 \text{ mol Al}} \right. = 0.167 \text{ mol Al}_2\text{S}_3$$

$$\frac{8.00 \text{ g S}}{} \left| \frac{1 \text{ mol S}}{32.1 \text{ g S}} \right. = 0.249 \text{ mol S}$$

3 moles S yield 1 mole Al_2S_3

$$\frac{0.249 \text{ mol S}}{} \left| \frac{1 \text{ mol Al}_2\text{S}_3}{3 \text{ mol S}} \right. = 0.0830 \text{ mol Al}_2\text{S}_3$$

(c) 0.0830 mole of Al_2S_3 is less than 0.167 mole of Al_2S_3. Using all of the sulfur would produce less product than using all of the aluminum. Therefore, sulfur is the limiting reactant and aluminum is in excess.

⅓ mol of Al requires ½ mol of S. Since only ¼ mol of S is available, S is the limiting reactant.

Thus, using sulfur as the limiting reactant, 0.0830 times the formula mass of aluminum sulfide will give the mass of aluminum sulfide produced.

$$\frac{0.0830 \text{ mol Al}_2\text{S}_3}{} \left| \frac{150 \text{ g Al}_2\text{S}_3}{1 \text{ mol Al}_2\text{S}_3} \right. = 12.5 \text{ g Al}_2\text{S}_3$$

12.5 g of Al_2S_3 will be produced from 8.00 g of sulfur and an excess of aluminum.

EXAMPLE: Alternate Method

An alternate method for solving this problem is as follows.

Solving process:

(a) $$2Al(c) + 3S(c) \rightarrow Al_2S_3(c)$$

(b) According to the equation, 2 moles Al require 3 moles S

$$\frac{9.00 \text{ g Al}}{} \left| \frac{1 \text{ mol Al}}{27.0 \text{ g Al}} \right| \frac{3 \text{ mol S}}{2 \text{ mol Al}} = 0.500 \text{ mol S}$$

Since we have only

$$\frac{8.00 \text{ g S}}{} \left| \frac{1 \text{ mol S}}{32.1 \text{ g S}} \right. = 0.249 \text{ mol S}$$

sulfur is the limiting reactant. If we had more than 0.500 mole of sulfur, aluminum would have been the limiting reactant.

PROBLEMS

19. $2NaBr(aq) + 2H_2SO_4(aq) + MnO_2(c) \rightarrow Br_2(l) + MnSO_4(aq) + 2H_2O(l) + Na_2SO_4(aq)$. What mass of bromine could be produced from 2.10 g of NaBr and 9.42 g of H_2SO_4?

20. $2Ca_3(PO_4)_2(c) + 6SiO_2(c) + 10C(c) \rightarrow P_4(g) + 6CaSiO_3(c) + 10CO(g)$. What volume of carbon monoxide gas is produced from 4.14 g $Ca_3(PO_4)_2$ and 1.20 g SiO_2? (Assume STP.)

21. $H_2S(g) + I_2(aq) \rightarrow 2HI(aq) + S(c)$. What mass of sulfur is produced by 4.11 g of I_2 and 317 cm³ of H_2S at STP?

22. $2Cl_2(g) + HgO(c) \rightarrow HgCl_2(c) + Cl_2O(g)$. What volume of Cl_2O can be produced from 116 cm³ of Cl_2 at STP and 7.62 g HgO?

19:9 NONSTANDARD CONDITIONS

It is important to keep in mind when working problems of the type described in Sections 19:5 through 19:8 that pressure and temperature affect the volume of a gas. Thus, the equality 22.4 dm³ = 1 mol is true only at STP. If a problem involves a gas under conditions other than standard conditions, it is necessary, before changing gas volume to moles of gas, to calculate the gas volume under standard conditions. The secret to success in these problems is to remember that the central step (moles of given to moles of requested) must take place at STP. Thus, if you are given a volume of gas at other than STP, you must convert to STP before performing the moles to moles step in the solving process. On the other hand, if you are requested to find the volume of a gas at conditions other than STP, you must convert the volume after the moles to moles step. Let us look at some examples.

Problems must be reviewed for conditions other than STP.

EXAMPLE: Mass-Gas Volume

What volume of chlorine gas at 24°C and 99.2 kPa would be required to react with 2.51 g of silver according to the equation

$$2Ag(c) + Cl_2(g) \rightarrow 2AgCl(c)$$

Solving process:

In order to solve this problem, we calculate the volume needed at STP, then we convert to the conditions stated. The solution is

$$\frac{2.51 \text{ g Ag}}{} \left| \frac{1 \text{ mol Ag}}{108 \text{ g Ag}} \right| \frac{1 \text{ mol Cl}_2}{2 \text{ mol Ag}} \left| \frac{22.4 \text{ dm}^3 \text{ Cl}_2}{1 \text{ mol Cl}_2} \right| \frac{297 \text{ K}}{273 \text{ K}} \left| \frac{101.3 \text{ kPa}}{99.2 \text{ kPa}} \right. = 0.289 \text{ dm}^3 \text{ Cl}_2$$

Students need to be reminded that corrections are not needed if the mass of the gas is used instead of the volume.

Must be at STP if a gas is involved in a mass-volume problem.

EXAMPLE: Gas Volume-Mass

What mass of mercury(II) chloride will react with 0.567 dm^3 of ammonia at 27°C and 102.7 kPa according to the equation

$$HgCl_2(aq) + 2NH_3(ag) \rightarrow Hg(NH_2)Cl(c) + NH_4Cl(aq)?$$

Solving process:

In this problem, we must change the volume of ammonia to standard conditions before converting it to moles. The solution is

Must be at STP if a gas is involved in a mass-volume problem.

$$\frac{0.567 \text{ dm}^3 \text{ NH}_3}{} \left| \frac{273 \text{ K}}{300 \text{ K}} \right| \frac{102.7 \text{ kPa}}{101.3 \text{ kPa}} \left| \frac{1 \text{ mol NH}_3}{22.4 \text{ dm}^3 \text{ NH}_3} \right| \frac{1 \text{ mol HgCl}_2}{2 \text{ mol NH}_3} \left| \frac{271 \text{ g HgCl}_2}{1 \text{ mol HgCl}_2} \right.$$

= 3.16 g HgCl$_2$

The same procedure can be used to solve limiting reactant problems. If one of the given materials is a gas at other than STP, its volume must be converted to STP before computing the number of moles in the sample. If the answer to the problem is the volume of a gas at other than STP, the volume must be computed at STP and then converted to the required conditions.

In solving volume-volume problems, the situation is changed slightly. Suppose both original and final gas volumes are measured at the same temperature and pressure. We would first correct the volumes to STP and then convert back to the original conditions. The corrections would all divide out. Thus, as long as the temperature and pressure remain the same, a volume-volume problem need not be worked at STP.

A volume-volume problem need not be worked at STP as long as the temperature and pressure do not change.

EXAMPLE: Volume-Volume (standard conditions)

What volume of oxygen at 100°C and 105.5 kPa is required to burn 684 m^3 of methane at the same temperature and pressure according to the equation $CH_4(g) + 2O_2(g) \rightarrow CO_2(g) + 2H_2O(g)$?

Solving process:

This procedure is observed because we do not convert to
moles.

$$\frac{684 \text{ m}^3 \text{ CH}_4 \quad \left| \quad 2 \text{ m}^3 \text{ O}_2 \right.}{1 \text{ m}^3 \text{ CH}_4} = 1370 \text{ m}^3 \text{ O}_2$$

What happens if the given substance in a volume-volume problem is at a different temperature and pressure from the required substance? The volume of the given substance must then be changed to correspond to the conditions of the required substance. The problem may now be solved as a regular volume-volume problem.

EXAMPLE: Volume-Volume

What volume of oxygen at 26°C and 102.5 kPa is required to burn 684 m^3 of methane at 100°C and 107.5 kPa?

Solving process:

$$\frac{684 \text{ m}^3 \text{ CH}_4 \quad \left| \quad 299 \text{ K} \quad \right| \quad 107.5 \text{ kPa} \quad \left| \quad 2 \text{ m}^3 \text{ O}_2 \right.}{373 \text{ K} \quad \left| \quad 102.5 \text{ kPa} \quad \right| \quad 1 \text{ m}^3 \text{ CH}_4} = 1150 \text{ m}^3 \text{ O}_2$$

19:10   GASES AND WORK

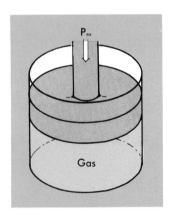

FIGURE 19-3. The compression or expansion of the gas depends on the external pressure on the piston.

$w > 0$ when gas does work on its surroundings (expansion).

$w < 0$ when work is done on the gas (compression).

Consider a gas confined in a cylinder containing a friction-less piston, as shown in Figure 19-3. If the external pressure (P_{ex}) on the piston is greater than the gas pressure, the gas will be compressed. Compression will cease when the internal gas pressure has risen enough to equal the external pressure. When such a change occurs, work has been done on the confined gas. In the same way, if the internal pressure exceeds the external pressure, the gas will expand. In that case, the gas has done work on its surroundings.

This work is represented by w which is a symbol for the work done by the gas. Thus, if the gas does work on its surroundings, w will be a positive quantity. On the other hand, if work is done on the gas (as in the first example), w will be a negative quantity.

The actual amount of work done by or on a gas depends on the conditions under which expansion or contraction takes place. Specifically, w depends upon whether the volume change occurred in an adiabatic system or an **isothermal** (constant temperature) system. It also depends upon the difference between the external and internal pressures during the change.

Chemists define a reversible expansion or contraction of a gas as an ideal change. Specifically, the change takes place be-cause of an infinitesimal pressure difference between the internal and external pressure. If the pressure difference is infinitesimal, then the process would take infinitely long! Reversible changes do not occur in practice, but they are convenient to use to find the ideal amount of work in a change. In actual practice we deal with irreversible changes.

Consider an isothermal reversible change in pressure or volume. Such a change represents the maximum work attainable from a system (or the minimum work to be done on a system). This work may be found from

$$w = -2.303\,nRT \, log \, \frac{V_2}{V_1} = -2.303\,nRT \, log \, \frac{P_1}{P_2}$$

use $R = 8.31$ J/mol·K

A type of ideal change often approached in the laboratory is an adiabatic reversible change where

$$w = C_v \Delta T$$

where C_v is the heat capacity at constant volume. For an ideal gas C_v does not vary with temperature.

The most practical change is the irreversible change against a constant pressure, for example, the atmosphere. In that case

$$w = -P_{ex} \Delta V.$$

The important factor to keep in mind about gases and work is that the work done by or on a gas will change the total energy of the gas. Only when a chemist takes into consideration this energy change can a change in a gas be completely described.

Work done by or on a gas will change the total energy of the gas.

You may have to review the use of logarithms before assigning these problems. See Appendix B.

PROBLEMS

23. One mole of gas at 25°C expands from 9.92 dm³ to 44.5 dm³. What work does the gas do on the surroundings if the expansion takes place
    a. as an isothermal reversible change?
    b. against a constant external pressure of 10.0 kPa?

24. A gas expands by an adiabatic reversible change. The heat capacity (constant volume) of the gas is 12.5 J/mol·K. The change causes a decrease in temperature of 8.48 K. What work is done by the gas?

25. At 98°C and 30.0 kPa, 1.80 mol of gas expands from 0.492 m³ to 0.151 m³. What work does the gas do on the surroundings?

26. A gas expands by an adiabatic reversible change. The heat capacity of the gas is 34.2 J/mol·K. This change causes a temperature change of 80.0 K. What work is done by the gas?

23. a. −3720 J
    b. −346 J
    Note: kPa·dm³ = J
24. 106 J/mol
25. 6230 J
26. 2740 J/mol

Amadeo Avogadro (1776–1856)

The theories of Amadeo Avogadro were overlooked due to the short-sightedness of his compatriots. He is best known for his hypothesis that equal volumes of gases, under identical conditions of pressure and temperature, contain the same number of molecules. However, this hypothesis was discounted by the scientific community until very late in his lifetime.

He also carried out investigations in other areas of science. Avogadro was particularly interested in electricity and heat. He investigated the effects of varying amounts of heat on the temperature of a substance. These experiments led him to measure the expansion of substances when heated and the pressure of the vapor of mercury at various temperatures.

CHEMICAL TECHNOLOGY: Chemicals from the Sea

Commercial production of chemicals from seawater is currently limited to bromine, magnesium, salt, natural gas, petroleum, and sulfur. The ocean and its underlying crust contain a wealth of minerals. Obtaining most of these substances, however, has not been economically feasible. Now that we face exhaustion of some land resources, scientists are seeking ways of recovering the wealth of the sea and its basins.

Seafloor sand and gravel is being dredged in coastal regions. These materials are used in the building industry, highway construction, and railroad track maintenance.

Ocean mining involves some formidable problems. The average depth of the ocean is 4400 meters! Many of the rich deposit areas exist along the ocean floor rather than near the coasts. Special equipment must be designed to withstand corrosion as well as the tremendous pressures that exist at these depths. In spite of these problems, there is great interest in ocean mining. A particularly rich mineral area exists on the eastern Pacific Ocean floor, just north of the equator. Mining in this area concerns a scattering of potato-sized lumps of metal oxides. The principal elements present are manganese and iron, and the lumps are usually referred to as manganese nodules. Not only is manganese a valuable product itself, but the nodules also contain cobalt, copper, and nickel in quantities sufficient to recover.

A number of companies and countries have developed undersea mining capabilities to recover these nodules. The costs are enormous. Mineral recovery from beneath the sea costs two to three hundred times as much as recovery of the same mineral on land. A political issue may develop in deciding to whom these ocean floor deposits belong.

One method for mining the nodules consists of a long cable lined with huge buckets. The cable looks like a huge necklace suspended from the ore ship. The ship dredges the ocean floor as nodules and other sediment fill the buckets. The cable is cycled continuously through the ship to unload the mined materials. Other methods, using hydraulic pumps are also being investigated.

The near future will probably show a significant increase in coastal mining for minerals that have washed down rivers to the sea. Such operations are being used to mine diamonds, tin ore, gold, and other dense minerals. These deposits are easier to recover in that they can be obtained by dredging shallow coastal areas.

Obtaining petroleum from the sea is now an essential industry. The first offshore oil drilling occurred off the Louisiana coast in 1945. Now over one hundred companies are engaged in exploration and drilling in all parts of the world. As with mineral mining, the construction costs are enormous. However, due to increasing import costs and rising demand, offshore drilling is still economically feasible even though it may take some time to reach the break-even point.

Most early exploration and drilling occurred in shallow waters adjacent to onshore fields. Drilling operations were conducted from platforms built-up from the seafloor. As petroleum demand further increased, open sea drilling became more common.

A new technology has developed to cope with the problems associated with deep ocean work. Various platform designs are necessary to maintain stability under hazardous weather conditions. The condition of the ocean floor as well as the depth of the well are also important considerations in design. Special diving equipment has been developed to allow divers to work at various depths in completing and maintaining a well. If the composition of the gas mixture divers breathe is carefully controlled, they can remain submerged in special pressure chambers for up to a week.

Engineers are experimenting with designs for undersea drilling stations. These stations would be totally enclosed and contain living quarters for personnel.

It is obvious that the ocean contains a number of important resources that will be a significant part of resource utilization and technological development in the future.

SUMMARY

1. Avogadro's principle: *At equal temperatures and pressures, equal volumes of gases contain equal numbers of molecules.*　19:1
2. The molar volume of a gas is the volume occupied by 1 mole of the gas at STP; its value is 22.4 dm^3 for all gases.　19:2
3. The ideal gas equation is $PV = nRT$, where P = pressure, V = volume, n = number of moles, R = a constant, and T = kelvin temperature.　19:3
4. The molecular mass of a gas may be determined by using a modified form of the ideal gas equation.　19:4
5. A limiting reactant is a reactant which is completely consumed in a reaction. Any remaining reactants are said to be in excess.　19:8
6. In solving problems involving gas volumes, consideration must be given 19:9 to the change of gas volume with change in pressure and temperature.
19:10 7. A gas which expands or is compressed does work or has work done on it.

PROBLEMS

27. 99.7 kPa
28. 39.6 g/mol
29. 20.0 dm^3 CO_2
30. 35.0 dm^3 O_2
31. 14.0 dm^3 SO_2
32. 0.313 mol CO_2
33. 11.4 g NiS
34. 8.23 g $Ca(OH)_2$
35. 58.5 g NaCl
36. 6.72 dm^3 CO_2
37. 7.16 dm^3 CO_2

27. What pressure will be exerted by 0.400 mole of a gas in a 10.0 dm^3 vessel at 27°C?

28. What is the molecular mass of a gas if 500 cm^3 have a mass of 1.00 g at −23°C and 105.0 kPa?

29. The burning of ethane (C_2H_6) produces CO_2 and water vapor as the only products. 10.0 dm^3 of ethane would produce how many dm^3 of CO_2? (All substances are gases measured at the same temperature and pressure.)

30. How many dm^3 of O_2 would be required for the completion of the reaction described in Problem 29?

31. Carbon disulfide will burn to produce CO_2 and SO_2. How many dm^3 of SO_2 at STP can be produced from 7.00 dm^3 of CS_2 vapor?

32. How many moles of CO_2 would be produced in Problem 31?

33. How many grams of nickel(II) sulfide can be produced by the reaction of 10.0 g of nickel with 4.00 g of sulfur?

34. 7.00 grams of CaO react with 2.00 g of water. How many grams of calcium hydroxide will be formed?

35. How many grams of sodium chloride could be produced from the reaction of 23.0 g of sodium with 22.4 dm^3 of chlorine?

36. Using the equation $Fe_2O_3(c) + 3CO(g) \rightarrow 2Fe(c) + 3CO_2(g)$, determine how many dm^3 of CO_2 at STP can be produced from 16.0 g of Fe_2O_3 and 10.0 dm^3 of CO.

37. In Problem 36, if the gas were collected at 27°C and 104.5 kPa pressure, what volume would it occupy?

38. What would be the density of the CO_2 gas collected under the conditions stated in Problem 37?

39. At 31°C and 60.0 kPa, 0.638 mol of gas expands from 10.1 dm^3 to 23.3 dm^3. What work does the gas do on the surroundings?

40. A gas expands by an adiabatic reversible change. The heat capacity of the gas is 20.8 J/mol·K. This change causes a temperature change of 91.1 K. What work is done by the gas?

38. 1.84 g/dm³
39. −1350 J
40. 1.90 × 10³ J/mol

REVIEW

1. If a sample of gas occupies 642 cm^3 at 93.9 kPa, what volume will it occupy at 109.0 kPa if the temperature remains constant?

2. If a sample of gas collected over water at 50°C occupies 62.5 cm^3 at a total pressure of 114.9 kPa, what volume will the dry gas occupy at 50°C and 97.8 kPa?

3. If a sample of gas occupies 286 cm^3 at 98.1 kPa and 42°C, what volume will it occupy at 42.2 kPa and 60°C?

4. Compute the relative rates of diffusion for oxygen and argon at the same temperature.

5. What is the density of a gas at STP if 1.34 g of the gas occupy 343 cm^3 at 24°C and 99.0 kPa?

6. Define an ideal gas. The particles of an ideal gas occupy zero volume and have no attractive forces.

7. Compute the ratio of the velocity of hydrogen molecules to helium atoms at the same temperature.

8. Compute the ratio of the velocity of neon atoms to nitrogen molecules at the same temperature.

9. If 60.0 dm^3 of gas at 7°C are heated to 312°C, what is the new volume of the gas (pressure is constant)?

1. 553 cm³
2. 65.6 cm³
3. 703 cm³
4. 1.12 O₂/Ar
5. 4.35 g/dm³

7. 1.41 H₂/He
8. 1.18 Ne/N₂
9. 125 dm³

ONE MORE STEP

1. Investigate the part played by Cannizzaro in gaining acceptance for Avogadro's principle.

2. Molecular masses of materials are often found today by using a mass spectrograph, which we have already discussed (Chapter 8). Find out how a "time-of-flight" spectrometer works.

3. How would knowledge of chemistry help an iron foundry?

4. If a student performs an experiment to determine the molecular mass of a gaseous compound using the modified ideal gas equation, $M = mRT/PV$, and forgets to correct for the fact that the gas was collected over water, would the results be high or low?

5. How much work is done by a gas which expands against zero external pressure?

A volcanic eruption can be considered an exothermic reaction. This activity is the result of a surplus of energy within the earth. The expulsion of this energy puts the volcano at a lower energy and a higher degree of disorder. When these states are achieved the volcanic activity stops. The occurrence of a chemical reaction depends on the energy and disorder of the reactants and products. What conditions are necessary for a reaction to occur? How can these conditions be altered to obtain products which are higher in energy than the reactants? How does disorder affect a reaction?

Alpha

ENERGY AND DISORDER

20

Chapter 20 introduces the student to thermodynamics through a study of state functions.

Demonstration—The thermite reaction demonstrates the energy associated with a chemical reaction. See the Teacher's Guide for preparation details.

In the last several chapters, we have been studying macroscopic amounts of matter. We have been interested in physical properties and physical changes. Where chemical reactions were involved, we looked at the quantitative relationships among the reactants and products. Now, we will consider what makes reactions occur.

We have noted that reactions which are exothermic generally take place spontaneously (without help). On the other hand, those that are endothermic are generally not spontaneous. In everyday life, we can see that changes in nature are usually "downhill." That is, nature tends to go from a state of higher energy to one of lower energy. Also, natural processes tend to go from an orderly state to a disorderly one. However, there are some exceptions.

How is it possible for products to form which are at a higher energy or a more ordered state than the reactants? In this chapter we will find the answer to such questions. However, keep in mind that unless otherwise stated we will be concerned with reactions taking place at constant temperature and pressure. Reactions taking place at a constant temperature are isothermal processes. Reactions that take place at constant pressure are **isobaric processes.**

20:1 ENTHALPY

In Chapter 7, the term enthalpy (H) was defined as heat content. Chemists often work with the change in the enthalpy of a system. The change in enthalpy or heat content is given the symbol ΔH. In an exothermic reaction, the products have less heat content than the reactants. ΔH is therefore negative. In an endothermic reaction, ΔH is positive.

GOAL: You will gain an understanding of the relationship among entropy, enthalpy, and free energy and their effect on chemical reactions.

Natural processes:
High energy → low energy
Order → disorder

Isothermal: Constant temperature
Isobaric: Constant pressure

Remind students that ΔH values are relative: The free elements are taken to have $\Delta H_f° = 0$.

Change in enthalpy = ΔH

Exothermic: $\Delta H < 0$
Endothermic: $\Delta H > 0$

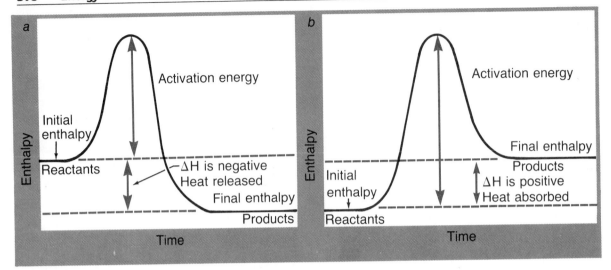

FIGURE 20-1. The products of an exothermic reaction (a) are lower in energy than the reactants. The products of an endothermic reaction (b) are higher in energy than the reactants.

Demonstration — A simple demonstration of a change where energy is absorbed can be done by pouring 25 cm³ of water into a 150 cm³ beaker half full of NH_4NO_3.

FIGURE 20-2. The billiard balls can be used as a model to show that processes tend to go from an ordered to disordered state.

20:2 ENTROPY

Highly exothermic reactions tend to take place spontaneously. However, weak exothermic and endothermic reactions can also occur spontaneously. Sometimes these reactions will proceed under stronger reaction conditions such as a temperature increase.

Consider the reaction of steam on very hot carbon to form carbon monoxide and hydrogen.

$$C(c) + H_2O(g) + energy \rightarrow H_2(g) + CO(g)$$

The products have a higher heat content than the reactants. Therefore, since heat energy is absorbed in this process, ΔH is positive. It has been determined experimentally that if 1 mole of carbon reacts with 1 mole of steam then, $\Delta H = 131$ kJ. We have observed in previous sections that most spontaneous reactions seem to have negative ΔH. Since ΔH is positive in this reaction, some additional factor must be at work.

This additional factor is the degree of disorder or **entropy**. We have seen in Chapter 16 that there is a very orderly arrangement of atoms in crystalline solids. In liquids, there is somewhat less order. Gases lack any orderly arrangement. The degree of disorder, or entropy, is represented by the symbol S.

Change in entropy is symbolized as ΔS. A positive value for ΔS means an increase in the degree of disorder. That is to say, the system becomes less ordered. Such a change (positive ΔS) occurs when a solid is converted to a liquid or a gas. When the opposite reaction occurs (liquid or gas is converted to a solid), ΔS is negative.

20:3 FREE ENERGY

The combination of H and S is called **free energy**. It is represented by G; thus, ΔG represents the change in free energy. These quantities are defined by the following relationships.

$$G = H - TS$$

$$\Delta G = \Delta H - T\Delta S$$

where T is the temperature in kelvin (absolute temperature).

It can be shown, both by theory and by experiment, that in a spontaneous change, ΔG is always negative. If a reaction takes place at low temperatures and involves little change in entropy, then the term $T\Delta S$ will be negligible. In such a reaction ΔG is largely a function of ΔH, the change in enthalpy. Thus, most reactions occurring at room temperature have a negative ΔH.

Highly endothermic reactions can occur only if $T\Delta S$ is large. Thus, the temperature is high, or there is a large increase in entropy. In the endothermic reaction of carbon with steam, both of these conditions occur. ΔS is positive because the orderly arrangement of carbon in the solid is converted to the disorderly

You may also wish to present the concept of entropy in terms of probability.

Entropy (S) is a measure of disorder in a system.

Increase in disorder:
$$\Delta S > 0$$
Decrease in disorder:
$$\Delta S < 0$$

Entropy, S, is derived from the second law of thermodynamics by Clausius, in 1850 (places limits on conversion of heat into work, forbids perpetual motion).

Change in free energy = ΔG

The term ΔG is often called Gibbs free energy. Josiah Gibbs (see page 407) was the first to suggest that any reaction which can do useful work at a constant temperature and pressure is spontaneous.

Spontaneous reaction:
$$\Delta G < 0$$

Endothermic reactions occur when $T\Delta S$ is large.

FIGURE 20-3. In the formation of CO_2, the degree of disorder increases resulting in a positive entropy change for the reaction.

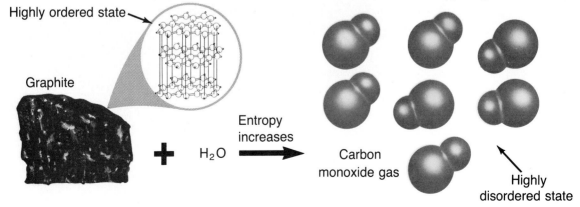

Highly ordered state

Graphite

$+$ H_2O → Entropy increases

Carbon monoxide gas

Highly disordered state

arrangement in CO gas. T is high because the reaction only takes place at red heat (600-900°C) or higher. If the temperature decreases, the reaction stops and goes into reverse.

If ΔH and ΔS have the same sign, there will be some temperature at which ΔH and $T \Delta S$ will be numerically equal, and ΔG will be exactly zero. This state is the thermodynamic definition of a system in equilibrium. At equilibrium, the value of the free energy G, not ΔG, is at a minimum for the system.

All spontaneous processes proceed toward equilibrium. For example, a ball rolls down a hill and not up. The bottom of the hill is where the ball has the least potential energy. Chemical potential energy, technically called free energy, is least when a system is at equilibrium.

An interesting result of the entropy contribution to the free energy equation is that molecules like H_2, O_2, and N_2, which are stable on earth, do not exist on the sun and stars. To see why they do not consider the case of N_2. In order to decompose one mole of N_2 molecules, much energy must be supplied.

$$N_2 + energy \rightarrow 2N \qquad energy = \Delta H = +941 \text{ kJ}$$

Since ΔH has such a large positive value, at ordinary temperatures N_2 is a very stable molecule. This stability is a direct result of $T \Delta S$ being small in comparison to the large positive ΔH (which makes ΔG positive). A gas composed of separate nitrogen atoms has a greater entropy than one made of N_2 molecules. The pairing of nitrogen atoms is a kind of order. Therefore, the decomposition of these molecules represents an increase in entropy (a positive ΔS). If N_2 molecules are exposed to higher temperatures (like those near the sun), the value of $T \Delta S$ is greater than 941 kJ and thus ΔG is negative. As a result, nitrogen exists near the sun only as discrete atoms.

FIGURE 20-4. Nitrogen exists as discrete atoms near the stars rather than as molecules.

Reproduced by permission from the Hale Observatories

20:4   STANDARD STATES

All three quantities (enthalpy, entropy, and free energy) depend on temperature. Thus, chemists have had to agree on a standard set of conditions for measuring these quantities. The conditions chosen are 298.15 K and 101.325 kPa. The pressure is specified because the quantities also depend on pressure in some reactions.

Enthalpy, entropy, and free energy depend on temperature.

Standard thermodynamic measurement conditions: 298 K and 101.325 kPa.

You may wish to introduce the concept of "state functions" here. A state function of a system depends only upon the physical state of the system and not how the system arrived at that state.

20:5   CALCULATIONS ON FREE ENERGY

Appendix A-6 lists the standard free energies of formation (ΔG_f°), enthalpies of formation (ΔH_f°), and entropies (S°) of some substances. The superscript "$^\circ$" shows these values have been obtained for standard conditions. The subscript "$_f$" shows they are values for the formation of one mole of the compound from the elements. We already know from Chapter 7 that the enthalpy change for a reaction is found by

$$\Delta H^\circ_{(reaction)} = \Delta H_f^\circ{}_{(products)} - \Delta H_f^\circ{}_{(reactants)}$$

In a like manner, we may compute the free energy and entropy changes for a reaction.

$$\Delta G^\circ_{(reaction)} = \Delta G_f^\circ{}_{(products)} - \Delta G_f^\circ{}_{(reactants)}$$

$$\Delta S^\circ_{(reaction)} = S^\circ{}_{(products)} - S^\circ{}_{(reactants)}$$

EXAMPLE: *Entropy Change*

What is the change in entropy for the reaction between methane and oxygen under standard measurement conditions. The equation for the reaction is $CH_4(g) + 2O_2(g) \rightarrow CO_2(g) + 2H_2O(l)$.

Solving process:

(a) It is best to organize the data you will use from Appendix A-6 into a table.

More extensive tables are available in many reference books, e.g. *The Handbook of Chemistry and Physics.*

Value	CH$_4$	O$_2$	CO$_2$	H$_2$O
ΔG_f° (kJ/mol)	−50.8	0	−394.4	−237
ΔH_f° (kJ/mol)	−74.8	0	−393.5	−286
ΔS° (J/mol K)	186	205.0	214	70.0

(b) To find ΔG use the following equations. It is important to have a balanced chemical equation.

$$\Delta G^\circ_{(reaction)} = \Delta G_f^\circ{}_{(products)} - \Delta G_f^\circ{}_{(reactants)}$$

$$[CO_2 + 2H_2O] - [2O_2 + CH_4]$$

Multiply each ΔG_f° by the number of moles from the balanced equation. Substitute these values into the equation used to determine ΔG°(reaction).

$$\frac{1 \text{ mol } CO_2}{} \left| \frac{(-394.4 \text{ kJ})}{\text{mol } CO_2} \right. = -394.4 \text{ kJ}$$

$$\frac{2 \text{ mol } H_2O}{} \left| \frac{(-237 \text{ kJ})}{\text{mol } H_2O} \right. = -474.4 \text{ kJ}$$

$$\frac{2 \text{ mol } O_2}{} \left| \frac{0 \text{ kJ}}{\text{mol } O_2} \right. = 0$$

$$\frac{1 \text{ mol } CH_4}{} \left| \frac{(-50.8 \text{ kJ})}{\text{mol } CH_4} \right. = -50.8 \text{ kJ}$$

ΔG°(reaction) $= [(-394.4 \text{ kJ}) + (-474.4 \text{ kJ})] - [(0) + (-50.8 \text{ kJ})]$

ΔG°(reaction) $= -818 \text{ kJ}$

(c) To find ΔH°:

$$\Delta H^\circ_{(reaction)} = \Delta H_f^\circ_{(products)} - \Delta H_f^\circ_{(reactants)}$$

$$[CO_2 + 2H_2O] - [2O_2 + CH_4]$$

Multiply each ΔH_f° by the number of moles from the balanced equation.

$$\frac{1 \text{ mol } CO_2}{} \left| \frac{(-393.5 \text{ kJ})}{\text{mol } CO_2} \right. = -393.5 \text{ kJ}$$

$$\frac{2 \text{ mol } H_2O}{} \left| \frac{(-286 \text{ kJ})}{\text{mol } H_2O} \right. = -572 \text{ kJ}$$

$$\frac{2 \text{ mol } O_2}{} \left| \frac{0 \text{ kJ}}{\text{mol } O_2} \right. = 0$$

$$\frac{1 \text{ mol } CH_4}{} \left| \frac{(-74.8 \text{ kJ})}{\text{mol } CH_4} \right. = -74.8 \text{ kJ}$$

ΔH°(reaction) $= [(-393.5 \text{ kJ}) + (-572 \text{ kJ})] - [(0) + (-74.8 \text{ kJ})]$

ΔH°(reaction) $= -891 \text{ kJ}$

(d) To find ΔS°:

$$S^\circ = -\frac{(\Delta G^\circ - \Delta H^\circ)}{T}$$

$$T = 25^\circ C + 273 = 298 \text{ K}$$

$$\Delta S^\circ = -\left[\frac{(-818 \text{ kJ}) - (-891 \text{ kJ})}{298 \text{ K}} \right] \left[\frac{(1000 \text{ J})}{1 \text{ kJ}} \right]$$

$$\Delta S^\circ = -245 \text{ J/K}$$

(e) We can check the entropy change by using the standard entropies.

$$\Delta S^\circ_{(reaction)} = S^\circ_{(products)} - S^\circ_{(reactants)}$$
$$[CO_2 + 2H_2O] - [2O_2 + CH_4]$$

Multiply each S° by the number of moles from the balanced equation.

$$\dfrac{1 \text{ mol } CO_2}{} \; \left| \; \dfrac{214 \text{ J}}{\text{mol} \cdot \text{K } CO_2} \right. = 214 \text{ J/K}$$

$$\dfrac{2 \text{ mol } H_2O}{} \; \left| \; \dfrac{70.0 \text{ J}}{\text{mol} \cdot \text{K } H_2O} \right. = 140 \text{ J/K}$$

$$\dfrac{2 \text{ mol } O_2}{} \; \left| \; \dfrac{205.0 \text{ J}}{\text{mol} \cdot \text{K } O_2} \right. = 410.0 \text{ J/K}$$

$$\dfrac{1 \text{ mol } CH_4}{} \; \left| \; \dfrac{186 \text{ J}}{\text{mol} \cdot \text{K } CH_4} \right. = 186 \text{ J/K}$$

$$\Delta S^\circ = [(214 \text{ J/K}) + (140 \text{ J/K})] - [(410.0 \text{ J/K}) + (186 \text{ J/K})]$$
$$\Delta S^\circ = -242 \text{ J/K}$$

EXAMPLE: Unknown Property

What is the standard entropy of bismuth(III) sulfide? Use the equations: $2Bi(c) + 3S(c) \rightarrow Bi_2S_3(c)$ and $\Delta G = \Delta H - T\Delta S$.

Solving process:
(a) Organize your data.

Value	Bi	S	Bi$_2$S$_3$
ΔG_f° (kJ/mol)	0	0	−164
ΔH_f° (kJ/mol)	0	0	−183
S° (J/mol · K)	56.9	31.9	?

(b) To find ΔG°:

$$\Delta G^\circ = \dfrac{1 \text{ mol } Bi_2S_3}{} \; \left| \; \dfrac{(-164 \text{ kJ})}{\text{mol } Bi_2S_3} \right. = -164 \text{ kJ}$$

Spontaneous reaction:
$\Delta G < 0$

(c) To find ΔH°:

$$\Delta H^\circ = \dfrac{1 \text{ mol } Bi_2S_3}{} \; \left| \; \dfrac{(-183 \text{ kJ})}{\text{mol } Bi_2S_3} \right. = -183 \text{ kJ}$$

Exothermic reaction:
$\Delta H < 0$

(d) To find ΔS°:

$$\Delta S^\circ = -\dfrac{(\Delta G^\circ - \Delta H^\circ)}{T} \text{ where } T = 298 \text{ K}$$

Decrease in disorder:
$\Delta S < 0$

$$\Delta S^\circ = \left[\frac{(+164 \text{ kJ}) - (-183 \text{ kJ})}{298 \text{ K}} \right] \left[\frac{1000 \text{ J}}{1 \text{ kJ}} \right] = -63.8 \text{ J/K}$$

(e) To find $S^\circ \text{ Bi}_2\text{S}_3$

$$\Delta S^\circ = S^\circ \text{ Bi}_2\text{S}_3$$

$$\left[\left(\frac{2 \text{ mol Bi}}{} \middle| \frac{56.9 \text{ J}}{\text{mol} \cdot \text{K Bi}} \right) + \left(\frac{3 \text{ mol S}}{} \middle| \frac{31.9 \text{ J}}{\text{mol} \cdot \text{K S}} \right) \right]$$

$S^\circ \text{ Bi}_2\text{S}_3 = \Delta S^\circ + 113.8 \text{ J/K} + 95.7 \text{ J/K}$

$\qquad = (-63.8 \text{ J/K}) + (113.8 \text{ J/K}) + (95.7 \text{ J/K}) = 146 \text{ J/K}$

By checking with Appendix A-6, we can verify that the answer is correct.

PROBLEMS

1. -47 kJ, yes
2. -542 kJ, yes
3. 26 800 J/K
4. 204 kJ

1. Compute the free energy change for the reaction
$$\text{BaCl}_2(aq) + \text{H}_2\text{SO}_4(aq) \rightarrow \text{BaSO}_4(c) + 2\text{HCl}(aq)$$
Is the reaction spontaneous?

2. Compute the free energy change for the reaction
$$2\text{HF}(g) \rightarrow \text{H}_2(g) + \text{F}_2(g)$$
Is the reaction spontaneous?

3. Compute S° for Ca(OH)_2 from the reaction
$$\text{Ca}(c) + 2\text{H}_2\text{O}(l) \rightarrow \text{Ca(OH)}_2(c) + \text{H}_2(g)$$

4. Compute ΔG_f° for H from the reaction
$$\text{H}_2(g) \rightarrow 2\text{H}(g)$$

20:6   ENERGY

We have learned (Section 1:5) that energy can be changed from one form to another. For example, under the proper conditions, energy may be converted to work. Recall the law of conservation of energy. The total amount of energy in an isolated system (such as the universe) remains constant except for nuclear changes.

Work can also be converted into energy. For instance, work is done in moving a book from the floor to a table. The book's energy is increased by an amount equal to the work done on it. It has a greater potential energy on the table than on the floor.

If a system undergoes a change, its internal energy changes according to the equation.

$$\Delta E = q - w$$

In this equation, q is defined as the heat received from the surroundings, and w is the work performed by the system on the

FIGURE 20-5. As the book is raised from the floor to the table, it gains potential energy.

Hickson-Bender Photography

surroundings. In the last chapter, we saw that expansion or compression of a gas involved work. Another common form of work in chemistry is generation or consumption of electricity. ΔE is the internal energy change. In changing, a system is said to go from one state to another state. Usually, there is more than one path from state 1 to state 2.

For example, consider the change of a definite quantity of liquid water at 100°C to steam at 104°C. One way of accomplishing such a change is to heat the water at constant pressure so that it boils at 100°C and continue heating until the steam reaches 104°C. An alternate path is to increase the pressure on the water to 116.7 kPa and heat. At that pressure water boils at 104°C. Thus, the liquid water is heated to 104°C and then vaporized to steam. The pressure is then reduced to 101.3 kPa.

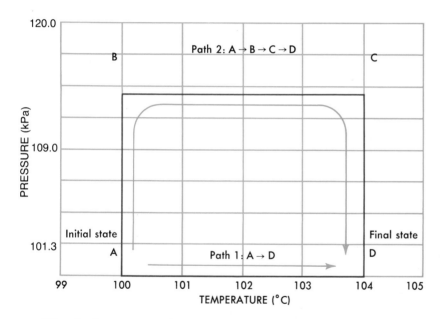

FIGURE 20-6. The overall change in internal energy remains the same when a given amount of water is heated from 100°C to steam at 104°C by two different processes.

The final states, in both cases, were the same. A basic law of science is that the change in internal energy of a system is independent of the path in going from state to state. ΔE depends only on the conditions of the two states not the path followed between them. Thus, in the preceding example, ΔE is the same in both cases since the final states are equivalent. Both q and w, however, do depend on the path.

ΔE is independent of the path in going from A to B.

Some other quantities used in working with energy are also independent of the path as is ΔE. These include ΔS, ΔH, and ΔG as well as others we have not studied. Each of these quantities is called a state function. A **state function** is one which is independent of how the change is accomplished.

A state function depends only upon the physical state of the system and is independent of the pathway used to arrive at that state (ΔE, ΔS, ΔH, and ΔG).

The total amount of energy in an isolated system is constant.

This is an adiabatic system.

Emphasize *q* from surroundings and *w* on surroundings.

An isolated system is a special case. In an isolated system there can be no interchange with the surroundings. Therefore, both q and w must be zero. As a result, ΔE is zero and the law of conservation of energy is demonstrated mathematically for an isolated system.

PROBLEMS

5. 30 kJ

6. 224 kJ

5. A system receives 419 kJ of heat from its surroundings and does 389 kJ of work on the surroundings. What is the change in its internal energy?

6. A system gives off 196 kJ of heat to the surroundings and the surroundings do 420 kJ of work on the system. What is the change in the internal energy of the system?

20:7 RELATION TO CHEMICAL SYSTEMS

How is the internal energy related to the other thermodynamic quantities we have studied? The strict definition of enthalpy is

$$H = E + PV \ or \ \Delta H = \Delta E + \Delta(PV)$$

$\Delta H = \Delta E + \Delta(PV)$

Note that $\Delta(PV)$ represents work done by the system.

where P = pressure, and V = volume.

Most of the changes observed by chemists occur in open vessels in the laboratory. Thus, pressure is constant (equal to atmospheric pressure). It can be shown mathematically that if

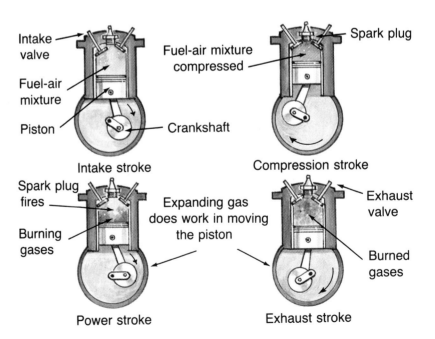

FIGURE 20-7. The internal energy of an automobile engine depends on the changes in pressure and volume that occur during combustion.

pressure is held constant, then $\Delta H = q$. Under such conditions, then, the enthalpy change is just the heat absorbed from the surroundings. Note that if q is negative, then heat must have been given up to the surroundings. In other words, a negative ΔH represents an exothermic reaction.

Under normal laboratory conditions, ΔH equals the heat absorbed from the surroundings. $\Delta H = q$

PROBLEMS

7. If the internal energy of a system changes by 418 kJ and the pressure-volume product changes by -616 kJ, what is the change in enthalpy of the system?

8. If the enthalpy of a system changes by -845 kJ and the internal energy changes by -489 kJ, what is the change in the pressure-volume product for the system?

7. -198 kJ
8. -356 kJ

Josiah Willard Gibbs   (1839–1903)

One of the great American theorists, J. Willard Gibbs was born and raised in New Haven, Connecticut. In 1871, he became professor of mathematical physics at Yale, where he remained until his death.

Gibb's principal contribution to science was his thermodynamic theory. In this work, he related the behavior of systems in equilibrium to the volume, energy, and degree of order present. He extended his theory to heterogeneous systems undergoing reaction, to which no previous theory had been applied.

Although recognized as the work of genius in America, his theories were not really appreciated in Europe.

Gibbs also made contributions in mathematics and electromagnetic theory.

CHEMICAL TECHNOLOGY: Liquefying Air

Several of the gases comprising air have extensive industrial and commercial uses. These gases are obtained from the process of liquefying air.

Before air can be liquefied, it is filtered to remove soot and other small dirt particles which would clog the equipment used later in the process. The filtered air is then compressed to about

10 megapascals (MPa). As a result of being compressed, the temperature of the air rises. This heat is removed in a device called a heat exchanger. A heat exchanger consists of a series of tubes passing through a cylindrical vessel. One fluid passes through the tubes. The other fluid flows through the vessel surrounding the tubes. Heat flows from the hotter fluid to the cooler fluid.

The compressed air is cooled with water, and further compressed to about 15 MPa. This air is cooled once more to room temperature with water in the heat exchanger. The air then goes through a series of heat exchangers using a refrigerant such as Freon or ammonia and/or some of the cold gas from the end of the process. At an early stage, water vapor and carbon dioxide are condensed and removed.

Some of the cold gas is used to run one or more compressors. In the process of doing that work, the gas uses some of its internal energy. Thus, its temperature drops even further. Most of the cold, compressed gas is allowed to expand through a valve. Recall from Chapter 18 that this expansion results in a temperature decrease. A large part of the gas is liquefied through the Joule-Thomson effect.

The liquid and extremely cold gas then enters a two-stage distillation column. In the column, the air is separated into high-purity nitrogen, oxygen, and other fractions. The high-purity products are sold and low-purity nitrogen gas is used as a coolant in the heat exchangers. The other liquid fraction passes to a specialized distillation unit where neon, argon, krypton, and xenon are produced. During distillation, each component is removed at its boiling point.

FIGURE 20-8. Air is liquefied through a stepwise process similar to that shown here.

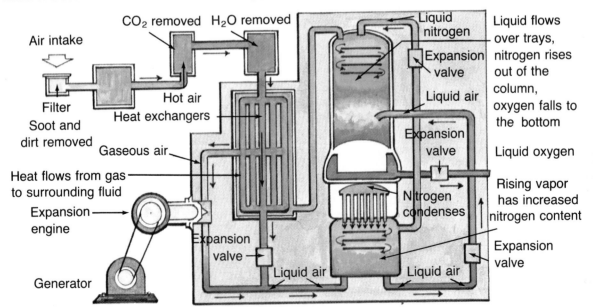

SUMMARY

1. Enthalpy is the heat content in a system. 20:1
2. Entropy is the degree of disorder of a system. 20:2
3. When the enthalpy change and entropy change differ, the net effect is found from the equation $\Delta G = \Delta H - T\Delta S$. In this equation G is free energy, H is enthalpy, T is the absolute temperature, and S is the entropy. 20:3
4. Spontaneous changes have negative free energy changes. 20:3
5. When ΔG is zero, the system is at equilibrium. 20:3
6. The change in a thermodynamic quantity (ΔH, ΔG, or ΔS) for a reaction is the sum of the quantities of the products less the sum of the quantities of the reactants. 20:5
7. The change in the internal energy of a system is the heat absorbed from the surroundings less the work done on the surroundings ($\Delta E = q - w$). 20:6
8. The thermodynamic quantities ΔG, ΔH, ΔS, and ΔE are "state" quantities. That is, these quantities depend only on the conditions in one state compared to another. The change is independent of the path chosen in going from one state to another. 20:4
9. The change in enthalpy is related to the internal energy by the equation: $\Delta H = \Delta E + \Delta (PV)$. 20:7
10. For a constant pressure process, $\Delta H = q$. 20:7

PROBLEMS

9. Using Appendix A-6, decide whether the following reactions should occur spontaneously or not. That is, will ΔG be negative?
   a. $PbBr_2 + Cl_2 \rightarrow PbCl_2 + Br_2$
   b. $H_2O(l) \rightarrow H_2O(g)$
   c. $2C_4H_{10} + 13O_2 \rightarrow 8CO_2 + 10H_2O$
   d. $Cu_2S + S \rightarrow 2CuS$
   e. $CuS + 2O_2 \rightarrow CuSO_4$

   9. a. spontaneous, −54 kJ
   b. not spontaneous, 8 kJ
   c. spontaneous, −5490 kJ
   d. spontaneous, −21.2 kJ
   e. spontaneous, −608 kJ

10. Using Appendix A-6, compute the one thermodynamic quantity missing from the table for the following substances.
    a. $Hg_2Cl_2 + Cl_2 \rightarrow 2HgCl_2$
    b. $3Be + N_2 \rightarrow Be_3N_2$
    c. $2H_2O_2 \rightarrow 2H_2O + O_2$
    d. $2NO + O_2 \rightarrow 2NO_2$

    10. a. 245 J/mol·K
    b. 32.6 J/mol·K
    c. 99.9 J/mol·K
    d. −186 kJ/mol

11. A system received 622 kJ of energy from its surroundings and did 813 kJ of work on the surroundings. What was the change in its internal energy?

12. A system gave off 262 kJ of energy to its surroundings and the surroundings did 160 kJ work on the system. What was the change in its internal energy?

13. If the internal energy of a system changes by 632 kJ and the pressure-volume product changes by 681 kJ, what is the change in enthalpy for the system?

14. The enthalpy change for a system was −926 kJ, while the pressure-volume product changed by 816 kJ. What was the change in internal energy?

11. −191 kJ
12. −102 kJ
13. 1313 kJ
14. −1742 kJ

REVIEW

1. 124 cm³
2. 244 cm³
3. 93.6 cm³
4. CO_2

7. 10 dm³
8. 3.94 g Al
9. 79.6 g NaCl
10. 248 g Na₃AlO₃

1. If a sample of gas occupies 163 cm³ at 52.4 kPa, what volume will it occupy at 68.7 kPa, temperature constant?

2. If a sample of gas occupies 258 cm³ at 97°C, what volume will it occupy at 77°C, pressure constant?

3. If a gas occupies 94.5 dm³ at 46°C, what volume will it occupy at 43°C? (Pressure constant)

4. Which gas would diffuse faster, CO_2 or UF_6?

5. In what two ways do real gases differ from an ideal gas?

6. What is Avogadro's principle?

7. What volume will be occupied by 0.161 mole of gas at 43.3 kPa and 52°C?

8. What mass of aluminum is required to react with 4.90 dm³ of chlorine according to the equation $2Al + 3Cl_2 \rightarrow 2AlCl_3$?

9. What mass of sodium chloride is obtained from the reaction of 49.5 g HCl with 91.8 g NaOH? ($HCl + NaOH \rightarrow NaCl + H_2O$)

10. What mass of sodium aluminate is obtained from the reaction of 134 g Al(OH)₃ with 635 g NaOH?
$$Al(OH)_3 + 3NaOH \rightarrow Na_3AlO_3 + 3H_2O$$

11. Use the phase diagram of oxygen to find the following.
    a. triple point temperature
    b. triple point pressure
    c. normal boiling point
    d. normal melting point
    e. critical point temperature and pressure

5. Real gases occupy a finite volume and exert an attractive force on each other.
6. Equal volumes of gases at the same temperature and pressure contain the same number of molecules.

FIGURE 20-9. Use with Review 11.

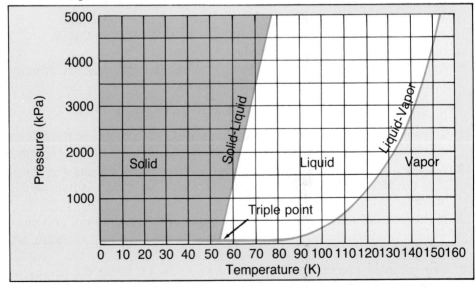

12. How much energy is required to heat 8.16 g of ice at $-16°C$ to steam at $102°C$?

13. A gas collected over water at $21°C$ and 103 kPa is dried. What volume does it occupy when dry if it occupied 37.0 dm³ when wet?

14. If a gas occupies 629 cm³ at $24°C$ and 101.0 kPa, what volume will it occupy at STP?

15. What is the density of a gas at STP if 8.02 g of it occupy 1.20 dm³ at 103.1 kPa and $8°C$?

16. What is the molecular mass of a gas if 2.20 g of it occupy 2.13 dm³ at $20°C$ and 107.1 kPa?

17. How many dm³ of hydrogen can be obtained from 21.0 g Zn?
$$Zn + 2HCl \rightarrow ZnCl_2 + H_2$$

18. What volume of hydrogen chloride gas can be obtained from 93.0 dm³ of chlorine?
$$H_2 + Cl_2 \rightarrow 2HCl$$

19. What volume of hydrogen at $6°C$ and 123.0 kPa can be obtained from 10.1 g Mn?
$$Mn + 2H_2O \rightarrow Mn(OH)_2 + H_2$$

12. 24 800 J
13. 28.0 dm³
14. 576 cm³
15. 6.76 g/dm³
16. 23.5 g/mol
17. 7.19 dm³
18. 186 dm³
19. 3.47 dm³

ONE MORE STEP

1. Prepare a report for the class on the difference between heat capacity and heat content.

2. What is meant by the thermodynamic quantity "work function" (Helmholtz free energy)?

3. Under certain conditions, the change in internal energy is equal to the heat absorbed from the surroundings. What are the conditions?

4. Under what conditions is the maximum work realizable from a chemical system?

3. constant volume
4. reversible

READINGS

Hanst, Philip L., "Noxious Trace Gases in the Air." *Chemistry*, Vol. 51, No. 1 (January-February 1978), pp. 8-15; Vol. 51, No. 2 (March 1978), pp. 6-12.

Strauss, Howard J., and Kaufman, Milton, *Handbook for Chemical Technicians*. New York: McGraw-Hill Book Co., 1976, Chapter 5.

Wicken, Jeffrey S., "The Chemically Organizing Effects of Entropy Maximization." *Journal of Chemical Education*, Vol. 53, No. 10 (October 1976), pp. 623-625.

The study of the oceans involves a knowledge of the chemistry of solutions. Dissolved solutes in ocean water provide the nutrients necessary for ocean life to exist. These same solutes have changed chemically the materials in the sunken ship. Ocean solutes are now being considered as a source of mineral deposits. Tapping this resource depends on a knowledge of solution chemistry. What causes a solute to dissolve? How can solutes be recovered from a solution? What type of solution is the ocean?

M. Timothy O'Keefe/Tom Stack and Associates

Chapter 21 classifies homogeneous mixtures into nine groups of solutions. The properties of each group are discussed. Molality and mole fraction calculations are introduced along with molarity which was covered in Chapter 5.

SOLUTIONS

21

Demonstration—Prepare a solution of a colored salt such as K_2CrO_4, $KMnO_4$, or $CuSO_4$. Prepare a suspension by mixing some soil and water. Filter both preparations and discuss the results. Ask the students which would be easier to remove from drinking water, chemical pollution or solids such as mud and algae.

What do we mean by solution? In Chapter 3, we referred to heterogeneous matter and homogeneous matter. Homogeneous matter is the same throughout. It is often made of only one substance—a compound or an element. Homogeneous matter may also be made of a mixture of several substances. Such a homogeneous mixture is called a solution. Most, but not all, solutions consist of a solid dissolved in a liquid. The particles in a true solution are molecules, atoms, or ions which will pass easily through the pores of filter paper. Solutions cannot be separated into their components by filtration.

The substance which occurs to the greater extent in a solution is said to do the dissolving and is called the **solvent.** The less abundant substance is said to be dissolved and is called the **solute.**

GOAL: You will gain an understanding of the characteristics of solutions and ways of expressing their concentrations.

A solution is a homogeneous mixture.

The more abundant substance in a solution is called the solvent.

21:1 THE SOLVENT

The most common solvent is water. Using water as a typical solvent, let us look at the mechanism of solvent action. Water molecules are very polar. Because they are polar they are attracted to other polar molecules and to ions. Table salt, $NaCl$, is an ionic compound made of sodium and chloride ions. If a salt crystal is put in water, the polar water molecules are attracted to ions on the crystal surfaces. The water molecules gradually surround and isolate the surface ions. The ions become hydrated, Figure 21-1. The attraction between the hydrated sodium and chloride ions and the remaining crystal ions becomes so small that the hydrated ions are no longer held by the crystal. They gradually move away from the crystal into solution. This separation of ions from each other is called **dissociation.** The surrounding of solute particles by solvent particles is called **solvation.**

Polar water molecules are attracted to ions and other polar molecules.

Dissociation is the separation of ions from each other.

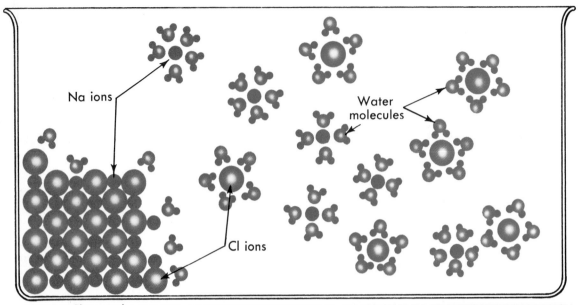

NaCl crystal

FIGURE 21-1. Table salt dissolves in water because polar water molecules gradually surround and isolate the sodium and chloride ions.

The process by which solute particles are surrounded by solvent particles is called solvation, or in the case of water, hydration.

Chemical reaction between solute and solvent is called solvolysis. If water is involved, the reaction is called hydrolysis. Be careful not to confuse the terms solvolysis and hydrolysis, which imply chemical reactions, with solvation and hydration, which imply no chemical change.

The dissociation of ions in solution leads to a factor which is important to keep in mind any time you are working with a solution of an ionic material. When the ions are dissociated, each ion species in the solution acts as though it were present alone. Thus, a solution of sodium chloride acts as a solution of sodium ions and chloride ions. There is no characteristic behavior of "sodium chloride" in solution because there really is no sodium chloride in solution. There is simply a solution containing both sodium ions and chloride ions uniformly mixed.

21:2 SOLVENT-SOLUTE COMBINATIONS

Four simple solution situations can be considered. They are listed in Table 21-1. Not all possible combinations of substances will fit into these four rigid categories. However, we will now consider these four as sample cases for studying solutions.

Table 21-1

Solvent-Solute Combinations		
Solvent Type	**Solute Type**	**Is Solution Likely?**
Polar	Polar	yes
Polar	Nonpolar	no
Nonpolar	Polar	no
Nonpolar	Nonpolar	yes

(1) *Polar solvent-Polar solute.*
The mechanism of solution involving a polar solvent and a polar solute is the one we have already described for salt and water. The polar solvent particles solvate the polar solute particles. They attach themselves due to the polar attraction. The intracrystalline forces are reduced so much that the surface particles are carried away by the solvent particles. In water, this process is called hydration.

dispersion forces only

(2) *Polar solvent-Nonpolar solute.*
Because these solvent particles are polar, they are attracted to each other. However, the solute particles in this case are nonpolar and have little attraction for particles of the solvent. Thus, solution to any extent is unlikely, as we see if we try to dissolve wax in water.

(3) *Nonpolar solvent-Polar solute.*
Reasoning similar to that of the second case applies here. The solvent particles are nonpolar and thus have little attraction for the solute particles. In addition, the solute particles in this case are polar and are attracted to each other. Again, solution to any extent is unlikely, as we see if we try to dissolve salt in benzene.

(4) *Nonpolar solvent-Nonpolar solute.*
Only van der Waals forces exist among the nonpolar solvent particles. The same is true for the nonpolar solute particles. Thus, all particles in the solution are subject only to van der Waals forces, and solution can occur. Random motion of solute molecules will cause some of them to leave the surface of the solute. There can be solvation in such cases, but the forces involved are far weaker than those in solutions involving polar compounds. The nonpolar particles are simply randomly dispersed. Thus, wax will dissolve in benzene.

Not all nonpolar substances are soluble in each other, however. Let us consider the most common type of solution: A solid dissolved in a liquid. The solubility of nonpolar solid in a nonpolar liquid depends upon two factors. These factors are its melting point and its heat of fusion. What do they have to do with solubility? When the solid dissolves, a liquid solution results. The solid is undergoing a phase change. Solids with low melting points and low heats of fusion will be more soluble than those with high melting points and high heats of fusion.

Table 21-2 lists a number of common solvents in order of increasing ability to dissolve highly polar and ionic materials. Compare the order here with that in Table 14-1, page 277.

Table 21-2

Ionic Dissolving Ability		
	Name	**Formula**
	Cyclohexane	C_6H_{12}
	Carbon tetrachloride	CCl_4
	Benzene	C_6H_6
	Toluene	C_7H_8
	Ethoxyethane	$C_4H_{10}O$
increasing	Ethyl acetate	$C_4H_8O_2$
	1-Butanol	$C_4H_{10}O$
	1-Propanol	C_3H_8O
	Propanone	C_3H_6O
	Ethanol	C_2H_6O
	Methanol	CH_4O
↓	Water	H_2O

21:3 SOLIDS, LIQUIDS, AND GASES IN SOLUTION

Since there are three common physical states of matter (solid, liquid, and gas), there are nine possible combinations of solvent-solute pairs. These combinations are given below.

There are nine possible combinations of solvent-solute pairs.

Table 21-3

Possible Solution Combinations		
Solvent	**Solute**	**Common Example**
gas	gas	oxygen-helium (deep-sea diver's gas)
gas	liquid	air-water (humidity)
gas	solid	air-naphthalene (mothballs)
liquid	gas	water-carbon dioxide (carbonated beverage)
liquid	liquid	acetic acid-water (vinegar)
liquid	solid	water-salt (seawater)
solid	gas	palladium-hydrogen (gas stove lighter)
solid	liquid	silver-mercury (dental amalgam)
solid	solid	gold-silver (ring)

Miscible: Mutually soluble

Immiscible liquids separate into layers on standing.

The property of mutual solubility of two liquids is called miscibility. If two liquids are mutually soluble in all proportions, they are said to be completely miscible. Ethylene glycol (automobile antifreeze) and water are two such liquids. Water and carbon tetrachloride, however, do not appreciably dissolve in each other and are, therefore, immiscible. Two liquids such as ethyl ether ($C_4H_{10}O$) and water, which dissolve in each other to some extent but not completely, are referred to as partially miscible.

A number of metals (such as gold and silver) are mutually soluble and form solid—solid solutions. Such solid metal—metal solutions constitute one type of alloy.

Some alloys are solid metal-metal solutions.

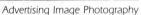
a
Advertising Image Photography

b
Hickson-Bender Photography

FIGURE 21-2. Oil and water are immiscible unless the system is agitated (a). Miscible liquids are soluble in all proportions (b).

21:4 SOLUTION EQUILIBRIUM

When crystals are first placed in a solvent, many particles may leave the surface and go into solution. As the number of solute particles in solution increases, some of the dissolved particles return to the surface of the crystal. Eventually the number of particles leaving the crystal surface equals the number returning to the surface. This point is called **solution equilibrium.**

At a specific temperature, there is a limit to the amount of solute that will dissolve in a given quantity of solvent. For instance, at 20°C, a maximum of 64.2 grams of nickel(II) chloride will dissolve in 100 cm^3 of water. This quantity is called the solubility of the substance at 20°C. This solubility can be changed by altering the temperature. A solution in which undissolved substance is in equilibrium with the dissolved substance is called a **saturated solution.** A solution containing less than the saturated amount of solute for that temperature is an **unsaturated solution.**

Larger amounts of solute can usually be dissolved in a solvent at a temperature higher than room temperature. If the hot solution is then cooled, an unstable solution is formed. This solution contains more solute than a saturated solution can hold. The solution is called a **supersaturated solution.** Supersaturation is possible because solids will not crystallize unless there is a special surface upon which to start crystallization. A container which has a smooth interior and which contains a dust-free solution has no such surfaces. However, a supersaturated solution will crystallize almost instantly if a crystal of the solute is

FIGURE 21-3. This supersaturated solution of sodium thiosulfate (a) can be made to crystallize by the addition of a seed crystal (b).

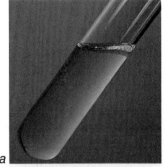
a
Hickson-Bender Photography

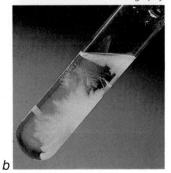
b
Hickson-Bender Photography

The formation of an insoluble solid as a result of a chemical reaction is called precipitation.

Demonstration—Place a petri dish on the overhead projector. To a small amount of H_2O in the dish, add a crystal of $KMnO_4$ and slowly stir the solution. Discuss what is happening at the particle level when solution equilibrium is reached.

introduced. How could you find out if a solution is saturated, unsaturated, or supersaturated?

Precipitation reactions are an important tool of the analytical chemist. The differing solubilities of substances can be used to separate them from mixtures. If a solution contains two ionic compounds, they may be separated by choosing a reactant that will precipitate only one ion. For example, consider a mixture of sodium nitrate and barium chloride. A chemist wishes to know what percentage of the mixture is $BaCl_2$, and thus finds the mass of the mixture before dissolving it in water. Once dissolved, the barium ions could be precipitated with sulfate ions from a soluble sulfate such as sulfuric acid. On the other hand, the chloride ions could be precipitated with silver ions from a soluble silver salt such as silver nitrate (see Table A-7 of the Appendix). The product is collected, dried, and massed. By solving a mass-mass problem, the chemist can find the amount, and thereby the percentage of $BaCl_2$ in the original mixture.

21:5 SOLUTION RATE

Solution rate is affected by
  1. surface area exposed to fresh solvent
  2. kinetic energy of particles

The rate of solution is affected by the surface area of the crystal which is exposed to fresh solvent. When the area of an exposed surface is increased, more solute particles are subjected to solvation. The surface area can be increased by breaking the crystal to be dissolved into very small particles. The surface area can also be increased by stirring the mixture as the solute is dissolving. In this way, the solvent which is saturated with solute is moved away from the surface of the solid solute. Fresh solvent can then come into contact with the solid surface.

Solution rate is also a function of the kinetic energy of both the solute and solvent particles. The faster the solvent particles are moving, the more rapidly they will circulate among the crystal

FIGURE 21-4. Solution rate can be increased by stirring (a), increasing the surface area of the solute (b), or heating (c).

a

F. Bernard Daniel

b

F. Bernard Daniel

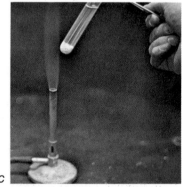

c

F. Bernard Daniel

particles. This motion has the same effect as increasing the surface area. If a solute particle's kinetic energy is increased, once it is solvated, it will move away from the solid material more rapidly. This motion exposes fresh surface, thus increasing solution rate. Finally, with increased kinetic energy, particles are more easily removed from the crystal. The kinetic energy of a system is increased by heating the mixture.

Kinetic energy can be increased by heating the system.

You may wish to review the discussion of ΔH, ΔG, and ΔS in Chapter 20.

21:6 HEAT OF SOLUTION

The reaction involving the solution of most solids in water is endothermic (ΔH positive). Recall from Chapter 20 that the free energy difference (ΔG) for a change is negative if the reaction proceeds spontaneously. For ΔG to be negative in the equation $\Delta G = \Delta H - T \Delta S$, ΔS must be positive if ΔH is positive. The solid has a high degree of order in the crystalline form. When dissolved, the particles are randomly distributed throughout the solution. The random distribution represents more disorder than the crystal. We see, then, that ΔS is positive, as predicted.

When gases dissolve in water, the hydrated molecules represent a higher degree of order than the random distribution in the gas. ΔS for the dissolving of a gas is, therefore, negative. Soluble gases, then, must have a negative ΔH. Experiment shows that the dissolving of gases is, in fact, an exothermic process. There are a few solids with a negative ΔH of solution. For these substances the degree of hydration is so high that more order exists in the solution than in the separate solid and liquid.

Using our knowledge of enthalpy change in solutions, we can predict the effect of temperature on solubility. Most solids having positive heats of solution ($\Delta H > 0$), are more soluble in hot water than in cold. However, gases, with negative heats of solution, ($\Delta H < 0$) are more soluble in cold water.

The solution of most solids in water is endothermic, ΔH is positive.

Demonstration—Add water to a small beaker containing NH_4NO_3. It absorbs 619 J per cm^3 of H_2O. Add water to a beaker containing $CaCl_2$. It gives off 490 J per cm^3 of H_2O. Pass the two beakers around the class. Discuss how hot and cold packs used for athletic injuries could be made.

Demonstration—Most solids are more soluble in hot water than in cold. Calcium acetate is an exception. Make a saturated solution of this substance. $Ca(C_2H_3O_2)_2$ will come out of solution when heated. Discuss the shape of its solubility curve (solubility vs. temperature).

21:7 EFFECTS OF PRESSURE

Pressure has little effect on solutions unless the solute is a gas. The amount of gas which dissolves in a given amount of solvent is greater at high pressure than it is at low pressure. *The mass of a gas which will dissolve in a liquid at a given temperature varies directly with the partial pressure of that gas.* This statement is Henry's Law, named in honor of William Henry, the English chemist who first discovered this relationship.

More gas will dissolve at high pressure than at low pressure. (Henry's Law)

21:8 SOLUTION PROPORTIONS

Solutions may also be classified on the basis of the relative amounts of solvent and solute present. If a relatively large amount of solute is present per unit volume, the solution is a concentrated solution. If only a relatively small amount of the solute is present per unit volume, the solution is a dilute solution. This terminology is less exact than indicating the degree of saturation or the ratio of solute to solvent.

"Concentrated" and "dilute" are inexact terms.

21:9 MOLAR SOLUTIONS

In Chapter 5 we learned about a precise concentration unit called molarity. We found that a one-molar ($1M$) solution contains 1 mole of solute in 1 dm^3 of solution. If 1 mole of sodium chloride is dissolved in enough water to make 1 dm^3 of solution, the solution is a 1-molar solution of sodium chloride. Sodium chloride is in the form of dissociated ions in solution. Therefore, the solution can also be said to be 1-molar in sodium ions and 1-molar in chloride ions.

A 1 molar ($1M$) solution contains one mol of solute per dm^3 of solution.

$$M = \frac{\text{moles of solute}}{dm^3 \text{ of solution}}$$

Molarity is the most common concentration unit in chemistry. Measurement of the volume of solutions is fast and convenient. If the solution measured has a known molarity, a measurement of volume is also a measurement of a number of particles. Each unit of volume contains a known number of ions or molecules. Multiplying the concentration in molarity (moles per dm^3) by the volume (dm^3) will give you the number of particles (in moles).

For a known molarity, a measurement of volume is a measure of the number of particles.

Whenever the concentration of solute in a solution is known with some degree of precision, the solution is called a standard solution.

The concentration of a standard solution is known with some precision.

A 1 formal ($1F$) solution contains one gram-formula mass of solute per dm^3 of solution. Some references reserve the term molar for solutions of substances which actually occur as molecules (sugar). We will not use the term formal.

EXAMPLE: Ion Concentration

What are the concentrations of ions in a $1.00M$ solution of $Al(NO_3)_3$? $Al(NO_3)_3(c) \rightarrow Al^{3+}(aq) + 3NO_3^-(aq)$

Solving process:
A $1.00M$ solution of $Al(NO_3)_3$ contains a concentration of aluminum ions equal to $1.00M$ and a concentration of nitrate ions equal to $3.00M$.

EXAMPLE: Number of Ions

How many moles of ions of each type are present in 200 cm^3 of $0.100M$ $MgCl_2$? $MgCl_2(c) \rightarrow Mg^{2+}(aq) + 2Cl^-(aq)$

Solving process:

$$\frac{200 \text{ cm}^3 \text{ soln}}{} \left| \frac{0.100 \text{ mol MgCl}_2}{1000 \text{ cm}^3 \text{ soln}} \right| \frac{1 \text{ mol Mg}^{2+}}{1 \text{ mol MgCl}_2} = 0.0200 \text{ mol Mg}^{2+}$$

assumes 100% dissociation

$$\frac{200 \text{ cm}^3 \text{ soln}}{} \left| \frac{0.100 \text{ mol MgCl}_2}{1000 \text{ cm}^3 \text{ soln}} \right| \frac{2 \text{ mol Cl}^-}{1 \text{ mol MgCl}_2} = 0.0400 \text{ mol Cl}^-$$

PROBLEM

1. Calculate the molarity of the ion designated in the following solutions.
   a. Br^- for 316 g $MgBr_2$ in 859 cm^3 solution
   b. Ca^{2+} for 8.28 g $Ca(C_5H_9O_2)_2$ in 414 cm^3 solution

1. a. 4.00M
   b. 0.0826M

21:10 MOLAL SOLUTIONS

Sometimes, it is convenient to express concentration in terms of moles of solute per kilogram of solvent. A solution which contains 1 mole of solute in each 1000 grams of solvent is called a one-molal ($1m$) solution. This solution differs from a 1-molar ($1M$) solution, which contains 1 mole of solute in 1 dm^3 of solution. Molality is most useful in studying the colligative properties of solutions which will be covered in Chapter 22.

A 1 molal ($1m$) solution contains one mole of solute in 1 kg (1000 g) of solvent.

$$m = \frac{\text{moles of solute}}{\text{kilogram of solvent}}$$

Molal solutions are useful in studying colligative properties.

EXAMPLE: Molality

If 52.0 grams of K_2CO_3 are dissolved in 518 grams of H_2O, what is the molality of the solution?

Solving process:

Formula mass of $K_2CO_3 = 2(39.1 \text{ g}) + 12.0 \text{ g} + 3(16.0 \text{ g}) = 138 \text{ g}$

Divide solute by solvent and convert to the proper units.

$$\frac{52.0 \text{ g K}_2\text{CO}_3}{518 \text{ g H}_2\text{O}} \left| \frac{1 \text{ mol K}_2\text{CO}_3}{138 \text{ g K}_2\text{CO}_3} \right| \frac{1000 \text{ g H}_2\text{O}}{1 \text{ kg H}_2\text{O}} = 0.726m$$

PROBLEM

2. Calculate the molality of the following solutions.
   a. 199 g $NiBr_2$ in 500 g water
   b. 92.3 g KF in 1000 g water

2. a. 1.82m NiBr$_2$
   b. 1.59m KF

21:11 MOLE FRACTION

Another method of describing concentration used frequently in organic chemistry is mole fraction. The mole fraction shows the comparison of moles of solute to moles of solution.

The mole fraction is a comparison of moles of solute to the total number of moles of solution.

The mole fraction is most commonly used by organic chemists in fractional distillation calculations.

EXAMPLE: Mole Fraction

What is the mole fraction of alcohol in a solution made of 2 moles of ethanol and 8 moles of water?

Solving process:

(a) Find the total number of moles

2 moles ethanol + 8 moles water = 10 moles solution

(b) The mole fraction of ethanol is

$$\frac{2 \text{ mol ethanol}}{10 \text{ mol solution}} = 0.2$$

Any size sample of this solution will have an ethanol mole fraction of 0.2. The sum of the mole fractions of all components of a solution must equal 1.

Sum of the mole fractions of all components = 1

PROBLEM

3. a. 0.923 mole fraction C_2H_6O
0.0770 mole fraction C_4H_4O

3. Calculate the mole fraction for each component in the following solutions.

    a. 12.3 g of C_4H_4O in 100 g of C_2H_6O

    b. 56.3 g of $C_{12}H_{22}O_{11}$ in 300 g H_2O

b. 0.988 mole fraction H_2O
0.00976 mole fraction $C_{12}H_{22}O_{11}$

Agnes Pockels (1862–1935)

Agnes Pockels was the daughter of an Austrian army officer. Although she attended high school for some time, she was largely self-taught. In her late teens, she made her first observations on the changes in surface tension of water contaminated by oil. Her first paper was printed under the sponsorship of Lord Rayleigh nearly ten years later when she was 29.

Most of her experimentation was done at home with homemade apparatus. Among other makeshift devices, she developed the Pockels' trough which was used to measure surface tension.

At 69, she won the Laura-Leonard prize for her work in the properties of surface layers and films. One year later she received her first degree, an honorary doctorate. An extension of her work in surface chemistry led to the Nobel Prize for Irving Langmuir in 1932.

CHEMICAL TECHNOLOGY: Seawater

From where did the ocean come? Why is there no ocean on the moon? Why is the ocean salty? We know that molecules are constantly in motion. Air molecules, if they are traveling fast enough, may escape Earth's gravitational attraction and fly off into space. The moon, with small gravitational force, has never been able to hold an atmosphere or moisture.

The speed of molecules is determined by their mass and temperature. Scientists have determined that Earth was quite hot at its early stage of formation. Any water present at that time would have vaporized and been lost to space. Our present ocean has accumulated as a result of water emerging from the interior of Earth, principally as a result of volcanic action.

Water vapor was emitted by erupting volcanoes, and as Earth cooled, the water vapor condensed into clouds and eventually fell as rain. The rain dissolved certain minerals as it fell on the original crystalline rocks of Earth's surface. These erosional effects (weathering) produced a flow of water which contained dissolved minerals, and this solution accumulated to form the ocean. We call the solution seawater or salt water since sodium ions and chloride ions are the main solutes. Small quantities of seawater solute continue to be added from volcanoes as well as rain and stream erosion. Since erosional and volcanic processes continue, why do the concentrations remain relatively constant? Solutes are being removed from the ocean as well as those which are added. The minerals in the sea are constantly forming sediment on the seafloor.

This sediment is the result of chemical reactions within seawater and living organisms in the sea which use solutes in the sea. When these organisms die, their remains sink to the bottom. It is generally assumed by scientists today that seawater represents a state of equilibrium between the addition of new salts and the precipitation of solutes.

Table 21-4

Composition of Seawater					
Element	Form of occurrence	Grams per kilogram of seawater	Element	Form of occurrence	Grams per kilogram of seawater
Chlorine	Cl^-	19.4	Bromine	Br^-	0.0673
Sodium	Na^+	10.8	*Carbon	HCO_3^-, CO_3^{2-}	0.0281
Sulfur	SO_2^{2-}	2.71	Strontium	Sr^{2+}	0.0079
Magnesium	Mg^{2+}	1.29	Boron	H_3BO_3	0.0045
Calcium	Ca^{2+}	0.412	Silicon	H_4SiO_4	0.0030
Potassium	K^+	0.399	Fluorine	F^-	0.0013
70 other elements have been found in smaller amounts.			*Concentrations are subject to wide local variation.		

SUMMARY

1. Polar solvents tend to dissolve polar solutes; nonpolar solvents tend to dissolve nonpolar solutes. 21:1-21:2
2. When ionic compounds dissolve, the ions dissociate. 21:1
3. A solution is said to reach solution equilibrium when the rates of particles leaving and returning to the solution are equal. When solution equilibrium is reached, the solution is said to be saturated with the solute. 21:4
4. If a relatively large amount of solute is present per unit volume, the solution is a concentrated solution. 21:8
5. The rate of solution is affected by the surface area of crystal exposed and the kinetic energy of solute and solvent. 21:5
6. Heat of solution is the enthalpy change which occurs when one substance is dissolved in another. Most solids have positive heats of solution. Gases have negative heats of solution. 21:6
7. Henry's law: The mass of a gas which will dissolve in a liquid at a given temperature varies directly with the partial pressure of that gas. 21:7
21:9-21:11 8. Molarity, molality, and mole fraction are common concentration units.

PROBLEMS

4. a. not soluble
   b. not soluble
   c. miscible
   d. not soluble
   e. not soluble
   f. miscible

5. a. slightly soluble
   b. soluble
   c. soluble
   d. not soluble
   e. soluble

4. Predict the solubility of the first substance in the second on the basis of comparative polarities.
   a. RbF in ethanol
   b. CuS in water
   c. Ethanol in water
   d. NCl_3 in C_6H_6
   e. Gasoline in water
   f. Benzene in hexane

5. Predict the solubility of the following in water on the basis of comparative polarities.
   a. CuF_2 b. $ScCl_3$ c. Rb_2S d. ThS_2 e. CsI

6. Calculate the molarity of the following solutions.
   a. 31.1 g $Al_2(SO_4)_3$ in 756 cm^3 solution
   b. 59.5 g $CaCl_2$ in 100 cm^3 solution
   c. 313.5 g $LiClO_3$ in 250 cm^3 solution

6. a. 0.120M
   b. 5.36M
   c. 13.9M

7. Calculate the molality of the following solutions.
   a. 98.0 g $RbBr$ in 824 g water
   b. 85.2 g $SnBr_2$ in 140 g water
   c. 10.0 g $AgClO_3$ in 201 g water

7. a. 0.721m
   b. 2.19m
   c. 0.260m

8. Calculate the mole fraction for each component in the following solutions.
   a. 54.3 g of $C_{10}H_8$ in 600 g $C_4H_{10}O$ 0.0498 $C_{10}H_8$; 0.951 $C_4H_{10}O$
   b. 67.4 g of C_9H_7N in 200 g C_2H_6O 0.107 C_9H_7N; 0.893 C_2H_6O

c. 0.0292 $C_5H_{10}O_5$; 0.0280 CH_6ON_4; 0.944 H_2O

   c. 5.48 g of $C_5H_{10}O_5$ and 3.15 g of CH_6ON_4 in 21.2 g H_2O

9. Compute the masses of solute needed to make the following solutions.
   a. 1.000 dm^3 of 0.780M $Sc(NO_3)_3$
   b. 200 cm^3 of 0.301M $Er_2(SO_4)_3$
   c. 100 cm^3 of 0.626M VBr_3
   d. 250 cm^3 of 0.0965M $DyCl_3$

9. a. 180 g $Sc(NO_3)_3$
   b. 37.5 g $Er_2(SO_4)_3$
   c. 18.2 g VBr_3
   d. 6.49 g $DyCl_3$

e. 500 cm^3 of $0.0978M$ $IrCl_4$ h. 200 cm^3 of $0.0469M$ KHC_2O_4
f. 1.00 dm^3 of $0.0130M$ YBr_3 i. 250 cm^3 of $0.274M$ $UO_2(NO_3)_2 \cdot 6H_2O$
g. 100 cm^3 of $0.528M$ Li_2SO_4 j. 500 cm^3 of $0.512M$ HSO_3F

10. Compute the mass of solute needed to add to the given amounts of solvent.

   a. $Fe_2(C_2O_4)_3$ to be added to 1000 g of water for a $0.851m$ solution   320 g Fe₂(C₂O₄)₃

   b. $VOBr_3$ to be added to 1000 g water for a $0.534m$ solution   164 g VOBr₃

   c. $C_7H_4O_2Br_2$ to be added to 200 g of C_2H_6O so that the mole fraction of the solvent is 0.510   1170 g C₇H₄O₂Br₂

   d. $C_{14}H_{16}N_2$ to be added to 1000 g of $C_4H_{10}O$ so that the mole fraction of the solute is 0.363   1630 g C₁₄H₁₆N₂

   e. $LiMnO_4$ to be added to 1000 g of water for a $0.614m$ solution   77.4 g LiMnO₄

11. Iodine crystals are relatively insoluble in water, however they do dissolve in carbon tetrachloride. Explain why. Both iodine and CCl₄ are nonpolar substances. Water is polar.

12. Using Table A-7 of the Appendix, select a reagent that will precipitate one of the metals ions in each of the following mixtures.

   a. $AgNO_3$ and $NaNO_3$ c. $BaCl_2$ and KNO_3

   b. $FeCl_3$ and $NaCl$ d. KCl and $CuSO_4$

12. a. $Cl^- \rightarrow AgCl(c)$
   b. $OH^- \rightarrow Fe(OH)_3(c)$
   c. $SO_4^{2-} \rightarrow BaSO_4(c)$
   d. $OH^- \rightarrow Cu(OH)_2(c)$

13. A chemist has a 5 gram mixture of silver and potassium nitrates. To isolate the silver, HCl is added. The dry AgCl precipitate has a mass of 3.5 grams. What was the mass of $AgNO_3$ in the original mixture? 4.14 g AgNO₃

14. What is the relationship between ΔH and solubility for solids and gases?

15. How does molarity differ from molality? Explain using the equations for each.

   15. Molarity $= \dfrac{\text{moles}}{\text{dm}^3 \text{ of solution}}$, Molality $= \dfrac{\text{moles}}{\text{kilogram solvent}}$,

   considers the volume of the solution   considers the mass of the solvent only

REVIEW

1. Compute the enthalpy change for the reaction:

$$Cu(c) + 2H_2SO_4(aq) \rightarrow CuSO_4(c) + SO_2(g) + 2H_2O(l)$$

2. Compute the free energy change for the reaction:

$$P_4O_{10}(c) + 6H_2O(l) \rightarrow 4H_3PO_4(l)$$

if $\Delta H = -454.3$ kJ and $\Delta S = 3.76$ J/K at 25°C.

3. What is meant by the expression "standard states?"

4. Define the quantities "q" and "w".

14. Most solids having positive heats of solution are more soluble in hot water than cold. Gases with negative heats of solution are more soluble in cold water.

1. $\Delta H = 177$ kJ
2. $\Delta G = -453$ kJ
3. Standard states: A reference set of conditions used in thermodynamic calculations.
4. q = heat received from the surroundings
   w = work done on the surroundings

ONE MORE STEP

1. Obtain an unknown substance from your instructor and attempt to identify it experimentally by determining its solubility curve.

2. Try to make a supersaturated solution of $Na_2S_2O_3$.

3. Measure the heat of solution of anhydrous sodium phosphate at several different concentrations. See if you can determine how the molar heat of solution varies with temperature.

The vapor pressure of a substance in solution is dependent on the number of particles in the solution. Vapor pressure is a colligative property. Changes in vapor pressure are used on a large scale at a petroleum refinery. The distillation process involves separating the components of a mixture by the differences in their vapor pressures. What are the other colligative properties? What are some other applications of colligative behavior?

Jim McNee/Tom Stack and Associates

COLLIGATIVE AND COLLOIDAL PROPERTIES

22

Demonstration—Fill two 400 cm³ beakers with ice and water. Place a thermometer in each beaker. Stir and wait until both beakers are at constant temperature, then add 50 g NaCl to one of the beakers. Stir both beakers equally and wait until the temperature is constant again. Ask students why the temperature dropped in the one beaker. Use this discussion to introduce the term colligative properties and the effect of solutes on the properties of solutions.

When a solute is dissolved in a solvent, there is a change in certain properties of the solvent. On the other hand, when particles too large to dissolve are dispersed throughout a liquid, the solvent's properties remain unchanged. In this chapter, we want to investigate those properties of solvents which are changed by solutes. We also want to look at the behavior of those particles which are too large to dissolve and have no effect on the liquid. Throughout the first six sections of this chapter, we will be dealing with an ideal solution. In Chapter 18, we were able to define an ideal gas. Unfortunately, we cannot define an ideal solution completely at this point. For the time being, we will just say that the particles of solute in an ideal solution have no effect on each other.

GOAL: You will gain an understanding of the properties of solutions that depend upon the number of particles, size of the particles, and the type of particles in the solution.

22:1 RAOULT'S LAW

Colligative properties are determined by the number of particles in solution rather than by the type of particle in solution. The properties so affected are vapor pressure, freezing point, boiling point, and the rate of diffusion through a membrane. Consider a solute dissolved in a liquid solvent. Some of the solute particles take up space on the liquid surface normally occupied by solvent particles. These solute particles decrease the opportunity for solvent particles to escape (evaporate) from the liquid surface. Thus, if the solute is nonvolatile, the vapor pressure of a solution is always less than that of the pure solvent at the same temperature. The lowering of the vapor pressure of the solvent varies directly as the mole fraction of dissolved solute. *Any nonvolatile solute at a specific concentration lowers the vapor pressure of a solvent by an amount which is characteristic of that solvent.* The characteristics of the solute are not involved. Ionic

Colligative properties depend on the number of particles in solution.

Colligative properties
1. vapor pressure
2. freezing point
3. boiling point
4. rate of diffusion through a membrane

All ionic and molecular solids having low vapor pressures are said to be nonvolatile.

Assuming a nonvolatile solvent.

compounds and molecular compounds with high melting points are typical nonvolatile solutes. To determine the vapor pressure of a solution, we must correct the vapor pressure of the pure solvent for the presence of the solute. The equation used for correcting the vapor pressure is

$$vapor\ pressure = vapor\ pressure \times mole\ fraction$$
(solution)   (solvent)   (solvent)

This expression is a mathematical statement of **Raoult's law** named for Francis Raoult, a French chemist. He first stated the principle that *the vapor pressure of a solution varies directly as the mole fraction of solvent.* Raoult's law holds in an ideal solution. We can now define an ideal solution as one in which all intermolecular attractions are the same. In other words, solute-solute, solvent-solvent, and solute-solvent attractions are all essentially the same.

An ideal solution: All intermolecular attractions are the same.

In the case of a volatile solute, Raoult's law is often inadequate to predict the behavior of the solution. However, there are many solutions whose behavior approaches the ideal closely enough to be treated as such. Each volatile component of an ideal solution has a vapor pressure which can be determined by Raoult's law.

EXAMPLE: Raoult's Law

Consider a solution composed of 1.00 mole of benzene, C_6H_6, and 1.00 mole of toluene, $C_6H_5CH_3$. The mole fraction of each component in the solution is 0.500. Thus, the number of benzene molecules in the solution equals the number of toluene molecules. At 25°C, benzene has a vapor pressure of 12.7 kPa, and toluene has a vapor pressure of 3.79 kPa. What is the vapor pressure of the resulting solution?

Solving process:

The vapor pressure is the sum of the individual pressure of benzene and toluene. The vapor pressure of benzene in the solution is

$$(0.500)(12.7\ kPa) = 6.35\ kPa$$

The vapor pressure of toluene in the solution is

$$(0.500)(3.79\ kPa) = 1.90\ kPa$$

Thus, the vapor pressure of the resulting solution is 8.25 kPa.

The ratio of molecules in the liquid will not always be the same ratio in the vapor.

liquid ratio 1 : 1
vapor ratio 3.34 : 1

Note especially that the vapor phase is much richer in the more volatile component (benzene) than is the liquid phase. The vapors of the two substances are in the same volume and at the same temperature. Thus, the ratio of their pressures must be equal to the ratio of the number of vapor molecules of each. This ratio is 6.35/1.90 or 3.34/1.

PROBLEMS

1. Find the vapor pressure of a water solution in which the mole fraction of $HgCl_2$ (a nonvolatile solute) is 0.181 at 28°C. Use the vapor pressure of water table in Chapter 18 page 362.

2. Find the total vapor pressure of a solution of ethanal (mole fraction 0.300, vapor pressure at 18°C = 86.3 kPa) in methanol at 18°C. (Vapor pressure of methanol at 18°C = 11.6 kPa).

1. 3.10 kPa
2. 34.0 kPa

22:2   FRACTIONAL DISTILLATION

We take advantage of the difference in vapor pressures of two components of a solution in the process of fractional distillation. If we plot the boiling point of mixtures of benzene and toluene, we obtain a graph as shown in the lower curve of Figure 22-1a. The boiling point of each mixture is, of course, the temperature at which the sum of the two vapor pressures equals 101.3 kPa. At each of these points, however, the vapor phase would be richer in the more volatile component. Let us calculate the composition of the vapor in equilibrium with the liquid at each of these points, and plot the data on the same graph (upper curve of Figure 22-1a).

Fractional distillation depends upon vapor pressure difference.

FIGURE 22-1. The lower curve in (a) represents the boiling point and composition of a benzene-toluene mixture of varying proportions. The upper curve represents the vapor concentrations. The stepwise line in (b) indicates how a benzene-toluene mixture can be separated into its components by fractional distillation.

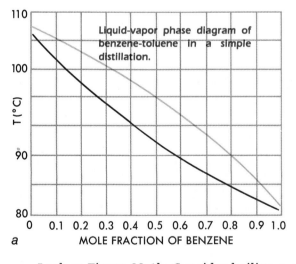

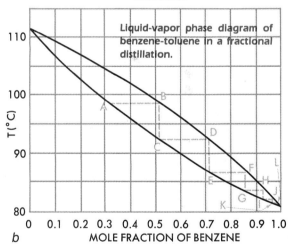

Look at Figure 22-1b. Consider boiling a solution of benzene and toluene in which the mole fraction of benzene is 0.3. It will boil at the temperature represented by point *A*. The vapor in equilibrium with that solution will have the composition represented by point *B* which is at the same temperature. It is richer in benzene than the original solution because benzene is more volatile than toluene. If we condense this vapor, we will obtain

A fractionating tower works on the principle of condensing and revaporizing the already vaporized substance many times as it flows through the tower.

a solution which will boil at point *C*. It will produce a vapor of composition *D*. This process can be continued until nearly pure benzene is obtained as vapor, and almost pure toluene remains behind. It is possible to construct a distillation apparatus in which separate distillations for each step are not necessary. The structure of the apparatus is such that each step takes place in a separate section of the equipment. In the laboratory, a fractional distillation apparatus is often used in separating volatile liquids. In industry, a fractionating tower is used for the same purpose on a commercial scale. Petroleum is separated into useful products by fractional distillation.

Table 22-1

Petroleum Distillation Fractions	
Name	**Boiling point range (°C)**
Gasoline	60–280
Jet fuel	190–450
Kerosene	350–550
Diesel fuel	430–700
Fuel oil	550–800
Lubricating oil	600–1000

FIGURE 22-2. The packing material in this distillation column (a) increases the surface area of the column. Thus, this column has the separating capabilities of one many times its height. A fractionating tower is used in industry to separate petroleum into its components (b).

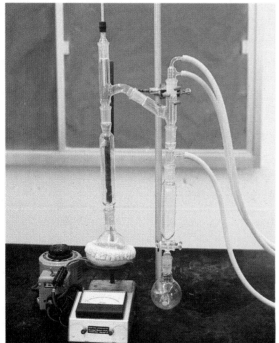

a

Robert C. Smoot

b

Marathon Oil Company

22:3 BOILING POINT AND FREEZING POINT

The presence of nonvolatile solute particles at the surface causes the boiling point of a solution to be raised. The boiling point of a liquid is the temperature at which the vapor pressure of the liquid equals the atmospheric pressure. In a solution, then, a higher temperature is needed to put enough solvent particles into the vapor phase to equal atmospheric pressure. The boiling point of a solution is, therefore, higher than that of the pure solvent.

How does the addition of a nonvolatile solute affect the freezing point of a solution? The freezing point is the temperature at which the vapor pressure of the solid and liquid are equal. Since the addition of solute particles lowers the vapor pressure, the vapor pressures of the solid and liquid will be equal at a lower temperature. Solutions, then, will freeze at a lower temperature than the pure solvent alone.

The boiling point of a liquid is the temperature at which the vapor pressure of the liquid equals the atmospheric pressure.

The boiling point of a solution is higher than the boiling point of the pure solvent.

The freezing point of a liquid is the temperature at which the vapor pressures of the solid and liquid are equal.

The freezing point of a solution is lower than the freezing point of the pure solvent.

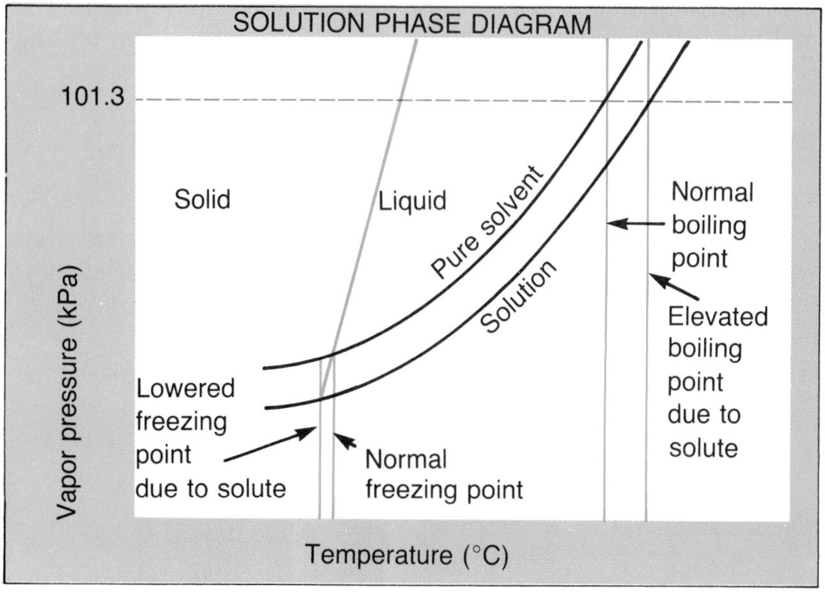

FIGURE 22-3. The addition of solute particles lowers the vapor pressure of a solvent and causes it to freeze at a lower temperature and boil at a temperature higher than normal.

In summary, *the addition of a nonvolatile solute to a liquid causes both a boiling point elevation and a freezing point depression.* Both boiling point elevation and freezing point depression occur because the vapor pressure of the solvent is lowered by the solute. These changes depend only on the concentration of the solute particles, and not upon the chemical composition of the solute. We will now consider some general quantitative statements which can be made about these changes.

BP elevation and FP depression depend on concentration of the solute particles.

22:4 CALCULATING FREEZING AND BOILING POINTS

It has been found experimentally that 1 mole of nonvolatile solute particles will raise the boiling temperature of 1 kg of water 0.512 C°. The same concentration of solute will lower the freezing point of 1 kg of water 1.86 C°. These two figures are the molal boiling point constant and molal freezing point constant for water. The corresponding constants for some other common solvents are given in Table A-8 of the Appendix. A 1m solution of sugar in water contains 1 mol of solute particles per 1 kg of water. However, a 1m solution of salt contains 2 mol of solute particles (1 mol of Na^+ and 1 mol of Cl^- ions). A 1m solution of calcium chloride contains 3 mol of solute particles per 1 kg of water (1 mol of Ca^{2+} and 2 mol of Cl^- ions). The 1m sugar solution freezes 1.86 C° below the freezing point of pure water. However, the 1m salt solution freezes about 2(1.86 C°) below the freezing point of pure water. The 1m solution of calcium chloride freezes approximately 3(1.86 C°) below the freezing point of pure water. The multiple lowering of the freezing point and elevation of the boiling point by ionic substances supports the theory of dissociation.

EXAMPLE: Freezing Point Depression and Boiling Point Elevation

If 85.0 grams of sugar are dissolved in 392 grams of water, what will be the boiling point and freezing point of the resulting solution? The molecular formula of sugar is $C_{12}H_{22}O_{11}$.

Solving process:
(a) Determine the number of moles of solute. The mass of one mole of $C_{12}H_{22}O_{11}$ equals 342 g.
Since there are 85.0 g of sugar present, the number of moles of sugar in 392 g of water is found by

$$\frac{85.0 \text{ g } C_{12}H_{22}O_{11}}{} \left| \frac{1 \text{ mol } C_{12}H_{22}O_{11}}{342 \text{ g } C_{12}H_{22}O_{11}} \right. = 0.248 \text{ mol of } C_{12}H_{22}O_{11}$$

(b) Convert this quantity to mol/1000 g of water. The result is the molality of the solution.

$m = \dfrac{\text{moles of solute}}{\text{kilogram of solvent}}$

$$\frac{0.248 \text{ mol } C_{12}H_{22}O_{11}}{392 \text{ g water}} \left| \frac{1000 \text{ g water}}{1 \text{ kg water}} \right. = 0.633 \, m \text{ solution}$$

(c) Determine the boiling point elevation. The boiling point is raised 0.512 C° for each mole of sugar added to 1000 g of water. Therefore, the boiling point is

$$100°C + (0.633)(0.512 \text{ C}°) = (100 + 0.324)°C = 100.324°C$$

(d) Determine the freezing point depression. The freezing point is lowered 1.86 C° for each mole of sugar added to 1000 g of water. Therefore, the freezing point is

$$0°C - (0.633)(1.86 \text{ C°}) = (0 - 1.18)°C = -1.18°C$$

Let us review what we have done. To determine the change in the freezing point, we multiplied the freezing point constant by the molality. We used a similar process for determining the boiling point elevation. To aid in remembering this process, we can write two equations representing the mathematical steps we have performed.

$$\Delta T_{FP} = (m)(K_{FP})$$

$$\Delta T_{BP} = (m)(K_{BP})$$

We may use these equations in solving boiling and freezing point problems. They may also be used in solving molecular mass problems as will be seen in the next section.

EXAMPLE: Freezing Point Depression and Boiling Point Elevation

If 26.4 grams of nickel(II) bromide are dissolved in 224 grams of water, what will be the boiling point and freezing point of the resulting solutions? (Assume 100% dissociation and no interaction between ions.)

Solving process:

(a) Determine the number of moles of solute. The formula mass of one mole of $NiBr_2$ is 58.7 g + 2(79.9 g) = 219 g. The number of moles of $NiBr_2$ is

$$\frac{26.4 \text{ g NiBr}_2}{} \quad \frac{1 \text{ mol NiBr}_2}{219 \text{ g NiBr}_2} = 0.121 \text{ mol NiBr}_2$$

(b) Determine the molality of the solution. Since the mass of water is 224 g, the molality equals

$$\frac{0.121 \text{ mol}}{224 \text{ g water}} \quad \frac{1000 \text{ g water}}{1 \text{ kg water}} = 0.540m \text{ NiBr}_2$$

However, the molality in total particles is three times this number 3(0.540) or 1.62m because

$$NiBr_2(c) \rightarrow Ni^{2+}(aq) + 2Br^-(aq)$$

(c) Determine the boiling point.

$$\text{Boiling point} = 100°C + \Delta T_{BP} = 100°C + (m)(K_{BP})$$

$$= 100°C + (1.62m)(0.512 \text{ C°}) = 100.829°C$$

$\Delta T_{BP} = m \cdot K_{BP}$

(d) Determine the freezing point.

$$\Delta T_{FP} = m \cdot K_{FP}$$

Freezing point $= 0°C - \Delta T_{FP} = 0°C - (m)(K_{FP})$

$$= 0°C - (1.62m)(1.86 \ C°) = -3.01°C$$

See Table A-8 in the Appendix
for constants.

PROBLEM

3. a. FP = −3.50°C
        BP = 100.964°C

  b. FP = −6.45°C
      BP = 101.78°C

  c. FP = −5.19°C
      BP = 101.43°C

  d. FP = −12.5°C
      BP = 103.44°C

  e. FP = −6.7°C
      BP = 219°C

3. Compute the boiling and freezing points of the following
   solutions.
   a. 47.7 grams $C_7H_{11}NO_7S$ *(4-nitro-2-toluenesulfonic acid
      dihydrate)* in 100 grams H_2O (nonionizing solute).
   b. 100 grams $C_{10}H_8O_6S_2$ *(1,5-naphthalenedisulfonic acid)*
      in 100 grams H_2O (nonionizing solute)
   c. 21.6 grams $NiSO_4$ in 100 grams H_2O (assume 100% ioniza-
      tion)
   d. 100 grams $Mg(ClO_4)_2$ in 200 grams H_2O (assume 100%
      ionization)
   e. 41.3 grams $C_{15}H_9NO_4$ *(2-methyl-1-nitroanthraquinone)*
      in 100 grams $C_6H_5NO_2$ *(nitrobenzene)*

**FIGURE 22-4. This drawing
shows an apparatus used in
molecular mass determinations
based on freezing point depression.**

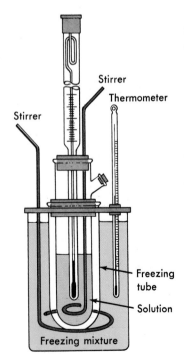

22:5 EXPERIMENTAL DETERMINATION OF MOLECULAR MASS

Molecular mass of a solute may be determined by using boiling point elevation or freezing point depression. A known mass
of the solute is added to known mass of a solvent. The resulting
shift in the boiling or freezing point is then measured.

EXAMPLE: Molecular Mass Determination

99.0 grams of nonionizing solute are dissolved in 669 grams of
water, and the freezing point of the resulting solution is −0.96°C.
What is the molecular mass of the solute?

Solving process:
(a) Determine the molality of the solution.

$$\Delta T_{FP} = (m)(K_{FP}) \qquad m = \frac{\Delta T_{FP}}{K_{FP}}$$

$$m = \frac{0.96 \ C°}{} \ \left| \ \frac{1m}{1.86 \ C°} \right. = 0.516 \ \text{mol/kg}$$

(b) Calculate the molecular mass.

$$\frac{99.0 \ \text{g solute}}{669 \ \text{g water}} \ \left| \ \frac{1000 \ \text{g}}{1 \ \text{kg}} \right. \ \left| \ \frac{1 \ \text{kg}}{0.516 \ \text{mol}} \right. = 287 \ \text{g/mol}$$

molality   *convert*   *convert*
                  to grams   *to moles*

PROBLEM

See Table A-8 in the Appendix for constants.

4. Calculate the molecular mass of the nonionic solutes. Use Table A-8 of the Appendix if necessary.

   a. 6.70 grams of solute in 983 grams of water lower the freezing point to $-0.430°C$.

   b. 42.1 grams of solute in 189 grams of water raise the boiling point to $100.680°C$.

   c. 20.8 grams of solute in 128 grams of acetic acid lower the freezing point to $13.5°C$.

   d. 10.4 grams of solute in 164 grams of phenol lower the freezing point to $36.3°C$.

   e. 2.53 grams of solute in 63.5 grams of nitrobenzene lower the freezing point to $3.40°C$.

4. a. 29.5 g/mol
   b. 168 g/mol
   c. 206 g/mol
   d. 94.6 g/mol
   e. 134 g/mol

22:6 OSMOTIC PRESSURE

There is another colligative property which is of great importance in living systems. Consider Figure 22-5. Two liquids are separated by a thin film called a membrane. One liquid is a pure solvent and the other liquid is a solution (with the same solvent). The membrane separating the liquids is a special kind of membrane called a semipermeable membrane. Semipermeable membranes will allow small particles (ions and molecules) to pass through, but will stop large molecules. As a result of an unequal passing of particles, a pressure difference builds up between the two sides of the membrane. This pressure is called the **osmotic pressure** of the solution. Osmotic processes are very important in the human body. Absorption of the products of digestion and the operation of the kidney as a waste remover are two osmotic processes vital to life.

Osmosis: Diffusion through a semipermeable membrane.

Osmotic pressure (π): Pressure difference between two sides of membrane.

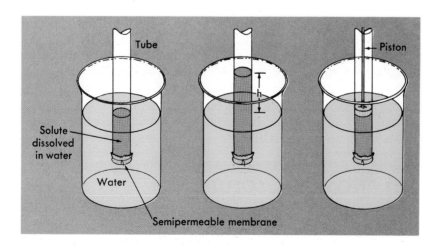

FIGURE 22-5. Osmotic pressure can be measured as the force applied to the piston to oppose the osmotic flow through the membrane.

Demonstration — Osmotic pressure can be shown by using a carrot or potato in a beaker of H_2O. Bore a large hole in the top, add 10 cm^3 of saturated sugar solution. Then stopper the hole with a 1-hole rubber stopper fitted with a 30 cm length of glass tubing. The water will go up the tube slowly. Allow at least 1 day before observing the results.

Since osmotic pressure is a colligative property, it can be expressed in an equation such as

$$\pi = (m)(K_{osm})$$

However, the constant for osmosis is highly temperature dependent. As a result, osmotic pressure is expressed in the form

$$\pi = MRT$$

In this equation, π is the osmotic pressure, M is the molarity of the solution, R is the ideal gas constant, and T is the kelvin temperature.

EXAMPLE: Osmotic Pressure

What osmotic pressure would be exerted by a solution which is 1.82M at 18°C?

Solving process:

$$\pi = MRT$$

Since the units of R are dm$^3 \cdot$kPa/mol$\cdot$K, we will express our molarity as 1.82 mol/1.00 dm^3.

$$\pi = \frac{1.82 \text{ mol}}{1.00 \text{ dm}^3} \ \left| \ \frac{8.31 \text{ dm}^3 \cdot \text{kPa}}{\text{mol} \cdot \text{K}} \ \right| \ \frac{291 \text{ K}}{} = 4.40 \times 10^3 \text{ kPa}$$

PROBLEMS

5. 18.6 grams of a solute with molecular mass 8940 grams are dissolved in enough water to make 1.00 dm^3 of solution at 25°C. What is the osmotic pressure of the solution?

6. 96.0 grams of a solute are dissolved in enough water to make 1.00 dm^3 of solution at 25°C. The osmotic pressure of the resulting solution is 15.8 kPa. What is the molecular mass of the solute?

7. 81.0 grams of a solute with molecular mass 4010 grams are dissolved in enough water to make 1.00 dm^3 of solution at 20.0°C. What is the osmotic pressure of the solution?

8. 200 grams of a solute are dissolved in enough water to make 1.00 dm^3 of solution at 21.0°C. The osmotic pressure of the resulting solution is 100 kPa. What is the molecular mass of the solute?

22:7 NONIDEAL SOLUTIONS

Chemists generally make the assumption that ionic compounds are completely dissociated in water solution. However, data obtained from colligative property experiments seem to

5. 5.15 kPa
6. 15 000 g/mol
7. 49.2 kPa
8. 4890 g/mol

contradict the assumption. The same indication comes from measurements of the solubility of certain compounds. The reasons for the deviation of these solutions from ideal behavior is the attractive force between oppositely charged ions. All real solutions deviate slightly from Raoult's law. However, except for this section, we are assuming that all solutions are ideal. In other words, we assume they obey Raoult's law.

Let us look at a specific case of deviation from Raoult's law. One mole of sodium chloride should produce 1 mole each of sodium ions and chloride ions. Therefore, you would expect a $2m$ solution of NaCl would lower the freezing point of the water by 4(1.86 C°) or 7.44 C°. Salt actually lowers the freezing point only about three-quarters of this amount. This difference between theory and experiment is explained by assuming that the solute is completely dissociated into ions and that these ions interact. A more detailed explanation of ion interaction in solution is given by the Debye-Hückel theory which is covered on page 510.

The actual ion effectiveness in freezing point depression and boiling point elevation is known as the **activity** of the ion. In dealing with a nonideal solution, chemists use activities in place of concentrations. As the solution becomes more concentrated, each ion individually becomes less effective through interaction with its neighboring ions.

22:8 COLLOIDS AND PHASES

In 1861, Thomas Graham, an English chemist, tested the passage of different substances through a parchment membrane. He found that one group of substances passed readily through the membrane, and another group did not pass through it at all. He called the first group **crystalloids** and the second group colloids. The name **colloid** means gluelike, and glue was one of the substances which did not pass readily through the membrane. Graham thought the ability or inability to pass through the membrane was due to particle size. It was later discovered that any substance could be used to produce a colloid. Included were some of those substances Graham had classified as crystalloids. Colloids are now defined as mixtures composed of two phases of matter, the dispersed phase and the continuous phase. They are intermediate class between suspensions and solutions. Colloid particles are larger than the single atoms, ions, or molecules of solutions. They are smaller than the particles of suspensions, which can be seen through a microscope and which settle out of suspension on standing. Colloids include materials labeled as emulsions, aerosols, foams, and gels.

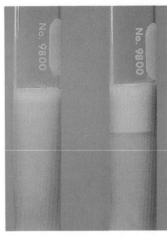

National Bureau of Standards

Hickson-Bender Photography

FIGURE 22-6. Smoke particles are too small to settle out on standing. Milk is a colloid that can be separated into its components using a centrifuge.

Larry Hamill

FIGURE 22-7. Gels and foams are classified as colloids.

22:9   COLLOIDAL SIZE

Colloidal particles are too small to be seen with a microscope. In 1912, Richard Zsigmondy, a German professor of chemistry, designed the ultramicroscope. Using the ultramicroscope, it is possible to "see" colloidal particles. If a finely ground substance is placed in water, one of three things will happen. First, it may form a true solution which is simply a dispersion of atoms, molecules, or ions of the substance into a solvent. The size limit of the particles in a true solution is about 1 nm.

Second, the particles may remain larger than 100 nm. These particles are large enough to be seen with a microscope. They are strongly affected by gravity and gradually fall to the bottom of the container. Since the particles are temporarily suspended and settle out upon standing, this mixture is called a **suspension.**

Particles from 1 to 100 nm in size usually remain dispersed throughout the medium. Such a mixture is called a colloid. Colloids are neither homogeneous nor heterogeneous. They represent a transition between homogeneous solutions and heterogeneous suspensions. However, they are considered heterogeneous (with the medium as one phase and the dispersed substance as a separate phase).

Table 22-2

Comparison of Solutions, Suspensions, and Colloids		
Type	**Particle size**	**Permanence**
Solution	<1 nm	permanent
Suspension	>100 nm	settle out
Colloid	<100 nm but > 1 nm	permanent

Actually, it is not enough to refer to colloids as being composed of particles in the above size range. Substances show unusual properties even when only one of the three dimensions of the particles is in the colloidal range. Included are thin sheets as well as minute particles. Colloid chemistry is defined as the study of the properties of matter whose particles are colloidal in size in at least one dimension.

Table 22-3

Properties of Solutions, Colloids, and Suspensions		
Solutions	**Colloids**	**Suspensions**
Do not settle out	Do not settle out	Settle out on standing
Pass unchanged through ordinary filter paper	Pass unchanged through ordinary filter paper	Separated by ordinary filter paper
Pass unchanged through membrane	Separated by a membrane	Separated by a membrane
Do not scatter light	Scatter light	Scatter light
Affect colligative properties	Do not affect colligative properties	Do not affect colligative properties

22:10 PROPERTIES OF COLLOIDS

If a beam of light is allowed to pass through a true solution, some of the light will be absorbed, and some will be transmitted. The particles in solution are not large enough to scatter the light. However, if light is passed through a colloid, the light is scattered by the larger, colloidal particles. The beam becomes visible from the side. This effect, called the **Tyndall effect,** is used in Zsigmondy's ultramicroscope. You may be familiar with this effect in seeing the beam of a searchlight in the night air (suspended water droplets in air). You may also have observed it as the sunbeam coming through a hole in the blinds (suspended dust particles in the air).

The table may be used to derive experimental methods of differentiating the three kinds of mixtures.

Tyndall effect: The scattering of light by colloid particles.

Demonstration—In a darkened room, pass a spot light beam through a large beaker containing 700 cm³ of H_2O and 5 g of sodium thiosulfate to which 5 cm³ of concentrated HCl has just been added. As colloidal sulfur forms, scattered blue light can be seen, 90° from the beam. On the wall, the spot light beam will change colors as in a sunset. Discuss how colloids in the air affect a sunset.

FIGURE 22-8. A light beam passes through a solution, but a colloid scatters the light (a). The Tyndall effect can be seen as light passes through fog (b).

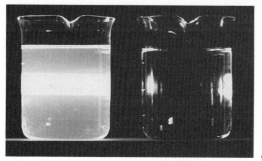

a   *b*

Hickson-Bender Photography   Ruth Fridenstine

Colloids have another interesting property. If you could look through an ultramicroscope, you would notice that the colloidal particles are in continuous motion. This motion, called **Brownian motion,** is a random motion of the particles. This motion is caused by their constant bombardment by the smaller molecules of the medium. The motion is the result of the collision of many molecules with the particle. It is as if a large crust of bread is moved back and forth as first one fish and then another hits the bread from opposite sides. Brownian motion is named in honor of Robert Brown, a biologist. Brown first noticed it while observing the motion of particles in a suspension of pollen grains in water.

As noted in Chapter 17, particles on the surface of a liquid are subject to unbalanced forces. Atoms, ions, or molecules at the surface of solids are also subject to unbalanced forces. As a result, solid and liquid surfaces tend to attract and hold substances with which they come into contact. This phenomenon is called **adsorption.** The stationary phase in chromatography operates through adsorption. Colloidal particles, because of their small size, have an extremely large ratio of surface to mass. A cube with a volume of 1 cm^3 has a surface area of 6 cm^2. If that cube is cut into 1000 smaller cubes of equal size, the surface area of that same amount of matter is now 60 cm^2. If we subdivide these cubes until they measure 10 nm on edge, the surface area has risen to 6 000 000 000 cm^2! Such a large surface area makes colloidal particles excellent adsorbing materials, or adsorbents. Dispersed particles have the property of adsorbing charge on the surface.

If a colloid is subjected to an electric field, a migration of the particles can be observed. The positive particles are attracted to the cathode. The negative particles are attracted to the anode. This migration, called **electrophoresis,** is evidence that colloid particles are charged. The separation of amino acids and peptides obtained in protein analysis is accomplished rapidly using electrophoresis. The process is also common in nucleic acid research.

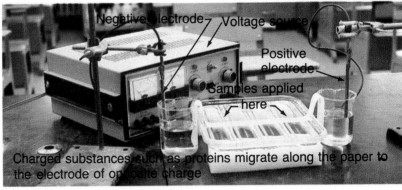

FIGURE 22-9. An electrophoresis apparatus is used in separating mixtures containing charged particles. Negative particles move toward the anode. Positive particles move toward the cathode.

Robert C. Smoot

Thomas Graham (1805–1869)

Thomas Graham, known as the "father of colloid chemistry," was strongly opposed in his scientific pursuits early in life. Graham's father was insistent that his son be a clergyman and withdrew funds for his education when he persisted in the study of science.

He formulated the law that today bears his name. It relates the relative rates of diffusion of dissimilar gases. The study of diffusion and effusion of gases led Graham to investigate the passage of materials through membranes. When he discovered that some substances would diffuse through a membrane and others would not, he attempted to classify all materials as either crystalloids or colloids. The process of separating materials by passing them through a membrane is called dialysis and is used today in both industrial and research laboratories.

CHEMICAL TECHNOLOGY: Explosives

When someone mentions explosives, most of us immediately think of weapons of war. However, large quantities of explosives are used by industry. Mining and quarrying are two industries using explosives.

Explosives are substances which react quite rapidly and produce large quantities of heat and large volumes of gases. These products exert a considerable force on their surroundings. One way of classifying explosives is by their sensitivity. The sensitivity of an explosive is the ease with which it may be detonated, or set off.

Explosives of moderate sensitivity often require more sensitive explosives called primers or detonators to set them off. Moderately sensitive explosives, on the other hand, may act as boosters to set off a low sensitivity explosive. A typical series might be a primer of mercury(II) fulminate, $Hg(OCN)_2$, a booster of tetryl, $(NO_2)_3C_6H_2CH_3NNO_2$, and a main charge of TNT, $CH_3C_6H_2(NO_2)_3$. Such an explosive might be used to crack rock near a water table when drilling a water well.

Another way of classifying explosives is based on brisance, which is the rate at which the explosion occurs. Most industrial applications call for a moderate brisance to obtain a shattering effect. A 40% TNT/60% $C_3H_6N_6O_6$ (RDX) mixture provides a very high brisance for military shells.

RDX

Tetryl

TNT

$$CH_2-O-NO_2$$
$$|$$
$$CH-O-NO_2$$
$$|$$
$$CH_2-O-NO_2$$
Nitroglycerin

Picric Acid

The most common industrial explosive is a mixture of 94% ammonium nitrate pellets and 6% fuel oil. This mixture has moderate brisance and low sensitivity. Thus it requires a booster. Dynamite is another popular industrial explosive. Dynamite consists of 20–60% nitroglycerine, some sodium nitrate as an oxidizer, and a mixture of sawdust, starch, and other carbon-containing substances which will absorb the oily nitroglycerine. Dynamite sensitivity is fairly high, so it needs only a detonator, but not a booster. It is useful for removing stumps, digging ditches, and similar localized jobs.

SUMMARY

1. The vapor pressure of a solution is the sum of the vapor pressures of its components. The vapor pressure of a component of a solution is its normal vapor pressure multiplied by its mole fraction in the solution. 22:1

2. Many substances can be separated by taking advantage of the difference 22:2 in their vapor pressures. The process used is called fractional distillation.

3. Solutes affect the vapor pressure, boiling point, freezing point, and osmotic pressure of a solvent. 22:1

4. Changes in boiling and freezing points may be calculated from the relations
$$\Delta T_{FP} = (m)(K_{FP}) \text{ and } \Delta T_{BP} = (m)(K_{BP}) \quad \text{22:3-22:5}$$

5. Osmotic pressure can be computed from $\pi = MRT$. 22:6

6. Ideal solutions obey Raoult's law. 22:1, 22:7

22:9 7. Colloid particles range between 1 and 100 nm in at least one dimension.

8. A colloid is composed of two phases: the dispersed phase and the continuous phase. 22:8

9. Colloids possess some unusual properties. They can scatter light (Tyndall effect), undergo constant random motion (Brownian motion), and act as excellent adsorbing materials. 22:10

PROBLEMS

9. What are colligative properties?

    9. vapor pressure
    freezing point
    boiling point
    osmosis

10. What is the relationship between Raoult's law and ideal solutions?

11. Define a nonvolatile solute.

12. How does the addition of a nonvolatile solute cause the freezing point of the solvent to be depressed? lowers vapor pressure

13. How does a colloid differ from a suspension? particle size is smaller

14. What is the vapor pressure of a solution composed of 133 grams of citric acid, $C_6H_8O_7$, (nonvolatile solute) in 100 grams of water at 60°C? 17.7 kPa

15. What is the vapor pressure at 24°C of a solution of 6.05 grams of benzene, C_6H_6, (vapor pressure = 12.1 kPa) and 1.60 grams of chloroform, $CHCl_3$, (vapor pressure = 25.2 kPa)? 14.0 kPa

16. Calculate the boiling point and the freezing point of the following solutions of molecular substances.
    a. 97.5 grams of $C_{12}H_{22}O_{11}$ *(sucrose)* in 185 grams of water
    b. 14.0 grams of $C_{10}H_8$ *(naphthalene)* in 25.0 grams of C_6H_6
    c. 500 grams of $C_{20}H_{27}NO_{11} \cdot 3H_2O$ *(amygdalin trihydrate)* in 500 grams of water
    d. 250 grams of $C_7H_4BrNO_4$ *(3-bromo-2-nitrobenzoic acid)* in 500 grams C_6H_6
    e. 60.0 grams of C_9H_{18} *(propylcyclohexane)* in 100 grams of acetic acid

16. a. BP = 100.788°C,
FP = −2.86°C
b. BP = 91.2°C,
FP = −15.9°C
c. BP = 101.00°C,
FP = −3.65°C
d. BP = 85.2°C,
FP = −4.5°C
e. BP = 119°C,
FP = 14.7°C

17. What is the molecular mass of a nonionic solute, if 5.60 grams of it in 104 grams of water lower the freezing point to −0.603°C? 166 g/mol

18. Find the osmotic pressure exerted by 8.10 grams of solute of molecular mass 1310 grams in 1.00 dm^3 of water at 22°C. 15.2 kPa

REVIEW

1. What is the molality of a solution made from 100 grams of water and 20.0 grams of $Fe_2(C_2O_4)_3$? 0.532 m

2. How would you prepare a 0.560 m solution of Li_2S from 250 cm^3 of water? dissolve 6.43 g Li_2S in 250 g H_2O

3. What is the mole fraction of acetone, $(CH_3)_2CO$, in a solution of 50 grams of acetone and 50 grams of water? 0.237 mole fraction acetone

ONE MORE STEP

1. Try to separate a solution of two liquids by distillation, with and without a fractionating column. See your instructor about technique and possible mixtures to use.

2. An ultracentrifuge can be used to separate colloids. Prepare a report to the class on the use of this apparatus in characterizing colloids.

3. Find out what methods are now being used industrially to remove dust from stack gases and reduce air pollution.

4. Find three examples of protective colloids.

5. Describe the structure of protoplasm in terms of solutions, liquid crystals, and colloids.

READINGS

Mysels, Karol J., "Solvent Tension or Solvent Dilution." *Journal of Chemical Education*, Vol. 55, No. 1 (January 1978), pp. 21-22.

Sarquis, Jerry, "Colloidal Systems." *Journal of Chemical Education*, Vol. 57, No. 8 (August 1980), pp. 602-605.

The light in the test tube is produced during a chemical reaction. In this case, the energy produced by the reaction is in the form of visible light. This reaction differs from a combustion reaction in that it is not exothermic. The light produced is referred to as cold light. The reaction is highly specific and a catalyst is required for it to occur. What is the function of a catalyst? How is a reaction changed by a catalyst? What conditions govern the rate of a reaction? Why might scientists be interested in the large scale production of cold light?

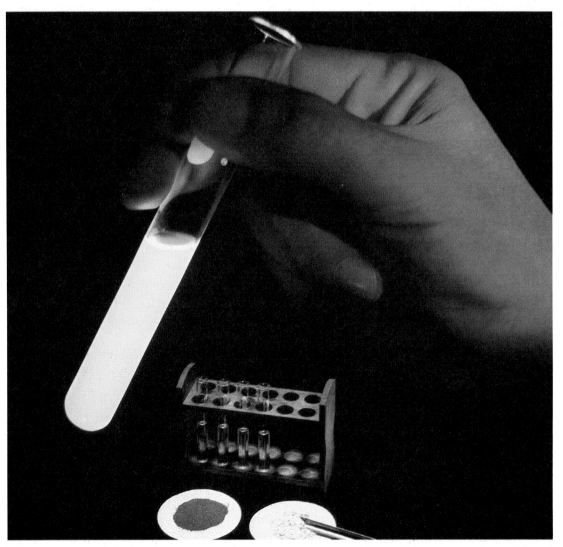

Hickson-Bender Photography

REACTION RATE AND CHEMICAL EQUILIBRIUM

23

Chapter 23 begins with the study of reaction rates and the factors that affect the rate of a chemical reaction. The quantitative study of equilibrium is then presented.

Demonstration—Clock Reaction. This demonstration can be used to introduce the study of reaction rate, reaction mechanisms, and the rate determining step. It is dramatic for students to see two solutions mixed and then turn blue-black after 6-7 seconds. The system then remains at equilibrium. For preparation details see the Teacher's Guide.

In studying the properties of matter, chemists wish to find out both the physical and the chemical characteristics of a substance. They want to be able to describe the behavior of a given substance with many other substances. Does it react? We have found that the change in free energy for a reaction can be used to answer that question. Of great importance, especially to the industrial chemist, is the answer to the question: How fast does it react?

Josiah Willard Gibbs discovered the relationship between entropy and enthalpy called the free energy. The amount of free energy after a spontaneous reaction is less than before the reaction.

Consider the reaction

$$2TiO \rightarrow 2Ti + O_2 \qquad \Delta G° = +495 \text{ kJ}$$

Since the free energy change is positive, the reaction does not take place. Titanium(II) oxide does not spontaneously decompose at room temperature. It is said to be **thermodynamically stable.**

As we have seen, a negative free energy change (ΔG is negative) indicates a reaction will proceed spontaneously. However, some spontaneous reactions take place so slowly that it takes hundreds of years for any observable change to occur. For example, the ΔG for combustion of glucose, a common sugar, is

$$C_6H_{12}O_6(c) + 6O_2(g) \rightarrow 6CO_2(g) + 6H_2O(l) \qquad \Delta G = -2870 \text{ kJ}$$

However, at room temperature, the reaction proceeds so slowly that sugar is said to be kinetically stable. Therefore, to predict whether a given spontaneous reaction will be useful, we must know the rate at which the reaction occurs as well as at what point equilibrium is established.

GOAL: You will gain an understanding of the factors which affect the rate of a reaction and the relationship of these factors to chemical equilibrium.

The free energy change is the maximum work that can be obtained from a system.

A thermodynamically stable substance does not decompose spontaneously (ΔG is positive).

The free energy decreases (ΔG is negative) in a spontaneous reaction because the system is changing to a more stable state.

A kinetically stable reaction proceeds very slowly at room temperature.

Consider what happens when we add an ice cube to a beaker of water. The temperature of the water drops. Heat is absorbed as the ice cube gets smaller and solid ice is converted into liquid water. We may represent this process by an equation.

$$solid + heat \rightarrow liquid$$

If we use a thermos bottle instead of a beaker and our ice cube is large enough, the temperature of the water will drop to 0°C. After the temperature reaches 0°C, we observe no further melting of the ice. If we now add a piece of metal which has been chilled to −20°C, we may be surprised to find that the ice cube grows larger! Evidently the process can go either way. At 0°C an equilibrium exists.

At 0°C, an ice-water mixture is in equilibrium.

$$solid + heat \rightleftarrows liquid$$

The relative amounts of solid and liquid can be changed by adding or removing a small amount of heat without changing the temperature. We say that the water-ice mixture is in equilibrium.

23:1 REVERSIBLE REACTIONS

Remind students that chemical equations are algebraic and subject to the same laws as other algebraic equations.

A chemist studies the structure of matter and the properties which result from this structure. Some of these properties are chemical reactions. Actually, the study of chemical reactions is the study of the breaking and forming of chemical bonds. The formation of chemical bonds is a complex subject. So far we have discussed only the simplest chemical reactions, those which go to completion. A reaction goes to completion when all of one of the reactants is used completely and the reaction stops. Reactions of this kind go from reactants to products. Not all reactions go to completion. Consider the following reaction.

Not all reactions go to completion.

$$H_2(g) + I_2(g) \rightarrow 2HI(g)$$

The arrow means the reaction is read from left to right, but this equation is only partially correct. The bond between the hydrogen and iodine in the hydrogen iodide molecule is a weak bond. Therefore, hydrogen iodide breaks easily into hydrogen gas and iodine vapor. The following equation represents this reaction.

$$H_2(g) + I_2(g) \leftarrow 2HI(g)$$

Notice the direction in which the arrow points. This reaction is read from right to left. We now combine the two equations.

$$H_2(g) + I_2(g) \rightleftarrows 2HI(g) \qquad \text{(reversible reaction)}$$

The first reaction is said to go from left to right. The second reaction is said to go from right to left. The combined equation represents a **reversible reaction.** Note that this use of the word reversible is different from the use in Chapter 18 concerning work.

FIGURE 23-1. The rate for the reaction $H_2 + I_2 \rightleftarrows 2HI$ can be expressed as the rate of appearance of the product, HI, or the rate at which the reactants, H_2 and I_2, disappear.

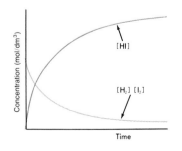

Concentration (mol/dm³)

[HI]

[H₂] [I₂]

Time

23:2 REACTION RATE

Suppose the product of a reversible reaction decomposes faster than the reactants form the product. Then there will always be more reactant than product. Here is an example. HI decomposes to H_2 and I_2 more rapidly than H_2 unites with I_2 to form HI. There will always be more hydrogen and iodine than hydrogen iodide. Consider a flask containing hydrogen, iodine, and hydrogen iodide. The hydrogen iodide is decomposing rapidly, more rapidly than H_2 and I_2 can combine to produce it. The rate of disappearance of hydrogen iodide is defined to be the reaction rate.

$$H_2(g) + I_2(g) \leftarrow 2HI(g) \text{ (rate of disappearance of HI)}$$

(Notice this reaction is the reverse reaction read from right to left.) The rate of appearance of hydrogen iodide is defined as the rate of the reaction from left to right.

$$H_2(g) + I_2(g) \rightarrow 2HI(g) \text{ (rate of appearance of HI)}$$

Reaction rate is usually defined in terms of the rate of disappearance of one of the reactants. It can also be defined as the rate of appearance of one of the products. The usual units for reaction rates are $mol/dm^3/s$. What we are actually measuring is the rate of change of concentration. If we know the two reaction rates, we can predict whether product or reactant will be in the higher concentration at equilibrium. We will now consider some factors which affect reaction rates.

Reaction rate is the rate of disappearance of reactant or rate of appearance of product.

23:3 NATURE OF REACTANTS

The nature of the reactants involved in a reaction will determine the kind of reaction that occurs. Reactions with bond rearrangement or electron transfer take longer than reactions without these changes. Ionic reactions (such as double displacement and neutralization reactions) occur almost instantaneously. They are rapid because ions of one charge are attracted by those of opposite charge and ions collide frequently.

In a reaction between ions, no electron transfer is involved. Reactions between neutral molecules are slower than ionic reactions because electron transfer and bond rearrangement must occur. As pointed out in Chapter 15, most molecular collisions are elastic. The molecules simply rebound and move away unchanged. However, some collisions do have enough energy to cause changes in the electron clouds of the colliding molecules. When the change occurs, the colliding molecules may form an **activated complex.** The energy required to form the activated complex is known as the **activation energy.** If the activation energy is high, few collisions have enough energy to form the activated complex. As a

Reaction rate depends upon the nature of the reactants.

Ionic reactions involve no electron transfer, and are rapid.

The activated complex forms when molecules collide with enough energy to change their electron clouds.
The activation energy is the energy required to form the activated complex.

Emphasize that most reactions occur in a series of steps called the reaction mechanism. Often several different mechanisms are possible for the same overall reaction. Where a catalyst is involved, the mechanism for the catalyzed reaction is always different from the mechanism for the uncatalyzed one.

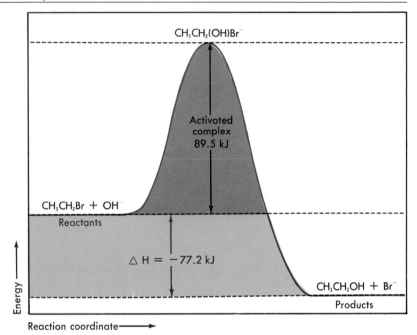

FIGURE 23-2. Activation energy is that energy which must be attained in order for a collision between the reactants to result in the formation of an activated complex.

result, the reaction may be so slow that it cannot be detected. Consider the following reaction.

$$CH_3CH_2Br + OH^- \rightarrow CH_3CH_2OH + Br^-.$$

The activated complex is $CH_3CH_2(OH)Br^-$. From Figure 23-2 we can see that the activation energy is 89.5 kJ per mole of CH_3CH_2Br. We can also see that the enthalpy change for the reaction is −77.2 kJ. We can now see why some substances are kinetically stable even though many of their reactions may have negative free energy changes. These reactions have very high activation energies. Consequently, unless very strong reaction conditions are used, the reactions do not take place.

FIGURE 23-3. The Hindenberg explosion was a reaction between hydrogen in the ship and oxygen in the air. It is believed that lightening or some other electric spark caused the reaction.

UPI

For example, hydrogen and oxygen can be kept in the same container at room temperature for ages without reacting to form water. Although the molecules collide, the activation energy will not be reached. If, however, the mixture is heated to 800°C, or a flame or spark is introduced, a violent reaction occurs. The heat, flame, or spark furnishes the activation energy.

Most reactions occur in a series of steps. Each step normally involves the collision of only two particles. Steps involving three or more particles are unlikely. There is little chance of three or more particles colliding with the proper position and energy to cause a reaction.

Most reactions occur in a series of steps.

If a reaction consists of several steps such as the following

$$A \rightarrow B$$

$$B \rightarrow C$$

$$C \rightarrow final\ product$$

one of the steps will be slower than all the others. This step is called the **rate determining step.** The other faster steps will not affect the rate. The series of reaction steps that must occur for a reaction to go to completion is called the **reaction mechanism.**

23:4 CONCENTRATION

Concentration refers to the quantity of matter that exists in a unit volume. For instance, in Chapter 5 we discussed the concentration in mol/dm^3 of solution. We referred to this concentration as the molarity of the solution. For a reaction to take place, the particles must collide. If the number of particles per unit volume is increased, the chance of their colliding is also increased. Reconsider the equation

Demonstration—Burn sulfur or charcoal in a bottle of air and then in a bottle of oxygen gas. The concentration of O_2 is increased, and so is the rate of the reaction.

Reaction rate depends upon concentration (molarity) of the reactants.

$$H_2(g) + I_2(g) \rightarrow 2HI(g)$$

If we keep the concentration of the hydrogen molecules the same, we would expect doubling the concentration of iodine to double the number of collisions between iodine and hydrogen molecules. In turn, the reaction rate would double. Actual experiment confirms that the rate of reaction varies directly as the concentration of iodine. Written in equation form, it is

Suggestion: Concentration has been discussed in Chapters 5 and 21. Review these discussions and spend extra time on the discussion of concentration in this chapter. It is important that students have a good grasp of the concept of concentration before proceeding further.

$$rate_1 = k_1[I_2]$$

where the brackets around the $I_2([\ \ ])$ mean "mol/dm^3."

What if the concentration of iodine remains constant, and the concentration of hydrogen is allowed to vary? We can say that the number of collisions and, therefore, the reaction rate, varies directly as the concentration of hydrogen molecules. We write

[ ] mean mol/dm^3

$$rate_2 = k_2[H_2]$$

If we allow the concentration of both iodine and hydrogen to vary, what will happen? If we double the concentration of hydrogen and also double the concentration of iodine, there will be four times as many molecules. What will the reaction rate be? There will be four times as many molecules per unit volume and four times as many collisions. The reaction rate is found to be quadrupled. We conclude, then, that *the reaction rate varies directly as the product of the concentrations of hydrogen and iodine.* We write

$$rate = k[H_2][I_2]$$

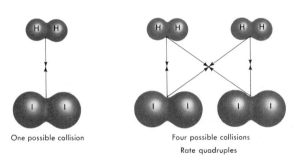

One possible collision   Four possible collisions
                                  Rate quadruples

The dependence of the rate on the increased number of particles in the activation energy range is given by the Arrhenius equation:

$$k = Ae^{-E_a/RT}$$

where k = specific
      rate constant
  A = a constant for a
      particular reaction
  e = base of natural
      logarithms
E_a = activation energy
  R = gas constant
  T = absolute
      temperature
The slope of a plot of ln k vs. $1/T$ is used to determine E_a.

FIGURE 23-4. An increase in the concentration (number of particles) of the reactants increases the number of effective collisions to form products.

In this case, the constant k depends upon the size, speed, and kind of molecule involved in the reaction. Each reaction has only one value of k for a given temperature; this k is called the **specific rate constant** of the reaction. It should be pointed out here that the actual mechanism of this reaction involves the breaking of the I-I bond before collision. However, it can be demonstrated mathematically that the same rate expression results.

An increase in the pressure on a gas results in a decrease in the volume occupied by the molecules. Since there are more molecules per unit volume, there has been an increase in concentration. Increasing the pressure on a gas, then, will also increase reaction rate.

Chemical reactions which take place at the interface between two phases are called **heterogeneous reactions.** An example of a heterogeneous reaction is zinc (a solid) dissolving in sulfuric acid (a liquid). The reaction takes place on the surface of the zinc which is the interface between the two phases. If more surface is exposed, the reaction will take place more rapidly. Because of the unusual properties of surface molecules, their bonds are more easily broken. They react more readily than molecules within a solid. Increasing the surface area increases the number of surface molecules in the same space (increases concentration). Increasing surface area, then, increases the rate of a reaction.

Specific rate constant, k, has one value for a given temperature.

An increase in the pressure of a gas has the effect of increasing the concentration, and thus the reaction rate (at constant temperature).

A heterogenous reaction involves two or more phases.

Demonstration—Attempt to light a pile of lycopodium powder or corn starch. Then dust the powder or starch into the flame. **CAUTION:** there will be a flare up of the burner flame. This demonstration is better seen in a darkened room.

Increasing the surface available will increase the reaction rate.

23:5 TEMPERATURE

Reaction rate is determined by the frequency of collision between molecules and increases as the frequency of collision increases. According to the kinetic theory, the speed (kinetic energy) of molecules increases as the temperature increases. Increased kinetic energy means that more collisions will occur and the reaction rate will increase. However, the increase in reaction rate depends less on the increase in the number of collisions than it does on another factor. This other factor is the increase in the number of molecules which have reached activation energy. Note from the graph in Figure 23-5 that molecules must collide with a kinetic energy sufficient to react. Otherwise a collision will not lead to reaction. On the graph, the area under the curve indicates the number of molecules present. At temperature T_1 few molecules have attained activation energy. At temperature T_2, $(T_2 > T_1)$ many more molecules have reached the activation energy. The same number of molecules is present at this higher temperature. However, the fraction of molecules that have attained the activation energy is greater at the higher temperature T_2.

Reaction rate depends upon the temperature of the reactants.

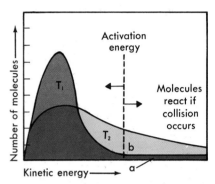

FIGURE 23-5. A ten degree increase in temperature from T_1 to T_2 will double or triple the number of molecules that have sufficient energy to react.

Demonstration—Add an Alka-Seltzer® tablet to each of 3 flasks. One has ice H_2O, one has H_2O at room temperature, and one has H_2O that has been heated. Stopper each flask with a one-hole rubber stopper that has been fitted with a glass tube and a balloon. The rate of expansion of the balloons can easily demonstrate the effect of temperature on the rate of a reaction.

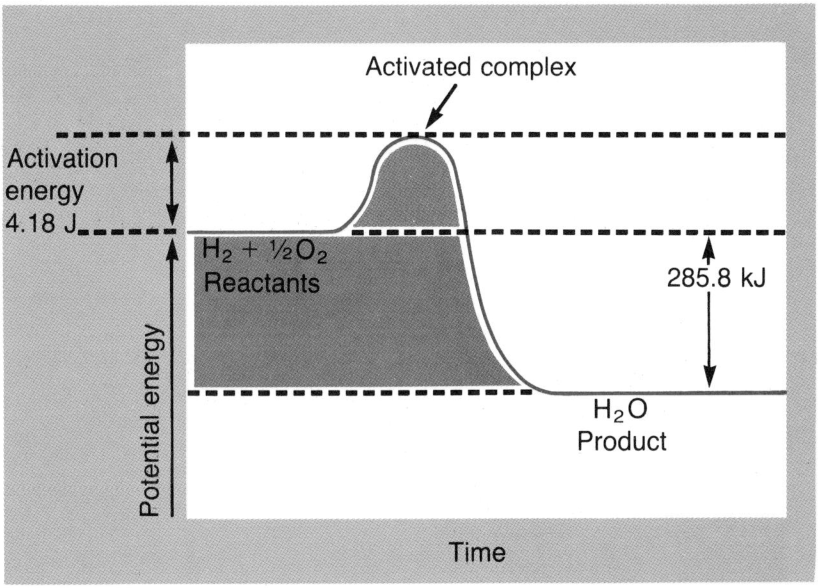

FIGURE 23-6. For the water reaction, the energy of the reactants rises as they collide and their kinetic energy is converted to potential energy.

Figure 23-6 is a graph which shows the energy changes involved in the reaction of hydrogen with oxygen. This graph can be thought of as a map of the potential energy possessed by the atoms and molecules taking part in a reaction. The gases, H_2 and

O_2, are considered to have no potential energy (0 kJ). As two molecules approach, the kinetic energy of motion is transformed into the potential energy of repulsion of electron clouds. As more and more kinetic energy is transformed into potential energy, the line of the graph, which represents potential energy, rises. If the molecules have enough kinetic energy to approach close enough to react chemically, they are said to be activated. **Activated molecules** form an activated complex. From here, the reaction must go downhill in either direction. The activated complex may fall back on the left side and break into H_2 and O_2 molecules, or it may react (fall down on the right side). The chance of falling either way is equal. If the activated complex does react, heat will be released and a molecule of water will be formed. The effect of raising the temperature is to produce more activated complexes through collision. Thus, with the increase in number of activated complexes, the number that will react will also increase.

An increase in temperature will increase the rate of any reaction. More activated complexes are formed because the number of collisions having the required activation energy increases.

23:6 CATALYSIS

A substance which increases a reaction rate without being permanently changed is called a catalyst. **Catalysis** is the process of increasing rates of reaction by the presence of a catalyst. The catalyst remains (apparently) chemically unaffected throughout the reaction. It changes the reaction mechanism in such a way that the activation energy required is less than in the uncatalyzed reaction. We will discuss two kinds of catalysts: the heterogeneous (or contact) catalyst, and the homogeneous catalyst.

The reaction of sulfur dioxide gas with oxygen gas

$$2SO_2(g) + O_2(g) \rightarrow 2SO_3(g)$$

is extremely slow at room temperature. If these two gases are brought into contact in the presence of solid vanadium(V) oxide (V_2O_5), the reaction is rapid. Vanadium(V) oxide is called the catalyst in this reaction. Notice that vanadium(V) oxide is a solid and the reactants are gases. The V_2O_5 lowers the required activation energy by providing a surface on which the activated complex can form.

A reaction in which the reactants and catalysts are not in the same state is a **heterogeneous reaction.** The catalyst is called a **heterogeneous catalyst.** This kind of catalyst has a surface on which the substances can react. Platinum and other finely divided metals and metallic oxides are common examples of this kind of catalyst. Most heterogeneous catalysts work by adsorbing one of the reactants. It might be correct to think of the contact

a

Courtesy of Bell Laboratory

b

Courtesy of Bell Laboratory

c

Janet Adams

FIGURE 23-7. This crystalline catalyst is being tested for use in automobile pollution control (a). The honeycomb shape of this catalyst provides more surface area for a reaction to occur (b). The catalytic convertor allows for more complete combustion thereby reducing the amounts of pollutants released in exhaust (c).

catalyst as taking part in the reaction. **Adsorption** is the adherence of one substance to the surface of another. In the process of adsorbing a molecule, such as O_2, the catalytic surface attracts the O_2 molecule. This attraction weakens the O-O bond to the point where the other reactant can break the O-O bond. The reaction then proceeds. Catalytic converters on automobile exhaust systems employ a contact catalyst.

Adsorption is the adherence of one substance to the surface of another.

A **homogeneous catalyst** exists in the same phase as the reactants. This kind of catalyst does enter into the reaction, but is returned unchanged in a final step of the reaction. It forms an intermediate compound or compounds which react more readily than the uncatalyzed reactants. They react more readily because they require less activation energy. As an example of homogeneous catalysis, consider the hydrolysis of sucrose (cane sugar). The reaction is

A homogeneous catalyst exists in the same phase as reactants.

$$C_{12}H_{22}O_{11}(aq) + H_2O(l) \rightarrow C_6H_{12}O_6(aq) + C_6H_{12}O_6(aq)$$

Sucrose   Glucose   Fructose

The reaction is normally very slow. If, however, the solution is made acidic, the presence of the acid causes the reaction to proceed readily. In the reaction, all substances are in aqueous solution (the same phase). Thus the reaction is a homogeneous one, and the acid is a homogeneous catalyst. The acid lowers the required activation energy by attacking the oxygen atom linking the two sugar molecules.

Catalysts are used a great deal in industry, as well as in the chemical laboratory. Other substances called **inhibitors** are also used to affect reaction rates. These substances do not "slow up" a reaction. Rather they "tie up" a reactant or catalytic substance in a complex, so that it will not react. Preservatives used in foods and medical preparations are included to avoid spoilage. These substances are examples of inhibitors.

Inhibitors slow up reaction rates by tying up a reactant.

23:7 REACTION MECHANISM

At a given temperature, the rate of a reaction varies directly as the product of the concentrations of the reactants in the slowest step. For the reaction $H_2(g) + I_2(g) \rightarrow 2HI(g)$, the rate expression was rate $= k[H_2][I_2]$. For the general reaction $A + B \rightarrow C$, the rate expression would be rate $= k[A][B]$. Hydrogen iodide decomposes into hydrogen and iodine. The equation is $2HI(g) \rightarrow H_2(g) + I_2(g)$. This reaction might be written $HI + HI \rightarrow H_2 + I_2$. The rate expression (if it is a one-step reaction) would be rate $= k[HI][HI]$, or $rate = k[HI]^2$. Note that the coefficient in the equation became the exponent in the rate expression. For the equation $mA + nB \rightarrow C$, the rate expression takes the form $rate = k[A]^m[B]^n$. In this expression m and n are coefficients (also exponents) and A and B are reactants. The exponents of the concentration factors are spoken of as the order of the expression. Remember, this generalization is true only for single-step reactions, or the rate-determining step in a sequence.

The coefficient in the equation becomes the exponent in the rate expression.

For a single step reaction, the exponents of concentration factors are the order of the expression.

How do we know if a reaction is a single-step? The only way to obtain accurate rate information is experimentally. As a result, the observation of reaction rates has given scientists an insight into the mechanisms of reactions. The reaction

$$C_2H_4Br_2(l) + 3I^-(aq) \rightarrow C_2H_4(l) + 2Br^-(aq) + I_3^-(aq)$$

has been shown to obey the rate expression rate $= k[C_2H_4Br_2][I^-]$. Thus, the reaction is first order with respect to $C_2H_4Br_2$ and first order with respect to I^-.

Overall, then, the reaction is second order. However, the reaction should be third order in I^- if it is a single-step reaction.

In that case, four particles ($C_2H_4Br_2$ and $3I^-$) would have to collide all at once in the right orientation to react. This collision is very unlikely. Therefore, the rate data tell us that we need to consider multiple-step mechanisms. The rate determining step, according to the data, involves only one I^- with the $C_2H_4Br_2$. There are a large number of possible mechanisms which would agree with the observed rate law. Consider just one

$$C_2H_4Br_2 + I^- \rightarrow C_2H_4Br^- + IBr \qquad \text{(slow)}$$
$$C_2H_4Br^- \rightarrow C_2H_4 + Br^- \qquad \text{(fast)}$$
$$IBr + I^- \rightarrow Br^- + I_2 \qquad \text{(fast)}$$
$$I_2 + I^- \rightarrow I_3^- \qquad \text{(fast)}$$

See if you can devise other mechanisms for this reaction which will agree with the rate data.

Reactants must collide with the proper activation energy and collision geometry (orientation) in order to form products.

Reaction rate depends on the rate determining (slowest) step.

The reaction mechanism is the series of steps that occur during a reaction.

EXAMPLE: Rate Law

What is the rate law for the following reaction?

$$H_2O_2 + 2HI \rightarrow 2H_2O + I_2$$

Trial	[H₂O₂]	[HI]	Rate
1	$0.1M$	$0.1M$	0.0076 mol/dm^3/s
2	$0.1M$	$0.2M$	0.0152 mol/dm^3/s
3	$0.2M$	$0.1M$	0.0152 mol/dm^3/s

Solving process:
(a) By comparing trials 1 and 2 we can see that doubling the [HI] doubles the rate. Thus there is a direct relationship:
   rate $\propto$ [HI].
(b) By comparing trials 1 and 3 we see that doubling the [H₂O₂] also doubles the rate and we again have a direct relationship:
   rate $\propto$ [H₂O₂].
(c) The rate law is, then, *rate* $= k[H_2O_2][HI]$.

PROBLEMS

1. Assume that NO(g) and H_2(g) react according to the rate law: *rate* $= k[NO]^2[H_2]$. How does the rate change if
   a. the concentration of H_2 is doubled?
   b. the volume of the enclosing vessel is suddenly halved?
   c. the temperature is decreased?
2. For the reaction $H_2(g) + I_2(g) \rightarrow 2HI(g)$, the following data were obtained.

1. a. doubled
   b. eight times faster
   c. slows down

Experiment	Initial [H$_2$]	Initial [I$_2$]	Initial rate of formation of HI
1	1.0M	1.0M	0.20 mol/dm^3/s
2	1.0M	2.0M	0.40 mol/dm^3/s
3	2.0M	2.0M	0.80 mol/dm^3/s

2. a. Rate = k[H$_2$][I$_2$]
      k = 0.2 (dm^3)^2/mol·s
   b. 0.05 mol/s

a. Write the rate law for this reaction, and calculate the value of the rate constant.

b. What would be the initial rate of formation of HI if the initial concentrations of H$_2$ and I$_2$ were each 0.50M?

3. Rate = k[CH$_3$COCH$_3$]

3. The reaction CH$_3$COCH$_3$ + I$_2$ $\xrightarrow{\text{acid}}$ CH$_3$COCH$_2$I + HI is run under carefully controlled conditions in the presence of an excess of acid. The following data were obtained.

Initial concentration		Initial rate
[CH$_3$COCH$_3$]	[I$_2$]	
0.100M	0.100M	1.16 $\times$ 10^{-7} mol/dm^3/s
0.0500M	0.100M	5.79 $\times$ 10^{-8} mol/dm^3/s
0.0500M	0.500M	5.78 $\times$ 10^{-8} mol/dm^3/s

4. There are several possible mechanisms that will agree with the rate law expression. See Teacher's Guide.
   I$_2$ + H$^+$ → HI + I$^+$
   catalyzed step
   HI → H$^+$ + I$^-$
   catalyst regenerated
   CH$_3$COCH$_3$ + I$^-$ →
   CH$_3$COCH$_2^-$ + HI
   slowest step
   CH$_3$COCH$_2^-$ + I$^+$ →
   CH$_3$COCH$_2$I

Write the rate law for the reaction.

4. It has been determined that the reaction of Problem 3 is also first order with respect to the acid catalyst. Propose a mechanism for the slow step consistent with the data.

23:8 EQUILIBRIUM CONSTANT

We have seen that the reaction of H$_2$ and I$_2$ to form HI is an equilibrium reaction. As the reaction proceeds, the reaction rate of the hydrogen and iodine reaction decreases. As H$_2$ and I$_2$ are used, fewer collisions between H$_2$ and I$_2$ molecules occur per unit time. The reverse reaction, the collision of two HI molecules to form H$_2$ and I$_2$, does not occur initially because the concentration of HI is zero.

However, as the concentration of HI increases, the reverse reaction, the decomposition of hydrogen iodide, steadily increases. Equilibrium is attained when the rates of the two opposing reactions are equal. The rates of the forward and reverse reactions of the hydrogen iodide reaction are written

$$rate\ of\ forward\ reaction = k_f[I_2][H_2]$$
$$rate\ of\ reverse\ reaction = k_r[HI]^2$$

FIGURE 23-8. Equilibrium is established when the rates of the forward and reverse reactions are equal.

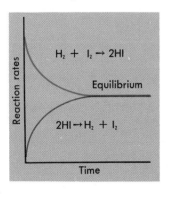

Reaction rates

H$_2$ + I$_2$ → 2HI

Equilibrium

2HI → H$_2$ + I$_2$

Time

At equilibrium, the two rates are equal, and

$$k_f[I_2][H_2] = k_r[HI]^2$$

At equilibrium, opposing reaction rates are equal.

Dividing both sides by $k_r[I_2][H_2]$

$$\frac{k_f[I_2][H_2]}{k_r[I_2][H_2]} = \frac{k_r[HI]^2}{k_r[I_2][H_2]}$$

We obtain

$$\frac{k_f}{k_r} = \frac{[HI]^2}{[I_2][H_2]}$$

Since both k_f and k_r are constants, the ratio k_f/k_r is a constant. This new constant is called the equilibrium constant (K_{eq}).

The ratio of two constants is a constant.

$$K_{eq} = \frac{[HI]^2}{[I_2][H_2]}$$

(Note that the equilibrium constant K_{eq} is capitalized to distinguish it from the specific rate constant k.)

Must we know the rate expressions for the forward and reverse reactions for every equilibrium condition? Guldberg and Waage, two Norwegian chemists, worked on the problem in 1867. They found that the numerator of the equilibrium expression contained the products, and the denominator the reactants. They also found that the exponents in the equilibrium expression were the same as coefficients from the chemical equation. Thus, it is possible to determine the equilibrium constant without knowing the reaction mechanism.

An equilibrium constant is the ratio of the rate expression of the forward reaction to the rate expression of the reverse reaction:

$$K_{eq} = \frac{k_f}{k_r}$$

For the general equation $mA + nB \rightarrow sP + rQ$, the equilibrium constant is

$$K_{eq} = \frac{[P]^s[Q]^r}{[A]^m[B]^n}$$

The law of mass action states that the exponents in the equilibrium constant are the coefficients from the chemical equation.

This K_{eq} establishes a relationship between the concentrations of the reactants and products of a reaction. If K_{eq} is very small (much less than 1), equilibrium will be established before much product is formed.

If K_{eq} is small (less than 1) very little product is formed.

If K_{eq} is large (much greater than 1), the reaction will approach completion. If product is desired, the reaction will be useful. For any reaction, K_{eq} remains constant only if the temperature remains constant. Thus, each reaction has a unique K_{eq} for every temperature.

If K_{eq} is large (greater than 1) the reaction is nearly complete.

For example, a K_{eq} of 1×10^{-8} would mean that equilibrium will be established before much product is formed. A K_{eq} of 1×10^8 would mean that equilibrium will be established only after a great deal of product is formed. Consider the following example of the reaction between carbon dioxide and hydrogen.

The K_{eq} is unique for any reaction at a given temperature.

$$CO_2(g) + H_2(g) \rightleftarrows CO(g) + H_2O(g)$$

At 1120°C, a measurement at equilibrium shows that the concentration of each substance is $0.01M$ except H_2O, which is $0.02M$. Substitution of the observed concentrations into the equilibrium expression results in a calculation of $K_{eq} = 2$.

$$K_{eq} = \frac{[CO][H_2O]}{[CO_2][H_2]} = \frac{[0.01][0.02]}{[0.01][0.01]} = 2$$

Thus the products are favored. On the other hand, consider the reaction: $PCl_5(g) \rightleftarrows PCl_3(g) + Cl_2(g)$. Measurement of its equilibrium constant at 200°C indicates a K_{eq} of 0.457. In this case, the reactant is favored.

EXAMPLE: Equilibrium Constants

What is the equilibrium constant for the following reaction if the final concentrations are $CH_3COOH = 0.302M$, $CH_3CH_2OH = 0.428M$, $H_2O = 0.654M$, and $CH_3CH_2OOCCH_3 = 0.655M$?

$$CH_3COOH + CH_3CH_2OH \rightleftarrows CH_3CH_2OOCCH_3 + H_2O$$

Solving process:

$$K_{eq} = \frac{[CH_3CH_2OOCCH_3][H_2O]}{[CH_3COOH][CH_3CH_2OH]} = \frac{[0.655][0.654]}{[0.302][0.428]} = 3.31$$

EXAMPLE: Equilibrium Concentration

What is the equilibrium concentration of SO_3 in the following reaction if the concentration of SO_2 and O_2 are each $0.0500M$ and $K_{eq} = 85.0$? The equation for the reaction is

$$2SO_2 + O_2 \rightleftarrows 2SO_3$$

Solving process:

$$K_{eq} = \frac{[SO_3]^2}{[SO_2]^2[O_2]}$$

$$85.0 = \frac{[x]^2}{[0.0500]^2[0.0500]}$$

$$x^2 = 0.0106$$

$$x = 0.103M$$

PROBLEMS

5. 1.69×10^{-3} *M*

5. At a given temperature, the K_{eq} for the gas phase reaction, $2HI(g) \rightleftarrows H_2(g) + I_2(g)$, is 1.40×10^{-2}. If the concentrations of both H_2 and I_2 at equilibrium are $2.00 \times 10^{-4}M$, find [HI].

6. At a given temperature, the reaction (all gases) $CO + H_2O \rightleftarrows$ $H_2 + CO_2$ produces the following concentrations: $CO = 0.200M$; $H_2O = 0.500M$; $H_2 = 0.32M$; $CO_2 = 0.42M$. Find the K_{eq} at that temperature.

7. If the temperature in the reaction in Problem 6 is changed, the K_{eq} becomes 2.40. By removing the H_2 and CO_2 and adding H_2O all concentrations except CO are adjusted to the values given in Problem 6. What is the new CO concentration?

8. Hydrogen sulfide decomposes according to the equation: $2H_2S(g) \rightleftarrows 2H_2(g) + S_2(g)$. At 1065°C, measurement of an equilibrium mixture of these three gases shows the following concentrations: $H_2S = 7.06 \times 10^{-3}M$, $H_2 = 2.22 \times 10^{-3}M$, and $S_2 = 1.11 \times 10^{-3}M$. What is the value of K_{eq} for this equation?

9. At 60.2°C, the equilibrium constant for the reaction, $N_2O_4(g) \rightleftarrows 2NO_2(g)$, is 8.75×10^{-2}. At this temperature, a vessel contains N_2O_4 at a concentration of $1.72 \times 10^{-2}M$ at equilibrium. What concentration of NO_2 does it contain?

6. 1.34
7. 0.112M
8. 1.10×10^{-4}
9. 3.88×10^{-2} M

23:9 LE CHATELIER'S PRINCIPLE

The conditions affecting equilibrium are temperature, pressure, and concentration of either reactants or products. If a system is in equilibrium and a condition is changed, then the equilibrium will shift toward restoring the original conditions. As you learned in Chapter 17, this statement is called Le Chatelier's principle. Le Chatelier first described the effect of stress (change of conditions) upon systems at equilibrium. His principle holds for reaction equilibrium as well. If stress is put on a reversible reaction at equilibrium, the equilibrium will shift in such a way to relieve the stress. Let us see how it applies.

Le Chatelier's principle: A system at equilibrium that undergoes a change will shift toward restoring the original conditions.

The reaction for the preparation of ammonia by the Haber process is

$$N_2(g) + 3H_2(g) \rightleftarrows 2NH_3(g) + heat$$

Let us consider the effect of concentration, pressure, and temperature on the equilibrium.

If the concentration of either of the reactants is increased, the number of collisions between reactant particles will increase. The result is an increase of the reaction rate toward the right. As the amount of NH_3 increases, the rate of the reverse reaction will also increase. However, the net result to the system as a whole is to shift the equilibrium toward the right. That is, more product is produced.

If the pressure is increased, the same effect is noted. That is, more product is formed. Consider the situation if the pressure is doubled. The concentrations of nitrogen, hydrogen, and ammonia are all doubled. The equilibrium expression for this reaction

Heat can be treated as a reactant or product in a reaction.

As the $[H_2]$ is increased, the $[N_2]$ decreases and the $[NH_3]$ increases. Thus the value of the equilibrium constant K_{eq} remains the same.

Increasing the concentration of reactant will produce a greater concentration of product.

Increased pressure on a reaction system with a gas phase has the same effect as increased concentration.

shows the concentration of ammonia is squared.

$$K_{eq} = \frac{[NH_3]^2}{[N_2][H_2]^3}$$

The reverse reaction must then speed up by a factor of 4. On the other hand, the concentration of hydrogen is cubed. Further, it is multiplied by the concentration of nitrogen. Doubling the pressure then should increase the rate of the forward reaction by $2^3 \times 2$, or 16 times! The net result is clearly an increase in product.

This observation applies only to ideal gases.

Pressure changes concentration, not K_{eq}.

In the reaction $H_2(g) + Cl_2(g) \rightleftarrows 2HCl(g)$, again all substances are gases. Pressure would not shift the equilibrium, as the rate in each direction would be affected the same way. Pressure, of course, has an effect only on the gases in a reaction. A reaction taking place in solution would be unaffected by pressure.

Both the forward and reverse reactions at equilibrium are speeded by an increase in temperature. However, their rates are increased by different amounts. Also, the value of the equilibrium constant itself is changed by a change in temperature. One easy way to predict the shift in an equilibrium subjected to a temperature change is to consider heat as a reactant or product.

Temperature change causes a change in K_{eq}.

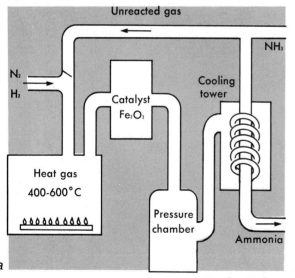

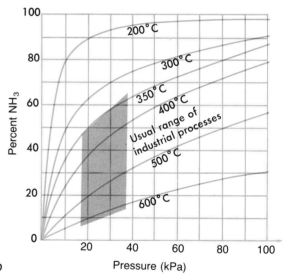

a

b

FIGURE 23-9. The Haber process is used in the production of ammonia (a). By controlling the pressure and temperature of the reaction system, the yield of ammonia can be increased (b).

In the Haber process:

$$N_2(g) + 3H_2(g) \rightleftarrows 2NH_3(g) + heat$$

heat is produced when hydrogen and nitrogen react. If heat is considered to be a product, the addition of heat (a product) will increase the concentration of the product. The equilibrium will be shifted to the left. In the Haber process, the reverse action (the decomposition of ammonia) is favored by the addition of heat.

In industry, a desired chemical (such as ammonia) can sometimes be obtained by a reversible reaction. However, equilibrium is often attained before enough product is produced to make the process economical. In such circumstances, the equilibrium can be shifted to give a higher yield of product. The chemist determines what conditions will tend to produce the highest yield. The conditions which produce the highest yield are called the **optimum conditions.**

In the Haber process, there are five optimum conditions. First, a high concentration of hydrogen and nitrogen should be maintained. Second, ammonia should be removed as it is formed. Third, a temperature is used that is high enough to maintain a reasonable rate but low enough not to favor the reverse reaction. Fourth, a catalyst should be used to lower the required activation energy. Fifth, a high pressure should be maintained throughout the process. Each condition increases the yield by shifting the equilibrium to favor the product.

Optimum conditions are those which produce the highest yield of product.

The optimum conditions for the Haber process are
1. high concentration of H_2 and N_2
2. removal of NH_3
3. precise temperature control
4. use of a contact catalyst
5. high pressure

Each increases the yield through a shift of equilibrium to favor the products.

23:10 EQUILIBRIA AND GAS PHASE REACTIONS

Consider a system of gases in chemical equilibrium. The components of the system are in the same container, so they are all at the same temperature. If we solve the ideal gas equation for n/V:

$$PV = nRT$$

$$\frac{n}{V} = \frac{P}{RT}$$

The number of particles in a given volume n/V is the same as the concentration. Since R is a constant and T is the same for all components, then their pressure P must be in the same ratios as their concentrations n/V:

$$\frac{n}{v} = \frac{R}{RT} \qquad\qquad \frac{n'}{V'} = \frac{P'}{RT}$$

therefore,

$$\frac{n/V}{n'/V'} = \frac{P}{P'}$$

As a consequence, equilibrium constant expressions for gas phase reactions (K_p) can be written in terms of the partial pressures of the substances involved.

$$N_2 + 3H_2 \rightleftarrows 2NH_3$$

$$K_p = \frac{(pp\,NH_3)^2}{(pp\,N_2)(pp\,H_2)^3}$$

Equilibrium constant expressions for gas phase reactions, K_p, are written in terms of partial pressures.

23:11   FREE ENERGY AND EQUILIBRIUM

We saw in Chapter 20 that reactions with $\Delta G < 0$ would occur spontaneously, and those with $\Delta G > 0$ would not occur. In this chapter, we have seen that reactions with very small K_{eq} do not occur to an appreciable extent. We also found that those with very large K_{eq} go almost to completion. As you might expect, there is a connection between free energy and the equilibrium constant. We will not derive the relationship here, as it involves complex mathematics. Simply stated, free energy and equilibria are related by the expression

$$\Delta G = -RT(\ln K_{eq})$$

R = 0.008 31 kJ/mol·K.

Refer students to Appendix B if they have difficulty with logarithms.

In the expression, R is the universal gas constant, T is the absolute temperature, and $\ln$ is the base of natural logarithms. Expressed in terms of common logarithms, the equation becomes

$$\Delta G = -2.30RT(\log K_{eq})$$

EXAMPLE: Free Energy Change

The equilibrium constant for the reaction of CO_2 and H_2 to form CO and H_2O at 1112°C is 2. What is ΔG for this reaction? Use $\Delta G = -2.30RT(\log K_{eq})$, $R = 0.008\ 31$ kJ/mol·K, and log tables.

Solving process:

$$\Delta G = (-2.30)(0.008\ 31)(1393)(\log 2)$$
$$= (-2.30)(0.008\ 31)(1393)(0.301) = -8.01 \text{ kJ}$$

EXAMPLE: Free Energy Change

For the decomposition of PCl_5 at 200°C, the equilibrium constant was 0.457. What is the free energy change for this reaction?

Solving process:

$$\Delta G = (-2.30)(0.008\ 31)(473)(\log 0.457)$$
$$= (-2.30)(0.008\ 31)(473)(-0.340) = 3.07 \text{ kJ}$$

EXAMPLE: Equilibrium Constant

The free energy change for the reaction $CH_4(g) + 2O_2(g) \rightleftarrows CO_2(g) + 2H_2O(g)$ is -818.0 kJ at 25°C. What is K_{eq} for this reaction?

Solving process:

Solving the equation relating free energy to equilibrium for K_{eq}, we find that

$$\log K_{eq} = \frac{\Delta G}{-2.30\ RT}$$

$$log \, K_{eq} = \frac{-818.0}{(-2.30)(0.008 \, 31)(298)} = 143.618$$

using log tables, this value converts to

$$K_{eq} = 4.15 \times 10^{143}$$

The equilibrium constant is such a large number that we can safely assume that all the reactant is converted to product.

PROBLEMS

10. Calculate K_{eq} at 25°C for the reaction $CO + H_2 \rightleftarrows H_2CO$ if $\Delta G = +28.95$ kJ.

11. At 627°C, K_{eq} for the reaction $2SO_3 \rightleftarrows 2SO_2 + O_2$ is 3.16×10^{-4}. Compute ΔG for this reaction.

10. 8.26×10^{-6}

11. 60.2 kJ

Henry Louis Le Chatelier   (1850–1936)

Henry Le Chatelier began his professional career as a mining engineer before turning to the teaching of chemistry. It was his experience as an engineer, however, that dictated his scientific investigations.

His greatest contribution to science was the equilibrium principle. Commonly known as Le Chatelier's principle, it states that if a system in stable equilibrium is subjected to a stress, then the equilibrium will shift to relieve the stress.

In other fields, he developed the platinum-rhodium thermocouple for measuring high temperatures. He also designed a special microscope to study metals, and developed new abrasives to polish the surface of a metal to be examined.

CHEMICAL TECHNOLOGY: Cryogenics

Cryogenics is the study of matter at extremely low temperatures, usually below 80 K. The term is derived from the Greek word *kryo* meaning icy cold. The reduction of the temperature of a substance involves slowing the particles (lowering the kinetic energy of the system). As the particles of a substance slow down, the system not only decreases in temperature but also in disorder, or entropy. The decreased entropy leads to interesting phenomena at temperatures close to absolute zero. It also allows scientists to study matter at temperatures where disorder is relatively low.

The third law of thermodynamics states that the entropy of a system is zero at absolute zero. As a material is cooled toward absolute zero, some of its particles will reach the lowest possible energy level while most of the particles are still in energy levels above the minimum. Recall the kinetic energy distribution curves for a substance at T_1, Figure 17-1. It is these minimum energy particles which exhibit such unusual properties.

Liquid helium can be produced by the usual method of compression, cooling, and Joule-Thomson expansion. Liquid helium boils at 4.2 K. By reducing the pressure over liquid helium, the

FIGURE 23-10. The photograph shows a cascade nuclear refrigerator. The blue cylinder is a superconducting magnet assembly. The spins of copper nuclei have been cooled to 50 nanokelvins using this apparatus.

Photo by Professor Lounasmaa, Courtesy of *Physics Today*

more energetic particles are removed from the liquid, and the temperature again drops. Helium can be cooled to approximately 1 K in this manner. Helium does not freeze unless the pressure is quite high, for example, about 2.5 MPa at 1 K.

At a temperature of 2.18 K, helium undergoes a liquid-liquid phase transition from helium I, the high temperature form, to helium II, the lower temperature form. Helium II has some strange properties. It behaves as though it has a zero viscosity, allowing it to flow through incredibly small spaces, and creep up and over the sides of its container. This property is called superfluidity. Helium II also conducts heat well, its thermal conductivity being over 1000 times better than that of normal metals. These properties are attributed to the atoms which have reached the minimum energy level.

According to the third law of thermodynamics, absolute zero can never be reached. However, by making use of magnetic fields and the magnetic properties of atoms, it is possible to cool some materials to about 0.01 K. By working with the magnetic fields of nuclei, temperatures lower than 0.0001 K have been achieved. using nuclear refrigerators.

SUMMARY

1. A reversible reaction is a reaction in which products may reform reactants. 23:1

2. Reaction rate is the rate of disappearance of one of the reactants of a reaction or the rate of appearance of one of the products. 23:2

3. Four factors influence reaction rate: nature of reactants, concentration, temperature, and catalysis. 23:3-23:6

4. More reactive materials require less activation energy. Therefore, they react more rapidly. 23:3

5. Most reactions take place in a series of steps called the reaction mechanism. 23:3

6. Concentration is the quantity of matter present in a unit volume. The symbol [ ] means concentration in units of moles per cubic decimeter. 23:4

7. Increasing the concentration of a reactant increases the rate of reaction by increasing the number of collisions. Increasing the pressure of a gas or the surface area of a heterogeneous reactant has the same effect on the reaction rate. 23:4

8. Increasing the temperature increases the rate of reaction. There are more frequent collisions and more of the collisions involve sufficient energy to form the activated complex. 23:5

9. A catalyst is a substance which causes an increase in reaction rate without being permanently changed. 23:6

10. A reaction in which the reactants and catalyst are not in the same phase is a heterogeneous reaction. The catalyst used is called a heterogeneous catalyst. A homogeneous catalyst is one which is in the same phase as the reactants. 23:6

11. Analysis of rate data can give chemists an insight into reaction mechanisms. 23:7

12. At a given temperature, the rate of a single-step reaction varies directly as the product of the concentrations of the reactants. 23:7

13. The equilibrium constant, K_{eq}, is the ratio of the forward rate constant, k_f, divided by the reverse rate constant, k_r. 23:8

14. Le Chatelier's principle states that if an equilibrium system is subjected to stress, then the equilibrium will shift to relieve the stress. 23:9

15. Equilibrium constants for gas phase reactions can be expressed in terms of the partial pressures of the reactants and products. 23:10

16. The free energy change for a reaction is related to its equilibrium constant by the expression $\Delta G = -2.30RT(\log K_{eq})$. 23:11

PROBLEMS

b. 0.333
c. increases
d. shifts right
e. changes

12. Given $2NH_3(g) + H_2SO_4(g) \rightleftharpoons (NH_4)_2SO_4(g)$.
    12. a. $K_{eq} = \dfrac{[(NH_4)_2SO_4]}{[NH_3]^2[H_2SO_4]}$
    a. What is the equilibrium expression?
    b. If the concentrations in mol/dm^3 after the reaction of NH_3, H_2SO_4, and $(NH_4)_2SO_4$ are 2.00, 3.00, and 4.00, respectively, what is K_{eq}?
    c. If $[NH_3]$ is increased, what happens to $[(NH_4)_2SO_4]$?
    d. If pressure is added, what happens to the equilibrium?
    e. If heat is added, what happens to the value of K_{eq}?

13. Which of the following reactions would you expect to have the faster rate? (Assume the mechanism to be the same.) $H_2(g) + Cl_2(g) \rightarrow 2HCl(g)$ or $H_2(g) + Br_2(g) \rightarrow 2HBr(g)$ $H_2(g) + Cl_2(g) \rightarrow 2HCl(g)$ (Cl_2 is more active than Br_2)

14. The following reaction goes to completion. What effect would an increase in temperature have on its rate? $2NO(g) + H_2(g) \rightarrow N_2O(g) + H_2O(g) + 364\ 000$ J reaction rate increases

15. Why must a fire in a fireplace be started with paper and kindling? Why not light the logs directly?

16. On the same set of axes, show an energy diagram of a reaction, both catalyzed and uncatalyzed.

17. Assume the reaction of Problem 14 to be a single-step reaction. What would be the effect on the reaction rate if the hydrogen gas concentration were doubled? reaction rate doubles

18. How would an increase in pressure affect the rate of a reaction in which the products occupied less volume than the reactants? rate increases

19. The equilibrium constant for the reaction $2H_2O \rightleftharpoons 2H_2 + O_2$ at 2000 K is 6.45×10^{-8}. What is the free energy change for the reaction at that temperature? 275 kJ

15. A match cannot raise the temperature of a log to its kindling temperature.

20. The free energy change for the reaction $2CO_2 \rightleftarrows 2CO + O_2$ at $1000°C$ is 338 kJ. What is the equilibrium constant for the reaction at that temperature? 1.33×10^{-14}

1. the surrounding of solute particles by solvent particles
2. no, water is highly polar butter is nonpolar
3. crush solute, heat, stir
4. A constant volume of gas will dissolve in a given quantity of liquid.

REVIEW

1. Describe the process of solvation.

2. Would you expect water and butter to be miscible? Explain.

3. Describe three procedures which can be used to speed the solvation of a solute in a solvent.

4. Henry's law states that the mass of a gas which will dissolve in a liquid varies directly as the pressure of the gas. What statement can be made about the volume of a gas which will dissolve in a liquid as the pressure is changed?

5. What is the molarity of a solution which contains 16.0 g HIO_3 in 100 cm^3 of solution? $0.909M$

6. What effect does a nonvolatile solute have on the boiling point of a solvent? increases the boiling point

7. Why does a $1.00m$ solution of $NaCl$ have a freezing point slightly above the predicted $-3.72°C$? activity of the ions is slightly less than their concentrations

8. What is the vapor pressure at $25°C$ of a solution of 98.1 g $C_{12}H_{22}O_{11}$ in 100 g water? 3.01 kPa

9. What are the freezing and boiling points of a solution of 6.78 g $C_6H_{12}O_6$ in 30.0 g water? $FP = -2.33°C$ $BP = 100.64°C$

10. If 4.23 g of an unknown in 45.0 g water lower the freezing point to $-1.58°C$, what is the molecular mass of the unknown? 111 g

11. What osmotic pressure would be exerted by 4.70 g of a substance of molecular mass 6870 g dissolved in sufficient water to make 500 cm^3 of solution at $15°C$? 3.27 kPa

ONE MORE STEP

1. If K_{eq} for $2A + B \rightleftarrows 2C$ is 8, set up the expression used to calculate the concentration of C at equilibrium, if the starting conditions were one-half mole of A and B in a 10 dm^3 container.

2. Thermodynamic quantities ΔH, ΔS, and ΔG apply to the activated complex as well as the products and reactants. Investigate the relationship between the energy of activation and these thermodynamic quantities.

3. Prepare a class report on the step-by-step mechanism of a multistep reaction. Be sure to include information on the slowest step.

4. Find out what the mathematical relationship is between K_c (concentration) and K_p.

5. Enzymes in living systems are catalysts. Investigate their mechanisms.

6. To what extent does free energy depend upon temperature?

The properties of acids make them suitable for a variety of uses. Thus, the commercial production of acids is one of the largest chemical industries. Hydrofluoric acid is highly corrosive and must be handled carefully. One of its uses is in the glass etching process. What are some other chemical properties of acids? What precautions must be observed when handling acids? How does the presence of a base change the chemical activity of an acid?

Janet Adams

Chapter 24 begins with definitions of acids and bases by an introduction to three acid-base theories. It also includes a discussion of acid-base behavior, nomenclature, and some properties of salts.

ACIDS, BASES, AND SALTS

24

Many foods have distinctive tastes. Some are bitter. Other foods are sour or salty. It is now known that a lemon or a grapefruit has a sour taste because it contains a compound called an acid. Soaps that contain lye, a base, taste bitter. Salty foods taste salty because they contain a salt, sodium chloride. The presence of these compounds, called acids, bases, and salts, gives many of our foods their distinctive flavors.

It was discovered long ago that these substances, when dissolved in water, conduct an electric current. Because they conduct a current, they are called **electrolytes.** Why do electrolytes conduct an electric current? The definitions of an acid, base, and salt have undergone several modifications in the history of chemistry. As knowledge about chemistry expanded, definitions of these words were also expanded to cover larger groups of compounds. The first part of this chapter traces the development of the definitions of these terms.

24:1 ARRHENIUS THEORY

In 1887, a Swedish chemist, Svante Arrhenius, published a paper concerning acids and bases. He knew that solutions containing acids or bases conducted an electric current. Arrhenius tried to explain why. He concluded that these substances released charged particles when dissolved. He called these charged particles ions (wanderers). He concluded that acids were *substances which separated* (ionized) *in water solution to produce hydrogen ions* (H^+, or free protons). He also believed that bases were *substances which ionized to produce hydroxide ions* (OH^-) *in water solution.*

$$HCl \rightarrow H^+ + Cl^-$$

$$NaOH \rightarrow Na^+ + OH^-$$

GOAL: You will gain an understanding of the different acid-base theories; the properties of acids, bases, and salts; and the procedures for naming these substances.

Acids taste sour (lemon). Bases taste bitter (soap).

Acids, bases, and salts are electrolytes.
Electrolytes conduct a current.

The Arrhenius theory is the traditional approach. However, it still is adequate for most introductory chemistry.

The three classes of electrolytes are acids, bases, and salts. They conduct an electric current because they dissolve to form ions in solution.

Arrhenius theory: An acid produces H^+ in water solution; a base produces OH^- in water solution.

24:2 BRÖNSTED-LOWRY THEORY

The Brönsted-Lowry theory is the most prevalent of the three theories in inorganic chemistry.

Brönsted-Lowry theory: An acid is a proton donor; a base is a proton acceptor.

As the knowledge of catalysts and nonaqueous solutions increased, it became necessary to redefine the terms acid and base. In 1923, an English scientist, T. M. Lowry, and a Danish scientist, J. N. Brönsted, independently proposed a new definition. They stated that in a chemical reaction, *any substance which donates a proton is an acid* and *any substance which accepts a proton is a base.* When hydrogen chloride gas is dissolved in water, ions are formed.

$$\underset{\text{acid}}{\text{HCl(g)}} + \underset{\text{base}}{H_2O(l)} \rightarrow H_3O^+(aq) + Cl^-(aq)$$

Free protons are hydrated by water molecules to form H_3O^+, the hydronium ion.

In this reaction, hydrogen chloride is an acid, and water is a base. Notice that the hydrogen ion (H^+) has combined with a water molecule to form the polyatomic ion H_3O^+, which is called the **hydronium** (hi DROH nee uhm) **ion.** There is strong evidence that the hydrogen ion is never found free as H^+. The bare proton is so strongly attracted by the electrons of surrounding water molecules that H_3O^+ forms immediately. Consider the opposite reaction.

$$H_3O^+(aq) + Cl^-(aq) \rightarrow HCl(g) + H_2O(l)$$

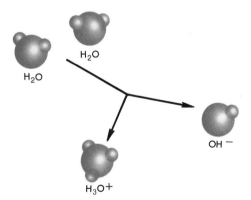

FIGURE 24-1. The reaction between two water molecules produces the hydronium ion, which is an acid, and the hydroxide ion, which is a base.

Bases have conjugate acids. Acids have conjugate bases.

In this reaction, the H_3O^+ ion is an acid. It acts as an acid because it donates a proton to the chloride ion, which is a base. The hydronium ion is said to be the conjugate acid of the base, water. The chloride ion is called the conjugate base of the acid, hydrochloric acid. In general, any acid-base reaction is described as:

acid + base → conjugate base + conjugate acid

The conjugate base is the remaining particle of the acid after a proton is released.

The conjugate acid of a base is formed when the base accepts a proton.

The **conjugate base** of an acid is the particle that remains after a proton has been released by the acid. The **conjugate acid** of a base is formed when the base acquires a proton from the acid. Table 24-1 contains a list of some anions and their conjugate acids.

Consider what happens when ammonia gas is added to water.

$$NH_3(g) + H_2O(l) \rightarrow NH_4^+(aq) + OH^-(aq)$$

$$\underset{\text{base}}{NH_3} + \underset{\text{acid}}{H_2O} \rightarrow \underset{\substack{\text{conjugate} \\ \text{acid}}}{NH_4^+} + \underset{\substack{\text{conjugate} \\ \text{base}}}{OH^-}$$

In this reaction, water acts as an acid because it donates a proton to the ammonia molecule. The ammonium ion is the conjugate acid of ammonia, a base, which receives a proton from water. Hydroxide ion is the conjugate base.

Table 24-1

Anions and Their Conjugate Acid		
Anion	**Name**	**Conjugate Acid**
CH_3COO^-	acetate	CH_3COOH
NH_3	ammonia	NH_4^+
CO_3^{2-}	carbonate	HCO_3^-
CN^-	cyanide	HCN
$H_2PO_4^-$	dihydrogen phosphate	H_3PO_4
HSO_4^-	hydrogen sulfate	H_2SO_4
HSO_3^-	hydrogen sulfite	H_2SO_3
NO_3^-	nitrate	HNO_3
ClO_4^-	perchlorate	$HClO_4$
S^{2-}	sulfide	HS^-
H_2O	water	H_3O^+

PROBLEM

1. Identify the acid, the base, conjugate acid, and conjugate base in the following reactions.

   a. $HNO_3 + NaOH \rightarrow H_2O + NaNO_3$

   b. $NaHCO_3 + HCl \rightarrow NaCl + H_2CO_3$

Acid	Base	$\rightarrow$	Conjugate Acid	Base
HNO_3	$NaOH$		H_2O	$NaNO_3$
HCl	$NaHCO_3$		H_2CO_3	$NaCl$

24:3 LEWIS THEORY

In 1923, the same year that Brönsted and Lowry proposed their theories, another new idea appeared. Gilbert Newton Lewis, an American chemist, proposed an even broader definition of acids and bases. The same type of reasoning as Brönsted's and Lowry's led to his proposals. However, Lewis focused on electron transfer instead of proton transfer. He defined *an acid as an electron-pair acceptor,* and *a base as an electron-pair donor.* This definition is more general than Brönsted's. It applies to solutions and reactions which do not even involve hydrogen or hydrogen ions. Consider the reaction between ammonia and boron trifluoride.

The Lewis theory is the most prevalent of the three theories in organic chemistry.

Lewis theory: An acid is an electron-pair acceptor; a base is an electron-pair donor.

$$BF_3(g) + NH_3(g) \rightarrow F_3BNH_3(g)$$

The electronic structures of boron trifluoride and ammonia are

$$\begin{matrix} & F & & & H \\ & \overset{..}{\underset{..}{B}} & & & \overset{..}{N} \\ F: & & & :N: & H \\ & F & & & H \end{matrix}$$

F:B̈ and :N̈:H

Note that boron has an empty orbital, and can accept two more electrons in its outer level. Since boron trifluoride can accept an electron pair, it is a Lewis acid. Now consider the structure of ammonia. Note that the nitrogen atom has an unshared electron pair, which can be donated to the boron. Ammonia is, therefore, a Lewis base because it can donate an electron pair. If we use dots to represent the electrons involved in the reaction, it can be written:

$$\underset{\substack{\text{Lewis} \\ \text{base}}}{H_3N\colon} + \underset{\substack{\text{Lewis} \\ \text{acid}}}{BF_3} \rightarrow \underset{\substack{\text{Addition} \\ \text{product}}}{H_3N\colon BF_3}$$

Consider again the reaction of ammonia gas and water.

$$\underset{\substack{\text{Lewis} \\ \text{base}}}{H\colon\overset{H}{\underset{H}{\overset{..}{N}}}\colon} + \underset{\substack{\text{Lewis} \\ \text{acid}}}{H-O-H} \rightarrow \left[H\colon\overset{H}{\underset{H}{\overset{..}{N}}}\colon H \right]^+ + OH^-$$

In the Lewis theory, as in the Brönsted-Lowry theory, many substances may act as acids or bases. For example:
base $NH_3 + H^+ \rightarrow NH_4^+$
acid $NH_3 \rightarrow H^+ + NH_2^-$
(amide)

The ammonia donates an electron pair and is the Lewis base. The hydrogen atom attached to the oxygen of the water molecule acts as the Lewis acid. Notice that ammonia is a base in all three theories.

Lewis acids are used frequently in the synthesis of organic compounds.

Lewis acids are used frequently in the synthesis of organic compounds. One such reaction is the Friedel-Crafts method of synthesis. The Lewis acid often used in this method is aluminum chloride. The electron-dot diagram for $AlCl_3$ is

$$\begin{matrix} & :\overset{..}{\underset{..}{Cl}}: & \\ :\overset{..}{\underset{..}{Cl}}: & \overset{..}{\underset{..}{Al}}: & \overset{..}{\underset{..}{Cl}}: \end{matrix}$$

We can see that the aluminum atom has an empty orbital which can accept an electron pair. For example, $AlCl_3$ can be used with chloromethane and benzene to form toluene ($C_6H_5CH_3$). When mixed with a compound such as CH_3Cl (chloromethane), the $AlCl_3$ picks up a Cl^- ion from the carbon compound.

$$CH_3Cl + AlCl_3 \rightarrow CH_3^+ + AlCl_4^-$$

$$\underset{}{H\colon\overset{H}{\underset{H}{\overset{..}{C}}}\colon\overset{..}{\underset{..}{Cl}}:} + \underset{}{\overset{:\overset{..}{\underset{..}{Cl}}:}{\underset{:\overset{..}{\underset{..}{Cl}}:}{\overset{..}{\underset{..}{Al}}:\overset{..}{\underset{..}{Cl}}:}} \rightarrow H\colon\overset{H}{\underset{H}{\overset{..}{C}}}\overset{\oplus}{} + \underset{}{\overset{:\overset{..}{\underset{..}{Cl}}:}{\underset{:\overset{..}{\underset{..}{Cl}}:}{:\overset{..}{\underset{..}{Cl}}:\overset{..}{\underset{..}{Al}}:\overset{..}{\underset{..}{Cl}}:}}{}^{\ominus}$$

If benzene is also present in the mixture, the CH_3^+ ion attacks the π electrons of the ring compound.

$$CH_3^+ + C_6H_6 \rightarrow C_6H_6CH_3^+$$

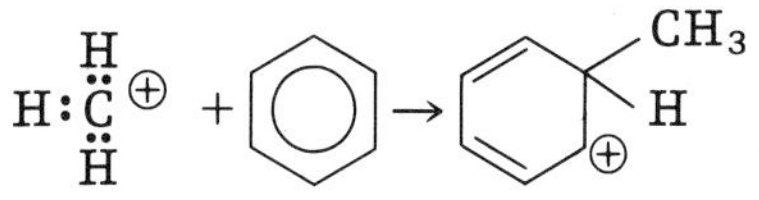

This second step is the rate determining step. In the third step of the reaction mechanism, the $AlCl_4^-$ ion reacts with the organic ion.

$$C_6H_6CH_3^+ + AlCl_4^- \rightarrow C_6H_5CH_3 + HCl + AlCl_3$$

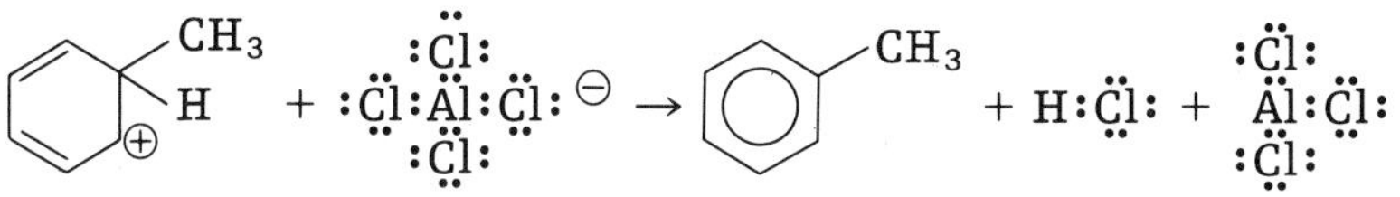

In this reaction $AlCl_3$ acts as a catalyst, returning unchanged at the last step.

Table 24-2

Summary of Acid-Base Theories		
Theory	**Acid Definition**	**Base Definition**
Arrhenius Theory	Any substance which releases H^+ ion in water solution.	Any substance which releases OH^- ions in water solution.
Brönsted-Lowry Theory	Any substance which donates a proton.	Any substance which accepts a proton.
Lewis Theory	Any substance which can accept an electron pair. H^+, **for example**	Any substance which can donate an electron pair.

Each succeeding theory is more inclusive.

A substance that is an acid or base under the Arrhenius theory is also an acid or base under the Lewis and the Brönsted-Lowry theories.

PROBLEMS

2. Classify the following substances as Lewis acids or Lewis bases.
   a. Cl^-
   b. CO_3^{2-}
   c. Na^+
   d. Br^-

2. a. base
   b. acid
   c. acid
   d. base

24:4 NAMING BINARY ACIDS

Binary acids are acids containing only two elements. If you look at Table 24-3, you will notice that the prefix is always *hydro-* and the suffix is always *-ic*.

To name a binary acid, we determine what stem to use by finding what element is combined with hydrogen. For instance,

Binary acids contain only 2 elements.

The names of binary acids begin with *hydro-* and end in *-ic*.

chlorine will have the stem -*chlor*-, and fluorine the stem -*fluor*-. To this stem, the prefix *hydro*- and the suffix -*ic* are added. There are a few exceptions to the rule that binary acids begin with *hydro*- and end with -*ic*. One example is hydrocyanic acid, HCN, which really is ternary. These exceptions must be learned separately, but HCN is the only one we will mention.

Table 24-3

Naming Binary Acids				
Binary Compound + Water	**Prefix**	**Stem**	**Suffix**	**Name**
Hydrogen chloride gas dissolved in water	Hydro-	-chlor-	-ic	Hydrochloric acid
Hydrogen iodide gas dissolved in water	Hydro-	-iod-	-ic	Hydroiodic acid
Hydrogen sulfide gas dissolved in water	Hydro-	-sulfur-	-ic	Hydrosulfuric acid

PROBLEM

3. a. hydrobromic
   b. hydrofluoric

3. Name the following binary acids.
   a. HBr (aq)
   b. HF (aq)

24:5 NAMING TERNARY ACIDS AND BASES

Ternary acids contain 3 elements.

Ternary acids are acids which contain three elements. Most of the ternary acids we will be working with have oxygen as the third element. We find the stem by determining what element is combined with oxygen and hydrogen in the acid molecule. We determine the prefix (if there is one) and the suffix by the number of oxygen atoms in each molecule.

The stem for naming ternary acids is derived from the element that is combined with hydrogen and oxygen in the acid molecule.

Generally, the most common form of the acid is given the suffix -*ic*. No prefix is used. Examples of common ternary acids are sulfur*ic* (H_2SO_4), chlor*ic* ($HClO_3$), and nitr*ic* (HNO_3).

If a second acid is formed containing the same three elements, but having less oxygen, this acid is given the suffix -*ous*. There is no prefix. Examples of these acids are sulfur*ous* (H_2SO_3), chlor*ous* ($HClO_2$), and nitr*ous* (HNO_2).

The name of a ternary acid indicates the number of oxygen atoms in each molecule.

If a third acid containing still less oxygen is formed, it is given the prefix *hypo*- and the suffix -*ous*. An example is hypochlorous acid ($HClO$).

You may wish to mention peroxy-acids and condensed acids at this point.

Acids containing more oxygen than the common form are named by adding the prefix *per*- to the common name. For example, *per*chloric acid ($HClO_4$). See the examples in Table 24-4.

Table 24-4

Naming Ternary Acids					
Compound	Number of Oxygen Atoms	Prefix	Stem	Suffix	Name of Acid
H_2SO_4	4	no prefix	sulfur-	-ic	sulfuric
H_2SO_3	3	no prefix	sulfur-	-ous	sulfurous
$HClO_4$	4	per-	-chlor-	-ic	perchloric
$HClO_3$	3	no prefix	chlor-	-ic	chloric
$HClO_2$	2	no prefix	chlor-	-ous	chlorous
$HClO$	1	hypo-	-chlor-	-ous	hypochlorous

*Suggestion: Emphasize that the number of oxygen atoms in the -*ic* acid must be memorized. This number cannot be predicted. However, once the -*ic* acid is known, the others may be predicted although they may not exist.

Acids
per-STEM-*ic* more oxygen
STEM-*ic* most common*
STEM-*ous* less oxygen
hypo-STEM-*ous* still less oxygen

It is not possible, without previous knowledge, to know which form of an acid is most common. If the name of one form is known, the other ternary acids containing the same elements can be named. Bromine forms only two acids with hydrogen and oxygen: $HBrO$ and $HBrO_3$. Instead of being named bromous and bromic acids, they are named hypobromous and bromic acids. The exception occurs because they contain the same number of oxygen atoms as hypochlorous and chloric acids. The same pattern is followed in naming the ternary acids of the other halogens.

Arrhenius bases are composed of metallic, or positively charged, ions and the negatively charged hydroxide ion. Bases are named by adding the word hydroxide to the name of the positive ion. Examples are sodium hydroxide, $NaOH$, and calcium hydroxide, $Ca(OH)_2$.

Bases are named by using the name of the metallic ion and the word hydroxide.

PROBLEMS

Encourage students to use Table 4-4 page 63.

4. Name the following acids.
   a. H_3BO_3 c. H_3PO_4 e. HIO_3
   b. HNO_2 d. H_3AsO_3
5. Write formulas for the following acids.
   a. carbonic acid   c. arsenic acid   e. hypoiodous acid
   b. nitric acid   d. selenic acid

4. a. boric acid
   b. nitrous acid
   c. phosphoric acid
   d. arsenious acid
   e. iodic acid
5. a. H_2CO_3
   b. HNO_3
   c. H_3AsO_4
   d. H_2SeO_4
   e. HIO

24:6   ACIDIC AND BASIC ANHYDRIDES

When sulfur dioxide is dissolved in water, sulfurous acid is formed. Any oxygen-containing substance which will produce an acid when dissolved in water is called an **acidic anhydride**.

$$SO_2(g) + H_2O(l) \rightarrow H_2SO_3(aq)$$

acidic anhydride + water → acid

Anhydride means without water.

An acid anhydride will form an acid with water. A basic anhydride will form a base when dissolved in water.

When sulfur-containing fuels such as coal and petroleum are burned, SO_2 is introduced into the atmosphere. Then, when water vapor condenses and rain falls, the SO_2 reacts with the water to produce sulfurous acid.

If sodium oxide is added to water, sodium hydroxide, a base, is formed. Any oxygen containing substance which will produce a base when dissolved in water is called a **basic anhydride.**

Note that an acid anhydride reacts with a basic anhydride to produce a salt. This reaction is a neutralization reaction but no water is produced.

$$Na_2O(c) + H_2O(l) \rightarrow 2NaOH(aq)$$
$$\underset{\text{anhydride}}{\text{basic}} + \text{water} \rightarrow \text{base}$$

Anhydride means without water, so anhydrides may be classified as acids or bases without water.

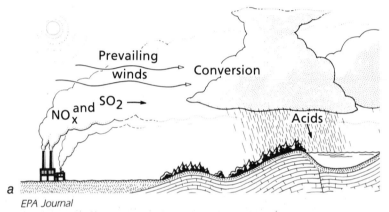

FIGURE 24-2. Acid rain is produced when sulfur and nitrogen oxides in the air dissolve in water (a). The action of CO_2 in water (carbonic acid) causes the formations in this cavern (b). The deterioration of stone is the result of acid rain (c).

EPA Journal

b Courtesy of Ohio Caverns

c W. Keith Turpie

PROBLEMS

6. Predict the acidic or basic nature of the following anhydrides.

    a. Li_2O **c.** CO_2 **e.** SeO_2

    b. MgO **d.** K_2O

7. Write formulas for the anhydrides of the following.

    a. $Ba(OH)_2$ **c.** H_6TeO_6 **e.** $Zn(OH)_2$

    b. HIO_4 **d.** $Al(OH)_3$

6. a. basic
   b. basic
   c. acidic
   d. basic
   e. acidic

7. a. BaO
   b. I_2O_7
   c. TeO_3
   d. Al_2O_3
   e. ZnO

24:7 ACID-BASE BEHAVIOR

Consider a compound having the formula HOX. If the element X is highly electronegative, it will have a strong attraction for the electrons it is sharing with the oxygen. As these electrons are pulled toward X, the oxygen, in turn, will pull strongly on the electrons it is sharing with the hydrogen. The hydrogen ion, or proton, would then be lost easily. In this case, HOX is behaving as an acid.

If the element X has a low electronegativity, the oxygen will tend to pull the shared electrons away from X. The hydrogen will remain joined to the oxygen. Since in this case the formation of hydroxide ion, OH^-, is likely, HOX is behaving as a base.

We know that nonmetals have high electronegativities and metals low electronegativities. We can conclude, then, that nonmetals will tend to form acids, and metals will tend to form bases.

Metals tend to form bases; nonmetals tend to form acids.

Some substances can react as either an acid or a base. If one of these substances is in the presence of a proton donor, then it reacts as a base. In the presence of a proton acceptor, it acts as an acid. Such a substance is said to be **amphoteric.** Water is the most common amphoteric substance.

Amphoteric: A substance which can act as either an acid or a base.

$$\underset{\substack{\text{proton} \\ \text{donor}}}{HCl} + \underset{\text{base}}{H_2O} \rightarrow H_3O^+ + Cl^-$$

$$\underset{\substack{\text{proton} \\ \text{acceptor}}}{NH_3} + \underset{\text{acid}}{H_2O} \rightarrow NH_4^+ + OH^-$$

24:8 DEFINITION OF A SALT

An acid is composed of positive hydrogen ions combined with negative nonmetallic ions. Metallic bases are composed of negative hydroxide ions combined with positive metallic ions. An Arrhenius acid reacts with an Arrhenius base to form a salt and water. The water is formed from the hydrogen ion of the acid and the hydroxide ion of the base. If the water is evaporated, the negative ions of the acid will unite with the positive ions of the

Demonstration — Mix equal volumes of 6*M* HCl and 6*M* NaOH. Evaporate the solution to dryness. Ask students how they might identify the product.

An acid-base neutralization reaction produces a salt.

a

Hickson-Bender Photography

b

FIGURE 24-3. Sodium nitrate is formed in the neutralization reaction of HNO_3 and NaOH (a). The salt can be isolated by boiling off the water leaving only $NaNO_3$ (b).

Review the various kinds of neutralization reactions now discussed.

acid + base
acid + basic anhydride
acid anhydride + base
acid anhydride + basic
         anhydride

base to form a new compound called a salt. It would appear that such a reaction should result in removal of all hydrogen and hydroxide ions from solution. The resulting solution should be neither an acid nor a base. We could say that the solution is **neutral** (neither acidic nor basic). The reaction of an acid and a base is called a **neutralization reaction.** A **salt** is a crystalline compound composed of the negative ion of an acid and the positive ion of a base. For example, if equivalent amounts of chloric acid and sodium hydroxide react, sodium chlorate and water are formed.

$$HClO_3(aq) + NaOH(aq) \rightarrow H_2O(l) + NaClO_3(aq)$$
$$\text{acid} \quad + \quad \text{base} \quad \rightarrow \quad \text{water} \quad + \quad \text{salt}$$

Salts may also result from the reactions of acidic or basic anhydrides with a corresponding base, acid, or anhydride.

$$Na_2O + H_2SO_4 \rightarrow Na_2SO_4 + H_2O$$

$$2NaOH + SO_3 \rightarrow Na_2SO_4 + H_2O$$

$$Na_2O + SO_3 \rightarrow Na_2SO_4$$

Although a salt is formed by neutralization, solutions of some salts in water are not neutral. It is possible to obtain salts which are acidic or basic. For example, if sodium hydroxide reacts with sulfuric acid the product, sodium hydrogen sulfate, is called an acidic salt.

$$H_2SO_4(aq) + NaOH(aq) \rightarrow H_2O(l) + NaHSO_4(aq)$$

It still contains an ionizable hydrogen atom. In a similar manner, partially neutralized bases form basic salts. Acidic or basic salts are not neutral in solution.

You may have already noted that there is a relationship between the name of an acid and the name of the salt it forms. Binary acids (prefix *hydro-*, suffix *-ic*) form salts ending in *-ide.* As an example, hydrochloric acid forms chloride salts. Ternary acids form salts in which *-ic* acids form *-ate* salts and *-ous* acids form *-ite* salts. Prefixes from the acid names remain in the salt names.

Table 24-5

Acid and Ion Names		
Acid		**Ion**
$HMnO_4$ permanganic acid	$\rightarrow$	MnO_4^- permanganate
H_2SO_4 sulfuric acid	$\rightarrow$	SO_4^{2-} sulfate
HNO_2 nitrous acid	$\rightarrow$	NO_2^- nitrite
HClO hypochlorous acid	$\rightarrow$	ClO^- hypochlorite

PROBLEMS

8. Name the following compounds.
   a. $NaHSO_4$ **b.** $KHC_4H_4O_6$ **c.** NaH_2PO_4 **d.** $NaHS$

9. Write formulas for the following compounds.
   a. sodium hydrogen carbonate
   b. sodium monohydrogen phosphate
   c. ammonium hydrogen sulfide
   d. potassium hydrogen sulfate

8. a. sodium hydrogen sulfate
   b. potassium hydrogen tartrate
   c. sodium dihydrogen phosphate
   d. sodium hydrogen sulfide

9. a. $NaHCO_3$
   b. Na_2HPO_4
   c. NH_4HS
   d. $KHSO_4$

24:9 STRENGTHS OF ACIDS AND BASES

Not all acids and bases are completely ionized in water solution. An acid (such as hydrochloric) which is considered to ionize completely into positive and negative ions is called a **strong acid.** A base (such as sodium hydroxide) which is completely dissociated into positive and negative ions is called a **strong base.**

Some acids and bases ionize only slightly in solution. The most important base of this kind is ammonia. In water solution, this base ionizes only partially into NH_4^+ and OH^-. The major portion of the ammonia molecules remain unreacted. Such a base is called a weak base. Acetic acid ionizes only slightly in water solution. It is called a weak acid. A **weak acid** or a **weak base** is one which ionizes only slightly in solution.

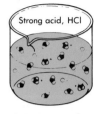

$$HCl + H_2O \rightarrow H_3O^+ + Cl^-$$

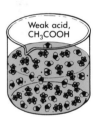

$$CH_3COOH + H_2O \rightleftharpoons H_3O^+ + CH_3COO^-$$

FIGURE 24-4. A strong acid, such as HCl, ionizes completely. A weak acid, such as CH_3COOH, ionizes slightly. In two solutions of equal concentration, fewer hydronium ions are present in solution for a weak acid than for a strong acid.

Strong acids are completely ionized in water solution.
Strong bases, in water, are completely dissociated into + and − ions.
Weak acids and bases ionize only slightly in water solution.

Demonstration—Using conductivity equipment, show the students the difference in conductivity of a strong and a weak acid of the same concentration and volume. A 15 or 25 watt light bulb or a *pH* meter could be used. Discuss the degree of ionization of the two acids.

Table 24-6

Relative Strengths of Some Acids and Bases		
Compound	**Formula**	**Relative Strength**
Hydrochloric acid	HCl	strong acid
Phosphorous acid	H_3PO_3	
Phosphoric acid	H_3PO_4	
Hydrofluoric acid	HF	
Hydroselenic acid	H_2Se	
Acetic acid	CH_3COOH	
Carbonic acid	H_2CO_3	
Hydrosulfuric acid	H_2S	
		neutral solution
Hypochlorite ion	ClO^-	
Cyanide ion	CN^-	
Ammonia	NH_3	
Carbonate ion	CO_3^{2-}	
Aluminum hydroxide	$Al(OH)_3$	
Phosphate ion	PO_4^{3-}	
Silicate ion	SiO_3^{2-}	
Hydroxide ion	OH^-	strong base

24:10   NET IONIC EQUATIONS

For reactions taking place in water, it is customary for chemists to write equations in the ionic form. In this method, only those ions taking part in the reaction are written. Other ions present in the solution but not involved in the reaction are known as **spectator ions** and are not included in the equation.

In writing net ionic equations, dissolved salts are considered in their ionic form. We list other substances as molecules or atoms. The following rule must be observed when writing net ionic equations. *Substances occurring in a reaction in molecular form are written as molecules. Those occurring as ions are written as ions.*

Weak acids and bases are written in molecular form while strong acids and bases should be written in the ionized form. An acid may contain more than one ionizable hydrogen atom. Such an acid is called a **polyprotic acid.** Below are listed some "thumb rules" for deciding whether to use ions or molecules in writing net ionic equations. These rules are not applicable in all cases but work well in most reactions. However, if your equation must be exact, you should use a handbook. The handbook will help you determine whether substances are to be written as ions or as molecules.

Rule 1. *Binary acids:* HCl, HBr, and HI are strong; all others (including HCN) are weak. Strong acids are written in ionic form.

Rule 2. *Ternary acids:* If the number of oxygen atoms in the molecule exceeds the number of hydrogen atoms by two or more, the acid is strong.

Weak: $HClO, H_3AsO_4, H_2CO_3, H_4SiO_4, HNO_2$

Strong: $HClO_3, HClO_4, H_2SO_4, HNO_3, H_2SeO_4$

Rule 3. *Polyprotic acids:* In the second and subsequent ionizations the acids are always weak, whether or not the original acid is strong or weak.

Rule 4. *Bases:* Hydroxides of the Groups IA and IIA elements (except beryllium) are strong. All others including ammonia, hydroxylamine, and organic bases are weak.

Rule 5. *Salts:* Salts are written in ionic form if soluble, and in molecular form if insoluble.   even though the undissolved crystal is probably ionic in structure

Ionic: $K^+ + Cl^-, Zn^{2+} + 2NO_3^-$

Molecular: $AgBr, BaSO_4$

Rule 6. *Oxides:* Oxides are always written in molecular form.

Rule 7. *Gases:* Gases are always written in molecular form.

Spectator ions are not involved in the reaction, and are not written in the net ionic equation.

Some substances are written as molecules; others as ions.

Polyprotic acids have more than one ionizable hydrogen atom.

Strong electrolytes are written in ionic form.

Weak electrolytes are written in molecular form.

It is often convenient to consider both protons of sulfuric acid as strong.

Soluble salts are written in ionic form; insoluble in molecular form.

EXAMPLE: Net Ionic Equations

Convert the following balanced equation to a net ionic equation.

$$H_2SiO_3 + 2NaOH \rightarrow Na_2SiO_3 + 2H_2O$$

Solving process:
According to Rule 2, since there are three oxygens and two hydrogens in silicic acid, it must be weak. Rule 4 tells us that NaOH is strong. The sodium silicate salt is soluble and we apply Rule 5. Water is an oxide and Rule 6 applies. Using these rules the ionic equation is written as

$$H_2SiO_3 + 2Na^+ + 2OH^- \rightarrow 2Na^+ + SiO_3^{2-} + 2H_2O$$

To make the equation a net ionic equation, we remove (by subtracting from both sides) those species which appear on each side. For our reaction, two sodium ions appear on each side and are removed. The net ionic equation is then:

$$H_2SiO_3 + 2OH^- \rightarrow SiO_3^{2-} + 2H_2O$$

EXAMPLE: Net Ionic Equations

Convert the following balanced equation to a net ionic equation.

$$2HCl + Ba(OH)_2 \rightarrow BaCl_2 + 2H_2O$$

Solving process:
Rule 1: HCl is strong
Rule 4: $Ba(OH)_2$ is strong
Rule 5: $BaCl_2$ is ionic (soluble)
Rule 6: H_2O is molecular

Ionic equation: $2H^+ + 2Cl^- + Ba^{2+} + 2OH^- \rightarrow Ba^{2+} + 2Cl^- + 2H_2O$
Net ionic equation: $2H^+ + 2OH^- \rightarrow 2H_2O$

Note that the net ionic equation should be further simplified by dividing through by 2 in order to put it in its lowest terms.

Final form: $H^+ + OH^- \rightarrow H_2O$

PROBLEMS See Teacher's Guide.

10. Reduce the following balanced equations to net ionic form.
    a. $4HCl(aq) + 2Cr(NO_3)_2(aq) + 2HgCl_2(aq) \rightarrow$
       $2CrCl_3(aq) + Hg_2Cl_2(c) + 4HNO_3(aq)$
    b. $2Mn(NO_3)_2(aq) + 5NaBiO_3(c) + 14HNO_3(aq) \rightarrow$
       $2NaMnO_4(aq) + 5Bi(NO_3)_3(aq) + 7H_2O(l) + 3NaNO_3(aq)$
    c. $2AgNO_3(aq) + H_2SO_4(aq) \rightarrow Ag_2SO_4(c) + 2HNO_3(aq)$
    d. $H_4SiO_4(aq) + 4NaOH(aq) \rightarrow Na_4SiO_4(aq) + 4H_2O(l)$
    e. $2CuSO_4(aq) + 2NH_4CNS(aq) + H_2SO_3(aq) + H_2O(l) \rightarrow$
       $2CuCNS(c) + (NH_4)_2SO_4(aq) + 2H_2SO_4(aq)$

24:11   IONIZATION CONSTANT

Acetic acid is a weak acid and ionizes only slightly. The equation of the ionization of acetic acid at equilibrium is

$$CH_3COOH(l) + H_2O(l) \rightleftarrows CH_3COO^-(aq) + H_3O^+(aq)$$

The equilibrium constant for this reaction is

$$K_{eq} = \frac{[products]}{[reactants]}$$

$$K_{eq} = \frac{[CH_3COO^-][H_3O^+]}{[CH_3COOH][H_2O]}$$

The CH_3COO^- and H_3O^+ ion concentrations are small, and the concentration of CH_3COOH is almost unaffected by the ionization. When acetic acid ionizes, hydrogen ions attach to a water molecule and form the hydronium ion (H_3O^+). However, acetic acid is a weak acid and ionizes only slightly. Thus, few hydrogen ions are formed. The concentration of water remains nearly constant (55.6 mol/dm^3—Section 25:2). Thus, we can multiply the concentration of water by the equilibrium constant and obtain the equation:

Ionization constant:
$K_{eq}[H_2O] = 55.6\ K_{eq}$

$$K_{eq}[H_2O] = \frac{[CH_3COO^-][H_3O^+]}{[CH_3COOH]}$$

Because $[H_2O]$ is constant, the product of the equilibrium constant and the concentration of water ($K_{eq}[H_2O]$) produces a new constant. This new constant is called the **ionization constant,** and is given the symbol K_a. For any weak acid (HA + $H_2O \rightleftarrows$ $H_3O^+ + A^-$), the ioniztion constant is:

Ionization constant (K_a) is a special case of an equilibrium constant.

$$K_a = \frac{[H_3O^+][A^-]}{[HA]}$$

Make it clear to students that the ionization constant is simply a special case of the equilibrium constant.

In a similar way we can write ionization constant expressions for weak bases (K_b). Ammonia is a weak base which reacts with water as follows:

$$NH_3 + H_2O \rightleftarrows NH_4^+ + OH^-$$

The ionization constant expression for ammonia is

$$K_b = \frac{[NH_4^+][OH^-]}{[NH_3]}$$

EXAMPLE: Ionization of a Weak Acid

What is the hydronium ion concentration of a 0.100M solution of formic acid (HCOOH)? Formic acid has an ionization constant of 1.78×10^{-4}.

Solving process:

$$HCOOH(l) + H_2O(l) \rightleftarrows H_3O^+(aq) + HCOO^-(aq)$$

$$K_a = \frac{[H_3O^+][HCOO^-]}{[HCOOH]} = 1.78 \times 10^{-4}$$

Let x represent $[H_3O^+]$ and $[HCOO^-]$. (The balanced equation shows that $[H_3O^+]$ is equal to $[HCOO^-]$ in this example.) If we let $x = [H_3O^+]$ or $[HCOO^-]$, then the concentration of formic acid $[HCOOH]$ is $(0.100 - x)$. Because x is so small when compared with the concentration of formic acid, $(0.100 - x)$ is approximately equal to $0.100M$.

Therefore,

$$1.78 \times 10^{-4} = \frac{x^2}{0.100}$$

$$\text{and } x^2 = (0.100)(1.78 \times 10^{-4}) = 1.78 \times 10^{-5} = 17.8 \times 10^{-6}$$

$$x = 4.22 \times 10^{-3} M$$

If x is sufficiently large compared to the acid concentration, the quadratic equation must be used to solve the problem.

EXAMPLE: H_3O^+ Concentration for a Weak Acid

What is the hydronium ion concentration in a $0.100M$ solution of $HClO_2$? $K_a HClO_2 = 1.10 \times 10^{-2}$

Solving process:

$$HClO_2 + H_2O \rightleftarrows H_3O^+ + ClO_2^-$$

$$K_a = \frac{[H_3O^+][ClO_2^-]}{[HClO_2]} = 1.10 \times 10^{-2}$$

Let $x = [H_3O^+] = [ClO_2^-]$ and $(0.1 - x) = [HClO_2]$

$$1.10 \times 10^{-2} = \frac{x^2}{(0.1 - x)}$$

$$x^2 = (0.1 - x)(1.10 \times 10^{-2})$$
$$x^2 = (1.10 \times 10^{-3}) - (1.10 \times 10^{-2})x$$

$$x^2 + (1.10 \times 10^{-2})x - (1.10 \times 10^{-3}) = 0$$

$$x = \frac{-(1.10 \times 10^{-2}) \pm \sqrt{(1.10 \times 10^{-2})^2 + 4(1.10 \times 10^{-3})}}{2}$$

$$x = \frac{-(1.10 \times 10^{-2}) \pm \sqrt{(1.21 \times 10^{-4}) + (4.40 \times 10^{-3})}}{2}$$

Problems requiring the use of the quadratic equation can be considered optional at this level. However, if you use them be sure to review the mathematical process for students.

Because K_a is 10^{-2} and $[HClO_2]$ is 10^{-1}, the difference is not 3 orders of magnitude. Thus, $(0.1 - x)$ is needed.

$ax^2 + bx + c = 0$

$x = \dfrac{-b \pm \sqrt{b^2 - 4ac}}{2a}$

In this equation:
$a = 1$
$b = 1.10 \times 10^{-2}$
$c = 1.10 \times 10^{-3}$

A good "rule of thumb" is to neglect x in $(0.1 - x)$ when it is added to or subtracted from a number that differs from the K value by three powers of ten or more. The use of the quadratic equation will not result in a significantly different answer.

$$x = \frac{-(1.10 \times 10^{-2}) \pm \sqrt{4.52 \times 10^{-3}}}{2}$$

$$x = \frac{-(1.10 \times 10^{-2}) \pm (6.72 \times 10^{-2})}{2}$$

$$x = \frac{-7.82 \times 10^{-2}}{2}, \quad \frac{5.62 \times 10^{-2}}{2}$$

$$x = -3.91 \times 10^{-2}, 2.81 \times 10^{-2}$$

A negative concentration is impossible. Thus,

$$x = [H_3O^+] = 2.81 \times 10^{-2} M$$

PROBLEMS

11. $1.78 \times 10^{-5} M$

11. What is the hydronium ion concentration in $0.0100M$ HClO? $K_a = 3.16 \times 10^{-8}$.

12. 3.03×10^{-6}

12. What is K_b for N_2H_4 (hydrazine) if a $0.500M$ solution has the following concentrations at equilibrium? $[N_2H_4] = 0.499M$, $[OH^-] = 1.23 \times 10^{-3}$, $[N_2H_5^+] = 1.23 \times 10^{-3}$

24:12   PERCENT OF IONIZATION

When a weak acid or base is dissolved in water, it ionizes only slightly. It is often desirable in such cases to know just how much of a substance is ionized. This amount is usually expressed in terms of percent, and is called the **percent of ionization.** For example, at room temperature, we found the hydronium ion concentration of $0.100M$ formic acid, HCOOH, to be $4.22 \times 10^{-3} M$. We know that

$$HCOOH + H_2O \rightleftarrows H_3O^+ + HCOO^-$$

Percent ionization can be calculated from the ratio obtained by comparing the concentration of the ions in solution to the concentration of the solute before it dissolved.

Thus, we can find the percent ionization of formic acid by dividing either $[H_3O^+]$ or $[HCOO^-]$ by $[HCOOH]$. Either $[H_3O^+]$ or $[HCOO^-]$ will show the correct ratio of dissociated ions because the two concentrations are equal.

EXAMPLE: Percent of Ionization

Find the percent of ionization of a $0.100M$ solution of formic acid if the hydronium ion concentration is $4.22 \times 10^{-3} M$.

Solving process:

$$Percent\ of\ ionization = \frac{[amount\ ionized]}{[original\ acid]} \times 100$$

$$= \frac{4.22 \times 10^{-3}}{0.100} \times 100 = 4.22\%$$

PROBLEMS

13. The ionization constant of acetic acid, CH_3COOH, is 1.76×10^{-5}. Find the percent of ionization of $0.100M$ acetic acid.

14. A solution of $1.00M$ HA in water ionizes 2.00%. Find K_a.

24:13 COMMON ION EFFECT

There are times when a chemist may wish to change the concentration of a specific ion in a solution. Such changes are often made by adding a new substance to the solution.

Acetic acid ionizes in a water solution to form acetate and hydronium ions. What will happen if we add some sodium acetate to the solution?

Sodium acetate dissociates into acetate (CH_3COO^-) and sodium ions.

$$NaC_2H_3O_2(c) \rightarrow Na^+(aq) + CH_3COO^-(aq)$$

Acetic acid ionizes into acetate and hydronium ions.

$$H_2O(l) + CH_3COOH(l) \rightleftarrows H_3O^+(aq) + CH_3COO^-(aq)$$

K_a for acetic acid is

$$\frac{[CH_3COO^-][H_3O^+]}{[CH_3COOH]} = 1.76 \times 10^{-5}$$

K_a is a constant, and does not change unless the temperature changes. If sodium acetate is added to an acetic acid solution, acetate ion concentration is increased and a shift in the equilibrium occurs. Because there are more particles of CH_3COO^-, there will be more collisions between CH_3COO^- and H_3O^+. Thus, the rate of reaction will increase toward acetic acid. Some of the excess acetate ions unite with hydronium ions to form molecular acetic acid and water. This reaction results in the removal of hydronium ions from solution (thus decreasing hydronium ion concentration). The acetic acid concentration increases slightly. A new equilibrium is established with more acetate ions and fewer hydronium ions. K_a remains unchanged.

The acetate ion is common to both acetic acid and sodium acetate. The effect of the acetate ion on the acetic acid and solution is called the **common ion effect.** The addition of a common ion increases the concentration of one of the products of the ionization. Thus, the equilibrium shifts toward the opposite side in accordance with Le Chatelier's principle. By adding acetate ions (sodium acetate), we have placed a stress on the system (a surplus of acetate ions). The system shifts so as to relieve that stress by reacting hydronium ions with the acetate ions. In the process acetate and hydronium ions are consumed and acetic acid molecules are produced.

An increase in acetate ion concentration will cause a decrease in hydrogen ion concentration.

The K_a remains the same if a common ion is added.

The common ion effect is a good example of Le Chatelier's principle.

A common ion causes equilibrium to shift toward the opposite side of the equation.

EXAMPLE: Common Ion Effect

What would be the hydronium ion concentration in a solution 0.100M in HOCN, cyanic acid, and 0.0500M in NaOCN, sodium cyanate? $K_a = 3.47 \times 10^{-4}$.

Solving process:
First, write the equation for the equilibrium system.

$$HOCN + H_2O \rightleftarrows H_3O^+ + OCN^-$$

Then write the expression for the ionization constant.

$$K_a = \frac{[H_3O^+][OCN^-]}{[HOCN]}$$

The hydronium ion is the quantity we seek, so we will let x represent that concentration. If x hydronium ions are produced, then x acid molecules ionized and x cyanate ions were produced from the acid. However, cyanate ions were also produced from the soluble sodium salt. Since sodium cyanate is soluble, we assume it dissociates completely. In that case, the salt contributes a concentration of 0.05M to the cyanate ion concentration. The total cyanate ion concentration would be 0.05 + x. If x acid molecules ionized and we started with 0.100, then at equilibrium the molecular acid concentration must be 0.100 − x.

$$3.47 \times 10^{-4} = \frac{(x)(x + 0.05)}{(0.100 - x)}$$

$$(3.47 \times 10^{-4})(0.100 - x) = (x)(x + 0.05)$$

$$(3.47 \times 10^{-5}) - (3.47 \times 10^{-4})x = x^2 + 0.05x$$

$$x^2 + (5.03 \times 10^{-2})x - (3.47 \times 10^{-5}) = 0$$

$ax^2 + bx + c = 0$

$x = \dfrac{-b \pm \sqrt{b^2 - 4ac}}{2a}$

$$x = \frac{-5.03 \times 10^{-2} \pm \sqrt{(5.03 \times 10^{-2})^2 + 4(3.47 \times 10^{-5})(1)}}{2}$$

$$x = \frac{-5.03 \times 10^{-2} \pm \sqrt{(2.53 \times 10^{-3}) + (1.39 \times 10^{-4})}}{2}$$

$$x = \frac{-5.03 \times 10^{-2} \pm \sqrt{2.67 \times 10^{-3}}}{2}$$

$$x = \frac{-5.03 \times 10^{-2} \pm 5.17 \times 10^{-2}}{2}$$

$$x = \frac{1.36 \times 10^{-3}}{2}$$

$$x = [H_3O^+] = 6.80 \times 10^{-4} M$$

PROBLEMS

For Problem 16 ignore x in $[0.106 - x]$

15. What is the hydronium ion concentration in a solution $0.150M$ in HNO_2 and $0.0300M$ in $NaNO_2$? Refer to Table A-9 of the Appendix for the K_a.

16. What is the hydronium ion concentration in a solution $0.106M$ in hypobromous acid and $0.00500M$ in $NaBrO$? $K_a = 2.40 \times 10^{-9}$.

17. Given a solution of the weak acid H_2CO_3, how could the hydronium ion concentration of this solution be reduced? How could the carbonate ion concentration of this same solution be reduced?

15. $2.3 \times 10^{-3}M$
16. $5.09 \times 10^{-8}M$
17. add $NaHCO_3$

24:14 POLYPROTIC ACIDS

Polyprotic acids have more than one ionizable hydrogen atom.

An acid containing more than one ionizable hydrogen atom is called a **polyprotic acid.** Sulfuric acid is an example of a polyprotic acid. In sulfuric acid, the hydrogen atoms leave the molecule one at a time. Sulfuric acid is a strong acid because the first hydrogen atom ionizes easily. The remaining hydrogen sulfate ion ionizes only slightly, and is considered a weak acid. The reaction can be represented by the following equations.

$$H_2SO_4(l) + H_2O(l) \rightarrow H_3O^+(aq) + HSO_4^-(aq) \quad \begin{array}{l}\text{ionizes readily}\\\text{(strong acid)}\end{array}$$

$$HSO_4^-(aq) + H_2O(l) \rightleftarrows H_3O^+(aq) + SO_4^{-2}(aq) \quad \begin{array}{l}\text{ionizes slightly}\\\text{(weak acid)}\end{array}$$

The first ionization of a polyprotic acid leaves behind a negative ion. Therefore, the attraction for hydrogen is increased. Because of this attraction, each successive ionization is more difficult and occurs to a lesser extent. Phosphoric acid is a triprotic acid (an acid containing three ionizable hydrogen atoms); it ionizes as follows.

The second ionization of a polyprotic acid contributes few hydrogen ions.

$$H_3PO_4(c) + H_2O(l) \rightleftarrows H_3O^+(aq) + H_2PO_4^-(aq) \qquad K_a = 7.11 \times 10^{-3}$$

$$H_2PO_4^-(aq) + H_2O(l) \rightleftarrows H_3O^+(aq) + HPO_4^{2-}(aq) \qquad K_a = 7.99 \times 10^{-8}$$

$$HPO_4^{-2}(aq) + H_2O(l) \rightleftarrows H_3O^+(aq) + PO_4^{3-}(aq) \qquad K_a = 4.80 \times 10^{-13}$$

Calculations involving diprotic acids are complex. We have three unknown quantities: hydronium ion, protonated anion, and anion. There is a large difference between the extent of first and second ionizations. Thus, it is usually possible to ignore the hydronium ion contributed by the second ionization.

PROBLEM

18. Calculate the ratio of the first ionization constant to the second ionization constant for each of the polyprotic acids listed in Table A-9. Do you see any pattern? **See Teacher's Guide.**

Gilbert Newton Lewis   (1875–1946)

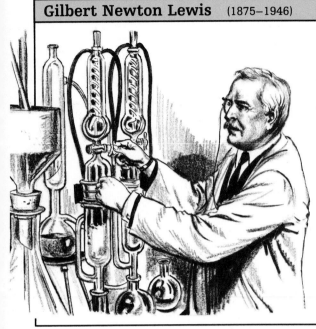

Following his education at the University of Nebraska and Harvard, Gilbert Newton Lewis began his professional career in an unusual way— as an employee of the Philippine government. Here he assumed the positions of Supervisor of Weights and Measures and chemist in the Bureau of Science.

Lewis was the first chemist to introduce the idea of the electron-pair bond. In so doing, he redefined the nature of acids and bases as being electron pair donors and acceptors. His theory also led to a clearer understanding of the concept of valence.

In addition to these accomplishments, Lewis was the first to isolate heavy hydrogen. His theory of excited electron states in organic compounds helped explain the phenomena of color, fluorescence, and phosphorescence.

CHEMICAL TECHNOLOGY: Acid Rain

The nonmetallic oxides produced by the burning of fossil fuels are all acidic anhydrides. Thus, when these gases contact water vapor or water droplets in the atmosphere, they react to produce these acids.

$SO_2 + H_2O \rightarrow H_2SO_3$ *sulfurous acid*

$SO_3 + H_2O \rightarrow H_2SO_4$ *sulfuric acid*

$2NO_2 + H_2O \rightarrow HNO_2 + HNO_3$ *nitrous and nitric acids*

$CO_2 + H_2O \rightarrow H_2CO_3$ *carbonic acid*

Rain formed from these water droplets is acidic. Acid rain has a number of harmful effects. One effect is the increase in the rate of deterioration of stone. Buildings constructed of stone are affected over time. The art work and carvings which decorate buildings and public areas are damaged. The fine detail on statuary is destroyed. Acid rain dissolves some compounds in the stone while the remaining substances become a powdery coating. In addition, the acid rain eats into the stone leaving tiny cracks. When water fills these cracks and freezes, its expansion causes cracking and breaking of the stone.

Acid rain also has adverse effects on living organisms. Acid rain has increased the acidity of numerous lakes in the north-eastern United States and Canada to such an extent that fish can no longer live in them. Acid rain also tends to dissolve vital minerals in the soil. These minerals are then washed away in run-off water. Crops grown in these depleted soils give poor yields if they grow at all. When the acidic run-off reaches waterways it further interferes with fish growth and development.

Correcting these problems by treating statues with preservatives and lakes with basic compounds such as lime is not really the answer. Removing the offending oxides from exhausts or the use of alternate energy sources is a much preferred course of action.

SUMMARY

1. There are three common acid-base theories: the Arrhenius theory, the Brönsted-Lowry theory, and the Lewis theory. 24:1-24:3
2. Metallic oxides tend to form basic anhydrides, while nonmetallic oxides tend to form acidic anhydrides. 24:6
3. A salt is a crystalline compound composed of the negative ion of an acid and the positive ion of a base. 24:8
4. A strong acid ionizes completely in a water solution. A weak acid ionizes only slightly in a water solution. 24:9
5. In net ionic equations, only the reacting species are shown. Spectator ions do not appear. 24:10
6. The ionization of a weak acid or base is an equilibrium process. 24:11
7. Percent ionization is the amount ionized divided by the original amount multiplied by 100. 24:12
8. A common ion represses the ionization of a weak electrolyte. 24:13
9. Polyprotic acids contain more than one ionizable hydrogen atom. Each successive ionization occurs to a lesser extent. 24:14

PROBLEMS

19. For each of the following reactions label the acid, base, conjugate acid, and conjugate base.
    a. $NH_3(g) + H_3O^+(aq) \rightarrow NH_4^+(aq) + H_2O(l)$
    b. $CH_3OH(l) + NH_2^-(aq) \rightarrow CH_3O^-(aq) + NH_3(g)$
    c. $OH^-(aq) + H_3O^+(aq) \rightarrow H_2O(l) + H_2O(l)$
    d. $NH_2^-(aq) + H_2O(l) \rightarrow NH_3(g) + OH^-(aq)$
    e. $H_2O(l) + HClO_4(aq) \rightarrow H_3O^+(aq) + ClO_4^-(aq)$

Acid	Base	Conjugate Acid	Conjugate Base
H_3O^+	NH_3	NH_4^+	H_2O
CH_3OH	NH_2^-	NH_3	CH_3O^-
H_3O^+	OH^-	H_2O	H_2O
H_2O	NH_2^-	NH_3	OH^-
$HClO_4$	H_2O	H_3O^+	ClO_4^-

20. Draw electron-dot formulas for each of the following substances. Decide if the substance would be a Lewis acid or base.
    a. $AlCl_3$ b. SO_3 c. PH_3 d. Xe   e. Zn^{+2}

21. Name the following acids.
    a. HBr(aq)
    b. $H_2Se(aq)$
    c. $HIO_3(aq)$
    d. H_2SeO_3 (H_2SO_3 is sulfurous acid)
    e. $H_2N_2O_2$ (HNO_3 is nitric acid and HNO_2 is nitrous acid)

21. a. hydrobromic
    b. hydroselenic
    c. iodic
    d. selenious
    e. hyponitrous

20. a. :Cl:
    :Cl:Al:Cl:
    acid

    b. :O:S::O
    acid

    c. H:P:H
    H
    base

    d. :Xe:
    base

    e. Zn^{2+}
    acid

22. a. H_3PO_3
    b. H_3PO_2
    c. H_2Te
    d. HIO_4
    e. HIO_3
    f. HCl

23. a. NaOH
    b. $Ca(OH)_2$
    c. HNO_3
    d. RbOH
    e. H_2TeO_3
    f. CsOH

24. a. Sc_2O_3
    b. Cs_2O
    c. I_2O_5
    d. Ga_2O_3
    e. CdO
    f. K_2O

26. a. sodium phosphate,
       Na_3PO_4
    b. potassium borate,
       K_3BO_3
    d. cadmium bromide,
       $CdBr_2$

c. chromium(III) perchlorate,
   $Cr(ClO_4)_3$

e. lithium silicate, Li_4SiO_4

34. $2.92 \times 10^{-2} M$
35. 29.2%
36. $1.8 \times 10^{-3} M$
37. $1 \times 10^{-13} M$
38. $8.30 \times 10^{-2} M$

22. Write formulas for the following acids.
    a. phosphorous acid
    b. hypophosphorous acid
    c. hydrotelluric acid
    d. periodic acid
    e. iodic acid
    f. hydrochloric acid

23. Write formulas for the acids or bases formed from the following anhydrides.
    a. Na_2O
    b. CaO
    c. N_2O_5
    d. Rb_2O
    e. TeO_2
    f. Cs_2O

24. Write formulas for the anhydrides of the following.
    a. $Sc(OH)_3$
    b. $CsOH$
    c. HIO_3
    d. $Ga(OH)_3$
    e. $Cd(OH)_2$
    f. KOH

25. Reduce the following complete equations to net ionic form.
    a. $6Cr(NO_3)_2 + 3CuSO_4 \rightarrow 3Cu + 4Cr(NO_3)_3 + Cr_2(SO_4)_3$
    b. $3H_2SO_4 + MnO_2 + 2KBr \rightarrow MnSO_4 + Br_2 + 2KHSO_4 + 2H_2O$
    c. $H_2SO_4 \rightarrow H_2O + SO_3$
    d. $P_4O_{10} + 6H_2O \rightarrow 4H_3PO_4$
    e. $4CuCNS + 7KIO_3 + 14HCl \rightarrow 4HCN + 4CuSO_4 + 7ICl + 7KCl + 5H_2O$

26. Give the name and formula of the salts obtained from complete neutralization reactions between the following acid-base pairs.
    a. sodium hydroxide and phosphoric acid
    b. potassium hydroxide and boric acid (H_3BO_3)
    c. chromium(III) hydroxide and perchloric acid
    d. cadmium hydroxide and hydrobromic acid
    e. lithium hydroxide and silicic acid (H_4SiO_4)

27. How does a Lewis acid differ from an Arrhenius acid?

28. Show the steps in the reaction whereby benzene reacts with ethyl chloride to give ethylbenzene in the presence of $AlCl_3$.

29. Why do metals tend to form bases rather than acids in water solution?

30. Why is H_2CO_3 considered a weak acid while H_2SO_4 is a strong acid?

31. In writing net ionic equations, why are insoluble salts shown in molecular form?

32. What is the common ion effect?

33. Why is the K_a for each succeeding ionization of phosphoric acid smaller?

34. What is the hydronium ion concentration in a $0.100M$ solution of $KHSO_4$? (See Table A-9 of the Appendix for K_a value.)

35. What is the percentage of ionization of the $HSO_4{}^-$ ion in Problem 34?

36. What is the benzoate ion concentration in a $0.0500M$ solution of benzoic acid, C_6H_5COOH?

37. What would be the hydronium ion concentration in a solution $0.100M$ in NaOH and $1.00M$ in NH_3?

38. What would be the hydrogen ion concentration in a $0.200M$ solution of oxalic acid, HOOCCOOH?

REVIEW

1. What is meant by a reversible reaction?

2. In what units is the concentration measured when writing rate expressions? molarity

3. What two effects does an increase in temperature have on reaction rate? more collisions/s

4. Describe the difference between homogeneous reactions and heterogeneous reactions. homogeneous—all reactants in the same phase   heterogeneous—reactants in

5. What is the relationship between the specific rate constants for a reversible reaction and the equilibrium constant for the same reaction?

6. What effect would an increase in pressure have on the following equilibrium?

$$CH_3 N_2 CH_3(g) \rightleftharpoons C_2 H_6(g) + N_2(g)$$

7. Would you expect methane gas, CH_4, to dissolve in water?

8. Differentiate among unsaturated, saturated, and supersaturated solutions.

9. What is the difference between concentrated and dilute solutions?

10. When $NH_4 NO_3$ is dissolved in water, the solution gets cold. Is the heat of solution of $NH_4 NO_3$ in water positive or negative?

11. From the following data, write the rate expression for the reaction $IO_3^- + 2Br^- + 2H^+ \rightarrow Br_2 + IO_2^- + H_2O$. There is a large excess of acid.

$[IO_3^-]$	$[Br^-]$	rate
0.0700	0.0700	0.00210 mol/dm^3/s
0.0350	0.0700	0.00105 mol/dm^3/s
0.0700	0.1400	0.00840 mol/dm^3/s

12. What is the hydronium ion concentration in a $0.250M$ solution of $C_6 H_5 OH$ with $K_a = 1.02 \times 10^{-10}$?

$$C_6 H_5 OH + H_2 O \rightleftharpoons H_3 O^+ + C_6 H_5 O^-$$

13. If the ΔG for a certain reaction is -55.6 kJ at $25°C$, what is the K_{eq} for the reaction?

1. A reaction whose products will react to produce the original reactants.

two or more phases

5. $\dfrac{k_f}{k_r} = K_{eq}$

6. shift left

7. No, it is nonpolar; water is polar.

9. number of ions per unit volume

10. positive
11. $R = k[IO_3^-][Br^-]^2$
12. $5.05 \times 10^{-6} M$
13. 5.78×10^9

ONE MORE STEP

1. What is meant by the "leveling effect" of water on very strong acids and very strong bases?

2. Find the names of the following acids. Why are they named as they are? $H_2 SO_5$, $H_2 S_2 O_7$, $H_2 S_2 O_8$, $HNCO$, $HSCN$

3. Inorganic acids are compounds containing ionizable hydrogen atoms. Inorganic bases are compounds containing hydroxide ions. What are the comparable compounds in organic chemistry?

You may have thought salt to be only the compound sodium chloride. However, the term salt represents a large class of chemical compounds. The mining and recovery of salts depends on their chemical properties. Yields and purities can be increased by changing the conditions under which a salt is crystallized. What factors control the amount of salt that can be recovered from a solution? What chemical processes may be used to purify the salt shown?

Joey Jacques

Chapter 25 includes a quantitative discussion of K_{sp}, K_w, and pH. Hydrolysis and buffers are presented as practical concepts. Indicators and titration calculations conclude the chapter.

SOLUTIONS OF ELECTROLYTES

25

Demonstration—Place 50 cm³ of 0.5 M Pb(NO₃)₂ in a 250 cm³ Erlenmeyer flask. Add 100 cm³ of 0.5 M Na₂SO₄. Stopper the flask and shake. Allow the white PbSO₄ to settle ($K_{sp} = 1.9 \times 10^{-8}$). Decant and discard the liquid. Wash the PbSO₄ twice using 50 cm³ of water for each washing. Discard the washings. To the white solid, add 100 cm³ of 0.5 M (NH₄)₂S or Na₂S. The black solid produced is PbS ($K_{sp} = 8.4 \times 10^{-28}$). This demonstration will help students realize that an insoluble precipitate is still very slightly soluble. As the equilibrium is disturbed, a majority of the Pb²⁺ ions from the PbSO₄ will be changed to PbS.

Thus far in our investigation of electrolytes we have dealt mainly with acids and bases. Solutions of salts also involve equilibria. It is possible, through a reaction called hydrolysis, for an apparently neutral salt to dissolve in water and produce an acidic or basic solution. In this chapter we will investigate the interaction between electrolytes and water.

GOAL: You will gain an understanding of the interaction of salts with water and acid-base solutions.

25:1 SOLUBILITY PRODUCT CONSTANT

Silver bromide is an ionic compound that is only slightly soluble in water. When an ionic compound is in a solution so concentrated that the solid is in equilibrium with its ions, the solution is saturated. The equilibrium equation for a saturated solution of silver bromide is

The ions in a saturated solution are in equilibrium with the undissolved solid.

$$\mathrm{AgBr(c)} \rightleftarrows \mathrm{Ag^+(aq)} + \mathrm{Br^-(aq)}$$

The equilibrium constant (K_{eq}) for this equilibrium system is

$$K_{eq} = \frac{[\mathrm{Ag^+}][\mathrm{Br^-}]}{[\mathrm{AgBr}]}$$

However, because we are dealing with a solid substance, the AgBr concentration is constant. Both sides of the equation can be multiplied by [AgBr], giving a new expression.

$$K_{eq}[\mathrm{AgBr}] = \frac{[\mathrm{Ag^+}][\mathrm{Br^-}][\mathrm{AgBr}]}{[\mathrm{AgBr}]}$$

$$K_{eq}[\mathrm{AgBr}] = [\mathrm{Ag^+}][\mathrm{Br^-}]$$

The concentration of a solid such as AgBr is a constant because the equilibrium between the solid and liquid is established at the surface of the solid. The number of ions per square centimeter of solid surface is dependent on the crystal structure which does not vary.

The solubility product constant is derived from a special case of equilibrium.

The term $K_{eq}[AgBr]$ is a constant. This new constant is called the **solubility product constant** K_{sp}.

$$K_{sp} = [Ag^+][Br^-]$$

At room temperature, K_{sp} of silver bromide is 7.70×10^{-13}. Consider some silver bromide dissolved in water and allowed to stand until the solution is at equilibrium. The product of the silver and bromide ion concentrations will then be 7.70×10^{-13}.

$$[Ag^+][Br^-] = 7.70 \times 10^{-13}$$

We can now determine the concentration of each ion using the following equation.

$$AgBr(c) \rightleftarrows Ag^+(aq) + Br^-(aq)$$

For every silver ion there is one bromide ion.

$$[Ag^+] = [Br^-]$$

or
$$[Ag^+][Ag^+] = 7.70 \times 10^{-13}$$

therefore,
$$[Ag^+]^2 = 7.70 \times 10^{-13}$$

$$[Ag^+] = 8.78 \times 10^{-7} M$$

In a saturated solution containing only silver bromide and water, the concentration of silver ions is 8.78×10^{-7} mol/dm^3. The concentration of bromide ions is also 8.78×10^{-7} mol/dm^3.

Suppose, however, that some potassium bromide solution is added. What will happen? KBr dissociates to K^+ and Br^- ions.

FIGURE 25-1. The addition of the common ion Br$^-$ to the AgBr equilibrium system decreases the Ag$^+$ concentration as more AgBr precipitates.

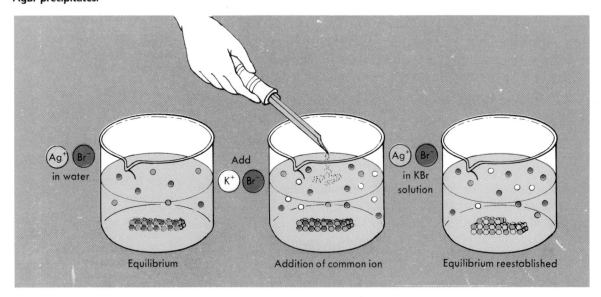

Equilibrium   Addition of common ion   Equilibrium reestablished

The increased number of bromide ions collide more frequently with silver ions. The equilibrium is thus shifted toward the solid silver bromide. When equilibrium is again established, the concentration of silver ion, $[Ag^+]$, has decreased. At the same time, the concentration of bromide ion, $[Br^-]$, has increased. Solid silver bromide has precipitated out, and the K_{sp}, 7.70×10^{-13}, has been reestablished. This reaction is an example of the common ion effect. The addition of a common ion removes silver ion from solution, and causes the equilibrium to shift toward the solid silver bromide. We could also say the addition of a common ion decreases the solubility of a substance in solution.

The addition of a common ion to a saturated solution causes precipitation of the solute.

The solubility of a substance is decreased by the addition of a common ion.

The result is predicted by the application of Le Chatelier's principle.

EXAMPLE: Common Ion

What will be the silver ion concentration in a saturated solution of silver bromide if 0.100 mol KBr is added to 1 dm^3 of the solution? Assume no increase in volume of the solution.

Students often need review on comparing (>, <) numbers expressed in scientific notation.

Solving process:
Potassium bromide is a soluble salt. Thus, it will contribute a bromide ion concentration of $0.100M$. The total bromide ion concentration will consist of $0.100M$ from the KBr plus some unknown amount from the AgBr. We will designate the amount of bromide ion from the AgBr as y. If the AgBr produces a bromide ion concentration of y, then it must also produce a silver ion concentration of y (AgBr $\rightarrow Ag^+ + Br^-$). Substituting these values in the solubility product expression gives us

$$7.70 \times 10^{-13} = y(0.100 + y)$$

We know that y will be small compared to 0.100 since silver bromide is almost insoluble. Thus, $0.100 + y$ is essentially equal to 0.100.

$$7.70 \times 10^{-13} = 0.100y$$
$$y = 7.70 \times 10^{-12}M$$

EXAMPLE: Solubility Product Constant

Suppose 500 cm^3 of $0.0200M$ NaCl are added to 500 cm^3 of $0.0100M$ $AgNO_3$. If the K_{sp} of AgCl is 1.56×10^{-10}, will any precipitate form?

Solving process:
The total volume of solution will be 1000 cm^3 since 500 cm^3 of each solution is used. Therefore, the concentrations of both the NaCl solution and the $AgNO_3$ solution will be halved.

$$[NaCl] = \frac{1}{2} \times 0.0200M = 0.0100M$$

$$[AgNO_3] = \frac{1}{2} \times 0.0100M = 0.00500M$$

Since both $NaCl$ and $AgNO_3$ dissociate completely

$$K_{sp} = [Ag^+][Cl^-]$$

$$= (0.00500)(0.0100) = 0.000\ 0500 = 5.00 \times 10^{-5}$$

However, the ion product cannot exceed the K_{sp}, 1.56×10^{-10}. Therefore, $AgCl$ will precipitate out of solution until

$$[Ag^+][Cl^-] = 1.56 \times 10^{-10}.$$

EXAMPLE: Solubility Product

The solubility product constant is the product of the molar concentrations of the ions in a saturated solution raised to the power of their coefficients in the balanced equation.

What is the iodate concentration in a saturated solution of copper(II) iodate? The K_{sp} of $Cu(IO_3)_2$ is 1.40×10^{-7}.

$$Cu(IO_3)_2 \rightleftarrows Cu^{2+} + 2IO_3^-$$

Solving process:
For every copper ion there are two iodate ions. If $[Cu^{2+}] = x$, then $[IO_3^-] = 2x$.

$$K_{sp} = [Cu^{2+}][IO_3^-]^2$$

$$1.40 \times 10^{-7} = x(2x)^2$$

$$1.40 \times 10^{-7} = x(4x^2)$$

$$1.40 \times 10^{-7} = 4x^3$$

$$x^3 = 0.35 \times 10^{-7} = 35.0 \times 10^{-9}$$

$$x = 5.92 \times 10^{-3}$$

$$[IO_3^-] = 2x = 11.84 \times 10^{-3}$$

PROBLEMS

1. $1.22 \times 10^{-8} M$

2. $K_{sp} = 4.00 \times 10^{-15}$

3. $3.42 \times 10^{-8} M$

4. $K_{sp} = 7.09 \times 10^{-9}$

1. The solubility product constant of silver iodide is 1.50×10^{-16}. What is $[Ag^+]$ in a solution at equilibrium?
2. If $[D^+]$ is $2.00 \times 10^{-5} M$ at equilibrium, what is the K_{sp} for D_2A?
3. What is the concentration of Be^{2+} in a saturated solution of $Be(OH)_2$? $K_{sp} = 1.60 \times 10^{-22}$
4. A saturated solution of PbI_2 has a lead ion concentration of 1.21×10^{-3}. What is K_{sp} for PbI_2?

25:2 IONIZATION OF WATER

Conductivity experiments have shown that water ionizes according to the equation

$$H_2O(l) + H_2O(l) \rightleftarrows H_3O^+(aq) + OH^-(aq)$$

Even though it does conduct a current, pure water is a poor conductor. An electric current is carried in a solution by the ions in the solution. Since pure water is a poor conductor of electricity, it must contain few ions. Thus, pure water must ionize only slightly. In pure water, the concentration of H_3O^+ is equal to the concentration of OH^-. Each molecule of H_2O that ionizes produces one ion each of H_3O^+ and OH^-.

Pure water ionizes only slightly.

Since water ionizes, it should be possible to find an equilibrium constant for this reaction.

$$K_{eq} = \frac{[H_3O^+][OH^-]}{[H_2O][H_2O]}$$

Conductivity experiments have indicated that pure water contains 1×10^{-7} mole of H_3O^+ (and the same amount of OH^-) per cubic decimeter. Therefore:

$$K_{eq} = \frac{(1.00 \times 10^{-7})(1.00 \times 10^{-7})}{[H_2O]^2}$$

In one experiment which consisted of 2 wires 1 cm apart and 1 cm beneath the surface, triple distilled water carried 3.5 milliamps at 115 volts. For comparison, a 0.1 M HCl solution under the same conditions carried a 120 milliamp current.

In pure water,
$[H_3O^+]=[OH^-]=1.00 \times 10^{-7}M$

We can find K_{eq} if we can arrive at some value for $[H_2O]$. Since water ionizes so slightly, we can approximate $[H_2O]$ in pure water by assuming that no ionization occurs. We assume that pure water contains only molecular H_2O.

Pure water is assumed to be molecular when calculating the K_{eq}.

One mole of water has mass 18.0 g (16.0 + 2.0). One dm^3 of pure water has mass 1000 g. The concentration of water in pure water is

These figures apply to water at room temperature. The K_w at other temperatures is slightly different.

$$[H_2O] = \frac{1 \text{ mol}}{18.0 \text{ g}} \left| \frac{1000 \text{ g}}{1.00 \text{ dm}^3} \right. = 55.6 \text{ mol/dm}^3$$

We can now find K_{eq} for water.

$$K_{eq} = \frac{(1.00 \times 10^{-7})(1.00 \times 10^{-7})}{(55.6)^2}$$

Because the value 55.6 mol/dm^3 is relatively constant, we can multiply both sides of the equation by $(55.6)^2$ and get a new constant

$$K_{eq}(55.6)^2 = [H_3O^+][OH^-] = 1.00 \times 10^{-14}$$

We will call this new constant $K_{eq}(55.6)^2$ the **ion product constant of water**, K_w.

K_w is the ion product constant of water.

$$K_w = [H_3O^+][OH^-] = 1.00 \times 10^{-14}$$

K_w is a constant for all dilute aqueous solutions. Although the concentrations of H_3O^+ and OH^- may change when substances are added to water, the product of $[H_3O^+]$ and $[OH^-]$ remains the same.

If an acid is added to water, the $[H_3O^+]$ increases and the $[OH^-]$ decreases.

If a base is added to water, the $[OH^-]$ increases and $[H_3O^+]$ decreases.

EXAMPLE: Concentration of Hydroxide Ion in Solution

What is the $[OH^-]$ in a water solution with $[H_3O^+] = 1.00 \times 10^{-5}$?

Solving process:

If an acid, HA, is added to water,

$$HA + H_2O \rightarrow H_3O^+ + A^-$$

an excess of hydronium ion is produced. Collisions between H_3O^+ and OH^- also increase.

$$H_3O^+ + OH^- \rightarrow H_2O + H_2O$$

As the $[H_3O^+]$ increases, the $[OH^-]$ decreases, and K_w remains 1.00×10^{-14}. If the $[H_3O^+]$ is increased to 10^{-5} by the addition of acid, the $[OH^-]$ must decrease.

$$[H_3O^+][OH^-] = 1.00 \times 10^{-14}$$

$$\text{and } [OH^-] = \frac{1.00 \times 10^{-14}}{[H_3O^+]}$$

$$[OH^-] = \frac{1.00 \times 10^{-14}}{1.00 \times 10^{-5}} = 1.00 \times 10^{-9}$$

If a base is added to water, the equilibrium shifts in the opposite direction, and the solution becomes more basic.

$$OH^-(aq) + H_3O^+(aq) \rightarrow H_2O(l) + H_2O(l)$$

H_3O^+ is removed from solution, and the ion product constant remains 1.00×10^{-14}.

PROBLEMS

5. $[OH^-] = 1.47 \times 10^{-5} M$

6. $[H_3O^+] = 1.92 \times 10^{-12} M$

5. What is the hydroxide ion concentration in a solution with hydronium ion concentration $6.80 \times 10^{-10} M$?

6. What is the hydronium ion concentration in a solution with hydroxide ion concentration $5.21 \times 10^{-3} M$?

25:3   pH SCALE

The ionization of water is so slight that it is almost never considered in the actual production or use of acids and bases. Why, then, was it introduced? Knowledge of the ion product constant for water has enabled chemists to develop a simple acidity scale, called the pH scale. The scale can be used to indicate the basicity as well as the acidity of any water solution. The **pH scale** is a measure of hydronium ion concentration.

The pH scale is a simplified way of stating the concentration of H_3O^+ ions in solution.

The concentration of H_3O^+ is expressed as powers of 10, from 10^{-14} to 10^0. This method is a convenient way to indicate the $[H_3O^+]$. We could simplify this expression even further by writing only the exponent. For instance, 10^{-7} would be written as $^{-7}$. However, the negative sign is undesirable. If $[H_3O^+] = 10^{-7}$, the log of $[H_3O^+] = -7$. If, however, we take the negative log of $[H_3O^+]$, we get the desired $+7$. The negative log of $[H_3O^+]$ is the pH.

Hydrogen ion concentration is measured by pH.

The pH of a neutral solution equals 7.
Acidic solution: pH < 7
Basic solution: pH > 7

EXAMPLE: pH Determination

The hydrogen ion concentration of a solution is $1 \times 10^{-7} M$. What is the pH of the solution?

Solving process:

$$pH = -\log[H_3O^+]$$

$$[H_3O^+] = 1 \times 10^{-7}$$

Therefore:

$$= -\log(1 \times 10^{-7}) = -\log(1.00 \times 10^{-7})$$
$$= -(\log 1.00 + \log 10^{-7}) = -[0 + (-7)] = 7$$

Note that a pH of 7 indicates a neutral solution ($[H_3O^+] = [OH^-]$).

Students should form the habit of deciding whether the solution will be acidic or basic before they work the problem. Then they should check to see whether their answer is in the correct range (>7 or <7).

EXAMPLE: pH Determination

One-tenth mole of HCl is added to enough water to make 1 dm^3 of solution. What is the pH of the solution? (Assume that the HCl is 100% ionized.)

Solving process:

$$[H_3O^+] = 0.1M = 1 \times 10^{-1} \text{ mol/dm}^3$$

$$pH = -\log[H_3O^+] = -\log(1.00 \times 10^{-1})$$
$$pH = -(\log 1.00 + \log 10^{-1}) = -[0 + (-1)] = 1$$

Note that as the hydronium ion concentration increases and a neutral solution is made more acidic, the pH goes from 7 toward 0. If the pH of a solution falls between 7 and 14, the solution is basic. Table 25-1 indicates the pH of several common solutions. Note for those solutions which exist in the body, the maintenance of the pH shown is vital to life.

Suppose we wished to know the pH of a solution which was basic or about which we knew only the hydroxide ion concentration. We can use the ion product constant of water to find the relationship between pH and hydroxide ion concentration.

If we take the logarithm of both sides of the ion product of water, we get

$$\log([H_3O^+][OH^-]) = \log 10^{-14}$$

$$\log[H_3O^+] + \log[OH^-] = -14$$

Multiplying both sides of the equation by -1

$$-\log[H_3O^+] + (-\log[OH^-]) = 14$$

If we now designate $-\log[OH^-]$ as pOH, and substitute

The sum of pH and pOH is 14.

$$pH + pOH = 14$$

Table 25-1

pH of Some Common Substances

Substance	pH		
0.1 *M* HCl	1	Acid	↑ Increasing acidity
Stomach contents	2		
Vinegar	2.9		
Soda pop	3		
Grapes	4		
Beer	4.5		
Pumpkin pulp	5		
Bread	5.5		
Intestinal contents	6.5		
Urine	6.6		
Bile	6.9		
Saliva	7	Neutral	
Blood	7.4	Base	↓ Increasing basicity
Eggs	7.8		
0.1 *M* $NH_3(aq)$	11.1		
0.1 *M* NaOH	13		

EXAMPLE: pH of Solution

Find the pH of a solution with H_3O^+ concentration $1.00 \times 10^{-5} M$.

Solving process:

$$\begin{aligned} pH &= -\log [H_3O^+] \\ &= -\log (1.00 \times 10^{-5}) \\ &= -(\log 1.00 + \log 10^{-5}) = -[0 + (-5)] = 5 \end{aligned}$$

EXAMPLE: pH of Solution

Find the pH of a solution with H_3O^+ concentration $4.37 \times 10^{-4} M$.

Solving process:

$$\begin{aligned} pH &= -\log [H_3O^+] = -\log(4.37 \times 10^{-4}) \\ &= -(\log 4.37 + \log 10^{-4}) = -[0.640 + (-4)] = 3.360 \end{aligned}$$

EXAMPLE: H_3O^+ Concentration

Find the concentration of H_3O^+ if the pH of a solution is 8.000.

Solving process:

$$pH = -\log [H_3O^+]$$
$$8.000 = -\log [H_3O^+]$$
$$-8.000 = \log [H_3O^+]$$
$$\text{antilog} -8.000 = [H_3O^+]$$
$$1.00 \times 10^{-8} = [H_3O^+]$$

EXAMPLE: H_3O^+ Concentration

Find the concentration of H_3O^+ if the pH of a solution is 2.300.

Solving process:

$$pH = -\log [H_3O^+]$$
$$-2.300 = \log [H_3O^+]$$
$$0.700 - 3 = \log [H_3O^+]$$
$$5.01 \times 10^{-3} = [H_3O^+]$$

PROBLEMS

7. Find the pH of solutions with the following H_3O^+ concentrations.
   a. $1.00 \times 10^{-3} M$ c. $6.59 \times 10^{-10} M$ e. $9.47 \times 10^{-8} M$
   b. $1.00 \times 10^{-6} M$ d. $7.01 \times 10^{-6} M$ f. $6.89 \times 10^{-14} M$

8. Find the H_3O^+ concentration of the following solutions.
   a. pH = 8   c. pH = 7.828   e. pH = 1.355
   b. pH = 4   d. pH = 9.821   f. pH = 3.68

7. a. 3.00   d. 5.15
   b. 6.00   e. 7.02
   c. 9.18   f. 13.2

8. a. $1 \times 10^{-8} M$
   b. $1 \times 10^{-4} M$
   c. $1.49 \times 10^{-8} M$
   d. $1.51 \times 10^{-10} M$
   e. $4.42 \times 10^{-2} M$
   f. $2.09 \times 10^{-4} M$

25:4 HYDROLYSIS

A salt is composed of positive ions from a base and negative ions from an acid. When a salt dissolves in water, it releases ions having an equal number of positive and negative charges. Thus, a solution of a salt should be neither acidic nor basic. Some salts do form neutral solutions, but others react with water (hydrolyze) to form acidic or basic solutions. There are four kinds of salt solutions we will discuss.

If potassium chloride is dissolved in water, a neutral solution results. Each ion from the salt, K^+ and Cl^-, is hydrated with no apparent reaction (except hydration). Water ionizes very slightly to form H_3O^+ and OH^- ions. The solution will, therefore, contain ions from the salt and ions from the water. In solution,

Hydrolysis is the reaction of a salt with water to produce an acidic or basic solution.

A neutral solution results when the salt produced from a strong acid and strong base is dissolved in water.

In hydrolysis, the H_3O^+ and OH^- ions are produced in solution and do not actually come from the dissolved salt but from ionized water molecules which form as the salt dissolves and upsets the equilibrium between the water ions.

An acidic solution results when the salt produced from a strong acid and a weak base is dissolved in water.

A basic solution results when the salt produced from a weak acid and a strong base is dissolved in water.

A mixture of a weak acid and a weak base does not always produce a neutral solution. A neutral solution occurs only when both ions hydrolyze to approximately the same degree. This problem does not arise with a solution of strong acid and base because both ionize completely.

The salt produced from a weak acid and a weak base may form an acidic, basic, or neutral solution.

the positive potassium ion could unite with the negative chloride ion or the negative hydroxide ion. However, potassium chloride is a salt which ionizes completely in water. Potassium hydroxide is a strong base which also ionizes completely. The same reasoning applies to Cl^- and H_3O^+. No reaction occurs. The four ions remain in solution as ions, and the solution is neutral. The ions produced by the salt of a strong acid and strong base do not react with water, and the $[H_3O^+]$ remains equal to the $[OH^-]$. Such a solution has a pH of 7. No hydrolysis occurs.

If we test a solution of aluminum chloride, a salt, we will find that the solution is acidic, not neutral as expected. With the exception of the metals of Groups IA and IIA, metallic hydroxides are all weak bases and in fact have low solubilities. The positive ions of such metals are strongly hydrated and give up a proton readily from the associated water molecule. When $AlCl_3$ is dissolved in water, the aluminum ions become hydrated.

$$AlCl_3(c) + 6H_2O(l) \rightarrow Al(H_2O)_6^{3+}(aq) + 3Cl^-(aq)$$

The hydrated aluminum ions then undergo hydrolysis. The reaction is

$$Al(H_2O)_6^{3+}(aq) + H_2O(l) \rightleftarrows Al(OH)(H_2O)_5^{2+}(aq) + H_3O^+(aq)$$

Since HCl is a strong acid, the H_3O^+ ions do not combine with the Cl^- ions, and the solution is acidic.

If we test a water solution of sodium carbonate, a salt, we will find the solution to be basic.

$$CO_3^{2-}(aq) + H_2O(l) \rightleftarrows HCO_3^-(aq) + OH^-(aq)$$

This reaction produces a large excess of hydroxide ions. Hydrogen carbonate ion, HCO_3^-, is an exceedingly weak acid, so that the reverse reaction proceeds only to a very slight extent.

$$HCO_3^-(aq) + H_2O(l) \rightleftarrows H_3O^+(aq) + CO_3^{2-}(aq)$$

Since more OH^- ions form than H_3O^+ ions, the solution becomes basic.

If the salt, ammonium acetate, is dissolved in water, ammonia and acetic acid are formed. Ammonia is a weak, slightly ionized base. Acetic acid is a weak, slightly ionized acid. Both H_3O^+ and OH^- ions are removed from solution. This reaction results in a neutral solution because acetic acid and ammonia are of the same degree of weakness. For other salts of two weak ions, you must know their relative degrees of weakness in order to predict the acidity of the solution. For example, a solution of NH_4CN would be basic. The acid, HCN, is far weaker than the base, NH_3. On the other hand, a solution of NH_4IO_3 would be acidic since HIO_3 is stronger as an acid than NH_3 is as a base. Remember that the action of a salt with water to form an acidic or basic solution is called **hydrolysis.**

Hydrolysis is the reaction of a salt with water to produce an acidic or basic solution.

PROBLEMS

9. Using Table 24-6, predict the acidic, basic, or neutral character of the solutions of the following salts.
   a. $CrBr_3$
   b. NH_4ClO_4
   c. $NiSO_4$
   d. GaI_3
   e. $MgC_4H_4O_6$

9. a. acidic
   b. acidic
   c. acidic
   d. acidic
   e. basic

25:5 BUFFERS

Many of the fluids in your body must be maintained within a very narrow pH range if you are to remain healthy. There are also many instances in laboratory and industrial chemistry when the maintenance of a certain pH is important. In both cases, the end is accomplished in the same way: the creation of a buffer system. A **buffer system** is a solution which can absorb moderate amounts of acid or base without a significant change in its pH.

A buffer system can absorb acids or bases without significant change in pH.

Consider the reaction of ammonia in water.

$$NH_3(g) + H_2O(l) \rightleftarrows NH_4^+(aq) + OH^-(aq)$$

If we look at the reverse reaction in this equilibrium, we can see that ammonium ions will react with a base. What happens when we dissolve ammonium ions (from ammonium chloride, for example) in water?

$$NH_4^+(aq) + H_2O(l) \rightleftarrows NH_3(aq) + H_3O^+(aq)$$

From this reverse reaction, we can see that ammonia molecules will react with acids. If we had a solution with sufficient quantities of each of these substances, ammonium ions and ammonia molecules, we would have our desired buffer solution. The ammonia molecules would react with any added acid, and the ammonium ions would react with any added base. Buffer solutions are prepared by using a weak acid or a weak base and one of its salts. Stated in general terms, the reactions would appear as follows.

Demonstration — Place equal volumes of $CaCO_3$ solution into two graduated cylinders. Buffer one of the cylinders with some sodium acetate solution, then add equal volumes of 3*M* acetic acid to both cylinders. Discuss the difference in the reaction observed.

For a weak acid:

$$HA + OH^- \rightarrow H_2O + A^-$$

$$A^- + H_3O^+ \rightarrow HA + H_2O$$

The weak acid, HA, will react with added base. The negative ion from the salt, A^-, will react with added acid.

For a weak base:

$$MOH + H_3O^+ \rightarrow M^+ + 2H_2O$$

$$M^+ + OH^- \rightarrow MOH$$

The weak base, MOH, will react with added acid. The positive ion from the salt, M^+, will react with added base.

Buffers are most efficient at neutralizing added acids or bases when the concentrations of weak acid (or base) and salt are equal. By choosing the correct weak acid (or base) we can prepare a buffer solution of almost any pH value. Note that there is a common ion between the weak electrolyte and its salt. The behavior of a buffer solution can always be predicted on the basis of Le Chatelier's Principle and our knowledge of the common ion effect.

Le Chatelier's Principle can be used to predict the behavior of a buffer solution.

Blood is buffered principally by HCO_3^- ion.

Blood is buffered principally by the hydrogen carbonate ion, HCO_3^-.

$$HCO_3^- + H_3O^+ \rightleftarrows H_2CO_3 + H_2O$$
$$HCO_3^- + OH^- \rightarrow H_2O + CO_3^{2-}$$

There is also buffering by the dihydrogen phosphate ion, $H_2PO_4^-$. The H_2CO_3, when it reaches the lungs, decomposes to form

$$H_2CO_3 \rightleftarrows H_2O + CO_2$$

CO_2 is then exhaled.

Athletes sometimes upset the buffering of their blood through a process called hyperventilation. In the excitement of a contest, they breathe more rapidly and deeply than they need to. When hyperventilation occurs, a person expels more CO_2 than necessary, upsetting the carbonic acid equilibrium. According to Le Chatelier's Principle, as the CO_2 is exhaled, more H_2CO_3 decomposes to replace the CO_2. As the H_2CO_3 is used, the equilibrium between carbonic acid and the hydrogen carbonate ion

Hyperventilation occurs when the buffering of the blood is upset.

$$HCO_3^- + H_3O^+ \rightleftarrows H_2CO_3 + H_2O$$

is upset and HCO_3^- is consumed in replacing the H_2CO_3.

Eventually, the HCO_3^- concentration drops to the point at which it is insufficient to maintain the blood pH at a safe level. Since using HCO_3^- also consumes H_3O^+, the blood pH is raised (becomes more basic). One response of the body to this condition is a constriction of the cerebral blood vessels. As the blood flow to the brain is reduced, the individual becomes dizzy, and can lapse into unconsciousness. At that point, the body's reflex mechanisms usually restore normal breathing.

Hyperventilation can be stopped by rebreathing the exhalations from a paper bag. The partial pressure of CO_2 is greater in the re-inhaled air, allowing less to escape from the blood. Gradually the blood pH returns to normal.

25:6 INDICATORS

In the laboratory, how do chemists know whether they are using an acidic, basic, or neutral solution? They could taste the solution to determine whether it was bitter or sour. However, this method is inexact as well as dangerous because most solutions are poisonous or corrosive. They could experiment to determine what reactions the solution undergoes, but the experiment might take too much time. The chemist generally uses a **pH meter** to determine the degree of acidity in a solution. This electronic device indicates the pH of a solution directly when its electrodes are immersed in the solution. We will investigate the operation of the pH meter in Chapter 27.

Natural indicators can be made from blueberry juice, red cabbage, carrots, and beets. Have your students determine the pH range over which they change color.

The chemist uses the pH meter to rapidly determine the degree of acidity of a solution.

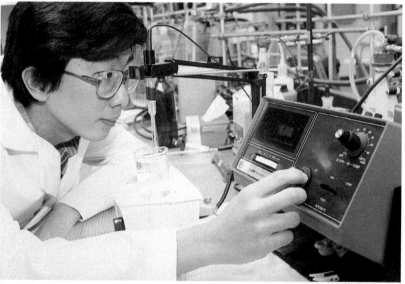

Doug Martin

As pH meters have become more common, the use of indicators has declined.

FIGURE 25-2. A pH meter provides a more accurate determination of the pH of a solution. Electrodes are immersed in the test solution and the pH is given by a digital readout.

There are times when a pH meter may not be available, or its use may not be convenient. Therefore, sometimes substances called indicators are employed. **Indicators** are weak organic bases and acids whose colors differ from the colors of their conjugate acids or bases. When indicators are added to a test solution, the color that results is related to the pH of the solution. A number of indicators and their color changes are listed in Table A-11 of the Appendix.

There are, however, limitations to the use of indicators. Solutions in which they are to be used successfully must be colorless. Otherwise, the color of the solution may mask the color changes of the indicator. Another important limitation is the ability of the human eye to distinguish a slight color change. For any given indicator, we can notice a color change over only a very

Indicators are used to determine pH through color change.

Table A-11 of the Appendix provides additional information on the pH ranges for indicators.

The ability of the human eye to distinguish color changes is the limiting factor in precision measurement of pH with indicators.

Indicators are useful only in colorless solutions, and over narrow pH ranges.

narrow range of the pH scale. To test for pH over a wide range of the pH scale, many indicators must be used. However, given a definite pH, any change in $[H_3O^+]$ or $[OH^-]$ can be detected by the use of one properly chosen indicator.

25:7 TITRATION

Analytical chemists often need to find the concentration of a solution. **Titration** is an analytical method in which a standard solution is used to determine the concentration of another solution. A standard solution is one for which the concentration is known.

Titration is a quantitative process in which a standard solution is used to determine the concentration of another solution.

A standard solution is one for which the concentration is known.

Titration is a form of volumetric analysis.

If an acid is added to a base, a neutralization reaction occurs. The acid unites with the base to form a salt and water.

$$acid + base \xrightarrow[\text{reaction}]{\text{neutralization}} salt + water$$

For example, acetic acid can be neutralized by sodium hydroxide to form sodium acetate and water. By adding an indicator, we can see at exactly what point complete neutralization occurs.

Hickson-Bender Photography

J. R. Schnelzer

Mike Sanderson

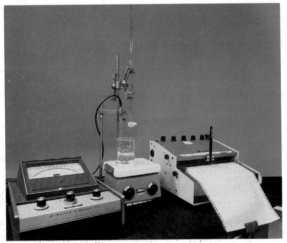

a   b   c

FIGURE 25-3. A pH meter is attached to a chart recorder (a). The burets used in titrations are graduated (b). The volume is measured by reading the level at the bottom of the meniscus. The chart recorder provides a graph of pH versus volume of titrating solution (c).

To carry out a titration, a buret is filled with a standard solution. A small amount of indicator is added to a measured amount of the solution of unknown concentration to be titrated. The buret is opened and the standard solution is allowed to flow (with stirring) into the solution to be titrated. Eventually a color change occurs. The color change indicates the neutralization point. At that point (the endpoint) an equivalent amount of standard solution has been added to the solution titrated.

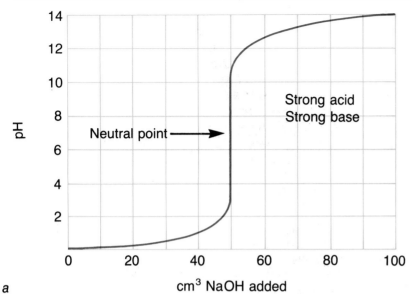

The endpoint occurs when an equivalent amount of standard solution has been added to the titrated solution.

The endpoint can be determined with a pH meter (graph) or an indicator (color change).

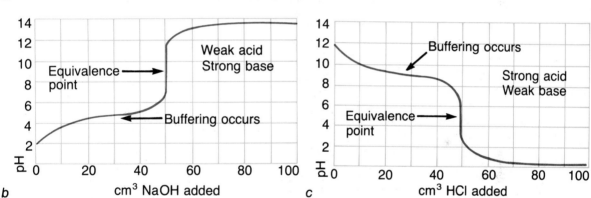

The endpoint may also be detected using a pH meter. If the pH meter is connected to a chart recorder, a graph of pH versus cm^3 of titrating solution added is obtained. The endpoint corresponds to the middle of that portion of the graph showing a very large change in pH with the addition of a small amount of titrating solution. The graph shown in Figure 25-4 is for the titration of a strong acid by a strong base. Weak electrolytes show a slightly different shape, shifted toward the pH of the stronger reactant.

The moles of standard solution can be calculated by multiplying the volume of standard solution used by its molarity.

$$\underset{\text{standard solution}}{moles} = \underset{\text{standard solution}}{volume} \times \underset{\text{standard solution}}{molarity}$$

The moles in the titrated solution of unknown concentration are then found using the coefficients in the balanced equation. Then,

FIGURE 25-4. The graph in (a) represents the titration of a strong acid and strong base. The graph in (b) shows the titration of a weak acid and strong base. The graph in (c) shows the titration of a strong acid and weak base.

dividing the moles of the titrated solution by the volume of that solution gives us the concentration of the titrated solution.

Normality—See Teacher's Guide for a suggested presentation if you desire to teach this concentration unit.

$$\underset{\text{titrated solution}}{\text{molarity } (M)} = \frac{\overset{\text{titrated solution}}{moles}}{\underset{\text{titrated solution}}{volume}}$$

Let us use an example to show how titration works. Suppose you wanted to find the molarity of vinegar. Such a solution is acidic because vinegar is dilute acetic acid derived from the fermentation of fruit juice. Let us use a standard NaOH solution that we know to be 0.500M. (You could prepare this solution quite easily.) We will use phenolphthalein as an indicator because of the reactants.

A buret used for titration is a carefully calibrated glass tube designed to deliver measured volumes.

Two burets, including the tip are filled with solution, one with acid and one with base, and the initial volumes recorded. A precise amount (20-25 cm³) of the vinegar solution is allowed to run into a beaker which contains a few drops of phenolphthalein. The phenolphthalein is colorless in acid solution.

Solution turns pink

While stirring constantly, the basic solution is allowed to run slowly into the beaker. You can tell when the acid is exactly neutralized. How? One drop of NaOH and then vinegar solution should alternately change the color. The volume used of each is recorded.

EXAMPLE: Titration

Suppose that we had used 15.0 cm³ of 0.500M NaOH and 25.0 cm³ of vinegar solution of unknown concentration. What is the molarity of the vinegar solution?

Solving process:
(a) The balanced equation for the neutralization is

Acid + Base → Salt + Water

$$NaOH(aq) + CH_3COOH(aq) \rightarrow CH_3COONa(aq) + H_2O(l)$$

(b) Since the concentration of the base is given, determine the moles of NaOH.

1000 cm³ = 1 dm³

$$\frac{15.0 \text{ cm}^3 \text{ soln}}{} \left| \frac{0.500 \text{ mol NaOH}}{1.00 \text{ dm}^3 \text{ soln}} \right| \frac{1 \text{ dm}^3}{1000 \text{ cm}^3} = 0.007\ 50 \text{ mol NaOH}$$

(c) Since the coefficients from the equation are all 1's, the moles of NaOH that react are equal to the moles of CH_3COOH that react

At endpoint moles H⁺ = moles OH⁻

$$0.007\ 50 \text{ mol NaOH} = 0.007\ 50 \text{ mol CH}_3\text{COOH}$$

(d) Determine the molarity of the acid.

$$\frac{0.007\ 50\ \text{mol CH}_3\text{COOH}}{25.0\ \text{cm}^3\ \text{soln}} \left| \frac{1000\ \text{cm}^3}{1\ \text{dm}^3} \right. = 0.300M\ \text{CH}_3\text{COOH}$$

EXAMPLE: Neutralization

How many cm^3 of $0.0200M$ KOH will exactly neutralize $15.0\ \text{cm}^3$ of $0.400M\ \text{H}_2\text{SO}_4$?

Solving process:

(a) The equation is

$$2\text{KOH(aq)} + \text{H}_2\text{SO}_4\text{(aq)} \rightarrow \text{K}_2\text{SO}_4\text{(aq)} + 2\text{H}_2\text{O(l)}$$

(b) $$\frac{15.0\ \text{cm}^3\ \text{soln}}{} \left| \frac{0.400\ \text{mol H}_2\text{SO}_4}{1.00\ \text{dm}^3\ \text{soln}} \right| \frac{1\ \text{dm}^3}{1000\ \text{cm}^3} = 0.006\ 00\ \text{mol H}_2\text{SO}_4$$

(c) Since 2 moles KOH are required for 1 mole H_2SO_4, 0.0120 (2 × 0.006 00) moles of KOH will be required.

(d) Therefore

$$\frac{0.0120\ \text{mol KOH}}{} \left| \frac{1.00\ \text{dm}^3\ \text{soln}}{0.200\ \text{mol KOH}} \right| \frac{1000\ \text{cm}^3}{1\ \text{dm}^3} = 60\ \text{cm}^3\ \text{KOH soln}$$

Svante August Arrhenius   (1859–1927)

In the beginning, the brilliant ideas of Svante August Arrhenius were rejected by his colleagues. His theory of electrolytic dissociation or ionization nearly caused his dismissal as a student at the University of Stockholm. Arrhenius was barely allowed to receive his doctorate degree. The significance of his work was not considered important by his advisors.

However, through perseverance and help, he was finally able to promote his ideas. Ironically, Arrhenius was granted the Nobel Prize for the theory that had once been viewed as an unsatisfactory doctoral thesis.

Throughout his life, Arrhenius continued to investigate and publish his conclusions on the electrolytic behavior of solutions. He was also interested in other phases of science; namely astronomy and biochemistry.

CHEMICAL TECHNOLOGY: Ion Activity and the Debye-Hückel Theory

Solutions of ions depart considerably from the behavior of ideal solutions. Recall from Chapter 21 that a general definition of an ideal solution is one in which the ions have no effect on each other. Weak force interactions between neutral molecules in a solution decrease as the sixth power of the distance between the molecules.

$$F \propto \frac{1}{d^6}$$

We assume that ionic compounds are completely dissociated in solution. The electrostatic interaction between ions varies as the reciprocal of the square of the distance between them as shown by the relationship

$$F \propto \frac{1}{d^2}$$

Ionic forces are obviously much longer range forces than weak forces.

Peter Debye and Eric Hückel developed a model to explain the behavior of ions in solution. The model could be used to predict the properties of many solutions. If electrical interactions alone are considered, then a solution might soon develop a high degree of order, similar to a crystal, where each positive ion is surrounded by negative ions. (Recall the model for sodium chloride on page 318.) However, in solution the ions are free to move and the normal thermal motion of the ions tends to distribute them in a random way. The properties of the solution, then, are a consequence of two opposing processes: electrostatically induced order and thermally induced disorder. An increase in order results in behavior that moves away from that of an ideal solution. The opposing process decreases order and the solution approaches ideal behavior.

In dealing with solutions, chemists use the concept of ionic strength which considers the total ion effectiveness of a solution. Ionic strength is represented as I in the following relationship

$$I = \frac{1}{2} \Sigma \, m_i z_i^2$$

I is the sum (Σ) of the molalities (m_i) of each ion in the solution multiplied by its charge (z_i) squared. Since each ion behaves in a less than ideal manner, chemists call its actual behavior level the activity (a) of the ion. Activity is also referred to as the effective concentration of an ion. The ratio of the activity to the concentration (molality) is called the activity coefficient (γ) of the ion.

$$\gamma = \frac{a}{m}$$

The value for an activity coefficient is less than one. It approaches one as the concentration of the ions in solution decreases. The higher the ionic strength of a solution, the stronger the interionic forces and the less ideal the solution will behave. The activity coefficients of the ions in solution are related to the ionic strength by

$$\log \gamma = -0.509 |z^+ z^-| (I)^{\frac{1}{2}}$$

γ is the geometric mean of the activity coefficients for the positive and negative ions. The charges on the ions are represented by z^+ and z^-. I is the ionic strength. Activity coefficients are difficult to calculate from experimental data. The activity of an ion depends not only on its own concentration but on the concentrations of all other ions that may be present in the solution. A more refined value can be obtained if additional factors are introduced to take into account the sizes of the ions, and thus the ease with which they move in the solution.

SUMMARY

1. The solubility product constant, K_{sp}, and the ion product constant for water, K_w, are special cases of the equilibrium constant. 25:1–25:2
2. The pH of a solution is equal to $-\log [H_3O^+]$. 25:3
3. Hydrolysis is the reaction of a salt with water to form an acidic or basic solution. 25:4
4. Buffer solutions are capable of absorbing moderate amounts of acid and/or base without a significant change in their pH value. 25:5
5. Indicators are weak acids and bases used to indicate the pH of a solution. 25:6
6. Acids and bases react with each other to form a salt and water. This type of reaction is called a neutralization reaction. 25:7
7. Titration is a laboratory process used to find the concentration of a substance in solution. 25:7

PROBLEMS

10. What volume of $0.196M$ LiOH is required to neutralize 27.3 cm^3 of $0.413M$ HBr? LiOH + HBr $\rightarrow$ LiBr + H$_2$O
11. If 75.0 cm^3 of $0.823M$ HClO$_4$ require 95.5 cm^3 of Ba(OH)$_2$ to reach the endpoint, what is the concentration of the Ba(OH)$_2$ solution. Ba(OH)$_2$ + 2HClO$_4$ $\rightarrow$ Ba(ClO$_4$)$_2$ + 2H$_2$O

10. 57.5 cm^3
11. 0.323M

12. increase the Cl⁻ concentra-
tion by adding a source of   15. reaction of salt with H_2O
Cl⁻ ions.   to form acid or base solution

512   **Solutions of Electrolytes**

12. A chemist wishes to precipitate as much Ag^+ as possible in the form of AgCl from a saturated solution of AgCl. How can the equilibrium between the precipitate and soluble ions be altered to allow more silver to precipitate?

13. 1×10^{-14}

13. What is the value for the ion product constant for water?

14. How does the pOH scale differ from the pH scale?

15. Define hydrolysis.

16. Why does the salt of a weak acid form a basic solution when added to water? more OH⁻ ions form than H_3O^+

17. The salt of a strong acid and strong base produces a neutral water solution. Will the salt of a weak acid and weak base also produce a neutral solution? Explain. may form acid, base, or neutral solution

18. What is the relationship between common ion effect and buffer solutions? buffers are made from solutions with common ions

19. How does rebreathing exhaled air help a person who is hyperventilating?

20. $1.40 \times 10^{-14} M$
21. $3.61 \times 10^{-5} M$
22. $7.41 \times 10^{-7} M$
23. 10.46
24. 10
25. 7.83
26. a. neutral
    b. basic
    c. acidic
    d. acidic
    e. neutral
27. 10.48
28. $0.0678 M$
29. $2.20 M$
30. $0.140 M$

20. The solubility product of MnS is 1.40×10^{-15}. What concentration of sulfide ion is needed in a $0.100M$ solution of $Mn(NO_3)_2$ to just precipitate MnS?

21. What is the hydronium ion concentration in a solution in which the hydroxide ion concentration is $2.77 \times 10^{-10} M$?

22. Find the hydroxide ion concentration of a solution with pOH = 6.13.

23. The K_{sp} of magnesium hydroxide is 1.20×10^{-11}. What is the pH of a saturated solution at equilibrium?

24. What is the pH of $0.0001M$ NaOH?

25. What is the pH of a $0.300M$ solution of HCN in which the CN⁻ concentration has been adjusted to $0.0100M$?

26. Predict whether each of the following salts in solution would form an acidic, a basic, or a neutral solution. Write the ionic equation for each.
    a. NaCl   b. K_2CO_3 c. $AlBr_3$ d. $HgCl_2$ e. $Ca(NO_3)_2$

27. What is the pH of a solution which is $0.0100M$ in HCN and $0.0150M$ in NaCN?

28. What is the concentration of a solution of NaOH if 21.2 cm³ of a $0.0800M$ solution of HCl is needed to neutralize 25.0 cm³ of the base?

29. If 86.2 cm³ of $0.765M$ sodium hydroxide neutralize 30.0 cm³ of hydrochloric acid solution, what is the concentration of the acid?

30. If 40.8 cm³ of $0.106M$ sulfuric acid neutralize 61.8 cm³ of potassium hydroxide solution, what is the concentration of the base?

REVIEW

1. $0.184 M$
2. $0.369 m$

1. What is the molarity of 1.00 dm³ of a solution containing 46.6 g $Hg(CN)_2$?

2. What is the molality of 0.944 g K_3AsO_4 dissolved in 10.0 g water?

3. What is the mole fraction of solute if 100 g $Rb_2C_4H_4O_6$ dissolve in 50.0 g H_2O?

4. What is the vapor pressure, at 30°C, of a solution of 39.5 g $C_6H_{12}O_6$ in 100 g H_2O?

5. What are the freezing and boiling points of a solution of 42.2 g $C_6H_{12}O_6$ in 200 g H_2O?

6. What is the molecular mass of a substance if 22.2 g of it dissolved in 250 g H_2O lower the freezing point of the solution to $-1.83°C$?

7. What would be the osmotic pressure of a solution of 7.10 g of a substance of molecular mass 1000 in sufficient water to make 500 cm^3 of solution at 0°C?   T = 25°C

8. Write the rate expression for the following reaction assuming it is a single-step reaction.

$$PCl_3 + Cl_2 \rightarrow PCl_5$$

9. Write the equilibrium constant expression for the following reaction.

$$HCO_3^- + OH^- \rightleftharpoons H_2O + CO_3^{2-}$$

10. Find the equilibrium constant for a reaction having $\Delta G = -8170$ J, T = 25°C.

11. From the following equation, label the acid, base, conjugate acid, and conjugate base. $$BH_3 + LiH \rightarrow BH_4^- + Li^+$$

12. Is Tl^+ a Lewis acid or base?

Answers (margin):

3. 0.101
4. 4.03 kPa
5. BP = 100.60°C
   FP = −2.19°C
6. 90.3 g
7. 35.2 kPa
8. $R = k[PCl_3][Cl_2]$
9. $K_{eq} = \dfrac{[CO_3^{2-}]}{[HCO_3^-][OH^-]}$
10. 2.72

11.
acid	base	conjugate base	conjugate acid
BH_3	LiH	BH_4^-	Li^+

ONE MORE STEP

1. Investigate the concept of hard and soft acids and bases.
2. What is the pH of a 0.100M solution of sodium acetate?
3. If NaCl is added slowly to a solution that is 1.00M in Ag^+ and 1.00M in Pb^{2+}, which salt will precipitate first?
4. In Problem 3, what will be the concentration of the metal ion whose salt precipitates first when the second salt starts to precipitate?
5. Look up the structural formula for a particular indicator and draw its structure in both the acidic and basic forms.

Answers (margin):

2. 8.88
3. AgCl

READINGS

Ember, Lois R., "Acid Pollutants: Hitchhikers Ride the Wind," *Chemical and Engineering News*, Vol. 59, No. 37 (September 14, 1981), pp. 20-31.

Giguere, Paul A., "The Great Fallacy of the H^+ Ion," *Journal of Chemical Education*, Vol. 56, No. 9 (September 1979), pp. 571-575.

Kolb, Doris, "The pH Concept," *Journal of Chemical Education*, Vol. 56, No. 1 (January 1979), pp. 49-53.

Likens, Gene A., "Acid Precipitation," *Chemical and Engineering News*, Vol. 54, No. 48 (November 22, 1976), pp. 29-44.

When you think of oxidation, you probably think of reactions involving oxygen, like the rusting of iron. However, the browning of many fruits and vegetables is also an oxidation process. When the plant tissue is damaged, chemical enzymes are produced. These enzymes act as catalysts in a reaction between compounds in the apple and oxygen in the air. One product is the brown pigments you observe. What is an oxidation-reduction reaction? In what ways are these reactions useful?

Hickson-Bender Photography

Chapter 26 involves the concept of redox reactions and using equations to represent the transfer of electrons between particles. Methods for balancing redox reactions are also presented.

OXIDATION–REDUCTION

26

Demonstration—Place 20 g of copper(II) chloride dihydrate in a 250 cm^3 beaker and dissolve in 175 cm^3 of H$_2$O. Loosely crumple a 10 cm × 10 cm piece of aluminum foil and place it in the solution. **CAUTION:** The reaction is exothermic; provide for adequate ventilation or use a fume hood. Ask students if an aluminum tank could be used to transport a CuCl$_2$ solution. Use this demonstration to introduce vocabulary and discuss how it relates to chemical spills and hazardous waste storage.

In one method of classifying chemical reactions there are basically two different types. In the first type, ions or molecules react with no apparent change in the electronic structure of the particles. In the second type, ions or atoms undergo changes of electronic structure. Electrons may be transferred from one particle to another. On the other hand, the sharing of the electrons may be somewhat changed. The second type of reaction involving electron changes is called an **oxidation-reduction reaction.** It is these "redox" reactions which we will now discuss. Before we indicate what oxidation-reduction reactions are, we will briefly indicate what they are not.

GOAL: You will gain an understanding of oxidation-reduction reactions to develop skill in balancing redox equations.

In oxidation-reduction reactions, a particle's electronic structure undergoes change.

Oxidation-reduction reactions are known as "redox" reactions.

Table 26-1

Two Reaction Types
Double displacement
$BaCl_2(aq) + Na_2SO_4(aq) \rightarrow BaSO_4(c) + 2NaCl(aq)$
$Ba^{2+} \rightarrow Ba^{2+}$
$Cl^- \rightarrow Cl^-$
$Na^+ \rightarrow Na^+$
$SO_4^{2-} \rightarrow SO_4^{2-}$
No change in charges
Redox
$16H^+(aq) + 2MnO_4^-(aq) + 5C_2O_4^{2-}(aq) \rightarrow 2Mn^{2+}(aq) + 8H_2O(l) + 10CO_2(g)$
$MnO_4^- \rightarrow Mn^{2+} (Mn^{7+} \rightarrow Mn^{2+})$
$C_2O_4^{2-} \rightarrow CO_2 (C^{3+} \rightarrow C^{4+})$
Changes in charges

In the $BaSO_4$ reaction in Table 26-1, the substances are all ionic. Since there is no change in the charge of these ions during the reaction, there are no electron changes. This reaction is not an oxidation-reduction reaction. The production of a precipitate ($BaSO_4$) is nearly always a result of a non-redox reaction. Most acid-base reactions are also the non-redox type.

Most Arrhenius acid-base reactions and most double displacement reactions are not redox reactions.

Since nearly every other kind of reaction is an oxidation-reduction reaction, redox reactions are important in the chemical laboratory. They are also important in life processes and in industry.

26:1   OXIDATION

The term oxidation was first applied to the combining of oxygen with other elements. There were many known instances of this behavior. Iron rusts and carbon burns. In rusting, oxygen combines slowly with iron to form Fe_2O_3. In burning, oxygen unites rapidly with carbon to form CO_2. Observation of these reactions gave rise to the terms "slow" and "rapid" oxidation.

Burning is another name for rapid oxidation.

a

Roger K. Burnard

b

Roger K. Burnard

FIGURE 26-1. The oxidation process is shown in the rusting of the oil rig (a) and the corrosion of the bronze statue (b).

Chemists recognize, however, that other nonmetallic elements unite with substances in a manner similar to that of oxygen. Hydrogen, antimony, and sodium all burn in chlorine, and iron will burn in fluorine. Since these reactions were similar, chemists formed a more general definition of oxidation. Electrons were removed from each free element by the reactants O_2 or Cl_2. Thus, **oxidation** is defined as the process by which electrons are apparently removed from an atom or ion.

Oxidation is now defined as the process by which electrons are removed from atoms or ions.

Table 26-2

Oxidation Reactions				
Oxidation Reaction	Free element	Oxi-dizing agent	Electrons trans-ferred	Oxida-tion product
$4Fe(c) + 3O_2(g) \rightarrow 2Fe_2O_3(c)$	Fe	O_2	$12e^-$*	Fe_2O_3
$C(c) + O_2(g) \rightarrow CO_2(g)$	C	O_2	$4e^-$	CO_2
$H_2(g) + Cl_2(g) \rightarrow 2HCl(g)$	H	Cl_2	$2e^-$	HCl
$2Sb(c) + 3Cl_2(g) \rightarrow 2SbCl_3(c)$	Sb	Cl_2	$6e^-$	$SbCl_3$
$2Na(c) + Cl_2(g) \rightarrow 2NaCl(c)$	Na	Cl_2	$2e^-$	NaCl

*12 moles of electrons are removed from 4 moles of Fe to form 2 moles of $Fe_2O_3(Fe^{3+})$.

26:2   REDUCTION

A reduction reaction was originally limited to the type of reaction in which ores were "reduced" from their oxides. Iron oxide was "reduced" to iron by carbon monoxide. Copper(II) oxide could be "reduced" to copper by hydrogen. In these reactions, oxygen is removed, and the free element is produced. The free element can be produced in other ways. An iron nail dropped into a copper(II) sulfate solution causes a reaction which produces free copper. An electric current passing through molten sodium chloride produces free sodium. The similarity between oxidation and reduction reactions led chemists to formulate a more generalized definition of reduction. By definition, **reduction** is the process by which electrons are apparently added to atoms or ions.

This new definition of oxidation allows the term to be applied as a general term for a specific kind of reaction.

Oxides were said to be "reduced" by the removal of oxygen.

All of these processes are reductions.

Reduction is defined as the process by which electrons are added to atoms or ions.

Bethlehem Steel Corporation

FIGURE 26-2. A blast furnace is used in the reduction of iron ore compounds to elemental iron.

Table 26-3

Reduction Reactions				
Reduction Reaction	Material reduced	Reducing agent	Electrons transferred	Reduction product
$Fe_2O_3(c) + 3CO(g) \rightarrow 2Fe(c) + 3CO_2(g)$	Fe^{3+}	CO	$6e^-$	Fe
$CuO(c) + H_2(g) \rightarrow Cu(c) + H_2O(g)$	Cu^{2+}	H_2	$2e^-$	Cu
$2Na^+Cl^-(l) \xrightarrow{\text{electric current}} 2Na(c) + Cl_2(g)$	Na^+	e^-	$2e^-$	Na
$3Cu^{2+}(aq) + 2Fe(c) \rightarrow 2Fe^{3+}(aq) + 3Cu(c)$	Cu^{2+}	Fe	$2e^-$	Cu

Tables 26-2 and 26-3 are merely examples of some redox reactions. Not all redox reactions produce or require free elements.

Oxidation and reduction occur at the same time in a reaction. The number of electrons lost must equal the number gained.

26:3   OXIDIZING AND REDUCING AGENTS

In an oxidation-reduction reaction, electrons are transferred. All the electrons exchanged in an oxidation-reduction reaction must be accounted for. It seems reasonable, therefore, that both oxidation and reduction must occur at the same time in a reaction. Electrons are lost and gained at the same time and the number lost must equal the number gained.

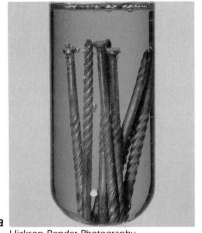
a
Hickson-Bender Photography

b
Hickson-Bender Photography

c
Hickson-Bender Photography

FIGURE 26-3. When iron nails are added to a copper (II) sulfate solution, copper begins to form. Note the color of the solution changes as the copper forms.

A reducing agent gives up electrons.

An oxidizing agent gains electrons.

The substance in the reaction which gives up electrons is called the **reducing agent.** The reducing agent contains the atoms which are oxidized (the atoms which lose electrons). Zinc is a good example of a reducing agent. It is oxidized to the zinc ion, Zn^{2+}. The substance in the reaction which gains electrons is called the **oxidizing agent.** It contains the atoms which are reduced (the atoms which gain electrons). Dichromate ion, $Cr_2O_7^{2-}$, is a good example of an oxidizing agent. It is reduced to the chromium(III) ion, Cr^{3+}.

If a substance gives up electrons readily, it is said to be a strong reducing agent. Its oxidized form, however, is normally a poor oxidizing agent. If a substance gains electrons readily, it is said to be a strong oxidizing agent. Its reduced form is a weak reducing agent. **Important**

26:4 OXIDATION NUMBERS

How is it possible to determine whether an oxidation-reduction reaction has taken place? We do so by determining whether any electron shifts have taken place during the reaction. To indicate electron changes, we look at the oxidation numbers of the atoms in the reaction. The oxidation number is the charge an atom appears to have when we assign a certain number of electrons to given atoms or ions. Any change of oxidation numbers in the course of a reaction indicates an oxidation-reduction reaction has taken place.

For example, suppose iron, as a reactant in a reaction, has an oxidation number of 2+. If iron appears as a product with an oxidation number other than 2+, say 3+, or 0, then a redox reaction has taken place. **It is helpful to review electron dot diagrams before studying this section.**

26:5 ASSIGNING OXIDATION NUMBERS

We have already seen in Chapters 4 and 10 how to predict possible oxidation numbers. Oxidation numbers are assigned according to the apparent charge of the element. To determine the apparent charge, you may find it helpful to consult the electron dot structure for the substance. However, the electron dot structure you draw will not give you the complete answer; it only helps you to visualize an atom, ion, or molecule.

Suppose you want to know the oxidation number of the sodium atom. The electron dot symbol is Na·, showing that the atom is not charged. The number of electrons is equal to the number of protons. The apparent charge of the sodium atom is 0, and its oxidation number is 0.

The sodium ion, however, is indicated in this manner: Na^+ showing that there is one more proton than electron. Since its apparent charge is 1+, its oxidation number is 1+.

Consider free chlorine, Cl_2, whose electronic structure is

$$:\ddot{C}l:\ddot{C}l:$$

Since each chlorine atom has the same electronegativity, the two chlorine atoms share the electrons equally. Thus, each is assigned seven electrons in the outer level, giving a net charge of 0 for each.

The oxidation-number is the charge an atom appears to have when assigned a certain number of electrons.

A change in oxidation number of an atom or ion indicates a redox reaction.

Sometimes a distinction is made between oxidation state and oxidation number. For instance, in MnO_2, O is in the 2− oxidation state but $O_2(O_2^{4-})$ in the compound has an oxidation number of 4−. However, this distinction is not always made. Instead, we may use the term oxidation number for a group of atoms meaning the algebraic sum of the oxidation numbers of the atoms in the group.

An ion's apparent charge is its oxidation number.

Free elements are assigned an oxidation number of zero.

Free chlorine (Cl_2), then, is assigned oxidation number 0.
Chlorine in hydrogen chloride

$$H:\overset{..}{\underset{..}{Cl}}:$$

has an oxidation number different from 0. The chlorine atom is more electronegative than the hydrogen atom. All the electrons shared are therefore arbitrarily assigned to the chlorine atom. Thus, the chlorine atom will have 18 electrons and 17 protons, and a resulting apparent charge of $1-$. Its oxidation number is $1-$. Hydrogen has had its electron assigned to chlorine, and will have one less electron than proton. The hydrogen atom's apparent charge will be $1+$ and its oxidation state will be $1+$.

Consider a possible electronic structure for sulfuric acid, H_2SO_4

$$H:\overset{..}{\underset{..}{O}}:\overset{\overset{..}{\underset{}{O}}:}{\underset{:\overset{..}{\underset{..}{O}}:}{S}}:\overset{..}{\underset{..}{O}}:H$$

It can be seen that the oxygen atoms share electrons with both sulfur and hydrogen atoms. Since oxygen is more electronegative than sulfur, the shared electrons are arbitrarily assigned to each oxygen atom. Thus, the sulfur atom is assigned six fewer electrons than it has protons. The sulfur atom, with a resulting apparent charge of $6+$, is assigned an oxidation number of $6+$. Each hydrogen atom, less electronegative than the oxygen atoms, will also have its electron assigned to oxygen. The hydrogen oxidation number in this compound is $1+$. Each oxygen atom has assigned to it all the shared electrons from either the sulfur or hydrogen atoms, or both. This assignment gives each oxygen atom a $2-$ oxidation number (ten electrons, eight protons). The total of the oxidation numbers of all the atoms in a compound must be zero. In H_2SO_4, one sulfur atom has an oxidation number $6+$, four oxygen atoms have the oxidation number $2-$, and two hydrogen atoms have $1+$. The apparent charge of the compound is zero.

In sulfur dichloride, SCl_2, sulfur has a different oxidation state. Consider a possible electronic structure

$$:\overset{..}{\underset{..}{Cl}}:$$
$$:\overset{}{\underset{}{S}}:\overset{..}{\underset{..}{Cl}}:$$

The sulfur atom shares only four electrons with chlorine. Sulfur has an oxidation state of $2+$ (14 electrons, 16 protons). Each chlorine has an oxidation state of $1-$ (18 electrons, 17 protons).

The oxidation number of an atom may change from compound to compound. Therefore, an electronic structure must be made for each new compound. The oxidation number can be determined from this electronic structure. Drawing electronic structures takes time. Fortunately, there is an easier way.

26:6   RULES FOR ASSIGNING OXIDATION NUMBERS

The following general rules have been made to enable you to determine the oxidation number more easily.

Rule 1. *The oxidation number of any free element is 0.* This statement is true for all atomic and molecular structures: monatomic, diatomic, or polyatomic.

Rule 2. *The oxidation number of a monatomic ion* (Na^+, Ca^{2+}, Al^{3+}, Cl^-) *is equal to the charge on the ion.* Some atoms have several different possible oxidation numbers. For example, iron can be either 2+ or 3+; tin, 2+ or 4+.

Rule 3. *The oxidation number of each hydrogen atom in most compounds is 1+.* There are some exceptions. In compounds such as lithium hydride (LiH), hydrogen, being the more electronegative atom, has an oxidation number of 1−.

Rule 4. *The oxidation number of each oxygen atom in most compounds is 2−* (H_2O). In peroxides, each oxygen is assigned 1− (Na_2O_2), (H_2O_2).

Rule 5. *The sum of the oxidation numbers of all the atoms in a particle must equal the apparent charge of that particle.*

Rule 6. *In compounds, the elements of Group IA and Group IIA and aluminum have positive oxidation numbers numerically equal to their group number in the periodic table.*

EXAMPLE: Oxidation Numbers

What are the oxidation numbers of the elements in Na_2SO_4?

According to rule 6, the oxidation number of sodium is 1+. According to rule 4, the oxidation number of oxygen is 2−. According to rule 5, the total of all oxidation numbers in the formula unit is 0. Letting x = oxidation number of sulfur, we have

$$2(1+) + x + 4(2-) = 0$$
$$x = 6+$$

EXAMPLE: Oxidation Numbers

What are the oxidation numbers of the elements in NO_3^-?

According to rule 4, the oxidation number of oxygen is 2−. According to rule 5, the total of the oxidation numbers in the ion is 1−. Letting x = the oxidation number of nitrogen, we have

$$x + 3(2-) = 1-$$
$$x = 5+$$

PROBLEM

1. a. 4+
   b. 7+
   c. 5+
   d. 4+
   e. 4+

   f. 6+
   g. 6+
   h. 2−
   i. 2+
   j. 0

1. In the following, give the oxidation number for the indicated atoms.

    a. S in Na_2SO_3
    b. Mn in $KMnO_4$
    c. N in $Ca(NO_3)_2$
    d. C in Na_2CO_3
    e. N in NO_2

    f. S in HSO_4^-
    g. S in $H_2S_2O_7$
    h. S in Al_2S_3
    i. Mn in $MnCl_2$
    j. C in $C_{12}H_{22}O_{11}$

26:7   IDENTIFYING OXIDATION-REDUCTION REACTIONS

Oxidation numbers can be used to determine whether oxidation and reduction (electron transfer) occur in a specific reaction. Even the simplest reaction may be a redox reaction. Let us see how it is possible to determine whether a reaction is actually a redox reaction.

The direct combination of sodium and chlorine to produce sodium chloride is a simple example.

$$2Na(c) + Cl_2(g) \rightarrow 2NaCl(c)$$

As a reactant, each sodium atom has an oxidation number of 0. In the product, the oxidation number of each sodium atom is 1+. Similarly, each chlorine atom as a reactant has an oxidation number of 0. As a product, each chlorine atom has an oxidation number of 1−. Since a change of oxidation number has occurred, an oxidation-reduction reaction has taken place.

$$2Na(c) + Cl_2(g) \rightarrow 2Na^+Cl^-(c)$$

A reaction in which the oxidation number of any element changes is an oxidation-reduction (redox) reaction.

The change in oxidation number can result only from a shift of electrons between atoms. This shift of electrons alters the apparent charge (the oxidation numbers).

A mnemonic device: Reduction reduces the oxidation number.

A gain of electrons means the substance is reduced. It also means that the apparent charge is algebraically lowered, and the oxidation number is lowered. In contrast, a loss of electrons is oxidation. When an atom is oxidized, its oxidation number increases.

The equation for a reaction can be used to determine whether the reaction is a redox reaction. It can also be used to find the substance oxidized, the substance reduced, and the oxidizing and reducing agents. Since the oxidation number of sodium in the equation

Oxidation number change can help determine:
   1. whether a reaction is redox
   2. reducing and oxidizing agents in the reaction
   3. elements that are oxidized or reduced

$$2Na(c) + Cl_2(g) \rightarrow 2NaCl(c)$$

changed from 0 to 1+, sodium is oxidized. Sodium is also the reducing agent. A reducing agent always loses electrons and is, therefore, always oxidized as it reduces the other substance.

EXAMPLE: Redox

For the following reaction, tell what is oxidized, what is reduced, and identify the oxidizing and reducing agents.

$$16H^+(aq) + 2MnO_4^-(aq) + 5C_2O_4^{2-}(aq) \rightarrow 2Mn^{2+}(aq) + 8H_2O(l) + 10CO_2(g)$$

Solving process:
Manganese is reduced ($7+ \rightarrow 2+$) and carbon is oxidized ($3+ \rightarrow 4+$). The permanganate ion (MnO_4^-) is the oxidizing agent because it contains manganese, and manganese is reduced. The oxalate ion ($C_2O_4^{2-}$) is the reducing agent; it contains carbon, which is oxidized.

PROBLEMS

reduced = X
oxidized = O

Some of the following unbalanced reactions are oxidation-reduction reactions, and some are not. In each case: **(a)** Is the reaction redox? **(b)** If yes, name the element reduced, the element oxidized, the oxidizing agent, and the reducing agent.

2. $BaCl_2(aq) + Na_2SO_4(aq) \rightarrow NaCl(aq) + BaSO_4(c)$
3. $H_2(g) + N_2(g) \rightarrow NH_3(g)$
4. $C(c) + H_2O(g) \rightarrow CO(g) + H_2(g)$
5. $AgNO_3(aq) + FeCl_3(aq) \rightarrow AgCl(c) + Fe(NO_3)_3(aq)$
6. $H_2CO_3(aq) \rightarrow H_2O(l) + CO_2(g)$
7. $MgSO_4(aq) + Ca(OH)_2(aq) \rightarrow Mg(OH)_2(aq) + CaSO_4(c)$
8. $H_2O_2(aq) + PbS(c) \rightarrow PbSO_4(c) + H_2O(l)$
9. $KCl(c) + H_2SO_4(aq) \rightarrow KHSO_4(aq) + HCl(g)$
10. $HNO_3(aq) + H_3PO_3(aq) \rightarrow NO(g) + H_3PO_4(aq) + H_2O(l)$
11. $HNO_3(aq) + I_2(c) \rightarrow HIO_3(aq) + NO_2(g) + H_2O(l)$
12. $Na_2S(aq) + AgNO_3(aq) \rightarrow Ag_2S(c) + NaNO_3(aq)$
13. $H^+(aq) + NO_3^-(aq) + Fe^{2+}(aq) \rightarrow H_2O(l) + NO(g) + Fe^{3+}(aq)$
14. $FeBr_2(aq) + Br_2(l) \rightarrow FeBr_3(aq)$
15. $S_2O_3^{2-}(aq) + I_2(c) \rightarrow S_4O_6^{2-}(aq) + I^-(aq)$
16. $H_2O_2(aq) + MnO_4^-(aq) \rightarrow O_2(g) + Mn^{2+}(aq)$

Note: The student is not asked to balance these unbalanced redox equations.

2. no

4. yes
   C oxidized, reducing agent
   H is reduced
   H_2O is oxidizing agent

	reducing agent	oxidizing agent
3.	hydrogen	nitrogen
4.	carbon	H_2O
8.	PbS	H_2O_2
10.	H_3PO_3	HNO_3
11.	I_2	HNO_3
13.	Fe^{2+}	NO_3^-
14.	$FeBr_2$	Br_2
15.	$S_2O_3^{2-}$	I_2
16.	H_2O_2	$Mn O_4^-$

26:8 HALF-REACTION METHOD

Balancing some oxidation reduction equations can be difficult and lengthy by the trial and error method. Let us look at an easier way.

The half-reaction method of balancing redox equations involves separating the equation into two equations called half-reactions. One of these half-reactions represents the oxidation that is taking place, and the other half-reaction represents the

Half-reactions can be used to balance redox equations.

Balancing redox equations involves separating the equation into two half reactions: one represents oxidation, one represents reduction.

reduction. The number of electrons gained in the process of reduction must equal the number of electrons lost in oxidation. You may add half-reactions involving equal numbers of electrons to obtain a balanced redox equation. A most important fact must be kept in mind while writing half-reactions: *Always write the formulas of molecules and ions as they actually occur.* For example, in the reaction involving nitric acid and phosphorous acid

$$HNO_3(aq) + H_3PO_3(aq) \rightarrow NO(g) + H_3PO_4(aq) + H_2O(l)$$

The half-reaction method of balancing equations more closely approximates what actually happens in reactions which take place in solution.

there are no actual N^{5+}, N^{2+}, P^{3+}, or P^{5+} ions. The substances must be represented in the form in which they actually occur. In this reaction, the actual ions and molecules are NO_3^-, NO, H_3PO_3, and H_3PO_4. We make one exception to this rule. We will represent H_3O^+ by H^+ to simplify balancing. You should always keep in mind that H^+ represents H_3O^+.

H^+ represents H_3O^+

Redox reactions are balanced by electrons, total charge, and atoms.

Each half-reaction and redox reaction can be balanced three ways, by electrons, by total charge, and by atoms. Any two of these three ways are sufficient to give an equation overall balance. The third method may be used as a check. In the following illustrations, we will use electrons and atoms to obtain the balanced equation. Then we will balance by charge as a check.

26:9 NITRIC ACID-PHOSPHOROUS ACID REACTION

Consider the nitric acid-phosphorous acid reaction.

$$HNO_3(aq) + H_3PO_3(aq) \rightarrow NO(g) + H_3PO_4(aq) + H_2O(l)$$

(a) Write the skeleton half-reaction for the reduction process.

$$NO_3^- \rightarrow NO$$

Nitrogen is reduced from oxidation number 5+ to 2+, and therefore, each nitrogen atom gains three electrons. Incorporating the electrons in the skeleton equation, we have balanced the half-reaction with respect to electrons.

Balance the number of electrons; total charge

$$NO_3^- + 3e^- \rightarrow NO$$

(b) Now we must balance the half-reaction with respect to atoms. Note that one nitrogen atom appears on each side of the equation, and the equation is balanced with respect to nitrogen. For oxygen however, there are three atoms on the left and only one on the right. It is, therefore, necessary to add two oxygen atoms to the right side of the half-reaction. From the information about the reaction taking place, we know that no oxygen is generated. Here is a second important rule for balancing redox reactions: In aqueous solutions, either H^+ and H_2O or OH^- and H_2O are always available. The nature of the reactants determines which pair of substances is present. In the reaction we are now considering, two acids are involved, and the available substances are H^+ and H_2O. (If a basic substance is present, the substances available are OH^- and H_2O.) The two oxygen atoms to be added to the right-hand side of the reduction half-reaction must be present in the form of water. The equation becomes

$$NO_3^- + 3e^- \rightarrow NO + 2H_2O$$

The half-reaction is now balanced with nitrogen and oxygen atoms. However, with the introduction of hydrogen on the right side, four hydrogen atoms must be placed on the left. In the acidic solution, hydrogen is in the form of hydrogen ions. Hydrogen must be added to the equation in ionic form.

$$NO_3^- + 3e^- + 4H^+ \rightarrow NO + 2H_2O$$

The half-reaction is now balanced with respect to electrons and to atoms. Let us check the balance by total charge. On the left we have one nitrate ion with a $1-$ charge, three electrons with $1-$ charges and four hydrogen ions with $1+$ charges. The sum of these charges shows a net left-hand charge of 0. On the right, nitrogen(II) oxide and water are both neutral molecules and the total charge is 0. The half-reaction is then balanced with respect to total charge.

(c) Repeat the same procedure with the oxidation half-reaction.

$$H_3PO_3 \rightarrow H_3PO_4$$

We calculate that the phosphorus atom changes in oxidation state from $3+$ in H_3PO_3 to $5+$ in H_3PO_4 as a result of losing two electrons. The half-reaction balanced with respect to electrons is then

$$H_3PO_3 \rightarrow H_3PO_4 + 2e^-$$

(d) The half-reaction is already balanced with respect to hydrogen and phosphorus. Adding one oxygen atom to the left side of the equation should balance it with respect to atoms. The oxygen must be added in the form of water, making the half-reaction

$$H_3PO_3 + H_2O \rightarrow H_3PO_4 + 2e^-$$

Now the hydrogen is out of balance, and two hydrogen atoms must be added to the right side in form H^+.

$$H_3PO_3 + H_2O \rightarrow H_3PO_4 + 2e^- + 2H^+$$

In checking charges, we see that each side is neutral.

In aqueous solutions, either H^+ and H_2O, or OH^- and H_2O are available.

Balance the total number of atoms.

In acid solution, hydrogen is in the form of hydrogen ions.

Remember H^+ stands for H_3O^+ in solution.

Balance the total charge.

Balance the number of electrons.

Balance the number of atoms.

Balance the charges.

(e) The two half-reactions are now balanced, but we have shown three electrons gained and only two electrons released. You know that the number of electrons lost must equal the number of electrons gained. Before adding the two half-reactions, it is necessary to have the same number of electrons in each half-reaction. In balancing oxidation-reduction reactions, you must find the least common multiple of the number of electrons lost and gained. In the example with which we are working, the least common multiple of electrons is 3 × 2 or 6. The reduction half-reaction must then be adjusted so that six electrons are gained by the substance being reduced. Similarly the oxidation half-reaction is adjusted so that six electrons are lost by the substance being oxidized. By multiplying the reduction half-reaction by 2 and the oxidation half-reaction by 3, we get

$$2(NO_3^- + 3e^- + 4H^+ \rightarrow NO + 2H_2O)$$

$$3(H_3PO_3 + H_2O \rightarrow H_3PO_4 + 2e^- + 2H^+)$$

$$2NO_3^- + 6e^- + 8H^+ \rightarrow 2NO + 4H_2O$$

$$3H_3PO_3 + 3H_2O \rightarrow 3H_3PO_4 + 6e^- + 6H^+$$

Balance the electrons in the two half-reactions and add.

Adding the two equations, we get

$$2NO_3^- + 6e^- + 8H^+ + 3H_3PO_3 + 3H_2O \rightarrow 2NO + 4H_2O + 3H_3PO_4 + 6e^- + 6H^+$$

Add two equations and simplify.

Note that electrons, hydrogen ions, and water molecules appear on both sides of the equation. By subtracting those quantities which appear on both sides of the equation, the equation may be simplified.

$$2NO_3^-(aq) + 2H^+(aq) + 3H_3PO_3(aq) \rightarrow 2NO(g) + H_2O(l) + 3H_3PO_4(aq)$$

If any electrons remain on either side, you have made a mistake. You will note that this equation is balanced with respect to electrons, atoms, and total charge.

26:10 SILVER-NITRIC ACID REACTION

Silver will react with nitric acid to produce silver nitrate, nitrogen(II) oxide, and water. Write and balance the equation for this reaction.

$$Ag(c) + HNO_3(aq) \rightarrow AgNO_3(aq) + NO(g) + H_2O(l)$$

The reduction half-reaction equation is the same as in the last reaction.

Reduction half-reaction

$$NO_3^- + 3e^- + 4H^+ \rightarrow NO + 2H_2O$$

The oxidation half-reaction is

$$Ag \rightarrow Ag^+ + e^-$$

Oxidation half-reaction

This equation is balanced with respect to electrons, atoms, and charge. The least common multiple of the electrons in both half-reactions is 3. So that $3e^-$ will appear on both sides of the equation, the oxidation half-reaction is multiplied by 3.

$$3Ag \rightarrow 3Ag^+ + 3e^-$$

Balance the electrons.

Add the two half-reactions and simplify.

Add the two half-reactions and simplify.

$$NO_3^-(aq) + 4H^+(aq) + 3Ag(c) \rightarrow NO(g) + 2H_2O(l) + 3Ag^+(aq)$$

This equation is the complete redox equation. It is balanced with respect to electrons, atoms, and charge.

26:11 IODINE-HYPOCHLOROUS ACID REACTION

Suppose one or more of the substances appears as two or more atoms per formula unit of reactant. What happens then? Consider the following reaction.

$$I_2(c) + HClO(aq) + H_2O(l) \rightarrow HIO_3(aq) + HCl(aq)(\textit{acidic})$$

The oxidation number of iodine changes from 0 to 5+, and the oxidation number of chlorine changes from 1+ to 1−. However, iodine is a diatomic molecule, so both atoms are oxidized. If one atom must lose five electrons to go from 0 to 5+, two atoms must lose ten electrons. Each chlorine is reduced from 1+ to 1− and must gain two electrons for each atom. The balancing of the oxidation half-reaction then proceeds as follows.

Skeleton	$I_2 \rightarrow 2IO_3^-$
Electrons	$I_2 \rightarrow 2IO_3^- + 10e^-$
Oxygen	$I_2 + 6H_2O \rightarrow 2IO_3^- + 10e^-$
Hydrogen	$I_2 + 6H_2O \rightarrow 2IO_3^- + 10e^- + 12H^+$
Check charge	$0 = 0$

Encourage students to check the charge.

The reduction half-reaction proceeds as follows.

Skeleton	$HClO \rightarrow Cl^-$
Electrons	$HClO + 2e^- \rightarrow Cl^-$
Oxygen	$HClO + 2e^- \rightarrow Cl^- + H_2O$
Hydrogen	$HClO + 2e^- + H^+ \rightarrow Cl^- + H_2O$
Check charge	$1- = 1-$

To obtain the overall redox equation, proceed as follows.

Electron least common multiple = 10

The reduction half-reaction is multiplied by 5 to obtain the correct number of electrons.

$$I_2 + 6H_2O \rightarrow 2IO_3^- + 10e^- + 12H^+$$

$$5HClO + 10e^- + 5H^+ \rightarrow 5Cl^- + 5H_2O$$

Adding and simplifying

The final reaction should be checked for both atomic balance and charge balance.

$$I_2(c) + 5HClO(aq) + H_2O(l) \rightarrow 2IO_3^-(aq) + 7H^+(aq) + 5Cl^-(aq)$$

26:12 REVIEW EXAMPLES

Consider the reduction of permanganate ion (MnO_4^-) to manganese(II) ion in acid solution. The reduction is accomplished with sulfur dioxide as the reducing agent, and sulfur is oxidized to sulfate ion. Balance the equation.

$$H^+(aq) + MnO_4^-(aq) + SO_2(g) \rightarrow Mn^{2+}(aq) + SO_4^{2-}(aq)$$

Taking the reduction half-reaction first, we obtain the following sequence of steps.

Skeleton	$MnO_4^- \rightarrow Mn^{2+}$
Electrons	$MnO_4^- + 5e^- \rightarrow Mn^{2+}$
Oxygen	$MnO_4^- + 5e^- \rightarrow Mn^{2+} + 4H_2O$
Hydrogen	$MnO_4^- + 5e^- + 8H^+ \rightarrow Mn^{2+} + 4H_2O$
Check charge	$2+ = 2+$

For the oxidation half-reaction

Skeleton	$SO_2 \rightarrow SO_4^{2-}$
Electrons	$SO_2 \rightarrow SO_4^{2-} + 2e^-$
Oxygen	$SO_2 + 2H_2O \rightarrow SO_4^{2-} + 2e^-$
Hydrogen	$SO_2 + 2H_2O \rightarrow SO_4^{2-} + 2e^- + 4H^+$
Check charge	$0 = 0$

For the complete equation the least common multiple for electrons = 10

Multiplying the equations appropriately

$$2MnO_4^- + 10e^- + 16H^+ \rightarrow 2Mn^{2+} + 8H_2O$$

$$5SO_2 + 10H_2O \rightarrow 5SO_4^{2-} + 10e^- + 20H^+$$

Adding and simplifying

$$2MnO_4^-(aq) + 5SO_2(g) + 2H_2O(l) \rightarrow 2Mn^{2+}(aq) + 5SO_4^{2-}(aq) + 4H^+(aq)$$

Consider the oxidation of oxalate ion to carbonate ion by permanganate ion, which in turn is reduced to manganese(IV) oxide. The reaction takes place in basic solution. Balance the reaction.

$$C_2O_4{}^{2-}(aq) + MnO_4{}^-(aq) + OH^-(aq) \rightarrow MnO_2(c) + CO_3{}^{2-}(aq) + H_2O(l)$$

The reduction half-reaction

Skeleton	$MnO_4{}^- \rightarrow MnO_2$
Electrons	$MnO_4{}^- + 3e^- \rightarrow MnO_2$
Oxygen	$2H_2O + MnO_4{}^- + 3e^- \rightarrow MnO_2 + 4OH^-$
Check charge	$4- = 4-$

The oxidation half-reaction

Skeleton	$C_2O_4{}^{2-} \rightarrow 2CO_3{}^{2-}$
Electrons	$C_2O_4{}^{2-} \rightarrow 2CO_3{}^{2-} + 2e^-$
Oxygen	$4OH^- + C_2O_4{}^{2-} \rightarrow 2CO_3{}^{2-} + 2H_2O + 2e^-$
Check charge	$6- = 6-$

For the overall redox reaction the least common multiple of electrons is 6. Multiply the manganese half-reaction by 2 and the oxalate half-reaction by 3.

$$4H_2O + 6e^- + 2MnO_4{}^- \rightarrow 2MnO_2 + 8OH^-$$

$$12OH^- + 3C_2O_4{}^{2-} \rightarrow 6CO_3{}^{2-} + 6e^- + 6H_2O$$

Add the half-reactions and simplify. The result is the overall redox reaction.

$$2MnO_4{}^- + 4OH^- + 3C_2O_4{}^{2-} \rightarrow 2MnO_2 + 6CO_3{}^{2-} + 2H_2O$$

PROBLEMS

Detailed discussions and answers to problems are given in the Teacher's Guide.

Balance the following equations.

17. $MnO_4{}^-(aq) + H_2SO_3(aq) + H^+(aq) \rightarrow Mn^{2+}(aq) + HSO_4{}^-(aq) + H_2O(l)$
18. $Cr_2O_7{}^{2-}(aq) + H^+(aq) + I^-(aq) \rightarrow Cr^{3+}(aq) + I_2(c) + H_2O(l)$
19. $NH_3(g) + O_2(g) \rightarrow NO(g) + H_2O(g)(basic)$
20. $As_2O_3(c) + H^+(aq) + NO_3{}^-(aq) + H_2O(l) \rightarrow H_3AsO_4(aq) + NO(g)$
21. $I_2(c) + H_2SO_3(aq) + H_2O(l) \rightarrow I^-(aq) + HSO_4{}^-(aq) \; H^+(aq)$
22. $H_3AsO_4(aq) + Zn(c) \rightarrow AsH_3(g) + Zn^{2+}(aq)$
23. $MnO_4{}^{2-}(aq) + H^+(aq) \rightarrow MnO_4{}^-(aq) + MnO_2(c)$
24. $MnO_4{}^-(aq) + SO_2(g) \rightarrow Mn^{2+}(aq) + SO_4{}^{2-}(aq) + H^+(aq)$
25. $NO_2(g) + OH^-(aq) \rightarrow NO_2{}^-(aq) + NO_3{}^-(aq)$
26. $HgS(c) + Cl^-(aq) + NO_3{}^-(aq) \rightarrow HgCl_4{}^{2-}(aq) + S(c) + NO(g)$

Jane Haldimond Marcet (1769–1845)

Although not a research chemist, Jane Marcet nonetheless had a profound effect on the chemists of her day and those that followed. Her book, *Conversations in Chemistry*, was first published early in the 1800's and was continually revised to reflect the new scientific breakthroughs through sixteen editions. At the time of the American Civil War, nearly 200 000 copies had been sold in England and the United States.

The book, written in dialogue form, provided experiments to illustrate chemical concepts and an approach that today would be labeled as discovery. Mrs. Marcet's work provided the chemical foundation for a young bookbindery clerk named Michael Faraday. Later during Faraday's distinguished career, he referred to *Conversations in Chemistry* as an "anchor in chemical knowledge."

CHEMICAL TECHNOLOGY: Extractive Metallurgy

Metallurgy is the science of extracting metals from their ores, refining the metals, and treating the metals by heat and/or pressure to achieve desired properties. Gold and metals in the platinum group are usually found free in nature. Some small quantities of silver and copper are also found free. All other ores are metal compounds. Most are oxides and sulfides, although some occur as carbonates, sulfates, silicates, and phosphates.

Oxide and sulfide ores are commercially most important. Sulfide ores are generally roasted as a first step. Roasting is heating the sulfide ore in the presence of air to convert it to sulfur dioxide and an oxide of the metal.

$$2PbS + 3O_2 \rightarrow 2PbO + 2SO_2$$

The reduction of an oxide to the free metal can be accomplished in several ways. One method is to use a more active metal to displace the desired metal from its oxide. Chromium is produced by this method.

$$Cr_2O_3 + 2Al \rightarrow Al_2O_3 + 2Cr$$

Another method is to use a gas which is a good reducing agent.

$$3CO + Fe_2O_3 \rightarrow 3CO_2 + 2Fe$$

Oxides may also be reduced by electricity. The electrode supplying the electrons is then the reducing agent as in the production of aluminum.

$$Al^{3+} + 3e^- \rightarrow Al$$

Reactive metals require special treatment. Zirconium, which occurs in the mineral zircon (zirconium silicate), is converted to zirconium carbide with coke. The carbide is then changed to zirconium tetrachloride with chlorine gas.

$$ZrSiO_4 + 4C \rightarrow ZrC + SiO + 3CO$$
$$ZrC + 4Cl_2 \rightarrow ZrCl_4 + CCl_4$$

Zirconium ores are always contaminated with hafnium which is removed in a water-organic process. The zirconium leaves the hafnium separation process as zirconyl chloride, $ZrOCl_2$, which is converted to the basic sulfate and then to the hydroxide.

$$ZrCl_4 + H_2O \rightarrow ZrOCl_2 + 2HCl$$
$$ZrOCl_2 + H_2SO_4 \rightarrow 2HCl + ZrOSO_4$$
$$ZrOSO_4 + 2NH_3 + 3H_2O \rightarrow Zr(OH)_4 + (NH_4)_2SO_4$$

The hydroxide is heated to produce the oxide, and then the oxide is treated with coke and chlorine to produce the tetrachloride again.

$$Zr(OH)_4 \rightarrow ZrO_2 + 2H_2O$$
$$ZrO_2 + 2C + 2Cl_2 \rightarrow ZrCl_4 + 2CO$$

Zirconium is then displaced by magnesium. As you might expect, zirconium is expensive.

$$ZrCl_4 + 2Mg \rightarrow Zr + 2MgCl_2$$

SUMMARY

1. An oxidation-reduction reaction involves an apparent transfer of electrons from one particle to another. Intro.-26:3
2. Oxidation is the process by which electrons are apparently removed from an atom or group of atoms. 26:1
3. Reduction is the process by which electrons are apparently added to atoms or groups of atoms. 26:2
4. Any substance in a reaction which loses electrons is a reducing agent. Any substance in a reaction which gains electrons is an oxidizing agent. 26:3
5. If a substance gives up electrons readily, it is a strong reducing agent. Its oxidized form is usually a poor oxidizing agent. If a substance acquires electrons readily, it is a strong oxidizing agent. Its reduced form is usually a poor reducing agent. 26:3
6. Oxidation number is the charge an atom appears to have when we assign a certain number of electrons to that atom. 26:4
7. Six rules for assigning oxidation numbers: 26:5-26:6
   a. The oxidation number of any free element is 0.

b. The oxidation number of any single-atom ion is equal to the charge on that ion.

c. The oxidation number of hydrogen is usually 1+.

d. The oxidation number of oxygen in most compounds is 2−.

e. The sum of the oxidation numbers of all the atoms in a particle must equal the apparent charge of that particle.

f. In compounds, elements of Group IA and Group IIA and aluminum have an oxidation number numerically equal to their group number in the periodic table.

8. In all chemical reactions, charge, number and kind of atoms, and number of electrons are conserved. Knowing these quantities, you can balance a redox equation. 26:7-26:12

9. Redox reactions are more easily balanced by splitting the equation into half-reactions. 26:8

PROBLEMS

Detailed discussions and answers to problems are given in the Teacher's Guide.

Students can refer to Section 24:10 for a review of net ionic equations.

Balance the following ten equations after putting them in net ionic form.

27. $Cu(c) + HNO_3(aq) \rightarrow Cu(NO_3)_2(aq) + NO(g) + H_2O(l)$

28. $Fe(NO_3)_2(aq) + HNO_3(aq) \rightarrow Fe(NO_3)_3(aq) + NO(g) + H_2O(l)$

29. $Zn(c) + HNO_3(aq) \rightarrow Zn(NO_3)_2(aq) + NO_2(g) + H_2O(l)$

30. $Sb(c) + H_2SO_4(aq) \rightarrow Sb_2(SO_4)_3(aq) + SO_2(g) + H_2O(l)$

31. $H_2S(g) + H_2SO_3(aq) \rightarrow S(c) + H_2O(l)$

32. $HCl(aq) + HNO_3(aq) \rightarrow HClO(aq) + NO(g)$

33. $Ag(c) + HClO_3(aq) + HCl(aq) \rightarrow AgCl(c) + H_2O(l)$

34. $KI(aq) + O_2(g) \rightarrow KI_3(aq) + H_2O(l)$

35. $HNO_3(aq) + H_2SO_4(aq) + Hg(l) \rightarrow Hg_2SO_4(c) + NO(g) + H_2O(l)$

36. $CO(g) + I_2O_5(g) \rightarrow CO_2(g) + I_2(g)$

37. In terms of this chapter, how do oxidation and reduction differ?

38. How many grams of K_2SO_3 can be oxidized to K_2SO_4 by 7.90 g of $KMnO_4$ which will be reduced to MnO_2?   11.9 g

39. How many cm^3 of 0.200M $KClO_3$ will be required to react completely with 20.0 cm^3 of 0.100M Cr_2O_3 to produce K_2CrO_4 and Cl^-?   10.0 cm³

37. oxidation = e^- loss
reduction = e^- gain

REVIEW

1. 3.54 × 10⁻⁷ M

1. The solubility product for $Cd_3(PO_4)_2$ is 2.50×10^{-33}. What is the concentration of Cd^{2+} in a saturated solution of $Cd_3(PO_4)_2$?

2. increases rate

2. What effect does an increase in pressure have on the rate of a reaction involving gases?

3. slowest step

3. Which step in a reaction mechanism determines the overall rate of the reaction?

4. Sr(OH)₂

4. What substance is produced from the anhydride SrO and water?

5. Reduce the following equation to net ionic form.

$$NaH_2PO_4 + HCl \rightarrow NaCl + H_3PO_4$$

6. If a solution of $0.100M$ propanoic acid (CH_3CH_2COOH) has a H_3O^+ concentration of $1.16 \times 10^{-3}M$, what is K_a for the acid?

7. What is the percent ionization in Problem 6?

8. What is the H_3O^+ concentration in a solution which is $0.100M$ in HF and $0.0100M$ in NaF?

6. $1.36 \times 10^{-5}M$
7. 1.16%
8. $3.53 \times 10^{-5}M$

9. At equilibrium, $[H^+]$ is 0.200, $[CHCl_2COO^-]$ is 0.200, and $[CHCl_2COOH]$ is 1.20. What is the K_{eq} for the reaction?

9. $K_{eq} = 3.33 \times 10^{-2}$

$$CHCl_2COOH \rightleftarrows CHCl_2COO^- + H^+$$

10. In the reaction in Problem 9, what is the percent ionization?

11. In Problem 9 if enough $CHCl_2COO^-$ were added as a common ion to make the concentration of $CHCl_2COO^-$ exactly $0.400M$, what would be the concentration of $CHCl_2COOH$?

10. 14.3%
11. $1.29M$

ONE MORE STEP

1. Assuming maximum appropriate values for oxidation numbers, assign formulas to hypothetical binary compounds of the following pairs of elements.

   a. Ba and N
   b. Cr and O
   c. Ca and P
   d. Sr and H
   e. Fr and C
   f. Li and O
   g. Fe and S
   h. Sc and F
   i. Ti and Cl

1. a. Ba_3N_2 d. SrH_2 g. Fe_2S_3
   b. CrO_3 e. Fr_4C h. ScF_3
   c. Ca_3P_2 f. Li_2O i. $TiCl_4$

2. Draw the electron dot diagram for the thiosulfate ion and assign oxidation numbers to each atom. What is unusual about this ion?

2. (electron dot diagram)

sulfur has two different oxidation states

3. Nitrogen exhibits nine oxidation numbers (including zero). Try to write a formula for a compound representing each state.

4. Using a chemical handbook investigate the compound Fe_3O_4. What color is it? What are the oxidation numbers of the elements composing it? What are its properties?

5. The reduction of ores to metals is still an important industrial process even though the word reduction has been broadened in meaning. Investigate the reduction of ilmenite and one other ore to the metals they contain. Ilmenite contains titanium. The other ore you select should be a substance containing some metal other than titanium.

READINGS

Conkling, John A., "Chemistry of Fireworks," *Chemical and Engineering News,* Vol. 59, No. 26 (June 29, 1981), pp. 24-32.

Machado, A. A. S. C., "The Use of Electron Balance in Ionic Equilibrium Calculations." *Journal of Chemical Education,* Vol. 53, No. 5 (May 1976), pp. 305-306.

By passing an electric current through a silver salt solution, silver can be plated out on this dish. Thus, objects are produced having the beauty and luster of silver at a much lower cost. The same dish made of pure silver would be quite expensive. This process is used in plating many metals for ornamental and protective purposes. What factors affect the amount of metal that can be plated during a given time period? What properties must a metal possess in order to make it suitable for plating? What are some other applications of electrochemistry?

Reed & Barton Silversmiths

ELECTROCHEMISTRY   **27**

Chapter 27 uses the topics discussed in Chapters 25 and 26 to develop an understanding of electrochemistry.

Demonstration—Set up a zinc-copper electrochemical cell before class. See the Teacher's Guide for complete preparation details. Discuss where the electricity comes from. This demonstration may be used to introduce some of the vocabulary in Chapter 27.

You press the button of your pocket flashlight and light (a form of radiant energy) is produced. You know already that the light results from the passage of an electric current through the flashlight bulb. Where does the electricity come from? The obvious answer is the battery. What then is a flashlight battery? How does it function?

GOAL: You will gain an understanding of how the relationship among electrolytes, energy, and electron changes in electrochemical reactions is put to practical use.

A battery is a cell in which a spontaneous redox reaction takes place. The battery produces a current because the electrons involved in the redox reaction are forced to travel through a wire or external circuit.

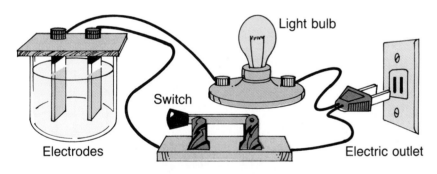

Light bulb

Switch

Electrodes

Electric outlet

Apparatus for testing conductivity

FIGURE 27-1. If a conductor is placed in the beaker, the bulb will light when the apparatus is plugged into the wall. The bulb will not light if a nonconductor is placed in the beaker.

A 7½ or 15 watt bulb will keep the current low enough to avoid a serious shock. Use bare filament bulbs (unfrosted glass) and try several different sizes till you find the one that best suits your purposes.

If we plug the apparatus in Figure 27-1 into an electric outlet, the bulb does not light because the circuit is not complete. Whenever we complete the circuit with a conducting substance, the bulb does light. In the circuit shown, a conducting substance in the beaker would complete the circuit. We now have an easy way of observing which substances are conductors of electricity. If we touch the two electrodes to a piece of copper or other metal, the bulb lights. Metals are conductors of electricity. Copper is one of the best conductors; for this reason it is used in electric equipment. If we touch the electrodes to a piece of glass or a sulfur crystal, the bulb does not light. Most nonmetallic solids, including

Metals conduct electricity.

Ag, Cu, and Al are the three most common metal conductors used in electric applications.

salts, are nonconductors. If we immerse the electrodes in pure water, benzene, alcohol, sugar solution or other solution of a nonpolar substance, the bulb does not light. These liquids are all nonconductors. However, if we add a small amount of sodium chloride (or any other salt), a small amount of hydrochloric acid, or sodium hydroxide, the bulb lights. These solutions are conductors of electricity. What materials conduct electricity in solution? Why do they conduct electricity?

Ionic or ionizable materials and metals conduct electricity because these substances contain charged particles which are free to move in an electric field.

Let us take pieces of two dissimilar metals and connect them to the terminals of a galvanometer. A **galvanometer** is an instrument for measuring electric current. The two pieces of metal are kept from making contact with each other and put into a salt solution. The galvanometer needle registers a flow of current. How is the current produced? If we place the two metal plates into separate beakers containing salt solutions, as shown in Figure 27-2, no current flows. When we add the salt bridge to the system as shown, a current is produced. The **salt bridge** is a U-tube containing an ionic substance in solution. What is the function of the salt bridge? It connects the two separate solutions without mixing them. Can the solutions be mixed and still be used to produce a current? In this chapter, we shall answer these and other related questions.

Current can be produced by two dissimilar metals immersed in a salt solution.

A salt bridge is a solution containing ions in a U-tube.

If the solutions are mixed, they will not conduct.

FIGURE 27-2. Current flows in (a) and (c). In (b) the circuit is not complete, thus no current flows.

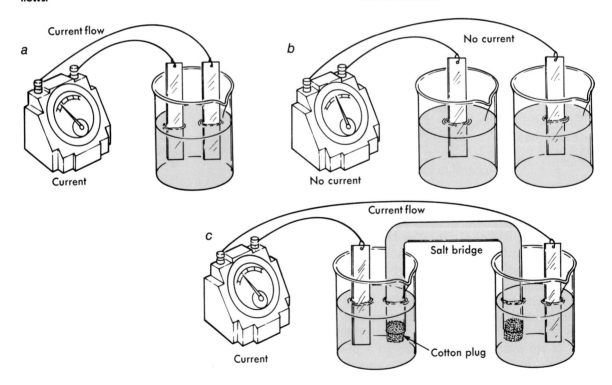

27:1 CONDUCTIVITY AND POTENTIAL DIFFERENCE

Metals, in general, are excellent conductors of electricity. This statement is true whether the metal is in the solid state or the liquid state. Mercury, a liquid at room temperature, is used in scientific apparatus because of its excellent electric conductivity. In Chapter 12, we found that the outer electrons of metal atoms are free to move if excited to the conduction band. If the potential energy of the electrons in the metal is raised, these electrons will flow to a point where their potential energy is lower. The flow or movement of electrons through a conductor is an **electric current.**

A difference in electric potential can be brought about in a number of ways. One way is to use a generator. Suppose we connect the two ends of a long wire to a generator. Electrons are added at one end of the wire and removed at the other end. When a potential energy difference is created at the ends of the wire, current flows. Energy is required to create a potential difference and work is done when a current is made to flow through a wire.

Metals are excellent conductors of electricity because their electrons are free to move when a small potential difference is created. In nonconducting substances, the outer electrons are tightly held. The forbidden zone represents a large energy gap. Very large potential differences are required to move electrons in these substances which we call insulators. However, even the best insulators break down and conduct a current if the potential difference is high enough.

Electric potential difference is measured in units called **volts.** The voltage (potential difference) produced by a generator or battery can be thought of as electric pressure. In fact, it is often easier to consider a generator or battery as an electron pump. The rate of electron flow, or current, is measured in **amperes** in SI (see Table A-1 of the Appendix for its definition).

27:2 ELECTROLYTIC CONDUCTION

Solid acids, bases, and salts (for example, oxalic acid) are nonconductors. When any one of these substances is dissolved in water, the resulting solution is a conductor. Those substances which are conductors in solution are known as electrolytes. Any substance which produces ions in solution is an electrolyte. Salts are ionic even in the solid state; but a salt must dissolve in order for the ions to separate from each other and become free to move. (Conduction also occurs in a melted salt.) Acids and bases may be either ionic or molecular substances. However, when they

Metallic conduction occurs by movement of free electrons to the conduction band.

An electric current is the movement of electrons through a conductor.

Work is done when electricity flows through a wire.

Rich Brommer

FIGURE 27-3. Electricity travels through wires when a potential difference exists between the two ends.

Electrolytes are substances whose solutions conduct electricity.

Molten salts and solutions of acids, bases, and salts will conduct electricity.

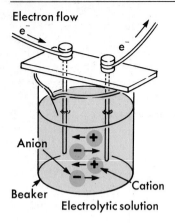

Electron flow

Anion

Beaker

Cation

Electrolytic solution

FIGURE 27-4. Anions in solution move toward the anode. Cations move toward the cathode.

dissolve in water, ions are formed. Electrolytic conduction is possible because ions move freely in the liquid state. If we connect the conductivity device to a direct current, one of the electrodes will be negative and the other electrode will be positive. It is customary to call the negative electrode the cathode and the positive electrode the anode. If we immerse the electrodes in an ionic solution, positive ions in the solution will be attracted to the cathode. For this reason, positive ions are called **cations.** Negative ions will be attracted toward the anode. Consequently, they are called **anions.** The movement of ions through a solution results in an electric current just as the movement of electrons in a metal results in a current.

27:3   ELECTRODE REACTIONS

What happens to a moving ion when it reaches the electrode to which it is attracted? We will consider molten sodium chloride, a system which contains only two kinds of ions and no other particles. We will use electrodes which are inert, that is, electrodes which do not react chemically with sodium or chloride ions. The positive sodium ions, or cations, are attracted to the cathode. The cathode is made negative by the action of a generator which, in effect, pumps electrons into it. The electrons in the cathode are in a state of high potential energy. The sodium ion has a positive charge. It has an attraction for electrons and an electron in a sodium atom would have a lower potential energy than an electron on the cathode. Thus, electrons move from the cathode (high potential energy) to the sodium ions (lower potential energy). At the cathode, the sodium ions will be converted into sodium atoms by the addition of an electron. This change is a chemical reaction and can be shown by an equation.

$$Na^+ + e^- \rightarrow Na$$

Note that this chemical change represents a gain of electrons. We found in Chapter 26 that electron gain is called reduction. The chemical change which occurs at the cathode is always reduction. In this case, the sodium ion is reduced to sodium metal.

Now consider what happens at the anode. The anode has a positive charge and negative ions are attracted to it. The anode is positive because the generator is, in effect, pumping electrons out of it. Thus, electrons in the anode may be said to exist in a state of low potential energy. Since the chloride ion has a negative charge, its outer electrons are in a state of higher potential. When chloride ions reach the anode, they give up electrons to the electron-deficient anode. Electrons move from a state of higher

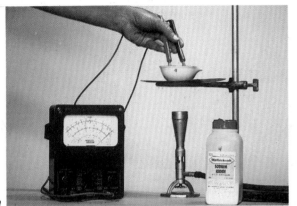

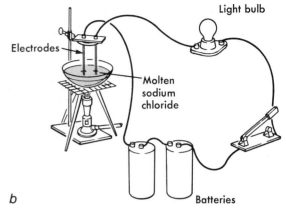

Hickson-Bender Photography

a

b

potential energy to a state of lower potential energy. We can show the chemical change which occurs at the anode by the following.

$$2Cl^- \rightarrow Cl_2 + 2e^-$$

Note that in this reaction chloride ions lose electrons to become chlorine atoms which then combine to form Cl_2 molecules. This reaction results in a loss of electrons. The name applied to a change in which electrons are lost is oxidation. The anode reaction is always oxidation.

We have shown the oxidation and reduction processes by separate equations because they take place at different points. However, these processes do not occur independently. The generator does not produce the electrons; it moves the electrons from one place to another. The electrons which the generator adds to the cathode are taken from the anode. The reduction process cannot occur without the oxidation process going on at the same time. The role of the generator is to raise the potential energy of the electrons on the cathode.

These electrode reactions are called half-reactions. The anode reaction involves a loss of electrons and the cathode reaction involves a gain of electrons. Therefore, the electrons must balance when we add the two half-reactions. The overall reaction for the electrolysis of sodium chloride is

$$2Na^+(l) + 2Cl^-(l) \rightarrow 2Na(l) + Cl_2(g)$$

The process by which an electric current produces a chemical change is called electrolysis. Electrolysis of molten sodium chloride is the usual commercial process by which metallic sodium is produced. Chlorine gas is produced at the same time as a by-product.

FIGURE 27-5. The conductivity of a molten salt can be shown by the reading on the voltmeter (a), or the illumination of the bulb (b).

At the anode, negative ions are oxidized by losing electrons.

Chemical change at the anode is oxidation.
Demonstration—On an overhead projector, place a few drops of phenolphthalein in a KI solution in a petri dish. Connect two pieces of Cu wire (electrodes) to a 1.5 V dry cell battery and dip the electrodes into the KI solution. Note the formation of I_2 (anode) and H_2 and OH^- (cathode).

In a cell, oxidation and reduction occur as separate half-reactions at the same time.

Electrolysis is the use of an electric current to produce a chemical change.

Demonstration — See the Teacher's Guide for preparation details on setting up an electrolysis apparatus for NaCl as described in the text. This process simulates the industrial process for the preparation of NaOH, Cl_2, and H_2.

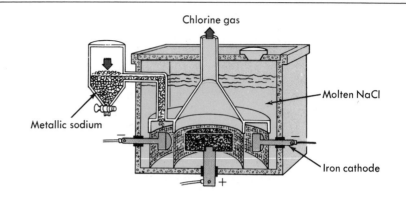

Chlorine gas

Molten NaCl

Metallic sodium

Iron cathode

FIGURE 27-6. A Downs cell is used in the industrial production of sodium.

If two different reactions are possible, the one which produces a lower potential difference is the one which occurs or at least predominates. For example, in the electrolytic refining of copper, only copper is deposited on the cathode because a considerable potential difference is required for the reduction of the more active metals which are present in the solution. Consequently, so long as any appreciable concentration of copper(II) ions is present, the iron(II) ion is not reduced.

27:4 ELECTROLYSIS OF A SALT SOLUTION

Another important commercial process involves the electrolysis of a concentrated sodium chloride solution. In this process, the anode reaction is exactly the same as that which occurs when molten sodium chloride is used. Chlorine gas is produced at the anode. The reaction at the cathode, however, will be different. Around the cathode, sodium ions and water molecules are present. An electron has a lower potential energy on a water molecule than on a sodium atom. Thus, electrons at the cathode are transferred to water molecules instead of sodium ions. When a water molecule acquires an extra electron, the electron is accepted by a hydrogen ion (a proton) which becomes a hydrogen atom. This change leaves a hydroxide ion. The hydrogen atoms produced combine to form H_2 molecules, and hydrogen gas bubbles from the solution at the cathode. The solution surrounding the cathode acquires a high concentration of sodium ions and hydroxide ions. If this solution is drained off and evaporated, the product is solid sodium hydroxide. This process is the most important one by which commercial sodium hydroxide is produced. Chlorine gas is also produced.

The half-reactions are

$$2Cl^- \rightarrow Cl_2 + 2e^-$$

$$2H_2O + 2e^- \rightarrow 2OH^- + H_2$$

The equation for the overall reaction may be written.

Electrolysis of a NaCl solution produces H_2, Cl_2, and OH^-.

$$2NaCl(aq) + 2H_2O(l) \rightarrow 2NaOH(aq) + H_2(g) + Cl_2(g)$$

It should be noted that sodium metal, chlorine gas, hydrogen gas, and sodium hydroxide are all produced from rock salt. Rock salt is a very cheap raw material. The costliest part of this operation is the electric power required.

In the processes we have just described, two kinds of electric conduction are involved. In the generator and the cables leading to the electrodes, conduction takes place by the movement of electrons through a metal. This conduction is known as **electronic** or **metallic conduction.** The electric path in electrolysis is completed through the liquid between the electrodes. This part of the conduction process takes place by the migration of ions and is called **electrolytic conduction.** Both kinds of conduction involve the movement of electric charge. For electrolytic conduction it is necessary that ions be present and that they be free to move. Ions move freely in solution or as molten solid. Solid salts do not conduct electricity. Note that all electrolytic operations involve both oxidation and reduction.

Electronic conduction: Movement of electrons through a metal.

Electrolytic conduction: Migration of ions through the liquid between the electrodes.

Molten salts or electrolytic solutions conduct electricity.

You may wish to point out that in most electrolytic processes there are side reactions which take place because of contaminants which are present.

27:5 VOLTAIC CELLS

The processes which we have described are examples in which electric energy is used to cause chemical changes. When you use a pocket flashlight, however, you are using a chemical process to produce electricity. In other words, you are converting chemical potential energy into electric energy. A device which makes such a conversion is known as a **voltaic cell.** An example of a simple voltaic cell is shown in Figure 27-7. In this cell, there are two compartments separated by a porous barrier or salt bridge which prevents the two solutions from mixing by diffusion. However, the barrier permits the migration of ions from one side of the cell to the other. The cathode in the left hand compartment consists of a strip of copper immersed in a copper(II) sulfate solution. Note that there is no external source of electrons (no generator). The anode, in the right hand compartment, consists of

Voltaic cells are often called galvanic cells.

A voltaic cell converts chemical energy into electrical energy.

FIGURE 27-7. A voltaic cell is also referred to as a galvanic cell.

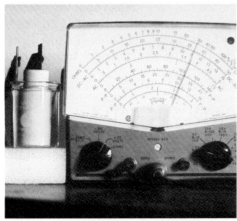

Robert C. Smoot

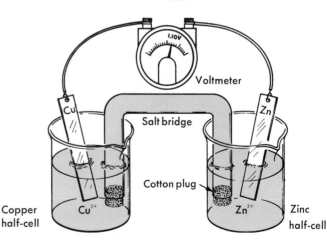

Voltmeter

Salt bridge

Cu

Zn

Cotton plug

Copper half-cell

Cu²⁺

Zn²⁺

Zinc half-cell

Reactions take place at separate electrodes. Electrons travel through the external circuit.

Electrons flow from the anode to the cathode in the external circuit.

a strip of zinc immersed in a zinc sulfate solution. If the two electrodes are connected through a precision voltmeter, an electric current flows and the voltmeter reads 1.10 volts. Electrons flow from the zinc anode through the voltmeter to the copper cathode. Chemical changes occur at the electrodes. Zinc is a more active metal than copper because its outer electrons have a higher potential energy than outer electrons in copper atoms. In other words, zinc has a greater tendency to give up electrons than copper. Electrons move from the zinc with its higher potential energy through the voltmeter to the copper with its lower potential energy. The anode half-reaction which occurs at the zinc electrode is

$$Zn \rightarrow Zn^{2+} + 2e^-$$

In the zinc-copper cell, zinc metal is oxidized at the anode and copper ion is reduced at the cathode.

Note that copper atoms are deposited on the surface of the zinc.

Since this change involves loss of electrons it is an oxidation reaction. Zinc metal is oxidized at the anode (the zinc bar in the zinc half-cell, in Figure 27-7). The copper cathode in the copper half-cell acquires excess electrons. It has a negative charge and copper ions move to it. The potential energy of electrons on the copper electrode is higher than the potential energy the electrons would have on the copper ions in the solution. The cathode transfers electrons to the copper ions and copper metal plates out on the cathode. The cathode reaction is

$$Cu^{2+} + 2e^- \rightarrow Cu$$

This process involves a gain of electrons and is a reduction reaction. Note that the operation of the cell involves both oxidation and reduction, but the two changes do not occur at the same electrode. Rather, the electrons travel through the external circuit (in this case, the voltmeter) and do electrical work.

Note that these changes can occur without producing an electric current. Consider a piece of zinc placed in a copper sulfate solution. Zinc metal is converted to Zn^{2+} ions, and Cu^{2+} ions are converted to copper metal. Energy is also produced but is released in the form of heat which is not available for practical use. No current is produced because the electrons are transferred directly from Zn atoms to Cu^{2+} ions.

Hickson-Bender Photography
FIGURE 27-8. Redox reactions can occur without the production of electricity. In this reaction, heat is released as copper ions are reduced.

This experiment indicates that if a useful current is to be produced, the two half-reactions must be separated.

27:6 STRUCTURE OF VOLTAIC CELLS

For a voltaic cell to operate, free movement of ions between the anode and cathode compartments is necessary.

A voltaic cell is a device used to produce electric energy from an oxidation-reduction reaction. The main feature of the voltaic cell is the porous barrier or salt bridge which separates the two solutions and keeps them from mixing freely. If this barrier is not porous to allow ions to migrate through it, the cell will not operate. Look at Figure 27-9. The anode compartment acquires an

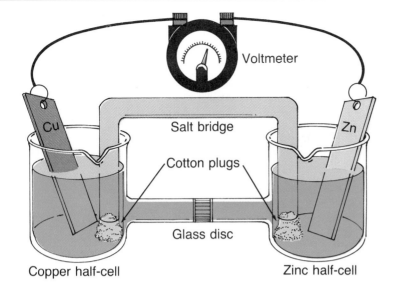

Copper half-cell   Zinc half-cell

Note: The porous barrier completes the circuit. It also permits the free passage of ions. This movement prevents the accumulation of an excess of ions of one sign in a half-cell.

FIGURE 27-9. The porous barrier between the two cells keeps the solutions from mixing. Without the barrier, the cell would not operate.

excess of zinc ions which are positive. In order to maintain neutrality, it must have negative ions to balance the positive zinc ions. At the same time, the cathode compartment uses copper ions. In order to maintain neutrality, it must lose negative ions. Sulfate ions move through the porous barrier from the cathode compartment to the anode compartment. In that way electric neutrality is maintained in the two compartments. The cell continues to operate as long as there is a potential energy difference between the half-cells. The two compartments in the cell are called half-cells because the reactions which occur in them are half-reactions.

The two compartments in the cell are called half-cells and their reactions are called half-reactions.

The two most commonly used types of voltaic cells are the dry cell and the lead storage cell. A flashlight battery is an example of a dry cell. An automobile battery is a lead storage cell.

Chemists have a shorthand method of representing cell reactions. The oxidation half-cell is written first. The reduced and oxidized species are separated by a vertical line. The zinc half-cell from the zinc-copper cell would be written

$$Zn|Zn^{2+}$$

The reduction half-cell is written in the reverse order.

$$Cu^{2+}|Cu$$

The two half-cells are separated by two vertical lines representing the salt bridge. The entire zinc-copper cell is thus shown as

$$Zn|Zn^{2+}\|Cu^{2+}|Cu$$

When using the shorthand method of representing cells place the anode on the left.
anode ‖ cathode

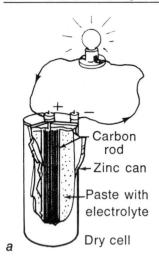

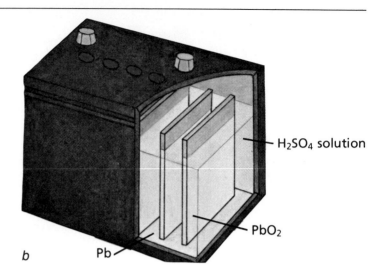

FIGURE 27-10. A dry cell (a) and an automobile battery (b) are both voltaic cells. The auto battery contains an electrolyte (H_2SO_4) in solution. The dry cell does not have an electrolyte in liquid form.

Note: The situation here is similar to measuring heat content as discussed in Section 7:5. The analogy used was "How high is a hill?" The height must be measured from some arbitrarily chosen point.

27:7 REDOX POTENTIALS

There is no way in which the potential energy of a single half-cell can be measured. However, the difference in potential between two half-cells in a voltaic cell can be measured by means of a voltmeter. This potential difference is a measure of the relative tendency of two substances to take on electrons. If we arbitrarily assign a potential of zero to the copper half-cell, we will say the zinc half-cell has a potential of -1.10 volts. The negative sign indicates that zinc ions are less likely to take on electrons than the copper ions. On the other hand, if we assign a potential of zero to the zinc half-cell, we will say that the copper half-cell

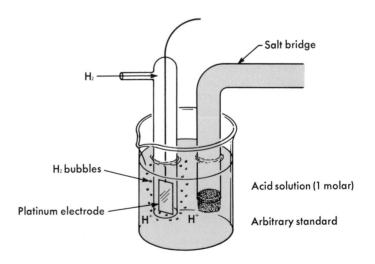

FIGURE 27-11. The apparatus shown is used in the reduction of hydrogen. The hydrogen reduction reaction is assigned a potential of zero for comparison purposes.

has a potential of +1.10 volts. In principle, any half-cell could be used for the reference half-cell. That is, any half-cell could be the one assigned zero potential. In practice, the zero potential is assigned to the hydrogen half-cell. The half-reaction is

$$H^+ + e^- \rightleftarrows \tfrac{1}{2}H_2$$

The hydrogen (reference) half-cell is assigned zero potential.

The hydrogen half-cell consists of a sheet of platinum whose surface has been specially treated. The platinum is immersed in a one molar ($1M$) ideal solution of H^+ ions. Hydrogen gas, from a cylinder, is bubbled into the solution around the platinum at a pressure of 101.325 kPa. The H_2 molecules are adsorbed on the platinum surface and form the electrode. The hydrogen half-cell is an ideal which can only be approached in practice.

27:8 STANDARD ELECTRODE POTENTIALS

If we use the hydrogen half-cell with the zinc half-cell, our voltmeter reads −0.76 volts. We assign this potential to the zinc half-cell. If we use the hydrogen half-cell with the copper half-cell, the voltmeter reads +0.34 volts. This potential is assigned to the copper half cell. In this way, potentials can be experimentally determined for almost all oxidation-reduction half-reactions. Some of these half-cell potentials are given in Table 27-1. Potentials are dependent on temperature, pressure, and concentration. The values given in the table are for a temperature of 25°C, a pressure of 101.325 kPa, and a $1M$ ionic concentration. A table of half-cell potentials is of great practical importance. It enables us to predict the direction for a large number of chemical reactions, the maximum voltage that can be produced by a particular voltaic cell, and the products of an electrolytic cell.

In Table 27-1, the substance on the left side of the arrow in each case is an oxidizing agent. It is an electron acceptor. The oxidizing agent with the highest positive potential is the strongest oxidizing agent. The oxidizing agents in this table are arranged in the order of increasing strength from top to bottom. Think of this series of substances as a list arranged in order of ability to attract electrons in competition with other oxidizing agents. The substance on the right side of the arrow in each case is a reducing agent. The strongest reducing agent is at the top of the table and the strength of the reducing agents decreases toward the bottom of the table. Let us see how this table can be used to predict the course of a particular reaction. Remember that electrons must flow from an electron donor (reducing agent) to an electron acceptor (oxidizing agent).

Demonstration—Place a clean penny in a petri dish on the overhead projector. Add $AgNO_3$ solution to the petri dish and observe the reaction. Refer to Table 27-1 to show students how they can use it to predict the products of the reaction.

Potentials vary with temperature, pressure, and concentration.

Half-cell potential tables are useful for predicting direction of chemical reactions.

Suggestion: Work with various combinations of half-reactions here so that use of the reduction potential table becomes a habit.

Electrons flow from donor (anode) to acceptor (cathode).

Electrons flow from donor (anode) to acceptor (cathode).

Table 27-1

Standard Reduction Potentials for Half-Reactions*

(Ionic concentrations, $1\,M$ in water at 25°C)

	Half-Reaction	Volts	
Weak	$Li^+ + e^- \rightarrow Li$	-3.05	**Strong**
oxidizing	$\frac{1}{2}Ca^{2+} + e^- \rightarrow \frac{1}{2}Ca$	-2.87	**reducing**
agents	$Na + e^- \rightarrow Na$	-2.71	**agents**
	$\frac{1}{2}Mg^{2+} + e^- \rightarrow \frac{1}{2}Mg$	-2.37	
	$\frac{1}{3}Al^{3+} + e^- \rightarrow \frac{1}{3}Al$	-1.66	
	$\frac{1}{2}Mn^{2+} + e^- \rightarrow \frac{1}{2}Mn$	-1.18	
	$\frac{1}{2}Cr^{2+} + e^- \rightarrow \frac{1}{2}Cr$	-0.91	
	$\frac{1}{3}H_3BO_3 + H^+ + e^- \rightarrow \frac{1}{3}B + H_2O$	-0.87	
	$\frac{1}{2}Zn^{2+} + e^- \rightarrow \frac{1}{2}Zn$	-0.76	
	$U^{4+} + e^- \rightarrow U^{3+}$	-0.61	
	$\frac{1}{3}Ga^{3+} + e^- \rightarrow \frac{1}{3}Ga$	-0.56	
	$CO_2 + H^+ + e^- \rightarrow \frac{1}{2}H_2C_2O_4$	-0.49	
	$\frac{1}{2}Fe^{2+} + e^- \rightarrow \frac{1}{2}Fe$	-0.44	
	$\frac{1}{2}Cd^{2+} + e^- \rightarrow \frac{1}{2}Cd$	-0.40	
	$\frac{1}{2}Co^{2+} + e^- \rightarrow \frac{1}{2}Co$	-0.28	
	$\frac{1}{2}Ni^{2+} + e^- \rightarrow \frac{1}{2}Ni$	-0.25	
	$\frac{1}{2}Sn^{2+} + e^- \rightarrow \frac{1}{2}Sn$	-0.14	
	$\frac{1}{2}Pb^{2+} + e^- \rightarrow \frac{1}{2}Pb$	-0.13	
	$H^+ + e^- \rightarrow \frac{1}{2}H_2(g)$	0.00	
	$\frac{1}{2}S + H^+ + e^- \rightarrow \frac{1}{2}H_2S(g)$	0.14	
	$\frac{1}{2}Sn^{4+} + e^- \rightarrow \frac{1}{2}Sn^{2+}$	0.15	
	$Cu^{2+} + e^- \rightarrow Cu^+$	0.16	
	$\frac{1}{2}SO_4^{2-} + 2H^+ + e^- \rightarrow \frac{1}{2}SO_2(aq) + H_2O$	0.17	
	$\frac{1}{2}Cu^{2+} + e^- \rightarrow \frac{1}{2}Cu$	0.34	
	$Cu^+ + e^- \rightarrow Cu$	0.52	
	$\frac{1}{2}I_2(c) + e^- \rightarrow I^-$	0.53	
	$HgCl_2 + e^- \rightarrow \frac{1}{2}Hg_2Cl_2 + Cl^-$	0.63	
	$Fe^{3+} + e^- \rightarrow Fe^{2+}$	0.77	
	$\frac{1}{2}Hg_2^{2+} + e^- \rightarrow Hg(l)$	0.79	
	$Ag^+ + e^- \rightarrow Ag$	0.80	
	$NO_3^- + 2H^+ + e^- \rightarrow NO_2 + H_2O$	0.80	
	$\frac{1}{2}Hg^{2+} + e^- \rightarrow \frac{1}{2}Hg$	0.85	
	$Hg^{2+} + e^- \rightarrow Hg^+$	0.92	
	$\frac{1}{3}NO_3^- + \frac{4}{3}H^+ + e^- \rightarrow \frac{1}{3}NO(g) + \frac{2}{3}H_2O$	0.96	
	$\frac{1}{2}Br_2(l) + e^- \rightarrow Br^-$	1.07	
	$\frac{1}{4}O_2 + H^+ + e^- \rightarrow \frac{1}{2}H_2O$	1.23	
	$\frac{1}{6}Cr_2O_7^{2-} + \frac{7}{3}H^+ + e^- \rightarrow \frac{1}{3}Cr^{3+} + \frac{7}{6}H_2O$	1.33	
	$\frac{1}{2}Cl_2(g) + e^- \rightarrow Cl^-$	1.36	
	$\frac{1}{3}Au^{3+} + e^- \rightarrow \frac{1}{3}Au$	1.50	
Strong	$\frac{1}{5}MnO_4^- + \frac{8}{5}H^+ + e^- \rightarrow \frac{1}{5}Mn^{2+} + \frac{4}{5}H_2O$	1.51	**Weak**
oxidizing	$\frac{1}{2}H_2O_2 + H^+ + e^- \rightarrow H_2O$	1.77	**reducing**
agents	$\frac{1}{2}F_2(g) + e^- \rightarrow F^-$	2.87	**agents**

*For additional values see Table A-12 of the Appendix.
Remember H^+ stands for H_3O^+ in solution.

FIGURE 27-12. Copper atoms are oxidized in a silver nitrate solution (a). No reaction occurs between copper and the zinc sulfate solution in (b).

As an example, consider what will happen if a strip of copper is immersed in a silver nitrate solution. A possible reaction could be written as

$$Cu(c) + 2Ag^+(aq) \rightarrow 2Ag(c) + Cu^{2+}(aq)$$

If this reaction is to occur, copper must give up electrons to silver ions. A glance at Table 27-1 shows that silver ions have a greater attraction for electrons than copper ions. This reaction may be done in the laboratory by immersing a small coil of fine copper wire in a silver nitrate solution. When silver ions are converted to silver atoms, a beautiful feathery deposit of metallic silver appears on the copper coil.

Suppose we immerse a strip of copper in a solution containing zinc ions. If a reaction is to occur, copper atoms must give up electrons to zinc ions. Table 27-1 shows that copper has a greater attraction for electrons than zinc. Thus, we can predict that copper atoms cannot give electrons to zinc ions. No reaction will occur.

Suggestion: Perform this experiment in the laboratory as a demonstration.

27:9 CELL POTENTIAL

Suppose we wish to find what voltage we could obtain from a cell using $Mg|Mg^{2+}$ and $Cu|Cu^{2+}$. We will assume that Mg will be oxidized and Cu^{2+} will be reduced. From Table 27-1, we see that

Magnesium has a higher potential than copper.

$$Mg^{2+} + 2e^- \rightarrow Mg \qquad -2.37 \text{ volts}$$

Thus, the oxidation reaction is

$$Mg \rightarrow Mg^{2+} + 2e^- \qquad +2.37 \text{ volts}$$

The reduction reaction is

$$Cu^{2+} + 2e^- \rightarrow Cu \qquad +0.34 \text{ volts}$$

The sum of the two potentials is $+2.71$ volts. This quantity is the voltage of the cell if the ion concentration in each compartment is one molar, and the temperature is 25°C. The direction of electron flow in the external circuit can be determined from the fact that the magnesium ion is losing electrons. Magnesium (the anode) gives up electrons which flow through the external circuit to the copper electrode. There the reduction reaction occurs. Would it be possible to construct a cell in which copper metal is used as the anode and magnesium ion is reduced at the cathode? Remember, a negative voltage indicates that the reverse reaction occurs.

If a reaction yields a negative voltage, the reverse reaction yields a positive voltage.

The standard reduction potential indicates a tendency of the half-reaction to gain electrons. The greater the voltage, the greater the tendency to gain electrons.

Note that the reduction potentials in Table 27-1 are expressed in volts. This voltage indicates how strong a tendency each half-reaction has to gain electrons. Lithium with a voltage of -3.05 has a weak tendency to gain an electron and fluorine at the bottom of the table has a strong tendency to gain an electron.

EXAMPLE: Cell Voltage

What voltage should be produced by the following cell?

$$\text{Fe} | \text{Fe}^{2+} \| \text{Br}_2 | \text{Br}^-$$

Solving process:
The table of standard reduction potentials lists the voltage for the two half-reactions as

$$\tfrac{1}{2}\text{Fe}^{2+} + e^- \rightarrow \tfrac{1}{2}\text{Fe} \qquad -0.44 \text{ V}$$

$$\tfrac{1}{2}\text{Br}_2 + e^- \rightarrow \text{Br}^- \qquad 1.07 \text{ V}$$

Since we have iron being oxidized to iron(II) ions, the voltage for that half-cell would be $+0.44$ V. The sum of the two half-cell voltages gives us the cell potential.

$$0.44 + 1.07 = 1.51 \text{ V}$$

PROBLEM

1. a. 0.32 volts
   b. 2.25 volts
   c. 2.00 V
   d. 1.04 V
   e. 0.46 V
   f. 1.49 V

1. Predict the voltages produced by the following cells. Use Table 27-1.
   a. $\text{Zn} | \text{Zn}^{2+} \| \text{Fe}^{2+} | \text{Fe}$
   b. $\text{Mn} | \text{Mn}^{2+} \| \text{Br}_2 | \text{Br}^-$
   c. $\text{H}_2\text{C}_2\text{O}_4 | \text{CO}_2 \| \text{MnO}_4^- | \text{Mn}^{2+}$
   d. $\text{Ni} | \text{Ni}^{2+} \| \text{Hg}_2^{2+} | \text{Hg}$
   e. $\text{Cu} | \text{Cu}^{2+} \| \text{Ag}^+ | \text{Ag}$
   f. $\text{Pb} | \text{Pb}^{2+} \| \text{Cl}^- | \text{Cl}_2$

27:10 PRODUCTS OF ELECTROLYSIS

In Section 27:4 we saw that there could be competition for reaction at the electrodes in an electrolytic cell. In the case examined there, the competition was between sodium ions and water molecules.

In order to predict which reactions will actually occur at an electrode, we use the table of reduction potentials. The energy required to cause an electrode reaction to occur varies directly with the negative voltage of that reaction. The reaction which requires the least amount of energy is associated with the least negative (most positive) voltage. Since most electrolysis reactions take place in water solution, we need to know the voltage required to oxidize and reduce water. In investigating the voltages involved in these reactions, we must remember that water dissociates slightly into H^+ and OH^-. In a neutral solution, both of these ions are found in a concentration of $10^{-7} M$. The reactions of interest to us are

Reduction of water:

$$2H_2O + 2e^- \rightleftarrows H_2 + 2OH^- \qquad -0.414 \text{ volts } (10^{-7}M \text{ OH}^-)$$

Oxidation of water:

$$2H_2O \rightleftarrows 4e^- + 4H^+ + O_2 \ -0.815 \text{ volts } (10^{-7}M \text{ H}^+)$$

In standard form:

$$\tfrac{1}{4}O_2 + H^+ + e^- \rightleftarrows \tfrac{1}{2}H_2O \ (10^{-7}M \text{ H}^+) \ +0.815 \text{ V}$$

$$\tfrac{1}{2}H_2O + e^- \rightleftarrows \tfrac{1}{2}H_2 + OH^- \ (10^{-7}M \text{ OH}^-) \ -0.414 \text{ V}$$

Let us assume we wish to predict the products of the electrolysis of a solution of potassium iodide in water. The possible reduction reactions are

$$K^+ + e^- \rightarrow K \qquad\qquad -2.93 \text{ V}$$

$$2H_2O + 2e^- \rightarrow H_2 + 2OH^- \quad -0.414 \text{ V}$$

The least negative value is the reduction of water, so the product at the cathode is hydrogen gas. The possible oxidations are

$$2I^- \rightarrow I_2 + 2e^- \qquad\qquad -0.53 \text{ V}$$

$$2H_2O \rightarrow 4e^- + 4H^+ + O_2 \quad -0.815 \text{ V}$$

The least negative value is the oxidation of iodide ion, so the product at the anode is iodine.

PROBLEM

2. Predict the products of the electrolysis of the following aqueous $1M$ solutions.
   a. Na_2SO_4
   b. $CuCl_2$
   c. CoF_2
   d. $Pb(NO_3)_2$
   e. $LiBr$
   f. $NaCl$

Margin notes

Reduction tables can be used to predict electrolysis products.

The voltage required to reduce water $= -0.414$ volts.

The voltage required to oxidize water $= -0.815$ volts.

The "least negative value" is the greater value on the number line.

2. a. H_2 and O_2
   b. Cu and O_2
   c. Co and O_2 e. H_2 and O_2
   d. Pb and O_2 f. H_2 and Cl_2

27:11   EFFECT OF CONDITIONS ON CELLS AND ENERGY

In the latter part of the nineteenth century, H. W. Nernst, a German chemist, worked with voltaic cells. He found the relationship between the voltage of a cell and the conditions under which it was operating. The voltage of a cell under standard conditions is called $E°$. The values in Table 27-1 are $E°$ values for $1M$ solutions at 25°C and 101.325 kPa pressure. If we now call the voltage of a cell at other than standard conditions E, we can use the relationship worked out by Nernst.

$$E = E° - \frac{RT}{nF} \ln \frac{(concentration\ of\ products)}{(concentration\ of\ reactants)}$$

Let us look at each of the factors in the equation. The value of R is the universal gas constant which we developed in the ideal gas equation (Section 19:3). However, in applying R to electric measurements it must be expressed in convenient units. These units will be different from the $dm^3 \cdot kPa/mol \cdot K$ used in gas calculations. Conversion to $J/mol \cdot K$ gives a value of 8.31. The value of T is the absolute temperature in K. The value of n is the number of electrons transferred in the balanced equation representing the change taking place in the cell. The value of F is a conversion factor from volts to joules per mole and is equal to 96 500. The symbol ln stands for the natural logarithm which we can replace with (2.30 log) to use common logarithms. If we combine the constants (R/F) 2.30, we obtain a value of 1.98×10^{-4}. If we combine standard temperature, 298 K, with the previous value, we obtain 0.0592. We may then write the Nernst equation in two simpler forms.

$$E = E° - \frac{1.98 \times 10^{-4}\,T}{n} \log \frac{(concentration\ of\ products)}{(concentration\ of\ reactants)}$$
$$\text{at nonstandard temperature}$$

or,

$$E = E° - \frac{0.0592}{n} \log \frac{(concentration\ of\ products)}{(concentration\ of\ reactants)}$$
$$\text{at standard temperature}$$

Let us now apply these equations to some sample problems.

EXAMPLE: Nonstandard Concentrations at Standard Temperature

What would be the voltage of a cell using $Ni | Ni^{2+}$ (2.50M) for one half-cell and $Ag | Ag^+$ (0.100M) for the other half-cell? Assume the pressure and temperature to be at standard values.

Solving process:
(a) Determine the equation for the total cell reaction. In a comparison between Ni^{2+} and Ag^+, silver has the greater tendency to gain electrons. On that basis, nickel is oxidized and silver is reduced.

$$Ni(c) + 2Ag^+(aq) \rightarrow Ni^{2+}(aq) + 2Ag(c)$$

Determine the balanced redox equation for the cell.

(b) Determine the values to be substituted into the Nernst equation.

$$E = E° - \frac{0.0592}{n} \log \frac{[Ni^{2+}]}{[Ag^+]^2}$$

$$E = E° - \frac{0.0592}{n} \log \frac{[products]}{[reactants]}$$

Solids having a constant concentration do not appear in the equation.

$\quad\quad\quad\quad$ Ni oxidation $\quad\quad$ Ag$^+$ reduction
From Table 27-1, $E° = +0.25$ volts $+ 0.80$ volts $= 1.05$ volts

$\quad\quad n = 2$ (the number of electrons transferred)

$$E = 1.05 \text{ V} - \frac{0.0592}{2} \log \frac{[2.50]}{[0.100][0.100]}$$

$$= 1.05 - 0.0296(\log 250)$$
$$= 1.05 - 0.0296(2.40)$$
$$= 1.05 - 0.07 = 0.98 \text{ volts}$$

Note that the concentration of silver ion is squared in the expression. The concentrations of reactants and products are handled in the Nernst equation exactly as they are in an equilibrium expression.

EXAMPLE: Different Concentrations at Nonstandard Temperature

What would be the voltage of a cell using $Zn|Zn^{2+}(2.00M)$ for one half-cell and $Cu|Cu^{2+}(0.500M)$ for the other half-cell at 45°C? The pressure is 101.325 kPa.

Solving process:

$$Zn(c) + Cu^{2+}(aq) \rightarrow Zn^{2+}(aq) + Cu(c)$$

$E° = 1.10$ volts (Section 27:8)

$$E = 1.10 - \frac{0.000198(318)}{2} \log \frac{[2.00]}{[0.500]} \quad \text{(The solids, having a constant concentration do not appear.)}$$

$$= 1.10 - 0.0315(\log 4)$$
$$= 1.10 - 0.0315(0.602)$$
$$= 1.10 - 0.02 = 1.08 \text{ volts}$$

PROBLEMS

3. What voltage could you expect (ideally) from the following cell at 25°C?

$$Pb \mid Pb^{2+}(0.100M) \parallel Sn^{4+}(0.150M) \mid Sn^{2+}(1.00M)$$

4. What voltage could you expect (ideally) from the following cell at 25°C?

$$Ni \mid Ni^{2+}(1.00M) \parallel Cu^{2+}(0.0100M) \mid Cu$$

5. What voltage could you expect (ideally) from the following cell at 18°C?

$$Fe \mid Fe^{2+}(0.152M) \parallel Ag^{+}(0.120M) \mid Ag$$

27:12   pH METER

The Nernst equation can be applied to half-cells as well as to an entire cell. Consider the hydrogen half-cell at standard temperature and pressure.

$$H^{+} + e^{-} \rightarrow \tfrac{1}{2}H_2$$

$$E = E° - 0.0592 \log \frac{1}{[H^{+}]}$$

Using the relationship $\log 1/x = -\log x$, we can rearrange the above equation.

$$E = E° + 0.0592 \log [H^{+}]$$

We know that $E°$ for the hydrogen half-cell is 0.00 volts. We also know that $-\log [H^{+}] = pH$. Substituting these values we get

$$E = -0.0592 \, pH$$

FIGURE 27-13. A pH meter is an analytical instrument used to measure electrically the hydrogen ion concentration of a solution. The voltage difference between the electrodes is measured in pH units.

Janet Adams

Thus E is a linear function of pH. By combining a reference electrode with a hydrogen electrode, we can measure the pH of a solution electrically. The reference electrode usually chosen is the saturated calomel* electrode because it has a known constant voltage. The meter measuring the voltage between the reference and hydrogen ion electrodes is calibrated to read directly in pH units. This calibration then saves the chemist the trouble of converting from volts to pH units.

E is a linear function of pH.

The pH meter makes use of a hydrogen ion electrode and a reference electrode.

27:13 ENERGY AND ELECTRIC CELLS

In Chapter 23 we saw that the free energy change for a reaction was related to the equilibrium constant for the reaction. The relationship was $\Delta G = -2.30RT \log K$. Perhaps you have already noticed the similarity between this expression and the Nernst equation. The Nernst equation may be written as

$$E = E^\circ - \frac{2.30RT}{nF} \log K$$

The value of F is a conversion factor from volts to joules per mole and is equal to 96 500.

At equilibrium, there is no net change, so E would equal zero. Solving the equation for $(2.30RT)\log K$ and substituting 0 for E, we obtain

$$2.30RT \log K = nFE^\circ$$

Substituting the equivalent expression in the free energy equation we get

$$\Delta G = -nFE^\circ$$

Recall $\Delta G = \Delta H - T\Delta S$

These relationships are important to a chemist. Voltages of cells, once they have been measured can be used to derive a great deal of other information. If the voltage is known, the free energy change for the reaction may be calculated. With other information, enthalpy and entropy changes can be found. Measurement of voltages may also be used to determine the equilibrium constant for reactions.

Voltages can be used to determine K_{eq}.

PROBLEMS

6. What is the free energy change for the following reaction at standard conditions?

$$2U^{3+} + Hg^{2+} \rightarrow 2U^{4+} + Hg$$

6. −282 kJ

7. What is the free energy change for the following reaction at standard conditions?

$$Zn + 2Hg^{2+} \rightarrow Zn^{2+} + Hg_2^{2+}$$

7. −324 kJ

*Calomel is Hg_2Cl_2.

27:14 QUANTITATIVE ASPECTS OF ELECTROCHEMISTRY

The equations for the electrode half-reactions can be balanced like any other chemical equation. They have the same quantitative significance. Consider the equation for the formation of sodium metal in the electrolysis of molten sodium chloride. It indicates that 1 mole of electrons is required to produce 1 mole of sodium atoms. However, other than in chemical reactions, electricity is not measured in moles. The more common unit for electricity is the coulomb. One coulomb (C) is the quantity of electricity produced by a current of one ampere flowing for one second. 96 500 coulombs is the equivalent of 1 mole of electrons. This quantity is a convenient unit for electrochemical calculations.

96 500 coulombs = 1 mole of electrons

One mole of sodium is 23 grams. To produce 23 grams of sodium by an electrolytic reaction, one mole of electrons must be used. One mole of electrons equals 96 500 coulombs. Since 1 coulomb is equal to a current of one ampere flowing for one second, 1 coulomb is equal to 1 ampere·second. The number of coulombs used in a reaction can be obtained by multiplying the number of amperes by the number of seconds. We could produce 23 grams of sodium by using a current of 10 amperes for 9650 seconds. Any combination of amperes and seconds which gives a product of 96 500 A·s will yield 23 g of sodium (one mol).

In the anode reaction for the electrolysis of sodium chloride, one chlorine molecule requires the release of two electrons. Thus, one mole of chlorine gas will require two moles of electrons.

The principles which we have just discussed are expressed in more concise form as Faraday's laws. They were proposed by Michael Faraday.

Since the amount of electricity produced is equal to the current in amperes multiplied by the time in seconds, we may say:

$$coulombs = amperes \times seconds$$

Further, we can write the following expression.

$$moles\ of\ electrons = \frac{ampere}{} \left| \frac{second}{} \right| \frac{1\ coulomb}{1\ ampere \cdot second} \left| \frac{1\ mole\ e^-}{96\ 500\ coulomb} \right.$$

From a balanced equation we obtain the relationship between the formula mass of a substance and the moles of electrons.

$$\frac{mass\ of\ substance}{per\ mole\ of\ electrons} = \frac{formula\ mass\ of\ substance}{moles\ of\ electrons\ transferred}$$

Combining the two expressions, we get the mathematical statement of Faraday's laws.

Demonstration—Plate copper metal on an electrode made from a pencil with the wood cut back. See the Teacher's Guide for details. After Cu has been plated, the cell can be reconnected to demonstrate an electrochemical cell producing a voltage.

One coulomb is the quantity of electricity produced by 1 ampere flowing for 1 second.

$1\ C = 1\ A \cdot s$

$$\textit{mass of substance} = \frac{\text{coulombs}}{} \left| \frac{1 \text{ mole } e^-}{96\,500 \text{ coulombs}} \right| \frac{\text{formula mass}}{\text{mole } e^-}$$

Note that the coefficient of the substance in the equation must be taken into account.

EXAMPLE: Faraday's Law Calculation

What mass of copper will be deposited by a current of 7.89 amperes flowing for a period of 1200 seconds?

Solving process:
The cathode reaction is

$$Cu^{2+}(aq) + 2e^- \rightarrow Cu(c)$$

and therefore 2 mol e^- plate out 63.5 g Cu(c). By combining the expressions, we obtain

$Cu^{2+} + 2e^- \rightarrow Cu$
2 moles of electrons will reduce 1 mole of Cu^{2+} to Cu.

$$\frac{7.89 \text{ A}}{} \left| \frac{1200 \text{ s}}{} \right| \frac{1 \text{ C}}{\text{A·s}} \left| \frac{1 \text{ mol } e^-}{96\,500 \text{ C}} \right| \frac{1 \text{ mol Cu}}{2 \text{ mol } e^-} \left| \frac{63.5 \text{ g Cu}}{1 \text{ mol Cu}} \right. = 3.12 \text{ g Cu}$$

EXAMPLE: Faraday's Law Calculation

What mass of Cr^{3+} ion is produced by a current of 0.713 ampere flowing for 12 800 seconds? The equation for the total reaction is

$$14H_3O^+(aq) + 6Fe^{2+}(aq) + Cr_2O_7^{2-}(aq) \rightarrow 6Fe^{3+}(aq) + 2Cr^{3+}(aq) + 21H_2O(l)$$

Solving process:
You must verify that the moles of electrons involved in the equation as written are equal to six $(Cr_2O_7^{2-} \rightarrow 2Cr^{3+})$. Then by substituting in the Faraday's Law equation the following expression is obtained.

Cr in $Cr_2O_7^{2-}$ has an oxidation number of 6+.

$$\frac{0.713 \text{ A}}{} \left| \frac{12\,800 \text{ s}}{} \right| \frac{1 \text{ C}}{\text{A·s}} \left| \frac{1 \text{ mol } e^-}{96\,500 \text{ C}} \right| \frac{2 \text{ mol Cr}^{3+}}{6 \text{ mol } e^-} \left| \frac{52.0 \text{ g Cr}^{3+}}{1 \text{ mol Cr}^{3+}} \right. = 1.64 \text{ g Cr}^{3+}$$

PROBLEMS

8. How many grams of silver will be deposited by a current of 1.00 A flowing for 9650 s?

9. A current of 5.00 A flows through a cell for 10.0 min. How many grams of silver could be deposited during this time? Write the cathode reaction.

10. What current must be used to plate 2.00 mol of copper on an electrode in 3.00 min?

11. What period of time was required if a current of 5.00 A was passed through a salt (sodium chloride) solution and 1.00 mol of chlorine was produced?

12. How many minutes would be necessary to deposit 0.400 g of calcium from a cell with a current of 10.0 A?

8. 10.8 g Ag
9. 3.36 g Ag, $Ag^+ + e^- \rightarrow Ag$
10. 2140 A
11. 10.7 h
12. 3.21 min

27:15 ELECTROANALYSIS

An immediate application of electrochemistry is its use in quantitative analysis. An example might serve to explain.

Platinum is usually used.

Suppose that it is necessary for you to determine the percentage of copper in a given water soluble copper compound. A sample of the compound of known mass could be dissolved in water and inert electrodes inserted. The mass of the cathode should be measured before the current is applied. As the current is passed through the cell, metallic copper plates onto the electrode of known mass. When the action is complete and current no longer flows, all the copper is plated. The mass of the electrode is again measured. The difference in mass (due to the copper) is compared to the mass of the sample to find the percentage of copper in the sample. Electroanalysis is a useful tool of the chemist.

EXAMPLE: Electroanalysis

What is the percentage of nickel in an alloy with the following analysis:

> Mass of alloy sample = 6.73 g
> Mass of cathode before depositing Ni = 19.142 g
> Mass of cathode after depositing Ni = 19.634 g

Solving process:

(a) Find the mass of nickel deposited.

$$19.634 - 19.142 = 0.492 \text{ g Ni}$$

(b) Find the percentage of nickel in this alloy.

$$\% = \frac{mass\ difference}{mass\ of\ sample} \times 100$$

$$\frac{0.492 \text{ g}}{6.73 \text{ g}} \times 100 = 7.31\% \text{ Ni}$$

PROBLEM

Brass is an alloy of Cu, Sn, and Pb.

13. A chemist must analyze for copper content, a sample of brass with mass 2.36 g. The alloy is dissolved in nitric acid, and the tin present is precipitated as SnO_2. The solution is then treated with sulfuric acid, precipitating the lead as $PbSO_4$. The resulting solution is prepared for electrolysis to determine the copper content. The mass of the cathode of the electrolysis apparatus is measured and found to be 26.203 grams. The electrolysis is run, the cathode is dried, and its mass is again measured. Its new mass is 28.273 g. What is the percentage of copper in the alloy?   87.7%

Michael Faraday (1791–1867)

The son of an English blacksmith, Michael Faraday was apprenticed early in life to a book-binder. As a result he could devote only his spare time to his pursuits in science. Largely self-educated, his real boost into the scientific world came through the sponsorship of Sir Humphrey Davy, an English chemist and physicist. Faraday's greatest work involved passing a current through different solutions and finding that it caused an electrolysis reaction. The relationship between the amount of current used and the amount of product formed was expressed in the form of two laws now known as Faraday's laws. He also discovered that an electric current creates a magnetic field.

In other areas, he discovered benzene and several organic chlorides. He did research on the physics of polarized light and the diffusion and liquefication of gases.

CHEMICAL TECHNOLOGY: Corrosion

The interaction of metals with their environment is called corrosion. Corrosion results in the deterioration of the metal in forming metal compounds. The cost of trying to prevent and correct this deterioration runs to many billions of dollars each year.

Water and oxygen are the chief reactants, but many other substances are involved. The pale green coating that copper and brass acquire (see Figure 26-1) involves carbon dioxide as well as oxygen and water. Dirt, salts used in treating icy streets, and other metals all increase the rate of corrosion. As in other chemical reactions, an increase in temperature increases the rate of corrosion.

Many corrosion processes, including rusting, are electrochemical processes. Consider an iron surface on which a piece of soot (carbon) has fallen, followed by a drop of water. Some carbon dioxide from the air dissolves in the water to form carbonic acid.

$$CO_2 + H_2O \rightarrow H_2CO_3$$

$$H_2CO_3 + H_2O \rightarrow H_3O^+ + HCO_3^-$$

The essential components of a voltaic cell are present—two electrodes (carbon and iron), and an electrolyte (a solution of H_3O^+

and HCO_3^-). The iron, being more active, acts as the anode. The carbon acts as the cathode.

$$Fe \rightarrow Fe^{2+} + 2e^- \qquad\qquad O_2 + 2H_2O + 4e^- \rightarrow 4OH^-$$

The Fe^{2+} ions can be oxidized by the air to Fe^{3+} ions, before or after combining with the OH^- ions. The $Fe(OH)_3$ formed soon becomes rust, $Fe_2O_3 \cdot xH_2O$, a hydrated iron(III) oxide.

Corrosion can be prevented in several ways. Some metals form a self-protecting layer of oxidized metal on the surface. This layer is impervious and protects the interior of the metal from further attack. Aluminum, nickel, and chromium are typical metals which exhibit this behavior. Metallurgists are learning how to create these types of layers on other metals. Coating or alloying corrosion-prone metals with self-protective metals is one way of fighting corrosion.

Metals may be coated with nonmetallic materials also. Grease, paint, and porcelain enamel have all been used to protect metals from corrosion. Another protective measure takes advantage of the electrochemical nature of corrosion. The metal to be protected is connected electrically to a more active metal. The connection may be a direct contact or by wire. When two metals in electric contact are subjected to an oxidizing agent, the more active metal is oxidized, while the less active metal remains unchanged. Zinc and magnesium are frequently used for this purpose in the shipping industry. Blocks of these more active metals are attached to the less active steel hull (see Figure 11-18).

SUMMARY

1. An electric current is carried through a metal by the movement of electrons. An electric current is carried through a solution or molten salt by the movement of positive and negative ions. 27:1

2. When two points with a potential difference are connected by a conductor, an electric current will flow. An electric current is the flow of electricity through a conductor. It passes from the point of higher potential to the point of lower potential. 27:1

3. Current is measured with an ammeter or galvanometer, and is expressed in amperes (A). 27:1

4. Voltage is the measure of potential difference. Voltage is measured with a voltmeter, and is expressed in volts (V). 27:1

5. Electrolyte solutions are electrically neutral, but contain ions which are free to move, as do molten ionic compounds. Cations are positive ions; anions are negative ions. 27:2

6. When ions migrating through an electrolytic cell reach an electrode, they undergo oxidation or reduction reactions. 27:3-27:4

7. A voltaic cell is a cell which produces an electric current and is composed of two dissimilar metals and an electrolyte. 27:5-27:6

8. Any oxidation-reduction reaction can (theoretically) be set up in such a way that current will be produced. 27:5

9. An oxidation-reduction reaction is a reversible reaction. Therefore, any change in temperature, pressure, or concentration will affect the flow of electric current. 27:11

10. The reduction potential of electrode reactions measures the relative strength of oxidizing and reducing agents. 27:7

11. The standard electrode potential series is a group of half-reactions arranged in order of their reduction potential. The hydrogen half-cell is the standard reference cell, and is assigned a voltage of 0.0000 V at standard conditions for convenience. 27:7-27:8

12. The table of standard electrode potentials can be used to predict the direction of reaction, the electromotive force of cells, and the products of electrolysis. 27:8-27:10

13. A reaction for which the reducing agent has less attraction for electrons than the oxidizing agent will occur spontaneously. 27:13

14. An electrolytic cell is a cell in which the electrons are forced to flow in a direction opposite to their normal flow. This flow-reversing process is called electrolysis. 27:10

15. In both electrolytic and electrochemical cells, oxidation occurs at the anode and reduction occurs at the cathode. 27:3-27:5, 27:10

16. The Nernst equation relates the voltage of a cell to the conditions under which the cell is operating. 27:11

$$E = E° - \frac{2.30RT}{nF} \log K$$

17. The relationship between hydrogen ion concentration and the voltage of the hydrogen half-cell can be used as the basis for the electrical measurement of pH. 27:12

18. The voltage generated by a cell and the free energy change of the reaction occurring in the cell are related by: 27:13

$$\Delta G = -nFE°$$

19. One coulomb is the quantity of electricity produced by a current of 1 ampere flowing for 1 second. 96 500 coulombs = 1 mole of electrons. 27:14

20. The mass of matter reacting in a cell is determined by formula mass and the amount of electricity which passes through the cell. 27:14-27:15

PROBLEMS

14. Which of the following reactions will proceed spontaneously?
    a. $Na + Cl_2 \rightarrow$?   c. $Cu + H_2 \rightarrow$?   e. $Zn + Pb^{2+} \rightarrow$?
    b. $Fe^{2+} + Cu \rightarrow$?   d. $Cu^{2+} + Ag^+ \rightarrow$?   f. $Fe + Pb^{2+} \rightarrow$?

    14. a. yes d. no
        b. no   e. yes
        c. no   f. yes

15. Explain how to determine whether a given electrode is an anode or a cathode. oxidation occurs at anode, reduction at cathode

16. How can an insulator be made to conduct a current?

17. Why does an ionic solid inhibit the flow of electric current?

18. How does electrolysis differ from electrolytic conduction?

19. If a particular metal is considered more active than another, what does that statement tell you concerning its electronic structure?

20. From each of the following pairs, select the better reducing agent.
    a. Cd, Fe
    b. Ca, Mg
    c. Pb, Zn
    d. Br^-, Cu

21. From each of the following pairs, select the better oxidizing agent.
    a. Ca^{2+}, Li^+
    b. Fe^{3+}, Hg_2^{2+}
    c. Cl_2, Hg^{2+}
    d. Cu^+, Cu^{2+}

22. How do electronic and electrolytic conduction differ?

23. What maximum voltage could you expect from a cell which consisted of $Al|Al^{3+}$ and $Ag|Ag^+$ half cells? Write the electrode reactions and the overall reaction.

24. What reaction would you expect at the electrodes of a Hooker cell (a device for the electrolysis of sodium chloride solution)?

25. The electrolysis of 10.0 grams of water would produce what volume of O_2 at STP? Give each electrode reaction.

26. What voltage could you expect from the following cell at 25°C?
    $Mg|Mg^{2+}(0.170M)||Cl_2|Cl^-(0.100M)$

27. What voltage would be obtained at 25°C from the following cell?
    $Cd|Cd^{2+}(0.500M)||Fe^{3+}(0.100M)|Fe^{2+}(0.200M)$

28. Using the standard reduction potential table compute the free energy change for the reaction: $Sn^{4+} + Fe \rightarrow Fe^{2+} + Sn^{2+}$
    See Teacher's Guide.

29. Find the equilibrium constant for the reaction in Problem 28.

30. What voltage would you expect to realize from a cell employing a reaction with a free energy change of -30 kJ? 0.311 V per e^- transferred

31. A platinum electrode has a mass of 7.493 g before being plated with nickel, and 9.417 g after the nickel is deposited. If the nickel was obtained from an alloy sample with mass 4.871 g, what percentage of the alloy is nickel?

32. How long must a current of 20.0 A be passed through a sodium chloride solution to produce 40.0 g of $NaOH$?

33. A silver ion solution is subjected to a current of 5.00 A for 2.00 h.
    a. Give the cathode reaction.
    b. How much silver would be plated out?

REVIEW

1. What is the modern definition of oxidation?

2. What does an oxidizing agent do?

3. Show oxidation numbers for the indicated atoms in the following compounds.
    a. U in UF_6
    b. Si in $Al_2(SiF_6)_3$
    c. Cl in $Pb(ClO_4)_2$ (lead is 2+)
    d. As in $Fe_3(AsO_4)_2$ (iron is 2+)

(Answer column, left margin:)

20. a. Fe
    b. Ca
    c. Zn
    d. Cu
21. a. Ca^{2+}
    b. Hg_2^{2+}
    c. Cl_2
    d. Cu^+

23. 2.46 V

25. 6220 cm³
26. 3.82 V
27. 1.16 V
28. −114 kJ

31. 39.5%
32. 1.34 h (80 min)
33. a. $Ag^+ + e^- \rightarrow Ag$
    b. 40.3 g

1. loss of electrons
2. gains electrons
3. a. 6+
   b. 4+
   c. 7+
   d. 5+

4. Balance by half-reactions:

$$Fe^{2+} + Cr_2O_7{}^{2-} \rightarrow Fe^{3+} + Cr^{3+} \ (in \ acid \ solution)$$

5. Define a Bronsted base.
6. What is the name of $H_2Te(aq)$?
7. What is the name of HClO?
8. What kind of elements tend to form bases?
9. What is the ionization constant for the dihydrogen pyrophosphate ion, if a 0.100M solution of the ion has a hydronium ion concentration of $1.58 \times 10^{-4}M$?
10. What is the percentage ionization in Problem 9?
11. Which ion would you expect to produce a more acidic solution, $H_4IO_6{}^-$ or $H_3IO_6{}^{2-}$?
12. What is the hydroxide ion concentration in a solution with hydronium ion concentration of $3.61 \times 10^{-6}M$?
13. What is the pH of the solution in Problem 12?

5. proton acceptor
6. hydrotelluric acid
7. hypochlorous acid
8. metallic

9. 2.50×10^{-7}
10. 0.158%
11. $H_4IO_6{}^-$
12. $2.77 \times 10^{-9}M$
13. 5.44

ONE MORE STEP

1. Trace the development of the search for an understanding of electricity from the first experience with static electricity to our present-day knowledge. You can find this information most easily in a history of science or in an encyclopedia.
2. Use the Nernst equation to compute the voltage of a cell in which one half-cell is made with Zn and 1.00M Zn^{2+} and the other half-cell is Zn and 0.100M Zn^{2+} at standard conditions.
3. Compute the voltage of a cell in which one half-cell is the hydrogen half-cell with hydrogen at a pressure of 203 kPa and the other half-cell is Zn and Zn^{2+} at 1.00M all other conditions are standard.
4. Some batteries carry a warning against recharging. See if you can discover what danger is involved and the reactions which produce that danger.
5. Investigate fuel cells as a source of electricity from chemical reactions.

2. 0.0296 V
3. 0.75 V

READINGS

Lauren, Paul M., "Sir Humphrey Davy's Battle with the Sea." *Chemistry,* Vol. 50, No. 7 (September 1977), pp. 14-17.
Smith, Wayne L., "Corrosion." *Chemistry,* Part I, Vol. 49, No. 1 (January-February 1976), pp. 14-16; Part II, Vol. 49, No. 5 (June 1976), pp. 7-9; Part III, Vol. 49, No. 8 (October 1976), pp. 10-12.
Strauss, Howard J., and Kaufman, Milton, *Handbook for Chemical Technicians.* New York: McGraw-Hill Book Co., 1976, Chapter 4.

The nucleus of an atom may become a major energy resource. Much research concerning the nucleus centers around controlling the energy produced in nuclear reactions. One such reaction involves combining low molecular mass nuclei to produce tremendous amounts of energy. This fusion process requires extremely high temperatures. Lasers are being used to excite the nucleus to a temperature where fusion can occur. The computer photograph showing a fusion explosion allows scientists to monitor the course of the reaction. What is a fusion reaction?

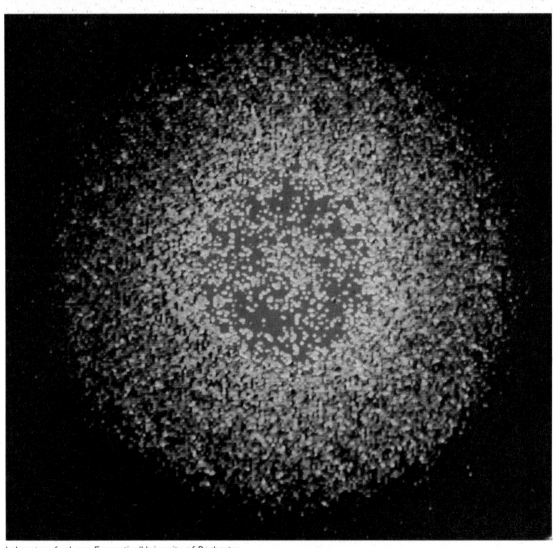

Laboratory for Laser Energetics/University of Rochester

Chapter 28 introduces the basic aspects of nuclear chemistry: elementary particles, particle accelerators, radioactivity, half-life, and nuclear reactions. Fission and fusion are presented in relation to their development and control.

NUCLEAR CHEMISTRY

28

Demonstration—Use a Geiger counter to show the presence of radioactive particles as background radiation and from a radioactive source such as uranyl nitrate. Discuss what causes the "click" the students hear. You may use a cloud chamber if a counter is not available. The tracks show up best under a strong light. See the Teacher's Guide for preparation details concerning a cloud chamber.

In 1896, Henri Becquerel, a French physicist, found that matter containing uranium exposes photographic film. This fact led Becquerel's assistants, Pierre and Marie Curie, to an important discovery. They found that rays are given off by the elements uranium and radium.

Uranium and radium can be found in nature in an ore called pitchblende. This ore is mined in Canada, Colorado, and Germany. If some of this ore is placed near, but not touching a charged electroscope, the leaves become discharged. Substances which have the same effects as uranium and radium are called radioactive substances. The whole phenomenon is called radioactivity.

GOAL: You will gain an understanding of natural and artificial nuclear reactions and the instruments used to study, control, and utilize radioactive materials and nuclear processes.

The air surrounding the radioactive source becomes ionized by the emitted rays. The air also becomes a conductor which discharges the electroscope leaves.

28:1 NUCLEAR STRUCTURE

The rays produced by radioactive materials are a mixture of several particles and quanta of energy. The particles and quanta are given off by the nuclei of radioactive atoms during spontaneous nuclear decay. We say the decay is spontaneous because we have no control over it. The amount of energy released in a nuclear change is very large. It is so large that it cannot be a result of an ordinary chemical change.

Albert Einstein was the first to explain the origin of this energy (Chapter 1). From his theory, we see that mass and energy are equivalent. This statement can be expressed in the equation

$$E = mc^2$$

E is the energy (in joules) released

m is the mass (in kilograms) of matter involved

c is a constant, the speed of light in meters per second

Radioactive materials produce particles and energy.

Nuclear decay is spontaneous.

Ordinary chemical reactions do not produce nearly as much energy as nuclear reactions produce.

Actually more accurately expressed: $\Delta E = \Delta mc^2$

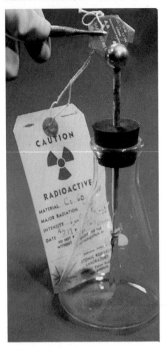

Craig Kramer

FIGURE 28-1. A radioactive substance will discharge the leaves of an electroscope.

Ordinary forces are not strong enough to hold a nucleus together.

Nucleons (protons and neutrons) have a property which corresponds to electron spin.

FIGURE 28-2. Uranium ore is mined in both underground and surface mines.

The energy-mass change in normal chemical reactions is too small to be measured. However, we are familiar with the nuclear changes which involve a mass-energy interconversion. The large amount of energy released in splitting the nuclei of uranium or plutonium is measurable.

The nucleus of the uranium-238 atom contains 92 protons and 146 neutrons. These particles are bound tightly in the nucleus. Acting alone, electrostatic attraction would allow the uncharged neutrons to float away. Since protons all have the same positive charge, electrostatic forces should cause them to fly apart. Gravitational force, which keeps us at the surface of the earth, is not strong enough to hold the nucleus together. What force, then, holds the nucleus together?

Ideas explaining nuclear structure differ, but scientists agree on certain facts.

(1) The **nuclear force** which holds protons and neutrons together is effective for very short distances only. This distance is about the same as the diameter of the nucleus.

(2) **Nucleons** (protons and neutrons) have a property which corresponds to the spin of electrons.

(3) Electrons do not exist in the nucleus, yet they can be emitted from the nucleus.

Dan Guravich 1978/Photo Researchers, Inc.

28:2 SUBATOMIC PARTICLES

Nuclear scientists divide subatomic particles into two broad classes, leptons and hadrons. Current theory holds that **leptons** ("light" particles) are truly elementary particles. The electron is the best known lepton.

For every particle, a mirror-image particle called an **anti-particle** exists, or is believed to exist. Thus, there is an anti-electron, called a positron, which is like an electron in every way

Leptons and hadrons are the two classes of subatomic particles.

Every particle has a mirror-image anti-particle (electron-positron).

except that it has a positive charge. Positrons are not common. They exist only until they collide with an electron. Such a collision is very likely in our world. When the collision occurs, both particles are destroyed and two quanta of energy are produced. It is interesting to note that there is at least one particle which is its own antiparticle. This particle is the neutral pion.

There are several other leptons. In order to account for the emission of electrons from the nucleus, a neutral particle called a **neutrino** was postulated. The neutrino has been identified and found to be essentially massless. The muon and the tau, both much more massive than the electron, make up the rest of the lepton family. There is a neutrino for the muon and one predicted for the tau. There are antiparticles for all these particles.

The **hadrons** are subdivided into two groups, the mesons and the baryons. Protons and neutrons are baryons, as are a number of other short-lived particles. There are several kinds of mesons.

Mesons and baryons are made of smaller particles called **quarks.** There exists experimental evidence for four kinds of quarks: "up," "down," "charmed," and "strange." Two other kinds are believed to exist, "top" and "bottom." The names convey nothing about the properties of the quarks. They are just labels to identify different particles. Each quark comes in three "colors," red, blue, and green. Again, the "color" label refers only to a distinguishing property, not an appearance. Each kind of quark, of course, has an antimatter counterpart, an antiquark.

Baryons are composed of three quarks, each of a different color. **Mesons** are composed of a quark and an antiquark of complementary color.

It is believed that quarks are held together by exchanging "particles" called **gluons.** The exchange of gluons between quarks is analogous to the exchange of photons by atoms. In a similar manner, the nucleons are held together in the nucleus by the exchange of pions. There are believed to be eight (or maybe nine) gluons, each of which is characterized by possessing one color and one anticolor.

The entire field of nuclear structure and the relationships of subatomic particles is a field of intense study. Much of the study is done using particle accelerators.

28:3 ACCELERATORS

Nuclear scientists use both linear and circular devices to accelerate particles. Both types operate using the charges on the particles. When the particle has achieved a very high speed (and

---

Elementary particles
Leptons (light particles)
Mesons (middle particles)
Baryons (heavier particles)

There are two groups of hadrons-mesons and baryons.

Mesons and baryons are made of smaller particles called quarks.

Baryons are composed of three different colored quarks.

Mesons are composed of a quark and antiquark of complementary colors.

The exchange of gluons between quarks holds them together.

Accelerators make use of magnetic fields and electromagnetic waves to accelerate charged particles.

FIGURE 28-3. In a linear accelerator, charged particles are accelerated by electromagnetic waves. Drift tubes prevent the faster waves from overtaking the particles.

thus a very high energy), it is aimed at a target material. The interaction which results as a consequence of the collision helps scientists understand the structure of the nucleus.

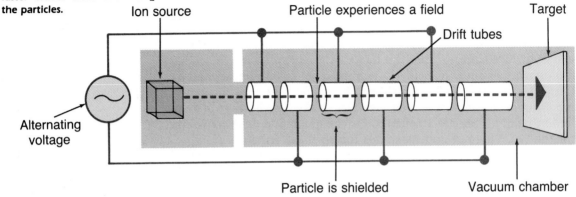

FIGURE 28-3. In a linear accelerator, charged particles are accelerated by electromagnetic waves. Drift tubes prevent the faster waves from overtaking the particles.

Courtesy of Stanford Linear Accelerator Center, Stanford Univ.

Department of Energy

a *b*

FIGURE 28-4. The linear accelerator at Stanford University is 2 miles long (a). The drift tube arrangement in the interior of the accelerator is shown (b).

In a linear accelerator a particle is introduced using a device similar to the mass spectrometer ion-beam generator, Figure 28-3. The charged particle in motion will be affected by an electromagnetic wave. A radio wave is used to "push," or accelerate, the particle down the "pipe" forming the core of the accelerator. The wave, however, is traveling at the speed of light. Since the particle is not traveling as fast, the wave tends to overtake the particle. If that were to happen, the particle would then decelerate. Therefore, there are uncharged tubes in the pipe called **"drift tubes."** The particle drifts through the tube until the next accelerating part of the radio wave is in the correct position.

Careful design of the drift tubes as well as control of the radio wave frequency is important to assure maximum acceleration. The exit of the particle from the drift tube and the arrival of the accelerating part of the wave must coincide.

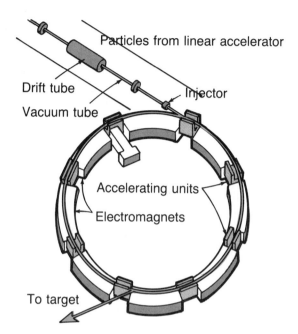

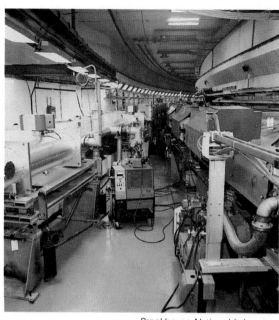

Brookhaven National Laboratory

In a circular accelerator, the "pipe" through which the particles move is in the shape of a circle, or slightly modified circle, Figure 28-5. Particles are accelerated by electric fields in several locations around the ring. The path of the particles is confined to the ring by huge magnets surrounding the ring. As the particles are accelerated, the magnetic field must be increased to keep the particles in the ring. Careful synchronization of acceleration and increasing magnetic fields is important. Hence, the device is called a **"synchrotron."**

Recently, some experiments have involved two rings whose beams collide head-on. An accelerator is used to produce a stream of particles which is stored in one ring. The accelerator can then generate a second stream to collide with those already in the storage ring.

FIGURE 28-5. The synchrotron is a circular accelerator. Magnets are used to control the path and acceleration of the particles.

28:4 RADIOACTIVITY

Scientists use a shorthand method of representing information about a particle. Each "corner" of a symbol for an element (or particle) is used to show some property of the particle. Let's look

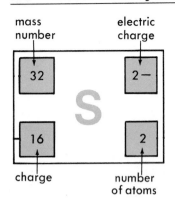

mass number

electric charge

32

2−

S

16

2

charge

number of atoms

Three types of natural radiation
1. alpha particles ($^4_2$He)
2. beta particles ($^0_{-1}e$)
3. gamma rays (γ)

One way radioactive nuclides decay is by positron emission.

K-capture is the process in which the nucleus captures an electron from the first energy level outside the nucleus.

Half-life is the length of time required for one-half of the atoms of a radioactive sample to decay.

at the example in Figure 28-6. We already know that the upper right-hand corner is used to show the electric charge on an ion. The lower right-hand corner is used to show the number of atoms in a formula unit. The upper left-hand corner is used for the mass number, or number of nucleons, in an atom or particle. In the lower left-hand corner, the charge on a particle or the nucleus of an atom is shown. Thus, an electron, which has a negligible mass and a 1− charge, is represented as $^0_{-1}e$. A sulfur nucleus or atom, depending on the case being discussed, is represented as $^{32}_{16}S$.

Three forms of radiation can come from naturally radioactive nuclei. Two of these types are made of particles. The third is made of rays (or beams) of quanta. The particles are alpha (α) and beta (β) particles. The rays are gamma (γ) rays. An **alpha particle** is a helium nucleus ($^4_2$He). It consists of two protons and two neutrons. A **beta particle** is an electron (β^- or $^0_{-1}e$). **Gamma rays** are very high energy X rays. The symbol for gamma radiation is γ. Nuclei which emit rays or particles are said to decay.

Scientists have created many radioactive nuclides that do not exist in nature. These substances are generated by bombarding stable nuclei with accelerated particles or exposing stable nuclei to neutrons in a nuclear reactor, Section 28:10. These artificially radioactive nuclides can decay by α, β, and γ rays as well as several other methods such as positron emission.

Most antiparticles have been formed and observed during the bombardment of normal nuclei in particle accelerators. They may also be formed in other ways. Other artificially radioactive nuclides decay by capturing one of the two 1s electrons outside the nucleus. The first energy level ($n = 1$) is sometimes called the K level. For this reason, this radioactive process is called K-capture.

28:5 HALF-LIFE

The rate at which many radioactive nuclides decay has been determined experimentally. The number of atoms which disintegrate in a unit of time varies directly as the number of atoms present. The length of time it takes for one-half of the atoms to disintegrate has been chosen as a standard for comparison purposes. This time interval is called the **half-life**. For example, the half-life of $^{131}_{56}Ba$ is 12 days. If we start with a given number n of atoms of $^{131}_{56}Ba$, then at the end of 12 days, $\frac{1}{2}n$ atoms will have disintegrated. At that time, we will have $\frac{1}{2}n$ atoms left. At the end of the next 12 days, half of the remaining atoms will have disintegrated and we will have $\frac{1}{4}n$ atoms left. In 12 more days, half of these atoms will have disintegrated and $\frac{1}{8}n$ atoms of $^{131}_{56}Ba$

will remain. How many atoms will remain at the end of another 12 days?

These half-life figures are determined experimentally for a large number of atoms of an individual nuclide. They predict the behavior of large numbers of atoms. At present, it is not possible to predict the exact instant when an individual atom will disintegrate.

Experimentally determined half-life figures are based on a large number of atoms.

Suggestion: The facts given in this chart can be used for practice writing of nuclear equations.

Table 28-1

Half-Life and Decay Mode of Selected Nuclides					
Nuclide	**Half-Life**	**Decay Mode**	**Nuclide**	**Half-Life**	**Decay Mode**
$^{3}_{1}H$	12.3 years	β^-	$^{129}_{55}Cs$	32.1 hours	K-capture and γ
$^{6}_{2}He$	0.802 seconds	β^-	$^{149}_{61}Pm$	53.1 hours	β^- and γ
$^{14}_{6}C$	5730 years	β^-	$^{145}_{64}Gd$	25 minutes	β^+ and γ
$^{19}_{8}O$	29.1 seconds	β^- and γ	$^{183}_{76}Os$	12.0 hours	K-capture and γ
$^{20}_{9}F$	11.6 seconds	β^- and γ	$^{212}_{82}Pb$	10.6 hours	β^- and γ
$^{26}_{14}Si$	2.1 seconds	β^+ and γ	$^{194}_{84}Po$	0.5 seconds	α
$^{39}_{17}Cl$	55.5 minutes	β^- and γ	$^{210}_{84}Po$	138 days	α
$^{49}_{21}Sc$	57.5 minutes	β^- and γ	$^{226}_{88}Fr$	1602 years	α and γ
$^{60}_{26}Fe$	3×10^5 years	β^-	$^{227}_{92}U$	1.3 minutes	α and γ
$^{71}_{30}Zn$	2.4 minutes	β^- and γ	$^{235}_{92}U$	7.1×10^8 years	α and γ
$^{84}_{34}Se$	3.2 minutes	β^-	$^{238}_{92}U$	4.51×10^9 years	α and γ
$^{87}_{37}Rb$	4.8×10^{10} years	β^-	$^{236}_{94}Pu$	2.85 years	α and γ
$^{91}_{42}Mo$	15.5 minutes	β^+ and γ	$^{242}_{94}Pu$	3.79×10^5 years	α
$^{100}_{46}Pd$	4.0 days	K-capture and γ	$^{244}_{100}Fm$	0.0033 seconds	Spontaneous fission

PROBLEMS

1. If you start with 5.32×10^9 atoms of $^{129}_{55}Cs$, how much time will pass before the amount is reduced to 5.20×10^6 atoms?
2. If you start with 5.80×10^{28} atoms of $^{242}_{94}Pu$, how many will remain in 3.03×10^6 years?
3. Define half-life.

1. 321 h
2. 2.27×10^{26} atoms
3. Half-life is the length of time required for one-half of the atoms of a radioactive sample to decay.

28:6 STABILITY OF NUCLIDES

Not all isotopes of an element are equally stable. It is possible, however, to estimate which nuclides will be most stable by applying three rules.

These are comparative rules, not absolute rules.

Rule 1. *The greater the binding energy per nucleon the more stable the nucleus.* The binding energy is the energy needed to separate the nucleus into individual protons and neutrons.

Consider the oxygen-16 nuclide. It contains eight protons, eight electrons, and eight neutrons. We can think of it as eight hydrogen atoms and eight neutrons. Each hydrogen atom has a mass of 1.007 825 2 amu. Each neutron has a mass of 1.008 665 2 amu. Thus, the total mass of an oxygen-16 atom should be 16.131 923 2 amu. However, the actual mass of the oxygen-16 atom is 15.994 915 0 amu. The difference between the calculated mass and the actual mass is called the **mass defect.**

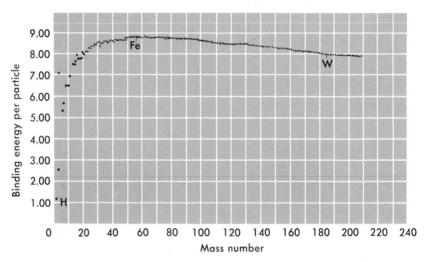

FIGURE 28-7. For heavy elements, the binding energy per particle decreases as mass increases. For lighter elements, the binding energy decreases as mass decreases.

mass of $8\,^1_1\text{H}$ atoms + mass of $8\,^1_0n$ = mass (expected) of $^{16}_8\text{O}$ atom

$$
\begin{aligned}
8(1.007\ 825\ 2\ \text{amu}) + 8(1.008\ 665\ 2\ \text{amu}) &= 16.131\ 923\ 2\ \text{amu} \\
\text{actual mass of } {}^{16}_{8}\text{O atom} &= \underline{15.994\ 915\ 0\ \text{amu}} \\
\text{mass defect} &= 0.137\ 008\ 2\ \text{amu}
\end{aligned}
$$

For an oxygen-16 atom, the mass defect is 0.137 008 2 amu. This mass has been converted to energy and released in the formation of the nucleus. Thus, it is also the energy that must be put back into the nucleus to separate the nucleons.

We can convert this mass defect of 0.137 008 2 amu into its energy equivalent using the equation

$$E = mc^2$$

$$E = \frac{0.137\ 008\ 2\ \cancel{\text{amu}}}{} \left| \frac{1.660\ 40 \times 10^{-17}\ \text{kg}}{1\ \cancel{\text{amu}}} \right| \frac{(2.997\ 93 \times 10^8\ \text{m})^2}{(\text{s})^2}$$

$$= 2.044\ 57 \times 10^{-11}\ \frac{\text{kg} \cdot \text{m}^{2}*}{\text{s}^2}$$

$$= 2.044\ 57 \times 10^{-11}\ \text{J}$$

*Recall that one joule is the energy required to maintain a force of one newton through a distance of one meter. A newton is equivalent to $\text{kg} \cdot \text{m/s}^2$. Thus
$$1\ \text{J} = (\text{kg} \cdot \text{m/s}^2)(\text{m}) = \text{kg} \cdot \text{m}^2/\text{s}^2$$

This energy ($E = 2.044\ 57 \times 10^{-11}$ J) is called the **binding energy.** If we divide the total binding energy by the total number of nucleons in the oxygen atom, we obtain the binding energy per nucleon.

Binding energy is the energy needed to separate the nucleus into individual particles.

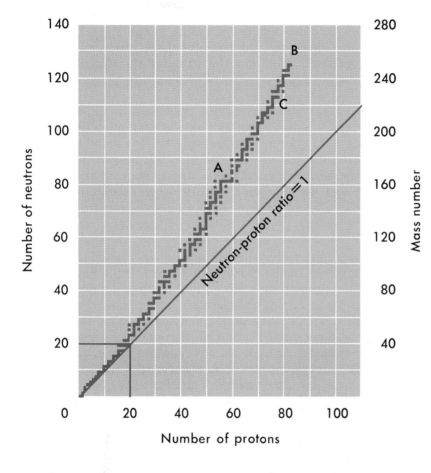

Note: Two kinds of nuclear change lead to greater binding energy: the break-up of large nuclei (fission) and combination of light nuclei (fusion).

FIGURE 28-8. Stable nuclei are represented by the shaded area. The nuclei in region *A* emit neutrons or beta particles. The nuclei in region *B* emit alpha particles. Those in *C* emit positrons or capture electrons.

Total nucleons = 8 protons + 8 neutrons = 16 nucleons

$$\text{Energy per nucleon} = \frac{2.044\ 57 \times 10^{-11}\ \text{J}}{1.6 \times 10^{1}\ \text{nucleons}}$$

$$= 1.277\ 85 \times 10^{-12}\ \frac{\text{J}}{\text{nucleon}}$$

The greater the binding energy per nucleon, the greater the stability of the nucleus. In Figure 28-8, the binding energy per nucleon is graphed against the mass number of known nuclides. Note that energy will be released in two reaction types involving the nucleus. It is released when two small nuclei join to form a medium-sized nucleus. It is also released when one large nucleus

The binding energy per particle is an indication of the stability of a nucleus.

The greater the binding energy, the greater the stability of the nucleus.

splits to form two medium-sized nuclei. In both cases the medium-sized nuclei have greater binding energies per nucleon than the nuclei from which they were produced.

Rule 2. *Nuclei of low atomic numbers with a 1:1 neutron-proton ratio are very stable.* In Figure 28-8, the ratio of neutrons to protons is plotted for the known stable nuclei. For low atomic numbers, the ratio has a value very close to one. However, as the atomic number increases, the value of the neutron-proton ratio steadily increases. The closer the value of the neutron-proton ratio of a nuclide is to the shaded area in this figure, the more stable it is.

Rule 3. *The most stable nuclei tend to contain an even number of both protons and neutrons.* Of the known stable nuclei, 57.8% have an even number of protons and an even number of neutrons. Those with an even number of one kind of nucleon but an odd number of the other are slightly less stable. Thus, 19.8% of stable nuclei have an even number of neutrons but an odd number of protons, 20.9% of stable nuclei have an even number of protons and an odd number of neutrons. Only 1.5% of stable nuclei have both an odd number of neutrons and an odd number of protons.

In Figure 28-8, nuclei falling within the regions *A, B,* and *C* are all unstable. Those nuclei lying in region *A* have excess neutrons and become more stable either by emitting neutrons or, more commonly, beta particles. Nuclei falling within the *B* region are too large for stability and are usually alpha emitters. A nucleus in the *C* region has excess protons and can become stable by positron emission or by *K*-electron capture. Either the loss of a positron (β^+) or the capture of an electron (β^-) results in a new atom. This atom has the same mass number as the original atom but has an atomic number whose value is one unit lower. When a nucleus in the *B* region emits an alpha particle, its composition moves parallel to the 1:1 ratio line toward the *A* region. Note that in the heavy-element radioactivity series, several alpha emissions are always followed by beta emission. The beta emission moves the nucleus back into the *B* region.

28:7 TRANSMUTATIONS

Nuclear reactions can result in the change of one element into another. If a reaction changes the number of protons in the nucleus, an atom with a different atomic number is obtained. This change is called transmutation. The most common isotope of natural uranium is $^{238}_{92}U$. Uranium-238 decays by emitting an alpha particle. The resulting nuclide contains two fewer protons and two fewer neutrons than uranium-238. Thus, it has an atomic number of 90 and a mass number of 234. This new nuclide is a

---

Nuclei with a 1:1 neutron-proton ratio are stable.

Stable nuclei tend to contain an even number of both protons and neutrons.

Stability of a nuclide depends upon
1. the binding energy per particle.
2. the neutron-proton ratio.
3. an even number of both protons and neutrons.

Spontaneous fission is also observed in this region.

Binding energy may be increased by several kinds of nuclear reactions
1. α-particle emission
2. *K*-electron capture
3. β⁺ emission
4. β⁻ emission
5. neutron emission

A nuclear transmutation reaction occurs when an atom with a different atomic number is produced.

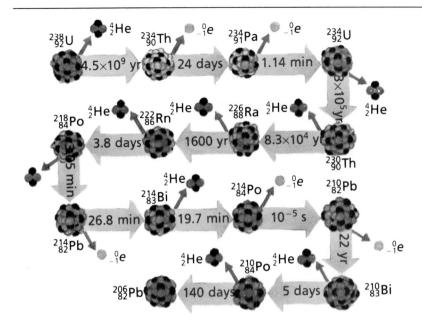

FIGURE 28-9. The nuclear decay of uranium-238 takes place in a series of steps. Note that each new product has a different half-life.

thorium atom, $^{234}_{90}$Th. By a natural process, uranium will transmute to thorium-234.

$$^{238}_{92}\text{U} \rightarrow {}^{234}_{90}\text{Th} + {}^{4}_{2}\text{He} \; (natural)$$

Thorium-234 decays by emitting a beta particle. Since the mass of an electron is negligible, the new nuclide also has the mass number 234, but has one more positive charge than before. Thus, its atomic number is 91. The new atom is $^{234}_{91}$Pa.

$$^{234}_{90}\text{Th} \rightarrow {}^{0}_{-1}\text{e} + {}^{234}_{91}\text{Pa}$$

The series of disintegrations that begins with $^{238}_{92}$U ends with $^{206}_{82}$Pb which is a stable nuclide as shown in Figure 28-9.

The earliest artificial transmutation was performed by Lord Rutherford in 1911. Rutherford bombarded nitrogen-14 with alpha particles. He obtained $^{17}_{8}$O and protons as products. This transmutation can be represented in equation form.

$$^{14}_{7}\text{N} + {}^{4}_{2}\text{He} \rightarrow {}^{17}_{8}\text{O} + {}^{1}_{1}\text{H} \; (artificial)$$

Equations representing nuclear changes are completed by keeping in mind two rules.

Rule 1. *Mass number is conserved in a nuclear change.* In other words, the sum of the mass numbers before the change must equal the sum of the mass numbers after the change.

Rule 2. *Electric charge is conserved in a nuclear change.* The total electric charges before and after a change must be equal.

Some elements undergo natural transmutation.

Students should be able to write and balance nuclear equations. Take the time necessary to allow them to acquire this skill.

In a nuclear equation mass number and electric charge are conserved.

EXAMPLE: Nuclear Equation

Complete the following nuclear equation.

$$^{18}_{9}\text{F} \rightarrow {}^{0}_{+1}e + ?$$

Solving process:

(a) Find the mass number of the unknown product. We know that the mass number is conserved in a nuclear reaction.

mass no. of $_{+1}^{0}e$ + mass no. of ? = 18

mass no. of ? = 18 − mass no. of $_{+1}^{0}e$

= 18 − 0 = 18

(b) Find the charge of the unknown product. We know that electric charge is conserved in a nuclear equation.

charge of $_{+1}^{0}e$ + charge of ? = 9

charge of ? = 9 − charge of $_{+1}^{0}e$

= 9 − 1 = 8+

Use the periodic table to determine the identity of an element.

(c) Determine the identity of the unknown product and complete the nuclear equation. Turn to the periodic table and find which nuclide has an 8+ charge. This nuclide is oxygen. The symbol for an oxygen atom with a mass number of 18 is $^{18}_{8}\text{O}$. Thus, the completed nuclear equation is

$$^{18}_{9}\text{F} \rightarrow {}^{0}_{+1}e + {}^{18}_{8}\text{O}$$

EXAMPLE: Nuclear Equation

Complete the following nuclear equation.

$$^{107}_{45}\text{Rh} \rightarrow {}^{107}_{46}\text{Pd} + ?$$

Solving process:

(a) Find the mass of the unknown product.

$$107 - 107 = 0$$

(b) Find the charge of the unknown product.

$$45 - 46 = -1$$

(c) Determine the identity of the unknown product and complete the nuclear equation. The unknown product has a charge of −1 and a mass of zero. The only particle which fits this description is an electron. The symbol for an electron is $_{-1}^{0}e$. Thus the completed nuclear equation is

$$^{107}_{45}\text{Rh} \rightarrow {}^{107}_{46}\text{Pd} + {}^{0}_{-1}e$$

PROBLEMS

Complete the following equations.

4. $^{27}_{12}\text{Mg}$ decays by beta-minus emission

4. $^{27}_{12}\text{Mg} \rightarrow {}^{0}_{-1}e + {}^{27}_{13}\text{Al}$

5. $^{49}_{24}$Cr decays by beta-plus emission

6. $^{76}_{36}$Kr decays by K-capture

7. $^{213}_{88}$Ra decays by alpha emission

8. $^{231}_{90}$Th decays by alpha emission

5. $^{49}_{24}$Cr $\rightarrow$ $^{0}_{+1}e + ^{49}_{23}$V

6. $^{76}_{36}$Kr $+ ^{0}_{-1}e$ $\rightarrow$ $^{76}_{35}$Br

7. $^{213}_{88}$Ra $\rightarrow$ $^{4}_{2}$He $+ ^{209}_{86}$Rn

8. $^{231}_{90}$Th $\rightarrow$ $^{4}_{2}$He $+ ^{227}_{88}$Ra

28:8 SYNTHETIC ELEMENTS

Elements with atomic numbers greater than 92 are called the transuranium elements. All of the synthesized transuranium elements have been produced by converting a lighter element into a heavier one. Such a change requires an increase in the number of protons in the nucleus. One of the processes of synthetic transmutation occurs as follows. A nuclear reactor produces a high concentration of neutrons which are "packed" into the nucleus of the element plutonium-239. As the mass number builds, a beta particle is emitted. When beta emission occurs, a neutron is converted into a proton with no significant loss of mass. This process produces an element with an atomic number greater than the original element. The process can be written

$$^{239}_{94}\text{Pu} + ^{1}_{0}n \rightarrow ^{240}_{94}\text{Pu}$$

$$^{240}_{94}\text{Pu} + ^{1}_{0}n \rightarrow ^{241}_{94}\text{Pu}$$

$$^{241}_{94}\text{Pu} \rightarrow ^{241}_{95}\text{Am} + ^{0}_{-1}e$$

Americium-241 in turn can be used as a target to produce another element with a higher atomic number. Fermium-256 ($^{256}_{100}$Fm) is the element with the highest atomic number reached in this manner.

A second method of synthesizing transuranium elements makes use of nuclear explosions which produce vast amounts of neutrons. Some neutrons are captured by uranium atoms. Successive electron emissions produce new elements. Fermium-256 is the element with the highest atomic number produced in this way also.

Elements with atomic numbers greater than 100 have been produced using other elements to bombard target elements. Mendelevium-256 was created by bombarding einsteinium-254 with alpha particles.

$$^{254}_{99}\text{Es} + ^{4}_{2}\text{He} \rightarrow ^{256}_{101}\text{Md} + 2^{1}_{0}n$$

Nobelium, atomic number 102, was created by using carbon ions and curium. The production of lawrencium, atomic number 103, made use of boron and californium. One way element 104 can be produced is the bombardment of plutonium by neon. Element 105 can be produced by the bombardment of californium with nitrogen. A heavy-ion accelerator in California is being prepared to accelerate particles as heavy as bromine nuclei.

Transuranium elements have atomic numbers greater than 92.

Some transuranium elements have been produced in nuclear reactors by bombarding plutonium-239 with neutrons.

Glenn T. Seaborg, who received credit for discovery of several transuranium elements, actually applied for and received a patent for elements he has produced. He assigned rights to these patents to the United States Government.

Other transuranium elements have been produced by bombarding target elements with other elements.

It is highly possible that elements with even greater atomic numbers can be produced. The elements produced thus far are characterized by low yields and extremely short half-lives. Only a few atoms of elements 103–107 were first prepared, and these had half-lives of seconds. However, nuclear scientists believe that elements with atomic numbers as high as 126 might be produced.

Eventually, it may be possible to produce synthetic elements with atomic numbers up to 126.

$$^{12}_{6}C + ^{244}_{96}Cm \rightarrow ^{254}_{102}No + 2^{1}_{0}n$$

$$^{11}_{5}B + ^{251}_{98}Cf \rightarrow ^{259}_{103}Lr + 3^{1}_{0}n$$

$$^{12}_{6}C + ^{249}_{98}Cf \rightarrow ^{257}_{104} + 4^{1}_{0}n$$

$$^{15}_{7}N + ^{249}_{98}Cf \rightarrow ^{260}_{105} + 4^{1}_{0}n$$

28:9   USES FOR RADIOACTIVE NUCLIDES

Radioactive nuclides can be used as tracers.

Some nonradioactive nuclides can also be used as tracers.

Since radioactive elements are easily detected by their radiation, they can be used as "tracers." Tracers have a number of practical applications in chemistry. In quantitative analysis, a small amount of a radioactive nuclide of the element sought is introduced into the sample. The proportion of the unstable nuclide recovered in the analytical process is measured. That ratio along with the actual total amount of substance recovered can be used to compute the original quantity of unknown.

Radioactive nuclides have also been used extensively to study the mechanisms of reactions. For example, the detecting of the step-by-step process of photosynthesis is greatly assisted using radioactive nuclides.

Half-life may be used to date objects.

Because of the low original concentration of $^{14}_{6}C$, the method is sensitive only for about four half-lives (23 000 years).

Naturally occurring radioactive nuclides can be used for dating certain objects. Using the time it takes for half of a nuclide sample to decay, we can date when living organisms died up to about 20 000 years ago. By the same technique, we can date the time of formation of rocks as far back as the origin of the earth.

Suppose we want to know what part of the human body utilizes a certain substance in our diet. Using a radioactive nuclide of an element in the substance, we would prepare some of the substance. We would have to use a very low level radiation if we were working with human beings. After a person eats or drinks the substance, we would examine the person's body with radiation detectors. The part of the body showing radioactivity from the nuclide used is located where the substance is concentrated in the body.

Radioactive nuclides (tracers) can be detected using a radiation detector.

28:10   FISSION

Fission is the breakup of a heavy nucleus into two approximately equal parts.

If a very heavy nucleus becomes too unstable, it breaks into two approximately equal parts. At the same time a large amount of energy is released. This process is called **fission.** A nucleus can be made unstable by bombardment with a number of particles, including neutrons.

The heaviest elements are the only ones which exhibit the phenomenon of fission. When a heavy nucleus breaks up, two heavy fragments plus one or more neutrons are emitted. One atom splits due to bombardment by a neutron. In the process of splitting, the atom gives off a neutron. In turn the neutron can cause a second atom to split. This process continues until a very large number of the atoms present have reacted. Thus, the emitted neutrons produce a chain reaction. Since a large energy change is involved in the fission process, a chain reaction can serve as an energy source for various purposes. A **nuclear reactor** is a device for controlling nuclear fission. Reactors can be designed to produce heat for electric power generation plants, or for propulsion units in ships and submarines. In nuclear reactors, the rate of the chain reaction is controlled very carefully. An uncontrolled nuclear chain reaction results in an explosion similar to a nuclear bomb, often incorrectly called an atomic bomb.

Fission reactions release very large amounts of energy.

Suggestion: Point out that mass-energy interconversion involves a nuclear reaction and that the popular term "atomic bomb" is inaccurate. Such a bomb should be called a nuclear bomb.

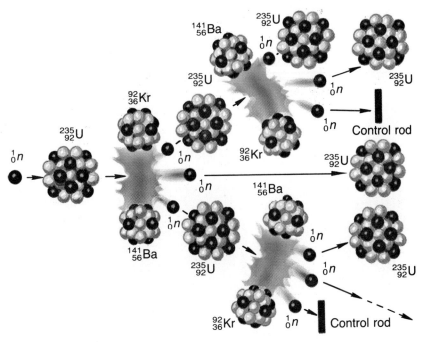

FIGURE 28-10. The fission process in a reactor consists of a chain of fission reactions. Control rods are used to break the chain and slow or stop the reaction.

In a nuclear reactor, a fissionable element is used as fuel. Uranium and plutonium (itself a product of a reactor) can be used as fuels. Not all isotopes will fission under appropriate conditions. Consequently, the chief fuels are $^{235}_{92}U$ and $^{239}_{94}Pu$. It is also possible to convert $^{232}_{90}Th$ to $^{233}_{92}U$ in a reactor and use it as a fuel. The neutrons being produced during fission are traveling too

Water and graphite are good moderators, causing neutrons to slow down as a result of collisions.

In a nuclear reactor, the rate of the reaction is regulated with control rods.

Water is the most widely used coolant preventing a reactor core from overheating.

fast to initiate efficiently the fission process in other atoms. As a result, most reactors contain a material called a **moderator** which causes the neutrons to slow down through collisions. Water and graphite are good moderators.

The reaction rate is controlled by rods composed of good neutron-absorbing materials. By inserting the rod (or withdrawing it somewhat), the reaction rate can be carefully adjusted to the desired level. The energy produced by the fissioning atoms is in the form of kinetic energy of the particles produced. As these particles collide with the materials in the reactor, their kinetic energy is gradually transferred to these other materials and the temperature of the whole system increases. It is necessary, then, to have a coolant to keep the reactor from overheating. Several substances have been tried as coolants, with water being the most popular. Liquid metals, such as Na, Na-K alloys, and gases such as He have been tried. The heat gained by the coolant is used to obtain useful work, such as running an electric generator.

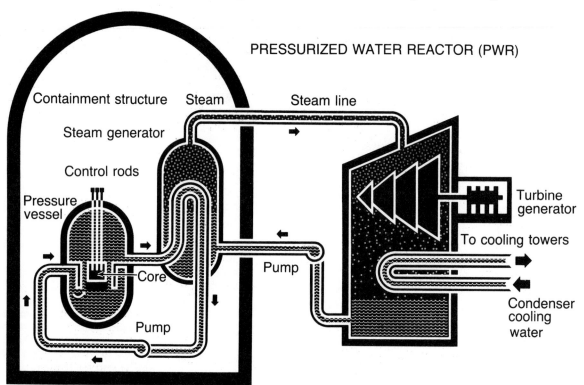

PRESSURIZED WATER REACTOR (PWR)

Containment structure   Steam   Steam line

Steam generator

Control rods

Pressure vessel

Core

Pump

Pump

Turbine generator

To cooling towers

Condenser cooling water

FIGURE 28-11. The diagram shows the parts of a pressurized water fission reactor. Reactors of this design are most common. Note that the cooling towers are not shown.

The whole reactor system is encased in protective materials because of the intense radioactivity. The **containment vessel** keeps radioactive materials from escaping into the environment. It also shields personnel in the plant from the radiation produced in the reactor.

U.S. Dept. of Energy

J. R. Schnelzer

The containment vessel encases the whole reactor system to prevent the escape of radio-active materials.

FIGURE 28-12. Fuel is being loaded into a fission reactor (a). Water, used as a coolant within the reactor, is channeled to cooling towers to prevent thermal pollution.

The demand for energy in the United States has outstripped our ability to produce new sources. Worldwide resources of fossil fuels such as petroleum and coal may last only a few decades. We have begun to utilize fission reactors as a source of electric power. However, they represent only a few percent of the total power production facilities in operation. Fission reactors do not represent an unlimited source of energy. However, they do offer a source of energy for the immediate future. As with other energy sources, there are problems associated with nuclear power. For example, what is to be done with the highly radioactive waste material? Can we be sure that strict safety measures will be maintained at reactor sites? European countries are aggressively pursuing nuclear power as a means of satisfying energy demands. The future of fission power reactors will have to be carefully considered by all people.

Nuclear reactor workers are permitted to receive up to 5 rem/yr of radiation. 100 rem/h results in radiation poisoning. 300–500 rem/h can result in death in 50% of the cases. Background radiation is about 0.1 rem/yr.

28:11 FUSION

The peak of the binding energy curve in Figure 28-7 occurs near the element iron, atomic number 26. We can see how both fission and the emission of small particles by atoms of high atomic number lead to more stable atoms. Note also that stability could be gained by the combination of the smallest nuclei into larger ones. A nuclear reaction in which two or more small nuclei combine to form one larger nucleus is called a **fusion reaction.** Note also that the slope of the binding energy curve is greater on the low atomic number side than it is on the high side. We should therefore expect fusion reactions to produce much greater amounts of energy per particle than fission reactions. This prediction is supported by observation.

In fusion reactions, two or more smaller nuclei combine to form a larger nucleus.

Fusion reactions release much larger amounts of energy than fission reactions.

Alternate fusion reactions for the sun

Bethe cycle for hot stars

$^{12}_{6}C + ^{1}_{1}H \rightarrow ^{13}_{7}N + h\nu$

$^{13}_{7}N \rightarrow ^{13}_{6}C + ^{0}_{+1}e + \nu$

$^{13}_{6}C + ^{1}_{1}H \rightarrow ^{14}_{7}N + h\nu$

$^{14}_{7}N + ^{1}_{1}H \rightarrow ^{15}_{8}O + h\nu$

$^{15}_{8}O \rightarrow ^{15}_{7}N + ^{0}_{+1}e + \nu$

$^{15}_{7}N + ^{1}_{1}H \rightarrow ^{12}_{6}C + ^{4}_{2}He$

Cooler cycle:

$^{1}_{1}H + ^{1}_{1}H \rightarrow ^{2}_{1}H + 2^{0}_{1}e^- + h\nu$

$^{1}_{1}H + ^{2}_{1}H \rightarrow ^{3}_{2}He + h\nu$

$^{3}_{2}He + ^{3}_{2}He \rightarrow ^{4}_{2}He + 2^{1}_{1}H + h\nu$

Scientists have harnessed the fission reaction in a controlled process on a small scale for limited power production. If we could harness the fusion reaction for power production, we would have a solution to energy problems for some time to come. Some of the difficult problems associated with fission reactions as a power source would also be eliminated. The availability of "fuel" for nuclear fusion reactions is much greater than for fission reactions. Also, fusion reactions which are useful for power production do not result in radioactive waste products.

The most likely reactions for fusion power generators are the following.

$$^{2}_{1}H + ^{2}_{1}H \rightarrow ^{3}_{2}He + ^{1}_{0}n$$

$$^{2}_{1}H + ^{2}_{1}H \rightarrow ^{3}_{1}H + ^{1}_{1}H$$

$$^{2}_{1}H + ^{3}_{1}H \rightarrow ^{4}_{2}He + ^{1}_{0}n$$

The last of these reactions is the most promising from the standpoint of power production. However, it does have drawbacks. Tritium ($^{3}_{1}H$) is a radioactive nuclide which occurs naturally in only tiny amounts. It can be produced by exposing lithium-6 to neutrons

$$^{6}_{3}Li + ^{1}_{0}n \rightarrow ^{4}_{2}He + ^{3}_{1}H$$

Isotopes of hydrogen

Tritium $^{3}_{1}H$

Deuterium $^{2}_{1}H$

A disadvantage is that the reactor itself will become radioactive as it is exposed to these radiations.

On the other hand, the reactions involving only deuterium ($^{2}_{1}H$) are free of radioactivity. Also, the supply of deuterium could provide the earth with energy for as long as 10^{12} years. Extraction of deuterium from water supplies would require only a small fraction of the power output of a fusion reactor.

The supply of naturally-occurring deuterium is estimated to be large enough to fuel fusion reactors for 10^{12} years.

Present technology promises practical fusion installations within your lifetime. If certain technical problems are solved, these reactors could appear in the near future. Let us look at some of these problems.

28:12   FUSION REACTORS

In order for two atomic nuclei to undergo fusion, they must come almost into contact. Recall that the nuclear force extends only about a distance equal to the diameter of the nucleus. However, since all nuclei are positively charged, they tend to repel each other strongly. In order for fusion reactions to occur, the reactants must be held in the temperature range of 10^8 to $10^{9}°C$ for a suitable time. The energy requirements to achieve these temperatures are quite high. The length of time required depends upon how closely packed the particles are during that time. At these high temperatures, matter is in the form of plasma. One

Matter must be in the form of plasma ($10^8°C$) for a fusion reaction to occur.

a

Nuclear Division, Union Carbide Corp.

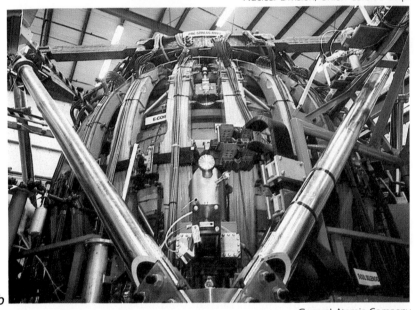

b

General Atomic Company

FIGURE 28-13. The magnetic field coils of a fusion reactor are shown in this interior view (a). Note that the fusion reactor (b) is much smaller than a fission reactor.

major problem in designing a fusion reactor is containing the fuel at that temperature. Containers made from usual materials cannot be used. The plasma would lose heat to them so rapidly that fusion temperatures would never be reached. Since plasmas are charged particles, they are affected by magnetic fields. By properly shaping a magnetic field, a plasma may be contained. As fusion occurs and the temperature rises, the pressure of a plasma causes it to expand. With charged particles in the plasma moving around at tremendous velocities, the plasma itself generates electric currents. Both of these effects make leakage from the magnetic "bottle" a difficult problem to solve. All of these problems are topics of present research. Who can predict what developments in this fascinating field will play in shaping our future!

Fusion reactions can be contained in "magnetic bottles."

Shirley Ann Jackson   (1946-   )

Shirley Jackson has a history of being first at a number of accomplishments. She was first in her high school graduating class and eventually became the first black woman to earn a doctorate degree at Massachusetts Institute of Technology. Following graduation from MIT, she did research at the Fermi National Accelerator Laboratory and at CERN in Geneva, Switzerland.

Although her interest was high energy physics, Dr. Jackson now works with microscopic solid state physics in the development of miniature physical systems such as electronic chips and microtransistors. Although she is currently employed by Bell Laboratories, she retains her tie to MIT through membership on the board of trustees. Dr. Jackson has been an example in providing opportunities for black students and women.

CHEMICAL TECHNOLOGY: Stellar Nucleosynthesis

In addition to the moon, stars, and planets we see in the sky, there are great clouds of gas and dust. About 75% of the matter in the universe is hydrogen and almost 25% is helium. All other elements make about 1% of the matter in the universe.

Let us consider why there are such massive amounts of these two light elements present in the universe. When a star forms, a cloud of hydrogen, helium, and dust contracts through the mutual gravitational attraction the particles have for one another. As these particles fall inward, they pick up speed and their temperatures are thus increased. Eventually, the core of the star is hot enough (10^7 K) to start the fusion reaction among hydrogen atoms to make helium. This process consists of a series of steps.

$$^1_1\text{H} + ^1_1\text{H} \rightarrow ^2_1\text{H} + ^0_1e + \gamma \qquad ^2_1\text{H} + ^1_1\text{H} \rightarrow ^3_2\text{He} \qquad ^3_2\text{He} + ^3_2\text{He} \rightarrow ^4_2\text{He} + 2^1_1\text{H}$$

As the hydrogen fuel is exhausted, the star continues to collapse. This collapse increases the density of the star and raises the temperature (10^8 K) to a range where helium fusion reactions begin.

$$^4_2\text{He} + ^4_2\text{He} \rightarrow ^8_4\text{Be} \quad \textit{unstable} \qquad ^8_4\text{Be} + ^4_2\text{He} \rightarrow ^{12}_6\text{C} \qquad ^{12}_6\text{C} + ^4_2\text{He} \rightarrow ^{16}_8\text{O}$$

Similar processes can continue in massive stars until iron nuclei are formed. Nuclei beyond iron consume energy when formed instead of producing it. As a consequence, the star starts a rapid collapse as the core turns to iron and the nuclear "fires" go out. The collapse of such a large amount of matter (at least four times the mass of the sun) produces an incredible amount of energy. The collapse finally ends in a catastrophic explosion of the entire star. In the process of the explosion, so much energy is available that all natural elements above iron are formed. The exploding star is called a supernova. All the naturally occurring elements above iron in the universe have been produced in supernova explosions.

The length of time required for a star to pass through these stages varies with the star's mass. Small stars burn their fuels slowly and last a long time, as long as 2×10^{10} years. On the other hand, super-massive stars burn quickly, lasting perhaps only 3×10^6 years.

SUMMARY

1. Radioactivity is the phenomenon of particle or quantum emission due to nuclear disintegration. Intro.
2. Radioactive decay is spontaneous; that is, it cannot be controlled. 28:1
3. Subatomic particles are divided into elementary particles called leptons and complex particles called hadrons. 28:2
4. Hadrons are believed to be made of particles called quarks. 28:2
5. Quarks and hadrons are thought to be held together by exchanging gluons and pions respectively. 28:2
6. Linear accelerators and synchrotrons are devices used by nuclear scientists to investigate nuclear structure by bombarding nuclei with high energy particles. 28:3
7. Naturally radioactive nuclides emit three kinds of radiation: alpha (helium nuclei), beta (electrons), and gamma (quanta of energy). 28:4
8. Many subatomic particles in addition to electrons and nucleons have been discovered. Some of these are classified as antimatter. 28:4
9. Each radioactive nuclide emits a characteristic radiation. Therefore, radioactive nuclides are extremely useful in the laboratory and in industry. 28:5, 28:9-28:12
10. The half-life of a radioactive substance is the time it takes for one-half of the atoms of a sample of the substance to disintegrate. 28:5
11. Three relationships can be used to predict the stability of nuclides: 28:6
    (a) the binding energy per particle
    (b) the neutron-proton ratio
    (c) an even number of both protons and neutrons

12. The calculated mass defect of an atom indicates the transformation of mass into binding energy. 28:6

13. Binding energy is the energy needed to separate the nucleus into individual protons and neutrons. 28:6

14. The changing of one element into another is called transmutation. 28:7

15. In completing nuclear equations, both mass number and electric charge must be conserved. 28:7-28:8

16. Fission is the splitting of a large, unstable nucleus into two smaller, approximately equal parts. 28:10

17. A nuclear reactor is a device for containing and controlling a fission reaction. 28:10

18. New elements may be synthesized by combining particles or nuclei with other nuclei. 28:7–28:8

19. Fusion is the combining of two or more small nuclei into one larger nucleus. 28:11

PROBLEMS

9. What are the differences among the three types of natural radiation?

10. What are the tests for stability of an isotope? binding energy, n/p ratio

11. What are some uses for radioactive nuclides? 11. chemical and medical tracers, dating, γ production

12. What are the differences between fusion and fission? 12. Fusion: joining of small nuclei to form one large nucleus.
Fission: splitting a large nucleus into smaller nuclei.

13. Complete the following equations.

   a. $^3_1H \rightarrow ? + ^0_{-1}e$

   b. $^{61}_{30}Zn \rightarrow ? + ^0_{+1}e$

   c. $^9_3Li \rightarrow ^9_4Be + ?$

   d. $^{240}_{96}Cm \rightarrow ? + ^4_2He$

   e. $^{199}_{84}Po + ^0_{-1}e \rightarrow ?$ (K-capture)

13. a. $^3_1H \rightarrow ^3_2He + ^0_{-1}e$

   b. $^{61}_{30}Zn \rightarrow ^{61}_{29}Cu + ^0_{+1}e$

   c. $^9_3Li \rightarrow ^9_4Be + ^0_{-1}e$

   d. $^{240}_{96}Cm \rightarrow ^{236}_{94}Pu \rightarrow ^4_2He$

   e. $^{199}_{84}Po + ^0_{-1}e \rightarrow ^{199}_{83}Bi$

14. How long will it take 6.00×10^{20} atoms of $^{71}_{30}Zn$ to disintegrate to 1.88×10^{19} atoms?

14. 12 min

REVIEW

1. What happens to a positive ion when it reaches the cathode?

1. it is reduced

2. Why is it necessary to separate the half-cells when constructing a voltaic cell? If mixed, they will not conduct.

3. Will Ni react with Zn^{2+}? (Use the table of standard reduction potentials.)

3. no
4. 0.15 V
5. 0.412 g

4. What voltage would you expect from a cell using $Co|Co^{2+}$ and $Pb|Pb^{2+}$ half-cells?

5. How many grams of Sn would be deposited from a Sn^{2+} solution by a current of 0.506 amperes flowing for 22.0 minutes?

6. What will be the products of the electrolysis of a water solution of $CuBr_2$?

7. What voltage could you expect from the following cell at 25°C?
$$Pb\,|\,Pb^{2+}(0.282M)\,\|\,F_2\,|\,F^-\,(0.0400M)$$

8. What voltage could you expect to obtain from a reaction with a free energy change of -26.6 kJ?

9. What is the modern definition of reduction?

10. What is the oxidation number of Br in $AgBrO_3$?

11. What is the oxidation number of Hg in $Hg(ClO_3)_2$? (Chlorine is 5+.)

12. How may an oxidation-reduction reaction be identified?

13. Balance: $Pb + PbO_2 + SO_4^{2-} \rightarrow PbSO_4$ (in acid solution).

14. Balance: $MnO_4^- + Cl^- \rightarrow Cl_2 + Mn^{2+}$ (in acid solution).

15. Balance: $MnO_4^- + I^- \rightarrow I_2 + MnO_2$ (in basic solution).

6. Cu and O_2
7. 3.06 V
8. 0.276 V per e^- transferred
9. gain of electrons
10. 5+
11. 2+
12. at least one element changes oxidation number

13. $Pb + 2SO_4^{2-} + PbO_2 + 4H^+ \rightarrow 2PbSO_4 + 2H_2O$
14. $16H^+ + 2MnO_4^- + 10Cl^- \rightarrow 2Mn^{2+} + 8H_2O + 5Cl_2$
15. $4H_2O + 2MnO_4^- + 6I^- \rightarrow 2MnO_2 + 8OH^- + 3I_2$

ONE MORE STEP

1. Using a Geiger counter or similar device and a radioactive source, determine (a) the change in radiation intensity with change in distance between source and detector, and (b) the shielding effect of paper, masonry, and metal.

2. Determine the difference between "weak" and "strong" interactions between nuclear particles.

3. Prepare a report on the differences and similarities of various accelerators: the cyclotron, the betatron, the synchrotron, and so on.

4. What progress has been made toward large-scale production of energy by nuclear fusion?

5. Investigate the use of $^{14}_{6}C$ for dating the age of once-living objects.

6. Investigate the dating of minerals by the use of naturally occurring radioactive nuclides.

7. Investigate the use of lasers to produce the temperatures necessary for fusion.

READINGS

Agnew, Harold M., "Gas-cooled Nuclear Power Reactors." *Scientific American,* Vol. 244, No. 6 (June 1981), pp. 55-63.

Anderson, Earl V., "Nuclear Energy: A Key Role Despite Problems." *Chemical and Engineering News,* Vol. 55, No. 10 (March 7, 1977), pp. 8-12.

Bunting, Roger K., "Element Number 61." *Chemistry,* Vol. 50, No. 5 (June 1977), pp. 16-18.

Rooth, Claes H., "Geosecs and Tritium Tracers." *Oceanus,* Vol. 20, No. 3 (Summer 1977), pp. 53-57.

Weinberg, Steven, "The Decay of the Proton." *Scientific American,* Vol. 244, No. 6 (June 1981), pp. 64-75.

Many of today's most common products are derived from organic sources. The manufacturing process for ribbon involves a knowledge of organic chemistry. The ribbon fiber is produced from organic compounds. The permanent press characteristics of this synthetic material depends on bonding and structure. The energy used to run the spinning machines probably comes from an organic source. What is organic chemistry? What are the characteristics of organic compounds? How are these compounds classified?

Putsee Vannucci/FPG

CLASSES OF ORGANIC COMPOUNDS

29

Chapter 29 is an introduction to organic chemistry. Nomenclature and the characteristics of hydrocarbons and functional derivatives are presented.

Demonstration—Mix a small amount of potassium permanganate with some concentrated sulfuric acid in an evaporating dish. Dip a glass rod into the mixture and immediately touch the rod with the attached mixture to the wick of an alcohol lamp. The alcohol ignites. Discuss the usefulness of organic compounds as fuels.

Early chemists observed that there were two types of substances—those from living matter and those from nonliving matter. These two types became known as organic substances and inorganic substances. It was found that all organic substances had some similar properties. Most organic compounds were found to decompose easily when heated. Most inorganic substances were observed to change very little, if any, when heated. Also, organic substances were thought to be produced only by living organisms.

Later chemists began to study organic substances in greater detail. They learned that nearly all organic compounds are made of chains and rings of carbon atoms. Chemists then learned to synthesize some simple organic compounds directly from inorganic substances! This amazing discovery marked the beginning of modern organic chemistry. Today, we define **organic chemistry** as the chemistry of carbon compounds.

GOAL: You will gain an understanding of how organic compounds are classified through a study of nomenclature, properties, and functional groups.

29:1 CLASSIFICATION OF HYDROCARBONS

One of the largest classifications of organic compounds is the group known as the hydrocarbons. These compounds are composed only of carbon and hydrogen. Almost all other organic compounds can be considered as derivatives of the simple hydrocarbons. If the carbon atoms are linked in chains, the compounds are called **aliphatic** (al ih FAT ihk) compounds. If the atoms are linked in rings, the compounds are called **cyclic** compounds.

Hydrocarbons are composed of hydrogen and carbon.

Aliphatic compounds have carbon atoms linked in chains.

The chain compounds may be further classified on the basis of the individual carbon-carbon bonds. A chain compound in which all carbon-carbon bonds are single bonds is called an **alkane** (AL kayn). This type of compound is also called a **saturated hydrocarbon** because each carbon-carbon bond is a single bond. Thus, additional atoms can be bonded to the original atoms in the compound only by breaking the compound into two or more fragments.

In saturated hydrocarbons each carbon-carbon bond is a single bond.

Table 29-1

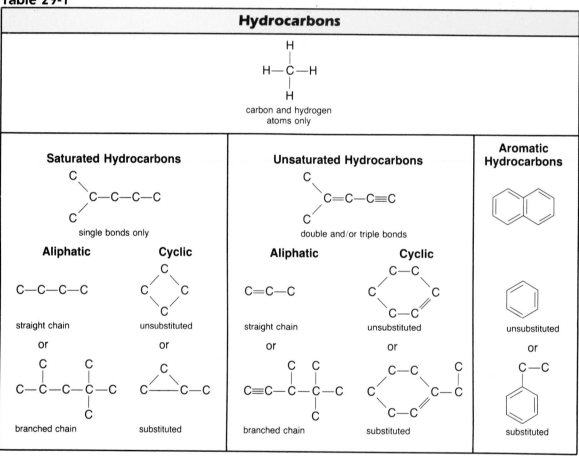

This series of compounds is also called the paraffin series.

29:2 ALKANES

The alkane series is the least complex set of hydrocarbons. The first four members of the alkane series and their formulas are methane, CH_4; ethane, C_2H_6; propane, C_3H_8; and butane, C_4H_{10}. After butane, the members of the alkane series are named using the Greek or Latin prefix for the number of carbon atoms. The word ending characteristic of this family is *-ane*.

Alkanes are saturated hydrocarbons.

Each alkane differs from the next by a —CH_2— group. You can think of this series as being formed by removing a hydrogen atom from one of the carbon atoms, adding a —CH_2— group, and replacing the hydrogen. For example:

$$CH_4 \quad + \quad CH_2 \quad \rightarrow \quad C_2H_6$$

Note that this equation does not represent the actual preparation of an alkane.

A series of compounds whose structures differ from each other by a specific structural unit is called a homologous (hoh MAHL uh guhs) series. In the case of the alkanes, the specific structural unit is —CH_2—. A general formula can be written for all of the members of a homologous series such as the alkanes. For the alkanes, the formula is C_nH_{2n+2}, when n is the number of carbon atoms in the compound.

The simplest alkane is methane. Methane contains one carbon atom and four hydrogen atoms. The structural formula for methane is shown on the right.

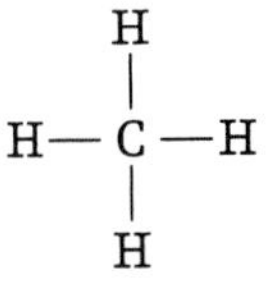

The structural formulas of the next three compounds in the alkane series are

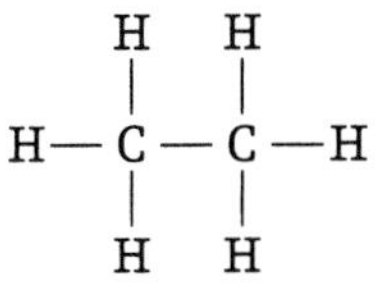

ethane 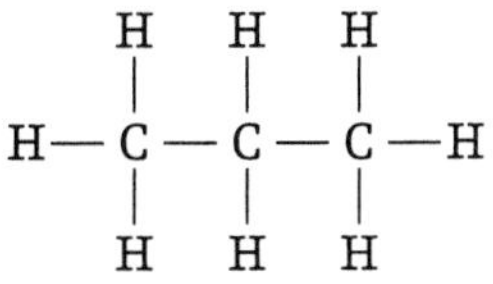   propane 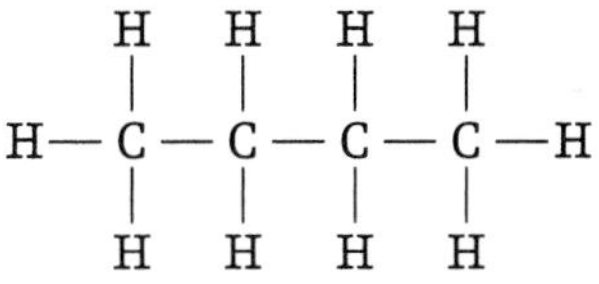   butane

If one hydrogen atom, together with its associated electron, is removed from a hydrocarbon molecule, a radical is left.

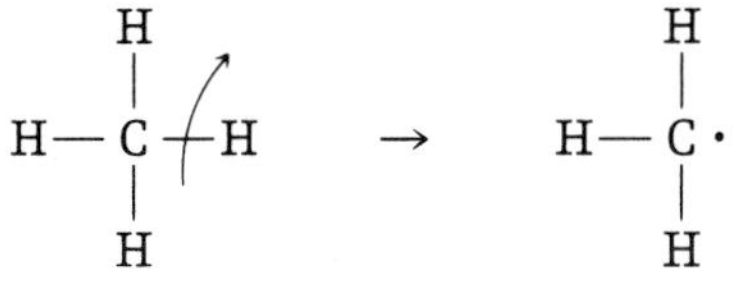

methane   methyl   propane   propyl
               radical   radical

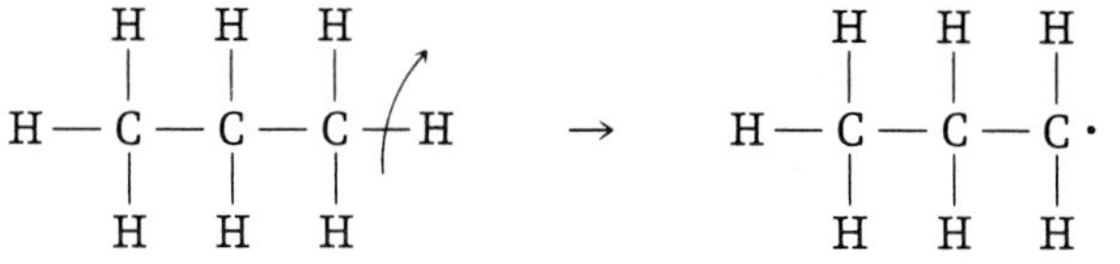

Radicals are named by substituting the ending -*yl* for the normal -*ane* ending of the parent compound.

There are general trends in physical and chemical properties within homologous series. For instance, as the molecular mass of the compounds in a series increases, the boiling point increases as shown in Table 29-2. Alkanes are soluble in nonpolar solvents.

Members of the alkane series differ by —CH_2—.

methylene group

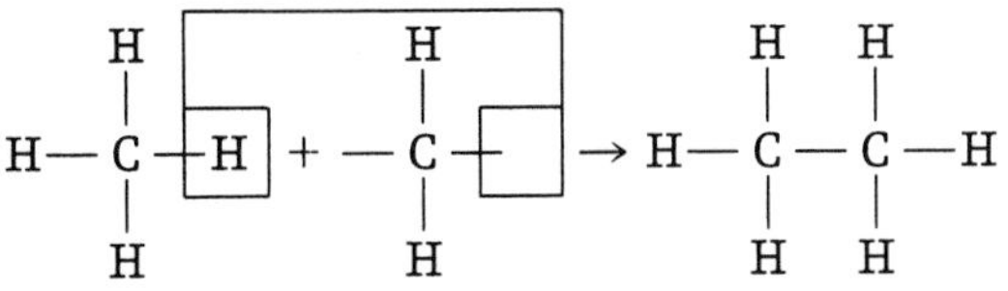

Note: These are conventionalized diagrams. The bonds in the actual molecules are arranged around the carbon atoms in such a way that the four bonds formed by each carbon are as far apart as possible. This results in a tetrahedral distribution of bonds.

Each member of a homologous series differs from each other member by a specific structural unit.

General formula for alkanes: C_nH_{2n+2}.

methane

A hydrocarbon radical is a hydrocarbon molecule from which a hydrogen atom has been removed.

propyl radical

Radicals are named by substituting the -*yl* ending for the normal -*ane* ending.

Table 29-2

Alkanes					
Name of Alkane	Formula	Melting Point, °C	Boiling Point, °C	Name and Formula of Radical	
Methane	CH_4	−183	−162	Methyl	CH_3-
Ethane	C_2H_6	−183	−89	Ethyl	C_2H_5-
Propane	C_3H_8	−188	−42	Propyl	C_3H_7-
Butane	C_4H_{10}	−138	−1	Butyl	C_4H_9-
Pentane	C_5H_{12}	−130	36	Pentyl	$C_5H_{11}-$
Hexane	C_6H_{14}	−95	69	Hexyl	$C_6H_{13}-$
Heptane	C_7H_{16}	−91	98	Heptyl	$C_7H_{15}-$
Octane	C_8H_{18}	−57	126	Octyl	$C_8H_{17}-$
Nonane	C_9H_{20}	−54	151	Nonyl	$C_9H_{19}-$
Decane	$C_{10}H_{22}$	−30	174	Decyl	$C_{10}H_{21}-$
—					
Dodecane	$C_{12}H_{26}$	−10	215	Dodecyl	$C_{12}H_{25}-$
—					
Hexadecane	$C_{16}H_{34}$	+19	288	Hexadecyl	$C_{16}H_{33}-$
Heptadecane	$C_{17}H_{36}$	+23	303	Heptadecyl	$C_{17}H_{35}-$

29:3 NAMING BRANCHED ALKANES

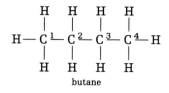

butane

butane

Carbon atoms in a structural formula of an organic compound are given position numbers.

Alkanes are named on the basis of the longest continuous chain of carbon atoms (parent chain).

Parent chain does not necessarily occur in a straight line.

For convenience in naming organic compounds, carbon atoms in a structural formula are given position numbers. In an unbranched chain molecule, the numbering of carbon atoms can begin at either end of the chain as shown on the left for butane.

Not all alkanes have unbranched chains of carbon atoms. In naming branched alkanes, we must first find the longest chain of carbon atoms. This chain is used as the basis of the compound name and is called the parent chain. The parent chain does not necessarily occur in a straight line. Look at the following structure.

The longest chain contains six carbon atoms. Thus, the parent chain is hexane (C_6H_{14}). The carbon atoms of the longest chain are given position numbers beginning at the end of the parent chain closer to the branch. The CH_3- group which is attached to the main chain is called a **branch** or **substituent.** The branch is named as a radical. We indicate, by number, the position of the carbon atom of the parent chain to which the branch (radical) is attached. In our example, the branch is attached to the third carbon. The branch is a methyl radical. The parent chain is hexane. The name of this compound is 3-methylhexane. The name is written with a hyphen between the substituent position number and the substituent name. The substituent and the parent are written as one word. Numbering of the carbon atoms of the parent alkane chain always begins at the end which will give the lowest position numbers to the substituents.

How do we name an alkane which has more than one branch? Consider the following example:

$$
\begin{array}{c}
\text{H} \\
| \\
\text{H}-\text{C}-\text{H} \\
\end{array}
$$

The parent chain is hexane. Both an ethyl group and a methyl group are attached to the parent chain. They are attached to the third carbon. The name of this alkane is 3-ethyl-3-methylhexane. Note that the radicals appear in the name in alphabetical order. Why is the name of this compound not 4-ethyl-4-methylhexane?

If there are two or more substituent groups which are alike, it is convenient to use prefixes such as *di-*, *tri-*, and *tetra-* instead of writing each substituent separately. A comma is placed between the position numbers of the substituents which are alike. For example, the name of the following compound is 2,3-dimethylhexane. Why is the name not 4,5-dimethylhexane?

Substituents or branch chains are attached to the main chain of carbon atoms.

Carbons of parent chain are numbered to give the lowest position numbers to branches.

A prefix is used to indicate two or more identical substituent groups.

Note that the number of positions and the number of groups must agree.

PROBLEMS

1. c

1. What is the correct name for this compound?

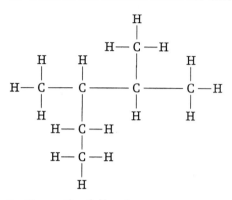

a. 2-ethyl-3-methylbutane
b. 2-methyl-3-ethylbutane
c. 2,3-dimethylpentane
d. 2-methylhexane

2. a. 2,2-dimethylbutane
b. hexane
c. 3-methylpentane
d. 2-methyl-3-ethylhexane

2. Name the following.

a.

c.

b.

d.

3. a.

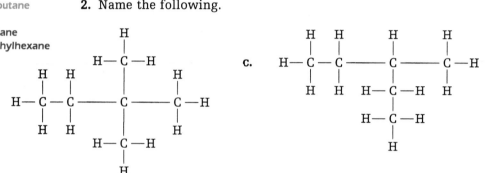

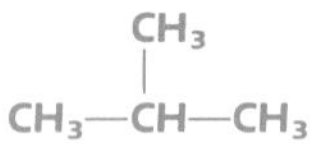

3. Write structural formulas for the following.
a. methylpropane
b. 2,3,4-trimethyloctane
c. 2-methyl-3-ethylhexane
d. 4-propyloctane

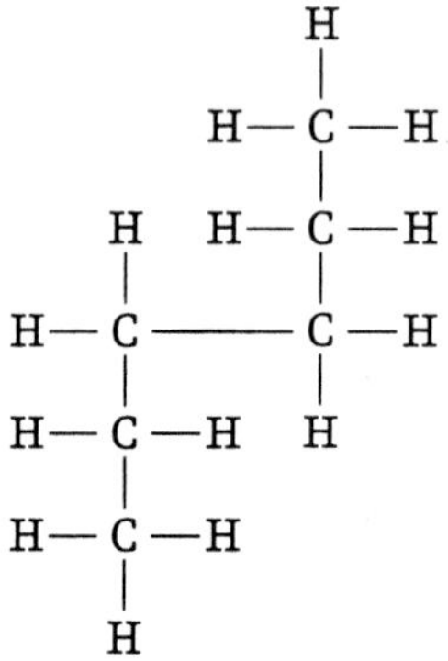

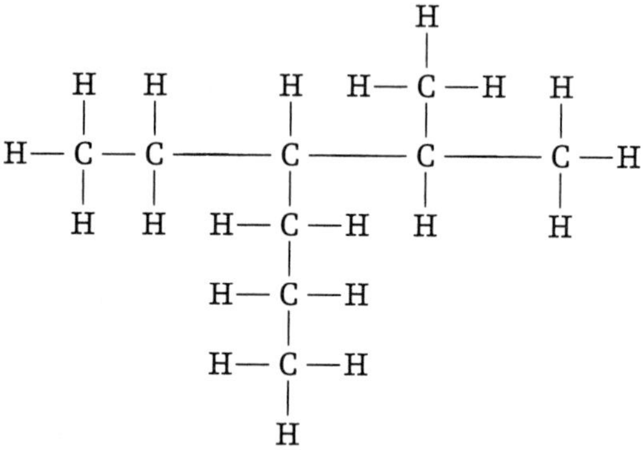

29:4 ISOMERS OF ALKANES

Isomers have the same formula but different molecular structures.

Note that only one structural diagram can be drawn for methane, ethane, or propane. There are, however, two possible structures for butane as shown on page 593.

Each of these two structures of butane is an isomer of butane. It is important for you at this point to review the information on isomers in Chapter 13. Most organic compounds have isomers. There is no known way of predicting exactly how many isomers most compounds can form. Pentane (C_5H_{12}), the next member of the alkane family, has three isomers. Hexane (C_6H_{14}) has five isomers. Heptane (C_7H_{16}) has nine. Isomers are named according to the longest chain and not according to the total number of carbon atoms in the molecule. The second structure of butane is named 2-methylpropane.

Our work will be easier if we modify the structural formulas to a condensed form. There can be only one bond between carbon and hydrogen atoms. In the condensed form of a structural formula, carbon atoms are still written separately. However, the hydrogen atoms that are attached to a carbon atom are grouped with that carbon atom. Thus, the isomers of pentane may be written as

butane

2-methylpropane

Isomers are named according to the longest chain of carbon atoms.

$$CH_3-CH_2-CH_2-CH_2-CH_3$$

pentane

$$CH_3-CH_2-\overset{\displaystyle CH_3}{\underset{\displaystyle |}{CH}}-CH_3$$

2-methylbutane

$$CH_3-\overset{\displaystyle CH_3}{\underset{\displaystyle \underset{\displaystyle CH_3}{|}}{\overset{\displaystyle |}{C}}}-CH_3$$

2,2-dimethylpropane

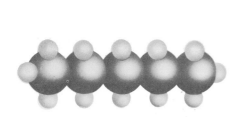

n-pentane

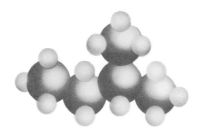

2-methylbutane

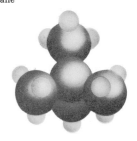

2,2-dimethylpropane

FIGURE 29-1. Note from the models for the isomers of pentane that the C—C bonds are not at 90° or 180° as shown by the structural formulas.

PROBLEMS

4. Name the following.

a. $CH_3-\overset{\displaystyle CH_3}{\underset{\displaystyle |}{CH}}-\overset{\displaystyle CH_3}{\underset{\displaystyle |}{CH}}-CH_2-CH_3$

b. $CH_3-CH_2-CH_2-CH_2-CH_2-CH_2-CH_2-CH_3$

c. $CH_3-CH_2-CH_2-CH_2-\overset{\displaystyle CH_3}{\underset{\displaystyle |}{CH}}-\overset{\displaystyle CH_3}{\underset{\displaystyle |}{\underset{\displaystyle CH_3}{C}}}-CH_3$

d. $CH_3-\overset{\displaystyle CH_3}{\underset{\displaystyle |}{CH}}-\overset{\displaystyle CH_3}{\underset{\displaystyle |}{CH}}-\overset{\displaystyle CH_3}{\underset{\displaystyle |}{CH}}-CH_2-CH_3$

4. a. 2,3-dimethylpentane
   b. octane
   c. 2,2,3-trimethylheptane
   d. 2,3,4-trimethylhexane

e. 2,2-dimethylbutane

e. $CH_3-\underset{\displaystyle \underset{CH_3}{|}}{\overset{\displaystyle \overset{CH_3}{|}}{C}}-CH_2-CH_3$

5. Draw structural formulas (condensed form) for the following.
  a. 2-methylheptane
  b. tetramethylbutane
  c. 2,2,4-trimethylpentane   See Teacher's Guide.
  d. 3-ethyl-2-methylpentane
  e. 3-ethylhexane

5. b. $CH_3-\underset{\displaystyle \underset{CH_3}{|}}{\overset{\displaystyle \overset{CH_3}{|}}{C}}-\underset{\displaystyle \underset{CH_3}{|}}{\overset{\displaystyle \overset{CH_3}{|}}{C}}-CH_3$

6. Hint: there are 5 isomers.

6. Draw structural formulas for all the isomers of hexane.

7. Name each isomer in Problem 6.   **7. a.** hexane
  b. 2-methylpentane
  c. 3-methylpentane
  d. 2,2-dimethylbutane
  e. 2,3-dimethylbutane

$H-\underset{\displaystyle \underset{CH_2CH_3}{|}}{\overset{\displaystyle \overset{CH_2CH_2CH_3}{|}}{C}}-CH_3$

3-methylhexane

$CH_3-\underset{\displaystyle \underset{CH_2CH_3}{|}}{\overset{\displaystyle \overset{CH_2CH_2CH_3}{|}}{C}}-H$

3-methylhexane

Optical isomers are mirror images of each other.

Asymmetric molecules of the same substance are optically active.

29:5   OPTICAL ACTIVITY

Another kind of isomerism concerns organic molecules of the same compound which are asymmetrical with respect to each other. They are mirror images. An **asymmetric carbon** atom is one attached to four different particles. As an example of asymmetrical objects, look at your hands. We think of our hands as being identical. Yet there is no way we can rotate our left hand in order to make it look exactly like our right hand. The left hand is a mirror image of the right hand. They have an asymmetrical relationship. So do the molecules of 3-methylhexane shown on the left. It is impossible to rotate the one to look exactly like the other. The two isomers are called **stereoisomers.** Stereoisomers have the same physical properties except in their behavior toward light. Asymmetrical molecules are said to be **optically active.** They have the property of rotating the plane in which polarized light is vibrating.

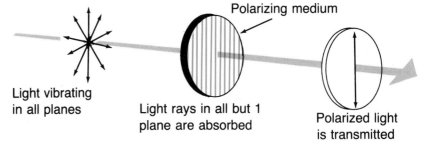

FIGURE 29-2. When light enters a polarizer, only those waves vibrating in one plane can pass through.

Light vibrating in all planes

Light rays in all but 1 plane are absorbed

Polarizing medium

Polarized light is transmitted

Polarized light vibrates in only one plane.

The electromagnetic waves in a beam of light vibrate in all directions, not just up and down or sideways. However, it is possible, using the proper kind of filter, to obtain light in which all the vibrations are taking place in the same plane. Such light is called **polarized light.**

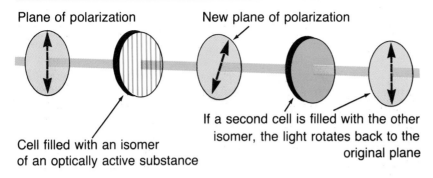

Plane of polarization

New plane of polarization

Cell filled with an isomer
of an optically active substance

If a second cell is filled with the other
isomer, the light rotates back to the
original plane

FIGURE 29-3. The polarimeter measures the rotation of polarized light as it passes through a solution containing an optically active substance.

An optically active substance will rotate the plane of polarized light when the light is passed through the substance. The amount of rotation is a characteristic of the substance through which the light is passing. This property is a useful analytical tool when an instrument called a **polarimeter** is used. It measures the amount of rotation of polarized light passing through a solution of an unknown substance. The technique is most useful in measuring unknown concentrations of solutions.

A polarimeter measures the amount that a compound rotates polarized light.

The sugars dextrose and levulose were named for their optical activity. Dextrose rotates light to the right and levulose rotates light to the left. In the example using 3-methylhexane, one form would rotate plane polarized light in one direction. The other form would rotate it in the other direction.

A dextrorotatory substance (Latin: *dexter*, right) rotates light to the right. A levorotatory substance (Latin: *laevus*, left) rotates light to the left.

29:6 NUCLEAR MAGNETIC RESONANCE

Chemists use a property of the atomic nucleus to distinguish among certain kinds of isomers. The technique is particularly useful for identifying structural, positional, and functional isomers. In Section 9:13 we found that nucleons have the property of spin. We know that a charged particle in motion creates a magnetic field. A spinning proton, then, should have a magnetic field, but a spinning neutron should not. It can be shown that both particles have a magnetic field! Just as electrons pair in orbitals, like nucleons also pair. If two neutrons pair, their spins will be opposite and their magnetic fields will cancel each other. However, for nuclei with unpaired nucleons, the nucleus as a whole should possess a magnetic field.

Spinning protons and neutrons have magnetic fields.

Nuclei with unpaired nucleons possess a magnetic field.

If a nucleus with a magnetic field is placed in an external magnetic field, two energy states are possible for the nucleus. The two fields are either aligned or opposed. The opposed fields represent a higher energy state. The energy required to "flip" the nucleus from one state to the other is affected by nearby atoms in the molecule. The energy can be measured by a process called **nuclear magnetic resonance** (NMR) **spectroscopy.**

The magnetic field of a nucleus when placed in an external magnetic field will be either aligned or opposed.

About two-thirds of the naturally occurring nuclei have magnetic fields. The hydrogen atom, with its single proton as a nucleus, has been by far the most widely studied through NMR spectroscopy. An NMR spectrum of an organic molecule will show several energy peaks. These peaks correspond to hydrogen atoms (protons) in different locations in the molecule. Each hydrogen atom with a different arrangement of the other atoms around it will give a separate peak.

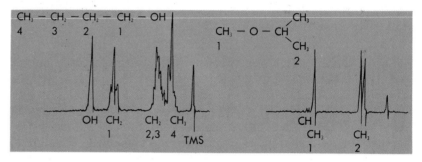

FIGURE 29-4. NMR spectroscopy can be used to identify a sample of organic isomers. The height of the peaks and the points at which they occur are characteristic of the structure of the molecule.

29:7 CYCLOALKANES

We have studied two forms of saturated hydrocarbons: straight-chain forms (alkanes) and branched-chain forms (also alkanes). There is a third form of saturated hydrocarbons; these cyclic forms are called cycloalkanes. Cycloalkanes contain only single bonds and have the general formula C_nH_{2n}. Cycloalkanes occur in petroleum in such forms as cyclopropane, cyclopentane, and cyclohexane.

Cycloalkanes are single-bond ring compounds.

General formula for cycloalkanes: C_nH_{2n}

In a structural formula for an organic molecule, a carbon atom is represented by the intersection of each pair of straight lines. All other bonds of the carbon atoms are to hydrogen atoms.

The formation of a ring causes bond strain in all cycloalkanes except cyclohexane.

A strained bond results when the molecular geometry shows the bonding electrons to be closer than the normal 109.5°.

These diagrams are somewhat unwieldy. Organic chemists use stylized drawings to represent cyclic compounds. In the symbols for cyclic compounds, a carbon atom is understood to be at the point where each pair of straight lines meets. Each carbon atom is understood to be bonded to enough hydrogen atoms to produce a total of four bonds. Standard symbols can be used to represent the first five cycloalkanes.

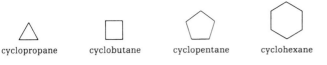

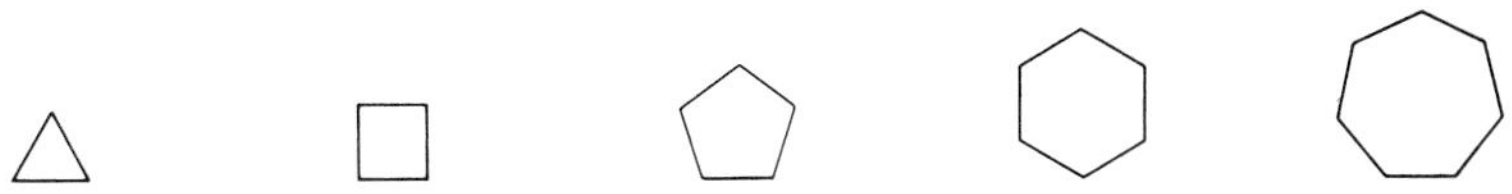

cyclopropane   cyclobutane   cyclopentane   cyclohexane   cycloheptane

In naming cycloalkanes, the ring carbons are numbered so as to give the substituents the lowest set of numbers. Some derivative compounds of the cycloalkanes are shown on the right.

Recall that the normal bond angles around a single-bonded carbon atom are 109.5°. The interior angle of an equilateral triangle is 60°. Thus, the C—C—C bond angle in cyclopropane is 60°. Bonding electrons forced that close exert a strong repelling force on each other. These bonds are called "strained" bonds and lead to a less stable molecule than a similar chain hydrocarbon. Other cycloalkanes also exhibit strained bonds.

Cyclohexane is an industrially important cycloalkane. It is produced from benzene (Section 13:7) and is used as a raw material in making nylon.

29:8 ALKENES

Some hydrocarbons contain multiple bonds between carbon atoms. These hydrocarbons may combine with other elements or compounds by adding on at the multiple bond. When addition occurs, the carbon chain remains unbroken. Thus, hydrocarbons which contain multiple bonds are called **unsaturated hydrocarbons.**

Unsaturated hydrocarbons containing double bonds between carbon atoms are called **alkenes** (AL keens) or olefins (OH leh fihns). Alkenes are another homologous series of hydrocarbons. The names of these compounds end in -ene. The -ene ending tells you that there is double bonding between carbon atoms.

The alkenes constitute a homologous series with the general formula C_nH_{2n}. The first five members of the alkene series are ethene, C_2H_4; propene, C_3H_6; butene, C_4H_8; pentene, C_5H_{10}; and hexene, C_6H_{12}. As with the alkanes, there are general trends in the physical and chemical properties of alkenes as the molecular mass increases.

Since the carbon atoms in an alkene are held together by two pairs of electrons, they are closer than two carbon atoms held by a single bond. The double bond is stronger than a single bond. Since the second pair of electrons (the pi bond) is further from the two nuclei than the sigma bond, the double bond is not twice as strong as a single bond. In addition, the greater π bond-nuclei distance makes a double bond more reactive than a single bond. The less tightly held π electrons are more easily attacked by a reactant. The arrangement of the π electron cloud off the axis

Demonstration—You can test for unsaturated bonds in bacon by placing 3-4 pieces of very crisp bacon in a flask that has been filled with Br_2 vapor. Shake well. In the stoppered flask, the color of Br_2 disappears. The glycerol part of fat molecules is converted into an unsaturated substance called acrolein

In cyclobutane, the internal angle is 100°.

CH₃

methylcyclopropane

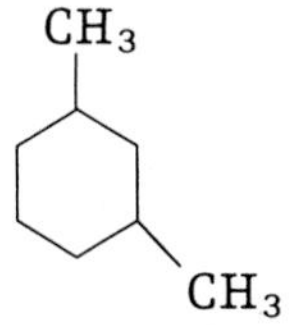

CH₃

CH₃

1,3-dimethylcyclohexane

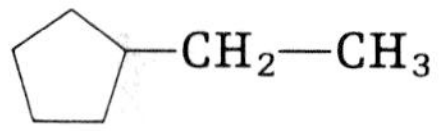

—CH₂—CH₃

ethylcyclopentane

Unsaturated hydrocarbons contain multiple bonds.

H   H
 C::C
H   H

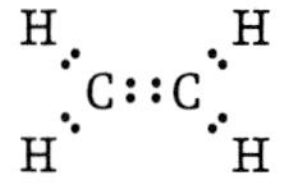

carbon-carbon double bond

Alkenes contain double bonds.

This term originated because in these compounds fewer than the four possible single carbon bonds are formed; i.e., not all bonds are single bonds.

General formula for alkenes: C_nH_{2n}.

Double bond is stronger than a single bond.

Demonstration — Show the presence and reactivity of a double bond by adding a few cm³ of bromine water to some cyclohexane, and then cyclohexene in separate test tubes. Use fume hood. Repeat adding Br_2(aq) to warm cottonseed oil.

(Figure 13-13) prevents free rotation of the atoms on either end of the bond. This rigidity allows for the possibility of geometric isomers.

29:9 NAMING ALKENES

With the introduction of double bonds, a new way of forming positional isomers is introduced. Butene in a straight chain can still have two isomers. These isomers are shown on the left.

Compounds with double bonds, which exist in isomeric form, are named by using a position number for the double bond. The number comes from the carbon atom on which the double bond begins, and is always placed before the name of the parent compound.

Alkenes are numbered so that the lowest position number is assigned to the first carbon atom to which the double bond is attached. The parent compound is named from the longest continuous chain containing a double bond. Thus, the name of the following alkene is 3-propyl-1-heptene.

$$\overset{1}{C}H_2$$
$$\overset{\|}{\underset{2}{C}H}$$
$$\overset{7}{C}H_3\!\!-\!\!\overset{6}{C}H_2\!\!-\!\!\overset{5}{C}H_2\!\!-\!\!\overset{4}{C}H_2\!\!-\!\!\overset{3}{C}H\!\!-\!\!CH_2\!\!-\!\!CH_2\!\!-\!\!CH_3$$

The double bond also makes possible another kind of isomerism: geometric isomerism. This type of isomerism was discussed in Chapter 13.

Two alkenes are commercially important, ethene (common name *ethylene*) and propene (common name *propylene*). In fact, ethene is the number one organic chemical in industry, over 10 million tons per year are produced! It is obtained chiefly as one product of the refining of petroleum (Section 30:6). It is used to produce plastics, antifreeze, synthetic fibers, and solvents. Propene is also a by-product of petroleum refining, and is used to manufacture plastics and synthetic fibers. Double bonds may also be found in cyclic compounds. A typical cycloalkene is cyclohexene shown on the left.

A single molecule may contain more than one double bond. In that case the *-ene* ending must be preceded by a prefix indicating the number of double bonds in the molecule. Thus, the compound $CH_2\!\!=\!\!CH\!\!-\!\!CH\!\!=\!\!CH_2$ is named 1,3-butadiene. 1,3-butadiene is produced from petroleum in large quantities to be used in the production of synthetic rubber.

1-butene

2-butene

cyclohexene

1,3-cyclohexadiene

29:10 ALKYNES

A third homologous series of hydrocarbons consists of molecules containing triple bonds between carbon atoms.

$$H:C::::C:H$$

carbon-carbon triple bond

Compounds with triple-bonded carbon atoms are called **alkynes** (AL kyns). Alkynes constitute a homologous series with the general formula C_nH_{2n-2}. They are important raw materials for industries producing synthetic materials such as plastics and fibers. Chemically, alkynes are very reactive. The alkynes are named just as the alkenes, except the ending *-yne* replaces *-ene.* *Acetylene* is the common name for ethyne, the first member of this series. Acetylene is commercially the most important member of the alkyne family. The first three members of the alkyne family are ethyne, C_2H_2; propyne, C_3H_4; and butyne, C_4H_6.

In naming alkynes, the numbering system for location of the triple bond and the substituent groups follows much the same pattern as was used for naming the alkenes. For example, the name of the following compound is 4,4-dimethyl-2-pentyne.

$$\overset{1}{C}H_3-\overset{2}{C}\equiv\overset{3}{C}-\overset{4}{\underset{\underset{CH_3}{|}}{\overset{\overset{CH_3}{|}}{C}}}-\overset{5}{C}H_3$$

29:11 AROMATIC HYDROCARBONS

To an organic chemist, one of the most important organic compounds is benzene, a cyclic hydrocarbon. Its structural formula can be written

The benzene ring is diagrammed as

In this structural representation, it is assumed that there is a carbon atom at each corner with one hydrogen atom attached. Note from Chapter 13 that the benzene ring has a conjugated

Alkynes contain triple bonds.

$$H-C\equiv C-H$$
ethyne (acetylene)

propyne

2-butyne

General formula for alkynes: C_nH_{2n-2}.

Alkynes are very chemically reactive.

The lowest possible positional number is assigned to the first triple-bonded carbon atom.

Compounds with two or more triple bonds are not alkynes. They belong to groups called alkadiynes, alkatriynes, etc. The second triple bond does not have much effect on the first unless they are relatively close in the chain.

The actual molecule is considered a resonance hybrid of these two structures.

The benzene ring contains a conjugated system of bonds.

Explain to students that it is not necessary for a compound to have a distinctive odor for it to be an aromatic compound. It is only necessary for the compound to include a benzene ring.

cyclohexane

Aromatic compounds are generally derived from benzene.

Naphthalene, $C_{10}H_8$, has a fused ring structure.

naphthalene

Anthracene, $C_{14}H_{10}$, forms when three benzene rings fuse together.

The radical formed from a benzene ring is the phenyl radical.

phenyl radical

system of double and single bonds in a continuous loop. Therefore, it possesses great stability. This diagram should not be confused with the symbol for cyclohexane. Cyclohexane is an alkane composed of only single bonds.

Thousands of compounds are derived from benzene. The study of benzene derivatives constitutes a whole branch of organic chemistry. Most of these compounds have rather distinctive odors. Thus, they are called **aromatic compounds.** Aromatic compounds are normally named as derivatives of benzene. Aromatic compounds occur in small quantities in some petroleum reserves. They occur to a large extent in coal tar obtained from the distillation of coal. Some compounds consist of a fused system of several rings. These compounds have properties similar to benzene. An example of a fused ring compound is naphthalene. The symbol for this fused ring system is shown on the left.

Chemists have found a number of compounds which exhibit behavior similar to benzene-containing compounds, but which do not contain a benzene ring. All of these aromatic compounds, both with and without benzene rings, have a common structural feature. This feature is a cyclic conjugated pi electron system containing $(4n + 2)$ pi electrons. The symbol n stands for any whole number. For benzene, with six pi electrons, $n = 1$. For naphthalene, with 10 pi electrons, $n = 2$.

The radical formed by removing a hydrogen atom from a benzene ring is called the phenyl radical. The symbol for the phenyl radical is shown on the left.

Some examples of benzene compounds are

CH$_3$	CH$_2$—CH$_3$	CH=CH$_2$	CH$_3$—CH—CH$_3$	CH$_3$
methylbenzene (toluene)	ethylbenzene	phenylethene (styrene)	2-phenylpropane (cumene)	1,4-dimethylbenzene (p-xylene)

Do not confuse the phenyl radical with the benzyl radical which is

Benzene, toluene, and xylene are synthesized from petroleum. Ethylbenzene and cumene are made from benzene, while styrene is made from ethylbenzene. All of these compounds are important to our economy. Benzene is used in making plastics, fibers, and in enriching gasoline. Toluene is also used to improve the quality of gasoline, as well as in the production of explosives and other chemicals. The explosive TNT is 2,4,6-trinitrotoluene. Ethylbenzene is converted almost entirely to styrene, which in turn, is a vital component of synthetic rubber, plastics, and paints. The compound p-xylene is a raw material for polyester fibers and cumene is used in making plastics. Other xylenes, 1,2- and

1,3-dimethylbenzenes, are used in producing chemicals, plastics, and in enriching gasoline. A very large part of our synthetic materials industry is based upon aromatic compounds containing a benzene ring.

Aromatic compounds are economically important to many chemical industries such as rubber, plastics, fibers, explosives, paint, and petroleum.

29:12 HALOGEN DERIVATIVES

Atoms other than carbon and hydrogen can be substituted for part of a hydrocarbon molecule. When this substitution occurs, the chemical reactivity of the hydrocarbon is generally increased. The nonhydrocarbon part of the molecule is called a functional group. Most of the chemical reactivity of the substituted hydrocarbon is due to the functional group.

One family of substituted hydrocarbon molecules has a halogen atom substituted for a hydrogen atom. For example, if we substitute a bromine atom for a hydrogen atom on methane, we obtain CH_3Br. The name of this compound is bromomethane. It is also possible to replace more than one hydrogen atom by halogen atoms. In the compound $CHCl_3$, three chlorine atoms have been substituted for three of the hydrogen atoms in a methane molecule. The name of this compound is trichloromethane. You may know this compound by its common name, *chloroform.* Chloroform has been widely used as a solvent. It was once used as an anesthetic. In the compound CCl_4, four chlorine atoms have been substituted for the four hydrogen atoms in a methane molecule. The common name of this tetrachloromethane compound is carbon tetrachloride. These compounds are named as derivatives of the hydrocarbons.

In large chains, we number the carbon atoms to avoid any confusion in naming the compounds. Suppose we have a chain which contains both a double bond and a halogen. In this case, begin the numbering at the end closer to the double bond. Thus, the name of the following compound is 1,4-dichloro-1-butene.

Substitutions in a hydrocarbon generally increase the reactivity.

$$Cl-\overset{\overset{\displaystyle Cl}{|}}{\underset{\underset{\displaystyle Cl}{|}}{C}}-Cl$$

tetrachloromethane

$$Cl-\overset{\overset{\displaystyle H}{|}}{\underset{\underset{\displaystyle Cl}{|}}{C}}-Cl$$

trichloromethane

$$H-\overset{\overset{\displaystyle H}{|}}{\underset{\underset{\displaystyle H}{|}}{C}}-Br$$

bromomethane

A halogen derivative has a halogen atom substituted for a hydrogen atom.

Substituted hydrocarbons are named with lowest possible position numbers for the substituents.

Note that the double bond has precedence over the halogen.

$$H-\overset{\overset{\displaystyle H}{|}}{\underset{\underset{\displaystyle Cl}{|}}{\overset{4}{C}}}-\overset{\overset{\displaystyle H}{|}}{\underset{\underset{\displaystyle H}{|}}{\overset{3}{C}}}-\overset{\overset{\displaystyle H}{|}}{\underset{\underset{\displaystyle H}{|}}{\overset{2}{C}}}=\overset{\overset{\displaystyle H}{|}}{\underset{\underset{\displaystyle Cl}{|}}{\overset{1}{C}}}-H$$

In aromatic compounds, it is necessary to indicate the relative positions of the various substituent groups on the ring. If two or more substituents are attached to the benzene ring, it is necessary to assign position numbers to the carbon atoms of the ring. The atoms in the benzene ring are numbered so as to give the smallest position numbers to the substituents. For example, the name of the compound shown on the right is 1,3-dibromobenzene, not 1,5-dibromobenzene.

1,3-dibromobenzene

In the naphthalene molecule, the 1-position is next to the atom without a hydrogen atom attached. There are four 1-positions possible in each molecule of naphthalene. The 1-position which gives the lowest numbers to substituents is always used. The numbering system for naphthalene is as follows.

naphthalene   2-chloronaphthalene   1,3-dibromonaphthalene

Several more examples which illustrate the naming of substituted hydrocarbons are

1-bromopropane   2-bromopropane   bromobenzene   1,3-dichlorobenzene

1,2-dichloroethane   chloroethene   4-chloro-2-pentene   1-iodonaphthalene
(ethylene dichloride)   (vinyl chloride)

1,2-dichloroethane (common name *ethylene dichloride*) is manufactured in large quantities from ethene. In turn, it is converted to chloroethene (common name *vinyl chloride*). The vinyl chloride is used to make a plastic, polyvinyl chloride (PVC), which is widely used in numerous applications, such as water and waste piping.

29:13   ORGANIC OXYGEN COMPOUNDS

Hundreds of thousands of organic compounds contain oxygen as well as hydrogen and carbon. Many of these compounds are familiar household items. Many more are important solvents and reactants in industry. Table 29-3 lists the names of the principal classes of oxygen-containing compounds. It also gives the general formula of the family. The symbol $R-$ represents any hydrocarbon radical. Thus, $R-OH$ is the general formula for alcohols. If $R-$ represents CH_3-, the alcohol has the formula CH_3OH. This alcohol is methanol. The endings in the third column indicate the method of naming compounds of each class.

Table 29-3

	Organic Compounds Containing Oxygen*		
Class	**General Formula**	**Ending**	**Example**
Alcohol	R—O—H	-ol	CH_3OH methanol
Ether	R—O—R'	-oxy-	$CH_3OCH_2CH_3$ methoxyethane
Aldehyde	R—$\overset{\overset{\textstyle O}{\|\|}}{C}$—H	-al	CH_3CH_2CHO propanal
Ketone	R—$\overset{\overset{\textstyle O}{\|\|}}{C}$—R'	-one	$CH_3COCH_2CH_3$ butanone
Acid	R—$\overset{\overset{\textstyle O}{\|\|}}{C}$—O—H	-oic acid	$CH_3CH_2CH_2CH_2COOH$ pentanoic acid
Ester	R—$\overset{\overset{\textstyle O}{\|\|}}{C}$—O—R'	-yl -oate	$CH_3CH_2CH_2OOCCH_3$ propyl ethanoate

*R— and R'— each represent a hydrocarbon radical. The two radicals may be the same, or they may be different.

29:14 ALCOHOLS AND ETHERS

Alcohols contain the hydroxyl group, —OH. Yet alcohols are neither acidic nor basic. The hydrogen atom is displaced only by active metals. Methanol, CH_3OH, is manufactured from CO and H_2 and is used extensively in producing plastics and fibers. Ethanol, CH_3CH_2OH, is produced from ethene and is one of our most important solvents as well as a raw material for further chemical manufactures. 2-propanol, $CH_3CHOHCH_3$, is produced from propene and is converted to acetone, an important solvent. 2-propanol with 30% water added is drugstore "rubbing alcohol".

The lower molecular mass alcohols are soluble in water through hydrogen bonding with the water. Alcohols with four or more carbon atoms, however, have such a large nonpolar part of the molecule that they are not soluble in water, a polar solvent.

It is possible to have more than one hydroxyl group in a single molecule.

$$\begin{array}{cc} CH_2 & \!\!\!\!-CH_2 \\ | & | \\ OH & OH \end{array}$$

This compound is called 1,2-ethanediol. Its common name is *ethylene glycol* and as such it is sold in large amounts as automobile cooling system antifreeze.

Alcohol molecules contain a hydroxyl functional group, R-OH represents an alcohol molecule.

Alcohols contain the hydroxyl group, R-OH, but they are neither acidic nor basic.

Lower molecular mass alcohols are water soluble due to hydrogen bonding with the water.

See the Teacher's Guide for demonstration of hydrogen bonding.

A single molecule, having two hydroxyl groups, has a name ending in *-diol*.

When hydroxyl groups are attached to the benzene ring, the resulting compounds tend to be slightly acidic. The simplest of these compounds is phenol

Phenol is produced from cumene and is used to make plastics, drugs, and fibers. Since aromatic hydroxyl compounds differ somewhat in properties from most alcohols, they are classed as **phenols.**

Ethoxyethane (diethyl ether) was used for many years as an anesthetic. The cyclic ether, ethylene oxide,

$$CH_2 \overset{}{\underset{O}{\diagdown \diagup}} CH_2$$

is synthesized from ethene. In addition to being converted to ethylene glycol, it is also used in making fibers, films, and detergents. Propylene oxide,

$$CH_3 - CH \overset{}{\underset{O}{\diagdown \diagup}} CH_2$$

produced from propene, is used in making plastics, cellophane, and hydraulic fluids.

29:15 ALDEHYDES AND KETONES

Methanal, better known as *formaldehyde,* is manufactured from methanol and is used to make plastics and adhesives. There are no other aldehydes of great industrial significance. Both aldehydes and ketones are characterized by the carbonyl group, $C=O$. The most important ketone is propanone, or acetone. Acetone is made from 2-propanol and used in plastics, solvents, and making other chemicals.

29:16 ACIDS AND ESTERS

Most organic acids are characterized by the carboxylic acid group, —COOH, and are weak acids. However, the strength of these acids is strongly influenced by other atoms in the molecule. Since the strength of the acid depends upon the breaking of the O—H bond by having the hydrogen ion removed by a water molecule, anything which would weaken that bond results in a stronger acid. The effect of one functional group on another functional group is called an **inductive effect.** If a chlorine atom bonds to a carboxylic acid molecule, the acid becomes stronger. Chlorine, with its high electronegativity, tends to attract electrons to itself from other parts of the molecule. The chlorine draws electrons away from the acid group. As an example, consider the K_a values for the acids in Table 29-4.

Table 29-4

Ionization Constants of Some Organic Acids		
Name	**Formula**	**Ionization Constant**
Acetic acid	CH_3COOH	1.74×10^{-5}
Chloroacetic acid	$ClCH_2COOH$	1.38×10^{-3}
Dichloroacetic acid	$Cl_2CHCOOH$	5.01×10^{-2}
Trichloroacetic acid	Cl_3CCOOH	2.29×10^{-1}

Organic acids in foods cranberries — benzoic acid, grapes — tartaric acid, citrus fruits — citric acid, sour milk — lactic acid, rhubarb — oxalic acid, green apples — malic acid

You have used ethanoic acid (*acetic acid*) in the laboratory. This acid is produced in large quantities from methanol and carbon monoxide. Vinegar is a 5% solution of acetic acid made by fermenting fruit or grain. Acetic acid is also used in the manufacture of fibers and plastics. Hexanedioic acid (*adipic acid*) is synthesized from cyclohexane in making nylon. What is its structure?

$HOOC(CH_2)_4COOH$, adipic acid

The compound, p-xylene is used to make the dicarboxylic acid, terephthalic acid.

COOH

COOH

Fibers, films, and bottles made of polyester all contain terephthalic acid.

It is possible to have anhydrides of organic acids just as for inorganic acids. Thus, acetic anhydride can be made from acetic acid and is used to produce rayon and plastics.

Anhydrides of organic acids also exist.

$$CH_3-\overset{O}{\overset{\|}{C}}-O-H + H-O-\overset{O}{\overset{\|}{C}}-CH_3 \rightarrow CH_3-\overset{O}{\overset{\|}{C}}-O-\overset{O}{\overset{\|}{C}}-CH_3 + H_2O$$

Esters can be considered as having been made from an acid and an alcohol. For example, consider the reaction between ethanol and ethanoic acid.

Esters can be considered as having been made from an acid and an alcohol.

$$CH_3CH_2-O-H + CH_3C\begin{smallmatrix}O\\\\O-H\end{smallmatrix} \rightarrow CH_3CH_2-O-C\begin{smallmatrix}O\\\\CH_3\end{smallmatrix} + H_2O$$

ethanol   acetic acid   ethyl acetate   water

Esters have the general formula
$$R-\overset{O}{\overset{\|}{C}}-O-R'$$

$C_3H_7COOC_2H_5$ is ethyl butyrate and has a pineapple odor.

Methyl salicylate has a wintergreen odor,

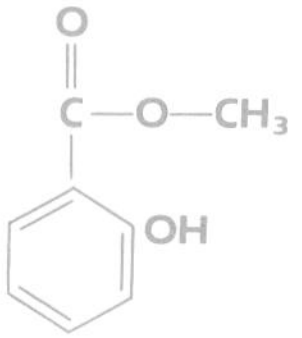

When they react, they produce water and ethyl acetate. The $^{18}_{8}O$ nuclide can be used to determine the path of oxygen in the reaction. Let us use some ethanol which contains $^{18}_{8}O$ atoms. This ethanol is then reacted with acetic acid containing the common $^{16}_{8}O$. The products are separated after the reaction and separately analyzed by mass spectrometer. We find the $^{18}_{8}O$ in the ethyl acetate. We now know that the oxygen in the water came from the acid, not from the alcohol.

Ethenyl ethanoate (*vinyl acetate*), $CH_3COOCH{=}CH_2$, is an ester produced from ethyne and ethanoic acid. It is used to make adhesives and paints.

You may want to prepare some esters as a demonstration or a lab. See the Teacher's Guide for preparation details.

29:17 ORGANIC NITROGEN COMPOUNDS

Many organic compounds of biological importance contain nitrogen. Because nitrogen has more than one oxidation level, it can combine with organic radicals in a number of ways.

$$\underset{\text{ammonia}}{H{-}\underset{\displaystyle H}{\underset{|}{N}}{-}H} \qquad \underset{\text{primary amine}}{H{-}\underset{\displaystyle H}{\underset{|}{N}}{-}R}$$

$$R{-}\underset{\displaystyle H}{\underset{|}{N}}{-}R' \qquad R{-}\underset{\displaystyle R''}{\underset{|}{N}}{-}R'$$

An amine contains nitrogen bonded to alkyl groups and/or hydrogen.

Amines are bases since the N atom possesses an unshared pair of electrons.

Amines are organic compounds in which a nitrogen atom is bound to alkyl groups and hydrogen atoms. Amines are derivatives of ammonia. If only one hydrogen atom of ammonia is replaced by an alkyl group, the compound is a primary amine. If two hydrogen atoms are replaced, the compound is a secondary amine. If all three are replaced, the compound is a tertiary amine. In general, chemists use the symbol *R*— to represent an alkyl group. General formulas for amines are shown on the left.

Amines are usually named as derivatives of ammonia. For example, the name of the following compound is diethylamine.

$$CH_3{-}CH_2{-}\underset{\displaystyle H}{\underset{|}{N}}{-}CH_2{-}CH_3$$

Amines may also be named as amino-substituted hydrocarbons. The carbon chain is numbered to give the amine group the lowest number. For example, the name of the following compound is 1,4-diaminobutane.

$$H_2N{-}\overset{1}{C}H_2{-}\overset{2}{C}H_2{-}\overset{3}{C}H_2{-}\overset{4}{C}H_2{-}NH_2$$

Amides are characterized by a carbonyl group and an amine group.

Use structural models to demonstrate how Wöhler rearranged the atoms of NH_4OCN to form urea, $(NH_2)_2CO$, by heating. He demonstrated that a "vital force" was not necessary to produce an organic compound.

$$\mathbf{NH_4OCN \rightarrow H_2NCONH_2}$$
ammonium cyanate → urea

Amides are characterized by a carbonyl group and an amine group. An amine-like compound of importance in both industry and living systems is urea, $H_2N{-}CO{-}NH_2$. Some organisms secrete their nitrogenous wastes in the form of urea. Commercially, urea is formed from ammonia and carbon dioxide. It is used as a fertilizer, a raw material for plastics production, and a livestock feed supplement.

Other important classes of nitrogen-containing compounds are listed in Table 29-5. *G*— is used in place of *R*— with amino acids. Some amino acids have other elements in addition to C and H so the symbol *G*— is used. For example, *G*— for aspartic acid represents HOOC—CH_2—. *G*— for methionine represents CH_3—S—CH_2—CH_2—.

Nitriles are characterized by a carbon-nitrogen triple bond. One important nitrile is propenenitrile (acrylonitrile). It is manufactured from propene, ammonia, and oxygen and is used in fibers, plastics, and synthetic rubber.

Table 29-5

Organic Compounds Containing Nitrogen		
Class	**General Formula**	**Example**
Amines	R—NH_2	$CH_3CH_2NH_2$ ethanamine
Amides	R—$\overset{\displaystyle O}{\overset{\displaystyle \|}{C}}$—$NH_2$	CH_3CONH_2 ethanamide
Amino acids	G—$\overset{\displaystyle NH_2}{\overset{\displaystyle \|}{CH}}$—COOH	$CH_3CH(NH_2)COOH$ alanine (2-aminopropanoic acid)
Nitriles	R—C≡N	$CH_3CH_2CH_2CN$ butanenitrile
Nitro compounds	R—NO_2	$C_6H_5NO_2$ nitrobenzene

Maria Goeppert Mayer (1906–1972)

Maria Goeppert Mayer was a seventh generation university professor in her family. She was the second woman to win a Nobel Prize in physics. Maria received her doctorate degree at the age of 24, in spite of the fact that she had to prepare herself to take the German University exams. At that time, the only school which prepared girls for the University had closed.

Maria worked with the major physicists and chemists of her time including Max Born. She was interested primarily in researching quantum theory, electrodynamics, spectroscopy, and crystal physics. She conceptualized a shell model for the atomic nucleus. She believed the relative stability of the nucleus could be explained by considering single particle orbits in various shells in the nucleus. For this proposal, she won the Nobel Prize in 1963 with two others.

At the time of her death, she was a faculty member at the University of California in San Diego.

CHEMICAL TECHNOLOGY: Synfuels

The limited supply of petroleum as a resource has led government and industry to investigate other hydrocarbon sources for use as fuels and raw materials for the chemical industry. Synfuels or synthetic fuels are derived from organic sources which are more difficult to convert or environmentally less acceptable than traditional fuels. Some of the sources being investigated are renewable: grains, sugars, and wood. The production of methanol and ethanol from these sources promises to be a major factor in increasing the supply of hydrocarbons for both fuels and industrial use in the immediate future.

Other sources are nonrenewable but important because they are found in large quantities. Tar sands, found mostly in Canada, contain hydrocarbon mixtures similar to the heaviest and thickest fractions of petroleum. Tar sands are chemically treated at extraction plants. Naphthalene is added and the mixture is moved to settling tanks. The sand is removed and the thick bitumen mixed with naphthalene is skimmed off the top. The bitumen-naphthalene mixture is separated by distillation. A thermal cracking process yields synthetic crude oil, coke, and some fuel gas.

Oil shales, found all over the world, also contain petroleum-like materials. Bitumen and kerogen can be thermally decomposed to yield oil, gas, and carbon. Major concentrations of oil shales are found in the United States. Note that the conversion of tar sands and oil shales to useable fuels requires a number of costly processes. However if the price of crude oil remains high, these processes become more economically feasible.

Coal is one of the most abundant raw materials in the world. Though coal is mostly carbon, it also contains small quantities of hydrogen, sulfur, and nitrogen. The most efficient fuels have a high hydrogen content. Therefore, the conversion of coal to a more useable fuel would involve the addition of hydrogen. There are two basic approaches in using coal to produce synthetic fuels. In one process, the coal is reacted with hydrogen in the presence of a catalyst to produce a liquid fuel directly. The general equation is

$$n C + (n + 1)H_2 \rightarrow C_n H_{2n+2}$$

Recall that the product has the general formula for members of the alkane series. An alternative method is to gasify the coal as the first step. In this process the coal is reacted with steam.

$$C + H_2O \rightarrow CO + H_2$$

The carbon monoxide and hydrogen produced can then be combined in the presence of a catalyst to form methane.

$$CO + 3H_2 \rightarrow CH_4 + H_2O$$

Methane can then be used directly as a fuel or be converted by an additional process to a liquid hydrocarbon fuel such as gasoline. By varying the catalyst used and the reaction conditions, carbon monoxide and hydrogen can react in another way to produce methanol.

$$CO + 2H_2 \rightarrow CH_3OH$$

Methanol can then be used as a reactant to produce a synthetic fuel or other chemical product.

The basic chemistry of these processes was researched decades earlier. Most of the work concerning synfuels was done in Germany. Widespread utilization of these processes depends upon the development of efficient, economical technologies. The descriptions given here are greatly simplified. Specific temperatures and pressures must be maintained during each step. Many side reactions occur producing unwanted by-products. Catalysts are contaminated in some reactions and must be replaced continuously. Impurities, in the reactants, produce polluting products. While some of these problems have been overcome, much still remains to be done.

SUMMARY

1. Unsaturated hydrocarbons contain one or more double or triple bonds. Saturated hydrocarbons are hydrocarbons which contain only single bonds between carbon atoms. 29:1

2. Straight-chain (aliphatic) carbon compounds are formed of carbon chains in which the atoms are covalently bound together. Cyclic carbon compounds are formed when the ends of a chain are bonded to each other. 29:1, 29:7

3. Hydrocarbons are carbon compounds which contain only carbon and hydrogen.
   (a) Alkanes are saturated hydrocarbons with chainlike molecules. 29:2
   (b) Cycloalkanes are saturated hydrocarbons with ringlike molecules. 29:7
   (c) Alkenes are hydrocarbons which contain a double bond between carbon atoms. 29:8
   (d) Alkynes are hydrocarbons which contain a triple bond between carbon atoms. 29:10
   (e) Aromatic hydrocarbons are hydrocarbons which contain a benzene ring or $(4n + 2)$ delocalized pi electrons. 29:11

4. A hydrocarbon radical is a hydrocarbon which has lost one hydrogen atom with its associated electron. It acts as a substituent to a carbon chain or ring. 29:11

5. A functional group is a nonhydrocarbon part of an organic molecule. 29:12

6. The principal classes of oxygen containing compounds are alcohols, ethers, aldehydes, ketones, acids, and esters. 29:13-29:16

7. The principal classes of nitrogen-containing compounds are amines, amides, amino acids, nitriles, and nitro compounds. 29:17

PROBLEMS

Detailed discussions and answers to problems are given in the Teacher's Guide.

8. What is a homologous series?

8. a series of compounds which differ by a specific structural unit

9. Write the general formula for alkenes. C_nH_{2n}

10. Write a formula for
   a. 6 carbon alkene   b. 8 carbon alkane   c. 10 carbon alkyne

10. a. C_6H_{12}
    b. C_8H_{18}
    c. $C_{10}H_{18}$

11. Write the general formula for an akyl radical.

11. C_nH_{2n+1}

12. What reasons can you cite as to why the boiling point of alkanes increases as a function of their molecular mass?

12. longer molecules have more surface over which weak forces interact

13. Write structural formulas for octane and nonane.

14. What is the chemical formula for the heptyl radical?

14. C_7H_{15}

15. Use position numbers to label the asymmetric carbon atom in the following.

   a.
   $$CH_2-CH-\underset{|}{\overset{\overset{\displaystyle CH_3}{|}}{CH}}-CH_3$$
   with Cl, Cl below

   a. $CH_2-CH-CH-CH_3$ (with CH_3 above the third carbon, and Cl below first and second carbons)

   b. $CH_3-CH_2-CH-CH_3$ (with Cl below third carbon)

16. What is a substituent group? branch or functional group attached to the parent chain

17. What rules are followed in labeling the positions of substituent groups in naming hydrocarbons?

18. Using the general formula for alkenes, write the formula for octene, heptene, and decene. $C_8H_{16}, C_7H_{14}, C_{10}H_{20}$

19. Which of the following compounds octane, pentene, heptyne would you predict to be most reactive? Why? heptyne

20. Write the formula for TNT, 2,4,6-trinitrotoluene.

21. Write the formula for 1,3-xylene.

22. Write the general formula for an alkyne.

22. C_nH_{2n-2}

23. Classify each of the following as a(n) amine, amide, nitrile, or amino acid.

23. a. amide
    b. amine
    c. nitrile
    d. amino acid

   a. (benzene ring)$-C\overset{\overset{\displaystyle O}{\parallel}}{\underset{\underset{\displaystyle NH_2}{}}{}}$

   b. (benzene ring)$-NH_2$

   c. (benzene ring)$-C\equiv N$

   d. (benzene ring)$-CH_2CHC\overset{\overset{\displaystyle O}{\parallel}}{\underset{\underset{\displaystyle NH_2}{|}}{}} OH$

24. Classify each of the following as a(n) alcohol, ether, aldehyde, or ketone.

a. $\langle\bigcirc\rangle$—CH_2CH_2OH

b. $\langle\bigcirc\rangle$—OH

c. $\langle\bigcirc\rangle$—$\overset{\overset{\displaystyle H}{|}}{C}{=}O$

d. $\langle\bigcirc\rangle$—$\overset{\overset{\displaystyle O}{||}}{C}$—$CH_3$

24. a. alcohol
b. alcohol
c. aldehyde
d. ketone

25. Classify each of the following as a(n) ester, carboxylic acid, aldehyde, or ether.

a. $\langle\bigcirc\rangle$—O—CH_3

b. $\underset{\overset{|}{OH}}{CH_2}$—$\underset{\overset{|}{OH}}{CH}$—$\underset{\overset{|}{OH}}{CH_2}$

c. $\langle\bigcirc\rangle\overset{\displaystyle COOH}{\underset{\displaystyle COOH}{}}$

d. CH_3—O—$\overset{\overset{\displaystyle CH_3}{|}}{\underset{\overset{|}{CH_3}}{C}}$—$CH_3$

25. a. ether
b. alcohol
c. carboxylic acid
d. ether

26. Make a list of the names of the first thirty alkanes. Use reference books suggested by your instructor.

27. Diagram the nine isomers of heptane.

28. Find out how many isomers there are of nonane and decane.

28. nonane = 35 isomers
decane = 75 isomers

29. Name the following.

a. CH_3—$\underset{\overset{|}{CH_3}}{CH}$—$CH_2$—$\underset{\overset{|}{\underset{\overset{|}{CH_3}}{CH_2}}}{CH}$—$CH_2$—$\overset{\overset{\displaystyle CH_3}{|}}{CH}$—$CH_2$—$CH_3$

b. CH_3—CH=CH—CH_2—CH_3

c. $\langle\bigcirc\rangle\overset{\displaystyle CH_2-CH_3}{\underset{\displaystyle CH_2-CH_3}{}}$

d. $\overset{\displaystyle CH_3\ CH_3}{\langle\text{hexagon}\rangle}$—$CH_3$

e. $CH{\equiv}C$—$\overset{\overset{\displaystyle CH_3}{|}}{\underset{\overset{|}{CH_3}}{C}}$—$CH_3$

29. a. 2,6-dimethyl-4-ethyloctane
b. 2-pentene
c. 1,2-diethylbenzene
d. 1,1,4-trimethylcyclohexane
e. 3,3-dimethyl-1-butyne

30. Draw the structural formula (condensed form) for the following.
  a. 3-ethylhexane
  b. 1,2,3,4,5,6-hexamethylcyclohexane
  c. 2-methylpropene
  d. 1-hexyne
  e. 2-methylnaphthalene

31. What is the molecular mass of the 40-carbon saturated hydrocarbon?

31. 562

32. Name the following compounds.
  a. CH_3—CH_2—CH_2—OH

32. a. 1-propanol

b. 2-methyl-2-propanol
c. 1-pentoxyhexane
d. butanal
e. 2-hexanone
f. butanoic acid
g. hexyl propanoate
h. 1-propanamine
   (1-aminopropane)

b.

$$CH_3-\overset{\overset{\displaystyle OH}{|}}{\underset{\underset{\displaystyle CH_3}{|}}{C}}-CH_3$$

c. $CH_3-CH_2-CH_2-CH_2-CH_2-O-CH_2-CH_2-CH_2-CH_2-CH_2-CH_3$

d. $CH_3-CH_2-CH_2-\overset{\overset{\displaystyle O}{||}}{C}-H$

e. $CH_3-\overset{\overset{\displaystyle O}{||}}{C}-CH_2-CH_2-CH_2-CH_3$

f. $CH_3-CH_2-CH_2-\overset{\overset{\displaystyle O}{||}}{C}-OH$

g. $CH_3-CH_2-CH_2-CH_2-CH_2-CH_2-O-\overset{\overset{\displaystyle O}{||}}{C}-CH_2-CH_3$

h. $CH_3-CH_2-CH_2-\overset{}{\underset{\underset{\displaystyle H}{|}}{N}}-H$

33. Draw condensed structural formulas for the following compounds.
    a. 1-butanol
    b. 2-methyl-1-propanol
    c. 1-propoxybutane
    d. ethanal
    e. 3-pentanone
    f. propyl methanoate
    g. trimethylamine
    h. propanoic acid
    i. propanamide
    j. nitromethane

34. What is the inductive effect? the effect of one functional group on another

35. How does the addition of functional groups affect the acidity of a carboxylic acid? element with high electronegativity increases acidity

36. How do you account for the difference in the Ka's for the following acids?

position and electronegativity of Cl substituent

   $CH_3CH_2CHClCOOH$ $ClCH_2CH_2CH_2COOH$
   (2-chlorobutanoic acid)   (4-chlorobutanoic acid)
   $K_a = 1.39 \times 10^{-3}$ $K_a = 2.96 \times 10^{-5}$

37. Write condensed structural formulas for the following compounds.
    a. cyclopentanone
    b. 3-pentene-2-one
    c. butyl butanoate
    d. ethyl chloroethanoate
    e. ethanenitrile
    f. 2-amino-3-phenyl propanal
    g. 1,2-dibromo-1-phenylethane
    h. hexadecane

38. Name the following compounds.

    a.
    $$CH_3-\overset{\overset{\displaystyle CH_3}{|}}{\underset{\underset{\displaystyle CH_3}{|}}{CH}}-CHO$$

    b. $CH_3-\overset{\overset{\displaystyle CH_3}{|}}{CH}-CH_2-CHO$

    c. HCOOH
    d. HOOC—COOH
    e. CH_3NH_2
    f. CH_3-Cl

38. a. 2-methylpropanal
    b. 2-methylbutanal
    c. methanoic acid (formic acid)
    d. ethanedioic acid (oxalic acid)
    e. methylamine
    f. chloromethane

39. Write structural formulas for the following.

    a. 1-phenylpropene   **d.** 1-bromopentane

    b. 1,2,4-trimethylbenzene **e.** 3-methyl-3-pentanol

    c. iodobenzene   **f.** 4-methylphenol

REVIEW

1. What is the current theory for the source of the nuclear force?

2. How do the different particles emitted by naturally radioactive materials differ in charge and mass?

3. Why is binding energy per particle an indication of nuclear stability?

4. Describe the mechanism of a fission chain reaction.

5. How would you recommend attempting to produce element 108?

6. Predict the voltage to be expected at 25°C from a cell constructed as follows: $Co|Co^{2+}(0.100M)\|Cu^{2+}(2.00M)|Cu$.

7. If a voltaic cell produces a potential difference of 1.00 volt, what is the equilibrium constant for the reaction taking place in the cell? What is the free energy change for the reaction? Assume one electron is transferred in the balanced equation.

8. A piece of metal alloy with mass 0.8128 grams is to be analyzed for its nickel content. The metal is dissolved in acid and any ions likely to interfere are removed by appropriate chemical treatment. The resulting solution is then subjected to electrolysis using a platinum cathode. The cathode has mass 12.3247 g before the electrolysis and 12.6731 g after the electrolysis. What is the percentage of nickel in the alloy?

9. The half life of an Ir isotope is 74.2 days. How long will it take 6.30×10^{11} atoms of that nuclide to disintegrate to 2.46×10^9 atoms?

10. Complete: $^{240}_{92}U \rightarrow {}^{0}_{-1}e + ?$

6. 0.66 V
7. −96.5 kJ
8. 42.86%
9. 594 days
10. $^{240}_{93}Np$

ONE MORE STEP

1. Investigate the industrial production methods and uses for the five organic chemicals produced in greatest volume in the United States.

2. Silicones are chemicals containing silicon as well as organic radicals. Find out how they are made, what they are used for, and what properties they have that lend themselves to these uses.

READINGS

Brown, William H., *Introduction to Organic Chemistry*, Boston: Willard Grant Press, 1975.

Strauss, Howard J., and Kaufman, Milton, *Handbook for Chemical Technicians*, New York: McGraw-Hill Book Co., 1976, Chapter 6.

The complex motion of an athlete can be broken down into a series of simpler movements. A photograph such as the one shown allows the athlete to analyze each step. The human body can be considered a complex chemical factory where thousands of reactions occur simultaneously. However, like the motion of the athlete, these processes can be broken down and classified to make their study easier. How are organic reactions classified? What are the four classes of biomolecules?

Thomas Zimmermann/Alpha

Chapter 30 begins with the study of five common types of organic reactions. The industrial and biological aspects of organic chemistry are covered in the last part of the chapter.

ORGANIC REACTIONS AND BIOCHEMISTRY

30

Demonstration—The preparation of nylon helps students understand and visualize organic reactions. Complete preparation instructions are in the Teacher's Guide. A relatively strong strand of nylon can be produced using these instructions. **CAUTION:** Wear plastic gloves and perform this demonstration only in an area with good ventilation.

There are thousands of "kinds" of organic reactions. However, just as in inorganic chemistry, by studying a few common types we can understand a great deal of the behavior of organic molecules.

30:1 OXIDATION

Hydrocarbons undergo oxidation in the presence of excess oxygen to form CO_2 and H_2O. However, at the high temperature necessary for oxidation of hydrocarbons, many different reactions take place at the same time. Hydrocarbon chains break into fragments. Carbon atoms change from one oxidation state to another. Oxygen atoms attach to the hydrocarbon fragments. Oxidation is complete when the only products are carbon dioxide and water.

Some hydrocarbons have very large heats of combustion. Thus, they are used commercially as fuels. Natural gas (methane) and bottled gas (butane containing some propane and ethane) are used in the home for heating and cooking. Ethyne is used in cutting and welding torches.

The heats of combustion for a number of common organic fuels are given in Table 30-1. The values are in units of kJ/mol. To find out which of several fuels would be the most economical, the price must be considered. If we know the price of the fuel per kilogram, we can convert the data as follows:

$$\frac{kJ}{mol} \left| \frac{1 \text{ mol}}{x \text{ g}} \right| \frac{1000 \text{ g}}{1 \text{ kg}} \left| \frac{1 \text{ kg}}{y \text{ dollars}} \right. = kJ \text{ per dollar}$$

If a gaseous fuel is being purchased, the sales unit may be a unit of volume. Then the temperature and pressure at which the volume is quoted must be known. From this information, the actual amount of matter may be computed from the ideal gas equation.

GOAL: You will gain an understanding of various organic reactions and practical and biological significance of some organic compounds.

Complete combustion of a hydrocarbon products are CO_2 and H_2O.

Fuels used commercially are hydrocarbons that have a very large heat of combustion.

Table 30-1

Heats of Combustion of Common Organic Fuels			
Fuel	Heat of Combustion (kJ/mol)	Fuel	Heat of Combustion (kJ/mol)
Benzene	3273	Propane	2202
Cyclohexane	3924	Butane	2879
Ethyne	1305	Ethanol	1371
Methane	882	Heptane	4811
Ethane	1541	2,2,4-Trimethylpentane	5456

PROBLEM

1. Complete and balance. (assume complete oxidation)

$$C_6H_{14} + O_2 \rightarrow \qquad 2C_6H_{14} + 19O_2 \rightarrow 12CO_2 + \quad 14H_2O$$

30:2 SUBSTITUTION REACTIONS

A reaction in which a hydrogen atom of a hydrocarbon is replaced by a functional group is called a **substitution reaction.** Alkane molecules react with chlorine in the presence of sunlight to produce chloro-substituted compounds. The product is a mixture of different isomers with very similar properties. Thus, this process is not a satisfactory way to prepare chlorine derivatives of alkanes. However, a number of aromatic compound substitution reactions can be controlled to produce specific products. For example, benzene reacts with nitric acid in the presence of concentrated sulfuric acid to form nitrobenzene.

benzene   nitric acid   nitrobenzene   water

Alkyl groups and halogen atoms also can be substituted easily onto a benzene ring.

In a second type of substitution reaction, one functional group replaces another. Alcohols undergo substitution reactions with hydrogen halides to form alkyl halides. For example, 2-propanol reacts with hydrogen iodide to form 2-iodopropane.

$$\underset{\text{2-propanol}}{CH_3{-}\overset{\displaystyle OH}{\overset{|}{CH}}{-}CH_3(l)} + \underset{\substack{\text{hydrogen}\\\text{iodide}}}{HI(aq)} \rightarrow \underset{\text{2-iodopropane}}{CH_3{-}\overset{\displaystyle I}{\overset{|}{CH}}{-}CH_3(l)} + \underset{\text{water}}{H_2O(l)}$$

Alkyl halides, in turn, react with ammonia to produce amines. For example, bromoethane reacts with ammonia to produce ethylamine.

$$CH_3—CH_2—Br(l) + NH_3(aq) \rightarrow CH_3—CH_2—NH_2(aq) + HBr(aq)$$

bromoethane ammonia   ethylamine   hydrogen bromide

Alkyl halides react with ammonia, NH_3, to produce amines.

PROBLEM

2. Complete and balance.

$$HOH + (CH_3)_3CI \rightarrow$$ HOH + (CH$_3$)$_3$CI → HI + (CH$_3$)$_3$COH

30:3 ADDITION REACTIONS

Each carbon atom contributes two electrons to a double bond. Suppose one bond is broken and the other remains intact. Each carbon atom then has available one electron to bond with some other atom. A number of substances will cause one bond of a double bond to break by adding on at the double bond. This type of reaction is called an **addition reaction.** An example is the addition of bromine to the double bond of ethene. The product of this reaction is 1,2-dibromoethane.

In addition reactions of alkenes, two species are added by breaking one bond of the double bond.

$$H_2C=CH_2(g) + Br_2(l) \rightarrow BrH_2C—CH_2Br(l)$$

ethene   bromine   1,2-dibromoethane

Atoms of many substances can be added at the double bond of an alkene. Common addition agents are the halogens (except fluorine), the hydrogen halides, and sulfuric acid. The double bonds in the benzene ring of aromatic compounds are so stabilized that addition reactions do not occur readily.

Addition reactions in more complex alkenes often lead to rearrangement of the molecule.

Bruce Charlton

FIGURE 30-1. A bromine solution is used in testing compounds for the presence of unsaturated bonds. Bromine loses its color in the presence of an unsaturated hydrocarbon, but will not react with a saturated hydrocarbon.

PROBLEM

$$CH_3CH_2CH\!=\!CH_2 + Br_2 \rightarrow CH_3CH_2BrHC\!-\!CH_2Br$$

3. Complete and balance.

$$CH_3CH_2CH\!=\!CH_2 + Br_2 \rightarrow$$

30:4   ELIMINATION REACTIONS

In elimination reactions, one product has a double bond.

HCl and HNO₂ are other substances which are often eliminated.

We have seen that under certain circumstances, atoms can be "added on" a double bond. It is also possible to remove certain atoms from a molecule to create a double bond. Such a reaction is known as an elimination reaction. In the most common elimination reactions, a water molecule is removed from an alcohol. A hydrogen atom is removed from one carbon atom, and a hydroxyl group is removed from the next carbon atom. For example, propene can be made from 1-propanol by the removal of water. Sulfuric acid is used as the dehydrating agent.

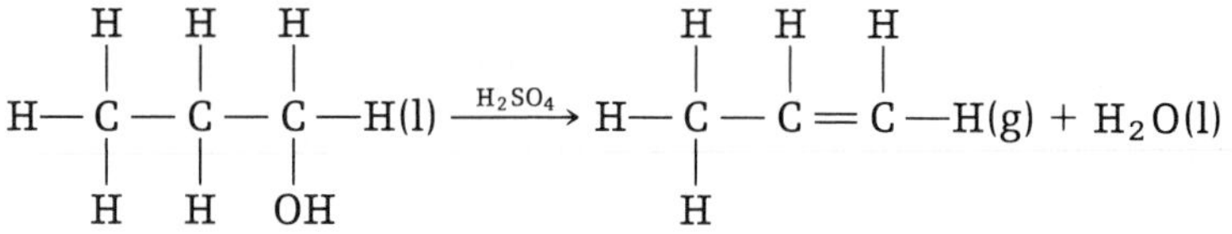

1-propanol   propene   water

PROBLEM

$$CH_3CH_2CH_2CH_2OH \rightarrow CH_3CH_2CH\!=\!CH_2 + H_2O$$

4. Complete and balance.

$$CH_3CH_2CH_2CH_2OH \xrightarrow{H_2SO_4}$$

Demonstration—It is easy to prepare soap. See the Teacher's Guide for details.

30:5   ESTERIFICATION AND SAPONIFICATION REACTIONS

The reaction of an alcohol and an organic acid produces an ester.

When an alcohol reacts with either an organic acid or an organic acid anhydride, an ester is formed. This type of reaction is called **esterification** (es tuhr uh fuh KAY shuhn). For example, in the reaction between ethanoic acid and methanol, methyl ethanoate and water are formed. Methyl ethanoate is an ester.

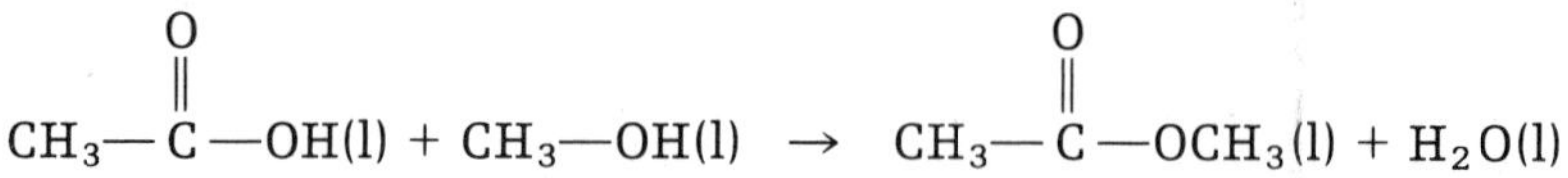

ethanoic acid   methanol   methyl ethanoate   water

Esters are split into alcohols and salts of carboxylic acids in saponification reactions.

An ester can be split into an alcohol and a carboxylic acid by hydrolysis. The hydrolysis reaction is the reverse of the reaction shown above. However, if a metallic base is used for the hydrolysis instead of water, the metallic salt of the carboxylic acid is obtained, not the acid. This process is called **saponification** (suh pahn uh fuh KAY shuhn). Saponification is the process used in making soaps. Since ancient times, soaps have been made from vegetable and animal oils and fats cooked in alkali bases (KOH, NaOH). Soap is a metallic salt of a fatty acid. The natural fat or oil is an ester. In the following saponification reaction, the natural fat is a glyceride ester. The products of the reaction are soap and glycerol (the alcohol of the glyceride).

A soap is a metallic salt of a fatty acid.

Fats are esters of glycerol.

$$
\begin{array}{l}
CH_2-O-\overset{\overset{\displaystyle O}{\|}}{C}-(CH_2)_{16}-CH_3{}^* \\[4pt]
CH-O-\overset{\overset{\displaystyle O}{\|}}{C}-(CH_2)_{16}-CH_3 + 3NaOH \rightarrow \begin{array}{ccc} CH_2 & CH & CH_2 \\ | & | & | \\ OH & OH & OH \end{array} + 3[CH_3-(CH_2)_{16}-COO^-Na^+] \\[4pt]
CH_2-O-\overset{\overset{\displaystyle O}{\|}}{C}-(CH_2)_{16}-CH_3
\end{array}
$$

fat (a glyceride ester)   base   glycerol   soap

PROBLEM

5. Complete and balance.
$$CH_3CH_2OH + CH_3CH_2CH_2COOH \rightarrow$$

$$CH_3CH_2OH + CH_3CH_2CH_2COOH \rightarrow CH_3CH_2CH_2\overset{\overset{\displaystyle O}{\|}}{C}-O-CH_2CH_3 + H_2O$$

30:6 PETROLEUM

The chief source of organic compounds is the naturally occurring mixture called petroleum. Other important sources are coal tar, natural gas, and fermentation of natural materials. Petroleum is a mixture of hydrocarbons containing small amounts of nitrogen, oxygen, and sulfur compounds. The hydrocarbons are mainly alkanes and cycloalkanes. The initial treatment of petroleum in a refinery is a fractional distillation. This treatment separates the mixture into portions having different boiling ranges. The chief fractions are petroleum ether (20°C–60°C), ligroin (60°C–100°C), gasoline (40–205°C), kerosene (175–325°C), gas oil (>275°C), and lubricating oil. The remainder is called asphalt.

The products from the distillation cannot be marketed as is. They must be refined to remove undesirable substances, particularly sulfur compounds. Additives are blended with gasoline and other products to improve their performance. Many by-products of gasoline production are used as raw materials for the production of plastics, synthetic fibers, and rubber.

The yield of gasoline can be improved in a number of ways. In one process, smaller molecules from the lower boiling fractions are joined to form larger molecules. In another process, the larger

Petroleum is the chief source of natural organic compounds.

Petroleum can be separated into portions with different boiling ranges by fractional distillation.

Cracking involves splitting large molecules of a higher boiling fraction into smaller molecules.

*A fat is an amorphous material, one that does not have a fixed melting point.

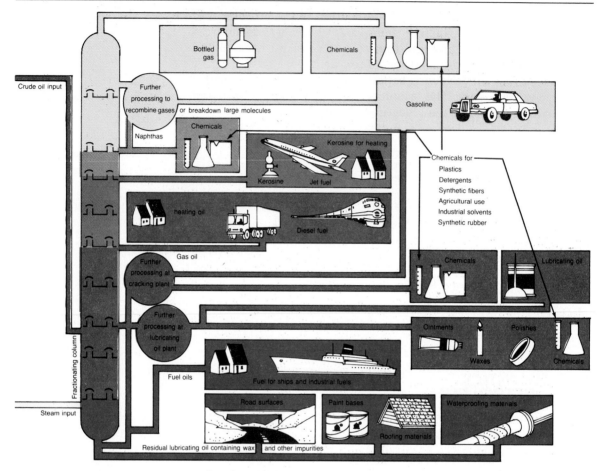

FIGURE 30-2. The products of petroleum fractionation and some of their uses are shown. Note from the diagram it should be obvious why the supply of petroleum is critical to the chemical industry.

The octane rating describes how evenly gasoline burns.

6. asphalt, lubricating oil, gas oil, kerosene, gasoline, ligroin, petroleum ether

Demonstration—It is easy to prepare synthetic rubber. The preparation produces a bad odor. See the Teacher's Guide for preparation details.

molecules of the higher boiling fractions are cracked, or broken, into smaller molecules.

Gasolines are rated on a scale known as **octane rating.** The basis for this scale is the property of some fuels to cause "knocking" in engines. The knocking occurs when some of the fuel explodes suddenly instead of burning evenly.

PROBLEM

6. Name five fractions obtained by distilling petroleum.

30:7 SYNTHETIC RUBBER

The producers of synthetic substitutes for rubber have built a thriving industry based on organic chemistry. No one synthetic material can as yet replace natural rubber. However, there are many synthetics that can perform a particular job as well as or better than natural rubber. The production of synthetic rubber depends primarily upon a chemical reaction called addition polymerization. In this reaction, a molecule called a monomer, which contains a double or triple bond, adds to other similar molecules. Chains (or cross-linked chains) of very large molecular size and mass are formed. For example, consider the reaction between two molecules of ethene.

$$CH_2{=}CH_2(l) + CH_2{=}CH_2(l) \rightarrow {-}CH_2{-}CH_2{-}CH_2{-}CH_2{-}(amor)$$

This process can continue almost indefinitely. The bonds at the end of a chain cross-link to other chains. Gigantic molecules are formed. Such molecules are called **polymers.** In this case, the polymer is named polyethene or polyethylene.

Natural rubber is a polymer of 2-methylbutadiene. The 2-methylbutadiene molecule is the monomer of natural rubber. Many types of synthetic rubber can be made from various monomers. Often they are made by polymerizing two or more substances containing double bonds.

By far the largest selling synthetic rubber is a copolymer of 1,3-butadiene and styrene. It is used chiefly in the production of automobile tires.

30:8 PLASTICS

The production of plastics has created another important organic chemical industry. Plastics can be produced by polymerization. Some common plastics made by addition polymerization are polyethylene, polypropylene, polyvinyl acetate, polystyrene, and acrylics.

Plastics can also be made by a similar process in which both the polymer and another product, usually water, result. In this type of reaction, the molecules actually condense. This type of reaction is called a condensation polymerization reaction. Other plastics such as cellophane and celluloid can be made by the chemical treatment of cellulose.

Structural diagrams for monomers and polymer units of some polymerization and condensation plastics are shown below.

Addition polymerization plastics:

$$CH{=}CH_2(l) \rightarrow \cdots {-}CH{-}CH_2{-}CH{-}CH_2{-}CH{-}CH_2 \cdots$$

phenylethene
or
styrene

polystyrene
(amor)

Synthetic rubber is a result of polymerization.

In addition polymerization, a molecule called a monomer adds to other monomers.

Polymerization is the joining together of molecules which contain double or triple bonds.

Note: Much of the early research in synthetics was done in Germany in the period prior to and during World War II.

An interesting exception is thiokol in which NaCl is the second product.

Plastics may be made by condensation reactions.

Demonstration — In a small beaker, prepare a paste of p-nitroaniline and concentrated H_2SO_4. Heat this mixture over a burner flame. The reaction produces a long plastic mass.

Condensation polymerization plastics:

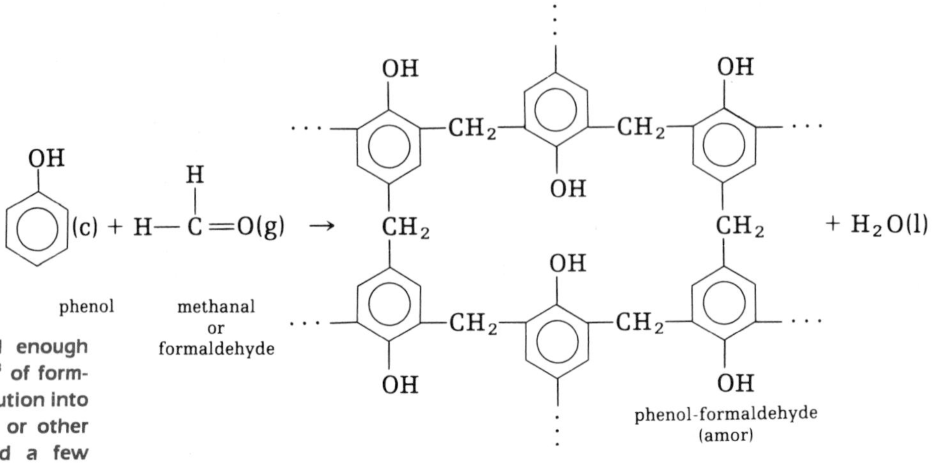

phenol   methanal
or
formaldehyde

phenol-formaldehyde
(amor)

Demonstration—Add enough urea to saturate 5 cm³ of form-aldehyde. Pour the solution into an aluminum film can or other similar container. Add a few drops of concentrated H_2SO_4. The reaction produces an instant plastic. **CAUTION:** The reaction is exothermic.

30:9   SYNTHETIC FIBERS

One of the earliest synthetic fibers was rayon. Rayon is simply reconstituted cellulose, which is the principal structural element of plants. Cellulose is a natural polymer of glucose, $C_6H_{12}O_6$.

Rayon is reconstituted cellulose.

Cellulose is a natural polymer of glucose, $C_6H_{12}O_6$.

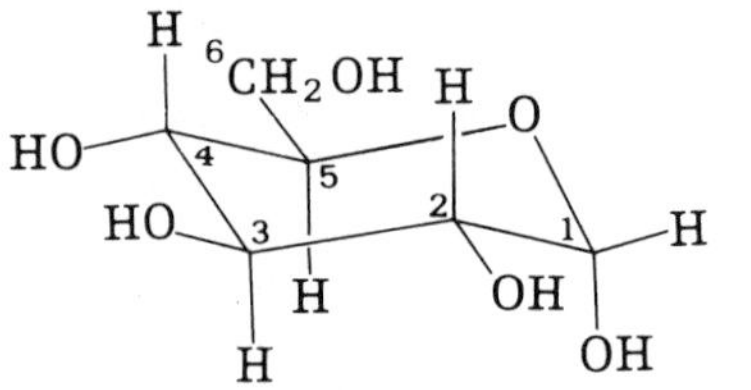

Glucose

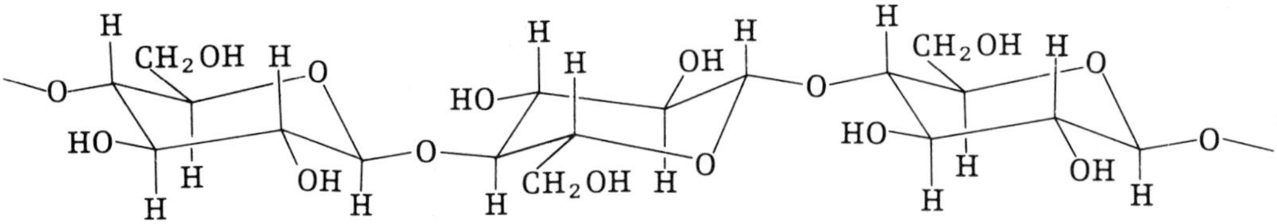

Cellulose

Cellulose in the form of purified wood pulp is soaked in a sodium hydroxide solution. The cellulose is converted to sodium cellulose whose structure is unknown. The sodium cellulose is then treated with carbon disulfide, CS_2, forming sodium cellulose xanthate which is soluble in sodium hydroxide solution. This solution, called "viscose," is squeezed through a small hole into a solution of sulfuric acid. The xanthate reacts with the sulfuric acid to regenerate the cellulose fiber.

Nylon is a name for a whole group of polyamide fibers. Nylon 66, made from adipic acid (hexanedioic acid) and hexamethylenediamine (1,6-diaminohexane), is the most common form. The amino group of the amine and the carboxyl group of the acid form an amide by condensation.

$$\underset{\text{H}}{\overset{\text{H}}{\underset{|}{\text{H}-\text{N}}}}-(\text{CH}_2)_6-\underset{\overset{|}{\text{H}}}{\text{N}}-\text{H} + \text{H}-\text{O}-\overset{\overset{\text{O}}{\|}}{\text{C}}-(\text{CH}_2)_4-\overset{\overset{\text{O}}{\|}}{\text{C}}-\text{O}-\text{H} \rightarrow \cdots -\underset{\overset{|}{\text{H}}}{\text{N}}-\overset{\overset{\text{O}}{\|}}{\text{C}}-\cdots + \text{H}_2\text{O}$$

Since each reactant has a functional group on each end, a polymer can be formed. The polymer is melted and forced through a small hole into a stream of cool air where the polymer solidifies to a fiber.

Nylon is the name for a group of polyamide fibers.

Joseph Sterling/Click, Chicago

FIGURE 30-3. Most synthetic fibers are produced in continuous filaments. The properties of the fiber depend on the spinning process used to give the filament its shape.

PROBLEM

7. What natural material is imitated by rayon? cellulose

30:10 PROTEINS

Approximately one half of your non-water mass consists of substances called proteins. These substances compose some structural parts of the body such as cartilage and tendons. However, more than three fourths of the protein in your body is used within the cells as catalysts! Biological catalysts are called enzymes. When we think of the word fuel, we think of burning a substance to obtain energy. Organisms, composed of cells, require energy. "Burning" fuels would destroy the cells. Thus, enzymes are present in the cells to enable reactions to occur at temperatures which are not injurious to the cells. **Proteins** are polymers made of **amino acids.** There are about 20 common amino acids. These acids are listed in Table 30-2.

Biological catalysts are called enzymes. These compounds are classified as proteins.

Enzymes are present in cells to enable reactions to occur at temperatures which do not injure cells.

Table 30-2

Amino Acids		

Amino acids have the form

$$
\begin{array}{c}
COOH \\
| \\
H\!-\!C\!-\!NH \\
| \\
G
\end{array}
$$

In the table, only the composition of G is represented.

Name	G	Symbol
Glycine	H—	Gly
Alanine	CH_3—	Ala
Valine	CH_3—CH— 	 CH_3	Val
Leucine	CH_3—CH—CH_2— 	 CH_3	Ley
Isoleucine	CH_3—CH_2—CH— 	 CH_3	Ile
Tryptophan	(indole ring)—CH_2—	Trp
Lysine	H_2N—CH_2—CH_2—CH_2—CH_2—	Lys

Arginine	H_2N—C—NH—CH_2—CH_2—CH_2—
	       ‖
	      NH
		Arg

Phenylalanine	(benzene ring)—CH_2—	Phe
Histidine	(imidazole ring)—CH_2—	His
Asparagine	O=C—CH_2— 	 NH_2	Asn
Glutamine	O=C—CH_2—CH_2— 	 NH_2	Gln
Serine	HO—CH_2—	Ser
Threonine	CH_3—CH— 	 OH	Thr
Aspartic acid	HOOC—CH_2—	Asp
Glutamic acid	HOOC—CH_2—CH_2—	Glu
Tyrosine	HO—(benzene ring)—CH_2—	Tyr
Methionine	CH_3—S—CH_2—CH_2—	Met
Cysteine	HS—CH_2—	Cys

Proline
 (an exception
 to the general
 formula)
	H_2C————CH_2
	
			 H_2C CH—COOH
			   \\ /
			     N
			
				     H
					Pro

In Section 29:17 we found that carboxylic acids reacted with amines to form amides,

$$\underset{\text{—}\,C\,\text{—}\,N\,\text{—}\,.}{\overset{\overset{\displaystyle O}{\|}\quad\overset{\displaystyle H}{|}}{}}$$

Amino acids are linked through the same condensation process. However, biochemists call the **amide link** a peptide bond. The new molecule formed from two amino acids is called a **dipeptide.** Three amino acids form a **tripeptide.** Many amino acids condense to a polypeptide. If a **polypeptide** has a biological function, it is called a protein.

Proteins differ from each other in several ways. The first difference, and most important, is the sequence, or order, of the amino acids composing the protein. Another way they differ is the way the polymer chain is coiled, folded, and twisted. Finally, the type of bonding holding the polymer in a particular shape can vary. Proteins contain from about 30 to several thousand amino acids. The 20 acids can form an enormous number of different proteins.

Reactions utilizing catalysts, as any reaction, consume or produce energy. Some of the energy produced appears as heat in the cell. However, most of the energy must be converted to some form other than heat or the cell will die. In cells, this "excess" energy is used to produce a product whose synthesis requires the input of energy. This compound is usually adenosine-5'-phosphate, or ATP for short. When an enzymatic reaction requiring energy occurs, some ATP can be decomposed to provide that energy. The structure of ATP is

PROBLEMS

8. What synthetic fiber imitates a protein? nylon

9. What is a peptide link?

Amino acids link because the carboxylic acid reacts with the amine to form a peptide bond.

Many amino acids condense to form a polypeptide.

Proteins differ in the order of amino acids, how the chain is coiled, folded or twisted, and in the type of bonding holding the polymer in a particular shape.

In cells, "excess energy" is used to produce ATP.

9. $\underset{\text{—}\,C\,\text{—}\,N\,\text{—}}{\overset{\overset{\displaystyle O}{\|}\quad\overset{\displaystyle H}{|}}{}}$

30:11 CARBOHYDRATES

Carbohydrates are also important to living systems. These compounds contain the elements carbon, hydrogen, and oxygen. Almost all carbohydrates are either simple sugars or condensation polymers of sugars. The most common simple sugar is glucose.

Carbohydrates are simple sugars or polymers of sugars.

Another common simple sugar is fructose.

Combining two simple sugars produces a disaccharide. In this case, combining glucose and fructose produces common table sugar, sucrose.

A disaccharide forms when two simple sugars combine.

There are a number of biologically important polysaccharides formed from the monomer, glucose. The chief storage form for carbohydrates in plants is starch, while in animals it is glycogen. Cellulose (Section 30:9) is yet another polymer of glucose.

Chief storage form for carbohydrates is starch in plants, and glycogen in animals.

Glycogen, starch, and cellulose differ simply in the way the monomers are bonded to each other. The links in the chain and the manner in which the chains are cross-linked determine which substance is produced by the condensation polymerization.

The process of breaking down carbohydrates to carbon dioxide and water is the chief energy source of an organism. Carbohydrate storage (starch/glycogen) is the energy reserve of the organism. The oxidation of glucose is the "burning" of the cell's "fuel." However, the enzymes in the cell permit this oxidation to take place under conditions that are healthy for the cell.

Carbohydrates break down in the organism to produce H_2O, CO_2, and energy.

PROBLEM

10. What is the principal function of carbohydrates in the body? energy source

30:12 LIPIDS

Proteins and carbohydrates tend to be more soluble in water than in nonpolar solvents. A general class of biologically important compounds made of those compounds more soluble in nonpolar solvents than in water is called the **lipids.** Lipids can be divided into several different groups.

Proteins and carbohydrates tend to be soluble in water.

Lipids (fats) are more soluble in nonpolar solvents than in water.

Fats are esters formed from glycerol and fatty acids (Section 30:5). Fatty acids are carboxylic acids with 12 to 20 carbon atoms in the chain. The number of carbons in the chain is an even number. The most abundant fatty acids are composed of 16-18 carbon atom chains. Some fatty acids are saturated while others have as many as four double bonds. In general, animal fats are saturated and plant oils are unsaturated. There are also a number of other lipids derived from glycerol in addition to fats. Many of these other lipids are used to build cell membranes.

Animal fats are saturated and plant oils are unsaturated.

Another class of lipids consists of compounds called steroids. All steroids contain the tetracyclic ring system

Steroids (lipids) have a tetracyclic ring system.

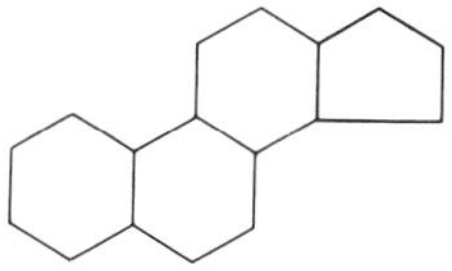

One steriod is cholesterol

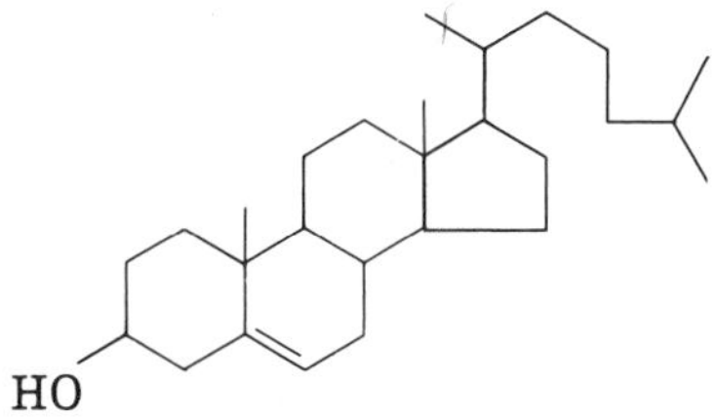

HO

which is found in bile. Cholesterol is an important constituent of cell membranes.

Some vitamins are lipids. **Vitamins** are substances used by cells to aid enzymatic reactions. The compounds chlorophyll and hemoglobin are also sometimes considered lipids. Chlorophyll is the green pigment used by plants in the process of converting carbon dioxide and water to carbohydrates. Hemoglobin is the red pigment utilized by humans and some other animals as an oxygen carrier.

Vitamins are lipids used by the cell to aid enzymatic reactions.

Chlorophyll is the green pigment used in plant photosynthesis.

Hemoglobin is the red pigment used as an oxygen carrier in animals.

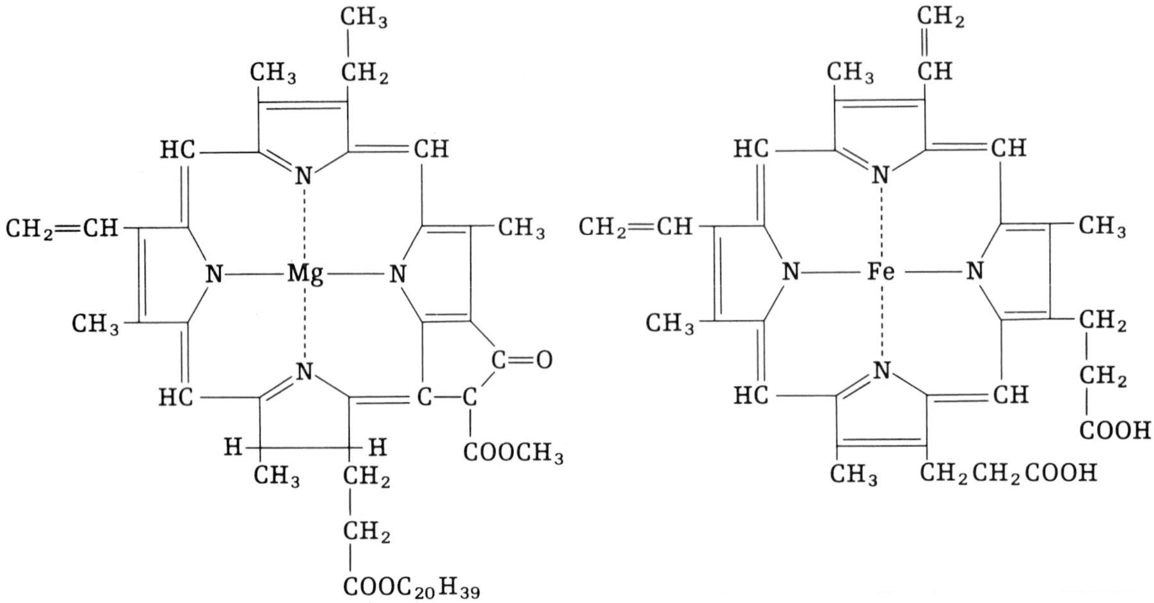

Chlorophyll a

Heme portion of hemoglobin

PROBLEMS

See Teacher's Guide.

11. Name three kinds of lipids which are structurally quite different.

12. How do animal fats differ from plant oils?

30:13 NUCLEIC ACIDS

Even though they are present in small quantities, nucleic acids are an important group of biological polymers. They determine our genetic inheritance through the process of replication or duplicating themselves. Within a cell, nucleic acids control the synthesis of enzymes.

Nucleic acids are polymers of nucleotides.

Each nucleotide has three parts: nitrogen base, a sugar, and a phosphate group.

Nucleic acids are polymers of units called nucleotides. Each **nucleotide** is composed of three parts: a nitrogen base, a sugar, and a phosphate group. Only two sugars are found in nucleic acids, ribose and deoxyribose.

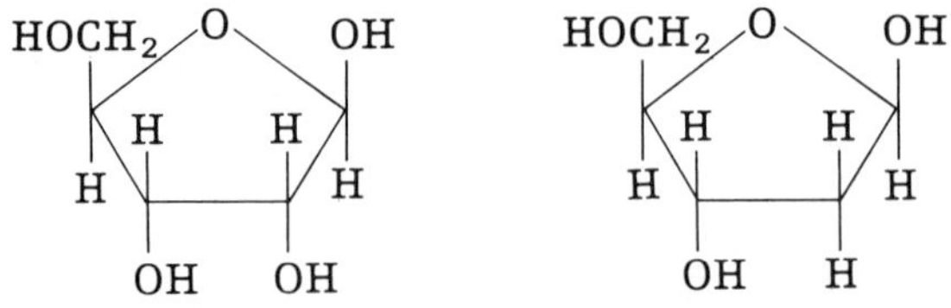

ribose

deoxyribose

DNA genetically transfers information to the next generation.

These two sugars give rise to two nucleic acids, ribonucleic acid (RNA) and deoxyribonucleic acid (DNA). Of the five nitrogen bases found in nucleic acids, DNA contains adenine, cytosine, guanine, and thymine. RNA also contains adenine, cytosine, and guanine, but substitutes uracil for thymine.

RNA is used to make enzymes.

The structures of adenine, cytosine, guanine, and thymine are shown.

adenine   cytosine   guanine   thymine

DNA is used genetically in transferring information from one generation to the next. Within a cell, the DNA is used to make several kinds of RNA. The RNA in turn is used to make enzymes. The process is quite a bit more complicated than what has been presented here, and not all of it is fully understood. Biochemical investigation is perhaps the most exciting area of emphasis in current research.

uracil

PROBLEM

13. How do RNA and DNA differ in terms of structure? In terms of function? RNA contains uracil instead of thymine. DNA transfers information genetically to next generation. RNA is used to make enzymes.

Percy Lavon Julian (1899–   )

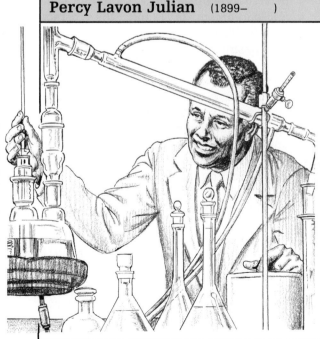

Percy Lavon Julian was born in Montgomery, Alabama. He attended a public school for black students and then went to a small state teachers school. In 1917, he enrolled in DePauw University where he majored in chemistry. He graduated as class valedictorian and as a member of Phi Beta Kappa. After receiving his master's degree from Harvard, he was awarded a fellowship to study chemistry in Vienna where he received his doctorate degree.

As an industrial chemist and director of research for a major company, his achievements included the extraction of soybean protein to produce an aero-foam for putting out fires. He did research on indoles, amino acids, and anti-fatigue drugs. He also synthesized progesterone, testosterone, and cortisone. In fact, Julian's synthesis put cortisone within the price range of the average arthritic patient for the first time.

CHEMICAL TECHNOLOGY: Genetic Engineering

There are many substances produced commercially by the action of microorganisms. Yeasts produce ethanol from grain and bacteria produce cheese from milk. Bacteria are also used in the production of propanone (acetone). Citric acid can be obtained from molds.

Biochemists have now developed methods for "custom tailoring" organisms to produce pharmaceuticals and substances of industrial importance. The substances produced by a microorganism are determined by its nucleic acids. By modifying the DNA of a microorganism, the substances it produces can be controlled.

Most DNA is found in cell chromosomes. Some DNA, however, is found outside the chromosomes in the form of long, continuous loops called plasmids. Using appropriate enzymes, a plasmid may be split open by breaking a chemical bond. Part of a DNA molecule from another organism may then be inserted and the loop is then closed. When the recombinant DNA plasmid is reinserted in the microorganism, the new section of nucleic acid leads to the production of the desired substance.

However, there are many problems to be overcome before the process described above can take place. Intensive research is done to identify the DNA section which is coded to produce the desired substance. Once a suitable host microorganism is found, the correct position for inserting the new section in the plasmid must be located. All cells have defense mechanisms to reject foreign DNA. The host cell must be "fooled" into accepting the new plasmid by chemically reducing the cell's defense mechanism. Enzymatic reactions in cells must be controlled chemically if the desired product is to be obtained in economical quantities.

Figure 30-4 shows a model for genesplicing using *Escherichia coli* bacteria *(E. coli)*. This microorganism is often used in recombinant DNA studies because of its comparatively simple genetic make-up. An enzyme is used to break the plasmid ring leaving two so-called "sticky ends." DNA from another microorganism is attached to the cleaved plasmid.

FIGURE 30-4. The model shows recombining the DNA of another organism to a cleaved plasmid.

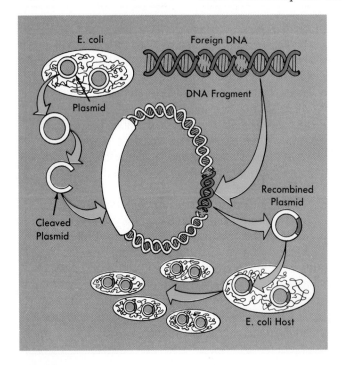

Biochemical production of insulin and interferon by re-combinant DNA microorganisms is a reality. Many new products in the health science field should appear in the future. The gene-splicing process itself provides us with a better understanding of growth and development. Scientists are hoping recombinant DNA research will provide answers to such problems as birth defects and cancer.

SUMMARY

1. Hydrocarbons may undergo oxidation, addition, substitution, or elimination reactions. 30:1-30:4

2. The formation of an ester from an alcohol and an acid or acid anhydride is called esterification. 30:5

3. The splitting of an ester into the alcohol and the salt of the acid is called saponification. 30:5

4. Petroleum is the principal source of organic chemicals. It is composed mostly of hydrocarbons. 30:6

5. Addition polymerization is a reaction in which many carbon molecules containing a double bond add to each other to form a chain or cross-linked chains of very great molecular size and mass. 30:7-30:8

6. Condensation polymerization is a reaction in which hundreds of small molecules react to produce a large molecule (polymer) and many small molecules, such as water. 30:8

7. Synthetic rubber, plastics, and synthetic fibers are all made by addition and condensation polymerization reactions. 30:7-30:9

8. The principal classes of chemical compounds of biological interest are proteins, carbohydrates, lipids, and nucleic acids. 30:10–30:13

9. Proteins are polymers of amino acids. They act as structural parts of the organism and as catalysts called enzymes. 30:10

10. Carbohydrates are the materials utilized by cells to produce energy. They contain carbon, hydrogen, and oxygen. 30:11

11. Lipids are soluble in nonpolar solvents. Lipid materials exist in many different forms from fats to pigments. 30:12

12. Nucleic acids control the behavior of cells and transfer genetic information from one generation to the next. 30:13

PROBLEMS

14. Predict the product of the reaction between ethene and hydrogen iodide. CH_3—CH_2I

15. Predict the structure of the copolymer of ethene and phenylethene.

16. Complete and balance equations for the following.

15. —CH—CH_2—CH_2—CH_2—(amor)

   a. chlorine + propene
   b. preparation of pentyl ethanoate
   c. complete combustion of benzene
   d. elimination of water from 1-butanol
   e. saponification of glyceryl trioctadecanoate with NaOH

17. What is the difference between addition polymerization and condensation polymerization?

18. Draw the structural formula for the tripeptide formed from alanine, valine, and tryptophan, in that order. Assume the acid group of alanine reacts.

19. Draw the structural diagram for the polypeptide formed from glycine, cysteine, tyrosine, and lysine, in that order. Assume the acid group of glycine reacts.

20. Why can only 20 amino acids form so many different proteins?

21. What is the principal function of proteins in the body? catalysts and structural components

22. What compound is produced with excess energy in a cell? ATP

23. What role do vitamins play in the cell? aid enzymatic reactions

REVIEW

1. Balance the following reaction.
$$Bi + NO_3^- + H^+ \rightarrow Bi^{3+} + NO + H_2O$$

2. What voltage should be generated by the following cell under standard conditions?
$$Co|Co^{2+}\|HgCl_2|Hg_2Cl_2$$

3. What products would you expect from the electrolysis of a solution of iron(II) sulfate?

4. What voltage would you expect from the following cell at standard temperature and pressure? (Assume $[H^+] = 1.00M$)
$$Cu|Cu^+\|MnO_4^-|Mn^{2+}(0.0100M)$$

5. What is the free energy change for a reaction if it shows a potential difference in a cell of 1.94 volts and $1e^-$ is transferred?

6. What mass of bromine will be produced by a current of 2.60 amperes flowing for 2.17 hours?

7. What is the amount of $^{100}_{46}Pd$ left at the end of 16 days if 270 g existed originally and the half-life is 4 days?

8. Complete: $^{129}_{55}Cs + _{-1}^{0}e \rightarrow ?$

9. Name the following compounds.

Br
|
a. CH_3—CH—CH_2—CH_3

b. CH_3—CH=CH_2

c. 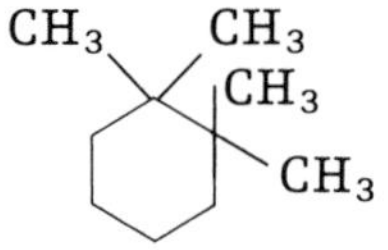 [structure: cyclohexane with CH₃ groups]

d. 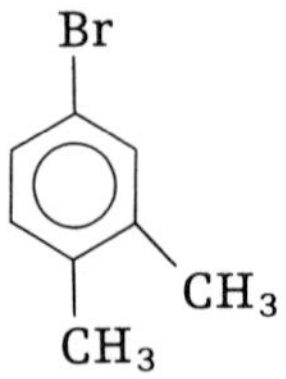 [structure: benzene ring with Br and CH₃ groups]

Answers in left margin:

2. 0.91 V
3. H_2 and SO_2
4. 1.01 V
5. −187 kJ
6. 16.8 g
7. 16.9 g
8. $^{129}_{54}Xe$

9. a. 2-bromobutane
   b. propene
   c. 1,1,2,2-tetramethylcyclohexane
   d. 1-bromo-3,4-dimethylbenzene

10. Write the formulas for the following.
    a. 1-bromo-1-chloropropene   **c.** 3-chlorocyclopropene
    b. ethene   **d.** 1-bromo-1,2-diphenylpropane

ONE MORE STEP

1. By reference work in the library, prepare a short report to your class on the mechanism of a well-known reaction in organic chemistry such as the Grignard or the Wurtz reaction.
2. Investigate the monomers which go into the production of Saran, Kodel, Acrilan, Dynel, and Mylar.
3. Find out what a Zwitterion is.
4. What is the difference between α-helix proteins and β-pleated proteins?
5. What is the biochemical role of nicotinamide adenine dinucleotide (NAD) in cell energy transfer?
6. The vitamin thiamine is converted in the cell to thiamin pyrophosphate. Find the structure of this molecule.
7. The citric acid cycle is the name for an important series of reactions in cells. Draw a series of equations describing the changes in the cycle.
8. Acidosis is a physiological condition brought on by the lack of cells ability to transport glucose across the cell membrane. It is a symptom of diabetes mellitus. Find out how the condition obtained its name.
9. Folic acid is one of the B vitamins. Find its structure.

READINGS

Blondin, George A., and Green, David E., "A Unifying Model of Bioenergetics." *Chemical and Engineering News,* Vol. 53, No. 45 (November 10, 1975), pp. 26-42.

Flavin, Christopher, "Petroleum: Too Valuable to Burn?" *SciQuest* Vol. 53, No. 9 (November 1980), pp. 18-21.

Harris, J. Milton, and Wamser, Carl C., *Fundamentals of Organic Reaction Mechanisms.* New York: John Wiley and Sons, 1976.

Jones, Maitland, Jr., "Carbenes." *Scientific American,* Vol. 234, No. 2 (February 1976), pp. 101-113.

Kelly, Myron W., "Adhesive Bonding." *Chemistry,* Vol. 49, No. 6 (July-August 1976), pp. 14-19.

Meloan, Clifton E., "DETERGENTS—Soaps and Syndets." *Chemistry,* Vol. 49, No. 7 (September 1976), pp. 6-10.

Sears, Jerry A., "Polymer Pioneers." *Chemistry,* Vol. 50, No. 7 (September 1977), pp. 6-10.

Uhlmann, D. R., and Kolbeck, A. G., "The Microstructure of Polymeric Materials." *Scientific American,* Vol. 233, No. 6 (December 1975), pp. 96-106.

Weisburger, Elizabeth L., "Cancer-Causing Chemicals." *Chemistry,* Vol. 50, No. 1 (January-February 1977), pp. 42-48.

APPENDIX A

Table A-1

Definitions of Standards

1 **ampere** is the constant current which, if maintained in two straight parallel conductors of infinite length, of negligible circular cross-section, and placed 1 meter apart in a vacuum, would produce a force of 2×10^{-7} newton per meter of length between these conductors.

1 **candela** is the luminous intensity, in the perpendicular direction, of a surface of $1/600\ 000\ m^2$ of a blackbody at the temperature of freezing platinum at a pressure of 101 325 pascals.

1 **cubic decimeter** is equal to 1 liter.

1 **kelvin** is $1/273.16$ of the thermodynamic temperature of the triple point of water.

1 **meter** is equal to 1 650 763.73 times the wavelength in a vacuum of the orange-red light of $^{86}_{36}$Kr. The transition is $2p_{10}5d_5$.

1 **mole** is the amount of substance containing as many elementary entities as there are atoms in 0.012 kilogram of carbon-12.

1 **second** is equal to 9 192 631 770 periods of the natural electromagnetic oscillation during that transition of ground state $^2S_{1/2}$ of cesium-133 which is designated $(F = 4, M = 0) \leftrightarrow (F = 3, M = 0)$

Avogadro's number = 6.02217×10^{23}

1 **electronvolt** = 1.60219×10^{-19} J

Faraday's constant = 96 486.7 C/mol e^-

Ideal gas constant = 8.31430 J/K·mol = 8.31430 dm^3·kPa/mol·K

Ideal gas volume at STP = 22.4136 dm^3

Planck's constant = 6.62620×10^{-34} J/Hz

Speed of light = $2.997\ 925 \times 10^8$ m/s

Table A-2

Symbols and Abbreviations	
α = rays from radioactive materials, helium nuclei	K_{eq} = equilibrium constant
β = rays from radioactive materials, electrons	K_{sp} = solubility product constant
γ = rays from radioactive materials, high-energy quanta	kg = kilogram
Δ = change in	M = molarity
λ = wavelength	m = mass, molality
ν = frequency	m = meter (*length*)
π = osmotic pressure	mol = mole (*amount*)
A = ampere (*electric current*)	min = minute (*time*)
°C = Celsius degree (*temperature*)	N = newton (*force*)
C = coulomb (*quantity of electricity*)	N_A = Avogadro's number
c = speed of light	n = number of moles
cd = candela (*luminous intensity*)	P = pressure, power
C_p = specific heat capacity	Pa = pascal (*pressure*)
D = density	$\bar{p}$ = momentum
E = energy, electromotive force	q = heat
F = force, Faraday	R = gas constant
G = free energy	S = entropy
g = gram (*mass*)	s = second (*time*)
H = enthalpy	T = temperature
Hz = hertz (*frequency*)	u = atomic mass unit
h = Planck's constant	V = volume
h = hour (*time*)	V = volt (*electromotive force*)
J = joule (*energy*)	v = velocity
K = kelvin (*temperature*)	W = watt (*power*)
K_a = ionization constant (acid)	w = work
K_b = ionization constant (base)	x = mole fraction

Table A-3

Some Properties of the Elements

Element	Symbol	Atomic Number (Z)	Atomic Mass (M)*	Melting Point (°C)	Boiling Point (°C)	Density (g/cm³)	Atomic Radius (nm)	First Ionization Energy (kJ/mol)	Standard Reduction Potential (V) (for elements from or to oxidation state indicated)	Heat of Fusion (kJ/mol)	Specific Heat Capacity (J/g·C°)	Heat of Vaporization (kJ/mol)	Abundance in Earth's Crust (%)	Major Oxidation States
Actinium	Ac	89	[227.02779]	1050	3200	10.07	0.188	666	(3+) −2.6	14.2	—	293	trace	3+
Aluminum	Al	13	26.98154	660	2467	2.70	0.143	578	—	10.7	0.900	284	8.8	3+
Americium	Am	95	[243.06139]	994	2607	13.67	0.184	579	(3+) −1.66	20.0	0.207	216	—	3+, 4+
Antimony	Sb	51	121.75	631	1750	6.69	0.136	834	(3+) −2.38	—	0.519	195	1×10^{-4}	3+, 5+
Argon	Ar	18	39.948	−189.2	−185.7	0.001784	0.191	1521	—	1.21	0.331	6.52	4×10^{-4}	—
Arsenic	As	33	74.9216	817 (2836 kPa)	613 (sublimes)	5.727	0.125	947	—	93.7	—	128 (sublimes)	5×10^{-4}	3+, 5+, 3−
Astatine	At	85	[209.98704]	302	337	—	0.14	917	(1−) +0.3	11.9	0.179	45.2	trace	
Barium	Ba	56	137.33	725	1640	3.5	0.217	503	(2+) −2.90	7.66	—	149	0.05	2+
Berkelium	Bk	97	[247.07032]	986	—	14.78	—	579	—	—	—	—	—	3+, 4+
Beryllium	Be	4	9.01218	1278	2970	1.8477	0.111	900	(2+) −1.85	14.6	1.83	295	0.001	2+
Bismuth	Bi	83	208.9808	271	1560	9.747	0.155	703	—	10.5	0.122	172	2×10^{-5}	3+, 5+
Boron	B	5	10.81	2079	3675	2.34	0.083	801	—	22.2	1.03	314	0.001	3+
Bromine	Br	35	79.904	−7.2	58.78	3.12	0.111	1140	(1−) +1.065	10.8	0.349	30.0	5×10^{-4}	1−
Cadmium	Cd	48	112.41	321	765	8.65	0.149	868	(2+) −0.4026	6.11	0.232	99.8	5×10^{-5}	2+
Calcium	Ca	20	40.08	839	1484	1.55	0.197	590	(2+) −2.76	9.33	0.652	162	3.64	2+
Californium	Cf	98	[251.07961]	900	—	14	—	—	—	—	—	—	—	3+
Carbon	C	6	12.011	3550	4827	2.267	0.077	1087	—	105	0.716	326	0.027	4+
Cerium	Ce	58	140.12	799	3426	6.657	0.183	528	(3+) −2.335	8.87	0.194	305	0.006	3+, 4+
Cesium	Cs	55	132.9054	28.4	678	1.873	0.265	376	(1+) −2.923	2.09	0.238	68.3	1×10^{-4}	1+
Chlorine	Cl	17	35.453	−101.00	−34.6	0.00298	0.099	1251	(1−) +1.3583	6.41	0.477	20.4	0.045	1−
Chromium	Cr	24	51.996	1857	2672	7.18	0.125	653	(2+) −0.557	15.3	0.448	305	0.01	2+, 3+, 6+
Cobalt	Co	27	58.9332	1495	2870	8.92	0.125	758	(2+) −0.28	15.2	0.446	389	0.0023	2+, 3+
Copper	Cu	29	63.546	1083	2567	8.96	0.128	745	(1+) +0.522 (2+) +0.3402	13.0	0.386	305	0.0054	1+, 2+
Curium	Cm	96	[247.07038]	1340	—	13.51	0.177	572	(3+) −2.35	17.2	0.173	251	3×10^{-4}	3+
Dysprosium	Dy	66	162.50	1412	2562	8.550	—	—	—	—	—	—	—	3+
Einsteinium	Es	99	[254.08805]	—	—	—	—	—	—	—	—	—	—	—
Erbium	Er	68	167.26	1497	2863	9.066	0.176	589	(3+) −2.30	17.2	0.168	293	2.4×10^{-4}	3+
Europium	Eu	63	151.96	822	1597	5.243	0.204	547	(3+) −2.41	10.5	0.156	176	1.2×10^{-4}	2+, 3+
Fermium	Fm	100	[257.09515]	—	—	—	—	—	—	—	—	—	—	—
Fluorine	F	9	18.998403	−219.62	−188.14	0.001580	0.072	1681	(1−) +2.87	1.02	0.824	6.86	0.065	1−
Francium	Fr	87	[223.01976]	27	677	—	0.27	—	—	—	—	—	—	1+
Gadolinium	Gd	64	157.25	1313	3266	7.900	0.180	592	(3+) −2.4	15.5	0.232	312	5.3×10^{-4}	3+
Gallium	Ga	31	69.737	29.78	2403	5.9037	0.122	579	(3+) −0.560	5.59	0.374	296	7×10^{-4}	3+
Germanium	Ge	32	72.59	937.4	2830	5.323	0.123	762	(2+) +0.23	34.7	0.322	285	1.5×10^{-4}	2+, 4+

*[ ] indicates mass of longest-lived isotope

Element	Symbol	Atomic Number (Z)	Atomic Mass (M)	Melting Point (°C)	Boiling Point (°C)	Density (g/cm³)	Atomic Radius (nm)	First Ionization Energy (kJ/mol)	Standard Reduction Potential (V) (for elements from or to oxidation state indicated)	Heat of Fusion (kJ/mol)	Specific Heat Capacity (J/g·°C)	Heat of Vaporization (kJ/mol)	Abundance in Earth's Crust (%)	Major Oxidation States
Gold	Au	79	196.9665	1064	2807	19.3	0.144	890	(3+)+1.42	12.7	0.128	310	5×10^{-7}	1+, 3+
Hafnium	Hf	72	178.49	2227	4602	13.3	0.156	675	(4+)−1.70	25.1	0.136	661	5×10^{-4}	4+
Helium	He	2	4.00260	−272.2 (2536 kPa)	−268.9	0.00017847	0.122	2372	—	0.0182	5.19	0.0820	—	
Holmium	Ho	67	164.9304	1474	2695	8.795	0.177	581	(3+)−2.32	17.2	0.165	251	1.2×10^{-4}	3+
Hydrogen	H	1	1.0079	−259.14	−252.87	0.00008987	0.053	1312	(1+) 0.0000	0.117	14.3	904	1×10^{-5}	1+
Indium	In	49	114.82	157	2080	7.31	0.163	558	(3+)−0.338	3.27	0.235	225	1×10^{-5}	1+, 3+
Iodine	I	53	126.9045	113.5	185.35	4.93	0.128	1008	(1−)+0.535	15.3	0.285	41.7	5×10^{-5}	1−
Iridium	Ir	77	192.22	2410	4130	22.42	0.136	878	(1−)+1.15	26.4	0.130	564	1×10^{-7}	2+, 3+, 4+
Iron	Fe	26	55.847	1535	2750	7.874	0.124	759	(2+)−0.409	14.9	0.448	354	5	2+, 3+
Krypton	Kr	36	83.80	−156.6	−152.30	0.0037493	0.198	1351	—	1.63	0.247	79.0	1.4×10^{-8}	
Lanthanum	La	57	138.9055	921	3457	6.145	0.188	538	(3+)−2.37	10.0	0.199	335	0.0018	3+
Lawrencium	Lr	103	[256.099]	—	—	—	—	—	—	—	—	—	—	
Lead	Pb	82	207.2	327.5	1740	11.35	0.175	716	(2+)−0.126	5.12	0.138	178	0.002	2+, 4+
Lithium	Li	3	6.941	180.54	1347	0.534	0.152	520	(3+)−3.045	4.60	3.48	136	0.005	1+
Lutetium	Lu	71	174.967	1663	3395	9.840	0.173	524	(3+)−2.25	19.2	0.137	247	5×10^{-5}	3+
Magnesium	Mg	12	24.305	649	1090	1.738	0.160	738	(2+)−2.375	9.04	1.01	132	2.1	2+
Manganese	Mn	25	54.9380	1244	1962	7.32	0.124	717	(2+)−1.029	14.4	0.480	225	0.085	2+, 4+, 6+, 7+
Mendelevium	Md	101	[258]	—	—	—	—	—	—	—	—	—	—	
Mercury	Hg	80	200.59	−38.84	356.58	13.546	0.160	1007	(2+)+0.851	2.33	0.139	58.5	5×10^{-6}	1+, 2+
Molybdenum	Mo	42	95.94	2617	4612	10.22	0.136	685	(3+)−0.2	27.6	0.248	594	1.5×10^{-4}	2+, 3+, 4+, 5+, 6+
Neodymium	Nd	60	144.24	1021	3068	6.90	0.182	530	(3+)−2.246	7.11	0.201	255	0.0024	3+
Neon	Ne	10	20.179	−248.7	−246.05	0.00089994	0.160	2081	—	0.324	1.03	1.77	5×10^{-7}	
Neptunium	Np	93	237.0482	640	3902	20.25	0.131	737	(3+)−1.86	10.9	0.124	230	—	3+, 4+, 6+
Nickel	Ni	28	58.71	1453	2732	8.90	0.125	737	(2+)−0.23	17.6	0.443	379	0.018	2+, 3+
Niobium	Nb	41	92.9064	2468	4742	8.57	0.143	664	(3+)−1.1	27.2	0.266	697	0.0020	3+, 4+, 5+
Nitrogen	N	7	14.0067	−209.86	−195.79	0.0012500	0.070	1402	—	0.721	1.04	5.58	0.0019	3−
Nobelium	No	102	[255.093]	—	—	—	—	—	—	—	—	—	—	
Osmium	Os	76	190.2	3045	5027	22.57	0.134	839	(2+)+0.85	29.3	0.130	28.6	5×10^{-6}	2+, 3+, 4+, 6+, 8+
Oxygen	O	8	15.9994	−218.4	−182.96	0.001429	0.066	1314	—	0.445	0.916	6.81	48.6	2−
Palladium	Pd	46	106.4	1552	3140	12.02	0.138	805	(2+)+0.83	17.2	0.245	372	—	2+, 3+, 4+
Phosphorus	P	15	30.97376	44.1	280	1.82	0.115	1012	—	2.51	0.724	49.8	0.12	3+, 5+, 3−
Platinum	Pt	78	195.09	1772	3827	21.447	0.138	868	(2+)+1.2	19.7	0.134	510	1×10^{-6}	2+, 4+, 6+
Plutonium	Pu	94	[244.06424]	639.5	3235	19.816	0.157	560	(3+)−2.02	12.6	0.137	334	—	3+, 4+, 6+
Polonium	Po	84	[208.98244]	254	962	9.32	0.167	812	(2+)+0.60	2.40	0.126	103	trace	2+, 4+
Potassium	K	19	39.0983	63.7	774	0.862	0.227	419	(1+)−2.924	2.40	0.748	79.0	2.59	1+
Praseodymium	Pr	59	140.9077	931	3512	6.64	0.183	523	(3+)−2.47	11.3	0.197	333	8.0×10^{-4}	3+, 4+
Promethium	Pm	61	[144.91279]	1168	2460	7.22	0.181	536	(3+)−2.42	12.6	0.185	293	—	3+

*[ ] indicates mass of longest-lived isotope

Element	Symbol	Atomic Number (Z)	Atomic Mass (M)*	Melting Point (°C)	Boiling Point (°C)	Density (g/cm³)	Atomic Radius (nm)	First Ionization Energy (kJ/mol)	Standard Reduction Potential (V) (for elements from or to oxidation state indicated)	Heat of Fusion (kJ/mol)	Specific Heat Capacity (J/g·°C)	Heat of Vaporization (kJ/mol)	Abundance in Earth's Crust (%)	Major Oxidation States
Protactinium	Pa	91	231.0359	1560	4027	15.37	0.161	—	—	14.6	0.121	481	trace	4+, 5+
Radium	Ra	88	226.0254	700	1140	5.5	0.220	509	(2+) −2.92	8.37	0.120	146	1×10^{-11}	2+
Radon	Rn	86	[222]	−71	−62	0.00973	0.22	1037	—	3.25	0.0937	18.1	4×10^{-17}	
Rhenium	Re	75	186.2	3180	5627	21.02	0.137	760	—	33.1	0.138	636	1×10^{-7}	3+, 4+, 5+, 6+, 7+
Rhodium	Rh	45	102.9055	1966	3727	12.41	0.135	720	(3+) +0.8	21.8	0.245	531	1×10^{-7}	2+, 3+, 4+
Rubidium	Rb	37	85.4678	39	688	1.532	0.248	403	(1+) −2.924	2.20	0.359	75.8	0.0034	1+
Ruthenium	Ru	44	101.07	2310	3900	12.41	0.133	711	—	25.5	0.238	568	4×10^{-8}	3+, 4+, 5+, 8+
Samarium	Sm	62	150.4	1077	1791	7.520	0.180	543	(3+) −2.41	10.9	0.188	293	6×10^{-4}	2+, 3+
Scandium	Sc	21	44.9559	1541	2831	2.989	0.16	631	(3+) −2.08	15.9	0.524	335	0.0022	3+
Selenium	Se	34	78.96	217	685	4.79	0.117	941	(2−) −0.78	5.10	0.272	59.7	9×10^{-6}	2−, 4+, 6+
Silicon	Si	14	28.0855	1410	2355	2.33	0.117	787	—	39.6	0.705	297	27.6	4+, 4−
Silver	Ag	47	107.868	961.9	2212	10.50	0.144	731	(1+) +0.7996	11.3	0.236	254	1×10^{-5}	1+
Sodium	Na	11	22.9898	97.81	882.9	0.971	0.192	496	(1+) −2.7109	2.64	1.23	97.9	2.83	1+
Strontium	Sr	38	87.62	769	1384	2.54	0.215	550	(2+) −2.89	9.16	0.296	141	0.0370	2+
Sulfur	S	16	32.06	112.8	444.7	2.07	0.104	1000	(2−) −0.508	1.23	0.736	10.5	0.05	2−, 4+, 6+
Tantalum	Ta	73	180.9479	2996	5425	16.65	0.143	761	—	31.4	0.140	753	2×10^{-4}	3+, 4+, 5+
Technetium	Tc	43	96.9062	2172	4877	11.50	0.136	702	—	23.0	0.243	502	—	4+, 5+, 6+, 7+
Tellurium	Te	52	127.60	449.5	989.8	6.24	0.143	869	(2−) −0.92	13.5	0.201	49.8	2×10^{-7}	2−, 4+, 6+
Terbium	Tb	65	158.9254	1356	3123	8.23	0.178	564	(3+) −2.39	16.3	0.182	293	1×10^{-4}	3+
Thallium	Tl	81	204.37	303.5	1457	11.85	0.170	589	(1+) −0.3363	4.31	0.129	162	7×10^{-5}	1+, 3+
Thorium	Th	90	232.0381	1750	4790	11.7	0.180	671	(4+) −1.90	15.6	0.123	544	0.0015	4+
Thulium	Tm	69	168.9342	1545	1947	9.321	0.175	596	(3+) −2.28	18.4	0.160	213	4.6×10^{-5}	2+, 3+
Tin	Sn	50	118.69	232	2270	7.31	0.141	709	(2+) −0.136	7.20	0.220	230	6×10^{-4}	2+, 4+
Titanium	Ti	22	47.90	1660	3287	4.54	0.145	658	(2+) −1.63	20.9	0.520	423	0.63	2+, 3+, 4+
Tungsten	W	74	183.85	3410	5660	19.3	0.137	770	—	35.2	0.134	885	1.5×10^{-4}	2+, 3+, 4+, 5+, 6+
Uranium	U	92	238.029	1132.3	3818	18.95	0.139	587	(3+) −1.80	15.5	0.116	460	2×10^{-5}	3+, 4+, 5+, 6+
Vanadium	V	23	50.9415	1890	3380	6.11	0.132	650	(2+) −1.18	17.6	0.484	459	0.01	2+, 3+, 4+, 5+
Xenon	Xe	54	131.30	−111.9	−107.1	0.0058971	0.218	1170	—	3.10	0.158	72.6	3×10^{-4}	
Ytterbium	Yb	70	173.04	819	1194	6.965	0.194	603	(3+) −2.27	9.20	0.132	155	0.0032	2+, 3+
Yttrium	Y	39	88.9059	1522	3338	4.469	0.181	616	(3+) −2.37	17.2	0.291	377	0.02	3+
Zinc	Zn	30	65.38	419.6	907	7.13	0.133	906	(2+) −0.763	6.67	0.386	115	0.023	2+
Zirconium	Zr	40	91.22	1852	4377	6.506	0.160	660	(4+) −1.53	23.0	0.278	418		2+, 3+
Element 104	(Rf)	104	[257]	—	—	—	—	—	—	—	—	—	—	
Element 105	(Ha)	105	[260]	—	—	—	—	—	—	—	—	—	—	
Element 106		106	[263]	—	—	—	—	—	—	—	—	—	—	
Element 107		107	[258]	—	—	—	—	—	—	—	—	—	—	

*[ ] indicates mass of longest-lived isotope

Table A-4

Major Formal Oxidation States of Polyatomic Ions			
1−	**2−**	**3−**	**4−**
Azide, N_3^-	Chromate, CrO_4^{2-}	Arsenite, AsO_3^{3-}	Hexacyanoferrate(II),
Benzoate, $C_7H_5O_2^-$	Dichromate, $Cr_2O_7^{2-}$	Citrate, $C_6H_5O_7^{3-}$	$Fe(CN)_6^{2-}$
Bromate, BrO_3^-	Hexachloroplatinate(IV),	Hexacyanoferrate(III),	Pyrophosphate, $P_4O_7^{4-}$
Chlorate, ClO_3^-	$PtCl_6^{2-}$	$Fe(CN)_6^{3-}$	
Formate, CHO_2^-	Molybdate, MoO_4^{2-}		
Hypophosphite, $PH_2O_2^-$	Peroxide, O_2^{2-}		
Metaphosphate, PO_3^-	Peroxydisulfate, $S_2O_8^{2-}$		
Nitrite, NO_2^-	Sulfite, SO_3^{2-}		
Periodate, IO_4^-	Tellurate, TeO_4^{2-}		
Permanganate, MnO_4^-	Tetraborate, $B_4O_7^{2-}$		
Peroxyborate, BO_3^-	Thiosulfate, $S_2O_3^{2-}$		
Thiocyanate, SCN^-	Tungstate, WO_4^{2-}		
Vanadate, VO_3^-			

Table A-5

Specific Heat Capacities (in $J/g \cdot C°$)					
Substance	**C_p**	**Substance**	**C_p**	**Substance**	**C_p**
AlF_3	0.987	CCl_3CCl_3	0.728	$MgCO_3$	0.837
BeO	1.05	CH_3COCH_3	2.18	$Mg(OH)_2$	1.31
CaC_2	1.00	CH_3CH_2OH	2.45	$MgSO_4$	0.929
$CaSO_4$	0.716	CH_3COOH	2.05	Na_2CO_3	1.14
CCl_4	0.856	HI	0.235	PCl_3	0.874
C_6H_6	1.74	ICl	0.661	SiC	0.686
C_6H_{14}	2.26	K_2CO_3	0.904	SiO_2	0.749
C_6H_5Br	0.989	$LiNO_3$	1.21	$TiCl_4$	0.803
$C_6H_5CH_3$	1.80			ZnS	0.469

Table A-6

Thermodynamic Properties (at standard states)						
$\Delta H_f°$ in kJ/mol			$\Delta G_f°$ in kJ/mol		$S°$ in J/mol·K	
concentration of aqueous solutions is $1M$						

Substance	$\Delta H_f°$	$\Delta G_f°$	$S°$	Substance	$\Delta H_f°$	$\Delta G_f°$	$S°$
Ag	0	0	42.7	H_3PO_3	−972	—	—
AgCl	−127	−110	96.1	H_3PO_4	−1280	−1120	110
AgCN	−146	−164	83.7	H_2S	−20.1	−33.0	206
Al	0	0	28.3	$H_2SO_3(aq)$	−614	−538	232
Al_2O_3	−1670	−1580	51.0	$H_2SO_4(aq)$	−908	−742	17.2
$BaCl_2(aq)$	−873	−823	121	$HgCl_2$	−230	−177	—
$BaSO_4$	−1470	−1350	132	Hg_2Cl_2	−265	−211	196
Be	0	0	9.54	Hg_2SO_4	−742	−624	201
Be_3N_2	−568	−512	—	I_2	0	0	117
Bi	0	0	56.9	K	0	0	63.6
$BiCl_3$	−379	−319	190	KBr	−392	−379	96.4
Bi_2S_3	−183	−164	146	$KMnO_4$	−813	−714	172
Br_2	0	0	152	KOH	−426	—	—
CH_4	−74.8	−50.8	186	LiBr	−350	—	—
C_2H_4	+52.3	+68.1	219	LiOH	−487	−444	50.2
C_2H_6	−84.7	−32.9	229	Mn	0	0	32.0
C_4H_{10}	−125	−15.7	310	$MnCl_2(aq)$	−555	−491	38.9
CO	−111	−137	198	$Mn(NO_3)_2(aq)$	−636	−451	218
CO_2	−393.5	−394.4	214	MnO_2	−521	−466	53.1
CS_2	+87.9	+63.6	151	MnS	−214	—	—
Ca	0	0	41.6	N_2	0	0	192
$Ca(OH)_2$	−987	−897	—	NH_3	−46.2	−16.6	193
Cl_2	0	0	223	NH_4Br	−270	−175	113
$CoCO_3$	−723	−650	—	NO	+90.4	—	211
CoO	−239	−213	43.9	NO_2	+33.8	+51.8	240
Cr_2O_3	−1130	−1050	81.2	Na	0	0	51.0
CsCl(aq)	−415	−371	188	NaBr	−360	—	—
$Cs_2SO_4(aq)$	−1400	−1310	283	NaCl	−411	−384	72.4
CuI	−67.8	−69.5	96.7	$NaNO_3(aq)$	−447	—	—
CuS	−53.1	−53.7	66.5	NaOH	−427	—	—
Cu_2S	−79.5	−86.2	121	$Na_2S(aq)$	−437	—	—
$CuSO_4$	−770	−662	113	Na_2SO_4	−1380	−1270	149
F_2	0	0	203	O_2	0	0	205
$FeCl_3$	−405	—	—	P_4O_6	−1640	—	—
FeO	−267	—	—	P_4O_{10}	−2980	−2700	229
Fe_2O_3	−822	−741	90.0	$PbBr_2$	−277	−260	162
H	+218	—	115	$PbCl_2$	−359	−314	136
H_2	0	0	131	S	0	0	31.9
HBr	−36.2	−53.2	198	SO_2	−297	−300	249
HCl	−92.3	−95.3	187	SO_3	−438	−368	95.6
HCl(aq)	−167	−131	56.5	SrO	−590	−560	54.4
HCN(aq)	+151	+172	94.1	Ti	0	0	30.3
HF	−269	−271	174	TiO_2	—	−853	50.2
HI	+25.9	+1.30	206	TlI	−50.2	−83.3	236
$H_2O(l)$	−286	−237	70.0	UCl_4	−1050	−962	198
$H_2O(g)$	−242	−229	189	UCl_5	−1100	−993	259
H_2O_2	—	−118	110	Zn	0	0	41.6
H_3PO_2	−609	—	—	$ZnCl_2(aq)$	−487	−410	3.72
				$ZnSO_4(aq)$	−1063	−892	−92.0

Table A-7

Solubility Rules
You will be working with water solutions, and it is helpful to have a few rules concerning what substances are soluble in water. The more common rules are listed below. 1. All common salts of the Group IA elements and ammonium ion are soluble. 2. All common acetates and nitrates are soluble. 3. All binary compounds of Group VIIA elements (other than F) with metals are soluble except those of silver, mercury(I), and lead. 4. All sulfates are soluble except those of barium, strontium, lead, calcium, silver, and mercury(I). 5. Except for those in Rule 1, carbonates, hydroxides, oxides, and phosphates are insoluble.

Table A-8

Molal Freezing and Boiling Point Constants (in C°/mol/1000 g solvent)				
Substance	Freezing point (°C)	Molal freezing point constant	Boiling point (°C)	Molal boiling point constant
Acetic Acid	16.604	−3.90	117.9	3.07
Benzene	5.5	−4.90	80.1	2.53
Camphor	179.8	−37.7	204	5.95
Cyclohexane	6.55	−20.0	80.74	2.79
Nitrobenzene	5.7	−7.00	210.8	5.24
Phenol	43	−7.40	181.75	3.56
Water	0.00	−1.86	100.00	0.512

Table A-9

Ionization Constants					
Substance	Ionization Constant	Substance	Ionization Constant	Substance	Ionization Constant
$HCOOH$	1.69×10^{-4}	H_2CO_3	4.30×10^{-7}	HS^-	1.10×10^{-13}
CH_3COOH	1.76×10^{-5}	HCO_3^-	5.61×10^{-11}	HSO_4^-	1.20×10^{-2}
$CH_2ClCOOH$	1.40×10^{-3}	HCN	4.93×10^{-10}	H_2SO_3	1.54×10^{-2}
$CHCl_2COOH$	3.32×10^{-2}	HF	3.53×10^{-4}	HSO_3^-	1.02×10^{-7}
CCl_3COOH	2.00×10^{-1}	HNO_2	4.60×10^{-4}	$HSeO_4^-$	1.20×10^{-2}
$HOOCCOOH$	5.90×10^{-2}	H_3PO_4	7.52×10^{-3}	H_2SeO_3	3.50×10^{-2}
$HOOCCOO^-$	6.40×10^{-5}	$H_2PO_4^-$	6.23×10^{-8}	$HSeO_3^-$	4.80×10^{-9}
CH_3CH_2COOH	1.34×10^{-5}	HPO_4^{2-}	2.20×10^{-13}	$HBrO$	2.06×10^{-9}
C_6H_5COOH	6.46×10^{-5}	H_3PO_3	1.00×10^{-2}	$HClO$	2.95×10^{-5}
H_3BO_3	7.30×10^{-10}	$H_2PO_3^-$	2.60×10^{-7}	HIO	2.30×10^{-11}
$H_2BO_3^-$	1.80×10^{-13}	H_3PO_2	7.94×10^{-2}	NH_3	1.77×10^{-5}
HBO_3^{2-}	1.60×10^{-14}	H_2S	1.32×10^{-7}	H_2NOH	1.07×10^{-8}

Table A-10

Solubility Product Constants (at 25°C)							
Substance	**K_{sp}**	**Substance**	**K_{sp}**	**Substance**	**K_{sp}**
AgBr	7.70×10^{-13}	$BaSO_4$	1.08×10^{-10}	$MnCO_3$	1.82×10^{-11}
$AgBrO_3$	5.77×10^{-5}	$CaCO_3$	8.70×10^{-9}	$NiCO_3$	6.61×10^{-9}
Ag_2CO_3	6.15×10^{-12}	CdS	3.60×10^{-29}	$PbCl_2$	1.62×10^{-5}
AgCl	1.56×10^{-10}	$Cu(IO_3)_2$	1.40×10^{-7}	PbI_2	1.39×10^{-8}
Ag_2CrO_4	9.00×10^{-12}	CuC_2O_4	2.87×10^{-8}	$Pb(IO_3)_2$	2.60×10^{-13}
$Ag_2Cr_2O_7$	2.00×10^{-7}	FeC_2O_4	2.10×10^{-7}	$SrCO_3$	1.60×10^{-9}
AgI	1.50×10^{-16}	FeS	3.70×10^{-19}	TlBr	3.39×10^{-6}
AgSCN	1.16×10^{-12}	Hg_2SO_4	7.41×10^{-7}	$ZnCO_3$	1.45×10^{-11}
$Al(OH)_3$	1.26×10^{-33}	Li_2CO_3	1.70×10^{-2}	ZnS	1.20×10^{-23}
$BaCO_3$	8.10×10^{-8}	$MgCO_3$	2.60×10^{-5}		

Table A-11

Acid-Base Indicators			
Indicator	**Acid Color**	**Range**	**Base Color**
Methyl violet	yellow	0.0–1.6	blue
Cresol red	red	1.0–2.0	yellow
Orange IV	red	1.4–2.6	yellow
Phloxine B	colorless	2.1–4.1	pink
2,4-Dinitrophenol	colorless	2.8–4.0	yellow
Methyl orange	red	3.2–4.4	yellow
α-Naphthyl red	red	4.0–5.6	yellow
Methyl red	red	4.8–6.0	yellow
4-Nitrophenol	colorless	5.4–6.6	yellow
Bromothymol blue	yellow	6.0–7.6	blue
Brilliant yellow	yellow	6.6–7.9	orange
Cresol red	yellow	7.0–8.8	red
2,6-Divanillylidenecyclohexanone	yellow	7.8–9.4	red
Ethyl bis(2,4-dinitrophenyl) acetate	colorless	8.4–9.6	blue
Thymolphthalein	colorless	9.4–10.6	blue
Alizarin yellow R	yellow	10.0–12.0	red
Malachite green hydrochloride	green-blue	10.2–12.5	colorless
Methyl blue	blue	10.6–13.4	pale violet
Orange G	yellow	11.5–14.0	pink
2,4,6-Trinitrotoluene	colorless	11.7–12.8	orange

Table A-12

Standard Reduction Potentials (at 25°C, 101.325 kPa, 1 M)		
Weak Oxidizing Agents		Strong Reducing Agents
Half-Reactions	**Volts**	
$Cs^+ + e^- \rightarrow Cs$	−2.92	
$Ba^{2+} + 2e^- \rightarrow Ba$	−2.90	
$Am^{3+} + 3e^- \rightarrow Am$	−2.38	
$Dy^{3+} + 3e^- \rightarrow Dy$	−2.35	
$Ce^{3+} + 3e^- \rightarrow Ce$	−2.34	
$Er^{3+} + 3e^- \rightarrow Er$	−2.30	
$Nd^{3+} + 3e^- \rightarrow Nd$	−2.25	
$H_2 + 2e^- \rightarrow 2H^-$	−2.23	
$Be^{2+} + 2e^- \rightarrow Be$	−1.85	
$Hf^{4+} + 4e^- \rightarrow Hf$	−1.70	
$SiF_6^{2-} + 4e^- \rightarrow Si + 6F^-$	−1.20	
$OCN^- + H_2O + 2e^- \rightarrow CN^- + 2OH^-$	−0.97	
$SiO_2 + 4H^+ + 4e^- \rightarrow Si + 2H_2O$	−0.84	
$2H_2O + 2e^- \rightarrow H_2 + 2OH^-$	−0.83	
$H_3PO_3 + 2H^+ + 2e^- \rightarrow H_3PO_2 + H_2O$	−0.50	
$Bi_2O_3 + 3H_2O + 6e^- \rightarrow 2Bi + 6OH^-$	−0.46	
$NO_2^- + H_2O + e^- \rightarrow NO + 2OH^-$	−0.46	
$Cr^{3+} + e^- \rightarrow Cr^{2+}$	−0.41	
$2H^+ (10^{-7}M) + 2e^- \rightarrow H_2$	−0.41	
$In^{3+} + 2e^- \rightarrow In^+$	−0.40	
$PbSO_4 + 2e^- \rightarrow Pb + SO_4^{2-}$	−0.36	
$H_3PO_4 + 2H^+ + 2e^- \rightarrow H_3PO_3 + H_2O$	−0.28	
$AgCN + e^- \rightarrow Ag + CN^-$	−0.02	
$UO_2^{2+} + e^- \rightarrow UO_2^+$	0.06	
$Sb_2O_3 + 6H^+ + 6e^- \rightarrow 2Sb + 3H_2O$	0.14	
$UO_2^{2+} + 4H^+ + 2e^- \rightarrow U^{4+} + 2H_2O$	0.33	
$VO^{2+} + 2H^+ + e^- \rightarrow V^{3+} + H_2O$	0.34	
$H_3AsO_4 + 2H^+ + 2e^- \rightarrow H_3AsO_3 + H_2O$	0.58	
$O_2 + 2H^+ + 2e^- \rightarrow H_2O_2$	0.68	
$O_2 + 4H^+ (10^{-7}M) + 4e^- \rightarrow 2H_2O$	0.82	
$ClO^- + H_2O + 2e^- \rightarrow Cl^- + 2OH^-$	0.90	
$NO_3^- + 3H^+ + 2e^- \rightarrow HNO_2 + H_2O$	0.94	
$VO_2^+ + 2H^+ + e^- \rightarrow VO^{2+} + H_2O$	1.00	
$ClO_4^- + 2H^+ + 2e^- \rightarrow ClO_3^- + H_2O$	1.19	
$2HNO_2 + 4H^+ + 4e^- \rightarrow N_2O + 3H_2O$	1.27	
$Au^{3+} + 2e^- \rightarrow Au^+$	1.42	
$ClO_3^- + 6H^+ + 5e^- \rightarrow \frac{1}{2}Cl_2 + 3H_2O$	1.47	
$HClO + H^+ + 2e^- \rightarrow Cl^- + H_2O$	1.49	
$PbO_2 + SO_4^{2-} + 4H^+ + 2e^- \rightarrow PbSO_4 + 2H_2O$	1.69	
$O_3 + 2H^+ + 2e^- \rightarrow O_2 + H_2O$	2.07	
$F_2 + 2H^+ + 2e^- \rightarrow 2HF$	3.03	

Strong Oxidizing Agents

Weak Reducing Agents

APPENDIX B

LOGARITHMS

A logarithm or log is an exponent. We will work with exponents given in terms of base 10.

$$N = b^x$$

$$\text{number} = \text{base}^{\text{exponent or logarithm}}$$

$$100 = 10^{2.0000}$$

For the log 2.000, the part of the numeral to the left of the decimal point is the characteristic. The part to the right of the decimal point is the mantissa.

$$\text{Log } 100 = 2.000$$
$$\text{characteristic} \quad \text{mantissa}$$

EXAMPLE: How to Find a Logarithm

Find the log of 657.

(a) Write the number in scientific notation, 6.57×10^2
(b) Look in the table under the column (N). Find the first two digits, (65)
(c) Look to the right and find the mantissa that is in the vertical column under the third digit of the number (7). It is .8176
(d) From the scientific notation, write the power of ten as the characteristic, to the left of the decimal point.
(e) Write the four digits from the table as the mantissa to the right of the characteristic and the decimal point, 2.8176

$$\text{thus } 657 = 10^{2.8176} \text{ or log } 657 = 2.8176$$

When given a logarithm and asked to find the number it represents, we use the table to find the first three digits for the number. We use the characteristic to determine where to locate the decimal point with respect to these digits.

EXAMPLE: How to Find the Antilogarithm

Given the logarithm 2.8176, find the number it represents (antilog).

(a) In the log table, find the mantissa that is closest to .8176
(b) We find by looking under the column (N) that this mantissa corresponds to 65. The third digit is found at the top of the column in which the mantissa appears, 7. (657)
(c) Write the three digits (657) in scientific notation, 6.57×10^x
(d) The characteristic will be the power of ten.

$$\text{antilog } 2.8176 = 6.57 \times 10^2 \text{ or } 657.$$

EXAMPLE: Logarithms of Numbers Less Than 1

Find the log 0.00657.

(a) Write the number in scientific notation, 6.57×10^{-3}

(b) Look in the table under the column N for the first two digits, 6.5, and to the right in the column under the third digit, 7, for the mantissa. Note that the mantissa is always a positive number, .8167

(c) From the scientific notation, we get the negative characteristic, −3.

(d) Add the negative characteristic and the positive mantissa. $(-3.0000) + (+.8167) = -2.1824$. This value is more commonly represented as 7.8167-10. However, the negative logarithm −2.1824 is more useful in *pH* calculations.

EXAMPLE: Antilog of a Negative Logarithm

Find the antilog of −2.1824.

(a) We ask ourselves what number would we add to the next, lesser integer, −3., to get the log −2.1824. It would be .8176.

$$
\begin{array}{r}
-3.0000 \\
\text{subtract} \quad -2.1824 \\
\hline
.8176
\end{array}
$$

We know that logarithm tables do not give mantissas for negative numbers. So, we have changed the −2.1824 into the sum of a negative characteristic and a positive mantissa. The characteristic is always the next negative number. The positive mantissa was determined by asking ourselves what positive number would we add to the negative characteristic to get −2.1824.

(b) $-2.1824 = -3. + .8176$

Antilog -2.1824 = antilog $-3. \times$ antilog $.8176$

We know the antilog of −3. is 10^{-3}. From the table, we find that the antilog .8176 = 6.57. Therefore the antilog of −2.1824 = 6.57×10^{-3}.

Table B-1

Logarithms of Numbers										
N	0	1	2	3	4	5	6	7	8	9
10	0000	0043	0086	0128	0170	0212	0253	0294	0334	0374
11	0414	0453	0492	0531	0569	0607	0645	0682	0719	0775
12	0792	0828	0864	0899	0934	0969	1004	1038	1072	1106
13	1139	1173	1206	1239	1271	1303	1335	1367	1399	1430
14	1461	1492	1523	1553	1584	1614	1644	1673	1703	1732
15	1761	1790	1818	1847	1875	1903	1931	1959	1987	2014
16	2041	2068	2095	2122	2148	2175	2201	2227	2253	2279
17	2304	2330	2355	2380	2405	2430	2455	2480	2504	2529
18	2553	2577	2601	2625	2648	2672	2695	2718	2742	2765
19	2788	2810	2833	2856	2878	2900	2923	2945	2967	2989
20	3010	3032	3054	3075	3096	3118	3139	3160	3181	3201
21	3222	3243	3263	3284	3304	3324	3345	3365	3385	3404
22	3424	3444	3464	3483	3502	3522	3541	3560	3579	3598
23	3617	3636	3655	3674	3692	3711	3729	3747	3766	3784
24	3802	3820	3838	3856	3874	3892	3909	3927	3945	3962
25	3979	3997	4014	4031	4048	4065	4082	4099	4116	4133
26	4150	4166	4183	4200	4216	4232	4249	4265	4281	4298
27	4314	4330	4346	4362	4378	4393	4409	4425	4440	4456
28	4472	4487	4502	4518	4533	4548	4564	4579	4594	4609
29	4624	4639	4654	4669	4683	4698	4713	4728	4742	4757
30	4771	4786	4800	4814	4829	4843	4857	4871	4886	4900
31	4914	4928	4942	4955	4969	4983	4997	5011	5024	5038
32	5051	5065	5079	5092	5105	5119	5132	5145	5159	5172
33	5185	5198	5211	5224	5237	5250	5263	5276	5289	5302
34	5315	5328	5340	5353	5366	5378	5391	5403	5416	5428
35	5441	5453	5465	5478	5490	5502	5514	5527	5539	5551
36	5563	5575	5587	5599	5611	5623	5635	5647	5658	5670
37	5682	5694	5705	5717	5729	5740	5752	5763	5775	5786
38	5798	5809	5821	5832	5843	5855	5866	5877	5888	5899
39	5911	5922	5933	5944	5955	5966	5977	5988	5999	6010
40	6021	6031	6042	6053	6064	6075	6085	6096	6107	6117
41	6128	6138	6149	6160	6170	6180	6191	6201	6212	6222
42	6232	6243	6253	6263	6274	6284	6294	6304	6314	6325
43	6335	6345	6355	6365	6375	6385	6395	6405	6415	6425
44	6435	6444	6454	6464	6474	6484	6493	6503	6513	6522
45	6352	6542	6551	6561	6571	6580	6590	6599	6609	6618
46	6628	6637	6646	6656	6665	6675	6684	6693	6702	6712
47	6721	6730	6739	6749	6758	6767	6776	6785	6794	6803
48	6812	6821	6830	6839	6848	6857	6866	6875	6884	6893
49	6902	6911	6920	6928	6937	6946	6955	6964	6972	6981
50	6990	6998	7007	7016	7024	7033	7042	7050	7059	7067
51	7076	7084	7093	7101	7110	7118	7126	7135	7143	7152
52	7160	7168	7177	7185	7193	7202	7210	7218	7226	7235
53	7243	7251	7259	7267	7275	7284	7292	7300	7308	7316
54	7324	7332	7340	7348	7356	7364	7372	7380	7388	7396

N	0	1	2	3	4	5	6	7	8	9
55	7404	7412	7419	7427	7435	7443	7451	7459	7466	7474
56	7482	7490	7497	7505	7513	7520	7528	7536	7543	7551
57	7559	7566	7574	7582	7589	7597	7604	7612	7619	7627
58	7634	7642	7649	7657	7664	7672	7679	7686	7694	7701
59	7709	7716	7723	7731	7738	7745	7752	7760	7767	7774
60	7782	7789	7796	7803	7810	7818	7825	7832	7839	7846
61	7853	7860	7868	7875	7882	7889	7896	7903	7910	7917
62	7924	7931	7938	7945	7952	7959	7966	7973	7980	7987
63	7993	8000	8007	8014	8021	8028	8035	8041	8048	8055
64	8062	8069	8075	8082	8089	8096	8102	8109	8116	8122
65	8129	8136	8142	8149	8156	8162	8169	8176	8182	8189
66	8195	8202	8209	8215	8222	8228	8235	8241	8248	8254
67	8261	8267	8274	8280	8287	8293	8299	8306	8312	8319
68	8325	8331	8338	8344	8351	8357	8363	8370	8376	8382
69	8388	8395	8401	8407	8414	8420	8426	8432	8439	8445
70	8451	8457	8463	8470	8476	8482	8488	8494	8500	8506
71	8513	8519	8525	8531	8537	8543	8549	8555	8561	8567
72	8573	8579	8585	8591	8597	8603	8609	8615	8621	8627
73	8633	8639	8645	8651	8657	8663	8669	8675	8681	8686
74	8692	8698	8704	8710	8716	8722	8727	8733	8739	8745
75	8751	8756	8762	8768	8774	8779	8785	8791	8797	8802
76	8808	8814	8820	8825	8831	8837	8842	8848	8854	8859
77	8865	8871	8876	8882	8887	8893	8899	8904	8910	8915
78	8921	8927	8932	8938	8943	8949	8954	8960	8965	8971
79	8976	8982	8987	8993	8998	9004	9009	9015	9020	9025
80	9031	9036	9042	9047	9053	9058	9063	9069	9074	9079
81	9085	9090	9096	9101	9106	9112	9117	9122	9128	9133
82	9138	9143	9149	9154	9159	9165	9170	9175	9180	9186
83	9191	9196	9201	9206	9212	9217	9222	9227	9232	9238
84	9243	9248	9253	9258	9263	9269	9274	9279	9284	9289
85	9294	9299	9304	9309	9315	9320	9325	9330	9335	9340
86	9345	9350	9355	9360	9365	9370	9375	9380	9385	9390
87	9395	9400	9405	9410	9415	9420	9425	9430	9435	9440
88	9445	9450	9455	9460	9465	9469	9474	9479	9484	9489
89	9494	9499	9504	9509	9513	9518	9523	9528	9533	9538
90	9542	9547	9552	9557	9562	9566	9571	9576	9581	9586
91	9590	9595	9600	9605	9609	9614	9619	9624	9628	9633
92	9638	9643	9647	9652	9657	9661	9666	9671	9675	9680
93	9685	9689	9694	9699	9703	9708	9713	9717	9722	9727
94	9731	9736	9741	9745	9750	9754	9759	9763	9768	9773
95	9777	9782	9786	9791	9795	9800	9805	9809	9814	9818
96	9823	9827	9832	9836	9841	9845	9850	9854	9859	9863
97	9868	9872	9877	9881	9886	9890	9894	9899	9903	9908
98	9912	9917	9921	9926	9930	9934	9939	9943	9948	9952
99	9956	9961	9965	9969	9974	9978	9983	9987	9991	9996

APPENDIX C

CHEMISTRY RELATED CAREERS

Most professional careers require some background in chemistry. Many careers depend heavily on the study of chemistry. Some of the fields in which chemistry plays a prominent part are listed below. If you are considering a chemistry-related career, you should realize that there are many aspects in each of these fields. For instance, within the field of chemistry itself, there are opportunities in sales, management, patent law, and technical writing. To pursue a professional career, you will need at least a bachelor's degree in your field. Some careers will require graduate study to obtain a master's degree or a doctor's degree. However, there are many opportunities in these fields for technologists and technicians. Technologists have a junior college education (associate degree) and technicians have a high school diploma. Technologists work with the professionals in the field, helping professionals carry out projects and programs. Technicians assist the professionals by carrying out the routine procedures which underlie the gathering of data necessary to a particular field.

Pure Sciences

Astronomer	studies the structure, motion, and evolution of the universe.
Biologist	studies the basic principles of plant and animal life.
Chemist	performs quantitative and qualitative tests to determine the structure and properties of materials.
Geologist	studies the composition, structure, and history of the earth.
Meteorologist	studies the physics and chemistry of the atmosphere, and forecasts weather.
Oceanographer	studies the physics, chemistry, geology, and biology of the oceans.
Physicist	researches the interaction of matter and energy.

Chemists

Analytical chemist	develops and improves the procedures for analyzing the structure and properties of substances.
Biochemist	studies the chemical effects of foods, drugs, and hormones on body processes.
Inorganic chemist	researches those substances which are relatively free of carbon such as ores, metals, and glass.
Organic chemist	researches those substances in which carbon is a major constituent; may specialize in agriculture, food, industry, textiles or a number of other fields.
Physical chemist	determines the physical properties of substances and other relationships involving energy and matter.

Applied Sciences

Agricultural Fields

Agronomist	develops new methods of raising field crops to insure more efficient production and better quality.

Forester	studies the growth, conservation, and harvesting of trees.
Horticulturist	researches the breeding, production, and processing of fruits, vegetables, and decorative plants.
Wood scientist	develops and improves methods of treating wood and wood by-products.

Engineering Fields

Biomedical engineer	may design artificial organs or develop more efficient hospital laboratory systems.
Ceramic engineer	processes non-metallic materials such as glass, tile, and porcelain into useful products.
Chemical engineer	designs, builds, and operates chemical production plants.
Environmental engineer	designs and maintains industrial structures with respect to the environment.
Metallurgical engineer	processes metallic materials into useful products.
Nuclear engineer	researches the development and control of nuclear energy.
Petroleum engineer	develops more efficient drilling and processing methods for oil and natural gas.

Technical Fields

Drafter, Surveyor	determines the measurements and specifications required for the development of a new product or structure.
Machinist	determines the tools, materials, and specifications required for the production of precision products.
Media technician	operates the light and sound equipment used in the production of films, radio and television broadcasts.
Photoengraver, Photographer	photographs and develops negatives for the design and production of publications.

Health Science

Dentist	examines and treats oral disease and abnormalities.
Dietician, Food Service	plans and prepares for the nutritional needs of individuals and groups.
Medical technologist	performs quantitative and qualitative tests to provide information for the treatment of disease.
Occupational and Physical Therapist	designs therapy programs to help patients overcome physical or emotional handicaps.
Pharmacologist, Pharmacist	researches the function, behavior, and preparation of drugs.
Veterinarian	diagnoses and treats diseases in animals.

This appendix contains just a small sample of chemistry-related careers. Additional information can be obtained from the American Chemical Society, the National Science Teachers Association, and the Manufacturing Chemists Association. *The Occupational Outlook Handbook, The Dictionary of Occupational Titles,* and college catalogues can provide more complete descriptions of many careers as well as the potential needs in each area.

GLOSSARY

absolute zero: The temperature at which all molecular motion should cease.

accuracy: The relationship between the graduations on a measuring device and the actual standard for the quantity being measured.

acid: A substance which produces hydrogen ions in water solution (Arrhenius). A proton donor (Brönsted). An electron-pair acceptor (Lewis).

acid anhydride: An oxygen containing substance which produces an acid when dissolved in water.

actinide: An element whose highest energy electron is in the 5f sublevel.

activated complex: The species formed when the reactants in a chemical reaction have collided with sufficient energy to meet the activation energy requirement.

activation energy: The energy required to start a chemical reaction.

activity (ion): The effective concentration of a species.

addition polymerization: The formation of a polymer from monomers by an addition reaction.

addition reaction: The adding on of a substance to the double bond of an alkene or the triple bond of an alkyne.

adiabatic: A process taking place without interchange of energy with its surroundings.

adsorption: The process of one substance being attracted and held to the surface of another.

alcohol: A class of organic compounds characterized by the presence of the hydroxyl group, $-OH$.

aldehyde: A class of organic compounds characterized by the presence of the carbonyl group ($>C=O$) on the end carbon of the chain (RCHO).

aliphatic: A subdivision of hydrocarbons characterized by open chains and nonaromatic rings.

alkali metal: An element from Group IA of the periodic table.

alkaline earth metal: An element from Group IIA of the periodic table.

alkane: An aliphatic compound having only single carbon-carbon bonds.

alkene: An aliphatic compound having a double carbon-carbon bond.

alkyne: An aliphatic compound having a triple carbon-carbon bond.

alloy: A mixture of two or more metals.

alpha particle: Helium nucleus.

amine: An organic compound derived from ammonia by replacement of one or more hydrogen atoms by organic radicals.

amino acid: An organic compound characterized by the presence of an amino group and a carboxylic acid group on the same carbon atom.

amorphous: A solid-appearing material without crystalline structure.

ampere: The unit of electric current equal to one coulomb per second.

amphoteric: A substance which can act as either an acid or a base.

amplitude: The displacement of a wave from the average position.

anhydrous: A substance without water of hydration.

anion: A negative ion.

anode: The positive electrode (general). The electrode at which oxidation occurs (electrochemical).

antibonding orbital: In molecular orbital theory, an orbital of the molecule which represents a higher energy than the atomic orbitals from which it was formed.

aromatic: A group of organic ring compounds having (4n + 2) pi electrons.

asymmetric: The property of not having symmetry.

atom: The smallest particle of an element which possesses the properties of that element.

atomic mass: The average mass of the atoms of an element.

atomic mass unit: One-twelfth the mass of the carbon-12 atom.

atomic number: The number of protons in the nucleus of an atom.

atomic radius: The radius of an atom without regard to surrounding atoms.

atomic theory: The body of knowledge concerning the existence of atoms and their characteristic structure.

Avogadro's number: The number of objects in a mole equal to 6.02×10^{23}.

Avogadro's hypothesis: The statement that equal volumes of gases at the same temperature and pressure contain the same number of molecules.

balance: A device used to measure mass.

band: A group of extremely closely spaced energy levels occupied by free electrons in a metal crystal.

barometer: A manometer used to measure the atmospheric pressure.

baryon: A subatomic particle classified as a large hadron.

base: A substance which produces hydroxide ions in water solution (Arrhenius). A proton acceptor (Brönsted). An electron-pair donor (Lewis).

basic anhydride: An oxygen containing substance which produces a base when dissolved in water.

beta particle: An electron.

bidentate: A ligand which attaches to the central ion in two locations.

binary: A compound containing two elements.

binding energy: The energy required to split the nucleus into separate nucleons.

Bohr atom: The planetary atom.

boiling point: The temperature at which the vapor pressures of the liquid and vapor phases of a substance are equal.

bond: The force holding atoms together in a compound.

bond angle: The angle between two bond axes extending from the same atom.

bond axis: The line connecting the nuclei of two bonded atoms.

bond character: The relative ionic or covalent character of a bond.

bond order: The number of electron pairs bonding two atoms as described by molecular orbital theory.

bond strength: The energy required to break a bond.

bonding orbital: In molecular orbital theory, a molecular orbital which is at a lower energy level than the atomic orbitals from which it was formed.

Boyle's law: The volume of a specific amount of gas varies inversely as the pressure if the temperature remains constant.

Brownian motion: The random motion of colloidal particles due to their bombardment by the molecules of the continuous phase.

buffer: A solution which can receive moderate amounts of either acid or base without significant change in its pH.

calorimeter: A device for measuring the change in enthalpy during a chemical change.

capillary rise: The tendency of a liquid to rise in a tube of small diameter due to the surface tension of the liquid.

carboxylic acid: A class of organic compounds characterized by the presence of the carboxyl group

$$\left(-C \underset{OH}{\overset{O}{\diagup}} \right)$$

catalyst: A substance which speeds a chemical reaction without being permanently changed itself.

catenation: The joining in chains of carbon atoms.

cathode: The negative electrode (general). The electrode at which reduction occurs (electrochemical).

cathode rays: The beam of electrons in a gas discharge tube.

cation: A positive ion.

cell potential: The voltage obtained from a voltaic cell.

cellulose: A biological polymer of glucose.

Celsius scale: The temperature scale based on the freezing point, 0°, and boiling point, 100°, of water.

chain reaction: A reaction in which the product from each step acts as a reactant for the next step.

chalcogen: An element from Group VIA of the periodic table.

Charles' law: The volume of a specific amount of gas varies directly as the absolute temperature if the pressure remains constant.

chemical change: A change in which one or more new substances with new properties are formed.

chemical properties: The properties characteristic of a substance when it is involved in a chemical change.

chemical reaction: A chemical change.

chemistry: The study and investigation of the structure and properties of matter.

chromatography: The separation of a mixture using a technique based upon differential adsorption.

closest-packing: A crystal structure particle arrangement in which the empty space between particles is minimized.

coefficient: A number placed before a formula in a balanced chemical equation to indicate the relative amount of the substance represented by the formula.

colligative properties: Properties of solutions which depend only on the number of particles present, without regard to type.

colloid: A dispersion of particles from 1 to 100 nm in at least one dimension, in a continuous medium.

column chromatography: A chromatographic technique utilizing a glass column packed with adsorbent.

common-ion effect: An equilibrium phenomenon in which an ion common to two or more substances in a solution shifts an equilibrium away from itself.

complex ion: A central positive ion surrounded by bonded ligands.

compound: Two or more elements combined by chemical bonds.

concentrated solution: A solution in which there is a high ratio between solute and solvent.

concentration: The ratio between the amount of solute and the amount of solvent in which the solute is dissolved.

condensation polymer: A polymer formed by a reaction in which a small molecule, usually water, is produced as the monomers form the polymer.

condensed state: The solid or liquid form of a substance.

conduction band: The group of extremely closely spaced energy levels in a metal which free electrons can occupy.

conductivity: A property involving the transport of electrons or heat from one point to another.

conjugate acid: The particle obtained after a base has gained a proton.

conjugate base: The particle remaining after an acid has donated a proton.

conjugated system: A series of alternating single and double bonds in an organic molecule.

contact catalyst: A catalyst which functions by adsorbing one of the reactants on its surface.

continuous phase: The dispersing medium in a colloid.

control rods: Neutron absorbing materials used to control the rate of reaction in a nuclear reactor.

coordinate covalent bond: A covalent bond in which both electrons of the shared pair were donated by the same atom.

coordination number: The number of ligands surrounding the central ion.

corrosion: The gradual electrochemical destruction of a metal by substances in the environment.

coulomb: A quantity of electricity equal to 1/96 500 of a mole of electrons.

covalent bond: A bond characterized by a shared pair of electrons.

covalent radius: The radius of an atom along the bond axis.

critical pressure: The pressure needed to liquefy a gas at a critical temperature.

critical temperature: The temperature above which no amount of pressure will liquefy a gas.

crystal: A solid in which the particles are arranged in a regular, repeating pattern.

crystallization: Separating a solid from a solution by evaporating the solvent, or by cooling.

cyclic compounds: Compounds in which the atoms are bonded in a ring.

cycloalkanes: Aliphatic hydrocarbons with the carbon atoms bonded in rings.

Dalton's law: In a mixture of gases the total pressure of the mixture is the sum of the partial pressures of each component gas.

De Broglie's hypothesis: Particles may have the properties of waves.

decomposition: A reaction in which a compound breaks into two or more simpler substances.

defect: An imperfection in a crystal lattice.

degenerate: Having the same energy.

dehydrating agent: A substance which can absorb water from other substances.

deliquescence: The absorption of water from the air by a solid to form a liquid solution.

delocalized electrons: Electrons which are free to move through the π cloud of p orbitals as in benzene.

density: Mass per unit volume.

desiccant: A dehydrating agent.

diagonal rule: A system for predicting the order of filling energy sublevels with electrons.

diffusion: The spreading of gas molecules throughout a given volume.

dipole-induced dipole force: An attraction between a dipole and a nonpolar molecule which has been induced to become a dipole.

dilute solution: A solution with a low ratio of solute to solvent.

dipole: A polar molecule.

dipole-dipole force: An attraction between dipoles.

dipole moment: The strength of a dipole expressed as charge multiplied by distance.

dislocation: A crystal defect.

dispersed phase: Colloidal particles distributed through-out the continuous phase.

dispersion force: The force between two particles due to the attraction of instantaneous separations of their charge centers.

dissociation: The separation of ions in solution.

distillation: The process of evaporating a liquid and condensing its vapor.

doping: Deliberate introduction of impurities into a crystal.

dot diagram: A pictorial representation of the location of outer level electrons in an atom, ion, or molecule.

double bond: A covalent bond in which two atoms share two pairs of electrons.

double displacement: A reaction in which the positive part of one compound combines with the negative part of another compound, and vice versa.

ductility: The property of a substance which enables it to be drawn into a fine wire.

dynamic equilibrium: An equilibrium in which two or more changes are taking place simultaneously, but at the same rate.

edge dislocation: A crystal defect in which a layer of atoms extends into the lattice between layers of unit cells.

efflorescence: The release of water molecules to the air by a hydrate.

effusion: The passage of gas molecules through small openings.

elastic: Collisions in which kinetic energy is conserved.

electrochemistry: The study of the interaction of electric current and atoms, ions, and molecules.

electrode potential: The reduction potential in volts of a half-reaction compared to the potential of the hydrogen half-reaction at 0.0000 V.

electrolysis: A chemical change produced by an electric current.

electrolyte: A substance whose aqueous solution conducts electricity.

electrolytic cell: A cell in which an electrolysis reaction is taking place.

electron: A subatomic particle representing the unit of negative charge.

electron affinity: The attraction of an atom for an electron expressed as the energy needed to remove an electron from a negative ion to restore neutrality.

electron cloud: The space effectively occupied by an electron in an atom.

electron configuration: A description of the energy level and sublevel for all the electrons in an atom.

electronegativity: The relative attraction of an atom for a shared pair of electrons.

electrophoresis: The migration of colloidal particles under the influence of an electric field.

element: A substance whose atoms have the same number of protons in the nucleus.

elimination reaction: An organic reaction in which a small molecule is removed from a larger molecule leaving a double bond in the larger molecule.

empirical formula: The formula giving the simplest ratio between the atoms of the elements present in a compound.

endothermic: A change which takes place with the absorption of heat.

endpoint: The point in a titration where equivalent numbers of moles of reactants are present.

energy: A property of matter which may be converted to work under the proper circumstances.

energy level: A specific amount of energy or group of energies which may be possessed by electrons in an atom.

energy sublevel: A specific energy which may be possessed by an electron in an atom.

enthalpy: That part of the energy of a substance which is due to the motion of its particles.

entropy: The degree of disorder in a system.

enzyme: A biological catalyst.

equation: A shorthand representation of a chemical change using symbols and formulas.

equilibrium: A state in which no net change takes place in a system.

equilibrium constant: A mathematical expression giving the ratio of the product of the concentrations of the substances produced to the product of the concentration of the reactants for a reaction.

ester: A class of organic compounds characterized by the presence of the $-C\overset{\textstyle O}{\underset{\textstyle O-}{\diagup}}$ group between two hydrocarbon radicals.

esterification reaction: The production of an ester by the reaction of an alcohol with an acid.

ether: A class of organic compounds characterized by the presence of $-O-$ between two hydrocarbon radicals.

evaporation: The process by which a molecule leaves the surface of a liquid or solid and enters the gaseous state.

exclusion principle: No two electrons in an atom may have the same set of quantum numbers.

exothermic: A change which produces heat.

factor-label method: A problem solving method in which units (labels) are treated as factors.

fat: A biological ester of glycerol and a fatty acid.

fission: The splitting of a nucleus into two approximately equal parts.

fluid: A material which flows (liquid or gas).

forbidden zone: The energy gap between the outer level band and the conduction band in crystals.

formula: A combination of atomic symbols and numbers indicating the elements and their proportions in a compound.

formula mass: The sum of the atomic masses of the atoms in a formula.

formula unit: The amount of a substance represented by its formula.

fractional crystallization: The separation of a mixture into its components through differences in solubility.

fractional distillation: The separation of a mixture into its components through differences in boiling points.

fractionation: Separating a whole into its parts.

free electrons: Electrons not bound to one atom or associated with one bond.

free energy: The chemical potential energy of a substance or system.

freezing point: The temperature at which the vapor pressures of the solid and liquid are equal.

frequency: The number of complete wave cycles per unit of time.

functional isomers: Organic compounds with the same formula, but with the nonhydrocarbon part of the molecule bonded in different ways.

fusion: The combining of two or more small nuclei into one larger nucleus.

galvanometer: An instrument used to detect an electric current.

gamma ray: A quanta of energy of very high frequency and very small wavelength.

gas: A physical state characterized by random motion of the particles which are far apart compared to their diameters.

gas chromatography: A chromatographic method in which a carrier gas (inert) distributes the vapor being analyzed in a packed column.

geometric isomers: Compounds with the same formula but different arrangement of substituents around a double bond.

gluon: A theoretical massless particle exchanged by quarks.

glycogen: A biological polymer of glucose.

Graham's law: The ratio of the relative rates of diffusion of gases is equal to the square root of the inverse ratio of their molecular masses.

ground state: All electrons in the lowest possible energy sublevels.

group: The members of a vertical column in the periodic table.

hadrons: A class of heavy subatomic particles.

half-cell: The part of an electrochemical cell in which either the oxidation or reduction reaction is taking place.

half-life: The length of time necessary for one-half an amount of a radioactive nuclide to disintegrate.

half-reaction: The oxidation or reduction reaction in a chemical reaction.

halogen: An element from Group VIIA of the periodic table.

heat: The form of energy due to motion of particles.

heat content: Enthalpy.

heat of formation: The amount of heat produced or consumed when a mole of a compound is formed from its elements.

heat of fusion: The heat required to change 1 gram of a substance from solid to liquid.

heat of reaction: The heat produced or consumed when a chemical change takes place in the amounts indicated by the equation involved.

heat of solution: The amount of heat produced or consumed when a substance is dissolved in water.

heat of vaporization: The heat needed to change 1 gram of a substance from liquid to gas.

Henry's law: The mass of a gas which will dissolve in a specific amount of a liquid varies directly with the pressure.

heterogeneous: Composed of different parts not uniformly dispersed.

homogeneous: Uniform throughout.

homologous series: A series of organic compounds which differ from each other by a specific structural unit.

hybrid orbitals: Equivalent orbitals formed from orbitals of different energies.

hydration: The adhering of water molecules to dissolved ions.

hydrate: A compound (crystalline) in which the ions are hydrated.

hydrocarbons: Compounds composed solely of carbon and hydrogen.

hydrogen bonding: An exceptionally strong type of dipole-dipole interaction due to the strong positive center in molecules in which hydrogen is bonded to a highly electronegative element (N, O, F).

hydrolysis: Reaction with water to form a weak acid or base.

hygroscopic: Absorbing water from the air.

ideal gas: A model in which gas molecules are treated as though they were geometric points exerting no force on each other.

ideal gas equation: $PV = nRT$

ideal solution: A solution obeying Raoult's law.

immiscible: Two liquids which will not dissolve in each other.

indicator: A weak organic acid whose conjugate base differs in color. Used to indicate the pH of a solution.

inertia: The tendency of an object to resist any change in its velocity.

infrared spectroscopy: A spectroscopic method useful in investigating the bonding in molecules.

inhibitor: A substance which prevents a reaction from taking place by forming a complex to tie up one of the reactants.

insulator: A substance having a large forbidden zone and which does not conduct.

intensive properties: Those properties of a substance which are independent of the amount of matter present.

interface: The area of contact between two phases.

ion: A particle with an electric charge.

ionic bond: The electrostatic attraction between ions of opposite charge.

ionic radius: The radius of an ion.

ionization constant: The equilibrium constant for the ionization of a weak electrolyte.

ionization energy: The energy required to remove an electron from an atom.

ion-product constant for water: The product of the hydronium and hydroxide ion concentrations, equal to 10^{-14}.

irreversible thermodynamic change: A change in volume or pressure in which some energy is lost to an entropy change.

isobaric: At constant pressure.

isomers: Two compounds having the same formula but different structures.

isomorphism: Two or more compounds having the same crystalline structure.

isothermal: At constant temperature.

isotopes: Two or more atoms of an element having the same number of protons but different numbers of neutrons.

joule: The SI unit of energy equal to $1 \text{ kg} \cdot \text{m}^2/\text{s}^2$.

Joule-Thomson effect: The cooling effect achieved by allowing a highly compressed gas to expand rapidly after passing through a small opening.

kelvin: The SI unit of temperature equal to 1/273.16 the thermodynamic temperature of the triple point of water.

ketone: A class of organic compounds characterized by the presence of the carbonyl group ($\diagup$C=O) between hydrocarbon radicals.

kilogram: The SI unit of mass.

kinetic energy: Energy due to motion.

kinetic theory: The group of ideas treating the interaction of matter and heat.

lanthanide: An element whose highest energy electron is in the $4f$ sublevel.

law of conservation of energy: Energy is conserved in all changes except nuclear reactions.

law of conservation of mass: Mass is conserved in all changes except nuclear reactions.

law of conservation of mass and energy: The total amount of mass and energy in the universe is constant.

law of definite proportions: The elements composing a compound are always present in the same proportions by mass.

law of multiple proportions: The masses of one element which combine with a specific mass of another element in a series of compounds. These masses are in the ratio of small whole numbers.

Le Chatelier's principle: If a stress is placed on a system at equilibrium, the system will shift so as to offset the stress.

leptons: A class of light subatomic particles.

ligand: A negative ion or polar molecule attached to a central ion in a complex.

limiting reactant: The reactant which is used completely in a reaction.

linear accelerator: A device for imparting a high energy to atomic or subatomic particles traveling in a straight line.

lipid: A biological molecule which is soluble in non-polar solvents.

liquefaction: Changing a gas to a liquid.

liquid: A state characterized by particles in such close proximity that their random motion appears to be a vibration about a moving point.

liquid crystal: A substance which has order in the arrangement of its particles in only one or two dimensions.

liter: A unit of volume equal to 1 dm³.

London forces: *see dispersion forces*

macromolecule: A crystal which consists of a single molecule with all component atoms bonded in a network fashion.

magnetohydrodynamics: The study of plasmas.

malleability: The property of a substance which allows it to be hammered into thin sheets.

manometer: A device for measuring gas pressure.

mass: The measure of the amount of matter.

mass defect: The difference between the mass of a nucleus and the sum of the masses of the particles from which it was formed.

mass number: The number of nucleons in an atom.

mass spectrometry: The separation of atoms or radicals on the basis of the varied effects of electric and magnetic fields on different masses.

matter: Anything which exhibits the property of inertia.

mean free path: The average distance a molecule travels between collisions.

melting point: The temperature at which the vapor pressures of the solid and liquid phases of a substance are equal.

meson: A subatomic particle classed as a hadron.

metal: An element which tends to lose electrons in chemical reactions.

metallic bond: A force holding metal atoms together and characterized by free electrons.

metalloid: An element which has properties characteristic of a metal and a nonmetal.

miscible: Two liquids which are mutually soluble in all proportions.

mixture: A combination of two or more substances.

mobile phase: The fluid containing the mixture to be analyzed in chromatography.

moderator: A substance used to slow neutrons in a nuclear reactor.

molal boiling point constant: A value characteristic of a solvent indicating the rise in the boiling point of 1 kilogram of the solvent if it contains 1 mole of particles.

molal freezing point constant: A value characteristic of a solvent indicating the drop in the freezing point of 1 kilogram of the solvent if it contains 1 mole of particles.

molality: A unit of concentration equal to the number of moles of solute in 1 kilogram of solvent.

molar heat capacity: The amount of heat required to change the temperature of 1 mole of a substance by 1 Celsius degree.

molar volume: The volume occupied by 1 mole of gas molecules at standard temperature and pressure and equal to 22.4 dm³.

molarity: A unit of concentration equal to the number of moles of solute in 1 dm³ of solution.

mole: Avogadro's number of objects $= 6.02 \times 10^{23}$.

mole fraction: A unit of concentration equal to the number of moles of solute in a mole of solution.

molecular formula: A formula indicating the actual number of each kind of atom contained in a molecule.

molecular mass: The mass of a molecule found by adding the atomic masses of the atoms comprising the molecule.

molecular orbital theory: A model of molecular structure based upon the formation of molecular orbitals from corresponding atomic orbitals.

molecule: A particle in which the constituent atoms are held together by covalent bonds.

momentum: The product of mass and velocity.

nematic substance: A liquid crystal with order in one dimension only.

net ionic equation: A chemical equation indicating only those substances taking part in the reaction and omitting spectator ions.

neutral: Neither acidic nor basic (electrolytes). Neither positive nor negative (electricity).

neutralization: The combining of an acid and a base until the amounts present correspond to the proportions shown by the equation for their reaction.

neutron: A neutral particle found in the nucleus of an atom and having a mass of approximately one atomic mass unit.

nitrile: A class of organic compounds characterized by the presence of the —CN group.

nitro: A class of organic compounds characterized by the presence of the —NO$_2$ group.

noble gas: Any element from Group VIIIA of the periodic table.

nonmetal: An element which tends to gain electrons in chemical reactions.

nonvolatile: A substance which has a high boiling point, strong intermolecular forces, and a low vapor pressure at room temperature.

nuclear magnetic resonance spectroscopy: A spectroscopic method based on the energy required to reorient a nucleus with a magnetic field with respect to an external magnetic field.

nucleic acid: A biological polymer involved in genetic transfer and cell metabolism.

nucleon: A particle found in the nucleus of an atom. A proton or neutron.

nuclide: An element containing a specific number of protons and a specific number of neutrons.

octahedral: A molecular or ionic shape in which six particles are clustered about a central particle at the vertices of a regular octahedron.

octane rating: A system of rating gasoline based upon the proportions of heptane and 2,2,4-trimethylpentane in the mixture.

octet rule: The tendency of atoms to react in such a way that they acquire eight electrons in their outer level. He with 2 electrons also conforms.

ohm: The unit of electric resistance. One volt will force 1 ampere through 1 ohm.

olefin: Another name for an alkene.

optical isomers: Mirror image molecules which rotate a plane of polarized light in opposite directions.

optically active: A property of substances characterized by their ability to rotate a plane of polarized light.

orbital: The space which can be occupied by 0, 1, or 2 electrons with the same energy level, energy sublevel, and spacial orientation.

organic: Related to carbon compounds.

organic oxidation reaction: The combustion of an organic compound to produce carbon dioxide and water.

osmotic pressure: The pressure developed across a semipermeable membrane by differential diffusion through the membrane.

oxidation: The loss of electrons.

oxidation number: The charge on an atom if the electrons in a compound are assigned in an arbitrary manner according to established rules.

oxidizing agent: A substance which tends to gain electrons.

packing: An adsorbent used in columns for column and gas chromatography.

pair repulsion: A model for molecular shape based upon the assumption that electron clouds will repel each other and be as far away from each other as possible.

paper chromatography: A chromatographic method based upon the movement of a solvent through paper by capillary action.

parent chain: The longest continuous chain of carbon atoms used for naming organic molecules.

partially miscible: Two liquids which are soluble in each other to a limited extent.

pascal: The SI unit of pressure equal to 1 N/m^2.

percentage composition: The proportion of an element present in a compound found by dividing the mass of the element present by the mass of the whole compound and multiplying by a hundred.

periodic law: The properties of the elements are a periodic function of their atomic numbers.

periodic table: A pictorial arrangement of the elements based upon their electron configurations.

petroleum: A natural mixture of organic compounds found in liquid form.

pH: The negative logarithm of the hydronium ion concentration.

phase: A physically distinct section of matter set off from the surrounding matter by physical boundaries.

phase diagram: A graphical representation of the vapor pressures of the solid and liquid forms of a substance.

photoelectric effect: The ejection of electrons from a surface which is exposed to light.

physical change: A change in which the substance or substances present after the change are the same chemically.

physical properties: The characteristics of a material as it is subjected to physical changes.

pi bond: A bond formed by the sideways overlap of *p* orbitals.

plasma: A high temperature physical state characterized by the separation of atoms into electrons and nuclei.

pOH: The negative logarithm of the hydroxide ion concentration.

polarimeter: A device for measuring the rotation of plane polarized light.

polarity: Unsymmetrical charge distribution.

polarized light: Light in which the field variations are all in the same plane.

polyatomic ion: A group of atoms bonded to each other covalently but possessing an overall charge.

polymer: A very large molecule made from simple units repeated many times.

polymerization: The reaction producing a polymer from monomers.

polymorphism: The property of existing in more than one crystalline form.

polyprotic acid: An acid with more than one ionizable hydrogen atom.

positional isomers: Two molecules having the same formula but differing in the position to which a substituent is attached to the parent chain.

positron: A subatomic particle identical to an electron except possessing a positive charge. The antiparticle of the electron.

potential difference: The difference in potential energy of electrons located at different points.

potential energy: Energy of an object due to its position.

precipitate: A solid produced from a reaction occurring in aqueous solution.

precision: The possible error in a measurement.

pressure: The force per unit area exerted by moving particles.

protein: A biological polymer of amino acids.

proton: A positive particle found in nuclei and having a mass of approximately 1 atomic mass unit.

quadridentate: A ligand which attaches to a central ion in four locations.

quantum number: A number describing a property of an electron in an atom.

quantum theory: The concept that energy is transferred in discrete units.

quark: A theoretical particle believed to be a constituent of a hadron.

radiant energy: Energy in transit between two objects.

radical: A fragment of a molecule. It is neutral yet at least one atom is lacking its octet of electrons.

radioactivity: The spontaneous disintegration of nuclei.

Raoult's law: The vapor pressure of a solution of a nonvolatile solute is the product of the vapor pressure of the pure solvent and the mole fraction of the solvent.

reaction mechanism: The actual step-by-step description of the interaction of atoms, ions, and molecules in a reaction.

reaction rate: The rate of disappearance of a reactant or the rate of appearance of a product.

redox reaction: A reaction involving the transfer of electrons.

reducing agent: A substance which tends to donate electrons.

reduction: The gain of electrons.

refraction: The bending of a beam of light as it passes from one medium to another.

refractometer: A device for measuring the refraction of light.

resonance: The phenomenon in which several equally valid dot diagrams can be drawn for a substance. The actual substance is an average of all the possible arrangements.

reversible chemical change: A change in which the products can be changed back into the original reactants, under the proper conditions.

reversible thermodynamic change: An ideal change in which the difference in pressure causing the change is infinitesimal.

salt: A compound formed from the positive ion of a base and the negative ion of an acid.

saponification reaction: The reaction of an ester with a strong base to form a soap and glycerol.

saturated hydrocarbon: A hydrocarbon in which all carbon-carbon bonds are single bonds.

saturated solution: A solution in which undissolved solute is in equilibrium with dissolved solute.

scientific notation: Expression of numbers in the form $M \times 10^n$ where $1.00 \leq M < 10$ and n is an integer.

screw dislocation: A crystal defect in which the unit cells are improperly aligned.

semiconductor: A device in which the electrons are involved in bonding, but which may be made to conduct under the proper conditions.

shielding effect: The decrease in the force between outer electrons and the nucleus due to the presence of other electrons between them.

SI units: The internationally accepted set of standards for measurement.

side chain: A hydrocarbon radical attached to the parent chain of an organic molecule.

sigma bond: A bond formed by the end-to-end overlap of atomic orbitals.

significant digits: Digits in the value of a measurement indicating the quantity to a precision justified by the measuring device and technique used to make the measurement.

single displacement: A reaction in which one element replaces another in a compound.

smectic substance: A liquid crystal having order in two dimensions.

solid: A physical state characterized by particles in such close proximity that their random motion appears to be vibration about a fixed point.

solubility: The quantity of a solute which will dissolve in a specific quantity of solvent at a specific temperature.

solubility product constant: The equilibrium constant for the dissolving of a slightly soluble salt.

solute: The substance present in lesser quantity in a solution.

solution: A homogeneous mixture composed of solute and solvent.

solution equilibrium: Solute is dissolving and crystallizing at the same rate.

solvation: The attaching of solvent particles to solute particles.

solvent: The substance present in the greater amount in a solution.

space lattice: The theoretical arrangement pattern of the unit cells in a crystal.

specific heat capacity: The amount of heat required to raise the temperature of 1 gram of a substance by 1 Celsius degree.

specific rate constant: A constant used to determine the rate of a reaction from the concentration of the reactants.

spectator ion: An ion present in a solution but not taking part in the reaction.

spin: A property of subatomic particles which corresponds most closely with our concept of rotation about an axis.

spontaneous: Occurring without outside influence.

square planar: An arrangement of particles in a complex ion in which the ligands are arranged in a plane with the central ion and form a square with the central ion in the center.

stability: The tendency (or lack of it) for a compound to disintegrate or decompose.

standard solution: A solution whose concentration is known with precision.

standard state: A reference set of conditions for thermodynamic measurements equal to 25°C, 101.325 kPa, and 1M.

standard temperature and pressure: A set of reference conditions for dealing with gases equal to 0°C and 101.325 kPa.

starch: A biological polymer of glucose.

state: A physical property of a phase designating it as solid, liquid, gas, or plasma.

state function: Thermodynamic quantity which is determined solely by the conditions, not the method of arriving at those conditions.

stationary phase: The adsorbent in chromatography.

stoichiometry: The solution of problems involving specific quantities of a substance or substances.

strong (acid or base): A completely ionized electrolyte.

structural isomers: Two compounds with the same formula but differing arrangements of the parent carbon chain.

sublimation: The change directly from solid to gas.

substituent: A hydrocarbon branch or nonhydrocarbon group attached to the parent chain or ring in organic compounds.

substitution reaction: A reaction in organic compounds in which a hydrogen atom or substituent is replaced by another substituent.

supercooled liquid: A liquid cooled below its normal freezing point without having changed state to the solid form. A metastable state.

supersaturated solution: A solution containing more solute than a saturated solution at the same temperature. A metastable state.

surface tension: The apparent "skin" effect on the surface of a liquid due to unbalanced forces on the surface particles.

suspension: A dispersion of particles larger than 100 nm throughout a continuous medium.

symmetry: The property of being balanced with respect to the relative positions of atoms or substituents on opposite sides of an imaginary center or axis.

synchrotron: A device for accelerating subatomic particles in a circular path.

synthesis: Formation of a compound from two or more simpler substances.

synthetic element: An element not occurring in nature produced by means of nuclear reactions.

technology: The application of scientific principles for practical use.

temperature: A measure of the average kinetic energy of molecules.

ternary: A compound formed from three elements.

tetrahedral: An arrangement in which four particles surround a central particle at angles of 109.5° to each other.

thermodynamics: The study of the interaction of heat and matter.

thermometer: A device for measuring temperature.

thin layer chromatography: A chromatographic method utilizing an adsorbent spread over a flat surface in a thin layer.

time: The interval between two occurrences.

titration: A laboratory technique for measuring the relative strength of solutions.

tracer: A nuclide used to follow a reaction or process.

transistor: An electronic device whose operation is based upon the behavior of certain crystals with deliberate built-in defects.

transition element: An element whose highest energy electron is in a *d* sublevel.

transmutation: The change of one element into another.

transuranium element: An element with Z > 92.

tridentate: A ligand which attaches to the central ion in three locations.

triple bond: A covalent bond in which two atoms share three pairs of electrons.

triple point: The temperature and pressure at which all three phases of a substance are in equilibrium.

Tyndall effect: The scattering of light by colloids.

ultraviolet spectroscopy: A spectroscopic technique using light of wavelength slightly less than visible light and lending evidence to the electronic structure of atoms and molecules.

uncertainty principle: The impossibility of measuring exactly both the position and the momentum of an object at the same time.

unit cell: The simplest unit of repetition in a crystal lattice.

unsaturated molecule: An organic molecule containing at least one double or triple bond.

unsaturated solution: A solution containing less solute than a saturated solution at the same temperature.

van der Waals forces: Weak forces of attraction between molecules.

van der Waals radii: The radius of an atom in the direction of adjacent nonbonded atoms.

vapor equilibrium: The state in which evaporation and condensation are taking place at the same rate.

vapor pressure: The pressure generated by a vapor in equilibrium with its liquid.

velocity: Speed expressed as a vector quantity.

viscosity: The resistance of a fluid to flow.

visible spectroscopy: A spectroscopic method useful in investigating the behavior of electrons in atoms.

volatile: A substance with a low boiling point, weak intermolecular forces, and a high vapor pressure at room temperature.

volt: The unit of electric potential difference.

voltaic cell: An electrochemical cell in which a chemical reaction generates an electric current.

wave: A periodic disturbance in a medium.

wave equation: A mathematical expression treating the electron as a wave and providing the amplitude of the wave at specific points in space with reference to the nucleus as the origin.

wavelength: The distance between corresponding crests or troughs in a wave.

wave-particle duality of nature: The property of particles behaving as waves as well as particles and the property of waves behaving as particles as well as waves.

weak (acids and bases): An electrolyte which is only slightly ionized.

weak forces: Attractive forces between molecules and consisting of dipole-dipole, dipole-induced dipole, and dispersion forces.

work: A force moving through a distance.

INDEX

International Atomic Masses

Element	Symbol	Atomic number	Atomic mass	Element	Symbol	Atomic number	Atomic mass
Actinium	Ac	89	227.02779*	Neodymium	Nd	60	144.24
Aluminum	Al	13	26.98154	Neon	Ne	10	20.179
Americium	Am	95	243.06139*	Neptunium	Np	93	237.0482
Antimony	Sb	51	121.75	Nickel	Ni	28	58.71
Argon	Ar	18	39.948	Niobium	Nb	41	92 9064
Arsenic	As	33	74.9216	Nitrogen	N	7	14.0067
Astatine	At	85	209.98704*	Nobelium	No	102	255.093*
Barium	Ba	56	137.33	Osmium	Os	76	190.2
Berkelium	Bk	97	247.07032*	Oxygen	O	8	15.9994
Beryllium	Be	4	9.01218	Palladium	Pd	46	106.4
Bismuth	Bi	83	208.9808	Phosphorus	P	15	30.97376
Boron	B	5	10.81	Platinum	Pt	78	195.09
Bromine	Br	35	79.904	Plutonium	Pu	94	244.06424*
Cadmium	Cd	48	112.41	Polonium	Po	84	208.98244*
Calcium	Ca	20	40.08	Potassium	K	19	39.0983
Californium	Cf	98	251.07961*	Praseodymium	Pr	59	140.9077
Carbon	C	6	12.011	Promethium	Pm	61	144.91279*
Cerium	Ce	58	140.12	Protactinium	Pa	91	231.0359*
Cesium	Cs	55	132.9054	Radium	Ra	88	226.0254
Chlorine	Cl	17	35.453	Radon	Rn	86	222*
Chromium	Cr	24	51.996	Rhenium	Re	75	186.2
Cobalt	Co	27	58.9332	Rhodium	Rh	45	102.9055
Copper	Cu	29	63.546	Rubidium	Rb	37	85.4678
Curium	Cm	96	247.07038*	Ruthenium	Ru	44	101.07
Dysprosium	Dy	66	162.50	Samarium	Sm	62	150.4
Einsteinium	Es	99	254.08805*	Scandium	Sc	21	44.9559
Erbium	Er	68	167.26	Selenium	Se	34	78.96
Europium	Eu	63	151.96	Silicon	Si	14	28.0855
Fermium	Fm	100	257.09515*	Silver	Ag	47	107.868
Fluorine	F	9	18.998403	Sodium	Na	11	22.9898
Francium	Fr	87	223.01976*	Strontium	Sr	38	87.62
Gadolinium	Gd	64	157.25	Sulfur	S	16	32.06
Gallium	Ga	31	69.737	Tantalum	Ta	73	180.9479
Germanium	Ge	32	72.59	Technetium	Tc	43	96.9062*
Gold	Au	79	196.9665	Tellurium	Te	52	127.60
Hafnium	Hf	72	178.49	Terbium	Tb	65	158.9254
Helium	He	2	4.00260	Thallium	Tl	81	204.37
Holmium	Ho	67	164.9304	Thorium	Th	90	232.0381
Hydrogen	H	1	1.0079	Thulium	Tm	69	168.9342
Indium	In	49	114.82	Tin	Sn	50	118.69
Iodine	I	53	126.9045	Titanium	Ti	22	47.90
Iridium	Ir	77	192.22	Tungsten	W	74	183.85
Iron	Fe	26	55.847	Uranium	U	92	238.029
Krypton	Kr	36	83.80	Vanadium	V	23	50.9415
Lanthanum	La	57	138.9055	Xenon	Xe	54	131.30
Lawrencium	Lr	103	256.099*	Ytterbium	Yb	70	173.04
Lead	Pb	82	207.2	Yttrium	Y	39	88.9059
Lithium	Li	3	6.941	Zinc	Zn	30	65.38
Lutetium	Lu	71	174.967	Zirconium	Zr	40	91.22
Magnesium	Mg	12	24.305	Element 104†		104	257*
Manganese	Mn	25	54.9380	Element 105†		105	260*
Mendelevium	Md	101	258*	Element 106†		106	263*
Mercury	Hg	80	200.59	Element 107†		107	258*
Molybdenum	Mo	42	95.94				

*The mass of the isotope with the longest known half-life.

† Names for elements 104–107 have not yet been approved by the IUPAC. The USSR has proposed Kurchatovium (Ku) for element 104, and Bohrium (Bh) for element 105. The United States has proposed Rutherfordium (Rf) for element 104, and Hahnium (Ha) for element 105.